BUS

BURNS

INDIANA STATUTES

ANNOTATED

CODE EDITION

TITLE 32

2002 REPLACEMENT VOLUME

Original Edition by
HARRISON BURNS

LexisNexis™

PREFACE

This 2002 replacement includes acts of the 2002 Regular Session. This volume is conformed to the Indiana Code as enacted by the 1976 Regular Session of the General Assembly, as amended. For the convenience of the user, the complete Code number, indicating title, article, chapter, and section of the Code, appears at the beginning of each section.

This volume contains notes taken from opinions appearing on LEXIS-NEXIS and filed by the Supreme Court of Indiana through 2002 Ind. LEXIS 124, February 8, 2002, and published in the North Eastern Reporter, 2d Series, through volume 761 N.E.2d. Notes have been taken from opinions filed by the Court of Appeals of Indiana through 2002 Ind. App. LEXIS 188, February 12, 2002, and through volume 761 N.E.2d. And, notes have been taken from opinions filed by the Indiana Tax Court through 2002 Ind. Tax LEXIS 6, February 5, 2002, and through volume 762 N.E.2d. Notes have been taken from Opinions of the Attorney General of Indiana, through opinion number 01-5. Also included in this volume are notes taken from the opinions of federal courts for cases arising in Indiana, appearing on LEXIS-NEXIS, and issued through January 10, 2002. Where available, citations have been provided to the Supreme Court Reporter (S.Ct.), Federal Reporter, 3d Series (F.3d), Federal Supplement, 2d Series (F. Supp. 2d), and Bankruptcy Reporter (Bankr.).

The annotations include references to the Indiana Law Journal, Indiana Law Review, Notre Dame Law Review, Res Gestae, Valparaiso University Law Review, and American Law Reports. These and other helpful notes and references have been reviewed, updated, and relocated where necessary. Cross reference notes providing directions to statutory material of similar and/or related subject matter located elsewhere in the Code are provided. Where a law has been repealed, the compiler's notes to that section contain a reference to any new or present provision on a similar subject, where applicable.

If you have questions or suggestions concerning Burns' Indiana Statutes, please write, call toll free 1-800-833-9844, fax toll free 1-800-643-1280, visit our website at www.lexis.com, or email us at customer.support@lexisnexis.com. Direct written inquiries to:

LexisNexis
Attn: Customer Service
    Burns' Indiana Statutes Annotated
1275 Broadway
Albany, NY 12204-2694

Please note that, for your convenience, there are postpaid cards at the back of each index volume for your suggestions.

LexisNexis™

June 2002

Prepared by the Editorial Staff of the Publisher:

Keith McKinell	Legal Analyst
Florence McCowin	Coordinating Editor
Stephen White	Indexing Legal Analyst
Andrea Stinnie	Indexing Coordinating Editor

USER'S GUIDE

In order to assist both the legal profession and the layman in obtaining the maximum benefit from Burns' Indiana Statutes Annotated, a User's Guide is included with the set. The Guide contains comments and information on the many features found in the Burns' Statutes volumes, which are intended to increase the usefulness of the set. See the supplement to the volume containing Titles 1, 2, and 3 for the complete User's Guide.

History of Burns' Statutes Annotated

For one hundred thirteen years, the Bench and Bar of Indiana have relied on Burns' Indiana Statutes Annotated, published first by The Bobbs-Merrill Company and now by LexisNexis. Bobbs-Merrill first became involved in 1889 with the publication of Elliott's Supplement to the Revised Statutes of 1881 by the Bowen-Merrill Company, a predecessor company. (The Revised Statutes of 1881 are an unenacted compilation sanctioned by the state of Indiana.)

From that time until the publication of the official Indiana Code, Burns' Indiana Statutes Annotated was the sole organized and indexed source of the official statute law of Indiana with the exception of Revised Statutes of Indiana published by E.D. Myers & Co., Chicago, Illinois in 1896, and Baldwin's 1934 Indiana Statutes published by the Baldwin Law Publishing Company, Cleveland, Ohio.

On November 3, 1892, Harrison Burns of Vincennes, Indiana, entered into an agreement which led to the publication of Burns' Annotated Indiana Statutes in three volumes in 1894. This work followed the organization of the Revised Statutes of 1881 but the sections were all assigned numbers continuously through the three volumes and it was completely annotated and fully indexed. Supplements were published in 1895 and 1897. Additional revisions by Judge Burns were required in 1908 and 1914 and the 1914 revision was supplemented in 1918 and 1921. A complete revision edited by Benjamin F. Watson was published in 1926 and supplemented in 1929.

In 1933 Bobbs-Merrill began publication of a new and improved edition of Burns' Annotated Indiana Statutes in 12 volumes, completely annotated, indexed and edited by the publisher's editorial staff. This edition contained a new section numbering system, provided for annual supplementation of each volume and for individual volume revision to keep the work current and up-to-date at all times. This edition was kept current by supplementation and revision and was the standard reference for Indiana Statutes until it was replaced by the present Burns' Code Edition beginning in 1972. The Burns' Code Edition, also completely annotated and indexed, was necessary to conform to the organization and numbering system of the Indiana Code of 1971 which was carried into the official Indiana Code of 1976.

In 1976, the Law Division of the Bobbs-Merrill Company was acquired by The Michie Company, and for a number of years the Burns' Code was published under the name Michie/Bobbs-Merrill. While there has been a continuity of editorial personnel working on Burns' Indiana Statutes Annotated, beginning in 1985 the Burns' Code was published under the name of The Michie Company, and, following subsequent acquisitions, is now published under the name of LexisNexis. It is the desire and goal of the Publishers to continue to provide an authoritative, useful and convenient edition of Indiana Statutes Annotated.

EFFECTIVE DATES OF ACTS AND STATUTES WITHOUT EFFECTIVE DATE PROVISIONS

Between 1979 and 1987, under IC 1-1-3-3, each act passed at a regular session of the general assembly took effect on September 1 next following its enactment, unless a different time was specified in the act. In 1987, IC 1-1-3-3 was amended to change the date to July 1. Prior to the adoption of IC 1-1-3-3, the effective date of acts which did not contain an emergency clause was the date of the last filing in the counties as shown by the proclamation of the governor under IC 1-1-3-2. The table below lists the effective dates for acts and statutes which did not contain other effective date provisions.

[R. = Regular Session; S. = Special Session]

1842-1843 Revised Statutes .... Approved Feb. 11, 1843—no effective date record
1851-1852 Special Acts .... November 6, 1852
1851-1852 Revised Statutes .... May 6, 1853
1853 .... July 24, 1853
1855 .... August 17, 1855
1857 .... August 24, 1857
1858 S. .... August 6, 1859
1859 .... August 6, 1859
1861 .... July 5, 1861
1861 S. .... September 7, 1861
1863 .... October 10, 1863
1865 .... September 2, 1865
1865 S. .... April 13, 1866
1867 .... June 6, 1867
1869 R. and S. .... August 16, 1869
1871 .... July 10, 1871
1872 S. .... July 7, 1873
1873 .... July 7, 1873
1875 R. and S. .... August 24, 1875
1877 R. and S. .... July 2, 1877
1879 R. and S. .... May 31, 1879
1881 R. and S. .... September 19, 1881
1883 .... June 5, 1883
1885 R. and S. .... July 18, 1885
1887 .... May 21, 1887
1889 .... May 10, 1889
1891 .... June 3, 1891
1893 .... May 18, 1893
1895 .... June 28, 1895
1897 .... April 14, 1897
1899 .... April 27, 1899
1901 .... May 15, 1901
1903 .... April 23, 1903
1905 .... April 15, 1905
1907 .... April 10, 1907
1908 S. .... November 20, 1908
1909 .... April 5, 1909
1911 .... April 21, 1911
1913 .... April 30, 1913
1915 .... April 26, 1915
1917 .... May 31, 1917
1919 .... May 15, 1919
1920 S. .... January 16, 1920
1920 S. .... November 13, 1920
1921 .... May 31, 1921
1921 S. .... December 14, 1921
1923 .... April 30, 1923

1925	April 25, 1925
1927	May 16, 1927
1929	May 21, 1929
1931	June 30, 1931
1932 S.	September 30, 1932
1933	May 22, 1933
1935	June 10, 1935
1936 S.	May 11, 1936
1937	June 7, 1937
1938 S.	Each act effective on date of approval
1939	June 14, 1939
1941	July 8, 1941
1943	November 3, 1943
1944 (1st S.S.)	April 11, 1944
1944 (2nd S.S.)	November 4, 1944
1945	December 12, 1945
1947	August 21, 1947
1949	September 10, 1949
1951	July 20, 1951
1951 S.	Each act effective on date of approval
1953	September 18, 1953
1955	June 30, 1955
1957	June 25, 1957
1959	July 20, 1959
1961	July 6, 1961
1963 R. and S.	August 12, 1963
1965	July 8, 1965
1965 (1st S.S.)	Each act effective on date of approval
1965 (2nd S.S.)	December 29, 1965
1967	July 26, 1967
1969	August 18, 1969
1971	September 2, 1971
1972	July 28, 1972
1973	July 26, 1973
1974	June 11, 1974
1975	July 29, 1975
1976	June 2, 1976
1977	August 29, 1977
1978	June 28, 1978
1979-1987	September 1
1988 and subsequent years	July 1

PARALLEL REFERENCE TABLES

The following Tables of Disposition and Derivation were prepared from tables compiled by the staff of the Indiana Legislative Council, Office of Code Revision. These tables indicate those sections of the Indiana Code prior to the enactment of P.L.2-2002 which correspond to the provisions of Title 32 as recodified by P.L.2-2002, as well as sections in Titles 24, 26, and 34 also affected by that legislation.

TABLE OF DISPOSITION

The following table lists prior sections of the Indiana Code and the corresponding Code number in Title 32, as recodified by P.L.2-2002, and provisions previously in Titles 24 and 34 now codified in Title 32. This table should make it convenient to trace a prior law citation to the citation for the new law.

Prior Provision	Current Provision	Prior Provision	Current Provision
24-4.6-2-1	32-21-5-1	24-5-9-17	32-32-2-20
24-4.6-2-2	32-21-5-2	24-5-9-18	32-32-2-21
24-4.6-2-3	32-21-5-3	24-5-9-19 part	32-32-2-12
24-4.6-2-4	32-21-5-4	24-5-9-19 part	32-32-2-22
24-4.6-2-5	32-21-5-5	24-5-9-20	32-32-2-23
24-4.6-2-6	32-21-5-6	24-5-9-21	32-32-1-1
24-4.6-2-7	32-21-5-7	24-5-9-22	32-32-3-1
24-4.6-2-8	32-21-5-8	24-5-9-23	32-32-3-2
24-4.6-2-9	32-21-5-9	24-5-9-24	32-32-3-3
24-4.6-2-10	32-21-5-10	24-5-9-25	32-32-3-4
24-4.6-2-11	32-21-5-11	24-5-9-26	32-32-3-5
24-4.6-2-12	32-21-5-12	24-5-9-27	32-32-3-6
24-4.6-2-13	32-21-5-13	24-5-9-28	32-32-3-7
24-4.6-2.1-1	32-21-6-1	24-5-9-29(a)	32-32-3-8
24-4.6-2.1-1.5	32-21-6-2	24-5-9-29(b)	32-32-2-19
24-4.6-2.1-2	32-21-6-3	24-5-9-30	32-32-3-9
24-4.6-2.1-3	32-21-6-4	24-5-9-31	32-32-3-10
24-4.6-2.1-4	32-21-6-5	24-5-9-32	32-32-3-11
24-4.6-2.1-5	32-21-6-6	24-5-9-33	32-32-3-12
24-5-9-1	32-32-2-2	24-5-9-34	32-32-3-13
24-5-9-2	32-32-2-3	24-5-9-35	32-32-3-14
24-5-9-3	32-32-2-4	24-5-9-36	32-32-3-15
24-5-9-4	32-32-2-5	24-5-11.5-1	32-27-1-1
24-5-9-5	32-32-2-6	24-5-11.5-2	32-27-1-2
24-5-9-6	32-32-2-7	24-5-11.5-3	32-27-1-3
24-5-9-7	32-32-2-8	24-5-11.5-4	32-27-1-4
24-5-9-8	32-32-2-9	24-5-11.5-5	32-27-1-5
24-5-9-9	32-32-2-10	24-5-11.5-6	32-27-1-6
24-5-9-10	32-32-2-11	24-5-11.5-7	32-27-1-7
24-5-9-11	32-32-2-13	24-5-11.5-8	32-27-1-8
24-5-9-12	32-32-2-14	24-5-11.5-9	32-27-1-9
24-5-9-13	32-32-2-15	24-5-11.5-10	32-27-1-10
24-5-9-14	32-32-2-16	24-5-11.5-11	32-27-1-11
24-5-9-15	32-32-2-17	24-5-11.5-12	32-27-1-12
24-5-9-16	32-32-2-18	24-5-11.5-13	32-27-1-13

Prior Provision	Current Provision	Prior Provision	Current Provision
24-5-11.5-14	32-27-1-14	32-1-4.5-2	32-17-8-2
24-5-11.5-15	32-27-1-15	32-1-4.5-3	32-17-8-3
32-1-1-1(a)	32-19-1-1	32-1-4.5-4	32-17-8-4
32-1-1-1(b)	32-19-1-2	32-1-4.5-5	32-17-8-5
32-1-1-1(c)	32-19-1-2	32-1-4.5-6	32-17-8-6
32-1-1-1(d)	32-19-1-2	32-1-5-1	32-20-3-1
32-1-1-2	32-19-1-4	32-1-5-2	32-20-3-2
32-1-1-3	32-19-2-1	32-1-5-3	32-20-3-3
32-1-1-4	32-19-1-5	32-1-5-4	32-20-4-1
32-1-1-5	32-19-1-3	32-1-5-5	32-20-4-2
32-1-1-6	32-19-2-2	32-1-5-6	32-20-4-3
32-1-1-7	32-19-1-6	32-1-5-7	32-20-1-2
32-1-1-8	32-19-3-1	32-1-5-8(a)	32-20-2-2
32-1-1-9	32-19-3-2	32-1-5-8(b)	32-20-2-3
32-1-1-10(a)	32-19-4-1	32-1-5-8(d)	32-20-2-4
32-1-1-10(b)	32-19-4-1	32-1-5-8(c)	32-20-2-5
32-1-1-10(c)	32-19-4-2	32-1-5-8(e)	32-20-2-6
32-1-1-10(d)	32-19-4-3	32-1-5-8(f)	32-20-2-7
32-1-1-10(e)	32-19-4-3	32-1-5-9 part	32-20-5-1
32-1-1-10(f)	32-19-4-4	32-1-5-9 part	32-20-5-2
32-1-2-2	32-22-1-1	32-1-5-10	32-20-1-1
32-1-2-3	32-22-2-1	32-1-6-1	Deleted
32-1-2-4	32-21-1-13	32-1-6-2(a)	32-25-2-7
32-1-2-5	32-21-1-14	32-1-6-2(b)	32-25-2-8
32-1-2-6	32-17-3-4	32-1-6-2(c)	32-25-2-9
32-1-2-7	32-17-2-1	32-1-6-2(d)	32-25-2-10
32-1-2-8	32-17-2-1	32-1-6-2(e)	32-25-2-11
32-1-2-9	32-17-2-2	32-1-6-2(f)	32-25-2-2
32-1-2-10	32-17-1-4	32-1-6-2(g)	32-25-2-3
32-1-2-11	32-21-3-3	32-1-6-2(h)	32-25-2-4
32-1-2-12	32-17-1-2	32-1-6-2(i)	32-25-2-5
32-1-2-13	32-21-1-15	32-1-6-2(j)	32-25-2-6
32-1-2-14	32-21-1-16	32-1-6-2(k)	32-25-2-12
32-1-2-15	32-29-1-5	32-1-6-2(l)	32-25-2-13
32-1-2-16	32-21-4-1	32-1-6-2(m)	32-25-2-14
32-1-2-16.3	32-21-4-2	32-1-6-2(n)	32-25-2-15
32-1-2-17	32-21-4-3	32-1-6-2(o)	32-25-2-16
32-1-2-18	32-21-2-3	32-1-6-2(p)	32-25-2-17
32-1-2-19	32-21-2-4	32-1-6-2(q)	32-25-2-18
32-1-2-20	32-21-2-5	32-1-6-2(r)	32-25-2-19
32-1-2-21	32-21-2-6	32-1-6-2(s)	32-25-2-20
32-1-2-23	32-21-2-7	32-1-6-3	32-25-1-1
32-1-2-24	32-21-2-8	32-1-6-4	32-25-3-1
32-1-2-26	32-21-2-9	32-1-6-5	32-25-4-1
32-1-2-27	32-21-2-10	32-1-6-6	32-25-4-2
32-1-2-28	32-21-2-11	32-1-6-7	32-25-4-3
32-1-2-29	32-21-2-12	32-1-6-8	32-25-9-1
32-1-2-30	32-17-1-1	32-1-6-9	32-25-8-5
32-1-2-31	32-21-3-1	32-1-6-10	32-25-6-1
32-1-2-32	32-21-3-4	32-1-6-11	32-25-8-6
32-1-2-33	32-17-1-3	32-1-6-12	32-25-7-1
32-1-2-34	32-17-2-3	32-1-6-12.1	32-25-7-2
32-1-2-35	32-17-2-4	32-1-6-12.2	32-25-7-3
32-1-2-36	32-17-2-5	32-1-6-13	32-25-7-4
32-1-2-37(a)	32-21-2-2	32-1-6-14	32-25-7-5
32-1-2-37(b)	32-21-2-13	32-1-6-15	32-25-8-3
32-1-4.5-1	32-17-8-1	32-1-6-15.1	32-25-8-13

Prior Provision	Current Provision	Prior Provision	Current Provision
32-1-6-15.2	32-25-7-6	32-2-3-2	32-21-9-2
32-1-6-15.3	32-25-8-14	32-2-3-3	32-21-9-3
32-1-6-15.4	32-25-6-2	32-2-3-4	32-21-9-4
32-1-6-15.5	32-25-8-15	32-2-4-1	32-21-1-11
32-1-6-15.6	32-25-8-4	32-2-5-1	32-21-1-12
32-1-6-16	32-25-5-1	32-2-7-1	32-18-2-1
32-1-6-17	32-25-8-7	32-2-7-2	32-18-2-2
32-1-6-18	32-25-8-9	32-2-7-3	32-18-2-3
32-1-6-19	32-25-8-10	32-2-7-4	32-18-2-4
32-1-6-20	32-25-8-11	32-2-7-5	32-18-2-5
32-1-6-21	32-25-8-12	32-2-7-6	32-18-2-6
32-1-6-22	32-25-4-4	32-2-7-7	32-18-2-7
32-1-6-23	32-25-5-2	32-2-7-8	32-18-2-8
32-1-6-24	32-25-6-3	32-2-7-9	32-18-2-9
32-1-6-25	32-25-8-1	32-2-7-10	32-18-2-10
32-1-6-26	32-25-8-2	32-2-7-11	32-18-2-11
32-1-6-27	32-25-8-8	32-2-7-12	32-18-2-12
32-1-6-28,	32-25-8-16	32-2-7-13	32-18-2-13
32-1-6-29		32-2-7-14	32-18-2-14
32-1-6-30	32-25-9-2	32-2-7-15	32-18-2-15
32-1-6-31	32-25-1-2	32-2-7-16	32-18-2-16
32-1-7-1	32-22-2-2	32-2-7-17	32-18-2-17
32-1-7-2	32-22-2-3	32-2-7-18	32-18-2-18
32-1-7-3	32-22-2-4	32-2-7-19	32-18-2-19
32-1-8-1	32-22-2-5	32-2-7-20	32-18-2-20
32-1-8-2	32-22-2-6	32-2-7-21	32-18-2-21
32-1-8-3	32-22-2-7	32-2-8-1	32-21-8-1
32-1-9-3	32-21-10-1	32-2-8-2	32-21-8-2
32-1-9-1	32-21-10-2	32-2-8-3	32-21-8-3
32-1-9-2	32-21-10-3	32-2-8-4	32-21-8-4
32-1-11-1	32-17-12-1	32-2-8-5	32-21-8-5
32-1-12-2,	32-22-1-2	32-2-8-6	32-21-8-6
32-1-12-3		32-3-1-1 part	32-17-6-1
32-1-13-1	32-22-1-3	32-3-1-1 part	32-17-6-2
32-1-13-2	32-22-1-4	32-3-1-1 part	32-17-6-3
32-1-17-1	32-22-1-5	32-3-1-1 part	32-17-6-4
32-1-20-1	32-21-7-1	32-3-1-1 part	32-17-6-5
32-1-20-2	32-21-7-2	32-3-1-1 part	32-17-6-6
32-1-21-1	32-17-10-1	32-3-2-1 part	32-17-7-1
32-1-21-2	32-17-10-2	32-3-2-1 part	32-17-7-2
32-1-21-3	32-17-10-3	32-3-2-1 part	32-17-7-3
32-2-1-1	32-21-1-1	32-3-2-1 part	32-17-7-5
32-2-1-2	32-21-1-2	32-3-2-1 part	32-17-7-6
32-2-1-3	32-21-1-3	32-3-2-2	32-17-7-7
32-2-1-4	32-21-1-4	32-3-2-3	32-17-7-8
32-2-1-5	32-21-1-5	32-3-2-4	32-17-7-9
32-2-1-6	32-21-1-6	32-3-2-5(a)	32-17-7-4
32-2-1-11	32-21-1-7	32-3-2-5(b)	32-17-7-10
32-2-1-12	32-21-1-8	32-3-2-5(c)	32-17-7-10
32-2-1-13	32-21-1-9	32-3-2-6	32-17-7-11
32-2-1.5-1	26-2-9-1	32-3-2-7	32-17-7-12
32-2-1.5-2	26-2-9-2	32-3-2-8	32-17-7-13
32-2-1.5-3	26-2-9-3	32-3-2-9	32-17-7-14
32-2-1.5-4	26-2-9-4	32-3-2-10	32-17-7-15
32-2-1.5-5	26-2-9-5	32-3-2-11	32-17-7-16
32-2-2-1	32-21-1-10	32-3-2-12	32-17-7-17
32-2-3-1	32-21-9-1	32-3-2-13	32-17-7-18

Prior Provision	Current Provision	Prior Provision	Current Provision
32-3-2-14	32-17-7-19	32-4-5-10	32-17-4-9
32-3-2-15	32-17-7-20	32-4-5-11	32-17-4-10
32-4-1.5-1(1)	32-17-11-1	32-4-5-12	32-17-4-11
32-4-1.5-1(2)	32-17-11-2	32-4-5-13	32-17-4-12
32-4-1.5-1(3)	32-17-11-3	32-4-5-14	32-17-4-13
32-4-1.5-1(4)	32-17-11-4	32-4-5-15	32-17-4-14
32-4-1.5-1(5)	32-17-11-5	32-4-5-16	32-17-4-15
32-4-1.5-1(6)	32-17-11-6	32-4-5-17	32-17-4-16
32-4-1.5-1(7)	32-17-11-7	32-4-5-18	32-17-4-17
32-4-1.5-1(8)	32-17-11-8	32-4-5-19	32-17-4-18
32-4-1.5-1(9)	32-17-11-9	32-4-5-20	32-17-4-19
32-4-1.5-1(10)	32-17-11-10	32-4-5-21	32-17-4-20
32-4-1.5-1(11)	32-17-11-11	32-4-5-22	32-17-4-21
32-4-1.5-1(12)	32-17-11-12	32-4-5-23	32-17-4-22
32-4-1.5-1(13)	32-17-11-13	32-4-6-1	32-17-4-23
32-4-1.5-1(14)	32-17-11-14	32-4-7-1	32-17-4-24
32-4-1.5-1(15)	32-17-11-15	32-4-8-1 part	32-17-5-1
32-4-1.5-2	32-17-11-16	32-4-8-1 part	32-17-5-2
32-4-1.5-3	32-17-11-17	32-4-8-1 part	32-17-5-3
32-4-1.5-4	32-17-11-18	32-4-8-1 part	32-17-5-4
32-4-1.5-5	32-17-11-19	32-4-8-2	32-17-5-5
32-4-1.5-6	32-17-11-20	32-4-8-3	32-17-5-6
32-4-1.5-7	32-17-11-21	32-5-1-1	32-23-1-1
32-4-1.5-8	32-17-11-22	32-5-1-2	32-23-1-2
32-4-1.5-9	32-17-11-23	32-5-1-3	32-23-1-3
32-4-1.5-10	32-17-11-24	32-5-1-4	32-23-1-4
32-4-1.5-11	32-17-11-25	32-5-2-1(a)	32-23-2-1
32-4-1.5-12	32-17-11-26	32-5-2-1(b)	32-23-2-2
32-4-1.5-13	32-17-11-27	32-5-2-1(c)	32-23-2-3
32-4-1.5-14	32-17-11-28	32-5-2-1(d)	32-23-2-4
32-4-1.5-15	32-17-11-29	32-5-2-2	32-23-2-5
32-4-1.6-1	32-17-9-2	32-5-2.5-1 part	32-23-4-1
32-4-1.6-2	32-17-9-3	32-5-2.5-1 part	32-23-4-2
32-4-1.6-3	32-17-9-4	32-5-2.5-1 part	32-23-4-3
32-4-1.6-4	32-17-9-5	32-5-2.5-2	32-23-4-4
32-4-1.6-5	32-17-9-6	32-5-2.5-3	32-23-4-5
32-4-1.6-6	32-17-9-7	32-5-2.6-1 part	32-23-5-2
32-4-1.6-7	32-17-9-8	32-5-2.6-1 part	32-23-5-3
32-4-1.6-8	32-17-9-9	32-5-2.6-1 part	32-23-5-4
32-4-1.6-9	32-17-9-10	32-5-2.6-2	32-23-5-5
32-4-1.6-10	32-17-9-11	32-5-2.6-3	32-23-5-6
32-4-1.6-11	32-17-9-12	32-5-2.6-4	32-23-5-7
32-4-1.6-12	32-17-9-13	32-5-2.6-5	32-23-5-1
32-4-1.6-13	32-17-9-14	32-5-2.6-6	32-23-5-1
32-4-1.6-14	32-17-9-15	32-5-2.6-7	32-23-5-8
32-4-1.6-15	32-17-9-1	32-5-3-1	32-23-3-1
32-4-2-1	32-17-3-1	32-5-6-1(a)	32-23-6-1
32-4-2-2	32-17-3-2	32-5-6-1(b)	32-23-6-2
32-4-3-1	32-17-3-3	32-5-7-1(a)	32-23-7-1
32-4-5-1	32-17-4-1	32-5-7-1(b)	32-23-7-2
32-4-5-2	32-17-4-2	32-5-7-1(c)	32-23-7-4
32-4-5-3	32-17-4-3	32-5-7-1(d)	32-23-7-5
32-4-5-4	32-17-4-4	32-5-7-1(e)	32-23-7-3
32-4-5-5	32-17-4-5	32-5-7-2	32-23-7-6
32-4-5-6	32-17-4-6	32-5-7-3	32-23-7-7
32-4-5-7	32-17-4-7	32-5-7-4	32-23-7-8
32-4-5-8	32-17-4-8	32-5-7-5	32-23-7-8

Prior Provision	Current Provision	Prior Provision	Current Provision
32-5-7-6	32-23-7-8	32-7-1-5	32-31-1-6
32-5-8-1 part	32-23-8-1	32-7-1-6	32-31-1-7
32-5-8-1 part	32-23-8-2	32-7-1-7	32-31-1-8
32-5-8-1 part	32-23-8-3	32-7-1-8	32-31-1-9
32-5-8-1 part	32-23-8-4	32-7-1-9	32-31-1-10
32-5-9-1 part	32-23-9-1	32-7-1-10	32-31-1-11
32-5-9-1 part	32-23-9-2	32-7-1-11	32-31-1-12
32-5-11-1	32-23-10-2	32-7-1-12	32-31-1-13
32-5-11-2	32-23-10-1	32-7-1-13	32-31-1-14
32-5-11-3	32-23-10-3	32-7-1-14	32-31-1-15
32-5-11-4	32-23-10-4	32-7-1-15	32-31-1-16
32-5-11-5	32-23-10-5	32-7-1-16	32-31-1-17
32-5-11-6	32-23-10-6	32-7-1-17	32-31-1-18
32-5-11-7	32-23-10-7	32-7-1-18	32-31-1-19
32-5-11-8	32-23-10-8	32-7-1-19	32-31-1-20
32-5-12-1	32-23-11-1	32-7-2-1 part	32-31-2-1
32-5-12-2	32-23-11-2	32-7-2-1 part	32-31-2-2
32-5-12-3	32-23-11-3	32-7-5-1	32-31-3-1
32-5-12-4	32-23-11-4	32-7-5-2	32-31-3-2
32-5-12-5	32-23-11-5	32-7-5-3	32-31-3-3
32-5-12-6	32-23-11-6	32-7-5-4	32-31-3-4
32-5-12-7	32-23-11-7	32-7-5-5	32-31-3-5
32-5-12-8	32-23-11-8	32-7-5-6	32-31-3-6
32-5-12-9	32-23-11-9	32-7-5-7	32-31-3-7
32-5-12-10	32-23-11-10	32-7-5-8	32-31-3-8
32-5-12-11	32-23-11-11	32-7-5-9	32-31-3-9
32-5-12-12	32-23-11-12	32-7-5-10	32-31-3-10
32-5-12-13	32-23-11-13	32-7-5-11	32-31-3-11
32-5-12-14	32-23-11-14	32-7-5-12	32-31-3-12
32-5-12-15	32-23-11-15	32-7-5-13	32-31-3-13
32-6-1.5-1	32-30-3-1	32-7-5-14	32-31-3-14
32-6-1.5-2	32-30-3-2	32-7-5-15	32-31-3-15
32-6-1.5-3	32-30-3-3	32-7-5-16	32-31-3-16
32-6-1.5-4	32-30-3-4	32-7-5-17	32-31-3-17
32-6-1.5-5	32-30-3-5	32-7-5-18	32-31-3-18
32-6-1.5-6	32-30-3-6	32-7-5-19	32-31-3-19
32-6-1.5-7	32-30-3-7	32-7-6-1	32-31-4-2
32-6-1.5-8	32-30-3-8	32-7-6-2(a)	32-31-4-1
32-6-1.5-9	32-30-3-9	32-7-6-2(b)	32-31-4-3
32-6-1.5-10	32-30-3-10	32-7-6-2(c)	32-31-4-3
32-6-1.5-11	32-30-3-11	32-7-6-2(d)	32-31-4-3
32-6-1.5-12	32-30-3-12	32-7-6-3	32-31-4-4
32-6-3-1	32-30-3-13	32-7-6-4	32-31-4-5
32-6-4-1	32-30-3-14	32-7-8-1	32-31-5-1
32-6-4-2	32-30-3-15	32-7-8-2	32-31-5-1
32-6-5-1	32-30-3-16	32-7-8-3	32-31-5-2
32-6-5-2	32-30-3-17	32-7-8-4	32-31-5-3
32-6-6-1	32-30-3-18	32-7-8-5	32-31-5-4
32-6-6-2	32-30-3-19	32-7-8-6	32-31-5-5
32-6-7-1	32-30-3-20	32-7-8-7	32-31-5-6
32-6-7-2	32-30-3-21	32-7-9-1	32-31-6-1
32-7-1-1	32-31-1-1	32-7-9-2	32-31-6-2
32-7-1-2 part	32-31-1-1	32-7-9-3	32-31-6-3
32-7-1-2 part	32-31-1-2	32-7-9-4	32-31-6-4
32-7-1-3 part	32-31-1-3	32-7-9-5	32-31-6-5
32-7-1-3 part	32-31-1-4	32-7-9-6	32-31-6-6
32-7-1-4	32-31-1-5	32-7-9-7	32-31-6-7

Prior Provision	Current Provision	Prior Provision	Current Provision
32-7-9-8	32-31-6-8	32-8-15.5-4	32-29-6-4
32-7-9-9	32-31-6-9	32-8-15.5-5	32-29-6-5
32-7-9-10	32-31-6-10	32-8-15.5-6	32-29-6-6
32-8-1-1	32-28-1-1	32-8-15.5-7	32-29-6-7
32-8-1-2	32-28-1-2	32-8-15.5-8	32-29-6-8
32-8-2-1	32-28-2-1	32-8-15.5-9	32-29-6-9
32-8-3-1	32-28-3-1	32-8-15.5-10	32-29-6-10
32-8-3-2	32-28-3-2	32-8-15.5-11	32-29-6-11
32-8-3-3	32-28-3-3	32-8-15.5-12	32-29-6-12
32-8-3-4	32-28-3-4	32-8-15.5-13	32-29-6-13
32-8-3-5	32-28-3-5	32-8-15.5-14	32-29-6-14
32-8-3-6	32-28-3-6	32-8-15.5-15	32-29-6-15
32-8-3-7	32-28-3-7	32-8-15.5-16	32-29-6-16
32-8-3-8	32-28-3-8	32-8-15.5-17	32-29-6-17
32-8-3-9	32-28-3-9	32-8-16-1	32-29-7-3
32-8-3-10	32-28-3-10	32-8-16-1.3 part	32-29-7-1
32-8-3-11	32-28-3-11	32-8-16-1.3 part	32-29-7-2
32-8-3-12	32-28-3-12	32-8-16-1.3 part	32-29-7-4
32-8-3-13	32-28-3-13	32-8-16-1.5	32-29-7-5
32-8-3-14	32-28-3-14	32-8-16-2	32-29-7-6
32-8-3-15	32-28-3-15	32-8-16-3	32-29-7-7
32-8-3-16	32-28-3-16	32-8-16-4	32-29-7-8
32-8-3-17	32-28-3-17	32-8-16-5	32-29-7-9
32-8-3-18	32-28-3-18	32-8-16-6	32-29-7-10
32-8-4-1	32-28-4-1	32-8-16-7	32-29-7-11
32-8-4-2	32-28-4-2	32-8-16-8	32-29-7-12
32-8-4-3	32-28-4-3	32-8-16-9	32-29-7-13
32-8-5-1	32-28-5-1	32-8-16-10	32-29-7-14
32-8-5-2	32-28-5-2	32-8-17-1 part	32-29-8-1
32-8-6-1	32-28-6-1	32-8-17-1 part	32-29-8-2
32-8-6-2	32-28-6-2	32-8-17-1 part	32-29-8-3
32-8-7-1	32-28-7-1	32-8-18-1	32-29-9-1
32-8-7-2	32-28-7-2	32-8-19-1(a)	32-29-10-1
32-8-7-3	32-28-7-3	32-8-19-1(b)	32-29-10-2
32-8-7-4	32-28-7-4	32-8-19-1(c)	32-29-10-3
32-8-8-1	32-28-8-1	32-8-19-1(d)	32-29-10-4
32-8-9-1	32-28-9-1	32-8-19-2	32-29-10-5
32-8-10-1	32-28-10-1	32-8-19-3	32-29-10-6
32-8-10-2	32-28-10-2	32-8-21-1	32-33-1-1
32-8-11-1	32-29-1-1	32-8-21-2	32-33-1-2
32-8-11-2	32-29-1-2	32-8-21-3	32-33-1-3
32-8-11-3	32-29-1-3	32-8-21-4	32-33-1-4
32-8-11-4	32-29-1-4	32-8-21-5	32-33-1-5
32-8-11-5	32-29-1-6	32-8-21-6	Deleted
32-8-11-6	32-29-1-7	32-8-22-1	32-33-2-1
32-8-11-7	32-29-1-8	32-8-22-2	32-33-2-2
32-8-11-8	32-29-1-9	32-8-22-3	32-33-2-3
32-8-11-9	32-29-1-10	32-8-22-4	32-33-2-4
32-8-11-10	32-29-1-11	32-8-22-5	32-33-2-5
32-8-12-1	32-29-2-1	32-8-22-6	32-33-2-6
32-8-12-2	32-29-2-2	32-8-22-7	32-33-2-7
32-8-13-1	32-29-3-1	32-8-22-8	32-33-2-8
32-8-14-1	32-29-4-1	32-8-23-1	32-33-3-1
32-8-15-1	32-29-5-1	32-8-23-2	32-33-3-2
32-8-15.5-1	32-29-6-1	32-8-23-3	32-33-3-3
32-8-15.5-2	32-29-6-2	32-8-23-4	32-33-3-4
32-8-15.5-3	32-29-6-3	32-8-23-5	32-33-3-5

Prior Provision	Current Provision	Prior Provision	Current Provision
32-8-24-1	32-28-12-1	32-8-35-3	32-33-14-3
32-8-24-2	32-28-12-2	32-8-36-1	32-33-15-1
32-8-24-2.3	32-28-12-3	32-8-36-2	32-33-15-2
32-8-24-3	32-28-12-4	32-8-36-3	32-33-15-3
32-8-24-4	32-28-12-5	32-8-36-4	32-33-15-4
32-8-24-5	32-28-12-6	32-8-37-1 part	32-33-16-1
32-8-24-6	32-28-12-7	32-8-37-1 part	32-33-16-2
32-8-25-1 part	32-28-11-1	32-8-37-2	32-33-16-3
32-8-25-1 part	32-28-11-2	32-8-37-3	32-33-16-4
32-8-26-1	32-33-4-1	32-8-37-4	32-33-16-5
32-8-26-2	32-33-4-2	32-8-37-5	32-33-16-6
32-8-26-3	32-33-4-3	32-8-37-6	32-33-16-7
32-8-26-4	32-33-4-4	32-8-37-7	32-33-16-8
32-8-26-5	32-33-4-5	32-8-37-8	32-33-16-9
32-8-26-6	32-33-4-6	32-8-38-1 part	32-33-5-1
32-8-26-7	32-33-4-7	32-8-38-1 part	32-33-5-2
32-8-26-8	32-33-4-8	32-8-38-2	32-33-5-3
32-8-27-2	32-33-6-1	32-8-38-3	32-33-5-4
32-8-28-1	32-33-7-2	32-8-38-4	32-33-5-5
32-8-28-2	32-33-7-3	32-8-38-5	32-33-5-6
32-8-28-3	32-33-7-4	32-8-38-6	32-33-5-7
32-8-28-4	32-33-7-5	32-8-38-7	32-33-5-8
32-8-28-5	32-33-7-6	32-8-39-1	32-28-13-1
32-8-28-6	32-33-7-1ʻ	32-8-39-2	32-28-13-2
32-8-29-1	32-33-8-1	32-8-39-2.2	32-28-13-3
32-8-30-1	32-33-9-1	32-8-39-2.7	32-28-13-4
32-8-30-2	32-33-9-2	32-8-39-3	32-28-13-5
32-8-30-3	32-33-9-3	32-8-39-4	32-28-13-6
32-8-30-4	32-33-9-4	32-8-39-5	32-28-13-7
32-8-30-5	32-33-9-5	32-8-39-5.5	32-28-13-8
32-8-30-6	32-33-9-6	32-8-39-6	32-28-13-9
32-8-30-8	32-33-9-7	32-8-40-1	32-34-10-1
32-8-30-9	32-33-9-8	32-8-40-2	32-34-10-2
32-8-31-1	32-33-10-5	32-8-40-3	32-34-10-3
32-8-31-2(a)	32-33-10-4	32-8-40-4	32-34-10-4
32-8-31-2(b)	32-33-10-3	32-8-40-5	32-34-10-5
32-8-31-2(c)	32-33-10-1	32-8-40-6	32-34-10-6
32-8-31-2(d)	32-33-10-2	32-8-40-7	32-34-10-7
32-8-31-3	32-33-10-6	32-8-40-8	32-34-10-8
32-8-31-4	32-33-10-7	32-9-1.5-1	32-34-1-1
32-8-31-5	32-33-10-8	32-9-1.5-2	32-34-1-2
32-8-31-6	32-33-10-9	32-9-1.5-3	32-34-1-52
32-8-31-7	32-33-10-10	32-9-1.5-4	32-34-1-3
32-8-32-1	32-33-11-1	32-9-1.5-5	32-34-1-4
32-8-32-2	32-33-11-2	32-9-1.5-6	32-34-1-5
32-8-32-3	32-33-11-3	32-9-1.5-7	32-34-1-6
32-8-32-4	32-33-11-4	32-9-1.5-7.5	32-34-1-7
32-8-32-5	32-33-11-5	32-9-1.5-8	32-34-1-8
32-8-32-7	32-33-11-6	32-9-1.5-9	32-34-1-9
32-8-32-6	32-33-11-7	32-9-1.5-10	32-34-1-10
32-8-33-1	32-33-12-1	32-9-1.5-11	32-34-1-11
32-8-33-2	32-33-12-2	32-9-1.5-12	32-34-1-12
32-8-34-1 part	32-33-13-1	32-9-1.5-13	32-34-1-13
32-8-34-1 part	32-33-13-2	32-9-1.5-14	32-34-1-14
32-8-34-1 part	32-33-13-3	32-9-1.5-15	32-34-1-15
32-8-35-1	32-33-14-1	32-9-1.5-16	32-34-1-16
32-8-35-2	32-33-14-2	32-9-1.5-17	32-34-1-17

Prior Provision	Current Provision	Prior Provision	Current Provision
32-9-1.5-18	32-34-1-18	32-9-3-21	32-34-8-21
32-9-1.5-19	32-34-1-19	32-9-3-22	32-34-8-22
32-9-1.5-20	32-34-1-20	32-9-3-23	32-34-8-23
32-9-1.5-21	32-34-1-21	32-9-3-24	32-34-8-24
32-9-1.5-22	32-34-1-22	32-9-3-25	32-34-8-25
32-9-1.5-23	32-34-1-23	32-9-3-26	32-34-8-26
32-9-1.5-24	32-34-1-24	32-9-3-27	32-34-8-27
32-9-1.5-25	32-34-1-25	32-9-3-28	32-34-8-28
32-9-1.5-26	32-34-1-26	32-9-3-29	32-34-8-23
32-9-1.5-27	32-34-1-27	32-9-4-1	32-34-8-29
32-9-1.5-28	32-34-1-28	32-9-5-1	32-34-9-2
32-9-1.5-29	32-34-1-29	32-9-5-2	32-34-9-3
32-9-1.5-30	32-34-1-30	32-9-5-3	32-34-9-4
32-9-1.5-31	32-34-1-31	32-9-5-4	32-34-9-5
32-9-1.5-32	32-34-1-32	32-9-5-5	32-34-9-6
32-9-1.5-33	32-34-1-33	32-9-5-6	32-34-9-1
32-9-1.5-34	32-34-1-34	32-9-5-7	32-34-9-7
32-9-1.5-35	32-34-1-35	32-9-5-8	32-34-9-8
32-9-1.5-36	32-34-1-36	32-9-5-9	32-34-9-9
32-9-1.5-37	32-34-1-37	32-9-5-13	32-34-9-10
32-9-1.5-38.1	32-34-1-38	32-9-5-14	32-34-9-11
32-9-1.5-40	32-34-1-39	32-9-5-15	32-34-9-12
32-9-1.5-41	32-34-1-40	32-9-5-16	32-34-9-13
32-9-1.5-42	32-34-1-41	32-9-6-1(1)	32-34-6-2
32-9-1.5-43	32-34-1-42	32-9-6-1(2)	32-34-6-3
32-9-1.5-44	32-34-1-43	32-9-6-2	32-34-6-5
32-9-1.5-45	32-34-1-51	32-9-6-3	32-34-6-6
32-9-1.5-46	32-34-1-44	32-9-6-4	32-34-6-6
32-9-1.5-47	32-34-1-45	32-9-6-5	32-34-6-1
32-9-1.5-48	32-34-1-46	32-9-6-6	32-34-6-4
32-9-1.5-49	32-34-1-47	32-9-6-7	32-34-6-7
32-9-1.5-50	32-34-1-48	32-9-7-1 part	32-34-7-2
32-9-1.5-51	Deleted	32-9-7-1 part	32-34-7-3
32-9-1.5-52	32-34-1-49	32-9-7-1 part	32-34-7-4
32-9-1.5-54	32-34-1-50	32-9-7-2	32-34-7-5
32-9-2-1	32-34-2-1	32-9-7-3	32-34-7-6
32-9-2-2	32-34-2-2	32-9-7-4	32-34-7-6
32-9-3-1	32-34-8-1	32-9-7-5	32-34-7-1
32-9-3-2	32-34-8-2	32-9-7-6	32-34-7-7
32-9-3-3	32-34-8-3	32-9-7-7	32-34-7-8
32-9-3-4	32-34-8-4	32-9-8-1	32-34-3-1
32-9-3-5	32-34-8-5	32-9-8-2	32-34-3-2
32-9-3-6	32-34-8-6	32-9-8-3	32-34-3-3
32-9-3-7	32-34-8-7	32-9-8-4	32-34-3-4
32-9-3-8	32-34-8-8	32-9-8-5	32-34-3-5
32-9-3-9	32-34-8-9	32-9-9-1	32-34-4-1
32-9-3-10	32-34-8-10	32-9-9-2	32-34-4-2
32-9-3-11	32-34-8-11	32-9-9-3	32-34-4-3
32-9-3-12	32-34-8-12	32-9-9-4	32-34-4-4
32-9-3-13	32-34-8-13	32-9-9-5	32-34-4-5
32-9-3-14	32-34-8-14	32-9-9-6	32-34-4-6
32-9-3-15	32-34-8-15	32-9-10-1	32-34-5-1
32-9-3-16	32-34-8-16	32-9-10-2	32-34-5-2
32-9-3-17	32-34-8-17	32-9-10-3	32-34-5-3
32-9-3-18	32-34-8-18	32-9-10-4	32-34-5-4
32-9-3-19	32-34-8-19	32-9-10-5	32-34-5-5
32-9-3-20	32-34-8-20	32-9-10-6	32-34-5-6

Prior Provision	Current Provision	Prior Provision	Current Provision
32-9-10-7	32-34-5-7	32-10-4-1	32-26-4-1
32-9-10-8	32-34-5-8	32-10-4-2	32-26-4-2
32-9-10-9	32-34-5-9	32-10-4-3	32-26-4-3
32-9-10-10	32-34-5-10	32-10-5-1	32-26-5-1
32-9-10-11	32-34-5-11	32-10-5-2	32-26-5-2
32-9-10-12	32-34-5-12	32-10-5-3	32-26-5-3
32-9-10-13	32-34-5-13	32-10-6-1	32-26-6-1
32-9-10-14	32-34-5-14	32-10-6-2	32-26-6-2
32-9-10-15	32-34-5-15	32-10-6-3	32-26-6-3
32-9-10-16	32-34-5-16	32-10-6-4	32-26-6-4
32-10-1-1	32-26-1-1	32-10-6-5	32-26-6-5
32-10-1-2	32-26-1-2	32-10-7-1	32-26-7-1
32-10-1-3	32-26-1-3	32-10-7-2	32-26-7-2
32-10-1-4	32-26-1-4	32-10-7-3	32-26-7-3
32-10-1-5	32-26-1-5	32-10-8-1	32-26-8-1
32-10-1-6	32-26-1-6	32-10-8-2	32-26-8-2
32-10-1-7	32-26-1-7	32-10-8-3	32-26-8-3
32-10-1-8	32-26-1-8	32-10-8-4	32-26-8-4
32-10-1-9	32-26-1-9	32-10-9-1	32-26-9-1
32-10-1-10	32-26-1-10	32-10-9-2	32-26-9-2
32-10-1-11	32-26-1-11	32-10-9-3	32-26-9-3
32-10-1-12	32-26-1-12	32-10-9-4	32-26-9-4
32-10-1-13	32-26-1-13	32-10-9-5	32-26-9-5
32-10-1-14	32-26-1-14	32-10-9-6	32-26-9-6
32-10-1-15	32-26-1-15	32-10-10-1	32-26-10-1
32-10-1-16	32-26-1-16	32-10-10-2	32-26-10-2
32-10-1-17	32-26-1-17	32-11-1-1	32-24-1-3
32-10-1-18	32-26-1-18	32-11-1-2	32-24-1-4
32-10-1-19	32-26-1-19	32-11-1-2.1 part	32-24-1-1
32-10-1-20	32-26-1-20	32-11-1-2.1 part	32-24-1-2
32-10-1-21	32-26-1-21	32-11-1-2.1 part	32-24-1-5
32-10-1-22	32-26-1-22	32-11-1-3	32-24-1-6
32-10-1-23	32-26-1-23	32-11-1-4	32-24-1-7
32-10-1-24	32-26-1-24	32-11-1-5	32-24-1-8
32-10-1-25	32-26-1-25	32-11-1-6	32-24-1-9
32-10-2-1	32-26-2-1	32-11-1-7	32-24-1-10
32-10-2-2	32-26-2-2	32-11-1-8	32-24-1-11
32-10-2-3	32-26-2-3	32-11-1-8.1	32-24-1-12
32-10-2-4	32-26-2-4	32-11-1-9	32-24-1-13
32-10-2-5	32-26-2-5	32-11-1-10	32-24-1-14
32-10-2-6	32-26-2-6	32-11-1-11	32-24-1-15
32-10-2-7	32-26-2-7	32-11-1-12	32-24-1-16
32-10-2-8	32-26-2-8	32-11-1-13	32-24-1-17
32-10-2-9	32-26-2-9	32-11-1.5-1(a)	32-24-2-1
32-10-2-10	32-26-2-10	32-11-1.5-1(b)	32-24-2-2
32-10-2-11	32-26-2-11	32-11-1.5-1(c)	32-24-2-4
32-10-2-12	32-26-2-12	32-11-1.5-2	32-24-2-5
32-10-2-13	32-26-2-13	32-11-1.5-3	32-24-2-6
32-10-2-14	32-26-2-14	32-11-1.5-4	32-24-2-7
32-10-2-15	32-26-2-15	32-11-1.5-5	32-24-2-8
32-10-2-16	32-26-2-16	32-11-1.5-6	32-24-2-9
32-10-2-17	32-26-2-17	32-11-1.5-7	32-24-2-10
32-10-2-18	32-26-2-18	32-11-1.5-8	32-24-2-11
32-10-2-19	32-26-2-19	32-11-1.5-9	32-24-2-12
32-10-2-20	32-26-2-20	32-11-1.5-10	32-24-2-13
32-10-3-1	32-26-3-1	32-11-1.5-11	32-24-2-14
32-10-3-2	32-26-3-2	32-11-1.5-12	32-24-2-15

Prior Provision	Current Provision	Prior Provision	Current Provision
32-11-1.5-13	32-24-2-16	32-13-1-15	32-36-1-15
32-11-2-1	32-24-3-1	32-13-1-16	32-36-1-16
32-11-2-2	32-24-3-2	32-13-1-17	32-36-1-17
32-11-2-3	32-24-3-3	32-13-1-18	32-36-1-18
32-11-2-4	32-24-3-4	32-13-1-19	32-36-1-19
32-11-2-5	32-24-3-5	32-13-1-20	32-36-1-20
32-11-2-6	32-24-3-6	32-14-1-1	32-37-1-1
32-11-3-1	32-24-4-1	32-14-2-1	32-37-2-1
32-11-3-2	32-24-4-2	32-14-2-2	32-37-2-2
32-11-3-3	32-24-4-3	32-14-2-3	32-37-2-3
32-11-3-4	32-24-4-4	32-14-2-4	32-37-2-4
32-11-4-1	32-24-5-1	32-14-2-5	32-37-2-5
32-11-4-2	32-24-5-2	32-14-3-1	32-37-3-1
32-11-4-3	32-24-5-3	32-14-3-2	32-37-3-2
32-11-4-4	32-24-5-4	32-14-4-1	32-37-4-1
32-11-4-5	32-24-5-5	32-14-5-1	32-37-5-1
32-11-6-1	32-24-6-1	32-15-1-1 part	32-30-1-1
32-11-6-1.5	32-24-6-2	32-15-1-1 part	32-30-1-2
32-11-6-2	Deleted	32-15-1-1 part	32-30-1-3
32-12-1-1	32-18-1-1	32-15-1-1 part	32-30-1-4
32-12-1-2	32-18-1-2	32-15-1-2	32-30-1-5
32-12-1-3	32-18-1-3	32-15-1-3	32-30-1-6
32-12-1-4	32-18-1-4	32-15-1-4	32-30-1-7
32-12-1-5	32-18-1-5	32-15-2-1	32-30-2-1
32-12-1-6	32-18-1-6	32-15-2-2	32-30-2-2
32-12-1-7	32-18-1-7	32-15-2-3	32-30-2-3
32-12-1-8	32-18-1-8	32-15-2-4	32-30-2-4
32-12-1-9	32-18-1-9	32-15-2-5	32-30-2-5
32-12-1-10	32-18-1-10	32-15-2-6	32-30-2-6
32-12-1-11	32-18-1-11	32-15-2-7	32-30-2-7
32-12-1-12	32-18-1-12	32-15-2-8	32-30-2-8
32-12-1-13	32-18-1-13	32-15-2-9	32-30-2-9
32-12-1-14	32-18-1-14	32-15-2-10	32-30-2-10
32-12-1-15	32-18-1-15	32-15-2-11	32-30-2-11
32-12-1-16	32-18-1-16	32-15-2-12	32-30-2-12
32-12-1-17	32-18-1-17	32-15-2-13	32-30-2-13
32-12-1-18	32-18-1-18	32-15-2-14	32-30-2-14
32-12-1-19	32-18-1-19	32-15-2-15	32-30-2-15
32-12-1-20	32-18-1-20	32-15-2-16	32-30-2-16
32-12-1-21	32-18-1-21	32-15-2-17	32-30-2-17
32-12-2-1	32-18-1-22	32-15-2-18	32-30-2-18
32-12-3-1 part	32-18-3-1	32-15-2-19	32-30-2-19
32-12-3-1 part	32-18-3-2	32-15-2-20	32-30-2-20
32-13-1-1	32-36-1-1	32-15-2-21	32-30-2-21
32-13-1-2	32-36-1-2	32-15-2-22	32-30-2-22
32-13-1-3	32-36-1-3	32-15-2-23	32-30-2-23
32-13-1-4	32-36-1-4	32-15-3-1	32-30-3.1-1
32-13-1-5	32-36-1-5	32-15-3-2	32-30-3.1-2
32-13-1-6	32-36-1-6	32-15-3-3	32-30-3.1-3
32-13-1-7	32-36-1-7	32-15-3-4	32-30-3.1-4
32-13-1-8	32-36-1-8	32-15-3-5	32-30-3.1-5
32-13-1-9	32-36-1-9	32-15-3-6	32-30-3.1-6
32-13-1-10	32-36-1-10	32-15-3-7	32-30-3.1-7
32-13-1-11	32-36-1-11	32-15-3-8	32-30-3.1-8
32-13-1-12	32-36-1-12	32-15-3-9	32-30-3.1-9
32-13-1-13	32-36-1-13	32-15-3-10	32-30-3.1-10
32-13-1-14	32-36-1-14	32-15-3-11	32-30-3.1-11

Prior Provision	Current Provision	Prior Provision	Current Provision
32-15-3-12	32-30-3.1-12	34-19-2-6	32-30-7-11
32-15-4-1	32-30-4-1	34-19-2-7	32-30-7-12
32-15-4-2	32-30-4-2	34-19-2-8	32-30-7-13
32-15-5-1	32-30-9-1	34-19-2-9	32-30-7-14
32-15-6-1	32-30-10-3	34-19-2-10	32-30-7-15
32-15-6-2	32-30-10-4	34-19-2-11	32-30-7-16
32-15-6-3	32-30-10-5	34-19-2-12	32-30-7-17
32-15-6-4	32-30-10-6	34-19-2-13	32-30-7-18
32-15-6-5	32-30-10-7	34-19-2-14	32-30-7-19
32-15-6-6	32-30-10-8	34-19-2-15	32-30-7-20
32-15-6-6.5 part	32-30-10-1	34-19-2-16	32-30-7-21
32-15-6-6.5 part	32-30-10-2	34-19-2-17	32-30-7-22
32-15-6-6.5 part	32-30-10-9	34-19-2-18	32-30-7-23
32-15-6-7	32-30-10-10	34-19-2-19	32-30-7-24
32-15-6-8	32-30-10-11	34-19-2-20	32-30-7-25
32-15-6-9	32-30-10-12	34-19-3-1	32-30-8-1
32-15-6-10	32-30-10-12	34-19-3-2	32-30-8-2
32-15-6-11	32-30-10-13	34-19-3-3	32-30-8-3
32-15-6-12	32-30-10-14	34-19-3-4	32-30-8-4
32-15-7-1	32-27-2-1	34-19-3-5	32-30-8-5
32-15-7-2	32-27-2-2	34-19-3-6	32-30-8-6
32-15-7-3	32-27-2-3	34-19-3-7	32-30-8-7
32-15-7-4	32-27-2-4	34-19-3-8	32-30-8-8
32-15-7-5	32-27-2-5	34-19-3-9	32-30-8-9
32-15-7-6	32-27-2-6	34-19-3-10	32-30-8-10
32-15-7-7	32-27-2-7	34-19-3-11	32-30-8-11
32-15-7-8	32-27-2-8	34-19-3-12	32-30-8-12
32-15-7-9	32-27-2-9	34-19-3-13	32-30-8-13
32-15-7-10	32-27-2-10	34-19-3-14	32-30-8-14
32-15-7-11	32-27-2-11	34-19-3-15	32-30-8-15
32-15-8-1	32-30-12-1	34-21-1-1	32-35-2-1
32-15-8-2	32-30-12-2	34-21-2-1	32-35-2-2
32-15-9-1 part	32-30-13-1	34-21-2-2	32-35-2-3
32-15-9-1 part	32-30-13-2	34-21-2-3	32-35-2-4
32-15-9-1 part	32-30-13-3	34-21-3-1	32-35-2-5
32-15-9-1 part	32-30-13-4	34-21-3-2	32-35-2-6
32-15-10-1	32-30-14-1	34-21-3-3	32-35-2-7
34-6-2-7	32-30-6-1	34-21-4-1	32-35-2-8
34-6-2-66	32-30-7-1	34-21-4-2	32-35-2-9
34-6-2-68	32-30-6-2	34-21-4-3	32-35-2-10
34-6-2-74	32-30-6-3	34-21-4-4	32-35-2-11
34-6-2-103	32-30-7-2	34-21-4-5	32-35-2-12
34-6-2-107	32-30-7-3	34-21-4-6	32-35-2-13
34-6-2-121	32-30-7-4	34-21-4-7	32-35-2-14
34-6-2-125	32-30-7-5	34-21-4-8	32-35-2-15
34-6-2-126	32-30-6-4	34-21-4-9	32-35-2-16
34-6-2-149	32-30-6-5	34-21-4-10	32-35-2-17
34-19-1-1	32-30-6-6	34-21-4-11	32-35-2-18
34-19-1-2	32-30-6-7	34-21-4-12	32-35-2-19
34-19-1-3	32-30-6-8	34-21-4-13	32-35-2-20
34-19-1-4	32-30-6-9	34-21-5-1	32-35-2-21
34-19-1-5	32-30-6-10	34-21-5-2	32-35-2-22
34-19-2-1	32-30-7-6	34-21-5-3	32-35-2-23
34-19-2-2	32-30-7-7	34-21-5-4	32-35-2-24
34-19-2-3	32-30-7-8	34-21-5-5	32-35-2-25
34-19-2-4	32-30-7-9	34-21-6-1	32-35-2-26
34-19-2-5	32-30-7-10	34-21-7-1	32-35-2-27

Prior Provision	Current Provision	Prior Provision	Current Provision
34-21-7-2	32-35-2-28	34-48-1-4	32-30-5-4
34-21-8-1	32-35-2-29	34-48-1-5	32-30-5-5
34-21-8-2	32-35-2-30	34-48-1-6	32-30-5-6
34-21-8-3	32-35-2-31	34-48-1-7	32-30-5-7
34-21-8-4	32-35-2-32	34-48-1-8	32-30-5-8
34-21-9-1	32-35-2-33	34-48-1-9	32-30-5-9
34-21-9-2	32-35-2-34	34-48-1-10	32-30-5-10
34-21-10-1	32-35-2-35	34-48-2-1	32-30-5-11
34-34-1-1	32-30-11-1	34-48-3-1	32-30-5-12
34-34-1-2	32-30-11-2	34-48-3-2	32-30-5-13
34-34-1-3	32-30-11-3	34-48-4-1	32-30-5-14
34-34-1-4	32-30-11-4	34-48-4-2	32-30-5-15
34-34-1-5	32-30-11-5	34-48-4-3	32-30-5-16
34-34-1-6	32-30-11-6	34-48-4-4	32-30-5-17
34-34-1-7	32-30-11-7	34-48-4-5	32-30-5-18
34-34-1-8	32-30-11-8	34-48-4-6	32-30-5-19
34-34-1-9	32-30-11-9	34-48-5-1	32-30-5-20
34-34-2-1	32-30-11-10	34-48-5-2	32-30-5-21
34-34-2-2	32-30-11-10	34-48-6-1	32-30-5-22
34-34-2-3	32-30-11-10	34-48-6-2	32-30-5-22
34-48-1-1	32-30-5-1	34-48-6-3	32-30-5-22
34-48-1-2	32-30-5-2	34-48-6-4	32-30-5-22
34-48-1-3	32-30-5-3		

TABLE OF DERIVATION

The following table lists current sections of the Indiana Code, in Title 32 as recodified by P.L.2-2002, and in Titles 26, and the corresponding prior Code number in Title 32 prior to recodifcation by P.L.2-2002, and in Titles 24 and 34. This table can be used to locate the prior law that a current provision is based upon.

Current Provision	Prior Provision	Current Provision	Prior Provision
26-2-9-1	32-2-1.5-1	32-17-4-17	32-4-5-18
26-2-9-2	32-2-1.5-2	32-17-4-18	32-4-5-19
26-2-9-3	32-2-1.5-3	32-17-4-19	32-4-5-20
26-2-9-4	32-2-1.5-4	32-17-4-20	32-4-5-21
26-2-9-5	32-2-1.5-5	32-17-4-21	32-4-5-22
32-16-1-1	NEW	32-17-4-22	32-4-5-23
32-16-1-2	NEW	32-17-4-23	32-4-6-1
32-16-1-3	NEW	32-17-4-24	32-4-7-1
32-16-1-4	NEW	32-17-5-1	32-4-8-1 part
32-16-1-5	NEW	32-17-5-2	32-4-8-1 part
32-16-1-6	NEW	32-17-5-3	32-4-8-1 part
32-16-1-7	NEW	32-17-5-4	32-4-8-1 part
32-16-1-8	NEW	32-17-5-5	32-4-8-2
32-16-1-9	NEW	32-17-5-6	32-4-8-3
32-17-1-1	32-1-2-30	32-17-6-1	32-3-1-1 part
32-17-1-2	32-1-2-12	32-17-6-2	32-3-1-1 part
32-17-1-3	32-1-2-33	32-17-6-3	32-3-1-1 part
32-17-1-4	32-1-2-10	32-17-6-4	32-3-1-1 part
32-17-2-1	32-1-2-7, 32-1-2-8	32-17-6-5	32-3-1-1 part
		32-17-6-6	32-3-1-1 part
32-17-2-2	32-1-2-9	32-17-7-1	32-3-2-1 part
32-17-2-3	32-1-2-34	32-17-7-2	32-3-2-1 part
32-17-2-4	32-1-2-35	32-17-7-3	32-3-2-1 part
32-17-2-5	32-1-2-36	32-17-7-4	32-3-2-5(a)
32-17-3-1	32-4-2-1	32-17-7-5	32-3-2-1 part
32-17-3-2	32-4-2-2	32-17-7-6	32-3-2-1 part
32-17-3-3	32-4-3-1	32-17-7-7	32-3-2-2
32-17-3-4	32-1-2-6	32-17-7-8	32-3-2-3
32-17-4-1	32-4-5-1	32-17-7-9	32-3-2-4
32-17-4-2	32-4-5-2	32-17-7-10	32-3-2-5(b), 32-3-2-5(c)
32-17-4-3	32-4-5-3		
32-17-4-4	32-4-5-4	32-17-7-11	32-3-2-6
32-17-4-5	32-4-5-5	32-17-7-12	32-3-2-7
32-17-4-6	32-4-5-6	32-17-7-13	32-3-2-8
32-17-4-7	32-4-5-7	32-17-7-14	32-3-2-9
32-17-4-8	32-4-5-8	32-17-7-15	32-3-2-10
32-17-4-9	32-4-5-10	32-17-7-16	32-3-2-11
32-17-4-10	32-4-5-11	32-17-7-17	32-3-2-12
32-17-4-11	32-4-5-12	32-17-7-18	32-3-2-13
32-17-4-12	32-4-5-13	32-17-7-19	32-3-2-14
32-17-4-13	32-4-5-14	32-17-7-20	32-3-2-15
32-17-4-14	32-4-5-15	32-17-8-1	32-1-4.5-1
32-17-4-15	32-4-5-16	32-17-8-2	32-1-4.5-2
32-17-4-16	32-4-5-17	32-17-8-3	32-1-4.5-3

Current Provision	Prior Provision	Current Provision	Prior Provision
32-17-8-4	32-1-4.5-4	32-18-1-7	32-12-1-7
32-17-8-5	32-1-4.5-5	32-18-1-8	32-12-1-8
32-17-8-6	32-1-4.5-6	32-18-1-9	32-12-1-9
32-17-9-1	32-4-1.6-15	32-18-1-10	32-12-1-10
32-17-9-2	32-4-1.6-1	32-18-1-11	32-12-1-11
32-17-9-3	32-4-1.6-2	32-18-1-12	32-12-1-12
32-17-9-4	32-4-1.6-3	32-18-1-13	32-12-1-13
32-17-9-5	32-4-1.6-4	32-18-1-14	32-12-1-14
32-17-9-6	32-4-1.6-5	32-18-1-15	32-12-1-15
32-17-9-7	32-4-1.6-6	32-18-1-16	32-12-1-16
32-17-9-8	32-4-1.6-7	32-18-1-17	32-12-1-17
32-17-9-9	32-4-1.6-8	32-18-1-18	32-12-1-18
32-17-9-10	32-4-1.6-9	32-18-1-19	32-12-1-19
32-17-9-11	32-4-1.6-10	32-18-1-20	32-12-1-20
32-17-9-12	32-4-1.6-11	32-18-1-21	32-12-1-21
32-17-9-13	32-4-1.6-12	32-18-1-22	32-12-2-1
32-17-9-14	32-4-1.6-13	32-18-2-1	32-2-7-1
32-17-9-15	32-4-1.6-14	32-18-2-2	32-2-7-2
32-17-10-1	32-1-21-1	32-18-2-3	32-2-7-3
32-17-10-2	32-1-21-2	32-18-2-4	32-2-7-4
32-17-10-3	32-1-21-3	32-18-2-5	32-2-7-5
32-17-11-1	32-4-1.5-1(1)	32-18-2-6	32-2-7-6
32-17-11-2	32-4-1.5-1(2)	32-18-2-7	32-2-7-7
32-17-11-3	32-4-1.5-1(3)	32-18-2-8	32-2-7-8
32-17-11-4	32-4-1.5-1(4)	32-18-2-9	32-2-7-9
32-17-11-5	32-4-1.5-1(5)	32-18-2-10	32-2-7-10
32-17-11-6	32-4-1.5-1(6)	32-18-2-11	32-2-7-11
32-17-11-7	32-4-1.5-1(7)	32-18-2-12	32-2-7-12
32-17-11-8	32-4-1.5-1(8)	32-18-2-13	32-2-7-13
32-17-11-9	32-4-1.5-1(9)	32-18-2-14	32-2-7-14
32-17-11-10	32-4-1.5-1(10)	32-18-2-15	32-2-7-15
32-17-11-11	32-4-1.5-1(11)	32-18-2-16	32-2-7-16
32-17-11-12	32-4-1.5-1(12)	32-18-2-17	32-2-7-17
32-17-11-13	32-4-1.5-1(13)	32-18-2-18	32-2-7-18
32-17-11-14	32-4-1.5-1(14)	32-18-2-19	32-2-7-19
32-17-11-15	32-4-1.5-1(15)	32-18-2-20	32-2-7-20
32-17-11-16	32-4-1.5-2	32-18-2-21	32-2-7-21
32-17-11-17	32-4-1.5-3	32-18-3-1	32-12-3-1 part
32-17-11-18	32-4-1.5-4	32-18-3-2	32-12-3-1 part
32-17-11-19	32-4-1.5-5	32-19-1-1	32-1-1-1(a)
32-17-11-20	32-4-1.5-6	32-19-1-2	32-1-1-1(b),
32-17-11-21	32-4-1.5-7		32-1-1-1(c),
32-17-11-22	32-4-1.5-8		32-1-1-1(d)
32-17-11-23	32-4-1.5-9	32-19-1-3	32-1-1-5
32-17-11-24	32-4-1.5-10	32-19-1-4	32-1-1-2
32-17-11-25	32-4-1.5-11	32-19-1-5	32-1-1-4
32-17-11-26	32-4-1.5-12	32-19-1-6	32-1-1-7
32-17-11-27	32-4-1.5-13	32-19-2-1	32-1-1-3
32-17-11-28	32-4-1.5-14	32-19-2-2	32-1-1-6
32-17-11-29	32-4-1.5-15	32-19-3-1	32-1-1-8
32-17-12-1	32-1-11-1	32-19-3-2	32-1-1-9
32-18-1-1	32-12-1-1	32-19-4-1	32-1-1-10(a),
32-18-1-2	32-12-1-2		32-1-1-10(b)
32-18-1-3	32-12-1-3	32-19-4-2	32-1-1-10(c)
32-18-1-4	32-12-1-4	32-19-4-3	32-1-1-10(d),
32-18-1-5	32-12-1-5		32-1-1-10(e)
32-18-1-6	32-12-1-6	32-19-4-4	32-1-1-10(f)

Current Provision	Prior Provision	Current Provision	Prior Provision
32-20-1-1	32-1-5-10	32-21-5-5	24-4.6-2-5
32-20-1-2	32-1-5-7	32-21-5-6	24-4.6-2-6
32-20-2-1	NEW	32-21-5-7	24-4.6-2-7
32-20-2-2	32-1-5-8(a)	32-21-5-8	24-4.6-2-8
32-20-2-3	32-1-5-8(b)	32-21-5-9	24-4.6-2-9
32-20-2-4	32-1-5-8(d)	32-21-5-10	24-4.6-2-10
32-20-2-5	32-1-5-8(c)	32-21-5-11	24-4.6-2-11
32-20-2-6	32-1-5-8(e)	32-21-5-12	24-4.6-2-12
32-20-2-7	32-1-5-8(f)	32-21-5-13	24-4.6-2-13
32-20-3-1	32-1-5-1	32-21-6-1	24-4.6-2.1-1
32-20-3-2	32-1-5-2	32-21-6-2	24-4.6-2.1-1.5
32-20-3-3	32-1-5-3	32-21-6-3	24-4.6-2.1-2
32-20-4-1	32-1-5-4	32-21-6-4	24-4.6-2.1-3
32-20-4-2	32-1-5-5	32-21-6-5	24-4.6-2.1-4
32-20-4-3	32-1-5-6	32-21-6-6	24-4.6-2.1-5
32-20-5-1	32-1-5-9 part	32-21-7-1	32-1-20-1
32-20-5-2	32-1-5-9 part	32-21-7-2	32-1-20-2
32-21-1-1	32-2-1-1	32-21-8-1	32-2-8-1
32-21-1-2	32-2-1-2	32-21-8-2	32-2-8-2
32-21-1-3	32-2-1-3	32-21-8-3	32-2-8-3
32-21-1-4	32-2-1-4	32-21-8-4	32-2-8-4
32-21-1-5	32-2-1-5	32-21-8-5	32-2-8-5
32-21-1-6	32-2-1-6	32-21-8-6	32-2-8-6
32-21-1-7	32-2-1-11	32-21-9-1	32-2-3-1
32-21-1-8	32-2-1-12	32-21-9-2	32-2-3-2
32-21-1-9	32-2-1-13	32-21-9-3	32-2-3-3
32-21-1-10	32-2-2-1	32-21-9-4	32-2-3-4
32-21-1-11	32-2-4-1	32-21-10-1	32-1-9-3
32-21-1-12	32-2-5-1	32-21-10-2	32-1-9-1
32-21-1-13	32-1-2-4	32-21-10-3	32-1-9-2
32-21-1-14	32-1-2-5	32-21-11-1	NEW
32-21-1-15	32-1-2-13	32-22-1-1	32-1-2-2
32-21-1-16	32-1-2-14	32-22-1-2	32-1-12-2, 32-1-12-3
32-21-2-1	NEW		
32-21-2-2	32-1-2-37(a)	32-22-1-3	32-1-13-1
32-21-2-3	32-1-2-18	32-22-1-4	32-1-13-2
32-21-2-4	32-1-2-19	32-22-1-5	32-1-17-1
32-21-2-5	32-1-2-20	32-22-2-1	32-1-2-3
32-21-2-6	32-1-2-21	32-22-2-2	32-1-7-1
32-21-2-7	32-1-2-23	32-22-2-3	32-1-7-2
32-21-2-8	32-1-2-24	32-22-2-4	32-1-7-3
32-21-2-9	32-1-2-26	32-22-2-5	32-1-8-1
32-21-2-10	32-1-2-27	32-22-2-6	32-1-8-2
32-21-2-11	32-1-2-28	32-22-2-7	32-1-8-3
32-21-2-12	32-1-2-29	32-23-1-1	32-5-1-1
32-21-2-13	32-1-2-37(b)	32-23-1-2	32-5-1-2
32-21-3-1	32-1-2-31	32-23-1-3	32-5-1-3
32-21-3-2	NEW	32-23-1-4	32-5-1-4
32-21-3-3	32-1-2-11	32-23-2-1	32-5-2-1(a)
32-21-3-4	32-1-2-32	32-23-2-2	32-5-2-1(b)
32-21-4-1	32-1-2-16	32-23-2-3	32-5-2-1(c)
32-21-4-2	32-1-2-16.3	32-23-2-4	32-5-2-1(d)
32-21-4-3	32-1-2-17	32-23-2-5	32-5-2-2
32-21-5-1	24-4.6-2-1	32-23-3-1	32-5-3-1
32-21-5-2	24-4.6-2-2	32-23-4-1	32-5-2.5-1 part
32-21-5-3	24-4.6-2-3	32-23-4-2	32-5-2.5-1 part
32-21-5-4	24-4.6-2-4	32-23-4-3	32-5-2.5-1 part

Current Provision	Prior Provision	Current Provision	Prior Provision
32-23-4-4	32-5-2.5-2	32-24-1-6	32-11-1-3
32-23-4-5	32-5-2.5-3	32-24-1-7	32-11-1-4
32-23-5-1	32-5-2.6-5,	32-24-1-8	32-11-1-5
	32-5-2.6-6	32-24-1-9	32-11-1-6
32-23-5-2	32-5-2.6-1 part	32-24-1-10	32-11-1-7
32-23-5-3	32-5-2.6-1 part	32-24-1-11	32-11-1-8
32-23-5-4	32-5-2.6-1 part	32-24-1-12	32-11-1-8.1
32-23-5-5	32-5-2.6-2	32-24-1-13	32-11-1-9
32-23-5-6	32-5-2.6-3	32-24-1-14	32-11-1-10
32-23-5-7	32-5-2.6-4	32-24-1-15	32-11-1-11
32-23-5-8	32-5-2.6-7	32-24-1-16	32-11-1-12
32-23-6-1	32-5-6-1(a)	32-24-1-17	32-11-1-13
32-23-6-2	32-5-6-1(b)	32-24-2-1	32-11-1.5-1(a)
32-23-7-1	32-5-7-1(a)	32-24-2-2	32-11-1.5-1(b)
32-23-7-2	32-5-7-1(b)	32-24-2-3	NEW
32-23-7-3	32-5-7-1(e)	32-24-2-4	32-11-1.5-1(c)
32-23-7-4	32-5-7-1(c)	32-24-2-5	32-11-1.5-2
32-23-7-5	32-5-7-1(d)	32-24-2-6	32-11-1.5-3
32-23-7-6	32-5-7-2	32-24-2-7	32-11-1.5-4
32-23-7-7	32-5-7-3	32-24-2-8	32-11-1.5-5
32-23-7-8	32-5-7-4,	32-24-2-9	32-11-1.5-6
	32-5-7-5,	32-24-2-10	32-11-1.5-7
	32-5-7-6	32-24-2-11	32-11-1.5-8
32-23-8-1	32-5-8-1 part	32-24-2-12	32-11-1.5-9
32-23-8-2	32-5-8-1 part	32-24-2-13	32-11-1.5-10
32-23-8-3	32-5-8-1 part	32-24-2-14	32-11-1.5-11
32-23-8-4	32-5-8-1 part	32-24-2-15	32-11-1.5-12
32-23-9-1	32-5-9-1 part	32-24-2-16	32-11-1.5-13
32-23-9-2	32-5-9-1 part	32-24-3-1	32-11-2-1
32-23-10-1	32-5-11-2	32-24-3-2	32-11-2-2
32-23-10-2	32-5-11-1	32-24-3-3	32-11-2-3
32-23-10-3	32-5-11-3	32-24-3-4	32-11-2-4
32-23-10-4	32-5-11-4	32-24-3-5	32-11-2-5
32-23-10-5	32-5-11-5	32-24-3-6	32-11-2-6
32-23-10-6	32-5-11-6	32-24-4-1	32-11-3-1
32-23-10-7	32-5-11-7	32-24-4-2	32-11-3-2
32-23-10-8	32-5-11-8	32-24-4-3	32-11-3-3
32-23-11-1	32-5-12-1	32-24-4-4	32-11-3-4
32-23-11-2	32-5-12-2	32-24-5-1	32-11-4-1
32-23-11-3	32-5-12-3	32-24-5-2	32-11-4-2
32-23-11-4	32-5-12-4	32-24-5-3	32-11-4-3
32-23-11-5	32-5-12-5	32-24-5-4	32-11-4-4
32-23-11-6	32-5-12-6	32-24-5-5	32-11-4-5
32-23-11-7	32-5-12-7	32-24-6-1	32-11-6-1
32-23-11-8	32-5-12-8	32-24-6-2	32-11-6-1.5
32-23-11-9	32-5-12-9	32-25-1-1	32-1-6-3
32-23-11-10	32-5-12-10	32-25-1-2	32-1-6-31
32-23-11-11	32-5-12-11	32-25-2-1	NEW
32-23-11-12	32-5-12-12	32-25-2-2	32-1-6-2(f)
32-23-11-13	32-5-12-13	32-25-2-3	32-1-6-2(g)
32-23-11-14	32-5-12-14	32-25-2-4	32-1-6-2(h)
32-23-11-15	32-5-12-15	32-25-2-5	32-1-6-2(i)
32-24-1-1	32-11-1-2.1 part	32-25-2-6	32-1-6-2(j)
32-24-1-2	32-11-1-2.1 part	32-25-2-7	32-1-6-2(a)
32-24-1-3	32-11-1-1	32-25-2-8	32-1-6-2(b)
32-24-1-4	32-11-1-2	32-25-2-9	32-1-6-2(c)
32-24-1-5	32-11-1-2.1 part	32-25-2-10	32-1-6-2(d)

Current Provision	Prior Provision	Current Provision	Prior Provision
32-25-2-11	32-1-6-2(e)	32-26-1-13	32-10-1-13
32-25-2-12	32-1-6-2(k)	32-26-1-14	32-10-1-14
32-25-2-13	32-1-6-2(l)	32-26-1-15	32-10-1-15
32-25-2-14	32-1-6-2(m)	32-26-1-16	32-10-1-16
32-25-2-15	32-1-6-2(n)	32-26-1-17	32-10-1-17
32-25-2-16	32-1-6-2(o)	32-26-1-18	32-10-1-18
32-25-2-17	32-1-6-2(p)	32-26-1-19	32-10-1-19
32-25-2-18	32-1-6-2(q)	32-26-1-20	32-10-1-20
32-25-2-19	32-1-6-2(r)	32-26-1-21	32-10-1-21
32-25-2-20	32-1-6-2(s)	32-26-1-22	32-10-1-22
32-25-3-1	32-1-6-4	32-26-1-23	32-10-1-23
32-25-4-1	32-1-6-5	32-26-1-24	32-10-1-24
32-25-4-2	32-1-6-6	32-26-1-25	32-10-1-25
32-25-4-3	32-1-6-7	32-26-2-1	32-10-2-1
32-25-4-4	32-1-6-22	32-26-2-2	32-10-2-2
32-25-5-1	32-1-6-16	32-26-2-3	32-10-2-3
32-25-5-2	32-1-6-23	32-26-2-4	32-10-2-4
32-25-6-1	32-1-6-10	32-26-2-5	32-10-2-5
32-25-6-2	32-1-6-15.4	32-26-2-6	32-10-2-6
32-25-6-3	32-1-6-24	32-26-2-7	32-10-2-7
32-25-7-1	32-1-6-12	32-26-2-8	32-10-2-8
32-25-7-2	32-1-6-12.1	32-26-2-9	32-10-2-9
32-25-7-3	32-1-6-12.2	32-26-2-10	32-10-2-10
32-25-7-4	32-1-6-13	32-26-2-11	32-10-2-11
32-25-7-5	32-1-6-14	32-26-2-12	32-10-2-12
32-25-7-6	32-1-6-15.2	32-26-2-13	32-10-2-13
32-25-8-1	32-1-6-25	32-26-2-14	32-10-2-14
32-25-8-2	32-1-6-26	32-26-2-15	32-10-2-15
32-25-8-3	32-1-6-15	32-26-2-16	32-10-2-16
32-25-8-4	32-1-6-15.6	32-26-2-17	32-10-2-17
32-25-8-5	32-1-6-9	32-26-2-18	32-10-2-18
32-25-8-6	32-1-6-11	32-26-2-19	32-10-2-19
32-25-8-7	32-1-6-17	32-26-2-20	32-10-2-20
32-25-8-8	32-1-6-27	32-26-3-1	32-10-3-1
32-25-8-9	32-1-6-18	32-26-3-2	32-10-3-2
32-25-8-10	32-1-6-19	32-26-4-1	32-10-4-1
32-25-8-11	32-1-6-20	32-26-4-2	32-10-4-2
32-25-8-12	32-1-6-21	32-26-4-3	32-10-4-3
32-25-8-13	32-1-6-15.1	32-26-5-1	32-10-5-1
32-25-8-14	32-1-6-15.3	32-26-5-2	32-10-5-2
32-25-8-15	32-1-6-15.5	32-26-5-3	32-10-5-3
32-25-8-16	32-1-6-28, 32-1-6-29	32-26-6-1	32-10-6-1
32-25-9-1	32-1-6-8	32-26-6-2	32-10-6-2
32-25-9-2	32-1-6-30	32-26-6-3	32-10-6-3
32-26-1-1	32-10-1-1	32-26-6-4	32-10-6-4
32-26-1-2	32-10-1-2	32-26-6-5	32-10-6-5
32-26-1-3	32-10-1-3	32-26-7-1	32-10-7-1
32-26-1-4	32-10-1-4	32-26-7-2	32-10-7-2
32-26-1-5	32-10-1-5	32-26-7-3	32-10-7-3
32-26-1-6	32-10-1-6	32-26-8-1	32-10-8-1
32-26-1-7	32-10-1-7	32-26-8-2	32-10-8-2
32-26-1-8	32-10-1-8	32-26-8-3	32-10-8-3
32-26-1-9	32-10-1-9	32-26-8-4	32-10-8-4
32-26-1-10	32-10-1-10	32-26-9-1	32-10-9-1
32-26-1-11	32-10-1-11	32-26-9-2	32-10-9-2
32-26-1-12	32-10-1-12	32-26-9-3	32-10-9-3
		32-26-9-4	32-10-9-4

Current Provision	Prior Provision	Current Provision	Prior Provision
32-26-9-5	32-10-9-5	32-28-6-2	32-8-6-2
32-26-9-6	32-10-9-6	32-28-7-1	32-8-7-1
32-26-10-1	32-10-10-1	32-28-7-2	32-8-7-2
32-26-10-2	32-10-10-2	32-28-7-3	32-8-7-3
32-27-1-1	24-5-11.5-1	32-28-7-4	32-8-7-4
32-27-1-2	24-5-11.5-2	32-28-8-1	32-8-8-1
32-27-1-3	24-5-11.5-3	32-28-9-1	32-8-9-1
32-27-1-4	24-5-11.5-4	32-28-10-1	32-8-10-1
32-27-1-5	24-5-11.5-5	32-28-10-2	32-8-10-2
32-27-1-6	24-5-11.5-6	32-28-11-1	32-8-25-1 part
32-27-1-7	24-5-11.5-7	32-28-11-2	32-8-25-1 part
32-27-1-8	24-5-11.5-8	32-28-12-1	32-8-24-1
32-27-1-9	24-5-11.5-9	32-28-12-2	32-8-24-2
32-27-1-10	24-5-11.5-10	32-28-12-3	32-8-24-2.3
32-27-1-11	24-5-11.5-11	32-28-12-4	32-8-24-3
32-27-1-12	24-5-11.5-12	32-28-12-5	32-8-24-4
32-27-1-13	24-5-11.5-13	32-28-12-6	32-8-24-5
32-27-1-14	24-5-11.5-14	32-28-12-7	32-8-24-6
32-27-1-15	24-5-11.5-15	32-28-13-1	32-8-39-1
32-27-2-1	32-15-7-1	32-28-13-2	32-8-39-2
32-27-2-2	32-15-7-2	32-28-13-3	32-8-39-2.2
32-27-2-3	32-15-7-3	32-28-13-4	32-8-39-2.7
32-27-2-4	32-15-7-4	32-28-13-5	32-8-39-3
32-27-2-5	32-15-7-5	32-28-13-6	32-8-39-4
32-27-2-6	32-15-7-6	32-28-13-7	32-8-39-5
32-27-2-7	32-15-7-7	32-28-13-8	32-8-39-5.5
32-27-2-8	32-15-7-8	32-28-13-9	32-8-39-6
32-27-2-9	32-15-7-9	32-29-1-1	32-8-11-1
32-27-2-10	32-15-7-10	32-29-1-2	32-8-11-2
32-27-2-11	32-15-7-11	32-29-1-3	32-8-11-3
32-28-1-1	32-8-1-1	32-29-1-4	32-8-11-4
32-28-1-2	32-8-1-2	32-29-1-5	32-1-2-15
32-28-2-1	32-8-2-1	32-29-1-6	32-8-11-5
32-28-3-1	32-8-3-1	32-29-1-7	32-8-11-6
32-28-3-2	32-8-3-2	32-29-1-8	32-8-11-7
32-28-3-3	32-8-3-3	32-29-1-9	32-8-11-8
32-28-3-4	32-8-3-4	32-29-1-10	32-8-11-9
32-28-3-5	32-8-3-5	32-29-1-11	32-8-11-10
32-28-3-6	32-8-3-6	32-29-2-1	32-8-12-1
32-28-3-7	32-8-3-7	32-29-2-2	32-8-12-2
32-28-3-8	32-8-3-8	32-29-3-1	32-8-13-1
32-28-3-9	32-8-3-9	32-29-4-1	32-8-14-1
32-28-3-10	32-8-3-10	32-29-5-1	32-8-15-1
32-28-3-11	32-8-3-11	32-29-6-1	32-8-15.5-1
32-28-3-12	32-8-3-12	32-29-6-2	32-8-15.5-2
32-28-3-13	32-8-3-13	32-29-6-3	32-8-15.5-3
32-28-3-14	32-8-3-14	32-29-6-4	32-8-15.5-4
32-28-3-15	32-8-3-15	32-29-6-5	32-8-15.5-5
32-28-3-16	32-8-3-16	32-29-6-6	32-8-15.5-6
32-28-3-17	32-8-3-17	32-29-6-7	32-8-15.5-7
32-28-3-18	32-8-3-18	32-29-6-8	32-8-15.5-8
32-28-4-1	32-8-4-1	32-29-6-9	32-8-15.5-9
32-28-4-2	32-8-4-2	32-29-6-10	32-8-15.5-10
32-28-4-3	32-8-4-3	32-29-6-11	32-8-15.5-11
32-28-5-1	32-8-5-1	32-29-6-12	32-8-15.5-12
32-28-5-2	32-8-5-2	32-29-6-13	32-8-15.5-13
32-28-6-1	32-8-6-1	32-29-6-14	32-8-15.5-14

Current Provision	Prior Provision	Current Provision	Prior Provision
32-29-6-15	32-8-15.5-15	32-30-2-23	32-15-2-23
32-29-6-16	32-8-15.5-16	32-30-3-1	32-6-1.5-1
32-29-6-17	32-8-15.5-17	32-30-3-2	32-6-1.5-2
32-29-7-1	32-8-16-1.3 part	32-30-3-3	32-6-1.5-3
32-29-7-2	32-8-16-1.3 part	32-30-3-4	32-6-1.5-4
32-29-7-3	32-8-16-1	32-30-3-5	32-6-1.5-5
32-29-7-4	32-8-16-1.3 part	32-30-3-6	32-6-1.5-6
32-29-7-5	32-8-16-1.5	32-30-3-7	32-6-1.5-7
32-29-7-6	32-8-16-2	32-30-3-8	32-6-1.5-8
32-29-7-7	32-8-16-3	32-30-3-9	32-6-1.5-9
32-29-7-8	32-8-16-4	32-30-3-10	32-6-1.5-10
32-29-7-9	32-8-16-5	32-30-3-11	32-6-1.5-11
32-29-7-10	32-8-16-6	32-30-3-12	32-6-1.5-12
32-29-7-11	32-8-16-7	32-30-3-13	32-6-3-1
32-29-7-12	32-8-16-8	32-30-3-14	32-6-4-1
32-29-7-13	32-8-16-9	32-30-3-15	32-6-4-2
32-29-7-14	32-8-16-10	32-30-3-16	32-6-5-1
32-29-8-1	32-8-17-1 part	32-30-3-17	32-6-5-2
32-29-8-2	32-8-17-1 part	32-30-3-18	32-6-6-1
32-29-8-3	32-8-17-1 part	32-30-3-19	32-6-6-2
32-29-9-1	32-8-18-1	32-30-3-20	32-6-7-1
32-29-10-1	32-8-19-1(a)	32-30-3-21	32-6-7-2
32-29-10-2	32-8-19-1(b)	32-30-3.1-1	32-15-3-1
32-29-10-3	32-8-19-1(c)	32-30-3.1-2	32-15-3-2
32-29-10-4	32-8-19-1(d)	32-30-3.1-3	32-15-3-3
32-29-10-5	32-8-19-2	32-30-3.1-4	32-15-3-4
32-29-10-6	32-8-19-3	32-30-3.1-5	32-15-3-5
32-29-11-1	NEW	32-30-3.1-6	32-15-3-6
32-30-1-1	32-15-1-1 part	32-30-3.1-7	32-15-3-7
32-30-1-2	32-15-1-1 part	32-30-3.1-8	32-15-3-8
32-30-1-3	32-15-1-1 part	32-30-3.1-9	32-15-3-9
32-30-1-4	32-15-1-1 part	32-30-3.1-10	32-15-3-10
32-30-1-5	32-15-1-2	32-30-3.1-11	32-15-3-11
32-30-1-6	32-15-1-3	32-30-3.1-12	32-15-3-12
32-30-1-7	32-15-1-4	32-30-4-1	32-15-4-1
32-30-2-1	32-15-2-1	32-30-4-2	32-15-4-2
32-30-2-2	32-15-2-2	32-30-5-1	34-48-1-1
32-30-2-3	32-15-2-3	32-30-5-2	34-48-1-2
32-30-2-4	32-15-2-4	32-30-5-3	34-48-1-3
32-30-2-5	32-15-2-5	32-30-5-4	34-48-1-4
32-30-2-6	32-15-2-6	32-30-5-5	34-48-1-5
32-30-2-7	32-15-2-7	32-30-5-6	34-48-1-6
32-30-2-8	32-15-2-8	32-30-5-7	34-48-1-7
32-30-2-9	32-15-2-9	32-30-5-8	34-48-1-8
32-30-2-10	32-15-2-10	32-30-5-9	34-48-1-9
32-30-2-11	32-15-2-11	32-30-5-10	34-48-1-10
32-30-2-12	32-15-2-12	32-30-5-11	34-48-2-1
32-30-2-13	32-15-2-13	32-30-5-12	34-48-3-1
32-30-2-14	32-15-2-14	32-30-5-13	34-48-3-2
32-30-2-15	32-15-2-15	32-30-5-14	34-48-4-1
32-30-2-16	32-15-2-16	32-30-5-15	34-48-4-2
32-30-2-17	32-15-2-17	32-30-5-16	34-48-4-3
32-30-2-18	32-15-2-18	32-30-5-17	34-48-4-4
32-30-2-19	32-15-2-19	32-30-5-18	34-48-4-5
32-30-2-20	32-15-2-20	32-30-5-19	34-48-4-6
32-30-2-21	32-15-2-21	32-30-5-20	34-48-5-1
32-30-2-22	32-15-2-22	32-30-5-21	34-48-5-2

Current Provision	Prior Provision	Current Provision	Prior Provision
32-30-5-22	34-48-6-1, 34-48-6-2, 34-48-6-3, 34-48-6-4	32-30-10-3 32-30-10-4 32-30-10-5 32-30-10-6	32-15-6-1 32-15-6-2 32-15-6-3 32-15-6-4
32-30-6-1	34-6-2-7	32-30-10-7	32-15-6-5
32-30-6-2	34-6-2-68	32-30-10-8	32-15-6-6
32-30-6-3	34-6-2-74	32-30-10-9	32-15-6-6.5 part
32-30-6-4	34-6-2-126	32-30-10-10	32-15-6-7
32-30-6-5	34-6-2-149	32-30-10-11	32-15-6-8
32-30-6-6	34-19-1-1	32-30-10-12	32-15-6-9, 32-15-6-10
32-30-6-7	34-19-1-2		
32-30-6-8	34-19-1-3	32-30-10-13	32-15-6-11
32-30-6-9	34-19-1-4	32-30-10-14	32-15-6-12
32-30-6-10	34-19-1-5	32-30-11-1	34-34-1-1
32-30-7-1	34-6-2-66	32-30-11-2 –	34-34-1-2
32-30-7-2	34-6-2-103	32-30-11-3	34-34-1-3
32-30-7-3	34-6-2-107	32-30-11-4	34-34-1-4
32-30-7-4	34-6-2-121	32-30-11-5	34-34-1-5
32-30-7-5	34-6-2-125	32-30-11-6	34-34-1-6
32-30-7-6	34-19-2-1	32-30-11-7	34-34-1-7
32-30-7-7	34-19-2-2	32-30-11-8	34-34-1-8
32-30-7-8	34-19-2-3	32-30-11-9	34-34-1-9
32-30-7-9	34-19-2-4	32-30-11-10	34-34-2-1, 34-34-2-2, 34-34-2-3
32-30-7-10	34-19-2-5		
32-30-7-11	34-19-2-6		
32-30-7-12	34-19-2-7	32-30-12-1	32-15-8-1
32-30-7-13	34-19-2-8	32-30-12-2	32-15-8-2
32-30-7-14	34-19-2-9	32-30-13-1	32-15-9-1 part
32-30-7-15	34-19-2-10	32-30-13-2	32-15-9-1 part
32-30-7-16	34-19-2-11	32-30-13-3	32-15-9-1 part
32-30-7-17	34-19-2-12	32-30-13-4	32-15-9-1 part
32-30-7-18	34-19-2-13	32-30-14-1	32-15-10-1
32-30-7-19	34-19-2-14	32-30-15-1	NEW
32-30-7-20	34-19-2-15	32-31-1-1	32-7-1-1, 32-7-1-2 part
32-30-7-21	34-19-2-16		
32-30-7-22	34-19-2-17	32-31-1-2	32-7-1-2 part
32-30-7-23	34-19-2-18	32-31-1-3	32-7-1-3 part
32-30-7-24	34-19-2-19	32-31-1-4	32-7-1-3 part
32-30-7-25	34-19-2-20	32-31-1-5	32-7-1-4
32-30-8-1	34-19-3-1	32-31-1-6	32-7-1-5
32-30-8-2	34-19-3-2	32-31-1-7	32-7-1-6
32-30-8-3	34-19-3-3	32-31-1-8	32-7-1-7
32-30-8-4	34-19-3-4	32-31-1-9	32-7-1-8
32-30-8-5	34-19-3-5	32-31-1-10	32-7-1-9
32-30-8-6	34-19-3-6	32-31-1-11	32-7-1-10
32-30-8-7	34-19-3-7	32-31-1-12	32-7-1-11
32-30-8-8	34-19-3-8	32-31-1-13	32-7-1-12
32-30-8-9	34-19-3-9	32-31-1-14	32-7-1-13
32-30-8-10	34-19-3-10	32-31-1-15	32-7-1-14
32-30-8-11	34-19-3-11	32-31-1-16	32-7-1-15
32-30-8-12	34-19-3-12	32-31-1-17	32-7-1-16
32-30-8-13	34-19-3-13	32-31-1-18	32-7-1-17
32-30-8-14	34-19-3-14	32-31-1-19	32-7-1-18
32-30-8-15	34-19-3-15	32-31-1-20	32-7-1-19
32-30-9-1	32-15-5-1	32-31-2-1	32-7-2-1 part
32-30-10-1	32-15-6-6.5 part	32-31-2-2	32-7-2-1 part
32-30-10-2	32-15-6-6.5 part	32-31-3-1	32-7-5-1

Current Provision	Prior Provision	Current Provision	Prior Provision
32-31-3-2	32-7-5-2	32-32-2-15	24-5-9-13
32-31-3-3	32-7-5-3	32-32-2-16	24-5-9-14
32-31-3-4	32-7-5-4	32-32-2-17	24-5-9-15
32-31-3-5	32-7-5-5	32-32-2-18	24-5-9-16
32-31-3-6	32-7-5-6	32-32-2-19	24-5-9-29(b)
32-31-3-7	32-7-5-7	32-32-2-20	24-5-9-17
32-31-3-8	32-7-5-8	32-32-2-21	24-5-9-18
32-31-3-9	32-7-5-9	32-32-2-22	24-5-9-19 part
32-31-3-10	32-7-5-10	32-32-2-23	24-5-9-20
32-31-3-11	32-7-5-11	32-32-3-1	24-5-9-22
32-31-3-12	32-7-5-12	32-32-3-2	24-5-9-23
32-31-3-13	32-7-5-13	32-32-3-3	24-5-9-24
32-31-3-14	32-7-5-14	32-32-3-4	24-5-9-25
32-31-3-15	32-7-5-15	32-32-3-5	24-5-9-26
32-31-3-16	32-7-5-16	32-32-3-6	24-5-9-27
32-31-3-17	32-7-5-17	32-32-3-7	24-5-9-28
32-31-3-18	32-7-5-18	32-32-3-8	24-5-9-29(a)
32-31-3-19	32-7-5-19	32-32-3-9	24-5-9-30
32-31-4-1	32-7-6-2(a)	32-32-3-10	24-5-9-31
32-31-4-2	32-7-6-1	32-32-3-11	24-5-9-32
32-31-4-3	32-7-6-2(b),	32-32-3-12	24-5-9-33
	32-7-6-2(c),	32-32-3-13	24-5-9-34
	32-7-6-2(d)	32-32-3-14	24-5-9-35
32-31-4-4	32-7-6-3	32-32-3-15	24-5-9-36
32-31-4-5	32-7-6-4	32-33-1-1	32-8-21-1
32-31-5-1	32-7-8-1,	32-33-1-2	32-8-21-2
	32-7-8-2	32-33-1-3	32-8-21-3
32-31-5-2	32-7-8-3	32-33-1-4	32-8-21-4
32-31-5-3	32-7-8-4	32-33-1-5	32-8-21-5
32-31-5-4	32-7-8-5	32-33-2-1	32-8-22-1
32-31-5-5	32-7-8-6	32-33-2-2	32-8-22-2
32-31-5-6	32-7-8-7	32-33-2-3	32-8-22-3
32-31-6-1	32-7-9-1	32-33-2-4	32-8-22-4
32-31-6-2	32-7-9-2	32-33-2-5	32-8-22-5
32-31-6-3	32-7-9-3	32-33-2-6	32-8-22-6
32-31-6-4	32-7-9-4	32-33-2-7	32-8-22-7
32-31-6-5	32-7-9-5	32-33-2-8	32-8-22-8
32-31-6-6	32-7-9-6	32-33-3-1	32-8-23-1
32-31-6-7	32-7-9-7	32-33-3-2	32-8-23-2
32-31-6-8	32-7-9-8	32-33-3-3	32-8-23-3
32-31-6-9	32-7-9-9	32-33-3-4	22 8 23-4
32-31-6-10	32-7-9-10	32-33-3-5	32-8-23-5
32-32-1-1	24-5-9-21	32-33-4-1	32-8-26-1
32-32-2-1	NEW	32-33-4-2	32-8-26-2
32-32-2-2	24-5-9-1	32-33-4-3	32-8-26-3
32-32-2-3	24-5-9-2	32-33-4-4	32-8-26-4
32-32-2-4	24-5-9-3	32-33-4-5	32-8-26-5
32-32-2-5	24-5-9-4	32-33-4-6	32-8-26-6
32-32-2-6	24-5-9-5	32-33-4-7	32-8-26-7
32-32-2-7	24-5-9-6	32-33-4-8	32-8-26-8
32-32-2-8	24-5-9-7	32-33-5-1	32-8-38-1 part
32-32-2-9	24-5-9-8	32-33-5-2	32-8-38-1 part
32-32-2-10	24-5-9-9	32-33-5-3	32-8-38-2
32-32-2-11	24-5-9-10	32-33-5-4	32-8-38-3
32-32-2-12	24-5-9-19 part	32-33-5-5	32-8-38-4
32-32-2-13	24-5-9-11	32-33-5-6	32-8-38-5
32-32-2-14	24-5-9-12	32-33-5-7	32-8-38-6

Current Provision	Prior Provision	Current Provision	Prior Provision
32-33-5-8	32-8-38-7	32-33-19-1	NEW
32-33-6-1	32-8-27-2	32-34-1-1	32-9-1.5-1
32-33-7-1	32-8-28-6	32-34-1-2	32-9-1.5-2
32-33-7-2	32-8-28-1	32-34-1-3	32-9-1.5-4
32-33-7-3	32-8-28-2	32-34-1-4	32-9-1.5-5
32-33-7-4	32-8-28-3	32-34-1-5	32-9-1.5-6
32-33-7-5	32-8-28-4	32-34-1-6	32-9-1.5-7
32-33-7-6	32-8-28-5	32-34-1-7	32-9-1.5-7.5
32-33-8-1	32-8-29-1	32-34-1-8	32-9-1.5-8
32-33-9-1	32-8-30-1	32-34-1-9	32-9-1.5-9
32-33-9-2	32-8-30-2	32-34-1-10	32-9-1.5-10
32-33-9-3	32-8-30-3	32-34-1-11	32-9-1.5-11
32-33-9-4	32-8-30-4	32-34-1-12	32-9-1.5-12
32-33-9-5	32-8-30-5	32-34-1-13	32-9-1.5-13
32-33-9-6	32-8-30-6	32-34-1-14	32-9-1.5-14
32-33-9-7	32-8-30-8	32-34-1-15	32-9-1.5-15
32-33-9-8	32-8-30-9	32-34-1-16	32-9-1.5-16
32-33-10-1	32-8-31-2(c)	32-34-1-17	32-9-1.5-17
32-33-10-2	32-8-31-2(d)	32-34-1-18	32-9-1.5-18
32-33-10-3	32-8-31-2(b)	32-34-1-19	32-9-1.5-19
32-33-10-4	32-8-31-2(a)	32-34-1-20	32-9-1.5-20
32-33-10-5	32-8-31-1	32-34-1-21	32-9-1.5-21
32-33-10-6	32-8-31-3	32-34-1-22	32-9-1.5-22
32-33-10-7	32-8-31-4	32-34-1-23	32-9-1.5-23
32-33-10-8	32-8-31-5	32-34-1-24	32-9-1.5-24
32-33-10-9	32-8-31-6	32-34-1-25	32-9-1.5-25
32-33-10-10	32-8-31-7	32-34-1-26	32-9-1.5-26
32-33-11-1	32-8-32-1	32-34-1-27	32-9-1.5-27
32-33-11-2	32-8-32-2	32-34-1-28	32-9-1.5-28
32-33-11-3	32-8-32-3	32-34-1-29	32-9-1.5-29
32-33-11-4	32-8-32-4	32-34-1-30	32-9-1.5-30
32-33-11-5	32-8-32-5	32-34-1-31	32-9-1.5-31
32-33-11-6	32-8-32-7	32-34-1-32	32-9-1.5-32
32-33-11-7	32-8-32-6	32-34-1-33	32-9-1.5-33
32-33-12-1	32-8-33-1	32-34-1-34	32-9-1.5-34
32-33-12-2	32-8-33-2	32-34-1-35	32-9-1.5-35
32-33-13-1	32-8-34-1 part	32-34-1-36	32-9-1.5-36
32-33-13-2	32-8-34-1 part	32-34-1-37	32-9-1.5-37
32-33-13-3	32-8-34-1 part	32-34-1-38	32-9-1.5-38.1
32-33-14-1	32-8-35-1	32-34-1-39	32-9-1.5-40
32-33-14-2	32-8-35-2	32-34-1-40	32-9-1.5-41
32-33-14-3	32-8-35-3	32-34-1-41	32-9-1.5-42
32-33-15-1	32-8-36-1	32-34-1-42	32-9-1.5-43
32-33-15-2	32-8-36-2	32-34-1-43	32-9-1.5-44
32-33-15-3	32-8-36-3	32-34-1-44	32-9-1.5-46
32-33-15-4	32-8-36-4	32-34-1-45	32-9-1.5-47
32-33-16-1	32-8-37-1 part	32-34-1-46	32-9-1.5-48
32-33-16-2	32-8-37-1 part	32-34-1-47	32-9-1.5-49
32-33-16-3	32-8-37-2	32-34-1-48	32-9-1.5-50
32-33-16-4	32-8-37-3	32-34-1-49	32-9-1.5-52
32-33-16-5	32-8-37-4	32-34-1-50	32-9-1.5-54
32-33-16-6	32-8-37-5	32-34-1-51	32-9-1.5-45
32-33-16-7	32-8-37-6	32-34-1-52	32-9-1.5-3
32-33-16-8	32-8-37-7	32-34-2-1	32-9-2-1
32-33-16-9	32-8-37-8	32-34-2-2	32-9-2-2
32-33-17-1	NEW	32-34-3-1	32-9-8-1
32-33-18-1	NEW	32-34-3-2	32-9-8-2

Current Provision	Prior Provision	Current Provision	Prior Provision
32-34-3-3	32-9-8-3	32-34-8-16	32-9-3-16
32-34-3-4	32-9-8-4	32-34-8-17	32-9-3-17
32-34-3-5	32-9-8-5	32-34-8-18	32-9-3-18
32-34-4-1	32-9-9-1	32-34-8-19	32-9-3-19
32-34-4-2	32-9-9-2	32-34-8-20	32-9-3-20
32-34-4-3	32-9-9-3	32-34-8-21	32-9-3-21
32-34-4-4	32-9-9-4	32-34-8-22	32-9-3-22
32-34-4-5	32-9-9-5	32-34-8-23	32-9-3-23,
32-34-4-6	32-9-9-6		32-9-3-29
32-34-5-1	32-9-10-1	32-34-8-24	32-9-3-24
32-34-5-2	32-9-10-2	32-34-8-25	32-9-3-25
32-34-5-3	32-9-10-3	32-34-8-26	32-9-3-26
32-34-5-4	32-9-10-4	32-34-8-27	32-9-3-27
32-34-5-5	32-9-10-5	32-34-8-28	32-9-3-28
32-34-5-6	32-9-10-6	32-34-8-29	32-9-4-1
32-34-5-7	32-9-10-7	32-34-9-1	32-9-5-6
32-34-5-8	32-9-10-8	32-34-9-2	32-9-5-1
32-34-5-9	32-9-10-9	32-34-9-3	32-9-5-2
32-34-5-10	32-9-10-10	32-34-9-4	32-9-5-3
32-34-5-11	32-9-10-11	32-34-9-5	32-9-5-4
32-34-5-12	32-9-10-12	32-34-9-6	32-9-5-5
32-34-5-13	32-9-10-13	32-34-9-7	32-9-5-7
32-34-5-14	32-9-10-14	32-34-9-8	32-9-5-8
32-34-5-15	32-9-10-15	32-34-9-9	32-9-5-9
32-34-5-16	32-9-10-16	32-34-9-10	32-9-5-13
32-34-6-1	32-9-6-5	32-34-9-11	32-9-5-14
32-34-6-2	32-9-6-1(1)	32-34-9-12	32-9-5-15
32-34-6-3	32-9-6-1(2)	32-34-9-13	32-9-5-16
32-34-6-4	32-9-6-6	32-34-10-1	32-8-40-1
32-34-6-5	32-9-6-2	32-34-10-2	32-8-40-2
32-34-6-6	32-9-6-3,	32-34-10-3	32-8-40-3
	32-9-6-4	32-34-10-4	32-8-40-4
32-34-6-7	32-9-6-7	32-34-10-5	32-8-40-5
32-34-7-1	32-9-7-5	32-34-10-6	32-8-40-6
32-34-7-2	32-9-7-1 part	32-34-10-7	32-8-40-7
32-34-7-3	32-9-7-1 part	32-34-10-8	32-8-40-8
32-34-7-4	32-9-7-1 part	32-35-1-1	NEW
32-34-7-5	32-9-7-2	32-35-2-1	34-21-1-1
32-34-7-6	32-9-7-3,	32-35-2-2	34-21-2-1
	32-9-7-4	32-35-2-3	34-21-2-2
32-34-7-7	32-9-7-6	32-35-2-4	34-21-2-3
32-34-7-8	32-9-7-7	32-35-2-5	34-21-3-1
32-34-8-1	32-9-3-1	32-35-2-6	34-21-3-2
32-34-8-2	32-9-3-2	32-35-2-7	34-21-3-3
32-34-8-3	32-9-3-3	32-35-2-8	34-21-4-1
32-34-8-4	32-9-3-4	32-35-2-9	34-21-4-2
32-34-8-5	32-9-3-5	32-35-2-10	34-21-4-3
32-34-8-6	32-9-3-6	32-35-2-11	34-21-4-4
32-34-8-7	32-9-3-7	32-35-2-12	34-21-4-5
32-34-8-8	32-9-3-8	32-35-2-13	34-21-4-6
32-34-8-9	32-9-3-9	32-35-2-14	34-21-4-7
32-34-8-10	32-9-3-10	32-35-2-15	34-21-4-8
32-34-8-11	32-9-3-11	32-35-2-16	34-21-4-9
32-34-8-12	32-9-3-12	32-35-2-17	34-21-4-10
32-34-8-13	32-9-3-13	32-35-2-18	34-21-4-11
32-34-8-14	32-9-3-14	32-35-2-19	34-21-4-12
32-34-8-15	32-9-3-15	32-35-2-20	34-21-4-13

Current Provision	Prior Provision	Current Provision	Prior Provision
32-35-2-21	34-21-5-1	32-36-1-9	32-13-1-9
32-35-2-22	34-21-5-2	32-36-1-10	32-13-1-10
32-35-2-23	34-21-5-3	32-36-1-11	32-13-1-11
32-35-2-24	34-21-5-4	32-36-1-12	32-13-1-12
32-35-2-25	34-21-5-5	32-36-1-13	32-13-1-13
32-35-2-26	34-21-6-1	32-36-1-14	32-13-1-14
32-35-2-27	34-21-7-1	32-36-1-15	32-13-1-15
32-35-2-28	34-21-7-2	32-36-1-16	32-13-1-16
32-35-2-29	34-21-8-1	32-36-1-17	32-13-1-17
32-35-2-30	34-21-8-2	32-36-1-18	32-13-1-18
32-35-2-31	34-21-8-3	32-36-1-19	32-13-1-19
32-35-2-32	34-21-8-4	32-36-1-20	32-13-1-20
32-35-2-33	34-21-9-1	32-37-1-1	32-14-1-1
32-35-2-34	34-21-9-2	32-37-2-1	32-14-2-1
32-35-2-35	34-21-10-1	32-37-2-2	32-14-2-2
32-36-1-1	32-13-1-1	32-37-2-3	32-14-2-3
32-36-1-2	32-13-1-2	32-37-2-4	32-14-2-4
32-36-1-3	32-13-1-3	32-37-2-5	32-14-2-5
32-36-1-4	32-13-1-4	32-37-3-1	32-14-3-1
32-36-1-5	32-13-1-5	32-37-3-2	32-14-3-2
32-36-1-6	32-13-1-6	32-37-4-1	32-14-4-1
32-36-1-7	32-13-1-7	32-37-5-1	32-14-5-1
32-36-1-8	32-13-1-8		

TABLE OF TITLES AND ARTICLES

DIVISION 1—GENERAL GOVERNMENT

DIVISION 2—EDUCATION

DIVISION 3—BUSINESS AND FINANCE

DIVISION 4—PROPERTY AND FAMILY LAW

DIVISION 5—COURTS AND JUDICIAL PROCEEDINGS

TABLE OF CONTENTS

TITLE 32

PROPERTY

Indiana Code

TITLE 32

PROPERTY

ARTICLE 1

ALIENATION OF PROPERTY

32-1-1-1 — 32-1-21-3. [Repealed.]

Compiler's Notes. This article, concerning the alienation of property, was repealed by P.L.2-2002, § 128, effective July 1, 2002.

IC 32-1-2-1, IC 32-1-2-22 and IC 32-1-2-25 were also repealed by Acts 1975, P.L. 111, § 13. IC 32-1-3 was also repealed by P.L.1-1989, § 75, effective July 1, 1989. IC 32-1-4 was also repealed by P.L.149-1991, § 6, effective July 1, 1991. IC 32-1-10 was also repealed by P.L.149-1991, § 6, effective July 1, 1991. IC 32-1-12-1 was also repealed by Acts 1975, P.L. 111, § 13. IC 32-1-14 was also repealed by Acts 1975, P.L. 111, § 13; and P.L.1-1993, § 226, effective May 4, 1993. IC 32-1-15 was also repealed by Acts 1973, P.L. 301, § 13 and P.L.3-1989, § 183, effective May 5, 1989. IC 32-1-16 was also repealed by Acts 1975, P.L 111, § 13; and P.L.1-1993, § 226, effective May 4, 1993. IC 32-1-17-2 was also repealed by Acts 1975, P.L. 111, § 13. IC 32-1-18 was also repealed by Acts 1975, P.L. 111, § 13; and by P.L.1-1992, § 167. IC 32-1-19 was also repealed by Acts 1985, P.L. 289, § 2.

ARTICLE 2

REQUIREMENT OF A WRITING

32-2-1-1 — 32-2-8-6. [Repealed.]

Compiler's Notes. This article, concerning written instruments, was repealed by P.L.2-2002, § 128, effective July 1, 2002. For present similar provisions, see IC 32-18-2 and IC 32-21.

IC 32-2-1-7 through IC 32-2-1-10 and IC

32-2-1-14 through IC 32-2-1-18 were also repealed by P.L.144-1994, § 4, effective July 1, 1994. IC 32-2-3-5 was also repealed by P.L.1-

1989, § 75, effective July 1, 1989. IC 32-2-6 was also repealed by P.L.1-1989, § 75, effective July 1, 1989.

ARTICLE 3

POWERS OF APPOINTMENT

32-3-1-1 — 32-3-2-15. [Repealed.]

Compiler's Notes. This article, concerning powers of appointment and disclaimers of property interests, was repealed by P.L.2-

2002, § 128, effective July 1, 2002. For present similar provisions, see IC 32-17-6 and IC 32-17-7.

ARTICLE 4

COTENANCIES AND PARTITION

32-4-1-1 — 32-4-8-3. [Repealed.]

Compiler's Notes. This article, concerning contenancies and partition, was repealed by P.L.2-2002, § 128, effective July 1, 2002. For present similar provisions, see IC 32-17.

IC 32-4-1 was also repealed by Acts 1975,

P.L. 288, § 51. IC 32-4-4 was also repealed by P.L.33-189, § 130, effective July 1, 1989. IC 32-4-5-9 was also repealed by P.L.33-1989, § 130, effective July 1, 1989.

ARTICLE 5

INTERESTS IN REALTY LESS THAN FEE SIMPLE

32-5-1-1 — 32-5-12-15. [Repealed.]

Compiler's Notes. This article, concerning interests in realty less than fee simple, was repealed by P.L.2-2002, § 128, effective July 1, 2002. For present similar provisions, see IC 32-23.

IC 32-5-3-2 through IC 32-5-3-7 were also

repealed by Acts 1973, P.L. 302, § 2. IC 32-5-4 was also repealed by P.L.1-1995, § 91, effective July 1, 1995. IC 32-5-5 was also repealed by P.L.1-1995, § 91, effective July 1, 1995. IC 32-5-10 was also repealed by P.L.1-1995, § 91, effective July 1, 1995.

ARTICLE 6

EJECTMENT AND QUIET TITLE

32-6-1-1 — 32-6-7-2. [Repealed.]

Compiler's Notes. This article, concerning ejectment and quiet title, was repealed by P.L.2-2002, § 128, effective July 1, 2002. For present similar provisions, see IC 32-30-2 and IC 32-30-3.

IC 32-6-1 was also repealed by Acts 1973, P.L. 303, § 2. IC 32-6-2 was also repealed by P.L.108-1985, § 1.

ARTICLE 7

LANDLORD-TENANT RELATIONS

32-7-1-1 — 32-7-9-10. [Repealed.]

Compiler's Notes. This article, concerning landlord-tenant relations, was repealed by P.L.2-2002, § 128, effective July 1, 2002. For present similar provisions, see IC 32-31.

IC 32-7-3 was also repealed by P.L.1-1990, § 293, effective March 20, 1990. IC 32-7-4 was also repealed by § 3207 of Acts 1978, P.L. 2, effective July 1, 1978.

ARTICLE 8

LIENS ON REALTY AND PERSONALTY

32-8-1-1 — 32-8-40-8. [Repealed.]

Compiler's Notes. This article, concerning liens and mortgages on realty and personalty, was repealed by P.L.2-2002, § 128, effective July 1, 2002. For present similar provisions, see IC 32-28 and IC 32-29.

IC 32-8-3-1, IC 32-8-3-5, IC 32-8-3-16, and IC 32-8-3-18 were amended by P.L.101-2002, §§ 1 to 4, effective July 1, 2002. Because of the repeal of this article by P.L.2-2002, effective July 1, 2002, these sections are not out.

IC 32-8-13-2 was also repealed by P.L.1-1989, § 75, effective July 1, 1989. IC 32-8-20 was also repealed by P.L.1-1989, § 75, effec-

tive July 1, 1989. IC 32-8-22-9 was also repealed by Acts 1980, P.L. 25, § 1, effective September 1, 1981. IC 32-8-27-1 was also repealed by § 3207 of Acts 1978, P.L. 2. IC 32-8-30-7 was also repealed by P.L.295-1983, § 6. IC 32-8-33-3 was also repealed by § 3207 of Acts 1978, P.L. 2.

IC 32-8-15.5-3 and IC 32-8-15.5-10 were also amended by P.L.1-2002, §§ 128 and 129, effective March 14, 2002. Because of the repeal of this article by P.L.2-2002, effective July 1, 2002, IC 32-8-15.5-1 through IC 32-8-15.5-17 are not set out.

ARTICLE 9

LOST AND UNCLAIMED PROPERTY

32-9-1-1 — 32-9-10-16. [Repealed.]

Compiler's Notes. This article, concerning lost and unclaimed property, was repealed by P.L.2-2002, § 128, effective July 1, 2002. For present similar provisions, see IC 32-34.

IC 32-9-1 was also repealed by P.L.31-1995, § 9, effective July 1, 1996. IC 32-9-1-7 was

also formerly repealed by P.L.210-1989, § 8, effective July 1, 1989. IC 32-9-1.5-38 and IC 32-9-1.5-39 were also repealed by P.L.127-2000, § 19. IC 32-9-5-10 through IC 32-9-5-12 were also repealed by § 3207 of Acts 1978, P.L. 2, effective July 1, 1978.

ARTICLE 10

FENCES

32-10-1-1 — 32-10-10-2. [Repealed.]

Compiler's Notes. This article, concerning fences, was repealed by P.L.2-2002, § 128, effective July 1, 2002. For present similar provisions, see IC 32-26.

IC 32-10-4-4 was also repealed by § 3207 of Acts 1978, P.L. 2, effective July 1, 1978. IC 32-10-5-4 was also repealed by § 3207 of Acts 1978, P.L. 2, effective July 1, 1978.

ARTICLE 11

EMINENT DOMAIN

32-11-1-1 — 32-11-6-2. [Repealed.]

Compiler's Notes. This article, concerning eminent domain, was repealed by P.L.2-2002, § 128, effective July 1, 2002. For present similar provisions, see IC 32-24.

IC 32-11-5 was also repealed by Acts 1975, P.L. 28, § 1.

ARTICLE 12

ASSIGNMENT FOR BENEFIT OF CREDITORS

32-12-1-1 — 32-12-3-1. [Repealed.]

Compiler's Notes. This article, concerning assignments for benefit of creditors, was repealed by P.L.2-2002, § 128, effective July 1, 2002. For present similar provisions, see IC 32-18.

ARTICLE 13

PUBLICITY

32-13-1-1 — 32-13-1-20. [Repealed.]

Compiler's Notes. This article, concerning rights of publicity, was repealed by P.L.2-2002, § 128, effective July 1, 2002. For present similar provisions, see IC 32-36.

IC 32-13-1-8 was amended by P.L.1-2002, § 130, effective March 14, 2002. Because of the repeal of this article by P.L.2-2002, § 128, effective July 1, 2002, this section is not set out.

ARTICLE 14

COPYRIGHT ROYALTIES

32-14-1-1 — 32-14-5-1. [Repealed.]

Compiler's Notes. This article, concerning copyright royalties, was repealed by P.L.2-2002, § 128, effective July 1, 2002. For present similar provisions, see IC 32-37.

ARTICLE 15

CAUSES OF ACTION CONCERNING REAL ESTATE

32-15-1-1 — 32-15-10-1. [Repealed.]

Compiler's Notes. This article, causes of action concerning real estate, was repealed by P.L.2-2002, § 128, effective July 1, 2002. For present similar provisions, see IC 32-27-2 and IC 32-30.

ARTICLE 16

EFFECT OF RECODIFICATION OF TITLE 32

CHAPTER.
1. EFFECT OF RECODIFICATION BY THE ACT OF THE
    2002 REGULAR SESSION OF THE GENERAL
    ASSEMBLY, 32-16-1-1 — 32-16-1-9.

CHAPTER 1

EFFECT OF RECODIFICATION BY THE ACT OF THE 2002 REGULAR SESSION OF
THE GENERAL ASSEMBLY

32-16-1-1. Prior property law. — As used in this chapter, "prior property law" refers to the statutes that are repealed or amended in the recodification act of the 2002 regular session of the general assembly as the statutes existed before the effective date of the applicable or corresponding provision of the recodification act of the 2002 regular session of the general assembly. [P.L.2-2002, § 1.]

Effective Dates. P.L.2-2002, § 1. July 1. 2002.

32-16-1-2. Purpose of recodification. — The purpose of the recodification act of the 2002 regular session of the general assembly is to recodify prior property law in a style that is clear, concise, and easy to interpret and apply. Except to the extent that:

(1) the recodification act of the 2002 regular session of the general assembly is amended to reflect the changes made in a provision of another bill that adds to, amends, or repeals a provision in the recodification act of the 2002 regular session of the general assembly; or

(2) the minutes of meetings of the code revision commission during 2001 expressly indicate a different purpose;

the substantive operation and effect of the prior property law continue uninterrupted as if the recodification act of the 2002 regular session of the general assembly had not been enacted. [P.L.2-2002, § 1.]

32-16-1-3. Application of certain sections to statutory construction. — Subject to section 2 [IC 32-16-1-2] of this chapter, sections 4 through 9 [IC 32-16-1-4 through IC 32-16-1-9] of this chapter shall be applied to the statutory construction of the recodification act of the 2002 regular session of the general assembly. [P.L.2-2002, § 1.]

32-16-1-4. Effect on prior law. — (a) The recodification act of the 2002 regular session of the general assembly does not affect:

(1) any rights or liabilities accrued;

(2) any penalties incurred;

(3) any violations committed;

(4) any proceedings begun;

(5) any bonds, notes, loans, or other forms of indebtedness issued, incurred, or made;

(6) any tax levies made or authorized;

(7) any funds established;

(8) any patents issued;

(9) the validity, continuation, or termination of any contracts, easements, or leases executed;

(10) the validity, continuation, scope, termination, suspension, or revocation of:

(A) permits;

(B) licenses;

(C) certificates of registration;

(D) grants of authority; or

(E) limitations of authority; or

(11) the validity of court decisions entered regarding the constitutionality of any provision of the prior property law;

before the effective date of the recodification act of the 2002 regular session of the general assembly (July 1, 2002). Those rights, liabilities, penalties, offenses, proceedings, bonds, notes, loans, other forms of indebtedness, tax levies, funds, patents, contracts, leases, permits, licenses, certificates of registration, grants of authority, or limitations of authority continue and shall be imposed and enforced under prior property law as if the recodification act of the 2002 regular session of the general assembly had not been enacted.

(b) The recodification act of the 2002 regular session of the general assembly does not:

(1) extend, or cause to expire, a permit, license, certificate of registration, or other grant or limitation of authority; or

(2) in any way affect the validity, scope, or status of a license, permit, certificate of registration, or other grant or limitation of authority;

issued under the prior property law.

(c) The recodification act of the 2002 regular session of the general assembly does not affect the revocation, limitation, or suspension of a permit, license, certificate of registration, or other grant or limitation of authority based in whole or in part on violations of the prior property law or the rules adopted under the prior property law. [P.L.2-2002, § 1.]

32-16-1-5. Construction relating to substantive changes from prior law. — The recodification act of the 2002 regular session of the general assembly shall be construed as a recodification of prior property law. Except as provided in section 2(1) and 2(2) [IC 32-16-1-2(1) and IC 32-16-1-2(2)] of this chapter, if the literal meaning of the recodification act of the 2002 regular session of the general assembly (including a literal application of an erroneous change to an internal reference) would result in a substantive change in the prior property law, the difference shall be construed as a typographical, spelling, or other clerical error that must be corrected by:

(1) inserting, deleting, or substituting words, punctuation, or other matters of style in the recodification act of the 2002 regular session of the general assembly; or

(2) using any other rule of statutory construction;

as necessary or appropriate to apply the recodification act of the 2002 regular session of the general assembly in a manner that does not result in a substantive change in the law. The principle of statutory construction that a court must apply the literal meaning of an act if the literal meaning of the act is unambiguous does not apply to the recodification act of the 2002 regular session of the general assembly to the extent that the recodification act of the 2002 regular session of the general assembly is not substantively identical to the prior property law. [P.L.2-2002, § 1.]

32-16-1-6. References to repealed or replaced sections. — Subject to section 9 [IC 32-16-1-9] of this chapter, a reference in a statute or rule to a statute that is repealed and replaced in the same or a different form in the recodification act of the 2002 regular session of the general assembly shall be treated after the effective date of the new provision as a reference to the new provision. [P.L.2-2002, § 1.]

32-16-1-7. References to recodified sections. — A citation reference in the recodification act of the 2002 regular session of the general assembly to another provision of the recodification act of the 2002 regular session of the general assembly shall be treated as including a reference to the provision of prior property law that is substantively equivalent to the provision of the recodification act of the 2002 regular session of the general assembly that is referred to by the citation reference. [P.L.2-2002, § 1.]

32-16-1-8. References to rules adopted under recodified sections. — (a) As used in the recodification act of the 2002 regular session of the general assembly, a reference to rules adopted under any provision of this title or under any other provision of the recodification act of the 2002 regular session of the general assembly refers to either:

(1) rules adopted under the recodification act of the 2002 regular session of the general assembly; or

(2) rules adopted under the prior property law until those rules have been amended, repealed, or superseded.

(b) Rules adopted under the prior property law continue in effect after June 30, 2002, until the rules are amended, repealed, or suspended. [P.L.2-2002, § 1.]

32-16-1-9. References to prior law in recodified sections. — (a) A reference in the recodification act of the 2002 regular session of the general assembly to a citation in the prior property law before its repeal is added in certain sections of the recodification act of the 2002 regular session of the general assembly only as an aid to the reader.

(b) The inclusion or omission in the recodification act of the 2002 regular session of the general assembly of a reference to a citation in the prior property law before its repeal does not affect:

(1) any rights or liabilities accrued;

(2) any penalties incurred;

(3) any violations committed;

(4) any proceedings begun;

(5) any bonds, notes, loans, or other forms of indebtedness issued, incurred, or made;

(6) any tax levies made;

(7) any funds established;

(8) any patents issued;

(9) the validity, continuation, or termination of contracts, easements, or leases executed;

(10) the validity, continuation, scope, termination, suspension, or revocation of:

(A) permits;

(B) licenses;

(C) certificates of registration;

(D) grants of authority; or

(E) limitations of authority; or

(11) the validity of court decisions entered regarding the constitutionality of any provision of the prior property law;

before the effective date of the recodification act of the 2002 regular session of the general assembly (July 1, 2002). Those rights, liabilities, penalties, offenses, proceedings, bonds, notes, loans, other forms of indebtedness, tax levies, funds, patents, contracts, leases, licenses, permits, certificates of registration, and other grants of authority continue and shall be imposed and enforced under prior property law as if the recodification act of the 2002 regular session of the general assembly had not been enacted.

(c) The inclusion or omission in the recodification act of the 2002 regular session of the general assembly of a citation to a provision in the prior property law does not affect the use of a prior conviction, violation, or noncompliance under the prior property law as the basis for revocation of a license, permit, certificate of registration, or other grant of authority under the recodification act of the 2002 regular session of the general assembly, as necessary or appropriate to apply the recodification act of the 2002 regular session of the general assembly in a manner that does not result in a substantive change in the law. [P.L.2-2002, § 1.]

ARTICLE 17

INTERESTS IN PROPERTY

CHAPTER 1

FEE SIMPLE INTEREST

32-17-1-1. "Grantor" defined. — As used in this chapter, "grantor" means every person by whom an estate or interest in land is:

(1) created;

(2) granted;

(3) bargained;

(4) sold;

(5) conveyed;

(6) transferred; or

(7) assigned.

[P.L.2-2002, § 2.]

Effective Dates. P.L.2-2002, § 2. July 1. 2002.

32-17-1-2. Conveyance in fee simple. — (a) A conveyance of land that is:

(1) worded in substance as "A.B. conveys and warrants to C.D." (insert a description of the premises) "for the sum of" (insert the consideration); and

(2) dated and signed, sealed, and acknowledged by the grantor;

is a conveyance in fee simple to the grantee and the grantee's heirs and assigns with a covenant as described in subsection (b).

(b) A conveyance in fee simple under subsection (a) includes a covenant from the grantor for the grantor and the grantor's heirs and personal representatives that the grantor:

(1) is lawfully seized of the premises;

(2) has good right to convey the premises;

(3) guarantees the quiet possession of the premises;

(4) guarantees that the premises are free from all encumbrances; and

(5) will warrant and defend the title to the premises against all lawful claims. [P.L.2-2002, § 2.]

Indiana Law Review. Private Rights and
Public Ways: Property Disputes and Rails-to-
Trails in Indiana, 30 Ind. L. Rev. 724 (1997).

NOTES TO DECISIONS

ANALYSIS

In general.
After-acquired title.
Conflict of laws.
Covenants of seizin.
Covenants of title.
—Condition of land.
—Effect of Marketable Title Act.
—Expenses.
—Failure of title.
—Notice.
—Partial eviction.
Covenants running with land.
Date.
Encumbrances.
General warranty deed.
Grant of fee simple.
Grantee's right of action.
Grantors with unequal interest.
Lawful claim.
Recitals in deeds and records.
Right of redemption.
Rules of construction.
Tenants in common.
Testamentary instruments contrasted.

In General.

A deed in the statutory form of a warranty
deed covenanted that the grantor was seized
of the premises, had a good right to convey,
and guaranteed the quiet provision thereof,
that the lands were free from encumbrances,
and that the grantor would warrant and defend the title against all lawful claims. Carver
v. Louthain, 38 Ind. 530 (1872); Coleman v.
Lyman, 42 Ind. 289 (1873); Kent v. Cantrall,
44 Ind. 452 (1873); Keiper v. Klein, 51 Ind.
316 (1875); Jackson v. Green, 112 Ind. 341, 14
N.E. 89 (1887); Worley v. Hineman, 6 Ind.
App. 240, 33 N.E. 260 (1892); Mauzy v. Flint,
42 Ind. App. 386, 83 N.E. 757 (1908); Maitlen
v. Maitlen, 44 Ind. App. 559, 89 N.E. 966
(1909); Ragle v. Dedman, 50 Ind. App. 359, 98
N.E. 367 (1912); Pence v. Rhonemus, 58 Ind.
App. 268, 108 N.E. 129 (1915).

Covenants in deeds could have been limited
as to the estate created or land conveyed.
Allen v. Kersey, 104 Ind. 1, 3 N.E. 557 (1885);
Ragle v. Dedman, 50 Ind. App. 359, 98 N.E.
367 (1912).

Where a quarter acre of land was conveyed
for school purposes, by a warranty deed which
provided that the land should revert to the
grantors or their heirs if it ceased to be used
for such purposes, and the grantors thereafter
conveyed the quarter section of land wherein
the quarter acre was located by warranty

deed to a third party, even if it was granted
that, upon breach of the condition subsequent, the right of reentry was in the original
grantors and their heirs, yet such heirs of the
original grantors by reentry would have acquired an after-acquired title to the part of
the land warranted to the heirs of the third
party, and were estopped from denying that
such heirs took title to the entire tract under
the warranty deed from their ancestors.
Higbee v. Rodeman, 129 Ind. 244, 28 N.E. 442
(1891); Fall Creek Sch. Tp. v. Shuman, 55 Ind.
App. 232, 103 N.E. 677 (1913); Hughes v.
Fifer, 218 Ind. 198, 31 N.E.2d 634 (1941).

The use of the words "conveys and warrants" in the statutory form of warranty deed
in Indiana created a conveyance in fee simple;
and the use of words of inheritance were
unnecessary. Crecelius v. New Albany Mach.
Mfg. Co., 4 F.2d 369 (7th Cir. 1924).

As a general rule, the mere manual tradition of a deed with no intention on the part of
the grantor of vesting any present estate
whatever in the grantee was not sufficient
delivery to make the deed effectual, and if the
grantor's intention by such tradition was to
vest title in the grantee only after the grant-
or's death, the deed must have been regarded
as testamentary in character. Stevenson v.
Harris, 124 Ind. App. 358, 118 N.E.2d 368
(1954).

Where a deed, executed conformably to the
statute, was delivered by the grantor to the
grantee, the law presumed it was done with
an intent on the part of the grantor to make it
effectual for the purposes therein expressed,
and while this presumption, like any others,
broke down in the face of evidence to the
contrary, such evidence must have been clear
and convincing. Stevenson v. Harris, 124 Ind.
App. 358, 118 N.E.2d 368 (1954).

After-Acquired Title.

Where one in possession and claiming the
title to certain land conveyed a one-sixth
interest in the same by warranty deed, and
the grantor later acquired title to such land,
such deed carried with it all the conditions
provided by this section, and a subsequent
decree quieting title to such land in the
grantor inured to the benefit of said grantee.
Sabinske v. Patterson, 100 Ind. App. 657, 196
N.E. 539 (1935).

Conflict of Laws.

The law of the state where land conveyed
was situated had to be looked to in determin-

Conflict of Laws. (Cont'd)
ing whether the deed of conveyance passed
any title to the vendee. Bethell v. Bethell, 54
Ind. 428, 23 Am. R. 650 (1876); Fisher v.
Parry, 68 Ind. 465 (1879); Jackson v. Green,
112 Ind. 341, 14 N.E. 89 (1887).

Covenants of Seizin.

If a grantor had neither possession nor
title, and the grantee was not put in possession, the covenant of seizin was broken as
soon as the deed was executed and a suit
would lie for the breach. Bethell v. Bethell, 54
Ind. 428, 23 Am. R. 650 (1876); Craig v.
Donovan, 63 Ind. 513 (1878); Fisher v. Parry,
68 Ind. 465 (1879); Jackson v. Green, 112 Ind.
341, 14 N.E. 89 (1887).

In an action for breach of covenants of
seizin, the burden of proof was on the plaintiff
to show want of title at the time of the
conveyance. Wine v. Woods, 158 Ind. 388, 63
N.E. 759 (1902).

Covenants of Title.

—Condition of Land.

Condition of the property, including the
presence of hazardous waste, does not constitute a defect in ownership precluding the
seller from conveying merchantable title. HM
Holdings, Inc. v. Rankin, 70 F.3d 933 (7th Cir.
1995).

—Effect of Marketable Title Act.

The Marketable Title Act (former IC 32-1-
5-1 to IC 32-1-5-10, repealed; see IC 32-20 for
similar provisions) relieves the covenants imposed by a warranty deed only to the extent
that a claim or interest is extinguished by the
Marketable Title Act. If a claim or interest is
not extinguished by the act, the act has no
effect on the guarantee contained in the deed.
McClaskey v. Bumb & Mueller Farms, Inc.,
547 N.E.2d 302 (Ind. App. 1989).

—Expenses.

The necessary expenses incurred for defending one's title were properly allowed
when it was shown that the covenantor had
notice of the suit, or where he himself de-
fended the action in the name of the grantee
defendant. Worley v. Hineman, 6 Ind. App.
240, 33 N.E. 260 (1892); Teague v. Whaley, 20
Ind. App. 26, 50 N.E. 41 (1898).

—Failure of Title.

When title failed to a portion of the land
conveyed by warranty deed, judgment against
vendor should have included interest on part
of the purchase money paid for such portion;
if note was given, it should have been regarded as having been credited, as of day on
which it was given, with price of portion, title

to which failed. Boatman v. Smith, 50 Ind. 403
(1875).

—Notice.

Where a grantor of real estate with covenants of warranty was not made a party to a
suit by one having an easement therein, the
grantee was required not only to notify him of
the pendency of the suit in order to bind him
by the judgment, he must also have asked
him to defend the title. Teague v. Whaley, 20
Ind. App. 26, 50 N.E. 41 (1898); Pence v.
Rhonemus, 58 Ind. App. 268, 108 N.E. 129
(1915).

Where there was a partial failure of title,
the purchaser could recover the pro rata value
of the portion of real estate omitted from the
deed, with interest from date of conveyance.
Equitable Trust Co. v. Milligan, 31 Ind. App.
20, 65 N.E. 1044 (1903).

—Partial Eviction.

Where the eviction was partial, the damages would bear the same proportion to the
whole purchase money, as the value of the
part to which the title failed bore to the whole
premises estimated at the price paid. Phillips
v. Reichert, 17 Ind. 120, 79 Am. Dec. 463
(1861); Hoot v. Spade, 20 Ind. 326 (1863);
McNally v. White, 154 Ind. 163, 54 N.E. 794
(1899), reh'g overruled, 154 Ind. 174, 56 N.E.
214 (1900).

Covenants Running with Land.

Covenants against encumbrances run with
the land, and a grantee could sue a remote
grantor for a breach of such covenant.
Dehority v. Wright, 101 Ind. 382 (1885);
Worley v. Hineman, 6 Ind. App. 240, 33 N.E.
260 (1893); Whittern v. Krick, 31 Ind. App.
577, 68 N.E. 694 (1903).

Covenants that run with land under a gen-
eral warranty deed. Maxon v. Lane, 102 Ind.
364, 1 N.E. 796 (1885); Conduitt v. Ross, 102
Ind. 166, 26 N.E. 198 (1885); Scott v. Stetler,
128 Ind. 385, 27 N.E. 721 (1891); Scott v.
Michaels, 129 Ind. 250, 28 N.E. 546 (1891);
Lake Erie & W.R.R. v. Priest, 131 Ind. 413, 31
N.E. 77 (1892); Worley v. Hineman, 6 Ind.
App. 240, 33 N.E. 260 (1893); Thiebaud v.
Union Furn. Co., 143 Ind. 340, 42 N.E. 741
(1896); Lake Erie & W.R.R. v. Power, 15 Ind.
App. 179, 43 N.E. 959 (1896); Lake Erie &
W.R.R. v. Griffin, 25 Ind. App. 138, 53 N.E.
1042 (1899), rehearing overruled, 25 Ind. App.
156, 57 N.E. 722 (1904); Chicago & S.E. Ry. v.
McEwen, 35 Ind. App. 251, 71 N.E. 926
(1904); Pittsburgh, C., C. & St. L. Ry v.
Wilson, 34 Ind. App. 324, 72 N.E. 666 (1904).

Covenants of warranty run with the land,
and subsequent purchasers could sue on covenants that were contained in deeds made by
grantors under which they held the land,
although such purchasers acquired title by

Covenants Running with Land. (Cont'd)
quitclaim deeds. Pence v. Rhonemus, 58 Ind.
App. 268, 108 N.E. 129 (1915).

Date.

A deed was good without a date. Thompson
v. Thompson, 9 Ind. 323, 68 Am. Dec. 638
(1857).

Encumbrances.

Joining in a conveyance by warranty deed
does not of itself estop such person from
asserting an equitable mortgage based on a
contractual promise to give a mortgage. Prell
v. Trustees of Baird & Warner Mtg. & Realty
Investors, 179 Ind. App. 642, 68 Ind. Dec. 193,
386 N.E.2d 1221 (1979).

General Warranty Deed.

Absent contrary agreement, there is a presumption that buyer receives title to property
by general warranty deed, and buyer takes
title free of any encumbrances; thus, absent
express contrary agreement, seller is responsible for any taxes and other obligations incurred before the date of sale. Wolvos v.
Meyer, 668 N.E.2d 671 (Ind. 1996).

Grant of Fee Simple.

Words in deed that vendors of property "do
grant and convey and warrant" granted the
vendee a fee simple estate. Tazian v. Cline,
673 N.E.2d 485 (Ind. App. 1996), aff'd, 686
N.E.2d 95 (Ind. 1997).

Deed granting a strip of land to railroad
granted a fee simple interest in the land to
railroad, not an easement, despite habendum
clause containing the phrase "for the uses and
purposes therein expressed." Tazian v. Cline,
686 N.E.2d 95 (Ind. 1997).

Grantee's Right of Action.

The grantee in a warranty deed could sue
his immediate or remote grantor for a breach
of covenants of the deed. McClure v. McClure,
65 Ind. 482 (1879); Worley v. Hineman, 6 Ind.
App. 240, 33 N.E. 260 (1893); Beasley v.
Phillips, 20 Ind. App. 182, 50 N.E. 488 (1898).

Defenses that a grantor might have set up
in an action on covenants by his immediate
grantee could have been set up as against a
remote grantee. Scott v. Stetler, 128 Ind. 385,
27 N.E. 721 (1891).

The grantee in a warranty deed may sue his
or her immediate grantor for breach of covenant in the deed. The grantee has the right to
remove an encumbrance and recover the
amount thereof from the grantor. Ticor Title
Ins. Co. v. Graham, 576 N.E.2d 1332 (Ind.
App. 1991).

Grantors with Unequal Interest.

If several grantors joined in a warranty
deed, all were bound by all the covenants of
the deed, although their interests in the land
conveyed were not equal. Ragle v. Dedman, 50
Ind. App. 359, 98 N.E. 367 (1912).

Lawful Claim.

Although the current state of the law gives
little choice to a grantee faced with an adverse claim and a grantor who refuses to
defend thereon, given the decision in *Keilbach
v. McCullough*, 669 N.E.2d 1052 (Ind. Ct.
App. 1996), and the long line of authority
supporting its holding, in the context of the
covenant of warranty, a "lawful claim" necessarily means a successful claim. Outcalt v.
Wardlaw, 750 N.E.2d 859 (Ind. App. 2001).

Recitals in Deeds and Records.

Notice had to be taken by purchasers of the
recitals in deeds and records which constituted their chain of title. Pierce v. Vansell, 35
Ind. App. 525, 74 N.E. 554 (1905).

Right of Redemption.

Property owner's warranty deed conveyed
the grantor's right to redemption to grantee,
which is derivative of the right to ownership,
and upon delivery of the deed, grantee acquired title to the property, but his interest
was subject to prior tax sale purchaser's lien
and right to exchange the tax sale certificate
for a tax deed. Atkins v. Niermeier, 671
N.E.2d 155 (Ind. App. 1996).

Rules of Construction.

Where words of inheritance were not used
in a deed, the entire instrument could have
been considered in determining the estate
granted. Long v. Horton, 126 Ind. App. 651,
133 N.E.2d 568 (1956).

Tenants in Common.

If several tenants in common of land joined
in a general warranty deed conveying the
land, a judgment against one of the grantors
which was a lien on his interest in the land
would have been included in the warranty,
and would have been a breach of the covenant
against encumbrances as against all of the
grantors. Ragle v. Dedman, 50 Ind. App. 359,
98 N.E. 367 (1912).

Deed which stated tenants in common conveyed their "respective" interests in real estate clearly stated their intent to convey and
warrant their own particular or several interests and included "words of severance" that
limited cotenant's warranty to his undivided
one-half interest. Windell v. Miller, 687
N.E.2d 585 (Ind. App. 1997).

Testamentary Instruments Contrasted.

An instrument having all the formalities of
a deed would have been construed as such,
and not as a will, where it appeared therefrom
that the maker intended to convey any inter-

Testamentary Instruments
  Contrasted. (Cont'd)
est whatever to vest on its execution. Kokomo Trust Co. v. Hiller, 67 Ind. App. 611, 116 N.E. 332 (1917).
  A recital reserving to the grantor, in an instrument in the form of a deed, the possession and control of lands during his lifetime amounted to a reservation of a life estate, and did not characterize the instrument as testamentary. Kokomo Trust Co. v. Hiller, 67 Ind. App. 611, 116 N.E. 332 (1917).

Collateral References. Provision in deed, or contract for sale of real property, discriminating against persons on account of race, color, or religion. 3 A.L.R.2d 466.
  Change of neighborhood in restricted district as affecting restrictive covenant; decisions since 1927. 4 A.L.R.2d 1111.
  Validity, construction, and effect of contractual provision regarding future revocation or modification of covenant restricting use of real property. 4 A.L.R.3d 570.
  Validity and effect of gift for charitable purposes which excludes otherwise qualified beneficiaries because of their race or religion. 25 A.L.R.3d 736.

  Meaning of terms "dwelling" or "dwelling house" or "house" as used in the conveyance or execption or reservation clauses. 38 A.L.R.3d 1419.
  Effect of residuary clause to pass property acquired by testator's estate after his death. 39 A.L.R.3d 1390.
  Specificity of description of premises as affecting enforceability of contract to convey real property — modern cases. 73 A.L.R.4th 135.
  Change in character of neighborhood as affecting validity or enforceability of restrictive covenant. 76 A.L.R.5th 337.

32-17-1-3. Estates tail abolished. — (a) Estates tail are abolished.

(b) An estate that under common law is a fee tail:

  (1) is considered a fee simple; and

  (2) if the estate is not limited by a valid remainder, is considered a fee simple absolute. [P.L.2-2002, § 2.]

NOTES TO DECISIONS

ANALYSIS

Conditional fee.
Fee simple.
Remainders.

Conditional Fee.
  When an estate was liable to be defeated by the happening of a contingency, it was not an estate tail, but a conditional fee. Outland v. Bowen, 115 Ind. 150, 17 N.E. 281 (1888).
  Where words were introduced into a deed after the words of conveyance in order to limit the estate, they had to be apt words for the purpose so that when taken in connection with the granting words of the deed, the meaning of the limitation would have been clear and irresistible on the face of the deed. Marsh v. Morris, 133 Ind. 548, 33 N.E. 290 (1893); Clark v. Hillis, 134 Ind. 421, 34 N.E. 13 (1893); Doren v. Gillum, 136 Ind. 134, 35 N.E. 1101 (1894); McIlhinny v. McIlhinny, 137 Ind. 411, 37 N.E. 147, 24 L.R.A. 489, 45 Am. St. R. 186 (1894); Chambers v. Chambers, 139 Ind. 111, 38 N.E. 334 (1894), overruled on other grounds, McAdams v. Bailey, 169 Ind. 518, 82 N.E. 1057 (1907); Granger v. Granger, 147 Ind. 95, 44 N.E. 189 (1896).

Fee Simple.
  A conveyance of land to a person, and the heirs of her body by person named, created a fee simple absolute in the grantee. Tipton v. LaRose, 27 Ind. 484 (1867); Lane v. Utz, 130 Ind. 235, 29 N.E. 772 (1892).
  Estates tail were abolished by statute, and what would have been an estate tail at common law was in this state a fee simple estate. Huxford v. Milligan, 50 Ind. 542 (1875); Granger v. Granger, 147 Ind. 95, 44 N.E. 189, 46 N.E. 80, 36 L.R.A. 186 (1896); Chamberlain v. Runkle, 28 Ind. App. 599, 63 N.E. 486 (1902); Teal v. Richardson, 160 Ind. 119, 66 N.E. 435 (1903); Lamb v. Medsker, 35 Ind. App. 662, 74 N.E. 1012 (1905); Lee v. Lee, 45 Ind. App. 645, 91 N.E. 507 (1910); Newhaus v. Brennan, 49 Ind. App. 654, 97 N.E. 938 (1912); Gibson v. Brown, 62 Ind. App. 460, 110 N.E. 716, 112 N.E. 894 (1915); Conover v. Cade, 184 Ind. 604, 112 N.E. 7 (1916); Quilliam v. Union Trust Co., 194 Ind. 521, 142 N.E. 214 (1924).
  Under a will devising land to testator's son for life "and after his death to his children surviving him in fee simple," the fee simple vested absolutely in the children of the life tenant at the death of the testator, subject to

Fee Simple. (Cont'd)

diminution to let in after-born children. Alsman v. Walters, 184 Ind. 565, 106 N.E. 879, 111 N.E. 921 (1914).

Where a will devised a homestead to testatrix's unmarried grandson "and when he is done with it, to be given to his oldest son and so on down to the latest generation to be kept in the Gardner name," the estate thus created was one in tail male which, by operation of this section, must have been adjudged a fee simple, it having been clearly apparent from the terms of the devise that testatrix intended to restrain the estate of inheritance to the eldest male descendants of the grandson. Gardner v. Grossman, 115 Ind. App. 135, 57 N.E.2d 440 (1944).

Remainders.

The statutes of this state contemplated that a valid remainder could have been limited after granting what would have been an estate tail at common law. Adams v. Merrill, 45 Ind. App. 315, 85 N.E. 114, 87 N.E. 36 (1908).

32-17-1-4. Lineal and collateral warranties abolished. — Lineal and collateral warranties with all their incidents are abolished. However, the heirs and devisees of a person who has made a covenant or agreement is answerable upon that covenant or agreement:

(1) to the extent of property descended or devised to the heirs and devisees; and

(2) in the manner prescribed by law.

[P.L.2-2002, § 2.]

NOTES TO DECISIONS

In General.

The heirs of a grantor could have been held liable only on the covenants in a deed made by him under the provisions of the statute regulating the settlement of decedents' estates. Hartman v. Lee, 30 Ind. 281 (1868); Blair v. Allen, 55 Ind. 409 (1876).

Heirs were liable on warranties contained in deeds of ancestors, since covenants of title were not personal, but ran with the land. Blair v. Allen, 55 Ind. 409 (1876); Harmon v. Dorman, 8 Ind. App. 461, 35 N.E. 1025 (1893); Wysong v. Nealis, 13 Ind. App. 165, 41 N.E. 388 (1895); Whittern v. Krick, 31 Ind. App. 577, 68 N.E. 694 (1903); Muller v. Fowler, 34 Ind. App. 66, 71 N.E. 512 (1904).

CHAPTER 2

ESTATE

32-17-2-1. Joint tenancy of estates vested in executors or trustees — Estates in common. — (a) This section does not apply to:

(1) mortgages;

(2) conveyances in trust; or

(3) conveyances made to husband and wife.

(b) Every estate vested in executors or trustees as executors shall be held by them in joint tenancy.

(c) Except as provided in subsection (b), a conveyance or devise of land or of any interest in land made to two (2) or more persons creates an estate in common and not in joint tenancy unless:

(1) it is expressed in the conveyance or devise that the grantees or devisees hold the land or interest in land in joint tenancy and to the survivor of them; or

(2) the intent to create an estate in joint tenancy manifestly appears from the tenor of the instrument. [P.L.2-2002, § 2.]

Effective Dates. P.L.2-2002, § 2. July 1. 2002.
Cross References. Form of quitclaim deed, IC 32-21-1-15.

Rights of survivors of joint tenants holding personalty, IC 32-17-11-17 — IC 32-17-11-19, IC 32-17-11-29.

NOTES TO DECISIONS

ANALYSIS

In general.
After-acquired title.
Bona fide purchasers.
Color of title.
Devise.
Husband and wife.
—Limitations.
—Survivorship.
Joint tenancy.
Mortgage.
Partnership.
Right of survivorship.
Tenancy by the entirety.
—Creation.
—Determination.
—Divorce.
—Effect.
—Judgment and execution.
Tenancy in common.

In General.
Want of title or encumbrances was not a defense to actions for purchase money when land was conveyed by a quitclaim deed. Shuler v. Hardin, 25 Ind. 386 (1865); Atherton v. Toney, 43 Ind. 211 (1873); Mullen v. Hawkins, 141 Ind. 363, 40 N.E. 797 (1895); Horner v. Lowe, 159 Ind. 406, 64 N.E. 218 (1902).

A quitclaim deed conveyed title as effectually as a deed with covenants. Rowe v. Beckett, 30 Ind. 154, 95 Am. Dec. 676 (1868); Davidson v. Coon, 125 Ind. 497, 25 N.E. 601, 9 L.R.A. 584 (1890).

A quitclaim deed operated simply to transfer whatever interest the grantor had at the time of its execution. Avery v. Akins, 74 Ind. 283 (1881); Bryan v. Uland, 101 Ind. 477, 1 N.E. 52 (1885); McClure v. Raben, 125 Ind. 139, 25 N.E. 179, 9 L.R.A. 477 (1890); Habig v. Dodge, 127 Ind. 31, 25 N.E. 182 (1894); Stephenson v. Boody, 139 Ind. 60, 38 N.E. 331 (1894); Hancock v. Wiggins, 28 Ind. App. 449, 63 N.E. 242 (1902); Sullenger v. Baecher, 55 Ind. App. 365, 101 N.E. 517, 102 N.E. 380 (1913).

General release of all interest of grantor in lands, with covenants of warranty, was only a quitclaim deed. Stephenson v. Boody, 139 Ind. 60, 38 N.E. 331 (1894).

Where vendor pointed out lines and corners of land to purchaser, but the deed was for less, the purchaser could recover the pro rata value of the portion of real estate omitted from the deed. Equitable Trust Co. v. Milligan, 31 Ind. App. 20, 65 N.E. 1044 (1903).

The fact that a deed to grantor's child and grandchild attempted to create a tenancy by entireties was not conclusive that the grantor was of such unsound mind that she did not understand the act in which she was engaged. Baker v. McCague, 118 Ind. App. 32, 75 N.E.2d 61 (1947).

After-Acquired Title.
A quitclaim deed did not estop the grantor from claiming under an after-acquired title. Nicholson v. Caress, 45 Ind. 479 (1874); Graham v. Graham, 55 Ind. 23 (1876); Avery v. Akins, 74 Ind. 283 (1881); Bryan v. Uland, 101 Ind. 477, 1 N.E. 52 (1885); McClure v. Raben, 125 Ind. 139, 25 N.E. 179, 9 L.R.A. 477 (1890); Haskett v. Maxey, 134 Ind. 182, 33 N.E. 358, 19 L.R.A. 379 (1893); Hancock v. Wiggins, 28 Ind. App. 449, 63 N.E. 242 (1902); McAdams v. Bailey, 169 Ind. 518, 82 N.E. 1057, 13 L.R.A. (n.s.) 1003, 124 Am. St. R. 240 (1907); Buckel v. Auer, 68 Ind. App. 320, 120 N.E. 437 (1918).

Consequently, the conveyance of an estate in expectancy by a quitclaim deed would not usually be operative. Avery v. Akins, 74 Ind. 283 (1881); McClure v. Raben, 125 Ind. 139, 25 N.E. 179, 9 L.R.A. 477 (1890); McAdams v. Bailey, 169 Ind. 518, 82 N.E. 1057, 13 L.R.A. (n.s.) 1003, 124 Am. St. R. 240 (1907); Farmers' Loan & Trust Co. v. Wood, 78 Ind. App. 147, 134 N.E. 899 (1922).

A recital in a deed without covenants that the grantor thereby intended to convey an interest specifically described and identified could have been effective through the principle of estoppel, to convey an after-acquired interest. McAdams v. Bailey, 169 Ind. 518, 82 N.E. 1057, 13 L.R.A. (n.s.) 1003, 124 Am. St. R. 240 (1907); Hight v. Carr, 185 Ind. 39, 112 N.E. 881 (1916); Buckel v. Auer, 68 Ind. App. 320, 120 N.E. 437 (1918).

Bona Fide Purchasers.
If a grantor in a warranty deed held title only by a quitclaim deed, his grantee was entitled to protection as an innocent purchaser. Meikel v. Borders, 129 Ind. 529, 29

Bona Fide Purchasers. (Cont'd)
N.E. 29 (1891); Rinehardt v. Reifers, 158 Ind. 675, 64 N.E. 459 (1902).

Grantees in quitclaim deeds could be innocent purchasers the same as other grantees. Smith v. McClain, 146 Ind. 77, 45 N.E. 41 (1896); Sullenger v. Baecher, 55 Ind. App. 365, 101 N.E. 517, 102 N.E. 380 (1913). But see Meikel v. Borders, 129 Ind. 529, 29 N.E. 29 (1891); Hancock v. Wiggins, 28 Ind. App. 449, 63 N.E. 242 (1902); Aetna Life Ins. Co. v. Stryker, 38 Ind. App. 312, 73 N.E. 953, 76 N.E. 822, 78 N.E. 245 (1905); Korporal v. Robinson, 38 Ind. App. 110, 78 N.E. 84 (1906).

The grantee in a quitclaim deed was to be considered a bona fide purchaser if the purchase was made in good faith for a fair price. Sullenger v. Baecher, 55 Ind. App. 365, 101 N.E. 517, 102 N.E. 380 (1913).

Color of Title.
If the grantor in a quitclaim deed had no title, and the grantee had notice thereof, the deed did not create color of title. Wright v. Tichenor, 104 Ind. 185, 3 N.E. 853 (1885).

Devise.
Where real estate was devised to three persons, who as trustees were to take charge of the same, a provision for sale and distribution failed when one of the persons named as trustee died before the testator. Hadley v. Hadley, 147 Ind. 423, 46 N.E. 823 (1897).

Tenants by the entirety could not dispose of the lands by will. Chaplin v. Leapley, 35 Ind. App. 511, 74 N.E. 546 (1905).

Where the husband devised to his wife a life estate in lands held by them as tenants by the entirety, and the widow elected to take the provisions of the will, she could not afterwards claim that such property descended to her by law. Young v. Biehl, 166 Ind. 357, 77 N.E. 406 (1906).

Husband and Wife.
Conveyance to a husband and wife "jointly" did not create a joint tenancy. Simons v. Bollinger, 154 Ind. 83, 56 N.E. 23, 48 L.R.A. 234 (1900).

A conveyance to a husband and wife did not make them joint tenants or tenants in common unless so expressed in the deed of conveyance. Richards v. Richards, 60 Ind. App. 34, 110 N.E. 103 (1915); Dotson v. Faulkenburg, 186 Ind. 417, 116 N.E. 577 (1917).

A mere option to purchase lands could not vest in the holders any title at all, whether by entireties or otherwise, so long as the option had not been exercised. Koehring v. Bowman, 194 Ind. 433, 142 N.E. 117 (1924).

A current lease of land from month to month, subject to termination at any time for nonpayment of rent or for violation of other conditions, conferred on the lessee an interest in the land but not an "estate" of any kind. Koehring v. Bowman, 194 Ind. 433, 142 N.E. 117 (1924).

The secret procuring by husband of deed to himself for property contracted for by both himself and wife did not affect the wife's equitable estate by entirety in the lands thus conveyed. Indiana Trust Co. v. Sherer, 96 Ind. App. 62, 180 N.E. 602 (1932).

—Limitations.
Where a conveyance was made to a husband and wife without any words limiting the estate, they held as tenants by the entirety, but where there were words of limitation so that it appeared that the grantor intended that the grantees should hold by halves, effect would have been given to the intent of the deed. Brown v. Brown, 133 Ind. 476, 32 N.E. 1128, 33 N.E. 615 (1893); Dodds v. Winslow, 26 Ind. App. 652, 60 N.E. 458 (1901).

—Survivorship.
Where a deed executed to a husband and wife was made to grantees in joint tenancy, and to the survivor of them, the condition of survivorship would not be defeated, as it was a rule of joint tenancies where the unity of title continued during their joint lives. Barden v. Overmeyer, 134 Ind. 660, 34 N.E. 439 (1893); Thornburg v. Wiggins, 135 Ind. 178, 34 N.E. 999, 22 L.R.A. 42, 41 Am. St. R. 422 (1893); Wilkins v. Young, 144 Ind. 1, 41 N.E. 68, 590, 55 Am. St. R. 162 (1895); Simons v. Bollinger, 154 Ind. 83, 56 N.E. 23, 48 L.R.A. 234 (1900).

Joint Tenancy.
A husband and wife, though not thus described in a deed of conveyance of real estate executed to them, took as tenants by entireties. Chandler v. Cheney, 37 Ind. 391 (1871); Nicholson v. Caress, 45 Ind. 479 (1874); Case v. Owen, 139 Ind. 22, 38 N.E. 395 (1894); Fowler v. Duhme, 143 Ind. 248, 42 N.E. 623 (1896).

If a deed used the word "jointly" in connection with the grantees in the granting clause, a joint tenancy was created. Case v. Owen, 139 Ind. 22, 38 N.E. 395, 47 Am. St. R. 253 (1894); Mundhenk v. Bierie, 81 Ind. App. 85, 135 N.E. 493 (1922).

Where a deed or devise was made to two or more grantees or devisees as joint tenants, and, for any reason, any one was incapable of taking, the whole estate went to the other grantees or devisees. McCord v. Bright, 44 Ind. App. 275, 87 N.E. 654 (1909).

This section and IC 32-1-2-8 emphasized two propositions: (1) joint tenancies had to be held in disfavor and refused, except when forced by clear and unmistakable words; and (2) the rule of the common law, as applicable

Joint Tenancy. (Cont'd)

to conveyances to husband and wife, should have remained undisturbed in this state. Finney v. Brandon, 78 Ind. App. 450, 135 N.E. 10 (1922).

Although joint tenancies were favored under the common law, the opposite presumption now prevails under this section. Richardson v. Richardson, 121 Ind. App. 523, 98 N.E.2d 190 (1951).

Where the language in the instrument used was "upon the death of one, the whole interest shall rest in the surviving sister," it was expressing the quality of survivorship as required by this act and manifestly created a joint tenancy. Hornung v. Biggs, 140 Ind. App. 349, 10 Ind. Dec. 27, 223 N.E.2d 359 (1967).

To create a joint tenancy between persons who are not legally husband and wife, it is necessary that their intention be declared expressly in the instrument or it must manifestly appear from the tenor of the instrument. Perez v. Gilbert, 586 N.E.2d 921 (Ind. App. 1992).

Mortgage.

Formerly, land that was held by a husband and wife jointly could not have been mortgaged to secure the debt of the husband, but could have been mortgaged by the husband and wife to secure her debt, or for the benefit of the common property. The rule that such lands could not be mortgaged to secure the debt of the husband was abrogated by the repeal of the law prohibiting the wife from becoming a surety. McLead v. Aetna Life Ins. Co., 107 Ind. 394, 8 N.E. 230 (1886); Fawkner v. Scottish Am. Mtg. Co., 107 Ind. 555, 8 N.E. 689 (1886); Crooks v. Kennett, 111 Ind. 347, 12 N.E. 715 (1887); McCormick Harvesting Mach. Co. v. Scovell, 111 Ind. 551, 13 N.E. 58 (1887); Wilson v. Logue, 131 Ind. 191, 30 N.E. 1079, 31 Am. St. R. 426 (1892); Harrison Bldg. & Deposit Co. v. Lackey, 149 Ind. 10, 48 N.E. 254 (1897); Grzesk v. Hibberd, 149 Ind. 354, 48 N.E. 361 (1897); Government Bldg. & Loan Inst. v. Denny, 154 Ind. 261, 55 N.E. 757 (1899); Abicht v. Searls, 154 Ind. 594, 57 N.E. 246 (1900).

When husband and wife owned real estate by entireties and mortgaged the same to borrow money, the wife was estopped from claiming that the mortgage was executed to secure money to pay the husband's debts, and therefore was void. Magel v. Milligan, 150 Ind. 582, 50 N.E. 564, 65 Am. St. 382 (1898).

Partnership.

Where a contract to purchase real estate by two individuals did not state that it was executed by a deceased and a surviving partner as partners, the burden was upon the surviving partner claiming a full interest in the contract under a partnership agreement, as against the deceased's partner's widow's claim of a one-half interest, to prove that the contract was an asset of the partnership by showing that the real estate became the property of the partnership through purchase with partnership funds. Winfrey v. State Life Ins. Co., 227 Ind. 449, 85 N.E.2d 821 (1949).

Right of Survivorship.

A deed to two persons as husband and wife, who were not legally married, did not create a right of survivorship, since the deed contained no other language expressing a desire to create a joint tenancy with rights of survivorship. Perez v. Gilbert, 586 N.E.2d 921 (Ind. App. 1992).

Tenancy by the Entirety.

—Creation.

A conveyance made to a husband and wife without definitely defining the estate created an estate of entirety, and neither could convey or encumber the property without the assent of the other, and the survivor took the entire estate. Davis v. Clark, 26 Ind. 424, 89 Am. Dec. 471 (1866); Arnold v. Arnold, 30 Ind. 305 (1868); Chandler v. Cheney, 37 Ind. 391 (1871); Jones v. Chandler, 40 Ind. 588 (1872); Carver v. Smith, 90 Ind. 222, 46 Am. R. 210 (1883); Hadlock v. Gray, 104 Ind. 596, 4 N.E. 167 (1886); Brown v. Brown, 133 Ind. 476, 32 N.E. 1128, 33 N.E. 615 (1893); Simons v. Bollinger, 154 Ind. 83, 56 N.E. 23, 48 L.R.A. 234 (1900); Sharpe v. Baker, 51 Ind. App. 547, 96 N.E. 627, 99 N.E. 44 (1911); Tharp v. Updike, 55 Ind. App. 452, 102 N.E. 855 (1913); Richards v. Richards, 60 Ind. App. 34, 110 N.E. 103 (1915); Dotson v. Faulkenburg, 186 Ind. 417, 116 N.E. 577 (1917).

Deeds to husbands and wives did not need to have so described them in order to have created a tenancy by entirety. Chandler v. Cheney, 37 Ind. 391 (1871); Hulett v. Inlow, 57 Ind. 412, 26 Am. R. 64 (1877); Thornburg v. Wiggins, 135 Ind. 178, 34 N.E. 999, 22 L.R.A. 42, 41 Am. St. R. 422 (1893); Richards v. Richards, 60 Ind. App. 34, 110 N.E. 103 (1915).

If lands were conveyed jointly to a husband, his wife and another, the husband and wife held one half of the land as tenants by entireties. Anderson v. Tannehill, 42 Ind. 141 (1873); Wilds v. Bogan, 55 Ind. 331 (1876); Hulett v. Inlow, 57 Ind. 412, 26 Am. R. 64 (1877).

A deed to a husband and wife and the heirs of their body created an estate by the entirety in fee simple. Waters v. Lyon, 141 Ind. 170, 40 N.E. 662 (1895).

Grantees had to be husband and wife at the time of conveyance to have created a tenancy by entirety. Pittsburgh, C., C. & St. L.R.R. v. O'Brien, 142 Ind. 218, 41 N.E. 528 (1895).

Tenancy by the Entirety. (Cont'd)

—Creation. (Cont'd)

Delivery of a deed to a husband creating an estate by entirety in him and his wife inured to her benefit. Tyler's Estate v. Tyler, 15 Ind. App. 132, 41 N.E. 965 (1895).

A conveyance to husband and wife "jointly" did not create a joint tenancy, but one of entireties. Simons v. Bollinger, 154 Ind. 83, 56 N.E. 23, 48 L.R.A. 234 (1900); Kiracofe v. Kiracofe, 80 Ind. App. 656, 142 N.E. 21 (1924).

If land was conveyed to a husband and wife, and there were no words used to indicate the estate created, they held the property as tenants by the entirety, but it could have been specified in such deeds that the grantees should hold the land in a different manner and have a different interest therein. Richards v. Richards, 60 Ind. App. 34, 110 N.E. 103 (1915); Dotson v. Faulkenburg, 186 Ind. 417, 116 N.E. 577 (1917).

Estates by entireties were not in harmony with any other part of the law of Indiana governing the legal rights of husband and wife, and the law authorizing their creation would not have been enlarged by construction. Koehring v. Bowman, 194 Ind. 433, 142 N.E. 117 (1924).

Estates by entireties did not exist as to personal property except when such property was directly derived from real estate held by that title, as crops produced by the cultivation of lands owned by entireties or proceeds arising from the sale of property so held. Koehring v. Bowman, 194 Ind. 433, 142 N.E. 117 (1924).

The secretly procuring by husband of deed to himself for property contracted for by both himself and wife did not affect the wife's equitable estate in the land thus conveyed. Indiana Trust Co. v. Sherer, 96 Ind. App. 62, 180 N.E. 603 (1932).

—Determination.

If a husband conveyed his interest in lands held by him and his wife jointly to her, she became vested with the entire estate. Enyeart v. Kepler, 118 Ind. 34, 20 N.E. 539, 10 Am. St. 94 (1889); Ramsey v. Yount, 68 Ind. App. 378, 120 N.E. 618 (1918).

Proceeds of sale of lands held as tenants by entirety were held by such tenants in severalty. Fogleman v. Shively, 4 Ind. App. 197, 30 N.E. 909, 51 Am. St. 213 (1892).

On the death of husband or wife holding an estate by the entirety, the survivor took all in fee. Baker v. Cailor, 206 Ind. 440, 186 N.E. 769 (1933).

—Divorce.

If a husband and wife were divorced while holding lands as tenants by entireties, they became tenants in common of the lands. Lash v. Lash, 58 Ind. 526 (1877); Sharpe v. Baker, 51 Ind. App. 547, 96 N.E. 627, 99 N.E. 44 (1911); Kiracofe v. Kiracofe, 80 Ind. App. 656, 142 N.E. 21 (1924); Van Horn v. Lindsay, 103 Ind. App. 420, 8 N.E.2d 409 (1937).

—Effect.

Crops raised on lands held jointly by a husband and wife were held in the same manner as the lands were held. Patton v. Rankin, 68 Ind. 245, 34 Am. R. 254 (1879); Sharpe v. Baker, 51 Ind. App. 547, 96 N.E. 627, 99 N.E. 44 (1911).

Separate contracts affecting title to land held as tenants by entirety could not be made by a husband or wife. Dyer v. Eldridge, 136 Ind. 654, 36 N.E. 522 (1894).

—Judgment and Execution.

Lands held jointly by husband and wife could not be sold on execution for the separate debt of either. Chandler v. Cheney, 37 Ind. 391 (1871); Jones v. Chandler, 40 Ind. 588 (1872); Mercer v. Coomler, 32 Ind. App. 533, 69 N.E. 202, 102 Am. St. 252 (1903); Baker v. Cailor, 206 Ind. 440, 186 N.E. 769 (1933).

If a joint judgment was recovered against a husband and wife upon a claim for which both were personally liable, land owned by them as tenants by the entirety could have been sold on execution to satisfy such judgment. Sharpe v. Baker, 51 Ind. App. 547, 96 N.E. 627, 99 N.E. 44 (1911).

A conveyance of real estate to husband and wife created an estate by the entirety which was immune to seizure in satisfaction of the individual debts of either. Eilts v. Moore, 117 Ind. App. 27, 68 N.E.2d 795 (1946).

The wife of a judgment debtor who was in possession and occupying real estate conveyed to them as tenants by the entireties was a necessary party defendant to proceedings supplementary to execution wherein it was sought to subject the real estate to the lien of the judgment against her husband alone, and hence a judgment therein that the husband was the sole owner of the real estate and ordering it applied to the satisfaction of such judgment against him was a nullity as to the wife and did not affect whatever rights she had under the deed to her and her husband. Eilts v. Moore, 117 Ind. App. 27, 68 N.E.2d 795 (1946).

The question of whether a deed by which one of two joint tenants and his wife conveyed a portion of the joint realty to the other joint tenant and his wife as tenant by the entireties was merely a partition deed allotting to such joint tenant his share to be held in severalty, and creating no new or additional estate by the entireties, was one concerning which a court could make no valid finding in a proceeding supplementary to execution against the grantee to which his wife was not made a party. Eilts v. Moore, 117 Ind. App. 27, 68 N.E.2d 795 (1946).

Tenancy in Common.

A conveyance to two or more persons created a tenancy in common unless the conveyance or the law provided otherwise. Nicholson v. Caress, 45 Ind. 479 (1874); McMillan v. Hadley, 78 Ind. 590 (1881); Stevens v. Reynolds, 143 Ind. 467, 41 N.E. 931, 52 Am. St. R. 422 (1895); Fowler v. Duhme, 143 Ind. 248, 42 N.E. 623 (1895); Taylor v. Stephens, 165 Ind. 200, 74 N.E. 980 (1905).

If the interests of several grantees were not specially designated, they took the estate as tenants in common. Fountain County Coal & Mining Co. v. Beckleheimer, 102 Ind. 76, 1 N.E. 202, 52 Am. Rep. 645 (1885).

A devise of land to persons equally and jointly created a tenancy in common. Taylor v. Stephens, 165 Ind. 200, 74 N.E. 980 (1905).

When real estate is conveyed by deed to a man and a woman as "husband and wife" when in fact the parties are not married, they hold title to the property as tenants in common and not as joint tenants. Perez v. Gilbert, 586 N.E.2d 921 (Ind. App. 1992).

Collateral References. Interest of spouse in estate by entireties as subject to satisfaction of his or her individual debt. 75 A.L.R.2d 1172.

Construction of provision in real estate mortgage, land contract, or other security instrument for release of separate parcels of land as payments are made. 41 A.L.R.3d 7.

Judgment lien or levy of execution on one joint tenant's share or interest as severing joint tenancy. 51 A.L.R.4th 906.

32-17-2-2. Quitclaim deeds. — A deed of release or quitclaim passes all the estate that the grantor (as defined in IC 32-17-1-1) may convey by a deed of bargain and sale. [P.L.2-2002, § 2.]

32-17-2-3. Future estates — Remainders. — (a) A freehold estate and a chattel real may be created to begin at a future day.

(b) An estate for life:

(1) may be created in a term of years with or without the intervention of a precedent estate; and

(2) a remainder may be limited on the estate for life.

(c) A remainder of a freehold or a chattel real, either contingent or vested, may be created, expectant on the termination of a term of years. [P.L.2-2002, § 2.]

NOTES TO DECISIONS

ANALYSIS

In general.
Contingent remainders.
Personal property.
Retention of interest.
Trust estate.

In General.

Lands could be devised to vest in fee in the devisee on the death of persons who survived the testator. Rush v. Rush, 40 Ind. 83 (1872).

Conveyances could be made to one person for life, then to go to others for life on the happening of certain contingencies, and then to go to others in fee. Owen v. Cooper, 46 Ind. 524 (1874); Hadlock v. Gray, 104 Ind. 596, 4 N.E. 167 (1886); Amos v. Amos, 117 Ind. 19, 19 N.E. 539 (1889); McIlhinny v. McIlhinny, 137 Ind. 411, 37 N.E. 147, 24 L.R.A. 489, 45 Am. St. R. 186 (1893); Adams v. Alexander, 159 Ind. 175, 64 N.E. 597 (1902).

A deed could be made to take effect on the death of the grantor. Spencer v. Robbins, 106 Ind. 580, 5 N.E. 726 (1886); Kelley v. Shimer, 152 Ind. 290, 53 N.E. 233 (1899).

Conveyance by an heir, without covenants of warranty, of his expectant interest in land owned by and in the possession of the parent at the time of the conveyance, could have been enforced against the heir after he inherited the title. McClure v. Raben, 125 Ind. 139, 25 N.E. 179, 9 L.R.A. 477 (1890); McClure v. Raben, 133 Ind. 507, 33 N.E. 275, 35 Am. St. R. 558 (1893); Chambers v. Chambers, 139 Ind. 111, 38 N.E. 334 (1894), overruled on other grounds, McAdams v. Bailey, 169 Ind. 518, 82 N.E. 1057 (1907); McAdams v. Bailey, 169 Ind. 518, 82 N.E. 1057, 13 L.R.A. (n.s.) 1003, 124 Am. St. R. 240 (1907); Hight v. Carr, 185 Ind. 39, 112 N.E. 881 (1916).

Contingent Remainders.

Where a testator devised certain property

Contingent Remainders. (Cont'd)
in trust for two grandchildren as a class, providing that the profits only were to be used for their education and support, and that if either should die before having children born to him his share should go to the survivor, and that if both died without having children born to either of them, their share of the estate should be distributed to the other beneficiaries of the will, and a construction of the whole instrument evidenced an intention to put the property beyond the control of the grandchildren, such grandchildren took a life estate with contingent remainder in their children, or, this failing, remainder in fee to the testator's other children, within the rule of a spendthrift trust. McCoy v. Houck, 180 Ind. 634, 99 N.E. 97 (1912).

Where a deed reserved in grantors a life estate and provided that thereafter the grantee should hold the land for and during his natural life only, with remainder to his children then living and to the descendants of those that might be dead, and in the event that grantee should die without leaving children or descendants of children, the brothers and sisters of grantee should take it, and further provided that if the grantee predeceased the grantor the land should revert back to the grantor, no particular estate was necessary to support the contingent remainders of grantee's children and they were unaffected by a deed by the grantee to grantor executed before their birth, and when the grantee, who survived the grantor, died leaving children and grandchildren, the remain-

ders vested. Rouse v. Patrick, 221 Ind. 517, 49 N.E.2d 528 (1943).

Personal Property.
A remainder could be created in personal property as well as real estate. Spence v. Second Nat'l Bank, 126 Ind. App. 125, 130 N.E.2d 667 (1955).

Retention of Interest.
Deeds could have been executed whereby the grantor reserved to himself a life estate in the lands. Cates v. Cates, 135 Ind. 272, 34 N.E. 957 (1893); Wilson v. Carrico, 140 Ind. 533, 40 N.E. 50, 49 Am. St. R. 213 (1895); Kelley v. Shimer, 152 Ind. 290, 53 N.E. 233 (1899); Haines v. Weirick, 155 Ind. 548, 58 N.E. 712, 80 Am. St. R. 251 (1900); Adams v. Alexander, 159 Ind. 175, 64 N.E. 597 (1902).

Lands could be conveyed and the possession and enjoyment thereof postponed until after the death of the grantor. Emmons v. Harding, 162 Ind. 154, 70 N.E. 142 (1904).

Trust Estate.
A trust agreement containing no provision by which the donor reserved authority to revoke the trust was irrevocable and the fact that the trust agreement provided in the granting clause that the transfer was to be at the time of his demise did not affect the fact that the estate transferred was immediately and irrevocably transferred, such transfer being intended to commence at a future date not rendering it invalid or testamentary in character. Bircher v. Wasson, 133 Ind. App. 27, 180 N.E.2d 118 (1962).

Collateral References. Creation of express trust in property to be acquired in future. 3 A.L.R.3d 1416.

Validity, construction, and effect of contractual provision regarding future revocation or modification of covenant restricting use of real property. 4 A.L.R.3d 570.

Bequest or devise referring to services to be

rendered by donee to testator during latter's lifetime as absolute or conditional gift. 22 A.L.R.3d 771.

Divorce property distribution: Treatment and method of valuation of future interest in real estate or trust property not realized during marriage. 62 A.L.R.4th 107.

32-17-2-4. Contingent remainder. — A remainder may be limited on a contingency. If the contingency occurs, the contingency abridges or determines the precedent estate. [P.L.2-2002, § 2.]

NOTES TO DECISIONS

ANALYSIS

In general.
Common law rule.
Contingent remainder based on contingent remainder.

In General.
It was a well-settled doctrine that the

courts would so construe a will, when not inconsistent with the intention of the testator, as to prevent the title to real estate from remaining contingent; and unless there were plain indications of a contrary intent, would consider the entire title as vested in those claiming under the will, rather than in abeyance. Wright v. Charley, 129 Ind. 257, 28 N.E.

In General. (Cont'd)

706 (1891); Essick v. Caple, 131 Ind. 207, 30 N.E. 900 (1892); Boling v. Miller, 133 Ind. 602, 33 N.E. 354 (1893); Corey v. Springer, 138 Ind. 506, 37 N.E. 322 (1894), overruled on other grounds, 111 N.E. 914 (Ind. 1916); Hoss v. Hoss, 140 Ind. 551, 39 N.E. 255 (1894); Fowler v. Duhme, 143 Ind. 248, 42 N.E. 623 (1896); Moore v. Gary, 149 Ind. 51, 48 N.E. 630 (1897); Aldred v. Sylvester, 184 Ind. 542, 111 N.E. 914 (1916); Nickerson v. Hoover, 70 Ind. App. 343, 115 N.E. 588 (1917).

Where grantor conveyed realty to his step-mother for life with remainder to the "heirs" of his father, who was then alive, the remainder, if construed as contingent, and the word "heirs" accepted in its technical sense, would have been such as was expressly provided for by statute, where the father predeceased the life tenant. Miller v. Harland, 78 Ind. App. 56, 130 N.E. 134 (1921).

Common Law Rule.

This statute was directly the reverse of the common law rule, for under that rule an executory devise could only have been limited upon events certain to happen. McCoy v. Houck, 180 Ind. 634, 99 N.E. 97 (1912).

Contingent Remainder Based on Contingent Remainder.

While a remainder could have been limited on a contingency, which in case it happened, would operate to abridge or determine the precedent estate, such contingent remainder could not be created on a prior remainder unless the provision of the instrument creating such contingent remainder expressly provided that the contingent remainder had to take effect in the event that the person or persons to whom the first remainder was limited should die under the age of 21 years, or upon some contingency by which the estate of the first remaindermen could have been determined before such first remaindermen attained their full age. Finney v. Brandon, 78 Ind. App. 450, 135 N.E. 10 (1922).

Collateral References. Forfeiture of life estate for waste. 16 A.L.R.3d 1344.

Time to which condition of remainderman's death refers, under gift or grant to one for life or term of years and then to remainderman, but if remainderman dies without issue, then over to another. 26 A.L.R.3d 407.

Implication of right of life tenant to entrench upon or dispose of corpus from language contemplating possible diminution or elimination of gift over. 31 A.L.R.3d 6.

Implication of right of life tenant to entrench upon or dispose of corpus from language relating to the extent of his dominion over the corpus, of the beneficial purpose of the provision for the life tenant. 31 A.L.R.3d 169.

32-17-2-5. Conveyance of greater estate than possessed by tenant for life or years. — A conveyance made by a tenant for life or years that purports to grant or convey a greater estate than the tenant possesses or can lawfully convey:

(1) does not result in a forfeiture of the tenants's estate; and

(2) passes to the grantee or alienee all the estate that the tenant may lawfully convey. [P.L.2-2002, § 2.]

NOTES TO DECISIONS

In General.

Where a deed reserved in grantors a life estate and provided that thereafter the grantee should hold the land for and during his natural life only, with remainder to his children then living and to the descendants of those that might be dead, and in the event the grantee should die without leaving children or descendants of children, the brothers and sisters of grantee should take it, and further provided that if the grantee predeceased the grantor, the land should revert back to the grantor, a conveyance by the grantee back to the grantor and a conveyance thereafter by grantor to others conveyed only the grantee's life estate, and hence the children of grantee, who were born after such conveyances, took vested remainder interests after the death of grantee, who survived the grantor, and such decision did not impair the obligation of a contract. Rouse v. Paidrick, 221 Ind. 517, 49 N.E.2d 528 (1943).

A deed, reserving the right to the use,

In General. (Cont'd)

occupation, rents, issues and profits of the land for grantor's life and conveying the real estate to grantee for life with remainder to his children living at his death, but providing that if grantee left no children surviving him the remainder was to go to brothers and sisters, and if grantee predeceased grantor title was to revert to grantor, conveyed only a life estate to grantee; and a deed of grantee thereafter, purporting to convey back to grantor the fee simple title, conveyed only grantee's life estate, and subsequent deed of grantor to another conveyed only the two life estates and did not cut off the remainder to grantee's children who were born subsequent to grantor's death, but who survived the grantee; and the fact that the original grantee lived 42 years after grantor's death and that the subsequent grantee remained in possession under claim of ownership for a period of 49 years, did not enlarge such grantee's estate beyond the life of the first grantee. Rouse v. Paidrick, 221 Ind. 517, 49 N.E.2d 528 (1943).

Common Law Rule.

The common law rule that one owning a life estate upon which contingent remainders were based, and who tortiously attempted to convey a greater estate than he had, forfeited the life estate resulting in destruction of the contingent remainder, has had no application in Indiana since 1852 upon passage of this section. Rouse v. Paidrick, 221 Ind. 517, 49 N.E.2d 528 (1943).

Oil and Gas Leases.

Where lease owner obtained his oil lease before the restoration clause entered the chain of title, lessee did not hold the lease subject to the clause and remained free by virtue of the priority of his lease to do anything he wanted with his oil wells. A conveyance of property is invalid to the extent the seller tries to convey an interest greater than he has and the conveyance of a fee simple does not extinguish an existing lease. Youngs v. Old Ben Coal Co., 243 F.3d 387 (7th Cir. 2001).

CHAPTER 3

TENANCY

32-17-3-1. Estate by the entireties — Intention to create tenancy in common. — (a) This section applies to a written contract in which a husband and wife:

(1) purchase real estate; or

(2) lease real estate with an option to purchase.

(b) Except as provided in subsection (d), a contract described in subsection (a) creates an estate by the entireties in the husband and wife. The interest of neither party is severable during the marriage.

(c) Upon the death of either party to the marriage, the survivor is considered to have owned the whole of all rights under the contract from its inception.

(d) If:

(1) a contract described in subsection (a) expressly creates a tenancy in common; or

(2) it appears from the tenor of a contract described in subsection (a) that the contract was intended to create a tenancy in common;

the contract shall be construed to create a tenancy in common. [P.L.2-2002, § 2.]

Effective Dates. P.L.2-2002, § 2. July 1. 2002.

NOTES TO DECISIONS

ANALYSIS

Contract to sell.
Four unities.
Parties.
Release.

Contract to Sell.

A contract for the sale of tenants by the entirety property is valid where signed by only one spouse if the spouse signed as an agent for the other spouse, but no agency relationship is present where the contracting spouse was not authorized by the other to sign, and the other spouse did not subsequently ratify the act. McIntosh v. Turner, 486 N.E.2d 565 (Ind. App. 1985), rehearing denied, 489 N.E.2d 116 (Ind. App. 1986).

Four Unities.

The four unities essential to establish a tenancy by the entireties are: (1) unity of estate; (2) unity of possession; (3) unity of control; and (4) unity in conveying or encumbering. Barnes v. Luttrull, 557 N.E.2d 692 (Ind. App. 1990).

Parties.

Holder of mortgage was not required to join any party whose interest attached after the mortgage foreclosure suit was filed. Mid-West Fed. Sav. Bank v. Kerlin, 672 N.E.2d 82 (Ind. App. 1996).

Release.

A conveyance of one spouse's interest in a tenancy by the entirety to the other spouse is "technically" a release. Lee Supply Corp. v. Agnew, 818 F.2d 1284 (7th Cir. 1987).

Husband's release to his wife of the proceeds from the sale of their house, held in tenancy by the entirety, never left a divided interest in the husband which could be subject to execution by his creditors. Lee Supply Corp. v. Agnew, 818 F.2d 1284 (7th Cir. 1987).

Collateral References. 41 Am. Jur. 2d Husband and Wife, §§ 55-60.

41 C.J.S. Husband and Wife, § 42.

Estate by entireties as affected by statute declaring nature of tenancy under grant or devise to two or more persons. 32 A.L.R.3d 570.

Felonious killing of one cotenant or tenant by the entireties by the other as affecting the latter's right in the property. 42 A.L.R.3d 1116.

32-17-3-2. Estate by the entireties — Effect of divorce. — If a husband and wife are divorced while a contract described in section 1(a) [IC 32-17-3-1(a)] of this chapter is in effect, the husband and wife own the interest in the contract and the equity created by the contract in equal shares. [P.L.2-2002, § 2.]

NOTES TO DECISIONS

ANALYSIS

Effect of divorce.
Tenants in common.

Effect of Divorce.

The presumptive tenancy by the entireties of spouses in realty became a tenancy in common in equal shares upon divorce of the parties, in the absence of any determination of their property rights by the court decreeing the divorce. Lewis v. Romine, 128 Ind. App. 564, 151 N.E.2d 156 (1958).

Tenants in Common.

Where dissolution of marriage was granted in Arizona and real property in Indiana was not disposed of by such decree, the parties became tenants in common in their interest in the land which was being bought on contract from husband's parents. Blake v. Hosford, 180 Ind. App. 175, 68 Ind. Dec. 458, 387 N.E.2d 1335 (1979).

Collateral References. Abandonment, desertion, or refusal to support on part of surviving spouse as affecting marital rights in deceased spouse's estate. 13 A.L.R.3d 446.

Adultery on part of surviving spouse as affecting marital rights in deceased spouse's estate. 13 A.L.R.3d 486.

Power of divorce court to deal with real property located in another state. 34 A.L.R.3d 962.

Mutual mistake as to tax consequences as ground for relief against property settlement. 39 A.L.R.3d 1376.

Power of incompetent spouse's guardian or representative to sue for granting or vacation of divorce or annulment of marriage, or to make a compromise or settlement in such suit. 32 A.L.R.5th 673.

32-17-3-3. Estate by the entireties — Effect of death on unpaid portion of purchase price. — If:

(1) a husband and wife execute a title bond or contract for the conveyance of real estate owned by them as tenants by the entireties; and

(2) one (1) of the spouses dies:

(A) during the continuance of the marriage; and

(B) before the whole of the agreed purchase price has been paid;

the interest of the deceased spouse in the unpaid part of the purchase price passes to the surviving spouse in the same right as the surviving spouse's rights of survivorship in real estate held as tenants by the entireties. [P.L.2-2002, § 2.]

Indiana Law Review. 1994 Developments in Property Law, 28 Ind. L. Rev. 1041 (1995).

NOTES TO DECISIONS

ANALYSIS

Construction.
Joint tenancy.
Nature of survivor's interest.

Construction.

The provisions of this section specifically clothed the interest of the surviving spouse in the unpaid purchase price due under contract of conditional sale with the same mantle of protection as that accorded the interest of said spouse in the real estate held as tenants by the entirety. State v. Estate of Weinstein, 141 Ind. App. 395, 11 Ind. Dec. 59, 228 N.E.2d 23, reh'g denied, 141 Ind. App. 399, 229 N.E.2d 741, 11 Ind. Dec. 216 (1967).

Joint Tenancy.

Where property held by the entireties was sold by husband and wife to son and his wife and after balance of purchase price was paid to father, the father deposited such amount in a certificate of deposit in the joint names of himself and his son, the father, in the absence of fraud, thereby changed the character of the proceeds from the entirety property to personalty held in joint tenancy. Anuszkiewicz v. Anuszkiewicz, 172 Ind. App. 279, 56 Ind. Dec. 424, 360 N.E.2d 230 (1977).

Nature of Survivor's Interest.

Upon the death of her husband, a wife was the sole owner of the right to the unpaid balances of sale prices of real estate owned by her and her husband as tenants by the entirety and sold by them on conditional sale contracts, such ownership existing not by virtue of a transfer but by virtue of the original grant, she holding no more and no less than on the day of the grant. State v. Estate of Weinstein, 141 Ind. App. 395, 11 Ind. Dec. 59, 228 N.E.2d 23, reh'g denied, 141 Ind. App. 399, 229 N.E.2d 741, 11 Ind. Dec. 216 (1967).

Collateral References. 41 Am. Jur. 2d Husband and Wife, § 72.

32-17-3-4. Joint deed of conveyance — Power of attorney. — (a) A joint deed of conveyance by a husband and wife is sufficient to convey and pass any interest described in the deed of either or both of them in land held by them as:

(1) tenants in common;

(2) joint tenants; or

(3) tenants by the entireties.

(b) An executed and recorded power of attorney by one (1) spouse to the other spouse authorizing the conveyance by the attorney in fact of any interest owned:

(1) individually by the grantor (as defined in IC 32-17-1-1) of the power of attorney; or

(2) with the grantor's spouse;

enables the attorney in fact through the exercise of the power of attorney to effectively convey the interest in land by individually making a deed of conveyance. [P.L.2-2002, § 2.]

Cross References. Insane husband or wife, conveyance, IC 32-22-1-5.

Rights of survivors of joint tenants holding personalty, IC 32-17-11-17 — IC 32-17-11-19, IC 32-17-11-29.

NOTES TO DECISIONS

ANALYSIS

After-acquired title.
Covenants in deeds.
Estoppel.
Joinder of husband.
Leases.
Power of attorney.
Separate deeds.
Wife's inchoate interest.

After-Acquired Title.

If a husband and wife made a warranty deed conveying all her estate in lands, she could not set up an after-acquired title to the property. King v. Rea, 56 Ind. 1 (1877); Johnson v. Bedwell, 15 Ind. App. 236, 43 N.E. 246 (1896).

Covenants in Deeds.

A married woman was bound by covenant in deed and was estopped from asserting an inchoate interest, on the death of her husband, against the grantee. Littell v. Hoagland, 106 Ind. 320, 6 N.E. 645 (1886); De Haven v. Musselman, 123 Ind. 62, 24 N.E. 171 (1890); Miller v. Miller, 140 Ind. 174, 39 N.E. 547 (1895); Johnson v. Bedwell, 15 Ind. App. 236, 43 N.E. 246 (1896); Dickey v. Kalfsbeck, 20 Ind. App. 290, 50 N.E. 590 (1898); Nichol v. Hays, 20 Ind. App. 369, 50 N.E. 768 (1898).

Estoppel.

Where a married woman joined with her husband in the conveyance of lands held in her own right, which purported to convey the entire estate therein, she was estopped from afterwards setting up any title to such lands, whether it existed at the time of making the conveyance, or was subsequently acquired by her. King v. Rea, 56 Ind. 1 (1877); Wertz v. Jones, 134 Ind. 475, 34 N.E. 1 (1893); Duckwall v. Kisner, 136 Ind. 99, 35 N.E. 697 (1893); Cole v. Temple, 142 Ind. 498, 41 N.E. 942 (1895); Magel v. Milligan, 150 Ind. 582, 50 N.E. 564, 65 Am. St. 382 (1898); Guynn v. Wabash County Loan & Trust Co., 53 Ind. App. 391, 101 N.E. 738 (1913); Cressler v. Brewer, 186 Ind. 185, 114 N.E. 449 (1916).

Joinder of Husband.

A husband could not be compelled to join in a deed conveying the lands of the wife unless he had contracted to do so. Stevens v. Parish, 29 Ind. 260, 95 Am. Dec. 636 (1868).

Leases.

A lease by a married woman of her lands to a gas and oil company for the purpose of operating wells was not an encumbrance or conveyance thereof within the meaning of the statute prohibiting a married woman from encumbering or conveying her lands without her husband joining in the execution thereof. Columbian Oil Co. v. Blake, 13 Ind. App. 680, 42 N.E. 234 (1895), overruled on other grounds, Shirk v. Stafford, 31 Ind. App. 247, 67 N.E. 542 (1903); Heal v. Niagara Oil Co., 150 Ind. 483, 50 N.E. 482 (1898); Kokomo Natural Gas & Oil Co. v. Matlock, 177 Ind.

Leases. (Cont'd)
225, 97 N.E. 787, 39 L.R.A. (n.s.) 675 (1912);
Spiro v. Robertson, 57 Ind. App. 229, 106 N.E.
726 (1914).

Leases by wife for abstraction of oil and gas
were valid although her husband did not join
in the execution thereof. Heal v. Niagara Oil
Co., 150 Ind. 483, 50 N.E. 482 (1898); Kokomo
Natural Gas & Oil Co. v. Matlock, 177 Ind.
225, 97 N.E. 787, 39 L.R.A. (n.s.) 675 (1912);
Spiro v. Robertson, 57 Ind. App. 229, 106 N.E.
726 (1914).

Power of Attorney.

Where a husband and wife executed a
power of attorney to sell the real estate of the
wife, but the manner of conveyance was not
prescribed, the deed executed by the attorney
was good, although the attorney failed to
insert in the deed and subscribe thereto the
name of the husband, since it was apparent
that the attorney intended to execute the
power fully and the purchase money was
received and retained by the husband and
wife. Ellison v. Branstrator, 153 Ind. 146, 54
N.E. 433 (1899).

Separate Deeds.

The separate deeds of a husband and wife
did not convey her lands. Baxter v. Bodkin, 25
Ind. 172 (1865).

The separate deed of a married woman was
void and conveyed no right or title. Shumaker
v. Johnson, 35 Ind. 33 (1871); Mattox v.
Hightshue, 39 Ind. 95 (1872); Kinnaman v.
Pyle, 44 Ind. 275 (1873); Luntz v. Greve, 102

Ind. 173, 26 N.E. 128 (1885); Price v. Brittain,
80 Ind. App. 294, 137 N.E. 620 (1923).

A husband could convey land directly to his
wife. Brookbank v. Kennard, 41 Ind. 339
(1872); Merchants' & Laborers' Bldg. Ass'n v.
Scanlan, 144 Ind. 11, 42 N.E. 1008 (1896);
Heiney v. Lontz, 147 Ind. 417, 46 N.E. 665
(1897); State Bank v. Backus, 160 Ind. 682, 67
N.E. 512 (1903); Ramsey v. Yount, 68 Ind.
App. 378, 120 N.E. 618 (1918).

The husband's interest in his wife's lands
could not be separately conveyed. Huffman v.
Copeland, 139 Ind. 221, 38 N.E. 861 (1894);
Unger v. Mellinger, 37 Ind. App. 639, 77 N.E.
814, 117 Am. St. R. 348 (1906); Buckel v. Auer,
68 Ind. App. 320, 120 N.E. 437 (1918).

Wife's Inchoate Interest.

A deed of a husband and wife did not convey
her interest in his lands when he retained his
interest in the lands. McCormick v. Hunter,
50 Ind. 186 (1875); Hudson v. Evans, 81 Ind.
596 (1882); Paulus v. Latta, 93 Ind. 34 (1883);
Snoddy v. Leavitt, 105 Ind. 357, 5 N.E. 13
(1886); Rupe v. Hadley, 113 Ind. 416, 16 N.E.
391 (1888); Davenport v. Gwilliams, 133 Ind.
142, 31 N.E. 790, 22 L.R.A. 244 (1892);
Huffman v. Copeland, 139 Ind. 221, 38 N.E.
861 (1894); Geisendorff v. Cobbs, 47 Ind. App.
573, 94 N.E. 236 (1911); Buckel v. Auer, 68
Ind. App. 320, 120 N.E. 437 (1918).

Married women could not, by their separate
deeds, convey their inchoate interests in the
lands of their husbands. Howlett v. Dilts, 4
Ind. App. 23, 30 N.E. 313 (1892); Buckel v.
Auer, 68 Ind. App. 320, 120 N.E. 437 (1918).

CHAPTER 4

PARTITION PROCEEDINGS

32-17-4-1. Persons who may compel proceedings. — (a) The following persons may compel partition of land held in joint tenancy or tenancy in common as provided under this chapter:

(1) A person that holds an interest in the land as a joint tenant or tenant-in-common either:

    (A) in the person's own right; or

    (B) as executor or trustee.

(2) If the sale of the estate of a decedent who held an interest in the land as a joint tenant or tenant in common is necessary, the decedent's administrator or executor.

(b) A trustee, an administrator, or an executor may be made a defendant in an action for the partition of real estate to answer as to any interest the trustee, administrator, or executor has in the real estate. [P.L.2-2002, § 2.]

Effective Dates. P.L.2-2002, § 2. July 1. 2002.

Cross References. Partition, fee simple and life estate, IC 32-17-5-1.

Partition, title in question, rules applicable, IC 32-30-2-21.

Quieting title or partition proceedings, parties unknown, procedure, IC 32-30-3-14.

Responsibilities and powers of a guardian, IC 29-3-8-1, IC 29-3-8-2.

NOTES TO DECISIONS

ANALYSIS

In general.
Assignees and trustees.
Buildings.
Cotenants.
Decedents' estates.
Enforcement of divorce decree.
Equitable adjustment to shares.
Guardians.
Interests of joint tenants.
Lienholders.
Life estates and remaindermen.
Married women.
Parties.
Possession rule.
Tenants in common.

In General.

Partition was only authorized by the statute among persons holding lands as joint tenants or tenants-in-common, or their representatives. School Corp. v. Russellville Lodge of Masons, 140 Ind. 422, 39 N.E. 549 (1895); Irvin v. Buckles, 148 Ind. 389, 47 N.E. 822 (1897).

Any joint tenant, tenant-in-common, or an administrator or executor, could sue for partition of lands. Weaver v. Gray, 37 Ind. App. 35, 76 N.E. 795 (1906).

A party holding either a legal or an equitable title to the land could institute partition proceedings. McClure v. Raber, 106 Ind. App. 359, 19 N.E.2d 891 (1939).

In partition proceedings, all persons holding liens or claims upon the land in question could properly be made parties thereto, and the court had power to hear and adjust all the equities between them, and, when the property was not divisible, to order sale and distribution of the proceeds according to the rights of the several parties. McClure v. Raber, 106 Ind. App. 359, 19 N.E.2d 891 (1939).

One who acquired a fee-simple title to an undivided one half of real estate by purchase, wholly independent of the will of his cotenant, during the cotenant's life had an absolute statutory right to compel partition of the real estate, in the absence of any condition or restriction on her right to partition or any other method of alienation by immediate conveyance to her or by any remote device or grant from which her title stemmed, and such right was not curtailed in any degree by the fact that part of the land sought to be partitioned was subject to a life estate pursuant to the cotenant's will. Myers v. Brane, 115 Ind. App. 144, 57 N.E.2d 594 (1944).

Assignees and Trustees.

Trustees holding an undivided title in lands could have partition thereof. Locke v. Barbour, 62 Ind. 577 (1878).

Assignees of insolvent debtors could have partition of lands conveyed to them when the court so directed in the execution of the trust. Jewett v. Perrette, 127 Ind. 97, 26 N.E. 685 (1891).

Trustee in bankruptcy took the absolute title to the real estate of the bankrupt, and had the right to partition against the wife of

Assignees and Trustees. (Cont'd)
the bankrupt. Harlin v. American Trust Co., 67 Ind. App. 213, 119 N.E. 20 (1918).

Buildings.

Where separate portions of buildings were owned by different persons, partition or partition sale could not have been had where the complaint did not disclose what the respective interests held by the parties were, as partition could only have been granted where the parties held as joint tenants or as tenants in common. School Corp. v. Russelville Lodge of Masons, 140 Ind. 422, 39 N.E. 549 (1895).

Cotenants.

The right of a cotenant to division or partition of the common real estate was one of the incidents of the cotenancy, together with the right to a sale of the whole tract in the event that the land was indivisible. McClure v. Raber, 106 Ind. App. 359, 19 N.E.2d 891 (1939).

Where a cotenant brought partition proceedings, one holding a mortgage on the undivided interest of one of the cotenants could properly have been made a party defendant. McClure v. Raber, 106 Ind. App. 359, 19 N.E.2d 891 (1939).

In partition proceeding by former husband against former wife, where court entered a decree and judgment ordering partition and sale and former wife appealed, appellee was entitled to a partition of the real estate in question, the judgment of the court below was not contrary to law and was sustained by sufficient evidence. Gemberling v. Novak, 128 Ind. App. 468, 147 N.E.2d 240 (1958).

Where two parcels of adjoining land were owned by cotenants, none of which had any interest in the other parcel, and a single building was constructed covering both parcels, one co-owner could bring action for partition against the other co-owners of the parcel in which he had an interest but he could not bring an action in partition against the owners of the other parcel for partition or sale of the building. Burford v. Burford, 182 Ind. App. 640, 72 Ind. Dec. 286, 396 N.E.2d 394 (1979).

Decedents' Estates.

An administrator could not prevent partition, even though the land was needed to pay debts. Cole v. Lafontaine, 84 Ind. 446 (1882).

A sale of real estate by an administrator under an order of the court was a judicial sale. Pierce v. Vansell, 35 Ind. App. 525, 74 N.E. 554 (1905); Stormont v. Stormont, 75 Ind. App. 240, 128 N.E. 660 (1920); Rodebeck v. Richardson, 83 Ind. App. 186, 144 N.E. 41 (1924).

Partition of lands contrary to the intention of a testator was forbidden by former IC 32-4-5-5 (repealed; see this chapter for similar provisions). Walling v. Scott, 50 Ind. App. 23, 96 N.E. 481 (1911), rehearing overruled, 97 N.E. 388 (1912); Jones v. Jones, 84 Ind. App. 176, 149 N.E. 108, rehearing denied, 84 Ind. App. 183, 150 N.E. 65 (1925).

The fact that decedent's real estate might have been subject to sale for the payment of his debts did not affect the rights of heirs as tenants in common to maintain partition, since the partition might have been made subject to the right of sale for the payment of debts. Hancock v. Maynard, 72 Ind. App. 661, 126 N.E. 451 (1920).

The purchaser of an heir's interest in realty may maintain a partition suit against the other tenants in common and the personal representative who is in possession of the property prior to final settlement of the estate and where the proceeds of the sale were made subject to the needs of the estate, the sale was not premature. Helvey v. O'Neill, 153 Ind. App. 635, 33 Ind. Dec. 341, 288 N.E.2d 553 (1972).

Enforcement of Divorce Decree.

Considering the divorce decree and judgment as a whole which provided that each of the parties shall have a lien on the described real estate for his or her respective interest, and furthermore definitely and unequivocally adjudicated that such real estate was to be divided "65% in value to plaintiff and 35% in value to defendant," in the partition proceeding by husband, the rights of the parties, whether legal or equitable, were equally within the cognizance and protecting power of the court. Gemberling v. Novak, 128 Ind. App. 468, 147 N.E.2d 240 (1958).

Equitable Adjustment to Shares.

Regardless of who provided the money to purchase the land, the creation of a joint tenancy relationship entitles each party to an equal share of the proceeds of the sale upon partition. Equitable adjustments to cotenants' equal shares are allowed when the cotenants hold the property as tenants in common, not when they hold as joint tenants. Cunningham v. Hastings, 556 N.E.2d 12 (Ind. App. 1990).

Guardians.

A guardian could institute an action for partition in the ward's behalf and prosecute it in his own name. Bowen v. Swander, 121 Ind. 164, 22 N.E. 725 (1889).

Interests of Joint Tenants.

Once a joint tenancy relationship is found to exist between two people in a partition action, it is axiomatic that each person owns a one-half interest. Cunningham v. Hastings, 556 N.E.2d 12 (Ind. App. 1990).

Lienholders.

Parties holding a lien on any of the undivided interests by mortgage, judgment, or otherwise, if made parties to the suit, were bound by the partition proceedings, and limited in their claims to the share set off in severalty to the party under whom they claimed. McClure v. Raber, 106 Ind. App. 359, 19 N.E.2d 891 (1939).

Life Estates and Remaindermen.

Even before the enactment of former IC 32-4-6-1 (repealed; see this chapter for similar provisions), a person owning a life estate in land and an undivided portion thereof in fee could have the latter portion set off. Lynch v. Leurs, 30 Ind. 411 (1868); Tower v. Tower, 141 Ind. 223, 40 N.E. 747 (1895).

Joint tenants and tenants in common of a life estate could have partition thereof. Russell v. Russell, 48 Ind. 456 (1874); Swain v. Hardin, 64 Ind. 85 (1878); Shaw v. Beers, 84 Ind. 528 (1882); Hawkins v. McDougal, 125 Ind. 597, 25 N.E. 807 (1890); Tower v. Tower, 141 Ind. 223, 40 N.E. 747 (1895); Smith v. Andrews, 50 Ind. App. 602, 98 N.E. 734 (1912); Coquillard v. Coquillard, 62 Ind. App. 426, 113 N.E. 474 (1916).

Before the enactment of former IC 32-4-6-1 (repealed; see this chapter for similar provisions), remaindermen could not, during the existence of a life estate, maintain an action for partition. Nicholson v. Caress, 59 Ind. 39 (1877); Schori v. Stephens, 62 Ind. 441 (1878); Coon v. Bean, 69 Ind. 474 (1880); Stout v. Dunning, 72 Ind. 343 (1880); Tower v. Tower, 141 Ind. 223, 40 N.E. 747 (1895); Smith v. Andrews, 50 Ind. App. 602, 98 N.E. 734 (1912). This was because the right of possession was required to be in the plaintiff to give him the right of partition. Schori v. Stephens, 62 Ind. 441 (1878); Stout v. Dunning, 72 Ind. 343 (1880); Tower v. Tower, 141 Ind. 223, 40 N.E. 747 (1895); Fry v. Hare, 166 Ind. 415, 77 N.E. 803 (1906); Shetterly v. Axt, 37 Ind. App. 687, 76 N.E. 901, 77 N.E. 865 (1906); Smith v. Andrews, 50 Ind. App. 602, 98 N.E. 734 (1912); Coquillard v. Coquillard, 62 Ind. App. 489, 113 N.E. 481 (1916).

One owning a life estate in an undivided portion could maintain partition against the remaindermen and have the value of his or her life estate set off to him or her. Shaw v. Beers, 84 Ind. 528 (1882); Tower v. Tower, 141 Ind. 223, 40 N.E. 747 (1895); Smith v. Andrews, 50 Ind. App. 602, 98 N.E. 734 (1912).

Married Women.

On the vesting of the legal title of lands of a married man under a judicial sale, his wife could have her portion set off. Taylor v. Stockwell, 66 Ind. 505 (1879); Roberts v. Shroyer, 68 Ind. 64 (1879); Ketchum v. Schicketanz, 73 Ind. 137 (1880); McCracken v. Kuhn, 73 Ind. 149 (1880); Caywood v. Medsker, 84 Ind. 520 (1882); Straughan v. White, 88 Ind. 242 (1882); Richardson v. Schultz, 98 Ind. 429 (1884); Foltz v. Wert, 103 Ind. 404, 2 N.E. 950 (1885); Elliott v. Cale, 113 Ind. 383, 14 N.E. 708 (1887), rehearing overruled, 113 Ind. 411, 16 N.E. 390 (1888); Whitney v. Marshall, 138 Ind. 472, 37 N.E. 964 (1894); Harlin v. American Trust Co., 67 Ind. App. 213, 119 N.E. 20 (1918).

Bankruptcy, transfer of the property of the bankrupt to the trustee was a judicial sale, entitling former's wife to partition. Roberts v. Shroyer, 68 Ind. 64 (1879); Ketchum v. Schicketanz, 73 Ind. 137 (1880); McCracken v. Kuhn, 73 Ind. 149 (1880); Haggerty v. Byrne, 75 Ind. 499 (1881); Lawson v. DeBolt, 78 Ind. 563 (1881); Leary v. Shaffer, 79 Ind. 567 (1881); Straughan v. White, 88 Ind. 242 (1882); Mattill v. Baas, 89 Ind. 220 (1883); Ragsdale v. Mitchell, 97 Ind. 458 (1884); Mayer v. Haggerty, 138 Ind. 628, 38 N.E. 42 (1894); Bowers v. Lillis, 187 Ind. 1, 115 N.E. 930 (1917); Harlin v. American Trust Co., 67 Ind. App. 213, 119 N.E. 20 (1918).

The grantee of a married woman in such cases could have partition. Hollenback v. Blackmore, 70 Ind. 234 (1880); Youst v. Hayes, 90 Ind. 413 (1883).

Heirs of married woman, when land was sold at judicial sale, had right to partition. Summit v. Ellett, 88 Ind. 227 (1882); Elliott v. Cale, 113 Ind. 383, 14 N.E. 708 (1887), rehearing overruled, 113 Ind. 411, 16 N.E. 390 (1888); Currier v. Elliott, 141 Ind. 394, 39 N.E. 554 (1895); Herrick v. Flinn, 146 Ind. 258, 45 N.E. 187 (1896).

If a widow holding lands derived from her husband remarried, she could have partition of the lands although she could not convey the same. Klinesmith v. Socwell, 100 Ind. 589 (1885); Helt v. Helt, 152 Ind. 142, 52 N.E. 699 (1899).

A guardian's ex parte sale of real estate was a judicial sale within the meaning of the statute that vested title in the wife as to her inchoate interest on the judicial sale of her husband's real estate. Sell v. Keiser, 49 Ind. App. 101, 96 N.E. 812 (1911); Huffman v. Huffman, 51 Ind. App. 330, 99 N.E. 769 (1912).

If land of an insane husband was sold under an order of court, the inchoate interest of the wife became vested as an absolute interest, and she could have partition. Huffman v. Huffman, 51 Ind. App. 330, 99 N.E. 769 (1912); Lawler v. Bear, 188 Ind. 308, 122 N.E. 660 (1919).

A sale of lands in a proceeding to set aside a conveyance as fraudulent was within the meaning of the statute which vested title in the wife as to her inchoate interest on the judicial sale of her husband's real estate, and

Married Women. (Cont'd)
the wife could have partition on the execution of a deed to the purchaser. Darby v. Vinnedge, 53 Ind. App. 525, 100 N.E. 862 (1913).

A married woman could maintain an action in partition against her husband. Pavy v. Pavy, 121 Ind. App. 194, 98 N.E.2d 224 (1951).

Parties.
In a partition proceeding, all persons interested should have been made parties to the suit; if they were not, their interest would not be affected by the proceedings. McClure v. Raber, 106 Ind. App. 359, 19 N.E.2d 891 (1939).

Possession Rule.
Persons did not need to be in possession of lands to be entitled to partition. Godfrey v. Godfrey, 17 Ind. 6, 79 Am. Dec. 448 (1861); Shetterly v. Axt, 37 Ind. App. 687, 76 N.E. 901, 77 N.E. 865 (1906).

The rule that the plaintiff must have been entitled to possession was modified by IC 32-4-6-1. Smith v. Andrews, 50 Ind. App. 602, 98 N.E. 734 (1912); Coquillard v. Coquillard, 62 Ind. App. 489, 113 N.E. 481 (1916).

In order to maintain an action for partition, either legal or equitable title and the right to possession must be in the party maintaining the action. Hurwich v. Zoss, 170 Ind. App. 542, 54 Ind. Dec. 425, 353 N.E.2d 549 (1976).

Tenants in Common.
Where a childless second wife elected to take under the law instead of under the will of her deceased husband, she and the son of the deceased husband, who held the remainder in the real estate, became tenants in common of the decedent's land, and either could maintain a partition proceeding against the other as to such real estate. Tom v. Tom, 107 Ind. App. 599, 26 N.E.2d 410 (1940).

In partition proceedings by former husband against former wife, where the court entered a decree and judgment ordering partition and sale and former wife appealed, such judgment for divorce proceeding was sufficient to vest interests in the real estate in the parties upon the dissolution of the marriage, and lower court was not in error in holding and determining that the parties' interests were sufficiently in rapport with titles of tenancy in common as to justify the court to order partition. Gemberling v. Novak, 128 Ind. App. 468, 147 N.E.2d 240 (1958).

Collateral References. 59A Am. Jur. 2d Partition, §§ 76-180.

68 C.J.S. Partition, §§ 61-150.

Timber rights as subject to partition. 21 A.L.R.2d 618.

Partition as affected by lease given by part only of cotenants. 49 A.L.R.2d 797.

Relief against cotenant for rents and profits or use and occupation as an incident of or adjustment in partition. 51 A.L.R.2d 388.

Compensation in partition proceedings for improvements made or placed on premises of another by mistake. 57 A.L.R.2d 263.

Spouse of living coowner of interest in property as necessary or proper party to partition action. 57 A.L.R.2d 1166.

Grant of part of cotenancy land, taken from less than all cotenants, as subject of protection through partition. 77 A.L.R.2d 1376.

Contractual provisions as affecting right to judicial partition. 37 A.L.R.3d 962.

Judgment lien or levy of execution on one joint tenant's share or interest as severing joint tenancy. 51 A.L.R.4th 906.

32-17-4-2. Petition for partition — Location of filing — Contents. — (a) A person described in section 1(a) [IC 32-17-4-1(a)] of this chapter may file a petition to compel partition in the circuit court or court having probate jurisdiction of the county in which the land or any part of the land is located.

(b) A petition filed under subsection (a) must contain the following:

(1) A description of the premises.

(2) The rights and titles in the land of the parties interested.

[P.L.2-2002, § 2.]

Cross References. Partition, fee simple and life estate, IC 32-17-4-23.

NOTES TO DECISIONS

In General.

The statute conferred jurisdiction on circuit courts and courts having probate jurisdiction. Coquillard v. Coquillard, 62 Ind. App. 426, 113 N.E. 474 (1916).

Allegations in General.

The petition should have set forth the interest of each of the parties in the lands. Lease v. Carr, 5 Blackf. 353 (1840); Wintermute v. Reese, 84 Ind. 308 (1882); School Corp. v. Russelville Lodge of Masons, 140 Ind. 422, 39 N.E. 549 (1895).

Petitions for partition did not need to allege possession of the lands, it having been sufficient to state the interest of each of the owners. Godfrey v. Godfrey, 17 Ind. 6, 79 Am. Dec. 448 (1861); Shetterly v. Axt, 37 Ind. App. 687, 76 N.E. 901, 77 N.E. 865 (1906).

The petition could have been so framed that the title of all parties claiming an interest in the premises could have been settled. Elston v. Piggott, 94 Ind. 14 (1884); Luntz v. Greve, 102 Ind. 173, 26 N.E. 128 (1885); Spencer v. McGonagle, 107 Ind. 410, 8 N.E. 266 (1886); Fordice v. Lloyd, 27 Ind. App. 414, 60 N.E. 367 (1901).

Complaint could allege indivisibility of property and pray for sale. Blake v. Minkner, 136 Ind. 418, 36 N.E. 246 (1894).

Allegations of Title.

The derivation of the title of the parties did not need to be set forth in the petition, it only having been necessary to state the interest of each. Blakely v. Boruff, 71 Ind. 93 (1880); Utterback v. Terhune, 75 Ind. 363 (1881); Pipes v. Hobbs, 83 Ind. 43 (1882).

An allegation that the parties were the owners in fee of the lands meant that they were the owners in fee simple. McMahan v. Newcomer, 82 Ind. 565 (1882).

If the plaintiff set forth the manner of his deriving title, the facts had to show that he had title. Spencer v. McGonagle, 107 Ind. 410, 8 N.E. 266 (1886).

Deeds by which title was derived could not be made a part of the complaint by filing them as exhibits. Jewett v. Perrette, 127 Ind. 97, 26 N.E. 685 (1891); Shetterly v. Axt, 37 Ind. App. 687, 76 N.E. 901, 77 N.E. 865 (1906); O'Mara v. McCarthy, 45 Ind. App. 147, 90 N.E. 330 (1910); Harger v. Warner, 185 Ind. 691, 114 N.E. 407 (1916).

Title in the plaintiff had to be alleged at the time of commencing suit. Brown v. Brown, 133 Ind. 476, 32 N.E. 1128, 33 N.E. 615 (1893).

The same was true of a will through which the title was derived. Shetterly v. Axt, 37 Ind. App. 687, 76 N.E. 901, 77 N.E. 865 (1906).

An allegation that the plaintiff and defendant were the owners as tenants in common amounted to an averment that they were the owners and in possession. Shetterly v. Axt, 37 Ind. App. 687, 76 N.E. 901, 77 N.E. 865 (1906).

Amendment of Complaint.

A complaint in partition could have been amended so as to conform to the report of the commissioners. Bower v. Bowen, 139 Ind. 31, 38 N.E. 326 (1894).

Cross Complaint.

A cross complaint for partition need only have shown a right of action at the time the pleading was filed. Shetterly v. Axt, 37 Ind. App. 687, 76 N.E. 901, 77 N.E. 865 (1906).

Description of Land.

A description of real estate was sufficient to pass title when the land could have been identified by extrinsic evidence. Threlkeld v. Allen, 133 Ind. 429, 32 N.E. 576 (1892).

Parties.

All persons claiming an interest in the lands should have been made parties to the action. Milligan v. Poole, 35 Ind. 64 (1871); Clark v. Stephenson, 73 Ind. 489 (1881); Schissel v. Dickson, 129 Ind. 139, 28 N.E. 540 (1891).

Wives of owners of lands were not necessary parties to actions for partition. Haggerty v. Wagner, 148 Ind. 625, 48 N.E. 366, 39 L.R.A. 384 (1897); Sarver v. Clarkson, 156 Ind. 316, 59 N.E. 933 (1901); Staser v. Gaar, Scott & Co., 168 Ind. 131, 79 N.E. 404 (1906); Wagner v. Carskadon, 28 Ind. App. 573, 60 N.E. 731, 61 N.E. 976 (1901).

If a husband and wife were separated, he was not a necessary party to an action for partition against her. Littell v. Burns, 29 Ind. App. 572, 64 N.E. 938 (1902).

It was proper to make those holding liens on undivided interests in the land parties to the action. A. Kiefer Drug Co. v. DeLay, 63 Ind. App. 639, 115 N.E. 71 (1917).

This section had no application to the rights of persons not affected by the will. Myers v.

Parties. (Cont'd)
Brane, 115 Ind. App. 144, 57 N.E.2d 594 (1944).

Superior Courts.
The Allen County Superior Court had jurisdiction of actions for the partition of real estate situated within such county. Romy v. State ex rel. Brannan, 32 Ind. App. 146, 67 N.E. 998 (1903).

The Madison Superior Court had jurisdiction of a civil action for the partition of a decedent's real estate and to quiet title thereto, in view of former IC 33-5-33-6 (see now IC 33-5-33.1-4). Hancock v. Maynard, 72 Ind. App. 661, 126 N.E. 451 (1920).

Venue.
If the lands were located in different counties, suit could have been brought in either county. Shull v. Kennon, 12 Ind. 34 (1859); Hyatt v. Cochran, 69 Ind. 436 (1880); Jones v. Levi, 72 Ind. 586 (1880).

It did not need to be expressly alleged that the lands were located in the county where suit was brought. Godfrey v. Godfrey, 17 Ind. 6, 79 Am. Dec. 448 (1861).

32-17-4-3. Procedure. — The proceedings, practice, and pleadings for an action under this chapter are the same as in civil suits, except as otherwise provided in this chapter. [P.L.2-2002, § 2.]

NOTES TO DECISIONS

ANALYSIS

In general.
Administrator.
All rights settled.
Claims for improvements.
Cross complaint.
Defenses.
Jury trial.
Mortgages and liens.
New trial.
Rents and profits.

In General.
A partition proceeding is in the nature of a judicial proceeding; it begins with a complaint and results in a judicial decree of partition. Ashbrook v. Hoffman, 617 F.2d 474 (7th Cir. 1980).

Administrator.
An administrator could not intervene and have the lands ordered sold to pay the debts of his decedent. Douthitt v. Smith, 69 Ind. 463 (1880); Clayton v. Blough, 93 Ind. 85 (1884).

A decree in partition procured by the heirs, pending the settlement of a decedent's estate, did not preclude the administrator from asserting liens held by the estate against the realty partitioned, the administrator not having been made a party to the proceedings. Green v. Brown, 146 Ind. 1, 44 N.E. 805 (1896).

All Rights Settled.
All legal and equitable rights of the parties to the lands could have been settled in the action. Martindale v. Alexander, 26 Ind. 104, 89 Am. Dec. 458 (1866); Milligan v. Poole, 35 Ind. 64 (1871); Schee v. McQuilken, 59 Ind. 269 (1877); Finley v. Cathcart, 149 Ind. 470,

48 N.E. 586 (1897), rehearing overruled, 149 Ind. 489, 49 N.E. 381, 63 Am. St. R. 292 (1898); Coquillard v. Coquillard, 62 Ind. App. 426, 113 N.E. 474 (1916).

Claims for Improvements.
Claims for improvements made by one tenant could have been set up and adjusted. Martindale v. Alexander, 26 Ind. 104, 89 Am. Dec. 458 (1866); Elrod v. Keller, 89 Ind. 382 (1882); Carver v. Coffman, 109 Ind. 547, 10 N.E. 567 (1887); Parish v. Camplin, 139 Ind. 1, 37 N.E. 607 (1894); Pulse v. Osborn, 30 Ind. App. 631, 64 N.E. 59 (1902).

A claim of defendants in a suit for partition, for the value of improvements made on the real estate, had to be presented by cross petition, and should have been filed before the judgment of partition and the appointment of the commissioners; but it was not error for the court to entertain the petition after the commissioners had filed the report of partition. Stafford v. Nutt, 35 Ind. 93 (1871); Elrod v. Keller, 89 Ind. 382 (1882); Alleman v. Hawley, 117 Ind. 532, 20 N.E. 441 (1889).

Cross Complaint.
Defendants to the action could, by cross complaint, set up their claims and have their titles quieted. Randles v. Randles, 63 Ind. 93 (1878); Schafer v. Schafer, 68 Ind. 374 (1879); McFerran v. McFerran, 69 Ind. 29 (1879); Ferris v. Reed, 87 Ind. 123 (1882).

Defenses.
The defendant could set up as a defense that he was either the legal or equitable owner of the entire estate. Davis v. Davis, 43 Ind. 561 (1873).

The defendant could set up in bar of the action a prior parol partition. Moore v. Kerr,

Defenses. (Cont'd)
46 Ind. 468 (1874); Hauk v. McComas, 98 Ind. 460 (1884); Savage v. Lee, 101 Ind. 514 (1885).

Jury Trial.
A trial by jury could have been demanded. Kitts v. Willson, 106 Ind. 147, 5 N.E. 400 (1886); Abernathy v. Allen, 132 Ind. 84, 31 N.E. 534 (1892); Peden v. Cavins, 134 Ind. 494, 34 N.E. 7, 39 Am. St. 276 (1893).

Mortgages and Liens.
A defendant could set up by counterclaim a mortgage on the land, and have the same foreclosed. Conyers v. Mericles, 75 Ind. 443 (1881).

Liens on the lands held by the parties could be adjudicated in actions for partition. Schissel v. Dickson, 129 Ind. 139, 28 N.E. 540 (1891).

New Trial.
The time and manner for making motions for new trials, in actions for partition, was governed by the provisions of the Civil Code. Jones v. Jones, 91 Ind. 72 (1883); Van Buskirk v. Stover, 162 Ind. 448, 70 N.E. 520 (1904).

Rents and Profits.
As a general rule, a cotenant could have been required to account only in case he had received rents from third persons or had taken and held possession in hostility to his cotenants and to their exclusion. Crane v. Waggoner, 27 Ind. 52, 89 Am. Dec. 493 (1866); Winings v. Wood, 53 Ind. 187 (1876); Humphries v. Davis, 100 Ind. 369 (1885); Carver v. Coffman, 109 Ind. 547, 10 N.E. 567 (1887); Carver v. Fennimore, 116 Ind. 236, 19 N.E. 103 (1888); Bowen v. Swander, 121 Ind. 164, 22 N.E. 725 (1889); Davis v. Hutton, 127 Ind. 481, 26 N.E. 187, 26 N.E. 1006 (1891); Schissel v. Dickson, 129 Ind. 139, 28 N.E. 540 (1891); Ryason v. Dunten, 164 Ind. 85, 73 N.E. 74 (1905); Overturf v. Martin, 170 Ind. 308, 84 N.E. 531 (1908), overruled on other grounds, Stauffer v. Kesler, 191 Ind. 702, 127 N.E. 803 (1920); Geisendorff v. Cobbs, 47 Ind. App. 573, 94 N.E. 236 (1911); Porter v. Mooney, 64 Ind. App. 479, 116 N.E. 60 (1917).

If a tenant in common occupied land under a bona fide claim of entire ownership, he would only have been liable to account for the rental value of the premises as they were at the time he took possession. Carver v. Fennimore, 116 Ind. 236, 19 N.E. 103 (1888); Hannah v. Carver, 121 Ind. 278, 23 N.E. 93 (1889); Porter v. Mooney, 64 Ind. App. 479, 116 N.E. 60 (1917).

In an action for partition, when the tenant in possession asked an allowance for improvements made while in possession, the cotenant could answer setting up the facts as to the receipt of rents by the tenant in possession due the cotenant, and such facts could have been taken into account in making the adjustment. Peden v. Cavins, 134 Ind. 494, 34 N.E. 7, 39 Am. St. R. 276 (1893); Geisendorff v. Cobbs, 47 Ind. App. 573, 94 N.E. 236 (1911).

Rents and advances could have been taken into account in settlement of claims in actions for partition. Barnett v. Thomas, 36 Ind. App. 441, 75 N.E. 868, 114 Am. St. R. 385 (1905); Porter v. Mooney, 64 Ind. App. 479, 116 N.E. 60 (1917).

In an action by a part of the heirs of an intestate against one of them for partition, in which they asked for an accounting for the rents and profits, where the defendant, with the consent and approval of his cotenants, had used the rents and profits in making improvements on the land, the charge against the occupying tenant should have been based on the actual condition of the real estate from year to year. Porter v. Mooney, 64 Ind. App. 479, 116 N.E. 60 (1917).

Where the venue of an action for partition and to quiet title to real estate was changed from the county wherein the real estate was situated, and the action was tried and judgment entered, the venue was properly changed back to the county where the real estate was situated and where the action first originated pursuant to an agreement of the parties entered in the consent judgment where the action was tried, and defendants, having acquiesced by voluntary agreements in such change, could not successfully assail it, even though the action of the court in granting it was erroneous. Hoffman v. Hoffman, 115 Ind. App. 277, 57 N.E.2d 591, 58 N.E.2d 201 (1944).

In an action for partition and to quiet title to real estate, a judgment ordering sale of the land as an indivisible had sufficient finality to support an appeal to the appellate court (Court of Appeals), even though, after entry of the judgment, the lower court had further duties to perform before the litigation could be considered finally disposed of and the cause was a pending action to the extent that the venue thereof could be changed by agreement of the parties back to the county where the action first originated. Hoffman v. Hoffman, 115 Ind. App. 277, 57 N.E.2d 591, 58 N.E.2d 201 (1944).

32-17-4-4. Judgments. — (a) If:

    (1) upon trial of any issue;

    (2) upon default; or

(3) by consent of parties;
the court determines that partition should be made, the court shall award an interlocutory judgment that partition be made to parties who desire partition.

(b) In issuing a judgment under subsection (a), the court shall:
(1) specify the share assigned to each party; and
(2) take into consideration advancements to heirs of a person dying intestate.

(c) If the court issues a judgment under subsection (a), any part of the premises remaining after the partition belongs to the persons entitled to the premises, subject to a future partition.

(d) If:
(1) upon trial of any issue;
(2) upon default; or
(3) by confession or consent of parties;
the court determines that the land for which partition is demanded cannot be divided without damage to the owners, the court may order the whole or any part of the premises to be sold as provided under section 12 [IC 32-17-4-12] of this chapter. [P.L.2-2002, § 2.]

Cross References. Advancements, charging of, IC 29-1-2-10, IC 29-1-17-5.

NOTES TO DECISIONS

ANALYSIS

In general.
Advancements.
Complaint.
Judicial power.
Orders.
—Authority and effect.
Review on appeal.

In General.
It was only where land could not have been divided without damage to the owners that a court could order a sale of the whole or any part thereof as a means of accomplishing the primary object of the proceedings. Pavy v. Pavy, 121 Ind. App. 194, 98 N.E.2d 224 (1951).

Advancements.
Advancements should have been taken into consideration in decreeing partition. Kepler v. Kepler, 2 Ind. 363 (1850); Nicholson v. Caress, 59 Ind. 39 (1877); Scott v. Harris, 127 Ind. 520, 27 N.E. 150 (1891); New v. New, 127 Ind. 576, 27 N.E. 154 (1891); Purner v. Koontz, 138 Ind. 252, 36 N.E. 1094 (1894); Brown v. Brown, 139 Ind. 653, 39 N.E. 152 (1894); Green v. Brown, 146 Ind. 1, 44 N.E. 805 (1896).
Upon dividing land in partition, advancements should have been taken into consideration and apportionments made by commis-

sioners and their acts were not judicial but were computations based on the judgment of partition defining the share of each tenant. Scott v. Harris, 127 Ind. 520, 27 N.E. 150 (1891).

Complaint.
Where the cause of action stated in the original complaint was simply that of partition, which was amended so as to state a cause of action in ejectment, the amended complaint stated a different cause of action, and did not relate back to the filing of the original complaint, so as to have defeated the statute of limitations. Blake v. Minkner, 136 Ind. 418, 36 N.E. 246 (1894).

Judicial Power.
In considering a petition for partition, the trial court does not have the power to order one tenant to sell his interest to the other, while allowing the tenant in possession the right to retain the entire tract. Janik v. Janik, 474 N.E.2d 1054 (Ind. App. 1985).

Orders.

—Authority and Effect.
The order for partition should have specified the interest of each of the parties in the lands. Lease v. Carr, 5 Blackf. 353 (1840).
If a portion of the land could have been

Orders. (Cont'd)

—Authority and Effect. (Cont'd)
divided without injury, such portion should have been ordered set off. Lucas v. Peters, 45 Ind. 313 (1873).

The order for partition settled and determined the rights of the parties. Wright v. Nipple, 92 Ind. 310 (1883); Fleenor v. Driskill, 97 Ind. 27 (1884); Irvin v. Buckles, 148 Ind. 389, 47 N.E. 822 (1897).

An order for partition did not estop one of defaulting defendants from asserting title to the portion set off to a codefendant. Finley v. Cathcart, 149 Ind. 470, 48 N.E. 586 (1897), rehearing overruled, 149 Ind. 489, 49 N.E. 381, 63 Am. St. R. 292 (1898).

Authority of the trial court, without the appointment of commissioners, to determine the issue as to the susceptibility of the real estate to division without damage thereto was not limited by former IC 32-4-5-13 (repealed; see this chapter for similar provisions). Crumrine v. Crumrine, 77 Ind. App. 76, 131 N.E. 230 (1921).

The mere appointment of a commissioner, conveyance not having been executed by him, did not prevent the original owners, or one of them to whom the other conveyed his interest, from maintaining an action against a third person for possession of the premises. Gowan v. Greathouse, 78 Ind. App. 98, 134 N.E. 898 (1922).

Where neither the court, commissioners, nor the parties were aware of the fact that the decree of partition entered would operate to cut one foot off the end of the barn, the barn should have been allowed to have been moved, for it was the duty of the commissioners in making the partition to set off the one third in a manner that would not damage the owners of the tract involved. Livengood v. Munns, 108 Ind. App. 27, 27 N.E.2d 92 (1940).

Review on Appeal.
An appeal did not lie from an interlocutory judgment decreeing partition. Davis v. Davis, 36 Ind. 160 (1871); Rennick v. Chandler, 59 Ind. 354 (1877).

An appeal could have been taken from a judgment ordering a sale of lands, or decreeing a lien on the same. Rennick v. Chandler, 59 Ind. 354 (1877); Fleenor v. Driskill, 97 Ind. 27 (1884); Kreitline v. Franz, 106 Ind. 359, 6 N.E. 912 (1886); Barnett v. Thomas, 36 Ind. App. 441, 75 N.E. 868, 114 Am. St. R. 385 (1905); Stauffer v. Kesler, 191 Ind. 702, 127 N.E. 803 (1920).

A judgment as to all the matters in issue, with the usual order of partition, was final and an appeal could have been taken therefrom. Mayer v. Haggerty, 138 Ind. 628, 38 N.E. 42 (1894).

An appeal could not have been taken from an interlocutory order of partition, but where the title of each of the cotenants was directly put in issue and adjudicated, an order for the sale of the property as indivisible constituted a final judgment, and, after a motion for a new trial had been ruled upon, an appeal would lie. Jones v. Jones, 84 Ind. App. 176, 149 N.E. 108 (1925), rehearing denied, 84 Ind. App. 183, 150 N.E. 65 (1926).

Although the order appealed was denominated an "interlocutory" decree, it was final and appealable, since it ordered a sale of the real estate. Hawkins v. Hawkins, 160 Ind. App. 5, 41 Ind. Dec. 396, 309 N.E.2d 177 (1974).

32-17-4-5. No partition contrary to intention of testator. — Notwithstanding section 4 [IC 32-17-4-4] of this chapter, a court may not order or affirm partition of any real estate contrary to the intention of a testator expressed in the testator's will. [P.L.2-2002, § 2.]

NOTES TO DECISIONS

ANALYSIS

In general.
Applicability.
Consent of beneficiaries.
Constructive conversion in will.
Will silent on partition.

In General.
When real estate was devised, partition thereof could not have been made contrary to the directions in the will. Brown v. Brown, 43 Ind. 474 (1873); Kepley v. Overton, 74 Ind. 448 (1881); Jones v. Jones, 84 Ind. App. 176, 149 N.E. 108 (1925), rehearing denied, 84 Ind. App. 183, 150 N.E. 65 (1926).

Where a deceased wife devised certain of her real estate to her husband for life, and directed that on his death the real estate be sold and the proceeds distributed between decedent's sister and brother, the heirs of the deceased sister and brother were not entitled to partition of the real estate between themselves. Duckwall v. Lease, 106 Ind. App. 664, 20 N.E.2d 204 (1939).

Applicability.
The provision of this section pertaining to

Applicability. (Cont'd)
partition of real estate devised by will in a manner not provided by the testator did not affect the rights of parties who were not affected by the will. Tom v. Tom, 107 Ind. App. 599, 26 N.E.2d 410 (1940).

A childless second wife was not prevented by this section from maintaining partition proceedings against the testator's son as remainderman, contrary to the testator's intention as disclosed by the will. Tom v. Tom, 107 Ind. App. 599, 26 N.E.2d 410 (1940).

Predecessor section to this section did not apply where the defendants were not affected by the will, not named in the will, and not bound by its terms, although the defendants were heirs to the testator, as grandchildren of the beneficiaries. Dwyer v. Allyn, 596 N.E.2d 903 (Ind. App. 1992).

Consent of Beneficiaries.
If a will directed land to be sold and the proceeds divided, one of the beneficiaries could not have the land divided without the consent of the other beneficiaries. Walling v. Scott, 50 Ind. App. 23, 96 N.E. 481 (1911), rehearing overruled, 97 N.E. 388 (1912).

Constructive Conversion in Will.
The fiction of constructive conversion of real estate by provision in will that the real estate be sold and the proceeds divided between designated persons rested on the proposition that in the absence of intervening interests or rights the testator's intention, so far as it affects the beneficiary, would control. Duckwall v. Lease, 106 Ind. App. 664, 20 N.E.2d 204 (1939).

Will Silent on Partition.
Where there was no expression in the testatrix's will indicating a desire that the land not be partitioned this section was no bar to partition. Berkebile v. Barnett, 159 Ind. App. 491, 41 Ind. Dec. 87, 307 N.E.2d 490 (1974).

32-17-4-6. Appointment of commissioners. — Upon judgment of partition, the court shall appoint three (3) individuals as commissioners who:

    (1)　are disinterested resident freeholders;

    (2)　reside and own land in the county in which court is held; and

    (3)　are not related to any of the parties;

who shall make partition of the land in accordance with the judgment of the court. [P.L.2-2002, § 2.]

NOTES TO DECISIONS

ANALYSIS

In general.
Discretion.
Failure to act.
Immunity for official acts.

In General.
Where partition had been accomplished by the trial court under IC 29-1-17-11, it was not necessary to appoint commissioners for partition under this section. Berkebile v. Barnett, 159 Ind. App. 491, 41 Ind. Dec. 87, 307 N.E.2d 490 (1974).

Commissioners are appointed by a court, their duties are defined by statute, and the court reviews their conduct. Ashbrook v. Hoffman, 617 F.2d 474 (7th Cir. 1980).

The commissioners serve as instruments or arms of the court leading to the issuance of a judicial decree of partition. Ashbrook v. Hoffman, 617 F.2d 474 (7th Cir. 1980).

The statute governing the appointment of a commissioner to sell land does not require that the commissioner be disinterested, unlike the statute regarding commissioners for the partition of land, since there is not the same risk that an interested commissioner could prejudice one cotenant while physically partitioning land, due to the necessarily adverse interests of cotenants. Cohen v. Meyer, 701 N.E.2d 1253 (Ind. App. 1998).

Discretion.
The partition commissioners, under the supervision of the court, exercise discretion in the conduct of quasi-judicial proceedings. Ashbrook v. Hoffman, 617 F.2d 474 (7th Cir. 1980).

Failure to Act.
If the commissioners appointed failed to act, others could have been appointed. McCormick v. Taylor, 5 Ind. 436 (1854).

Immunity for Official Acts.
Partition commissioners are sufficiently related to the judicial process to entitle them to quasi-judicial absolute immunity for their official acts. Ashbrook v. Hoffman, 617 F.2d 474 (7th Cir. 1980).

32-17-4-7. Oath of commissioners. — (a) Before discharging their duties, the commissioners appointed under section 6 [IC 32-17-4-6] of this chapter shall take an oath to faithfully perform the duties of their trust.

(b) The oath described in subsection (a) must:

(1) if taken in open court, be entered in the court's order book; and

(2) if not taken in open court, be endorsed on the warrant issued to the commissioners to make the partition. [P.L.2-2002, § 2.]

NOTES TO DECISIONS

ANALYSIS

County surveyor.
Omission of seal to warrant.

County Surveyor.

If the county surveyor was a commissioner, he could administer the oath to the other commissioners. Wilcox v. Monday, 83 Ind. 335 (1882).

Omission of Seal to Warrant.

The omission of the seal of the court to the warrant issued to the commissioners was immaterial, and the writ would have been deemed amended. Crane v. Kimmer, 77 Ind. 215 (1881).

32-17-4-8. Shares of multiple parties set off together. — Two (2) or more persons may, if they choose, have their shares set off together. [P.L.2-2002, § 2.]

32-17-4-9. Report of commissioners. — (a) The commissioners shall report to the court regarding their activities under this chapter.

(b) The commissioners shall make the report required under this section:

(1) in open court; or

(2) by signing and swearing to the report before a person authorized to administer oaths.

(c) A report filed under this section must specify the shares assigned to each party by:

(1) divisions;

(2) lots;

(3) metes and bounds; or

(4) plats.

[P.L.2-2002, § 2.]

NOTES TO DECISIONS

ANALYSIS

Authority of courts and commissioners.
Corrections by report.
Description of land.
Majority report.
Partition proper.
Precatory recommendations.

Authority of Courts and Commissioners.

Trial courts and commissioners may go beyond the express provisions of the partition statutes in order to accomplish an equitable division, and have the power to award owelty in order to equalize the value of each party's interest. Culley v. McFadden Lake Corp., 674 N.E.2d 208 (Ind. App. 1996).

Corrections by Report.

The commissioners could correct by their report inaccurate descriptions of the lands, and the court could order such descriptions corrected in the other proceedings. Randles v. Randles, 63 Ind. 93 (1878).

The commissioners had no authority to change the lines between the lands divided and the adjacent lands. Brown v. Anderson, 90 Ind. 93 (1883).

Description of Land.

If the lands were so described that they could have been located by a survey, it was sufficient. Boyd v. Doty, 8 Ind. 370 (1856); Miller v. City of Indianapolis, 123 Ind. 196, 24 N.E. 228 (1890).

The report should have described the lands set off with such certainty as would enable the same to have been located. Duling v. Johnson, 32 Ind. 155 (1869).

Majority Report.

A majority of the commissioners could make a report. Griffy v. Enders, 60 Ind. 23 (1877).

Partition Proper.

Where trial court found land could be partitioned, partition would benefit both parties and the land did not have to be sold, and where commissioners testified that, after trying several different partition plans, their recommendation was the most equitable and owelty awarded one party was a nominal amount compared to the total value of the land, trial court did not err in partitioning the land and awarding owelty. Culley v. McFadden Lake Corp., 674 N.E.2d 208 (Ind. App. 1996).

Precatory Recommendations.

Commissioners' statement, that if parties could not agree to partition they recommended land be sold and interest divided, served only as guidance and not as a requirement, and trial court was not required to obtain the consent of all of the parties before adopting commissioners' report. Culley v. McFadden Lake Corp., 674 N.E.2d 208 (Ind. App. 1996).

32-17-4-10. Confirmation of reports. — If the court confirms a report filed under section 9 [IC 32-17-4-9] of this chapter, the court shall:

(1) spread the report on the order book;

(2) enter a judgment of partition in accordance with the report; and

(3) record the report and judgment in a separate book kept for that purpose. [P.L.2-2002, § 2.]

NOTES TO DECISIONS

ANALYSIS

In general.
Authority of courts and commissioners.
Clarification of report.
Partition proper.
Precatory recommendations.
Title, effect of judgment.
When title in issue.
Widow.

In General.

If a party died pending the action, a decree setting off to such part a portion of the lands was a nullity. Harness v. Harness, 63 Ind. 1 (1878).

Judgment in former action as to partition, dower and rents, was conclusive. Beaver v. Irwin, 6 Ind. App. 285, 33 N.E. 462 (1893).

The purchaser holding title by virtue of sheriff's deed was entitled to have his title quieted against parties to partition proceeding, they, by such proceeding, having received their due proportion of the land that had descended. Brown v. Grepe, 135 Ind. 4, 34 N.E. 312 (1893).

Decree of partition in accordance with the interest of parties set forth in partition was an adjudication of the rights of the parties. Irvin v. Buckles, 148 Ind. 389, 47 N.E. 822 (1897).

In an action by a tenant in common for the partition of his half in the real estate so held, no issue was raised between the defendants as to their respective interest, as between each other, where defendants did not appear to such action, but were defaulted, and a defendant therein was not estopped from asserting title to the portion of real estate set off to her codefendant while she held by an unrecorded deed of conveyance made prior to the partition proceeding. Finley v. Cathcart, 149 Ind. 470, 48 N.E. 586 (1897), rehearing overruled, 149 Ind. 489, 49 N.E. 381, 63 Am. St. R. 292 (1898); Pence v. Long, 38 Ind. App. 63, 77 N.E. 961 (1906).

Authority of Courts and Commissioners.

Trial courts and commissioners may go beyond the express provisions of the partition statutes in order to accomplish an equitable division, and have the power to award owelty in order to equalize the value of each party's interest. Culley v. McFadden Lake Corp., 674 N.E.2d 208 (Ind. App. 1996).

Clarification of Report.

Where commissioners recommended awarding plaintiffs a collective one-third interest, and trial court revised the commissioners' report to award each plaintiff a one-sixth interest, trial court merely clarified the commissioners' recommended partition scheme,

Clarification of Report. (Cont'd)
and did not disturb the commissioners' distribution or change the meaning of their report. Culley v. McFadden Lake Corp., 674 N.E.2d 208 (Ind. App. 1996).

Partition Proper.
Where trial court found land could be partitioned, partition would benefit both parties and the land did not have to be sold, and where commissioners testified that, after trying several different partition plans, their recommendation was the most equitable and owelty awarded one party was a nominal amount compared to the total value of the land, trial court did not err in partitioning the land and awarding owelty. Culley v. McFadden Lake Corp., 674 N.E.2d 208 (Ind. App. 1996).

Precatory Recommendations.
Commissioners' statement, that if parties could not agree to partition they recommended land be sold and interest divided, served only as guidance and not as a requirement, and trial court was not required to obtain the consent of all of the parties before adopting commissioners' report. Culley v. McFadden Lake Corp., 674 N.E.2d 208 (Ind. App. 1996).

Title, Effect of Judgment.
Judgment of partition did not ordinarily settle any question of title, but simply allotted to each a share of the land to be held in severalty and divested of the title of his cotenants; but it settled the rights of the parties at the time of the entry of judgment. Avery v. Akins, 74 Ind. 283 (1881); Crane v. Kimmer, 77 Ind. 215 (1881), overruled on other grounds, Green v. Brown, 146 Ind. 1, 44 N.E. 805 (1896); Hanna v. Scott, 84 Ind. 71 (1882); L'Hommedieu v. Cincinnati, W. & M. Ry., 120 Ind. 435, 22 N.E. 125 (1889); Isbell v. Stewart, 125 Ind. 112, 25 N.E. 160 (1890); Haskett v. Maxey, 134 Ind. 182, 33 N.E. 358, 19 L.R.A. 379 (1893); Stephenson v. Boody, 139 Ind. 60, 38 N.E. 331 (1894); Finley v. Cathcart, 149 Ind. 470, 48 N.E. 586, 49 N.E. 381, 63 Am. St. R. 292 (1897); Thompson v. Henry, 153 Ind. 56, 54 N.E. 109 (1899).

The judgment had no effect on after-acquired titles. Thorp v. Hanes, 107 Ind. 324, 6 N.E. 920 (1886).

If the title to the lands was directly put in issue, the judgment of partition was conclusive as to the rights of the parties. Thorp v. Hanes, 107 Ind. 324, 6 N.E. 920 (1886); Watson v. Camper, 119 Ind. 60, 21 N.E. 323 (1889); L'Hommedieu v. Cincinnati, W. & M. Ry., 120 Ind. 435, 22 N.E. 125 (1889); Isbell v. Stewart, 125 Ind. 112, 25 N.E. 160 (1890); Branson v. Studebaker, 133 Ind. 147, 33 N.E. 98 (1892); Finley v. Cathcart, 149 Ind. 470, 48 N.E. 586 (1897), rehearing overruled, 149 Ind. 489, 49 N.E. 381, 63 Am. St. R. 292 (1898).

When Title in Issue.
Ordinarily, the title was not in issue in a partition suit, but the pleadings could have been so drawn as to have put the title in issue. Isbell v. Stewart, 125 Ind. 112, 25 N.E. 160 (1890); Davis v. Lennen, 125 Ind. 185, 24 N.E. 885 (1890); Hawkins v. Taylor, 128 Ind. 431, 27 N.E. 1117 (1891); Thompson v. McCorkle, 136 Ind. 484, 34 N.E. 813 (1893), motion overruled, 36 N.E. 211, 43 Am. St. R. 334 (1894); Mayer v. Haggerty, 138 Ind. 628, 38 N.E. 42 (1894); Green v. Brown, 146 Ind. 1, 44 N.E. 805 (1896); Heritage v. Heritage, 52 Ind. App. 76, 99 N.E. 442 (1912).

When the title to the real estate, or any part thereof, was bona fide in question, proof thereof could have been made under an answer of general denial. Hawkins v. Taylor, 128 Ind. 431, 27 N.E. 1117 (1891); Shetterly v. Axt, 37 Ind. App. 687, 76 N.E. 901, 77 N.E. 865 (1906).

It was presumed that title was not in issue in partition proceedings. Green v. Brown, 146 Ind. 1, 44 N.E. 805 (1896); Pence v. Long, 38 Ind. App. 63, 77 N.E. 961 (1906); Heritage v. Heritage, 52 Ind. App. 76, 99 N.E. 442 (1912).

Widow.
In a suit for partition by one of the children of the deceased husband against the widow and the other children, if the title was not directly put in issue by the pleading, a decree adjudging the widow was entitled to an estate for life was not conclusive of her interest. Habig v. Dodge, 127 Ind. 31, 25 N.E. 182 (1890).

A judgment by default decreeing partition of lands inherited by a remarrying widow and the children of her former marriage merely allotted the lands, and such widow took her share subject to the law of descent casting the inheritance thereof on such children in case of her death during the subsequent marriage. Pence v. Long, 38 Ind. App. 63, 77 N.E. 961 (1906).

32-17-4-11. Setting aside of reports. — (a) Before confirming a report filed under section 9 [IC 32-17-4-9] of this chapter, the court may, if the court determines that good cause exists, set aside the report.

(b) If the court sets aside a report under subsection (a):

(1) the court may:

(A) recommit the duty of partition to the same commissioners; or

(B) appoint other commissioners in the same manner as the original commissioners; and

(2) the commissioners shall perform the duties described in this chapter. [P.L.2-2002, § 2.]

NOTES TO DECISIONS

Analysis

Clarification of report.
Method of questioning report.
Setting aside report required.
Trial by court.

Clarification of Report.

Where commissioners recommended awarding plaintiffs a collective one-third interest, and trial court revised the commissioners' report to award each plaintiff a one-sixth interest, trial court merely clarified the commissioners' recommended partition scheme, and did not disturb the commissioners' distribution or change the meaning of their report. Culley v. McFadden Lake Corp., 674 N.E.2d 208 (Ind. App. 1996).

Method of Questioning Report.

To question the correctness of the report of the commissioners, exceptions thereto should have been filed, and if overruled, exceptions taken to the ruling and such ruling assigned as error. Kern v. Maginniss, 55 Ind. 459 (1877); Clark v. Stephenson, 73 Ind. 489 (1881).

Under the earlier law, the exceptions and action of the court had to be shown by a bill of exceptions. Clark v. Stephenson, 73 Ind. 489 (1881); Radcliff v. Radford, 96 Ind. 482 (1882).

Merely excepting to the report of the commissioners presented no question. Quick v. Brenner, 101 Ind. 230 (1885).

Setting Aside Report Required.

Where commissioners, in dividing land, valued the various parts according to their possible use, and with respect to one area valued it for a use for which it could not be used and comply with the zoning laws, the court could not make any adjustments in the commissioner's report but the report would have to be set aside and further proceedings taken pursuant to this section. Gilstrap v. Gilstrap, 73 Ind. Dec. 181, 397 N.E.2d 1277 (Ind. App. 1979).

Trial by Court.

Exceptions to report of commissioners were triable by the court only. Dillman v. Cox, 23 Ind. 440 (1864).

The report of commissioners was regarded in the same light as a verdict, and should only have been set aside for the same reason that a verdict would have been. Lucas v. Peters, 45 Ind. 313 (1873).

In proceedings to review judgment of partition, if the court found the partition as made was unequal, it could not render a judgment requiring monetary compensation, but rather should have required another partition and if that was unsuccessful then order sold such portion as was not susceptible of division. Lucas v. Peters, 45 Ind. 313 (1873).

The truth of the exceptions must have been shown to have been available. Parks v. Kimes, 100 Ind. 148 (1885); Van Buskirk v. Stover, 162 Ind. 448, 70 N.E. 520 (1904).

32-17-4-12. Court ordered sale of land. — (a) If the commissioners report to the court that the whole or part of the land of which partition is demanded can not be divided without damage to the owners, the court may order the whole or any part of the land to be sold at public or private sale on terms and conditions prescribed by the court.

(b) If the court orders a sale under this section, the order shall provide for reasonable public notice of the sale.

(c) If the court orders a sale under this section but does not order the sale to be made for cash, the court shall require that the purchaser make a cash payment of at least one-third (⅓) of the purchase price to the commissioner appointed under section 14 [IC 32-17-4-14] of this chapter at the time of the sale.

(d) Land sold under this section may not be sold for less than:

(1) if sold at public sale, two-thirds (⅔) of its appraised value; and

(2) if sold at private sale, its appraised value.
The court shall determine the appraised value of the land in the same manner as in cases of sales of land on execution.

(e) If only a part of land is sold under this section, the remainder may be partitioned as provided under this chapter.

(f) If the value of land ordered by the court to be sold at private sale does not exceed one thousand dollars ($1,000), the land may, in the discretion of the court, be sold without any notice of sale being had or given.

(g) In all cases, the purchaser of land sold under this section has rights in all crops planted on the land after the sale.

(h) The court may:

(1) approve reports of sale by commissioners in partition proceedings; and

(2) order the deed delivered to the purchaser.
[P.L.2-2002, § 2.]

Cross References. Decedents' estates, vacation of sale, resale, IC 29-1-15-16.

NOTES TO DECISIONS

ANALYSIS

Advertising of sale.
Amount of bid.
Appointment of commissioner.
Collateral attack.
Commissioner's report.
Determination of court.
Division of proceeds.
Duties of commissioner for sale.
Estoppel.
Immunity for official acts.
Liens.
New trial.
Nonjoinder of parties.
Oral contract of sale.
Parties.
Payment of taxes.
Report and confirmation.
Review on appeal.
Sale free of liens.
Setting aside sale.
Value of land.
Wife's or widow's interest.

Advertising of Sale.
Any inadequacy in the advertisement is reviewable on appeal but will not subject the commissioners to a federal civil damages suit. Ashbrook v. Hoffman, 617 F.2d 474 (7th Cir. 1980).

Amount of Bid.
At a partition sale, the bid of $2,550, not the amount of such bid plus the 1932 taxes agreed to be paid by the bidder, was the amount bid, in determining whether the subsequent bid exceeded the original bid by ten per cent, as

required by statute in order to set aside the sale under original bid. Broo v. Duncan, 97 Ind. App. 597, 187 N.E. 680 (1933).

Appointment of Commissioner.
Where a trial court appointed a real estate agent as commissioner for the sale of property under the partition statute, neither the appointment nor the commission rate was an abuse of discretion in that there was evidence that the agent could obtain a higher price than was otherwise offered, and would be responsible for all costs of sale. Cohen v. Meyer, 701 N.E.2d 1253 (Ind. App. 1998).

Collateral Attack.
A judgment confirming the sale could not have been collaterally attacked. McLead v. Applegate, 127 Ind. 349, 26 N.E. 830 (1891); Eller v. Evans, 128 Ind. 156, 27 N.E. 418 (1891).

Commissioner's Report.
If the commissioners reported the land indivisible, it should have been stated that no share could have been set off without injury to the parties. Lake v. Jarrett, 12 Ind. 395 (1859); Lucas v. Peters, 45 Ind. 313 (1873).

The report of the commissioners that the lands could not have been divided should only have been set aside on proof of the falsity thereof. Patterson v. Blake, 12 Ind. 436 (1859).

The making of an interlocutory order for partition and the appointment of commissioners did not prevent the making of an order for sale if the commissioners reported the land

Commissioner's Report. (Cont'd)
indivisible. Roach v. Baker, 130 Ind. 362, 30 N.E. 310 (1892).

If the commissioners reported that the property was not divisible, and the court ordered the property sold, the correctness of the action of the court could not have been raised by an exception to such report. Roach v. Baker, 130 Ind. 362, 30 N.E. 310 (1892).

Determination of Court.
This section did not limit the authority of the trial court, without the appointment of commissioners, to determine the issue as to the susceptibility of the real estate to division without damage thereof, under former IC 32-4-5-4 (repealed; for similar provisions see IC 32-17-4-4). Crumrine v. Crumrine, 77 Ind. App. 76, 131 N.E. 230 (1921).

Division of Proceeds.
The proceeds of sale should have been divided among the parties according to their respective interests. Chisham v. Way, 73 Ind. 362 (1881).

Duties of Commissioner for Sale.
The duties of a commissioner for sale of lands in a partition proceeding were determined by statute and orders of court, and the commissioner was an instrument or arm of the court, acting for and primarily answerable to the court. Bryan v. Yoder, 225 Ind. 57, 71 N.E.2d 474 (1947).

Estoppel.
The plaintiffs, having acquiesced in the order of sale, arising out of partition proceedings, more than thirty years, and having received and retained the purchase-money paid for it, was estopped from claiming any interest in the land as against the purchaser at the sale or those claiming under him. Eller v. Evans, 128 Ind. 156, 27 N.E. 418 (1891).

Immunity for Official Acts.
Complaints concerning the disposal of the proceeds of sale where it is not alleged that the proceeds were misappropriated; improper participation in the bidding process; and an alleged unlawful cover-up of wrongdoing in the sale; all these relate to the conduct of the quasi-judicial partition proceeding and are activities for which the commissioners are absolutely immune. Ashbrook v. Hoffman, 617 F.2d 474 (7th Cir. 1980).

Liens.
Persons holding liens on an undivided interest in the land could have the share of the proceeds of sale of the debtor applied on the liens. Milligan v. Poole, 35 Ind. 64 (1871); Arnold v. Butterbaugh, 92 Ind. 403 (1884); Huffman v. Darling, 153 Ind. 22, 53 N.E. 939

(1899); A. Kiefer Drug Co. v. DeLay, 63 Ind. App. 639, 115 N.E. 71 (1917).

Liens on undivided portions of land would follow the share of the person owing the debt. Milligan v. Poole, 35 Ind. 64 (1871); Huffman v. Darling, 153 Ind. 22, 53 N.E. 939 (1899); Globe Mercantile Co. v. Perkeypile, 189 Ind. 31, 125 N.E. 29 (1920).

If the purchaser paid liens, he could be subrogated to the rights of the party who should have paid the liens in the proceeds of sale. Spray v. Rodman, 43 Ind. 225 (1873); Dunning v. Seward, 90 Ind. 63 (1883).

Unless otherwise decreed, the purchaser of lands took the same subject to liens. Wood v. Winings, 58 Ind. 322 (1877).

The court could order the lands sold free of liens, and the liens transferred to the proceeds of sale. Fouty v. Morrison, 73 Ind. 333 (1881).

In an action for partition, the various estates and interests of the common owners were transferred to the fund arising from a sale of the land. Coquillard v. Coquillard, 62 Ind. App. 426, 113 N.E. 474 (1916).

New Trial.
A motion for a new trial in partition, to have been available, must have been made during the term at which the finding was made or verdict rendered, except in special cases or by consent. Jones v. Jones, 91 Ind. 72 (1883).

Nonjoinder of Parties.
If all the owners of the lands were not made parties, the sale could have been set aside. Harlan v. Stout, 22 Ind. 488 (1864).

Oral Contract of Sale.
An alleged oral contract of sale with a commissioner appointed in a partition proceeding was not effectual where it was never reported to the court by the commissioner, never confirmed by the court, and deed was never ordered as provided by law. Bryan v. Yoder, 225 Ind. 57, 71 N.E.2d 474 (1947).

Parties.
Where three persons owned tract of land as tenants in common and two of such persons had entered into a contract of sale of their interests to another, such other person should have been made a party to the proceeding for partition. Gilstrap v. Gilstrap, 73 Ind. Dec. 181, 397 N.E.2d 1277 (Ind. App. 1979).

Payment of Taxes.
Judgment in partition directing sale and directing payment to plaintiff of one-half of taxes paid by him was proper where plaintiff owned one-half interest and defendants owned one-half interest in lands. Hosanna v. Odishoo, 208 Ind. 132, 193 N.E. 599, reh'g denied, 208 Ind. 144, 195 N.E. 72 (1935).

Report and Confirmation.

Report to and confirmation by the court was necessary to complete a commissioner's sale in a partition proceeding, and without such report and confirmation, the sale was ineffectual. Bryan v. Yoder, 225 Ind. 57, 71 N.E.2d 474 (1947).

Review on Appeal.

An appeal would lie from an order decreeing the sale of the lands. Hunter v. Miller, 17 Ind. 88 (1861); Rennick v. Chandler, 59 Ind. 354 (1877); Benefiel v. Aughe, 93 Ind. 401 (1884); Fleenor v. Driskill, 97 Ind. 27 (1884); Kreitline v. Franz, 106 Ind. 359, 6 N.E. 912 (1886); Barnett v. Thomas, 36 Ind. App. 441, 75 N.E. 868, 114 Am. St. R. 385 (1905); Stauffer v. Kesler, 191 Ind. 702, 127 N.E. 803 (1920).

An order to sell in partition because the land could not be partitioned without damage was not appealable under former § 2-3218 (since repealed; see now Rule AP. 4) or former § 4-214 (since repealed), but such order of sale was a final judgment under IC 34-1-47-1. Stauffer v. Kesler, 191 Ind. 702, 127 N.E. 803 (1920); Heppe v. Heppe, 199 Ind. 566, 149 N.E. 890 (1925).

Sale Free of Liens.

Judgment in partition directing sale free of liens asserted in complaint and cross-complaint and directing payment thereof from proceeds was held proper as against contention that the complaint did not state facts entitling plaintiff to foreclosure of his lien. Hosanna v. Odishoo, 208 Ind. 132, 193 N.E. 599, reh'g denied, 208 Ind. 144, 195 N.E. 72 (1935).

Setting Aside Sale.

An order setting aside a partition sale of real estate, because of the subsequent "final judgment" as to the purchaser, "final judgment" as to the purchaser, even though such purchaser's intervention in the suit and motion to confirm the sale was not the proper procedure. Broo v. Duncan, 97 Ind. App. 597, 187 N.E. 680 (1933).

When stockholders of an insolvent corporation objected to a receiver's sale of corporate assets, they should have followed the procedure outlined in this section. Cooper v. Morris, 210 Ind. 162, 200 N.E. 222 (1936).

Value of Land.

Parties to partition proceeding could not bind trial court by stipulating land's value. Bechert v. Bechert, 435 N.E.2d 573 (Ind. App. 1982).

Wife's or Widow's Interest.

A second wife who had no children, there being children of the first marriage of the husband, was entitled to the value of her life estate out of the proceeds of sale. Russell v. Russell, 48 Ind. 456 (1874); Swain v. Hardin, 64 Ind. 85 (1878).

When lands were sold, the widow of a former owner was entitled to her share of the proceeds, although she might have been prevented from conveying the lands by reason of her remarriage. Small v. Roberts, 51 Ind. 281 (1875); Klinesmith v. Socwell, 100 Ind. 589 (1885).

The wife of the owner of land did not need to be a party in order to divest her inchoate interest by a sale of the land. Haggerty v. Wagner, 148 Ind. 625, 48 N.E. 366, 39 L.R.A. 384 (1897); Wagner v. Carskadon, 28 Ind. App. 573, 60 N.E. 731, 61 N.E. 976 (1901); Staser v. Gaar, Scott & Co., 168 Ind. 131, 79 N.E. 404 (1906).

The wife of a man whose interest in land was sold in partition proceedings was entitled to one-third of the purchase-money due her husband as against his general creditors. Staser v. Gaar, Scott & Co., 168 Ind. 131, 79 N.E. 404 (1906).

32-17-4-13. Confirmation of partial partition. — If the court confirms partial partition:

(1) the shares assigned are full shares; and

(2) the residue reserved for sale is discharged from all title or claim of the parties receiving assignment of their shares under the partition. [P.L.2-2002, § 2.]

NOTES TO DECISIONS

Interests in Remainder.

Default by defendants and the setting off of the share of plaintiff did not determine the interests of the several defendants in the remainder of the land. Finley v. Cathcart, 149 Ind. 470, 48 N.E. 586 (1897), rehearing overruled, 149 Ind. 489, 49 N.E. 381, 63 Am. St. R. 292 (1898).

32-17-4-14. Appointment of commissioner to conduct sale. — (a) If the court orders a sale under section 12 [IC 32-17-4-12] of this chapter, the court shall appoint a commissioner, other than a commissioner appointed to make partition, to conduct the sale.

(b) A commissioner appointed under this section shall file a bond payable to the state of Indiana in an amount determined by the court, conditioned for the faithful discharge of the duties of the commissioner's trust. [P.L.2-2002, § 2.]

Cross References. Real property, sale by fiduciary under order of court, bond, IC 30-3-3-1.

NOTES TO DECISIONS

ANALYSIS

Action on bond.
Demand.
Discretion of court.
Interest.
Limitations.
Parties.
Vacancy.

Action on Bond.

If the commissioner failed to pay over the proceeds of sale in proper time, or converted the money or notes to his own use, suit would lie on his bond. Maxedon v. State ex rel. Simpson, 24 Ind. 370 (1865); Owen v. State ex rel. Owen, 25 Ind. 107 (1865); Williams v. State ex rel. Johnson, 87 Ind. 527 (1882); Coggeshall v. State ex rel. Corder, 112 Ind. 561, 14 N.E. 555 (1887).

The duties of a commissioner appointed to make the sale of land in a partition proceeding were determined by the statutes and orders of the court, and he was an instrument of the court primarily answerable thereto, and only became liable on his bond when he failed to faithfully discharge the duties of his trust. A. Kiefer Drug Co. v. DeLay, 63 Ind. App. 639, 115 N.E. 71 (1917).

Demand.

No demand was necessary before suit on the bond of the commissioner. Ferguson v. State ex rel. Hagans, 90 Ind. 38 (1883).

Discretion of Court.

Where two commissioners appointed by the court could not agree upon the sale of partitioned land, it was not an abuse of the trial court's discretion to order one commissioner to execute a commissioner's deed, since the sale of land in partition was a judicial sale, and the commissioner was only an arm of the court, acting for and primarily answerable to the court. McFall v. Fouts, 139 Ind. App. 597, 8 Ind. Dec. 668, 218 N.E.2d 138 (1966).

Interest.

When the commissioner failed to properly pay over the purchase-money, he was chargeable with interest. Ferguson v. State ex rel. Hagans, 90 Ind. 38 (1883).

Limitations.

Suit on such bond was not barred until 20 years after the action accrued. Owen v. State ex rel. Owen, 25 Ind. 107 (1865).

Parties.

The successor of a commissioner could not, as relator, sue on the bond of the former commissioner, the persons in interest having been the proper relators. Maxedon v. State ex rel. Simpson, 24 Ind. 370 (1865).

Where, in a partition proceeding, an order was made for the sale of land and it was sold in accordance with the order, one holding a judgment against one of the parties in partition who was not himself a party and who did not file a transcript with the clerk until after the entry of the order of sale could not recover on the commissioner's bond because the commissioner, even though notified of the judgment creditor's claim, did not pay him the amount thereof. A. Kiefer Drug Co. v. DeLay, 63 Ind. App. 639, 115 N.E. 71 (1917).

The statute governing the appointment of a commissioner to sell land does not require that the commissioner be disinterested, unlike the statute regarding commissioners for the partition of land, since there is not the same risk that an interested commissioner could prejudice one cotenant while physically partitioning land, due to the necessarily adverse interests of cotenants. Cohen v. Meyer, 701 N.E.2d 1253 (Ind. App. 1998).

Vacancy.

If the position of commissioner became vacant, another commissioner could have been appointed. Coggeshall v. State ex rel. Corder, 112 Ind. 561, 14 N.E. 555 (1887).

32-17-4-15. Sale of land — Execution of conveyance — Mortgage.

— (a) If the court determines that:

(1) land is sold under section 12 [IC 32-17-4-12] of this chapter for cash; or

(2) land is sold under section 12 of this chapter for partial credit and that the first or cash payment of the purchase price is paid;

the court shall order the commissioner appointed under section 14 [IC 32-17-4-14] of this chapter, or some other person, to execute a conveyance to the purchaser.

(b) A conveyance made under this section bars all claims of the prior owners of the land as if the prior owners had executed the conveyance.

(c) If partial credit is given for land sold under section 12 of this chapter, the court shall, at the time the court orders the conveyance to be made under this section, also order and direct that, concurrently with the execution of the conveyance, the purchaser shall execute to the commissioner a mortgage upon the land to secure the deferred payments of the purchase price of the land.

(d) The commissioner shall place a mortgage executed under this section upon record as required by law. [P.L.2-2002, § 2.]

NOTES TO DECISIONS

ANALYSIS

Action for purchase money.
Oral contract of sale.
Possession.
Reference to records.

Action for Purchase Money.

The commissioner could sue for the purchase money without tendering a deed. Swain v. Morberly, 17 Ind. 99 (1861).

On obtaining a judgment for the purchase money, the commissioner could have the land ordered resold. Rout v. King, 103 Ind. 555, 3 N.E. 249 (1885).

Oral Contract of Sale.

An alleged oral contract of sale with a commissioner appointed in a partition proceeding was not effectual where it was never reported to the court by the commissioner, never confirmed by the court, and deed was never ordered as provided by law. Bryan v. Yoder, 225 Ind. 57, 71 N.E.2d 474 (1947).

Possession.

The purchaser of the lands was not entitled to the possession thereof until he obtained a deed. Stout v. McPheeters, 84 Ind. 585 (1882); Deputy v. Mooney, 97 Ind. 463 (1884).

The mere appointment of a commissioner, conveyance not having been executed by him, did not prevent the original owners, or one of them to whom the other conveyed his interest, from maintaining an action against a third person for possession of the premises. Gowan v. Greathouse, 78 Ind. App. 98, 134 N.E. 898 (1922).

A purchaser of land at a partition sale was not entitled to possession until he obtained a deed, and he was not entitled to a deed until the purchase money was paid or secured. Bryan v. Yoder, 225 Ind. 57, 71 N.E.2d 474 (1947).

Reference to Records.

The deed of a commissioner in partition, which gave the title of the cause and recited that it was made in pursuance to an order and judgment of court therein and appropriate entry citations, was sufficient to put subsequent purchasers or mortgagees from the grantee upon inquiry. Singer v. Scheible, 109 Ind. 575, 10 N.E. 616 (1887).

Collateral References. Rights and remedies of one purchasing at partition sale where there was misrepresentation or mistake as to acreage or location of boundaries of tract sold. 69 A.L.R.2d 254.

32-17-4-16. Commissioner may not purchase land. — Commissioners appointed to make partition, or to sell, may not purchase the land partitioned or sold by the commissioners. [P.L.2-2002, § 2.]

32-17-4-17. Payment of proceeds by commissioner. — The commissioner shall pay the proceeds of a sale under this chapter after payment of just costs and expenses to the persons entitled to the proceeds according to their respective shares, under the direction of the court. [P.L.2-2002, § 2.]

NOTES TO DECISIONS

ANALYSIS

In general.
Demand.
Payment to parties.
Valuation of improvements or repairs.

In General.
The court should order the distribution of the proceeds of sale among the parties according to their interests. Chisham v. Way, 73 Ind. 362 (1881).

In partition suits it was proper to make those who held liens on undivided interests in the land parties to the action, and the court had power to protect their interests and, in case of sale, to provide for the payment or satisfaction of such liens out of funds derived from the sale of such interests to the extent that the net proceeds from the sale were sufficient so to do. A. Kiefer Drug Co. v. DeLay, 63 Ind. App. 639, 115 N.E. 71 (1917).

The mere fact that a judgment was of record and appeared unsatisfied was not conclusive evidence that it was unpaid or that there was not some valid reason why funds in the hands of the commissioner in a partition proceeding should not have been applied to such a judgment against an heir of the lands sold. A. Kiefer Drug Co. v. DeLay, 63 Ind. App. 639, 115 N.E. 71 (1917).

Demand.
The commissioner should have paid to the parties their shares as fixed by the order of the court without demand. Ferguson v. State ex rel. Hagans, 90 Ind. 38 (1883).

Payment to Parties.
If the money was paid to the clerk of the court, the parties entitled thereto could have recovered the same. Hunt v. Milligan, 57 Ind. 141 (1877).

The commissioner should have paid the moneys to the parties entitled thereto, and not to the clerk of the court, except by order of the court. Coggeshall v. State ex rel. Corder, 112 Ind. 561, 14 N.E. 555 (1887).

Valuation of Improvements or Repairs.
Improvements or repairs effected by a cotenant in exclusive possession should be valued not at cost, but by the amount of increase in the fair market value of the property at the time of partition. Janik v. Janik, 474 N.E.2d 1054 (Ind. App. 1985).

32-17-4-18. Number of commissioners — Filling of vacancies. — (a) Any two (2) of the persons named as commissioners to make partition may perform the duties required by this chapter.

(b) The court may fill a vacancy of a commissioner. [P.L.2-2002, § 2.]

NOTES TO DECISIONS

In General.
Two of the commissioners could make a valid report, either over the objection or in the absence of the other. Griffy v. Enders, 60 Ind. 23 (1877).

32-17-4-19. Report of commissioners — Effect of vacancy. — (a) The occurrence of a vacancy does not invalidate the previous acts of the commissioners.

(b) A successor commissioner shall take up and continue the proceedings, which are as valid as if the proceedings had been done by the commissioners first appointed. [P.L.2-2002, § 2.]

32-17-4-20. Provisions for allowances. — The court shall provide an allowance, in an amount that the court determines to be reasonable:

(1) to the commissioners for their services; and

(2) for surveying, marking, chaining, platting, and executing the necessary conveyances. [P.L.2-2002, § 2.]

32-17-4-21. Award and assignment of costs. — (a) All costs and necessary expenses, including reasonable attorney's fees for plaintiff's attorney, in an amount determined by the court, shall be awarded and enforced in favor of the parties entitled to the costs and expenses against the partitioners.

(b) The court shall assign costs and expenses awarded under subsection (a) against each partitioner as the court may determine in equity, taking into consideration each partitioner's relative interest in the land or proceeds apportioned. [P.L.2-2002, § 2.]

NOTES TO DECISIONS

ANALYSIS

In general.
Applicability.
Attorney fees.
Credit for mortgage payments.
Entitlement to set off.

In General.

The costs could have been apportioned according to the interests of the parties. Jenkins v. Dalton, 27 Ind. 78 (1866); Wilcox v. Monday, 83 Ind. 335 (1882).

This section only related to costs incident to the partition proceedings proper, and costs made in litigating the question of title should have been taxed to the losing party. Merrill v. Shirk, 128 Ind. 503, 28 N.E. 95 (1891).

Where an action to quiet title was joined with an action for partition, the taxation of costs was governed by statute and the successful party was entitled to recover his costs, and the court had no discretion to refuse it. Merrill v. Shirk, 128 Ind. 503, 28 N.E. 95 (1891).

Applicability.

Former IC 32-4-5-22 (repealed; see this section for similar provisions) was not intended to apply when all sides are represented by counsel, the matters stated in the complaint are contested by the defendant, and the defendant derives no benefit from plaintiff's counsel's services. Lux v. Schroeder, 645 N.E.2d 1114 (Ind. App. 1995).

Attorney Fees.

Prior to the amendment of this section in 1893, attorney fees could not have been taxed as a portion of the costs. Hutts v. Martin, 134 Ind. 587, 33 N.E. 676 (1893).

Attorney's fee of defendant could not have been fixed by the court and made a lien on the land set-off. Hutts v. Martin, 134 Ind. 587, 33 N.E. 676 (1893).

The statute providing for the taxing of attorney fees in a partition proceeding against all of the parties was not mandatory, but such taxation was to have been awarded in such proportions against each of the parties as the court determined. Bell v. Shaffer, 154 Ind. 413, 56 N.E. 217 (1900).

In partition proceedings, where plaintiff and defendants were both represented by counsel, the court should have refused to award attorney fees to plaintiff's counsel. Bell v. Shaffer, 154 Ind. 413, 56 N.E. 217 (1900); Burger v. Schnaus, 61 Ind. App. 614, 112 N.E. 246 (1916); Tieben v. Hapner, 62 Ind. App. 650, 111 N.E. 644, 113 N.E. 310 (1916).

When defendants contested the claims of the plaintiff, no part of the fees of the attorney for the plaintiff should have been taxed as costs in the action. Osborne v. Eslinger, 155 Ind. 351, 58 N.E. 439, 80 Am. St. 240 (1900); Saint Clair v. Marquell, 161 Ind. 56, 67 N.E. 693 (1903); Tieben v. Hapner, 62 Ind. App. 650, 111 N.E. 644, 113 N.E. 310 (1916).

It was error for the court to allow more as an attorney fee in an action for partition than was demanded in the complaint when any of the defendants made default. Deputy v. Dollarhide, 42 Ind. App. 554, 86 N.E. 344 (1908).

Under this statute, the trial court had a discretion as to the allowance of an attorney fee in behalf of the plaintiff in a partition suit to have been taxed as costs in the case. Burger v. Schnaus, 61 Ind. App. 614, 112 N.E. 246 (1908).

A petition by plaintiff in a partition suit,

Attorney Fees. (Cont'd)

subsequent to a decree of sale, for an allowance of attorney fees to have been taxed as costs could not have been stricken from the files without consideration on the merits, though relief thereon might have been denied, under this statute. Brown v. Conlin, 73 Ind. App. 630, 128 N.E. 360 (1920).

Credit for Mortgage Payments.

Court erred in crediting co-tenant-wife for mortgage payments made by her pursuant to a divorce decree, which were made at a time when she was in exclusive possession of the home and when co-tenant-husband had no right to compel partition and derived no benefit from his investment in the home. Janik v. Janik, 474 N.E.2d 1054 (Ind. App. 1985).

Entitlement to Set Off.

If the tenant in possession makes a claim for improvements or other expenses, his co-tenant is entitled to set off rents and profits for the use and occupation for the period of his possession. Janik v. Janik, 474 N.E.2d 1054 (Ind. App. 1985).

Collateral References. Allowance and apportionment of counsel fees partition action or suit. 94 A.L.R.2d 575.

32-17-4-22. Review of partition. — Upon showing sufficient cause, a party to proceedings under this chapter who was not served with summons may, not more than one (1) year after a partition is confirmed, appear and open the proceedings, and obtain a review of the partition. [P.L.2-2002, § 2.]

NOTES TO DECISIONS

ANALYSIS

Defective service.
Equalizing division.
Infants.
Jury trial.

Defective Service.

Defendants who were not served with process and who did not appear in an action for partition could, within one year after the partition, appear and have the proceedings reviewed upon showing good cause therefor. Deputy v. Dollarhide, 42 Ind. App. 554, 86 N.E. 344 (1908).

If the jurat to an affidavit filed as proof of publication of notice to nonresident defendants was not signed by an officer, a judgment by default against such defendants was void, and they could have had such judgment reviewed. Deputy v. Dollarhide, 42 Ind. App. 554, 86 N.E. 344 (1908).

Equalizing Division.

In proceedings to review judgment of parti- tion, if the court found that the partition as made was unequal, it could not render a judgment requiring monetary compensation to those who had received less, but should have required another partition or failing that, the court should then have ordered such portion to have been sold as was not susceptible of division. Lucas v. Peters, 45 Ind. 313 (1873).

Infants.

Under this statute, a minor could not maintain an action of review until after arriving of age, and then only for cause shown. Brown v. Keyser, 53 Ind. 85 (1876); Bundy v. Hall, 60 Ind. 177 (1877).

The guardian of an infant defendant was not authorized hereunder to maintain proceedings in review. Bundy v. Hall, 60 Ind. 177 (1877).

Jury Trial.

Jury trial could not be demanded on proceedings for review. Allen v. Anderson, 57 Ind. 388 (1877).

32-17-4-23. Compelling partition of interest in land subject to a life estate. — A:

(1) person that owns:

(A) an undivided interest in fee simple in any lands; and

(B) a life estate in:

(i) the remaining part of the land; or

(ii) any part of the remaining portion of the land; or

(2) person that owns a fee in the land described in subdivision (1) that is subject to the undivided interest in fee and the life estate in the land;

may compel partition of the land and have the fee simple interest in the land set off and determined in the same manner as land is partitioned under Indiana law. [P.L.2-2002, § 2.]

NOTES TO DECISIONS

ANALYSIS

In general.
Tenants in common.

In General.

Since the enactment of this statute, a person owning an undivided interest in the fee of land which was subject to a life estate, and who also owned all or part of the life estate, could have partition. Smith v. Andrews, 50 Ind. App. 602, 98 N.E. 734 (1912); Coquillard v. Coquillard, 62 Ind. App. 489, 113 N.E. 481 (1916).

One who acquired a fee-simple title to an undivided one-half of real estate by purchase, wholly independent of the will of his cotenant, during the cotenant's life had an absolute statutory right to compel partition of the real estate, in the absence of any condition or restriction on her right to partition or any other method of alienation by immediate conveyance to her or by any remote device or grant from which her title stemmed, and such

right was not curtailed in any degree by the fact that part of the land sought to be partitioned was subject to a life estate pursuant to the cotenant's will. Myers v. Brane, 115 Ind. App. 144, 57 N.E.2d 594 (1944).

The rule requiring ouster by one cotenant of another in order to commence the statute of limitations would seem logically to apply with equal force between a tenant in possession and a remainderman given the right by statute to bring an action for partition. Piel v. DeWitt, 170 Ind. App. 63, 53 Ind. Dec. 663, 351 N.E.2d 48 (1976).

Either actual possession or the right to immediate possession is generally required to maintain an action for partition of real estate. Bronson v. Bronson, 448 N.E.2d 1231 (Ind. App. 1983).

Tenants in Common.

Possession as a tenant in common does not satisfy the possession requirement for purposes of partition. Bronson v. Bronson, 448 N.E.2d 1231 (Ind. App. 1983).

32-17-4-24. Party under 18 years of age — Submission of plat by commissioners. — (a) In a proceeding for the partition of real estate:

(1) in a state court; and

(2) in which a person less than eighteen (18) years of age is a party in interest;

the commissioners appointed to make the partition may lay off into lots or out-lots, streets, and alleys, any land included in the partition and may make a plat of the lots or out-lots, streets, and alleys and submit the plat to the court for approval or rejection.

(b) If a plat submitted under subsection (a) is approved by the court:

(1) the commissioners appointed to make the partition shall acknowledge the plat in open court;

(2) the plat must be recorded as other similar plats of like nature are recorded; and

(3) the plat is legally valid as if the plat were made by a legal proprietor of the lands who is at least eighteen (18) years of age.

(c) The court shall determine, upon the return by the commissioners of a plat described in subsection (b), whether it is in the interest of the parties for the land that is the subject of the partition proceeding to be laid off into lots or out-lots, streets, and alleys. If the court determines that it is in the interest of the parties, the appointed commissioners may partition the land as in other cases without detriment to the interested parties. If partition of the land is not practicable without detriment to the interested parties, the lots or out-lots may be sold by order of the court. [P.L.2-2002, § 2.]

Cross References. Personal representative of decedent's estate may plat into lots, IC 29-1-15-22.

NOTES TO DECISIONS

In General.
Commissioners appointed to make partition could lay off the lands into lots, streets and alleys, and guardians of minors could consent thereto. City of Indianapolis v. Kingsbury, 101 Ind. 200, 51 Am. R. 749 (1884).

This statute expressly gave them such authority when a minor was a party in interest. City of Indianapolis v. Kingsbury, 101 Ind. 200, 51 Am. R. 749 (1884).

————

Collateral References. 59A Am. Jur. 2d Partition, § 112.
68 C.J.S. Partition, § 84.

CHAPTER 5

PARTITION INVESTMENT LIMITATIONS

32-17-5-1. Applicability. — This chapter applies to a person that is entitled to:
(1) an estate in real estate for life or years;
(2) an estate tail;
(3) a fee simple;
(4) a conditional, base, or qualified fee;
(5) a particular, limited, or conditional estate in real estate; or
(6) an interest in personal property;
and any other person is entitled to a vested or contingent remainder, an executory devise, or any other vested or contingent interest in the same real estate or personal property. [P.L.2-2002, § 2.]

Effective Dates. P.L.2-2002, § 2. July 1. 2002.

Collateral References. 59A Am. Jur. 2d Partition, §§ 42-44.
68 C.J.S. Partition, §§ 214-222.

32-17-5-2. Application for court action. — On application of a party in interest described in section 1 [IC 32-17-5-1] of this chapter, the circuit court may, if all the parties are:
(1) parties to the proceedings and before the court; or
(2) properly served with notice as in other civil actions;

decree a sale, exchange, or lease of the real estate, or sale or exchange of the personal property, if the court considers a sale, exchange, or lease to be advantageous to the parties concerned. [P.L.2-2002, § 2.]

32-17-5-3. Investment of proceeds. — If the court decrees a sale, exchange, or lease under section 2 [IC 32-17-5-2] of this chapter, the court shall direct the investment of the proceeds of the:
(1) sale;
(2) terms of the instrument of exchange or lease; or
(3) limitations of the reversion and rents and income;
so as to inure as by the original grant, devise, or condition to the use of the same parties who would be entitled to the property sold or leased or the income of the personal property. [P.L.2-2002, § 2.]

32-17-5-4. Decree binding on all parties. — If all persons in being are parties who would be entitled to the property sold or leased or the income of the personal property if the contingency had happened at the date of the commencement of the proceedings, a decree under section 2 [IC 32-17-5-2] of this chapter is binding on any person that claims an interest in the real estate or personal property:
(1) under any party to the decree;
(2) under any person from whom a party to the decree claims; or
(3) from, under, or by the original:
(A) deed;
(B) will; or
(C) instrument;
by which the particular, limited, or conditional estate with remainders or executory devisees was created. [P.L.2-2002, § 2.]

32-17-5-5. Jurisdiction — Proceedings commenced by complaint — Appointment of guardian ad litem. — (a) The circuit court:
(1) of the county in which a will, deed, or instrument:
(A) is probated or recorded; and
(B) under or from which a party claims or derives the party's interest in the real or personal property that is the subject of the will, deed, or instrument; or
(2) that has jurisdiction of a trust from which the property is derived;
has jurisdiction to hear and determine the rights of the parties under this chapter. Proceedings under this chapter are commenced by complaint as in other civil actions.
(b) For an infant defendant who is a member of the class for whom property that is the subject of a proceeding under this chapter is held:
(1) in reversion;
(2) in remainder; or
(3) upon condition;
the court shall appoint a special guardian ad litem who is not related to any of the parties interested in the property. The living members stand for and represent the whole class, and the parties stand for and represent the full title and whole interest in the property. [P.L.2-2002, § 2.]

32-17-5-6. Direction of investment in securities. — If the proceeds under section 3 [IC 32-17-5-3] of this chapter are invested in personal property, the court may, in the court's decree, direct additional investment:

    (1) in securities; and

    (2) upon terms and conditions;

that the court considers to be in the best interests of the parties. [P.L.2-2002, § 2.]

CHAPTER 6

POWERS OF APPOINTMENT-RENUNCIATION OR EXERCISE

32-17-6-1. Applicability. — This chapter applies to a person who holds a power of appointment under any of the following:

    (1) A last will and testament of a decedent.

    (2) A deed.

    (3) An indenture of trust inter vivos.

    (4) An insurance policy.

    (5) Any other contract or instrument.

[P.L.2-2002, § 2.]

Effective Dates. P.L.2-2002, § 2. July 1. 2002.

Cross References. Powers generally, IC 30-1-9-14, IC 30-1-9-15, IC 30-1-9-17 — IC 30-1-9-19, IC 30-4-2-9.

Collateral References. 62 Am. Jur. 2d Powers of Appointment and Alienation, §§ 25-103.

72 C.J.S. Powers, §§ 14-16.

32-17-6-2. Execution of written instrument. — A person described in section 1 [IC 32-17-6-1] of this chapter may execute an appropriate written instrument to, in whole or in part:

    (1) renounce the person's right of appointment; or

    (2) exercise the person's power of appointment one (1) or more times. [P.L.2-2002, § 2.]

32-17-6-3. Renoucement final and irrevocable. — A renouncement of a right of appointment is final and irrevocable unless the right to revoke the renouncement or to repossess the right of appointment is expressly reserved in the instrument of renouncement. [P.L.2-2002, § 2.]

32-17-6-4. Subsequent revocation of appointment. — Unless a person exercising a power of appointment expressly renounces and surrenders the right to revoke an appointment in the instrument of appointment, the person may subsequently revoke the appointment and may periodically:

    (1) exercise;

(2) revoke the exercise of; and

(3) reexercise the power of appointment.
[P.L.2-2002, § 2.]

32-17-6-5. Exercise of right revokes prior appointments. — A subsequent exercise of a right of appointment is a revocation of all prior appointments to the extent that the subsequent appointment conflicts or is inconsistent with any prior appointments. [P.L.2-2002, § 2.]

32-17-6-6. Last unrevoked appointment effective and controlling. — The last unrevoked exercise of a power of appointment is effective and controlling. [P.L.2-2002, § 2.]

CHAPTER 7

DISCLAIMING PROPERTY INTERESTS

32-17-7-1. "Creation of interest" defined. — As used in this chapter, "creation of the interest" means the date on which the person creating the interest does not have a power to:

(1) revoke the transfer; or

(2) determine by any means the recipient of the interest or of its benefits. [P.L.2-2002, § 2.]

Effective Dates. P.L.2-2002, § 2. July 1. 2002.

32-17-7-2. "Fiduciary" defined. — As used in this chapter, "fiduciary" means any trustee, personal representative, or other person acquiring an interest for the benefit of others. [P.L.2-2002, § 2.]

32-17-7-3. "Interest" defined. — (a) As used in this chapter, "interest" means a present or future interest that is either equitable or legal.

(b) The term includes a power in trust and a power to consume, appoint, or apply an interest for any purpose. [P.L.2-2002, § 2.]

32-17-7-4. "Joint tenancy" defined. — (a) As used in this chapter, "joint tenancy" means any interest with the right of survivorship.

(b) The term includes a:

(1) tenancy by the entireties;

(2) multiple party account (as defined in IC 32-17-11-5) with the right of survivorship; and

(3) joint interest of spouses under IC 32-17-11-29.

[P.L.2-2002, § 2.]

32-17-7-5. "Person" defined. — (a) As used in this chapter, "person" means any individual, corporation, organization, or other entity that is entitled to possess, enjoy, or exercise power over an interest.

(b) The term includes a trustee and a person succeeding to a disclaimed interest. [P.L.2-2002, § 2.]

32-17-7-6. "Property" defined. — (a) As used in this chapter, "property" means tangible or intangible property, regardless of its location, that is either real or personal.

(b) The term includes:

(1) the right to receive proceeds under a life insurance policy or annuity; and

(2) an interest in an employee benefit plan.

[P.L.2-2002, § 2.]

NOTES TO DECISIONS

ANALYSIS

Property.
—Contributions to savings and profit-sharing programs.

Property.

—Contributions to Savings and Profit-Sharing Programs.
A bankruptcy estate includes the debtor's right to withdraw his contributions from an employee savings and profit-sharing program which is part of an Employee Retirement Income Security Act (ERISA) qualified plan. In re Berndt, 34 Bankr. 515 (Bankr. N.D. Ind. 1983).

32-17-7-7. Persons who may disclaim interest. — (a) A person to whom an interest devolves by whatever means may disclaim the interest in whole or in part as provided in this chapter.

(b) The personal representative, guardian, or conservator of a person to whom an interest devolves may disclaim the interest on behalf of the person.

(c) A disclaimer must:

(1) be in writing;

(2) describe the property and the interest in the property to be disclaimed; and

(3) be signed by the person to whom the interest devolves or the person's personal representative, guardian, or conservator. [P.L.2-2002, § 2.]

Res Gestae. Probate and Property: Assignment of an interest in decedent's estate, 43 (No. 3) Res Gestae 17 (1999).

NOTES TO DECISIONS

ANALYSIS

Effect for inheritance tax purposes.
Relation back.

Effect for Inheritance Tax Purposes.
Under former IC 29-1-6-4, a renunciation by beneficiary could have no effect on the valuation of such beneficiary's interest for inheritance tax purposes. In re Estate of Newell, 77 Ind. Dec. 360, 408 N.E.2d 552 (Ind. App. 1980).

Relation Back.
Under former IC 29-1-6-4, a renunciation related back for all purposes to the date of death of the decedent, and therefore inheritance tax could not be assessed against the person renouncing. In re Estate of Wisely, 74 Ind. Dec. 706, 402 N.E.2d 14 (Ind. App. 1980).

32-17-7-8. Requirements for disclaimer — Intestacy or testamentary instrument. — (a) This section applies to a disclaimer of an interest that:

(1) has devolved from a decedent either:
   (A) by the laws of intestacy; or
   (B) under a testamentary instrument, including a power of appointment exercised by a testamentary instrument; and
(2) is not an interest with the right of survivorship.

(b) Subject to subsections (c) and (d), a disclaimer described in subsection (a) is effective only if it is:

(1) filed in a court in which proceedings concerning the decedent's estate:
   (A) are pending; or
   (B) if no proceedings are pending, could be pending if commenced; and
(2) delivered in person or mailed by first class United States mail to:
   (A) the personal representative of the decedent; or
   (B) the holder of the legal title to the property to which the interest relates.

(c) A disclaimer of an interest in real property is effective under subsection (b) only if it is recorded in each county where the real property is located.

(d) A disclaimer is effective under this section only if the requirements of subsection (b) and, if applicable, subsection (c) are accomplished not later than nine (9) months after:

(1) if a present interest is disclaimed, the death of the person; or
(2) if a future interest is disclaimed, the later of:
   (A) the event by which the final taker of the interest is ascertained; or
   (B) the day on which the disclaimant becomes twenty-one (21) years of age.

(e) If a provision has not been made for another devolution, an interest disclaimed under this section devolves as follows:

(1) If the disclaimant is a fiduciary, as if the disclaimed interest had never been created in the disclaimant.

(2) In all other cases, as if the disclaimant had predeceased the person.

(f) A disclaimer under this section relates back for all purposes that relate to the interest disclaimed to the time immediately before the death of the person. [P.L.2-2002, § 2.]

NOTES TO DECISIONS

In General.
The disclaimer relates back to a time immediately before a decedent's death and the interest disclaimed devolves as if the disclaimant predeceased the decedent. The effect of the disclaimer is the same as if the disclaimed interest had never been created in the disclaimant. As a result, the disclaimed interest is not transferred to the disclaimant at the decedent's death. As there is no transfer of an interest to the disclaimant, there is nothing to which a lien can attach. Consequently, creditors of the disclaimant and his estate have no claim against or right in the disclaimed property. National City Bank v. Oldham, 537 N.E.2d 1193 (Ind. App. 1989).

32-17-7-9. Disclaimer reuqirements — Life insurance policy or annuity. — (a) This section applies to a disclaimer of an interest that has devolved under a life insurance policy or annuity.

(b) A disclaimer described in subsection (a) is effective only if it is:

(1) delivered in person; or

(2) mailed by first class United States mail;

to the issuer of the policy or annuity not later than nine (9) months after the death of the insured or annuitant.

(c) If a provision has not been made for another devolution, an interest disclaimed under this section devolves as follows:

(1) If the disclaimant is a fiduciary, as if the disclaimed interest had never been created in the disclaimant.

(2) In all other cases, as if the disclaimant had predeceased the insured or annuitant.

(d) A disclaimer under this section relates back for all purposes that relate to the interest disclaimed to the time immediately before the death of the insured or annuitant. [P.L.2-2002, § 2.]

32-17-7-10. Disclaimer requirements — Interest in a joint tenancy. — (a) This section applies to a disclaimer of an interest in a joint tenancy created by any means, including:

(1) an intestacy;

(2) a testamentary instrument; or

(3) the exercise of a power of appointment by a testamentary instrument.

(b) A disclaimer described in subsection (a) is effective only if the requirements of section 12 [IC 32-17-7-12] of this chapter are accomplished not later than nine (9) months after the event by which the final taker of the entire interest is ascertained.

(c) If a provision has not been made for another devolution, an interest disclaimed under this section devolves as follows:

(1) If the disclaimant is a fiduciary, as if the disclaimed interest had never been created in the disclaimant.

(2) In all other cases, as if the disclaimant had died immediately before the creation of the interest.

(d) A disclaimer under this section relates back for all purposes that relate to the interest disclaimed to the time immediately before the creation of the interest. [P.L.2-2002, § 2.]

32-17-7-11. Disclaimer requirements — Interests devolving by other means. — (a) This section applies to a disclaimer of an interest that has devolved by means other than those described in sections 8, 9, and 10 [IC 32-17-7-8, IC 32-17-7-9, and IC 32-17-7-10] of this chapter, including an interest that has devolved under:

(1) a nontestamentary instrument; or

(2) the exercise of a power of appointment by a nontestamentary instrument.

(b) A disclaimer described in subsection (a) is effective only if the requirements of section 12 [IC 32-17-7-12] of this chapter are accomplished not later than nine (9) months after:

(1) if a present interest is disclaimed, the creation of the interest; or

(2) if a future interest is disclaimed, the later of:

(A) the event by which the final taker of the interest is ascertained; or

(B) the day on which the disclaimant becomes twenty-one (21) years of age.

(c) If no provision has been made for another devolution, an interest disclaimed under this section devolves as follows:

(1) If the disclaimant is a fiduciary, as if the disclaimed interest had never been created in the disclaimant.

(2) In all other cases, as if the disclaimant had died immediately before the creation of the interest.

(d) A disclaimer under this section relates back for all purposes that relate to the interest disclaimed to the time immediately before the creation of the interest. [P.L.2-2002, § 2.]

32-17-7-12. Delivery of disclaimer — Recording disclaimer. — (a) A disclaimer of an interest under section 10 or 11 [IC 32-17-7-10 or IC 32-17-7-11] of this chapter is effective only if it is delivered in person or mailed by first class United States mail either to:

(1) the transferor of the interest or the transferor's personal representative; or

(2) the holder of the legal title to the property to which the interest relates.

(b) A disclaimer of an interest in real property under section 10 or 11 of this chapter is effective only if it is recorded in each county where the real property is located. [P.L.2-2002, § 2.]

NOTES TO DECISIONS

Certificates of Deposit.

A bank should properly be considered the holder of legal title to certificates of deposit issued by that bank to joint tenants with the right of survivorship, and thus is the party to whom a disclaimer ought to be given. Indiana Dep't of State Revenue v. Estate of Parker, 485 N.E.2d 1387 (Ind. App. 1985).

32-17-7-13. Future interests. — (a) This section applies to a future interest that would have taken effect in possession or enjoyment if it had not been disclaimed.

(b) If a provision has not been made for another devolution, a future interest described in subsection (a) takes effect for all purposes as if the disclaimant had died before the event by which the final taker of the interest is ascertained. [P.L.2-2002, § 2.]

32-17-7-14. Disclaimer irrevocable. — (a) When a disclaimer becomes effective, it:

(1) constitutes an unqualified and irrevocable refusal to accept the disclaimed interest; and

(2) is binding upon the disclaimant and all persons claiming through or under the disclaimant.

(b) A written waiver of the right to disclaim in whole or in part:

(1) is irrevocable upon signing by the disclaimant, or the disclaimant's personal representative, guardian, or conservator;

(2) bars the right, to the extent set forth in the waiver, to disclaim after the waiver becomes irrevocable; and

(3) is binding upon the person waiving and all persons claiming through or under the person waiving. [P.L.2-2002, § 2.]

32-17-7-15. Events barring right to disclaimer. — The right to disclaim an interest is barred after any of the following events:

(1) An assignment, conveyance, encumbrance, pledge, or transfer of the interest.

(2) A contract for any of the events listed in subdivision (1).

(3) A sale or other disposition of the interest under judicial process. [P.L.2-2002, § 2.]

NOTES TO DECISIONS

ANALYSIS

Applicability.
Encumbrance.

Applicability.

This section has no application to events occurring prior to the event creating the interest which the disclaimant later attempts to renounce. National City Bank v. Oldham, 537 N.E.2d 1193 (Ind. App. 1989).

Where an heir executed a renunciation of her interest in corporate stock under this section, and the executrix and owner of the remaining stock agreed to sell the stock, the trial court correctly dismissed the heir's complaint, alleging fraud and misrepresentation in procuring her renunciation, because the person who actually sold the corporate assets was one who did not have a right to renounce the property; for this statute to apply, plaintiff-appellant would have had to have been the person who sold the corporate assets. Schmidt v. Collins, 556 N.E.2d 933 (Ind. App. 1990) (decided under former IC 29-1-6-4).

Encumbrance.

Judgment lien on testator's property which arose before his death was not an "encumbrance" within the meaning of this section, and heir who later executed a disclaimer never gained an interest in the estate which could become encumbered. National City Bank v. Oldham, 537 N.E.2d 1193 (Ind. App. 1989).

32-17-7-16. Right to disclaim barred by acceptance. — The right to disclaim an interest or a benefit under an interest is barred by an acceptance of the interest or benefit, to the extent that the interest or benefit is accepted. [P.L.2-2002, § 2.]

NOTES TO DECISIONS

In General.

Heir's execution of an affidavit for transfer of real estate on the tax transfer books, relating to residential property which his father had devised him, did not constitute an acceptance of any interest he had in the property, and he was not barred from making a disclaimer. National City Bank v. Oldham, 537 N.E.2d 1193 (Ind. App. 1989).

As a general rule, a party to an instrument concerning interest in real estate is bound by the instrument whether or not it is recorded. Book v. Hester, 695 N.E.2d 597 (Ind. App. 1998).

Where owners of dominant property had actual notice of disclaimer they had made in prior quiet title action with respect to prescriptive easement, they were estopped from later claiming prejudice by fact that disclaimer was not recorded. Book v. Hester, 695 N.E.2d 597 (Ind. App. 1998).

32-17-7-17. Spendthrift provisions. — The right to disclaim exists regardless of a spendthrift provision or similar restriction on the interest of the person disclaiming. [P.L.2-2002, § 2.]

32-17-7-18. Rights not abridged by chapter. — This chapter does not abridge the right of any person to assign, convey, release, disclaim, or renounce an interest arising under this chapter or any other law. [P.L.2-2002, § 2.]

32-17-7-19. Official commentary. — A court may consult the official comments published by the probate code study commission to determine the underlying reasons, purposes, and policies of this chapter and may use the official comments as a guide in the construction and application of this chapter. [P.L.2-2002, § 2.]

32-17-7-20. Continuance of right to disclaim under prior law. — If the right to disclaim an interest exists on July 1, 1983, under IC 29-1-6-4 (repealed), IC 30-4-2-3 (repealed), or IC 30-4-2-4 (repealed), the interest may be disclaimed by complying with this chapter:

(1) if a present interest is disclaimed, before April 1, 1984; or

(2) if a future interest is disclaimed, not later than nine (9) months after the later of:

(A) the event by which the final taker of the interest is ascertained; or

(B) the day on which the disclaimant becomes twenty-one (21) years of age. [P.L.2-2002, § 2.]

CHAPTER 8
UNIFORM STATUTORY RULE AGAINST PERPETUITIES

32-17-8-1. Applicability — Date — Prior law. — (a) Except as provided in subsection (b), this chapter applies to a nonvested property interest or a power of appointment that is created on or after May 8, 1991. For purposes of this section, a nonvested property interest or a power of appointment created by the exercise of a power of appointment is created when the power is irrevocably exercised or when a revocable exercise becomes irrevocable.

(b) If a nonvested property interest or a power of appointment was created before May 8, 1991, and:

(1) is determined in a judicial proceeding commenced on or after May 8, 1991, to violate this state's rule against perpetuities as that rule existed before May 8, 1991; or

(2) may violate this state's rule against perpetuities as that rule existed before May 8, 1991;

a court upon the petition of an interested person shall reform the disposition by inserting a savings clause that most closely preserves the transferor's plan of distribution and is within the limits of the rule against perpetuities applicable when the nonvested property interest or power of appointment was created. [P.L.2-2002, § 2.]

Effective Dates. P.L.2-2002, § 2. July 1. 2002.

Indiana Law Journal. Organizing the Townhouse in Indiana, 40 Ind. L.J. 419.

NOTES TO DECISIONS

ANALYSIS

Nondonative transfer.
Reformation of contract.
—Refusal.
Violation of rule under former law.

Nondonative Transfer.

Pre-emptive right to purchase additional acres in contract for purchase of land was a nonvested property interest arising out of a nondonative transfer, and as a result the Uniform Statutory Rule Against Perpetuities, former IC 32-1-4.5-1 to former IC 32-1-4.5-6 (repealed; for similar provisions see IC 32-17-8-1 to 32-17-8-6), was inapplicable to that pre-emptive right provision. Buck v. Banks, 668 N.E.2d 1259 (Ind. App. 1996).

Reformation of Contract.

—Refusal.

Trial court did not err in refusing to reform pre-emptive right to purchase additional acres provision in contract of sale of land so as to bring it within the rule against perpetuities, pursuant to subsection (b), where the portion of the contract pertaining to the original purchase had been fully performed, leaving nothing to be reformed. Buck v. Banks, 668 N.E.2d 1259 (Ind. App. 1996).

Agreement executed in 1970 would not be reformed pursuant to subdivision (b)(2), because Uniform Statutory Rule Against Perpetuities did not apply to the agreement, and because there was no nondonative transfer. Wedel v. American Elec. Power Serv. Corp., 681 N.E.2d 1122 (Ind. App. 1997), transfer denied, 698 N.E.2d 1184 (Ind. 1998).

Violation of Rule under Former Law.

Provision in contract for sale of land entered in 1958 unambiguously provided that pre-emptive right to purchase additional acres extended to the parties' heirs, executors, administrators and assigns and, in doing so, violated the Indiana common law rule against perpetuities, which was codified at former IC 32-1-4-1 to IC 32-1-4-6 when the contract was made. Buck v. Banks, 668 N.E.2d 1259 (Ind. App. 1996).

Agreement executed in 1970 would not be reformed pursuant to former IC 32-1-4.5-1(b)(2) (repealed; for similar provisions see IC 32-17-8-1), because Uniform Statutory Rule Against Perpetuities did not apply to the agreement, and because there was no nondonative transfer. Wedel v. American Elec. Power Serv. Corp., 681 N.E.2d 1122 (Ind. App. 1997), transfer denied, 698 N.E.2d 1184 (Ind. 1998).

Collateral References. 61 Am. Jur. 2d Perpetuities and Restraints on Alienation, §§ 1-99.

70 C.J.S. Perpetuities, §§ 1-77.

Revocation or termination of trust, or withdrawal of funds or invasion of corpus thereof, settlor's reservation of right of, as affecting operation of rule against perpetuities. 7 A.L.R.2d 1089.

Rule limiting duration of restraints on alienation as applicable to covenant in deed restricting use of property. 10 A.L.R.2d 824.

Application of rule against perpetuities to trust for dissemination or preservation of material of historical or other educational interest or value. 12 A.L.R.2d 849.

Validity, under rule against perpetuities, of gift in remainder to creator's great grandchildren, following successive life estates to children and grandchildren. 18 A.L.R.2d 671.

Option created by will to purchase real estate as affected by rule against perpetuities. 44 A.L.R.2d 1228.

Restraints on alienation by option created by will to purchase real estate. 44 A.L.R.2d 1228.

Application of rule against perpetuities to limitation over on discontinuance of use for which premises are given or granted, or the commencement of a prohibited use. 45 A.L.R.2d 1154.

Effect of applying rule against perpetuities to limitation over on discontinuance of use for which premises are given or granted, or the commencement of a prohibited use. 45 A.L.R.2d 1158.

Perpetual nonparticipating royalty interest in oil and gas as violating rule against perpetuities. 46 A.L.R.2d 1268.

Rule against perpetuities as affecting validity of trust for maintenance or care of private cemetery, burial lot, tomb, or monument. 47 A.L.R.2d 603.

Separability for purposes of rule against perpetuities of gifts to several persons by one description. 56 A.L.R.2d 450.

Lease for term of years, or contract therefor, as violating rule against perpetuities. 66 A.L.R.2d 733.

Rule against perpetuities as affecting validity, as charitable trust, of gift to church, church society, or trustees or officers thereof, without declaration or restriction as to its use or purpose. 81 A.L.R.2d 827.

Application of doctrine of equitable approximation to cut down, to a permissible time period, the time of a testamentary gift that violates rule against perpetuities. 95 A.L.R.2d 807.

Doctrine that gift which might be void under rule against perpetuities will be given effect where contingency actually occurs within period of rule. 20 A.L.R.3d 1094.

Disposition of property of inter vivos trust falling in after death of settlor, who left will making no express disposition of the trust property. 30 A.L.R.3d 1318.

Preemptive rights to realty as violation of rule against perpetuities or rule concerning restraint on alienation. 40 A.L.R.3d 920.

Validity of restraint on alienation, of an estate in fee, ending not later than expiration of a life or lives in being. 42 A.L.R.2d 1243.

32-17-8-2. Applicability — Property interests — Powers. — This chapter does not apply to the following:

(1) A nonvested property interest or a power of appointment arising out of a nondonative transfer, except a nonvested property interest or a power of appointment arising out of any of the following:

(A) A premarital or postmarital agreement.

(B) A separation or divorce settlement.

(C) A spouse's election.

(D) A similar arrangement arising out of a prospective, an existing, or a previous marital relationship between the parties.

(E) A contract to make or not to revoke a will or trust.

(F) A contract to exercise or not to exercise a power of appointment.

(G) A transfer in satisfaction of a duty of support.

(H) A reciprocal transfer.

(2) A fiduciary's power relating to the administration or management of assets, including the power of a fiduciary to sell, lease, or mortgage property, and the power of a fiduciary to determine principal and income.

(3) A power to appoint a fiduciary.

(4) A discretionary power of a trustee to distribute principal before termination of a trust to a beneficiary having an indefeasibly vested interest in the income and principal.

(5) A nonvested property interest held by a charity, government, or governmental agency or subdivision, if the nonvested property interest is preceded by an interest held by another charity, government, or governmental agency or subdivision.

(6) A nonvested property interest in or a power of appointment with respect to a trust or other property arrangement forming part of a pension, a profit sharing, a stock bonus, a health, a disability, a death benefit, an income deferral, or other current or deferred benefit plan for one (1) or more employees, independent contractors, or their beneficiaries or spouses, to which contributions are made for the purpose of distributing to or for the benefit of the participants or their beneficiaries or spouses the property, income, or principal in the trust or other property arrangement, except a nonvested property interest or a power of appointment that is created by an election of a participant or a beneficiary or spouse.

(7) A property interest, power of appointment, or arrangement that was not subject to the common law rule against perpetuities or is excluded by another Indiana statute.

(8) A:

(A) provision for the accumulation of an amount of the income of a trust estate reasonably necessary for the upkeep, repair, or proper management of the subject of the estate;

(B) direction in a trust that provides for the allocation wholly or in part to the principal of the trust of stock dividends or stock rights derived from shares held in a trust;

(C) provision for a sinking or reserve fund; or

(D) statutory provision directing an accumulation.
[P.L.2-2002, § 2.]

32-17-8-3. Valid nonvested property interests — Powers of appointment. — (a) A nonvested property interest is valid if:

(1) when the interest is created, the interest is certain to vest or terminate not later than twenty-one (21) years after the death of an individual then alive; or

(2) the interest either vests or terminates within ninety (90) years after the interest's creation.

(b) A general power of appointment not presently exercisable because of a condition precedent is valid if:

(1) when the power is created, the condition precedent is certain to be satisfied or become impossible to satisfy not later than twenty-one (21) years after the death of an individual then alive; or

(2) the condition precedent either is satisfied or becomes impossible to satisfy within ninety (90) years after the condition precedent's creation.

(c) A nongeneral power of appointment or a general testamentary power of appointment is valid if:

(1) when the power is created, the power is certain to be irrevocably exercised or otherwise to terminate not later than twenty-one (21) years after the death of an individual then alive; or

(2) the power is irrevocably exercised or otherwise terminates within ninety (90) years after the power's creation.

(d) In determining whether a nonvested property interest or a power of appointment is valid under subsection (a)(1), (b)(1), or (c)(1), the possibility that a child will be born to an individual after the individual's death is disregarded. [P.L.2-2002, § 2.]

32-17-8-4. Time of creation of interest. — (a) Except as provided in subsections (b) and (c) and in section 1(a) [IC 32-17-8-1(a)] of this chapter, the time of creation of a nonvested property interest or a power of appointment is determined under general principles of property law.

(b) For purposes of this chapter, if there is a person who alone can exercise a power created by a governing instrument to become the unqualified beneficial owner of:

(1) a nonvested property interest; or

(2) a property interest subject to a power of appointment described in section 3(b) or 3(c) [IC 32-17-8-3(b) or IC 32-17-8-3(c)] of this chapter;

the nonvested property interest or power of appointment is created when the power to become the unqualified beneficial owner terminates.

(c) For purposes of this chapter, a nonvested property interest or a power of appointment arising from a transfer of property to a previously funded trust or other existing property arrangement is created when the nonvested property interest or power of appointment in the original contribution was created. [P.L.2-2002, § 2.]

32-17-8-5. Construction — Clause providing for invalid nonvesting property interest. — (a) This section applies to a clause in a governing instrument that:

(1) purports to:

(A) postpone the vesting or termination of any interest or trust until;

(B) disallow the vesting or termination of any interest or trust beyond;

(C) require all interests or trusts to vest or terminate not later than; or

(D) operate in any similar fashion upon;

the occurrence of an event described in subdivision (2); and

(2) takes effect upon the later of the following occurrences:

(A) The expiration of a period that exceeds twenty-one (21) years or that might exceed twenty-one (21) years after the death of the survivor of lives in being at the creation of the trust or other property arrangement.

(B) The death of, or the expiration of a period not exceeding twenty-one (21) years after the death of, the survivor of specified lives in being at the creation of the trust or other property arrangement.

(b) If a clause described in subsection (a) appears in an instrument creating a trust or other property arrangement, then, in measuring a period from the creation of a trust or other property arrangement, the portion of the clause that pertains to the period that exceeds twenty-one (21) years or that might exceed twenty-one (21) years after the death of the survivor of lives in being at the creation of the trust or other property arrangement is not valid. The court shall construe the clause as becoming effective upon:

(1) the death of; or

(2) the expiration of the period not exceeding twenty-one (21) years after the death of;

the survivor of the specified lives in being at the creation of the trust or other property arrangement. [P.L.2-2002, § 2.]

NOTES TO DECISIONS

ANALYSIS

In general.
Acceleration of interest.
Charitable bequests.
Charitable trusts.
Construction of will.
Corporate stock.
Gifts favored.
Intestate succession.
Legatee predeceasing testator.
Partial invalidity.
Rule not violated.
Rule violated.
Valid bequests.

In General.

Under a prior similar provision, permanent investment of funds, with directions to use the income for a designated purpose, did not violate the section. Board of Comm'rs v. Dinwiddie, 139 Ind. 128, 37 N.E. 795 (1894).

An unlawful suspension of the power of alienation for a longer period than any lives in being was created by a will forbidding absolute devisees of land to alienate the same for twenty-five years after the execution of the will. Fowler v. Duhme, 143 Ind. 248, 42 N.E. 623 (1896).

Where will expressed the testator's wish that the wife during her life should have the entire benefit of the estate, it was deemed, in view of the statute relating to provisions for the accumulation of personal property, that he intended the wife to receive all the income even though it exceeded the amount stipulated, greatly. Porter v. Union Trust Co., 182 Ind. 637, 108 N.E. 117, 1917D Ann. Cas. 427 (1915).

Under a prior similar provision, absolute ownership of personal property was suspended under that section only when no person was in existence who by his act, or when no persons were in existence who, by their joint acts, could confer an absolute title thereto. Groub v. Blish, 88 Ind. App. 309, 152 N.E. 609, 153 N.E. 895 (1926).

Both former IC 23-14-16-1 (repealed) and former IC 17-2-51-1 (repealed) provided different methods of creating a cemetery trust, and a trust created pursuant to either section was not violative of the statute against perpetuities. McClarnon v. Stage, 215 Ind. 157, 19 N.E.2d 252 (1939).

A prior similar provision was not applicable to a gift to an orphans' home contained in a will executed in 1913. In re Lowe's Estate, 117 Ind. App. 554, 70 N.E.2d 187 (1946).

Where trial court dismissed action to construe will on ground that complaint failed to state a cause of action, appellate court could not determine arguments made on appeal as to the time for vesting of property since not passed on by the lower court, and where it was found that complaint stated a cause of action, cause was reversed and remanded. Bailey v. Bailey, 134 Ind. App. 603, 180 N.E.2d 544 (1962).

Acceleration of Interest.

Where an attempted prior interest failed because it was a trust interest limited to last for a duration not permitted by applicable law, then, in the absence of a manifestation of a contrary intent, the succeeding interest was accelerated in favor of the person described in the limitation as entitled thereto, ascertained in accordance with the facts existing at the time when the attempted prior interest, if valid, would have become a present interest, and if the succeeding interest was otherwise effectively created subject to a condition not fulfilled at the time when the attempted prior interest, if valid, would have become a present interest, the succeeding interest was accelerated as soon as such condition precedent was fulfilled in favor of the person described in the limitation as entitled thereto, ascertained in accordance with the facts then existing. Sipe v. Merchants Trust Co., 109 Ind. App. 566, 34 N.E.2d 968 (1941).

Charitable Bequests.

A gift to charity in the first instance, then

Charitable Bequests. (Cont'd)

over to other charities upon the happening of a contingency, which might or might not take place within lives in being, did not violate a prior similar provision. Herron v. Stanton, 79 Ind. App. 683, 147 N.E. 305 (1920).

Charitable bequests did not fall within the statute prohibiting the alienation of property, but, if such bequest were a part of a scheme to create a trust for 30 years, the same were invalid. Phillips v. Heldt, 33 Ind. App. 388, 71 N.E. 520 (1904). See also Long v. Union Trust Co., 280 F. 686 (7th Cir. 1922).

The rule against perpetuities did not apply to gifts for charitable uses where the title vested immediately in the charity and a direction for accumulation did not necessarily affect the validity of the gift. Barr v. Geary, 82 Ind. App. 5, 142 N.E. 622 (1924).

A charitable devise did not fall within the provision of the statute prohibiting the creation of perpetuities. Scobey v. Beckman, 111 Ind. App. 574, 41 N.E.2d 847 (1942).

A provision in a will bequeathing to the board of trustees of a church certain real estate to be used as a parsonage for the church constituted a charitable use and was not violative of the statute against perpetuities. Scobey v. Beckman, 111 Ind. App. 574, 41 N.E.2d 847 (1942).

Under prior similar provisions, the statute making effective the common law rule against perpetuities, which provided that no limitation or condition shall suspend the absolute ownership of personal property longer than until the termination of lives in being at the time of the execution of the instrument containing such limitation or condition or, if in a will, of lives in being at the death of the testator, was applicable to a bequest to an orphans' home contained in a will executed in 1913. In re Lowe's Estate, 117 Ind. App. 554, 70 N.E.2d 187 (1946).

Under a prior similar provision, where a will provided a trust for certain life annuities, including one for testator's wife, and provided that upon the death of the annuitants, all of such trust estate should be reduced to cash and, after paying all charges and expenses, the balance be given in specified proportions to certain enumerated benevolent and religious institutions, including an orphans' home, the bequest to such orphans' home did not violate that statute. In re Lowe's Estate, 117 Ind. App. 554, 70 N.E.2d 187 (1946).

Charitable Trusts.

A devise or bequest in trust for certain churches was a valid charitable trust and not subject to the limitations of this act. Bailey v. Bailey, 142 Ind. App. 119, 12 Ind. Dec. 340, 232 N.E.2d 372 (1967).

Construction of Will.

Under statute providing that no condition should suspend absolute ownership of personal property longer than until the termination of lives in being, where there were no grandchildren in being at the time of the death of a testator, a provision of his will that a trustee should hold, for the benefit of testator's grandchildren, all property not specifically bequeathed was imperative and the trust failed for lack of a beneficiary. Shriver v. Montgomery, 181 Ind. 108, 103 N.E. 945 (1914).

Corporate Stock.

Under a prior similar provision, a contract by minority of stockholders of a corporation for the sale of their stock to the majority stockholders, on terms covering a period of 20 years, with an agreement to issue participation certificates therefor, was not violative of the section embodying the rule against perpetuities. Groub v. Blish, 88 Ind. App. 309, 152 N.E. 609, 153 N.E. 895 (1926).

Gifts Favored.

Under a prior similar provision, a devise by a wife in trust to the children of the two sons of the testatrix's deceased husband, and to the children of the brothers and sisters of the testatrix, the estate to be divided into two equal parts, one for the children of the said sons, and the other for the children of the brothers and sisters of the testatrix, was held to vest on the death of the son last surviving, and on the death of the last brother or sister of the testatrix, and did not come within the section providing a rule against perpetuities. Swain v. Bowers, 91 Ind. App. 307, 158 N.E. 598 (1927).

Where the language of a trust agreement, executed in connection with a gift inter vivos, was susceptible of two constructions, one violating a statute, and the other sustaining the agreement and effecting the donor's intention, thereby sustaining the gift, the latter construction should have been adopted. Warner v. Keiser, 93 Ind. App. 547, 177 N.E. 369 (1931).

Intestate Succession.

Where an intended testamentary trust that was of an entire estate violated the rule against perpetuities and the will made no alternative provision, the testator's property passed by intestate succession. Merrill v. Wimmer, 481 N.E.2d 1294 (Ind. 1985).

Legatee Predeceasing Testator.

The death of legatees prior to the death of a testator could render a will valid which would have been void under the statute against perpetuities had such legatees survived the testator. Murphey v. Brown, 159 Ind. 106, 62 N.E. 275 (1901).

Partial Invalidity.

Under a prior similar provision, if the provisions of a will constituted and created such a single, entire, inseparable and indivisible trust scheme as would have invalidated the provisions for distribution at the termination of the trust if the trust itself was invalid under the statute, the bequest would lapse and the property would pass by the law of descent. Sipe v. Merchants Trust Co., 109 Ind. App. 566, 34 N.E.2d 968 (1941).

Where a will created a trust for a period of five years, and in a subsequent item provided for distribution of the trust property at the expiration of the trust to certain named beneficiaries, the provision creating the trust, if invalid under a prior similar provision, could have been stricken and the remainder left standing, since the provision for final distribution was not such an inseparable part of the trust scheme as to have rendered it invalid also, and such provision would have stood accelerated into present possession. Sipe v. Merchants Trust Co., 109 Ind. App. 566, 34 N.E.2d 968 (1941).

Rule Not Violated.

Testamentary scheme did not violate the rule against perpetuities. Brown v. American Fletcher Nat'l Bank, 519 N.E.2d 166 (Ind. App. 1988).

Rule Violated.

Trust provisions held to violate rule against perpetuities. Merrill v. Wimmer, 481 N.E.2d 1294 (Ind. 1985).

Valid Bequests.

A will directing money to be put at interest, and to be paid to legatees, as they respectively reach full age, was valid. Dyson v. Repp, 29 Ind. 482 (1869).

Bequests of money, with directions to invest the same and use the income for a specific purpose, were valid. Board of Comm'rs v. Dinwiddie, 139 Ind. 128, 37 N.E. 795 (1894).

A devise in trust providing that such sums be used from the income of the estate as the beneficiaries' best interest might require did not constitute a trust for "accumulation" within a prior similar provision. Swain v. Bowers, 91 Ind. App. 307, 158 N.E. 598 (1927).

Collateral References. 61 Am. Jur. 2d Perpetuities and Restraints on Alienation, §§ 1-99.

70 C.J.S. Perpetuities, §§ 1-77.

Revocation or termination of trust, or withdrawal of funds or invasion of corpus thereof, settlor's reservation of right of, as affecting operation of rule against perpetuities. 7 A.L.R.2d 1089.

Rule limiting duration of restraints on alienation as applicable to covenant in deed restricting use of property. 10 A.L.R.2d 824.

Validity, under rule against perpetuities, of gift in remainder to creator's great grandchildren, following successive life estates to children and grandchildren. 18 A.L.R.2d 671.

Validity of restraint on alienation, of an estate in fee, ending not later than expiration of a life or lives in being. 42 A.L.R.2d 1243.

Option created by will to purchase real estate as affected by rule against perpetuities. 44 A.L.R.2d 1214.

Restraints on alienation by option created by will to purchase real estate. 44 A.L.R.2d 1214.

Application of rule against perpetuities to limitation over on discontinuance of use for which premises are given or granted, or the commencement of a prohibited use. 45 A.L.R.2d 1154.

Effect of applying rule against perpetuities to limitation over on discontinuance of use for which premises are given or granted, or the commencement of a prohibited use. 45 A.L.R.2d 1154.

Perpetual nonparticipating royalty interest in oil and gas as violating rule against perpetuities. 46 A.L.R.2d 1268.

Rule against perpetuities as affecting validity of trust for maintenance or care of private cemetery, burial lot, tomb, or monument. 47 A.L.R.2d 596.

Separability for purposes of rule against perpetuities of gifts to several persons by one description. 56 A.L.R.2d 446.

Lease for term of years, or contract therefor, as violating rule against perpetuities. 66 A.L.R.2d 733.

Rule against perpetuities as affecting validity, as charitable trust, of gift to church, church society, or trustees or officers thereof, without declaration or restriction as to its use or purpose. 81 A.L.R.2d 819.

Application of doctrine of equitable approximation to cut down, to a permissible time period, the time of a testamentary gift that violates rule against perpetuities. 95 A.L.R.2d 807.

Doctrine that gift which might be void under rule against perpetuities will be given effect where contingency actually occurs within period of rule. 20 A.L.R.3d 1094.

Disposition of property of inter vivos trust falling in after death of settlor, who left will making no express disposition of the trust property. 30 A.L.R.3d 1318.

Preemptive rights to realty as violation of rule against perpetuities or rule concerning restraint on alienation. 40 A.L.R.3d 920.

Validity, as for a charitable purpose, of trust for publication or distribution of particular books or writings. 34 A.L.R.4th 419.

Oil and gas royalty as real or personal property. 56 A.L.R.4th 539.

32-17-8-6. Reform of disposition by court. — Upon the petition of an interested person, a court shall reform a disposition in the manner that most closely preserves the transferor's plan of distribution and is within the ninety (90) years allowed by section 3(a)(2), 3(b)(2), or 3(c)(2) [IC 32-17-8-3(a)(2), IC 32-17-8-3(b)(2), or IC 32-17-8-3(c)(2)] of this chapter if:

(1) a nonvested property interest or a power of appointment becomes invalid under section 3 [IC 32-17-8-3] of this chapter;

(2) a class gift is not but might become invalid under section 3 of this chapter and the time has arrived when the share of any class member is to take effect in possession or enjoyment; or

(3) a nonvested property interest that is not validated by section 3(a)(1) [IC 32-17-7-3(a)(1)] of this chapter can vest but not within ninety (90) years after the interest's creation. [P.L.2-2002, § 2.]

CHAPTER 9

UNIFORM ACT ON TRANSFER ON DEATH SECURITIES

32-17-9-1. Applicability. — This chapter applies to registrations of securities:

(1) in beneficiary form regardless of the date of registration; and

(2) by persons who die after June 30, 1997.

[P.L.2-2002, § 2.]

Effective Dates. P.L.2-2002, § 2. July 1. 2002.

32-17-9-2. "Beneficiary form" defined. — As used in this chapter, "beneficiary form" means a registration form for a security that indicates:

(1) the present owner of the security; and

(2) the intention of the owner regarding the person who will become the owner of the security upon the death of the owner. [P.L.2-2002, § 2.]

32-17-9-3. "Register" defined. — As used in this chapter, "register" means:

(1) to issue a certificate showing the ownership of a certificated security; or

(2) in the case of an uncertificated security, to initiate or transfer an account showing ownership of securities. [P.L.2-2002, § 2.]

32-17-9-4. "Registering entity" defined. — (a) As used in this chapter, "registering entity" means a person who originates or transfers a security title by registration.

(b) The term includes:

(1) a broker maintaining security accounts for customers; and

(2) a transfer agent or other person acting for or as an issuer of securities. [P.L.2-2002, § 2.]

32-17-9-5. "Security" defined. — (a) As used in this chapter, "security" means a share, participation, or other interest in property, in a business, or in an obligation of an enterprise or other issuer.

(b) The term includes a certificated security, an uncertificated security, and a security account. [P.L.2-2002, § 2.]

32-17-9-6. "Security account" defined. — As used in this chapter, "security account" means:

(1) a reinvestment account associated with a security, a securities account with a broker, a cash balance in a brokerage account, cash, interest, earnings, or dividends earned or declared on a security in an account, a reinvestment account, or a brokerage account, whether or not credited to the account before the owner's death; or

(2) a cash balance or other property held for or due to the owner of a security as a replacement for or product of an account security, regardless of whether the cash was credited to the account before the owner's death. [P.L.2-2002, § 2.]

32-17-9-7. Persons who may obtain registration — Tenancy. —
(a) Only individuals whose registration of a security shows:

(1) sole ownership by one (1) individual; or

(2) multiple ownership by two (2) or more individuals with right of survivorship, rather than as tenants in common;

may obtain registration in beneficiary form.

(b) Multiple owners of a security registered in beneficiary form hold as:

(1) joint tenants with right of survivorship; or

(2) tenants by the entireties;

and not as tenants in common. [P.L.2-2002, § 2.]

32-17-9-8. Securities that may be registered in beneficiary form. —
(a) A security may be registered in beneficiary form if the form is authorized by this or a similar statute of:

(1) the state of:

(A) organization of the issuer or registering entity;

(B) the location of the registering entity's principal office; or

(C) the office of its transfer agent or its office making the registration; or

(2) the state listed as the owner's address at the time of registration.

(b) Notwithstanding subsection (a), a registration governed by the law of a jurisdiction in which this or similar legislation:

(1) is not in force; or

(2) was not in force when a registration in beneficiary form was made; is presumed to be valid and authorized as a matter of contract law. [P.L.2-2002, § 2.]

32-17-9-9. Designation of beneficiary required. — A security, whether evidenced by certificate or account, is registered in beneficiary form when the registration includes a designation of a beneficiary to take the ownership at the death of the owner or the deaths of all multiple owners. [P.L.2-2002, § 2.]

32-17-9-10. Required language. — To be effective, registration in beneficiary form must be shown by:

(1) the words "transfer on death" or the abbreviation "T.O.D."; or

(2) the words "pay on death" or the abbreviation "P.O.D.";

after the name of the registered owner and before the name of a beneficiary. [P.L.2-2002, § 2.]

32-17-9-11. No effect until death of owner — Cancellation. — (a) The designation of a T.O.D. beneficiary on a registration in beneficiary form has no effect on ownership until the owner's death.

(b) A registration of a security in beneficiary form may be canceled or changed at any time by the sole owner or all of the then surviving owners without the consent of the beneficiary. [P.L.2-2002, § 2.]

32-17-9-12. Effect of death. — (a) On the death of a sole owner or the last to die of all multiple owners, ownership of securities registered in beneficiary form passes to the beneficiary or beneficiaries who survive all owners.

(b) On proof of death of all owners and compliance with the applicable requirements of the registering entity, a security registered in beneficiary form may be reregistered in the name of the beneficiary or beneficiaries who survived the death of all owners.

(c) Until division of the security after the death of all owners, multiple beneficiaries surviving the death of all owners hold their interests as tenants in common.

(d) If a beneficiary does not survive the death of all owners, the security belongs to the estate of the deceased sole owner or the estate of the last to die of all multiple owners. [P.L.2-2002, § 2.]

32-17-9-12.1. Liability for creditor claims and statutory allowances. — The liability of a beneficiary for creditor claims and statutory allowances is determined under IC 32-17-13. [P.L.165-2002, § 13.]

Effective Dates. P.L.165-2002, § 13. July
1, 2002.

32-17-9-13. Registering entities — Requests for registration. —
(a) A registering entity is not required to offer or to accept a request for
security registration in beneficiary form. If a registering entity offers
registration in beneficiary form, the owner requesting registration in
beneficiary form assents to the protections given to the registering entity by
this chapter.

(b) By accepting a request for registration of a security in beneficiary
form, the registering entity agrees that the registration will be implemented
on the death of the deceased owner as provided in this chapter.

(c) A registering entity is discharged from all claims to a security by the
estate, creditors, heirs, or devisees of a deceased owner if the registering
entity registers a transfer of the security in accordance with section 11 [IC
32-17-9-11] of this chapter and does so in good faith reliance on:

    (1) the registration;

    (2) this chapter; and

    (3) information provided to it by:

        (A) affidavit of the personal representative of the deceased owner;

        (B) the surviving beneficiary;

        (C) the surviving beneficiary's representatives; or

        (D) other information available to the registering entity.

(d) The protections of this chapter do not extend to a reregistration or
payment made after a registering entity has received written notice from
any claimant to any interest in the security objecting to implementation of
a registration in beneficiary form. No other notice or other information
available to the registering entity affects the registering entity's right to
protection under this chapter.

(e) The protection provided by this chapter to the registering entity of a
security does not affect the rights of beneficiaries in disputes between
themselves and other claimants to ownership of the security transferred or
its value or proceeds. [P.L.2-2002, § 2.]

32-17-9-14. Transfer not testamentary. — (a) A transfer on death
resulting from a registration in beneficiary form is effective by reason of the
contract regarding the registration between the owner and the registering
entity and this chapter and is not testamentary.

(b) This chapter does not limit the rights of creditors of security owners
against beneficiaries and other transferees under other laws of Indiana.
[P.L.2-2002, § 2.]

32-17-9-15. Terms and conditions for receiving requests. — (a) A
registering entity offering to accept registrations in beneficiary form may
establish the terms and conditions under which it will receive requests:

    (1) for registrations in beneficiary form; and

    (2) for implementation of registrations in beneficiary form, including
requests for cancellation of previously registered TOD beneficiary

designations and requests for reregistration to effect a change of beneficiary.

(b) The terms and conditions established under subsection (a) may provide for the following:

(1) Proving death.

(2) Avoiding or resolving any problems concerning fractional shares.

(3) Designating primary and contingent beneficiaries.

(4) Substituting a named beneficiary's descendants to take in the place of the named beneficiary if the beneficiary has died. Substitution may be indicated by appending to the name of the primary beneficiary the letters LDPS, standing for "lineal descendants per stirpes". This designation substitutes a deceased beneficiary's descendants who survive the owner for a beneficiary who fails to survive the owner, the descendants to be identified and to share in accordance with the law of the beneficiary's domicile at the owner's death governing inheritance by descendants of an intestate.

(c) In addition to the items described in subsection (b), terms and conditions established under subsection (a) may also include:

(1) other forms of identifying beneficiaries who are to take on one (1) or more contingencies; and

(2) rules for providing proofs and assurances needed to satisfy reasonable concerns by registering entities regarding conditions and identities relevant to accurate implementation of registrations in beneficiary form.

(d) The following are illustrations of registrations in beneficiary form that a registering entity may authorize:

(1) Sole owner-sole beneficiary: John S. Brown T.O.D. (or P.O.D.) John S. Brown, Jr.

(2) Multiple owners-sole beneficiary: John S. Brown, Mary B. Brown, JT TEN, T.O.D. John S. Brown, Jr.

(3) Multiple owners-primary and secondary (substituted) beneficiaries as follows:

(A) John S. Brown, Mary B. Brown, JT TEN, T.O.D. John S. Brown, Jr. SUB BENE Peter Q. Brown.

(B) John S. Brown, Mary B. Brown, JT TEN, T.O.D. John S. Brown, Jr. LDPS. [P.L.2-2002, § 2.]

CHAPTER 10

LIMITATIONS ON POSSIBILITY OF REVERTER OR RIGHTS OF ENTRY FOR A BREACH OF A CONDITION SUBSEQUENT

32-17-10-1. Applicability. — This chapter does not apply to the following:

(1) A conveyance made for the purpose of extinguishing a possibility of reverter or a right of entry.

(2) The rights of:

(A) a mortgagee based on the terms of the mortgage;

(B) a trustee or beneficiary under a trust deed in the nature of a mortgage based on the terms of the trust deed;

(C) a grantor under a vendor's lien reserved in a deed;

(D) a lessor under a lease for a term of years; or

(E) a person with a separate property interest in coal, oil, gas, or other minerals. [P.L.2-2002, § 2.]

Effective Dates. P.L.2-2002, § 2. July 1. 2002.

Indiana Law Review. 1993 Developments in Indiana Property Law, 27 Ind. L. Rev. 1285 (1994).

32-17-10-2. Thirty-year time restriction. — A possibility of reverter or right of entry for breach of a condition subsequent concerning real property is invalid after thirty (30) years from the date the possibility of reverter or right of entry is created, notwithstanding a period of creation longer than thirty (30) years:

(1) if the breach of the condition has not occurred; and

(2) despite whether the possibility of reverter or right of entry was created before, on, or after July 1, 1993. [P.L.2-2002, § 2.]

32-17-10-3. Commencement of action after June 30, 1994. — A person may not commence an action for recovery of any part of real property after June 30, 1994, based on a possibility of reverter or right of entry for a breach of a condition subsequent if:

(1) the breach of the condition occurred before July 1, 1993; and

(2) the possibility of reverter or right of entry was created before July 1, 1963. [P.L.2-2002, § 2.]

CHAPTER 11

MULTIPLE PARTY ACCOUNTS

32-17-11-1. "Account" defined. — (a) As used in this chapter, "account" means a contract of deposit of funds between a depositor and a financial institution.

(b) The term includes a checking account, savings account, certificate of deposit, share account, and other like arrangement. [P.L.2-2002, § 2.]

Effective Dates. P.L.2-2002, § 2. July 1. 2002.
Indiana Law Review. 1992 Developments in Indiana Property Law, 26 Ind. L. Rev. 1113 (1993).

1993 Developments in Indiana Property Law, 27 Ind. L. Rev. 1285 (1994).
Res Gestae. Probate & Property, 36 Res Gestae 476 (1993).

NOTES TO DECISIONS

Individual Retirement Account.
This chapter applies to an Individual Retirement Account. Graves v. Summit Bank, 541 N.E.2d 974 (Ind. App. 1989).
Dissolution of a marriage, during which the husband had designated the wife as benefi-

ciary to his Individual Retirement Account, had no legal effect upon the IRA beneficiary designation, which the husband had not changed. Graves v. Summit Bank, 541 N.E.2d 974 (Ind. App. 1989).

Collateral References. 10 Am. Jur. 2d Banks, §§ 367-376.
9 C.J.S. Banks and Banking, § 286.

Payable-on-death savings account or certificate of deposit as will. 50 A.L.R.4th 272.

32-17-11-2. "Beneficiary" defined. — As used in this chapter, "beneficiary" means a person named in a trust account as one for whom a party to the account is named as trustee. [P.L.2-2002, § 2.]

32-17-11-3. "Financial institution" defined. — (a) As used in this chapter, "financial institution" means any organization authorized to do business in Indiana under IC 28 or federal law relating to financial institutions.

(b) The term includes the following:
(1) Banks and trust companies.
(2) Building and loan associations.
(3) Industrial loan and investment companies.
(4) Savings banks.
(5) Credit unions.
[P.L.2-2002, § 2.]

32-17-11-4. "Joint account" defined. — As used in this chapter, "joint account" means an account payable on request to one (1) or more of two (2) or more parties whether or not mention is made of any right of survivorship. [P.L.2-2002, § 2.]

NOTES TO DECISIONS

Joint Bank Account.
Joint bank account does not qualify as common law gift because donor does not sur-

render dominion. Rogers v. Rogers, 437 N.E.2d 92 (Ind. App. 1982).

32-17-11-5. "Multiple party account" defined. — (a) As used in this chapter, "multiple party account" means any of the following types of accounts:

(1) A joint account.

(2) A P.O.D. account.

(3) A trust account.

(b) The term does not include accounts established for deposit of funds of a partnership, joint venture, or other association for business purposes, or accounts controlled by one (1) or more persons as the duly authorized agent or trustee for a corporation, unincorporated association, charitable or civic organization, or a regular fiduciary or trust account where the relationship is established other than by deposit agreement. [P.L.2-2002, § 2.]

32-17-11-6. "Net contribution" defined. — As used in this chapter, "net contribution" of a party to a joint account as of any given time means the sum of:

(1) all deposits made by or for the party; minus

(2) all withdrawals made by or for the party that have not been paid to or applied to the use of any other party; plus

(3) a pro rata share of any interest or dividends included in the current balance.

The term includes any proceeds of deposit life insurance added to the account by reason of the death of the party whose net contribution is in question. [P.L.2-2002, § 2.]

32-17-11-7. "Party" defined. — (a) As used in this chapter, "party" means a person who, by the terms of the account, has a present right, subject to request, to payment from a multiple party account. A P.O.D. payee or beneficiary of a trust account is a party only after the account becomes payable to the payee or beneficiary by reason of the payee's or beneficiary's surviving the original payee or trustee.

(b) Unless the context otherwise requires, the term includes a guardian, conservator, personal representative, or assignee, including an attaching creditor, of a party. The term also includes a person identified as a trustee of an account for another whether or not a beneficiary is named.

(c) The term does not include:

(1) any named beneficiary unless the beneficiary has a present right of withdrawal; or

(2) a person who is merely authorized to make a request as the agent of another. [P.L.2-2002, § 2.]

NOTES TO DECISIONS

Party.

Signatory was a party, not a third-party beneficiary to the account, where, by her signature, she obligated herself, jointly and severally with decedent, to pay any amounts chargeable to the account by the bank for which there were insufficient funds in the account. Rubsam v. Estate of Pressler, 537 N.E.2d 520 (Ind. App. 1989).

Limited agency relationship in the creation of the account did not make a signatory an agent, rather than a party, where there was no evidence that the signatory's unlimited right of withdrawal was merely for the conve-

Party. (Cont'd)
nience of decedent, or as her agent. Rubsam v.

Estate of Pressler, 537 N.E.2d 520 (Ind. App. 1989).

32-17-11-8. "Payment" defined. — As used in this chapter, "payment" of sums on deposit includes the following:
(1) Withdrawal.
(2) Payment on check or other directive of a party.
(3) Any pledge of sums on deposit by a party.
(4) Any set-off, reduction, or other disposition of all or part of any account pursuant to a pledge. [P.L.2-2002, § 2.]

32-17-11-9. "Proof of death" defined. — As used in this chapter, "proof of death" includes a death certificate, an affidavit of death, or a record or report that is prima facie proof of death under IC 29-2-6, IC 29-2-7 (before its repeal), or IC 29-2-14. [P.L.2-2002, § 2.]

32-17-11-10. "P.O.D. account" defined. — As used in this chapter, "P.O.D. account" means an account payable on request to:
(1) one (1) person during the person's lifetime and on the person's death to at least one (1) P.O.D. payee; or
(2) one (1) or more persons during their lifetimes and on the death of all of them to one (1) or more P.O.D. payees. [P.L.2-2002, § 2.]

32-17-11-11. "P.O.D. payee" defined. — As used in this chapter, "P.O.D. payee" means a person designated on a P.O.D. account as one to whom the account is payable on request after the death of one (1) or more persons. [P.L.2-2002, § 2.]

32-17-11-12. "Request" defined. — As used in this chapter, "request" means:
(1) a proper request for withdrawal; or
(2) a check or order for payment;
that complies with all conditions of the account, including special requirements concerning necessary signatures and regulations of the financial institution. If the financial institution conditions withdrawal or payment on advance notice, for purposes of this section, the request for withdrawal or payment is treated as immediately effective and a notice of intent to withdraw is treated as a request for withdrawal. [P.L.2-2002, § 2.]

32-17-11-13. "Sums on deposit" defined. — As used in this chapter, "sums on deposit" means the balance payable on a multiple party account, including interest, dividends, and any deposit life insurance proceeds added to the account by reason of the death of a party. [P.L.2-2002, § 2.]

32-17-11-14. "Trust account" defined. — (a) As used in this chapter, "trust account" means an account in the name of at least one (1) party as trustee for at least one (1) beneficiary if:
(1) the relationship is established by the form of the account and the deposit agreement with the financial institution; and

(2) there is no subject of the trust other than the sums on deposit in the account.

It is not essential that payment to the beneficiary be mentioned in the deposit agreement.

(b) The term does not include the following:

(1) A regular trust account under a testamentary trust.

(2) A trust agreement that has significance apart from the account.

(3) A fiduciary account arising from a fiduciary relation such as attorney-client. [P.L.2-2002, § 2.]

32-17-11-15. "Withdrawal" defined. — As used in this chapter, "withdrawal" includes payment to a third person pursuant to a check or other directive of a party. [P.L.2-2002, § 2.]

32-17-11-16. Applicability. — (a) The provisions of sections 17, 18, and 19 [IC 32-17-11-17, IC 32-17-11-18, and IC 32-17-11-19] of this chapter concerning beneficial ownership as between parties, or as between parties and P.O.D. payees or beneficiaries of multiple party accounts:

(1) apply only to controversies between:

(A) the parties or the P.O.D. payees or beneficiaries of multiple party accounts; and

(B) creditors and other successors of:

(i) the parties; or

(ii) the P.O.D. payees or beneficiaries of multiple party accounts; and

(2) do not affect the power of withdrawal of the parties or the P.O.D. payees or beneficiaries of multiple party accounts as determined by the terms of account contracts.

(b) The provisions of sections 22 through 27 [IC 32-17-11-22 through IC 32-17-11-27] of this chapter govern the liability and set-off rights of financial institutions that make payments under sections 22 through 27 of this chapter. [P.L.2-2002, § 2.]

32-17-11-17. Ownership of accounts. — (a) Unless there is clear and convincing evidence of a different intent, during the lifetime of all parties, a joint account belongs to the parties in proportion to the net contributions by each party to the sums on deposit.

(b) A P.O.D. account belongs to the original payee during the original payee's lifetime and not to the P.O.D. payee or payees. If at least two (2) parties are named as original payees, subsection (a) governs the rights of the parties during their lifetimes.

(c) Unless:

(1) a contrary intent is manifested by the terms of the account or the deposit agreement; or

(2) there is other clear and convincing evidence of an irrevocable trust;

a trust account belongs beneficially to the trustee during the trustee's lifetime. If at least two (2) parties are named as trustee on the account, subsection (a) governs the beneficial rights of the trustees during their lifetimes. If there is an irrevocable trust, the account belongs beneficially to the beneficiary. [P.L.2-2002, § 2.]

Cross References. Bank and trust companies, joint accounts, IC 28-1-20-1.1.

Indiana Law Review. 1992 Developments in Indiana Property Law, 26 Ind. L. Rev. 1113 (1993).

1995 Developments in Property Law, 29 Ind. L. Rev. 1035 (1996).

Res Gestae. Tax traps for gift givers, 40 (No. 8) Res Gestae 32 (1997).

NOTES TO DECISIONS

ANALYSIS

Certificates of deposit.
Joint bank account.
—Evidence of different intent.
—Gift.
—Guardian's duty respecting joint account.
—Presumption.
—Withdrawal.
Name of account.
Removal of name of party.

Certificates of Deposit.

Where one joint owner made all of the contributions to a certificate of deposit, collected all of the interest, and retained full control, and there was no evidence of an inter vivos gift, the certificate was not subject to garnishment to satisfy a debt of the other owner. Browning & Herdrich Oil Co. v. Hall, 489 N.E.2d 988 (Ind. App. 1986).

Joint Bank Account.

—Evidence of Different Intent.

Where money deposited in joint account originated from husband, the fact that wife handled all of finances, made all deposits and withdrawals, and had complete control over the passbook because of husband's gambling problem was not evidence of intent to make the wife a donee-beneficiary of the husband's half of the account. United States v. Capital Sav. Ass'n, 576 F. Supp. 790 (N.D. Ind. 1983).

—Gift.

Mere fact that money is deposited in joint bank account to credit of owner and another is not sufficient to show intent to make a gift to the other, because donor does not surrender dominion. Rogers v. Rogers, 437 N.E.2d 92 (Ind. App. 1982); Browning & Herdrich Oil Co. v. Hall, 489 N.E.2d 988 (Ind. App. 1986).

—Guardian's Duty Respecting Joint Account.

Where ward had contributed all the money in joint account, the entire account belonged to her during her lifetime and the funds could have been withdrawn at any time, and thus, her guardian had an affirmative duty to take

control of the account. Kuehl v. Terre Haute First Nat'l Bank, 436 N.E.2d 1160 (Ind. App. 1982).

—Presumption.

This section creates a rebuttable presumption that, during the lifetime of the parties, the proceeds in a joint account belong to the joint tenants in the proportion that they contributed to the account. Rollings v. Smith, 716 N.E.2d 502 (Ind. App. 1999).

—Withdrawal.

One of two joint tenants of money deposited in joint bank account cannot, by withdrawing money without other's knowledge and consent, divest the other of his joint ownership therein. Rogers v. Rogers, 437 N.E.2d 92 (Ind. App. 1982).

Presumption that the funds in a joint account will belong to the survivor at the death of a joint owner did not come into play where the funds were withdrawn prior to the death of one owner; whether the sole contributor to joint funds intended to make a present gift to the other owner was a question for consideration by the trial court. Shourek v. Stirling, 621 N.E.2d 1107 (Ind. 1993).

Name of Account.

The name of the account has no legal significance. It may be indicative of the ownership, but the name does not create a conclusive presumption of ownership. Rubsam v. Estate of Pressler, 537 N.E.2d 520 (Ind. App. 1989).

Removal of Name of Party.

Where a certificate of deposit was purchased in three names, and the question of how and why a widow's and her deceased husband's names were removed was necessarily one of credibility with the third person claiming that the certificate was given to him and the widow denying the same, because there was evidence from which the court could conclude no gift was intended, the trial court's judgment was affirmed. Goins v. Estate of Goins, 615 N.E.2d 897 (Ind. App. 1993).

Collateral References. Joint bank account as subject to attachment, garnishment, or execution by creditor of one joint depositor. 85 A.L.R.5th 527.

32-17-11-18. Rights of survivorship. — (a) Sums remaining on deposit at the death of a party to a joint account belong to the surviving party or parties as against the estate of the decedent unless there is clear and convincing evidence of a different intention at the time the account is created. If there are at least two (2) surviving parties, their respective ownerships during lifetime are:

(1) in proportion to their previous ownership interests under section 17 [IC 32-17-11-17] of this chapter; and

(2) augmented by an equal share for each survivor of any interest the decedent may have owned in the account immediately before the person's death.

The right of survivorship continues between the surviving parties.

(b) If the account is a P.O.D. account, on death of the original payee or of the survivor of at least two (2) original payees, any sums remaining on deposit belong to the P.O.D. payee or payees who survive the original payee. If at least two (2) P.O.D. payees survive, there is no right of survivorship between the P.O.D. payees unless the terms of the account or deposit agreement expressly provide for survivorship.

(c) If the account is a trust account, on death of the trustee or the survivor of at least two (2) trustees, any sums remaining on deposit belong to the person or persons named as beneficiaries who survive the trustee, unless there is clear and convincing evidence of a contrary intent. If at least two (2) beneficiaries survive, there is no right of survivorship between the beneficiaries unless the terms of the account or deposit agreement expressly provide for survivorship.

(d) Except as provided in subsections (a) through (c), the death of any party to a multiple party account has no effect on beneficial ownership of the account other than to transfer the rights of the decedent as part of the decedent's estate.

(e) A right of survivorship arising:

(1) from the express terms of the account; or

(2) under:

(A) this section;

(B) a beneficiary designation in a trust account; or

(C) a P.O.D. payee designation;

cannot be changed by will. [P.L.2-2002, § 2.]

Indiana Law Review. 1993 Developments in Indiana Property Law, 27 Ind. L. Rev. 1285 (1994).

1994 Developments in Property Law, 28 Ind. L. Rev. 1041 (1995).

1995 Developments in Property Law, 29 Ind. L. Rev. 1035 (1996).

Res Gestae. Probate & Property, 36 Res Gestae 476 (1993).

Rules, rulings for the trial lawyer, 37 Res Gestae 576 (1994).

Divorce & family law, 38 Res Gestae 40 (1994).

NOTES TO DECISIONS

Bank Account.

A father and son had the right to create a joint tenancy with right of survivorship in a bank account, and a joint bank account agreement executed for that purpose was not void for lack of consideration since the son's declaration of intention as evidenced by the agreement, consummated by his subsequent deposits, constituted a series of gifts in praesenti of a joint interest with right of survivorship in the money involved. Hibbard v. Hibbard, 118 Ind. App. 292, 73 N.E.2d 181 (1947).

Signatures of mother and daughter to a written instrument creating a joint account with the right of survivorship was a contract with the depository and could not have been varied by parol evidence in the absence of fraud, duress or undue influence and the contract executed in connection with the account would have been given full effect. Estate of Harvey v. Huffer, 125 Ind. App. 478, 126 N.E.2d 784 (1955).

When a constructive trust is sought to be imposed upon joint bank accounts, the burden is placed upon the subordinate party to prove undue influence and that the dominant party received an undue advantage; it is not until the subordinate party proves such that the burden of proof shifts. Reiss v. Reiss, 516 N.E.2d 7 (Ind. 1987).

The statutory presumption that sums remaining on deposit belonged to surviving party prevailed where the estate failed to prove by clear and convincing evidence that a confidential relationship existed between the survivor and his sister. Reiss v. Reiss, 516 N.E.2d 7 (Ind. 1987).

Distribution to Survivor.

Where an account was for joint tenancy with a right of survivorship, upon the death of a joint tenant the account should go to the survivor and not be divided equally between the survivor and the guardian of the decedent joint tenant's estate. Walters v. Murat, 460 N.E.2d 1011 (Ind. App. 1984).

No Joint Account Found.

Where depositor in bank, knowing he was terminally ill, authorized another person to make withdrawals from his account, judgment of trial court that such person was not entitled to share in such account after the depositor's death was proper, although there was also evidence from which the court might have found the parties intended to create a joint account, where there was also evidence sustaining the trial court's determination that only a power of attorney was created. Cooper v. La Porte Bank & Trust Co., 415 N.E.2d 778 (Ind. App. 1981).

Presumptions.

The legislative enactment of the survivorship presumption by unmistakable implication replaces the common law presumption of undue influence. It follows that the common law presumption of undue influence arising between parties with certain relationships no longer exist under the Non-Probate Transfer Act. Subsection (a) of this section creates the presumption that a survivor to a joint account is the intended receiver of the proceeds in the account; in order to defeat this presumption, a party challenging the survivor's right to the proceeds must present clear and convincing evidence that the decedent at the account's creation did not intend the joint tenant to receive the proceeds or that the intent of the decedent changed before death and the decedent by written order informed the financial institution of this change. Rogers v. National City Bank, 622 N.E.2d 476 (Ind. 1993).

Since proceeds in a joint account presumptively belong to the survivor, relative did not present clear and convincing evidence that deceased did not intend for his spouse to receive the proceeds of their joint account. Rogers v. National City Bank, 622 N.E.2d 476 (Ind. 1993).

The law no longer recognizes a presumption of undue influence in a transaction between spouses based on the confidential relationship of husband and wife and a showing that the dominant spouse benefited from the transaction; rather, the burden of proof remains with the spouse seeking to set aside the transaction to establish that the other spouse exercised undue influence. Womack v. Womack, 622 N.E.2d 481 (Ind. 1993).

Former IC 32-4-1.5-4 (repealed; see this section for similar provisions) created the presumption that a survivor to a joint account is the intended receiver of the proceeds in the account. Shourek v. Stirling, 652 N.E.2d 865 (Ind. App. 1995).

Undue Influence.

—Not Shown.

Undue influence was not shown where, although husband testified that he expected repayment of the purchase price of a house from wife, the evidence established that he

Undue Influence. (Cont'd)

—Not Shown. (Cont'd)
did not require wife to sign any written document evidencing the debt as he had done when his children borrowed money from him, that he personally executed the note securing the purchase of the property, and that he obtained the cashier's check for the purchase price balance, and that additionally, husband testified during cross-examination, "[n]o one pressured me" into the transaction. Womack v. Womack, 622 N.E.2d 481 (Ind. 1993).

Collateral References. Joint lease of safe-deposit box as evidence in support or denial of gift inter vivos of contents thereof. 40 A.L.R.3d 462.

Withdrawal of Funds by Survivor.
Presumption that the funds in a joint account will belong to the survivor at the death of a joint owner did not come into play where the funds were withdrawn prior to the death of one owner; whether the sole contributor to joint funds intended to make a present gift to the other owner was a question for consideration by the trial court. Shourek v. Stirling, 621 N.E.2d 1107 (Ind. 1993).

Creation of joint savings account or savings certificate as gift to survivor. 43 A.L.R.3d 971.

32-17-11-19. Rights of survivorship — Determined by form of account. — (a) The provisions of section 18 [IC 32-17-11-18] of this chapter as to rights of survivorship are determined by the form of the account at the death of a party.

(b) The form of an account may be altered by written order given by a party to the financial institution to:

(1) change the form of the account; or

(2) stop or vary payment under the terms of the account.

(c) An order or request described in subsection (b) must be:

(1) signed by a party;

(2) received by the financial institution during the party's lifetime; and

(3) not countermanded by another written order of the same party during the party's lifetime. [P.L.2-2002, § 2.]

Indiana Law Review. 1992 Developments in Indiana Property Law, 26 Ind. L. Rev. 1113 (1993).

NOTES TO DECISIONS

ANALYSIS

Alteration.
—Requirements.
Deposit agreement.
Negligence of bank.
Presumptions.
Undue influence.
—Not shown.

Alteration.

—Requirements.
A joint account can be terminated only by mutual agreement of the joint tenants or the form of ownership altered only by written order received by the financial institution during the party's lifetime. Graves v. Kelley, 625 N.E.2d 493 (Ind. App. 1993).

Deposit Agreement.
The deposit agreement of a joint account establishes a party's right to withdraw funds and governs the relationship between the bank and the joint tenants. Graves v. Kelley, 625 N.E.2d 493 (Ind. App. 1993).

Negligence of Bank.
Where decedent had orally requested that his wife's name be removed from four certificates of deposit, his estate, which alleged that the bank had negligently failed to transfer the certificates to decedent's individual name, had the burden of establishing a duty owed from the bank to decedent, the failure of the bank to conform its conduct to the requisite standard of care, and injury to decedent prox-

Negligence of Bank. (Cont'd)
imately resulting from such failure. Voss v. Lynd, 583 N.E.2d 1239 (Ind. App. 1992).

Presumptions.

The legislative enactment of the survivorship presumption by unmistakable implication replaced the common law presumption of undue influence. It followed that the common law presumption of undue influence arising between parties with certain relationships no longer existed under the Non-Probate Transfer Act. Subsection (a) of the predecessor to this section created the presumption that a survivor to a joint account is the intended receiver of the proceeds in the account; in order to defeat this presumption, a party challenging the survivor's right to the proceeds must present clear and convincing evidence that the decedent at the account's creation did not intend the joint tenant to receive the proceeds or that the intent of the decedent changed before death and the decedent by written order informed the financial institution of this change. Rogers v. National City Bank, 622 N.E.2d 476 (Ind. 1993).

Since proceeds in a joint account presumptively belong to the survivor, relative did not present clear and convincing evidence that deceased did not intend for his spouse to receive the proceeds of their joint account.

Rogers v. National City Bank, 622 N.E.2d 476 (Ind. 1993).

The law no longer recognizes a presumption of undue influence in a transaction between spouses based on the confidential relationship of husband and wife and a showing that the dominant spouse benefited from the transaction; rather, the burden of proof remains with the spouse seeking to set aside the transaction to establish that the other spouse exercised undue influence. Womack v. Womack, 622 N.E.2d 481 (Ind. 1993).

Undue Influence.

—Not Shown.

Undue influence was not shown where, although husband testified that he expected repayment of the purchase price of a house from wife, the evidence established that he did not require wife to sign any written document evidencing the debt as he had done when his children borrowed money from him, that he personally executed the note securing the purchase of the property, and that he obtained the cashier's check for the purchase price balance, and additionally, husband testified during cross-examination, "[n]o one pressured me" into the transaction. Womack v. Womack, 622 N.E.2d 481 (Ind. 1993).

32-17-11-20. Transfers resulting from survivorship. — Any transfers resulting from the application of section 18 [IC 32-17-11-18] of this chapter are:

(1) effective by reason of:
    (A) the account contracts involved; and
    (B) this chapter; and
(2) not to be considered as:
    (A) testamentary; or
    (B) subject to IC 29.

[P.L.2-2002, § 2.]

Res Gestae. Probate & Property, 36 Res Gestae 476 (1993).

32-17-11-21. [Repealed.]

Compiler's Notes. This section, relating to the effect of insufficient estate funds on multiple party accounts, as enacted by P.L. 2-2002, § 2, effective July 1, 2002, was re-

pealed by P.L.165-2002, § 15, effective July 1, 2002. For present similar provisions, see IC 32-17-13.

32-17-11-21.1. Liability for creditor claims and statutory allowances. — The liability of a surviving party, P.O.D. payee, or beneficiary for creditor claims and statutory allowances is determined under IC 32-17-13. [P.L.165-2002, § 12.]

Effective Dates. P.L.165-2002, § 12. July
1, 2002.

32-17-11-22. Financial institutions — Multiple party accounts. —

(a) Financial institutions may enter into multiple party accounts to the same extent that they may enter into single party accounts.

(b) Any multiple party account may be paid, on request, to any one (1) or more of the parties.

(c) For purposes of establishing net contributions, a financial institution is not required to inquire as to:

(1) the source of funds received for deposit to a multiple party account; or

(2) the proposed application of any sum withdrawn from an account. [P.L.2-2002, § 2.]

Res Gestae. Tax traps for gift givers, 40
(No. 8) Res Gestae 32 (1997).

32-17-11-23. Payment from joint account to incapacitated or deceased persons. —

(a) Except as provided in subsection (b), any sums in a joint account may be paid, on request, to any party without regard to whether any other party is incapacitated or deceased at the time the payment is demanded.

(b) Payment may not be made to the personal representative or heirs of a deceased party unless:

(1) proofs of death are presented to the financial institution showing that the decedent was the last surviving party; or

(2) there is no right of survivorship under section 18 [IC 32-17-11-18] of this chapter. [P.L.2-2002, § 2.]

NOTES TO DECISIONS

Analysis

Negligence of bank.
Notice of adverse claim.

Negligence of Bank.

Where decedent had orally requested that his wife's name be removed from four certificates of deposit, his estate, which alleged that the bank had negligently failed to transfer the certificates to decedent's individual name, had the burden of establishing a duty owed from the bank to decedent, the failure of the bank to conform its conduct to the requisite standard of care, and injury to decedent proximately resulting from such failure. Voss v. Lynd, 583 N.E.2d 1239 (Ind. App. 1992).

Notice of Adverse Claim.

Former IC 28-1-20-1 (see now IC 28-1-20-1.1) provided means by which party to multiple-party account could put bank on notice of adverse claim, so that if bank made payment to another party while on notice, it did so at its peril. Kuehl v. Terre Haute First Nat'l Bank, 436 N.E.2d 1160 (Ind. App. 1982).

32-17-11-24. Persons to whom P.O.D. account may be paid. —

A P.O.D. account may be paid, on request:

(1) to any original party to the account;

(2) upon presentation to the financial institution of proof of death showing that the P.O.D. payee survived all persons named as original payees, the P.O.D. payee, or the personal representative or heirs of a deceased P.O.D. payee; and

(3) if proof of death is presented to the financial institution showing that a deceased original payee was the survivor of all other persons named on the account either as an original payee or as P.O.D. payee, the personal representative or heirs of the decedent. [P.L.2-2002, § 2.]

32-17-11-25. Persons to whom trust account may be paid. — A trust account may be paid, on request:

(1) to any trustee;

(2) unless the financial institution has received written notice that the beneficiary has a vested interest not dependent upon the beneficiary surviving the trustee, if proof of death is presented to the financial institution showing that the decedent was the survivor of all other persons named on the account either as trustee or beneficiary, to the personal representative or heirs of a deceased trustee; and

(3) upon presentation to the financial institution of proof of death showing that the beneficiary or beneficiaries survived all persons named as trustee, to the beneficiary or beneficiaries. [P.L.2-2002, § 2.]

32-17-11-26. Financial institutions — Discharge from claims. — (a) Payment made under section 22, 23, 24, or 25 [IC 32-17-11-22, IC 32-17-11-23, IC 32-17-11-24, or IC 32-17-11-25] of this chapter discharges the financial institution from all claims for amounts paid whether or not the payment is consistent with the beneficial ownership of the account as between parties, P.O.D. payees, or beneficiaries, or their successors.

(b) The protection provided under this section does not extend to payments made after a financial institution has received written notice from any party able to request present payment to the effect that withdrawals in accordance with the terms of the account should not be permitted.

(c) Unless a notice described in subsection (b) is withdrawn by the person giving it, the successor of any deceased party must concur in any demand for withdrawal if the financial institution is to be protected under this section.

(d) No other notice or any other information shown to have been available to a financial institution affects the institution's right to the protection provided under this section.

(e) The protection provided under this section does not affect the rights of parties in disputes between themselves or their successors concerning the beneficial ownership of funds in or withdrawn from multiple party accounts. [P.L.2-2002, § 2.]

NOTES TO DECISIONS

Notice of Adverse Claim.

Former IC 28-1-20-1 (see now IC 28-1-20-1.1) provided means by which party to multiple-party account could put bank on notice of adverse claim, so that if bank made payment to another party while on notice, it did so at its peril. Kuehl v. Terre Haute First Nat'l Bank, 436 N.E.2d 1160 (Ind. App. 1982).

32-17-11-27. Financial institutions — Right to set off. — (a) Without qualifying any other statutory right to set off or lien and subject to any contractual provision, if a party to a multiple party account is indebted to a financial institution, the financial institution has a right to set off against the account in which the party has, or had immediately before the party's death, a present right of withdrawal.

(b) The amount of the account subject to set off as described in subsection (a) is that proportion to which the debtor is, or was immediately before the debtor's death, beneficially entitled.

(c) In the absence of proof of net contributions, the amount of the account subject to set off as described in subsection (a) is an equal share with all parties having present rights of withdrawal. [P.L.2-2002, § 2.]

32-17-11-28. Provisions not invalidated. — (a) Any of the following provisions in an insurance policy, contract of employment, bond, mortgage, promissory note, deposit agreement, pension plan, trust agreement, conveyance, or any other written instrument effective as a contract, gift, conveyance, or trust is considered to be nontestamentary, and this title and IC 29 do not invalidate the instrument or any provision:

(1) That money or other benefits due to, controlled, or owned by a decedent before the person's death shall be paid after the person's death to a person designated by the decedent in either the instrument or a separate writing, including a will, executed at the same time as the instrument or subsequently.

(2) That any money due or to become due under the instrument shall cease to be payable in event of the death of the promisee or the promisor before payment or demand.

(3) That any property that is the subject of the instrument shall pass to a person designated by the decedent in either the instrument or a separate writing, including a will, executed at the same time as the instrument or subsequently.

(b) This section does not limit the rights of creditors under other Indiana laws. [P.L.2-2002, § 2.]

Collateral References. Payable-on-death savings account or certificate of deposit as will. 50 A.L.R.4th 272.

Effect of Uniform Probate Code § 6-201, providing that certain instruments attempting to pass property at death shall be deemed nontestamentary. 81 A.L.R.4th 1122.

32-17-11-29. Tenancy in common — Survivorship among spouses. — (a) This section does not apply to an account.

(b) Except as provided in subsection (c), personal property that is owned by two (2) or more persons is owned by them as tenants in common unless expressed otherwise in a written instrument.

(c) Upon the death of either husband or wife:
(1) household goods:
(A) acquired during marriage; and
(B) in possession of both husband and wife; and
(2) any:
(A) promissory note;
(B) bond;
(C) certificate of title to a motor vehicle; or

(D) other written or printed instrument;
    evidencing an interest in tangible or intangible personal property in the name of both husband and wife;
becomes the sole property of the surviving spouse unless a clear contrary intention is expressed in a written instrument. [P.L.2-2002, § 2.]

NOTES TO DECISIONS

In General.
Property held by joint tenants only went to the survivor when the instrument creating the estate so expressly provided. Johnson v. Johnson, 128 Ind. 93, 27 N.E. 340 (1891).

If personal estate was bequeathed to two persons, and no provision was made as to survivorship, and one of the legatees died, the other legatee took but one half of the bequest. Thieme v. Union Trust Co., 32 Ind. App. 522, 70 N.E. 276 (1904).

Personal property held in joint tenancy did not go to the survivor unless it was so expressly stipulated in the instrument creating the estate. Hibbard v. Hibbard, 118 Ind. App. 292, 73 N.E.2d 181 (1947).

Personal property held in joint tenancy did not go to the survivor unless the instrument creating the estate expressly so provided. Salvation Army, Inc. v. Hart, 239 Ind. 1, 154 N.E.2d 487 (1958).

Although this section provides for a right of survivorship in certain cases, it does not prohibit a joint tenant from entering a contract into which she is obligated to sell what would pass to her under the right of survivorship. Stech v. Panel Mart, Inc., 434 N.E.2d 97 (Ind. App. 1982).

Where personal property is not disposed of in marriage dissolution decree joint tenancy is severed, ex-spouses become owners as tenants in common, and one spouse may not dispose of property without permission of other and delivery of half-share of value. Poulson v. Poulson, 691 N.E.2d 504 (Ind. App. 1998).

Husband and Wife.

—In General.
If notes were made payable to a husband and wife, the survivor would have been entitled to but one half of such notes. Collyer v. Cook, 28 Ind. App. 272, 62 N.E. 655 (1902).

Where a note or a note and mortgage was made payable to a husband and wife, it was a general rule that they owned each an undivided one-half interest, even though the consideration for the note and mortgage was a separate property of the husband, since it was presumed the husband intended to make his wife a gift of a one-half interest. Salvation Army, Inc. v. Hart, 239 Ind. 1, 154 N.E.2d 487 (1958).

—Income Tax Refund.
An income tax refund check payable jointly to a husband and wife is the property of the survivor. Rubeck v. American Fletcher Nat'l Bank & Trust Co., 489 N.E.2d 985 (Ind. App. 1986).

—Possessory Interest.
Because a husband's removal of a gun collection from the marital residence upon spouses' separation did not destroy wife's possessory interest and present right to possession, both spouses remained joint tenants with right of survivorship. Lutz v. Lemon, 715 N.E.2d 1268 (Ind. App. 1999).

Proceeds.
Persons who own property as joint tenants with the right of survivorship also hold the proceeds derived from that property as joint tenants with the right of survivorship if the instrument representing the proceeds expressly provides that the proceeds are to be held with the right of survivorship. Graves v. Kelley, 625 N.E.2d 493 (Ind. App. 1993).

Collateral References. Rights and remedies of co-owners of copyright. 3 A.L.R.3d 1301.

Rights in proceeds of insurance on property held jointly with right of survivorship, where one of joint owners dies pending payment of proceeds. 4 A.L.R.3d 427.

CHAPTER 12

CONTRACTS CONCERNING UNITED STATES LANDS

32-17-12-1. Contract may not be voided. — A contract for valid consideration:

(1) to sell any interest, real or supposed, in any land belonging to the United States;

(2) for the occupancy of land belonging to the United States; or

(3) for any improvement made on land belonging to the United States; may not be voided by either party or the party's heirs, executors, administrators, or assigns if the nature and extent of the interest were, at the time of contract, known to the party, and the party's consent to the interest was obtained without fraud, conspiracy, or misrepresentation. [P.L.2-2002, § 2.]

Effective Dates. P.L.2-2002, § 2. July 1. 2002.
Collateral References. 63A Am. Jur. 2d Public Lands, §§ 1, 12-14, 56, 58.

73A C.J.S. Public Lands, §§ 36-57.

CHAPTER 13

LIABILITY OF NONPROBATE TRANSFEREES FOR CREDITOR CLAIMS AND
STATUTORY ALLOWANCES

32-17-13-1. "Nonprobate transfer" defined. — (a) As used in this chapter, "nonprobate transfer" means a valid transfer, effective at death, by a transferor:

(1) whose last domicile was in Indiana; and

(2) who immediately before death had the power, acting alone, to prevent transfer of the property by revocation or withdrawal and:

(A) use the property for the benefit of the transferor; or

(B) apply the property to discharge claims against the transferor's probate estate.

The term does not include transfer of a survivorship interest in a tenancy by the entireties real estate, transfer of a life insurance policy or annuity, or payment of the death proceeds of a life insurance policy or annuity.

(b) With respect to a security described in IC 32-17-9, "nonprobate transfer" means a transfer on death resulting from a registration in beneficiary form by an owner whose last domicile was in Indiana.

(c) With respect to a nonprobate transfer involving a multiple party account, a nonprobate transfer occurs if the last domicile of the depositor whose interest is transferred under IC 32-17-11 was in Indiana. [P.L.165-2002, § 11.]

Effective Dates. P.L.165-2002, § 11. July 1, 2002.

32-17-13-2. Liability of nonprobate transferees. — (a) Except as otherwise provided by statute, a transferee of a nonprobate transfer is subject to liability to a decedent's probate estate for:
> (1) allowed claims against the decedent's probate estate; and
> (2) statutory allowances to the decedent's spouse and children;
> to the extent the decedent's probate estate is insufficient to satisfy those claims and allowances.

(b) The liability of the nonprobate transferee may not exceed the value of nonprobate transfers received or controlled by the nonprobate transferee.

(c) The liability of the nonprobate transferee does not include the net contributions of the nonprobate transferee. [P.L.165-2002, § 11.]

32-17-13-3. Order of liability. — Nonprobate transferees are liable for the insufficiency described in section 2 [IC 32-17-13-2] of this chapter in the following order:
> (1) As provided in the decedent's will or other governing instrument.
> (2) To the extent of the value of the nonprobate transfer received or controlled by the trustee of trusts that can be amended, modified, or revoked by the decedent during the decedent's lifetime. If there is more than one (1) such trust, in proportion to the relative value of the trusts.
> (3) Other nonprobate transferees in proportion to the values received. [P.L.165-2002, § 11.]

32-17-13-4. Abatement. — Unless otherwise provided by the trust instrument, interest of beneficiaries in all trusts incurring liabilities under this chapter shall abate as necessary to satisfy the liability as if all of the trust instruments were a single will and the interests were devises under it. [P.L.165-2002, § 11.]

32-17-13-5. Apportionment. — (a) A provision made in an instrument may direct the apportionment of the liability among the nonprobate transferees taking under that or any other governing instrument.

(b) If a provision in an instrument conflicts with a provision in another instrument, the later provision prevails. [P.L.165-2002, § 11.]

32-17-13-6. Forum. — Upon due notice to a nonprobate transferee, the liability imposed by this chapter is enforceable in proceedings in Indiana in the county where:
> (1) the transfer occurred;
> (2) the transferee is located; or
> (3) the probate action is pending.

[P.L.165-2002, § 11.]

32-17-13-7. Notice — Failure to commence proceeding. — (a) A proceeding under this chapter may not be commenced unless the personal representative of the decedent's estate has received a written demand for the proceeding from the surviving spouse or a surviving child, to the extent that statutory allowances are affected, or a creditor.

(b) If the personal representative declines or fails to commence a proceeding after demand, a person making demand may commence the proceeding in the name of the decedent's estate at the expense of the person making the demand and not of the estate.

(c) A personal representative who declines in good faith to commence a requested proceeding incurs no personal liability for declining. [P.L.165-2002, § 11.]

32-17-13-8. Statute of limitations. — A proceeding under this chapter must be commenced not later than nine (9) months after the person's death, but a proceeding on behalf of a creditor whose claim was allowed after proceedings challenging disallowance of the claim may be commenced within sixty (60) days after final allowance of the claim. [P.L.165-2002, § 11.]

32-17-13-9. Payment or delivery of assets — Release from liability. — Unless written notice asserting that a decedent's probate estate is insufficient to pay allowed claims and statutory allowances has been received from the decedent's personal representative, the following rules apply:

(1) Payment or delivery of assets by a financial institution, registrar, or another obligor to a nonprobate transferee under the terms of the governing instrument controlling the transfer releases the obligor from all claims for amounts paid or assets delivered.

(2) A trustee receiving or controlling a nonprobate transfer is released from liability under this section on any assets distributed to the trust's beneficiaries. Each beneficiary, to the extent of the distribution received, becomes liable for the amount of the trustee's liability attributable to that asset imposed by sections 2 and 3 [IC 32-17-13-2 and IC 32-17-13-3] of this chapter. [P.L.165-2002, § 11.]

ARTICLE 18

INTERESTS OF CREDITORS IN PROPERTY

CHAPTER 1

ASSIGNMENT OF REAL AND PERSONAL PROPERTY FOR THE BENEFIT OF CREDITORS

32-18-1-1. Debtor in embarrassed or failing circumstances. — (a) A debtor who is in embarrassed or failing circumstances may make a general assignment of all the debtor's property in trust for the benefit of all the debtor's bona fide creditors.

(b) Except as provided in this chapter, an assignment described in subsection (a) that is made after March 19, 1859, is considered fraudulent and void.

(c) A debtor who is:

(1) in embarrassed or failing circumstances; and

(2) making a general assignment of all the debtor's property as provided in this chapter;

may select the debtor's trustee. The trustee shall serve and qualify, unless creditors representing an amount of at least one-half (½) of the liabilities of the debtor petition the court for the removal of the trustee and the appointment of another trustee. If the petition is filed, the judge of the circuit or superior court in which the debtor resides shall immediately remove the trustee and appoint a suitable disinterested party to act as trustee in place of the removed trustee.

(d) This chapter may not be construed to prevent a debtor from preferring a particular creditor by an assignment not made under this chapter that:

(1) conveys less than all of the debtor's property;

(2) is made for the benefit of less than all of the debtor's creditors; or

(3) is made by other means;

if the action is taken in good faith and not as a part of, or in connection with, a general assignment made under this chapter. However, a corporation may not prefer any creditor if a director of the corporation is a surety on the indebtedness preferred or has been a surety on the indebtedness within four (4) months before the preference. [P.L.2-2002, § 3.]

Effective Dates. P.L.2-2002, § 3. July 1. 2002.

Cross References. Distribution of assets to secured creditors under Uniform Liquidation Act, IC 30-2-7.

NOTES TO DECISIONS

ANALYSIS

In general.
Constitutionality.
Bank deposits and trust funds.
Bankruptcy Act.
Conditions in assignment.
Corporations.
Fraudulent intent.
Husband and wife.
Mortgage of property.
Partnerships.
Preferences in general.
Return of surplus to debtor.
Secret trust.

In General.

All assignments under the statute had to be general and embrace all the property of the debtor. Krug v. McGilliard, 76 Ind. 28 (1881); Henderson v. Pierce, 108 Ind. 462, 9 N.E. 449 (1886); Seibert v. Milligan, 110 Ind. 106, 10 N.E. 929 (1887).

Unintentional omission of some of the property of the debtor would not render the assignment void. Krug v. McGilliard, 76 Ind. 28 (1881); Seibert v. Milligan, 110 Ind. 106, 10 N.E. 929 (1887).

Specifying the creditors who were to have been paid rendered an assignment special. West v. Graff, 23 Ind. App. 410, 55 N.E. 506 (1899).

Although an agreement was called a "trust," it could, nevertheless, have been a voluntary assignment, vulnerable upon bankruptcy. In re Dautz, 272 F. 348 (D. Ind. 1921).

Constitutionality.

The last clause of the 1929 amendment to the predecessor statute to this section came within the title of this act and did not violate the "one subject" rule, Art. 4, § 19, of the Indiana Constitution. Vale v. Gary Nat'l Bank, 16 Ind. Dec. 473, 406 F.2d 39 (7th Cir. 1969).

Bank Deposits and Trust Funds.

The beneficiary of an express or constructive trust could follow the funds so long as they could have been ascertained, and when the ascertainment failed, he could follow the property into which the trust funds were converted or invested, and in case of insolvency he could have had a preference decreed. Winstandley v. Second Nat'l Bank, 13 Ind. App. 544, 41 N.E. 956 (1895).

Bank deposits were transferred to an assignee on an assignment by the depositor for the benefit of his creditors. Union Sav. Bank & Trust Co. v. Indianapolis Lounge Co., 20 Ind. App. 325, 47 N.E. 846 (1897).

Bankruptcy Act.

Operation of state law on assignments for benefit of creditors was suspended by federal Bankruptcy Act, and state courts were without jurisdiction or authority to administer estates of bankrupts or insolvents. In re Smith, 92 F. 135 (D. Ind. 1899). See, however, Pobreslo v. Joseph M. Boyd Co., 287 U.S. 518, 53 S. Ct. 20, 77 L. Ed. 469 (1933), construing a Wisconsin statute and holding that voluntary assignments for benefit of creditors were not inconsistent with the Bankruptcy Act, although they could have been set aside under that act.

Conditions in Assignment.

Condition in an assignment that the creditors participating in the assets should thereby release all claims against the assigning debtor was void. Fairbanks, Morse & Co. v. Gardner, 72 Ind. App. 647, 126 N.E. 338 (1920).

Corporations.

A corporation, unless restrained by law or its charter, could make an assignment under this section. De Camp v. Alward, 52 Ind. 468 (1876); Bristol Milling & Mfg. Co. v. Probasco, 64 Ind. 406 (1878); Ward v. Polk, 70 Ind. 309 (1880); Hill v. Nisbet, 100 Ind. 341 (1885); Wright v. Hughes, 119 Ind. 324, 21 N.E. 907, 12 Am. St. 412 (1889); Parke County Coal Co. v. Terre Haute Paper Co., 129 Ind. 73, 26 N.E. 884 (1891); Levering v. Bimel, 146 Ind. 545, 45 N.E. 775 (1897).

A corporation could prefer a creditor the same as an individual. Parke County Coal Co. v. Terre Haute Paper Co., 129 Ind. 73, 26 N.E. 884 (1891); Levering v. Bimel, 146 Ind. 545, 45 N.E. 775 (1897); Nappanee Canning Co. v. Reid, Murdoch & Co., 159 Ind. 614, 64 N.E. 870, 59 L.R.A. 199 (1902).

A corporation could prefer certain creditors, although stockholders and officers other than directors were sureties for the debts preferred. Henderson v. Indiana Trust Co., 143 Ind. 561, 40 N.E. 516 (1895); Levering v. Bimel, 146 Ind. 545, 45 N.E. 775 (1897); Smith v. Wells Mfg. Co., 148 Ind. 333, 46 N.E. 1000 (1897); Clapp v. Allen, 20 Ind. App. 263, 50 N.E. 587 (1898); Swift & Co. v. Dyer-Veatch Co., 28 Ind. App. 1, 62 N.E. 70 (1901); Nappanee Canning Co. v. Reid, Murdoch &

Corporations. (Cont'd)

Co., 159 Ind. 614, 64 N.E. 870, 59 L.R.A. 199 (1902); City Nat'l Bank v. Goshen Woolen Mills Co., 163 Ind. 214, 71 N.E. 652 (1904); D.L. Adams Co. v. Federal Glass Co., 180 Ind. 576, 103 N.E. 414 (1913); Fricke v. Angemeier, 53 Ind. App. 140, 101 N.E. 329 (1913).

Fraudulent Intent.

Fraudulent intent was not inferred from the mere fact of preference. Lewis v. Citizens' Bank, 98 Ind. App. 655, 190 N.E. 453 (1934).

The question of fraudulent intent was one of fact. Lewis v. Citizens' Bank, 98 Ind. App. 655, 190 N.E. 453 (1934).

In the absence of a finding of fraudulent intent, the appellate court (Court of Appeals) would presume that the conveyance was not fraudulent. Lewis v. Citizens' Bank, 98 Ind. App. 655, 190 N.E. 453 (1934).

The omission of the trial court to find fraud was equivalent to a finding that fraud did not exist. Lewis v. Citizens' Bank, 98 Ind. App. 655, 190 N.E. 453 (1934).

The conveyance by a judgment debtor of a portion of his real estate to certain of his creditors as tenants in common, although he was at the time in an embarrassing or failing condition, was held not fraudulent and void under this section. Lewis v. Citizens' Bank, 98 Ind. App. 655, 190 N.E. 453 (1934).

Husband and Wife.

The fact that the person whose debt was preferred was a wife or other near relative did not affect the validity of such preference if the indebtedness was bona fide. Schaeffer v. Fithian, 17 Ind. 463 (1861); Kyger v. F. Hull Skirt Co., 34 Ind. 249 (1870); Sims v. Rickets, 35 Ind. 181, 9 Am. R. 679 (1871); Goff v. Rogers, 71 Ind. 459 (1880); Hogan v. Robinson, 94 Ind. 138 (1884); Hoes v. Boyer, 108 Ind. 494, 9 N.E. 427 (1886); Jones v. Snyder, 117 Ind. 229, 20 N.E. 140 (1889); Laird v. Davidson, 124 Ind. 412, 25 N.E. 7 (1890); Dillen v. Johnson, 132 Ind. 75, 30 N.E. 786 (1892); Fulp v. Beaver, 136 Ind. 319, 36 N.E. 250 (1894); Adams v. Curtis, 137 Ind. 175, 36 N.E. 1095 (1894); Nappanee Canning Co. v. Reid, Murdoch & Co., 159 Ind. 614, 64 N.E. 870, 59 L.R.A. 199 (1902).

A husband could prefer his wife where she agreed to release him from the obligations of an antenuptial contract whereby she was to receive a certain sum out of his estate at his death as her share thereof as his widow if the sum agreed on in the postnuptial settlement was not grossly unjust to his creditors. Clow v. Brown, 37 Ind. App. 172, 72 N.E. 534 (1904).

Mortgage of Property.

A failing debtor contemplating an assignment could prefer some of his creditors by executing mortgages on his property. Stix v. Sadler, 109 Ind. 254, 9 N.E. 905 (1887); Gilbert v. McCorkle, 110 Ind. 215, 11 N.E. 296 (1887); Carnahan v. Schwab, 127 Ind. 507, 26 N.E. 67 (1891); John Shillito Co. v. McConnell, 130 Ind. 41, 26 N.E. 832 (1891); Peed v. Elliott, 134 Ind. 536, 34 N.E. 319 (1893); Simmons Hdwe. Co. v. Thomas, 147 Ind. 313, 46 N.E. 645 (1897); West v. Graff, 23 Ind. App. 410, 55 N.E. 506 (1899).

A mortgage to secure preferred creditors could not have been executed as a part of the assignment. John Shillito Co. v. McConnell, 130 Ind. 41, 26 N.E. 832 (1891); Peed v. Elliott, 134 Ind. 536, 34 N.E. 319 (1893).

If a mortgage was not accepted until after the assignment was made, it would not relate back prior to the assignment so as to make the mortgagees preference creditors. Reagan v. First Nat'l Bank, 157 Ind. 623, 61 N.E. 575 (1901), reh'g overruled, 157 Ind. 673, 62 N.E. 701 (1902).

Partnerships.

A partnership could make an assignment for the benefit of its creditors the same as an individual. Blake v. Faulkner, 18 Ind. 47 (1862); Garnor v. Frederick, 18 Ind. 507 (1862); Ex parte Hopkins, 104 Ind. 157, 2 N.E. 587 (1885); Callahan v. Heinz, 20 Ind. App. 359, 49 N.E. 1073 (1898); Nappanee Canning Co. v. Reid, Murdoch & Co., 159 Ind. 614, 64 N.E. 870, 59 L.R.A. 199 (1902).

An assignment made by partners needed to include only the partnership property. Blake v. Faulkner, 18 Ind. 47 (1862); Garnor v. Frederick, 18 Ind. 507 (1862); Ex parte Hopkins, 104 Ind. 157, 2 N.E. 587 (1885).

Receiver for partnership before assignment had right of possession of property. Needham v. Wright, 140 Ind. 190, 39 N.E. 510 (1895).

One member of a partnership could not make an assignment without the consent or a ratification by other members. Callahan v. Heinz, 20 Ind. App. 359, 49 N.E. 1073 (1898).

The partnership could, notwithstanding its insolvency, have applied assets of the partnership to the payment or securing of debts of the individuals composing the firm. Nappanee Canning Co. v. Reid, Murdoch & Co., 159 Ind. 614, 64 N.E. 870, 59 L.R.A. 199 (1902).

Preferences in General.

The statute regulating assignments by failing debtors did not prevent such debtors from making sale of their property to pay preferred creditors. Wilcoxon v. Annesley, 23 Ind. 285 (1864); Keen v. Preston, 24 Ind. 395 (1865); Wright v. Mack, 95 Ind. 332 (1884); Cushman v. Gephart, 97 Ind. 46 (1884); Hays v. Hostetter, 125 Ind. 60, 25 N.E. 134 (1890); Carnahan v. Schwab, 127 Ind. 507, 26 N.E. 67 (1891); West v. Graff, 23 Ind. App. 410, 55 N.E. 506 (1899); Nappanee Canning Co. v. Reid, Murdoch & Co., 159 Ind. 614, 64 N.E.

Preferences in General. (Cont'd)
870, 59 L.R.A. 199 (1902); State Bank v. Backus, 160 Ind. 682, 67 N.E. 512 (1903); Larch v. Holz, 53 Ind. App. 56, 101 N.E. 127 (1913); Young v. Merle & Heaney Mfg. Co., 184 Ind. 403, 110 N.E. 669 (1915).

An assignment for the benefit of a portion of the creditors of the debtor was valid unless it was actually fraudulent. Cushman v. Gephart, 97 Ind. 46 (1884); Grubbs v. Morris, 103 Ind. 166, 2 N.E. 579 (1885).

If the assignment was made in good faith, and some of the creditors were preferred, such provision could have been disregarded and the assignment upheld. Henderson v. Pierce, 108 Ind. 462, 9 N.E. 449 (1886); Redpath v. Tutewiler, 109 Ind. 248, 9 N.E. 911 (1887); Schwab v. Lemon, 111 Ind. 54, 12 N.E. 87 (1887); Grubbs v. King, 117 Ind. 243, 20 N.E. 142 (1889); West v. Graff, 23 Ind. App. 410, 55 N.E. 506 (1899).

Preference between creditors could not have been made when an assignment was made for the benefit of all creditors. John Shillito Co. v. McConnell, 130 Ind. 41, 26 N.E. 832 (1891); Peed v. Elliott, 134 Ind. 536, 34 N.E. 319 (1893).

An embarrassed or failing debtor could lawfully prefer one or more of his creditors by payment, mortgage, pledge, or deed in exclusion of the others, and, if the debt was a bona fide and honest one, the said preferences would not have been set aside "when such action is taken in good faith" and in the absence of a fraudulent intent; this rule was not affected by this section. Lewis v. Citizens' Bank, 98 Ind. App. 655, 190 N.E. 453 (1934).

The proscription in this section against preferences to corporate directors is limited to suretyship situations. Abrahamson v. Levin, 162 Ind. App. 304, 44 Ind. Dec. 624, 319 N.E.2d 351 (1975).

Return of Surplus to Debtor.
The debtor could sell his property to pay his debts with the stipulation that the surplus, if any, had to be returned to him. Keen v. Preston, 24 Ind. 395 (1865); Dessar v. Field, 99 Ind. 548 (1884).

A debtor could convey his property to trustees to be disposed of for his benefit and the benefit of his creditors. Robbins v. Magee, 76 Ind. 381 (1881).

If only certain creditors were to have been paid, and surplus returned to the debtor, the assignment would have been void. Thompson v. Parker, 83 Ind. 96 (1882).

Secret Trust.
A secret trust, created for the benefit of the debtor, rendered the assignment void. Caldwell v. Williams, 1 Ind. 405 (1849); McFarland v. Birdsall, 14 Ind. 126 (1860).

Collateral References. 6 Am. Jur. 2d Assignments for Benefit of Creditors, §§ 1-6.

6A C.J.S. Assignments for Benefit of Creditors, §§ 1-7.

Validity of corporation's assignment for benefit of creditors as affected by president's lack of authority from directors to make the same. 10 A.L.R.2d 711.

Right to reformation of contract or instrument as affected by intervening rights of third persons. 79 A.L.R.2d 1180.

Debtor's transfer of assets to representation of creditors as effectuating release of unsecured claims, in absence of express agreement to that effect. 8 A.L.R.3d 903.

"Wages" within meaning of priority provisions of Bankruptcy Act (11 U.S.C. § 507(a)(3)) or of state insolvency laws. 17 A.L.R.3d 374.

Amount of attorneys' compensation in absence of contract or statute fixing amount. 57 A.L.R.3d 475.

Amount of attorneys' compensation in matters involving guardianship and trusts. 57 A.L.R.3d 550.

Excessiveness or adequacy of attorneys' fees in matters involving real estate — modern cases. 10 A.L.R.5th 448.

Excessiveness or inadequacy of attorney's fees in matters involving commercial and general business activities. 23 A.L.R.5th 241.

32-18-1-2. Indenture — Oath. — (a) An assignment under this chapter must be:

(1) by indenture; and

(2) signed and acknowledged before a person who is authorized to take the acknowledgment of deeds.

(b) The indenture must, within ten (10) days after the execution, be filed with the recorder of the county in which the assignor resides. The recorder shall record the indenture of assignment the same as deeds are recorded.

(c) The indenture of assignment must:

(1) contain a full description of all real estate assigned; and

(2) be accompanied by a schedule containing a particular enumeration and description of all the personal property assigned.

(d) The assignor shall make oath before a person authorized to administer oaths. The oath must:

(1) verify the indenture and schedule and contain a statement of all the property, rights, and credits belonging to the assignor, or of which the assignor has knowledge, and that the assignor has not, directly or indirectly, transferred or reserved a sum of money or article of property for the assignor's own use or the benefit of another person; and

(2) indicate the assignor has not acknowledged a debt or confessed a judgment to a person for a sum greater than was justly owing to the person, or with the intention of delaying or defrauding the assignor's creditors.

(e) An assignment under this chapter may not convey to the assignee an interest in property assigned until the assignment is recorded as provided in this section. [P.L.2-2002, § 3.]

NOTES TO DECISIONS

ANALYSIS

Bank deposits.
Exempt property.
Foreign assignments.
Fraud.
Omission of property.
Partnerships.
Possession of trustee.
Recording.

Bank Deposits.

Deposits in bank made by a debtor were transferred to an assignee by a general assignment. Union Sav. Bank & Trust Co. v. Indianapolis Lounge Co., 20 Ind. App. 325, 47 N.E. 846 (1897); Gray v. Covert, 25 Ind. App. 561, 58 N.E. 731, 81 Am. St. 117 (1900).

Exempt Property.

A reservation in good faith in an assignment by the assignor, of "so much property as may be exempt from execution," did not avoid the deed. Garnor v. Frederick, 18 Ind. 507 (1862).

Foreign Assignments.

An assignment, made in another state, in accordance with the law of that state, was upheld in Indiana when it was not contrary to the law or policy of this state. Pitman v. Marquardt, 20 Ind. App. 431, 50 N.E. 894 (1898).

Fraud.

Goods obtained by debtor by fraud could have been recovered from the assignee of the debtor. Cooper v. Perdue, 114 Ind. 207, 16 N.E. 140 (1888); Peninsular Stove Co. v. Ellis, 20 Ind. App. 491, 51 N.E. 105 (1898).

Omission of Property.

Omission made unintentionally of some of the property of the debtor from the deed of assignment did not render the same void. Krug v. McGilliard, 76 Ind. 28 (1881); Seibert v. Milligan, 110 Ind. 106, 10 N.E. 929 (1887).

If personal property was omitted from the schedule, the assignee could take possession thereof, and it would become assets in his hands the same as if it were described in the schedule. Hasseld v. Seyfort, 105 Ind. 534, 5 N.E. 675 (1886).

Partnerships.

Under the voluntary assignment law of 1859, an assignment by copartners for the payment of partnership debts, which embraced all of their joint property, was valid, although it did not embrace any of the individual property by any of the partners. Blake v. Faulkner, 18 Ind. 47 (1862); Garnor v. Frederick, 18 Ind. 507 (1862); Ex parte Hopkins, 104 Ind. 157, 2 N.E. 587 (1885).

One member of a partnership could not make an assignment without the consent or a ratification by the other members. Callahan v. Heinz, 20 Ind. App. 359, 49 N.E. 1073 (1898).

Possession of Trustee.

Exclusive possession of the property assigned should have been given to the trustee. Caldwell v. Williams, 1 Ind. 405 (1849); Nutter v. Harris, 9 Ind. 88 (1857).

Assignee could recover from the assignor possession of the real estate conveyed. Taylor

Possession of Trustee. (Cont'd)
v. Bruner, 130 Ind. 482, 30 N.E. 635, 30 Am.
St. 247 (1892).

Recording.
The schedule of personal property required
to accompany the deed of assignment did not
need to be recorded. Black v. Weathers, 26
Ind. 242 (1866).
Under the express terms of the statute, no
title to the property assigned passed to the
assignee until such assignment was recorded
as required by the statute. New v. Reissner,
56 Ind. 118 (1877); Forkner v. Shafer, 56 Ind.
120 (1877); Switzer v. Miller, 58 Ind. 561
(1877); Eden v. Everson, 65 Ind. 113 (1878);
Foster v. Brown, 65 Ind. 234 (1879); State ex

rel. Braden v. Krug, 82 Ind. 58 (1882); Miller
v. Swhier, 40 Ind. App. 465, 79 N.E. 1092
(1907).
Deeds of assignment conveying real estate
had to be recorded in each county where the
lands were situate in order to have been
notice to third parties. Switzer v. Miller, 58
Ind. 561 (1877).
An averment in a pleading that the deed of
assignment has been "duly" recorded has been
held sufficient. Jewett v. Perrette, 127 Ind. 97,
26 N.E. 685 (1891).
Deeds of assignment when recorded vested
in the assignee title to property conveyed by
the debtor to defraud his creditors. Doherty v.
Ramsey, 1 Ind. App. 530, 27 N.E. 879, 50 Am.
St. 223 (1891).

32-18-1-3. Filings. — (a) Not later than fifteen (15) days after the
execution of the assignment, the trustee shall file a copy of the assignment
and schedule in the office of the clerk of the circuit court of the county in
which the debtor resides. The trustee shall state under oath, before
execution of the trust:

> (1) that the trustee will faithfully execute the trust, and the property
> assigned has been actually delivered into the trustee's possession for
> the uses declared in the assignment; and
>
> (2) what the probable value of the assigned property is.

(b) The trustee shall, at the time the assignment and schedule is filed
under subsection (a), file with the clerk a written undertaking to the state
with at least one (1) sufficient surety. The bond to be approved by the clerk:

> (1) must be in a sum double the amount of the value of the property
> assigned; and
>
> (2) conditioned for the faithful discharge of the duties of the trustee's
> trust.

The bond must be for the use of a person injured by the action of the trustee.
[P.L.2-2002, § 3.]

Cross References. Duties of trustee defined, IC 32-18-1-11.

NOTES TO DECISIONS

Analysis

Action on bond.
Liability on bond.

Action on Bond.
Suits on the bond of an assignee should
have been brought in the name of the state on
the relation of the interested party. Jackson v.
Rounds, 59 Ind. 116 (1877).

Liability on Bond.
Trustees were liable on their bonds for any
neglect of their duties resulting in damage to
creditors. State ex rel. Puett v. Musser, 4 Ind.
App. 407, 30 N.E. 944 (1892).
Assignee was liable for refusal to surrender
goods obtained by debtor by fraud. Peninsular
Stove Co. v. Ellis, 20 Ind. App. 491, 51 N.E.
105 (1898).

Collateral References. Validity of corporation's assignment for benefit of creditors as

affected by president's lack of authority from
directors to make the same. 10 A.L.R.2d 711.

Good will as passing by implication under
assignment of business for benefit of creditors. 65 A.L.R.2d 502.

32-18-1-4. Minuting of filing. — The clerk of the circuit court shall
minute the filing of the copy of indenture, schedule, and undertaking in the
proper book under section 3 [IC 32-18-1-3] of this chapter. [P.L.2-2002, § 3.]

32-18-1-5. Failure of trustee to comply. — (a) If the trustee fails to
comply with the provisions of sections 1 through 4 [IC 32-18-1-1 through IC
32-18-1-4] of this chapter, the judge of the circuit court or the clerk of the
circuit court may, at the instance of the assignor or a creditor, by petition:
     (1) remove the trustee; and
     (2) appoint another suitable person as trustee.
  (b) A replacement trustee shall:
     (1) comply with the requirements specified in this chapter;
     (2) immediately take possession and control of the property assigned;
     and
     (3) enter upon the execution of the trust, as provided in this chapter.
     [P.L.2-2002, § 3.]

Cross References. Removal of trustee, IC
32-18-1-18.

32-18-1-6. Notice of trustee's appointment — Inventory. —
(a) Immediately after complying with the requirements set forth in this
chapter, the trustee shall give notice of the trustee's appointment by
publication, three (3) weeks successively, in a newspaper printed and
published in the county. If a newspaper is not printed and published in the
county, the trustee shall:
     (1) place written notice in at least five (5) of the most public places in
     the county; and
     (2) publish notice in a newspaper printed and published in the nearest
     county, for the time and in the manner mentioned in reference to
     publication in the county where the assignor resides.
  (b) The trustee shall, within thirty (30) days after beginning the duties of
the trust, make and file, under oath, a full and complete inventory of all the
property, real and personal, the rights, credits, interests, profits, and
collaterals that the trustee obtains, or of which the trustee may have
obtained knowledge as belonging to the assignor. If:
     (1) any property not mentioned in an inventory comes into the trustee's
     hands; or
     (2) the trustee obtains satisfactory information of the existence of
     property not mentioned in an inventory;
the trustee shall file an additional inventory of the property as described in
this section. [P.L.2-2002, § 3.]

NOTES TO DECISIONS

Omitted Property.

If personal property was omitted from the schedule required to accompany the deed of assignment, the assignee could take possession thereof, and his title would be superior to the claims of execution creditors whose judgments were rendered after such taking possession. Hasseld v. Seyfort, 105 Ind. 534, 5 N.E. 675 (1886).

32-18-1-7. Appraisal — Oath. — The trustee, not more than twenty (20) days after filing the inventory mentioned in section 6 [IC 32-18-1-6] of this chapter, shall cause the property mentioned in the inventory to be appraised by two (2) reputable householders of the neighborhood. The appraisers, before proceeding to discharge their duty, must take and subscribe an oath that they will honestly appraise the property mentioned in the inventory filed by the trustee. The oath must be filed, together with the appraisement, with the clerk of the circuit court. [P.L.2-2002, § 3.]

32-18-1-8. Appraisal — Requirements. — The appraisers shall, in the presence of the trustee:

(1) appraise each article mentioned in the inventory at its true value; and

(2) set down opposite each article respectively the value fixed by them in dollars and cents. [P.L.2-2002, § 3.]

32-18-1-9. Set off to assignor. — (a) If the assignor is a resident householder of Indiana, the appraisers shall set off to the assignor articles of property or so much of the real estate mentioned in the inventory as the assignor may select, not to exceed three hundred dollars ($300).

(b) The appraisers shall, in an appraisement, specify what articles of property and the value of the property, or what part of the real estate and its value, they have set apart to the assignor. [P.L.2-2002, § 3.]

NOTES TO DECISIONS

ANALYSIS

In general.
Allowance from proceeds of sale.
Effect of fraudulent transfers.
Householder at time of assignment.
Partnerships.

In General.

Debtors could retain the amount of property that was allowed by law as exempt from execution. Garnor v. Frederick, 18 Ind. 507 (1862); O'Neil v. Beck, 69 Ind. 239 (1879).

The amount allowed to the debtor as exempt from the assignment was increased to $600 by Acts 1879 (Spec. Sess.), ch. 50, § 1, p. 127 (total exemption raised to $1,000 by Acts 1933, IC 34-2-28-1). O'Neil v. Beck, 69 Ind. 239 (1879).

Allowance from Proceeds of Sale.

A debtor could not claim the amount allowed him as exempt out of the proceeds of the sale of the property assigned. He had to make his claim for exemption in the manner provided for in this section. Graves v. Hinkle, 120 Ind. 157, 21 N.E. 328 (1889).

If a debtor properly designated property claimed as exempt, and the assignee failed to have the same set off, the debtor could claim the proceeds of the sale of such property. Doherty v. Ramsey, 1 Ind. App. 530, 27 N.E. 879, 50 Am. St. 223 (1891).

Promise by assignee to allow claim for exemption out of proceeds of sale of property was enforceable by debtor, assignor. Faulkner v. Jones, 13 Ind. App. 381, 41 N.E. 830 (1895).

Effect of Fraudulent Transfers.

A fraudulent transfer of property by the debtor did not defeat his right to claim the amount allowed him as exempt. Doherty v. Ramsey, 1 Ind. App. 530, 27 N.E. 879, 50 Am. St. 223 (1891).

Householder at Time of Assignment.

The debtor had to be a householder at the time of making the assignment in order to have been entitled to claim an exemption. Miller v. Swhier, 40 Ind. App. 465, 79 N.E. 1092 (1907).

If a person not a householder made an assignment which was recorded, he was not entitled to an exemption, although he became a householder before the property was appraised. Miller v. Swhier, 40 Ind. App. 465, 79 N.E. 1092 (1907).

Partnerships.

A partner could not claim any exemption in the partnership property. Love v. Blair, 72 Ind. 281 (1880); Smith v. Harris, 76 Ind. 104

(1881); State ex rel. Talbott v. Emmons, 99 Ind. 452 (1885); Ex parte Hopkins, 104 Ind. 157, 2 N.E. 587 (1885); Sharpe v. Baker, 51 Ind. App. 547, 96 N.E. 627 (1911).

Where partners made a voluntary assignment of the partnership property, they were not entitled to any exemption of such property until the partnership debts were fully paid. Ex parte Hopkins, 104 Ind. 157, 2 N.E. 587 (1885).

If a partner purchased the interest of his partner in a stock of merchandise and then made an assignment for the benefit of his creditors, such partner, if a resident householder, could claim the statutory exemption. Fairfield Shoe Co. v. Olds, 176 Ind. 526, 96 N.E. 592 (1911).

32-18-1-10. Sale of property. — (a) The trustee, as soon as possible after an appraisement is filed, shall collect the rights and credits of the assignor. Except for property set off by the assignor as exempt, the trustee shall sell at public auction the appraised property after giving thirty (30) days notice of the time and place of sale:

(1) by publication in a newspaper printed and published in the county; or

(2) if a newspaper is not printed and published in the county, by posting written or printed notices in at least five (5) of the most public places in the county.

(b) The trustee shall sell the appraised property to the highest bidder for cash, or upon credit, the trustee taking notes with security to be approved by the trustee, waiving relief from valuation or appraisement laws, payable not more than twelve (12) months after the date, with interest.

(c) The trustee must make a full return, under oath, of the sale to the clerk of the circuit court. The clerk shall file the return with the other papers in the case. However, a court may, upon the sworn petition of the trustee, a creditor, or the assignor, for good cause shown, extend the time for selling the property, or any part of the property, for as much time as the court determines will serve the best interests of the creditors. The court may extend the credit on sales for not more than two (2) years.

(d) The court may, upon the sworn petition of the trustee or of a majority of the creditors showing that the property may deteriorate in value by delay or that it will be beneficial to the creditors to have an early sale order the property sold upon notice of the time, place, and terms of sale, and in a manner the court determines is best.

(e) The court may authorize the property sold at private sale at not less than its appraised value if it is shown that a private sale would be beneficial to the creditors of the assignor. The court shall supervise the estate of the assignor and may make all necessary orders in the interest of the creditors for its control and management by the trustee before the sale. In the interest of all parties, the court may upon petition of the assignee, if the wife of the assignor is a party to the petition, order partition of the land of the assignor, before sale, between the assignee and wife of the assignor. The court shall set off to the wife her inchoate one-third (⅓) in the land before sale. If the court finds that the land cannot be partitioned without detriment to the interest of the creditors of the assignor, the court may make an order directing the sale of all the land conveyed to the assignee by the assignor, including the wife's one-third (⅓) inchoate interest. The one-third (⅓) of the money for which the land is sold shall be paid to the wife of the assignor when collected. The assignee shall, after sale, compel the trustee to report the money in the trustee's hands for distribution, and shall compel the money to be paid into court for distribution if the assets are shown to be sufficient to pay a ten percent (10%) dividend upon the indebtedness. The distribution may be ordered from time to time when, on application of any person interested, it is shown to the court that there is sufficient funds in the hands of the trustee to pay the dividend of ten percent (10%). [P.L.2-2002, § 3.]

Cross References. Distribution of assets to secure creditors under Uniform Liquidation Act, IC 30-2-7.

NOTES TO DECISIONS

ANALYSIS

Accounting by trustee.
Actions by trustee.
—In general.
—Pleadings.
—Setting aside fraudulent conveyance.
Assignee for benefit of creditors.
Attempted amendments.
Order for sale of property.
Sale of lands.
—Approval by court.
—Debtor's wife.
—Defenses.
—Jurisdiction.
—Liens.
—Value.
Sale of personalty and realty.

Accounting by Trustee.
An assignee was chargeable with interest on the funds in his hands from the time he should have secured an order for the distribution of the same. If trust funds were used to purchase claims against the estate, the profit made by such purchase had to be accounted for. Manhattan Cloak & Suit Co. v. Dodge, 120 Ind. 1, 21 N.E. 344 (1889).

Actions by Trustee.

—In General.
If an assignee wrongfully refused to bring suit when it should have been done, the creditors could institute the suit. Wright v. Mack, 95 Ind. 332 (1884).
An assignee could sue to have partition of the lands conveyed only when so ordered by the court, and when it would have been to the

best interest of the trust. Jewett v. Perrette, 127 Ind. 97, 26 N.E. 685 (1891).
Assignees could sue to recover the possession of real estate included in the deed of assignment. Taylor v. Bruner, 130 Ind. 482, 30 N.E. 635 (1892).
The assignee of an insolvent bank could not maintain an action to enforce the double liability of shareholders provided by statute, such action having been enforceable only by the creditors. Runner v. Dwiggins, 147 Ind. 238, 46 N.E. 580, 36 L.R.A. 645 (1897).

—Pleadings.
When the assignee sued, he should have alleged that the deed of assignment had been duly recorded. Foster v. Brown, 65 Ind. 234 (1879); Wheeler v. Hawkins, 101 Ind. 486 (1885). See Jewett v. Perrette, 127 Ind. 97, 26 N.E. 685 (1891).
Deed of assignment was not the foundation of a pleading by the assignee, and it was not necessary to make it a part of the pleading. Cooper v. Perdue, 114 Ind. 207, 16 N.E. 140 (1888); Jewett v. Perrette, 127 Ind. 97, 26 N.E. 685 (1891).

—Setting Aside Fraudulent Conveyance.
Assignee was the proper party to have brought an action to recover property fraudulently conveyed by the debtor. Foster v. Brown, 65 Ind. 234 (1879); Cooper v. Perdue, 114 Ind. 207, 16 N.E. 140 (1888); Voorhees v. Carpenter, 127 Ind. 300, 26 N.E. 838 (1891); Franklin Nat'l Bank v. Whitehead, 149 Ind. 560, 49 N.E. 592, 39 L.R.A. 725, 63 Am. St. 302 (1898); Searles v. Little, 153 Ind. 432, 55 N.E. 93 (1899).
After the settlement of the trust and dis-

Actions by Trustee. (Cont'd)

—Setting Aside Fraudulent Conveyance. (Cont'd)
charge of the assignee, a creditor could not sue to set aside a fraudulent conveyance made by the debtor before the assignment, even though the fraud was not discovered until after the settlement of the trust. Voorhees v. Carpenter, 127 Ind. 300, 26 N.E. 838 (1891).

Assignee for Benefit of Creditors.
It is the duty of an assignee for the benefit of creditors to administer the trust to the best advantage and to protect it, for which purpose he could employ and pay for necessary assistance, including an attorney. In re Davis, 204 Ind. 227, 183 N.E. 547 (1932).

Attempted Amendments.
This section was an amendment of Acts 1875, ch. 117, p. 166, by Acts 1881 (Spec. Sess.), ch. 4, p. 74. Attempts were made in 1893 and 1897 to amend this section, but both attempted amendments were held void. Peele v. Ohio & Ind. Oil Co., 158 Ind. 374, 63 N.E. 763 (1902).

Order for Sale of Property.
This section gave the court broad authority and placed no limitation as to notice, terms, or conditions so far as private sales authorized or ratified by it were concerned. Southworth v. Stout, 112 Ind. App. 429, 44 N.E.2d 225 (1942).

A provision of an order of private sale of property assigned by a corporation for the benefit of creditors that the purchaser assume all debts and liabilities except liability for any claim based on preferred stock, and that he be permitted to apply upon any portion of his bid preferred stock at a valuation equal to the amount each share would receive on distribution of the proceeds of the sale, was not objectionable on the ground that the court was without authority to order the sale for other than cash or credit. Southworth v. Stout, 112 Ind. App. 429, 44 N.E.2d 225 (1942).

A preferred stockholder could not complain because he had to look for payment of his claim to the purchaser of the assets of the corporation, pursuant to an order of sale of the property which had been assigned for the benefit of creditors. Southworth v. Stout, 112 Ind. App. 429, 44 N.E.2d 225 (1942).

Sale of Lands.

—Approval by Court.
Title to land sold by an assignee did not vest in the purchaser until the court approved the sale. Chase v. VanMeter, 140 Ind. 321, 39 N.E. 455 (1894).

—Debtor's Wife.
Wife of a debtor who made an assignment became vested with one-third interest in his land when the same was sold. Lawson v. DeBolt, 78 Ind. 563 (1881); Wright v. Gelvin, 85 Ind. 128 (1882); Chase v. VanMeter, 140 Ind. 321, 39 N.E. 455 (1894); Willson v. Miller, 30 Ind. App. 586, 66 N.E. 757 (1903); Evansville Imp. Co. v. Gardner, 75 Ind. App. 401, 128 N.E. 471 (1920).

The assignment itself did not transfer any title to the debtor's wife, and she had no absolute interest in lands of the debtor until the same were sold. Hall v. Harrell, 92 Ind. 408 (1884); Taylor v. Bruner, 130 Ind. 482, 30 N.E. 635 (1892); Willson v. Miller, 30 Ind. App. 586, 66 N.E. 757 (1903).

The debtor's wife could have her third set off to her by partition. Evansville Imp. Co. v. Gardner, 75 Ind. App. 401, 128 N.E. 471 (1920).

—Defenses.
A purchaser of property from an assignee for creditors could not interpose as a defense to an action by such assignee for the collection of notes given in payment for such property the failure of the assignee to report the sale to the court, without alleging an offer to return the property. Breyfogle v. Stotsenburg, 148 Ind. 552, 47 N.E. 1057 (1897).

—Jurisdiction.
The court of the county where the debtor resided and made the assignment had power to authorize the sale of lands situate in other counties. Lawson v. DeBolt, 78 Ind. 563 (1881).

Courts having jurisdiction of the assignment could authorize the sale of the lands at private sale on credit. Lawson v. DeBolt, 78 Ind. 563 (1881).

—Liens.
Liens on property sold by the assignee were transferred to the funds arising from the sale. Stix v. Sadler, 109 Ind. 254, 9 N.E. 905 (1887); Hamrick v. Loring, 147 Ind. 229, 45 N.E. 107 (1896).

Threatened injury to the rights of the mortgagees in the mortgaged property could have been enjoined. Where mortgaged property in the hands of an assignee was threatened to have been sold, to the injury of the mortgagee, the threatened sale could have been enjoined until the debt secured by the mortgage became due. Ades v. Levi, 137 Ind. 506, 37 N.E. 388 (1894).

—Value.
Real estate could have been sold for less

Sale of Lands. (Cont'd)

—Value. (Cont'd)
than two thirds of its appraised value although the sale was private. Evansville Imp. Co. v. Gardner, 75 Ind. App. 401, 128 N.E. 471 (1920).

Sale of Personalty and Realty.
Under this section, the court was not obliged to order sale of the personal property and then turn the real estate back to an assignor corporation merely because there was sufficient personal property to pay all but preferred creditors of the corporation. Southworth v. Stout, 112 Ind. App. 429, 44 N.E.2d 225 (1942).

The purpose of former IC 32-12-3-1 (repealed; for similar privisions see IC 32-18-3-

1), concerning sale of real estate assigned for the benefit of creditors and authorizing a resale in the event a bond was furnished guaranteeing a bidder for not less than ten percent more than the amount bid at the previous sale, was to give creditors the benefit of the best available sale price for the real estate, and this section, giving the court the right to sell personalty and realty as an entirety, sought to give creditors in the proper case the advantages to be obtained from selling a business as a going concern, and, when the two sections were read and construed together, it was clear that former IC 32-12-3-1 (repealed; for similar privisions see IC 32-18-3-1) not intended to limit the broad powers given the court by this section. Southworth v. Stout, 112 Ind. App. 429, 44 N.E.2d 225 (1942).

32-18-1-11. Report by trustee. — The trustee shall, within six (6) months after beginning the duties of the trust, report to the judge of the circuit court, under oath:

    (1) the amount of money in the trustee's hands from:

        (A) the sale of property; and

        (B) collections; and

    (2) the amount still uncollected.

The trustee shall also, in the report, list all claims of creditors that have been presented to the trustee against the assignor. The trustee shall denote the claims that the trustee concludes should be allowed and those that the trustee determines not to allow. [P.L.2-2002, § 3.]

32-18-1-12. Report —Appearance docket of court. — The clerk of the court shall spread the report and list upon the appearance docket of the court. The clerk shall distinguish between the claims the trustee has determined to allow and the claims the trustee has refused to allow. In all cases in which the trustee has refused to allow a claim, and in which a creditor objects to the allowance of the claim of another creditor, the judge may order the case to stand for trial at the next term of the court. The trial shall be governed by the rules regulating the trials of similar actions in the circuit court. If, after trial of the claim, the court is satisfied that the claim is valid and just, the court shall order the claim to be allowed and paid as other similar claims are paid. The court shall also make an order with respect to costs as the court considers just. [P.L.2-2002, § 3.]

Cross References. Preference of claims for labor, IC 22-2-10-1.

NOTES TO DECISIONS

ANALYSIS

In general.
Actions by creditors.
Foreign creditors.
Trust funds.

Wage claims.

In General.
The rules applicable to the enforcement of claims against decedents' estates were appli-

In General. (Cont'd)

cable generally to claims presented against estates of insolvent debtors. Gifford v. Black, 22 Ind. 444 (1864).

It was necessary to state the nature and amount only of claims presented to the trustee. Fosdyke v. Nixon, 107 Ind. 138, 8 N.E. 11 (1886).

Assignees of claims were entitled to the distributive share thereof. Fosdyke v. Nixon, 107 Ind. 138, 8 N.E. 11 (1886).

Actions by Creditors.

The making of an assignment by an insolvent debtor did not prohibit his creditors from suing and obtaining personal judgments on their claims. Lawrence v. McVeagh, 106 Ind. 210, 6 N.E. 327 (1886); Second Nat'l Bank v. Townsend, 114 Ind. 534, 17 N.E. 116 (1888); New Albany Mfg. Co. v. Sulzer, 29 Ind. App. 89, 63 N.E. 873 (1902).

Creditors who filed claims which were not paid could sue the debtor afterwards. New Albany Mfg. Co. v. Sulzer, 29 Ind. App. 89, 63 N.E. 873 (1902).

Foreign Creditors.

A foreign creditor could not by attachment proceedings sequester the property in another state, which had been voluntarily assigned by a debtor in this state for the benefit of all his creditors, and at the same time prosecute his claim against the assignee in this state, and have the claim allowed, and share in the funds which the assignee had in his hands for the payment of debts. Combs v. New Albany Rail Mill Co., 146 Ind. 688, 46 N.E. 16 (1897); Cowen v. Failey, 149 Ind. 382, 49 N.E. 270 (1898).

Trust Funds.

The beneficiary of an express or constructive trust could follow the funds so long as they could be ascertained, and when ascertainment failed he could follow the property into which the trust funds had been converted or invested, and in case of insolvency he could have a preference decreed. Winstandley v. Second Nat'l Bank, 13 Ind. App. 544, 41 N.E. 956 (1895).

Wage Claims.

Where plaintiff was a laborer within the meaning of the statute, he was entitled to have his claim for wages declared a preferred claim payable before a distribution of the assets among the general creditors. Pendergast v. Yandes, 124 Ind. 159, 24 N.E. 724, 8 L.R.A. 849 (1890); Shull v. Fontanet Mining Ass'n, 128 Ind. 331, 26 N.E. 790 (1891); Eversole v. Chase, 127 Ind. 297, 26 N.E. 835 (1891); Terre Haute & I.R.R. v. Baker, 4 Ind. App. 66, 30 N.E. 431 (1892); Bell v. Hiner, 16 Ind. App. 184, 44 N.E. 576 (1896), overruled on other grounds, Board of Comm'rs v. Crone, 36 Ind. App. 283, 75 N.E. 826 (1905).

The statute, giving a preference to the claims of mechanics and laborers when a debtor made an assignment for the benefit of his creditors, did not give such claims a preference over debts secured by mortgage. McDaniel v. Osborn, 166 Ind. 1, 75 N.E. 647, 2 L.R.A. (n.s.) 615, 117 Am. St. R. 354 (1905).

Contractors furnishing materials and erecting buildings were not laborers. Anderson Driving Park Ass'n v. Thompson, 18 Ind. App. 458, 48 N.E. 259 (1897).

Collateral References. Priority under 31 U.S.C. § 191, as between claim of United States and employee's claim for wages. 36 A.L.R.2d 1203.

Preference prohibitions as affecting validity of provision in deed or transfer to assignee for benefit of creditors for payment of attorneys' fees. 79 A.L.R.2d 513.

Statutory priority as affecting validity of provision in deed or transfer to assignee for benefit of creditors for payment of attorneys' fees. 79 A.L.R.2d 513.

Validity of provision in deed or transfer to assignee for benefit of creditors for payment of attorneys' fees. 79 A.L.R.2d 513.

32-18-1-13. Liens and encumbrances on property. — (a) A part of the property assigned on which there are liens or encumbrances may be sold by the trustee subject to the liens or encumbrances.

(b) However, if the trustee is satisfied that the general fund would be materially increased by the payment of the liens or encumbrances, the trustee shall make application, by petition, to the judge of the circuit court for an order to pay the liens and encumbrances before selling the property. Before the holder of any lien or encumbrance is entitled to receive any part of the holder's debt from the general fund, the holder shall proceed to enforce the payment of the debt by sale, or otherwise, of the property on which the lien or encumbrance exists. For the residue of the claim, the holder of the lien or encumbrance shall share pro rata with the other creditors, if entitled to do so under Indiana law. [P.L.2-2002, § 3.]

Cross References. Distribution of assets to secure creditors under Uniform Liquidation Act, IC 30-2-7.

NOTES TO DECISIONS

ANALYSIS

Attachment liens.
Composition of claim.
Enforcement of liens.
Execution liens.
Foreign corporations.
Improper payment.
Judgment liens.
Liability of trustee.
Mortgages subsequent to assignment.
Payment from proceeds of sale.
Taxes.
Wife of debtor.

Attachment Liens.

Liens acquired by attachment proceedings before the assignment had preference over general debts. Woolson v. Pipher, 100 Ind. 306 (1885).

Composition of Claim.

If a creditor holding a lien agreed to accept a sum less than the amount due in satisfaction thereof, he was bound by the agreement. Pfaffenberger v. Platter, 114 Ind. 473, 16 N.E. 835 (1888).

Enforcement of Liens.

Suits to enforce liens on the property assigned did not need to have been instituted in the court where the assignment was pending. Gilbert v. McCorkle, 110 Ind. 215, 11 N.E. 296 (1887).

Execution Liens.

Liens of executions were not divested by the assignment, and the officer could take possession of the property and sell the same. Griffin v. Wallace, 66 Ind. 410 (1879); Marsh v. Vawter, 71 Ind. 22 (1880); State ex rel. Braden v. Krug, 82 Ind. 58 (1882).

When personal property was omitted from the schedule and was afterwards surrendered to the trustee as a part of the estate, he could as against executions subsequently issued and levied, retain and dispose of it in the execution of the trust. Hasseld v. Seyfort, 105 Ind. 534, 5 N.E. 675 (1886).

Foreign Corporations.

A mortgage executed by an insolvent corporation on lands in this state to secure pre-ferred creditors was not a part of a deed of assignment made by mortgagor where the deed of assignment was declared invalid as to the mortgaged property. Nathan v. Lee, 152 Ind. 232, 52 N.E. 987, 43 L.R.A. 820 (1899); Nappanee Canning Co. v. Reid, Murdoch & Co., 159 Ind. 614, 64 N.E. 870, 59 L.R.A. 199 (1903).

Improper Payment.

Assignee had no right to apply the funds on a mortgage that was invalid as a lien, and an order of court affirming the payment did not validate the same. Lockwood v. Slevin, 26 Ind. 124 (1866).

When payment of claim of mortgagee was made by mistake, in order to maintain an action of foreclosure, the mortgagee was required to repay the amount mistakenly paid to him by the trustee. Rumley Co. v. Moore, 151 Ind. 24, 50 N.E. 574 (1898).

Judgment Liens.

Judgments rendered after the assignment did not become liens on lands not included in the deed of assignment. Seibert v. Milligan, 110 Ind. 106, 10 N.E. 929 (1887).

Liability of Trustee.

An action would lie against the trustee for breach of trust upon failure to obey court order for sale of property and distribution of proceeds, resulting in actual loss to creditor. State ex rel. Puett v. Musser, 4 Ind. App. 407, 30 N.E. 944 (1892).

Mortgages Subsequent to Assignment.

Mortgages executed by the debtor but which were not accepted until after the assignment were not prior liens. Reagan v. First Nat'l Bank, 157 Ind. 623, 61 N.E. 575 (1901), reh'g overruled, 157 Ind. 673, 62 N.E. 701 (1902).

Payment from Proceeds of Sale.

If a mortgagee consented that the assignee could sell the mortgaged property and pay the mortgage out of the proceeds thereof, the mortgage did not need to have been foreclosed before such payment was made. Stix v. Sadler, 109 Ind. 254, 9 N.E. 905 (1887).

If property having liens thereon was sold by

Payment from Proceeds of Sale. (Cont'd) the assignee, the liens were transferred to the fund and the court could direct priority of payment. Hamrick v. Loring, 147 Ind. 229, 45 N.E. 107 (1896).

Taxes.
  Assignee was required to pay taxes only on lands sold when he was authorized to sell the lands free of liens. Burns v. Gavin, 118 Ind. 320, 20 N.E. 799 (1889).

Wife of Debtor.
  Wife of debtor could not have the personal estate in the hands of assignee applied in satisfaction of a mortgage on lands of debtor, in order to protect the inchoate interest of the wife in such lands. Gough v. Clift, 81 Ind. 371 (1882).

Collateral References. Priority under 31 U.S.C. § 191, as between claim of United States and employee's claim for wages. 36 A.L.R.2d 1203.
  Statutory priority as affecting validity of provision in deed or transfer to assignee for benefit of creditors for payment of attorneys' fees. 79 A.L.R.2d 513.
  Validity of provision in deed or transfer to assignee for benefit of creditors for payment of attorneys' fees. 79 A.L.R.2d 513.

32-18-1-14. Confirmation of report — Distribution of money by clerk.

— If the court confirms the report made as provided under section 11 [IC 32-18-1-11] of this chapter and if no contested claims are standing on the docket as provided under section 12 [IC 32-18-1-12] of this chapter, the court shall order the trustee to pay all money in the trustee's hands to the clerk of the court. The clerk, after deducting the costs incident to the execution of the trust, including an allowance to the trustee as the court considers just, shall:

  (1) distribute the money among the creditors according to this chapter; and

  (2) take receipts from each creditor.

[P.L.2-2002, § 3.]

NOTES TO DECISIONS

In General.
  Assignees of claims could receive the distributive shares thereof. Fosdyke v. Nixon, 107 Ind. 138, 8 N.E. 11 (1886).
  Assignee was chargeable with interest on the funds in his hands from the time he ought to have procured an order for distributing the same. Manhattan Cloak & Suit Co. v. Dodge, 120 Ind. 1, 21 N.E. 344, 6 L.R.A. 369 (1889).

  Where an assignee sold mortgaged property, the lien of the mortgage was transferred to the fund arising from the sale, and on petition of the parties claiming under the mortgage, the court could direct the distribution thereof according to priorities. Hamrick v. Loring, 147 Ind. 229, 45 N.E. 107 (1896).

32-18-1-15. Examination of assignors and transferees.

— (a) If a creditor or the trustee, by verified petition, asks the court for the examination of the assignor or any person to whom any part of the person's property has been transferred within six (6) months before the assignment, the circuit or superior court may issue an order for the examination of:

  (1) the assignor;

  (2) a person or officer of a corporation to whom a transfer is believed to have been fraudulently made;

  (3) a a person or officer of an association to whom a transfer is believed to have been fraudulently made; and

(4) a person alleged to have been concerned in the transfer.

(b) A person described in subsection (a) may be brought before the court and, on oath, be compelled to answer all questions put to the person pertinent to the alleged transaction. The court may stay further transfers and subject property that has been fraudulently withheld or transferred to the operation of the general trust. The assignor or person shall be interrogated or be compelled to answer all questions concerning the disposition of the property of the assignor. The assignor may be interrogated and compelled to answer all questions concerning the management of the assignor's business and affairs for the six (6) months before the assignment. The assignor shall be compelled to produce all books, papers, and accounts in reference to the assignor's business affairs during the six (6) months preceding the assignment. [P.L.2-2002, § 3.]

32-18-1-16. Oath of claimant. — A person who files a claim with the trustee must make oath that the claim is just and lawful and no part of the claim is for usurious interest. If a claim or part of a claim is for usurious interest, it must be deducted from the claims before they are allowed. The trustee may administer an oath to a creditor in reference to the validity and justice of a claim. [P.L.2-2002, § 3.]

32-18-1-17. Compounding and compromising of debts. — A trustee may compound or compromise a debt or claim belonging to the assignor that cannot be otherwise recovered without endangering the recovery of the claim or debt. [P.L.2-2002, § 3.]

32-18-1-18. Final report to the court. — (a) The trustee shall, at the expiration of one (1) year after entering upon the duties of the trust or at the next term of the court after the expiration of one (1) year after entering upon the duties of the trust, make a final report to the court.

(b) After a hearing and determination, if the judge is satisfied with and approves the report, the judge shall order the trustee to be discharged from the trust. However, the judge may, for good cause shown, grant further time to the trustee to file a final account. [P.L.2-2002, § 3.]

NOTES TO DECISIONS

Employment of Attorney.

An assignee for the benefit of creditors had the duty to administer the trust to the best advantage, and could employ and pay for necessary assistance, including an attorney. In re Davis, 204 Ind. 227, 183 N.E. 547 (1932).

32-18-1-19. Trustee — Removal — Filling of vacancies. — (a) The judge of the circuit court may, upon the petition of a creditor or the assignor, remove a trustee under this chapter for good cause shown and appoint a successor.

(b) If a vacancy occurs by death, resignation, or removal of a trustee from Indiana, the judge may fill the vacancy and shall order a trustee who is removed to surrender all property in the trustee's hands belonging to the trust to the successor. The court may require a trustee removed under this section to pay to the clerk of the court all money in the trustee's hands, and on or before the next term, the trustee shall make and file a full and final report showing the condition of the trust and the trustee's management of the trust while under the trustee's control. If the court is satisfied with the report and the trustee has fully complied with this chapter and paid all money in the trustee's hands to the clerk of the court, the court may discharge the trustee. [P.L.2-2002, § 3.]

32-18-1-20. Appeal. — This chapter may not be construed to prevent a party aggrieved by an order or decree of the court under this chapter from having an appeal as in other civil actions. [P.L.2-2002, § 3.]

NOTES TO DECISIONS

In General.
An appeal could not be taken from an order of the court sustaining exceptions to the final report of the assignee, and refusing to approve the same. Cravens v. Chambers, 55 Ind. 5 (1876).

32-18-1-21. Fees — Clerk of court — Appraisers. — (a) For whatever services the clerk of the circuit court is required to perform under this chapter, the clerk is allowed the same fees as are allowed the clerk by law for similar services in other civil proceedings.

(b) The appraisers under this chapter are entitled to one dollar ($1) per day each for their services.

(c) The judge shall remunerate the trustee for the trustee's services in executing the trust out of the general fund as the judge considers just and proper. [P.L.2-2002, § 3.]

NOTES TO DECISIONS

Attorney for Trustee.
Assignee for benefit of creditors could employ an attorney and pay his compensation and expenses, when necessary in administering the trust. In re Davis, 204 Ind. 227, 183 N.E. 547 (1932).

32-18-1-22. Surviving partners. — (a) A surviving partner of a firm doing business in Indiana has full power to make assignments under this chapter. [P.L.2-2002, § 3.]

Compiler's Notes. As enacted by P.L.2-2002, § 3, this section contains a subsection (a) designation, but no subsection (b).

NOTES TO DECISIONS

In General.
A partnership assignment needed only to include partnership property. Blake v. Faulkner, 18 Ind. 47 (1862); Garnor v. Frederick, 18 Ind. 507 (1862); Ex parte Hopkins, 104 Ind. 157, 2 N.E. 587 (1885).

The making of an assignment by a surviving partner did not invalidate a chattel mortgage executed by such partner prior to the assignment. First Nat'l Bank v. Parsons, 128 Ind. 147, 27 N.E. 486 (1891).

Collateral References. 6 Am. Jur. 2d Assignments for Benefit of Creditors, § 14.

6A C.J.S. Assignments for Benefit of Creditors, § 47.

CHAPTER 2

UNIFORM FRAUDULENT TRANSFER ACT

32-18-2-1. Applicability. — (a) This chapter applies to all transfers made and obligations incurred after June 30, 1994.

(b) This chapter does not apply to a transfer made or an obligation incurred before July 1, 1994. [P.L.2-2002, § 3.]

Effective Dates. P.L.2-2002, § 3. July 1. 2002.

Indiana Law Review. The Indiana Uniform Fraudulent Transfer Act Introduction, 28 Ind. L. Rev. 1195 (1995).

Res Gestae. Indiana enacts Uniform Fraudulent Transfer Act, 38 Res Gestae 20 (1994).

Rules and rulings for the trial lawyer, 41 (No. 1) Res Gestae 33 (1997).

32-18-2-2. "Asset" defined. — (a) As used in this chapter, "asset" means property of a debtor.

(b) The term does not include any of the following:

(1) Property, to the extent the property is encumbered by a valid lien.

(2) Property, to the extent the property is generally exempt under law other than federal bankruptcy law.

(3) An interest in property held in tenancy by the entireties to the extent the interest is not subject to process by a creditor holding a claim against only one (1) tenant. [P.L.2-2002, § 3.]

32-18-2-3. "Claim" defined. — As used in this chapter, "claim" means a right to payment, whether the right is:

(1) reduced to judgment or not;

(2) liquidated or unliquidated;

(3) fixed or contingent;

(4) matured or unmatured;

(5) disputed or undisputed;

(6) legal or not;

(7) equitable or not; or

(8) secured or unsecured.
[P.L.2-2002, § 3.]

32-18-2-4. "Creditor" defined. — As used in this chapter, "creditor" means a person who has a claim. [P.L.2-2002, § 3.]

NOTES TO DECISIONS

In General.
Under prior similar provisions, persons having claims arising out of torts or contracts were creditors. Pennington v. Clifton, 11 Ind. 162 (1858); Rhodes v. Green, 36 Ind. 7 (1871); Shean v. Shay, 42 Ind. 375, 13 Am. R. 366 (1873); Bishop v. Redmond, 83 Ind. 157 (1882).

A wife who obtained a judgment for alimony was the creditor of the husband. Plunkett v. Plunkett, 114 Ind. 484, 16 N.E. 612, 17 N.E. 562 (1888).

32-18-2-5. "Debt" defined. — As used in this chapter, "debt" means liability on a claim. [P.L.2-2002, § 3.]

32-18-2-6. "Debtor" defined. — As used in this chapter, "debtor" means a person who is liable on a claim. [P.L.2-2002, § 3.]

32-18-2-7. "Lien" defined. — (a) As used in this chapter, "lien" means a charge against or an interest in property to secure payment of a debt or performance of an obligation.
(b) The term includes any of the following:
(1) A security interest created by agreement.
(2) A judicial lien obtained by legal or equitable process or proceedings.
(3) A common law lien.
(4) A statutory lien.
[P.L.2-2002, § 3.]

32-18-2-8. "Person" defined. — As used in this chapter, "person" means an individual, a partnership, a corporation, a limited liability company, an association, an organization, a government, a governmental subdivision or agency, a business trust, an estate, a trust, or any other legal or commercial entity. [P.L.2-2002, § 3.]

32-18-2-9. "Property" defined. — As used in this chapter, "property" means anything that can be the subject of ownership. [P.L.2-2002, § 3.]

32-18-2-10. "Transfer" defined. — (a) As used in this chapter, "transfer" means any mode of disposing of or parting with an asset or an interest in an asset, whether the mode is direct or indirect, absolute or conditional, or voluntary or involuntary.
(b) The term includes payment of money, release, lease, and creation of a lien or other encumbrance. [P.L.2-2002, § 3.]

32-18-2-11. "Valid lien" defined. — As used in this chapter, "valid lien" means a lien that is effective against the holder of a judicial lien subsequently obtained by legal or equitable process or proceedings. [P.L.2-2002, § 3.]

32-18-2-12. Exceptions to definitions — Insolvency. — (a) For purposes of this section, assets do not include property that has been:

    (1) transferred, concealed, or removed with intent to hinder, delay, or defraud creditors; or

    (2) transferred in a manner making the transfer voidable under this chapter.

(b) For purposes of this section, debts do not include an obligation to the extent it is secured by a valid lien on property of the debtor not included as an asset under this section.

(c) A debtor is insolvent if the sum of the debtor's debts is greater than all of the debtor's assets at a fair valuation.

(d) A debtor who is generally not paying the debtor's debts as they become due is presumed to be insolvent. This presumption imposes upon the party against whom the presumption is directed the burden of proving that the nonexistence of insolvency is more probable than its existence.

(e) A partnership is insolvent if the sum of the partnership's debts is greater than the aggregate, at a fair valuation, of all of the partnership's assets and the sum of the excess of the value of each general partner's nonpartnership assets over each general partner's nonpartnership debts. [P.L.2-2002, § 3.]

32-18-2-13. When value given. — (a) Value is given for a transfer or an obligation if, in exchange for the transfer or obligation, property is transferred or an antecedent debt is secured or satisfied. Value does not include an unperformed promise made otherwise than in the ordinary course of the promisor's business to furnish support to the debtor or another person.

(b) For purposes of sections 14(2) and 15 [IC 32-18-2-14(2) and IC 32-18-2-15] of this chapter, a person gives a reasonably equivalent value if the person acquires an interest of the debtor in an asset through a regularly conducted, noncollusive foreclosure sale or execution of a power of sale for the acquisition or disposition of the interest of the debtor upon default under a mortgage, deed of trust, or security agreement.

(c) A transfer is made for present value if the exchange between the debtor and the transferee is intended by the debtor and transferee to be contemporaneous and is in fact substantially contemporaneous. [P.L.2-2002, § 3.]

NOTES TO DECISIONS

No Fraudulent Intent.

    Although the evidence indicated that several badges of fraud may have been present in the transfer in question, the trial court specifically found that there was no fraudulent intent, and although the trial court's findings could have been more specific, they were supported by the evidence, and the findings supported the trial court's conclusion that the transfer of stock and the release of the loan was not fraudulent. Indianapolis Ind. Aamco Dealers Adver. Pool v. Anderson, 746 N.E.2d 383 (Ind. App. 2001).

32-18-2-14. Fraudulent transfers and obligations — Intent. — A transfer made or an obligation incurred by a debtor is fraudulent as to a creditor, whether the creditor's claim arose before or after the transfer was made or the obligation was incurred, if the debtor made the transfer or incurred the obligation:

(1) with actual intent to hinder, delay, or defraud any creditor of the debtor; or

(2) without receiving a reasonably equivalent value in exchange for the transfer or obligation, and the debtor:

(A) was engaged or was about to engage in a business or a transaction for which the remaining assets of the debtor were unreasonably small in relation to the business or transaction; or

(B) intended to incur or believed or reasonably should have believed that the debtor would incur debts beyond the debtor's ability to pay as the debts became due. [P.L.2-2002, § 3.]

NOTES TO DECISIONS

ANALYSIS

In general.
Declarations of vendor.
Good faith and fair consideration.
Intent.

In General.

Every sale of goods in the possession of the vendor was presumed fraudulent as to his creditors unless immediate delivery of the goods was made to the vendee, but such presumption could have been rebutted. Jones v. Gott, 10 Ind. 240 (1858); Geisendorff v. Eagles, 70 Ind. 418 (1879); Rose v. Colter, 76 Ind. 590 (1881); Powell v. Stickney, 88 Ind. 310 (1882); Cable Co. v. McElhoe, 58 Ind. App. 637, 108 N.E. 790 (1915).

Lands, fraudulently conveyed could have been attached; but it must have been shown that the purchaser was a party to the fraud. Johnston v. Field, 62 Ind. 377 (1878).

Conveyances made to defraud creditors were valid as to all persons except such creditors. Etter v. Anderson, 84 Ind. 333 (1882); Kitts v. Willson, 130 Ind. 492, 29 N.E. 401 (1891); Reed v. Robbins, 58 Ind. App. 659, 108 N.E. 780 (1915).

Lands conveyed to defraud creditors were subject to execution to satisfy a subsequent judgment for costs if other property could not then have been found liable to execution. Stevens v. Works, 81 Ind. 445 (1882).

Lands conveyed to defraud creditors could have been sold on execution before the conveyance was set aside, but in order to protect his title, the purchaser must have shown facts to justify setting such conveyance aside. Hanna v. Aebker, 84 Ind. 411 (1882); Eve v. Louis, 91 Ind. 457 (1883); Pennington v. Flock, 93 Ind. 378 (1884); Milburn v. Phillips,

136 Ind. 680, 34 N.E. 983, 36 N.E. 360 (1893); McNally v. White, 154 Ind. 163, 54 N.E. 794 (1899), reh'g overruled, 154 Ind. 174, 56 N.E. 214 (1900).

Where a debtor, who at the time had less property than he would be entitled to under exemption laws, purchase real estate which he conveyed to his wife and children, such conveyance would not be set aside as fraudulent. Faurote v. Carr, 108 Ind. 123, 9 N.E. 350 (1886).

If a debtor had a conditional fee in lands, the same could have been sold on execution. Greer v. Wilson, 108 Ind. 322, 9 N.E. 284 (1886).

Where a person purchases and pays for lands and takes title in the name of another, the conveyance is presumed fraudulent as to the creditors of the person paying the purchase-money. Eiler v. Crull, 112 Ind. 318, 14 N.E. 79 (1887); Jones v. Snyder, 117 Ind. 229, 20 N.E. 140 (1888); Pence v. Rhonemus, 58 Ind. App. 268, 108 N.E. 129 (1915); Koehler v. Koehler, 75 Ind. App. 510, 121 N.E. 450 (1919).

Where a husband gave money to his wife in order to defraud his creditors and his wife accepted the money with knowledge of the fraudulent intent and without giving any consideration, she was chargeable as a trustee and could be compelled to account as such at the suit of her husband's creditors. Blair v. Smith, 114 Ind. 114, 15 N.E. 817, 5 Am. St. R. 593 (1888).

Under the express provisions of the statute, land fraudulently conveyed by the execution debtor was subject to a judgment against him. Blair v. Smith, 114 Ind. 114, 15 N.E. 817, 5 Am. St. R. 593 (1888).

Conveyances had to be adjudged fraudulent

In General. (Cont'd)

before the land could be sold without appraisement when an appraisement was otherwise required. Milburn v. Phillips, 136 Ind. 680, 34 N.E. 983, 36 N.E. 360 (1893).

It is not fraudulent to transfer exempt property with the intent to remove it beyond the reach of creditors. Isrigg v. Pauley, 148 Ind. 436, 47 N.E. 821 (1897).

Where a debtor who is a householder transfers his property to another in order to defraud his creditors and his transferee has notice of this intent, the debtor's creditors may not reach that property if the value of the transferee wife's interest therein together with the debtor's exemption and all liens on the property senior to such creditors equals or exceeds the value of the property transferred. Marmon v. White, 151 Ind. 445, 51 N.E. 930 (1898).

Where a party seeking to set aside a conveyance of real property as fraudulent filed a lis pendens notice and the property was reconveyed during the suit and mortgaged by the owner the mortgagees were bound by the decree declaring the conveyance fraudulent. Wild v. Noblesville Bldg., Loan Fund & Sav. Ass'n, 153 Ind. 5, 53 N.E. 944 (1899).

A conveyance to defraud existing creditors was not fraudulent as to subsequent creditors where there was no intent to defraud the latter. Stumph v. Bruner, 89 Ind. 556 (1883); Petree v. Brotherton, 133 Ind. 692, 32 N.E. 300 (1892).

A presumption of fraud, when goods sold were not delivered to the purchaser, arose only in favor of creditors of the vendor or subsequent purchasers in good faith. Warner v. Warner, 30 Ind. App. 578, 66 N.E. 760 (1903).

The failure of the holder of installment contracts to show the insolvency of the debtors at any particular time was not fatal to its action to set aside certain conveyances as fraudulent, because the transfers were accompanied by fraudulent intent, as determined by certain "badges of fraud," including the transfer of large amounts of valuable assets to family members without consideration, retaining assets of highly questionable value, such as accounts receivable. Jackson v. Farmers State Bank, 481 N.E.2d 395 (Ind. App. 1985).

Declarations of Vendor.

Where the continued possession and management, by the husband, of property sold to his wife, showed that the sale was prima facie fraudulent, the declarations of the husband, while in possession as agent of his wife, to the effect that the sale was made to defeat the claims of certain creditors, was admissible to show fraud. Higgins v. Spahr, 145 Ind. 167, 43 N.E. 11 (1896).

Good Faith and Fair Consideration.

If the sale was made in good faith for a fair consideration, the continuance of the vendor in possession as agent of the vendee did not render the sale void. South Branch Lumber Co. v. Stearns, 2 Ind. App. 7, 28 N.E. 117 (1891).

Intent.

Where the designated evidence in the record did not raise a question of material fact as to fraudulent intent, in that there was no evidence that the disputed transaction was out of the ordinary, summary judgment was appropriate. Garza v. Lorch, 705 N.E.2d 468 (Ind. App. 1998).

Although the evidence indicated that several badges of fraud may have been present in the transfer in question, the trial court specifically found that there was no fraudulent intent, and although the trial court's findings could have been more specific, they were supported by the evidence, and the findings supported the trial court's conclusion that the transfer of stock and the release of the loan was not fraudulent. Indianapolis Ind. Aamco Dealers Adver. Pool v. Anderson, 746 N.E.2d 383 (Ind. App. 2001).

32-18-2-15. Fraudulent transfers and obligations — Claims arising before transfer or obligation. — A transfer made or an obligation incurred by a debtor is fraudulent as to a creditor whose claim arose before the transfer was made or the obligation was incurred if:

(1) the debtor made the transfer or incurred the obligation without receiving a reasonably equivalent value in exchange for the transfer or obligation; and

(2) the debtor:

(A) was insolvent at that time; or

(B) became insolvent as a result of the transfer or obligation. [P.L.2-2002, § 3.]

NOTES TO DECISIONS

No Fraudulent Transfer.

Although the evidence indicated that several badges of fraud may have been present in the transfer in question, the trial court specifically found that there was no fraudulent intent, and although the trial court's findings could have been more specific, they were supported by the evidence, and the findings supported the trial court's conclusion that the transfer of stock and the release of the loan was not fraudulent. Indianapolis Ind. Aamco Dealers Adver. Pool v. Anderson, 746 N.E.2d 383 (Ind. App. 2001).

32-18-2-16. Perfection — Priority of interests in transferred property. — The following apply for purposes of this chapter:

(1) A transfer is made:

(A) with respect to an asset that is real property other than a fixture (but including the interest of a seller or purchaser under a contract for the sale of the asset), when the transfer is so far perfected that a good faith purchaser of the asset from the debtor against whom applicable law permits the transfer to be perfected cannot acquire an interest in the asset that is superior to the interest of the transferee; and

(B) with respect to an asset that is not real property or that is a fixture, when the transfer is so far perfected that a creditor on a simple contract cannot acquire a judicial lien (other than under this chapter) that is superior to the interest of the transferee.

(2) If applicable law permits a transfer to be perfected under subdivision (1) and the transfer is not so perfected before the commencement of an action for relief under this chapter, the transfer is considered made immediately before the commencement of the action.

(3) If applicable law does not permit a transfer to be perfected under subdivision (1), the transfer is made when it becomes effective between the debtor and the transferee.

(4) A transfer is not made until the debtor has acquired rights in the asset transferred.

(5) An obligation is incurred:

(A) if oral, when it becomes effective between the parties; or

(B) if evidenced by a writing, when the writing executed by the obligor is delivered to or for the benefit of the obligee. [P.L.2-2002, § 3.]

32-18-2-17. Actions for relief against a transfer of obligation. — (a) In an action for relief against a transfer or an obligation under this chapter, a creditor, subject to the limitations in section 18 [IC 32-18-2-18] of this chapter, may obtain any of the following:

(1) Avoidance of the transfer or obligation to the extent necessary to satisfy the creditor's claim.

(2) An attachment or other provisional remedy against the asset transferred or other property of the transferee in accordance with the procedure prescribed by IC 34-25-2-1 or any other applicable statute providing for attachment or other provisional remedy against debtors generally.

(3) Subject to applicable principles of equity and in accordance with applicable rules of civil procedure, any of the following:

(A) An injunction against further disposition by the debtor or a transferee, or both, of the asset transferred, its proceeds, or of other property.

(B) Appointment of a receiver to take charge of the asset transferred or of the property of the transferee.

(C) Any other relief the circumstances require.

(b) If a creditor has obtained a judgment on a claim against the debtor, the creditor, if the court orders, may levy execution on the asset transferred or its proceeds. [P.L.2-2002, § 3.]

NOTES TO DECISIONS

Proceedings Supplemental.

Proceedings supplemental are not an inappropriate vehicle to employ to set aside alleged fraudulent transfers, and a judgment creditor may proceed against a garnishee defendant where he has property of the judgment debtor, regardless of whether the judgment debtor himself could have pursued the garnishee defendant or whether the garnishee defendant was a party to the underlying lawsuit, and the proceedings supplemental are continuation of the original action which properly remain with the trial court which rendered the judgment. Stuard v. Jackson & Wickliff Auctioneers, Inc., 670 N.E.2d 953 (Ind. App. 1996).

32-18-2-18. Voidability of transfers. — (a) A transfer or an obligation is not voidable under section 14(1) [IC 32-18-2-14(1)] of this chapter against a person who took in good faith and for a reasonably equivalent value or against any subsequent transferee or obligee.

(b) Except as otherwise provided in this chapter, to the extent a transfer is voidable in an action by a creditor under section 17(a)(1) [IC 32-18-2-17(a)(1)] of this chapter, the creditor may recover judgment for the value of the asset transferred, as adjusted under subsection (c), or the amount necessary to satisfy the creditor's claim, whichever is less. The judgment may be entered against:

(1) the first transferee of the asset or the person for whose benefit the transfer was made; or

(2) any subsequent transferee other than a good faith transferee who took for value or from any subsequent transferee.

(c) If the judgment under subsection (b) is based upon the value of the asset transferred, the judgment must be for an amount equal to the value of the asset at the time of the transfer, subject to adjustment as the equities may require.

(d) Notwithstanding voidability of a transfer or an obligation under this chapter, a good faith transferee or obligee is entitled, to the extent of the value given the debtor for the transfer or obligation, to:

(1) a lien on or a right to retain any interest in the asset transferred;

(2) enforcement of any obligation incurred; or

(3) a reduction in the amount of the liability on the judgment.

(e) A transfer is not voidable under section 14(2) or section 15 [IC 32-18-2-14(2) or IC 32-18-2-15] of this chapter if the transfer results from:

(1) termination of a lease upon default by the debtor when the termination is permitted by the lease and applicable law; or

(2) enforcement of a security interest in compliance with Article 9 of the Uniform Commercial Code. [P.L.2-2002, § 3.]

Compiler's Notes. Article 9 of the Uniform Commercial Code, referred to in subsection (e)(2), as revised in 2000, may be found at IC 26-1-9.1.

NOTES TO DECISIONS

In General.

Such conveyances were usually binding upon every person except creditors of the grantor. Springer v. Drosch, 32 Ind. 486, 2 Am. R. 365 (1870); O'Neil v. Chandler, 42 Ind. 471 (1873); Garner v. Graves, 54 Ind. 188 (1876); Kitts v. Willson, 130 Ind. 492, 29 N.E. 401 (1891); Kitts v. Willson, 140 Ind. 604, 39 N.E. 313 (1894).

A conveyance to defraud creditors was generally binding upon a subsequent grantee of the same grantor. Anderson v. Etter, 102 Ind. 115, 26 N.E. 218 (1885).

The conveyance by a debtor of all his property, without consideration, to a person who had notice of all the facts was by statute made fraudulent as to the creditors of the person making such conveyance. D.L. Adams Co. v. Federal Glass Co., 180 Ind. 576, 103 N.E. 414 (1913).

A conveyance for the purpose of hindering or delaying creditors was not absolutely void, but was voidable only at the suit of the injured party. Leasure v. Leasure, 86 Ind App. 499, 157 N.E. 11, 158 N.E. 925 (1927).

Former IC 32-2-1-14 allowed the court to set aside transfers made with intent to defraud one's creditors. Warsco v. Graves, 70 Bankr. 535 (N.D. Ind. 1987).

Action to Declare Trust.

In an action under former IC 30-1-9-6 and former IC 30-1-9-7 to declare a trust in favor of creditors, the defendant had the burden of overcoming the prima facie case which the plaintiff made on proof of a conveyance to defendant on a consideration paid by another as to whom plaintiff was a creditor at the time of the transfer, and it was not necessary for the plaintiff either to allege or prove the insolvency of the debtor at such time. Pence v. Rhonemus, 58 Ind. App. 268, 108 N.E. 129 (1915).

Bankruptcy.

A deed and contemporaneous agreement shown to have been executed with the intent on the part of both grantor and grantee to defraud the grantor's creditors could have been set aside in an action by a trustee in bankruptcy. Dobbs v. Royer, 81 Ind. App. 383, 142 N.E. 131 (1924).

Consideration.

When a grantee paid a valuable consideration, he had to be connected with the fraud of the grantor before the conveyance would have been set aside. McCormick v. Hyatt, 33 Ind. 546 (1870); Pinnell v. Stringer, 59 Ind. 555 (1877); Johnston v. Field, 62 Ind. 377 (1878); Brown v. Rawlings, 72 Ind. 505 (1880); First Nat'l Bank v. Carter, 89 Ind. 317 (1883); Jewett v. Meech, 101 Ind. 289 (1885); Carnahan v. McCord, 116 Ind. 67, 18 N.E. 177 (1888); Scott v. Davis, 117 Ind. 232, 20 N.E. 139 (1889); Hays v. Montgomery, 118 Ind. 91, 20 N.E. 646 (1889); State ex rel. Harrison v. Osborn, 143 Ind. 671, 42 N.E. 921 (1896); Hedrick v. Hall, 155 Ind. 371, 58 N.E. 257 (1900).

If there was in reality a valuable consideration and sufficient consideration for a conveyance, it was immaterial whether the amount was stipulated in the deed or not and where it was charged that the conveyance was fraudulent, the nature and amount of consideration was important with reference to the good faith of the transaction. Lowry v. Howard, 35 Ind. 170, 9 Am. R. 676 (1871); Parton v. Yates, 41 Ind. 456 (1872); Pence v. Croan, 51 Ind. 336 (1875); Sherman v. Hogland, 54 Ind. 578 (1876); Spaulding v. Blythe, 73 Ind. 93 (1880); Wooters v. Osborn, 77 Ind. 513 (1881); Phelps v. Smith, 116 Ind. 387, 17 N.E. 602, 19 N.E. 156 (1888); Nichols,

Consideration. (Cont'd)
Shepard & Co. v. Burch, 128 Ind. 324, 27 N.E. 737 (1891).

It was not necessary for the purpose of setting aside a fraudulent conveyance to a volunteer, who paid no consideration, to allege and prove notice to the grantee of the fraudulent intent of the grantor. York v. Rockwood, 132 Ind. 358, 31 N.E. 1110 (1892); Roberts v. F. & M. Bank, 136 Ind. 154, 36 N.E. 128 (1894); Pierce v. Hower, 142 Ind. 626, 42 N.E. 223 (1895); First Nat'l Bank v. Smith, 149 Ind. 443, 49 N.E. 376 (1898); Bass v. Citizens' Trust Co., 32 Ind. App. 583, 70 N.E. 400 (1904).

Precedent debt was held good consideration for conveyance where there was evidence tending to show good faith. Snyder v. Jetton, 137 Ind. 449, 37 N.E. 143 (1894).

A conveyance in nominal consideration of $1.00 and agreement that grantee take care of grantor was without consideration was void against one who was a creditor of grantor at the time of the conveyance and whose claim was reduced to a judgment a few weeks thereafter. Spiers v. Whitesell, 27 Ind. App. 204, 61 N.E. 28 (1901).

If property was conveyed for an inadequate consideration, the conveyance could have been declared fraudulent as to creditors of the vendor, and the rights of the vendee protected to the extent of the purchase-money paid. Jameson v. Dilley, 27 Ind. App. 429, 61 N.E. 601 (1901).

A purchaser of land from one who had been divorced from his wife could not have been affected by alleged fraud on the part of the vendor in procuring a colorable jurisdiction of the person of his wife in the divorce proceeding, in the absence of a showing that at the time of the purchase the purchaser had knowledge of the fraud. Friebe v. Elder, 181 Ind. 597, 105 N.E. 151 (1914).

Purchasers of land under a judgment of a court of general jurisdiction, when there was nothing on the face of the judgment to show that it was void, were protected as innocent purchasers, and a person could have been an innocent purchaser by purchasing property from a person who had notice of an intent to defraud creditors by a former grantor of the property if the last purchaser had no notice of the fraudulent intent. Young v. Wiley, 183 Ind. 449, 107 N.E. 278 (1914).

Creditors.
Creditors only could have the conveyance set aside. Springer v. Drosch, 32 Ind. 486, 2 Am. R. 356 (1870); O'Neil v. Chandler, 42 Ind. 471 (1873); Edwards v. Haverstick, 53 Ind. 348 (1876); Garner v. Graves, 54 Ind. 188 (1876); Anderson v. Etter, 102 Ind. 115, 26 N.E. 218 (1885).

A voluntary conveyance in fraud of credi-
tors could have been set aside at the suit of subsequent creditors when it was executed to defraud subsequent as well as existing creditors. Petree v. Brotherton, 133 Ind. 692, 32 N.E. 300 (1892); Gable v. Columbus Cigar Co., 140 Ind. 563, 38 N.E. 474 (1894).

Effect Between Parties.
A conveyance, fraudulent as to creditors, could have been valid between the parties and have been enforced as between them, and especially in favor of a third person to whom a promise had been made, growing out of such transaction. Moore v. Meek, 20 Ind. 484 (1863); Edwards v. Haverstick, 53 Ind. 348 (1876); Mattill v. Baas, 89 Ind. 220 (1883); Seivers v. Dickover, 101 Ind. 495 (1884); Anderson v. Etter, 102 Ind. 115, 26 N.E. 218 (1885); Henry v. Stevens, 108 Ind. 281, 9 N.E. 356 (1886); Rupe v. Hadley, 113 Ind. 416, 16 N.E. 391 (1888); Kitts v. Willson, 130 Ind. 492, 29 N.E. 401 (1892); Kitts v. Willson, 140 Ind. 604, 39 N.E. 313 (1894).

Evidence Sufficient for Fraudulent Transfer.
The evidence sustained a finding of a fraudulent transfer although the debtor set forth legitimate business purposes for the transactions, because a pure motive on the part of the debtor in making a fraudulent transfer will not cleanse the transaction. Jackson v. Russell, 533 N.E.2d 153 (Ind. App. 1989), cert. denied, 494 U.S. 1004, 110 S. Ct. 1297, 108 L. Ed. 2d 474 (1990).

Executors and Administrators.
Administrators or executors could have brought action under decedents' act for purpose of procuring order to sell land and setting aside conveyances as in fraud of creditors. Galentine v. Wood, 137 Ind. 532, 35 N.E. 901 (1893).

A genuine issue of fact precluded a summary judgment where it was necessary for the factfinder to weigh the evidence and judge the credibility of witnesses in order to determine whether the personal representative of an estate transferred stock for estate planning purposes or whether there was a concurrence of the "badges of fraud" sufficient to make a finding of fraudulent intent. Jones v. Central Nat'l Bank, 547 N.E.2d 887 (Ind. App. 1989).

Fraudulent Intent.
The party alleging fraud had to prove it. Stewart v. English, 6 Ind. 176 (1855); Morgan v. Olvey, 53 Ind. 6 (1876); Fulp v. Beaver, 136 Ind. 319, 36 N.E. 250 (1894); Bruner v. Brown, 139 Ind. 600, 38 N.E. 318 (1894); Adams v. Laugel, 144 Ind. 608, 42 N.E. 1017 (1896); Smith v. Roseboom, 13 Ind. App. 284, 41 N.E. 552 (1895).

Fraud could not be presumed, but it might

Fraudulent Intent. (Cont'd)
have been inferred from facts or circumstances proved. Kane v. Drake, 27 Ind. 29 (1866); Farmer v. Calvert, 44 Ind. 209 (1873); Levi v. Kraminer, 2 Ind. App. 594, 28 N.E. 1028 (1891); Dobbs v. Royer, 81 Ind. App. 383, 142 N.E. 131 (1924).

A fraudulent intent was a question of fact to have been established by proof as other questions of fact. Leasure v. Coburn, 57 Ind. 274 (1877); Goff v. Rogers, 71 Ind. 459 (1880); Lockwood v. Harding, 79 Ind. 129 (1881); Morris v. Stern, 80 Ind. 227 (1881); Powell v. Stickney, 88 Ind. 310 (1882); Fisher v. Syfers, 109 Ind. 514, 10 N.E. 306 (1887); Fulp v. Beaver, 136 Ind. 319, 36 N.E. 250 (1894); Phillips v. Kennedy, 139 Ind. 419, 38 N.E. 410, 39 N.E. 147 (1894); Levi v. Bray, 12 Ind. App. 9, 39 N.E. 754 (1895); Personette v. Cronkhite, 140 Ind. 586, 40 N.E. 59 (1895); Wyatt v. Brown, 14 Ind. App. 232, 42 N.E. 948 (1896); American Varnish Co. v. Reed, 154 Ind. 88, 55 N.E. 224 (1899); Roehm v. Reed, 23 Ind. App. 547, 55 N.E. 772 (1899); Stout v. Price, 24 Ind. App. 360, 55 N.E. 964, 56 N.E. 857 (1900); De Ruiter v. De Ruiter, 28 Ind. App. 9, 62 N.E. 100, 91 Am. St. R. 107 (1901); Tyler v. Davis, 37 Ind. App. 557, 75 N.E. 3 (1905); Leasure v. Leasure, 86 Ind. App. 499, 157 N.E. 11, 158 N.E. 925 (1927).

Fraud was a question of fact, and could not be presumed, or inferred, as a matter of law. Phelps v. Smith, 116 Ind. 387, 17 N.E. 602, 19 N.E. 156 (1888); Rockland Co. v. Summerville, 139 Ind. 695, 39 N.E. 307 (1894); Wyatt v. Brown, 14 Ind. App. 232, 42 N.E. 948 (1896); National State Bank v. Sandford Fork & Tool Co., 157 Ind. 10, 60 N.E. 699 (1901).

Where the issue was whether certain property in dispute was sold with intent to cheat creditors of the owners thereof, the person claiming the property by virtue of such sale could be asked if he had an intent to cheat, hinder or delay the creditors in making the purchase. Wilson v. Clark, 1 Ind. App. 182, 27 N.E. 310 (1891).

Acts that would have worked a fraud would have been held to constitute fraud regardless of the intent. Personette v. Cronkhite, 140 Ind. 586, 40 N.E. 59 (1895).

Conveyances having the effect of hindering, delaying, or defrauding creditors were fraudulent, without regard to the intent of the grantor. Personette v. Cronkhite, 140 Ind. 586, 40 N.E. 59 (1895).

Fraud was never presumed as a matter of law, but must have been established by proof, and when averred must have been proved and found as a question of fact. Wills v. Mooney-Mueller Drug Co., 50 Ind. App. 193, 97 N.E. 449 (1912); Vermillion v. First Nat'l Bank, 59 Ind. App. 35, 105 N.E. 530 (1914), rehearing overruled, 59 Ind. App. 54, 108 N.E. 370 (1915).

An intent to defraud creditors by the conveyance of property was a question of fact that had to be proved, and while the intent might have been inferred from facts and cirumstances proved, the ultimate fact had to be found to exist by the court or jury trying the case. Vermillion v. First Nat'l Bank, 59 Ind. App. 35, 105 N.E. 530 (1914), rehearing overruled, 59 Ind. App. 54, 108 N.E. 370 (1915).

In an action to set aside a fraudulent conveyance, fraudulent intent must have been found in order to sustain a decree setting aside the conveyance, and absence of finding as to fraudulent intent was equivalent to finding for defendant, since plaintiff had burden on that question. Hosanna v. Odishoo, 208 Ind. 132, 193 N.E. 599, reh'g denied, 208 Ind. 144, 195 N.E. 72 (1935).

In an action to set aside a fraudulent conveyance, and for partition and for accounting with respect to the same subject matter but having been three different causes of action, a judgment for plaintiff not supported by finding of fraudulent intent was not based upon the issues relating to setting aside conveyances as fraudulent. Hosanna v. Odishoo, 208 Ind. 132, 193 N.E. 599, reh'g denied, 208 Ind. 144, 195 N.E. 72 (1935).

In an action to set aside a conveyance, neither age, improvidence, lack of consideration, nor a combination of all three was sufficient grounds for relief, but there must also have been present some wrongful act on the part of the grantee, such as fraud or undue influence, to warrant the court of equity setting aside the deed. Deckard v. Kleindorfer, 108 Ind. App. 485, 29 N.E.2d 997 (1940), overruled on other grounds, Colbo v. Buyer, 235 Ind. 518, 134 N.E.2d 45 (1956).

Where owners of 24 acres of real estate who owed delinquent federal taxes and were hopelessly insolvent sold it to petitioner for $11,500 and there was evidence that potential buyers had offered to pay $36,000 for the property and that two financially responsible persons had actually attempted to purchase the property for $1,500 per acre, the tax court correctly determined that the conveyance was fraudulent under this section. Nader v. Commissioner, 323 F.2d 139 (7th Cir. 1963).

Direct and positive proof of an intent to defraud creditors was not required in order to make a transfer of property subject to creditors' rights. Nader v. Commissioner, 323 F.2d 139 (7th Cir. 1963).

Statutory requirement of proof of actual intent to defraud creditors was not applicable to cases involving constructive fraud. Nader v. Commissioner, 323 F.2d 139 (7th Cir. 1963).

The failure of the holder of installment contracts to show the insolvency of the debtors at any particular time was not fatal to its action to set aside certain conveyances as

Fraudulent Intent. (Cont'd)
fraudulent, because the transfers were accompanied by fraudulent intent, as determined by certain "badges of fraud," including the transfer of large amounts of valuable assets to family members without consideration, retaining assets of highly questionable value, such as accounts receivable. Jackson v. Farmers State Bank, 481 N.E.2d 395 (Ind. App. 1985).

As no single indicium constitutes a showing of fraudulent intent per se, the facts must be taken together to determine how many badges of fraud exist and if together they amount to a pattern of fraudulent intent. This determination rests, in the first instance, with the trier of fact. Johnson v. Estate of Rayburn, 587 N.E.2d 182 (Ind. App. 1992).

—Burden of Proof.
The burden of proof was on the party alleging the fraud. A.D. Baker Co. v. Berry, 80 Ind. App. 591, 141 N.E. 623 (1923); LaPorte Prod. Credit Ass'n v. Kalwitz, 567 N.E.2d 1202 (Ind. App. 1991).

In order to sustain decree setting aside a conveyance of judgment debtor's property, fraudulent intent must have been found as a fact and failure to find such fact was equivalent to a finding against plaintiff, who had the burden of proof on that question. Hosanna v. Odishoo, 208 Ind. 132, 193 N.E. 599, reh'g denied, 208 Ind. 144, 195 N.E. 72 (1935).

An action to recover damages resulting from defendant's fraudulent conduct whereby plaintiff was induced to purchase a certain peanut vender did not come within the class of cases controlled by the provisions of this section, since the fraud referred to in such section must have been deemed to have reference only to actions involving the question of fraudulent intent where the rights of the parties depended in some manner on some provision of the act of which said section was a part. Ray Stringer Co. v. Dillon, 105 Ind. App. 194, 12 N.E.2d 365 (1938).

In action by a judgment creditor against a judgment debtor to set aside as fraudulent an assignment of corporate stock by such debtor, plaintiff had the burden of showing that the assignment of stock was made with intent to hinder, delay, or defraud creditors, although made without consideration. Deming Hotel Co. v. Sisson, 216 Ind. 587, 24 N.E.2d 912 (1940).

In action by a judgment creditor to set aside a conveyance by the debtor in fraud of creditor, it was not enough to prove that executions issued against the debtor were returned unsatisfied, but the proof must also have shown that the debtor did not have left sufficient property subject to execution to pay the judgment. Deming Hotel Co. v. Sisson, 216 Ind. 587, 24 N.E.2d 912 (1940).

In action by judgment creditor to set aside a conveyance made by a judgment debtor, proof of the debtor's insolvency at the time judgment was rendered did not shift to the debtor the burden of proving that he was solvent at the time of the conveyance. Deming Hotel Co. v. Sisson, 216 Ind. 587, 24 N.E.2d 912 (1940).

In action by a judgment creditor of a partnership to have an assignment of bonds made by the partnership member set aside as a fraud of the assignor's creditors, plaintiff was required to prove that at the time of the assignment the partnership was insolvent, or in such danger of insolvency that the assignor would have been bound to have knowledge of such danger. Deming Hotel Co. v. Sisson, 216 Ind. 587, 24 N.E.2d 912 (1940).

Contracts by which aged and infirm persons conveyed all or a substantial part of their property to others in consideration of an agreement for support, maintenance, and care during their declining years constituted a class by themselves and would have been enforced without reference to the form or phraseology of the writing by which they were expressed, or whether by the strict letter of the law a forfeiture of the estate was expressly provided for. Deckard v. Kleindorfer, 108 Ind. App. 485, 29 N.E.2d 997 (1940), overruled on other grounds, Colbo v. Buyer, 235 Ind. 518, 134 N.E.2d 45 (1956).

A judgment creditor seeking to set aside a transfer of real estate as fraudulent clearly has the burden of proof to show that the transfer was made with the intent to hinder, delay, or defraud the creditor. Kourlias v. Hawkins, 153 Ind. App. 411, 32 Ind. Dec. 670, 287 N.E.2d 764 (1972).

—Evidence of Fraud.
Where it was in question whether an act was done to defraud creditors, it was competent to prove directly by the actor what his actual intent was. Sedgwick v. Tucker, 90 Ind. 271 (1883); Over v. Schiffling, 102 Ind. 191, 26 N.E. 91 (1885); Wilson v. Clark, 1 Ind. App. 182, 27 N.E. 310 (1891).

Fraud being difficult to prove, a wide scope was given to the evidence. Hoffman v. Henderson, 145 Ind. 613, 44 N.E. 629 (1896).

Evidence of dealings and declarations of grantor subsequent to the conveyance, as tending to show fraud upon his part, was admissible in evidence as against the grantor in the trial of an action to set aside such conveyance as fraudulent. Vansickle v. Shenk, 150 Ind. 413, 50 N.E. 381 (1898).

Reputation of a grantor for honesty could not have been proved to determine the question of fraud. Vansickle v. Shenk, 150 Ind. 413, 50 N.E. 381 (1898).

In action by judgment creditor to have an assignment of corporate bonds set aside as a fraud on the debtor's creditors, special find-

Fraudulent Intent. (Cont'd)

—Evidence of Fraud. (Cont'd)
ings of facts which did not find such fraudulent intent did not support a judgment setting aside the conveyance because of fraud. Deming Hotel Co. v. Sisson, 216 Ind. 587, 24 N.E.2d 912 (1940).

In action by judgment creditor to set aside an assignment of bonds by the judgment debtor as a fraud on the debtor's creditors, a special finding by the court that the assignment was made without intent to defraud his judgment creditor, held to sustain the judgment in favor of the defendant. Deming Hotel Co. v. Sisson, 216 Ind. 587, 24 N.E.2d 912 (1940).

In an action by a grantor to set aside his conveyance on the ground of failure of consideration and constructive fraud, the court sat as a court of equity, and if the least scintilla of fraud was found the court would interfere. Deckard v. Kleindorfer, 108 Ind. App. 485, 29 N.E.2d 997 (1940), overruled on other grounds, Colbo v. Buyer, 235 Ind. 518, 134 N.E.2d 45 (1956).

As no single indicium constitutes a showing of fraudulent intent per se, the facts must be taken together to determine how many badges of fraud exist and if together they amount to a pattern of fraudulent intent. This determination rests, in the first instance, with the trier of fact. Johnson v. Estate of Rayburn, 587 N.E.2d 182 (Ind. App. 1992).

Defendant was held as a matter of law to have intended to defraud the United States where he established a trust, made himself and his family the sole beneficiaries of the trust, transferred property to the trust with little consideration, and assigned nearly all his assets to the trust in an attempt to defer his income. United States v. Smith, 950 F. Supp. 1394 (N.D. Ind. 1996).

Fraudulent intent is a question of fact, and a conveyance will not be deemed fraudulent merely because it was accomplished without the exchange of valuable consideration. United States v. Smith, 950 F. Supp. 1394 (N.D. Ind. 1996).

—Finding of Fraud.
Finding of fraud to have been sufficient must have found the existence of fraud as a fact. Sickman v. Wilhelm, 130 Ind. 480, 29 N.E. 908 (1892); Morgan v. Worden, 145 Ind. 600, 32 N.E. 783 (1892); Fulp v. Beaver, 136 Ind. 319, 36 N.E. 350 (1895); Levi v. Bray, 12 Ind. App. 9, 39 N.E. 754 (1895); First Nat'l Bank v. Dovetail Body & Gear Co., 143 Ind. 550, 40 N.E. 810, 52 Am. St. 435 (1895); Waterbury v. Miller, 13 Ind. App. 197, 41 N.E. 383 (1895); Stout v. Price, 24 Ind. App. 360, 55 N.E. 964, 56 N.E. 857 (1900); National State Bank v. Sandford Fork & Tool Co., 157 Ind. 10, 60 N.E. 599 (1901); Wills v. Mooney-Mueller Drug Co., 50 Ind. App. 193, 97 N.E. 449 (1912).

—Findings at Time of Transaction.
A finding that conveyances of land owned by a husband, so as to vest the title in such husband and his wife jointly, were without consideration, was insufficient in the absence of a finding of fraud as a fact, to support the conclusion that such conveyances were fraudulent as against a mortgagee who subsequently and without notice thereof took a new mortgage to secure the husband's debt. Miller v. Engler, 54 Ind. App. 689, 103 N.E. 358 (1913).

In action by a judgment creditor to have an assignment of bonds set aside as a fraud of the judgment debtors, good faith of the transaction must have been determined as of the time of such transaction. Deming Hotel Co. v. Sisson, 216 Ind. 587, 24 N.E.2d 912 (1940).

—Summary Judgment.
A genuine issue of fact precluded a summary judgment where it was necessary for the factfinder to weigh the evidence and judge the credibility of witnesses in order to determine whether the personal representative of an estate transferred stock for estate planning purposes or whether there was a concurrence of the "badges of fraud" sufficient to make a finding of fraudulent intent. Jones v. Central Nat'l Bank, 547 N.E.2d 887 (Ind. App. 1989).

Grantee.
The grantee in a fraudulent conveyance, who paid a valuable consideration, could not be affected thereby, unless he had notice of the fraudulent purpose of the grantor. Brown v. Rawlings, 72 Ind. 505 (1880); Sherman v. Hogland, 73 Ind. 472 (1880); Bishop v. Redmond, 83 Ind. 157 (1882); Barkley v. Tapp, 87 Ind. 25 (1882); First Nat'l Bank v. Carter, 89 Ind. 317 (1883); Seager v. Aughe, 97 Ind. 285 (1884); Jewett v. Meech, 101 Ind. 289 (1885); Hunsinger v. Hofer, 110 Ind. 390, 11 N.E. 463 (1887); Phelps v. Smith, 116 Ind. 387, 17 N.E. 602, 19 N.E. 156 (1888); Carnahan v. McCord, 116 Ind. 67, 18 N.E. 177 (1888); Scott v. Davis, 117 Ind. 232, 20 N.E. 139 (1889); Hays v. Montgomery, 118 Ind. 91, 20 N.E. 646 (1889); Goldman v. Biddle, 118 Ind. 492, 21 N.E. 43 (1889); Jameson v. Dilley, 27 Ind. App. 429, 61 N.E. 601 (1901).

If a deed was made and accepted for fraudulent purposes, it could have been overthrown no matter what might have been the consideration paid therefor or how pure the motive that induced it. Gable v. Columbus Cigar Co., 140 Ind. 563, 38 N.E. 474 (1894); O'Kane v. Terrell, 144 Ind. 599, 43 N.E. 869 (1896).

A person who took a conveyance of property with intention of aiding the grantor in de-

Grantee. (Cont'd)

frauding his creditors was liable to the creditors to the extent of the property he received; even though he subsequently disposed of the property, the vendee was a trustee for the creditors. Doherty v. Holliday, 137 Ind. 282, 32 N.E. 315, 36 N.E. 907 (1894).

A grantee in a fraudulent conveyance was entitled to a decree quieting title as against an interloper and trespasser without any claim to the property or any part thereof. Leasure v. Leasure, 86 App. 499, 157 N.E. 11, 158 N.E. 925 (1927).

Lack of Consideration.

Grantees who paid no consideration did not need to have notice of the fraud in order that the conveyance could have been set aside. Roberts v. F. & M. Bank, 136 Ind. 154, 36 N.E. 128 (1894); Milburn v. Phillips, 136 Ind. 680, 34 N.E. 983, 36 N.E. 360 (1894); Pierce v. Hower, 142 Ind. 626, 42 N.E. 223 (1895); First Nat'l Bank v. Smith, 149 Ind. 443, 49 N.E. 376 (1898).

When land was conveyed for an inadequate consideration to a purchaser who had no notice of an intention to defraud, the conveyance could have been set aside in favor of the creditors of the vendor and the rights of the vendee protected to the extent of the consideration paid. Jameson v. Dilley, 27 Ind. App. 429, 61 N.E. 601 (1901).

Non-Statutory Cause of Action.

Indiana law recognizes a non-statutory cause of action for fraudulent conveyance such that debtor's transfer of property to her daughter where badges of fraud were present could be avoided by bankruptcy trustee. Miller v. McKinley (In re Delagrange), 65 Bankr. 97 (N.D. Ind. 1986), aff'd, 820 F.2d 229 (7th Cir. 1987).

Notice of Fraud.

If the grantee had notice of the fraud, the conveyance could have been set aside, although full consideration was paid. Bray v. Hussey, 24 Ind. 228 (1865); Harrison v. Jaquess, 29 Ind. 208 (1867); Bishop v. Redmond, 83 Ind. 157 (1882); Milburn v. Phillips, 136 Ind. 680, 34 N.E. 983, 36 N.E. 360 (1894); Gable v. Columbus Cigar Co., 140 Ind. 563, 38 N.E. 474 (1894); O'Kane v. Terrell, 144 Ind. 599, 43 N.E. 869 (1896).

If the grantee had notice of the fraud before payment of the purchase money, the conveyance could have been set aside to the extent of the unpaid purchase-money. Rhodes v. Green, 36 Ind. 7 (1871); Seager v. Aughe, 97 Ind. 285 (1884).

Grantees who had notice of the fraud held the property, or its proceeds, in trust for creditors. Doherty v. Holliday, 137 Ind. 282,

32 N.E. 315 (1892), rehearing overruled, 36 N.E. 907 (1894).

Partnership.

—Joint Debt.

Where a partner without the consent of his copartners applied partnership funds to the payment of his individual debt in the discharge of a mortgage lien and then conveyed his property to his wife who had knowledge of the fraud, such partner was a trustee of the firm for the partnership funds and the real estate was subject to the trust. Hanna v. McLaughlin, 158 Ind. 292, 63 N.E. 475 (1902).

To entitle holder of joint and several notes to a judgment setting aside a fraudulent conveyance of real estate by one of the makers, in a joint action on the notes, he had to show that the other coobligors were insolvent. Geiser Mfg. Co. v. Lee, 33 Ind. App. 38, 66 N.E. 701 (1903).

Preferences to Creditors.

A mortgage executed by an insolvent corporation to secure the payment of preferred stock, to the exclusion of general creditors, was void as to such creditors. Reagan v. First Nat'l Bank, 157 Ind. 623, 61 N.E. 575, 62 N.E. 701 (1901).

Preference of creditors with fraudulent intent could not have been set aside unless such creditors participated in fraudulent intent. Jordan v. Lynch Land Co., 83 Ind. App. 33, 147 N.E. 318 (1925).

Sale to Pay Debts.

A person in embarrassed circumstances could sell his property for the purpose of discharging his debts for such consideration as he might have agreed to accept, and if there was nothing illegal in the transaction it would have stood as against his creditors. Lowry v. Howard, 35 Ind. 170, 9 Am. R. 676 (1871); Hogan v. Robinson, 94 Ind. 138 (1884); Hoes v. Boyer, 108 Ind. 494, 9 N.E. 427 (1886); Cornell v. Gibson, 114 Ind. 144, 16 N.E. 130, 5 Am. St. R. 605 (1888); Jones v. Snyder, 117 Ind. 229, 20 N.E. 140 (1889); Laird v. Davidson, 124 Ind. 412, 25 N.E. 7 (1890); Carnahan v. Schwab, 127 Ind. 507, 26 N.E. 67 (1891); McCormick v. Smith, 127 Ind. 230, 26 N.E. 825 (1891); John Shillito Co. v. McConnell, 130 Ind. 41, 26 N.E. 832 (1891); Peed v. Elliott, 134 Ind. 536, 34 N.E. 319 (1893); Heiney v. Lontz, 147 Ind. 417, 46 N.E. 665 (1897); West v. Graff, 23 Ind. App. 410, 55 N.E. 506 (1899).

In the absence of fraudulent intent, a conveyance by debtor to wife to pay debt would not have been set aside as against creditors. Dillen v. Johnson, 132 Ind. 75, 30 N.E. 786 (1892); Fulp v. Beaver, 136 Ind. 319, 36 N.E. 250 (1894); Adams v. Curtis, 137 Ind. 175, 36

Sale to Pay Debts. (Cont'd)
N.E. 1095 (1894); Heiney v. Lontz, 147 Ind. 417, 46 N.E. 665 (1897); Schreeder v. Werry, 35 Ind. App. 84, 73 N.E. 832 (1905).

Estoppel of wife. Stoner v. American Trust Co., 81 Ind. App. 635, 142 N.E. 126 (1924).

Subsequent Purchasers.
Where the grantee of real estate, who was a

purchaser for a valuable consideration and in good faith, conveyed the real estate to the wife of the grantor, the wife took title free of demands of husband's creditors, though she might have had notice of fraud imputed to her husband, no money of husband having been put into the purchase. Evans v. Nealis, 69 Ind. 148 (1879); Studabaker v. Langard, 79 Ind. 320 (1881).

Collateral References. Assumption of mortgage as consideration for conveyance attacked as in fraud of creditors. 6 A.L.R.2d 270.

Cotenant's capacity to maintain suit to set aside conveyance of interest of another cotenant because of fraud. 7 A.L.R.2d 1317.

Right of creditor to set aside transfer of property as fraudulent as affected by the fact that his claim is barred by the statute of limitations. 14 A.L.R.2d 598.

Necessary parties defendant. 24 A.L.R.2d 395.

Right of creditors to attack as fraudulent a conveyance by third person to debtor's spouse. 35 A.L.R.2d 8.

Right of subsequent creditors to attack as fraudulent a conveyance by third person to debtor's spouse. 35 A.L.R.2d 8.

Conveyance or transfer in consideration of legal services, rendered or to be rendered as fraudulent as against creditors. 45 A.L.R.2d 500.

Admissibility of testimony of transferee as to his knowledge, purpose, intention, or good faith on issue whether conveyance was in fraud of transferor's creditors. 52 A.L.R.2d 418.

Accountability of grantee for rents and profits of fraudulently conveyed real property as subject to credits for expenditures for taxes, improvements, and the like. 60 A.L.R.2d 93.

Right of tort claimant, prior to judgment, to attack conveyance or transfer as fraudulent. 73 A.L.R.2d 749.

Conveyance as fraudulent where made in contemplation of possible liability for future tort. 38 A.L.R.3d 597.

Inclusion of funds in savings bank trust (Totten trust) in determining surviving spouse's interest in decedent's estate. 64 A.L.R.3d 187.

Excessiveness or inadequacy of attorney's fees in matters involving commercial and general business activities. 23 A.L.R.5th 241.

32-18-2-19. Statute of limitations. — A cause of action with respect to a fraudulent transfer or obligation under this chapter is extinguished unless brought as follows:

(1) If brought under section 14(1) [IC 32-18-2-14(1)] of this chapter, an action is extinguished unless brought not later than the later of the following:

(A) Four (4) years after the transfer was made or the obligation was incurred.

(B) One (1) year after the transfer or obligation was or could reasonably have been discovered by the claimant.

(2) If brought under section 14(2) or 15(1) [IC 32-18-2-14(2) or IC 32-18-2-15(1)] of this chapter, an action is extinguished unless it is brought not later than four (4) years after the transfer was made or the obligation was incurred. [P.L.2-2002, § 3.]

NOTES TO DECISIONS

Applicability.
When seeking to void a fraudulent conveyance, the United States is not bound by a state statute of limitations. United States v. Smith, 950 F. Supp. 1394 (N.D. Ind. 1996).

Federal law, not state law, controls the time

within which the government must bring suit to set aside an allegedly fraudulent conveyance in the course of efforts to collect federal taxes. United States v. Cody, 961 F. Supp. 220 (S.D. Ind. 1997).

32-18-2-20. Principles of law and equity to supplement chapter. — Unless superseded by this chapter, the principles of law and equity, including the law merchant and the law relating to principal and agent, equitable subordination, estoppel, laches, fraud, misrepresentation, duress, coercion, mistake, insolvency, or other validating or invalidating cause, supplement this chapter. [P.L.2-2002, § 3.]

32-18-2-21. Applicability and construction to effectuate general purpose. — This chapter shall be applied and construed to effectuate its general purpose to make uniform the law with respect to the subject of this chapter among states enacting it. [P.L.2-2002, § 3.]

CHAPTER 3
RESALE OF INSOLVENT DEBTORS' REAL ESTATE

SECTION.
32-18-3-1. Filing of bond.
32-18-3-2. Resale of real estate.

32-18-3-1. Filing of bond. — In a sale of real estate by:
(1) a receiver; or
(2) an assignee or trustee under IC 32-18-1;
a person may, before the confirmation of the sale by the proper court, file with the clerk of the court, or in open court, a bond in the sum sufficient to secure the sale. The surety for the bond must be approved by the clerk or the court. [P.L.2-2002, § 3.]

Effective Dates. P.L.2-2002, § 3. July 1.
2002.

32-18-3-2. Resale of real estate. — If on resale of the real estate, or any part of the real estate, the real estate sells for ten percent (10%) more than the amount bid at the previous sale, the court may not confirm the sale but order the real estate resold. If on resale the additional sum is not realized, the person posting the bond is liable for the difference. It is the duty of the receiver, assignee, or trustee to institute and prosecute the suit, which is for the use and benefit of the trust. [P.L.2-2002, § 3.]

NOTES TO DECISIONS

Sale of Real and Personal Property.
When real and personal property assigned for the benefit of creditors was ordered sold as an entirety, the bid could only have been raised, pursuant to this section, by increasing by the required ten percent the amount offered for the entirety. Southworth v. Stout, 112 Ind. App. 429, 44 N.E.2d 225 (1942).

The purpose of this section, concerning sale of real estate assigned for the benefit of creditors and authorizing a resale in the event a bond was furnished guaranteeing a bidder for not less than ten percent more than the amount bid at the previous sale, was to give creditors the benefit of the best available sale price for the real estate, and IC 32-12-1-10, giving the court the right to sell personalty and realty as an entirety, sought to give creditors in the proper case the advantages to be obtained from selling a business as a going concern, and, when the two sections were read and construed together, it was clear that this section was not intended to limit the broad powers given the court by former IC 32-12-1-10 (repealed; for similar provisions see IC 32-18-1-10). Southworth v. Stout, 112 Ind. App. 429, 44 N.E.2d 225 (1942).

Collateral References. 6 Am. Jur. 2d Assignments for Benefit of Creditors, §§ 125-134.

6A C.J.S. Assignments for Benefit of Creditors, §§ 93-100.

ARTICLE 19

DESCRIBING REAL PROPERTY; INDIANA COORDINATE SYSTEM

CHAPTER 1

DESIGNATION OF INDIANA COORDINATE SYSTEM; ZONES

32-19-1-1. Coordinates established by National Ocean Survey/National Geodetic Survey. — The systems of plane coordinates that have been established by the National Ocean Survey/National Geodetic Survey (formerly the United States Coast and Geodetic Survey) or its successors for defining and stating the positions or locations of points on the surface of the earth within Indiana are known and designated as the "Indiana coordinate system of 1927" and the "Indiana coordinate system of 1983". [P.L.2-2002, § 4.]

Effective Dates. P.L.2-2002, § 4. July 1. 2002.
Collateral References. 23 Am. Jur. 2d Deeds, §§ 48-64.

26 C.J.S. Deeds, §§ 29, 30.
Sufficiency, under statute of frauds, of description or designation of property in real estate brokerage contract. 30 A.L.R.3d 935.

32-19-1-2. Counties in east and west zones. — (a) For the purpose of the use of the systems described in section 1 [IC 32-19-1-1] of this chapter, Indiana is divided into an east zone and a west zone.

(b) The area included in the following counties constitutes the east zone:
Adams
Allen
Bartholomew
Blackford
Brown

Cass
Clark
Dearborn
Decatur
DeKalb
Delaware
Elkhart
Fayette
Floyd
Franklin
Fulton
Grant
Hamilton
Hancock
Harrison
Henry
Howard
Huntington
Jackson
Jay
Jefferson
Jennings
Johnson
Kosciusko
LaGrange
Madison
Marion
Marshall
Miami
Noble
Ohio
Randolph
Ripley
Rush
St. Joseph
Scott
Shelby
Steuben
Switzerland
Tipton
Union
Wabash
Washington
Wayne
Wells
Whitley.
(c) The area included in the following counties constitutes the west zone:
Benton

Boone
Carroll
Clay
Clinton
Crawford
Daviess
Dubois
Fountain
Gibson
Greene
Hendricks
Jasper
Knox
Lake
LaPorte
Lawrence
Martin
Monroe
Montgomery
Morgan
Newton
Orange
Owen
Parke
Perry
Pike
Porter
Posey
Pulaski
Putnam
Spencer
Starke
Sullivan
Tippecanoe
Vanderburgh
Vermillion
Vigo
Warren
Warrick
White.
[P.L.2-2002, § 4.]

32-19-1-3. Descriptions of Indiana coordinate systems — Use of coordinate systems. — (a) To more precisely describe the Indiana coordinate system of 1927, the following descriptions by the National Ocean Survey/National Geodetic Survey are adopted:

(1) The "Indiana coordinate system of 1927, east zone" is a transverse Mercator projection of the Clarke spheroid of 1866, having a central

meridian 85 degrees 40 minutes west of Greenwich, on which meridian the scale is set at one part in 30,000 too small. The origin of coordinates is at the intersection of the meridian 85 degrees 40 minutes west of Greenwich and the parallel 37 degrees 30 minutes north latitude. This origin is given the coordinates: x = 500,000 feet and y = 0 feet.

(2) The "Indiana coordinate system of 1927, west zone" is a transverse Mercator projection of the Clarke spheroid of 1866, having a central meridian 87 degrees 05 minutes west of Greenwich, on which meridian the scale is set at one part in 30,000 too small. The origin of coordinates is at the intersection of the meridian 87 degrees 05 minutes west of Greenwich and the parallel 37 degrees 30 minutes north latitude. This origin is given the coordinates: x = 500,000 feet and y = 0 feet.

(b) To more precisely describe the Indiana coordinate system of 1983, the following description by the National Ocean Survey/National Geodetic Survey is adopted:

(1) The "Indiana coordinate system of 1983, east zone" is a transverse Mercator projection of the North American Datum of 1983, having a central meridian 85 degrees 40 minutes west of Greenwich, on which meridian the scale is set at one part in 30,000 too small. The origin of coordinates is at the intersection of the meridian 85 degrees 40 minutes west of Greenwich and the parallel 37 degrees 30 minutes north latitude. This origin is given the coordinates: x = 100,000 meters and y = 250,000 meters.

(2) The "Indiana coordinate system of 1983, west zone" is a transverse Mercator projection of the North American Datum of 1983, having a central meridian 87 degrees 05 minutes west of Greenwich, on which meridian the scale is set at one part in 30,000 too small. The origin of coordinates is at the intersection of the meridian 87 degrees 05 minutes west of Greenwich and the parallel 37 degrees 30 minutes north latitude. This origin is given the coordinates: x = 900,000 meters and y = 250,000 meters.

(c) To locate the position of the coordinate systems on the surface of the earth in Indiana, the following shall be used:

(1) The position of the Indiana coordinate system of 1927 shall be determined from horizontal geodetic control points established throughout Indiana in conformity with the standards of accuracy and specifications for first-order and second-order geodetic surveying as prepared and published by the Federal Geodetic Control Committee (FGCC) of the United States Department of Commerce, whose geodetic positions have been rigidly adjusted on the North American Datum of 1927, and whose coordinates have been computed on the Indiana coordinate system of 1927. Standards and specifications of the FGCC (or its successors) in force on the date of the survey apply.

(2) The position of the Indiana coordinate system 1983 shall be determined from horizontal geodetic control points established throughout Indiana in conformity with the standards of accuracy and specifications for first-order and second-order geodetic surveying as prepared and published by the Federal Geodetic Control Committee (FGCC) of the

United States Department of Commerce, whose geodetic positions have been rigidly adjusted on the North American Datum of 1983, and whose coordinates have been computed on the Indiana coordinate system of 1983. Standards and specifications of the FGCC (or its successors) in force on the date of the survey apply. [P.L.2-2002, § 4.]

32-19-1-4. Designation of east and west zones. — (a) As established for use in the east zone, the Indiana coordinate system of 1927 or the Indiana coordinate system of 1983:

 (1) shall be named; and

 (2) in any land description in which it is used, shall be designated the:

  (A) "Indiana coordinate system of 1927, east zone"; or

  (B) "Indiana coordinate system of 1983, east zone".

 (b) As established for use in the west zone, the Indiana coordinate system of 1927 or the Indiana coordinate system of 1983:

 (1) shall be named; and

 (2) in any land description in which it is used. shall be designated, the:

  (A) "Indiana coordinate system of 1927, west zone"; or

  (B) "Indiana coordinate system of 1983, west zone".

[P.L.2-2002, § 4.]

32-19-1-5. Land extending into both zones. — If a tract of land to be defined by a single description extends from one (1) into the other of the east zone or the west zone:

 (1) the positions of all points on the boundaries of the tract may be referred to as either the east zone or the west zone; and

 (2) the zone that is used must be specifically named in the description. [P.L.2-2002, § 4.]

32-19-1-6. Restrictions on use of terms, coordinate system of 1927. — (a) The use of the term "Indiana coordinate system of 1927" or "Indiana coordinate system of 1983" on any map, report of survey, or other document shall be limited to coordinates based on the Indiana coordinate system described in this chapter.

 (b) Beginning January 1, 1990, the Indiana coordinate system of 1927 may not be used, and only the Indiana coordinate system of 1983 may be used. [P.L.2-2002, § 4.]

CHAPTER 2

COORDINATES; GEODETIC CONTROL MONUMENTS

32-19-2-1. Distances. — (a) The plane coordinates of a point on the earth's surface, used to express the position or location of that point in the appropriate zone of the Indiana coordinate system described in IC 32-19-1, must consist of two (2) distances expressed in:

(1) U.S. Survey feet (1 meter = 39.37/12 feet) and decimals of a foot when using the Indiana coordinate system of 1927; and

(2) meters and decimals of a meter and United States Survey feet and decimals of a foot when using the Indiana coordinate system of 1983.

(b) The distance described in subsection (a) that gives the position in an east-and-west direction is called the "x-coordinate". The distance described in subsection (a) that gives the position in a north-and-south direction is called the "y-coordinate". These coordinates must be made to depend upon and conform to plane rectangular coordinate values for the monumented points of the North American Horizontal Geodetic Control Network as published by the National Ocean Survey/National Geodetic Survey or its successors, if the successor's plane coordinates have been computed on the Indiana coordinate system of 1927 or the Indiana coordinate system of 1983. Any station may be used for establishing a survey connection to the Indiana coordinate system of 1927 or the Indiana coordinate system of 1983. [P.L.2-2002, § 4.]

Effective Dates. P.L.2-2002, § 4. July 1. 2002.

32-19-2-2. Use of geodetic control monuments in defining land boundaries — Determining geodetic control monuments. — (a) Coordinates based on the Indiana coordinate system of 1927 or the Indiana coordinate system of 1983 purporting to define the position of a point on a land boundary may not be presented to be recorded in any public land records or deed records unless the recording document also contains:

(1) a description of the nearest first-order or second-order horizontal geodetic control monument from which the coordinates being recorded were determined; and

(2) the method of survey for the determination.

(b) If the position of the described first-order or second-order geodetic control monument is not published by the National Geodetic Survey (or its successors), the recording document must contain a certification signed by a land surveyor registered under IC 25-21.5 stating that the subject control monument and its coordinates were established and determined in conformance with the specifications given in IC 32-19-1-3.

(c) The publishing of the existing control stations or the acceptance with intent to publish the newly established control stations by the National Geodetic Survey constitutes evidence of adherence to the FGCC specifications. Horizontal geodetic control monuments shall be permanently monumented and control data sheets prepared and filed so that a densification of the control network is accomplished.

(d) The surveying techniques and positioning systems used to produce first-order or second-order geodetic precision shall be identified. Annotation must accompany state plane coordinate values when they are used to less than second-order precision. [P.L.2-2002, § 4.]

CHAPTER 3

DESCRIPTIONS OF LAND USING THE INDIANA COORDINATE SYSTEM

32-19-3-1. Descriptions by coordinates subsidiary. — If coordinates based on the Indiana coordinate system are used to describe any tract of land, which in the same document is also described by reference to any subdivision, line, or corner of the United States public land surveys:

(1) the description by coordinates shall be construed as supplemental to the basic description of the subdivision, line, or corner contained in the official plats and field notes filed of record; and

(2) in the event of any conflict, the description by reference to the subdivision, line, or corner of the United States public land surveys prevails over the description by coordinates. [P.L.2-2002, § 4.]

Effective Dates. P.L.2-2002, § 4. July 1.
2002.

32-19-3-2. No requirement to rely on coordinate description. — This article does not require a purchaser or mortgagee to rely on a description, any part of which depends exclusively upon the Indiana coordinate system. [P.L.2-2002, § 4.]

CHAPTER 4

GEODETIC ADVISER

32-19-4-1. Establishment of office. — (a) Purdue University shall establish the office of geodetic adviser for the state.

(b) The geodetic adviser is appointed by and serves at the discretion of Purdue University. Purdue University shall determine the amount of compensation for the geodetic adviser. [P.L.2-2002, § 4.]

Effective Dates. P.L.2-2002, § 4. July 1.
2002.

32-19-4-2. Duties. — (a) The geodetic adviser is responsible for the implementation of a new system of geodetic control monuments in the form of a high accuracy geodetic reference network that is part of the National Spatial Reference System and that meets the needs of geodetic and geographic information users.

(b) The geodetic adviser shall coordinate and assist in the following:

(1) The design of the geodetic reference network.

(2) The establishment of any geodetic reference monument.

(3) The maintenance of data base control stations, to the extent that funding is available.

(4) The establishment and implementation of quality control and quality assurance programs for the geodetic reference network.

(5) The assistance and training of users of the geodetic reference network. [P.L.2-2002, § 4.]

32-19-4-3. Funding. — (a) The state, a state agency (as defined in IC 4-13-1-1), or a unit (as defined in IC 36-1-2-23) may provide funding from available funds for the activities described in this chapter.

(b) A unit (as defined in IC 36-1-2-23) may pay the cost of any geodetic reference monument that is established within the boundaries of that unit.

(c) Money in the county surveyor's corner perpetuation fund collected under IC 36-2-7-10 or IC 36-2-19 may be used for purposes of this chapter. [P.L.2-2002, § 4.]

32-19-4-4. Prohibition on altering monuments. — A county legislative body may adopt an ordinance:

(1) prohibiting a person from moving, changing, or otherwise altering a monument that is part of the National Spatial Reference System; and

(2) prescribing a monetary penalty for violation of the ordinance.

Any money collected for a violation of the ordinance shall be deposited in the county surveyor's corner perpetuation fund. [P.L.2-2002, § 4.]

Cross References. Infraction and ordinance violation enforcement proceedings, IC 34-28-5.

ARTICLE 20

MARKETABLE TITLE FOR REAL PROPERTY

CHAPTER 1

PURPOSE AND APPLICATION

32-20-1-1. Liberal construction. — (a) This article shall be liberally construed to effect the legislative purpose of simplifying and facilitating land title transactions by allowing persons to rely on a record chain of title as described in IC 32-20-3-1, subject only to the limitations that are described in IC 32-20-3-2.

(b) However, this article does not change the law affecting the capacity to own land of a person claiming a marketable record title under this article. [P.L.2-2002, § 5.]

Effective Dates. P.L.2-2002, § 5. July 1.
2002.

32-20-1-2. Restrictions. — This article may not be construed to do the following:
(1) Extend the period to bring an action or to do any other required act under any statutes of limitations.
(2) Except as specifically provided in this article, affect the operation of any statutes governing the effect of the recording or the failure to record any instrument affecting land. [P.L.2-2002, § 5.]

CHAPTER 2

DEFINITIONS

32-20-2-1. Applicability of definitions. — The definitions in this chapter apply throughout this article. [P.L.2-2002, § 5.]

Effective Dates. P.L.2-2002, § 5. July 1.
2002.

32-20-2-2. Marketable record title. — "Marketable record title" means a title of record, as described in IC 32-20-3-1, that operates to extinguish interests and claims existing before the effective date of the root of title, as provided in IC 32-20-3-3. [P.L.2-2002, § 5.]

32-20-2-3. Muniments. — "Muniments" means the records of title transactions in the chain of title of a person that:
(1) purport to create the interest in land claimed by the person; and
(2) upon which the person relies as a basis for the marketability of the person's title;
commencing with the root of title and including all subsequent transactions. [P.L.2-2002, § 5.]

32-20-2-4. Person dealing with land. — "Person dealing with land" includes:
(1) a purchaser of an estate or interest in an estate;
(2) a mortgagee;
(3) a levying or attaching creditor;
(4) a land contract vendee; or
(5) a person seeking to:
  (A) acquire an estate or interest in an estate; or

(B) impose a lien on an estate.
[P.L.2-2002, § 5.]

32-20-2-5. Records. — "Records" includes all official public records that affect title to land. [P.L.2-2002, § 5.]

32-20-2-6. Root of title. — "Root of title" means that title transaction in the chain of title of a person:
    (1) that purports to create the interest claimed by the person;
    (2) upon which the person relies as a basis for the marketability of the person's title; and
    (3) that is the most recent to be recorded as of a date at least fifty (50) years before the time when marketability is being determined.
The effective date of the root of title is the date on which it is recorded. [P.L.2-2002, § 5.]

32-20-2-7. Title transaction. — "Title transaction" means any transaction affecting title to any interest in land, including the following:
    (1) Title by will or descent.
    (2) Title by tax deed.
    (3) Title by trustee's, referee's, guardian's, executor's, administrator's, commissioner's, or sheriff's deed.
    (4) Title by decree of a court.
    (5) Title by warranty deed, quitclaim deed, or mortgage.
[P.L.2-2002, § 5.]

CHAPTER 3

INTERESTS IN TITLE

32-20-3-1. Unbroken chain of title. — A person who has an unbroken chain of title of record to an interest in land for at least fifty (50) years has a marketable record title to that interest, subject to section 2 [IC 32-20-3-2] of this chapter. A person is considered to have this unbroken chain of title when:
    (1) the official public records disclose a title transaction of record that occurred at least fifty (50) years before the time the marketability is determined; and
    (2) the title transaction purports to create an interest in:
      (A) the person claiming the interest; or
      (B) a person from whom, by one (1) or more title transactions of record, the purported interest has become vested in the person claiming the interest;
with nothing appearing of record purporting to divest the claimant of the purported interest. [P.L.2-2002, § 5.]

Effective Dates. P.L.2-2002, § 5. July 1. 2002.

NOTES TO DECISIONS

<small>ANALYSIS</small>

In general.
Breach of contract to sell.
Condition of property.
Warranty deed.
—Effect on covenants.

In General.

Where the title insurance company was responsible for an error in the commitment for title insurance which caused the purchaser to be deeded property which the seller had previously conveyed to another, and where the insurance company was required to reimburse the purchaser the amount expended for said property, the appellate court held that, in view of the conflicting equities, it was not against the weight of the evidence for the trial court to conclude that the insurance company was not subrogated to the rights of the purchaser and that it had no right to demand reimbursement from the seller. Lawyers Title Ins. Corp. v. Capp, 174 Ind. App. 633, 59 Ind. Dec. 678, 369 N.E.2d 672 (1977).

Breach of Contract to Sell.

Where action was brought for breach of contract to convey marketable title to realty, Acts 1947, ch. 193, did not apply, because the action did not affect the title to real estate, even though defect involved was over 50 years old. Fouts v. Largent, 228 Ind. 547, 94 N.E.2d 448 (1950).

Condition of Property.

Condition of the property, including the presence of hazardous waste, does not constitute a defect in ownership precluding the seller from conveying merchantable title. HM Holdings, Inc. v. Rankin, 70 F.3d 933 (7th Cir. 1995).

Warranty Deed.

—Effect on Covenants.

This chapter relieves the covenants imposed by a warranty deed only to the extent that a claim or interest is extinguished by it. If a claim or interest is not extinguished, this chapter has no effect on the guarantee contained in the deed. McClaskey v. Bumb & Mueller Farms, Inc., 547 N.E.2d 302 (Ind. App. 1989).

Collateral References. 77 Am. Jur. 2d Vendor and Purchaser, §§ 131-189.

91 C.J.S. Vendor and Purchaser, §§ 189-200.

Common source of source of title doctrine. 5 A.L.R.3d 375.

Slander of title: sufficiency of plaintiff's interest in real property to maintain action. 86 A.L.R.4th 738.

32-20-3-2. Interests and rights superior to marketable record title.
— Marketable record title is subject to the following:

(1) All interests and defects that are inherent in the muniments of which the chain of record title is formed. However, a general reference in the muniments, or any one (1) of them, to:

(A) easements;

(B) use restrictions; or

(C) other interests created before the root of title;

is not sufficient to preserve them, unless specific identification is made in the muniments of a recorded title transaction that creates the easement, use restriction, or other interest.

(2) All interests preserved by:

(A) the filing of proper notice; or

(B) possession by the same owner continuously for at least fifty (50) years, in accordance with IC 32-20-4-1.

(3) The rights of any person arising from adverse possession or adverse user, if the period of adverse possession or adverse user was wholly or partly subsequent to the effective date of the root of title.

(4) Any interest arising out of a title transaction recorded after the effective date of the root of title from which the unbroken chain of title of record is started. However, the recording shall not revive or give validity to any interest that has been extinguished before the time of the recording by the operation of section 3 [IC 32-20-3-3] of this chapter.

(5) The exceptions stated in IC 32-20-4-3 concerning:

    (A) rights of reversioners in leases;

    (B) rights of any lessee in and to any lease; and

    (C) easements and interests in the nature of easements.

(6) All interests of the department of environmental management in land used for the disposal of hazardous wastes arising from the recording of a restrictive covenant under IC 13-22-3-3. [P.L.2-2002, § 5.]

Collateral References. Circumstances justifying delay in rescinding land contract after learning of ground of rescission. 1 A.L.R.3d 542.

Variance between offer and acceptance in regard to title as affecting consummation of contract for sale of real property. 16 A.L.R.3d 1424.

Zoning or other public restrictions on the use of property as affecting rights and remedies of parties to contract for the sale thereof. 39 A.L.R.3d 362.

Surviving spouse's right to marital share as affected by valid contract to convey by will. 85 A.L.R.4th 418.

32-20-3-3. Marketable title taken free and clear. — Subject to section 2 [IC 32-20-3-2] of this chapter, marketable record title is held by its owner and is taken by a person dealing with the land free and clear of all interests, claims, or charges whose existence depends upon any act, transaction, event, or omission that occurred before the effective date of the root of title. All the interests, claims, or charges, however denominated, whether:

    (1) legal or equitable;

    (2) present or future; or

    (3) asserted by a person who is:

        (A) sui juris or under a disability;

        (B) within or outside Indiana;

        (C) natural or corporate; or

        (D) private or governmental;

are void. [P.L.2-2002, § 5.]

CHAPTER 4

NOTICE OF CLAIM

32-20-4-1. Requirement to file notice. — (a) A person claiming an interest in land may preserve and keep effective that interest by filing for record during the fifty (50) year period immediately following the effective date of the root of title of the person whose record title would otherwise be marketable, a notice in writing, verified by oath, setting forth the nature of the claim. A disability or lack of knowledge of any kind on the part of anyone does not suspend the running of the fifty (50) year period. Notice may be filed for record by the claimant or by a person acting on behalf of any claimant who is:

(1) under a disability;

(2) unable to assert a claim on the claimant's behalf; or

(3) one (1) of a class whose identity cannot be established or is uncertain at the time of filing the notice of claim for record.

(b) If the same record owner of any possessory interest in land has been in possession of the land continuously for a period of at least fifty (50) years, during which period:

(1) title transaction with respect to the interest does not appear of record in the record owner's chain of title;

(2) notice has not been filed by the record owner or on behalf of the record owner as provided in subsection (a); and

(3) possession continues to the time when marketability is being determined;

the period of possession is considered equivalent to the filing of the notice immediately preceding the termination of the fifty (50) year period described in subsection (a).

(c) If:

(1) a person claims the benefit of an equitable restriction or servitude that is one (1) of a number of substantially identical mutual restrictions on the use of tracts in a platted subdivision, the plat of which is recorded as provided by law; and

(2) the subdivision plan provides for an association, corporation, committee, or other similar group that is empowered to determine whether the restrictions are to be terminated or continued at the expiration of a stated period not exceeding fifty (50) years, and, by the terms of this provision, it is determined that:

(A) the restrictions are not to be terminated; or

(B) the restrictions are to be continued because no determination to terminate has been made;

then the officer or other person authorized to represent the association, corporation, committee, or other similar group may preserve and keep in effect all the restrictions by filing a notice as provided in subsection (a) on behalf of all owners of land in the subdivision for the benefit of whom the restrictions exist. [P.L.2-2002, § 5.]

Effective Dates. P.L.2-2002, § 5. July 1. 2002.
Indiana Law Review. Private Rights and Public Ways: Property Disputes and Rails-to-Trails in Indiana, 30 Ind. L. Rev. 724 (1997).

32-20-4-2. Requirements of filing. — (a) To be effective and to be entitled to be recorded, the notice referred to in section 1 [IC 32-20-4-1] of this chapter must contain the following:

(1) An accurate and full description of all land affected by the notice in specific terms. However, if the claim is founded upon a recorded instrument, then the description in the notice may be the same as that contained in the recorded instrument.

(2) The name and address of the claimant.

(3) The name and address of the person preparing the notice if other than the claimant.

This notice must be filed for record in the office of the recorder of a county where the land described is situated.

(b) A county recorder shall accept all notices presented to the recorder that describe land located in the county that the recorder serves. The recorder shall enter and record full copies of the notice in the same way that deeds are recorded. Each recorder shall charge the same fees for recording a notice as are charged for recording deeds.

(c) Each recorder shall index the notices in the same manner that deeds are indexed. Until the notice is recorded and correctly indexed, a notice does not comply with section 1 of this chapter regarding notice. [P.L.2-2002, § 5.]

Collateral References. Sufficiency, under statute of frauds, of description or designation of property in real estate brokerage contract. 30 A.L.R.3d 935.

32-20-4-3. Failure to file. — (a) Failure to file the notice required under this chapter does not bar:

(1) a lessor or the lessor's successor as a reversioner of the lessor's right to possession on the expiration of any lease; or

(2) a lessee or the lessee's successor of the lessee's rights in and to any lease.

(b) Failure to file the notice required under this chapter does not bar or extinguish any easement, interest in the nature of an easement, or any rights appurtenant to an easement granted, excepted, or reserved by the instrument creating the easement or interest, including any rights for future use, if the existence of the easement or interest is evidenced by the location beneath, upon, or above any part of the land described in the instrument of any pipe, valve, road, wire, cable, conduit, duct, sewer, track, pole, tower, or other physical facility and whether or not the existence of the facility is observable. However, equitable restrictions or servitudes on the use of land are not considered easements or interests in the nature of easements as that phrase is used in this section. [P.L.2-2002, § 5.]

CHAPTER 5

SLANDER OF TITLE

32-20-5-1. May not use filing of notices to slander title. — A person may not use the privilege of filing notices under this article to slander the title to land. [P.L.2-2002, § 5.]

Effective Dates. P.L.2-2002, § 5. July 1. 2002.

32-20-5-2. Penalties. — In any action to quiet title to land, if the court finds that a person has filed a claim only to slander title to land, the court shall:

(1) award the plaintiff all the costs of the action, including attorney's fees that the court allows to the plaintiff; and

(2) decree that the defendant asserting the claim shall pay to the plaintiff all damages that the plaintiff may have sustained as the result of the notice of claims having been filed for record. [P.L.2-2002, § 5.]

ARTICLE 21

CONVEYANCE PROCEDURES FOR REAL PROPERTY

CHAPTER 1

STATUTE OF FRAUDS; WRITING REQUIREMENTS

32-21-1-1. Applicability. — (a) This section does not apply to a lease for a term of not more than three (3) years.

(b) A person may not bring any of the following actions unless the promise, contract, or agreement on which the action is based, or a memorandum or note describing the promise, contract, or agreement on which the action is based, is in writing and signed by the party against whom the action is brought or by the party's authorized agent:

(1) An action charging an executor or administrator, upon any special promise, to answer damages out of the executor's or administrator's own estate.

(2) An action charging any person, upon any special promise, to answer for the debt, default, or miscarriage of another.

(3) An action charging any person upon any agreement or promise made in consideration of marriage.

(4) An action involving any contract for the sale of land.

(5) An action involving any agreement that is not to be performed within one (1) year from the making of the agreement.

(6) An action involving an agreement, promise, contract, or warranty of cure concerning medical care or treatment. However, this subdivision does not affect the right to sue for malpractice or negligence. [P.L.2-2002, § 6.]

Effective Dates. P.L.2-2002, § 6. July 1. 2002.

Cross References. Contracts for sale of goods for price of $500 or more, IC 26-1-2-201.

Insane husband or wife, conveyance, IC 32-22-1-5.

Married women conveying land, IC 32-17-3-4.

Seal, unnecessary, IC 32-21-1-12.

Teachers' contracts required to be in writing, IC 20-6.1-4-3.

Indiana Law Review. 1993 Developments in Indiana Property Law, 27 Ind. L. Rev. 1285 (1994).

Res Gestae. Rules, rulings for the trial lawyer, 39 (No. 3) Res Gestae 34 (1995).

Valparaiso University Law Review. Tenancy by the Entirety as an Asset Shield: An Unjustified Safe Haven for Delinquent Child Support Obligors, 29 Val. U.L. Rev. 1057 (1995).

NOTES TO DECISIONS

ANALYSIS

General Provisions
In general.
Assignment.
Constructive trusts.
Contract based on statutory mandate.
Devise of land.
Employment contracts.
Execution of contract.
Fraud.
Incorporation by reference.
Judicial sales.
Land sale.
Loan agreements.
Modification or rescission.
Offer to purchase containing parol terms.
Parol evidence.
Partial performance.
Pleading and practice.
Presumption.
Promise to indemnify.
Promissory estoppel.
Renewal of surety bond.
Sufficiency of allegations.
Sufficiency of memorandum.
—In general.

—Correspondence.

Executor or Administrator
In general.

Agreement to Answer for Debt of Another
In general.
Agency.
Assumption of debt.
Bills and notes.
Building or construction contractors.
Corporations.
Credit to third person.
Decedents' estates.
Guaranty.
Indemnification agreement.
Joint obligors.
Legal disability of third person.
Loan of property.
Mortgage.
Property delivered to third person.

Agreement in Consideration of Marriage
In general.
Antenuptial contracts.

Sale of Lands
In general.
Acknowledgment.

Action against real estate salesman.
Antenuptial contracts.
Auction sales.
Boundary agreements.
Brokerage agreement.
Buildings.
Certificate of sale.
—Contract to transfer.
Conflict of laws.
Consideration.
Contingent remainder.
Contract dependent upon vendor obtaining title.
Contract to furnish purchase price.
Cotenants.
Deeds.
—In general.
—Notations.
—Titles.
Delivery.
Delivery by leaving for record.
Delivery in escrow.
Description of land.
Designation of grantee.
Destruction of deed.
Devises.
Disposition of property not covered by divorce decree.
Easements.
Estoppel.
Evidence.
—Evidence of ownership.
Foreign contracts.
Grantor's signature.
Leases.
Married women.
Mistake.
Mortgages.
Notes secured by purchase money mortgage.

Oil and gas.
Parol modification.
Part performance.
—In general.
—Payment of purchase price.
—Possession and improvements.
Pleading.
Possession.
Promissory estoppel.
—Detrimental reliance.
Reconveyances.
Record titles.
Restrictions in deed.
Right of possession.
Sand, gravel, and soil.
Services as consideration.
Sufficiency of memorandum.
Surrender and release.
Tenants by entireties.
Timber.

Agreement Not to Be Performed Within One Year

In general.
Agreement to make will.
Employment contracts.
Leases.
Marriage contract.
Modification or rescission.
—Monthly payments.
Partnership contracts.
Part performance.
Performance dependent upon contingency.
Real estate contracts.
Sale of lands.
Severable contracts.
Teachers' contracts.

Agreement of Cure

Legislative intent.

GENERAL PROVISIONS

In General.

An action could have been maintained on a contract required by the statute to be in writing, although the original signed copy was unavailable when the pleading was drawn. Wilkinson v. First Nat'l Bank, 214 Ind. 513, 14 N.E.2d 530 (1938).

In order to take a case out of the operation of the statute of frauds, the person to whom the conveyance was to have been made must have changed his position in reliance on such contract. Brown v. Freudenberg, 106 Ind. App. 692, 17 N.E.2d 865 (1938).

A list of descriptions clipped to the back of an executed lease might have been sufficient to identify the lands intended to be leased in a suit by the lessor for the cancellation of the lease. Maier v. Continental Oil Co., 120 F.2d 237 (7th Cir.), cert. denied, 314 U.S. 652, 62 S. Ct. 101, 86 L. Ed. 523 (1941).

Contracts governed by the statute of frauds, like other contracts, were to have been read in the light of surrounding circumstances. Maier v. Continental Oil Co., 120 F.2d 237 (7th Cir.), cert. denied, 314 U.S. 652, 62 S. Ct. 101, 86 L. Ed. 523 (1941).

An action was maintainable for restitution on a quantum meruit basis for any benefit furnished a defendant, who refused to perform his part of the contract, by a plaintiff who had partly performed the agreement, which was unenforceable because of the statute of frauds, when the latter was not in default in continuing performance. Matthews v. Continental Roll & Steel Foundry Co., 121 F.2d 594 (3d Cir. 1941).

The statute of frauds does not govern the formation of contracts but only the enforceability of contracts which have been formed. Young v. Bryan, 178 Ind. App. 702, 59 Ind. Dec. 133, 368 N.E.2d 1, 368 N.E.2d 3 (1977).

The statute of frauds is an affirmative defense. Dawson v. St. Vincent Hosp. & Health

GENERAL PROVISIONS (Cont'd)

In General. (Cont'd)
Care Ctr., Inc., 426 N.E.2d 1328 (Ind. App. 1981).

A writing that sets forth the subject matter and terms of a contract with sufficient certainty, without recourse to parol evidence, satisfies the statute of frauds. Newman v. Huff, 632 N.E.2d 799 (Ind. App. 1994).

Assignment.
Where the statute of frauds applies, the general rule is that an assignment must likewise be in writing. Dominion Invs. v. Yasechko, 767 F. Supp. 1460 (N.D. Ind. 1991).

Constructive Trusts.
Constructive trusts were raised by the courts, in proper cases, in defiance of the statute of frauds, on the principle that the statute could not have been invoked to aid in the perpetration of a fraud, or to shield one who had perpetrated a fraud. Koehler v. Koehler, 75 Ind. App. 510, 121 N.E. 450 (1919).

Contract Based on Statutory Mandate.
This section was applicable to common law agreements only, unless the parties thereto provided otherwise. Miller v. State ex rel. McDonald, 87 Ind. App. 264, 159 N.E. 551 (1928).

A road contractor's bond required by former IC 8-20-1-65 did not come within the provisions of this section of the statute of frauds, since the statute did not apply to contracts required by statute. Miller v. State ex rel. McDonald, 87 Ind. App. 264, 159 N.E. 551 (1928).

Devise of Land.
Where father orally agreed to devise farmland to his son and son farmed the land relying on such promise and evidence showed such performance on the part of the son, such evidence was sufficient to take such oral contract out of the statute of frauds. Satterthwaite v. Estate of Satterthwaite, 420 N.E.2d 287 (Ind. App. 1981).

Employment Contracts.
The factors the employee cited as requiring upholding of the oral employment contract under a theory of promissory estoppel were merely the kind of adverse consequences which normally attend an involuntary termination of employment. Neither the benefit of the bargain itself, nor mere inconvenience, nor incidental expenses short of a reliance injury so substantial and independent that it constituted unjust and unconscionable injury and loss, was sufficient to remove the claim from the operation of the statute. Thus, the employee could not recover against the employer for the alleged breach of an oral employment contract. Mehling v. Dubois County Farm Bureau Coop. Ass'n, 601 N.E.2d 5 (Ind. App. 1992).

An employee did not suffer an injury which was unjust or unconscionable when he took employment with employer where he did not give up his residence, and continued to own a building and equipment connected with his business, and thus, he could not avoid operation of the Statute of Frauds. Keating v. Burton, 617 N.E.2d 588 (Ind. App. 1993).

Under Indiana law, an oral promise of employment that is unenforceable under the statute of frauds may be enforceable under the doctrine of promissory estoppel. Wright v. Associated Ins. Cos., 29 F.3d 1244 (7th Cir. 1994).

While death may serve as a contingency constituting performance in a lifetime employment contract, death does not constitute performance in contracts involving employment until retirement, where the parties intend that the employee will retire only after a number of years greater than one, and this section applies to such a contract. Wior v. Anchor Indus., Inc., 669 N.E.2d 172 (Ind. 1996).

Execution of Contract.
A refusal to reduce a contract to writing was not sufficient to take the case out of the statute. Caylor v. Roe, 99 Ind. 1 (1884); Caldwell v. School City of Huntington, 132 Ind. 92, 31 N.E. 566 (1892).

Acceptance of contract by a party and action thereon by him constituted an execution of the contract. Thiebaud v. Union Furn. Co., 143 Ind. 340, 42 N.E. 741 (1896); Terre Haute & I.R.R. v. State ex rel. Ketcham, 159 Ind. 438, 65 N.E. 401 (1902), rev'd on other grounds, 194 U.S. 579, 24 S. Ct. 767, 48 L. Ed. 1124 (1904); American Quarries Co. v. Lay, 37 Ind. App. 386, 73 N.E. 608 (1905); Neal v. Baker, 198 Ind. 393, 153 N.E. 768 (1926).

Fraud.
The mere breach or violation of an oral agreement which was within the statute of frauds, by one of the parties thereto, or his refusal to perform it, was not of itself a fraud either in equity or at law from which the courts would have given relief or which would have enabled the other party to assert rights and defenses based on the contract. Hurd v. Ball, 128 Ind. App. 278, 143 N.E.2d 458 (1957), transfer denied, 237 Ind. 665, 148 N.E.2d 194 (1958).

Incorporation by Reference.
The statute of frauds may be satisfied by several writings though one only is signed if the signed writing refers to the unsigned

GENERAL PROVISIONS (Cont'd)

Incorporation by Reference. (Cont'd)
writing so as to make it a part of the instrument which refers to it, and inasmuch as a note sufficiently identified and referred to the additional advance, it and the payment schedule therein were incorporated into the note so that the co-signer's signature on the note operated as a signature on the additional advance as well. Holmes v. Rushville Prod. Credit Ass'n, 170 Ind. App. 509, 54 Ind. Dec. 395, 353 N.E.2d 509 (1976), vacated, 170 Ind. App. 517, 355 N.E.2d 417, reinstated, 170 Ind. App. 509, 357 N.E.2d 734, 55 Ind. Dec. 468 (1977), transfer denied, 267 Ind. 454, 371 N.E.2d 379, 60 Ind. Dec. 413 (1978).

Judicial Sales.
Judicial sales made by and under the supervision of a court are not within the statute of frauds, and are binding on the purchaser without any written contract or memorandum of sale, it being the confirmation of the sale by the court which takes it out of the statute. Geist v. Diversified Fin. Planners, Inc., 570 N.E.2d 1327 (Ind. App. 1991).

Land Sale.
Although the statute of frauds rendered unenforceable an oral contract for the sale of land, a seller could not hide behind the statute solely to preclude a purchaser from recovering the portion of the purchase price paid by the latter. Lacey v. Morgan, 152 Ind. App. 119, 30 Ind. Dec. 625, 282 N.E.2d 344 (1972).

Oral contracts for the conveyance of real property are voidable, not void. Perkins v. Owens, 721 N.E.2d 289 (Ind. App. 1999).

Loan Agreements.
The Indiana statute of frauds does not explicitly cover an agreement to lend funds in exchange for a mortgage interest. Blue Valley Turf Farms, Inc. v. Realestate Mktg. & Dev., Inc., 424 N.E.2d 1088 (Ind. App. 1981).

Modification or Rescission.
If a contract was required to be in writing, it could only have been changed or modified by a written instrument. Bradley v. Harter, 156 Ind. 499, 60 N.E. 139 (1901); Burgett v. Loeb, 43 Ind. App. 657, 88 N.E. 346 (1909).

Rights created under a contract which had to be in writing could have been released or surrendered only by a written instrument. Heller v. Dailey, 28 Ind. App. 555, 63 N.E. 490 (1902); Ramage v. Wilson, 37 Ind. App. 532, 77 N.E. 368 (1906).

A lease for three years, which was required to be in writing, could not have been changed or modified by an oral agreement. Miller Jewelry Co. v. Dickson, 111 Ind. App. 676, 42 N.E.2d 398 (1942).

Offer to Purchase Containing Parol Terms.
Offer to purchase real estate, which admittedly contained parol terms, was a parol contract for purposes of statute of frauds and broker's commission statute and was, therefore, unenforceable by broker in action for payment of commission. Shrum v. Dalton, 442 N.E.2d 366 (Ind. App. 1982).

Parol Evidence.
While parol evidence was not generally admissible to show the connection between signed and unsigned writings relied upon to constitute a memorandum within the meaning of the statute of frauds, it was admissible to identify unsigned writings referred to in the signed writing. Foltz v. Evans, 113 Ind. App. 596, 49 N.E.2d 358 (1943).

Partial Performance.
Where one party to an oral contract in reliance on that contract has performed his part of the agreement to such an extent that repudiation of the contract would lead to an unjust or fraudulent result, equity will disregard the requirement of a writing and enforce the oral agreement. Summerlot v. Summerlot, 77 Ind. Dec. 676, 408 N.E.2d 820 (Ind. App. 1980).

Where one party to an oral agreement has partially performed in reliance on the contract and it would be perpetrating a fraud upon him to allow the other party to repudiate the contract, equity removes the agreement from the statute of frauds and enforces the contract. Tolliver v. Mathas, 538 N.E.2d 971 (Ind. App. 1989).

For the doctrine of part performance to remove an alleged oral contract from the statute of frauds there must be some indicia that the alleged part performance relates back to an oral contract for sale entered into by the parties. Nelson v. Blackwell, 227 Bankr. 859 (Bankr. S.D. Ind. 1998).

Where it was solely the belief of one party that there was to be a sale of real estate, where he had not paid the purchase price, nor made a down payment, where his possession of the property began pursuant to a lease, and where repairs made to the property to make it habitable were pursuant to the landlord's offer to waive payment of rent for two and half months, the doctrine of part performance did not remove the alleged oral contract for sale from the statute of frauds. Nelson v. Blackwell, 227 Bankr. 859 (Bankr. S.D. Ind. 1998).

Circumstances generally held sufficient to invoke the doctrine of part performance as an exception to the statute of frauds are some combination of (1) payment of the purchase price or a part thereof, (2) possession, and (3) lasting and valuable improvements on the

GENERAL PROVISIONS (Cont'd)

Partial Performance. (Cont'd)
land. Perkins v. Owens, 721 N.E.2d 289 (Ind. App. 1999).

To the extent that the plaintiffs ever "possessed" the disputed property, their possession was the same after entry into their respective oral contracts as before, and where "improvements" to the property consisted of mowing and building a non-permanent utility barn, payment of the purchase price, standing alone, was insufficient to remove the case from the statute of frauds, and the trial court was without jurisdiction to challenge the validity of a deed given to the defendant. Perkins v. Owens, 721 N.E.2d 289 (Ind. App. 1999).

Partial payment alone is not sufficient to constitute partial performance and removal from the statute of frauds; circumstances generally held sufficient to invoke the doctrine of part performance as an exception to the statute of frauds are some combination of the following: payment of the purchase price or a part thereof; possession; and lasting and valuable improvements on the land. Marathon Oil Co. v. Collins, 744 N.E.2d 474 (Ind. App. 2001).

Pleading and Practice.
In an action to enforce a contract which, under the statute of frauds, had to be in writing, it could have been contended on the trial that the contract was invalid without pleading the statute of frauds. Suman v. Springate, 67 Ind. 115 (1879); Dixon v. Duke, 85 Ind. 434 (1882); Indiana Trust Co. v. Finitzer, 160 Ind. 647, 67 N.E. 520 (1903); Graham v. Henderson Elevator Co., 60 Ind. App. 697, 111 N.E. 332 (1916).

Parties and privies alone had the right to plead statute of frauds. Jackson v. Stanfield, 137 Ind. 592, 36 N.E. 345, 37 N.E. 14, 23 L.R.A. 588 (1894); Krotz v. A.R. Beck Lumber Co., 34 Ind. App. 577, 73 N.E. 273 (1905); Cannon v. Castleman, 164 Ind. 343, 73 N.E. 689 (1905).

In an action for specific performance of an oral contract allegedly entered into between the mother and decedent for the benefit of an illegitimate child, a demurrer to the complaint based on the statute of frauds would have been proper and would have been sustainable where the complaint clearly brought the contract within the purview of the statute of frauds. Hurd v. Ball, 128 Ind. App. 278, 143 N.E.2d 458 (1957), transfer denied, 237 Ind. 665, 148 N.E.2d 194 (1958).

A motion for summary judgment in an action by appellant to enjoin appellees from interfering with an alleged oral easement should have been denied, for while such an easement was an interest in land and within

the provisions of the statute of frauds, this statute did not make a parol contract for an interest in land void, but merely voidable. Whether or not an oral agreement existed and if so whether it was enforceable under an exception to the rules of the statute of frauds presented a genuine issue of material facts. Dubois County Mach. Co. v. Blessinger, 149 Ind. App. 594, 27 Ind. Dec. 312, 274 N.E.2d 279 (1971).

Only parties and privies have the right to plead the statute of frauds as a defense. Pioneer Lumber & Supply Co. v. First-Merchants Nat'l Bank, 169 Ind. App. 406, 23 Ind. Dec. 244, 349 N.E.2d 219 (1976); Blue Valley Turf Farms, Inc. v. Realestate Mktg. & Dev., Inc., 424 N.E.2d 1088 (Ind. App. 1981).

In order to preserve the defense of the statute of frauds on appeal, the party must either have set forth the defense in a responsive pleading or show that the defense was litigated by the parties. Lawshe v. Glen Park Lumber Co., 176 Ind. App. 344, 62 Ind. Dec. 338, 375 N.E.2d 275 (1978).

Presumption.
When the complaint in a suit for the specific performance of a contract to convey land was silent as to whether the contract was oral or in writing, it was presumed to have been oral. Horner v. McConnell, 158 Ind. 280, 63 N.E. 472 (1902); Crafton v. Carmichael, 29 Ind. App. 320, 64 N.E. 627 (1902); Bell v. Bitner, 33 Ind. App. 6, 70 N.E. 549 (1902); Yoe v. Newcomb, 33 Ind. App. 615, 71 N.E. 256 (1904); Featherstone Foundry & Mach. Co. v. Criswell, 36 Ind. App. 681, 75 N.E. 30 (1905); Wabash R.R. v. Grate, 53 Ind. App. 583, 102 N.E. 155 (1913); McKenna v. Smith, 77 Ind. App. 372, 133 N.E. 510 (1922); Sachs v. Blewett, 206 Ind. 151, 185 N.E. 856 (1933).

Promise to Indemnify.
Where the plaintiff/third party promised the go-kart race organizers (the debtors) to indemnify them against claims made by other drivers (the creditors) against the race organizers, because plaintiff/third party made her promise to indemnify to the debtors and not the creditors, the "in writing" requirement of the statute of frauds did not apply, because the statute applies only if the promise to indemnify is made by the third party directly to the creditor. Beaver v. Grand Prix Karting Ass'n, 246 F.3d 905 (7th Cir. 2001).

Promissory estoppel.
Plaintiff's claim of promissory estoppel did not operate to remove a case from the statute of frauds because the promise relied upon was the very promise that the statute of frauds declared unenforceable if not in writing. Revealed Water Prods. v. Arrowhead Plastic Eng'g, Inc., No. IP 99-0069-CT/G, decided

GENERAL PROVISIONS (Cont'd)

Promissory estoppel. (Cont'd)
9/29/00, — F. Supp. 3d —, 2000 U.S. Dist. LEXIS 14646 (S.D. Ind. 2000).

Renewal of Surety Bond.
Renewal of a surety bond was in legal effect a new contract of surety, and hence came within the statute of frauds, and must be in writing. Peters v. Bechdolt, 100 Ind. App. 395, 192 N.E. 116 (1934).

Complaint which failed to allege that renewal of surety bond was in writing, as it had to be to be enforceable, did not state a cause of action. Peters v. Bechdolt, 100 Ind. App. 395, 192 N.E. 116 (1934).

Sufficiency of Allegations.
The allegations of the amended complaint were, as a matter of law, sufficient to state a claim for which relief could be granted as against the defendant-appellee's motion to dismiss by invocation of the provisions of the statute of frauds as found in the statute. Gladis v. Melloh, 149 Ind. App. 466, 27 Ind. Dec. 131, 273 N.E.2d 767 (1971).

Sufficiency of Memorandum.

—In General.
Contracts partly written and partly in parol were verbal contracts. Board of Comm'rs v. Shipley, 77 Ind. 553 (1881); Pulse v. Miller, 81 Ind. 190 (1881); Gordon v. Gordon, 96 Ind. 134 (1884); Louisville, N.A. & C. Ry. v. Reynolds, 118 Ind. 170, 20 N.E. 711 (1889); Carskaddon v. City of South Bend, 141 Ind. 596, 39 N.E. 667, 41 N.E. 1 (1895); Lingeman v. Shirk, 15 Ind. App. 432, 43 N.E. 33 (1896); Stauffer v. Linenthal, 29 Ind. App. 305, 64 N.E. 643 (1902); Zimmerman v. Zehendner, 164 Ind. 466, 73 N.E. 920 (1905); Miller v. Sharp, 52 Ind. App. 11, 100 N.E. 108 (1912); Tishbein v. Paine, 52 Ind. App. 441, 100 N.E. 766 (1913); Washburn-Crosby Milling Co. v. Brown, 56 Ind. App. 104, 104 N.E. 997 (1914); Graham v. Henderson Elevator Co., 60 Ind. App. 697, 111 N.E. 332 (1916); Moore v. Ohl, 65 Ind. App. 691, 116 N.E. 9 (1917); Peters v. Martin, 69 Ind. App. 436, 122 N.E. 16 (1919).

Resolution of city council verbally accepted did not constitute a written contract. Carskaddon v. City of South Bend, 141 Ind. 596, 39 N.E. 667, 41 N.E. 1 (1895).

The memorandum required by the statute of frauds could consist of several writings, if each writing was signed by the party to be charged, and the writings indicated that they related to the same transaction. Block v. Sherman, 109 Ind. App. 330, 34 N.E.2d 951 (1941).

The memorandum required by the statute of frauds could consist of several writings, though one writing only was signed, if the signed writing was annexed to the other writing by the party to be charged, or the signed writing referred to the unsigned writing so as to make it a part of the instrument which refered to it. Block v. Sherman, 109 Ind. App. 330, 34 N.E.2d 951 (1941).

Where a signed instrument and an unsigned one were relied upon to satisfy the statute of frauds, the connection between the two instruments had to appear by internal evidence derived from the signed instrument, and this connection could not be shown by parol evidence concerning the intentions or actions of the parties, and the signed instrument had to so clearly and definitely refer to the unsigned one that by force of the reference the unsigned one became a part of the signed instrument. Block v. Sherman, 109 Ind. App. 330, 34 N.E.2d 951 (1941).

Two instruments, one signed and the other unsigned, could not have been considered together to form a memorandum sufficient to satisfy the statute of frauds, where they were not attached and there was no reference in the signed instrument to the unsigned one, despite the fact that they were written in the person's own handwriting, delivered on the same date, and both recited the same purchase price and same down payment, since it would have been necessary to resort to parol evidence to show the connection between the two papers. Block v. Sherman, 109 Ind. App. 330, 34 N.E.2d 951 (1941).

A memorandum, in order to have made enforceable a contract within the statute of frauds, might have been any document or writing, formal or informal, signed by the party to have been charged, or by his agent actually or apparently authorized thereunto, which stated with reasonable certainty, each party to the contract either by his own name, or by such a description as would have served to identify him, or by the name or description of his agent, and the land, goods, or other subject-matter to which the contract related, and the terms and conditions of all the promises constituting the contract and by whom and to whom the promises were made. Block v. Sherman, 109 Ind. App. 330, 34 N.E.2d 951 (1941).

A memorandum, in order to have satisfied the statute of frauds, had to contain all the essential stipulations and undertakings of the prior verbal agreement which it embodied and, if any of these stipulations were omitted, then the memorandum, although the parts which it did contain might have, by themselves, made a complete contract, was not a note or memorandum of the agreement as required by the statute, and could not be enforced at law or in equity. Block v. Sherman, 109 Ind. App. 330, 34 N.E.2d 951 (1941).

While, in order to satisfy the statute of

GENERAL PROVISIONS (Cont'd)

Sufficiency of Memorandum. (Cont'd)

—In General. (Cont'd)
frauds, the time and place of performance were not always necessary terms of a valid memorandum, because in their absence the law supplied these by implication, but where a time for performance was expressly agreed upon as a part of the contract, and thus made a condition, it had to appear as a constituent part of the memorandum. Block v. Sherman, 109 Ind. App. 330, 34 N.E.2d 951 (1941).

Where a signed receipt, relied upon to satisfy the statute of frauds, showed nothing concerning the assumption of taxes, completion of the abstract, or time of payment of the balance of the purchase price, although such matters were shown by the complaint to have been embodied in the parol agreement between the parties, the receipt was not a sufficient memorandum and the complaint was bad on demurrer. Block v. Sherman, 109 Ind. App. 330, 34 N.E.2d 951 (1941).

A notation on the back of a ten-year lease that read "canceled new lease," together with a check given rental agents which contained the words "rent for Dec/34," did not constitute a sufficient memorandum to take an oral agreement to move from the premises to other premises in the same building out of the statute of frauds, since it did not appear that the cancellation was signed, and since the two instruments could not have been considered together because the check did not refer to the cancellation, the cancellation was not dated, and contemporaneous delivery of the two instruments was not alleged. Miller Jewelry Co. v. Dickson, 111 Ind. App. 676, 42 N.E.2d 398 (1942).

A written memorandum could consist of several writings if each was signed by the party to be charged and the writings indicated that they related to the same transaction; and could have consisted of several writings though only one was signed, if the signed writing was annexed to the other writings by the party to have been charged, or the signed writing referred to the unsigned writing so as to have made it a part of the instrument which referred to it. Foltz v. Evans, 113 Ind. App. 596, 49 N.E.2d 358 (1943).

A resolution of the Indiana state toll bridge commission duly enacted, placed of record, and signed by the chairman as required by it, constituted a sufficient memorandum to take a contract for legal services not performable within one year out the prohibition of the statute of frauds. Indiana State Toll Bridge Comm'n v. Minor, 236 Ind. 193, 139 N.E.2d 445 (1957).

A contract required by the statute of frauds to be in writing must be totally in writing to be enforceable. A contract which is partly written and partly oral is a parol contract, and does not satisfy the statutory requirement of a written contract. Thus where a receipt is only a part of a predominantly parol contract for the sale of land, this agreement must be considered a parol land sale contract and its terms, even those terms which were reduced to writing, are rendered unenforceable by the statute. Kopis v. Savage, 498 N.E.2d 1266 (Ind. App. 1986).

Agreement to sell cottage was enforceable despite its lack of certain written terms and conditions, including an express promise to convey title and a provision for the payment of real estate taxes, where memorandum did correctly identify the parties, the real estate, the purchase price and the closing date, and included seller's signature. Johnson v. Sprague, 614 N.E.2d 585 (Ind. App. 1993).

—Correspondence.
Correspondence between the parties might have been sufficient to establish the contract as required by the statute. Wills v. Ross, 77 Ind. 1, 40 Am. R. 279 (1881); Thames Loan & Trust Co. v. Beville, 100 Ind. 309 (1885); Witty v. Michigan Mut. Life Ins. Co., 123 Ind. 411, 24 N.E. 141, 8 L.R.A. 365, 18 Am. St. 327 (1890); Austin v. Davis, 128 Ind. 472, 26 N.E. 890, 12 L.R.A. 120, 25 Am. St. 456 (1891); Olcott v. McClure, 50 Ind. App. 79, 98 N.E. 82 (1912).

A letter signed by the writer containing an offer of employment and setting forth the terms thereof, and telegraphic acceptance by the recipient were held to have been a sufficient memorandum under the statute of frauds. Keithly v. Craig, 79 Ind. App. 403, 135 N.E. 156 (1922).

A letter written and signed by husband and wife, to a girl who had formerly lived with and cared for them, asking her to return and live with them the remainder of their lives, and stating that, if she would do so, "everything will all be yours after our death," was held not a sufficient memorandum to take the case out of the statute of frauds. Neal v. Baker, 198 Ind. 393, 153 N.E. 768 (1926).

A memorandum satisfying the statute of frauds might have consisted of several letters providing that they fully expressed the contract, were signed by the parties writing them, and were unified by proper reference. Highland Inv. Co. v. Kirk Co., 96 Ind. App. 5, 184 N.E. 308 (1933).

In an action on a contract required by statute to be in writing, a substituted contract offered by plaintiff to defendant, in a letter written to defendant, was not sufficient memorandum of an oral agreement, in the absence of proof that such offer was accepted by defendant. Maglaris v. Claude Neon Fed. Co., 101 Ind. App. 156, 198 N.E. 462 (1935).

Executor or Administrator

In General.
Contracts entered into by executors and administrators after the deaths of the decedents were not within the statute of frauds. Holderbaugh v. Turpin, 75 Ind. 84, 39 Am. R. 124 (1881); Bott v. Barr, 95 Ind. 243 (1884).

Where there was no consideration to support the promise contained in a letter to settle the balance of a claim against an estate, the administrator was not liable thereon. Vogel v. O'Toole, 2 Ind. App. 196, 28 N.E. 209 (1891).

Agreement to Answer for Debt of Another

In General.
A contract to answer for the debt of another had to be in writing. Smith v. Stevens, 3 Ind. 332 (1852); Berkshire v. Young, 45 Ind. 461 (1874); Langford v. Freeman, 60 Ind. 46 (1877); Catlett v. Trustees of M.E. Church, 62 Ind. 365, 30 Am. R. 197 (1878); Cheesman v. Wiggins, 122 Ind. 352, 23 N.E. 945 (1890); Parker v. Dillingham, 129 Ind. 542, 29 N.E. 23 (1891); Southern Ind. Loan & Sav. Inst. v. Roberts, 42 Ind. App. 653, 86 N.E. 490 (1908); Knight & Jillson Co. v. Castle, 172 Ind. 97, 87 N.E. 976, 27 L.R.A. (n.s.) 573 (1909); Mossburg v. United Oil & Gas Co., 43 Ind. App. 465, 87 N.E. 992 (1909); Wainright Trust Co. v. United States Fid. & Guar. Co., 63 Ind. App. 309, 114 N.E. 470 (1916), overruled on other grounds, Everley v. Equitable Sur. Co., 190 Ind. 274, 130 N.E. 227 (1921).

A promise made by one to pay a debt he owed to a third person was not a promise to pay the debt of another, although it operated to pay a debt owing by the promisee. Nelson v. Hardy, 7 Ind. 364 (1856); Day v. Patterson, 18 Ind. 114 (1862); Lamb v. Donovan, 19 Ind. 40 (1862); Hardy v. Blazer, 29 Ind. 226, 92 Am. Dec. 347 (1867); Davis v. Calloway, 30 Ind. 112, 95 Am. Dec. 671 (1868); Crim v. Fitch, 53 Ind. 214 (1876); Wolke v. Flemming, 103 Ind. 105, 2 N.E. 325, 53 Am. R. 495 (1885); Parker v. Dillingham, 129 Ind. 542, 29 N.E. 23 (1891).

To have made a promise to answer for the debt of another fell within the statute, the person for whom the promise was made had to be liable to the person to whom the promise was made, and continue liable after the making of the promise. Downey v. Hinchman, 25 Ind. 453 (1865); Ellison v. Wisehart, 29 Ind. 32 (1867); Crosby v. Jeroloman, 37 Ind. 264 (1871); Hyatt v. Bonham, 19 Ind. App. 256, 49 N.E. 361 (1898).

If money was paid upon a promise of repayment, such promise was not within the statute, although such payment was for the benefit of a third person. Elson v. Spraker, 100 Ind. 374 (1885).

The statute did not apply to promises in respect to debts created at the instance and for the benefit of the promisor. New Amsterdam Cas. Co. v. Madison County Trust Co., 81 Ind. App. 157, 142 N.E. 727 (1924).

The renewal of a surety bond was in effect a new contract of suretyship, and was required to be in writing. Peters v. Bechdolt, 100 Ind. App. 395, 192 N.E. 116 (1934).

Where a contract was entered into between two persons for the benefit of a third person, the third person could have maintained a suit upon the contract in his own name to enforce it. Hauser v. George, 100 Ind. App. 346, 195 N.E. 592 (1935).

Where the purchaser of property agreed, as consideration therefor, to pay the purchase-money to a third person in satisfaction of a debt owing by the seller to such person, such an agreement was not a promise to pay the debt of another as contemplated by this section. Hauser v. George, 100 Ind. App. 346, 195 N.E. 592 (1935).

Parol evidence was admissible to apply a written contract of guaranty to a lease, and to show that they were executed contemporaneously, even though the guaranty bore an earlier date. Smith v. Ostermeyer Realty Co., 102 Ind. App. 164, 197 N.E. 743 (1935).

Where a trust company guaranteed the payment of certain bonds, such guaranty applied also to other bonds issued in substitution for the original bonds which were not sold, and was not within the inhibition of the statute of frauds. New Albany Trust Co. v. Nadorff, 108 Ind. App. 229, 27 N.E.2d 116 (1940).

Where the contract was one not in writing entered into by two persons for the benefit of a third, namely the appellant, it was held to be within the inhibition of the statute of frauds. Hurd v. Ball, 128 Ind. App. 278, 143 N.E.2d 458 (1957), transfer denied, 237 Ind. 665, 148 N.E.2d 194 (1958).

Agency.
An agreement by an agent that he would be responsible for uncollectible accounts for goods sold by him was within the statute. Smock v. Brush, 62 Ind. 156 (1878).

One who bid in hogs at an auction after disclosing that he was bidding for another but without disclosing the indentity of his principal was liable for the bid price without any agreement in writing to pay the bid price. Bottorff v. Ault, 10 Ind. Dec. 122, 374 F.2d 832 (7th Cir. 1967).

AGREEMENT TO ANSWER FOR DEBT OF
  ANOTHER (Cont'd)

Assumption of Debt.
A promise made by the purchaser of property to pay the purchase-money to a third person to satisfy a debt owing by the seller was not a promise to pay the debt of another. Gwaltney v. Wheeler, 26 Ind. 415 (1866); Woodward v. Wilcox, 27 Ind. 207 (1866); Snyder v. Robinson, 35 Ind. 311, 9 Am. R. 738 (1871); Helms v. Kearns, 40 Ind. 124 (1872); McDill v. Gunn, 43 Ind. 315 (1873); Haggerty v. Johnston, 48 Ind. 41 (1874); Carter v. Zenblin, 68 Ind. 436 (1879); Bateman v. Butler, 124 Ind. 223, 24 N.E. 989 (1890); Collins v. Stanfield, 139 Ind. 184, 38 N.E. 1091 (1894); Dickson v. Conde, 148 Ind. 279, 46 N.E. 998 (1897); Deering & Co. v. Armstrong, 14 Ind. App. 44, 42 N.E. 372 (1895); Bedford Belt Ry. v. Winstandley, 16 Ind. App. 143, 44 N.E. 556 (1896); Baltes Land, Stone & Oil Co. v. Sutton, 32 Ind. App. 14, 69 N.E. 179 (1903); Southern Ind. Loan & Sav. Inst. v. Roberts, 42 Ind. App. 653, 86 N.E. 490 (1908); Gregory v. Arms, 48 Ind. App. 562, 96 N.E. 196 (1911).

Assumption of a debt of vendor as part of purchase-money of property was not a promise to pay the debt of another. Lowe v. Hamilton, 132 Ind. 406, 31 N.E. 1117 (1892); Gregory v. Arms, 48 Ind. App. 562, 96 N.E. 196 (1911).

Assumption of debt and release of original debtor was not within the statute of frauds. Hyatt v. Bonham, 19 Ind. App. 256, 49 N.E. 361 (1898).

This section did not relieve one, to whom had been assigned purchase-money notes secured by a chattel mortgage on a threshing machine, from liability, under the contract of warranty by the seller to deliver another machine or return the amount paid, when such machine had not come up to the warranty, although the agreement to assume the obligation could have been oral. Emerson-Brantingham Implement Co. v. Tooley, 81 Ind. App. 460, 141 N.E. 890 (1923).

Grantee who as part consideration for conveyance assumes to discharge lien upon land conveyed was personally liable to holder of lien if grantor was personally liable. The holder of such lien could sue grantee to enforce personal liability, since grantee's promise was not within statute of frauds. Harvey v. Lowry, 204 Ind. 93, 183 N.E. 309 (1932).

Bills and Notes.
Verbal acceptances of orders or bills of exchange were not within the statute of frauds. Miller v. Neihaus, 51 Ind. 401 (1875); Louisville, E. & St. L. Ry. v. Caldwell, 98 Ind. 245 (1884).

A promise made on the transfer of a note to pay whatever amount could not be collected from the maker was within the statute. Hassinger v. Newman, 83 Ind. 124, 43 Am. R. 64 (1882).

A bank's agreement to pay purchaser of notes and mortgages, whether the makers pay or not, was a "promise to answer for debts and defaults of others" within the statute of frauds. Bank of Linn Grove v. Stults, 93 Ind. App. 129, 176 N.E. 707 (1931).

Building or Construction Contractors.
Where the owner of property undertook to pay for work and materials to have been subsequently done and furnished by a subcontractor in order to secure the completion of a building where the principal contractor had failed to carry on the work, the promise was an original one, and not within the statute of frauds. Board of Comm'rs v. Cincinnati Steam-Heating Co., 128 Ind. 240, 27 N.E. 612, 12 L.R.A. 502 (1891); Parker v. Dillingham, 129 Ind. 542, 29 N.E. 23 (1891).

This section required a contractor's bond to be in writing, since it was a special promise to answer for the default of another. Wainright Trust Co. v. United States Fid. & Guar. Co., 63 Ind. App. 309, 114 N.E. 470 (1916), overruled on other grounds, Everley v. Equitable Sur. Co., 190 Ind. 274, 130 N.E. 227 (1921).

A highway contractor's promise to pay laborers and others employed by materialmen was held not promise to pay debt of another under the statute of frauds. Davis Constr. Co. v. Petty, 91 Ind. App. 147, 168 N.E. 769 (1929).

Corporations.
The parol agreement of a corporation, on purchasing the property of another company, to assume a contract executed by the latter to employ an injured servant, which it was not otherwise bound to assume, was within the statute of frauds. Cox v. Baltimore & O.S.W.R.R., 180 Ind. 495, 103 N.E. 337 (1913).

Corporation president's oral promise guaranteeing the repayment of the corporation's debt was not enforceable under an estoppel argument put forth by the creditor as an exception to the statute of frauds where president had obtained no personal benefit as the result of his promise to guarantee the debt. Luson Int'l Distribs., Inc. v. Mitchell, 939 F.2d 493 (7th Cir. 1991).

Credit to Third Person.
When any credit was given to a third person, then a promise to pay by another had to be in writing. Wills v. Ross, 77 Ind. 1, 40 Am. R. 279 (1881); Miller v. State ex rel. Prather, 35 Ind. App. 379, 74 N.E. 260 (1905).

An oral promise to answer for the debt of another was collateral and within this section of the statute, if credit was given to the third person to any extent, so that he was in any

AGREEMENT TO ANSWER FOR DEBT OF
ANOTHER (Cont'd)

Credit to Third Person. (Cont'd)
degree independently and originally liable for
the goods delivered to him. Symons v. Burton,
83 Ind. App. 631, 149 N.E. 460 (1925).

Decedents' Estates.
A widow's promise to pay debts of decedent,
if no administration was had, did not bind
her. Keadle v. Siddens, 5 Ind. App. 8, 31 N.E.
539 (1892).

Recovery against an heir for services rendered heir, as distinguishable from those rendered decedent, was not barred by the statute
of frauds which was applicable to promise to
answer for debt of another. Horning v. Moyer,
96 Ind. App. 374, 185 N.E. 303 (1933).

Guaranty.
A guaranty that a third person was liable
upon a note executed by him was not a promise to pay the debt of such person. King v.
Summitt, 73 Ind. 312, 38 Am. R. 145 (1881);
Hassinger v. Newman, 83 Ind. 124, 43 Am. R.
64 (1882).

Verbal guaranty of performance founded on
new consideration was an original promise.
Voris v. Star City Bldg. & Loan Ass'n, 20 Ind.
App. 630, 50 N.E. 779 (1898).

No action can be prosecuted upon a guaranty to answer for the debt of another unless
the promise is in writing, and signed by the
party to be charged. Montgomery, Zukerman,
Davis, Inc. v. Diepenbrock, 698 F. Supp. 1453
(S.D. Ind. 1988).

Indemnification Agreement.
A sub-subcontractor's oral agreement with
the subcontractor to indemnify the subcontractor for any liability the latter might incur
under its written indemnification agreement
with the contractor does not fall within the
statute of frauds. Henry C. Beck Co. v. Fort
Wayne Structural Steel Co., 701 F.2d 1221
(7th Cir. 1983).

Joint Obligors.
A complaint for contribution between joint
adventurers upon the implied obligation of
defendant to reimburse plaintiff to the extent
the latter discharged that portion of their
joint obligation which should have been paid

by defendant was not open to the objection
that it sought to recover upon a special promise to answer for the debt of another. Gates v.
Fauvre, 74 Ind. App. 382, 119 N.E. 155 (1918).

Oral contract to pay for legal services rendered to debtor's son was enforceable. Walker
v. Elkin, 758 N.E.2d 972 (Ind. App. 2001).

Legal Disability of Third Person.
A promise to pay a debt of a person who was
not bound by reason of a legal disability did
not fall within the statute. King v. Summitt,
73 Ind. 312, 38 Am. R. 145 (1881).

Loan of Property.
A promise made that property loaned to a
third person would be returned was within
the statute. Hayes v. Burkam, 51 Ind. 130
(1875).

Mortgage.
A mortgage may secure the debt of another
without the mortgagor assuming personal liability for the debt. Given this point, such a
mortgage satisfies the statute of frauds where
the nature of the obligation is in writing and
the mortgagor signs the document. Gallagher
v. Central Ind. Bank, 448 N.E.2d 304 (Ind.
App. 1983).

Property Delivered to Third Person.
A promise to pay for property purchased by
the promisor, but delivered to another, was
not within the statute. Kernodle v. Caldwell,
46 Ind. 153 (1873); Johnson v. Hoover, 72 Ind.
395 (1880); Wills v. Ross, 77 Ind. 1, 40 Am. R.
279 (1881); Boyce v. Murphy, 91 Ind. 1, 46 Am.
R. 567 (1883); Lance v. Pearce, 101 Ind. 595
(1885); Cox v. Peltier, 159 Ind. 355, 65 N.E. 6
(1902).

A parol promise to pay for goods that were
supplied to another person, on his order, was
within the statute of frauds, and could not be
enforced. Indiana Trust Co. v. Finitzer, 160
Ind. 647, 67 N.E. 520 (1903).

Where plaintiff sued both the promisor and
the persons to whom the goods were delivered, and took judgment against the latter, it
conclusively showed that the party to whom
the goods were delivered was liable primarily,
and that the promisor's agreement was
merely a collateral undertaking. Symons v.
Burton, 83 Ind. App. 631, 149 N.E. 460 (1925).

AGREEMENT IN CONSIDERATION OF MARRIAGE

In General.
A promise made to release a debt in consid-
eration of marriage had to be in writing.
Flenner v. Flenner, 29 Ind. 564 (1868);
Brenner v. Brenner, 48 Ind. 262 (1874); Smith

v. Hunt, 50 Ind. App. 592, 98 N.E. 841 (1912).

A simple contract of marriage was not
within the statute of frauds. Short v. Stotts,
58 Ind. 29 (1877); Caylor v. Roe, 99 Ind. 1
(1884); Vaughan v. Smith, 177 Ind. 111, 96

AGREEMENT IN CONSIDERATION OF
    MARRIAGE (Cont'd)

In General. (Cont'd)
N.E. 594, 1914C Ann. Cas. 1092 (1911).

Antenuptial Contracts.
Antenuptial contracts were not within this clause, but were within the next clause when they related to real estate. Rainbolt v. East, 56 Ind. 538, 26 Am. R. 40 (1877).

Antenuptial contracts in consideration of marriage were within the statute of frauds and had to be in writing. Caylor v. Roe, 99 Ind. 1 (1884); Davis v. Cox, 178 Ind. 486, 99 N.E. 803 (1912).

SALE OF LANDS

In General.

When parol contracts for the sale of lands were executed, they were as valid as if originally in writing. Fisher v. Wilson, 18 Ind. 133 (1862); Huston v. Stewart, 64 Ind. 388 (1878); Hinkle v. Fisher, 104 Ind. 84, 3 N.E. 624 (1885).

Parol contracts for the sale of lands were not void, but there was no remedy for their enforcement. Mather v. Scoles, 35 Ind. 1 (1870); Wills v. Ross, 77 Ind. 1, 40 Am. R. 279 (1881); Day v. Wilson, 83 Ind. 463, 43 Am. R. 76 (1882); Schierman v. Beckett, 88 Ind. 52 (1882).

Vendee could not defeat collection of purchase-money due under a parol contract of sale if the vendor was able and willing to convey the land. Washington Glass Co. v. Mosbaugh, 19 Ind. App. 105, 49 N.E. 178 (1898).

An action would not lie for breach of a verbal contract for the purchase of land. Crumpacker v. Jeffrey, 63 Ind. App. 621, 115 N.E. 62 (1917).

A parol contract for conveyance of real estate was held to come within the inhibition of the statute of frauds. Donnelly v. Fletemeyer, 94 Ind. App. 337, 176 N.E. 868, rehearing denied, 94 Ind. App. 944, 179 N.E. 190 (1931).

This section referred to oral agreements for the sale of real estate which had not been carried out. Sachs v. Blewett, 206 Ind. 151, 185 N.E. 856, 91 A.L.R. 1285 (1933).

Where nothing was done by the parties to an oral agreement to sell real estate to take it out of the inhibition of the statute of frauds, it bound no one. Robrock v. Ditzler, 113 Ind. App. 332, 47 N.E.2d 163 (1943).

In an action for breach of contract to convey real estate, wherein plaintiff specifically pleaded a written contract to convey and attached copy thereof to the complaint and made it a part thereof, any reference to an oral agreement was merely in explanation of her acceptance of a deed conveying less than all the real estate for which she had contracted and to which she was entitled thereunder, and hence the action was on a written agreement, and not an oral one, and was not barred by the statute of frauds. Thompson v. Reising, 114 Ind. App. 456, 51 N.E.2d 488 (1943).

An oral agreement between one of several vendors and a broker whereby such vendor agreed to partially reimburse the broker if he would make up the difference between the offered and asking price for the real estate was not a "contract for the sale of lands" nor a "contract for the payment of commissions," within the meaning of the statute of frauds. Nelson v. Shelley, 114 Ind. App. 530, 52 N.E.2d 849 (1944).

In an action on an oral contract whereby plaintiff was to receive a one-eighth share in oil and gas leasehold estate which he might procure for defendant, an allegation that defendant voluntarily conveyed to plaintiff a one-thirty-second interest in a described lease was insufficient to plead a waiver of the benefit of the statute of frauds, where such averment tended to show an entirely different contract than the one sued on in the complaint. Callihan v. Bander, 117 Ind. App. 467, 73 N.E.2d 360 (1947).

Provision in statute of frauds relating to sale of lands did not affect contract for sale of bowling alley where sale of interest in real estate was not involved. Kavanaugh v. England, 232 Ind. 54, 110 N.E.2d 329 (1953).

The statute of frauds required that a contract for the sale of lands had to be in writing in order to be enforceable. Gates v. Petri, 127 Ind. App. 670, 143 N.E.2d 293 (1957).

A verbal contract for the sale of land was not, in itself, void, the statute merely providing that no action could have been brought upon it. Genda v. Hall, 129 Ind. App. 643, 154 N.E.2d 527 (1958).

A written contract for the sale of real estate did not meet the requirements of the statute of frauds when it described the land involved as "137 acres" in a certain township in a particular county in the state of Indiana and such contract would not have been specifically enforced. Wilson v. Wilson, 134 Ind. App. 655, 1 Ind. Dec. 433, 190 N.E.2d 667 (1963).

Acknowledgment.

Deeds were valid between the parties without an acknowledgment. Hubble v. Wright, 23 Ind. 322 (1864); Mays v. Hedges, 79 Ind. 288 (1881); Bever v. North, 107 Ind. 544, 8 N.E. 576 (1886); Wine v. Woods, 109 Ind. 291, 10 N.E. 399 (1887); Bereolos v. Roth, 74 Ind. App. 100, 124 N.E. 410 (1919).

SALE OF LANDS (Cont'd)

Action Against Real Estate Salesman.

An unsigned purchase agreement was properly admitted in an action by buyers against a salesman since the buyers sought damages for fraud based on certain misrepresentations that the salesman had made concerning the status of title to the land they purchased, and since only the parties to a contract or their privies, which did not include the salesman, may rely on the statute of frauds. Riehle v. Moore, 601 N.E.2d 365 (Ind. App. 1992).

Antenuptial Contracts.

A contract made between a man and woman contemplating marriage, fixing the interest that each would have in the lands of the other upon death, had to be in writing. Rainbolt v. East, 56 Ind. 538, 26 Am. R. 40 (1877).

Auction Sales.

When lands were sold at auction, a memorandum made by the clerk of the sale was sufficient. Hart v. Woods, 7 Blackf. 568 (1845).

Sales of real estate by auction were within the statute of frauds, unless expressly exempted. Sachs v. Blewett, 206 Ind. 151, 185 N.E. 856, 91 A.L.R. 1285 (1933).

The fact that the highest bidder at an auction sale of real estate made bid with no intention of complying therewith did not constitute fraud, warranting recovery of damages after resale of the property at a reduced price, where the bidders' contract to purchase was unenforceable under the statute of frauds. Sachs v. Blewett, 206 Ind. 151, 185 N.E. 856, 91 A.L.R. 1285 (1933).

Boundary Agreements.

An agreement between adjoining landowners as to boundary lines which had the effect of transferring title to land was within the statute of frauds. Fuelling v. Fuesse, 43 Ind. App. 441, 87 N.E. 700 (1909).

Brokerage Agreement.

Where a real estate brokerage agreement clearly conditioned its becoming effective upon written acceptance by the broker, the absence of undisputed evidence that the condition was complied with or waived renders the grant of summary judgment on the contract inappropriate. Merri-Bowl, Inc. v. Hazifotis, 547 N.E.2d 1093 (Ind. App. 1989).

Buildings.

An agreement for the use of a building forming a part of the realty fell within the statute. Brumfield v. Carson, 33 Ind. 94, 5 Am. R. 184 (1870).

Certificate of Sale.

—Contract to Transfer.

A contract for the sale or transfer of a certificate of sale of land, executed by a sheriff, had to be in writing under the statute of frauds. Cox v. Roberts, 25 Ind. App. 252, 57 N.E. 937 (1900).

Conflict of Laws.

A deed conveying real estate in this state had to conform to the law of this state. Bethell v. Bethell, 54 Ind. 428, 23 Am. R. 650 (1876); Fisher v. Parry, 68 Ind. 465 (1879); Robards v. Marley, 80 Ind. 185 (1881); Swank v. Hufnagle, 111 Ind. 453, 12 N.E. 303, 13 N.E. 105 (1887); Cochran v. Benton, 126 Ind. 58, 25 N.E. 870 (1890); Nathan v. Lee, 152 Ind. 232, 52 N.E. 987, 43 L.R.A. 820 (1899); Mauzy v. Flint, 42 Ind. App. 386, 83 N.E. 757 (1908); Sinclair v. Gunzenhauser, 179 Ind. 78, 98 N.E. 37 (1912).

A deed executed in another state, though differing in form from that authorized by statute in this state, could convey to the grantee the title to real estate in this state. Ingram v. Jeffersonville, N.A. & S. Rapid Transit Co., 65 Ind. App. 532, 116 N.E. 12 (1917).

Consideration.

As between the parties, a deed was good without any consideration. Thompson v. Thompson, 9 Ind. 323, 68 Am. Dec. 638 (1857); Randall v. Ghent, 19 Ind. 271 (1862); McCaw v. Burk, 31 Ind. 56 (1869); Aldrich v. Amiss, 178 Ind. 303, 99 N.E. 419 (1912); Wenger v. Clay Tp., 61 Ind. App. 640, 112 N.E. 402 (1916); Keller v. Cox, 67 Ind. App. 381, 118 N.E. 543 (1918).

A statement in a deed that the consideration had been paid could have been contradicted. Lamb v. Donovan, 19 Ind. 40 (1862).

The real consideration of a deed could have been shown by parol though it contradicted the deed. Mather v. Scoles, 35 Ind. 1 (1870); Stearns v. Dubois, 55 Ind. 257 (1876); Levering v. Shockey, 100 Ind. 558 (1885); Hays v. Peck, 107 Ind. 389, 8 N.E. 274 (1886); Nichols, Shepard & Co. v. Burch, 128 Ind. 324, 27 N.E. 737 (1890); Smith v. McClain, 146 Ind. 77, 45 N.E. 41 (1896); Lowry v. Downey, 150 Ind. 364, 50 N.E. 79 (1898); Indianapolis S.R.R. v. Wycoff, 51 Ind. App. 159, 95 N.E. 442 (1911).

Recitals in deeds as to consideration were prima facie evidence of the payment thereof. McConnell v. Citizens' State Bank, 130 Ind. 127, 27 N.E. 616 (1891); Milburn v. Phillips, 136 Ind. 680, 34 N.E. 983 (1893), rehearing overruled, 36 N.E. 360 (1894).

Release by wife of her inchoate interest in land was a good consideration for a conveyance to her. Merchants' & Laborers' Bldg.

SALE OF LANDS (Cont'd)

Consideration. (Cont'd)
Ass'n v. Scanlan, 144 Ind. 11, 42 N.E. 1008 (1896).

Parol evidence as to the consideration could not be received to destroy a deed as an instrument of conveyance. Smith v. McClain, 146 Ind. 77, 45 N.E. 41 (1896); Lowry v. Downey, 150 Ind. 364, 50 N.E. 79 (1898); Burk v. Brown, 58 Ind. App. 410, 108 N.E. 252 (1915).

Though written contracts could not be enlarged or altered by prior or contemporaneous agreements, nevertheless, the consideration mentioned in a deed or mortgage was always open to modification or contradiction by parol testimony. Gemmer v. Hunter, 35 Ind. App. 501, 74 N.E. 586 (1905).

Contingent Remainder.
Livery of seizin not having been required, a contingent remainder did not require a present estate to support it. Rouse v. Paidrick, 221 Ind. 517, 49 N.E.2d 528 (1943).

Contract Dependent upon Vendor Obtaining Title.
If a person made a parol promise to convey land to another when the promisor obtained title to the land, such promise was within the statute of frauds, and an action would not lie for a breach thereof. Mather v. Scoles, 35 Ind. 1 (1870); Boruff v. Hudson, 138 Ind. 280, 37 N.E. 786 (1894); Collins v. Green, 40 Ind. App. 630, 82 N.E. 932 (1907); Meyer v. E.G. Spink Co., 76 Ind. App. 318, 124 N.E. 757 (1919), rehearing overruled, 127 N.E. 455 (Ind. App. 1920).

Contract to Furnish Purchase Price.
A contract to furnish money with which land was to have been purchased and conveyed to a corporation had to be in writing as a "contract for the sale and conveyance of real estate" under this section. Meyer v. E.G. Spink Co., 76 Ind. App. 318, 124 N.E. 757 (1919), rehearing overruled, 127 N.E. 455 (Ind. App. 1920).

Cotenants.
Where two persons purchased property as tenants in common, one furnishing the entire purchase price with a right to a lien on the interest of the other until the payment of such person's share, and after the death of such other person the one furnishing the purchase price brought suit for partition and discharge of the lien, it was no defense that such lien was not in writing as required by this section since there was no contention that the entire purchase price was not advanced as alleged, and it would have been proper for the court to adjust the equities between the cotenants.

Andrews v. Harris, 127 Ind. App. 352, 141 N.E.2d 761 (1957).

Deeds.

—In General.
An instrument that conveyed the title to land was a deed. Reynolds v. Davidson's Adm'r, 27 Ind. 296 (1866).

—Notations.
Where deed contained notation following acknowledgment to effect that, in case of death of grantee, land would revert to named person who had furnished consideration for the property, such notation did not qualify the fee, even if notation was part of the deed. Ferguson v. Mix, 125 Ind. App. 251, 123 N.E.2d 909 (1955).

—Titles.
Titles created by deeds were commonly called record or legal titles, as distinguished from equitable titles, and it was the policy of the law to protect them, and such titles were the highest evidence of ownership and not easily defeated. Sheets v. Stiefel, 117 Ind. App. 584, 74 N.E.2d 921 (1947).

Delivery.
There could have been a delivery of a deed either by actions or by words, but to constitute a delivery, the deed had to pass into the possession or under the control of the grantee, with the consent of the grantor. Dearmond v. Dearmond, 10 Ind. 191 (1858); Berry v. Anderson, 22 Ind. 36 (1864); Somers v. Pumphrey, 24 Ind. 231 (1865); Burkholder v. Casad, 47 Ind. 418 (1874); Stokes v. Anderson, 118 Ind. 533, 21 N.E. 331, 4 L.R.A. 313 (1888); Schaefer v. Purviance, 160 Ind. 63, 66 N.E. 154 (1903); Franklin Ins. Co. v. Feist, 31 Ind. App. 390, 68 N.E. 188 (1903); Indiana Trust Co. v. Byram, 36 Ind. App. 6, 72 N.E. 670 (1904), reh'g denied, 36 Ind. App. 25, 73 N.E. 1094 (1905); Townsend v. Millican, 53 Ind. App. 11, 101 N.E. 112 (1913); Reed v. Robbins, 58 Ind. App. 659, 108 N.E. 780 (1915); Kokomo Trust Co. v. Hiller, 67 Ind. App. 611, 116 N.E. 332 (1917); Petre v. Petre, 69 Ind. App. 57, 121 N.E. 285 (1918); McColley v. Binkley, 69 Ind. App. 352, 121 N.E. 847 (1919).

A deed only took effect from the time of its delivery. Love v. Wells, 25 Ind. 503, 87 Am. Dec. 375 (1865); Tharp v. Jarrell, 66 Ind. 52 (1879); Vaughan v. Godman, 94 Ind. 191 (1883), overruled on other grounds, Bellin v. Bloom, 217 Ind. 656, 28 N.E.2d 53 (1940); Fitzgerald v. Goff, 99 Ind. 28 (1884); Quick v. Milligan, 108 Ind. 419, 9 N.E. 392, 58 Am. Rep. 49 (1886); Rogers v. Eich, 146 Ind. 235, 45 N.E. 93 (1896); McColley v. Binkley, 69 Ind. App. 352, 121 N.E. 847 (1919); Nation v.

SALE OF LANDS (Cont'd)

Delivery. (Cont'd)

Green, 188 Ind. 697, 123 N.E. 163 (1919); Yost v. Miller, 74 Ind. App. 673, 129 N.E. 487 (1921).

Possession by a grantee of a deed was presumptive evidence of its delivery and acceptance. Burkholder v. Casad, 47 Ind. 418 (1874); Vaughan v. Godman, 94 Ind. 191 (1883), overruled on other grounds, Bellin v. Bloom, 217 Ind. 656, 28 N.E.2d 53 (1940); McFall v. McFall, 136 Ind. 622, 36 N.E. 517 (1894); Petre v. Petre, 69 Ind. App. 57, 121 N.E. 285 (1918).

A delivery to one grantee was a delivery to all of the grantees. Stout v. Dunning, 72 Ind. 343 (1880); Henry v. Anderson, 77 Ind. 361 (1881); Tyler's Estate v. Tyler, 15 Ind. App. 132, 41 N.E. 965 (1895).

The use of the word "executed," in connection with the execution of a deed, implied a delivery of the deed. Smith v. James, 131 Ind. 131, 30 N.E. 902 (1892); Pool v. Davis, 135 Ind. 323, 34 N.E. 1130 (1893).

The intention of the grantor was the controlling factor in determining whether or not there had been a delivery of the deed otherwise executed. Osborne v. Eslinger, 155 Ind. 351, 58 N.E. 439, 80 Am. St. 240 (1900); Petre v. Petre, 69 Ind. App. 57, 121 N.E. 285 (1918); McColley v. Binkley, 69 Ind. App. 352, 121 N.E. 847 (1919).

To constitute a delivery of a deed, it was necessary that the grantor should intend to give present effect to the instrument. Osborne v. Eslinger, 155 Ind. 351, 58 N.E. 439, 80 Am. St. 240 (1900); McCord v. Bright, 44 Ind. App. 275, 87 N.E. 654 (1909); Pethtel v. Pethtel, 45 Ind. App. 664, 90 N.E. 102 (1909); Townsend v. Millican, 53 Ind. App. 11, 101 N.E. 112 (1913); Smithson v. Bouse, 67 Ind. App. 66, 118 N.E. 970 (1918); McColley v. Binkley, 69 Ind. App. 352, 121 N.E. 847 (1919).

A deed had to contain words of grant, release, or transfer, showing intent to actually transfer grantor's interest in order to pass title and be valid. Bercot v. Velkoff, 111 Ind. App. 323, 41 N.E.2d 686 (1942).

A deed had to be signed by the grantor, or someone whom he directed to sign for him, or his authorized agent, have been attested and acknowledged in conformity to statutory requirements, and delivered by the grantor to the grantee or to someone in his behalf and accepted by the grantee. Bercot v. Velkoff, 111 Ind. App. 323, 41 N.E.2d 686 (1942).

Delivery by Leaving for Record.

Leaving a deed by the grantor at the recorder's office for record was a sufficient delivery. Mallett v. Page, 8 Ind. 364 (1856); Somers v. Pumphrey, 24 Ind. 231 (1865); Taylor v. McClure, 28 Ind. 39 (1867); Vaughan v.

Godman, 103 Ind. 499, 3 N.E. 257 (1885); Colee v. Colee, 122 Ind. 109, 23 N.E. 687, 17 Am. St. 345 (1889).

Leaving a deed for record by the grantor was presumptive evidence of a delivery, but such presumption could have been rebutted. Fireman's Fund Ins. Co. v. Dunn, 22 Ind. App. 332, 53 N.E. 251 (1899); Franklin Ins. Co. v. Feist, 31 Ind. App. 390, 68 N.E. 188 (1903); Allen v. Powell, 65 Ind. App. 601, 115 N.E. 96 (1917); Petre v. Petre, 69 Ind. App. 57, 121 N.E. 285 (1918); Wainwright Trust Co. v. Stern, 72 Ind. App. 116, 125 N.E. 578 (1920).

Delivery in Escrow.

A deed could have been delivered by the grantor to a third party to be delivered to the grantee on the death of the grantor. Hockett v. Jones, 70 Ind. 227 (1880); Squires v. Summers, 85 Ind. 252 (1882); Owen v. Williams, 114 Ind. 179, 15 N.E. 678 (1882); Smiley v. Smiley, 114 Ind. 258, 16 N.E. 585 (1888); Goodpaster v. Leathers, 123 Ind. 121, 23 N.E. 1090 (1890); Dinwiddie v. Smith, 141 Ind. 318, 40 N.E. 748 (1895); Stout v. Rayl, 146 Ind. 379, 45 N.E. 515 (1896); Osborne v. Eslinger, 155 Ind. 351, 58 N.E. 439, 80 Am. St. 240 (1900); Saint Clair v. Marquell, 161 Ind. 56, 67 N.E. 693 (1903); McCord v. Bright, 44 Ind. App. 275, 87 N.E. 654 (1909); Newman v. Fidler, 177 Ind. 220, 97 N.E. 785 (1912); Kokomo Trust Co. v. Hiller, 67 Ind. App. 611, 116 N.E. 332 (1917); Smithson v. Bouse, 67 Ind. App. 66, 118 N.E. 970 (1918); McColley v. Binkley, 69 Ind. App. 352, 121 N.E. 847 (1919).

Performance of conditions of deed placed in escrow were sufficient to convey title. Chicago, I. & E. Ry. v. Linn, 30 Ind. App. 88, 65 N.E. 552 (1902); Farmers' Mut. Fire Ins. Co. v. Olson, 74 Ind. App. 449, 129 N.E. 234 (1920).

Description of Land.

A deed in general terms conveying all lands of the grantor could have been sufficient. Woods v. Polhemus, 8 Ind. 60 (1856); Symmes v. Brown, 13 Ind. 318 (1859); Barnes v. Bartlett, 47 Ind. 98 (1874); Knowlton v. Dolan, 151 Ind. 79, 51 N.E. 97 (1898).

A conveyance of land on a highway carried with it the fee to the center of the road. Cox v. Louisville, N.A. & C.R.R., 48 Ind. 178 (1874); Warbritton v. Demorett, 129 Ind. 346, 27 N.E. 730, 28 N.E. 613 (1891); Board of Comm'rs v. Indianapolis Natural Gas Co., 134 Ind. 209, 33 N.E. 972 (1893); Western Union Tel. Co. v. Krueger, 36 Ind. App. 348, 74 N.E. 25 (1905); Brackney v. Boyd, 71 Ind. App. 592, 123 N.E. 695, 125 N.E. 238 (1919).

The description of land in a deed was sufficient if it furnished the means by which the land could have been identified. Rucker v. Steelman, 73 Ind. 396 (1881); Scheible v. Slagle, 89 Ind. 323 (1883); Trentman v. Neff,

SALE OF LANDS (Cont'd)

Description of Land. (Cont'd)
124 Ind. 503, 24 N.E. 895 (1890); Thain v. Rudisill, 126 Ind. 272, 26 N.E. 46 (1890); Edens v. Miller, 147 Ind. 208, 46 N.E. 526 (1897); Griffin v. Durfee, 29 Ind. App. 211, 64 N.E. 237 (1902); Maris v. Masters, 31 Ind. App. 235, 67 N.E. 699 (1903); Elsea v. Adkins, 164 Ind. 580, 74 N.E. 242, 108 Am. St. R. 320 (1905); Warner v. Marshall, 166 Ind. 88, 75 N.E. 582 (1905); Pilliod v. Angola Ry. & Power Co., 46 Ind. App. 719, 91 N.E. 829 (1910); Ault v. Clark, 62 Ind. App. 55, 112 N.E. 843 (1916); Koons v. Burkhart, 68 Ind. App. 30, 119 N.E. 820 (1918).

Possession taken under a written lease that did not sufficiently describe the lands leased, and the making of lasting and valuable improvements thereon, were sufficient to take the lease out of the operation of the statute of frauds. Weaver v. Shipley, 127 Ind. 526, 27 N.E. 146 (1891); Maris v. Masters, 31 Ind. App. 235, 67 N.E. 699 (1903).

Where a deed specified a certain number of acres to be taken off a certain side of a larger tract of land, it would have been construed to mean that parallel lines had to fix the boundaries without mentioning them. Collins v. Dresslar, 133 Ind. 290, 32 N.E. 883 (1892); Koons v. Burkhart, 68 Ind. App. 30, 119 N.E. 820 (1918).

Where the township and range were given, but not the county and state, the court took judicial knowledge as to the latter, for purposes of land description in contract for sale and conveyance of the same. Tewksbury v. Howard, 138 Ind. 103, 37 N.E. 355 (1894); Columbian Oil Co. v. Blake, 13 Ind. App. 680, 42 N.E. 234 (1895), overruled on other grounds, Shirk v. Stafford, 31 Ind. App. 247, 67 N.E. 542 (1903).

If there was no sufficient description of land in a deed, it would have been void for uncertainty. Wilson v. Johnson, 145 Ind. 40, 38 N.E. 38, 43 N.E. 930 (1894); Edens v. Miller, 147 Ind. 208, 46 N.E. 526 (1897).

Parol evidence could have been received to complete a description and identify property covered by a contract of sale where the description given was consistent, but incomplete, but would not have been received where such completion would have required a contradiction or alteration of the description given or the introduction of a new one. McKenna v. Smith, 77 Ind. App. 372, 133 N.E. 510 (1922); Dowd v. Andrews, 77 Ind. App. 627, 134 N.E. 294 (1922); Neal v. Baker, 198 Ind. 393, 153 N.E. 768 (1926).

In an action for breach of contract for exchange of land which was incompletely described, it was not necessary to the sufficiency of the complaint that it have alleged that defendant owned but one tract of land which would answer to the description contained in the contract, as the ownership of other land would have been a matter of defense. Dowd v. Andrews, 77 Ind. App. 627, 134 N.E. 294 (1922).

A description of the land as "part of the west half of the northeast quarter of section 26, 12, 3 containing 43.62 acres, more or less" was too indefinite and uncertain to make the contract a sufficient memorandum under the statute. Thompson v. Griffith, 79 Ind. App. 60, 133 N.E. 596 (1922).

Where legal description was omitted from contract for sale of realty, it was void for insufficiency, and complaint for reformation which inserted description based on monuments to be established did not make description sufficient to allow specific performance of contract. Cripe v. Coates, 124 Ind. App. 246, 116 N.E.2d 642 (1954).

Designation of Grantee.
Deeds had to contain words of conveyance and name a grantee in existence at the time of the execution of the deed. Harriman v. Southam, 16 Ind. 190 (1861), overruled on other grounds, Snyder v. Studebaker, 19 Ind. 462 (1862); Davis v. Davis, 43 Ind. 561 (1872); Glass v. Glass, 71 Ind. 392 (1880); Hummelman v. Mounts, 87 Ind. 178 (1882); Lyles v. Lescher, 108 Ind. 382, 9 N.E. 365 (1886).

Deeds to heirs of living persons without naming the heirs conveyed no title. Winslow v. Winslow, 52 Ind. 8 (1875); Outland v. Bowen, 115 Ind. 150, 17 N.E. 281, 7 Am. St. 420 (1888); Booker v. Tarwater, 138 Ind. 385, 37 N.E. 979 (1894); Shoe v. Heckley, 78 Ind. App. 586, 134 N.E. 214 (1922).

If a deed so described the grantee that he could have been identified, it was sufficient. Hoover v. Malen, 83 Ind. 195 (1882).

Where the word "heirs" was used in a deed or contract for the conveyance of land, coupled with other explanatory words, the courts would give to it a construction conforming to the manifest purpose of the parties. Stevens v. Flannagan, 131 Ind. 122, 30 N.E. 898 (1892); Essick v. Caple, 131 Ind. 207, 30 N.E. 900 (1892); Tinder v. Tinder, 131 Ind. 381, 30 N.E. 1077 (1892); Booker v. Tarwater, 138 Ind. 385, 37 N.E. 979 (1894); Griffin v. Ulen, 139 Ind. 565, 39 N.E. 254 (1894); Granger v. Granger, 147 Ind. 95, 44 N.E. 189 (1896), rehearing overruled, 147 Ind. 101, 46 N.E. 80, 36 L.R.A. 186, 190 (1897); Moore v. Gary, 149 Ind. 51, 48 N.E. 630 (1897); Lamb v. Medsker, 35 Ind. App. 662, 74 N.E. 1012 (1905); Miller v. Harland, 78 Ind. App. 56, 130 N.E. 134 (1921).

Destruction of Deed.
A party could not prove in support of his title the contents of a deed which had been destroyed by his own voluntary act or con-

SALE OF LANDS (Cont'd)

Destruction of Deed. (Cont'd)
sent. Speer v. Speer, 7 Ind. 178, 63 Am. Dec. 418 (1855); Schaeffer v. Fithian, 17 Ind. 463 (1861); Old Nat'l Bank v. Findley, 131 Ind. 225, 31 N.E. 62 (1892); Gibbs v. Potter, 166 Ind. 471, 77 N.E. 942 (1906).

Devises.
A contract to devise lands had to be in writing. Wallace v. Long, 105 Ind. 522, 5 N.E. 666, 55 Am. R. 222 (1886); Schoonover v. Vachon, 121 Ind. 3, 22 N.E. 777 (1889).

Parol promise by a devisee to a testator to convey land to another was within the statute. Orth v. Orth, 145 Ind. 184, 42 N.E. 277 (1895), reh'g overruled, 145 Ind. 206, 44 N.E. 17, 32 L.R.A. 298, 57 Am. St. R. 185 (1896).

Part performance by promisee on parol promise to devise land took case out of the statute of frauds. Horner v. Clark, 27 Ind. App. 6, 60 N.E. 732 (1901); Horner v. McConnell, 158 Ind. 280, 63 N.E. 472 (1902).

The statute of frauds did not apply to an oral agreement to devise land in consideration of the devisee excluding notes payable to third persons when the devise was made and the devisee took possession of the land after the death of the testator. Ballard v. Camplin, 161 Ind. 16, 67 N.E. 505 (1903).

A decedent's oral contract to execute a will making claimant against his estate his legatee was within the statute of frauds, but where consideration was services, recovery could have been had on quantum meruit. Hensley v. Hilton, 191 Ind. 309, 131 N.E. 38 (1921).

In an action against a decedent's estate to recover for services rendered upon decedent's parol contract to convey land in consideration of such services, recovery could have been had upon a quantum meruit for services rendered pursuant to such contract, regardless of whether plaintiff fully performed all services specified therein. Miller v. Kifer, 75 Ind. App. 198, 130 N.E. 278 (1921).

In a devisee's action to quiet title to real estate, by decedent's wife, contested by decedent's daughter claiming under an oral agreement with the decedent, to give the real estate to the daughter if she and her husband would move onto the farm and improve it, which they did, and lived on the farm for 15 years until after the decedent's death, the daughter's claim was not precluded as a collateral attack on the will, where the decedent reserved only a life estate in the real estate. Ault v. Miller, 203 Ind. 487, 181 N.E. 35 (1932).

Verbal agreement embracing the promise to devise by will was within the statute of frauds and was not enforceable. Hurd v. Ball, 128 Ind. App. 278, 143 N.E.2d 458 (1957), transfer denied, 237 Ind. 665, 148 N.E.2d 194 (1958).

Suit on an oral contract to make a will devising real property in consideration of forbearance on the part of plaintiff to claim a one-half interest in the personal estate of the father and permitting such person to reside rent free on property in which plaintiff had an interest was barred by the statute of frauds where there was no taking of possession by plaintiff of the property involved in the contract during the lifetime of the deceased. Genda v. Hall, 129 Ind. App. 643, 154 N.E.2d 527 (1958).

A contract to devise land had to be in writing. Genda v. Hall, 129 Ind. App. 643, 154 N.E.2d 527 (1958).

Oral contract to devise and bequeath real estate and personal property was within the fourth section of the statute of frauds. Robison v. Page, 129 Ind. App. 289, 156 N.E.2d 389 (1959).

Where plaintiff went to live with the decedent on alleged oral contract that decedent would bequeath all her property to plaintiff, and deceased remained in possession of the real estate until her death, plaintiff did not take possession of the real estate in question so as to remove the alleged oral contract from the operation of the statute of frauds. Robison v. Page, 129 Ind. App. 289, 156 N.E.2d 389 (1959).

Disposition of Property Not Covered by Divorce Decree.
Where parties orally agreed as to disposition of property which was not covered by divorce decree, a letter written by wife to husband's parents that farm was to go to children when husband died, but not stating that she would transfer her interest in farm to husband, was not sufficient to remove agreement from statute of frauds. Blake v. Hosford, 180 Ind. App. 175, 68 Ind. Dec. 458, 387 N.E.2d 1335 (1979).

Easements.
An oral promise to grant an easement in lands was within the statute of frauds. Richter v. Irwin, 28 Ind. 26 (1867).

Easements are interests in land and, with the exception of prescriptive easements, contracts to grant or reserve easements are subject to the requirements of the statute of frauds. This general rule, however, does not apply when an easement is created by a deed which the grantee does not sign. Chase v. Nelson, 507 N.E.2d 640 (Ind. App. 1987).

Estoppel.
A conveyance executed by a married woman could not be avoided by her after her husband's death on the ground that she had executed it under a misapprehension of her

SALE OF LANDS (Cont'd)

Estoppel. (Cont'd)
legal rights, since an acknowledgment before a magistrate of the conveyance estopped her. McNelly v. Rucker, 6 Blackf. 391 (1843).

Evidence.
Where the court, as a furtherance of the pretrial conference, determined to hear evidence as to the nature and value of such property devised and bequeathed by decedent's will for the purpose of determining the presented legal question as to the application of the statute of frauds, it was not an abuse of discretion of the court. Hurd v. Ball, 128 Ind. App. 278, 143 N.E.2d 458 (1957), transfer denied, 237 Ind. 665, 148 N.E.2d 194 (1958).

Where defendant sought to prove parol contract for sale of land, had shown possession of land and improvements by defendant, verdict for defendant was improper where answers of the jury to interrogatories showed that there was no proof to show whether the possession of the land was before or after the parol contract and that there was no proof of the terms of the contract. Otterman v. Hollingsworth, 140 Ind. App. 281, 7 Ind. Dec. 603, 214 N.E.2d 189 (1966).

—Evidence of Ownership.
Titles to property granted by deeds in the form required by statute are the best evidence of ownership of real property. Viccaro v. City of Fort Wayne, 449 N.E.2d 1161 (Ind. App. 1983).

Foreign Contracts.
Foreign contracts void under the law at the place of execution could not be enforced in this state. Cochran v. Ward, 5 Ind. App. 89, 29 N.E. 795, 31 N.E. 581, 51 Am. St. R. 229 (1892).

Grantor's Signature.
The signing of a deed by the Christian name alone could have been a sufficient execution when the surname of the grantor was otherwise shown. Zann v. Haller, 71 Ind. 136, 36 Am. R. 193 (1880).

Where the grantor's name was signed to a deed by some other person at the grantor's request, the signing was a sufficient subscribing within the meaning of the statute. Ashwell v. Miller, 54 Ind. App. 381, 103 N.E. 37 (1913).

Leases.
If a lease is made for a term certain, with the privilege of another term, and both terms exceed three years, the latter term would have been within the statute. Schmitz v. Lauferty, 29 Ind. 400 (1868).

A lease for more than three years had to be in writing. Schmitz v. Lauferty, 29 Ind. 400 (1868); Railsback v. Walke, 81 Ind. 409 (1882); Nash v. Berkmeir, 83 Ind. 536 (1882); Heller v. Dailey, 28 Ind. App. 555, 63 N.E. 490 (1902); Remm v. Landon, 43 Ind. App. 91, 86 N.E. 973 (1909); Soroka v. Knott, 90 Ind. App. 649, 168 N.E. 703 (1929).

A parol lease of lands for more than three years when possession was taken would constitute a tenancy from year to year. Railsback v. Walke, 81 Ind. 409 (1882); Nash v. Berkmeir, 83 Ind. 536 (1882).

Parol leases of lands not exceeding three years were not within the statute of frauds. Lowman v. Sheets, 124 Ind. 416, 24 N.E. 351, 7 L.R.A. 784 (1890).

Under this section, a verbal agreement for a lease of realty, with the privilege of renewal for 15 years, was void. Ramer v. State, 190 Ind. 124, 128 N.E. 440 (1920).

A written contract, which might have been made by parol, could have been modified by a parol agreement, if the modification was based upon a valuable consideration, and this rule was applicable to written leases for a term not exceeding three years. Anderson v. Miller, 76 Ind. App. 681, 133 N.E. 29 (1921).

A list of descriptions clipped to the back of an executed lease could have been sufficient to identify the lands intended to be leased in a suit by the lessor for the cancellation of the lease. Maier v. Continental Oil Co., 120 F.2d 237 (7th Cir.), cert. denied, 314 U.S. 652, 62 S. Ct. 101, 86 L. Ed. 523 (1941).

In an action for the possession of real estate, wherein plaintiffs claimed possession by virtue of a deed to them by defendants which recited that possession should be given on a named date, an alleged oral agreement, made prior to the execution of the deed, that possession of the real estate was to be conferred upon defendants so long as plaintiff should own it, was not enforceable as a lease for a term not exceeding three years, as an exception to the statute of frauds and the statute of conveyance requiring conveyances of interests in land to be in writing, since in order to come within the exception, it must have affirmatively appeared that the term of the lease did not exceed three years. Guckenberger v. Shank, 110 Ind. App. 442, 37 N.E.2d 708 (1941).

Married Women.
A promise made to a married woman to convey to her a tract of land in consideration of her joining in a conveyance of the lands of her husband was within the statute. Green v. Groves, 109 Ind. 519, 10 N.E. 401 (1887).

A parol contract of a married woman for the sale of lands could not have been taken out of the statute by part performance. Percifield v. Black, 132 Ind. 384, 31 N.E. 955 (1892).

The contract of a married woman for the

SALE OF LANDS (Cont'd)

Married Women. (Cont'd)
sale of her lands could not have been enforced unless such contract was signed by her husband. Knepper v. Eggiman, 177 Ind. 56, 97 N.E. 161 (1912).

A married woman could execute a valid lease for a greater period than three years without her husband joining therein. Spiro v. Robertson, 57 Ind. App. 229, 106 N.E. 726 (1914).

Mistake.
Where there had been an agreement actually entered into which the parties had attempted to put in writing but failed to do so because of a mistake either of themselves or of the scrivener, courts having jurisdiction in matters of equitable cognizance had power to reform the instrument in such manner as to make it express the true agreement. Cripe v. Coates, 124 Ind. App. 246, 116 N.E.2d 642 (1954).

Mortgages.
An agreement to execute a mortgage on lands had to be in writing. Irwin v. Hubbard, 49 Ind. 350, 19 Am. R. 679 (1874).

Notes Secured by Purchase Money Mortgage.
Where a vendor of land took the purchaser's notes secured by mortgage, as part of the purchase price, the parties by subsequent parol agreement could modify the obligation represented by the notes. McCoun v. Shipman, 75 Ind. App. 212, 128 N.E. 683 (1920).

Oil and Gas.
Contracts for the sale of all the oil and gas in land had to be in writing. Heller v. Dailey, 28 Ind. App. 555, 63 N.E. 490 (1902).

The grant of all the gas and oil in and under a tract of land was a grant of an interest in the land and had to be in writing. Heller v. Dailey, 28 Ind. App. 555, 63 N.E. 490 (1902); Johnson v. Sidey, 59 Ind. App. 678, 109 N.E. 934 (1915); Wenger v. Clay Tp., 61 Ind. App. 640, 112 N.E. 402 (1916).

Oil and gas leasehold estates were within the statute of frauds. Callihan v. Bander, 117 Ind. App. 467, 73 N.E.2d 360 (1947).

Parol Modification.
If a written contract for the sale of land required payment therefor to be made in money, an oral agreement to accept lands in payment could not have been enforced. Bradley v. Harter, 156 Ind. 499, 60 N.E. 139 (1901); McCoy v. McCoy, 32 Ind. App. 38, 69 N.E. 193, 102 Am. St. R. 223 (1903).

If a contract concerning land was required

to be in writing, the surrender of any right or release of liability under such a contract must also have been in writing. Heller v. Dailey, 28 Ind. App. 555, 63 N.E. 490 (1902).

Contracts for the sale of land could not be altered or modified by parol agreement, and thereafter, as so modified, enforced. Hetrick v. Ashburn, 86 Ind. App. 496, 142 N.E. 386 (1924).

An oral agreement for the extension of time for the payment of an instalment of the purchase price of real estate was ineffective to change the written agreement by accelerating the time for future payments. Nagdeman v. Cawley, 89 Ind. App. 196, 162 N.E. 68 (1928).

Where a dispute arose as to the rate of interest to be paid on promissory notes secured by mortgage, and the parties orally agreed upon a rate of interest less than that named in the notes and mortgage, and the makers carried out such oral agreement by paying the rate of interest agreed upon until all the principal and interest called for by the notes and such oral agreement were fully paid, such performance took the oral agreement out of the statute of frauds. Purity Maid Prods. Co. v. American Bank & Trust Co., 105 Ind. App. 541, 14 N.E.2d 755 (1938).

A contract in writing, which left some essential term thereof to be shown by parol, was only a parol contract, and was therefore not enforceable under the statute of frauds. Sheldmyer v. Bias, 112 Ind. App. 522, 45 N.E.2d 347 (1942).

In an action based upon a parol contract for conveyance of real estate, wherein a letter containing a promise to give a deed was introduced in evidence, but did not constitute a sufficient memorandum of the agreement to take it out of the statute of frauds, parol evidence was not admissible to show the consideration for the promise to give a deed, since parol evidence could have been used only to apply such a contract to its subject-matter, or to explain latent ambiguities, but to supply facts to show the circumstances of the contract, or to supply any of its essential terms. Sheldmyer v. Bias, 112 Ind. App. 522, 45 N.E.2d 347 (1942).

An oral agreement extending the terms of a written lease which gave an option to lessor to purchase and retain a boiler installed by lessees to a month-to-month basis was not in contravention of this section, nor of § 33-105 (since repealed; see now IC 26-1-2-201) relating to contracts for the sale of personal property of the value of more than $500, for the reason that an option to purchase goods was not a contract within the meaning of such sections. Calwell v. Bankers Trust Co., 113 Ind. App. 345, 47 N.E.2d 170 (1943).

Where a contract was required by law to be in writing, it could only be modified by a

SALE OF LANDS (Cont'd)

Parol Modification. (Cont'd)
written instrument. Gates v. Petri, 127 Ind. App. 670, 143 N.E.2d 293 (1957).

An instruction which instructed as a matter of law that a written agreement could be changed or modified by a subsequent oral agreement upon sufficient consideration was an erroneous misstatement of the law relating to agreements concerning the sale of lands in Indiana. Gates v. Petri, 127 Ind. App. 670, 143 N.E.2d 293 (1957).

Part Performance.

—In General.
Parol contracts for the sale of lands could not be enforced when there was not such a part performance as would take the same out of the statute of frauds. Thompson v. Elliott, 28 Ind. 55 (1867); Cuppy v. Hixon, 29 Ind. 522 (1868); Parker v. Heaton, 55 Ind. 1 (1876); Carlisle v. Brennan, 67 Ind. 12 (1879); Rucker v. Steelman, 73 Ind. 396 (1881); Switzer v. Hauk, 89 Ind. 73 (1883); Jackson v. Myers, 120 Ind. 504, 22 N.E. 90, 23 N.E. 86 (1889).

A parol agreement that in consideration of the surrender by the natural parent of child to have been adopted by another, such adopted child would inherit land, was within the statute of frauds, and was not taken out by performance on the part of the child by living with the adopted parents in conformity with the agreement. Wright v. Green, 67 Ind. App. 433, 119 N.E. 379 (1918).

Where an oral agreement between the parties to a contract, modifying the same, had been so far complied with by one side, as to cause noncompliance by the other side to operate as a fraud on the party complying, the statute of frauds did not apply. Purity Maid Prods. Co. v. American Bank & Trust Co., 105 Ind. App. 541, 14 N.E.2d 755 (1938).

Actual, open, and exclusive possession of real estate purchased under an oral contract was not essential requirement in all cases, in order to warrant a decree for specific performance of the contract. Brown v. Freudenberg, 106 Ind. App. 692, 17 N.E.2d 865 (1938).

In order to take a parol contract for the sale of real estate out of the statute of frauds, it must have been shown, among other things, that the purchaser went into possession under the contract of sale. Brown v. Freudenberg, 106 Ind. App. 692, 17 N.E.2d 865 (1938).

Where the purchaser of real estate which the vendor agreed to convey to the purchaser in consideration of the rendition of personal services by the purchaser to the vendor, if the grantee took such possession of the property as was consistent with the existing conditions imposed by the contract, and the contract was

fully performed, specific performance should not have been denied for the sole reason that the possession taken was not exclusive. Brown v. Freudenberg, 106 Ind. App. 692, 17 N.E.2d 865 (1938).

An oral contract by an aunt to convey certain real estate on which she was residing to a niece, if the niece and family would move into the premises with her and take care of the real estate and of the aunt, the possession of the real estate by the niece and family jointly with the aunt and exclusive possession for a considerable time after the marriage of the aunt and her residence in another state, and until her death, was held sufficient to take the oral contract out of the statute of frauds, notwithstanding the niece and family were temporarily out of possession for a while with the consent of the aunt, but subsequently resumed possession. Brown v. Freudenberg, 106 Ind. App. 692, 17 N.E.2d 865 (1938).

So long as an oral contract to convey real estate in consideration of the rendition of personal services by the purchaser remained executory, the court would refuse to decree a specific performance of the contract. Brown v. Freudenberg, 106 Ind. App. 692, 17 N.E.2d 865 (1938).

Before possession of real estate could have been considered as part performance of a contract sufficient to take it out of the operation of the statute of frauds, it had to be clearly shown that the possession relied upon was in consequence of the contract. Guckenberger v. Shank, 110 Ind. App. 442, 37 N.E.2d 708 (1941).

Where real estate was conveyed by warranty deed which contained an express stipulation that the grantees should have possession on a named date, and an alleged oral contract to the effect that possession was to be conferred upon the grantees so long as the grantors should continue to own it, the contract was unenforceable under the statute of frauds, as there was no part performance on the part of the grantors in remaining in possession after the date specified in the deed as to take the case out of the operation of such statute and render it a tenancy from year to year, since their continuation in possession was not in consequence of any contract. Guckenberger v. Shank, 110 Ind. App. 442, 37 N.E.2d 708 (1941).

A parol agreement for conveyance of real estate could not be specifically enforced, nor could it be the foundation of an action for damages, where the complaint contained no allegation concerning the value of services performed by plaintiff, and it did not allege any facts such as the taking of possession of the real estate that would constitute part performance sufficient to withdraw the agreement from the operation of the statute of

SALE OF LANDS (Cont'd)

Part Performance. (Cont'd)

—In General. (Cont'd)
frauds. Sheldmyer v. Bias, 112 Ind. App. 522, 45 N.E.2d 347 (1942).

In an action on an oral contract whereby plaintiff was to receive a one-eighth share in oil and gas leasehold estates which he might procure for defendant, an allegation subsequent to the acquisition of interests in certain leasehold estates defendant entered upon them and took possession of same, for and on his own behalf, individually, and as trustee for plaintiff, to the extent of plaintiff's one-eighth interest therein, was not an averment of such facts as to part performance as to remove the contract from the operation of the statute of frauds. Callihan v. Bander, 117 Ind. App. 467, 73 N.E.2d 360 (1947).

Not every act of part performance would move a court of equity, though legal remedies were inadequate, to enforce an oral agreement affecting rights in land. Hurd v. Ball, 128 Ind. App. 278, 143 N.E.2d 458 (1957), transfer denied, 237 Ind. 665, 148 N.E.2d 194 (1958).

A verbal contract for the sale of land may be removed from the operation of the statute of frauds by the doctrine of part performance, and whether there was performance sufficient to invoke this doctrine is a question which requires of the circumstances of each case. Young v. Bryan, 178 Ind. App. 702, 59 Ind. Dec. 133, 368 N.E.2d 1, 368 N.E.2d 3 (1977).

Acceptance of check (not cashed), standing alone, is not sufficient to show part performance so as to take contract out of the statute of frauds. DuPont Feedmill Corp. v. Standard Supply Corp., 182 Ind. App. 459, 72 Ind. Dec. 84, 395 N.E.2d 808 (1979).

—Payment of Purchase Price.
Payment of purchase-money alone would not take a parol contract for the sale of lands out of the statute of frauds. Mather v. Scoles, 35 Ind. 1 (1870); Suman v. Springate, 67 Ind. 115 (1879); Green v. Groves, 109 Ind. 519, 10 N.E. 401 (1887).

Payment of the purchase price was not sufficient part performance to take out of the operation of the statute of frauds an oral contract for the sale of land. King v. Hartley, 71 Ind. App. 1, 123 N.E. 728 (1919).

Purchaser's payment of the purchase price, standing alone, is insufficient to remove a case from the statute of frauds as part performance of the contract. Lux v. Schroeder, 645 N.E.2d 1114 (Ind. App. 1995).

—Possession and Improvements.
Possession had to be taken under and by virtue of the contract, as a continuance of possession had when the contract as made was not sufficient. Johnston v. Glancy, 4 Blackf. 94, 28 Am. Dec. 45 (1835); Carlisle v. Brennan, 67 Ind. 12 (1879); Green v. Groves, 109 Ind. 519, 10 N.E. 401 (1887); Swales v. Jackson, 126 Ind. 282, 26 N.E. 62 (1890); Waymire v. Waymire, 141 Ind. 164, 40 N.E. 523 (1895); Riley v. Haworth, 30 Ind. App. 377, 64 N.E. 928 (1902).

An entry into possession of lands, payment of the purchase-money, and the making of improvements under a parol contract of purchase, took the contract out of the statute of frauds. Atkinson v. Jackson, 8 Ind. 31 (1856); Stater v. Hill, 10 Ind. 176 (1858); Watson v. Mahan, 20 Ind. 223 (1863); Hixon v. Cuppy, 33 Ind. 210 (1870); Law v. Henry, 39 Ind. 414 (1872); Haddon v. Haddon, 42 Ind. 378 (1873); Fall v. Hazelrigg, 45 Ind. 576, 15 Am. R. 278 (1874); Lafollett v. Kyle, 51 Ind. 446 (1875); Mauck v. Melton, 64 Ind. 414 (1878); Barnes v. Union Sch. Tp., 91 Ind. 301 (1883); O'Brien v. Knotts, 165 Ind. 308, 75 N.E. 594 (1905); McFarland v. Stansifer, 36 Ind. App. 486, 76 N.E. 124 (1905); Timmonds v. Taylor, 48 Ind. App. 531, 96 N.E. 331 (1911).

Where entry for purposes of inspection was cursory and the taking of possession quite limited, possession was not taken under the contract nor with the vendor's consent and there was no right of recovery of the purchase price. Barnett v. Washington Glass Co., 12 Ind. App. 631, 40 N.E. 1102 (1895).

An action would lie to compel the execution of a lease for more than three years under an oral agreement to execute the lease where the lessee had taken possession of the leased premises and had expended money on the faith of such agreement. Saint Joseph Hydraulic Co. v. Globe Tissue Paper Co., 156 Ind. 665, 59 N.E. 995 (1901).

Where a tenant in common in possession of land orally agreed to purchase the interest of a cotenant, the mere fact that he remained in possession was insufficient to take the case out of the statute of frauds. King v. Hartley, 71 Ind. App. 1, 123 N.E. 728 (1919).

Where a father orally agreed to grant his son the use and possession of a farm during grantor's life on condition that the son dispose of his business and move upon the farm, make improvements, and furnish the father a home, the taking possession of the farm by the son pursuant to the contract, and the making of valuable improvements with the father's knowledge and consent, was sufficient part performance to take the case out of the statute of frauds. Hoppes v. Hoppes, 190 Ind. 166, 129 N.E. 629 (1921).

In an action by the wife of decedent to quiet title to real estate devised to the wife by decedent, but claimed by decedent's daughter under an oral agreement with decedent that if she and her husband would move onto the

SALE OF LANDS (Cont'd)

Part Performance. (Cont'd)

**—Possession and
Improvements.** (Cont'd)
farm and improve it he would give the land to
the daughter, and they did move onto it and
improved it and lived thereon for 15 years
until after decedent's death, the fact that the
daughter's husband occupied the realty under
a lease from plaintiff would not prevent the
daughter from claiming it. Ault v. Miller, 203
Ind. 487, 181 N.E. 35 (1932).

Pleading.
Agreements to purchase land had to be
presumed oral and within the statute of
frauds, in the absence of contrary allegation
in the pleading. McKenna v. Smith, 77 Ind.
App. 372, 133 N.E. 510 (1922); Sachs v.
Blewett, 206 Ind. 151, 185 N.E. 856, 188 N.E.
674 (1933).

Possession.
In order that an oral agreement to convey
real estate in return for personal services
rendered in caring for the grantor on the
premises be taken out of the statute of frauds,
only such possession need have been taken as
was consistent with the existing conditions
and circumstances imposed by the contract.
Jackson v. First Nat'l Bank & Trust Co., 115
Ind. App. 313, 57 N.E.2d 946 (1944).
In order that an oral agreement to convey
real estate be taken out of the statute of
frauds where the one claiming ownership was
not already in possession at the time of its
execution, possession must have been taken
under and pursuant to its provisions, but the
possession need not always have been exclusive. Jackson v. First Nat'l Bank & Trust Co.,
115 Ind. App. 313, 57 N.E.2d 946 (1944).

Promissory Estoppel.
If the only "injustice" identified by plaintiff
was defendant's refusal to abide by the terms
of an oral agreement to convey real estate,
such could not constitute the requisite "injustice" necessary to invoke the doctrine of promissory estoppel. Lux v. Schroeder, 645 N.E.2d
1114 (Ind. App. 1995).
Defendant's oral promise that if plaintiff
were to move back to Indiana, she would
"always have the 135 house" did not constitute a contract for the sale of land, therefore,
the statute of frauds did not apply. Brown v.
Branch, 733 N.E.2d 17 (Ind. App. 2000).

—Detrimental Reliance.
Although a boyfriend's oral promise to give
his real property to his girlfriend fell within
Statute of Frauds, the girlfriend did not show
promissory reliance resulting in infliction of

injury or loss sufficient to remove promise
from the statute's operation. Brown v. Branch,
758 N.E.2d 48 (Ind. 2001).

Reconveyances.
No authority exists for the proposition that
an agreement to reconvey real estate is not a
contract for the sale of land subject to the
statute of frauds. Lux v. Schroeder, 645
N.E.2d 1114 (Ind. App. 1995).

Record Titles.
Titles granted in the manner prescribed
herein were called record or legal titles, as
distinguished from equitable titles and it was
the policy of the law to protect them. Record
titles were the highest evidence of ownership.
Hughes v. Cook, 126 Ind. App. 103, 130
N.E.2d 330 (1955).

Restrictions in Deed.
Restrictions in a deed accepted by the
grantee satisfied the statute of frauds and
imposed the undertakings in the deed upon
the grantees. Brendonwood Common v.
Franklin, 76 Ind. Dec. 37, 403 N.E.2d 1136
(Ind. App. 1980).

Right of Possession.
Any contract which sought to confer the
right to possession of real estate was one
which sought to convey an interest in land
and was required to be in writing.
Guckenberger v. Shank, 110 Ind. App. 442, 37
N.E.2d 708 (1941).
Where owners of adjoining lots entered into
an oral agreement whereby the boundary
lines of the lots, which were not in dispute,
were changed, and in accordance therewith
caused a replat of the lots to be made and
recorded, such agreement was insufficient to
change the boundary lines so as to make the
owners of the lots owners as shown by the
replat, in the absence of any deeds or conveyances between the lot owners in connection
with such replatting. Bercot v. Velkoff, 111
Ind. App. 323, 41 N.E.2d 686 (1942).

Sand, Gravel, and Soil.
The execution of a contract in the form of a
deed, duly signed, acknowledged, and recorded, granting to a party a perpetual right
to take and remove from certain described
land sand, gravel, and soil, was a conveyance
of an interest in the land. Wenger v. Clay Tp.,
61 Ind. App. 640, 112 N.E. 402 (1916).

Services as Consideration.
Parol promises to convey lands in consideration of the performance of services fell
within the statute. Hershman v. Pascal, 4 Ind.
App. 330, 30 N.E. 932 (1892); Smith v. Lotton,
5 Ind. App. 177, 31 N.E. 816 (1892).

SALE OF LANDS (Cont'd)

Sufficiency of Memorandum.

A receipt acknowledging the receipt of the purchase-money was not a sufficient memorandum. Patterson v. Underwood, 29 Ind. 607 (1868); Wilstach v. Heyd, 122 Ind. 574, 23 N.E. 963 (1890).

A memorandum made by a sheriff on the sale of lands had to be signed by him in order to take the sale out of the statute of frauds. Ruckle v. Barbour, 48 Ind. 274 (1874).

A memorandum in reference to the sale of lands had to set out the contract with such certainty that its terms could have been understood from the writing itself. Ridgway v. Ingram, 50 Ind. 145, 19 Am. R. 706 (1874); Lee v. Hills, 66 Ind. 474 (1879); Wilstach v. Heyd, 122 Ind. 574, 23 N.E. 963 (1890); Briggs v. Watson, 80 Ind. App. 529, 139 N.E. 197 (1923).

City council accepting oral offer to sell land, and verbal acceptance of proposition of city to buy, did not constitute a written contract. Carskaddon v. City of South Bend, 141 Ind. 596, 39 N.E. 667, 41 N.E. 1 (1895).

If a contract for the sale of land was signed by the landowner, and was delivered to and accepted by the other party, such contract was binding although not signed by the purchaser. Burke v. Mead, 159 Ind. 252, 64 N.E. 880 (1902); Doxey's Estate v. Service, 30 Ind. App. 174, 65 N.E. 757 (1902). Compare with Harter v. Morris, 72 Ind. App. 189, 123 N.E. 23, 123 N.E. 719 (1919).

This section was not satisfied as to a contract for exchange of lands by one of the parties signing his acceptance to such contract without delivering it. Harter v. Morris, 72 Ind. App. 189, 123 N.E. 23, 123 N.E. 719 (1919).

Letters not completely expressing the terms of the contract, whereby plaintiff was to purchase a lot and erect a building for leasing to defendant, and leaving the matters open for further negotiations, did not satisfy the statute of frauds. Highland Inv. Co. v. Kirk Co., 96 Ind. App. 5, 184 N.E. 308 (1933).

A letter written by an aunt to her nephew, which contained the statement, "Remember will give you the same kind of deed to South bungalow," was insufficient as a memorandum of the essentials of a verbal agreement between the parties for conveyance of real estate. Sheldmyer v. Bias, 112 Ind. App. 522, 45 N.E.2d 347 (1942).

A memorandum, in order to make enforceable a contract within the statute of frauds, must have stated with reasonable certainty the terms and conditions of all the provisions constituting the contract, and by whom and to whom the promises were made, and, if any of the essential stipulations or undertakings of the verbal bargain were omitted, then the memorandum was insufficient and the agreement could not have been enforced at law or in equity. Sheldmyer v. Bias, 112 Ind. App. 522, 45 N.E.2d 347 (1942).

A memorandum of a contract for the sale of a real estate had to embrace all the essential terms of the contract, for if an essential term of the contract was left to be shown by parol, it was a parol contract and therefore not enforceable under the statute of frauds. Foltz v. Evans, 113 Ind. App. 596, 49 N.E.2d 358 (1943).

Where a written proposition to purchase a lot on which a house was being built referred to plans and specifications which were introduced in evidence and identified by testimony as those referred to, such exhibits, though not signed by the parties, did not constitute a term of the contract not incorporated in the writing, but, together with the proposition, constituted a written memorandum of a contract to purchase the real estate within the meaning of the statute of frauds. Foltz v. Evans, 113 Ind. App. 596, 49 N.E.2d 358 (1943).

Where defendant was already on the land, and no written contract or memorandum had been produced concerning a sale of real estate, a parol contract to sell this land could find no exception to this act and such parol contract could not stand. Otterman v. Hollingsworth, 140 Ind. App. 281, 7 Ind. Dec. 603, 214 N.E.2d 189 (1966).

Surrender and Release.

A grant of an interest in land which was required to be in writing could have been surrendered and released only by a written instrument. Heller v. Dailey, 28 Ind. App. 555, 63 N.E. 490 (1902); Ramage v. Wilson, 37 Ind. App. 532, 77 N.E. 368 (1906).

Tenants by Entireties.

To constitute a valid contract, the minds of the parties must have met on the identities of the person with whom they were dealing. Where the lands were a farm, owned by the husband and wife, and holding the land as tenants by entireties, neither party could, in any manner, contract to dispose of the said farm without the written consent of the other. Gates v. Petri, 127 Ind. App. 670, 143 N.E.2d 293 (1954).

Timber.

A contract for the sale of growing trees was a contract for the sale of an interest in land and had to be in writing in order to make it binding on either party. Owens v. Lewis, 46 Ind. 488, 15 Am. R. 295 (1874); Armstrong v. Lawson, 73 Ind. 498 (1881); Hostetter v. Auman, 119 Ind. 7, 20 N.E. 506 (1889); Watson v. Adams, 32 Ind. App. 281, 69 N.E. 696 (1904).

SALE OF LANDS (Cont'd)

Timber. (Cont'd)

When standing timber was cut and taken possession of under an oral contract of sale, an action to recover the purchase price was not barred by the statute of frauds. Whicker v. Wallace, 81 Ind. App. 84, 140 N.E. 919 (1923).

AGREEMENT NOT TO BE PERFORMED WITHIN ONE YEAR

In General.

This clause applied only to contracts that were not to be performed within a year according to the agreement of the parties, and was not applicable to contracts that could, or could not, have been performed within a year. Wiggins v. Keizer, 6 Ind. 252 (1855); Wilson v. Ray, 13 Ind. 1 (1859); Hill v. Jamieson, 16 Ind. 125, 79 Am. Dec. 414 (1861); Indiana & I.C. Ry. v. Scearce, 23 Ind. 223 (1864); Bell v. Hewitt's Ex'rs, 24 Ind. 280 (1865); Frost v. Tarr, 53 Ind. 390 (1876); Parker v. Siple, 76 Ind. 345 (1881); Hinkle v. Fisher, 104 Ind. 84, 3 N.E. 624 (1885); Piper v. Fosher, 121 Ind. 407, 23 N.E. 269 (1890); Durham v. Hiatt, 127 Ind. 514, 26 N.E. 401 (1891); Pennsylvania Co. v. Dolan, 6 Ind. App. 109, 32 N.E. 802, 51 Am. St. R. 289 (1892); American Quarries Co. v. Lay, 37 Ind. App. 386, 73 N.E. 608 (1905); Decatur v. McKean, 167 Ind. 249, 78 N.E. 982 (1906); Timmonds v. Taylor, 48 Ind. App. 531, 96 N.E. 331 (1911); Freas v. Custer, 201 Ind. 159, 166 N.E. 434 (1929).

Whenever the contract could not have been performed within a year, it fell within the statute. Groves v. Cook, 88 Ind. 169, 45 Am. R. 462 (1882); Shumate v. Farlow, 125 Ind. 359, 25 N.E. 432 (1890); Meyer v. E.G. Spink Co., 76 Ind. App. 318, 124 N.E. 757 (1919), rehearing overruled, 127 N.E. 455 (Ind. App. 1920).

Under this section, a contract to furnish funds to acquire and improve real estate and for sale of stock in a corporation which could not have been performed within one year had to be in writing. Meyer v. E.G. Spink Co., 76 Ind. App. 318, 124 N.E. 757 (1919), rehearing overruled, 127 N.E. 455 (1920).

Where an oral agreement was one that by its terms was not to be performed within one year, it was unenforceable. Hurd v. Ball, 128 Ind. App. 278, 143 N.E.2d 458 (1957), transfer denied, 237 Ind. 665, 148 N.E.2d 194 (1958).

Where no time is fixed for the performance of an oral agreement or where performance depends upon a contingency which may or may not happen within one year, the agreement does not violate the statute of frauds. Wright Mfg. Corp. v. Scott, 172 Ind. App. 154, 56 Ind. Dec. 306, 360 N.E.2d 2 (1977), aff'd, 176 Ind. App. 365, 375 N.E.2d 278 (1978).

Agreement to Make Will.

A verbal agreement in which decedent agreed to bequeath and devise by will to an illegitimate child and which could have been performed within one year, was not within the provisions of this section. Hurd v. Ball, 128 Ind. App. 278, 143 N.E.2d 458 (1957), transfer denied, 237 Ind. 665, 148 N.E.2d 194 (1958).

Employment Contracts.

Contracts for personal service for an indefinite period did not fall within this clause. Pennsylvania Co. v. Dolan, 6 Ind. App. 109, 32 N.E. 802, 51 Am. St. R. 289 (1892).

A contract in parol by a railroad company to give an injured employee employment so long as he proved a competent and worthy man in consideration of his forbearing to sue the company was not within the statute of fraud. Cox v. Baltimore & O.S.W.R.R., 180 Ind. 495, 103 N.E. 337, 50 L.R.A. (n.s.) 453 (1913).

An employment for service for one year to begin in the future was within the statute. Board of Comm'rs v. Howell, 21 Ind. App. 495, 52 N.E. 769 (1899); Griffith v. Hammer, 73 Ind. App. 159, 126 N.E. 855 (1920).

Parol evidence was inadmissible to show the existence of a contract for the rendition of personal services not to have been performed in one year from the making thereof. Butler Univ. v. Weaver, 97 Ind. App. 151, 180 N.E. 875 (1932).

An oral contract of employment which might or might not have been performed within one year does not come within the provisions of this section. Holcomb & Hoke Mfg. Co. v. Younge, 103 Ind. App. 439, 8 N.E.2d 426 (1937).

The word "year," as used in this section and subdivision, meant a calendar year, and, in computing such period of time, there must have been exclusion of the first day and an inclusion of the last day, since the rule disregarded fractions of a day in making the computations. Holcomb & Hoke Mfg. Co. v. Younge, 103 Ind. App. 439, 8 N.E.2d 426 (1937).

Where an oral contract of employment required the employee to commence work on November 4, 1930, and it was to have expired November 4, 1931, it did not come within the statute of frauds, since the term of the contract was for only one year. Holcomb & Hoke Mfg. Co. v. Younge, 103 Ind. App. 439, 8 N.E.2d 426 (1937).

In action by an employee for breach of an oral contract of employment for one year, the question whether the one-year period was to have been counted from the date of the mak-

AGREEMENT NOT TO BE PERFORMED WITHIN ONE YEAR (Cont'd)

Employment Contracts. (Cont'd)
ing of the contract or from the date that the employee began his services for the employer, which was several days after making the contract, was a question of fact for the jury. Holcomb & Hoke Mfg. Co. v. Younge, 103 Ind. App. 439, 8 N.E.2d 426 (1937).

A contract of employment for a period of five years was within the statute of frauds. Montgomery Ward & Co. v. Guignet, 112 Ind. App. 661, 45 N.E.2d 337 (1942).

The fact that an oral employment contract for a period of five years was partially performed did not remove it from the operation of the statute of frauds. Montgomery Ward & Co. v. Guignet, 112 Ind. App. 661, 45 N.E.2d 337 (1942).

This section effectually prevented the implication of a new employment contract for a like period and consideration when the original written contract was for a period of more than one year. Jenkins v. King, 224 Ind. 164, 65 N.E.2d 121, 163 A.L.R. 397 (1946).

Where an employment contract provided that the employee was to receive a stated amount per year for a period of two years, after which a new agreement should be made and contained a covenant that in the event the employee should leave the services of the employer he would not, for a period of five years, engage in the business of soliciting or writing insurance of any kind in the county where the employer was located, and the employee served out the full term so provided, and continued to work thereafter without any written or other express contract for a period of 23 months, his so leaving the employment was not a breach of the covenant, and hence, he could not have been enjoined from immediately engaging in the insurance business in such county. Jenkins v. King, 224 Ind. 164, 65 N.E.2d 121, 163 A.L.R. 397 (1946).

An agreement to employ plaintiff in a stated position at a stipulated salary for 18 months and to transfer him to another area at the same salary if employment was not continued beyond 18 months was within the statute. ITT Cannon Elec., Inc. v. Brady, 141 Ind. App. 506, 11 Ind. Dec. 399, 230 N.E.2d 114 (1967).

A contract for lifetime employment is not governed by the statute of frauds since by its own terms it is capable of being performed within one year because the employee's life may end in one year. Kiyose v. Trustees of Ind. Univ., 166 Ind. App. 34, 48 Ind. Dec. 738, 333 N.E.2d 886 (1975).

Where the parties expressly stipulated to a payment arrangement which was not capable of being fully performed within one year, the agreement was governed by the statute of frauds and was unenforceable because the agreement was not memorialized in a writing and signed by the party charged with making the payments. Wallem v. CLS Indus., 725 N.E.2d 880 (Ind. App. 2000).

Leases.
Oral lease for a period of more than three years could have been taken out of operation of this act by part performance. Sourbier v. Claman, 101 Ind. App. 679, 200 N.E. 721 (1936).

Marriage Contract.
A parol contract of marriage not to be performed within a year fell within the statute. Paris v. Strong, 51 Ind. 339 (1875); Vaughan v. Smith, 177 Ind. 111, 96 N.E. 594, 1914C Ann. Cas. 1092 (1911).

Modification or Rescission.
The fifth clause of this section applies to a contract to refrain from practicing medicine for five years in a specified area in consideration of cash payments although payments could have been completed within one year and the termination, relinquishment, or modification of such contract must be in writing and may not be accomplished by subsequent oral agreement. Modisett v. Jally, 153 Ind. App. 173, 32 Ind. Dec. 398, 286 N.E.2d 675 (1972).

—Monthly Payments.
A contract for the instalment of an electric sign which called for payment of monthly instalments over a period of three years, and for the rendition of services by the party installing the sign in keeping it in proper repair during the three-year period, and wherein the other party agreed to keep and use the sign for such period, and providing that the contract should be deemed renewed for another period of three years, unless terminated by thirty days' notice, came within the statute of frauds. Maglaris v. Claude Neon Fed. Co., 101 Ind. App. 156, 198 N.E. 462 (1935).

Where, by oral agreement between the vendor and purchaser of real estate for a certain sum, the purchaser executed eleven promissory notes for payment of the purchase price, the payments to have been made monthly until the full purchase price was paid, and the entire indebtedness could have been paid within a year from the date of the oral agreement, there having been no express stipulation by the parties that the debt should not have been paid within a year, such agreement as to payment did not come within the provisions of this section, subdivision 5, and action could have been brought thereon. Purity Maid Prods. Co. v. American Bank & Trust Co., 105 Ind. App. 541, 14 N.E.2d 755 (1938).

AGREEMENT NOT TO BE PERFORMED WITHIN ONE YEAR (Cont'd)

Partnership Contracts.

Where an oral partnership agreement was completely executed, and a subsequent written contract was executed to cover ownership of stock in a corporation in which the partnership was interested, which did not attempt to cover the terms of the oral agreement but was merely supplementary thereto, both contracts could have been enforced in an action for a dissolution of the partnership and for an accounting, as against a contention that the oral agreement was within the statute of frauds because it could not have been performed within one year. Kist v. Coughlin, 222 Ind. 639, 57 N.E.2d 199, modified on other grounds, 222 Ind. 639, 57 N.E.2d 586 (1944).

Part Performance.

The contract must have been such as could have been performed by both parties within a year in order to have taken it out of the statute. Wilson v. Ray, 13 Ind. 1 (1859); Meyer v. E.G. Spink Co., 76 Ind. App. 318, 124 N.E. 757 (1919), rehearing overruled, 127 N.E. 455 (Ind. App. 1920).

If the contract was performed fully by one of the parties, the fact that the other could not perform within a year did not bring it within the statute. Haugh v. Blythe's Ex'rs, 20 Ind. 24 (1863); Groves v. Cook, 88 Ind. 169, 45 Am. R. 462 (1882); Piper v. Fosher, 121 Ind. 407, 23 N.E. 269 (1890); Lowman v. Sheets, 124 Ind. 416, 24 N.E. 351, 7 L.R.A. 784 (1890); Meyer v. E.G. Spink Co., 76 Ind. App. 318, 124 N.E. 757 (1919), rehearing overruled, 127 N.E. 455 (Ind. App. 1920).

The doctrine of part performance had no application to contracts that could not have been performed within a year. Wolke v. Fleming, 103 Ind. 105, 2 N.E. 325, 53 Am. R. 495 (1885).

Where plaintiff and defendant, tenants of adjoining tracts of land, verbally agreed with each other and with their common landlord that the hay crop should be grown the first year on plaintiff's land and the second year on defendant's, the hay and seed to be divided in specified proportions, and the agreement as to the first year's crop was fully performed, by plaintiff, defendant could not defeat an action for conversion of plaintiff's share of the crop raised during the second year on the ground that the contract as to the crop could not be performed within a year and was not in writing, and there had been no part performance within a year as to the second year's crop. Shank v. Kuhn, 74 Ind. App. 264, 128 N.E. 775 (1920).

When an indefinite and uncertain contract of present employment was acted upon until services were performed by one party and accepted by the other, the court could take into account all that was said and done by the parties in rendering the services, accepting the same, and making payments therefor, insofar as they tended to explain the uncertainties in the written contract, or to supply omissions therein. Lester v. Hinkle, 193 Ind. 605, 141 N.E. 463 (1923).

Part performance of a contract for personal services that could not have been fully performed within a year did not take it out of the statute of frauds. Butler Univ. v. Weaver, 97 Ind. App. 151, 180 N.E. 875 (1932).

In an action for rent, under a ten-year lease, answers that defendant complied with an oral agreement to give up the premises and take different premises in the same building, in return for which the rent was to have been reduced, and that a check given rental agents, marked for rent for a given month, was cashed, were insufficient to show that the parol modification of the written lease was so far performed that it was taken out of the statute of frauds, and hence a noncompliance of the oral agreement operated as a fraud upon defendant, on the theory of estoppel, since there was nothing in the answers to indicate that a compliance with the oral agreement on the part of defendant operated to its detriment. Miller Jewelry Co. v. Dickson, 111 Ind. App. 676, 42 N.E.2d 398 (1942).

Performance Dependent upon Contingency.

If the performance of the contract depended upon a contingency that could or could not happen within a year, the contract was not within the statute. Marley v. Noblett, 42 Ind. 85 (1873); Cole v. Wright, 70 Ind. 179 (1880); American Quarries Co. v. Lay, 37 Ind. App. 386, 73 N.E. 608 (1905).

The fact that settlement agreement might not be performed within one year was insufficient alone to make it subject to the requirements of the Statute of Frauds. Silkey v. Investors Diversified Servs., Inc., 690 N.E.2d 329 (Ind. App. 1997).

Real Estate Contracts.

Receipts with the words "Rent to Own" were not sufficient as a matter of law to constitute a written agreement for the sale of real property, since they did not specify, inter alia, the selling price, interest rate, or term of the alleged agreement. Nelson v. Blackwell, 227 Bankr. 859 (Bankr. S.D. Ind. 1998).

The fifth clause of this section had no reference to contracts concerning real estate, and therefore did not affect oral lease of restaurant. Sourbier v. Claman, 101 Ind. App. 679, 200 N.E. 721 (1936).

Sale of Lands.

This clause did not apply to contracts rela-

AGREEMENT NOT TO BE PERFORMED WITHIN ONE YEAR (Cont'd)

Sale of Lands. (Cont'd)
tive to the sale of real estate. Fall v. Hazelrigg, 45 Ind. 576, 15 Am. R. 278 (1874); Baynes v. Chastain, 68 Ind. 376 (1879); Railsback v. Walke, 81 Ind. 409 (1882); Cochran v. Ward, 5 Ind. App. 89, 29 N.E. 795, 31 N.E. 581, 51 Am. St. R. 229 (1892); Timmonds v. Taylor, 48 Ind. App. 531, 96 N.E. 331 (1911).

Severable Contracts.
If several contracts were made at the same time, and some were to have been performed within a year and some not, and such contracts were severable, those not falling within the statute could have been enforced. Lowman v. Sheets, 124 Ind. 416, 24 N.E. 351, 7 L.R.A. 784 (1890).

Teachers' Contracts.
A contract made by a school corporation with a teacher to teach school for more than a year had to have been in writing. Caldwell v. School City of Huntington, 132 Ind. 92, 31 N.E. 566 (1892).

AGREEMENT OF CURE

Legislative Intent.
The intent of the legislature in adding clause "Sixth" former IC 32-2-1-1 (repealed; now see this section for similar provisions) was not to provide for a limitation on actions for such incidental home nursing services rendered by lay persons, but to provide a limitation on actions involving providers of professional medical care and services. Crump v. Coleman, 181 Ind. App. 414, 70 Ind. Dec. 490, 391 N.E.2d 867 (1979).

Collateral References. 72 Am. Jur. 2d Statute of Frauds, §§ 1, 26-43, 179-192.

37 C.J.S. Frauds, Statute of, §§ 1-3, 68.

Restrictions on use of real property. 5 A.L.R.2d 1316.

Performance as taking contract, not to be performed within a year, out of statute of frauds. 6 A.L.R.2d 1053.

Sale, or contract for sale, of standing timber as within provision of statute of frauds respecting sale or contract of sale of real property. 7 A.L.R.2d 517.

Check as payment. 8 A.L.R.2d 251.

Delivery of a memorandum as necessary to its effectiveness to satisfy the statute of frauds. 12 A.L.R.2d 508.

Statute of frauds as affecting enforceability as between the parties of agreement to purchase property at judicial or tax sale for their joint benefit. 14 A.L.R.2d 992.

Failure to object to parol evidence or voluntary introduction thereof, as waiver of defense of statute of frauds. 15 A.L.R.2d 1330.

Sufficiency of memorandum of lease agreement to satisfy the statute of frauds, as regards terms and conditions of lease. 16 A.L.R.2d 621.

Agency to purchase personal property for another as within statute of frauds. 20 A.L.R.2d 1140.

Sufficiency of description or designation of land in contract or memorandum of sale, under statute of frauds. 23 A.L.R.2d 6.

Necessity and sufficiency of statement of consideration in contract or memorandum of sale of land, under statute of frauds. 23 A.L.R.2d 164.

Rights of parties under oral agreement to buy or bid in land for another. 27 A.L.R.2d 1285.

Oral contract for personal services as long as employee is able to continue in work, to do satisfactory work, or the like, as within statute of frauds relating to contracts not to be performed within year. 28 A.L.R.2d 878.

Validity of oral promise or agreement not to revoke will. 29 A.L.R.2d 1229.

Oral acceptance of written offer by party sought to be charged as satisfying statute of frauds. 30 A.L.R.2d 972.

What constitutes part performance sufficient to take agreement in consideration of marriage out of operation of statute of frauds. 30 A.L.R.2d 1419.

Erasure: effect of attempted cancellation or erasure in memorandum otherwise sufficient to satisfy statute of frauds. 31 A.L.R.2d 1112.

Application of statute of frauds to promise not to make a will. 32 A.L.R.2d 370.

Agreement to drop or compromise will contest or withdraw objections to probate, as within statute of frauds. 42 A.L.R.2d 1319.

Statute of frauds as affecting option for repurchase by vendor. 44 A.L.R.2d 342.

Statute of frauds as affecting question when real estate owned by partner before formation of partnership will be deemed to have become asset of firm. 45 A.L.R.2d 1009.

Promissory estoppel as to statute of frauds. 48 A.L.R.2d 1069.

Vendee's liability for use and occupancy of premises, where vendor disaffirms land contract unenforceable under statute of frauds. 49 A.L.R.2d 1169.

Contract to support, maintain, or educate a child as within provision of statute of frauds relating to contracts not to be performed within a year. 49 A.L.R.2d 1293.

Necessity of writing to create right by private grant or reservation to hunt or fish on another's land. 49 A.L.R.2d 1395.

Solid mineral royalty as real or personal property for purposes of statute of frauds. 68 A.L.R.2d 728.

Mutual promises to marry as made in or upon consideration of marriage within statute of frauds. 75 A.L.R.2d 633.

Validity of oral surrender of written lease as affected by partial execution. 78 A.L.R.2d 933.

Doctrine of part performance with respect to renewal option in lease not complying with statute of frauds. 80 A.L.R.2d 425.

Application of statute of frauds to general bonus or profit-sharing plan. 81 A.L.R.2d 1086.

Buyer's note as payment within contemplation of statute of frauds. 81 A.L.R.2d 1355.

Enforceability, under statute of frauds provision as to contracts not to be performed within a year, of oral employment contract for more than one year but specifically made terminable upon death of either party. 88 A.L.R.2d 701.

Application of statute of frauds to water well-drilling contract. 90 A.L.R.2d 1346.

Will, or instrument in form of will, as memorandum containing identification or description of subject-matter sufficient to satisfy statute of frauds with respect to contract to devise or bequeath. 94 A.L.R.2d 921.

What 12-month period constitutes "year" or "calendar year" as used in public enactment, contract, or other written instrument. 5 A.L.R.3d 584.

Deed to railroad company as conveying fee or easement. 6 A.L.R.3d 973.

Procuring signature by fraud as forgery. 11 A.L.R.3d 1074.

"Out of pocket" or "benefit of bargain" as proper rule of damages for fraudulent representations inducing contract for the transfer of property. 13 A.L.R.3d 875.

Concealment of or misrepresentation as to prior marital status as ground for annulment of marriage. 15 A.L.R.3d 759.

Statute excluding testimony of one person because of death of another as applied to testimony in respect of lost or destroyed instructment. 18 A.L.R.3d 606.

Price fixed in contract violating statute of frauds as evidence of value in action on quantum meruit. 21 A.L.R.3d 9.

Infant's misrepresentation as to his age as estopping him from disaffirming his voidable transaction. 29 A.L.R.3d 1270.

Sufficiency, under statute of frauds, of description or designation of property in real estate brokerage contract. 30 A.L.R.3d 935.

Brokerage contracts: Sufficiency, under statute of frauds, of description or designation of property in real estate brokerage contract. 30 A.L.R.3d 935.

Part performance as affecting applicability of statute of frauds to promise not to make a will. 32 A.L.R.2d 370.

Applicability of statute of frauds to agreement to rescind contract for sale of land. 42 A.L.R.3d 242.

Circumstances excusing lessee's failure to give timely notice of exercise of option to renew or extend lease. 27 A.L.R.4th 266.

Sufficiency as to method of giving oral or written notice exercising option to renew or extend lease. 29 A.L.R.4th 903.

What constitutes timely notice of exercise of option to renew or extend lease. 29 A.L.R.4th 956.

Waiver or estoppel as to notice requirement for exercising option to renew or extend lease. 32 A.L.R.4th 452.

Sufficiency as to parties giving or receiving notice of exercise of option to renew or extend lease. 34 A.L.R.4th 857.

Oil and gas royalty as real or personal property. 56 A.L.R.4th 539.

Sufficiency of showing, in establishing boundary by parol agreement, that boundary was uncertain or in dispute before agreement. 72 A.L.R.4th 132.

Applicability of statute of frauds to promise to pay for legal services furnished to another. 84 A.L.R.4th 994.

32-21-1-2. Consideration need not be in writing. — The consideration that is the basis of a promise, contract, or agreement described in section 1 [IC 32-21-1-1] of this chapter does not need to be in writing but may be proved. [P.L.2-2002, § 6.]

NOTES TO DECISIONS

ANALYSIS

In general.
Antenuptial contracts.

Parol evidence.

In General.
The statute provided that the contract did

In General. (Cont'd)

not need to state the consideration. Hiatt v. Hiatt, 28 Ind. 53 (1867); Knapp v. Beach, 52 Ind. App. 573, 101 N.E. 37 (1913).

Antenuptial Contracts.

Antenuptial contracts did not need to state a consideration, as marriage was a sufficient consideration to support a promise. Moore v. Harrison, 26 Ind. App. 408, 59 N.E. 1077 (1901).

Parol Evidence.

If the consideration stated in a contract required by the statute of frauds to be in writing was indefinite and uncertain, parol evidence was admissible to explain the same. Burke v. Mead, 159 Ind. 252, 64 N.E. 880 (1902).

When the consideration was stated in a deed in general terms, either party could show by parol or documentary evidence the true consideration for its execution. Powell v. Nusbaum, 136 N.E. 571 (1922).

32-21-1-3. Conveyance of an existing trust. — A conveyance of an existing trust in land, goods, or things in action is void unless the conveyance is in writing and signed by the party making the conveyance or by the party's lawful agent. [P.L.2-2002, § 6.]

Collateral References. Disposition of property of inter vivos trust falling in after death of settlor, who left will making no express disposition of the trust property. 30 A.L.R.3d 1318.

"Pour-over" provisions from will to inter vivos trust. 12 A.L.R.3d 56.

32-21-1-4. Trust may arise or be extinguished by implication of law. — Nothing contained in any Indiana law may be construed to prevent any trust from arising or being extinguished by implication of law. [P.L.2-2002, § 6.]

Cross References. Resulting trusts, IC 30-1-9-6 — IC 30-1-9-8.

NOTES TO DECISIONS

In General.

A guardian who purchased and improved a lot or tract of land with his ward's money, taking title in his own name, created a resulting or implied or constructive trust in the lot or tract in favor of the ward. Ray v. Ferrel, 127 Ind. 570, 27 N.E. 159 (1891); Mull v. Bowles, 129 Ind. 343, 28 N.E. 771 (1891); Hill v. Pollard, 132 Ind. 588, 32 N.E. 564 (1892); Prow v. Prow, 133 Ind. 340, 32 N.E. 1121 (1893); Jackson v. Landers, 134 Ind. 529, 34 N.E. 323 (1893); Myers v. Jackson, 135 Ind. 136, 34 N.E. 810 (1893); Orb v. Coapstick, 136 Ind. 313, 36 N.E. 278 (1894), overruled on other grounds, Pugh v. Highley, 152 Ind. 252, 53 N.E. 171 (1899); Toney v. Wendling, 138 Ind. 228, 37 N.E. 598 (1894); Meredith v. Meredith, 150 Ind. 299, 50 N.E. 29 (1898); Alexander v. Spaulding, 160 Ind. 176, 66 N.E. 694 (1903); Richards v. Wilson, 185 Ind. 335, 112 N.E. 780 (1916).

Resulting trusts were recognized in Indiana. Auten v. Sevier, 136 Ind. App. 434, 4 Ind. Dec. 156, 202 N.E.2d 274 (1964).

Collateral References. Resulting trust in property conveyed by third person to debtor's spouse and attacked by creditors as fraudulent. 35 A.L.R.2d 8.

32-21-1-5. No abridgement of right of specific performance. — Nothing contained in any Indiana statute may be construed to abridge the powers of courts to compel the specific performance of agreements in cases of part performance of the agreements. [P.L.2-2002, § 6.]

NOTES TO DECISIONS

ANALYSIS

Burden of proof.
Inadequacy of consideration.
Leases.
Part performance of parol contract.

Burden of Proof.

Burden of proof in actions to enforce specific performance of contracts rested upon the plaintiff to show compliance with the statute of frauds. Luzader v. Richmond, 128 Ind. 344, 27 N.E. 736 (1891); Waymire v. Waymire, 141 Ind. 164, 40 N.E. 523 (1895).

Inadequacy of Consideration.

Inadequacy of consideration was not alone a sufficient cause for refusing specific performance of a contract. Hamilton v. Hamilton, 162 Ind. 430, 70 N.E. 535 (1904).

Leases.

Specific performance of a written contract to execute a lease for more than three years could have been decreed when the lessee took possession under the contract and paid rent. Saint Joseph Hydraulic Co. v. Globe Tissue Paper Co., 156 Ind. 665, 59 N.E. 995 (1901).

Part Performance of Parol Contract.

Payment of the purchase money for land was not such a part performance of a parol contract of sale as would have taken the contract out of the statute of frauds. Mather v. Scoles, 35 Ind. 1 (1870); Suman v. Springate, 67 Ind. 115 (1879); Green v. Groves, 109 Ind. 519, 10 N.E. 401 (1887); Riley v. Haworth, 30 Ind. App. 377, 64 N.E. 928 (1902).

If possession of land was taken under a written contract of sale, the consideration to have been paid in money, and a subsequent parol agreement was made to accept land in payment instead of money, there was no such part performance of the parol agreement as would have taken the same out of the statute of frauds. Bradley v. Harter, 156 Ind. 499, 60 N.E. 139 (1901).

In order that having taken possession of land under a parol contract of sale took the case out of the statute of frauds, the possession had to have been open, absolute, and with the consent of the vendor. Riley v. Haworth, 30 Ind. App. 377, 64 N.E. 928 (1902).

32-21-1-6. Actions concerning character, credit, or ability. — An action may not be brought against a person for a representation made by the person concerning the character, conduct, credit, ability, trade, or dealings of any other person, unless the representation is in writing and signed by the person or by the person's lawful agent. [P.L.2-2002, § 6.]

NOTES TO DECISIONS

ANALYSIS

In general.
Conspiracy to obtain property.
Corporations.
Estoppel.
Innocent purpose.
Miscellaneous representations.
Representations in violation of fiduciary relationship.

In General.

Representations had to be made in writing in order to create a liability under this section. Cook v. Churchman, 104 Ind. 141, 3 N.E. 759 (1885); Heintz v. Mueller, 19 Ind. App. 240, 49 N.E. 293 (1898), overruled on other grounds, Grover v. Cavenaugh, 40 Ind. App. 340, 92 N.E. 104 (1907).

Conspiracy to Obtain Property.

Conspiracy to obtain money or goods by making false representations as to credit or character of persons was within the provisions of the statute of frauds. Cook v. Churchman, 104 Ind. 141, 3 N.E. 759 (1885); Mendenhall v. Stewart, 18 Ind. App. 262, 47 N.E. 943 (1897).

The obtaining of property by fraudulent representations and conspiracy was not within this section. Hodgin v. Bryant, 114 Ind. 401, 16 N.E. 815 (1888).

Corporations.

This section applied to representations made as to corporations the same as to natural persons. Heintz v. Mueller, 19 Ind. App. 240, 49 N.E. 293 (1898), overruled on other grounds, Grover v. Cavenaugh, 40 Ind. App. 340, 92 N.E. 104 (1907).

False representations made by officers and agents of a corporation as to the financial condition of the corporation to induce persons to purchase stock in the corporation did not fall within the provisions of this section.

Corporations. (Cont'd)
Grover v. Cavanagh, 40 Ind. App. 340, 82 N.E. 104 (1907).

Estoppel.
The statute of frauds, more particularly this section, should not prevent an answer in equitable estoppel from being interposed as a defense in mechanic's lien cases against a mechanic lienholder. Voorhees-Jontz Lumber Co. v. Bezek, 137 Ind. App. 382, 6 Ind. Dec. 145, 209 N.E.2d 380 (1965).

Innocent Purpose.
Where false representations as to the credit or financial standing of a third party, not to induce the plaintiff to deal with such third party and to extend credit to him, but to induce the person to whom the representations were made to enter into a contract with the defendant, they did not come within the statute. Grover v. Cavanagh, 40 App. 340, 82 N.E. 104 (1907).

Miscellaneous Representations.
This section did not apply to representa-

tions as to the amount of capital invested in a business. Saint John v. Hendrickson, 81 Ind. 350 (1882).

Representations made by a person concerning the value of patent rights and bank stock in order to induce investments therein did not fall within this section. Coulter v. Clark, 160 Ind. 311, 66 N.E. 739 (1903).

False representations as to the character and value of property were not included within this section, and did not need to be in writing to constitute a cause of action. Stauffer v. Hulwick, 176 Ind. 410, 96 N.E. 154, 1914A Ann. Cas. 951 (1911).

Representations in Violation of Fiduciary Relationship.
Statute of frauds did not cover oral representations made in violation of fiduciary relationship between bank and depositor. Teeling v. Indiana Nat'l Bank, 436 N.E.2d 855 (Ind. App. 1982).

Collateral References. Interest of or benefit to person making representation as affecting applicability of statute requiring representations as to credit, etc., of another to be in writing. 32 A.L.R.2d 743.

32-21-1-7. Conveyance revocable at will of grantor void. — If a conveyance of or charge upon an estate contains a provision for revocation at the will of the grantor, the provision is void as to subsequent purchasers from the grantor, for a valuable consideration, of the estate or interest subject to the provision, even though the provision is not expressly revoked. [P.L.2-2002, § 6.]

NOTES TO DECISIONS

In General.
A trust once created and accepted without reservation of power could only be revoked by the consent of all parties in interest. Ewing v. Jones, 130 Ind. 247, 29 N.E. 1057, 15 L.R.A. 75 (1892); Ewing v. Wilson, 132 Ind. 223, 31

N.E. 64, 19 L.R.A. 767 (1892), overruled on other grounds, Colbo v. Buyer, 235 Ind. 518, 134 N.E.2d 45 (1956); Brunson v. Henry, 140 Ind. 455, 39 N.E. 256 (1894); Ewing v. Bass, 149 Ind. 1, 48 N.E. 241 (1897).

Collateral References. Applicability of statute of frauds to agreement to rescind contract for sale of land. 42 A.L.R.3d 242.

32-21-1-8. Conveyance revocable at will of person other than grantor valid. — If the power to revoke a conveyance of any interest in land, and to reconvey the interest, is given to any person other than the grantor in the conveyance, and the person given the power conveys the interest to a purchaser for a valuable consideration, the subsequent convey-ance is valid. [P.L.2-2002, § 6.]

32-21-1-9. Conveyance before power of revocation vests valid. — If a conveyance to a purchaser under either section 7 or 8 [IC 32-21-1-7 or IC 32-21-1-8] of this chapter is made before the person making the conveyance is entitled to execute the person's power of revocation, the conveyance is valid from the time the power of revocation vests in the person. [P.L.2-2002, § 6.]

32-21-1-10. Contract for procurement of purchaser. — A contract for the payment of any sum of money or thing of value, as a commission or reward for the finding or procuring by one (1) person of a purchaser for the real estate of another, is not valid unless the contract is in writing and signed by the owner of the real estate or the owner's legally appointed and duly qualified representative. For purposes of this section, any general reference to the real estate that is sufficient to identify the real estate is a sufficient description of the real estate. [P.L.2-2002, § 6.]

Cross References. License requirement, IC 25-34.1-3-3.1.
Valparaiso University Law Review. Tenancy by the Entirety as an Asset Shield:

An Unjustified Safe Haven for Delinquent Child Support Obligors, 29 Val. U.L. Rev. 1057 (1995).

NOTES TO DECISIONS

ANALYSIS

In general.
Constitutionality.
Agents.
Amount of compensation.
Applicability.
Cancellation.
Conduct and authority of broker.
Contingent contracts.
Contract between brokers.
Contract not performed.
Description of lands.
Divisible contracts.
Division of commissions.
Exchange of land.
Execution after services performed.
Execution before services completed.
Foreign contracts.
Fraud.
Gift of land.
Identification of property.
Listing contract.
Married women.
Misrepresentation.
Offer to purchase containing parol terms.
Option.
Oral contract for commission.
Purpose.
Revoked offer.
Services performed.
Sufficiency of memorandum.

Summary judgment.
—Inappropriate.
Trial.

In General.
Since the enactment of this statute in 1901, no recovery could be had for services rendered in the sale of real estate unless a contract in writing promising to pay for such service had been executed by the owner or his duly autho-rized representative. Beahler v. Clark, 32 Ind. App. 222, 68 N.E. 613 (1903); Zimmerman v. Zehendner, 164 Ind. 466, 73 N.E. 920 (1905); Isphording v. Wolfe, 36 Ind. App. 250, 75 N.E. 598 (1905); Provident Trust Co. v. Darrough, 168 Ind. 29, 78 N.E. 1030 (1906); Phillips v. Jones, 39 Ind. App. 626, 80 N.E. 555 (1907); Price v. Walker, 43 Ind. App. 519, 88 N.E. 78 (1909); Wysong v. Sells, 44 Ind. App. 238, 88 N.E. 954 (1909); Waddle v. Smith, 58 Ind. App. 587, 108 N.E. 537 (1915); Luther v. Bash, 61 Ind. App. 535, 112 N.E. 110 (1916); Peters v. Martin, 69 Ind. App. 436, 122 N.E. 16 (1919); Smitley v. Nau, 143 Ind. App. 113, 14 Ind. Dec. 693, 238 N.E.2d 681 (1968).

There could be no recovery under the quan-tum meruit. Beahler v. Clark, 32 Ind. App. 222, 68 N.E. 613 (1903); Zimmerman v. Zehendner, 164 Ind. 466, 73 N.E. 920 (1905); Fullenwider v. Goben, 176 Ind. 312, 95 N.E. 1010 (1911); Phillips v. Jones, 39 Ind. App. 626, 80 N.E. 555 (1907).

In General. (Cont'd)

A contract to pay a broker a commission for procuring a purchaser of land had to be wholly in writing under this statute. Luther v. Bash, 61 Ind. App. 535, 112 N.E. 110 (1916); Peters v. Martin, 69 Ind. App. 436, 122 N.E. 16 (1919).

A parol contract to pay a commission on sale of land was within this section and had to be in writing, notwithstanding a feature in the contract outside of the commission. Bryan v. Mayo, 188 Ind. 548, 124 N.E. 873 (1919).

An oral agreement between a vendor of a farm and brokers whereby vendor agreed to transfer title to one-half of the growing crops to the brokers as a portion of their commission for the sale of the farm was void and unenforceable. Ax v. Schloot, 116 Ind. App. 366, 64 N.E.2d 668 (1946).

This section applied to all contracts that contained an agreement for compensation, remuneration, or pay for such services. Belleville Lumber & Supply Co. v. Chamberlin, 120 Ind. App. 12, 84 N.E.2d 60 (1949).

A broker could not recover compensation for services rendered by him without a written contract of employment, and even where such a contract existed, its terms could have been revoked through the lapse of time. Smitley v. Nau, 143 Ind. App. 113, 14 Ind. Dec. 693, 238 N.E.2d 681 (1968).

When no written contract exists between broker and seller there can be no recovery on theory of partial performance or quantum meruit. Gerardot v. Emenhiser, 173 Ind. App. 353, 58 Ind. Dec. 17, 363 N.E.2d 1072 (1977).

In order to recover a commission under the terms of a written contract for the sale of realty a broker is required to prove either an actual sale and transfer of property or that he procured a purchaser who was ready, willing and able to purchase the property on terms specified in the contract or that through the broker's procurement a third party had entered into a valid executory contract with vendors for the purchase of such property. Gerardot v. Emenhiser, 173 Ind. App. 353, 58 Ind. Dec. 17, 363 N.E.2d 1072 (1977).

Where the personal representative never filed a written instrument with the trial court renouncing all claims for the compensation provided by the will, and where he stated in the final accounting hearing that he considered his agreement to serve as personal representative to be a contract entered into with the estate requiring the payment provided for in the will, he was required to submit an itemized billing statement and to remit to the estate any funds for which a satisfactory accounting could not be made. Grimm v. Kruse, 705 N.E.2d 483 (Ind. App. 1999).

Constitutionality.

This statute was constitutional. Selvage v. Talbott, 175 Ind. 648, 95 N.E. 114, 33 L.R.A. (n.s.) 973, 1913C Ann. Cas. 724 (1911).

Agents.

A contract providing for a commission for the sale of real estate signed by an agent of the owner of the real estate was valid and enforceable even though the authority of the agent was not in writing. Brown v. Poulos, 78 Ind. Dec. 869, 411 N.E.2d 712 (Ind. App. 1980).

Amount of Compensation.

A contract to pay a commission for the sale of land had to fix the amount of the commission to have been paid. Phillips v. Jones, 39 Ind. App. 626, 80 N.E. 555 (1907); Doney v. Laughlin, 50 Ind. App. 38, 94 N.E. 1027 (1911); Morton v. Gaffield, 51 Ind. App. 28, 98 N.E. 1007 (1912); Vogel v. Ensor, 76 Ind. App. 91, 131 N.E. 416 (1921).

Where an owner of real estate signed an agreement to pay a broker two per cent of the cash or property received in exchange for the land, the owner was liable to the broker who procured a purchaser, the owner refusing to convey after acceptance of terms by the prospective purchaser, although the exact amount of the broker's commission was not ascertainable without the aid of parol evidence. Luther v. Bash, 61 Ind. App. 535, 112 N.E. 110 (1916).

A contract for a commission was within the provision of this statute where it provided for a rate fixed by a real estate exchange, although such rate was a minimum rate. Stockberger v. Zane, 73 Ind. App. 4, 125 N.E. 65 (1919).

In a suit on the contract for a commission payable according to a rate fixed by a real estate exchange, evidence of the minutes of such real estate exchange fixing rates was admissible, notwithstanding this section. Stockberger v. Zane, 73 Ind. App. 4, 125 N.E. 65 (1919).

Written contract fixing minimum price at which owner would sell and providing that he would pay all over that amount as commission satisfied the requirements of this section. Brown v. Ogle, 75 Ind. App. 90, 130 N.E. 147 (1921).

An oral agreement between one of several vendors and a broker whereby such vendor agreed to partially reimburse the broker if he would make up the difference between the offered and asking price for the real estate was not a "contract for the sale of lands" nor a "contract for the payment of commissions," within the meaning of the statute of frauds. Nelson v. Shelley, 114 Ind. App. 530, 52 N.E.2d 849 (1944).

Applicability.

A contract by which one person agreed to

Applicability. (Cont'd)
purchase land of another when he obtained title to the land was not within the purview of this section. Collins v. Green, 40 Ind. App. 630, 82 N.E. 932 (1907).

A complaint predicating the right of recovery on an alleged parol contract, providing that plaintiff should receive as compensation for his services in fertilizing of unproductive farm any excess of the market value of the land over a stipulated figure, did not state a cause of action within this section. Welty v. Taylor, 63 Ind. App. 674, 115 N.E. 257 (1917).

An oral promise by one person to pay another a certain sum of money out of the proceeds of a sale of land was not within this section of the statute. Hetrick v. Ashburn, 86 Ind. App. 496, 142 N.E. 386 (1924).

A written letter containing a counterproposal to an offer relayed by real estate broker with a statement that the writer of the letter expects an answer by a certain date and that if he does not receive an answer he will count it as a negative reply, and no answer was made by such date although a completely different offer was made by the broker thereafter, there was no written agreement within the meaning of this section. Gerardot v. Emenhiser, 173 Ind. App. 353, 58 Ind. Dec. 17, 363 N.E.2d 1072 (1977).

The statute of frauds is inapplicable to employment contracts between real estate purchasers and their brokers. Panos v. Prentiss, 460 N.E.2d 1014 (Ind. App. 1984).

This section is inapplicable where a claim is based on a brokerage agreement involving the sale of personal property. Abex Corp. v. Vehling, 443 N.E.2d 1248 (Ind. App. 1983).

This section is applicable only to contracts with the owners of the real estate, not between a principal broker and his associate. Otto v. Pelis, 640 N.E.2d 712 (Ind. App. 1994).

Cancellation.
Cancellation of the contract by the broker defeated his right to the commission. Irwin v. State Brokerage Co., 82 Ind. App. 687, 147 N.E. 531 (1925).

Conduct and Authority of Broker.
If an agent employed to sell land was guilty of fraud, to the injury of his employer, he was liable, although the contract of employment was not in writing. Bragg v. Eagan, 51 Ind. App. 513, 98 N.E. 835 (1912).

An agent who was employed to sell land for a commission could not act as the agent of the landowner in signing the name of such owner to a contract authorizing the agent to sell the land and promising to pay the agent a commission for making the sale. Lowe v. Mohler, 56 Ind. App. 593, 105 N.E. 934 (1914).

Contingent Contracts.
Where only written contract was landown-er's acceptance of a proposition which contained a reservation that the offer was contingent on the purchaser's ability to obtain financing, and financing was not obtained and agent returned earnest money, agent could not recover commission although property was subsequently sold to such purchaser in the absence of a showing of fraud. Frash v. Eisenhower, 176 Ind. App. 659, 63 Ind. Dec. 5, 376 N.E.2d 1201 (1978).

Contract Between Brokers.
Where plaintiff and defendant, neither of whom owned any interest in an elevator, entered into an oral agreement to obtain a certain elevator for the purpose of resale, by the terms of which defendant was to obtain an option to purchase it and plaintiff was to find a purchaser therefor and the profits from the transaction were to be divided equally between them, and pursuant to such arrangement a profit of $8,000 resulted, but defendant paid plaintiff only $2,000 thereof, plaintiff could maintain an action in assumpsit for money had and received for the balance of the money to which he was entitled, since this statute was applicable only to contracts with owners of real estate. Clark v. Ward, 117 Ind. App. 307, 70 N.E.2d 755 (1947).

Contract Not Performed.
Trial court properly sustained demurrer where realtor brought suit for recovery of commission on sale, since amount received upon sale was less than amount specified in written agreement between realtor and owner, and contract to sell was therefore not performed. Ward v. Potts, 228 Ind. 228, 91 N.E.2d 643 (1950).

Description of Lands.
The following description was held sufficient: "I hereby agree to pay *** for trading my 615-acre farm at H." Herr v. McConnell, 67 Ind. App. 529, 119 N.E. 496 (1918).

A contract authorizing an agent to sell lands and promising to pay a commission therefor did not need to specifically describe the land, and such description could have been supplied by parol. Morton v. Gaffield, 51 Ind. App. 28, 98 N.E. 1007 (1921).

A city lot was presumed to be located in the city where the agreement was dated. Sowers v. Schommer, 82 Ind. App. 479, 144 N.E. 851 (1924).

Divisible Contracts.
Where part of an oral contract was within the statute of frauds, the whole contract, if it was entire and indivisible, was nonenforceable, but if the contract was divisible, then that part which was not within the statute could have been enforced. Belleville Lumber

Divisible Contracts. (Cont'd)
& Supply Co. v. Chamberlin, 120 Ind. App. 12, 84 N.E.2d 60 (1949).

An oral contract for the supervision of the development of a subdivision and for the sale of houses therein was an entire and indivisible contract within this section. Belleville Lumber & Supply Co. v. Chamberlin, 120 Ind. App. 12, 84 N.E.2d 60 (1949).

Division of Commissions.

The statute providing that contracts promising to pay commissions for sales of land had to be executed in writing by owners of the land did not render void contracts between brokers for a division of the commission when a sale was effected. Provident Trust Co. v. Darrough, 168 Ind. 29, 78 N.E. 1030 (1906).

Exchange of Land.

A broker could not recover a commission for bringing about an exchange of land under this section unless his contract was in writing; a "purchaser" included one who acquired title to land in an exchange of lands. Elmore v. Brinneman, 70 Ind. App. 222, 123 N.E. 248 (1919); Lewis v. Popejoy, 70 Ind. App. 590, 123 N.E. 646 (1919).

Execution After Services Performed.

If a written agreement promising to pay a commission for the sale of land was executed after the service had been rendered, it was valid. Doney v. Laughlin, 50 Ind. App. 38, 94 N.E. 1027 (1911); Miller v. Farr, 178 Ind. 36, 98 N.E. 805 (1912); Waddle v. Smith, 58 Ind. App. 587, 108 N.E. 537 (1915); Andrews v. Peters, 82 Ind. App. 200, 145 N.E. 579 (1924); Hatfield v. Thurston, 87 Ind. App. 541, 161 N.E. 568 (1928).

Execution Before Services Completed.

If an agreement to pay a commission for the sale of land was to pay the commission when the sale was completed, there must have been a complete and enforceable contract for a sale before the commission was due. Waddle v. Smith, 58 Ind. App. 587, 108 N.E. 537 (1915).

Foreign Contracts.

A contract executed in another state promising to pay a commission for the sale of land could have been enforced in this state although not in writing. Henning v. Hill, 80 Ind. App. 363, 141 N.E. 66 (1923).

Fraud.

Fraudulent representations of a person as to his ownership of land would not render him liable to pay a commission for the sale of the land under a parol contract. Fullenwider v. Goben, 176 Ind. 312, 95 N.E. 1010 (1911).

This section must not be so construed as to enable the landowner to commit imposition and fraud upon an agent where there was substantial compliance with the statute. Brown v. Ogle, 75 Ind. App. 90, 130 N.E. 147 (1921).

Gift of Land.

Where a donor engaged another to obtain a proposition in writing from a named association for the purchase of real estate, it being agreed that it was not to be obtained for any sale or actual purchase but for the purpose of enabling the donor to make a gift of the real estate only, the delivery of the proposition by the person so engaged to the donor was the "finding or procuring of a purchaser" within the meaning of this section. Borinstein v. Katzow, 222 Ind. 548, 55 N.E.2d 260 (1944).

Identification of Property.

The test of whether the description of the property is sufficient is whether from the information found within the four corners of the listing agreement, a reasonable man could locate the correct property. Day v. West, 176 Ind. App. 15, 61 Ind. Dec. 520, 373 N.E.2d 935 (1978).

Listing Contract.

The time element in a listing contract may neither be waived nor modified except by written instrument. Barrick Realty Co. v. Bogan, 422 N.E.2d 1306 (Ind. App. 1981).

Married Women.

A married woman could alone execute contract promising to pay commission for the sale of her separate lands. Isphording v. Wolfe, 36 Ind. App. 250, 75 N.E. 598 (1905).

Misrepresentation.

Where a broker told vendors that 1949 law required that property must be listed and a commission paid in order to sell or exchange real estate, such statement was not misrepresentation of the law to indicate bad faith sufficient to vitiate the written agreement between the parties, since the statute of frauds did require such listing, although the 1949 Act pertaining to licensing of real estate brokers did not. Lemons v. Barton, 134 Ind. App. 214, 186 N.E.2d 426 (1962).

Offer to Purchase Containing Parol Terms.

Offer to purchase real estate, which admittedly contained parol terms, was a parol contract for purposes of statute of frauds and broker's commission statute and was, therefore, unenforceable by broker in action for payment of commission. Shrum v. Dalton, 442 N.E.2d 366 (Ind. App. 1982).

Option.

An agreement employing a person to pro-

Option. (Cont'd)

cure for his employer an option to purchase real estate did not need to be in writing. Pierson v. Donham, 55 Ind. App. 636, 104 N.E. 606 (1914).

Specific contractual provisions describing the rights of the parties in the event of a grant of an option to purchase are required before brokers can collect commissions under given listing agreements, absent a written extension of time for performance or fraud on the part of the principal. Estate of Saemann v. Tucker Realty, 529 N.E.2d 126 (Ind. App. 1988).

Oral Contract for Commission.

Real estate broker could not bring suit for damages resulting from tortious interference with contractual relations when based on oral contract for commission in sale of real estate. William S. Deckelbaum Co. v. Equitable Life Assurance Soc'y, 419 N.E.2d 228, modified on other grounds, 422 N.E.2d 301 (Ind. App. 1981).

Purpose.

The purpose of this section is to prevent disputes over the terms of a commission contract for finding a purchaser for real estate. The statute is to protect owners against fraud; it is not to be used by owners to perpetrate a fraud on the one seeking a commission. In furtherance of these policies, performance by the finder or broker may take the agreement out of the provisions of this section. (Decided under former IC 32-2-2-1.) First Fed. Sav. Bank v. Galvin, 616 N.E.2d 1048 (Ind. App. 1993).

Revoked Offer.

This section, as a statute of frauds, was designed to prevent a verbal commission agreement from being actionable, because of the potential for fraud. There is no requirement that a commission clause be part of an unrevoked offer for the sale of land. Niepokoj v. Schulz, 514 N.E.2d 643 (Ind. App. 1987).

Services Performed.

Where evidence disclosed that real estate agent secured a buyer for property, that buyers signed a purchase agreement and paid earnest money, that buyers had made a loan application at the bank which was ready to be closed and owner of property refused to sign agreement contending he wanted to retain pipeline easement and mineral rights but never objected because of financial reasons, there was no evidence from which it could be concluded that the real estate agent did not perform the services contemplated and thus he should have recovered his commission. Day v. West, 176 Ind. App. 15, 61 Ind. Dec. 520, 373 N.E.2d 935 (1978).

Where there was no evidence that the personal representative was required to fulfill any unusual or additional duties during the course of a property auction, the court erred in awarding him a real estate commission in addition to the amount provided for in the testator's will. Grimm v. Kruse, 705 N.E.2d 483 (Ind. App. 1999).

Sufficiency of Memorandum.

The provision of the statute requiring contracts agreeing to pay a commission for the sale of land to be in writing could have been complied with by letters between the parties. Olcott v. McClure, 50 Ind. App. 79, 98 N.E. 82 (1912).

A correspondence in regard to compensation for services of broker in which the minds of the parties did not meet did not constitute a contract in writing under this section. Peters v. Martin, 69 Ind. App. 436, 122 N.E. 16 (1919).

Where a principal and broker failed to agree in writing as to a commission, the principal's contract with third party, procured by the broker, stating that the broker's commission would be not to exceed $500 did not sufficiently fix the amount within this section. Peters v. Martin, 69 Ind. App. 436, 122 N.E. 16 (1919).

A broker's contract for commission in the sale of real estate when in writing, as required by this section, and signed by the parties to be charged was sufficient, although not signed by the broker. Andrews v. Peters, 82 Ind. App. 200, 145 N.E. 579 (1924).

This section did not require that the terms of the sale had to be set out in the commission contract. Sowers v. Schommer, 82 Ind. App. 479, 144 N.E. 851 (1924).

Only the contract to pay commission for the sale of land, and not the terms of sale, were required to be in writing and signed by the owner. Bollero v. Wintermute, 91 Ind. App. 1, 168 N.E. 40 (1929).

Where there was written evidence of an agreement by an owner to pay a commission to one of its employees for finding a purchaser for certain property and the employee had performed his part of the bargain, the agreement to pay him a commission could be enforced where the employee sent a letter to the owner stating that its president had agreed to pay him a seven percent (7%) commission for finding a buyer, where the owner never contradicted this representation, where the minutes of the Senior Loan Committee supported this representation of the agreement, and where the owner clearly agreed to pay the employee a commission and the employee performed his part of the bargain, and this section did not operate to prevent enforcement of the agreement against the owner.

Sufficiency of Memorandum. (Cont'd)
First Fed. Sav. Bank v. Galvin, 616 N.E.2d 1048 (Ind. App. 1993).

Summary Judgment.

—Inappropriate.
Where a real estate brokerage agreement clearly conditioned its becoming effective upon written acceptance by the broker, the absence of undisputed evidence that the con-dition was complied with or waived rendered the grant of summary judgment on the contract inappropriate. Merri-Bowl, Inc. v. Hazifotis, 547 N.E.2d 1093 (Ind. App. 1989).

Trial.
When the facts found by the trial court necessarily lead to the conclusion that the agreement was in writing, such facts were treated as found. Andrews v. Peters, 82 Ind. App. 200, 145 N.E. 579 (1924).

Collateral References. 12 Am. Jur. 2d Brokers, §§ 38-41.

37 C.J.S. Frauds, Statute of, §§ 62, 63.

Statutory necessity and sufficiency of written statement as to amount of compensation in broker's contract to promote purchase, sale or exchange of real estate. 9 A.L.R.2d 747.

Right to recover on quantum meruit for broker's services in buying or selling real estate where contract is not in writing as required by statute in relation to brokers. 41 A.L.R.2d 905.

Agreement between brokers as within statute requiring agreements for commissions for the sale of real estate to be in writing. 44 A.L.R.2d 741.

Joint adventure agreement for acquisition, development, or sale of land as within provision of statute of frauds governing broker's agreement for commission on real estate sale. 48 A.L.R.2d 1042.

Authority of real estate broker to bind employer by representations to purchaser as to the character or condition of the property. 58 A.L.R.2d 10.

Real estate broker's right to commission as affected by failure or refusal of customer (prospect) to comply with valid contract. 74 A.L.R.2d 437.

Skill and care required of real estate broker. 94 A.L.R.2d 468.

Sufficiency, under statute of frauds, of description or designation of property in real estate brokerage contract. 30 A.L.R.3d 935.

Modern view as to right of real estate broker to recover commission from seller-principal where buyer defaults under valid contract of sale. 12 A.L.R.4th 1083.

Real-estate broker's right to recover commission from seller where sale fails because of seller's failure to deliver good title — modern cases. 28 A.L.R.4th 1007.

Liability for tortious interference with prospective contractual relations involving sale of business, stock, or real estate. 71 A.L.R.5th 491.

32-21-1-11. Execution in foreign country. — If executed in a foreign country, conveyances, mortgages, and other instruments in writing that would be admitted to record under the recording laws of this state must be acknowledged by the grantor or person executing the instrument and proved before any diplomatic or consular officer of the United States, duly accredited, or before any officer of the foreign country who, by the laws of that country, is authorized to take acknowledgments or proof of conveyances. If the acknowledgment or proof is in the English language and attested by the official seal of the officer acknowledging it, the instrument may be admitted to record. However, if the acknowledgment or proof is in a language other than English or is not attested by an official seal, then the instrument must be accompanied by a certificate of a diplomatic or consular officer of the United States attesting:

(1) that the instrument is duly executed according to the laws of the foreign country;

(2) that the officer certifying the acknowledgment or proof had legal authority to do so; and

(3) to the meaning of the instrument, if the instrument is made in a foreign language. [P.L.2-2002, § 6.]

32-21-1-12. No requirement for seal or ink scroll.

— It is not necessary to affix a private seal or ink scroll necessary to validate a conveyance of land or an interest in land executed by a natural person, business trust, or corporation. It is not necessary for the officer taking the acknowledgment of the conveyance to use an ink scroll or seal unless the officer is required by law to keep an official seal. [P.L.2-2002, § 6.]

NOTES TO DECISIONS

In General.

IC 34-1-16-3 did not dispense with the necessity of a seal when a seal was expressly required by statute. Conkey v. Conder, 137 Ind. 441, 37 N.E. 132 (1894).

Since the enactment of this statute, private seals did not need to be used by natural persons in executing conveyances. Heller v. Dailey, 28 Ind. App. 555, 63 N.E. 490 (1902).

32-21-1-13. Conveyance by deed — Requirements — Exceptions.

— Except for a bona fide lease for a term not exceeding three (3) years, a conveyance of land or of any interest in land shall be made by a deed that is:
(1) written; and
(2) subscribed, sealed, and acknowledged by the grantor (as defined in IC 32-17-1-1) or by the grantor's attorney. [P.L.2-2002, § 6.]

32-21-1-14. Conveyance by attorney.

— A conveyance of land by attorney is not good unless the attorney is empowered by a written instrument that is subscribed, sealed, and acknowledged by the attorney's principal in the same manner that is required for a conveyance by the attorney's principal. [P.L.2-2002, § 6.]

NOTES TO DECISIONS

ANALYSIS

In general.
Contracts for commissions.
Husband and wife.
Marriage.

In General.

A purchaser was not bound to accept the deed of an attorney in fact where the vendor was so situated as to be capable of conveying by his own act. Dawson v. Shirley, 6 Blackf. 531 (1843).

A power of attorney to convey lands in this state must be executed in the same manner as a conveyance, and the deed under the power must be executed in the same manner as other deeds, and both instruments must be acknowledged and recorded according to the statutory requirements. Butterfield v. Beall, 3 Ind. 203 (1851).

Defects in the acknowledgment of a power of attorney did not affect the validity of a contract of sale executed by such attorney. Joseph v. Fisher, 122 Ind. 399, 23 N.E. 856 (1890).

It had to appear that an attorney who executed a conveyance had authority to exe-

In General. (Cont'd)
cute the instrument. Ramage v. Wilson, 37 Ind. App. 532, 77 N.E. 368 (1906).

Contracts for Commissions.
An agent of a landowner could validly sign a contract for the payment of a commission for obtaining purchaser for real estate even though the authorization of the agent was not in writing. Brown v. Poulos, 78 Ind. Dec. 869, 411 N.E.2d 712 (Ind. App. 1980).

Husband and Wife.
Where a husband and wife executed a power of attorney to sell the real estate of the wife, a deed executed by such attorney con-veyed the title of the wife, although the attorney-in-fact failed to insert in the deed, and subscribe thereto, the name of the husband, since it was apparent that the attorney intended to execute the power fully and effectually, and the purchase money was received and retained by the husband and wife. Ellison v. Branstrator, 153 Ind. 146, 54 N.E. 433 (1899).

Marriage.
The marriage of a man did not revoke a power of attorney previously given by him to convey lands. Joseph v. Fisher, 122 Ind. 399, 23 N.E. 856 (1890).

32-21-1-15. Quitclaim deeds. — A conveyance of land that is:
(1) worded in substance as "A.B. quitclaims to C.D." (here describe the premises) "for the sum of" (here insert the consideration); and
(2) signed, sealed, and acknowledged by the grantor (as defined in IC 32-17-1-1);
is a good and sufficient conveyance in quitclaim to the grantee and the grantee's heirs and assigns. [P.L.2-2002, § 6.]

Cross References. Title conveyed by quit-claim deed, IC 32-17-2-1.

NOTES TO DECISIONS

ANALYSIS

In general.
After-acquired titles.
—Expectant estates.
Bona fide purchasers.
Interest conveyed.

In General.
Quitclaim deeds conveyed title as effectively as warranty deeds. Rowe v. Beckett, 30 Ind. 154, 95 Am. Dec. 676 (1868); Davidson v. Coon, 125 Ind. 497, 25 N.E. 601, 9 L.R.A. 584 (1890).

General release of all interest of grantor in lands, with covenants of warranty, was only a quitclaim deed. Stephenson v. Boody, 139 Ind. 60, 38 N.E. 331 (1894).

Where boundaries to land purported to have been conveyed by quitclaim deed were pointed out, but deed did not convey all of such land, the purchaser could recover the pro rata value of the portion of real estate omitted from the deed. Equitable Trust Co. v. Milligan, 31 Ind. App. 20, 65 N.E. 1044 (1903).

The use of the word "assign" as an operative word of conveyance was sufficient to meet the requirements of the statute concerning quitclaim deeds. Reagan v. Dugan, 112 Ind. App. 479, 41 N.E.2d 841 (1942).

After-Acquired Titles.

—Expectant Estates.
Grantors in quitclaim could assert after-acquired title. Nicholson v. Caress, 45 Ind. 479 (1874); Graham v. Graham, 55 Ind. 23 (1876); Avery v. Akins, 74 Ind. 283 (1881); Bryan v. Uland, 101 Ind. 477, 1 N.E. 52 (1884); Haskett v. Maxey, 134 Ind. 182, 33 N.E. 358, 19 L.R.A. 379 (1892); McAdams v. Bailey, 169 Ind. 518, 82 N.E. 1057, 13 L.R.A. (n.s.) 1003, 124 Am. St. 240 (1907); Buckel v. Auer, 68 Ind. App. 320, 120 N.E. 437 (1918).

Conveyances and releases by quitclaim deeds of expectant estates were looked upon with suspicion and presumed fraudulent and not enforceable unless they were clearly made to appear to have been perfectly fair transactions. Avery v. Akins, 74 Ind. 283 (1881); McClure v. Raben, 125 Ind. 139, 25 N.E. 179, 9 L.R.A. 477 (1890); McAdams v. Bailey, 169 Ind. 518, 82 N.E. 1057, 13 L.R.A. (n.s.) 1003, 124 Am. St. R. 240 (1907); Farmers' Loan & Trust Co. v. Wood, 78 Ind. App. 147, 134 N.E. 899 (1922).

Bona Fide Purchasers.
If the grantee in a quitclaim deed made a warranty deed in conveying said land, his grantee was entitled to protection as an innocent purchaser. Meikel v. Borders, 129 Ind.

Bona Fide Purchasers. (Cont'd)
529, 29 N.E. 29 (1891); Rinehardt v. Reifers, 158 Ind. 675, 64 N.E. 459 (1902).

Grantees in quitclaim deeds could have been bona fide or innocent purchasers. Smith v. McClain, 146 Ind. 77, 45 N.E. 41 (1896); Sullenger v. Baecher, 55 Ind. App. 365, 101 N.E. 517, 102 N.E. 380 (1913). But see Meikel v. Borders, 129 Ind. 529, 29 N.E. 29 (1891); Hancock v. Wiggins, 28 Ind. App. 449, 63 N.E. 242 (1902); Aetna Life Ins. Co. v. Stryker, 38 Ind. App. 312, 73 N.E. 953, 76 N.E. 822 (1905), rehearing overruled, 38 Ind. App. 327, 78 N.E. 245 (1906); Korporal v. Robinson, 38 Ind. App. 110, 78 N.E. 84 (1906).

The grantee in a quitclaim deed was to have been considered a bona fide purchaser if the purchase was made in good faith for a fair price. Sullenger v. Baecher, 55 Ind. App. 365, 101 N.E. 517, 102 N.E. 380 (1913).

Interest Conveyed.
A quitclaim deed conveyed only such inter-est in the land described therein as the grantor held at the time of the conveyance. Sabinske v. Patterson, 100 Ind. App. 657, 196 N.E. 539 (1935).

Where, after foreclosure of a mortgage and entry of deficiency judgment, the mortgagors executed an instrument assigning all their right, title, and interest in the real estate and their right to purchase it at foreclosure sale or to redeem therefrom, and therein consented to the purchase by the assignee from any holder of title and relinquished any and all rights they had in and to the property, such instrument conveyed all the right, title, and interest which the mortgagors had in the real estate to the assignee, who, being the owner thereof, was possessed of the statutory right to redeem from the foreclosure sale. Reagan v. Dugan, 112 Ind. App. 479, 41 N.E.2d 841 (1942).

32-21-1-16. No specific language to create estate of inheritance. — It is not necessary to use the words "heirs and assigns of the grantee" to create in the grantee an estate of inheritance. If it is the intention of the grantor (as defined in IC 32-17-1-1) to convey any lesser estate, the grantor shall express that intention in the deed. [P.L.2-2002, § 6.]

NOTES TO DECISIONS

ANALYSIS

In general.
Appurtenances.
Former law.
Rules of construction.
Words of inheritance.

In General.
When the word "heirs" was used in a deed in connection with the grantee in its ordinary legal signification, a fee simple estate was vested in the grantee. Shimer v. Mann, 99 Ind. 190, 50 Am. R. 82 (1884); Taney v. Fahnley, 126 Ind. 88, 25 N.E. 882 (1890); Lane v. Utz, 130 Ind. 235, 29 N.E. 772 (1892); Teal v. Richardson, 160 Ind. 119, 66 N.E. 435 (1903); Newhaus v. Brennan, 49 Ind. App. 654, 97 N.E. 938 (1912).

Estates that were created by deeds under the rule in Shelley's Case. Earnhart v. Earnhart, 127 Ind. 397, 26 N.E. 895, 22 Am. St. R. 652 (1891); Jackson v. Jackson, 127 Ind. 346, 26 N.E. 897 (1891); Lane v. Utz, 130 Ind. 235, 29 N.E. 772 (1892); Perkins v. McConnell, 136 Ind. 384, 36 N.E. 121 (1894); McIlhinny v. McIlhinny, 137 Ind. 411, 37 N.E. 147, 24 L.R.A. 489, 45 Am. St. R. 186 (1894); Granger v. Granger, 147 Ind. 95, 44 N.E. 189 (1896), rehearing overruled, 147 Ind. 101, 46 N.E. 80, 36 L.R.A. 186, 190 (1897); Chamberlain v. Runkle, 28 Ind. App. 599, 63 N.E. 486 (1902); McCllen v. Lehker, 70 Ind. App. 435, 123 N.E. 475 (1919).

Fee simple estate could have been conveyed and a life estate reserved to grantor. Cates v. Cates, 135 Ind. 272, 34 N.E. 957 (1893); Timmons v. Timmons, 49 Ind. App. 21, 96 N.E. 622 (1911); Kokomo Trust Co. v. Hiller, 67 Ind. App. 611, 116 N.E. 332 (1917).

The use of the words "conveys and warrants" in the statutory form of warranty deed in Indiana created a conveyance in fee simple; and the use of words of inheritance were unnecessary. Crecelius v. New Albany Mach. Mfg. Co., 4 F.2d 369 (7th Cir. 1924).

Under this section, when the granting clause of a deed was general or indefinite respecting the estate in the lands conveyed, it could have been defined, qualified, and controlled by the habendum. Claridge v. Phelps, 105 Ind. App. 344, 11 N.E.2d 503 (1937).

Appurtenances.
Under the provisions of this section, in granting a right-of-way which would have become appurtenant to land, it was not necessary to use the words "heirs and assigns." Cleveland, C., C. & St. L. Ry. v. Griswold, 51 Ind. App. 497, 97 N.E. 1030 (1912).

Former Law.

Deeds executed prior to the statutes of 1852, containing no words of inheritance, and deeds executed under the common law, not containing the word "heir" or "heirs," did not convey a fee simple estate. Nelson v. Davis, 35 Ind. 474 (1871); Nicholson v. Caress, 59 Ind. 39 (1877); Fountain County Coal & Mining Co. v. Beckleheimer, 102 Ind. 76, 1 N.E. 202, 52 Am. R. 645 (1885); Lamb v. Medsker, 35 Ind. App. 662, 74 N.E. 1012 (1905).

Rules of Construction.

A deed had to be strictly construed against the grantor because he had the advantage of drafting it, so generally the grantee was entitled to the greatest estate possible under the language used. Long v. Horton, 126 Ind. App. 651, 133 N.E.2d 568 (1956).

Where there was any inconsistency between the granting clause and the habendum clause of a deed, the granting clause prevailed as the most dependable expression of the grantor's intention. Long v. Horton, 126 Ind. App. 651, 133 N.E.2d 568 (1956).

Words of Inheritance.

It was not necessary to use the words "heirs and assigns of the grantee" in a deed in order to have created in the grantee an estate of inheritance. Chamberlain v. Runkle, 28 Ind. App. 599, 63 N.E. 486 (1902); Adams v. Merrill, 45 Ind. App. 315, 85 N.E. 114 (1908), reh'g overruled, 45 Ind. App. 327, 87 N.E. 36 (1909).

Where words of inheritance were not used in a deed, the entire instrument could have been considered in determining the estate granted. Long v. Horton, 126 Ind. App. 651, 133 N.E.2d 568 (1956).

CHAPTER 2

RECORDING PROCESS

32-21-2-1. "Grantor" defined. — As used in this chapter, "grantor" has the meaning set forth in IC 32-17-1-1. [P.L.2-2002, § 6.]

Effective Dates. P.L.2-2002, § 6. July 1. 2002.

32-21-2-2. "Tract" defined. — As used in this chapter, "tract" means an area of land that is:

(1) under common fee simple ownership;

(2) contained within a continuous border; and

(3) a separately identified parcel for property tax purposes.
[P.L.2-2002, § 6.]

32-21-2-3. Requirements for recording. — For a conveyance, a mortgage, or an instrument of writing to be recorded, it must be:

(1) acknowledged by the grantor; or

(2) proved before a:

(A) judge;

(B) clerk of a court of record;

(C) county auditor;

(D) county recorder;

(E) notary public;

(F) mayor of a city in Indiana or any other state;

(G) commissioner appointed in a state other than Indiana by the governor of Indiana;

(H) minister, charge d'affaires, or consul of the United States in any foreign country;

(I) clerk of the city county council for a consolidated city, city clerk for a second class city, or clerk-treasurer for a third class city;

(J) clerk-treasurer for a town; or

(K) person authorized under IC 2-3-4-1.

[P.L.2-2002, § 6.]

Cross References. Attaching certificate to deed, IC 32-21-1-9.

Disputing truth of certificate, IC 32-21-1-11.

Explanation of instrument by officer, IC 32-21-1-8.

False attestation by officer, IC 35-44-1-2.

Foreign countries, acknowledgments in, IC 32-21-1-11.

Form of acknowledgment, IC 32-21-1-7.

Notaries disqualified to act, IC 33-16-2-7.

Powers, IC 33-16-2-5.

Prosecuting attorneys taking acknowledgments, IC 33-14-5-1, IC 33-14-5-2.

NOTES TO DECISIONS

ANALYSIS

In general.
Corporations.
Correction of certificate.
Effect of acknowledgment.
Illegal or defective acknowledgment.
Joint parties.
Mechanic's liens.
Necessity of acknowledgment.
Sufficiency of acknowledgment.
—Completion.
—Corporations.
—Defective.
—Identity of acknowledgers.
—Illustrative cases.
—Married women.
—Presence.

In General.

All courts of this state took judicial notice of the statute which entitled a deed of conveyance to be recorded. Peak v. State, 240 Ind. 334, 163 N.E.2d 584 (1960).

Corporations.

A notary who was a stockholder in a corporation could not take the acknowledgment of an instrument executed to the corporation. Kothe v. Krag-Reynolds Co., 20 Ind. App. 293, 50 N.E. 594 (1898).

Correction of Certificate.

The certificate of the officer to an acknowledgment could have been corrected by him at any time. Westhafer v. Patterson, 120 Ind. 459, 22 N.E. 414, 16 Am. St. 330 (1889). See

also, Jordan v. Corey, 2 Ind. 385, 52 Am. Dec. 516 (1850).

Effect of Acknowledgment.

If a deed was apparently acknowledged properly, it was prima facie proof of its execution. Carver v. Carver, 97 Ind. 497 (1884); Krom v. Vermillion, 143 Ind. 75, 41 N.E. 539 (1895).

Illegal or Defective Acknowledgment.

The only effect of an illegal or defective acknowledgment was to render the recording of the instrument of no effect. It was good between the parties and as to those having notice of it without acknowledgment or recording. Hubble v. Wright, 23 Ind. 322 (1864); Mays v. Hedges, 79 Ind. 288 (1881); Givan v. Doe ex dem. Tout, 7 Blackf. 210 (1844); Bever v. North, 107 Ind. 544, 8 N.E. 576 (1886); Wine v. Woods, 109 Ind. 291, 10 N.E. 399 (1887); Westhafer v. Patterson, 120 Ind. 459, 22 N.E. 414, 16 Am. St. R. 330 (1889); Davidson v. State, 135 Ind. 254, 34 N.E. 972 (1893); Blair v. Whittaker, 31 Ind. App. 664, 69 N.E. 182 (1903); Bereolos v. Roth, 74 Ind. App. 100, 124 N.E. 410 (1919); Cypress Creek Coal Co. v. Boonville Mining Co., 194 Ind. 187, 142 N.E. 645 (1924).

The Act of 1875 legalized certain defective acknowledgments taken outside of the state. Steeple v. Downing, 60 Ind. 478 (1878); Cole v. Wright, 70 Ind. 179 (1880).

Generally, it was only subsequent purchasers for value who could take advantage of defective acknowledgments. Westhafer v.

Illegal or Defective
Acknowledgment. (Cont'd)
Patterson, 120 Ind. 459, 22 N.E. 414, 16 Am.
St. R. 330 (1889); Bryant v. Richardson, 126
Ind. 145, 25 N.E. 807 (1890).

Any mere informality in, or omission from,
the certificate of acknowledgment did not
invalidate the conveyance. Bryant v.
Richardson, 126 Ind. 145, 25 N.E. 807 (1890).

If the acknowledgment of an instrument
was illegal, the record of such instrument was
not constructive notice to anyone. Kothe v.
Krag-Reynolds Co., 20 Ind. App. 293, 50 N.E.
594 (1898); Bledsoe v. Ross, 59 Ind. App. 609,
109 N.E. 53 (1915).

Joint Parties.
One of the parties to a deed or other instrument could not take the acknowledgment of
the other parties thereto. Hubble v. Wright,
23 Ind. 322 (1864); Kothe v. Krag-Reynolds
Co., 20 Ind. App. 293, 50 N.E. 594 (1898).

Mechanic's Liens.
The acknowledgment requirement for filings regarding alienation of property, found in
this section, do not apply to mechanic's liens.
Eyster v. S.A. Birnbaum Contracting, Inc.,
662 N.E.2d 201 (Ind. App. 1996).

Necessity of Acknowledgment.
Any conveyance, mortgage or other instrument which was recorded without being duly
acknowledged or proved was not constructive
notice to anyone. Deming v. State ex rel.
Miller, 23 Ind. 416 (1864); Watkins v. Brunt,
53 Ind. 208 (1876); Sanders v. Muegge, 91 Ind.
214 (1883); Reeves v. Hayes, 95 Ind. 521
(1884); Carver v. Carver, 97 Ind. 497 (1884);
Walters v. Hartwig, 106 Ind. 123, 6 N.E. 5
(1886); Kothe v. Krag-Reynolds Co., 20 Ind.
App. 293, 50 N.E. 594 (1898); Sinclair v.
Gunzenhauser, 179 Ind. 78, 98 N.E. 37 (1912);
Carmichael v. Arms, 51 Ind. App. 689, 100
N.E. 302 (1912); Bledsoe v. Ross, 59 Ind. App.
609, 109 N.E. 53 (1915); Bereolos v. Roth, 74
Ind. App. 100, 124 N.E. 410 (1919); Starz v.
Kirsch, 78 Ind. App. 431, 136 N.E. 36 (1922).

Under the express terms of this section, to
entitle any conveyance, mortgage, or instrument of writing to have been recorded, it must
have been acknowledged or proved as required by statute. Carver v. Carver, 97 Ind.
497 (1884); Bledsoe v. Ross, 59 Ind. App. 609,
109 N.E. 53 (1915); Bereolos v. Roth, 74 Ind.
App. 100, 124 N.E. 410 (1919).

Sufficiency of Acknowledgment.

—Completion.
While the form of the acknowledgment itself may deviate as long as it is substantially
the same as found in former IC 32-1-2-23
(repealed; see IC 32-21-1-7 for similar provi-

sions), the completion of the acknowledgment
of the document sought to be acknowledged
must be strictly complied with. Baldin v. Calumet Nat'l Bank, 135 Bankr. 586 (Bankr.
N.D. Ind. 1991).

—Corporations.
Where mortgage revealed a single corporate grantor, signed by representatives of the
corporation, as evidenced by the corporate
titles next to the individuals' respective
names, and an acknowledgment signed by the
same individuals, both of whom happened to
be designated as husband and wife, the lack
of any direct reference in the acknowledgment to the corporate grantor was insufficient
to render the mortgage invalid. United States
v. Arnol & Mildred Shafer Farms, Inc., 107
Bankr. 605 (N.D. Ind. 1989).

—Defective.
Recording of a mortgage with a defective
acknowledgment was in effect no recording at
all and thus did not provide constructive
notice, even though the deed was in fact
received for recording by the county recorder.
Baldin v. Calumet Nat'l Bank, 135 Bankr. 586
(Bankr. N.D. Ind. 1991).

—Identity of Acknowledgers.
Pursuant to Indiana law, a proper acknowledgment must provide the identity of the
acknowledgers, and state that they are the
same parties that executed the underlying
instrument as well. Baldin v. Calumet Nat'l
Bank, 135 Bankr. 586 (Bankr. N.D. Ind.
1991).

—Illustrative Cases.
A certificate of acknowledgment of a deed in
the following words, "personally came A.B.,
the executor of the annexed deed, and acknowledged it," was held to have been sufficient. Davar v. Cardwell, 27 Ind. 478 (1867);
Brown v. Corbin, 121 Ind. 455, 23 N.E. 276
(1890); Bryant v. Richardson, 126 Ind. 145, 25
N.E. 807 (1890); Indiana Natural Gas & Oil
Co. v. Leer, 34 Ind. App. 61, 72 N.E. 283
(1904); Guyer v. Union Trust Co., 55 Ind. App.
472, 104 N.E. 82 (1914).

Where deeds to real estate in Indiana were
executed in another state and acknowledged
and certified under the seal of a notary public,
the acknowledgments were not invalidated by
the manner in which they were taken, nor by
the form of the certificate used by the notary.
Ingram v. Jeffersonville, N.A. & S. Rapid
Transit Co., 65 Ind. App. 532, 116 N.E. 12
(1917).

—Married Women.
The acknowledgments of married women
were to have been taken the same as those of

Sufficiency of Acknowledgment. (Cont'd)

—Married Women. (Cont'd)
other persons. Hubble v. Wright, 23 Ind. 322 (1864).

—Presence.
Persons must have been personally present before the officer taking the acknowledgment of a deed. Woods v. Polhemus, 8 Ind. 60 (1856); Mays v. Hedges, 79 Ind. 288 (1881).

Collateral References. Notice by recording of instrument not entitled to be recorded because of insufficiency of acknowledgment. 59 A.L.R.2d 1299.

Disqualification of attorney, otherwise qualified, to take oath or acknowledgment from client. 21 A.L.R.3d 483.

32-21-2-4. Acknowledgement in county other than recording. —
(a) This section applies when a conveyance, mortgage, or other instrument that is required to be recorded is acknowledged in any county in Indiana other than the county in which the instrument is required to be recorded.

(b) The acknowledgment must be:

(1) certified by the clerk of the circuit court of the county in which the officer resides; and

(2) attested by the seal of that court.

However, an acknowledgment before an officer having an official seal, if the acknowledgment is attested by that official seal, is sufficient without a certificate. [P.L.2-2002, § 6.]

32-21-2-5. Acknowledgement outside Indiana but inside United States. — To record in Indiana a conveyance that is acknowledged outside Indiana but within the United States, the conveyance must be:

(1) certified by the clerk of any court of record of the county in which the officer receiving the acknowledgment resides; and

(2) attested by the seal of that court.

However, an acknowledgment before an officer having an official seal that is attested by the officer's official seal is sufficient without a certificate. [P.L.2-2002, § 6.]

NOTES TO DECISIONS

In General.
Deeds acknowledged in other states before officers having no seals, and not certified by the clerk of a court, of record, and which had been recorded in this state, were legalized by Acts 1875, ch. 42, p. 61. Steeple v. Downing, 60 Ind. 478 (1878); Cole v. Wright, 70 Ind. 179 (1880).

A duly certified copy of a deed recorded in another state could have been admitted in evidence without such copy bearing an impress of the seal of the officer taking the acknowledgment of such deed. Benefiel v. Aughe, 93 Ind. 401 (1884).

Where deeds to real estate in Indiana were executed in another state and acknowledged and certified under the seal of a notary public, the acknowledgments were not invalidated by the manner in which they were taken, nor by the form of the certificate used by the notary. Ingram v. Jeffersonville, N.A. & S. Rapid Transit Co., 65 Ind. App. 532, 116 N.E. 12 (1917).

32-21-2-6. Proving deed. — A deed may be proved according to the rules of common law before any officer who is authorized to take acknowledgments. A deed that is proved in the manner provided in this section is entitled to be recorded. [P.L.2-2002, § 6.]

Cross References. Acknowledgments in foreign countries, IC 32-21-1-11.

32-21-2-7. Form of acknowledgement. — The following or any other form substantially the same is a good or sufficient form of acknowledgment of a deed or mortgage:

"Before me, E.F. (judge or justice, as the case may be) this _____ day of _____, A.B. acknowledged the execution of the annexed deed, (or mortgage, as the case may be.)"
[P.L.2-2002, § 6.]

Cross References. Attachment of certificate to deed, IC 32-21-1-9.

Explanation of instrument by person taking acknowledgment, IC 32-21-1-8.

False attestation by officer, IC 35-44-1-2.

Signing blank forms, penalty, IC 35-44-1-2.

NOTES TO DECISIONS

ANALYSIS

In general.
Chattel mortgages.
Correction of certificate.
Effect of acknowledgment.
Sufficiency of acknowledgment.
—Completion.
—Corporations.
—Defective.

In General.

A certificate of acknowledgment of a deed in the following words "personally came A.B., the executor of the annexed deed, and acknowledged it," was held to have been sufficient. Davar v. Cardwell, 27 Ind. 478 (1867); Brown v. Corbin, 121 Ind. 455, 23 N.E. 276 (1890); Bryant v. Richardson, 126 Ind. 145, 25 N.E. 807 (1890); Indiana Natural Gas & Oil Co. v. Leer, 34 Ind. App. 61, 72 N.E. 283 (1904); Guyer v. Union Trust Co., 55 Ind. App. 472, 104 N.E. 82 (1914); Ingram v. Jeffersonville, N.A. & S. Rapid Transit Co., 65 Ind. App. 532, 116 N.E. 12 (1917).

A certificate of acknowledgment merely stating that the mortgagors signed the mortgage was insufficient. Guyer v. Union Trust Co., 55 Ind. App. 472, 104 N.E. 82 (1914).

It was not a breach of his official bond for a justice of the peace to execute, under his official seal, a certificate that a promissory note was signed by a certain person in his presence, when in fact it was not so signed, since, under Const., Art. 7, § 14, his powers were only statutory, and there was no statutory requirement or authority for the acknowledgment of a promissory note. State ex rel. Coppage v. Reichard, 59 Ind. App. 338, 109 N.E. 438 (1915).

Where the chattel mortgage showed that the mortgagor was known to the notary who took the acknowledgment to be the person who executed the instrument of his free act, for the purpose of mortgaging the property named therein, it was sufficient for the purposes of this section, as against a subsequent execution purchaser who had actual knowledge of the mortgage. Voigt v. Ludlow Typograph Co., 213 Ind. 329, 12 N.E.2d 499 (1938).

Chattel Mortgages.

The acknowledgment of the execution of a chattel mortgage must have been in substantial compliance with the form of acknowledgments provided by statute, and if such a mortgage not properly acknowledged was recorded, the record was not notice of its existence to any person, and was not binding upon anyone except the parties to the mortgage. Guyer v. Union Trust Co., 55 Ind. App. 472, 104 N.E. 82 (1914).

A certificate of acknowledgment of a chattel mortgage was not sufficient to justify the record of the instrument, where, in addition to its bad form and failure to state the names of the parties acknowledging, and whether they acknowledged before the officer, it failed to give the state and county in which it was acknowledged or in which the notary had his appointment. Wartell v. Peters Hotel Co., 70 Ind. App. 444, 123 N.E. 480 (1919).

Correction of Certificate.

An officer taking an acknowledgment had the right, and it was his duty, to correct mistakes in his certificate. Jordan v. Corey, 2 Ind. 385, 52 Am. Dec. 516 (1850); Woods v. Polhemus, 8 Ind. 60 (1856); Westhafer v. Patterson, 120 Ind. 459, 22 N.E. 414, 16 Am. St. R. 330 (1889).

Effect of Acknowledgment.

A certificate of acknowledgment in proper

Effect of Acknowledgment. (Cont'd)
form was prima facie evidence of the execution of the instrument. Carver v. Carver, 97 Ind. 497 (1884); Krom v. Vermillion, 143 Ind. 75, 41 N.E. 539 (1895).

Sufficiency of Acknowledgment.

—Completion.
While the form of the acknowledgment itself may deviate as long as it is substantially the same as found in this section, the completion of the acknowledgment of the document sought to be acknowledged must be strictly complied with. Baldin v. Calumet Nat'l Bank, 135 Bankr. 586 (Bankr. N.D. Ind. 1991).

—Corporations.
Where mortgage revealed a single corporate grantor, signed by representatives of the corporation, as evidenced by the corporate titles next to the individuals' respective names, and an acknowledgment signed by the same individuals, both of whom happened to be designated as husband and wife, the lack of any direct reference in the acknowledgment to the corporate grantor was insufficient to render the mortgage invalid. United States v. Arnol & Mildred Shafer Farms, Inc., 107 Bankr. 605 (N.D. Ind. 1989).

—Defective.
Recording of a mortgage with a defective acknowledgment was in effect no recording at all and thus did not provide constructive notice, even though the deed was in fact received for recording by the county recorder. Baldin v. Calumet Nat'l Bank, 135 Bankr. 586 (Bankr. N.D. Ind. 1991).

Collateral References. Measure of damages for false or incomplete certificate by notary public. 13 A.L.R.3d 1039.

32-21-2-8. Duty of public officer to explain deed to grantor. — (a) If before a public officer authorized to receive acknowledgment of deeds:

(1) the grantor of a deed intends to sign the deed with the grantor's mark; and

(2) in all other cases when the public officer has good cause to believe that the contents and purport of the deed are not fully known to the grantor;

it is the duty of the public officer before signature to fully explain to the grantor the contents and purport of the deed.

(b) The failure of the public officer to comply with subsection (a) does not affect the validity of a deed. [P.L.2-2002, § 6.]

Cross References. Penalty for failure to make explanation, IC 35-44-1-2.

NOTES TO DECISIONS

In General.
The signing of the name of a person to an instrument by his authority was a sufficient signing of the instrument. Nye v. Lowry, 82 Ind. 316 (1881); Kennedy v. Graham, 9 Ind. App. 624, 35 N.E. 925 (1893), rehearing denied, 37 N.E. 25 (1894); Crumrine v. Crumrine's Estate, 14 Ind. App. 641, 43 N.E. 322 (1896); Ashwell v. Miller, 54 Ind. App. 381, 103 N.E. 37 (1913).

The failure of an officer to discharge the duty imposed on him by this section did not invalidate the deed. Fitzgerald v. Goff, 99 Ind. 28 (1884); Leslie v. Merrick, 99 Ind. 180 (1884).

32-21-2-9. Certificate of acknowledgement. — A certificate of the acknowledgment of a conveyance or other instrument in writing that is required to be recorded, signed, and sealed by the officer taking the acknowledgment shall be written on or attached to the deed. When by law the certificate of the clerk of the proper county is required to accompany the acknowledgment, the certificate shall state that:

(1) the officer before whom the acknowledgment was taken was, at the time of the acknowledgment, acting lawfully; and

(2) the clerk's signature to the certificate of acknowledgment is genuine. [P.L.2-2002, § 6.]

NOTES TO DECISIONS

ANALYSIS

In general.
False certificate.
—Indictment.

In General.

An officer who took an acknowledgment may, at any time, correct mistakes in the certificate of acknowledgment, and it is his duty to make such corrections, which duty may be enforced. Woods v. Polhemus, 8 Ind. 60 (1856); Westhafer v. Patterson, 120 Ind. 459, 22 N.E. 414, 16 Am. St. R. 330 (1889). See also, Jordan v. Corey, 2 Ind. 385, 52 Am. Dec. 516 (1850).

If the official character of an officer who took an acknowledgment was stated in the body of the certificate of acknowledgment, such character need not have been stated after the signature of the officer to such certificate. Indiana Natural Gas & Oil Co. v. Leer, 34 Ind. App. 61, 72 N.E. 283 (1904).

A chattel mortgage was not invalid on the ground that it did not contain a description of the property sought to be mortgaged where the mortgaged property was referred to as contained in a schedule of property attached thereto and marked "Exhibit A," which schedule appeared after the notary's certificate of acknowledgment. Voigt v. Ludlow Typograph Co., 213 Ind. 329, 12 N.E.2d 499 (1938).

False Certificate.

—Indictment.

In an indictment for making a false certificate as a notary public to a deed where the entire certificate of the notary was set out verbatim in the indictment, the necessity of alleging a conclusion as to its legal significance was eliminated. Peak v. State, 240 Ind. 334, 163 N.E.2d 584 (1960).

32-21-2-10. Book of deeds kept by recorder. — A recorder of deeds shall keep a book having each page divided into five (5) columns that are headed as follows:

Date of Reception.	Names of Grantors.	Names of Grantees.	Description of Land.	Vol. and Page Where Recorded.

The recorder shall enter in this book all deeds and other instruments left with the recorder to be recorded. The recorder shall note in the first column the day and hour of receiving the deed or instrument and shall note the other particulars in the appropriate columns. A deed or instrument is considered recorded at the time the date of reception is noted by the recorder. [P.L.2-2002, § 6.]

NOTES TO DECISIONS

ANALYSIS

In general.
Highway easements.

In General.

Instruments were deemed recorded from the time they were entered in the entry book. Kessler v. State ex rel. Wilson, 24 Ind. 313 (1865), overruled on other grounds, Gilchrist v. Gough, 63 Ind. 576 (1878); Sinclair v. Gunzenhauser, 179 Ind. 78, 98 N.E. 37 (1912).

Instruments duly recorded and indexed were notice to subsequent purchasers whether the instruments were entered in the entry book or not. Nichol v. Henry, 89 Ind. 54 (1883).

The entry books kept by county recorders

In General. (Cont'd)
were not parts of the records of such offices, and did not constitute notice of the contents of records. Sinclair v. Gunzenhauser, 179 Ind. 78, 98 N.E. 37, 100 N.E. 376 (1912).

The entry book of a recorder was only notice of the time of the receipt of the instruments for record, and of the existence of the instrument. Sinclair v. Gunzenhauser, 179 Ind. 78, 98 N.E. 37 (1912).

Highway Easements.
Statutory provision for recording of high-way easements (former IC 8-13-22-1) was construed in pari materia with provisions that the recorder keep a record of instruments, date and time of reception, names of grantors and grantees, description of lands involved, volume and page of the record where recorded (former IC 17-3-39-3 and former 32-1-2-27 (repealed; for similar provisions see IC 32-21-1-10) and a grant of right-of-way to the state was constructive notice to the world when duly recorded. State v. Young, 238 Ind. 452, 151 N.E.2d 697 (1958).

32-21-2-11. Recording of deed and certificate of acknowledgement — Record as evidence. — (a) This section applies to a conveyance or other instrument entitled by law to be recorded.

(b) The recorder of the county in which the land included in a conveyance or other instrument is situated shall record the deed or other instrument together with the requisite certificate of acknowledgment or proof endorsed on the deed or other instrument or annexed to the deed or other instrument.

(c) Unless a certificate of acknowledgment is recorded with a deed, the record of the conveyance or other instrument or a transcript may not be read or received in evidence. [P.L.2-2002, § 6.]

NOTES TO DECISIONS

Record as Evidence.
A record of a deed was proper evidence, and neither the original nor a certified copy was required. Bowers v. Van Winkle, 41 Ind. 432 (1872); Patterson v. Dallas, 46 Ind. 48 (1874); Embree v. Emerson, 37 Ind. App. 16, 74 N.E. 44, 1110 (1905).

Certified copies of the records of deeds were admissible in evidence. Abshire v. State ex rel. Wilson, 53 Ind. 64 (1876); Mills v. Snypes, 10 Ind. App. 19, 37 N.E.422 (1894).

The record of a deed not entitled to have been recorded could not be used as evidence. Westerman v. Foster, 57 Ind. 408 (1877); Starnes v. Allen, 151 Ind. 108, 45 N.E. 330 (1896), rehearing overruled, 51 N.E. 78 (1898).

If the execution of a deed was denied under oath, it could not be used as evidence until its execution was proved, but a proper acknowledgment of the deed was prima facie evidence of its execution. Carver v. Carver, 97 Ind. 497 (1884); Krom v. Vermillion, 143 Ind. 75, 41 N.E. 539 (1895).

The notice of a mechanic's lien had to be recorded in the "Miscellaneous Record Book" of the recorder's office and entry in another book was not admissible to prove the contents of a notice of a mechanic's lien unless it was shown that no proper record of the lien was made, that the original was lost, and that the copy in such record was a true copy. Adams v. Buhler, 131 Ind. 66, 30 N.E. 883 (1892).

If the acknowledgment to an instrument was illegal, the record of such deed was not competent evidence. Kothe v. Krag-Reynolds Co., 20 Ind. App. 293, 50 N.E. 594 (1898).

32-21-2-12. Certificate of acknowledgement and record rebuttable. — The:

(1) certificate of the acknowledgment of a conveyance or instrument of writing;

(2) the record; or

(3) the transcript of the record;

is not conclusive and may be rebutted and the force and effect of it contested by a party affected by the conveyance or instrument. [P.L.2-2002, § 6.]

NOTES TO DECISIONS

Analysis

In general.
Jurat on mortgage.

In General.

  The acknowledgment of a deed was prima facie, but not conclusive, evidence of the execution of the deed. Carver v. Carver, 97 Ind.

497 (1884); Krom v. Vermillion, 143 Ind. 75, 41 N.E. 539 (1895).

Jurat on Mortgage.

  Although a jurat on a mortgage is not conclusive as to the validity of its execution, it is substantial and probative evidence of its due execution. Moehlenkamp v. Shatz, 72 Ind. Dec. 368, 396 N.E.2d 433 (Ind. App. 1979).

32-21-2-13. Division of tract for tax purposes. — (a) If the auditor of the county or the township assessor under IC 6-1.1-5-9 and IC 6-1.1-5-9.1 determines it necessary, an instrument transferring fee simple title to less than the whole of a tract that will result in the division of the tract into at least two (2) parcels for property tax purposes may not be recorded unless the auditor or township assessor is furnished a drawing or other reliable evidence of the following:

  (1) The number of acres in each new tax parcel being created.

  (2) The existence or absence of improvements on each new tax parcel being created.

  (3) The location within the original tract of each new tax parcel being created.

  (b) Any instrument that is accepted for recording and placed of record that bears the endorsement required by IC 36-2-11-14 is presumed to comply with this section. [P.L.2-2002, § 6.]

CHAPTER 3

EFFECT OF RECORDING

32-21-3-1. "Conveyance" defined. — As used in this chapter, "conveyance" means:

  (1) an instrument of writing concerning land or an interest in land, except a last will and testament;

  (2) a lease for a term not exceeding three (3) years; or

  (3) an executory contract for the sale and purchase of land;

for purposes of the acknowledgment or proof of the instrument, lease, or contract, the recording of the instrument, lease, or contract, and the force and effect of that recording. [P.L.2-2002, § 6.]

Effective Dates. P.L.2-2002, § 6. July 1. 2002.

Cross References. Leases for less than three years, IC 32-21-1-1.

Recording leases, IC 32-21-4-1.

NOTES TO DECISIONS

In General.

An instrument acknowledging the nonpayment of purchase money for lands, and giving the vendor possession thereof until the money was paid, conveyed an interest in lands and could have been recorded. Melross v. Scott, 18 Ind. 250 (1862).

All courts of this state took judicial notice of the statute which entitled a deed of conveyance to have been recorded. Peak v. State, 240 Ind. 334, 163 N.E.2d 584 (1960).

Agreement to Reconvey.

An agreement executed contemporaneously with a deed, providing for the cancellation of the deed and a reconveyance of the property, was not a conveyance within the meaning of the statute requiring deeds of conveyance to be recorded. Raub v. Lemon, 61 Ind. App. 59, 108 N.E. 631 (1915).

Applicability.

This section applied only to such instruments in writing as affected the title to land, or some interest therein, and not to those which merely evidenced personal covenants. Starz v. Kirsch, 78 Ind. App. 431, 136 N.E. 36 (1922).

Executory Contracts.

Executory contracts for the sale of lands when properly executed and acknowledged could have been recorded. Case v. Bumstead, 24 Ind. 429 (1865).

Leases.

A lease of real estate for a term of years was not a conveyance of land, but was personal estate and passed to the personal representative of the lessee on his death. Spiro v. Robertson, 57 Ind. App. 229, 106 N.E. 726 (1914).

Oil and Gas.

The grant of all the gas and oil in and under a tract of land was a grant of an interest in land and could have been recorded. Heller v. Dailey, 28 Ind. App. 555, 63 N.E. 490 (1902); Johnson v. Sidey, 59 Ind. App. 678, 109 N.E. 934 (1915); Wenger v. Clay Tp., 61 Ind. App. 640, 112 N.E. 402 (1916).

Collateral References. Conveyance of land as including mature but unharvested crops. 51 A.L.R.4th 1263.

32-21-3-2. "Grantor" defined. — As used in this chapter, "grantor" has the meaning set forth in IC 32-17-1-1. [P.L.2-2002, § 6.]

32-21-3-3. Conveyance not valid unless recorded. — A conveyance of any real estate in fee simple or for life, a conveyance of any future estate, or a lease for more than three (3) years after the making of the lease is not valid and effectual against any person other than:

(1) the grantor;

(2) the grantor's heirs and devisees; and

(3) persons having notice of the conveyance or lease;

unless the conveyance or lease is made by a deed recorded within the time and in the manner provided in this chapter. [P.L.2-2002, § 6.]

Cross References. Priority determined by time of recording, IC 32-21-4-1.

NOTES TO DECISIONS

Highway easement.
Judicial sales.
Leases.
Liens.
Notice.
Occupying claimants.
Priority of record.
Quieting title.
Validity between parties.
Wife's inchoate interest.

Acknowledgment.

If any instrument was recorded without being acknowledged or proved, it was not constructive notice to anyone. Deming v. State ex rel. Miller, 23 Ind. 416 (1864); Watkins v. Brunt, 53 Ind. 208 (1876); Sinclair v. Gunzenhauser, 179 Ind. 78, 98 N.E. 37 (1912); Bledsoe v. Ross, 59 Ind. App. 609, 109 N.E. 53 (1915).

If the acknowledgment of a deed was void, the record thereof was not constructive notice to any person. Kothe v. Krag-Reynolds Co., 20 Ind. App. 293, 50 N.E. 594 (1898); Bledsoe v. Ross, 59 Ind. App. 609, 109 N.E. 53 (1915).

Agreement to Reconvey.

An agreement executed contemporaneously with a deed of conveyance, providing for the cancellation of the deed and a reconveyance of the property, was not a conveyance within the meaning of the statute requiring deeds of conveyance to have been recorded. Raub v. Lemon, 61 Ind. App. 59, 108 N.E. 631 (1915).

Easement.

The language of this section and former IC 32-1-2-16 (repealed; for similar provisions see IC 32-21-4-1) was sufficiently broad to include within its terms the granting of an easement. State v. Anderson, 241 Ind. 184, 170 N.E.2d 812 (1960).

Estoppel.

Married woman who failed to have deed recorded and who joined husband in mortgage was estopped from denying the validity of the transaction as against a mortgagee in good faith and for a valuable consideration. Michener v. Bengel, 135 Ind. 188, 34 N.E. 664 816 (1893).

Highway Easement.

Purchaser of property was not bound by highway easement acquired by state highway department where such easement was not recorded under the provisions of the recording laws but only filed with the state highway department under former IC 8-13-5-2. State v. Anderson, 241 Ind. 184, 170 N.E.2d 812 (1960).

Judicial Sales.

Purchasers at judicial sales had the same rights as against unrecorded deeds as other purchasers. Dawkins v. Kions, 53 Ind. 164 (1876); Pierce v. Spear, 94 Ind. 127 (1884); Sills v. Lawson, 133 Ind. 137, 32 N.E. 875 (1892). See also, Hosier v. Hall, 2 Ind. 556, 54 Am. Dec. 460 (1851).

Leases.

An unacknowledged and unrecorded lease for more than three years was valid as between parties and persons with notice. Bereolos v. Roth, 74 Ind. App. 100, 124 N.E. 410 (1919).

Liens.

The recital in a deed that a part of the purchase money was unpaid, and that it was evidenced by certain notes and that a lien therefor was retained, constituted sufficient notice to a subsequent purchaser of the vendor's lien, although such purchaser had no actual notice. Wiseman v. Hutchinson, 20 Ind. 40 (1863); Warford v. Hankins, 150 Ind. 489, 50 N.E. 468 (1898).

Judgments against grantors rendered after the execution of deeds were not liens on the lands, although the deeds were not recorded. Runyan v. McClellan, 24 Ind. 165 (1865); Pierce v. Spear, 94 Ind. 127 (1884).

Failure to record a deed did not extend the rights of the general creditors of the grantor. Hutchinson v. First Nat'l Bank, 133 Ind. 271, 30 N.E. 952, 36 Am. St. R. 537 (1892); State Bank v. Backus, 160 Ind. 682, 67 N.E. 512 (1903); Tansel v. Smith, 49 Ind. App. 263, 93 N.E. 548, 94 N.E. 890 (1911); Larrance v. Lewis, 51 Ind. App. 1, 98 N.E. 892 (1912).

The right to assert a mechanic's lien was not affected by the failure of a purchaser of the real estate to have his deed recorded, whereby notice of the transfer was not acquired until the work was begun. Jeffersonville Water Supply Co. v. Riter, 138 Ind. 170, 37 N.E. 652 (1894).

Notice.

The record of an instrument which was not entitled to be recorded was not constructive notice. Brown v. Budd, 2 Ind. 442 (1850); Watkins v. Brunt, 53 Ind. 208 (1876); Sanders v. Muegge, 91 Ind. 214 (1883); Reeves v. Hayes, 95 Ind. 521 (1884); Water v. Hartwig, 106 Ind. 123, 6 N.E. 5 (1886); Kothe v. Krag-Reynolds Co., 20 Ind. App. 293, 50 N.E. 594 (1898); Sinclair v. Gunzenhauser, 179 Ind. 78, 98 N.E. 37 (1912); Carmichael v. Arms, 51 Ind. App. 689, 100 N.E. 302 (1912); Bledsoe v. Ross, 59 Ind. App. 609, 109 N.E. 53 (1915); Bereolos v. Roth, 74 Ind. App. 100, 124 N.E. 410 (1919); Starz v. Kirsch, 78 Ind. App. 431, 136 N.E. 36 (1922).

Deeds had to be recorded in the recorder's office in order to have been notice to subsequent purchasers without actual notice.

Notice. (Cont'd)

Rosser v. Bingham, 17 Ind. 542 (1861); Sinclair v. Gunzenhauser, 179 Ind. 78, 98 N.E. 37 (1912).

Deeds recorded after the time fixed by law constituted notice to all persons thereafter. Meni v. Rathbone, 21 Ind. 454 (1863); Trisler v. Trisler, 38 Ind. 282 (1871); Brannon v. May, 42 Ind. 92 (1873); Gilchrist v. Gough, 63 Ind. 576, 30 Am. R. 250 (1878); Brower v. Witmeyer, 121 Ind. 83, 22 N.E. 975 (1889); Shirk v. Thomas, 121 Ind. 147, 22 N.E. 976, 16 Am. St. R. 381 (1889), overruled on other grounds, Pugh v. Highley, 152 Ind. 252, 53 N.E. 171 (1899).

Where a mortgage was left for record with the recorder, and was entered by him in the entry book, it was deemed to have been recorded from the date of its reception, as noted in the entry book, and no injury could result to anyone from a failure of the recorder actually to record the instrument. Kessler v. State ex rel. Wilson, 24 Ind. 313 (1865), overruled on other grounds, Gilchrist v. Gough, 63 Ind. 576, 30 Am. R. 250 (1878); Nichol v. Henry, 89 Ind. 54 (1883); Sinclair v. Gunzenhauser, 179 Ind. 78, 98 N.E. 37 (1912).

The record of a deed was notice only to those who claimed under or through the grantor by whom the deed was executed. Corbin v. Sullivan, 47 Ind. 356 (1874); Hazlett v. Sinclair, 76 Ind. 488, 40 Am. R. 254 (1881); Stockwell v. State ex rel. Johnson, 101 Ind. 1 (1884); Sinclair v. Gunzenhauser, 179 Ind. 78, 98 N.E. 37 (1912).

Where, in an action to quiet title, on the ground that plaintiff acquired title by an unrecorded lost deed, the evidence established the fact that defendants, who allegedly purchased the real estate after plaintiff received the deed, were not purchasers in good faith for a valuable consideration and without notice of plaintiff's title was proper. Armstrong v. Azimow, 118 Ind. App. 213, 76 N.E.2d 692 (1948).

Occupying Claimants.

A purchaser of land who failed to acquire title because of a prior recorded deed, but who in good faith took possession and expended large sums of money in making improvements, was held a bona fide occupant entitled under the Occupying Claimant Act, to recover for such improvements. Harmon v. Scott, 78 Ind. App. 554, 133 N.E. 141 (1921).

Priority of Record.

A deed not recorded in time could have been superseded by a subsequent deed to a person without notice. Orth v. Jennings, 8 Blackf. 420 (1847); Baily v. Baily, 38 Ind. 442 (1871); Meikel v. Borders, 129 Ind. 529, 29 N.E. 29 (1891); Sills v. Lawson, 133 Ind. 137, 32 N.E. 875 (1892).

Quieting Title.

In an action to quiet title against a subsequent purchaser, it had to be alleged that the deed of the plaintiff was recorded before that of such purchaser, or that such purchaser had notice of the claim of the plaintiff. Union Central Life Ins. Co. v. Dodds, 155 Ind. 365, 58 N.E. 258 (1900); Dodds v. Winslow, 26 Ind. App. 652, 60 N.E. 458 (1901).

Validity Between Parties.

Deeds were valid between the parties without being acknowledged or recorded. Hubble v. Wright, 23 Ind. 322 (1864); Mays v. Hedges, 79 Ind. 288 (1881); Wine v. Woods, 109 Ind. 291, 10 N.E. 399 (1887); Blair v. Whittaker, 31 Ind. App. 664, 69 N.E. 182 (1903); Bereolos v. Roth, 74 Ind. App. 100, 124 N.E. 410 (1919).

Wife's Inchoate Interest.

If a married man lost his interest in lands by failing to have his deed recorded, the inchoate interest of his wife was also divested. Alexander v. Herbert, 60 Ind. 184 (1877).

Collateral References. Record of instrument which comprises or includes an interest or right that is not a proper subject of record. 3 A.L.R.2d 577.

Agreement between real estate owners restricting use of property as within contemplation of recording laws. 4 A.L.R.2d 1419.

Statute excluding testimony of one person because of death of another as applied to testimony in respect of lost or destroyed instrument. 18 A.L.R.3d 606.

Presumptions and burden of proof as to time of alteration of deed. 30 A.L.R.3d 571.

32-21-3-4. Letters of attorney and executory contracts. — The following may be recorded in the county where the land to which the letter or contract relates is situated:

(1) Letters of attorney containing a power to a person to:

(A) sell or convey land; or

(B) sell and convey land as the agent of the owner of the land.

(2) An executory contract for the sale or purchase of land when proved or acknowledged in the manner prescribed in this chapter for the proof or acknowledgment of conveyances.

The record when recorded and the certified transcript of the record may be read in evidence in the same manner and with the same effect as a conveyance. [P.L.2-2002, § 6.]

Cross References. Executing power of attorney, IC 32-21-1-14.

Recording powers of attorney, IC 30-5.

CHAPTER 4

PRIORITY OF RECORDED TRANSACTIONS

32-21-4-1. Location of recording — First in time priority. — (a) A:

(1) conveyance or mortgage of land or of any interest in land; and

(2) a lease for more than three (3) years;

must be recorded in the recorder's office of the county where the land is situated.

(b) A conveyance, mortgage, or lease takes priority according to the time of its filing. The conveyance, mortgage, or lease is fraudulent and void as against any subsequent purchaser, lessee, or mortgagee in good faith and for a valuable consideration if the purchaser's, lessee's, or mortgagee's deed, mortgage, or lease is first recorded. [P.L.2-2002, § 6.]

Effective Dates. P.L.2-2002, § 6. July 1. 2002.

Cross References. Recording necessary

for validity against third persons, IC 32-21-3-3.

NOTES TO DECISIONS

ANALYSIS

In general.
Actual notice.
Applicability.
Assignments.
—Rights of creditors.
Bankruptcy.
Burden of proof.
Chain of title.
Corporation seal.
Deeds recorded in other records.
Entry book.
Execution levy.
General creditors.
Highway right-of-way.
Indexes.
Instruments not entitled to record.
Interest in land.
Knowledge of contents.

Leases and assignments.
Mineral interests.
Mortgages.
Patents for swamp lands.
Priority of deeds.
Purchasers at execution sales.
Purchasers at tax sales.
Purchasers of equitable titles.
Quitclaim deeds.
Record as notice.
Subsequent purchasers.
Sufficient notice.
Time of filing and recording.
Validity between parties.

In General.

     This section which gave precedence to the purchaser whose conveyance was first recorded could not be avoided by a court of

In General. (Cont'd)

equity; but the rule that would charge a purchaser with knowledge of the possession of an equitable claimant, regardless of the diligence and care with which the prospective purchaser examined the land and sought to discover whether there was a claimant in possession, could and should have been avoided. Mishawaka, St. Joseph Loan & Trust Co. v. Neu, 209 Ind. 433, 196 N.E. 85 (1935).

This section was for the protection of subsequent purchasers, lessees, or mortgagees, and the terms of the recording statute could not be extended to include general creditors within its protection. Gratzinger v. Arehart, 209 Ind. 547, 198 N.E. 787 (1935).

Deeds, mortgages and leases of real estate for period of more than three years, when properly acknowledged and placed on record as required by statute, were constructive notice of their existence, and charged subsequent grantee with notice of all that was shown by record, including recitals in instrument so recorded. C. Callahan Co. v. Lafayette Consumers Co., 102 Ind. App. 319, 2 N.E.2d 994 (1936).

The purpose of this section and a former section, requiring the recording of mortgages, was to give persons subsequently dealing with the mortgaged property notice of the mortgage lien. Lincoln Nat'l Bank & Trust Co. v. Nathan, 215 Ind. 178, 19 N.E.2d 243 (1939).

The purpose of the recording statute is to give subsequent purchasers constructive notice of prior conveyances. In re Herr, 79 Bankr. 793 (Bankr. N.D. Ind. 1987).

Recording acts impart constructive notice only to those who claim through or under the grantor in question, and not prior grantees. Ashland Pipeline Co. v. Indiana Bell Tel. Co., 505 N.E.2d 483 (Ind. App. 1987).

A purchaser of real estate is presumed to have examined the records of such deeds as constitute the chain of title thereto under which he claims, and is charged with notice, actual or constructive, of all facts recited in such records showing encumbrances, or the nonpayment of purchase-money. A record outside the chain of title does not provide notice to bona fide purchasers for value. Szakaly v. Smith, 544 N.E.2d 490 (Ind. 1989).

Actual Notice.

Actual notice of the existence of unrecorded instruments had the same effect as the recording thereof. Wilson v. Hunter, 30 Ind. 466 (1868); Walters v. Hartwig, 106 Ind. 123, 6 N.E. 5 (1886); Carmichael v. Arms, 51 Ind. App. 689, 100 N.E. 302 (1912).

Where a bank's mortgage described a different tract of land than the property under dispute, and had therefore been recorded out of the chain of title for that property, the public records did not place a subsequent mortgagor on notice, whether constructive, actual, or inquiry, of the first mortgage. Keybank Nat'l Ass'n v. NBD Bank, 699 N.E.2d 322 (Ind. App. 1998).

Applicability.

Former IC 32-1-2-16 (repealed; see this section for similar provisions) applied to the conveyance, mortgage or lease of lands, but not to a public highway right-of-way established by law. Mattingly v. Warrick County Drainage Bd., 743 N.E.2d 1245 (Ind. App. 2001).

Assignments.

—Rights of Creditors.

Where a savings and trust company borrowed money and issued bonds evidencing such indebtedness, and set aside first real estate mortgages as a fund to secure such indebtedness, the fact that the mortgages were assigned of record to another bank and trust company, without designating that they were held in trust for payment of the bonds, did not place the creditors of the assignee in any better position as against the general creditors of the assignor. Gratzinger v. Arehart, 209 Ind. 547, 198 N.E. 787 (1935).

Grantee of lessor, although bona fide purchaser for value, was bound to take notice of recorded lease and its assignment when duly entered of record. C. Callahan Co. v. Lafayette Consumers Co., 102 Ind. App. 319, 2 N.E.2d 994 (1936).

Bankruptcy.

Where, pursuant to antenuptial agreement, the husband conveyed land to his wife, and within a few days, and before the deed was recorded an involuntary petition in bankruptcy was filed against the husband, the rights of the trustee in bankruptcy did not take priority over the rights of the wife. Robertson v. Schlotzhauer, 243 F. 324 (7th Cir. 1917).

Burden of Proof.

Where a mortgage was assigned but never recorded, and a senior mortgage was foreclosed and the real estate sold without making the assignee of the junior mortgage a party, it was held in an action by the assignee to enforce the junior mortgage that the burden was on the plaintiff to prove that the purchaser had notice of knowledge of the assignment at time of purchase. Citizens State Bank v. Julian, 153 Ind. 655, 55 N.E. 1007 (1899).

Chain of Title.

Where the easement agreement was recorded one minute after the conveyance was recorded, the easement agreement was not

Chain of Title. (Cont'd)
within plaintiff's chain of title, and he could not be deemed to have constructive notice of its existence. Hartig v. Stratman, 729 N.E.2d 237 (Ind. App. 2000).

Corporation Seal.
The secretary of a corporation was the proper custodian of the corporate seal, and when he affixed it to a deed or other instrument, the presumption was that he did so rightfully by the direction of the corporation. Ellison v. Branstrator, 153 Ind. 146, 54 N.E. 433 (1899).

Deeds Recorded in Other Records.
Deeds executed as mortgages were not affected by being recorded in the deed records. Scobey v. Kiningham, 131 Ind. 552, 31 N.E. 355 (1892).

The statute required deeds to be recorded in deed records, and recording a deed in any other record was not notice of the deed or its contents. Sinclair v. Gunzenhauser, 179 Ind. 78, 98 N.E. 37 (1912).

Deeds of trust should have been recorded in the deed records, and the recording of such a deed in the miscellaneous records was not constructive notice of its existence. Sinclair v. Gunzenhauser, 179 Ind. 78, 98 N.E. 37 (1912).

Entry Book.
The entry book kept by the recorder constituted notice of the date of filing, the names of the parties, and the description of the land, but not the contents of the instrument. Gilchrist v. Gough, 63 Ind. 576, 30 Am. R. 240 (1878); Nichol v. Henry, 89 Ind. 54 (1883); Sinclair v. Gunzenhauser, 179 Ind. 78, 98 N.E. 37 (1912).

Instruments duly recorded and indexed were notice to subsequent purchasers although such instruments were not entered in the entry book. Nichol v. Henry, 89 Ind. 54 (1883); Sinclair v. Gunzenhauser, 179 Ind. 78, 98 N.E. 37 (1912).

Execution Levy.
The general principle of real property law that the time of perfection determines priority is expressly modified by former IC 34-1-4-8, which provides that an execution levy shall not have "any force or effect as against bona fide purchasers or encumbrancers of the same" until the lis pendens notice is filed. Geller v. Meek, 496 N.E.2d 103 (Ind. App. 1986).

General Creditors.
Failure to record instruments affected only the class of persons mentioned in the statute, and had no effect on general creditors. Hutchinson v. First Nat'l Bank, 133 Ind. 271, 30 N.E. 952, 36 Am. St. 537 (1892); Schmidt v.

Zahrndt, 148 Ind. 447, 47 N.E. 335 (1897); Tansel v. Smith, 49 Ind. App. 263, 93 N.E. 548, 94 N.E. 890 (1911).

Highway Right-of-Way.
Where the state sought to enjoin the defendants from interfering with the removal of an advertising sign located on alleged state highway right-of-way, defendants were entitled to summary judgment, since the 1926 instrument which granted the alleged right-of-way had never been recorded, and because the defendants, who purchased the two parcels in 1952 and 1953 did not have actual knowledge of the existence of the right-of-way and constructive notice was not attributable to the defendants. State v. Cinko, 155 Ind. App. 357, 35 Ind. Dec. 335, 292 N.E.2d 847 (1973).

Former IC 32-1-2-16 (repealed; see this section for similar provisions) did not require that a public highway right of way established by law be recorded in recorder's office, and it was clearly legislative intent that the general recording statute not apply to roads established by law under the 1905 Highway Act. Worldcom Network Servs., Inc. v. Thompson, 698 N.E.2d 1233 (Ind. App. 1998).

Indexes.
Indexes kept by recorders were not notice of the contents of the instrument referred to. Gilchrist v. Gough, 63 Ind. 576, 30 Am. R. 250 (1878); Nichol v. Henry, 89 Ind. 54 (1883); Sinclair v. Gunzenhauser, 179 Ind. 78, 98 N.E. 37 (1912).

Instruments Not Entitled to Record.
The record of an instrument which was not entitled to be recorded was the same as if it had not been recorded and was not constructive notice to anyone. Brown v. Budd, 2 Ind. 442 (1850); Watkins v. Brunt, 53 Ind. 208 (1876); Sanders v. Muegge, 91 Ind. 214 (1883); Reeves v. Hayes, 95 Ind. 521 (1884); Walters v. Hartwig, 106 Ind. 123, 6 N.E. 5 (1886); Kothe v. Krag-Reynolds Co., 20 Ind. App. 293, 50 N.E. 594 (1898); Sinclair v. Gunzenhauser, 179 Ind. 78, 98 N.E. 37 (1912); Carmichael v. Arms, 51 Ind. App. 689, 100 N.E. 302 (1912); Bledsoe v. Ross, 59 Ind. App. 609, 109 N.E. 53 (1915); Bereolos v. Roth, 74 Ind. App. 100, 124 N.E. 410 (1919); Starz v. Kirsch, 78 Ind. App. 431, 136 N.E. 36 (1922).

Interest in Land.
The phrase "or any interest therein," as used in this section, and following the word "lands," must have been construed to have included a classification of property other than real property. Lincoln Nat'l Bank & Trust Co. v. Nathan, 215 Ind. 178, 19 N.E.2d 243 (1939).

If certain property constituted an interest in real estate, even though such property

Interest in Land. (Cont'd)
might have been classed as personalty, it was properly mortgaged by a real estate mortgage, and recorded in the county where the property was located in view of former IC 34-1-67-1. Lincoln Nat'l Bank & Trust Co. v. Nathan, 215 Ind. 178, 19 N.E.2d 243 (1939).

A mortgage on property which constituted an interest in real estate, even though such property might have been classed as personalty, could not have been held invalid as against third persons with notice, on the ground that it had not been recorded pursuant to the provisions of the chattel mortgage statute. Lincoln Nat'l Bank & Trust Co. v. Nathan, 215 Ind. 178, 19 N.E.2d 243 (1939).

A mortgage on elevators constructed on lands owned by railroad, under contract between the railroad and the owners of the elevators, providing for removal of the elevators on 30 days' notice by the railroad, constituted an "interest in real estate" within the meaning of this section, and was properly recorded in the county where the elevators were situated. Lincoln Nat'l Bank & Trust Co. v. Nathan, 215 Ind. 178, 19 N.E.2d 243 (1939).

Knowledge of Contents.
A purchaser of real estate was bound to know the contents of a deed or other title paper which formed a link in the chain of title. Lowry v. Smith, 97 Ind. 466 (1844); Wiseman v. Hutchinson, 20 Ind. 40 (1863); Croskey v. Chapman, 26 Ind. 333 (1866); Colman v. Watson, 54 Ind. 65 (1876); Hazlett v. Sinclair, 76 Ind. 488, 40 Am. R. 254 (1881); State ex rel. Lowry v. Davis, 96 Ind. 539 (1884); Stockwell v. State ex rel. Johnson, 101 Ind. 1 (1884); Singer v. Scheible, 109 Ind. 575, 10 N.E. 616 (1887); Smith v. Lowry, 113 Ind. 37, 15 N.E. 17 (1888); Wagner v. Winter, 122 Ind. 57, 23 N.E. 754 (1890); Pierce v. Vansell, 35 Ind. App. 525, 74 N.E. 554 (1905); Oglebay v. Todd, 166 Ind. 250, 76 N.E. 238 (1905); Larrance v. Lewis, 51 Ind. App. 1, 98 N.E. 892 (1912); Simmons v. Parker, 61 Ind. App. 403, 112 N.E. 31 (1916).

Leases and Assignments.
Notice had to be taken of recorded leases and assignments. American Window Glass Co. v. Indiana Natural Gas & Oil Co., 37 Ind. App. 439, 76 N.E. 1006 (1906).

Mineral Interests.
The recording of a deed of conveyance made in compliance with this section is not sufficient to satisfy the statement of claim provisions of the Dormant Mineral Interests Act former IC 32-5-11 (repealed; for similar provisions see IC 32-23-10-2 et seq.). McCoy v. Richards, 581 F. Supp. 143 (S.D. Ind. 1983), aff'd, 771 F.2d 1108 (7th Cir. 1985).

Mortgages.
If a person obtained a deed to land and failed to have it recorded within the time fixed by statute, and the grantor devised the land to another person, who, with the knowledge and consent of the grantee in the deed, mortgaged the land, such deed was void as to the mortgagee. Guynn v. Wabash County Loan & Trust Co., 53 Ind. App. 391, 101 N.E. 738 (1913).

The lien of a mortgage which was not acknowledged nor recorded and which was executed without notice to the mortgagee of a prior vendor's lien was superior to vendor's lien, where the warranty deed of the vendor recited payment in full of the purchase price. Heuring v. Stiefel, 85 Ind. App. 102, 152 N.E. 861 (1926).

Reconstruction finance corporation was not required to purchase loan by a bank under "blanket participation agreement" where mortgages securing loan were not recorded until after disbursement, since loan was not secured by "validly pledged collateral" at the time of disbursement, even though mortgages were recorded at the time of the demand by the bank of reconstruction finance corporation to purchase participation in loan. Central Nat'l Bank v. Reconstruction Fin. Corp., 134 F. Supp. 873 (N.D. Ill. 1955).

Patents for Swamp Lands.
Patents for swamp lands issued by this state were to have been recorded in the office of secretary of state, and did not need to have been recorded in the county where the lands were situated. Mason v. Cooksey, 51 Ind. 519 (1875); Nitche v. Earle, 88 Ind. 375 (1882).

Priority of Deeds.
Where deeds for interests in the same real estate from a father to his son and from the son to his father were all executed on the same date and were filed for record on the same day and at the same hour, no priority existed between them under this section. Sodders v. Jackson, 112 Ind. App. 179, 44 N.E.2d 310 (1942).

Purchasers at Execution Sales.
Failure to record a deed did not make judgments afterwards rendered against the grantor liens on the lands, but purchasers at sheriffs' sales under such judgments were protected the same as other subsequent purchasers without notice. Runyan v. McClellan, 24 Ind. 165 (1865); Pierce v. Spear, 94 Ind. 127 (1884).

Purchasers at execution sales were protected against prior unrecorded deeds the same as other subsequent purchasers. Dawkins v. Kions, 53 Ind. 164 (1876); Pierce v. Spear, 94 Ind. 127 (1884); Sills v. Lawson, 133 Ind. 137, 32 N.E. 875 (1892); Union Cent. Life Ins. Co. v. Dodds, 155 Ind. 365, 58 N.E. 258

Purchasers at Execution Sales. (Cont'd) (1900); Dodds v. Winslow, 26 Ind. App. 652, 60 N.E. 458 (1901).

Purchasers at Tax Sales.

Purchasers of land under foreclosure proceedings for delinquent taxes held the land as against deed for the land that was not recorded within the time fixed by law. Bliss v. Gallagher, 60 Ind. App. 454, 109 N.E. 215 (1915).

Purchasers of Equitable Titles.

The purchaser of an equitable title did not obtain preference over an unrecorded deed. Wright v. Shepherd, 47 Ind. 176 (1874).

Quitclaim Deeds.

Grantees in quitclaim deeds could have been good faith purchasers, but the burden was upon them to show the fact in order that they could have had a preference over other purchasers. Sullenger v. Baecher, 55 Ind. App. 365, 101 N.E. 517, 102 N.E. 380 (1913).

Where warranty deed was of record, a subsequent grantee of quitclaim deed could not have been a bona fide purchaser for value since he was deemed to have had either actual or constructive notice of the rights of third persons. Coons v. Baird, 148 Ind. App. 250, 24 Ind. Dec. 287, 265 N.E.2d 727 (1971).

Record as Notice.

The record of a deed was only notice to those who claim through or under the grantor. Corbin v. Sullivan, 47 Ind. 356 (1874); Hazlett v. Sinclair, 76 Ind. 488, 40 Am. R. 254 (1881); Stockwell v. State ex rel. Johnson, 101 Ind. 1 (1884); Sinclair v. Gunzenhauser, 179 Ind. 78, 98 N.E. 37 (1912).

The record of a deed was only notice of what appeared of record, and was not notice of any portion of the instrument not recorded. Gilchrist v. Gough, 63 Ind. 576, 30 Am. R. 250 (1878); State ex rel. Lowry v. Davis, 96 Ind. 539 (1884); Lowry v. Smith, 97 Ind. 466 (1884); Osborn v. Hocker, 160 Ind. 1, 66 N.E. 42 (1903); Osborn v. Hall, 160 Ind. 153, 66 N.E. 457 (1903).

If in recording an instrument, the land was not described as the same was described in the instrument, such record was not notice to a subsequent purchaser or mortgagee of the land described in the instrument. State ex rel. Graham v. Walters, 31 Ind. App. 77, 66 N.E. 182, 99 Am. St. 244 (1903).

Where husband's mother executed deed to him and his wife as tenants by entireties, which deed was withheld from record beyond the period of 45 days formerly allowed by this section before amendment, and until after the mother's death, the subsequent execution of mortgage by the husband and wife to secure repayment of moneys borrowed by the hus-

band, with the wife's knowledge, bound wife by an estoppel in pais. Cressler v. Brewer, 186 Ind. 185, 114 N.E. 449 (1916).

Deeds, mortgages, and leases of real estate for a period of more than 3 years, if properly acknowledged and recorded, were constructive notice of their existence and of recitals contained therein. Willard v. Bringolf, 103 Ind. App. 16, 5 N.E.2d 315 (1936).

The effect of a record of a conveyance or mortgage of lands or of any interest as notice was not to have been extended beyond the terms of this section. Sodders v. Jackson, 112 Ind. App. 179, 44 N.E.2d 310 (1942).

Under the Chandler Act, a transfer to a mortgagee was made and became effective when it became valid against a bona fide creditor, which, under this section, was when it was recorded. In re Cox, 132 F.2d 881 (7th Cir. 1943).

The recording of an instrument in its proper book is fundamental to the scheme of providing constructive notice of title through the records. Keybank Nat'l Ass'n v. NBD Bank, 699 N.E.2d 322 (Ind. App. 1998).

A person charged with the duty of searching the records of a particular tract of property is not on notice of any adverse claims which do not appear in the chain of title, because the recording statute would then be a snare, rather than a protection. Keybank Nat'l Ass'n v. NBD Bank, 699 N.E.2d 322 (Ind. App. 1998).

Subsequent Purchasers.

Purchasers of lands had to take notice of properly recorded deeds and mortgages, and of all facts such records disclosed. Martin v. Cauble, 72 Ind. 67 (1880); Singer v. Scheible, 109 Ind. 575, 10 N.E. 616 (1886); Smith v. Lowry, 113 Ind. 37, 15 N.E. 17 (1888); Gregory v. Arms, 48 Ind. App. 562, 96 N.E. 196 (1911).

Sufficient Notice.

Whatever fairly puts a reasonable, prudent person on inquiry is sufficient notice to cause that person to be charged with actual notice, where the means of knowledge are at hand and he omits to make the inquiry from which he would have ascertained the existence of a deed or mortgage. Keybank Nat'l Ass'n v. NBD Bank, 699 N.E.2d 322 (Ind. App. 1998).

Time of Filing and Recording.

Deeds were deemed recorded from the time they were noted in the entry book of the recorder. Kessler v. State ex rel. Wilson, 24 Ind. 313 (1865), overruled on other grounds, Gilchrist v. Gough, 63 Ind. 576 (1878); Sinclair v. Gunzenhauser, 179 Ind. 78, 98 N.E. 37 (1912).

Indorsements made by the recorder on instruments might have been evidence of the time of filing of such instruments for record.

Time of Filing and Recording. (Cont'd)
Moore v. Glover, 115 Ind. 367, 16 N.E. 163 (1888).

Validity Between Parties.

Deeds were valid between the parties without being acknowledged or recorded. Hubble v. Wright, 23 Ind. 322 (1864); Mays v. Hedges, 79 Ind. 288 (1881); Wine v. Woods, 109 Ind. 291, 10 N.E. 399 (1887); Blair v. Whittaker, 31 Ind. App. 664, 69 N.E. 182 (1903); Bereolos v. Roth, 74 Ind. App. 100, 124 N.E. 410 (1919);

Cypress Creek Coal Co. v. Boonville Mining Co., 194 Ind. 187, 142 N.E. 645 (1924).

Unrecorded deeds and mortgages were valid as against every person except subsequent purchasers, lessees, and mortgagees in good faith and for a valuable consideration. Sills v. Lawson, 133 Ind. 137, 32 N.E. 875 (1892); State Bank v. Backus, 160 Ind. 682, 67 N.E. 512 (1903); Tansel v. Smith, 49 Ind. App. 263, 93 N.E. 548, 94 N.E. 890 (1911); Larrance v. Lewis, 51 Ind. App. 1, 98 N.E. 892 (1912).

Collateral References. Restrictive covenant omitted from deed imposed by general plan of subdivision. 4 A.L.R.2d 1364.

Grantee from whose deed restrictive covenant, imposed by general plan of subdivision, has been omitted. 4 A.L.R.2d 1368.

Rights as between purchaser of timber under unrecorded instrument and subsequent vendee of land. 18 A.L.R.2d 1150.

Relative rights to real property as between purchasers from or through decedent's heirs and devisees under will subsequently sought to be established. 22 A.L.R.2d 1107.

Personal covenant in recorded deed as enforceable against grantee's lessee or successor. 23 A.L.R.2d 520.

Necessity that mortgage covering oil and

gas lease be recorded as real estate mortgage, and/or filed or recorded as chattel mortgage. 34 A.L.R.2d 902.

Relative rights in real property as between purchasers from or through decedent's heirs or devisees and unknown surviving spouse. 39 A.L.R.2d 1082.

Priority as between mechanic's lien and purchase money mortgage as affected by recording. 73 A.L.R.2d 1407.

Sufficiency of designation of taxpayer in recorded notice of federal tax lien. 3 A.L.R.3d 633.

Covenant restricting use of land, made for purpose of guarding against competition, as running with land. 25 A.L.R.3d 897.

32-21-4-2. Security interest must be recorded — Interest perfected upon recording — Exceptions. — (a) This section applies to an instrument regardless of when the instrument was recorded, except that this section does not divest rights that vested before May 1, 1993.

(b) An assignment, a mortgage, or a pledge of rents and profits arising from real estate that is intended as security, whether contained in a separate instrument or otherwise, must be recorded under section 1 [IC 32-21-4-1] of this chapter.

(c) When an assignment, a mortgage, or a pledge of rents and profits is recorded under subsection (b), the security interest of the assignee, mortgagee, or pledgee is immediately perfected as to the assignor, mortgagor, pledgor, and any third parties:

(1) regardless of whether the assignment, mortgage, or pledge is operative:

(A) immediately;

(B) upon the occurrence of a default; or

(C) under any other circumstances; and

(2) without the holder of the security interest taking any further action.

(d) This section does not apply to security interests in:

(1) farm products;

(2) accounts or general intangibles arising from or relating to the sale of farm products by a farmer;

(3) timber to be cut; or

(4) minerals or the like (including oil and gas);
that may be perfected under IC 26-1-9.1. [P.L.2-2002, § 6.]

32-21-4-3. Defeasible deeds. — (a) This section applies when:
(1) a deed purports to contain an absolute conveyance of any estate in land; and
(2) is made or intended to be made defeasible by a:
(A) deed of defeasance;
(B) bond; or
(C) other instrument.
(b) The original conveyance is not defeated or affected against any person other than:
(1) the maker of the defeasance;
(2) the heirs or devisees of the maker of the defeasance; or
(3) persons having actual notice of the defeasance;
unless the instrument of defeasance is recorded in the manner provided by law within ninety (90) days after the date of the deed. [P.L.2-2002, § 6.]

NOTES TO DECISIONS

In General.
Possession by a grantor after the execution of a deed was not notice of an unrecorded defeasance held by him, as actual notice must have been had of an unrecorded defeasance to have rendered it effectual against subsequent purchasers. Crassen v. Swoveland, 22 Ind. 427 (1864); Tuttle v. Churchman, 74 Ind. 311 (1880).
An unrecorded defeasance was good as against a subsequent grantee who was a mere volunteer, although he had no notice of the defeasance. Wilson v. Wilson, 86 Ind. 472 (1882).
A deed of real property, though absolute on its face, given to secure a loan, executed contemporaneously with a written agreement on the part of the grantee, to reconvey on repayment, was a mortgage as between the parties, and if the grantee, before default by the grantor, conveyed the property to an innocent purchaser who ousted the grantor from possession, the first grantee was liable in damages. Loeb v. McAlister, 15 Ind. App. 643, 41 N.E. 1061 (1895), reh'g overruled, 15 Ind. App. 647, 44 N.E. 378 (1896).
Actual notice of an unrecorded defeasance, or notice of facts that would cause a prudent person to make inquiry as to the existence of such instrument, prevented a subsequent purchaser from being a good faith purchaser. Weeks v. Hathaway, 45 Ind. App. 196, 90 N.E. 647 (1910).

CHAPTER 5

RESIDENTIAL REAL ESTATE SALES DISCLOSURE

32-21-5-1. Applicability. — (a) This chapter applies only to a sale of, an exchange of, an installment sales contract for, or a lease with option to buy residential real estate that contains not more than four (4) residential dwelling units.

(b) This chapter does not apply to the following:

(1) Transfers ordered by a court, including transfers:

(A) in the administration of an estate;

(B) by foreclosure sale;

(C) by a trustee in bankruptcy;

(D) by eminent domain;

(E) from a decree of specific performance;

(F) from a decree of divorce; or

(G) from a property settlement agreement.

(2) Transfers by a mortgagee who has acquired the real estate at a sale conducted under a foreclosure decree or who has acquired the real estate by a deed in lieu of foreclosure.

(3) Transfers by a fiduciary in the course of the administration of the decedent's estate, guardianship, conservatorship, or trust.

(4) Transfers made from at least one (1) co-owner solely to at least one (1) other co-owner.

(5) Transfers made solely to any combination of a spouse or an individual in the lineal line of consanguinity of at least one (1) of the transferors.

(6) Transfers made because of the record owner's failure to pay any federal, state, or local taxes.

(7) Transfers to or from any governmental entity.

(8) Transfers involving the first sale of a dwelling that has not been inhabited.

(9) Transfers to a living trust.

[P.L.2-2002, § 6.]

Effective Dates. P.L.2-2002, § 6. July 1. 2002.

Indiana Law Review. 1993 Developments in Indiana Property Law, 27 Ind. L. Rev. 1285 (1994).

Survey of Tort Law Developments in 1994: The Good, The Bad and The Ugly, 28 Ind. L. Rev. 1097 (1995).

32-21-5-2. "Buyer" defined. — As used in this chapter, "buyer" means a transferee in a transaction described in section 1 [IC 32-21-5-1] of this chapter. [P.L.2-2002, § 6.]

32-21-5-3. "Closing" defined. — As used in this chapter, "closing" means a transfer of an interest described in section 1 [IC 32-21-5-1] of this chapter by a deed, installment sales contract, or lease. [P.L.2-2002, § 6.]

32-21-5-4. "Defect" defined. — As used in connection with disclosure forms required by this chapter, "defect" means a condition that would have a significant adverse effect on the value of the property, that would significantly impair the health or safety of future occupants of the property, or that if not repaired, removed, or replaced would significantly shorten or adversely affect the expected normal life of the premises. [P.L.2-2002, § 6.]

32-21-5-5. "Disclosure form" defined. — As used in this chapter, "disclosure form" refers to a disclosure form prepared under section 8 [IC 32-21-5-8] of this chapter or a disclosure form that meets the requirements of section 8 of this chapter. [P.L.2-2002, § 6.]

32-21-5-6. "Owner" defined. — As used in this chapter, "owner" means the owner of residential real estate that is for sale, exchange, lease with an option to buy, or sale under an installment contract. [P.L.2-2002, § 6.]

32-21-5-7. Adoption of disclosure form — Contents. — The Indiana real estate commission established by IC 25-34.1-2-1 shall adopt a specific disclosure form that contains the following:
    (1) Disclosure by the owner of the known condition of the following areas:
        (A) The foundation.
        (B) The mechanical systems.
        (C) The roof.
        (D) The structure.
        (E) The water and sewer systems.
        (F) Other areas that the Indiana real estate commission determines are appropriate.
    (2) A notice to the prospective buyer that contains substantially the following language:

"The prospective buyer and the owner may wish to obtain professional advice or inspections of the property and provide for appropriate provisions in a contract between them concerning any advice, inspections, defects, or warranties obtained on the property.".

(3) A notice to the prospective buyer that contains substantially the following language:

"The representations in this form are the representations of the owner and are not the representations of the agent, if any. This information is for disclosure only and is not intended to be a part of any contract between the buyer and owner.".

(4) A disclosure by the owner that an airport is located within a geographical distance from the property as determined by the Indiana real estate commission. The commission may consider the differences between an airport serving commercial airlines and an airport that does not serve commercial airlines in determining the distance to be disclosed. [P.L.2-2002, § 6.]

32-21-5-8. Owner may prepare disclosure form. — An owner may prepare or use a disclosure form that contains the information required in the disclosure form under section 7 [IC 32-21-5-7] of this chapter and any other information the owner determines is appropriate. [P.L.2-2002, § 6.]

32-21-5-9. Disclosure form not a warranty. — A disclosure form is not a warranty by the owner or the owner's agent, if any, and the disclosure form may not be used as a substitute for any inspections or warranties that the prospective buyer or owner may later obtain. [P.L.2-2002, § 6.]

32-21-5-10. Disclosure to be given to buyer and appraiser — Signed form necessary for closing. — (a) An owner must complete and sign a disclosure form and submit the form to a prospective buyer before an offer for the sale of the residential real estate is accepted.

(b) An appraiser retained to appraise the residential real estate for which the disclosure form has been prepared shall be given a copy of the form upon request. This subsection applies only to appraisals made for the buyer or an entity from which the buyer is seeking financing.

(c) Before closing, an accepted offer is not enforceable against the buyer until the owner and the prospective buyer have signed the disclosure form. After closing, the failure of the owner to deliver a disclosure statement form to the buyer does not by itself invalidate a real estate transaction. [P.L.2-2002, § 6.]

32-21-5-11. Liability for errors in disclosure. — The owner is not liable for any error, inaccuracy, or omission of any information required to be delivered to the prospective buyer under this chapter if:

(1) the error, inaccuracy, or omission was not within the actual knowledge of the owner or was based on information provided by a public agency or by another person with a professional license or special knowledge who provided a written or oral report or opinion that the owner reasonably believed to be correct; and

(2) the owner was not negligent in obtaining information from a third party and transmitting the information. [P.L.2-2002, § 6.]

32-21-5-12. Owner must alert buyer to changes in disclosure at closing. — (a) An owner does not violate this chapter if the owner subsequently discovers that the disclosure form is inaccurate as a result of any act, circumstance, information received, or agreement subsequent to the delivery of the disclosure form. However, at or before settlement, the owner is required to disclose any material change in the physical condition of the property or certify to the purchaser at settlement that the condition of the property is substantially the same as it was when the disclosure form was provided.

(b) If at the time disclosures are required to be made under subsection (a) an item of information required to be disclosed is unknown or not available to the owner, the owner may state that the information is unknown or may use an approximation of the information if the approximation is clearly identified, is reasonable, is based on the actual knowledge of the owner, and is not used to circumvent the disclosure requirements of this chapter. [P.L.2-2002, § 6.]

32-21-5-13. Buyer may nullify contract due to defects arising after offer. — (a) Notwithstanding section 12 [IC 32-21-5-12] of this chapter, if a prospective buyer receives a disclosure form or an amended disclosure form after an offer has been accepted that discloses a defect, the prospective buyer may after receipt of the disclosure form and within two (2) business days nullify the contract by delivering a written rescission to the owner or the owner's agent, if any.

(b) A prospective buyer is not liable for nullifying a contract under this section and is entitled to a return of any deposits made in the transaction. [P.L.2-2002, § 6.]

CHAPTER 6

PSYCHOLOGICALLY AFFECTED PROPERTIES

32-21-6-1. "Agent" defined. — As used in this chapter, "agent" means a real estate agent or other person acting on behalf of the owner or transferee of real estate or acting as a limited agent. [P.L.2-2002, § 6.]

Effective Dates. P.L.2-2002, § 6. July 1. 2002.

32-21-6-2. "Limited agent" defined. — As used in this chapter, "limited agent" means an agent who, with the written and informed consent of all parties to a real estate transaction, is engaged by both the seller and buyer or both the landlord and tenant. [P.L.2-2002, § 6.]

32-21-6-3. "Psychologically affected property" defined. — As used in this chapter, "psychologically affected property" includes real estate or a dwelling that is for sale, rent, or lease and to which one (1) or more of the following facts or a reasonable suspicion of facts apply:
　(1) That an occupant of the property was afflicted with or died from a disease related to the human immunodeficiency virus (HIV).
　(2) That an individual died on the property.
　(3) That the property was the site of:
　　(A) a felony under IC 35;
　　(B) criminal gang (as defined in IC 35-45-9-1) activity;
　　(C) the discharge of a firearm involving a law enforcement officer while engaged in the officer's official duties; or
　　(D) the illegal manufacture or distribution of a controlled substance.
　[P.L.2-2002, § 6.]

32-21-6-4. "Tranferee" defined. — As used in this chapter, "transferee" means a purchaser, tenant, lessee, prospective purchaser, prospective tenant, or prospective lessee of the real estate or dwelling. [P.L.2-2002, § 6.]

32-21-6-5. Disclosure not required. — An owner or agent is not required to disclose to a transferee any knowledge of a psychologically affected property in a real estate transaction. [P.L.2-2002, § 6.]

32-21-6-6. Owner or agent not liable for refusal to disclose. — An owner or agent is not liable for the refusal to disclose to a transferee:

(1) that a dwelling or real estate is a psychologically affected property; or

(2) details concerning the psychologically affected nature of the dwelling or real estate.

However, an owner or agent may not intentionally misrepresent a fact concerning a psychologically affected property in response to a direct inquiry from a transferee. [P.L.2-2002, § 6.]

CHAPTER 7

ADVERSE POSSESSION

32-21-7-1. Claimant must pay all taxes and special assessments. — In any suit to establish title to land or real estate, possession of the land or real estate is not adverse to the owner in a manner as to establish title or rights in and to the land or real estate unless the adverse possessor or claimant pays and discharges all taxes and special assessments due on the land or real estate during the period the adverse possessor or claimant claims to have possessed the land or real estate adversely. However, this section does not relieve any adverse possessor or claimant from proving all the elements of title by adverse possession required by law. [P.L.2-2002, § 6.]

Effective Dates. P.L.2-2002, § 6. July 1. 2002.

Indiana Law Review. 1994 Developments in Property Law, 28 Ind. L. Rev. 1041 (1995).

NOTES TO DECISIONS

ANALYSIS

Adverse possession.
After acquiring record title holder.
Applicability.
Boundary disputes.
Constructive notice of possession.
—Violation of condition in deed.
Dominion over land.
—Swamp.
Fence erection rendering tax requirement inapplicable.
Possession of realty.
Proof.
Property not assessed.
Tax duplicates.
Transferability of adverse possession rights.

Adverse Possession.

An additional element of adverse possession imposed by statute provides that the adverse claimant must have paid all taxes and assessments on the real estate during the period of adverse possession; however, the statutory element does not apply where there is a boundary dispute due to the erection of a fence. Rieddle v. Buckner, 629 N.E.2d 860 (Ind. App. 1994).

After Acquiring Record Title Holder.

The tax payment requirement is a means of giving notice to the record title holder that someone else is claiming his land, and where land had passed by adverse possession prior

After Acquiring Record Title
Holder. (Cont'd)
to its acquisition by record title holder, notice was not an issue and it was not necessary to show payment of taxes. Berrey v. Jean, 74 Ind. Dec. 502, 401 N.E.2d 102 (Ind. App. 1980).

Applicability.
Where the 20-year statutory period of adverse possession of realty had been completed before the enactment of this statute, it was not applicable. Cooper v. Tarpley, 112 Ind. App. 1, 41 N.E.2d 640 (1942).

The language of former IC 32-1-20-1 (repealed; see this section for similar provisions) clearly limited it to suits for adverse possession to acquire title to land. Larch v. Larch, 564 N.E.2d 313 (Ind. App. 1990).

Boundary Disputes.
The purpose of the tax payment requirement is to give notice to the true owner, and where the land involved in dispute is a boundary dispute the tax payment requirement is inapplicable. Ford v. Eckert, 77 Ind. Dec. 98, 406 N.E.2d 1209 (Ind. App. 1980).

Former IC 32-1-20-1 (repealed; see this section for similar provisions), requiring the payment of taxes, did not apply in the case of a boundary dispute, where tax statements did not serve notice of the adverse interest because the adjoining landowners continued to pay taxes on their adjoining land and the improvements thereon. Davis v. Sponhauer, 574 N.E.2d 292 (Ind. App. 1991).

An adverse claimant must pay all the taxes and special assessments due on the real estate during the period of adverse possession; however, this statutory requirement does not apply where the disputed area is contiguous to property owned by the adverse claimant and he has paid taxes according to the tax duplicate, even though the tax duplicate does not include the disputed strip. Clark v. Aukerman, 654 N.E.2d 1183 (Ind. App. 1995).

Constructive Notice of Possession.

—Violation of Condition in Deed.
Where a deed creates a fee simple determinable, with a possibility of reverter in the event the land user fails to maintain a particular structure on the land, and it is common knowledge that the land user no longer maintains such a structure, thus violating the condition in the deed, this requires a finding of constructive notice of adverse possession as a matter of law. Poole v. Corwin, 447 N.E.2d 1150 (Ind. App. 1983).

Dominion Over Land.

—Swamp.
The claimants' failure to utilize swampy property for purposes other than a lawn was not fatal where the land was not spacious enough for much development, was in a depressed area, and was not leveled off to make it the same elevation as the surrounding land. Snowball Corp. v. Pope, 580 N.E.2d 733 (Ind. App. 1991).

Fence Erection Rendering Tax Requirement Inapplicable.
In circumstances where boundary disputes arise due to the erection of fences or other structures, the supplementary element of tax payments to acquire the land by adverse possession is inapplicable, since the erection of the fence or other structure becomes the notice to the adjoining landowner and the tax duplicate would not show the particular land so as to serve as notice. Kline v. Kramer, 179 Ind. App. 592, 68 Ind. Dec. 120, 386 N.E.2d 982 (1979).

Where fence was erected over the boundary line and all the elements of adverse possession were established, except for the payment of taxes, the party claiming by adverse possession acquired the land although no taxes were paid. Connors v. Augustine, 77 Ind. Dec. 394, 407 N.E.2d 1186 (Ind. App. 1980).

Where the parties each possessed land up to the fence line even though the actual boundary between the two parcels was the section line, the disputed area was contiguous to the property owned by plaintiff, and plaintiff paid taxes on the contiguous property which he owned, the exception to the statutory requirement was applicable, and plaintiffs were not required to pay the taxes on the disputed tract. Clark v. Aukerman, 654 N.E.2d 1183 (Ind. App. 1995).

Possession of Realty.
Where the owner of land in which there was an entrance to a cave extending into the land of an adjoining owner trespassed upon the adjoining owner's property through a subterranean passage, under circumstances that the adjoining owner did not know or by the exercise of reasonable care could not have known of such secret occupancy, the occupancy having been for 20 years or more, such trespasser could not by having so done obtained a fee-simple title to the portion of the cave which extended into the adjoining owner's land. Marengo Cave Co. v. Ross, 212 Ind. 624, 10 N.E.2d 917 (1937).

Proof.
Cross-complainants in an action to quiet title who alleged ownership by adverse possession and unlawful claims by plaintiffs which clouded their title had the burden of proving that they and their grantees had been in actual, visible, notorious and exclusive possession, under claim of ownership, and hostile

Proof. (Cont'd)
to the owner of the record title and the world at large, and which possession was continuous for the full statutory period, and that taxes and special assessments legally levied during such period had been paid. Sheets v. Stiefel, 117 Ind. App. 584, 74 N.E.2d 921 (1947).

Property Not Assessed.
Where the land was taken off the assessment rolls and no taxes were assessed it need not be shown that any taxes were paid. Longabaugh v. Johnson, 163 Ind. App. 108, 45 Ind. Dec. 475, 321 N.E.2d 865 (1975).

Tax Duplicates.
The courts took judicial notice of the fact that complete legal descriptions of real estate were not set out on the tax duplicates issued by county and city treasurers. Echterling v. Kalvaitis, 235 Ind. 141, 126 N.E.2d 573 (1955); Nasser v. Stahl, 126 Ind. App. 709, 134 N.E.2d 567 (1956); Smith v. Brown, 126 Ind. App. 545, 134 N.E.2d 823 (1956).

Where continuous and open and notorious adverse possession had been established for 20 years to a contiguous and adjoining strip of land, and taxes had been paid according to the tax duplicate, although the strip of land was not especially set out therein and the taxes were not paid by the claimant, adverse possession was established. Echterling v. Kalvaitis, 235 Ind. 141, 126 N.E.2d 573 (1955); Nasser v. Stahl, 126 Ind. App. 709, 134 N.E.2d 567 (1956); Smith v. Brown, 126 Ind. App. 545, 134 N.E.2d 823 (1956).

Where adverse possession was established to a contiguous and adjoining strip of land and taxes paid according to the tax duplicate, although the duplicate did not expressly include that strip, adverse possession was established to that strip even though the taxes were not paid by the adverse claimant, and the absence of color of title affected only the extent of possession. Penn Cent. Transp. Co. v. Martin, 170 Ind. App. 519, 54 Ind. Dec. 402, 353 N.E.2d 474 (1976).

Where plaintiffs sought to quiet title to strip of land lying between adjoining landowners by adverse possession, and each of the parties had paid taxes on their respective lands as shown by the tax duplicates, the fact that the specific strip of land was not indicated on plaintiff's tax duplicate did not prevent plaintiff from acquiring such strip by adverse possession. Dowell v. Fleetwood, 420 N.E.2d 1356 (Ind. App. 1981).

Transferability of Adverse Possession Rights.
Where land is being sold under land sales contract, payment of taxes by the vendor is sufficient to save the adverse possession rights of the vendee as against an adjoining landowner. Dowell v. Fleetwood, 420 N.E.2d 1356 (Ind. App. 1981).

Collateral References. 3 Am. Jur. 2d Adverse Possession, §§ 165-169.

2 C.J.S. Adverse Possession, §§ 210-225.

32-21-7-2. Property of state or political subdivision not subject to adverse possession. — Title to real property owned by the state or a political subdivision (as defined in IC 36-1-2-13) may not be alienated by adverse possession. [P.L.2-2002, § 6.]

Compiler's Notes. P.L.86-1998, § 2, effective July 1, 1998, enacted prior to the 2002 recodification of this title by P.L.2-2002, provides: "A cause of action based on adverse possession may not be commenced against a political subdivision (as defined in IC 36-1-2-13) after June 30, 1998."

Collateral References. 3 Am. Jur. 2d Adverse Possession, §§ 1, 4, 205-210.

2 C.J.S. Adverse Possession, §§ 10-20.

CHAPTER 8

TAX SALE SURPLUS DISCLOSURE

32-21-8-1. Applicability. — This chapter applies to a transfer of property made after June 30, 2001, that transfers ownership of the property from a delinquent taxpayer to another person after the property is sold at a tax sale under IC 6-1.1-24 and before the tax sale purchaser is issued a tax sale deed under IC 6-1.1-25-4. [P.L.2-2002, § 6.]

Effective Dates. P.L.2-2002, § 6. July 1. 2002.

32-21-8-2. Disclosure required. — A taxpayer must file a tax sale surplus fund disclosure form in duplicate with the county auditor before the taxpayer may transfer title to property if:
  (1) the taxpayer owes delinquent taxes on the property;
  (2) the property was sold at a tax sale under IC 6-1.1-24; and
  (3) a part of the tax sale purchaser's bid on the property was deposited into the tax sale surplus fund under IC 6-1.1-24-7. [P.L.2-2002, § 6.]

32-21-8-3. Contents of disclosure. — A tax sale surplus fund disclosure form must contain the following information:
  (1) The name and address of the taxpayer transferring the property.
  (2) The name and address of the person acquiring the property.
  (3) The proposed date of transfer.
  (4) The purchase price for the transfer.
  (5) The date the property was sold at a tax sale under IC 6-1.1-24.
  (6) The amount of the tax sale purchaser's bid that was deposited into the tax sale surplus fund under IC 6-1.1-24-7. [P.L.2-2002, § 6.]

32-21-8-4. Signature and acknowledgement. — The tax sale surplus fund disclosure form must be signed by the taxpayer transferring the property and acknowledged before an officer authorized to take acknowledgments of deeds. [P.L.2-2002, § 6.]

32-21-8-5. Receipt of form by auditor. — The county auditor shall:
  (1) stamp the tax sale surplus fund disclosure form to indicate the county auditor's receipt of the form; and
  (2) remit the duplicate to the taxpayer.
[P.L.2-2002, § 6.]

32-21-8-6. Form prescribed by state board of accounts. — The state board of accounts shall prescribe the tax sale surplus fund disclosure form required by this chapter. [P.L.2-2002, § 6.]

CHAPTER 9
WRITTEN INSTRUMENTS BY MEMBERS OF THE ARMED FORCES

32-21-9-1. Scope — Certification. — (a) In addition to the acknowledgment of written instruments and the performance of other notarial acts in the manner and form otherwise authorized by the laws of this state, a person:

(1) who is serving in or with the armed forces of the United States wherever located;

(2) who is serving as a merchant seaman outside the limits of the United States included within the fifty (50) states and the District of Columbia; or

(3) who is outside the limits of the United States by permission, assignment, or direction of any department or office of the United States government in connection with any activity pertaining to the prosecution of any war in which the United States is engaged;

may acknowledge any instruments, attest documents, subscribe oaths and affirmations, give depositions, execute affidavits, and perform other notarial acts before any commissioned officer with the rank of second lieutenant or higher in the active services of the Army of the United States or the United States Marine Corps or before any commissioned officer with the rank of ensign or higher in the active service of the United States Navy or the United States Coast Guard, or with equivalent rank in any other component part of the armed forces of the United States.

(b) The commissioned officer before whom a notarial act is performed under this section shall certify the instrument with the officer's official signature and title in substantially the following form:

With the Armed Forces (or other component part of   )
)ss
the armed forces) of the United States at[1] _____   )
The foregoing instrument was acknowledged this _____
day of _____ 20_____ by[2] _____ serving (in) the armed forces of the
                                                (with)
United States) _____ (as a merchant seaman outside the limits of the United States) (as a person not in the armed forces, but outside the limits of the United States by permission, assignment, or direction of a department of the United States Government in connection with an activity pertaining to the prosecution of the war), before me, a commissioned officer in the active service of the (Army of the United States) (United States Marine Corps) (United States Navy) (United States Coast Guard) (or equivalent rank in any other component part of the armed forces).

(Signature of officer)

_____

Rank and Branch

Footnote 1. In the event that military considerations preclude disclosure of the place of execution or acknowledgment the words "an undisclosed place" may be supplied instead of the appropriate city or county, state, and country.

Footnote 2. If by a natural person or persons, insert name or names; if by a person acting in a representative or official capacity or as attorney-in-fact, then insert name of person acknowledging the instrument, followed by an accurate description of the capacity in which he acts including the name of the person, corporation, or other entity represented. [P.L.2-2002, § 6.]

Effective Dates. P.L.2-2002, § 6. July 1. 2002.
Cross References. Acknowledgments for instruments required to be recorded, IC 32-21-2, IC 32-21-3.

Collateral References. 37 C.J.S. Frauds, Statute of, § 172.

32-21-9-2. Prima facie evidence. — An acknowledgment or other notarial act made substantially in the form prescribed by section 1 [IC 32-21-9-1] of this chapter is prima facie evidence:

(1) that the person named in the instrument as having acknowledged or executed the instrument:

(A) appeared in person before the officer taking the acknowledgment;

(B) was personally known to the officer to be the person whose name was subscribed to the instrument; and

(C) acknowledged that the person signed the instrument as a free and voluntary act for the uses and purposes set forth in the instrument;

(2) if the acknowledgment or execution is by a person in a representative or official capacity, that the person acknowledging or executing the instrument acknowledged it to be the person's free and voluntary act in such capacity or the free and voluntary act of the principal, person, or entity represented; and

(3) if the acknowledgment or other notarial act is by a person as an officer of a corporation, that the person was known to the officer taking the acknowledgment or performing any other notarial act to be a corporate officer and that the instrument was executed and acknowledged for and on behalf of the corporation by the corporate officer with proper authority from the corporation, as the free and voluntary act of the corporation. [P.L.2-2002, § 6.]

32-21-9-3. No requirement to state place of execution. — An instrument acknowledged or executed as provided in this chapter is not invalid because of a failure to state in the instrument the place of execution or acknowledgment. [P.L.2-2002, § 6.]

32-21-9-4. Evidentiary value. — An acknowledgment or other notarial act made substantially as provided in this chapter constitutes prima facie proof of the facts recited in the instrument and, without further or other authentication, entitles any document so acknowledged or executed to be filed and recorded in the proper offices of record and received in evidence before the courts of this state, to the same extent and with the same effect as documents acknowledged or executed in accordance with any other provision of law now in force or that may be enacted. [P.L.2-2002, § 6.]

CHAPTER 10

CONVEYANCES IN WHICH THE GRANTOR AND ANOTHER ARE NAMED AS GRANTEES

32-21-10-1. "Person" and "Persons" defined. — As used in this chapter:

(1) "person" includes a person who may be married; and

(2) "persons" includes persons who may be married to each other. [P.L.2-2002, § 6.]

Effective Dates. P.L.2-2002, § 6. July 1. 2002.

32-21-10-2. Conveyance to grantors and other persons — Effect of transfer. — (a) A person who owns real property or an interest in real property that the person has the power to convey may effectively convey the property or interest by a conveyance naming as grantees that person and one (1) or more other persons.

(b) Two (2) or more persons who own real property or an interest in real property that the persons have the power to convey may effectively convey the property or interest by a conveyance naming as grantees one (1) or more of those persons and one (1) or more other persons.

(c) A conveyance under subsection (a) or (b) has the same effect as to whether it creates an estate in:

(1) severalty;

(2) joint tenancy with right of survivorship;

(3) tenancy by the entirety; or

(4) tenancy in common;

as if the conveyance were a conveyance from a stranger who owned the property or interest to the persons named as grantees in the conveyance. [P.L.2-2002, § 6.]

Collateral References. 23 Am. Jur. 2d Deeds, § 35.

Risk of loss by casualty pending contract for conveyance of real property — modern cases. 85 A.L.R.4th 233.

32-21-10-3. Conveyance to subset of grantors — Effect of transfer. — (a) Two (2) or more persons who own real property or an interest in real property that they have power to convey may effectively convey the property or interest by a conveyance naming as grantee or grantees one (1) or more of those persons.

(b) A conveyance under subsection (a) has the same effect, as to whether it creates an estate in:

(1) severalty;

(2) joint tenancy with right of survivorship;

(3) tenancy by the entirety; or

(4) tenancy in common;

as if the conveyance were a conveyance from a stranger who owned the property or interest to the person or persons named as grantee or grantees in the conveyance. [P.L.2-2002, § 6.]

CHAPTER 11
RESPONSIBLE PROPERTY TRANSFER LAW

SECTION.
32-21-11-1. Delivery of disclosure document.

32-21-11-1. Delivery of disclosure document. — In addition to any other requirements concerning the conveyance of real property, a transferor of property (as defined in IC 13-11-2-174) may be required to deliver a disclosure document under IC 13-25-3 to each of the other parties to a transfer of the property at least thirty (30) days before the transfer. [P.L.2-2002, § 6.]

Effective Dates. P.L.2-2002, § 6. July 1. 2002.

ARTICLE 22
CONVEYANCE LIMITATIONS OF REAL PROPERTY

CHAPTER 1
LIMITATIONS ON PERSONS WHO MAY CONVEY REAL PROPERTY

32-22-1-1. Persons who may not convey property. — Except as provided in section 3 [IC 32-22-1-3] of this chapter, a:

(1) mentally incompetent person; or

(2) person less than eighteen (18) years of age;

may not alienate land or any interest in land. [P.L.2-2002, § 7.]

Effective Dates. P.L.2-2002, § 7. July 1. 2002.

Cross References. Disaffirmance by infants, return of consideration, IC 32-22-1-2.

Insane persons, deed by husband or wife, IC 32-22-1-5.

NOTES TO DECISIONS

ANALYSIS

Mentally incompetent persons.
—In general.
—Assignments of expectancies.
—Disaffirmance.
—Effect of insanity.
—Married women.
—Old age or infirmity.
—Ratification.
—Return of consideration.
Minors.
—Disaffirmance.
—Return of consideration.

Mentally Incompetent Persons.

—In General.

A person who alleged unsoundness of mind at a particular time had to establish by the preponderance of evidence that he was not of sound mind at the given time; but when it appeared that a person was, at a given time, of unsound mind, unless the unsoundness was occasioned by some temporary cause, the legal presumption arose that that state of mind continued until the contrary was made to appear by evidence. Crouse v. Holman, 19 Ind. 30 (1862); Wray v. Wray, 32 Ind. 126 (1869); Stumph v. Miller, 142 Ind. 442, 41 N.E. 812 (1895); Raymond v. Wathen, 142 Ind. 367, 41 N.E. 815 (1895); Wells v. Wells, 197 Ind. 236, 150 N.E. 361 (1926).

"Persons of unsound mind," as used in this section, were persons who lacked sufficient mental capacity to make conveyances when measured according to the standard fixed by the courts. Humphrey v. Harris, 48 Ind. App. 469, 96 N.E. 38 (1911).

The capacity of persons to take title to and hold land, or to transmit the same by conveyance, devise, or descent, was regulated by the law of the state where the property was situated. Donaldson v. State ex rel. Honan, 182 Ind. 615, 101 N.E. 485 (1913).

—Assignments of Expectancies.

A court of equity may specifically enforce assignments of expectancies where such a transfer is considered an executory contract for a transfer of future interests and common honesty requires that they should be carried out. McAdams v. Bailey, 169 Ind. 518, 82 N.E. 1057 (1907).

—Disaffirmance.

It was formerly held in all cases that deeds made by persons who had not been judicially declared insane had to be disaffirmed before an action would lie to recover the land. Nichol v. Thomas, 53 Ind. 42 (1876); Schuff v. Ransom, 79 Ind. 458 (1881); Fay v. Burditt, 81

Ind. 433, 42 Am. R. 142 (1882); Ashmead v. Reynolds, 127 Ind. 441, 26 N.E. 80 (1890); Voris v. Harshbarger, 11 Ind. App. 555, 39 N.E. 521 (1894); Aetna Life Ins. Co. v. Sellers, 154 Ind. 370, 56 N.E. 97, 77 Am. St. 481 (1900); Downham v. Holloway, 158 Ind. 626, 64 N.E. 82, 92 Am. St. Ind. 330 (1902). It is now held that the law does not require it when the one procuring the conveyance knew of the grantor's mental infirmity. Barkley v. Barkley, 182 Ind. 322, 106 N.E. 609, 1915B L.R.A. 678 (1914).

When a person of unsound mind was brought into court as a defendant to answer as to any interest he might have had in real estate theretofore conveyed by him, the filing of an answer and cross complaint by the guardian of such person was a sufficient disaffirmance of such conveyance. Hull v. Louth, 109 Ind. 315, 10 N.E. 270, 58 Am. R. 405 (1886).

Complaint was not bad on a motion in arrest of judgment for failure to allege a disaffirmance. Lange v. Dammier, 119 Ind. 567, 21 N.E. 749 (1889).

—Effect of Insanity.

The deeds of persons who had not been judicially declared of unsound mind were voidable but not void. Somers v. Pumphrey, 24 Ind. 231 (1865); Musselman v. Cravens, 47 Ind. 1 (1874); Nichol v. Thomas, 53 Ind. 42 (1876); Freed v. Brown, 55 Ind. 310 (1876); Schuff v. Ransom, 79 Ind. 458 (1881); Downham v. Holloway, 158 Ind. 626, 64 N.E. 82, 92 Am. St. R. 330 (1902); Studabaker v. Faylor, 170 Ind. 498, 83 N.E. 747, 127 Am. St. R. 397 (1908).

The contracts and deeds of persons who had been judicially declared insane were void. Devin v. Scott, 34 Ind. 67 (1870); Musselman v. Cravens, 47 Ind. 1 (1874); Copenrath v. Kienby, 83 Ind. 18 (1882); Redden v. Baker, 86 Ind. 191 (1882); Spaulding v. Harvey, 129 Ind. 106, 28 N.E. 323, 13 L.R.A. 619, 28 Am. St. R. 176 (1891).

—Married Women.

If an insane married woman joined her husband in the conveyance of lands, such conveyance did not affect her interest in such lands. Gray v. Turley, 110 Ind. 254, 11 N.E. 40 (1887).

—Old Age or Infirmity.

One was not incapacitated to make and execute a deed merely because of advanced years or by reason of physical infirmities unless such age and the infirmities resulting therefrom impaired one's mental faculties until he was unable to properly, intelligently, and fairly protect and preserve his property

Mentally Incompetent Persons. (Cont'd)

—Old Age or Infirmity. (Cont'd)
rights. Deckard v. Kleindorfer, 108 Ind. App. 485, 29 N.E.2d 997 (1940), overruled on other grounds, Colbo v. Buyer, 235 Ind. 518, 134 N.E.2d 45 (1956).

—Ratification.
A guardian of an insane person was powerless to convey lands of his ward without a court order or to ratify a prior conveyance by his ward, without such an order. Funk v. Rentchler, 134 Ind. 68, 33 N.E. 364, 898 (1892).

—Return of Consideration.
An action would lie to recover lands conveyed by an insane person without a return of the consideration. Nichol v. Thomas, 53 Ind. 42 (1877); Physio-Medical College v. Wilkinson, 108 Ind. 314, 9 N.E. 167 (1886); Hull v. Louth, 109 Ind. 315, 10 N.E. 270, 58 Am. R. 405 (1887).

Return of consideration was required when contracts were fair and persons who dealt with insane person acted in good faith. Fay v. Burditt, 81 Ind. 433, 42 Am. R. 142 (1881); Copenrath v. Kienby, 83 Ind. 18 (1882); Boyer v. Berryman, 123 Ind. 451, 24 N.E. 249 (1890); Louisville, N.A. & C. Ry. v. Herr, 135 Ind. 591, 35 N.E. 556 (1893); Voris v. Harshbarger, 11 Ind. App. 555, 39 N.E. 521 (1894); Thrash v. Starbuck, 145 Ind. 673, 44 N.E. 543 (1896); Aetna Life Ins. Co. v. Sellers, 154 Ind. 370, 56 N.E. 97, 77 Am. St. R. 481 (1900); Wells v. Wells, 197 Ind. 236, 150 N.E. 361 (1926).

Minors.

—Disaffirmance.
The deeds of minors were voidable but not void, and, on arrival of age, the deed had to be disaffirmed before a suit would lie to recover the lands. Law v. Long, 41 Ind. 586 (1873); Scranton v. Stewart, 52 Ind. 68 (1875); Buchanan v. Hubbard, 119 Ind. 187, 21 N.E. 538 (1889); Shroyer v. Pittenger, 31 Ind. App. 158, 67 N.E. 475 (1903); Wainwright Trust Co. v. Prudential Life Ins. Co., 80 Ind. App. 37, 134 N.E. 913 (1922).

A written notice given by a married woman after her arrival at age that she disaffirmed an executed contract was a sufficient act of disaffirmance, and such an act of disaffir-

mance done within three and a half years after the female grantor's arrival at age was within a reasonable time. Scranton v. Stewart, 52 Ind. 68 (1875); Riggs v. Fisk, 64 Ind. 100 (1878); Long v. Williams, 74 Ind. 115 (1881); Sims v. Bardoner, 86 Ind. 87, 44 Am. R. 263 (1882); Richardson v. Pate, 93 Ind. 423, 47 Am. R. 374 (1883); Shroyer v. Pittenger, 31 Ind. App. 158, 67 N.E. 475 (1903).

A minor could disaffirm a deed although not entitled to the possession of the land. Long v. Williams, 74 Ind. 115 (1881).

It was a question of fact whether or not a deed was disaffirmed by a minor within a reasonable time after arrival at age. Stringer v. Northwestern Mut. Life Ins. Co., 82 Ind. 100 (1882).

Mere acquiescence by a minor in the conveyance of lands did not amount to an affirmance of the deed until his right of action was barred by the statute of limitations. Sims v. Bardoner, 86 Ind. 87, 44 Am. R. 263 (1882); Sims v. Smith, 86 Ind. 577 (1882); Applegate v. Conner, 93 Ind. 185 (1883); Buchanan v. Hubbard, 96 Ind. 1 (1884).

The heirs of an infant grantor could disaffirm his deed after his death. Gillenwater v. Campbell, 142 Ind. 529, 41 N.E. 1041 (1895).

—Return of Consideration.
Minors could disaffirm their deeds and sue to recover the lands without returning the purchase money. Miles v. Lingerman, 24 Ind. 385 (1865); Law v. Long, 41 Ind. 586 (1873); Dill v. Bowen, 54 Ind. 204 (1876); Shroyer v. Pittenger, 31 Ind. App. 158, 67 N.E. 475 (1903).

Where the specific property received by the minor as consideration remained in his hands and was capable of return, he was bound to give it up. Buchanan v. Hubbard, 119 Ind. 187, 21 N.E. 538 (1889).

Where a minor conveyed real estate and on arriving of age disaffirmed his deed and sold the land to another who brought suit to quiet title and have the former deed declared void, and the defendant answered by way of estoppel but made no allegation as to representation of age or that he was misled, the answer in estoppel was fatally defective. Bradshaw v. Van Winkle, 133 Ind. 134, 32 N.E. 877 (1892); Shaul v. Rinker, 139 Ind. 163, 38 N.E. 593 (1894); Gillenwater v. Campbell, 142 Ind. 529, 41 N.E. 1041 (1895).

Collateral References. Guardian's power to make lease for infant ward beyond minority or term of guardianship. 6 A.L.R.3d 570.

Capacity of infant to act as executor or administrator, and effect of improper appointment. 8 A.L.R.3d 590.

Mental condition which will justify the appointment of guardian, committee, or conservator of the estate for an incompetent or spendthrift. 9 A.L.R.3d 774.

Oil and gas royalty as real or personal property. 56 A.L.R.4th 539.

32-22-1-2. Disaffirmance — Return of consideration. — (a) This section does not apply to any sale or contract made and entered into before September 19, 1881.

(b) In all sales of real estate by a person less than eighteen (18) years of age, the person may not disaffirm the sale without first restoring to the purchaser the consideration received in the sale, if the person falsely represented himself or herself to the purchaser to be at least eighteen (18) years of age and the purchaser acted in good faith, relied upon the person's representations in the sale, and had good cause to believe the person to be at least eighteen (18) years of age. [P.L.2-2002, § 7.]

NOTES TO DECISIONS

ANALYSIS

In general.
Heirs of infant married woman.
Method of showing disaffirmance.
Return of consideration.
Time for disaffirmance.

In General.

If the grantee of an infant married woman sought to have his title confirmed, she could have, by a counterclaim, disaffirmed the deed and recovered her interest in the land. McClanahan v. Williams, 136 Ind. 30, 35 N.E. 897 (1893).

Prior to the enactment of former IC 32-1-12-1, minors were required to return only the consideration received on disaffirming deeds when they made false representations as to being of age. Bradshaw v. Van Winkle, 133 Ind. 134, 32 N.E. 877 (1892); Shaul v. Rinker, 139 Ind. 163, 38 N.E. 593 (1894); Gillenwater v. Campbell, 142 Ind. 529, 41 N.E. 1041 (1895).

The provisions of this section applied to mortgages executed by infants on lands, as well as to deeds. United States Sav. Fund & Inv. Co. v. Harris, 142 Ind. 226, 40 N.E. 1072, 41 N.E. 451 (1895).

If an infant married woman asserted in a deed executed by her that she was 21 years old, and the grantee relied on such statement, such woman could not disaffirm a deed and recover the land unless she returned the consideration received by her. Ackerman v. Hawkins, 45 Ind. App. 483, 88 N.E. 616 (1909).

Heirs of Infant Married Woman.

The heirs of an infant married woman could disaffirm a deed executed by her. Gillenwater v. Campbell, 142 Ind. 529, 41 N.E. 1041 (1895).

Method of Showing Disaffirmance.

A voidable deed could have been disaffirmed by entry on the land, by a written notice of disaffirmance, by a subsequent conveyance, or by any other equally emphatic act, declaratory of an intention to disaffirm. Scranton v. Stewart, 52 Ind. 68 (1875); Riggs v. Fisk, 64 Ind. 100 (1878); Long v. Williams, 74 Ind. 115 (1881); Sims v. Bardoner, 86 Ind. 87, 44 Am. R. 263 (1882); Shroyer v. Pittenger, 31 Ind. App. 158, 67 N.E. 475 (1903).

Return of Consideration.

Prior to the enactment of a prior similar provision, an infant married woman on disaffirming a deed could recover the land without returning the consideration received. Miles v. Lingerman, 24 Ind. 385 (1865); Law v. Long, 41 Ind. 586 (1873); Carpenter v. Carpenter, 45 Ind. 142 (1873); State ex rel. Hutson v. Joest, 46 Ind. 235 (1874); Dill v. Bowen, 54 Ind. 204 (1876); Richardson v. Pate, 93 Ind. 423, 47 Am. R. 374 (1883); Shirk v. Shultz, 113 Ind. 571, 15 N.E. 12 (1888); Shipley v. Smith, 162 Ind. 526, 70 N.E. 803 (1904).

Since the enactment of a prior similar provision, if any consideration was received by the party disaffirming, and the husband was of full age and joined in the deed, she had to return the consideration received for executing the deed. United States Sav. Fund & Inv. Co. v. Harris, 142 Ind. 226, 40 N.E. 1072, 41 N.E. 451 (1895); Gillenwater v. Campbell, 142 Ind. 529, 41 N.E. 1041 (1895); Blair v. Whittaker, 31 Ind. App. 664, 69 N.E. 182 (1903); Ackerman v. Hawkins, 45 Ind. App. 483, 88 N.E. 616 (1909).

Infant married women could disaffirm a mortgage so as to escape a personal liability without returning the consideration. United States Sav. Fund & Inv. Co. v. Harris, 142 Ind. 226, 40 N.E. 1072, 41 N.E. 451 (1895); Gillenwater v. Campbell, 142 Ind. 529, 41 N.E. 1041 (1895).

An infant who with her adult husband had executed a lease of her land for a period of two years and received the first year's rent during her minority, could, upon arriving at her majority, a few days after the commencement of

Return of Consideration. (Cont'd)
the second year of the lease, disaffirm the same, and recover possession of the real estate, without restoring the rent received for the first year. Shipley v. Smith, 162 Ind. 526, 70 N.E. 803 (1904).

If no consideration were received, it was not necessary to show a return of consideration on a disaffirmance of the deed. Shroyer v. Pittenger, 31 Ind. App. 158, 67 N.E. 475 (1903); Ackerman v. Hawkins, 45 Ind. App. 483, 88 N.E. 616 (1909).

Where, upon reaching majority, plaintiff filed a complaint for rescission of her deed made in infancy, alleging no consideration, defendant was not entitled to judgment because there was no offer to repay, since the former section provided that the court should, in such case, decree the amount to be a lien against the land. Bilskie v. Bilskie, 69 Ind. App. 595, 122 N.E. 436 (1919).

Time for Disaffirmance.
An infant married woman had to disaffirm

her deeds within a reasonable time after arrival of age. Scranton v. Stewart, 52 Ind. 68 (1875); Sims v. Bardoner, 86 Ind. 87, 44 Am. R. 263 (1882); Shroyer v. Pittenger, 31 Ind. App. 158, 67 N.E. 475 (1903).

An infant married woman could, after arrival of age, and during coverture, disaffirm her deeds made during minority, and sue to have her title quieted. Sims v. Bardoner, 86 Ind. 87, 44 Am. R. 263 (1882); Sims v. Smith, 86 Ind. 577 (1882).

An infant married woman could disaffirm her deed at any time before her right of action to recover the lands was barred. Sims v. Bardoner, 86 Ind. 87, 44 Am. R. 263 (1882); Richardson v. Pate, 93 Ind. 423, 47 Am. R. 374 (1883).

Infant married women joining in deeds conveying lands of their husbands could not disaffirm the deeds during the lives of such husbands. McClanahan v. Williams, 136 Ind. 30, 35 N.E. 897 (1893).

Collateral References. 42 Am. Jur. 2d Infants, §§ 58, 75, 82, 83.
43 C.J.S. Infants, §§ 126, 128.

Infant's misrepresentation as to his age as estopping him from disaffirming his voidable transactions. 29 A.L.R.3d 1270.

32-22-1-3. Married to persons over 18. — Any person who is:

(1) less than eighteen (18) years of age; and

(2) married to a person who is at least eighteen (18) years of age;

may convey, mortgage, or agree to convey any interest in real estate or may make any contract concerning the interest, with the consent of the circuit, superior, or probate court of the county where the person resides, upon payment of the fee required under IC 33-19-5-4. [P.L.2-2002, § 7.]

NOTES TO DECISIONS

In General.
If a married woman under age joined her husband in the conveyance of his real estate without the consent of her parents, such deed would have been voidable, but not void under former section which required such consent. Scranton v. Stewart, 52 Ind. 68 (1875).

A married woman over 18 and under 21 years of age could convey her interest in the lands of her husband by joining with him in a deed as provided in 1 R.S. 1852, ch. 23, § 24 (since repealed). Fisher v. Payne, 90 Ind. 183 (1883).

Prior to the enactment of the former section, joinder by an infant married woman in the conveyance of the lands of her husband

did not convey her interest in such lands. Applegate v. Conner, 93 Ind. 185 (1883).

Since the enactment of the former section, it has been competent for an infant married woman to join her adult husband in the conveyance of his real estate. Bakes v. Gilbert, 93 Ind. 70 (1884); Kennedy v. Hudkins, 140 Ind. 570, 40 N.E. 52 (1894); United States Sav. Fund & Inv. Co. v. Harris, 142 Ind. 226, 40 N.E. 1072, 41 N.E. 451 (1895).

Infant married women could join their adult husbands in executing mortgages on lands of their husbands. Bakes v. Gilbert, 93 Ind. 70 (1884); United States Sav. Fund & Inv. Co. v. Harris, 142 Ind. 226, 40 N.E. 1072, 41 N.E. 451 (1895).

Collateral References. 42 Am. Jur. 2d
Infants, §§ 58, 75, 83.
  43 C.J.S. Infants, § 139-141.

32-22-1-4. Judicial consent. — A judge may give consent under section 3 [IC 32-22-1-3] of this chapter to a conveyance or mortgage and to any note secured by the mortgage, agreement, or contract if the judge determines that it would benefit the person described in section 3 of this chapter and that it would be prejudicial to the spouse of the person if the execution of the instrument were prevented. The judge shall endorse the judge's consent on the instrument and sign it, and the instrument so certified is valid for all purposes as if the married person were at least eighteen (18) years of age. However, the judge has the power, in the judge's discretion, to examine witnesses concerning the propriety or necessity of executing the instrument. [P.L.2-2002, § 7.]

NOTES TO DECISIONS

Consent of Court.
  Prior to Acts 1907, ch. 76, an infant married woman could convey her real estate by deed in which her husband joined, without the consent of the judge of the circuit court, subject to disaffirmance on coming of age. Reese v. Cochran, 10 Ind. 195 (1858); Johnson v. Rockwell, 12 Ind. 76 (1859); Scranton v. Stewart, 52 Ind. 68 (1875); Losey v. Bond, 94 Ind. 67 (1884).

  Collateral References. Capacity of infant to act as executor or administrator, and effect of improper appointment. 8 A.L.R.3d 590.

32-22-1-5. Mentally incompetent spouse. — (a) If a person owning real estate desires to sell the real estate or a part of the real estate and the person's spouse is, at the time, mentally incompetent, the person, upon complying with this section, may sell and convey the real estate by deed without the joinder of the mentally incompetent spouse. The conveyance has the same effect as would the joint deed of both spouses.

  (b) Before a deed is made under this section, the owner intending to sell the real estate shall, by petition, apply to the court having probate jurisdiction in the county where the real estate or a part of the real estate to be sold is situated, alleging that the owner's spouse is mentally incompetent and that the incompetency is probably permanent. Upon the filing of the petition, notice shall be given to the person alleged to be mentally incompetent, either by service of process, as provided by law for service of process against incompetent persons in other civil actions, or, if the person alleged to be incompetent is by affidavit shown to be a nonresident of Indiana, by publication.

  (c) After notice and upon or after the return day of the notice, the legally appointed guardian, if any, of the person alleged to be mentally incompetent or, if there is no guardian, a guardian ad litem for the person appointed by the court, shall make any proper defense to the application. The matter of the petition shall be submitted to the court, and if the allegations are proved to the satisfaction of the court, the court shall make and enter a finding that the person alleged to be incompetent is incompetent, and that the incompetency is probably permanent.

(d) Upon the filing by the petitioner with the clerk of the court of a bond, in an amount and with surety approved by the court, that is payable to the state and conditioned to:

(1) keep the mentally incompetent spouse from becoming a county charge; and

(2) account to the spouse, upon restoration to competency, if the spouse demands it, fifty percent (50%) of the purchase money received for the real estate upon sale;

the court shall enter an order authorizing the whole title to be conveyed by the petitioner without the joinder of the mentally incompetent spouse.

(e) A deed made under an order of court under this section has the same effect as the deed of an unmarried person competent to convey real estate.

(f) If it is shown to the satisfaction of the court having probate jurisdiction in the county in which lands authorized to be sold under this section are located that:

(1) the lands were sold under an order authorizing the sale;

(2) the entire proceeds of the sale were invested in other real estate located in Indiana;

(3) the land purchased with the proceeds of the sale was of no less value than the land sold under the order;

(4) the title to the land purchased with the proceeds of the sale was taken in the name of the person having a mentally incompetent spouse; and

(5) the mentally incompetent spouse will not suffer any loss as a result of the investment described in subdivision (2);

the court shall enter an order discharging the bond described in subsection (d) and releasing the sureties from all liabilities on the bond. [P.L.2-2002, § 7.]

Cross References. Disaffirmance by infants, return of consideration, IC 32-22-1-2.

Insane persons, deeds by husband or wife, IC 32 22 1 5.

NOTES TO DECISIONS

In General.

On compliance with the statute, the husband or wife of an insane person could convey land. Teeter v. Newcom, 130 Ind. 28, 29 N.E. 391 (1891); Hallett v. Hallett, 8 Ind. App. 305, 34 N.E. 740 (1893).

This section did not constitute a limitation upon statutes concerning partition. Pavy v. Pavy, 121 Ind. App. 194, 98 N.E.2d 224 (1951).

Collateral References. Admissibility, in civil case, of expert or opinion evidence as to proposed witness' inability to testify. 11 A.L.R.3d 1360.

Actionability of imputing to private person mental disorder or incapacity, or impairment of mental faculties. 23 A.L.R.3d 652.

Estate by entireties as affected by statute declaring nature of tenancy under grant or devise to two or more persons. 32 A.L.R.3d 570.

CHAPTER 2

RIGHTS OF ALIENS TO HOLD AND CONVEY REAL PROPERTY

32-22-2-1. Title derived before statehood. — The title of any resident of Indiana who was in actual possession of any land on or before November 1, 1851, or the title of any person holding under the resident may not be defeated or prejudiced by:

(1) the alienism of the resident; or

(2) the alienism of any other person through whom the resident's title was derived. [P.L.2-2002, § 7.]

Effective Dates. P.L.2-2002, § 7. July 1. 2002.

NOTES TO DECISIONS

ANALYSIS

Aliens.
Indians.

Aliens.

An alien who was a bona fide resident of the United States could have held and conveyed real estate. Murray v. Kelly, 27 Ind. 42 (1866); State ex rel. Att'y Gen. v. Witz, 87 Ind. 190 (1882).

At common law, an alien could have taken, held and conveyed real estate against all except the state, but the title of an alien to real estate was liable to be divested by an inquest of office prosecuted on behalf of the state. Halstead v. Board of Commr's, 56 Ind. 363 (1877); Donaldson v. State ex rel. Honan, 182 Ind. 615, 101 N.E. 485 (1913).

The right of aliens to convey land, or to acquire the same by descent, was regulated by statute. Donaldson v. State ex rel. Honan, 182 Ind. 615, 101 N.E. 485 (1913).

Indians.

An Indian who was a bona fide resident of the United States, though not a citizen thereof, could convey or devise real estate. Parent v. Walmsly's Adm'r, 20 Ind. 82 (1863); Steeple v. Downing, 60 Ind. 478 (1878).

32-22-2-2. Rights of aliens who have declared intention to become citizens — Rights of all aliens. — All aliens residing in Indiana who have declared their intention to become citizens of the United States, conformably to the laws of the United States, may acquire and hold real estate in the same manner as citizens of Indiana. Any alien, whether the alien resides in Indiana or elsewhere, may:

(1) make loans of money and take and accept mortgages upon real estate within Indiana to secure the payment of the loans or of any bona fide indebtedness owing from any person to a the alien; and

(2) take, hold, transmit, and convey any real estate acquired, held, or obtained by the process of laws:

(A) in the collection of debts; or

(B) by any procedure for the enforcement of any lien or claim on the lien, whether created by mortgage or otherwise;

as fully as a citizen of Indiana may take, hold, transmit, or convey the real estate. [P.L.2-2002, § 7.]

Cross References. Curing title of land held by aliens prior to November 1851, IC 32-22-1-2.

NOTES TO DECISIONS

In General.

Under Acts 1861, ch. 4, p. 5, nonresident aliens could acquire real estate by devise or descent, and might hold or convey the same during a period of eight years after the settlement of the estate of the decedent testator. State ex rel. Att'y Gen. v. Witz, 87 Ind. 190 (1882).

At common law, an alien had no inheritable blood, and could neither take land by descent, nor transmit it to others. Lehman v. State ex rel. Miller, 45 Ind. App. 330, 88 N.E. 365 (1909); Donaldson v. State ex rel. Honan, 182 Ind. 615, 101 N.E. 485 (1913). See also Murray v. Kelly, 27 Ind. 42 (1866).

Where no inquest has been instituted, an alien may convey or mortgage land owned by him. Lehman v. State ex rel. Miller, 45 Ind. App. 330, 88 N.E. 365 (1909); Donaldson v. State ex rel. Honan, 182 Ind. 615, 101 N.E. 485 (1913). See also Halstead v. Board of Comm'rs, 56 Ind. 363 (1877).

Aliens could hold and convey lands only upon such terms and conditions as could have been prescribed by law. Lehman v. State ex rel. Miller, 45 Ind. App. 330, 88 N.E. 365 (1909); Donaldson v. State ex rel. Honan, 182 Ind. 615, 101 N.E. 485 (1913).

Under Acts 1881 (Spec. Sess.), ch. 8, p. 84, the real estate of a nonresident alien did not descend to his heirs. Donaldson v. State ex rel. Honan, 182 Ind. 615, 101 N.E. 485 (1913).

Collateral References. 3A Am. Jur. 2d Aliens and Citizens, §§ 10-42.

3 C.J.S. Aliens, §§ 16-46.

32-22-2-3. Rights of aliens who have not declared intention to become citizens. — (a) Except as provided in section 4 [IC 32-22-2-4] of this chapter, all aliens residing in Indiana who have not declared their intention to become citizens of the United States may:

(1) acquire and hold land by devise and descent only; and

(2) convey land acquired and held under subdivision (1):

(A) not later than five (5) years after the date the land is acquired; or

(B) if subsection (c) applies, not later than the date on which the land escheats to the state under subsection (c).

(b) Except as provided in subsection (c), land acquired by an alien under subsection (a) escheats to the state five (5) years after the date the land is acquired if the land is not conveyed during those five (5) years.

(c) If:

(1) land is acquired and held by an alien under subsection (a);

(2) the acquisition of the land by the alien by devise or descent is subject to the settlement of the estate of the decedent from whom the land is acquired; and

(3) the final settlement of the estate of the decedent from whom the land is acquired occurs more than five (5) years after the date of death of the decedent;

the land escheats to the state two (2) years after the date of the final settlement of the estate.

(d) If an alien, during the pendency of the settlement of the estate as described in subsection (c), becomes a naturalized citizen of the United States and of the state in which the alien resides, the alien:

(1) is relieved of all disabilities of aliens as to ownership of real estate;

(2) may continue to hold real estate acquired by devise or descent; and

(3) may further acquire and hold real estate in the same manner and with the same power as a citizen of the United States. [P.L.2-2002, § 7.]

NOTES TO DECISIONS

Validity of Section.
This section was not in conflict with the treaty between the United States and Switzerland regulating the rights of the citizens of each country, and land held by an alien citizen at his death could have escheated to the state if the provisions of this section were not complied with. Lehman v. State ex rel. Miller, 45 Ind. App. 330, 88 N.E. 365 (1909).

32-22-2-4. Real estate acquired for enforcement of lien or collection of debts. — (a) Sections 2 and 3 [IC 32-22-2-2 and IC 32-22-2-3] of this chapter do not prevent the holder of any lien upon or interest in real estate from taking a valid title to real estate:

(1) in which the holder has the interest; or

(2) upon which the holder has the lien.

(b) Except as provided in subsection (c), nothing in this chapter prevents any alien, whether the alien resides in Indiana or elsewhere, from taking, holding, transmitting, or conveying any real estate in Indiana that is acquired, held, or obtained by the process of law:

(1) in the collection of debts; or

(2) by any procedure for the enforcement of any lien or claim on the lien, whether created by mortgage or otherwise;

as fully as a citizen of Indiana may take, hold, transmit, or convey the real estate.

(c) An alien may not hold real estate acquired as described in subsection (b) for more than five (5) years. [P.L.2-2002, § 7.]

32-22-2-5. Rights of natural persons who are aliens. — (a) Natural persons who are aliens, whether they reside in the United States or any foreign country, subject to sections 6 and 7 [IC 32-22-2-6 and IC 32-22-2-7] of this chapter, may:

(1) acquire real estate by purchase, devise, or descent;

(2) hold and enjoy real estate; and

(3) convey, devise, transmit, mortgage, or otherwise encumber real estate;

in the same manner and with the same effect as citizens of Indiana or the United States.

(b) The title of any real estate inherited, mortgaged, conveyed, or devised is not affected by the alienage of any person from or through whom the title is claimed or derived. [P.L.2-2002, § 7.]

Cross References. Curing title of land held by alien prior to November, 1851, IC 32-22-1-2.

Collateral References. 3A Am. Jur. 2d Aliens and Citizens, §§ 10-42.
3 C.J.S. Aliens, §§ 16-46.

32-22-2-6. Acquisition of lands in excess of 320 acres. — (a) If an alien acquires land in Indiana in excess of three hundred and twenty (320) acres, the alien shall, not later than five (5) years after acquiring the excess or becoming eighteen (18) years of age, unless the alien becomes a citizen of the United States, convey all lands acquired by the alien in Indiana. If the alien dies within the five (5) year period without having conveyed, this chapter does not prevent the alien's heirs or devisees from inheriting or taking the unconveyed lands by devise from or through the alien. If an alien acquires the excess above three hundred and twenty (320) acres and the excess remains unconveyed at the end of five (5) years after the acquisition of the excess:

    (1) the excess escheats to the state; and

    (2) the attorney general shall file an information in the circuit or superior court of the county in which the land is situated:

        (A) alleging the ground upon which recovery is claimed; and

        (B) making all persons interested parties to the information.

  (b) The attorney general shall, at the time of filing the information referred to in subsection (a), file in the office of the clerk of the court a notice containing:

    (1) the title of the court;

    (2) the names of all the parties to the suit, if known, and if not known, then by the designation of "unknown heirs", as is provided in suits to quiet title;

    (3) a description of the real estate; and

    (4) a statement of the nature of the action.

The clerk shall record the notice in lis pendens records as of the date and hour of filing, and the land and all of the land owned by the alien and described in the information and notice shall, upon hearing and judgment, upon the information, escheat to the state.

  (c) Any person, firm, or corporation, who, before the filing of the information and notice, in good faith and for a valuable consideration has acquired, or except for the alienage of the person or persons from or through whom claim is made, would have acquired, by deed, mortgage, contract, legal proceeding, or otherwise, any right, title, interest, or lien to, in, or upon the land, or any part of the land, is not prejudiced or affected by the alienage of the person or persons, and the right, title, interest, or lien is in all respects as valid as if the alienage of the person or persons did not exist, and may be set by the owner or owners of the land and is fully protected in any proceeding for the recovery or to enforce the escheat of the land to the state. [P.L.2-2002, § 7.]

Cross References. Escheat of estates, IC 29-1-2-1(8), IC 29-1-17-12.

Collateral References. 27 Am. Jur. 2d Escheat, § 12.

32-22-2-7. Applicability. — This chapter does not affect:

(1) the title to any real estate recovered or conveyed before March 6, 1905, by or under the authority of the state as escheated land;

(2) litigation pending on March 6, 1905, involving the escheat of land to the state; or

(3) the title of the state to any land to which the state has claimed, asserted, or attempted to assert title before March 6, 1905, by an action in any court of Indiana. [P.L.2-2002, § 7.]

ARTICLE 23

CONVEYANCE OF PROPERTY INTERESTS LESS THAN FEE SIMPLE

CHAPTER 1

EASEMENTS: BY PRESCRIPTION

32-23-1-1. Adverse use. — The right-of-way, air, light, or other easement from, in, upon, or over land owned by a person may not be acquired by another person by adverse use unless the use is uninterrupted for at least twenty (20) years. [P.L.2-2002, § 8.]

Effective Dates. P.L.2-2002, § 8. July 1. 2002.
Indiana Law Review. 1993 Developments in Indiana Property Law, 27 Ind. L. Rev. 1285 (1994).

NOTES TO DECISIONS

ANALYSIS

Easements.
—In general.
—Abandonment.
—Continuous use.
—Dedication.
—Drains.
—Duty owed to business invitee.
—Exclusive use.
—Extension by implication.
—Lateral support.
—Legal disabilities.
—License.
—Light and air.
—Married women.
—Notice of easement.
—Overflow of lands.
—Parol grant.
—Party walls.
—Permissive use.
—Presumption.
—Quieting title.
—Stairways.
—Tacking.
—Twenty years' use.
Ways.
—In general.
—Adverse use.

Easements.

—In General.

Where the grantor conveyed property to the grantee, reserving to the grantee an easement in favor of a third party who was a stranger to the deed, the court held that the deed properly created an easement in favor of the third party. Brademas v. Hartwig, 175 Ind. App. 4, 59 Ind. Dec. 760, 369 N.E.2d 954 (1977).

In order to establish a prescriptive easement, the evidence must show an actual, hostile, open, continuous and adverse use for 20 years under claim of right or with knowledge and acquiescences of the owner. Searcy v. Lagrotte, 175 Ind. App. 498, 61 Ind. Dec. 142, 372 N.E.2d 755 (1978).

Members of the general public cannot, by routine and regular use, create a prescriptive easement on behalf of a landholder; rather, it is the owner in fee who must establish that he and his successors in interest have met the elements of a prescriptive easement. Greenco, Inc. v. May, 506 N.E.2d 42 (Ind. App. 1987).

—Abandonment.

An easement could have been lost by nonuser. Town of Freedom v. Norris, 128 Ind. 377, 27 N.E. 869 (1891).

When an easement was created by express grant, lapse of time and occupation by the owner of the servient fee did not extinguish it unless there was an absolute denial of the right to the easement and the occupation was so adverse and hostile that the owner of the easement could have maintained an action for obstructing his enjoyment of it. Seymour Water Co. v. Lebline, 195 Ind. 481, 144 N.E. 30, 145 N.E. 764 (1924).

Intention to abandon and put an end to an easement was a necessary element of abandonment thereof. Kammerling v. Grover, 9 Ind. App. 628, 36 N.E. 922 (1894); Seymour Water Co. v. Lebline, 195 Ind. 481, 144 N.E. 30, 145 N.E. 764 (1924).

The question as to whether there had been an abandonment was ordinarily one of fact for the jury. Skelton v. Schenetzky, 82 Ind. App. 432, 144 N.E. 144 (1924).

Where the prescriptive period was interrupted by the planting of a garden on most of the tract by tenant of owner and later planting and maintenance of grass by the owner, the trial court properly denied a prescriptive easement and quieted title in the owner of the tract. Pugh v. Conway, 157 Ind. App. 44, 37 Ind. Dec. 510, 299 N.E.2d 214 (1973).

—Continuous Use.

Where the users of an alleged easement used the property as an access road to their property according to the nature of its use and in a manner consistent with their property's normal purposes, which was farming and farm related business, intermissions in the use of the property, in light of the undeveloped nature of the users' property, were reasonable in duration and consistent with continuous use. In addition, public use attributable to the users supported their continuity of use. Bauer v. Harris, 617 N.E.2d 923 (Ind. App. 1993).

Where the users of an alleged easement used the property both for personal access to their property and for access by their business invitees and lessees, where over the years they leased portions of their property for various business pursuits, and where on every occasion, their customers and lessees crossed the property at the site of the claimed easement to reach the leased portions of their property, lessees and business customers used the driveway across the other property at their express or implied direction, and accordingly, that use was attributable to them for the purpose of establishing an easement; their activities on their property, including leasing the property for farming and operation of a granary, evidenced an intent to use the property for access, not an intent to abandon use. The use by their customers and lessees was derivative of their claim of right to an easement, and that use was attributable to them and ratified their claim. Bauer v. Harris, 617 N.E.2d 923 (Ind. App. 1993).

—Dedication.

A nonuser, of an easement dedicated for a public use, for the purpose intended, for a period of thirty years, due to an abandonment of commerce upon the stream, was taken as an abandonment of the easement. Town of Freedom v. Norris, 128 Ind. 377, 27 N.E. 869 (1891).

To constitute a dedication to the use of the public, a clear intention so to do must have been shown and also an acceptance by the public or the proper local authorities of such dedication. City of Hammond v. Standard Oil Co., 79 Ind. App. 356, 138 N.E. 769 (1923).

—Drains.

Parties to a joint construction of a drain were entitled only to such rights as the orig-

Easements. (Cont'd)

—Drains. (Cont'd)
inal construction of the drain gave to them and one party might have enforced this right had he not voluntarily put himself in a position where enforcement of the right by injunction would have given him the benefit of the wrong he committed and allowed the water wrongfully turned into the drain to flow into it. McAllister v. Henderson, 134 Ind. 453, 34 N.E. 221 (1893).

Whether neither the owner of servient land or the owner of dominant land were aware of a field title drainage system that existed under both parcels of land, until the construction of a subdivision destroyed the field tile drainage system, there was no easement by prescription. Powell v. Dawson, 469 N.E.2d 1179 (Ind. App. 1984), rehearing denied, 512 N.E.2d 194 (Ind. App. 1987).

—Duty Owed to Business Invitee.
A permitted use, within the scope of the granted easement, cannot be adverse so as to ripen into an easement by prescription. Naderman v. Smith, 512 N.E.2d 425 (Ind. App. 1987).

—Exclusive Use.
Where the users of an alleged easement did not rely upon the general public's use of the easement, but instead relied upon their own use of it for personal and business purposes to establish their claim, the fact that the general public also used the easement did not render the users' use nonexclusive. Bauer v. Harris, 617 N.E.2d 923 (Ind. App. 1993).

In the context of a prescriptive easement, the term "exclusive use" means an independent claim of right, a use which does not depend upon use by others; it does not mean a use which excludes others entirely. Bauer v. Harris, 617 N.E.2d 923 (Ind. App. 1993).

—Extension by Implication.
The presence of other utilities in the area adjacent to state road did not establish an easement in favor of long distance telephone carrier; a prescriptive easement is limited to the purpose for which it is created and cannot be extended by implication. Contel of Ind., Inc. v. Coulson, 659 N.E.2d 224 (Ind. App. 1995).

—Lateral Support.
The owners of lands had the right of lateral support of adjoining lands, but not as to buildings erected on lands, unless such right had been acquired by prescription. Moellering v. Evans, 121 Ind. 195, 22 N.E. 989, 6 L.R.A. 449 (1889); Payne v. Moore, 31 Ind. App. 360, 66 N.E. 483, 67 N.E. 1005 (1903).

Adjacent landowners had right of support

of land on division lines and whenever a party made improvements which endangered the land of his neighbor, he had to supply walls or other sufficient substitutes for the support which he removed. Block v. Haseltine, 3 Ind. App. 491, 29 N.E. 937 (1892); Bohrer v. Dienhart Harness Co., 19 Ind. App. 489, 49 N.E. 296 (1898); Payne v. Moore, 31 Ind. App. 360, 66 N.E. 483, 67 N.E. 1005 (1903).

—Legal Disabilities.
An easement could not be acquired by prescription against a person under disabilities, but when a disability was relied upon, it had to be affirmatively set up as a defense. Palmer v. Wright, 58 Ind. 486 (1876); Davidson v. Nicholson, 59 Ind. 411 (1877); Fankboner v. Corder, 127 Ind. 164, 26 N.E. 766 (1891).

—License.
If an expense was incurred under a parol license, such license could not be revoked when the licensee would have been injured. Hodgson v. Jeffries, 52 Ind. 334 (1876); Nowlin v. Whipple, 79 Ind. 481 (1881); Nowlin v. Whipple, 120 Ind. 596, 22 N.E. 669, 6 L.R.A. 159 (1889); Ferguson v. Spencer, 127 Ind. 66, 25 N.E. 1035 (1890); Messick v. Midland Ry., 128 Ind. 81, 27 N.E. 419 (1891); Harlan v. Logansport Natural Gas Co., 133 Ind. 323, 32 N.E. 930 (1893); Buck v. Foster, 147 Ind. 530, 46 N.E. 920, 62 Am. St. R. 427 (1897); Knoll v. Baker, 34 Ind. App. 124, 72 N.E. 480 (1904).

When the use was under a license and merely permissive, an easement could not be acquired by lapse of time. Nowlin v. Whipple, 120 Ind. 596, 22 N.E. 669, 6 L.R.A. 159 (1889); Conner v. Woodfill, 126 Ind. 85, 25 N.E. 876, 22 Am. St. 568 (1890); Clay v. Pittsburgh, C., C. & St. L. Ry., 164 Ind. 439, 73 N.E. 904 (1905).

—Light and Air.
The doctrine of prescriptive right to ancient windows was never in force in America as a part of the common law. Keiper v. Klein, 51 Ind. 316 (1875); Stein v. Hauck, 56 Ind. 65, 26 Am. R. 10 (1877).

A conveyance of land with buildings having windows overlooking other lands of the grantor did not prevent him from building on his other lands so as to obstruct such windows. Keiper v. Klein, 51 Ind. 316 (1875).

—Married Women.
An easement could have been acquired in the lands of a married woman without a deed. Robinson v. Thrailkill, 110 Ind. 117, 10 N.E. 647 (1887).

—Notice of Easement.
Notice of an easement could have been inferred from the fact that it was visible from inspection of the land. Hodgson v. Jeffries, 52

Easements. (Cont'd)

—Notice of Easement. (Cont'd)
Ind. 334 (1876); Robinson v. Thrailkill, 110 Ind. 117, 10 N.E. 647 (1887).

Notice of easements furnished by deeds was notice to all persons claiming under such deeds. Hazlett v. Sinclair, 76 Ind. 488, 40 Am. R. 254 (1881).

—Overflow of Lands.
The right to overflow lands had to have been acquired by grant or prescription. Snowden v. Wilas, 19 Ind. 10, 81 Am. Dec. 370 (1862).

Ice on overflowed land belonged to the owner of the fee to the land. Brookville & Metamora Hydraulic Co. v. Butler, 91 Ind. 134, 46 Am. R. 580 (1883).

In an action for obstructing water, which flowed to plaintiff's mill, a complaint which alleged that the right to overflow certain land with the water which defendant obstructed, and to use the water, was acquired by continuous adverse use by plaintiff for a period of more than twenty years, stated a good cause of action. Terre Haute & I.R.R. Co. v. Zehner, 15 App. 273, 42 N.E. 756 (1896), aff'd, 166 Ind. 149, 76 N.E. 169, 3 L.R.A. (n.s.) 277 (1905).

Riparian owner, in a suit by him to acquire title, prevailed over the defendant, who had succeeded to the rights of a canal, since the latter, a user by flowage, evidenced no broader claim than a right of flowage which was a right of mere easement. Indianapolis Water Co. v. Kingan & Co., 155 Ind. 476, 58 N.E. 715 (1900).

—Parol Grant.
A parol grant of a right was not binding unless possession was taken thereunder. Richter v. Irwin, 28 Ind. 26 (1867); Robinson v. Thrailkill, 110 Ind. 117, 10 N.E. 647 (1887).

If a parol grant was made for a consideration and use was had thereof for a number of years, it could not have been revoked because it was not in writing. Nowlin v. Whipple, 79 Ind. 481 (1881); Robinson v. Thrailkill, 110 Ind. 117, 10 N.E. 647 (1886); Dodge v. Johnson, 32 Ind. App. 471, 67 N.E. 560 (1903).

A revoked parol license to enjoy an easement over land was revocable by the licensor at any time while it remained executory, but an executed parol license to use another's land, granted upon a consideration, or upon the faith of which money had been expended, could not have been revoked. Messick v. Midland Ry., 128 Ind. 81, 27 N.E. 419 (1891); Buck v. Foster, 147 Ind. 530, 46 N.E. 920, 62 Am. St. R. 427 (1897).

If a judgment was obtained because of a revocation of a parol license, no rights could afterwards have been claimed under the li-cense. Oster v. Broe, 161 Ind. 113, 64 N.E. 918 (1902).

—Party Walls.
Agreement to pay for use of party wall was a mere personal covenant and not a covenant running with the land. Bloch v. Isham, 28 Ind. 37, 92 Am. Dec. 287 (1867).

Where party wall was constructed, with agreement by half owner to pay upon use of wall, erection of building making use of wall as one side of building, but not making use of joist holes, was held use of wall under agreement. Greenwald v. Kappes, 31 Ind. 216 (1869).

No liability to pay for use of party wall existed when consent to the erection of such wall was given on express condition that half owner should not be liable for, nor chargeable with, any part of the cost or value of such wall. Eckleman v. Miller, 57 Ind. 88 (1877).

Covenant to pay one-half of cost of party wall upon use of wall ran with the land. Conduitt v. Ross, 102 Ind. 166, 26 N.E. 198 (1885).

When grantor restricted, in deed, height of building to two stories, and two story building containing party wall was erected, grantor could not extend height of party wall above second story for his own exclusive use. Fidelity Lodge, No. 59, I.O.O.F. v. Bond, 147 Ind. 437, 45 N.E. 338 (1896), rehearing overruled, 147 Ind. 444, 46 N.E. 825 (1897).

Right to use party wall and build did not carry with it the right to destroy wall and half owners were not required to anticipate the depriving of the wall of the easement of lateral support. Briggs v. Klosse, 5 Ind. App. 129, 31 N.E. 208, 51 Am. St. R. 238 (1892); Cartwright v. Adair, 27 Ind. App. 293, 61 N.E. 240 (1901); Payne v. Moore, 31 Ind. App. 360, 66 N.E. 483, 67 N.E. 1005 (1903).

—Permissive Use.
Use which is merely permissive or which is exercised under a mere license cannot ripen into an easement. Fleck v. Hann, 658 N.E.2d 125 (Ind. App. 1995).

—Presumption.
The presumption of a grant arises from proof of an uninterrupted adverse use for the requisite period; however, the presumption may be defeated by proof that the use was by permission. Larch v. Larch, 564 N.E.2d 313 (Ind. App. 1990).

Once open and continuous use of another's land commences with knowledge on the part of the owner, such use is presumed to be adverse to the owner. Larch v. Larch, 564 N.E.2d 313 (Ind. App. 1990).

Unexplained use of an easement for 20 years is presumed to be under a claim of right, adverse, and sufficient to establish title by

Easements. (Cont'd)

—Presumption. (Cont'd)
prescription unless that use is contradicted or explained. Fleck v. Hann, 658 N.E.2d 125 (Ind. App. 1995).

—Quieting Title.
An action could have been maintained to quiet title to an easement. Sanxay v. Hunger, 42 Ind. 44 (1873); Davidson v. Nicholson, 59 Ind. 411 (1877); McAllister v. Henderson, 134 Ind. 453, 34 N.E. 221 (1893); Corns v. Clouser, 137 Ind. 201, 36 N.E. 848 (1894).

—Stairways.
A reservation of such a right-of-way over a stairway and hall as might "be necessary to the proper use and occupancy of the upper story" of a building, did not carry an interest in the soil, and the destruction of the building by fire without the fault of the owner, extinguished the right. Shirley v. Crabb, 138 Ind. 200, 37 N.E. 130 (1894); Dodge v. Johnson, 32 Ind. App. 471, 67 N.E. 560 (1903).

—Tacking.
Statutory period need not be maintained by one adverse user; continuity of use for the requisite 20-year period may be established by tacking the adverse use of predecessors in title. Fleck v. Hann, 658 N.E.2d 125 (Ind. App. 1995).

—Twenty Years' Use.
After an uninterrupted use of an easement for 20 years a grant was presumed. Postlethwaite v. Payne, 8 Ind. 104 (1856).

Ways.

—In General.
A way was an incorporeal hereditament and consisted in the right of passing over the lands of another. It could have arisen from grant, prescription or necessity, and was attached to the person using it, or was annexed to the land and passed with a conveyance thereof. Sanxay v. Hunger, 42 Ind. 44 (1873); Moore v. Crose, 43 Ind. 30 (1873); Ross v. Thompson, 78 Ind. 90 (1881); Steel v. Grigsby, 79 Ind. 184 (1881).

—Adverse Use.
To obtain a right-of-way by adverse use, such use must have been continuous, uninterrupted, and under a claim of right, with the acquiescence of the owner of the land over which the way passed, for a period of 20 years. Palmer v. Wright, 58 Ind. 486 (1876); Davidson v. Nicholson, 59 Ind. 411 (1877); McCardle v. Barricklow, 68 Ind. 356 (1878); Hill v. Hagaman, 84 Ind. 287 (1882); Parish v. Kaspare, 109 Ind. 586, 10 N.E. 109 (1887);

Faukboner v. Corder, 127 Ind. 164, 26 N.E. 766 (1891); Harding v. Cowgar, 127 Ind. 245, 26 N.E. 799 (1891); Bales v. Pidgeon, 129 Ind. 548, 29 N.E. 34 (1891); Davis v. Cleveland C., C. & St. L. Ry., 140 Ind. 468, 39 N.E. 495 (1895); Mitchell v. Bain, 142 Ind. 604, 42 N.E. 230 (1895); Kibbey v. Richards, 30 Ind. App. 101, 65 N.E. 541, 96 Am. St. R. 333 (1902); Gascho v. Lennert, 176 Ind. 677, 97 N.E. 6 (1912).

An uninterrupted use of a way under a claim of title for 20 years established as easement, although the original claim was unfounded. Parish v. Kaspare, 109 Ind. 586, 10 N.E. 109 (1887).

Adverse use of land, over which way was claimed, for more than twenty years extinguished the easement in the way and it could not have been revived by a grantee of the claim of easement by a reference to the reservation in the deed of conveyance to the holder of the easement. McKinney v. Lanning, 139 Ind. 170, 38 N.E. 601 (1894).

Where right to use of easement was granted by deed such use was not adverse to that of the feeholder and fact that plaintiffs were only ones using such easement for period of 20 years did not give them the rights to exclusive use, and feeholder could also grant easement rights to others. Brown v. Heidersbach, 172 Ind. App. 434, 56 Ind. Dec. 565, 360 N.E.2d 614 (1977).

Once open and continuous use of another's land commences with knowledge on the part of the owner, a rebuttable presumption arises that such use is adverse. Searcy v. Lagrotte, 175 Ind. App. 498, 61 Ind. Dec. 142, 372 N.E.2d 755 (1978).

While it is not necessary that the use be exercised constantly and without permission, use of the property must be shown to be continuous for the requisite statutory period. Umbreit v. Chester B. Stem, Inc., 176 Ind. App. 53, 61 Ind. Dec. 566, 373 N.E.2d 1116 (1978).

Where party failed to establish when the actual possessory use of the easement began, it was shown that no one had lived on the property for which the easement was sought from 1925 until 1975, that party had no personal knowledge of the road prior to 1974 and failed to call his immediate predecessor in title as a witness and no evidence as to prior title, finding against the establishment of the easement was proper. Umbreit v. Chester B. Stem, Inc., 176 Ind. App. 53, 61 Ind. Dec. 566, 373 N.E.2d 1116 (1978).

Where it is undisputed in the record that a roadway's location has shifted over the years and both parties and their witnesses testified it has gradually changed location, but they disagree in which direction it has moved, no one definite location for the roadway for the prescriptive 20-year period has been shown

Ways. (Cont'd)

—Adverse Use. (Cont'd)
by the evidence, and defendant has not sustained his burden to prove his adverse use thereof for the 20-year statutory period. Jochem v. Kerstiens, 498 N.E.2d 1241 (Ind. App. 1986).

Open and continuous use raises rebuttable presumption that the use is adverse. Popp v. Hardy, 508 N.E.2d 1282 (Ind. App. 1987).

Where the use of an alleged easement was inconsistent with the property owners' title to the property in all respects, it could be inferred from the users' conduct in inviting customers to enter their property by using the driveway and by leasing their property to others that they claimed the right to use the driveway across the owners' property for access by their customers and lessees. Therefore, the trial court's findings of fact gave rise to the rebuttable presumption that the use was adverse and under a claim of right. Bauer v. Harris, 617 N.E.2d 923 (Ind. App. 1993).

—Complaint to Establish.
In a suit to establish a right to the easement of a right-of-way across certain lands, the complaint was defective if it did not contain a description of the land over which the easement was claimed. Bayless v. Price, 131 Ind. 437, 31 N.E. 88 (1892).

—Conveyance of Way.
An appurtenant way could have been conveyed only by a deed conveying the estate. Moore v. Crose, 43 Ind. 30 (1873).

An executor could not grant a right-of-way over the lands of his testator. Hankins v. Kimball, 57 Ind. 42 (1877).

There was no statutory authority that authorized a court to empower a guardian to donate the right-of-way for a railroad over his ward's lands, and a deed by a guardian for such right, without the prior approval by the court of a price agreed upon by the guardian, was void. Indiana, B. & W. Ry. v. Brittingham, 98 Ind. 294 (1884); Indiana, B. & W. Ry. v. Allen, 100 Ind. 409 (1885).

An agreement to supply a private way for loss of access to public highway as an inducement to join in petition for change of highway was contract for right of private way and was not void as against public policy. Corns v. Clouser, 137 Ind. 201, 36 N.E. 848 (1894).

—Eminent Domain.
The legislature could not authorize the establishment of a private way on making compensation to the landowner. Stewart v. Hartman, 46 Ind. 331 (1874); Blackman v. Halves, 72 Ind. 515 (1880); Logan v. Stogdale, 123 Ind. 372, 24 N.E. 135, 8 L.R.A. 58 (1890).

—Gates Across Way.
The owner of the fee of the lands could maintain a gate where the way intersected a public highway, except where the way had existed without such a gate for 20 years. Phillips v. Dressler, 122 Ind. 414, 24 N.E. 226, 17 Am. St. 375 (1890); Faukboner v. Corder, 127 Ind. 164, 26 N.E. 766 (1891).

Where parties to a grant with easement of right-of-way gave their contract a construction at variance somewhat from the letter of the conveyance and grant of easement by placement of gates on what was an unfenced right-of-way, the courts would have adopted that construction and would have held the parties to it. Frazier v. Myers, 132 Ind. 71, 31 N.E. 536 (1892).

The grant of a way, and the free and undisturbed use thereof, did not necessarily preclude the erection of gates across the way. Boyd v. Bloom, 152 Ind. 152, 52 N.E. 751 (1899).

—Grantees' Rights.
When the owner of lands annexed a right-of-way, or other easement, thereto, and conveyed the same, his grantees, near and remote, acquired an easement. John Hancock Mut. Life Ins. Co. v. Patterson, 103 Ind. 582, 2 N.E. 188, 53 Am. Rep. 550 (1885); Lammott v. Ewers, 106 Ind. 310, 6 N.E. 636, 55 Am. R. 546 (1886); Parish v. Kaspare, 109 Ind. 586, 10 N.E. 109 (1887); Robinson v. Thrailkill, 110 Ind. 117, 10 N.E. 647 (1887); Faukboner v. Corder, 127 Ind. 164, 26 N.E. 766 (1891); Bales v. Pidgeon, 129 Ind. 548, 29 N.E. 34 (1891); Steinke v. Bentley, 6 Ind. App. 663, 34 N.E. 97 (1893).

The grantee of a way was impliedly granted the right to put the same in such condition as to have made it useable. Mercurio v. Hall, 81 Ind. App. 554, 144 N.E. 248 (1924).

—Injunction.
The obstruction of a right-of-way could have been prohibited by injunction. Hall v. Hedrick, 125 Ind. 326, 25 N.E. 350 (1890); Harding v. Cowgar, 127 Ind. 245, 26 N.E. 799 (1891); Sheeks v. Erwin, 130 Ind. 31, 29 N.E. 11 (1891).

—Location.
Where one having an easement in the lands of another for a private way, and the same was to be located for the first time, the owner of the land over which it was to have passed had the right to choose it in a reasonable manner otherwise by the owner of the easement, also in a reasonable manner, and when once selected it could not have been changed by either party without the consent of the other. Ritchey v. Welsh, 149 Ind. 214, 48 N.E. 1031, 40 L.R.A. 105 (1898); Thomas v. McCoy, 30 Ind. App. 555, 66 N.E. 700 (1903).

Ways. (Cont'd)

—Necessity.
A right-of-way over lands had to arise from necessity, and not from convenience. Anderson v. Buchanan, 8 Ind. 132 (1856); Steel v. Grigsby, 79 Ind. 184 (1881).

A way from necessity could only have been claimed when the same person had at some time been possessed of the lands over which, and to which, the way passed. Stewart v. Hartman, 46 Ind. 331 (1874); Logan v. Stogdale, 123 Ind. 372, 24 N.E. 135, 8 L.R.A. 58 (1890); Ellis v. Bassett, 128 Ind. 118, 27 N.E. 344, 25 Am. St. R. 421 (1891).

—Partition.
If a way existed prior to a division of lands by partition proceedings, such partition would not divest the right to the way. Ellis v. Bassett, 128 Ind. 118, 27 N.E. 344, 25 Am. St. R. 421 (1891); Ritchey v. Welsh, 149 Ind. 214, 48 N.E. 1031, 40 L.R.A. 105 (1898); Kaiser v. Somers, 80 Ind. App. 89, 138 N.E. 20 (1923).

—Pipelines.
Where right-of-way through land of grantor to lay a natural gas pipeline was signed by grantor alone, and which was accepted by grantee and the written instrument was duly recorded, the instrument was a contract entered into by both the parties, and could not have been annulled by one of them only.

Harlan v. Logansport Natural Gas Co., 133 Ind. 323, 32 N.E. 930 (1893).

—Public Ways.
A private easement could exist in a way which was also a public highway. Ross v. Thompson, 78 Ind. 90 (1881).

The statute providing for the acquiring of a private way by use did not apply to highways. Pitser v. McCreery, 172 Ind. 663, 88 N.E. 303, 89 N.E. 317 (1909).

—Railroads.
Railroad companies acquired only an easement in lands acquired for a right-of-way. Quick v. Taylor, 113 Ind. 540, 16 N.E. 588 (1888); Cincinnati, I., St. L. & C. Ry. v. Geisel, 119 Ind. 77, 21 N.E. 470 (1889); Smith v. Holloway, 124 Ind. 329, 24 N.E. 886 (1890); Chicago & W.M. R.R. v. Huncheon, 130 Ind. 529, 30 N.E. 636 (1892); Cleveland, C., C. & St. L. Ry. v. Smith, 177 Ind. 524, 97 N.E. 164 (1912); Meyer v. Pittsburgh, C., C. & St. L. Ry., 63 Ind. App. 156, 113 N.E. 443 (1916).

—Rights of Servient Owner.
The owner of the fee of lands over which a right-of-way existed could make all lawful use of the lands that was consistent with the use of the way. Julien v. Woodsmall, 82 Ind. 568 (1882); Brookville & Metamora Hydraulic Co. v. Butler, 91 Ind. 134, 46 Am. R. 580 (1883); Smith v. Holloway, 124 Ind. 329, 24 N.E. 886 (1890); Cleveland, C., C. & St. L. Ry. v. Smith, 177 Ind. 524, 97 N.E. 164 (1912).

Collateral References. 25 Am. Jur. 2d Easements, §§ 39-63.

28 C.J.S. Easements, §§ 17-22.

Loss of privat3e easement by nonuser or adverse possession. 25 A.L.R.2d 1265.

Acquisition of right of way by prescription as affected by change of location or deviation during prescriptive period. 80 A.L.R.2d 1095.

Adverse possession based on encroachment of building or other structure. 2 A.L.R.3d 1005.

Extent and reasonableness of use of private way in exercise of easement granted in general terms. 3 A.L.R.3d 1256.

Deed to railroad company as conveying fee or easement. 6 A.L.R.3d 973.

Way of necessity where property is accessible by navigable water. 9 A.L.R.3d 600.

Right of owners of parcels into which dominant tenement is or will be divided to use right-of-way. 10 A.L.R.3d 960.

Acquisition of title to land by adverse possession by state or other governmental unit or agency. 18 A.L.R.3d 678.

Right of servient owner to maintain, improve, or repair easement of way at expense of dominant owner. 20 A.L.R.3d 1026.

Locating easement of way created by necessity. 36 A.L.R.4th 769.

Scope of prescriptive easement for access (easement of way). 79 A.L.R.4th 604.

32-23-1-2. Notice of dispute by owner. — The owner of land described in section 1 [IC 32-23-1-1] of this chapter, or the agent or guardian of the owner, may give notice to a claimant of a right or easement described in section 1 of this chapter that the owner, or the agent or guardian of the owner, will dispute the claimant's claim to a right or easement by adverse use. [P.L.2-2002, § 8.]

32-23-1-3. Form of notice. — Notice provided to a claimant under section 2 [IC 32-23-1-2] of this chapter must be:

(1) in writing; and

(2) served by an officer on the:

(A) claimant, if the claimant can be found; or

(B) if the claimant cannot be found, on the claimant's agent or the claimant's guardian;

or if the claimant, the claimant's agent, and the claimant's guardian cannot be found, a copy of the written notice shall be posted, for not less than ten (10) days, in a conspicuous place on or adjoining the premises where the right is disputed. [P.L.2-2002, § 8.]

NOTES TO DECISIONS

Injunction.

An injunction would not lie to prevent the acquiring of an easement over land by use, as such a right could have been prevented by giving notice under the statute of an intention to dispute such right. Hart v. Hildebrandt, 30 Ind. App. 415, 66 N.E. 173 (1903).

A mandatory injunction may be obtained where there is more than the question of an easement involved as, for instance, the proper construction of a party wall. Evans v. Shephard, 81 Ind. App. 147, 142 N.E. 730 (1924).

32-23-1-4. Service of notice. — The service or notice required under section 3 [IC 32-23-1-3] of this chapter must be endorsed by the officer serving the notice, on the original paper, and returned to the party giving the notice. The party that gives the notice shall record the original paper and endorsement of service or notice in the recorder's office of the county where the land is located. The served or posted and recorded notice is, at the time of record, an interruption of the adverse use. [P.L.2-2002, § 8.]

CHAPTER 2

EASEMENTS IN GROSS: ALIENATION, INHERITANCE, ASSIGNMENT

32-23-2-1. "Easement in gross of commercial character" defined. — As used in this chapter, "easement in gross of a commercial character" means an easement:

(1) for the transmission or distribution of natural gas, petroleum products, or cable television signals;

(2) for the provision of telephone or water service; or

(3) for the transmission, distribution, or transformation of electricity. [P.L.2-2002, § 8.]

Effective Dates. P.L.2-2002, § 8. July 1. 2002.

32-23-2-2. Alienability of easements created after June 30, 1989. —

An easement in gross of a commercial character, including an easement acquired by eminent domain, that is created after June 30, 1989, may be alienated, inherited, or assigned in whole or in part unless the instrument creating the easement provides otherwise. [P.L.2-2002, § 8.]

Collateral References. 25 Am. Jur. 2d Easements, §§ 93-98.
28 C.J.S. Easements, §§ 45, 46.

32-23-2-3. Alienability of easements created before June 30, 1989.

— (a) This section does not apply to an easement in gross of a commercial character that is created after June 30, 1989.

(b) An easement in gross that was created after July 6, 1961, may be alienated, inherited, or assigned in whole or in part if the instrument that created the easement in real property states that the easement may be alienated, inherited, or assigned. [P.L.2-2002, § 8.]

32-23-2-4. No reinstatement of expired, terminated, or abandoned easement. —

This chapter does not revive or reinstate an expired, a terminated, or an abandoned easement in gross of a commercial character. [P.L.2-2002, § 8.]

32-23-2-5. Cross-references in plat. —

(a) An easement that is created after June 30, 1989, must cross-reference the original recorded plat. However, if the real property from which the easement is being created is not platted, the easement must cross-reference the most recent deed of record in the recorder's office. The recorder shall charge a fee for recording the easement in accordance with IC 36-2-7-10.

(b) When a release of easement is recorded in the office of the county recorder in the county where the property is situated, the release document must cross-reference the original easement document and reflect the name of the current owner of the property to whom the easement is being released as shown on the property tax records of the county. [P.L.2-2002, § 8.]

CHAPTER 3

EASEMENTS: WAY OF NECESSITY

32-23-3-1. Establishment. — If:

(1) land that belongs to a landowner in Indiana is shut off from a public highway because of the:

(A) straightening of a stream under Indiana law;

(B) construction of a ditch under Indiana law; or

(C) erection of a dam that is constructed by the state or by the United States or an agency or a political subdivision of the state or of the United States under Indiana law; and

(2) the owner of the lands described in subdivision (1) is unable to secure an easement or right-of-way on and over the land that is adjacent to the affected land, and intervening between the land and the public highways that are most convenient to the land because:

(A) an adjacent and intervening landowner refuses to grant an easement; or

(B) the interested parties cannot agree upon the consideration to be paid by the landowner that is deprived of access to the highway;

the landowner of the affected land shall be granted the right of easement established as a way of necessity as provided under IC 32-24-1. [P.L.2-2002, § 8.]

Effective Dates. P.L.2-2002, § 8. July 1. 2002.

NOTES TO DECISIONS

Subsequent Owners.

A subsequent owner of a peninsula, which peninsula had been cut off from access over other land when a dam was constructed, could not use this section to obtain an easement over the only unsubmerged land adjoining the peninsula for his own private benefit. Continental Enters., Inc. v. Cain, 180 Ind. App. 106, 68 Ind. Dec. 366, 387 N.E.2d 86 (1979).

Collateral References. 25 Am. Jur. 2d Easements, §§ 34-38.

28 C.J.S. Easements, §§ 35-44.

Extent and reasonableness of use of private way in exercise of easement granted in general terms. 3 A.L.R.3d 1256.

Abutting owner's right to damages for limitation of access caused by conversion of conventional road into limited-access highway. 42 A.L.R.3d 13.

Measure and elements of damage for limitation of access caused by conversion of conventional road into limited-access high-way. 42 A.L.R.3d 148.

CHAPTER 4

SOLAR EASEMENT

32-23-4-1. "Passive solar energy system" defined. — As used in this chapter, "passive solar energy system" means a structure specifically designed to retain heat that is derived from solar energy. [P.L.2-2002, § 8.]

Effective Dates. P.L.2-2002, § 8. July 1. 2002.

Collateral References. 25 Am. Jur. 2d Easements, § 24.

28 C.J.S. Easements, § 42.

32-23-4-2. "Solar easement" defined. — As used in this chapter, "solar easement" means an easement obtained for the purpose of exposure of a solar energy device or a passive solar energy system to the direct rays of the sun. [P.L.2-2002, § 8.]

32-23-4-3. "Solar energy device" defined. — As used in this chapter, "solar energy device" means an artifice, an instrument, or the equipment designed to receive the direct rays of the sun and convert the rays into heat, electricity, or another form of energy to provide heating, cooling, or electrical power. [P.L.2-2002, § 8.]

32-23-4-4. Easement created in writing — Subject to conveyance and recording requirements. — A solar easement:

(1) must be created in writing; and

(2) is subject to the conveyancing and recording requirements of this title. [P.L.2-2002, § 8.]

32-23-4-5. Contents of instrument creating easement. — An instrument that creates a solar easement must include the following:

(1) The vertical and horizontal angles, expressed in degrees, at which the solar easement extends over the real property that is subject to the solar easement, and a description of the real property to which the solar easement is appurtenant.

(2) Any terms and conditions under which the solar easement is granted or will be terminated. [P.L.2-2002, § 8.]

CHAPTER 5
UNIFORM CONSERVATION EASEMENT ACT

32-23-5-1. Applicability. — (a) This chapter applies to any interest created after September 1, 1984, that complies with this chapter, whether the interest is designated:

(1) as a conservation easement;

(2) as a covenant;

(3) as an equitable servitude;

(4) as a restriction;

(5) as an easement; or

(6) otherwise.

(b) This chapter applies to any interest created before September 1, 1984, if the interest would have been enforceable had the interest been created after September 1, 1984, unless retroactive application contravenes the constitution or laws of Indiana or the United States.

(c) This chapter does not invalidate any interest, whether designated:

(1) as a conservation easement;
(2) as a preservation easement;
(3) as a covenant;
(4) as an equitable servitude;
(5) as a restriction;
(6) as an easement; or
(7) otherwise;

if the designated interest is enforceable under another law of this state.

(d) This chapter shall be applied and construed to effectuate the general purpose of the chapter to make uniform the laws with respect to the subject of the chapter among the states that enact language consistent with this chapter. [P.L.2-2002, § 8.]

Effective Dates. P.L.2-2002, § 8. July 1. 2002.
Res Gestae. Conservation easements in
real estate development, 41 (No. 6) Res Gestae 24 (1997).

32-23-5-2. "Conservation easement" defined. — As used in this chapter, "conservation easement" means a nonpossessory interest of a holder in real property that imposes limitations or affirmative obligations with the purpose of:

(1) retaining or protecting natural, scenic, or open space values of real property;

(2) assuring availability of the real property for agricultural, forest, recreational, or open space use;

(3) protecting natural resources;

(4) maintaining or enhancing air or water quality; or

(5) preserving the historical, architectural, archeological, or cultural aspects of real property. [P.L.2-2002, § 8.]

32-23-5-3. "Holder" defined. — As used in this chapter, "holder" means:

(1) a governmental body that is empowered to hold an interest in real property under the laws of Indiana or the United States; or

(2) a charitable corporation, charitable association, or charitable trust, the purposes or powers of which include:

(A) retaining or protecting the natural, scenic, or open space values of real property;

(B) assuring the availability of real property for agricultural, forest, recreational, or open space use;

(C) protecting natural resources;

(D) maintaining or enhancing air or water quality; or

(E) preserving the historical, architectural, archeological, or cultural aspects of real property. [P.L.2-2002, § 8.]

32-23-5-4. "Third party right of enforcement" defined. — As used in this chapter, "third party right of enforcement" means a right that is:

(1) provided in a conservation easement to enforce any of the conservation easement's terms; and

(2) granted to a governmental body, charitable corporation, charitable association, or charitable trust that is eligible to be a holder but is not a holder. [P.L.2-2002, § 8.]

32-23-5-5. Rights of holder. — (a) Except as otherwise provided in this chapter, a conservation easement may be:
   (1) created;
   (2) conveyed;
   (3) recorded;
   (4) assigned;
   (5) released
   (6) modified;
   (7) terminated; or
   (8) otherwise altered or affected;
in the same manner as other easements.

   (b) A right or duty in favor of or against a holder and a right in favor of a person having a third party right of enforcement does not arise under a conservation easement before the conservation easement is accepted by the holder and the acceptance is recorded.

   (c) Except as provided in section 6(b) [IC 32-23-5-6(b)] of this chapter, a conservation easement is unlimited in duration unless the instrument creating the conservation easement provides otherwise.

   (d) An interest in real property is not impaired by a conservation easement if the interest exists at the time the conservation easement is created, unless the owner of the interest is a party to the conservation easement or consents to the conservation easement. [P.L.2-2002, § 8.]

32-23-5-6. Persons who may bring actions. — (a) An action that affects a conservation easement may be brought by:
   (1) an owner of an interest in the real property burdened by the easement;
   (2) a holder of the easement;
   (3) a person having a third party right of enforcement; or
   (4) a person authorized by other law.

   (b) This chapter does not affect the power of a court to modify or terminate a conservation easement in accordance with the principles of law and equity, or the termination of a conservation easement by agreement of the grantor and grantee. [P.L.2-2002, § 8.]

32-23-5-7. Validity of easement. — A conservation easement is valid even though:
   (1) the conservation easement is not appurtenant to an interest in real property;
   (2) the conservation easement can be or has been assigned to another holder;
   (3) the conservation easement is not of a character that has been recognized traditionally at common law;
   (4) the conservation easement imposes a negative burden;

(5) the conservation easement imposes affirmative obligations upon the owner of an interest in the burdened property or upon the holder;

(6) the benefit does not touch or concern real property; or

(7) there is no privity of estate or of contract. [P.L.2-2002, § 8.]

32-23-5-8. Assessment and taxation. — For the purposes of IC 6-1.1, real property that is subject to a conservation easement shall be assessed and taxed on a basis that reflects the easement. [P.L.2-2002, § 8.]

CHAPTER 6

EASEMENTS: WPA PROJECTS

32-23-6-1. Application for release of easement. — (a) If:

(1) a landowner in Indiana has had a pond or lake built on the landowner's real estate by the federal Works Progress Administration; and

(2) as a requisite to the building of the pond or lake, the landowner has given a lease in writing to the state relative to the building, upkeep, and use of the pond or lake;

the department of natural resources may, upon application in writing to the department of natural resources, release any easement the state may have to the real estate. [P.L.2-2002, § 8.]

Compiler's Notes. The Works Progress Administration was established by Executive Order of May 6, 1935 and its name changed to Works Projects Administration on July 1, 1939 by Reorganization Plan 1. Its liquidation was authorized December 4, 1942.

Effective Dates. P.L.2-2002, § 8. July 1. 2002.

Collateral References. 25 Am. Jur. 2d Easements, §§ 34-38.

28 C.J.S. Easements, §§ 35-44.

32-23-6-2. Filing of release. — A release under section 1 [IC 32-23-6-1] of this chapter may be filed with the recorder of the county in which the real estate is situated and recorded in the miscellaneous record in the recorder's office. [P.L.2-2002, § 8.]

CHAPTER 7

OIL AND GAS: ESTATES IN LAND

32-23-7-1. "Oil and gas" defined. — As used in this chapter, "oil and gas" means petroleum and mineral oils and gaseous substances of whatever character naturally lying or found beneath the surface of land. [P.L.2-2002, § 8.]

Effective Dates. P.L.2-2002, § 8. July 1. 2002.

Collateral References. 38 Am. Jur. 2d Gas and Oil, §§ 3, 4, 10-13.

58 C.J.S. Mines and Minerals, §§ 132-142.

Rights and remedies of owner or lessee of oil or gas land or mineral or royalty interest therein, in respect of waste of oil or gas through operations on other lands. 4 A.L.R.2d 198.

What constitutes oil or gas "royalty" or "royalties" within language of conveyance, exception, reservation, devise, or assignment. 4 A.L.R.2d 492.

Rights of tenants for years and remaindermen inter se in royalties or rents under oil or gas lease. 18 A.L.R.2d 98.

Oil and gas as "minerals" within deed, lease or license. 37 A.L.R.2d 1440.

Effect, as between lessor and lessee, of provision in mineral lease purporting to except or reserve a previously granted right-of-way or other easement through, over, or upon the premises. 49 A.L.R.2d 1191.

Royalty as real or personal property where instrument creating it amounts to sale of minerals in place. 68 A.L.R.2d 728.

Lessee's breach of implied obligation under oil or gas lease to explore and develop further after initial discovery of oil or gas, in absence of showing reasonable expectation of profit to lessee from further drilling. 79 A.L.R.2d 792.

Liability for property damage caused by vibrations attributable to oil or gas well operations. 79 A.L.R.2d 966.

Construction and effect of provision in oil or gas deed or lease for payment of damages for injury to "crops" or "growing crops." 87 A.L.R.2d 235.

Estoppel of oil and gas lessee to deny lessor's title. 87 A.L.R.2d 602.

What amounts to development or operation

for oil or gas within terms of habendum clause extending primary term while the premises are being "developed or operated." 99 A.L.R.2d 307.

Rights of parties to oil and gas lease or royalty deed after expiration of fixed term where production temporarily ceases. 100 A.L.R.2d 885.

Tenancy at will under oil and gas lease after expiration of fixed term where production temporarily ceases. 100 A.L.R.2d 942.

Sales as "isolated" or "successive," or the like, under state securities acts. 1 A.L.R.3d 614.

Right and measure of recovery for breach of obligation to drill exploratory oil or gas wells. 4 A.L.R.3d 284.

Guardian's power to make lease for infant beyond maturity or term of guardianship. 6 A.L.R.3d 570.

"Dry hole" as "well" within undertaking to drill well. 15 A.L.R.3d 450.

Construction of oil and gas lease provision giving lessee free use of water from lessor's land. 23 A.L.R.3d 1434.

Liability of one maintaining pipeline for transportation of gas or other dangerous substances for injury or property damage sustained by one using surface. 30 A.L.R.3d 685.

Liability in connection with fire or explosion incident to bulk storage, transportation, delivery, loading, or unloading of petroleum products. 32 A.L.R.3d 1169.

Rights, under oil and gas lease, deed, or sales contract, to "distillate," "condensate," or "natural gasoline." 38 A.L.R.3d 983.

Meaning of "paying quantities" in oil and gas lease. 43 A.L.R.3d 8.

Construction and application of "Mother Hubbard" or "cover-all" clause in gas and oil lease or deed. 80 A.L.R.4th 205.

32-23-7-2. "Oil and gas estate in land" defined. — As used in this chapter, "oil and gas estate in land" means the aggregate of all rights in land that affect the oil and gas in, on, under, or that may be taken from beneath the surface of the land. [P.L.2-2002, § 8.]

Cross References. Lapse of mineral interest, prevention, IC 32-23-10.

Collateral References. Oil and gas roy-

alty as real or personal property. 56 A.L.R.4th 539.

32-23-7-3. "Operations for oil and gas" defined. — As used in this chapter, "operations for oil and gas", unless otherwise indicated by the context of this chapter, means:

(1) the:
    (A) exploration;
    (B) testing;
    (C) surveying; or
    (D) other investigation;
of the potential of the land for oil and gas;
(2) the actual drilling or preparations for drilling of wells for oil and gas on the land; or
(3) any other actions directed toward the eventual production or attempted production of oil and gas from the land. [P.L.2-2002, § 8.]

32-23-7-4. "Person in interest" defined. — (a) As used in this chapter, "person in interest" means the owner of a beneficial interest in the oil and gas estate in land, whether the interest is held for life, for a term of years, or in fee.

(b) The term includes a lessee, licensee, or duly qualified agent of the owner.

(c) The term does not include a mortgagee or security assignee of the owner if the mortgagee or security assignee does not have a right to the control or operation of the premises for oil and gas. [P.L.2-2002, § 8.]

Collateral References. Rights and obligations, with respect to adjoining landowners, arising out of secondary recovery of gas, oil, and other fluid minerals. 19 A.L.R.4th 1182.

32-23-7-5. "Surface rights" defined. — As used in this chapter, "surface rights" means all rights relating to the occupancy, user, or ownership of the surface of land affected by this chapter. [P.L.2-2002, § 8.]

NOTES TO DECISIONS

ANALYSIS

Operations for oil and gas.
—Applicability.

in this section applies to IC 32-5-8-1. Barr v. Sun Exploration Co., 436 N.E.2d 821 (Ind. App. 1982).

Operations for Oil and Gas.

—Applicability.
The definition of "operations for oil and gas"

32-23-7-6. Rights and privileges transferred with interest in oil and gas. — A grant or reservation contained in an instrument that affects land in Indiana and that purports to convey or transfer an interest in the oil and gas in, on, under, or that may be produced from beneath the surface of the land transfers the following expressed rights and privileges in addition to any other rights naturally flowing from the character of the instrument in law to the named recipient:

(1) A person in interest in the oil and gas estate in land may enter the land for the purpose of:
    (A) exploring, prospecting, testing, surveying, or otherwise investigating the land to determine the potential of the land for oil or gas production; or

(B) otherwise conducting operations for oil and gas on the land;
whether or not the person is also the owner, lessee, or licensee of an
owner of an interest in the surface rights in the land.

(2) A person in interest in the oil and gas estate in land in Indiana may
enter the land to drill a well or test well on the land for the production
or attempted production of oil and gas regardless of whether the:

(A) person is also the owner, lessee, or licensee of an owner of an
interest in the surface rights in the land; and

(B) owner of the remaining rights in the land consents to the
entrance and drilling.

A person that drills a well under this subdivision shall provide an
accounting to the remaining or nonparticipating persons in interest in
the oil and gas estate in the land, for their respective proportionate
shares of the net profits arising from the operations conducted upon the
land for oil or gas. In calculating the profits, a reduction may not be
made from the gross proceeds of the production of oil and gas, except for
expenses that are reasonably or necessarily incurred in connection with
the drilling, completion, equipping, and operation of the wells drilled
upon the premises during the period in which the relationship of
cotenancy existed between the person drilling the well and the person
whose interest is sought to be charged with the respective proportionate
part of the cost of the drilling.

(3) A person who may enter and enters land in Indiana for the purpose
of exploring, prospecting, testing, surveying, or otherwise investigating
the potential of the land for oil and gas, or for the purpose of conducting
operations on the land for the production of oil and gas, is accountable
to the owner of the surface of the land for the actual damage resulting
from the person's activities on the land to:

(A) the surface of the land;

(B) improvements to the land; or

(C) growing crops on the land.

However, a person who enters land under this subdivision is not liable
for punitive damages. This subdivision does not increase damages
between a lessor and a lessee in a valid and subsisting oil and gas lease
that specifies damages if damages are not due other than damages that
are expressly provided by contract between cotenants or the lessees of
cotenants of a like estate in the land. This section does not authorize the
location of a well for oil and gas nearer than two hundred (200) feet to
an existing house, barn, or other structure (except fences) without the
express consent of the owner of the structure.

(4) The right to conduct operations for oil and gas upon land located in
Indiana includes the right to:

(A) install and maintain physical equipment on the land; and

(B) use the portion of the surface of the land that is reasonably
necessary for the operations;

subject to the payment of damages resulting from the installation only
of the equipment specified in this subdivision. [P.L.2-2002, § 8.]

32-23-7-7. Title — Tenancy of interests in oil and gas. —
(a) Interests in the oil and gas in, on, under, or that may be taken from
beneath the surface of land located in Indiana may be created:

    (1) for life;

    (2) for a term of years; or

    (3) in fee;

in the manner and to the extent that other interests in real estate and title
are created.

  (b) Title to the estates specified under subsection (a) may be vested in one
(1) or more persons by:

    (1) sole ownership;

    (2) tenancy in common;

    (3) joint tenancy;

    (4) tenancy by the entireties; or

    (5) another manner recognized under Indiana law.

  (c) Interests or estates specified in this section are freely alienable, in
whole or in part, in the same manner as are other interests in real estate.
[P.L.2-2002, § 8.]

Indiana Law Journal. The Power of a
Trustee to Execute Oil and Gas Leases, 33
Ind. L.J. 227.

**32-23-7-8. Rights of parties to contract — Rights and powers to
regulate not affected. —** (a) This chapter does not limit the rights of
parties to contract with regard to the oil and gas estate affecting lands in
Indiana:

    (1) to the extent permitted by; and

    (2) in a manner consistent with;

the nature of the estate in law as specified under this chapter.

  (b) This chapter is intended to declare the law of this state with regard to
the subject matter treated in this chapter as the law existed before March 5,
1951.

  (c) This chapter does not affect the rights or powers of any commission,
board, or authority duly constituted for the regulation of the oil and gas
industry in Indiana. [P.L.2-2002, § 8.]

CHAPTER 8

OIL AND GAS: CANCELLATION OF CONTRACTS AND LEASES FOR OIL AND GAS

32-23-8-1. Factors voiding contracts. — (a) Leases for oil and gas
that are recorded in Indiana are void:

    (1) after a period of one (1) year has elapsed since:

(A) the last payment of rentals on the oil and gas lease as stipulated in the lease or contract; or

(B) operation for oil or gas has ceased, both by the nonproduction of oil or gas and the nondevelopment of the lease; and

(2) upon the written request of the owner of the land, accompanied by the affidavit of the owner stating that:

(A) no rentals have been paid to or received by the owner or any person, bank, or corporation in the owner's behalf for a period of one (1) year after they have become due; and

(B) the leases and contracts have not been operated for the production of oil or gas for one (1) year. [P.L.2-2002, § 8.]

Effective Dates. P.L.2-2002, § 8. July 1. 2002.

NOTES TO DECISIONS

ANALYSIS

Applicability.
Cessation of operations.
Construction of lease.
Domestic use.
Failure to cancel lease.
Failure to pay.
Incorrect request.
Obligation to explore.

Applicability.
"Operations for oil and gas" as defined under former IC 32-5-7-1 (repealed) also applied to former IC 32-5-8-1 (repealed; see this section for similar provisions). Barr v. Sun Exploration Co., 436 N.E.2d 821 (Ind. App. 1982).

Cessation of Operations.
Both nonproduction of oil and gas and nondevelopment of lease must be shown to prove cessation of operations for oil and gas. Barr v. Sun Exploration Co., 436 N.E.2d 821 (Ind. App. 1982).
Temporary cessation of oil production does not terminate oil and gas lease. Barr v. Sun Exploration Co., 436 N.E.2d 821 (Ind. App. 1982).
Fact that no oil was produced for a period of over a year did not result in termination of oil and gas lease under former IC 32-5-8-1 (repealed; see this section for similar provisions) where activities to repair, maintain and operate the oil well toward eventual production or attempted production of oil were in evidence, and where owner of land on which well was located was employed as a pumper throughout the period in question. Barr v. Sun Exploration Co., 436 N.E.2d 821 (Ind. App. 1982).

Construction of Lease.
Where a gas and oil lease did not contain

the descriptions of the real estate involved, but there was attached to such lease a separate paper containing the descriptions, and the lease, preceding the blank space for descriptions, contained the words "described as follows" and "said described land," the references were sufficient, as they related to the subject-matter of the contract and were made as evidence of one agreement, and they should be construed as one transaction. Maier v. Continental Oil Co., 120 F.2d 237 (7th Cir.), cert. denied, 314 U.S. 652, 62 S. Ct. 101, 86 L. Ed. 523 (1941).

Domestic Use.
Continuous production of gas by the lessor for domestic use was not "production" for purposes of former IC 32-5-8-1 (repealed; see this section for similar provisions) to prevent the cancellation of the lease. Plymouth Fertilizer Co. v. Balmer, 488 N.E.2d 1129 (Ind. App. 1986).
The use of gas by the lessor for domestic purposes does not estop cancellation of the lease in lieu of rent as the purpose of the lease is production to produce royalties for the lessor. Plymouth Fertilizer Co. v. Balmer, 488 N.E.2d 1129 (Ind. App. 1986).

Failure to Cancel Lease.
Where plaintiff appealed from the denial of his claims for a brokerage fee and incidental damages arising from the aborted sale of real estate pursuant to a purchase agreement with defendant, and an oil and gas lease, having apparently been abandoned, existed on the subject property rendering its title unmarketable, even though plaintiff was successful in removing the lease by filing an affidavit signed by the heirs of the estate stating that the lease had not been developed and rents had not been paid for a period exceeding one year, the affidavit was not filed

Failure to Cancel Lease. (Cont'd)
until fifteen months after the scheduled closing, so that the title was defective at the time
of closing, thereby rendering the title unmer-
chantable. Salmon v. Perez, 545 N.E.2d 21
(Ind. App. 1989).

Failure to Pay.
Under former IC 32-5-8-1 (repealed; see
this section for similar provisions), a landowner could claim cancellation of the lease
when a one-year period has elapsed and the
lessee has not paid rentals as stipulated for in
the lease or contract, or the operator has not
conducted operations, both by not producing
oil, and by not developing the lease. The
statute did not provide for cancellation based
on failure to pay unless the provision is in the
contract or lease. Wilson v. Elliott, 589 N.E.2d
259 (Ind. App. 1992).

Incorrect Request.
Under former IC 32-5-8-1 (repealed; see
this section for similar provisions), only upon
written request of the owner will the county
recorder certify on the land title that the oil
and gas lease and contracts are invalid and
void. Logically, if the written request incor-
rectly identifies the land and the lease, the
county recorder cannot certify on the appropriate title which lease is null and void.
Wilson v. Elliott, 589 N.E.2d 259 (Ind. App.
1992).

Obligation to Explore.
Delay in performance of obligation to explore, under oil and gas lease, for over two
years and nine months entitled lessor to forfeiture. Bollenbacher v. Miller, 94 Ind. App.
409, 179 N.E. 556 (1932).
The obligation under an oil and gas lease to
explore and develop was such an essential
part of the contract, even though implied, that
it was treated as a condition which, if not
performed in a reasonable time, entitled the
grantor to claim a forfeiture and abandonment of the contract. Heeter v. Hardy, 118 Ind.
App. 256, 76 N.E.2d 590 (1948).
An abandoned oil and gas lease was void.
Heeter v. Hardy, 118 Ind. App. 256, 76 N.E.2d
590 (1948).

Collateral References. 38 Am. Jur. 2d
Gas and Oil, §§ 221-227.
58 C.J.S. Mines and Minerals, §§ 195-222.

Duty of oil or gas lessee to restore surface of
leased premises upon termination of operations. 62 A.L.R.4th 1153.

32-23-8-2. Certification of invalidity or cancellation. — (a) The recorder of the county in which real estate described in section 1 [IC 32-23-8-1] of this chapter is situated shall certify upon the face of the record of the oil and gas lease that:

(1) the leases and contracts are invalid and void by reason of nonpayment of rentals; and

(2) the oil and gas lease is canceled of record.

(b) The request and affidavit shall be recorded in the miscellaneous
records of the recorder's office. [P.L.2-2002, § 8.]

32-23-8-3. Voiding cancellation. — If, at any time after the cancella-
tion of a lease and contract and within the term provided in the lease or
contract, the lessee submits to the recorder:

(1) a receipt or a canceled check, or an affidavit, showing that the rental
has been paid; or

(2) an affidavit that:

(A) the lease has been operated within a period of one (1) year before
the cancellation, as stipulated in the lease or contract; and

(B) the affidavit of the lessor provided under this chapter is false or
fraudulent;

the cancellation is void, and the recorder shall so certify at the place where
the cancellation of the lease and contract has been entered. [P.L.2-2002,
§ 8.]

NOTES TO DECISIONS

Affidavit.

Filing an adequate affidavit is a condition precedent to having an oil and gas lease rendered void on the record title. Wilson v. Elliott, 589 N.E.2d 259 (Ind. App. 1992).

Because the owner of the oil and gas estate never filed an affidavit with the county re-corder that the lease had expired as a result of one year of nonproduction, the oil and gas lease was still in force when the contract was written for the removal of the wells. Youngs v. Old Ben Coal Co., 243 F.3d 387 (7th Cir. 2001).

32-23-8-4. Appeal of cancellation. — The owner of a lease that is canceled by a county recorder under this chapter may, not more than six (6) months after the date of cancellation of the lease, appeal the order and record of cancellation in the circuit court of the county in which the land is located. [P.L.2-2002, § 8.]

CHAPTER 9

OIL AND GAS: PURCHASE OF AND PAYMENT FOR CRUDE OIL

32-23-9-1. Time for payment. — (a) A person, firm, limited liability company, or corporation that purchases crude oil that is pumped from an oil well in Indiana shall pay for the crude oil:

(1) not more than sixty (60) days after the date of the examination and approval of abstracts of title that are furnished by owners of interests and that show good title in the owners of interests; and

(2) after the purchasers have received executed division orders from the owners of interests. [P.L.2-2002, § 8.]

Effective Dates. P.L.2-2002, § 8. July 1.
2002.

32-23-9-2. Penalty for failure to make payment. — If a person, firm, limited liability company, or corporation described in section 1 [IC 32-23-9-1] of this chapter:

(1) fails to pay for the crude oil:

(A) not more than sixty (60) days after the date of the examination and approval of title; and

(B) after the purchasers have received executed division orders from the owners of interests; or

(2) has failed to notify the known claimants of an interest of the purchaser's reason for nonpayment to the claimants of an interest;

the purchaser shall pay interest at the rate of six percent (6%) per year on the unpaid balance from the date on which the purchaser was required to pay for the crude oil under this chapter to the date of payment. [P.L.2-2002, § 8.]

CHAPTER 10
LAPSE OF MINERAL INTEREST

32-23-10-1. "Mineral interest" defined. — As used in this chapter, "mineral interest" means the interest that is created by an instrument that transfers, by:

(1) grant;
(2) assignment;
(3) reservation; or
(4) otherwise;

an interest of any kind in coal, oil and gas, and other minerals. [P.L.2-2002, § 8.]

Effective Dates. P.L.2-2002, § 8. July 1. 2002.

32-23-10-2. Time period — Consequence of lapse. — An interest in coal, oil and gas, and other minerals, if unused for a period of twenty (20) years, is extinguished and the ownership reverts to the owner of the interest out of which the interest in coal, oil and gas, and other minerals was carved. However, if a statement of claim is filed in accordance with this chapter, the reversion does not occur. [P.L.2-2002, § 8.]

NOTES TO DECISIONS

ANALYSIS

In general.
Constitutionality.
Common law rules for lapse.
No implied duty.
Purpose of chapter.
Quiet title action unnecessary.

In General.

While former IC 32-5-11 (repealed; see this chapter for similar provisions) undoubtedly extinguished the unused interests of lost and unknown owners, it could not fairly be read as decreeing a lapse only in those situations where the identity or whereabouts of the mineral interest owner was unknown to the surface rights owner. McCoy v. Richards, 623 F. Supp. 1300 (S.D. Ind. 1984), aff'd, 771 F.2d 1108 (7th Cir. 1986).

Constitutionality.

This act, providing for the lapsing of mineral interests, does not violate due process. Short v. Texaco, Inc., 273 Ind. 518, 76 Ind. Dec. 691, 406 N.E.2d 625 (1980), aff'd, 454 U.S. 516, 102 S. Ct. 781, 70 L. Ed. 2d 738 (1982).

The extinguishment of mineral interests under this act does not amount to an exercise by the state of its power of eminent domain and therefore does not amount to the taking of property without just compensation in violation of Ind. Const., Art. 1, § 21. Short v. Texaco, Inc., 273 Ind. 518, 76 Ind. Dec. 691, 406 N.E.2d 625 (1980), aff'd, 454 U.S. 516, 102 S. Ct. 781, 70 L. Ed. 2d 738 (1982).

Common Law Rules for Lapse.

The Dormant Mineral Interest Act provides one mechanism for declaring that leasehold interests have lapsed, supplementing, but not displacing, common law rules developed for termination of leasehold interests in minerals, and it is not the exclusive means of terminating such leasehold interests for lack

Common Law Rules for Lapse. (Cont'd) of use. Begley v. Peabody Coal Co., 978 F. Supp. 861 (S.D. Ind. 1997).

No Implied Duty.
Where lease authorizing lessee to mine provided for substantial income for the lessor in the absence of any mining and imposed no affirmative obligation to mine, there was no compelling equitable need for an implied obligation of diligent mining, the breach of which would support termination of the lease. Begley v. Peabody Coal Co., 978 F. Supp. 861 (S.D. Ind. 1997).

Purpose of Chapter.
The aim of former IC 32-5-11 (repealed; see this chapter for similar provisions) was to eliminate title problems resulting from long-held mineral interests which had remained inactive for extended periods of time. Kirby v. Ashland Oil, Inc., 463 N.E.2d 1127 (Ind. App. 1984).

Quiet Title Action Unnecessary.
A quiet title action is not necessary to effectuate the lapse of a mineral interest. McCoy v. Richards, 623 F. Supp. 1300 (S.D. Ind. 1984), aff'd, 771 F.2d 1108 (7th Cir. 1986).

Collateral References. 54 Am. Jur. 2d Mines and Minerals, §§ 141-145.
58 C.J.S. Mines and Minerals, § 132.

32-23-10-3. Factors determining use of interest. — (a) A mineral interest is considered to be used when:

(1) minerals are produced under the mineral interest;

(2) operations are conducted on the mineral interest for injection, withdrawal, storage, or disposal of water, gas, or other fluid substances;

(3) rentals or royalties are paid by the owner of the mineral interest for the purpose of delaying or enjoying the use or exercise of the rights;

(4) a use described in subdivisions 1 through 3 is carried out on a tract with which the mineral interest may be unitized or pooled for production purposes;

(5) in the case of coal or other solid minerals, there is production from a common vein or seam by the owners of the mineral interest; or

(6) taxes are paid on the mineral interest by the owner of the mineral interest.

(b) A use under or authorized by an instrument that creates a mineral interest continues in force all rights granted by the instrument. [P.L.2-2002, § 8.]

NOTES TO DECISIONS

Active Use Envisioned.
Former IC 32-5-11 (repealed; see this chapter for similar provisions) clearly envisioned an active use of mineral interests by the owner. Kirby v. Ashland Oil, Inc., 463 N.E.2d 1127 (Ind. App. 1984).

Payment of Taxes.
Payment of taxes by the owner of the mineral interest constitutes a "use" of the interest which continues it in force and preserves it from extinguishment. Consolidation Coal Co. v. Mutchman, 565 N.E.2d 1074 (Ind. App. 1990), reh'g denied, 589 N.E.2d 1163 (Ind. App. 1991).

Qualifying Uses.

—In General.
Former IC 32-5-11 (repealed; see this chapter for similar provisions) provided for three qualifying uses: (1) actual production by the

Qualifying Uses. (Cont'd)

—In General. (Cont'd)
owner; (2) payment of rents or royalties by the owner for purposes of delaying production; and (3) payment of taxes on the mineral interests by the owner. Kirby v. Ashland Oil, Inc., 463 N.E.2d 1127 (Ind. App. 1984).

—Lease Insufficient.
The mere act of leasing one's mineral interests is not a sufficient use to prevent a lapse. Kirby v. Ashland Oil, Inc., 463 N.E.2d 1127 (Ind. App. 1984).

Sale or Lease.
The sale or lease of an interest in minerals to another is not sufficient to establish a "use" on the part of the seller or lessor. McCoy v. Richards, 581 F. Supp. 143 (S.D. Ind. 1983), aff'd, 771 F.2d 1108 (7th Cir. 1985).

Since the express language of this section prohibits a finding that the sale or lease of a mineral interest is, of itself, a "use" of that mineral interest, the granting of oil and gas leases by property owners creates new mineral interests in the lessees and does not constitute a "use" sufficient to preserve the property owners' mineral interest. McCoy v. Richards, 623 F. Supp. 1300 (S.D. Ind. 1984), aff'd, 771 F.2d 1108 (7th Cir. 1985).

32-23-10-4. Statement of claim — Requirements. — (a) The statement of claim under section 2 [IC 32-23-10-2] of this chapter must:

(1) be filed by the owner of the mineral interest before the end of the twenty (20) year period set forth in section 2 of this chapter; and

(2) contain:

(A) the name and address of the owner of the mineral interest; and

(B) a description of the land on or under which the mineral interest is located.

(b) A statement of claim described in subsection (a) must be filed in the office of the recorder of deeds in the county in which the land is located.

(c) Upon the filing of a statement of claim within the time provided in this section, the mineral interest is considered to be in use on the date the statement of claim is filed. [P.L.2-2002, § 8.]

NOTES TO DECISIONS

ANALYSIS

Applicability of general recording requirements.
Two-year period.

Applicability of General Recording Requirements.
The recording of a deed of conveyance made in compliance with former IC 32-1-2-16 (repealed; see IC 32-21-4-1 for similar provisions), relating to recording requirements generally, was not sufficient to satisfy the statement of claim provisions of that chapter.

McCoy v. Richards, 581 F. Supp. 143 (S.D. Ind. 1983), aff'd, 771 F.2d 1108 (7th Cir. 1985).

Two-Year Period.
The two-year period after the effective date of Acts 1971, P.L.423, ending September 3, 1973, prescribed by former IC 32-5-11-4 (repealed; see IC 32-21-4-1 for similar provisions) constituted a reasonable time. Short v. Texaco, Inc., 273 Ind. 518, 76 Ind. Dec. 691, 406 N.E.2d 625 (1980), aff'd, 454 U.S. 516, 102 S. Ct. 781, 70 L. Ed. 2d 738 (1982).

32-23-10-5. Failure to file statement of claim. — Failure to file a statement of claim within the time provided in section 4 [IC 32-23-10-4] of this chapter does not cause a mineral interest to be extinguished if the owner of the mineral interest:

(1) was, at the time of the expiration of the period specified in section 4 of this chapter, the owner of ten (10) or more mineral interests in the county in which the mineral interest is located;

(2) made a diligent effort to preserve all the mineral interests that were not being used and, not more than ten (10) years before the expiration of the period specified in section 4 of this chapter, preserved other mineral interests in the county by filing statements of claim as required under this chapter;

(3) failed to preserve the mineral interest through inadvertence; and

(4) filed the statement of claim required under this chapter:

(A) not more than sixty (60) days after publication of notice as specified in section 6 [IC 32-23-10-6] of this chapter; and

(B) if a notice referred to in clause (A) is not published, not more than sixty (60) days after receiving actual knowledge that the mineral interest had lapsed. [P.L.2-2002, § 8.]

NOTES TO DECISIONS

Constitutionality.
Former IC 32-5-11-5 (repealed; see this section for similar provisions) did not violate the equal protection provisions of the constitu-tion. Short v. Texaco, Inc., 273 Ind. 518, 76 Ind. Dec. 691, 406 N.E.2d 625 (1980), aff'd, 454 U.S. 516, 102 S. Ct. 781, 70 L. Ed. 2d 738 (1982).

32-23-10-6. Notice of lapse. — (a) A person who succeeds to the ownership of a mineral interest may, upon the lapse of the mineral interest, give notice of the lapse of the mineral interest by:

(1) publishing notice in a newspaper of general circulation in the county in which the mineral interest is located; and

(2) if the address of the mineral interest owner is shown of record or can be determined upon reasonable inquiry, by mailing, not more than ten (10) days after publication, a copy of the notice to the owner of the mineral interest.

(b) The notice required under subsection (a) must state:

(1) the name of the owner of the mineral interest, as shown of record;

(2) a description of the land; and

(3) the name of the person giving the notice.

(c) If a copy of the notice required under subsection (a) and an affidavit of service of the notice are promptly filed in the office of the recorder in the county where the land is located, the record is prima facie evidence in a legal proceeding that notice was given. [P.L.2-2002, § 8.]

NOTES TO DECISIONS

Permissive Provisions.
The notice provisions of former IC 32-5-11-6 (repealed; see this section for similar provisions) are merely permissive. Ohning v. Buckskin Coal Corp., 528 N.E.2d 493 (Ind. App. 1988).
Landowners' interests in the coal underlying their properties were not subject to tax liens imposed for the unpaid taxes assessed to the former owner of lapsed mineral rights where the landowners were under no duty to notify anyone of their reversionary interest at the time the lapse occurred. Ohning v. Buckskin Coal Corp., 528 N.E.2d 493 (Ind. App. 1988).

32-23-10-7. Recording of statement of claim and service of notice of lapse. — Upon the filing of the statement of claim specified in section 4 [IC 32-23-10-4] of this chapter or the proof of service of notice specified in section 6 [IC 32-23-10-6] of this chapter in the recorder's office for the county where a mineral interest is located, the recorder shall:

(1) record the filing in a book to be kept for that purpose, to be known as the "dormant mineral interest record"; and

(2) indicate by marginal notation on the instrument creating the original mineral interest the filing of the statement of claim or affidavit of publication and service of notice. [P.L.2-2002, § 8.]

NOTES TO DECISIONS

Applicability of General Recording Requirements.

The recording of a deed of conveyance made in compliance with former IC 32-1-2-16 (repealed; see IC 32-21-4-1 for similar provisions), relating to recording requirements generally, was not sufficient to satisfy the statement of claim provisions of this chapter. McCoy v. Richards, 581 F. Supp. 143 (S.D. Ind. 1983), aff'd, 771 F.2d 1108 (7th Cir. 1985).

32-23-10-8. Waiver. — The provisions of this chapter may not be waived at any time before the expiration of the twenty (20) year period provided in section 2 [IC 32-23-10-2] of this chapter. [P.L.2-2002, § 8.]

CHAPTER 11

ABANDONED RAILROAD RIGHTS-OF-WAY

32-23-11-1. Applicability. — This chapter does not apply to a railroad right-of-way that is abandoned as part of a demonstration project for the relocation of railroad lines from the central area of a city as provided under Section 163 of the Federal-Aid Highway Act of 1973 (P.L.93-87, Title I, Section 163). [P.L.2-2002, § 8.]

Effective Dates. P.L.2-2002, § 8. July 1. 2002.

32-23-11-2. "Public utility" defined. — As used in this chapter, "public utility" has the meaning set forth in IC 8-1-8.5-1. [P.L.2-2002, § 8.]

32-23-11-3. "Railroad" defined. — (a) As used in this chapter, "railroad" refers to a railroad company.

(b) The term includes a person to whom any part of a right-of-way was transferred under the Regional Rail Reorganization Act of 1973 (45 U.S.C. 701 et seq.). [P.L.2-2002, § 8.]

NOTES TO DECISIONS

Constitutionality.
—Due process.

Constitutionality.

—Due Process.
Former IC 8-4-35 operated to extinguish a property right upon the mere lapsing of time, regardless of whether the state had been able to afford the aggrieved party a hearing before the extinguishing of the right pursuant to the statutory scheme. The state's ability to provide a timely hearing most of the time does not satisfy due process and does not justify the failure to guarantee a pre-deprivation hearing in all cases. Penn Cent. Corp. v. United States R.R. Vest Corp., 834 F. Supp. 1075 (N.D. Ind. 1993).

Any argument that any taking of a railroad's property under former IC 8-4-35 was its own fault because it failed to trigger its right to a hearing by filing a quiet title action failed where, even had the railroad taken all reasonable steps to obtain a hearing, there was no guarantee it would receive a hearing before its property entitlement would lapse pursuant to the operation of former IC 8-4-35. Penn Cent. Corp. v. United States R.R. Vest Corp., 834 F. Supp. 1075 (N.D. Ind. 1993).

The failure of Indiana law to guarantee a pre-deprivation hearing, coupled with the lack of any compelling interest that would make such a guarantee unpracticable, causes the procedure set forth in former IC 8-4-35 to violate the railroads' right to due process of law. Penn Cent. Corp. v. United States R.R. Vest Corp., 834 F. Supp. 1075 (N.D. Ind. 1993).

32-23-11-4. "Right-of-way" defined. — (a) As used in this chapter, "right-of-way" means a strip or parcel of real property in which a railroad has acquired an interest for use as a part of the railroad's transportation corridor.

(b) The term does not refer to any real property interest in the strip or parcel. [P.L.2-2002, § 8.]

NOTES TO DECISIONS

Construction of Conveyance.
Where the deed conveys a strip of land without limiting language the railroad has a fee simple, despite the caption of "right-of-way" placed on the deed, because the caption

on the cover of a deed does not create an ambiguity in a clearly worded conveyance. Clark v. CSX Transp., Inc., 737 N.E.2d 752 (Ind. App. 2000).

32-23-11-5. "Right-of-way fee" defined. — "Right-of-way fee" refers to the fee simple interest in the real property through which a right-of-way runs. [P.L.2-2002, § 8.]

NOTES TO DECISIONS

Constitutionality.
—Violative of due process.

Constitutionality.

—Violative of Due Process.
Former IC 8-4-35-4 through IC 8-4-35-7, which deemed railroad rights-of-way aban-

doned if the Interstate Commerce Commission authorized abandonment of railroad service over the right-of-way and the railroad removed its equipment from it, and then deemed the railroad's interest vested in the owner of fee simple real property with a deed containing a description of the real property that included the right-of-way or, if there is no such deed, in the owner of the adjoining fee, requiring only that the new owner file an

Constitutionality. (Cont'd)

—Violative of Due Process. (Cont'd) affidavit describing the right-of-way and stating that it was vested in him to establish record title and requiring the railroad to execute and deliver a quit claim deed within 180 days of receiving the affidavit, violated due process by failing to give the railroad opportunity for a hearing. The argument that the railroad might be able to get its property back by means of a quiet-title action under IC 34-1-48-20 did not alleviate the problem since there was no evidence that the railroad could obtain relief within 180 days. Penn Cent. Corp. v. United States R.R. Vest Corp., 955 F.2d 1158 (7th Cir. 1992).

Former IC 8-4-35 operated to extinguish a property right upon the mere lapsing of time, regardless of whether the state had been able to afford the aggrieved party a hearing before the extinguishing of the right pursuant to the statutory scheme. The state's ability to provide a timely hearing most of the time does not satisfy due process and does not justify the failure to guarantee a pre-deprivation hearing in all cases. Penn Cent. Corp. v. United States R.R. Vest Corp., 834 F. Supp. 1075 (N.D. Ind. 1993).

Any argument that any taking of a railroad's property under former IC 8-4-35 was its own fault because it failed to trigger its right to a hearing by filing a quiet title action failed where, even had the railroad taken all reasonable steps to obtain a hearing, there was no guarantee it would receive a hearing before its property entitlement would lapse pursuant to the operation of IC 8-4-35. Penn Cent. Corp. v. United States R.R. Vest Corp., 834 F. Supp. 1075 (N.D. Ind. 1993).

The failure of Indiana law to guarantee a pre-deprivation hearing, coupled with the lack of any compelling interest that would make such a guarantee unpracticable, caused the procedure set forth in former IC 8-4-35 to violate the railroad's right to due process of law. Penn Cent. Corp. v. United States R.R. Vest Corp., 834 F. Supp. 1075 (N.D. Ind. 1993).

32-23-11-6. Right-of-way considered abandoned. — (a) Except as provided in subsection (b) and in sections 7 and 8 [IC 32-23-11-7 and IC 32-23-11-8] of this chapter, a right-of-way is considered abandoned if any of subdivisions (1) through (3) apply:

(1) Before February 28, 1920, both of the following occurred:

(A) The railroad discontinued use of the right-of-way for railroad purposes.

(B) The rails, switches, ties, and other facilities were removed from the right-of-way.

(2) After February 27, 1920, both of the following occur:

(A) The Interstate Commerce Commission or the United States Surface Transportation Board issues a certificate of public convenience and necessity relieving the railroad of the railroad's common carrier obligation on the right-of-way.

(B) The earlier of the following occurs:

(i) Rails, switches, ties, and other facilities are removed from the right-of-way, making the right-of-way unusable for continued rail traffic.

(ii) At least ten (10) years have passed from the date on which the Interstate Commerce Commission or the United States Surface Transportation Board issued a certificate of public convenience and necessity relieving the railroad of its common carrier obligation on the right-of-way.

(3) The right-of-way was abandoned under the Regional Rail Reorganization Act of 1973 (45 U.S.C. 701 et seq.).

(b) A right-of-way is not considered abandoned if:

(1) rail service continues on the right-of-way; or

(2) the railroad has entered into an agreement preserving rail service on the right-of-way. [P.L.2-2002, § 8.]

Indiana Law Review. Trains, Trails, and Property Law: Indiana Law and the Rails-to-Trails Controversy, 31 Ind. L. Rev. 754 (1998).

NOTES TO DECISIONS

ANALYSIS

Constitutionality.
—Violative of due process.
Abandonment.
—Found.
Class actions.
Construction.
—Other facilities.
Easements.
—Extinguishment.
Fee simple interest.
—Not extinguished.
Scope of right-of-way.

Constitutionality.

—Violative of Due Process.
Former IC 8-4-35-4 through IC 8-4-35-7, which deemed railroad rights-of-way abandoned if the Interstate Commerce Commission authorized abandonment of railroad service over the right-of-way and the railroad removed its equipment from it, and then deemed the railroad's interest vested in the owner of fee simple real property with a deed containing a description of the real property that included the right-of-way or, if there is no such deed, in the owner of the adjoining fee, requiring only that the new owner file an affidavit describing the right-of-way and stating that it was vested in him to establish record title and requiring the railroad to execute and deliver a quit claim deed within 180 days of receiving the affidavit, violated due process by failing to give the railroad opportunity for a hearing. The argument that the railroad might be able to get its property back by means of a quiet-title action under IC 34-1-48-20 did not alleviate the problem since there was no evidence that the railroad could obtain relief within 180 days. Penn Cent. Corp. v. United States R.R. Vest Corp., 955 F.2d 1158 (7th Cir. 1992).

Former IC 8-4-35 operated to extinguish a property right upon the mere lapsing of time, regardless of whether the state had been able to afford the aggrieved party a hearing before the extinguishing of the right pursuant to the statutory scheme. The state's ability to provide a timely hearing most of the time does not satisfy due process and does not justify the failure to guarantee a pre-deprivation hearing in all cases. Penn Cent. Corp. v. United States R.R. Vest Corp., 834 F. Supp. 1075 (N.D. Ind. 1993).

An argument that any taking of a railroad's property under former IC 8-4-35 was its own fault because it failed to trigger its right to a hearing by filing a quiet title action failed where, even had the railroad taken all reasonable steps to obtain a hearing, there was no guarantee it would receive a hearing before its property entitlement would lapse pursuant to the operation of former IC 8-4-35. Penn Cent. Corp. v. United States R.R. Vest Corp., 834 F. Supp. 1075 (N.D. Ind. 1993).

The failure of Indiana law to guarantee a pre-deprivation hearing, coupled with the lack of any compelling interest that would make such a guarantee unpracticable, caused the procedure set forth in former IC 8-4-35 to violate the railroad's right to due process of law. Penn Cent. Corp. v. United States R.R. Vest Corp., 834 F. Supp. 1075 (N.D. Ind. 1993).

Abandonment.

—Found.
Railroad, having received authorization from the Interstate Commerce Commission to abandon, and having removed rails and ties, had abandoned railroad right-of-way as a matter of law. Consolidated Rail Corp. v. Lewellen, 682 N.E.2d 779 (Ind. 1997).

Class Actions.
Where quiet title claims all involved the well-established principle that where a railroad holds only an easement or lesser interest in the property upon which its tracks cross, the abandonment of the tracks triggers an extinguishment of the railroad's interest and ownership reverts to the fee simple owner or the adjoining fee simple owners, the trial court's determination that common questions of law and fact would predominate over questions affecting only individual plaintiffs was not clearly erroneous. CSX Transp., Inc. v. Clark, 646 N.E.2d 1003 (Ind. App. 1995).

Construction.

—Other Facilities.
The phrase "other facilities" includes only the railroad materials consistent with the materials listed in this section: rails, ties, and switches; trestles, bridges, culverts, drainage tiles, and subsurface ballast are not the same type of railroad materials as rails, ties, and switches. Consolidated Rail Corp. v. Lewellen, 682 N.E.2d 779 (Ind. 1997).

Easements.

—Extinguishment.
Where a railroad holds only an easement or

Easements. (Cont'd)

—Extinguishment. (Cont'd)
lesser interest in the property upon which its tracks cross, the abandonment of the tracks triggers an extinguishment of the railroad's interest and ownership reverts to the fee simple owner with a deed containing the property within its description or, if none, the adjoining fee simple owners. CSX Transp., Inc. v. Clark, 646 N.E.2d 1003 (Ind. App. 1995).

Where owners' title ran to the center of the right-of-way, subject to the burden of the railroad's easement, and upon abandonment, that title was no longer subject to the burden of the easement, owners did not have to file affidavits or record the titles contemplated by former IC 8-4-35-6 to become owners of the right-of-way. Calumet Nat'l Bank v. AT & T Co., 682 N.E.2d 785 (Ind. 1997).

Fee Simple Interest.

—Not Extinguished.
Where a railroad holds a fee simple interest in a railroad corridor, an abandonment does not trigger an extinguishment of the railroad's fee simple interest. CSX Transp., Inc. v. Clark, 646 N.E.2d 1003 (Ind. App. 1995).

Scope of Right-of-Way.
This section codified an established principle of common law, that where there is no language in any of the relevant deeds describing real property that includes the right-of-way, the title of the owners of land abutting railroad rights-of-way runs to the center of the right-of-way. Calumet Nat'l Bank v. AT & T Co., 682 N.E.2d 785 (Ind. 1997).

32-23-11-7. Trail use condition. — A right-of-way is not considered abandoned if the Interstate Commerce Commission or the United States Surface Transportation Board imposes on the right-of-way a trail use condition under 16 U.S.C. 1247(d). [P.L.2-2002, § 8.]

32-23-11-8. Right-of-way not considered abandoned. — (a) A right-of-way is not considered abandoned if the following conditions are met:
(1) The railroad sells the railroad's rights in the right-of-way before abandoning the right-of-way.
(2) The purchaser of the railroad's rights in the right-of-way is not a railroad.
(3) The purchaser purchases the right-of-way for use by the purchaser to transport goods or materials by rail.
(b) A railroad may discontinue rail service on the right-of-way without abandoning the right-of-way. [P.L.2-2002, § 8.]

32-23-11-9. Conveyance of held by railroad. — If a railroad conveys its interest in a right-of-way, the railroad conveys not more than the interest it holds at the time of the conveyance. [P.L.2-2002, § 8.]

32-23-11-10. Vesting of right-of-way fee. — (a) This section applies if a railroad does not own the right-of-way fee.
(b) If a railroad abandons its right to a railroad right-of-way, the railroad's interest vests in the owner of the right-of-way fee with a deed that contains a description of the real property that includes the right-of-way.
(c) If a deed described in subsection (b) does not exist, then the railroad's interest vests in the owner of the adjoining fee. The interest of the railroad that vests in the owner of the adjoining fee is for the part of the right-of-way from the center line of the right-of-way to the adjoining property line. [P.L.2-2002, § 8.]

Indiana Law Review. Trains, Trails, and Property Law: Indiana Law and the Rails-to-Trails Controversy, 31 Ind. L. Rev. 754 (1998).

NOTES TO DECISIONS

ANALYSIS

Constitutionality.
—Violative of due process.
Abandonment.
—Easements.
—Fee simple interest.
—Prior similar provision.
Class actions.

Constitutionality.

—Violative of Due Process.

Former IC 8-4-35-4 through IC 8-4-35-7, which deemed railroad rights-of-way abandoned if the Interstate Commerce Commission authorized abandonment of railroad service over the right-of-way and the railroad removed its equipment from it, and then deemed the railroad's interest vested in the owner of fee simple real property with a deed containing a description of the real property that included the right-of-way or, if there were no such deed, in the owner of the adjoining fee, requiring only that the new owner file an affidavit describing the right-of-way and stating that it was vested in him to establish record title and requiring the railroad to execute and deliver a quit claim deed within 180 days of receiving the affidavit, violated due process by failing to give the railroad opportunity for a hearing. The argument that the railroad might be able to get its property back by means of a quiet-title action under IC 34-1-48-20 did not alleviate the problem since there was no evidence that the railroad could obtain relief within 180 days. Penn Cent. Corp. v. United States R.R. Vest Corp., 955 F.2d 1158 (7th Cir. 1992).

Former IC 8-4-35 operated to extinguish a property right upon the mere lapsing of time, regardless of whether the state had been able to afford the aggrieved party a hearing before the extinguishing of the right pursuant to the statutory scheme. The state's ability to provide a timely hearing most of the time does not satisfy due process and does not justify the failure to guarantee a pre-deprivation hearing in all cases. Penn Cent. Corp. v. United States R.R. Vest Corp., 834 F. Supp. 1075 (N.D. Ind. 1993).

An argument that any taking of a railroad's property under former IC 8-4-35 was its own fault because it failed to trigger its right to a hearing by filing a quiet title action failed where, even had the railroad taken all reasonable steps to obtain a hearing, there was no guarantee it would receive a hearing before its property entitlement would lapse pursuant to the operation of IC 8-4-35. Penn Cent. Corp. v. United States R.R. Vest Corp., 834 F. Supp. 1075 (N.D. Ind. 1993).

The failure of Indiana law to guarantee a pre-deprivation hearing, coupled with the lack of any compelling interest that would make such a guarantee unpracticable, caused the procedure set forth in former IC 8-4-35 to violate the railroad's right to due process of law. Penn Cent. Corp. v. United States R.R. Vest Corp., 834 F. Supp. 1075 (N.D. Ind. 1993).

Abandonment.

—Easements.

Where a railroad holds only an easement or lesser interest in the property upon which its tracks cross, the abandonment of the tracks triggers an extinguishment of the railroad's interest and ownership reverts to the fee simple owner with a deed containing the property within its description or, if none, the adjoining fee simple owners. CSX Transp., Inc. v. Clark, 646 N.E.2d 1003 (Ind. App. 1995).

—Fee Simple Interest.

Where a railroad holds a fee simple interest in a railroad corridor, an abandonment does not trigger an extinguishment of the railroad's fee simple interest. CSX Transp., Inc. v. Clark, 646 N.E.2d 1003 (Ind. App. 1995).

—Prior Similar Provision.

Under former IC 8-4-35-8, in order to be valid, a license granted by a railroad company to a communications company had to be granted while the railroad company still had an interest in the right-of-way to convey; where the right-of-way had been abandoned, the railroad had no interest to license to the communications company, and the license was not valid. Calumet Nat'l Bank v. AT & T Co., 682 N.E.2d 785 (Ind. 1997).

Class Actions.

Where quiet title claims all involved the well-established principle that where a railroad holds only an easement or lesser interest in the property upon which its tracks cross, the abandonment of the tracks triggers an extinguishment of the railroad's interest and ownership reverts to the fee simple owner or the adjoining fee simple owners, the trial court's determination that common questions

32-23-11-11. Abandonment by railroad does not divest other interests in right-of-way. — (a) The vesting of a railroad's interest under section 10 [IC 32-23-11-10] of this chapter does not divest a valid public utility, communication, cable television, fiber optic, or pipeline easement, license, or legal occupancy if the railroad granted the easement before the date on which the railroad abandoned the right-of-way.

(b) This chapter does not deprive a public utility, communication company, cable television company, fiber optic company, or pipeline company of the use of all or part of a right-of-way if, at the time of abandonment, the company:

(1) is occupying and using all or part of the right-of-way for the location and operation of the company's facilities; or

(2) has acquired an interest for use of all or part of the right-of-way.

(c) This chapter does not do the following:

(1) Limit the right of the owner of a right-of-way fee to demand compensation from a railroad or a utility for the value of an interest taken and used or occupied after abandonment.

(2) Grant to the owner of a right-of-way fee the right to obtain duplicative compensation from a utility or pipeline company for the value of the use of any portion of the right-of-way that is subject to the terms of an agreement previously entered into between the utility or pipeline company and the owner of the right-of-way fee. For purposes of this subdivision, "pipeline" does not include a coal slurry pipeline. [P.L.2-2002, § 8.]

32-23-11-12. Action to establish rights. — (a) A person may bring an action to establish full rights of possession of the person's right-of-way fee in any part of a right-of-way that is burdened by an easement for railroad purposes not more than thirty (30) years after the right-of-way is abandoned under this chapter.

(b) A person may commence an action to establish the person's ownership of a right-of-way fee in any part of a right-of-way by enforcing a possibility of reverter or a right of entry under IC 32-17-10. [P.L.2-2002, § 8.]

32-23-11-13. Principles of ownership same as those for fee simple ownership. — Except as provided in section 14 [IC 32-23-11-14] of this chapter, the ownership of a right-of-way fee is determined under the same principles that fee simple ownership in property is otherwise determined under Indiana law. [P.L.2-2002, § 8.]

32-23-11-14. Principles of ownership — Exceptions. — For purposes of this chapter, the following are not adverse possessions or prescriptive easements to the owner and do not establish title or rights to the real property:

(1) Possession of a right-of-way by a nonrailroad purchaser under section 8 [IC 32-23-11-8] of this chapter.

(2) Possession of a right-of-way by a public utility or under a communication, cable television, fiber optic, or pipeline easement, license, or legal occupancy under section 11 [IC 32-23-11-11] of this chapter.

(3) Possession of a right-of-way by a responsible party (as defined in IC 8-4.5-1-17). [P.L.2-2002, § 8.]

32-23-11-15. Easement of necessity. — If a railroad owns a right-of-way fee that becomes landlocked after the right-of-way is abandoned, the railroad retains an easement of necessity in the abandoned right-of-way:

(1) from the landlocked property to the nearest public highway, road, or street; and

(2) to the extent necessary to reach and use the landlocked fee interest for its intended purpose. [P.L.2-2002, § 8.]

ARTICLE 24

EMINENT DOMAIN

CHAPTER 1

GENERAL PROCEDURES

32-24-1-1. "Condemnor" defined. — As used in section 5 [IC 32-24-1-5] of this chapter, "condemnor" means any person authorized by Indiana law to exercise the power of eminent domain. [P.L.2-2002, § 9.]

Effective Dates. P.L.2-2002, § 9. July 1. 2002.

32-24-1-2. "Owner" defined. — As used in section 5 [IC 32-24-1-5] of this chapter, "owner" means the persons listed on the tax assessment rolls as being responsible for the payment of real estate taxes imposed on the property and the persons in whose name title to real estate is shown in the records of the recorder of the county in which the real estate is located. [P.L.2-2002, § 9.]

32-24-1-3. Condemnation procedures. — (a) Any person that may exercise the power of eminent domain for any public use under any statute may exercise the power only in the manner provided in this article, except as otherwise provided by law.

(b) Before proceeding to condemn, the person:

(1) may enter upon any land to examine and survey the property sought to be acquired; and

(2) must make an effort to purchase for the use intended the land, right-of-way, easement, or other interest, in the property.

(c) If the land or interest in the land, or property or right is owned by a person who is an incapacitated person (as defined in IC 29-3-1-7.5) or less than eighteen (18) years of age, the person seeking to acquire the property may purchase the property from the guardian of the incapacitated person or person less than eighteen (18) years of age. If the purchase is approved by the court appointing the guardian and the approval is written upon the face of the deed, the conveyance of the property purchased and the deed made and approved by the court are valid and binding upon the incapacitated person or persons less than eighteen (18) years of age.

(d) The deed given, when executed instead of condemnation, conveys only the interest stated in the deed.

(e) If property is taken by proceedings under this article, the entire fee simple title may be taken and acquired if the property is taken for any purpose other than a right-of-way. [P.L.2-2002, § 9.]

Cross References. Acquisition of fee simple title for highway purposes, authority of department, IC 8-23-18-1.

Constitutional provision as to taking property, Ind. Const., Art. 1, § 21.

Highways, taking property for, IC 8-17-1-3, IC 8-23-7.

Lateral railroads, IC 8-4-10-1.

Railroads, appropriation of property, IC 8-4-1-15.

Relocation assistance for persons displaced by exercise of eminent domain for public improvement purposes, IC 8-23-17.

School corporations, eminent domain for schoolhouses, IC 20-5-23-1.

State toll bridge commission, IC 8-16-1-8.

NOTES TO DECISIONS

ANALYSIS

In general.
Constitutionality.
Abandonment of rights.
Action for damages against condemnor.
Alternate remedies.
Appeals.
Applicability.
Appropriating for another.
Archeological digs.
Attempt to purchase.
Canals.
Cemeteries.
Cities and towns.

Contracts and franchises.
Conveyance in lieu of condemnation.
Corporations.
Damages.
Electric companies.
Evidence of valuation.
Guardians.
Highway proceedings.
Injunction.
Interest.
Jurisdiction.
Lands already appropriated.
Legislative authority.
Legislative intent.

Lienholders.
Mill owners.
Objections.
Offer to purchase.
Payment by condemnor.
Pleadings.
Possession.
Prior statutes superseded.
Private use or benefit.
Purpose.
Railroad companies.
Railroad crossing another.
Right of entry.
Secondary easement by necessity.
Soil testing.
State and state agencies.
Telegraph companies.
Tenants.
Waiver.
Water companies.

In General.

The mode provided by statute for the taking of property under the right of eminent domain had to have been closely pursued, but not necessarily to the extent of exact or literal compliance. Darrow v. Chicago, L.S. & S.B. Ry., 169 Ind. 99, 81 N.E. 1081 (1907).

The Eminent Domain Act of 1905 superseded all other statutes prescribing condemnation procedure, save one mentioned in § 12 of the act. State v. Pollitt, 220 Ind. 593, 45 N.E.2d 480 (1942).

Eminent domain proceedings are statutory and fixed procedures must be followed by all parties. Lehnen v. State, 693 N.E.2d 580 (Ind. App. 1998).

Constitutionality.

This act did not deprive landowners of their property without just compensation, nor did it violate any provisions of the federal or state constitutions. Vandalia Coal Co. v. Indianapolis & L. Ry., 168 Ind. 144, 79 N.E. 1082 (1907); Smith v. Cleveland, C., C. & St. L. Ry., 170 Ind. 382, 81 N.E. 501 (1907); Schnull v. Indianapolis Union Ry., 190 Ind. 572, 131 N.E. 51 (1921); Sisters of Providence v. Lower Vein Coal Co., 198 Ind. 645, 154 N.E. 659 (1926), overruled on other grounds, Joint County Park Bd. v. Stegemoller, 228 Ind. 118, 89 N.E.2d 720 (1950).

Constitutionality of statutes and right of street and interurban railroad companies to appropriate lands under the right of eminent domain was upheld. Smith v. Cleveland, C., C. & St. L. Ry., 170 Ind. 382, 81 N.E. 501 (1907); Mull v. Indianapolis & Cincinnati Traction Co., 169 Ind. 214, 81 N.E. 657 (1907).

The provisions of this act as amended did not violate the due process clause of U. S. Const., Amend. 14, or any other federal or state constitutional provision. City of Lebanon v. Public Serv. Co., 214 Ind. 295, 14 N.E.2d 719, appeal dismissed, 305 U.S. 558, 59 S. Ct. 84, 83 L. Ed. 352, rehearing denied, 305 U.S. 671, 59 S. Ct. 143, 83 L. Ed. 435 (1938).

Due process of law was provided by these sections, which provided for determination of value of the property sought to be condemned, by three disinterested freeholders of the county, followed by a trial of the issues by a court of general jurisdiction, at the election of the parties aggrieved, and giving the right of appeal to the Supreme Court. Southern Ind. Gas & Elec. Co. v. City of Boonville, 215 Ind. 552, 20 N.E.2d 648 (1939).

Abandonment of Rights.

The parties waived or abandoned their rights under appropriation proceedings by their failure to have made demand for money awarded and failure to have taken possession. Coburn v. Sands, 150 Ind. 141, 48 N.E. 786 (1897).

Action for Damages Against Condemnor.

Where the condemnor enters upon lands pursuant to the rights granted by this section and causes damage or destruction to the realty, an action for damages lies against the condemnor and the suit may not be enjoined on the grounds that it obstructs the condemnor's rights under this section. Indiana & Mich. Elec. Co. v. Stevenson, 166 Ind. App. 157, 49 Ind. Dec. 464, 337 N.E.2d 150 (1975).

The destruction of corn and trees in making a preliminary survey, where there was evidence that the survey could have been made without such destruction, amounted to the taking of property in violation of Ind. Const., Art. 1, § 21, for which both compensatory and punitive damages could be awarded. Indiana & Mich. Elec. Co. v. Stevenson, 173 Ind. App. 329, 57 Ind. Dec. 738, 363 N.E.2d 1254 (1977).

Alternate Remedies.

Persons could have resorted to an action at law to recover damages instead of the remedy herein given. Lane v. Miller, 22 Ind. 104 (1864); Toney v. Johnson, 26 Ind. 382 (1866); Shortle v. Terre Haute & I.R.R., 131 Ind. 338, 30 N.E. 1084 (1892); Evansville & R.R.R. v. Charlton, 6 Ind. App. 56, 33 N.E. 129 (1893); Chicago & I. Coal Ry. v. Hall, 135 Ind. 91, 34 N.E. 704, 23 L.R.A. 231 (1893); Pittsburgh, C., C. & St. L. Ry. v. Harper, 11 Ind. App. 481, 37 N.E. 41 (1894).

Plaintiff could not seek another remedy while other proceedings for relief were pending. Ney v. Swinney, 36 Ind. 454 (1871); Rehman v. New Albany B. & T.R.R., 8 Ind. App. 200, 35 N.E. 292 (1893).

Appeals.

The 1907 amendment to § 4-214 (since repealed) provided that thereafter all appeals

Appeals. (Cont'd)
in condemnation proceedings for the appropriation of lands for public use had to be taken directly to the Supreme Court. Northern Ind. Pub. Serv. Co. v. Darling, 128 Ind. App. 456, 149 N.E.2d 702 (1958).

Applicability.
This chapter governs only eminent domain proceedings, and was therefore inapplicable where it was alleged that an easement grant required the trial court to appoint three appraisers to determine the damages resulting from a permanent injunction. Rees v. Panhandle E. Pipe Line Co., 452 N.E.2d 405 (Ind. App. 1983).

Appropriating for Another.
One person could not have appropriated land for the benefit of another. Swinney v. Fort Wayne, M. & C.R.R., 59 Ind. 205 (1877).

Archeological Digs.
The state highway commission's right to enter private property for the purpose of examination and survey under this section confers no license to engage in the process of conducting archeological digs. Indiana State Hwy. Comm'n v. Ziliak, 428 N.E.2d 275 (Ind. App. 1981), rehearing denied, 431 N.E.2d 842 (Ind. App. 1982).

Attempt to Purchase.
An effort to purchase the property sought to have been acquired was a condition precedent to the right to maintain an action to condemn. Indiana Serv. Corp. v. Town of Flora, 218 Ind. 208, 31 N.E.2d 1015 (1941).

The attempt to agree did not need to be pursued further than to develop the fact that an agreement to purchase was not possible at any price which the condemnor was willing to pay. Wampler v. Trustees of Ind. Univ., 241 Ind. 449, 172 N.E.2d 67 (1961).

The reviewing court had to assume, under the statutory obligation of a condemnor to first offer to purchase the easement, that the condemnor did make a good faith offer, which was identical with the demands in the condemnation action. Southern Ind. Gas & Elec. Co. v. Gerhardt, 241 Ind. 389, 172 N.E.2d 204 (1961).

Lack of good faith was not shown by a difference between the terms of the offer to purchase and the complaint for condemnation, or because the value of possible coal deposits was not included in the offered purchase price where the existence of such deposits was speculative. Wyatt-Rauch Farms, Inc. v. Public Serv. Co., 160 Ind. App. 228, 42 Ind. Dec. 115, 311 N.E.2d 441 (1974).

The effort to purchase, required as a condition precedent to the exercise of condemnation under this section, does not contemplate

an impossibility to purchase at any price, however large, but merely an unwillingness on the part of the owner to sell except at a price which in the petitioner's judgment is excessive, and in such an event the attempt to agree need not be pursued further than to develop the fact that an agreement to purchase is not possible at any price which the condemnor is willing to pay. City of Greenfield v. Hancock County Rural Elec. Membership Corp., 160 Ind. App. 529, 42 Ind. Dec. 488, 312 N.E.2d 867 (1974).

In an action to condemn property pursuant to the eminent domain act, an effort to purchase the property is a condition precedent, and the burden is on the party seeking to condemn to show a good faith effort to purchase and an inability to agree. J.M. Foster Co. v. Northern Ind. Pub. Serv. Co., 164 Ind. App. 72, 46 Ind. Dec. 570, 326 N.E.2d 584 (1975).

In an action to condemn property pursuant to the eminent domain act, failure to negotiate in good faith as a condition precedent centers around negotiations as to price, not the location of the property, as the decision as to the location of the particular property sought to be taken rests within the discretion of the condemnor. J.M. Foster Co. v. Northern Ind. Pub. Serv. Co., 164 Ind. App. 72, 46 Ind. Dec. 570, 326 N.E.2d 584 (1975).

Where school corporation knew of town's negotiations to obtain land, the school corporation's suit to condemn the land for the purpose of thwarting the action of the town was properly dismissed. Greater Clark County Sch. Corp. v. Public Serv. Co., 179 Ind. App. 331, 67 Ind. Dec. 258, 385 N.E.2d 952 (1979).

Canals.
Title was obtained when land was appropriated for the Wabash and Erie Canal. Water Works Co. v. Burkhart, 41 Ind. 364 (1872); Indianapolis Water Co. v. Kingan & Co., 155 Ind. 476, 58 N.E. 715 (1900).

Cemeteries.
The right to condemn real estate for cemetery purposes was based on conditions existing when the action was started. Peru Cem. Co. v. Mount Hope Cem., 224 Ind. 202, 65 N.E.2d 849 (1946).

Cities and Towns.
If a municipality made an offer to acquire a particular public utility property, or a specific part thereof, which offer was rejected by the owner, and if the municipality then undertook to condemn other or different property than that which it had offered to purchase, it could not be said that an effort was made to purchase that which it was sought to condemn.

Cities and Towns. (Cont'd)
Indiana Serv. Corp. v. Town of Flora, 218 Ind. 208, 31 N.E.2d 1015 (1941).

Where a public utility was operating its property under an indeterminate permit issued under IC 8-4-1-17 — IC 8-4-1-19, but prior thereto it had operated under a franchise from a city, in an action by the city to condemn the property, evidence as to the company's franchise, distinct from the value of its physical property, was properly excluded, where, under the act, the indeterminate permit continued until such time as the city should exercise its option to purchase, and the 1913 Act was amended in 1933 (IC 8-1-2-95) to the extent that if the city desired to purchase, the value of the property was to have been determined under the Eminent Domain Act instead of by the public service commission, and a contention that the indeterminate permit had a property value to have been determined by the public service commission, and if its value was determined in any other manner, the permit was not terminated but must have been purchased, could not have been sustained. Public Serv. Co. v. City of Lebanon, 219 Ind. 62, 34 N.E.2d 20 (1941), appeal dismissed, 315 U.S. 786, 62 S. Ct. 908, 86 L. Ed. 1191 (1942).

De facto officers of a town could maintain a condemnation action. Town of Markleville v. Markle, 242 Ind. 322, 179 N.E.2d 279 (1962).

This chapter expresses no requirement regarding authorization procedures necessary to commence condemnation proceedings, and municipalities that do not elect to proceed under this chapter must follow the municipal procedures prescribed by the provisions of the cities and towns law relating to condemnations, as special law that acts as an exception to the general law. City of Greenfield v. Hancock County Rural Elec. Membership Corp., 160 Ind. App. 529, 42 Ind. Dec. 488, 312 N.E.2d 867 (1974).

There is nothing to prevent this section from including cities and towns within its sphere. Vickery v. City of Carmel, 424 N.E.2d 147 (Ind. App. 1981).

City, which purchased a leasehold interest in lieu of condemnation, had no obligation to purchase a sublease interest where the sublease had terminated upon the city's purchase in view of language in the sublease providing that it would terminate if the master lease terminated "for any reason." P.C. Mgt., Inc. v. Page Two, Inc., 573 N.E.2d 434 (Ind. App. 1991).

Contracts and Franchises.
The obligation of a public utility franchise and the acceptance of the indeterminate permit was not impaired by the change in the statutory provisions with reference to the manner of determining the necessity of acquiring the property in question, or by modification of the methods of ascertaining its value for such purpose. Southern Ind. Gas & Elec. Co. v. City of Boonville, 215 Ind. 552, 20 N.E.2d 648 (1939).

Every contract, whether made between the state and an individual, or between individuals, had to yield to the right of eminent domain, whenever necessity for its exercise shall have occurred, since every contract was made in subordination to it. Southern Ind. Gas & Elec. Co. v. City of Boonville, 215 Ind. 552, 20 N.E.2d 648 (1939).

Where a city acquired a utility as a result of purchase pursuant to statute (IC 8-1-2-86 et seq.), which had been accepted by the city, which created a contract, the eminent domain statute would have been looked to merely as prescribing the procedure under which the compensation should have been determined. Public Serv. Co. v. City of Lebanon, 221 Ind. 78, 46 N.E.2d 480 (1943).

The compensation for additional improvements to utility property, purchased by a city pursuant to statute necessarily made after the assessment of damages for the original property, did not need to be determined and actually paid or tendered before possession passed, since the foundation of the city's right to acquire the property was contractual, and hence Ind. Const., Art. 1, § 21, relating to assessment and tender of compensation before the taking of private property, was not applicable. Public Serv. Co. v. City of Lebanon, 221 Ind. 78, 46 N.E.2d 480 (1943).

The acceptance of the provisions of the original Shively-Spencer Act (IC 8-1-2-86 et seq.), which provided that the necessity for the purchase of a utility should be determined by the circuit or superior court of the county, and that the compensation to be paid should be fixed by the public service commission, subject to judicial review, by the holder of an indeterminate permit, created a binding contract between it and the state which was in nowise dependent upon the power of eminent domain. Public Serv. Co. v. City of Lebanon, 221 Ind. 78, 46 N.E.2d 480 (1943).

Conveyance in Lieu of Condemnation.
A conveyance in lieu of actual condemnation of real property constitutes a condemnation proceeding because it indicates an intention to acquire the property by condemnation and is tantamount to a taking under the power of eminent domain. P.C. Mgt., Inc. v. Page Two, Inc., 573 N.E.2d 434 (Ind. App. 1991); Schwartz v. Castleton Christian Church, Inc., 594 N.E.2d 473 (Ind. App. 1992).

Corporations.
When a corporation sought to appropriate land under the right of eminent domain, it had to show, before appraisers were ap-

Corporations. (Cont'd)

pointed, that it was such a corporation as was entitled to exercise such right, and that it had made an effort to purchase the land desired. Slider v. Indianapolis & Louisville Traction Co., 42 Ind. App. 304, 85 N.E. 372 (1908).

Damages.

The law in force at the time land was taken governed as to the assessment of damages. Cincinnati, H. & I.R.R. v. Clifford, 113 Ind. 460, 15 N.E. 524 (1888).

Electric Companies.

An electric company had authority to operate a telephone line for its own use over the land taken by it for a right-of-way for its electric transmission line. Joliff v. Muncie Elec. Light Co., 181 Ind. 650, 105 N.E. 234 (1914).

A complaint to appropriate property for the use of a hydraulic electric plant, alleging that the plaintiff was organized under former Burns' Stat. 1926, §§ 5533 — 5543 (since repealed), was not open to the objection that it showed plaintiff to be a private corporation not charged with any public duty or subject to public regulation. Miller v. Southern Ind. Power Co., 184 Ind. 370, 111 N.E. 308 (1916).

An electric power company, organized under former Burns' Stat. 1926, §§ 5533 — 5543 (since repealed), was authorized to appropriate the fee of lands necessary to the carrying out of its objects. Pingry v. Indiana Hydroelectric Power Co., 197 Ind. 426, 151 N.E. 226 (1926).

Evidence showed good faith effort on part of electric company to purchase easement of ingress and egress to its transmission line over appellant's land. Moore v. Indiana & Mich. Elec. Co., 229 Ind. 309, 95 N.E.2d 210 (1950).

Even where an electric company had no property within the newly annexed area, a franchised utility's right to serve the annexed area could not be perfected without a condemnation action where the other electric company had a property interest outside the area, the value or usefulness of which would be substantially interfered with by the loss of the annexed area. Indiana & Mich. Elec. Co. v. Whitley County Rural Elec. Membership Corp., 160 Ind. App. 446, 42 Ind. Dec. 390, 312 N.E.2d 503 (1974).

Evidence of Valuation.

In condemnation proceeding, price paid for subject property by defendant-landowner seven years and two months prior to taking was not inadmissible solely on grounds of passage of such period of time. State v. Valley Dev. Co., 256 Ind. 278, 25 Ind. Dec. 230, 268 N.E.2d 73 (1971).

Guardians.

Guardians could not have consented to the appropriation of the lands of their wards. Indiana, B. & W.R.R. v. Allen, 100 Ind. 409 (1885).

Highway Proceedings.

Where the complaint filed by highway commission for condemnation of land alleged an effort to purchase the land sought, in the absence of an objection raising an issue of fact as to plaintiff's failure to make an effort to agree with the owners of the land touching the damages sustained or touching the purchase price of the land, exception by defendant to the court's ruling upon the objections which were filed presented no question on appeal as to the lack of an effort to purchase the land or agree upon damages. Root v. State, 207 Ind. 312, 192 N.E. 447 (1934).

An action for a writ of assessment of damages and the appointment of appraisers pursuant to the provisions of the eminent domain statute could not have been maintained against the state where the owners had executed an instrument dedicating to the public the land in question, and the state highway commission accepted the dedication without it having been revoked by the grantors, and immediately constructed a highway thereon. Smith v. State, 217 Ind. 643, 29 N.E.2d 786 (1940).

An action to review the administrative determination of the state highway department denying opening of a driveway to a filling station was not available to try out the issues that should have been involved in a proceeding in eminent domain. Huff v. Indiana State Hwy. Comm'n, 238 Ind. 280, 149 N.E.2d 299 (1958).

It could not have been successfully contended that the statutes of this state, namely the eminent domain act and the limited access statutes, did not authorize or give consent to a property owner or the owner of a leasehold's interest in real estate to bring action against the state for damages where the state through its highway department had taken away an abutting owner's existing right of access to a highway by making it into a limited access highway. State v. Marion Circuit Court, 238 Ind. 637, 153 N.E.2d 327 (1958).

Where property owner suffered inconvenience and annoyance when a divider strip was placed in the newly constructed highway, it did not amount to a compensable appropriation of the right of access, even though ingress and egress was made more circuitous and difficult, it did not constitute a "taking" of private property. State v. Ensley, 240 Ind. 472, 164 N.E.2d 342 (1960).

Injunction.

The use of property appropriated could not

Injunction. (Cont'd)

have been enjoined because of errors in the proceedings. Boyd v. Logansport, R. & N. Traction Co., 161 Ind. 587, 69 N.E. 398 (1904).

The exercise of the right of eminent domain could not have been defeated by injunction as the statute gave the landowner an adequate legal remedy. Halstead v. City of Brazil, 83 Ind. App. 53, 147 N.E. 629 (1925).

Interest.

There is no statutory authorization for the plaintiff in a condemnation action to receive interest. Tipmont Rural Elec. Membership Corp. v. City of Crawfordsville, 423 N.E.2d 697 (Ind. App. 1981).

Jurisdiction.

During the pendency of an action in which a court had jurisdiction to decide the issue of possession of real estate, another court of lesser or coordinate jurisdiction could not interfere therewith by another action in eject-ment or in equity to restrain or enjoin such possession. State v. Marion Circuit Court, 239 Ind. 327, 157 N.E.2d 481 (1959).

Lands Already Appropriated.

Appropriation of property under right of eminent domain that had already been appro-priated for public use could not have been accomplished where the first use was materi-ally impaired or destroyed. Cincinnati, W. & M. Ry. v. City of Anderson, 139 Ind. 490, 38 N.E. 167, 47 Am. St. 285 (1894); Steele v. Empsom, 142 Ind. 397, 41 N.E. 822 (1895); City of Terre Haute v. Evansville & T.H.R.R., 149 Ind. 174, 46 N.E. 77, 37 L.R.A. 189 (1897); Powell v. City of Greensburg, 150 Ind. 148, 49 N.E. 955 (1898); Indianapolis & V.R.R. v. Indianapolis & M. Rapid Transit Co., 33 Ind. App. 337, 67 N.E. 1013 (1903).

Land acquired by private persons for the purpose of being conveyed to a railroad com-pany for a right-of-way could have been ap-propriated by another company. Toledo & Ind. Traction Co. v. Indiana & C. I. Ry., 171 Ind. 213, 86 N.E. 54 (1908).

Legislative Authority.

It was a judicial question whether the tak-ing of property was for a public or private use, and a legislative declaration did not bind courts. Logan v. Stogsdale, 123 Ind. 372, 24 N.E. 135, 8 L.R.A. 58 (1890).

The legislature was the sole judge as to what persons might have exercised the right of eminent domain. Consumers' Gas Trust Co. v. Harless, 131 Ind. 446, 29 N.E. 1062, 15 L.R.A. 505 (1892).

The power to condemn land for a public use must have been conferred either by express or implied legislative authority. Indianapolis &

V.R.R. v. Indianapolis & M. Rapid Transit Co., 33 Ind. App. 337, 67 N.E. 1013 (1903).

A presumption existed in favor of the public character of a use declared by the legislature to be public, but was not conclusive upon the courts. Sexauer v. Star Milling Co., 173 Ind. 342, 90 N.E. 474, 26 L.R.A. (n.s.) 609 (1910).

Legislative Intent.

In passing the eminent domain act, it was the intention of the legislature to expedite such proceedings by turning the possession over to the condemnor upon the payment of the appraisal and pending any future litiga-tion in the case. State v. Marion Circuit Court, 239 Ind. 327, 157 N.E.2d 481 (1959).

Lienholders.

Where a city condemned real estate for street purposes and had paid the owner, it took the property for such purposes free of the lien of a previous judgment, but not from a mortgage lien. Gimbel v. Stolte, 59 Ind. 446 (1877); Coburn v. Sands, 150 Ind. 141, 48 N.E. 786 (1897).

Mill Owners.

Mill owners, who operated mills for the purpose of grinding grain for the general public, could exercise the right of eminent domain. Sexauer v. Star Milling Co., 173 Ind. 342, 90 N.E. 474, 26 L.R.A. (n.s.) 609 (1910).

Objections.

Former IC 32-11-1-5 (repealed; for similar provisions see IC 32-24-1-8) made provision for objection to eminent domain proceedings on account of lack of jurisdiction either of the subject matter or person, or because plaintiff had no right to exercise the power of eminent domain for the use sought, or for any other reason disclosed in the complaint or set up in such objections, and contemplated that causes which would have ordinarily consti-tuted grounds for plea in abatement, demur-rer, or answer, could have been presented in objections authorized by said section. Root v. State, 207 Ind. 312, 192 N.E. 447 (1934); Guerrettaz v. Public Serv. Co., 227 Ind. 556, 87 N.E.2d 721 (1949); Joint County Park Bd. v. Stegemoller, 228 Ind. 103, 88 N.E.2d 686 (1949), reh'g denied, 228 Ind. 118, 89 N.E.2d 720 (1950).

Offer to Purchase.

In condemnation proceedings under this section, the offer to purchase had to be the same as that which was sought by such pro-ceedings. Meyer v. Northern Ind. Pub. Serv. Co., 257 Ind. 67, 29 Ind. Dec. 230, 278 N.E.2d 561 (1972).

Where property manager of airport sent letter to owner of land offering to purchase his property for a specified amount, such letter

Offer to Purchase. (Cont'd)

constituted a good faith offer to purchase notwithstanding that the subsequent approval by the airport board was required where such approval was a mere formality. Highland Realty, Inc. v. Indianapolis Airport Auth., 182 Ind. App. 439, 72 Ind. Dec. 62, 395 N.E.2d 1259 (1979).

Payment by Condemnor.

Payment by party condemning land did not jeopardize right to have the amount of benefits or damages reviewed as provided by statute. If, upon trial of the issue, the award was increased, condemning party had to pay or tender the additional amount or its right to possession ceased: if reduced, it was entitled to judgment for the excess. Board of Comm'rs v. Blue Ribbon Ice Cream & Milk Corp., 231 Ind. 436, 109 N.E.2d 88 (1952).

Pleadings.

A complaint counting upon a special statute had to allege facts substantially bringing the plaintiff within the terms thereof and the evidence had to sustain the allegations. Morrison v. Indianapolis & W. Ry., 166 Ind. 511, 76 N.E. 961, 77 N.E. 744, 9 Ann. Cas. 587 (1906).

Matters affecting the jurisdiction of the person and in abatement could have been presented by unverified objection filed at the same time as other objections, which could have severally constituted a demurrer or answer. Joint County Park Bd. v. Stegemoller, 228 Ind. 103, 88 N.E.2d 686 (1949), reh'g denied, 228 Ind. 118, 89 N.E.2d 720 (1950).

Possession.

A court in which a condemnation proceeding was pending had the jurisdiction to determine the possession of the real estate pending the litigation if the issue was presented. If such court decided erroneously, then the remedy was through an appeal. State v. Marion Circuit Court, 239 Ind. 327, 157 N.E.2d 481 (1959).

Prior Statutes Superseded.

Except as provided in former IC 32-11-1-13 (repealed; for similar provisions, see IC 32-24-1), it would seem the procedure provided herein superseded that provided in prior statutes conferring the power of eminent domain for certain purposes on specified corporations and associations and providing the method by which it was to be exercised. Alberson Cem. Ass'n v. Fuhrer, 192 Ind. 606, 137 N.E. 545 (1923).

The procedure prescribed by former Acts 1889, ch. 157 (IC 18-5-6-1) (since repealed), relating to condemnation of additional land for cemetery purposes, has not been in force since this act became effective. Dyar v.

Albright Cem. Ass'n, 199 Ind. 431, 157 N.E. 545 (1927), overruled on other grounds, Joint County Park Bd. v. Stegemoller, 228 Ind. 118, 89 N.E.2d 720 (1950).

Private Use or Benefit.

Property could not have been authorized to be appropriated under the right of eminent domain for a purely private use or benefit. Wild v. Deig, 43 Ind. 455, 13 Am. R. 399 (1873); Stewart v. Hartman, 46 Ind. 331 (1874); Blackman v. Halves, 72 Ind. 515 (1880); Logan v. Stogsdale, 123 Ind. 372, 24 N.E. 135, 8 L.R.A. 58 (1890); Great W. Natural Gas & Oil Co. v. Hawkins, 30 Ind. App. 557, 66 N.E. 765 (1903).

Purpose.

The fundamental purpose of the statutory eminent domain scheme, former IC 32-11-1 (repealed; for similar provisions see IC 32-14-1) is to ensure land owners are given just compensation when their property is taken. Southern Ind. Gas & Elec. Co. v. Russell, 451 N.E.2d 673 (Ind. App. 1983).

The fundamental purpose of the eminent domain act is to ensure that holders of interest in property receive just compensation for property taken for public use. P.C. Mgt., Inc. v. Page Two, Inc., 573 N.E.2d 434 (Ind. App. 1991).

Railroad Companies.

Lands owned in fee simple by a railroad company could have been appropriated by another public-service company unless the railroad company had legally located its road thereon. Southern Ind. Ry. v. Indianapolis & L. Ry., 168 Ind. 360, 81 N.E. 65, 13 L.R.A. (n.s.) 197 (1907).

Lateral railroad companies could appropriate lands under this act. Westport Stone Co. v. Thomas, 175 Ind. 319, 94 N.E. 406, 35 L.R.A. (n.s.) 646 (1911).

A railroad company in condemning a right-of-way acquired only an easement. Cleveland, C., C. & St. L. Ry. v. Doan, 47 Ind. App. 322, 94 N.E. 598 (1911); Hoffman v. Zollman, 49 Ind. App. 664, 97 N.E. 1015 (1912); Meyer v. Pittsburgh, C., C. & St. L. Ry., 63 Ind. App. 156, 113 N.E. 443 (1916).

An interurban railroad that was compelled to permit cars of other companies to be transported over its tracks could appropriate land for its terminal notwithstanding it would have been used in part by such other companies, and by an express company handling goods carried over its road. Eckart v. Fort Wayne & N. Ind. Traction Co., 181 Ind. 352, 104 N.E. 762 (1914).

The procedure for the appropriation of a right-of-way for a lateral railroad under IC 8-4-10-1 was governed by this act. Sisters of Providence v. Lower Vein Coal Co., 198 Ind.

Railroad Companies. (Cont'd)
645, 154 N.E. 659 (1926), overruled on other grounds, Joint County Park Bd. v. Stegemoller, 228 Ind. 118, 89 N.E.2d 720 (1950).

Railroad Crossing Another.
Preliminary to the acquisition by a railroad of the right to cross another, the first railroad had to enter into negotiation with the second for the purpose of reaching an agreement as to compensation, and failing in that, had to institute condemnation proceedings. New Jersey, I. & I.R.R. v. New York Cent. R.R., 89 Ind. App. 205, 146 N.E. 111 (1925).

Right of Entry.
This section, while giving a condemnor the right to enter upon lands in order to survey and examine them prior to condemnation proceedings, does not permit the condemnor to destroy or damage trees, crops, brush or any other part of the realty in carrying out those activities. Indiana & Mich. Elec. Co. v. Stevenson, 166 Ind. App. 517, 49 Ind. Dec. 464, 337 N.E.2d 150 (1975).

Secondary Easement by Necessity.
The concept of a secondary easement by necessity is a common law concept which has been altered by this section's specific requirements as interpreted by the courts. Hagemeier v. Indiana & Mich. Elec. Co., 457 N.E.2d 590 (Ind. App. 1983).

Even if a utility can acquire an ingress-egress easement by necessity, the statutory requirements applicable to the actual right-of-way for a transmission line must prevail in relation to the utility's right to clear the condemnees' land. Hagemeier v. Indiana & Mich. Elec. Co., 457 N.E.2d 590 (Ind. App. 1983).

Soil Testing.
Defendant's request for access to the plaintiffs' property for soil testing was not an initiation of condemnation proceedings and did not entitle the plaintiffs to recovery of fees and expenses once defendant abandoned its efforts. Bradley v. Eagle-Union Community Sch. Corp., 647 N.E.2d 672 (Ind. App. 1995).

State and State Agencies.
A general statute, such as this act, should have had the same interpretation when the state was the condemnor as would have applied in actions brought by private corporations possessing the privilege of eminent domain. State v. Pollitt, 220 Ind. 593, 45 N.E.2d 480 (1942).

The words "or other body having the right to exercise the power of eminent domain," as used in this section, were broad enough to include the state or any of its administrative

agencies. State v. Pollitt, 220 Ind. 593, 45 N.E.2d 480 (1942).

The exercise of the right of eminent domain was prescribed by the constitution and regulated by statute, and when the legislature provided an exclusive method of procedure to condemn land, available alike to all bodies having the right to exercise the power of eminent domain, any such body seeking to exercise the right, even though it be the state itself by one of its administrative agencies was bound by the provisions of the statute. State v. Pollitt, 220 Ind. 593, 45 N.E.2d 480 (1942).

The state highway commission, in taking land for highway purposes, was an administrative agency of the state, and as such could act only within the limits of authority conferred by statute. State v. Pollitt, 220 Ind. 593, 45 N.E.2d 480 (1942).

Indiana Constitution, Art. 1, § 21 did not forbid legislation permitting the state to take private property without first tendering compensation, but the provision was not self-executing. Under it, the state could have taken property whether or not compensation was first assessed and tendered if the legislature saw fit to so provide, but no such legislation had been enacted. Board of Comm'rs v. Blue Ribbon Ice Cream & Milk Corp., 231 Ind. 436, 109 N.E.2d 88 (1952).

Where the eminent domain act, applicable to the state and all subdivisions and agencies thereof was created by the same legislature which, by separate act, established the procedure by which "any city" should exercise the right of condemnation, the court would have to assume that the legislature intended a special law to operate as an exception to the general law, as relating to actions by cities and towns; therefore, the special condemnation act was not superseded by conflicting portions of the general eminent domain act. Hagemann v. City of Mount Vernon, 238 Ind. 613, 154 N.E.2d 33 (1958).

Telegraph Companies.
A telegraph company had the right to appropriate land for the location and maintenance of its necessary poles and lines. Western Union Tel. Co. v. Louisville & N.R.R., 183 Ind. 258, 108 N.E. 951, 1917B Ann. Cas. 705 (1915).

Tenants.
Tenants of lands could have been made parties and damages could have been assessed for their interests. Douglas v. Indianapolis & N.W. Traction Co., 37 Ind. App. 332, 76 N.E. 892 (1906).

Waiver.
In condemnation proceedings, a failure to appeal from an interlocutory order was a

Waiver. (Cont'd)

waiver of any claimed error which could have been raised thereby; consequently, the issue of whether or not an effort was made to purchase the easement in question prior to the bringing of the suit was not before the reviewing court for consideration. Whitlock v. Public Serv. Co., 239 Ind. 680, 159 N.E.2d 280, 161 N.E.2d 169 (1959).

Water Companies.

The fact that a water company would prob-ably furnish water to the inhabitants of a city by selling the water to the city for distribution through the mains and pipes of its municipal water plant, or by leasing its waterworks to the city for use in connection with such plant, would not preclude its exercise of the power of eminent domain as a public utility. Matlock v. Bloomington Water Co., 196 Ind. 271, 146 N.E. 852, reh'g overruled, 196 Ind. 280, 148 N.E. 198 (1925).

Collateral References. 26 Am. Jur. 2d Eminent Domain, §§ 13-16.

27 Am. Jur. 2d Eminent Domain, §§ 375-384.

29A C.J.S. Eminent Domain, §§ 391-416.

Damage to private property by negligence of governmental agents as "taking," "damage," or "use" for public purposes in constitutional sense. 2 A.L.R.2d 707.

Compensation for damage from subterranean waters arising in connection with use of subsurface of street for tunnel purposes by municipality or public. 11 A.L.R.2d 180.

Constitutional rights of owner as against destruction of building by public authorities. 14 A.L.R.2d 73.

Condemnation of another railroad's property for purposes of spur track and the like. 35 A.L.R.2d 1326.

Validity, construction, and effect of statute authorizing eminent domain for urban redevelopment by private enterprise. 44 A.L.R.2d 1414.

Necessity of taking for cemetery purposes. 54 A.L.R.2d 1322.

Necessity of condemnation where private rights are affected by regulation of bathing, swimming, boating, fishing, or the like to protect public water supply. 56 A.L.R.2d 790.

Right to condemn property in excess of needs for a particular public purpose. 6 A.L.R.3d 297.

Power to condemn property or interest therein to replace other property taken for public use. 20 A.L.R.3d 862.

Right to enter land for preliminary survey or examination. 29 A.L.R.3d 1104.

Power of eminent domain as between state and subdivision or agency thereof, or as between different subdivisions or agencies themselves. 35 A.L.R.3d 1293.

Abutting owner's right to damages for limitation of access caused by conversion of conventional road into limited-access highway. 42 A.L.R.3d 13.

Measure and elements of damage for limitation of access caused by conversion of conventional road into limited-access highway. 42 A.L.R.3d 148.

Zoning regulations limiting use of property near airport as taking of property. 18 A.L.R.4th 549.

Sufficiency of condemnor's negotiations required as preliminary to taking in eminent domain. 21 A.L.R.4th 765.

Airport operations or flight of aircraft as constituting taking or damaging of property. 22 A.L.R.4th 863.

Eminent domain: Industrial park or similar development as public use justifying condemnation of private property. 62 A.L.R.4th 1183.

Measure of damages or compensation in eminent domain as affected by premises being restricted to particular educational, religious, charitable, or noncommercial use. 29 A.L.R.5th 36.

Construction and application of rule requiring public use for which property is condemned to be "more necessary" or "higher use" than public use to which property is already appropriated — state takings. 49 A.L.R.5th 769.

32-24-1-4. Complaint for damages. — (a) If the person seeking to acquire the property does not agree with the owner of an interest in the property or with the guardian of an owner concerning the damages sustained by the owner, the person seeking to acquire the property may file a complaint for that purpose with the clerk of the circuit court of the county where the property is located.

(b) The complaint must state the following:

(1) The name of the person seeking to acquire the property. This person shall be named as the plaintiff.

(2) The names of all owners, claimants to, and holders of liens on the property, if known, or a statement that they are unknown. These owners, claimants, and holders of liens shall be named as defendants.

(3) The use the plaintiff intends to make of the property or right sought to be acquired.

(4) If a right-of-way is sought, the location, general route, width, and the beginning and end points of the right-of-way.

(5) A specific description of each piece of property sought to be acquired and whether the property includes the whole or only part of the entire parcel or tract. If property is sought to be acquired by the state or by a county for a public highway or by a municipal corporation for a public use and the acquisition confers benefits on any other property of the owner, a specific description of each piece of property to which the plaintiff alleges the benefits will accrue. Plats of property alleged to be affected may accompany the descriptions.

(6) That the plaintiff has been unable to agree for the purchase of the property with the owner, owners, or guardians, as the case may be, or that the owner is mentally incompetent or less than eighteen (18) years of age and has no legally appointed guardian, or is a nonresident of Indiana.

(c) All parcels lying in the county and required for the same public use, whether owned by the same parties or not, may be included in the same or separate proceedings at the option of the plaintiff. However, the court may consolidate or separate the proceedings to suit the convenience of parties and the ends of justice. The filing of the complaint constitutes notice of proceedings to all subsequent purchasers and persons taking encumbrances of the property, who are bound by the notice. [P.L.2-2002, § 9.]

NOTES TO DECISIONS

ANALYSIS

Amendatory act.
—Effect.
Appeal.
Appraisers.
—Appointment.
—Disinterested.
Award of damages.
Burden of proof.
Cemetery associations.
Damages.
Description of land.
Description of lands to be taken.
Description of property right.
Efforts to purchase.
Electric companies.
Filing in open court.
Highway proceedings.
—Venue.
Interests in property.
Levee proceeding.

Nature of proceedings.
Necessity for taking.
Nonresidents.
Parties.
Presumption on appeal.
Questions to be determined.
Railroad companies.
Separate tracts of land.
Service on railroad agent.
Sufficiency in general.
Telephone companies.
Water companies.
Waiver of notice.

Amendatory Act.

—Effect.
The effect of the amendatory act was to broaden the Eminent Domain Act of 1905, and provide an orderly method of condemnation, where a court had a final voice as to what was just compensation for the property taken.

Amendatory Act. (Cont'd)

—Effect. (Cont'd)
City of Lebanon v. Public Serv. Co., 214 Ind. 295, 14 N.E.2d 719, appeal dismissed, 305 U.S. 558, 59 S. Ct. 84, 83 L. Ed. 352, rehearing denied, 305 U.S. 671, 59 S. Ct. 143, 83 L. Ed. 435 (1938).

Appeal.
While on appeal from a judgment dismissing a complaint in a condemnation action, the Supreme Court could not weigh the evidence to determine whether there was error in the court's decision that there was no necessity for the taking of the land, yet where it was undisputed that there had been a taking of a portion of land for a public purpose and that the remainder was necessary, there was no evidence to justify the court's decision and the judgment was reversed. Indianapolis Water Co. v. Lux, 224 Ind. 125, 64 N.E.2d 790 (1946).

Appraisers.

—Appointment.
Where issue was joined on electric power company's authority to take the fee of lands necessary to the carrying out of its objects, the trial court had jurisdiction to appoint appraisers to assess damages to landowners from the appropriation of the fee. Pingry v. Indiana Hydroelectric Power Co., 197 Ind. 426, 151 N.E. 226 (1926).

—Disinterested.
Fact that appraisers' report was prepared on stationery supplied by defendant's attorneys did not show that the appraisers were not disinterested. State v. Smith, 260 Ind. 555, 37 Ind. Dec. 325, 297 N.E.2d 809 (1973).

Award of Damages.
Award of damages for taking by condemnation made by a jury which was within the bounds of opinions given by witnesses was not reversed. Annee v. State, 256 Ind. 686, 26 Ind. Dec. 463, 271 N.E.2d 711, rehearing denied, 256 Ind. 691, 274 N.E.2d 260 (1971).

Burden of Proof.
Former IC 32-11-1-2 (repealed; see this section for similar provisions) placed the burden of proof on the condemnor to plead and, upon objection, to show that a good faith effort was made to purchase the property, but that the parties were unable to agree. City of Evansville ex rel. Dep't of Redevelopment v. Reising, 547 N.E.2d 1106 (Ind. App. 1989).

Cemetery Associations.
Where, in an action by a cemetery association to condemn real estate for cemetery purposes, the essential facts found were sufficient to entitle plaintiff to recover, a conclusion of law that the law was with the plaintiff was a sufficient basis for a judgment appointing appraisers. Young v. Bunnell Cem. Ass'n, 221 Ind. 173, 46 N.E.2d 825 (1943).

In an action by an imperfectly incorporated cemetery association, subsequently legalized by statute, to condemn real estate for cemetery purposes, allegations that the land was intended for use as a public cemetery and for public cemetery purposes were not conclusions and were sufficient under this section. Young v. Bunnell Cem. Ass'n, 221 Ind. 173, 46 N.E.2d 825 (1943).

In an action by an imperfectly incorporated cemetery association, subsequently legalized by statute, to condemn real estate for cemetery purposes, it was not necessary to set out in the complaint the statute under which it was sought to exercise the right of eminent domain. Young v. Bunnell Cem. Ass'n, 221 Ind. 173, 46 N.E.2d 825 (1943).

Damages.
The damages assessed and awarded by the appraisers, provided for in this section, were the compensation for the land taken. State v. Kraszyk, 240 Ind. 524, 167 N.E.2d 339 (1960).

Description of Land.
A notice by publication, omitting the county but giving the congressional township and range of the lands sought to have been condemned, was sufficient. Southern Ind. Ry. v. Indianapolis & L. Ry., 168 Ind. 360, 81 N.E. 65, 13 L.R.A. (n.s.) 197 (1907).

Description of Lands to Be Taken.
The application should have specifically described the lands taken. Indianapolis & V.R.R. v. Newsom, 54 Ind. 121 (1876); Midland Ry. v. Smith, 109 Ind. 488, 9 N.E. 474 (1886); Miller v. Southern Ind. Power Co., 184 Ind. 370, 111 N.E. 308 (1916).

Where land was described as bounded by a river, public highway or railroad, the description was sufficient. Cleveland v. Obenchain, 107 Ind. 591, 8 N.E. 624 (1886); McDonald v. Payne, 114 Ind. 359, 16 N.E. 795 (1888); Joliff v. Muncie Elec. Light Co., 181 Ind. 650, 105 N.E. 234 (1914).

The description of the land in the complaint was sufficient if it would have enabled one skilled in such matters to locate the land. Mull v. Indianapolis & Cincinnati Traction Co., 169 Ind. 214, 81 N.E. 657 (1907); Darrow v. Chicago, L.S. & S.B. Ry., 169 Ind. 99, 81 N.E. 1081 (1907); Joliff v. Muncie Elec. Light Co., 181 Ind. 650, 105 N.E. 234 (1914).

Description of Property Right.
Where a utility, seeking condemnation of another utility's property, failed to include a description of the franchise right affected in

Description of Property Right. (Cont'd)
its complaint, such failure to specify did not
evidence a defect in the good faith negotiation
required, as such franchise right was not
property for which the affected utility had a
right to compensation. Decatur County Rural
Elec. Membership Corp. v. Public Serv. Co.,
159 Ind. App. 346, 40 Ind. Dec. 604, 307
N.E.2d 96 (1974).

Where language in a condemnor's complaint did not contain criteria which would
enable a surveyor to determine the extent of
its rights to clear vegetation and other obstructions from the condemnees' lands adjoining a right-of-way, the complaint contained an
inadequate description of the right-of-way
and did not comply with this section.
Hagemeier v. Indiana & Mich. Elec. Co., 457
N.E.2d 590 (Ind. App. 1983).

Efforts to Purchase.
It should have been alleged in the complaint that the plaintiff had made efforts to
purchase the land sought to have been appropriated. Slider v. Indianapolis & Louisville
Traction Co., 42 Ind. App. 304, 85 N.E. 372,
reh'g overruled, 85 N.E. 372 (1908).

It was not error to sustain a demurrer to an
objection tendering the issue of inability to
agree for the purchase of the land, since such
issue was fully before the court under subdivision 6 of this section. Clinton Coal Co. v.
Chicago & E.I.R.R., 190 Ind. 465, 130 N.E.
798 (1921).

A power company which sought to condemn
a strip of land across a farm for the erection of
a transmission line was not required to pursue a route on a direct line from the starting
point to its terminal without deviation, but
could have made reasonable or necessary deviations. Guerrettaz v. Public Serv. Co., 227
Ind. 556, 87 N.E.2d 721 (1949).

An effort to purchase the property sought to
have been acquired was a condition precedent
to the right to maintain an action to condemn,
and the burden was on the condemnor to
show a good faith effort to purchase and an
inability to agree. Dahl v. Northern Ind. Pub.
Serv. Co., 239 Ind. 405, 157 N.E.2d 194
(1959).

A complaint which alleged that plaintiff
"has endeavored to purchase an easement for
a right of way" of the lands of the defendant
and "has been unable to agree with them for
the purchase thereof" was sufficient. Dahl v.
Northern Ind. Pub. Serv. Co., 239 Ind. 405,
157 N.E.2d 194 (1959).

Where the offer made by the appellee was
for the entire easement and no reply was
made thereto by any of the appellants, this
was sufficient to show that appellee was unable to agree with the appellants for the
purchase of the easement sought. Dahl v.

Northern Ind. Pub. Serv. Co., 239 Ind. 405,
157 N.E.2d 194 (1959).

Electric Companies.
It was not necessary for the complaint of an
electrical power transmission company to allege that lands sought to have been appropriated by it were not within an incorporated
city or town. Jones v. Indiana Power Co., 192
Ind. 67, 135 N.E. 332 (1922).

In a proceeding by a power company to
condemn a strip of land across a farm for the
erection of a transmission line, the burden
was upon the company to show clear legislative authority to appropriate the real estate
for the purpose named in the complaint.
Guerrettaz v. Public Serv. Co., 227 Ind. 556,
87 N.E.2d 721 (1949).

In a proceeding by a power company to
condemn a strip of land across a farm for the
erection of a transmission line, the complaint,
which specifically described the real estate
with its point of beginning, its course and
terminus, was not objectionable for failing to
state definitely where the line began or where
it ended. Guerrettaz v. Public Serv. Co., 227
Ind. 556, 87 N.E.2d 721 (1949).

Objection to failure of a franchised utility to
make the mortgagee of a rural electric membership corporation a party to a condemnation action brought by it against such mortgagor could have been made only by the
mortgagee itself and not by the mortgagor.
Kosciusko County Rural Elec. Membership
Corp. v. Northern Ind. Pub. Serv. Co., 248 Ind.
482, 11 Ind. Dec. 305, 229 N.E.2d 811 (1967).

Filing in Open Court.
Although the statute provided for filing the
complaint in the office of the clerk of the court,
it could have been filed in open court. Darrow
v. Chicago, L. S. & S.B. Ry., 169 Ind. 99, 81
N.E. 1081 (1907).

Highway Proceedings.

—Venue.
By analogy to the rule when the highway
commission was the moving party, venue of
action for damages for wrongfully taking land
for highway purposes was in the county
where the land was situated even though the
action was against the state highway commission. State v. Bragg, 207 Ind. 246, 192 N.E.
263 (1934).

Interests in Property.
The legislature did not intend that the
court separate the cause of action as to all the
various interests that might appear in the
various parcels of real estate. State v. Montgomery Circuit Court, 239 Ind. 337, 157
N.E.2d 577 (1959).

Levee Proceeding.

In a proceeding under this section by a township levee committee to condemn certain real estate for levee purposes, former IC 13-2-19-1 was held to vest in the levee committee the fullest discretion; and, if in its judgment the land sought to have been condemned was necessary for the repair, maintenance or protection of the levee, the committee had the power to condemn such land for such purpose. Hallett v. Calvert, 207 Ind. 25, 191 N.E. 77 (1934).

Nature of Proceedings.

Proceedings to condemn property in the exercise of the right of eminent domain were not, strictly speaking, civil actions, but were actions of a special character, based upon a statute by which they were authorized, in view of IC 8-1-2-1. City of Lebanon v. Public Serv. Co., 214 Ind. 295, 14 N.E.2d 719, appeal dismissed, 305 U.S. 558, 59 S. Ct. 84, 83 L. Ed. 352, rehearing denied, 305 U.S. 671, 59 S. Ct. 143, 83 L. Ed. 435 (1938).

Necessity for Taking.

The statute did not require the complaint to allege that there was a necessity for taking the land, but if it did, a general allegation that the land was necessary for the use of the plaintiff in its business was sufficient. Eckart v. Fort Wayne & N. Ind. Traction Co., 181 Ind. 352, 104 N.E. 762 (1914).

Nonresidents.

Publication of a notice for three successive weeks in a weekly newspaper was sufficient notice as to nonresidents, and the hearing could have been had at the end of five days after the last publication. Southern Ind. Ry. v. Indianapolis & L. Ry., 168 Ind. 360, 81 N.E. 65, 13 L.R.A. (n.s.) 197 (1907).

Nonresidents of the state were to have been given notice of the proceedings by publication. Gwinner v. Gary Connecting Rys., 182 Ind. 553, 103 N.E. 794 (1914).

Parties.

Failure of condemnor to name as a party the holder of a mineral lease on the condemned property was not a jurisdictional defect. Wyatt-Rauch Farms, Inc. v. Public Serv. Co., 160 Ind. App. 228, 42 Ind. Dec. 115, 311 N.E.2d 441 (1974).

Based upon the plain language of the statute, it appears that the legislature intended that only those record owners, as of the date of the filing of the complaint, should receive a copy of the summons and complaint; therefore, while the city could have elected to amend its complaint to include the new owner when it learned of the new owner's status as a subsequent purchaser, it was not required to

do so under the statute. MDM Invs. v. City of Carmel, 740 N.E.2d 929 (Ind. App. 2000).

Presumption on Appeal.

In a proceeding to condemn a public utility, which was appealed to the Supreme Court, such court was warranted in assuming, in the absence of some showing of fact, that the court appointed appraisers who were qualified as required by the statute. Southern Ind. Gas & Elec. Co. v. City of Boonville, 215 Ind. 552, 20 N.E.2d 648 (1939).

Questions to Be Determined.

A trial court is restricted in a condemnation proceeding to determining as objections to a taking: (1) Whether the proceedings are legal, (2) whether the department has the authority to condemn, (3) whether the property is being acquired for a private or public purpose, and (4) whether a condemnation is fraudulent, capricious or illegal. City of Evansville ex rel. Dep't of Redevelopment v. Reising, 547 N.E.2d 1106 (Ind. App. 1989).

A factual question as to whether an area is blighted cannot be raised in an eminent domain condemnation proceeding. Such questions relating to the factual situation upon which a declaratory resolution is based must be raised by remonstrance and appeal within the statutory framework provided by the legislature in the Redevelopment Act. City of Evansville ex rel. Dep't of Redevelopment v. Reising, 547 N.E.2d 1106 (Ind. App. 1989).

Railroad Companies.

A complaint by a railroad company for condemnation of a strip of land that belonged to another railroad company had to set out, by a specific description, the location, general route, width and termini of the proposed way. Southern Ind. Ry. v. Indianapolis & L. Ry., 168 Ind. 360, 81 N.E. 65, 13 L.R.A. (n.s.) 197 (1907).

The petitioner in a proceeding to condemn land for a railroad right-of-way was required to prove the averments of its petition, so far as to establish that it had the right to exercise the power of eminent domain for the use sought, without any answer being filed, and it was not error in such a proceeding for the court to overrule objections to the petition which were mere general denials of the facts alleged in the petition. Cottrell v. Chicago, T.H. & S.E. Ry., 192 Ind. 692, 138 N.E. 504 (1923).

The circuit court of a county had jurisdiction of proceedings to appropriate land therein for railroad right-of-way. Sisters of Providence v. Lower Vein Coal Co., 198 Ind. 645, 154 N.E. 659 (1926), overruled on other grounds, Joint County Park Bd. v. Stegemoller, 228 Ind. 118, 89 N.E.2d 720 (1950).

Railroad Companies. (Cont'd)

The owner of a right-of-way for an electric interurban railroad crossed by the proposed route of a lateral railroad was merely an owner of intervening lands concerning which neither allegation nor proof was required. Sisters of Providence v. Lower Vein Coal Co., 198 Ind. 645, 154 N.E. 659 (1926), overruled on other grounds, Joint County Park Bd. v. Stegemoller, 228 Ind. 118, 89 N.E.2d 720 (1950).

Separate Tracts of Land.

All lands in a county required for the same public use could have been included in the same proceedings, or separate proceedings could have been had for separate tracts. Vandalia Coal Co. v. Indianapolis & L. Ry., 168 Ind. 144, 79 N.E. 1082 (1907).

Service on Railroad Agent.

When the notice was served on the agent of a railroad company, the return of service should have stated that no officer of a higher grade could be found in the county. Southern Ind. Ry. v. Indianapolis & L. Ry., 168 Ind. 360, 81 N.E. 65, 13 L.R.A. (n.s.) 197 (1907).

Sufficiency in General.

Complaints under this section had to substantially comply with all of the provisions hereof. Morrison v. Indianapolis & W. Ry., 166 Ind. 511, 76 N.E. 961, 77 N.E. 744, 9 Ann. Cas. 587 (1906); Vandalia Coal Co. v. Indianapolis & L. Ry., 168 Ind. 144, 79 N.E. 1082 (1907); Slider v. Indianapolis & Louisville Traction Co., 42 Ind. App. 304, 85 N.E. 372, reh'g overruled, 85 N.E. 372 (1908).

Complaints which contain all the formal averments required by statute were sufficient. Sexauer v. Star Milling Co., 173 Ind. 342, 90 N.E. 474, 26 L.R.A. (n.s.) 609 (1910).

Telephone Companies.

Plaintiffs fulfilled their statutory obligation when they tendered to defendants a good faith offer to purchase easement. Defendant's failure to respond to the offer indicated a failure to agree on a purchase price, and the utilities thereafter instituted condemnation proceedings in accordance with statutory authority. Calumet Nat'l Bank v. AT & T Co., 647 N.E.2d 689 (Ind. App. 1995).

Water Companies.

Where, in an action by a water company to condemn land, there was evidence that the construction of a dam for the purpose of creating a reservoir raised the level of a stream approximately four and one-half feet where it flowed through defendants' land, and when the reservoir was full it permanently flooded a portion of such land and during the time of high water flooded a great part of the remainder, and that part of the land not flooded was necessary for a border around such reservoir, a necessity for the taking of the portion of the land not flooded was shown. Indianapolis Water Co. v. Lux, 224 Ind. 125, 64 N.E.2d 790 (1946).

Waiver of Notice.

Statutory notice as required by this section is not waived by entering a general appearance. Joint County Park Bd. v. Stegemoller, 228 Ind. 112, 89 N.E.2d 820 (1950).

Collateral References. Promissory statements of condemnor as to character of use or undertakings to be performed by it, propriety of pleading of. 7 A.L.R.2d 364.

Right of adjoining landowners to intervene in condemnation proceedings on ground that they might suffer consequential damages. 61 A.L.R.2d 1292.

Solid mineral royalty under mining lease as real or personal property for purpose of payment of damages in condemnation proceedings. 68 A.L.R.2d 728.

Right of lessee holding unexercised option to purchase the demised property to damages or compensation upon condemnation thereof. 85 A.L.R.2d 588.

Permissible modes of service of notice of proceedings. 89 A.L.R.2d 1404.

Inclusion or exclusion of first and last days in computing time for giving notice of eminent domain proceedings which must be given a certain number of days before a known future date. 98 A.L.R.2d 1331.

32-24-1-5. Offer to purchase property — Service of notice — Entry to restore services. — (a) As a condition precedent to filing a complaint in condemnation, and except for an action brought under IC 8-1-13-19 (repealed), a condemnor may enter upon the property as provided in this chapter and must, at least thirty (30) days before filing a complaint, make an offer to purchase the property in the form prescribed in subsection (c). The offer must be served personally or by certified mail upon:

(1) the owner of the property sought to be acquired; or

(2) the owner's designated representative.

(b) If the offer cannot be served personally or by certified mail, or if the owner or the owner's designated representative cannot be found, notice of the offer shall be given by publication in a newspaper of general circulation in the county in which the property is located or in the county where the owner was last known to reside. The notice must be in the following form:

NOTICE

TO: _____, _____ (owner(s)), _____ (condemnor) needs your property for a _____ _____ (description of project), and will need to acquire the following from you:

_____ (general description of the property to be acquired). We have made you a formal offer for this property that is now on file in the Clerk's Office in the _____ County Court House. Please pick up the offer. If you do not respond to this notice or accept the offer by _____ (a date 30 days from 1st date of publication) 20___, we shall file a suit to condemn the property.

_____

Condemnor

The condemnor must file the offer with the clerk of the circuit court with a supporting affidavit that diligent search has been made and that the owner cannot be found. The notice shall be published twice as follows:

(1) One (1) notice immediately.

(2) A subsequent publication at least seven (7) days and not more than twenty-one (21) days after the publication under subdivision (1).

(c) The offer to purchase must be in the following form:

UNIFORM PROPERTY OR EASEMENT
ACQUISITION OFFER

_____ (condemnor) is authorized by Indiana law to obtain your property or an easement across your property for certain public purposes. _____ (condemnor) needs (your property) (an easement across your property) for a _____ (brief description of the project) and needs to take _____ (legal description of the property or easement to be taken; the legal description may be made on a separate sheet and attached to this document if additional space is required) It is our opinion that the fair market value of the (property) (easement) we want to acquire from you is $_____, and, therefore, _____ (condemnor) offers you $_____ for the above described (property) (easement). You have twenty-five (25) days from this date to accept or reject this offer. If you accept this offer, you may expect payment in full within ninety (90) days after signing the documents accepting this offer and executing the easement, and provided there are no difficulties in clearing liens or other problems with title to land. Possession will be required thirty (30) days after you have received your payment in full.

HERE IS A BRIEF SUMMARY OF YOUR OPTIONS AND LEGALLY
PROTECTED RIGHTS:

    1. By law, _____ (condemnor) is required to make a good faith
effort to purchase (your property) (an easement across your property).

    2. You do not have to accept this offer.

    3. However, if you do not accept this offer, and we cannot come to an
agreement on the acquisition of (your property) (an easement),
_____ (condemnor) has the right to file suit to condemn and
acquire the (property) (easement) in the county in which the property is
located.

    4. You have the right to seek advice of an attorney, real estate
appraiser, or any other person of your choice on this matter.

    5. You may object to the public purpose and necessity of this project.

    6. If _____ (condemnor) files a suit to condemn and acquire
(your property) (an easement) and the court grants its request to
condemn, the court will then appoint three appraisers who will make an
independent appraisal of the (property) (easement) to be acquired.

    7. If we both agree with the court appraisers' report, then the matter is
settled. However, if either of us disagrees with the appraisers' report to
the court, either of us has the right to ask for a trial to decide what
should be paid to you for the (property) (easement) condemned.

    8. If the court appraisers' report is not accepted by either of us, then
_____ (condemnor) has the legal option of depositing the amount
of the court appraisers' evaluation with the court. And if such a deposit
is made with the court, _____ (condemnor) is legally entitled to
immediate possession of the (property) (easement). You may, subject to
the approval of the court, make withdrawals from the amount deposited
with the court. Your withdrawal will in no way affect the proceedings of
your case in court, except that, if the final judgment awarded you is less
than the withdrawal you have made from the amount deposited, you
will be required to pay back to the court the amount of the withdrawal
in excess of the amount of the final judgment.

    9. The trial will decide the full amount of damages you are to receive.
Both of us will be entitled to present legal evidence supporting our
opinions of the fair market value of the property or easement. The
court's decision may be more or less than this offer. You may employ, at
your cost, appraisers and attorneys to represent you at this time or at
any time during the course of the proceeding described in this notice.
(The condemnor may insert here any other information pertinent to this
offer or required by circumstances or law).

    10. If you have any questions concerning this matter you may contact
us at:

_____

_____

(full name, mailing and street address and phone of the condemnor)
This offer was made to the owner(s):

    _____ of _____,

    _____ of _____,

——————— of ——————,
——————— of ——————,
on the ——— day of ————— 20——,
                              BY:

————————————————————
                              (signature)

————————————————————
————   (printed name and title)
Agent of: ————————————————————
                              (condemnor)

If you decide to accept the offer of $———— made by ————
(condemnor) sign your name below and mail this form to the address
indicated above. An additional copy of this offer has been provided for
your file.

ACCEPTANCE OF OFFER

I (We), —————, ————, —————, owner(s) of the above
described property or interest in property, hereby accept the offer of
$———— made by ————— (condemnor) on this ———— day of
————, 20——.

————————————————————
————————————————————
————————————————————
————————————————————

NOTARY'S CERTIFICATE

STATE OF ————   )
)SS:
COUNTY OF ————   )
  Subscribed and sworn to before me this ———— day of ————, 20——.
My Commission Expires: —————

————————————————————
                              (Signature)

————————————————————
                              (Printed) NOTARY PUB-
                              LIC

(d) If the condemnor has a compelling need to enter upon property to
restore utility or transportation services interrupted by disaster or unforeseeable events, the provisions of subsections (a), (b), and (c) do not apply for
the purpose of restoration of utility or transportation services interrupted by
the disaster or unforeseeable events. However, the condemnor shall be
responsible to the property owner for all damages occasioned by the entry,
and the condemnor shall immediately vacate the property entered upon as
soon as utility or transportation services interrupted by the disaster or
unforeseeable event have been restored. [P.L.2-2002, § 9.]

NOTES TO DECISIONS

ANALYSIS

Application to state condemnations.
Fair market value.
Good faith.

Application to State Condemnations.

The provisions of former IC 32-41-1-3 (repealed; see this section for similar provisions) requiring a condemnor to make an offer based on the actual fair market value of the property as a condition precedent to condemnation, being the most recent expression of the legislature, superseded the earlier provision in former IC 32-11-1-9 (repealed; for similar provision see IC 32-24-1-13) relieving the state of the obligation to prove an offer to purchase. Decker v. State, 426 N.E.2d 151 (Ind. App. 1981).

Fair Market Value.

Evidence of the degree of acceptance of offers made to other landowners in the area which were based on the same schedules in no way indicated the fair market value of the property and could not establish a good faith

offer to purchase. Unger v. Indiana & Mich. Elec. Co., 420 N.E.2d 1250 (Ind. App. 1981).

This section did not require the condemnor to offer an irrefutable fair market value figure which would include all the damages as a precondition to the taking. Oxendine v. Public Serv. Co., 423 N.E.2d 612 (Ind. App. 1980).

Good Faith.

Where offer for easement through land was based on a schedule of a specified amount for a lineal foot plus another specified amount for each tower to be built, which schedule applied to all land in the area without taking into consideration the fair market value of the property, it was not a good faith offer as required by this section before bringing suit. Unger v. Indiana & Mich. Elec. Co., 420 N.E.2d 1250 (Ind. App. 1981).

Any condemnor, including the state, must have made a good faith offer to purchase in the particular manner described by former IC 32-24-1-3 (repealed; see this section for similar provisions) before attempting to exercise its eminent domain authority. Decker v. State, 426 N.E.2d 151 (Ind. App. 1981).

32-24-1-6. Notice of complaint. — (a) Upon the filing of a complaint under this chapter, the circuit court clerk shall issue a notice requiring the defendants to appear before the court on the day to be fixed by the plaintiff by indorsement on the complaint at the time of filing the complaint, and to show cause, if any, why the property sought to be condemned should not be acquired. The notice shall be substantially in the following form:

In the ＿＿＿＿＿＿ Court of Indiana.
To the Sheriff of ＿＿＿＿＿ County, Indiana:

You are hereby commanded to notify ＿＿＿＿＿＿, defendants, to appear before the ＿＿＿＿＿ Court of ＿＿＿＿＿ County, Indiana on the ＿＿＿ day of ＿＿＿, 20＿＿ , at ＿＿＿ o'clock, ＿＿ M. to show cause, if any, they have why the property sought to be acquired in the complaint of ＿＿＿＿＿＿ should not be acquired.

Witness my hand and the seal of the court affixed at ＿＿＿＿＿, Indiana, this ＿＿＿ day of ＿＿＿, 20＿＿.

Clerk of ＿＿＿＿＿ Court.

(b) The notice shall be served in the same manner as a summons is served in civil actions. Upon a showing by affidavit that any defendant is a nonresident of Indiana or that the defendant's name or residence is unknown, publication and proof of the notice may be made as provided in section 7 [IC 32-24-1-7] of this chapter. [P.L.2-2002, § 9.]

NOTES TO DECISIONS

ANALYSIS

Effect of notice.
Nonresidents.
Sufficiency.

Effect of Notice.

Persons not notified were not bound by the proceedings. Lane v. Miller, 17 Ind. 58 (1861); City of Ft. Wayne v. Fort Wayne & J.R.R., 149 Ind. 25, 48 N.E. 342 (1897).

The defendants were required to appear on the day named in the notice and show cause why the plaintiff had no right to condemn the land. Morrison v. Indianapolis & W. Ry., 166 Ind. 511, 76 N.E. 961, 77 N.E. 744, 9 Ann. Cas. 587 (1906).

The court, in condemnation proceedings, could retain jurisdiction obtained by service of statutory summons and notice, until rendition of final judgment. Sisters of Providence v. Lower Vein Coal Co., 198 Ind. 645, 154 N.E. 659 (1926), overruled on other grounds, Joint County Park Bd. v. Stegemoller, 228 Ind. 118, 89 N.E.2d 720 (1950).

Nonresidents.

Nonresidents of the state were to have been given notice of the proceedings by publication. Gwinner v. Gary Connecting Rys., 182 Ind. 553, 103 N.E. 794 (1914).

Sufficiency.

Notice in the form of civil summons to show cause for not condemning property was sufficient. Sisters of Providence v. Lower Vein Coal Co., 198 Ind. 645, 154 N.E. 659 (1926), overruled on other grounds, Joint County Park Bd. v. Stegemoller, 228 Ind. 118, 89 N.E.2d 720 (1950).

32-24-1-7. Proof of notice — Nonresident owners — Assessment of damages. — (a) The notice, upon its return, must show its:

(1) service for ten (10) days; or

(2) proof of publication for three (3) successive weeks in a weekly newspaper of general circulation printed and published in the English language in the county in which the property sought to be acquired is located.

The last publication of the notice must be five (5) days before the day set for the hearing.

(b) The clerk of the court in which the proceedings are pending, upon the first publication of the notice, shall send to the post office address of each nonresident owner whose property will be affected by the proceedings a copy of the notice, if the post office address of the owner or owners can be ascertained by inquiry at the office of the treasurer of the county.

(c) The court, being satisfied of the regularity of the proceedings and the right of the plaintiff to exercise the power of eminent domain for the use sought, shall appoint three (3) disinterested freeholders of the county to assess the damages, or the benefits and damages, as the case may be, that the owner or owners severally may sustain, or be entitled to, by reason of the acquisition. [P.L.2-2002, § 9.]

32-24-1-8. Objections to proceedings. — (a) A defendant may object to the proceedings:

(1) because the court does not have jurisdiction either of the subject matter or of the person;

(2) because the plaintiff does not have the right to exercise the power of eminent domain for the use sought; or

(3) for any other reason disclosed in the complaint or set up in the objections.

(b) Objections under subsection (a) must be:

(1) in writing;

(2) separately stated and numbered; and

(3) filed not later than the first appearance of the defendant.

(c) The court may not allow pleadings in the cause other than the complaint, any objections, and the written exceptions provided for in section 11 [IC 32-24-1-11] of this chapter. However, the court may permit amendments to the pleadings.

(d) If an objection is sustained, the plaintiff may amend the complaint or may appeal from the decision in the manner that appeals are taken from final judgments in civil actions. All the parties shall take notice and are bound by the judgment in an appeal.

(e) If the objections are overruled, the court shall appoint appraisers as provided for in this chapter. Any defendant may appeal the interlocutory order overruling the objections and appointing appraisers in the manner that appeals are taken from final judgments in civil actions upon filing with the circuit court clerk a bond:

(1) with the penalty that the court fixes;

(2) with sufficient surety;

(3) payable to the plaintiff; and

(4) conditioned for the diligent prosecution of the appeal and for the payment of the judgment and costs that may be affirmed and adjudged against the appellants.

The appeal bond must be filed not later than ten (10) days after the appointment of the appraisers.

(f) All the parties shall take notice of and be bound by the judgment in the appeal.

(g) The transcript must be filed in the office of the clerk of the supreme court not later than thirty (30) days after the filing of the appeal bond. The appeal does not stay proceedings in the cause. [P.L.2-2002, § 9.]

NOTES TO DECISIONS

ANALYSIS

In general.
Appeal.
—In general.
—Appraisers.
—Harmless error.
—Mandate.
—Order not stayed.
—Parties.
Appeal bond.
Applicability.
Authority of trial court.
Change of judge.
Construction.
Estoppel.
Federal courts.
Injunction.
Matters outside of issues.
Objections.
Order of condemnation.
Pleadings.
—In general.
—Amendments.
Separate and severable defenses.

Sustaining objections.
—Effect.

In General.

In an eminent domain proceeding by redevelopment commission of municipality, it was proper for the defendant to have determined the question of the motive for taking the property and whether the proceedings were in good faith or a subterfuge used to convey private property to a private individual for private use, and where to have such questions determined in the trial court was denied, the case would be reversed. Derloshon v. City of Fort Wayne ex rel. Dep't of Redevelopment, 250 Ind. 163, 13 Ind. Dec. 255, 234 N.E.2d 269 (1968); Hayden v. City of Fort Wayne ex rel. Dep't of Redevelopment, 250 Ind. 640, 14 Ind. Dec. 647, 238 N.E.2d 449 (1968).

A condemnation defendant may seek judicial review as to the legality of the proceedings and whether the condemning entity has the legal authority and right to condemn. City Chapel Evangelical Free Inc. v. City of South Bend, 744 N.E.2d 443 (Ind. 2001).

Appeal.

—In General.

Prior to the passage of this act, an appeal would not lie from an order appointing or refusing to appoint appraisers. Stoy v. Indiana Hydraulic Power Co., 166 Ind. 316, 76 N.E. 1057 (1906); Westport Stone Co. v. Thomas, 170 Ind. 91, 83 N.E. 617 (1908).

If a complaint were held insufficient on objections, an appeal could not have been taken when a final judgment was not rendered. Westport Stone Co. v. Thomas, 170 Ind. 91, 83 N.E. 617 (1908).

If appraisers were appointed, an appeal could have been taken from the action of the court appointing the appraisers and the right of the plaintiff to appropriate the land could have been tested on the appeal. Sexauer v. Star Milling Co., 173 Ind. 342, 90 N.E. 474, 26 L.R.A. (n.s.) 609 (1910).

Where the interlocutory order appointing appraisers was reversed, judgment after trial by jury on exceptions to report of appraisers had to be reversed. Western Union Tel. Co. v. Louisville & N.R.R., 185 Ind. 690, 114 N.E. 406 (1916).

The sustaining of a demurrer to a purported objection based upon a ground not specified by statute was not available error on appeal. Clinton Coal Co. v. Chicago & E.I.R.R., 190 Ind. 465, 130 N.E. 798 (1921).

The sufficiency of facts alleged in a complaint to constitute a cause of action could not have been questioned by an independent assignment of error on appeal. Jones v. Indiana Power Co., 192 Ind. 67, 135 N.E. 332 (1922).

The defendants in an eminent domain proceeding could appeal from the judgment of the court appointing appraisers and overruling objections to the taking of such action on the ground that plaintiff had no right to the exercise of such power for the use sought, and on the ground of want of jurisdiction. The court further held that this section was not repealed by § 2-3218 (since repealed; see now Rule AP. 4). Lowe v. Indiana Hydro-Electric Power Co., 194 Ind. 409, 143 N.E. 165 (1924).

In eminent domain proceedings, appeals by plaintiff were taken "in the manner that appeals are taken from final judgments in civil actions." Hallett v. Calvert, 207 Ind. 25, 191 N.E. 77 (1934).

An appeal from an order overruling a defendant's objections in an eminent domain proceeding was specifically authorized, but, except as to the time when the bond and transcript were to have been filed, the procedure was under the general statutes and rules relating to appeals, and not under those pertaining to interlocutory orders. Indiana Serv. Corp. v. Town of Flora, 218 Ind. 208, 31 N.E.2d 1015 (1941).

While the law looked with favor upon the right of litigants to have their cases reviewed, one who sought to take advantage of a method of appeal that was special in character and in derogation of the general regulations relating to that subject had to bring himself clearly within the proceeding which he undertook to invoke. Indiana Serv. Corp. v. Town of Flora, 218 Ind. 208, 31 N.E.2d 1015 (1941).

The school corporation Eminent Domain Act of 1907 supplemented but did not supersede or abrogate the general Eminent Domain Act of 1905, and objections and appeal from overruling thereof were authorized on the part of a holder of property already dedicated to a public use in an eminent domain action to condemn such property for school purposes. Cemetery Co. v. Warren Sch. Tp., 236 Ind. 171, 139 N.E.2d 538 (1957).

An order overruling objections to a condemnation is an interlocutory order, and the filing of an assignment of errors is the proper procedure in taking an appeal from such an order, and a motion to correct errors is not required. J.M. Foster Co. v. Northern Ind. Pub. Serv. Co., 164 Ind. App. 72, 46 Ind. Dec. 570, 326 N.E.2d 584 (1975).

An order overruling objections and appointing appraisers is interlocutory, and an appeal therefrom must be pursuant to the appellate rules governing interlocutory appeals rather than as provided in this section. Southern Ind. Rural Elec. Coop. v. Civil City of Tell City, 179 Ind. App. 217, 67 Ind. Dec. 117, 384 N.E.2d 1145 (1979).

The procedure for an appeal from an order overruling objections and appointing appraisers is governed by this section. The transcript should be accompanied with an assignment of errors specifying the errors relied upon. A Rule TR. 59 motion to correct errors is inappropriate, and the rules of appellate procedure applicable to interlocutory appeals apply concerning briefing deadlines and other matters. Frum v. Little Calumet River Basin Dev. Comm'n, 506 N.E.2d 492 (Ind. App. 1987).

—Appraisers.

The question whether the trial court should have appointed appraisers to assess damages resulting from the taking of plaintiff's land for highway purposes, was a question of fact, and the Supreme Court would not weigh the evidence to determine such question. State Hwy. Comm'n v. Sandbrink, 215 Ind. 71, 18 N.E.2d 382 (1939).

Orders appointing appraisers in condemnation proceedings were not embraced in Burns' § 2-3218 (since repealed; see now Rule AP. 4, authorizing appeals from specifically enumerated orders). Indiana Serv. Corp. v. Town of Flora, 218 Ind. 208, 31 N.E.2d 1015 (1941).

This section did not authorize an appeal from an order appointing appraisers, but that which was to have been reviewed by such

Appeal. (Cont'd)

—Appraisers. (Cont'd)
appeal was the decision sustaining the objections to the complaint and denying plaintiff's right to take the land. State v. Wood, 219 Ind. 424, 39 N.E.2d 448 (1942).

An action in which the trial court found that no objections to the complaint in condemnation had been filed and proceeded to appoint appraisers, to whose report exceptions were filed and pending, was not appealable under this section. Lake County Trust Co. v. Indiana Port Comm'n, 248 Ind. 362, 11 Ind. Dec. 133, 229 N.E.2d 457 (1967).

—Harmless Error.
An appeal could not have been taken from the overruling of objections to the complaint, as the ruling might have become harmless by reason of the court's refusing to appoint appraisers. Sexauer v. Star Milling Co., 173 Ind. 342, 90 N.E. 474, 26 L.R.A. (n.s.) 609 (1910).

Where evidence as to necessity of taking by interurban railroad company showed that the land was required for the convenient operation of the railroad, and disclosed nothing to warrant an inference that the land would have been used for any purpose other than a legitimate one, error in permitting a witness for the company to testify that in his opinion the condemnation was a necessity was harmless. Eckart v. Fort Wayne & N. Ind. Traction Co., 181 Ind. 352, 104 N.E. 762 (1914).

—Mandate.
Where, on appeal from a judgment in a condemnation proceeding, the Supreme Court declared that the judgment should have been reversed for the sole reason that the offer to purchase embraced only a portion of the property sought to be acquired, no mention having been made in the opinion as to the validity of the election authorizing the property's acquisition, and the lower court ordered the opinion and mandate spread of record and as a part of the same entry set aside its former order appointing appraisers, and adjudged that appellee's objections were in all things sustained, there was no basis for a contention that the mandate also adjudicated that the election was invalid. Flora v. Indiana Serv. Corp., 222 Ind. 253, 53 N.E.2d 161 (1944).

—Order Not Stayed.
The district court has no jurisdiction to stay and suspend a condemnation order pending an appeal. State ex rel. Ind. & Mich. Elec. Co. v. Sullivan Circuit Court, 456 N.E.2d 1019 (Ind. 1983).

—Parties.
When an appeal was taken from an interlocutory order appointing appraisers, all of the coparties of the appellant had to be made parties to the appeal. Lake Shore Sand Co. v. Lake Shore & M.S. Ry., 171 Ind. 457, 86 N.E. 754 (1908).

Under this statute, only the persons whose lands were about to be taken or whose interests therein were affected by the proceedings could appeal. State v. Wood, 219 Ind. 424, 39 N.E.2d 448 (1942).

The question as to whether the state had a statutory right to appeal from an interlocutory order appointing appraisers for the assessment of lands taken by the state for highway purposes was jurisdictional and could not have been waived. State v. Wood, 219 Ind. 424, 39 N.E.2d 448 (1942).

Appeal Bond.
Failure to file an appeal bond within the time limit prescribed by former IC 32-11-1-5 did not of itself require affirmance or dismissal on motion, as the statute was not jurisdictional but rather discretionary with the court since no appeal bond was necessary under Rule TR. 62 (D) (1) and former Rule AP. 6 (B) when the appeal was in the nature of an appeal from an interlocutory order and the appellee was not prejudiced by the late filing of the bond. Dzur v. Northern Ind. Pub. Serv. Co., 257 Ind. 674, 29 Ind. Dec. 233, 278 N.E.2d 563 (1972).

Where the transcript was not filed within the thirty-day period following the filing of the appeal bond, the court of appeals was without jurisdiction. Pouch v. Public Serv. Co., 165 Ind. App. 608, 48 Ind. Dec. 558, 333 N.E.2d 812 (1975).

That portion of this section which deals with the posting of bond is invalid since it is in direct contravention of Rule AP. 6, which provides that no appeal bond is necessary. Southern Ind. Rural Elec. Coop. v. Civil City of Tell City, 179 Ind. App. 217, 67 Ind. Dec. 117, 384 N.E.2d 1145 (1979).

Applicability.
This section applied only to regular condemnation proceedings and not to appeals by defendant-taker of land where land had already been taken and damages only were sought by plaintiff-landowner. Evansville-Vanderburgh Levee Auth. Dist. v. Towne Motel, Inc., 247 Ind. 161, 7 Ind. Dec. 475, 213 N.E.2d 705 (1966).

Authority of Trial Court.
In condemnation proceedings, the trial court had full authority under the statute to hear evidence and to grant full, true, and just compensation for all property taken. City of Lebanon v. Public Serv. Co., 214 Ind. 295, 14 N.E.2d 719, appeal dismissed, 305 U.S. 558, 59 S. Ct. 84, 83 L. Ed. 352, reh'g denied, 305 U.S. 671, 59 S. Ct. 143, 83 L. Ed. 435 (1938);

Authority of Trial Court. (Cont'd)
Public Serv. Co. v. City of Lebanon, 219 Ind.
62, 34 N.E.2d 20, 36 N.E.2d 852 (1941).

Change of Judge.
A motion for a change of judge in eminent
domain proceedings fell under IC 34-2-12-1
and was not a pleading which was not allowed
under this section. State ex rel. Indianapolis
Power & Light Co. v. Daviess Circuit Court,
246 Ind. 468, 5 Ind. Dec. 384, 206 N.E.2d 611
(1965), overruled, State ex rel. Chambers v.
Jefferson Circuit Court, 262 Ind. 337, 316
N.E.2d 353 (1974).

Construction.
The word "plaintiff" used in this section
referred to the state or corporation having the
sovereign power of eminent domain, and the
word "defendant" referred to the person
against whom the power was sought to have
been asserted. State v. Wood, 219 Ind. 424, 39
N.E.2d 448 (1942).
This statute was special in character, and
the party appealing thereunder had to bring
himself clearly within the procedure which he
undertook to invoke. State v. Wood, 219 Ind.
424, 39 N.E.2d 448 (1942).

Estoppel.
The owners of land, a part of which was
appropriated by the state highway commission for highway purposes, were not estopped
to maintain an action for appointment of
appraisers for assessment of damages caused
by the taking of the land for such purpose
where the state representatives undertook to
repair the injuries caused by the taking of
plaintiff's land, and promised to pay the landowner's damages caused by the taking of the
land, in view of former IC 32-11-1-12 (repealed; for similar provision see 32-24-1-16).
State Hwy. Comm'n v. Sandbrink, 215 Ind. 71,
18 N.E.2d 382 (1939).

Federal Courts.
In a proceeding by the United States to
condemn Indiana lands for use in connection
with a demonstration recreational project,
though the right of eminent domain had to be
exercised, as near as might be, in conformity
to the laws of this state, the federal conformity statutes were not intended to abrogate
the plain terms of the federal statute governing appeals, and the order of the district court
in overruling the landowner's objections to
the complaint and appointing appraisers was
not an order from which an appeal would lie
to the circuit court of appeals, though under
this section the order was an appealable one.
Dieckmann v. United States, 88 F.2d 902 (7th
Cir. 1937).

Injunction.
Where the defendant in a condemnation

action objected to the complaint and failed to
appeal upon his objections being overruled, he
could not raise the objections again by means
of a petition to enjoin the plaintiff from taking
the property. Thiesing Veneer Co. v. State, 254
Ind. 699, 23 Ind. Dec. 12, 262 N.E.2d 382
(1970).

Matters Outside of Issues.
The fact that a city seeking to condemn an
electric public service plant had contracted
with third persons for the purchase of bonds
to raise funds with which to pay for the utility
which it sought to condemn was of no concern
to the defendant utility. City of Lebanon v.
Public Serv. Co., 214 Ind. 295, 14 N.E.2d 719
(1938).
In a proceeding by city to condemn an
electric public utility plant serving the city,
under its power of eminent domain, it was a
matter of no concern to the utility that no
funds were appropriated, or that funds were
not available to pay for the property sought to
have been taken, when taken. City of Lebanon v. Public Serv. Co., 214 Ind. 295, 14
N.E.2d 719 (1938).

Objections.
Objections to the appropriation of land
could have been filed after the day named in
the summons for the defendants to have appeared. Morrison v. Indianapolis & W. Ry., 166
Ind. 511, 76 N.E. 961, 77 N.E. 744, 9 Ann. Cas.
587 (1906).
If objections to a complaint to condemn land
set up facts to defeat the right of the plaintiff
to condemn, such objections were regarded as
a plea or answer and could have been tested
by a demurrer. Toledo & Ind. Traction Co. v.
Indiana & C. I. Ry., 171 Ind. 213, 86 N.E. 54
(1908).
Objections filed to a complaint in condemnation proceedings were regarded as a demurrer insofar as they were directed to the
face of the complaint. Toledo & Ind. Traction
Co. v. Indiana & C. I. Ry., 171 Ind. 213, 86
N.E. 54 (1908).
All objections to complaints in proceedings
to appropriate lands had to be in writing and
point out specifically the objections made, and
a general denial of the allegations of the
complaint did not raise any issue. Westport
Stone Co. v. Thomas, 175 Ind. 319, 94 N.E.
406, 35 L.R.A. (n.s.) 646 (1911); Joliff v.
Muncie Elec. Light Co., 181 Ind. 650, 105 N.E.
234 (1914); Miller v. Southern Ind. Power Co.,
184 Ind. 370, 111 N.E. 308 (1916).
Objections filed to a complaint in condemnation proceedings could tender issues of law
or fact, but a single objection could not have
been used for both purposes. Miller v. Southern Ind. Power Co., 184 Ind. 370, 111 N.E. 308
(1916).
In a proceeding by a railroad company to

Objections. (Cont'd)

condemn land for a right-of-way, it was not error to overrule objections merely denying petitioner's right under the law or merely denying facts alleged in the petition. Cottrell v. Chicago, T.H. & S.E. Ry., 192 Ind. 692, 138 N.E. 504 (1923).

This section made provision for objection to eminent domain proceedings on account of lack of jurisdiction either of the subject matter or person, or because plaintiff had no right to exercise the power of eminent domain for the use sought, or for any other reason disclosed in the complaint or set up in such objections, and contemplated that causes which would have ordinarily constituted grounds for plea in abatement, demurrer, or answer, could have been presented in objections authorized by said section. Root v. State, 207 Ind. 312, 192 N.E. 447 (1934); Guerrettaz v. Public Serv. Co., 227 Ind. 556, 87 N.E.2d 721 (1949); Joint County Park Bd. v. Stegemoller, 228 Ind. 103, 88 N.E.2d 686 (1949), reh'g denied, 228 Ind. 118, 89 N.E.2d 720 (1950).

Since the objection contemplated by this section could serve the purpose of an answer or demurrer, or both, the objectors could introduce evidence in support of the allegations in their objections. Reuter v. Milan Water Co., 209 Ind. 240, 198 N.E. 442 (1935), overruled on other grounds, Joint County Park Bd. v. Stegemoller, 228 Ind. 118, 89 N.E.2d 720 (1950).

Where defendants appeared and filed objections that the court had no jurisdiction of the persons of the defendants, which objection served the purpose of a demurrer or answer or both, and did not move to quash the service of summons, on special appearance for that purpose, they thereby waived such objection. Reuter v. Milan Water Co., 209 Ind. 240, 198 N.E. 442 (1935), overruled on other grounds, Joint County Park Bd. v. Stegemoller, 228 Ind. 118, 89 N.E.2d 720 (1950).

Where, in a condemnation proceeding, the only question adjudicated was that the property was not necessary for the purpose for which it was sought to be condemned, all matters in the complaint not objected to, except the right of the petitioner to exercise the power of eminent domain for the use sought or taken, were admitted unless objected to. Indianapolis Water Co. v. Lux, 224 Ind. 125, 64 N.E.2d 790 (1946).

Where objections to the complaint denied that a joint county park board had been legally created and that it had power of eminent domain, but no facts were stated, the sustaining of the objections, treated as a demurrer, was error. Joint County Park Bd. v. Stegemoller, 228 Ind. 103, 88 N.E.2d 686 (1949), reh'g denied, 228 Ind. 118, 89 N.E.2d 720 (1950).

Under this section, statutory objections are to have been either demurrers or answers, but the same objection could not serve as both a demurrer and an answer. State ex rel. Joint County Park Bd. v. Verbarg, 228 Ind. 280, 91 N.E.2d 916 (1950).

A utility could not condemn a right-of-way over land for which it had no immediate plans for use solely on speculation for possible use in the future. Country Estates, Inc. v. Northern Ind. Pub. Serv. Co., 254 Ind. 108, 21 Ind. Dec. 275, 258 N.E.2d 54 (1970); Meyer v. Northern Ind. Pub. Serv. Co., 254 Ind. 112, 21 Ind. Dec. 278, 258 N.E.2d 57 (1970).

One of the objections made to the jurisdiction of the court may be that the condemnor failed to make a good faith effort to purchase. Unger v. Indiana & Mich. Elec. Co., 420 N.E.2d 1250 (Ind. App. 1981).

A trial court is restricted in a condemnation proceeding to determining as objections to a taking: (1) whether the proceedings are legal, (2) whether the department has the authority to condemn, (3) whether the property is being acquired for a private or public purpose, and (4) whether a condemnation is fraudulent, capricious or illegal. City of Evansville ex rel. Dep't of Redevelopment v. Reising, 547 N.E.2d 1106 (Ind. App. 1989).

Where landowner did not file any objections to the proceedings until her filing of pleadings, long after her first appearance, the trial court did not err in striking her pleadings that were not allowed under the eminent domain statute. Maharis v. Orange County, 685 N.E.2d 1131 (Ind. App. 1997).

An answer to a complaint for appropriation of real estate was improper where the answer merely denied that the land was necessary for the improvements set forth in the complaint, but failed to indicate with any particularity and reason why the property was not necessary. State v. Collom, 720 N.E.2d 737 (Ind. App. 1999).

Order of Condemnation.

An order for condemnation is an interlocutory order and need not contain a legal description of the property. Wyatt-Rauch Farms, Inc. v. Public Serv. Co., 160 Ind. App. 228, 42 Ind. Dec. 115, 311 N.E.2d 441 (1974).

Pleadings.

—In General.

Civil code could have been resorted to in matters of practice. Great W. Natural Gas & Oil Co. v. Hawkins, 30 Ind. App. 557, 66 N.E. 765 (1903).

Defendants could show cause why the plaintiff had no right to appropriate land before appraisers were appointed. Morrison v. Indianapolis & W. Ry., 166 Ind. 511, 76 N.E. 961, 77 N.E. 744, 9 Ann. Cas. 587 (1906);

Pleadings. (Cont'd)

—In General. (Cont'd)
Vandalia Coal Co. v. Indianapolis & L. Ry., 168 Ind. 144, 79 N.E. 1082 (1907).

No pleadings could have been filed by the defendant other than the written objections provided for in this section. Vandalia Coal Co. v. Indianapolis & L. Ry., 168 Ind. 144, 79 N.E. 1082 (1907).

Pleadings could have been amended by leave of court as in ordinary civil actions. Darrow v. Chicago, L.S. & S.B. Ry., 169 Ind. 99, 81 N.E. 1081 (1907).

Proceedings under this statute were summary in nature until the question of damages was reached, and the provisions of the code as to trial by jury and change of venue from the county were not applicable. Matlock v. Bloomington Water Co., 196 Ind. 271, 146 N.E. 852, reh'g overruled, 198 N.E. 280, 148 N.E. 198 (1925).

If proceeding was dismissed, the landowner was not entitled to recover incidental costs or damages. Howard v. Illinois Cent. R.R., 64 F.2d 267 (7th Cir. 1933).

It was not competent to allege, in defense of a proceeding to condemn property under the power of eminent domain, that the plaintiff would apply it to a use different from that for which it was being appropriated. Sisters of Providence v. Lower Vein Coal Co., 198 Ind. 645, 154 N.E. 659 (1926), overruled on other grounds, Joint County Park Bd. v. Stegemoller, 228 Ind. 118, 89 N.E.2d 720 (1950).

This act set out clearly and completely the procedure that was to be followed in condemnation proceedings under the power of eminent domain. Dyar v. Albright Cem. Ass'n, 199 Ind. 431, 157 N.E. 545 (1927), overruled on other grounds, Joint County Park Bd. v. Stegemoller, 228 Ind. 118, 89 N.E.2d 720 (1950).

—Amendments.
Amendments under former IC 32-11-1-6 (repealed; see this section for similar provisions) were proper only when necessary to make the complaint conform to the evidence. Continental Enters., Inc. v. Cain, 180 Ind. App. 106, 68 Ind. Dec. 366, 387 N.E.2d 86 (1979).

In action to obtain easement over the land of another, it was not error for trial court to deny plaintiff the right to amend pleading to allege a public purpose and to have title to easement vested in county where court denied motion on ground that evidence of public purpose had been taken into consideration when it made its finding that the easement sought was for a private purpose. Continental Enters., Inc. v. Cain, 180 Ind. App. 106, 68 Ind. Dec. 366, 387 N.E.2d 86 (1979).

Separate and Severable Defenses.
If, on appeal from the decisions of the court sustaining the objections to a complaint seeking to condemn real estate and denying plaintiff's right to take the land, the decision was sustained, the case was ended, but if it was reversed, appraisers were appointed, and the cause proceeded to final judgment from which either party could have appealed. State v. Wood, 219 Ind. 424, 39 N.E.2d 448 (1942).

In condemnation proceedings, separate and severable defenses could have been joined in written objections, any one of which, if well taken and established, was a sufficient answer to the complaint. Flora v. Indiana Serv. Corp., 222 Ind. 253, 53 N.E.2d 161 (1944).

Sustaining Objections.

—Effect.
In condemnation proceedings, where objections filed to the complaint went mostly to questions of fact, the sustaining of the objections had the same legal effect as the sustaining of a demurrer to the complaint in a civil action, in view of former IC 32-11-1-8. City of Lebanon v. Public Serv. Co., 214 Ind. 295, 14 N.E.2d 719, appeal dismissed, 305 U.S. 558, 59 S. Ct. 84, 83 L. Ed. 752, reh'g denied, 305 U.S. 671, 59 S. Ct. 143, 83 L. Ed. 435 (1938).

32-24-1-9. Appraisers — Oath — Duties. — (a) Each appraiser shall take an oath that:

(1) the appraiser has no interest in the matter; and

(2) the appraiser will honestly and impartially make the assessment.

(b) After the appraisers are sworn as provided in subsection (a), the judge shall instruct the appraisers as to:

(1) their duties as appraisers; and

(2) the measure of the damages and benefits, if any, they allow.

(c) The appraisers shall determine and report all of the following:

(1) The fair market value of each parcel of property sought to be acquired and the value of each separate estate or interest in the property.

(2) The fair market value of all improvements pertaining to the property, if any, on the portion of the property to be acquired.

(3) The damages, if any, to the residue of the property of the owner or owners caused by taking out the part sought to be acquired.

(4) The other damages, if any, that will result to any persons from the construction of the improvements in the manner proposed by the plaintiff.

(d) If the property is sought to be acquired by the state or by a county for a public highway or a municipal corporation for a public use that confers benefits on any property of the owner, the report must also state the benefits that will accrue to each parcel of property, set opposite the description of each parcel of property whether described in the complaint or not.

(e) Except as provided in subsection (f), in estimating the damages specified in subsection (c), the appraisers may not deduct for any benefits that may result from the improvement.

(f) In the case of a condemnation by the state or by a county for a public highway or a municipal corporation for public use, the appraisers shall deduct any benefits assessed from the amount of damage allowed, if any, under subsection (c)(3) and (c)(4) and the difference, if any, plus the damages allowed under subsection (c)(1) and (c)(2) shall be the amount of the award. However, the damages awarded may not be less than the damages allowed under subsection (c)(1) and (c)(2). Upon the trial of exceptions to the award by either party, a like measure of damages must be followed.

(g) For the purpose of assessing compensation and damages, the right to compensation and damages is considered to have accrued as of the date of the service of the notice provided in section 6 [IC 32-24-1-6] of this chapter, and actual value of compensation and damages at that date shall be:

(1) the measure of compensation for all property to be actually acquired; and

(2) the basis of damages to property not actually acquired but injuriously affected;

except as to the damages stated in subsection (c)(4). [P.L.2-2002, § 9.]

NOTES TO DECISIONS

Value of property.
—Evidence.
—Future value.
—Partial taking.

In General.

The appraisers should have taken into consideration and assessed all damages, both direct and consequential, which the landowner would have sustained from the appropriation of the property described in the complaint. Vandalia Coal Co. v. Indianapolis & L.Ry., 168 Ind. 144, 79 N.E. 1082 (1907).

In condemnation proceedings, the true measure of damages for land having a market value when appropriated was the fair market value for which the land could have been sold if the owner was willing to sell. Alberson Cem. Ass'n v. Fuhrer, 192 Ind. 606, 137 N.E. 545 (1923).

In a proceeding to condemn land for highway purposes, testimony showing the value of land, a small part of which was taken for highway purposes with improved road constructed through it, and the value of the tract before such construction, was incompetent. State v. Brubeck, 204 Ind. 1, 170 N.E. 81 (1930).

Testimony offered to show market value of land, before and after the appropriation, was properly excluded. State v. Reid, 204 Ind. 631, 185 N.E. 449, 86 A.L.R. 1442 (1933).

The measure of damages was the difference between the value of the whole tract before the taking and the value of the remainder, irrespective of any benefits conferred by the appropriation. State v. Reid, 204 Ind. 631, 185 N.E. 449, 86 A.L.R. 1442 (1933).

Constitutionality.

This section, construed as excluding consideration of benefits in determining the amount of compensation to have been paid for taking land for state highway, did not violate Ind. Const., Art. 1, § 21, requiring payment of just compensation. State v. Reid, 204 Ind. 631, 185 N.E. 449, 86 A.L.R. 1442 (1933).

Apportionment of Interests.

The appraisers must not only appraise the entire plot of ground, but where there are several interests therein, the appraisers must also apportion such interests, but an appraisal without such apportionment can be invalidated only by a proper plea. Best Realty Corp. v. State, 74 Ind. Dec. 435, 400 N.E.2d 1204 (Ind. App. 1980).

Assessment of Damages.

Damages in an eminent domain proceeding must be assessed at the time of the taking. City of Elkhart v. No-Bi Corp., 428 N.E.2d 43 (Ind. App. 1981).

Where there are no limitations on the mode of construction, damages will be assessed based on a lawful and non-negligent mode of construction most injurious to the condemnee. City of Elkhart v. No-Bi Corp., 428 N.E.2d 43 (Ind. App. 1981).

Cemetery Lots.

In determining the value of cemetery lots taken, it was proper to base such value on the net sales price of lots already sold in the affected area and on the net sales price of similar burial lots in other sections of the cemetery. State v. Lincoln Memory Gardens, Inc., 242 Ind. 206, 177 N.E.2d 655 (1961).

Compensation.

—Items Included.

This act as amended authorized the court to require additional investment and expenditures to have been included in the compensation. City of Lebanon v. Public Serv. Co., 214 Ind. 295, 14 N.E.2d 719, appeal dismissed, 305 U.S. 558, 59 S. Ct. 84, 83 L. Ed. 352, reh'g denied, 305 U.S. 671, 59 S. Ct. 143, 83 L. Ed. 435 (1938).

In an action by the state to condemn real estate for the purpose of widening, and in some places, changing, the right-of-way of a highway which ran through defendants' farm, it was proper for defendants to show, as an element of damage, that the improvement caused surface water to have been collected from a portion of land and to have been precipitated onto the remaining portion. State v. Ahaus, 223 Ind. 629, 63 N.E.2d 199 (1945).

In an action by the state to condemn real estate for the purpose of widening, and in certain places, changing, the right-of-way of a highway, every element of damage which would naturally and ordinarily result from the taking could have been considered in arriving at the amount of damages to have been awarded. State v. Ahaus, 223 Ind. 629, 63 N.E.2d 199 (1945).

The general rules as to the measure of damages, where all or a part of a tract of land was taken for widening a highway, were the same as in other cases where property was taken or damaged for a public use. State v. Ahaus, 223 Ind. 629, 63 N.E.2d 199 (1945).

In an action by the state to condemn real estate for the purpose of widening, and in some places, changing, the right-of-way of a highway which ran through defendants' farm, an instruction drawn on the theory of the accumulation of surface water and of the unlawful diversion of it onto land of another was not harmful to plaintiff, even though the evidence disclosed that the improvement caused the water to be collected from a portion of defendants' land and to be precipitated onto the remaining portion, since the changing of the flow of surface water could be considered as an element of damage. State v. Ahaus, 223 Ind. 629, 63 N.E.2d 199 (1945).

Compensation. (Cont'd)

—Items Included. (Cont'd)

Where, in a condemnation proceeding, there was no evidence as to what, if any, benefits from the improvements were conferred upon any lands involved which were not condemned, it was proper to refuse to give requested instructions that the benefits conferred, if any, to the residue of the lands could be considered as determining the question of compensatory damages. State v. Stabb, 226 Ind. 319, 79 N.E.2d 392 (1948), overruled on other grounds, State v. Heslar, 257 Ind. 307, 274 N.E.2d 261, 27 Ind. Dec. 377 (1971).

The alleged impairment of property owner's easement of ingress and egress caused by a divider strip in the center of a newly constructed highway was not caused by the condemnation and taking of land since it was taken in order to widen the highway. State v. Ensley, 240 Ind. 472, 164 N.E.2d 342 (1960).

The principle of substitution, that is, the price for which other property could be obtained for the same purpose, was not an element to have been considered in the assessment of damages in eminent domain proceedings. State v. Lincoln Memory Gardens, Inc., 242 Ind. 206, 177 N.E.2d 655 (1961).

Evidence of the cost of constructing a drive so as to have access to part of parcel of land left after condemnation proceedings was proper in assessment of damages. Crumpacker v. State, 266 Ind. 1, 26 Ind. Dec. 439, 271 N.E.2d 716 (1971).

Moving and relocation expenses were not a part of just compensation within the meaning of this section. Cheathem v. City of Evansville, 151 Ind. App. 181, 29 Ind. Dec. 251, 278 N.E.2d 602 (1972), cert. denied, 410 U.S. 966, 93 S. Ct. 1442, 35 L. Ed. 2d 700 (1973). But see State v. Rankin, 260 Ind. 228, 294 N.E.2d 604 (1973).

Although the owner of property abutting on a public highway has an easement of egress and ingress which cannot be substantially or materially interfered with or taken away without just compensation, where the impairment of access was caused not by the condemnation of a part of the property but by the construction of a median strip which diverted traffic, the property owner had no property right in the free flow of traffic and could claim no compensation for the fact that traffic was diverted or made to travel a more circuitous route. State v. Cheris, 153 Ind. App. 451, 33 Ind. Dec. 39, 287 N.E.2d 777 (1972); Cheathem v. City of Evansville, 151 Ind. App. 181, 29 Ind. Dec. 251, 278 N.E.2d 602 (1972), cert. denied, 410 U.S. 966, 93 S. Ct. 1442, 35 L. Ed. 2d 700 (1973).

In determining the appropriate amount of damages in an eminent domain action, all of the landowner's interest is compensable, including the rights of ingress, egress, and air space. Southern Ind. Gas & Elec. Co. v. Russell, 451 N.E.2d 673 (Ind. App. 1983).

Consequential Damages.

In an action by the state to condemn real estate for purpose of construction of a limited access highway, there could have been no award in conformity to a claim concerning "such other damages" from the construction of the improvement in the manner proposed by the plaintiff, pursuant to this section, as evidence was inadmissible which went to loss of profit when the whole tract was taken, as was evidence as to damages for destruction of property inadmissible. State v. Heslar, 257 Ind. 307, 27 Ind. Dec. 377, 274 N.E.2d 261 (1971), reh'g denied, 257 Ind. 625, 277 N.E.2d 796 (1972).

Construction.

Evidence as to the value of a business being conducted on land condemned was not admissible where there was only one owner whose property was being taken. Elson v. City of Indianapolis ex rel. Dep't of Redevelopment, 246 Ind. 337, 4 Ind. Dec. 652, 204 N.E.2d 857 (1965).

Deduction for Benefits.

Benefits accruing from the construction of railroads could not have been considered in assessing damages. Evansville, I. & C. S.L.R.R. v. Fitzpatrick, 10 Ind. 120 (1858); White Water Valley R.R. v. McClure, 29 Ind. 536 (1868); Chicago, I. & E. Ry. v. Curless, 27 Ind. App. 306, 60 N.E. 467 (1901); Chicago, I. & E.R.R. v. Winslow, 27 Ind. App. 316, 60 N.E. 466 (1901); Indianapolis N. Traction Co. v. Dunn, 37 Ind. App. 248, 76 N.E. 269 (1905); Union Traction Co. v. Pfeil, 39 Ind. App. 51, 78 N.E. 1052 (1906); Cleveland, C., C. & St. L. Ry. v. Smith, 192 Ind. 674, 138 N.E. 347 (1923); Sisters of Providence v. Lower Vein Coal Co., 198 Ind. 645, 154 N.E. 659 (1926), overruled on other grounds, Joint County Park Bd. v. Stegemoller, 228 Ind. 118, 89 N.E.2d 720 (1950).

Where part of plaintiff's property was condemned for highway construction, his sale of fill dirt from the residual property to the highway contractors did not constitute a special benefit such as could be considered and used as a setoff against damages to the residual land, since at the time he was served with notice of condemnation he had no substantial expectation that the residual property could in any way profit and had no agreement with the contractors that they should buy fill dirt from him. State v. Zehner, 175 Ind. App. 94, 60 Ind. Dec. 105, 369 N.E.2d 1103 (1977).

Defendants Withdrawing Claims.

In an eminent domain case, a defendant

**Defendants Withdrawing
   Claims.** (Cont'd)
could withdraw his claim for damages to the
residue and other damages and thus prevent
the state from introducing evidence of benefits resulting to the remaining land because, if
no claim was made for damages to the remaining land, the state had no right under
the statute to show that the value of such
remaining land was enhanced. State v. Furry,
252 Ind. 486, 18 Ind. Dec. 413, 250 N.E.2d 590
(1969).

Elements of Damages.
In condemnation suit for a highway, of city
land to be used for a sewage disposal system,
damages sustained to engineering and plans
which were in esse at the time of taking were
proper, but damages concerning extension of
the water main, increased diameter of water
main, bends around bridge foundation, and
highway permits were not proper elements of
damage. State v. City of Terre Haute, 250 Ind.
613, 14 Ind. Dec. 584, 238 N.E.2d 459 (1968).

One could not recover damages for intended
use to arise in the future. State v. City of Terre
Haute, 250 Ind. 613, 14 Ind. Dec. 584, 238
N.E.2d 459 (1968).

In an action by the state to condemn real
estate for purpose of construction of a limited
access highway, there could have been no
award pursuant to this section other than to
recompense a person for damages resulting
from the method of construction in a physical
sense. State v. Heslar, 257 Ind. 307, 27 Ind.
Dec. 377, 274 N.E.2d 261 (1971), reh'g denied,
257 Ind. 625, 277 N.E.2d 796 (1972).

In an action by the state to condemn real
estate for the purpose of construction of a
limited access highway, every element of damage which would naturally have resulted
should have been determined and reported in
arriving at the amounts of damages to have
been awarded in conformity to the provisions
of this section. State v. Heslar, 257 Ind. 307,
27 Ind. Dec. 377, 274 N.E.2d 261 (1971), reh'g
denied, 257 Ind. 625, 277 N.E.2d 796 (1972).

In eminent domain cases, the measure of
damages is the fair market value of the property at the time of taking. State v. Church of
Nazarene, 268 Ind. 523, 63 Ind. Dec. 38, 377
N.E.2d 607 (1978).

In order for the church to have been justly
compensated, the state had to respond in
damages for not only the market value of the
strip of land which was appropriated, but also
for damages resulting to the residue of the
property of the church, and as there was
simultaneous unity of title, unity of use, and
contiguity, the church was entitled to severance damages, the essence of which is the loss
in value to the remainder tract by reason of a
partial taking of land. State v. Church of

Nazarene, 268 Ind. 523, 63 Ind. Dec. 38, 377
N.E.2d 607 (1978).

The valuation of tract of land by witness
according to its value as building lots, although the land at that time was a single
tract, was not improper provided such utiliza-
tion of the tract could be made without en-
countering development expenses and there
would be no capital, skill, profit or other
elements involved in a sale for such purpose.
State v. Church of Nazarene, 268 Ind. 523, 63
Ind. Dec. 38, 377 N.E.2d 607 (1978).

When land which is taken by condemnation
has a fair market value at the time of its
appropriation, the measure of damages is the
fair market value for which the land could be
sold if the owner were willing to sell and a
buyer willing to buy, neither under compul-
sion to do so. City of Lafayette v. Beeler, 178
Ind. App. 281, 65 Ind. Dec. 423, 381 N.E.2d
1287 (1978).

A condemnee may be compensated for all
present and prospective damages which are
the natural and reasonable result of the taking. City of Elkhart v. No-Bi Corp., 428 N.E.2d
43 (Ind. App. 1981).

An owner cannot recover damages for an
intended specific use of property to arise in
the future, but this rule applies only to uses
not in esse at the time of the taking, so that
where property was already used as a warehouse, this use was in esse and was an intended specific future use only in the sense
that it would be used as a warehouse after the
taking as well as before, and since the property was used as a warehouse at the time of
the taking, any evidence of its future use as a
warehouse was not barred as evidence of an
intended specific future use. City of Elkhart v.
No-Bi Corp., 428 N.E.2d 43 (Ind. App. 1981).

Lost farming profits could not be considered
as an element of damages in condemnation
proceeding based on taking of agricultural
property. Town of Newburgh v. Pecka, 609
N.E.2d 1152 (Ind. App. 1993).

Because the landowners suffered damages
due to the closure of the city street that were
a natural or reasonable incident to the improvements to be made by the city, the landowners were entitled to present evidence with
regard to those damages and to have them
assessed in the condemnation case. The landowners were not required to institute and
maintain a separate action for inverse condemnation in order to recover damages for the
closure of the street. City of Hammond v.
Marina Entertainment Complex, Inc., 733
N.E.2d 958 (Ind. App. 2000).

Highway Proceedings.
When condemning land for highway purposes, the state was not a "municipal corporation" entitled to deduct benefits resulting
from the improvements, in assessing dam-

Highway Proceedings. (Cont'd)

ages. State v. Brubeck, 204 Ind. 1, 170 N.E. 81 (1930); State v. Reid, 204 Ind. 631, 185 N.E. 449, 86 A.L.R. 1442 (1933).

In a proceeding to condemn land for state highway, the measure of damages was the difference between the value of whole tract before taking and the value of the remainder, irrespective of benefits conferred by the appropriation, in view of this section, and Ind. Const., Art. 1, § 21. State v. Reid, 204 Ind. 631, 185 N.E. 449, 86 A.L.R. 1442 (1933).

In a proceeding to condemn land for state highways, the amount of damages could not have been measured by determining and comparing market values before and after the taking, since that would have permitted consideration of benefits, contrary to this section. State v. Reid, 204 Ind. 631, 185 N.E. 449, 86 A.L.R. 1442 (1933).

Improvements by Condemnor.

If proceedings were had against a person not the owner of the land, and the condemnor made improvements on the land, such improvements were not to have been considered as a part of the land in subsequent condemnation proceedings against the owner of the land. McClarren v. Jefferson Sch. Tp., 169 Ind. 140, 82 N.E. 73, 13 L.R.A. (n.s.) 417, 13 Ann. Cas. 978 (1907).

Instructions to Appraisers.

This section does not require that the appraisers be instructed "in writing." State v. Smith, 260 Ind. 555, 37 Ind. Dec. 325, 297 N.E.2d 809 (1973).

Interlocutory Orders Not Appealable.

The determination by the trial court on motion of defendant to determine the aggregate award of the appraisers that there was no ambiguity in the award and that it reflected damages in the amount of $60,000 was an interlocutory order not appealable under this section. Anthrop v. Tippecanoe Sch. Corp., 277 Ind. 169, 28 Ind. Dec. 649, 277 N.E.2d 169 (1972).

Judgment.

When the amount of the damages to have been paid by the condemnor was the only question involved, a judgment for the amount thereof was proper at whatever point in the proceeding that question had reached a finality. Southern Ind. Power Co. v. Cook, 182 Ind. 505, 107 N.E. 12 (1914).

Where the plaintiff had taken possession of the land, and the parties agreed upon the appraisers to assess the damages and they waived the right to file exceptions and right of appeal, and no exceptions were filed to the report of the appraisers fixing the amount of damages, the court could have rendered judg-

ment for the damages assessed, and the plaintiff could not have appealed from such judgment. Southern Ind. Power Co. v. Cook, 182 Ind. 505, 107 N.E. 12 (1914).

Jury Instructions.

It was not error to refuse to give instruction to jury which set forth the techniques of appraisal, since the proper method of appraisal was to be considered by the jury from witness' testimony along with all other evidence tending to prove damages. Board of Comm'rs v. Joeckel, 77 Ind. Dec. 165, 407 N.E.2d 274 (Ind. App. 1980).

Methods of Appraisal.

Three separate methods of appraisal are recognized in eminent domain cases: (1) the comparable sales approach; (2) the income or capitalization approach; and (3) when neither the comparable sales approach nor the income approach are applicable, the cost approach. Southern Ind. Gas & Elec. Co. v. Russell, 451 N.E.2d 673 (Ind. App. 1983).

Cost approach was an improper method of ascertaining the fair market value of easement rights appropriated by public utility. Southern Ind. Gas & Elec. Co. v. Russell, 451 N.E.2d 673 (Ind. App. 1983).

Oath of Appraisers.

Where there was no objection to the failure of appraisers to take an oath and there was no attempt to show the harm resulting from this defect, the oath requirement was satisfied by the appraisers' report which stated they were "duly sworn" by the court. State v. Smith, 260 Ind. 555, 37 Ind. Dec. 325, 297 N.E.2d 809 (1973).

Quantity of Estate.

Where issue was joined on electric power company's authority to take the fee of lands necessary to the carrying out of its objects, the trial court had jurisdiction to appoint appraisers to assess damages to landowners resulting from the appropriation of the fee. Pingry v. Indiana Hydroelectric Power Co., 197 Ind. 426, 151 N.E. 226 (1926).

Railroad Right-of-Way.

Future benefits that might accrue to the owner of land from the construction or operation of a railroad were excluded in the consideration and fixing of the amount of damages recoverable. Evansville, I. & C. S.L.R.R. v. Fitzpatrick, 10 Ind. 120 (1858); Lafayette Plankroad Co. v. New Albany & S.R.R., 13 Ind. 90, 74 Am. Dec. 246 (1859); White Water Valley R.R. v. McClure, 29 Ind. 536 (1868); Grand Rapids & I.R.R. v. Horn, 41 Ind. 479 (1873); Montmorency Gravel Rd. Co. v. Stockton, 43 Ind. 328 (1873); Baltimore, P. & C.R.R. v. Lansing, 52 Ind. 229 (1875); Swinney v. Fort

Railroad Right-of-Way. (Cont'd)
Wayne, M. & C.R.R., 59 Ind. 205 (1877);
Lafayette, M. & B.R.R. v. Murdock, 68 Ind.
137 (1879); Indiana, B. & W. Ry. v. Allen, 100
Ind. 409 (1885); Terre Haute & L.R.R. v.
Crawford, 100 Ind. 550 (1885); Chicago & I.
Coal Ry. v. Hunter, 128 Ind. 213, 27 N.E. 477
(1891); Chicago & W.M.R.R. v. Huncheon, 130
Ind. 529, 30 N.E. 636 (1892); Rehman v. New
Albany B. & T.R.R., 8 Ind. App. 200, 35 N.E.
292 (1893).

The damages recoverable for the condemnation of lands by interurban and electric
railroad companies for transmission lines
right-of-way included the value of the land
appropriated, together with such damages as
resulted from the proper construction operation of such lines. Union Traction Co. v. Pfeil,
39 Ind. App. 51, 78 N.E. 1052 (1906); Mull v.
Indianapolis & Cincinnati Traction Co., 169
Ind. 214, 81 N.E. 657 (1907); Indianapolis &
W. Ry. v. Hill, 172 Ind. 402, 86 N.E. 414
(1908); Toledo & C. Interurban Ry. v. Wilson,
44 Ind. App. 213, 86 N.E. 508 (1908), reh'g
overruled, 88 N.E. 864 (1909); Indianapolis &
W. Ry. v. Branson, 172 Ind. 383, 86 N.E. 834,
reh'g overruled, 88 N.E. 594 (1909).

In assessing damages for lands taken by a
railroad for a right-of-way, it was not proper
for the appraisers to allow any sum for damages because of annoyance or inconvenience
that might have resulted to the landowner
because of the operation of the railroad. Indianapolis & Cincinnati Traction Co. v.
Larrabee, 168 Ind. 237, 80 N.E. 413, 10 L.R.A.
(n.s.) 1003, 11 Ann. Cas. 695 (1907); Toledo &
C. Interurban Ry. v. Wagner, 171 Ind. 185, 85
N.E. 1025 (1908); Indianapolis & W. Ry. v.
Hill, 172 Ind. 402, 86 N.E. 414 (1908); Cleveland, C., C. & St. L. Ry. v. Smith, 192 Ind. 674,
138 N.E. 347 (1923).

Whether farm divided by railroad track was
operated as a single farm, or as two farms,
was a question for the jury upon assessing
damages for the taking of additional land by
the railroad. Cleveland, C., C. & St. L. Ry. v.
Smith, 177 Ind. 524, 97 N.E. 164 (1912);
Chicago & E.R.R. v. Hoffman, 67 Ind. App.
281, 119 N.E. 169 (1918).

This section authorized adjacent landowner
whose property was not acquired to recover
for damages resulting from construction of a
railroad only when the right-of-way was acquired by eminent domain, and not by purchase. Fink v. Cleveland, C., C. & St. L. Ry.,
181 Ind. 539, 105 N.E. 116 (1914).

The measure of damages in condemnation
proceedings for land taken by a railroad for
additional drainage purposes was the value of
the defendant's farm in its entirety before the
change of drainage and its value after such
change. Chicago & E.R.R. v. Hoffman, 67 Ind.
App. 281, 119 N.E. 169 (1918).

The rule that the price paid for a railroad

right-of-way settled future damages applied
only to damages which might reasonably have
been expected to result from the conveyance
and the construction and maintenance of the
road in a proper and lawful manner. Chicago
& E.R.R. v. Hoffman, 67 Ind. App. 281, 119
N.E. 169 (1918).

Time for Computation.
The statute provided that the value of the
land "at the date of the service of notice" as
provided in a preceding section "shall be the
measure of compensation." Fort Wayne &
S.W. Traction Co. v. Fort Wayne & W. Ry., 170
Ind. 49, 83 N.E. 665, 16 L.R.A. (n.s.) 537
(1908).

Where the landowner rejected the tender of
the appraisers' award, and successfully prosecuted his appeal, or in case the condemnor
appealed and thereby prevented such owner
from using the money thus tendered or paid
into court, he was entitled to interest upon
the full amount of the award as determined
on appeal from the time the condemnor took
possession. Schnull v. Indianapolis Union Ry.,
190 Ind. 572, 131 N.E. 51 (1921).

The valuation date provided in this section,
being the date of service of notice, applies to
an inverse condemnation action brought under IC 32-11-1-12. State v. Blackiston Land
Co., 158 Ind. App. 93, 39 Ind. Dec. 32, 301
N.E.2d 663 (1973).

Value of Property.
The "fair market value" was a determination of what the land could have been sold for
on the date of the taking if the owner were
willing to sell. Anything affecting the sale
value at that time was a proper matter for the
jury's consideration in attempting to arrive at
a "fair market value." Southern Ind. Gas &
Elec. Co. v. Gerhardt, 241 Ind. 389, 172
N.E.2d 204 (1961).

A mere offer to buy or sell property was not
a measure of the market value of similar
property. State v. Lincoln Memory Gardens,
Inc., 242 Ind. 206, 177 N.E.2d 655 (1961).

Neither an increase nor a decrease in the
market value of the property sought to have
been taken, which was brought about by the
same project for which the property was being
taken, could have been considered in determining the value of the property. State v.
Sovich, 253 Ind. 224, 19 Ind. Dec. 456, 252
N.E.2d 582 (1969).

In an action by the state to condemn real
estate for the purpose of construction of a
limited access highway, the measure of damages where a leasehold interest was taken
was the fair market value of the unexpired
term of the lease over and above the rent
stipulated to have been paid, in conformance
with the provisions of this section. State v.
Heslar, 257 Ind. 307, 27 Ind. Dec. 377, 274

Value of Property. (Cont'd)

N.E.2d 261 (1971), reh'g denied, 257 Ind. 625, 277 N.E.2d 796 (1972).

An expert witness was entitled to use the sale of a lot to the city in forming his opinion of damages in a suit involving state condemnation. Best v. State, 167 Ind. App. 378, 50 Ind. Dec. 346, 339 N.E.2d 82 (1975).

In a condemnation suit, a question asked of an expert witness on direct examination as to whether he determined the amount which the landowner had paid for the property was permissible where a motion of the landowner had been granted making inadmissible questions as to what the amount was. Best v. State, 167 Ind. App. 378, 50 Ind. Dec. 346, 339 N.E.2d 82 (1975).

—Evidence.

Owner of garage/warehouse that was condemned by the city was unable to prove that the building and his funeral parlor, located two blocks away, were contiguous or that the properties were so intertwined in use that the taking of the garage/warehouse tract neces- sarily injured the funeral home tract where the building was not necessary to operation of the funeral parlor, the funeral parlor would continue in business, the owner had leased another warehouse for use in his business, and the owner planned to purchase the leased warehouse. City of Mishawaka ex rel. Dep't of Redevelopment v. Fred W. Bubb Funeral Chapel, Inc., 469 N.E.2d 757 (Ind. App. 1984).

—Future Value.

The market value of the condemned land insofar as that value is presently enhanced by the property's adaptability for subdivision use may be shown, but the possible future value of each prospective lot may not be proven. City of Lafayette v. Beeler, 178 Ind. App. 281, 65 Ind. Dec. 423, 381 N.E.2d 1287 (1978).

—Partial Taking.

Where an award is made for a partial taking, full compensation equals the fair market value of the land taken plus the value of any damages to the residue. City of Elkhart v. No-Bi Corp., 428 N.E.2d 43 (Ind. App. 1981).

Collateral References. Quotient report or award by commissioners or the like. 39 A.L.R.2d 1208.

Distribution as between life tenant and remainderman of proceeds of condemned property. 91 A.L.R.2d 963.

Use or improvement of highway as establishing grade necessary to entitle abutting owner to compensation on subsequent change. 2 A.L.R.3d 985.

Valuation at time of original entry by condemnor or at time of subsequent initiation of condemnation proceedings. 2 A.L.R.3d 1038.

Compensable property right, restrictive covenant or right to enforcement thereof. 4 A.L.R.3d 1137.

Depreciation in value, from project for which land is condemned, as a factor in fixing compensation. 5 A.L.R.3d 901.

Zoning as a factor in determination of damages in eminent domain. 9 A.L.R.3d 291.

Deduction of benefits in determining compensation or damages in proceedings involving opening, widening, or otherwise altering highway. 13 A.L.R.3d 1149.

Charging landowner with rent or use value of land where he remains in possession after condemnation. 20 A.L.R.3d 1164.

Existence of restrictive covenant as element in fixing value of property condemned. 22 A.L.R.3d 961.

Rights and liabilities of parties to executory contract for sale of land taken by eminent domain. 27 A.L.R.3d 572.

Plotting or planning in anticipation of improvement as taking or damaging of property affected. 37 A.L.R.3d 127.

Eminent domain: compensability of loss of view from owner's property — state cases. 25 A.L.R.4th 671.

Eminent domain: unity or contiguity of separate properties sufficient to allow damages for diminished value of parcel remaining after taking of other parcel. 59 A.L.R.4th 308.

Referee's failure to file report within time specified by statute, court order, or stipulation as terminating reference. 71 A.L.R.4th 889.

32-24-1-10. Payment of damages — Certification. — (a) If the plaintiff pays to the circuit court clerk the amount of damages assessed under section 9 [IC 32-24-1-9] of this chapter, the plaintiff may take possession of and hold the interest in the property so acquired for the uses stated in the complaint, subject to the appeal provided for in section 8 [IC 32-24-1-8] of this chapter. But the amount of the benefits or damages is subject to review as provided in section 11 [IC 32-24-1-11] of this chapter.

(b) Upon payment by the plaintiff of the amount of the award of the court appointed appraisers, the plaintiff shall file or cause to be filed with the auditor of the county in which the property is located a certificate, certifying the amount paid to the circuit court clerk and including the description of the property being acquired. The auditor of the county shall then transfer the property being acquired to the plaintiff on the tax records of the county. [P.L.2-2002, § 9.]

NOTES TO DECISIONS

Acceptance of Damages.

The acceptance of the damages prevented the person accepting from controverting the rights of the plaintiff. Test v. Larsh, 76 Ind. 452 (1881); Baltimore, O. & C.R.R. v. Johnson, 84 Ind. 420 (1882); Morris v. Watson, 8 Ind. App. 1, 35 N.E. 405 (1893).

A landowner accepting payment of the appraisers' award was precluded from prosecuting his exceptions to the award, Schnull v. Indianapolis Union Ry., 190 Ind. 572, 131 N.E. 51 (1921).

Appeal.

—Order Not Stayed.

The district court has no jurisdiction to stay and suspend a condemnation order pending an appeal. State ex rel. Ind. & Mich. Elec. Co. v. Sullivan Circuit Court, 456 N.E.2d 1019 (Ind. 1983).

—Trial Court Authority.

A trial court does not have authority to grant relief from its order of condemnation while jurisdiction of the appeal of that order is vested in an appellate court. Coulson v. Indiana & Mich. Elec. Co., 471 N.E.2d 278 (Ind. 1984).

The trial court authority recognized as continuing unabated during the pendency of the appeal of an order of condemnation is the authority to conduct the further proceedings which "routinely follow an overruling of objections" and which lead to a trial upon exceptions to finally determine damages to the landowners. Coulson v. Indiana & Mich. Elec. Co., 471 N.E.2d 278 (Ind. 1984).

Application to Corporate Merger.

The predecessor statute to this section, by reason of former IC 23-1-5-7, applied to appraisal of stock of dissenting shareholder, and therefore corporation was properly required to deposit amount of assessor's award into court prior to trial or exception to appraiser's report. Apartment Properties Inc. v. Luley, 252 Ind. 201, 17 Ind. Dec. 384, 247 N.E.2d 71 (1969).

Change of Venue.

In view of the intent of the legislature to expedite condemnation proceedings by permitting the payment of the award and the taking of possession pending the ultimate determination of the issues involved, there was no reason offered why a change of venue should have held up or stayed such possession; therefore, the court held it was proper, pending the perfection of the change of venue and until the Grant Circuit Court took jurisdiction, to pay the amount of award to the court of the Delaware Superior Court where the cause was pending at the time the change of venue was requested. State ex rel. Keesling v. Grant Circuit Court, 238 Ind. 577, 153 N.E.2d 912 (1958).

Collateral Attack.

Condemnation proceedings wherein the court had jurisdiction of the parties and the subject matter were valid against collateral attack. Shedd v. Northern Ind. Pub. Serv. Co., 98 Ind. App. 42, 182 N.E. 278 (1932).

Highway Commission.

The eminent domain statute, including this section, was applicable to the state acting through the state highway commission. Thomas v. Lauer, 227 Ind. 432, 86 N.E.2d 71 (1949).

Injunction.

When the rights of parties could have been protected under this section, an injunction would not lie. Smith v. Goodknight, 121 Ind. 312, 23 N.E. 148 (1889); Halstead v. City of Brazil, 83 Ind. App. 53, 147 N.E. 629 (1925).

Void eminent domain proceedings could have been enjoined. City of Ft. Wayne v. Fort Wayne & J.R.R., 149 Ind. 25, 48 N.E. 342 (1897).

An injunction would lie to prevent the taking of land by a city for a street where the owner thereof had no notice of the condemnation proceedings and was not made a party thereto. City of Ft. Wayne v. Fort Wayne & J.R.R., 149 Ind. 25, 48 N.E. 342 (1897).

Jurisdiction.

The provisions of this section and IC 32-11-1-8 had to be construed together, and by such sections the propriety of further proceedings after the damages initially determined were paid and possession passed was contemplated, and hence the court had continuing jurisdiction to provide for full and just compensation to the owner of all the property, including extensions, additions, and capital expenditures, made after the proceedings were commenced. Public Serv. Co. v. City of Lebanon, 221 Ind. 78, 46 N.E.2d 480 (1943).

After a city's right to acquire public utility property was determined, the court could adjudge that the utility was entitled to a purchase-money lien on the property acquired by the city, for the sum fixed as compensation for additional improvements necessarily made after damages for the original property had been fixed, and could then proceed to determine the reasonable value of such improvements, and could, by appropriate orders, have seen that its judgment was carried out. Public Serv. Co. v. City of Lebanon, 221 Ind. 78, 46 N.E.2d 480 (1943).

Payment and Possession.

Damages must have been paid or tendered before the right to possession accrued. Indianapolis & C.R.R. v. Brower, 12 Ind. 374 (1859); Sidener v. Norristown, H. & St. L. Tpk. Co., 23 Ind. 623 (1864); Lake Erie & W. Ry. v. Kinsey, 87 Ind. 514 (1882).

Paying damages into court did not vest title to the land, but conferred only a right of possession. Lake Erie & W. Ry. v. Kinsey, 87 Ind. 514 (1882); Terre Haute & L.R.R. v. Crawford, 100 Ind. 550 (1885).

Where plaintiff was in possession of land before it commenced the condemnation proceeding, a judgment rendered upon the award of the appraisers for the amount thereof, and vesting the lands in the plaintiff upon its payment, was not erroneous. Southern Ind. Power Co. v. Cook, 182 Ind. 505, 107 N.E. 12 (1914).

In proceedings under this section, the state was neither bound to take possession of the condemned real estate nor to pay the award of damages prior to taking possession, but where the state, after the award was made and to which the state filed exceptions, elected to and did pay the damages as a condition precedent to exercising possessory rights, the payment was voluntary. State v. Pollitt, 220 Ind. 593, 45 N.E.2d 480 (1942).

The trial court had no power to stay the taking physical possession of the condemned property by the condemnor pending trial on the amount of damages nor to preserve the buildings and improvements upon the land for the purposes of viewing by a jury at a trial upon the amount of damages. State ex rel. City of Hammond v. LaPorte Circuit Court, 249 Ind. 494, 12 Ind. Dec. 634, 233 N.E.2d 471 (1968).

Possession Pending Appeal.

It could have been provided by law that the damages could have been paid into court and that possession could have been taken during pendency of appeal. Consumers' Gas Trust Co. v. Harless, 131 Ind. 446, 29 N.E. 1062, 15 L.R.A. 505 (1892).

The possession of the condemnor during the pendency of an appeal, and until compliance with the orders and judgment of the court, gave it no greater right than that of a licensee. Schnull v. Indianapolis Union Ry., 190 Ind. 572, 131 N.E. 51 (1921).

The water works company, after paying to the clerk of court the amount of the appraiser's award, held only as a licensee during an appeal from the old ruling of the exceptions and objections to the complaint; however, as licensee, such water company could occupy the real estate and possess the same to the extent necessary to the performance of its work. State ex rel. Keesling v. Grant Circuit Court, 238 Ind. 577, 153 N.E.2d 912 (1958).

When the state paid the amount of the appraiser's award into the hands of the clerk, it was thereby enabled to, and did, deprive the landowners of the use of their land. Since the appraiser's award was the compensation for the land, and if the landowners were satisfied therewith, such sum represented the land appropriated and immediately became the property of the state, and in order to maintain its right to possession was required to keep the tender of compensation good pending the final determination of the amount of damages due the landowners. State v. Kraszyk, 240 Ind. 524, 167 N.E.2d 339 (1960).

Public Utilities.

During proceedings by a city to acquire utility property pursuant to statute, and even after the damages for the property had been assessed and until the city paid the purchase

Public Utilities. (Cont'd)
price, it was incumbent on the utility to furnish adequate service to the community or run the risk of being mandated to do so or of losing its permit. Public Serv. Co. v. City of Lebanon, 221 Ind. 78, 46 N.E.2d 480 (1943).

Purpose.
By the enactment of this section, the legislature intended to expedite condemnation proceedings by permitting the payment of the award and the taking of possession of the property pending the ultimate determination of the issues involved. The condemnee could accept the money and thereby waive its exceptions to the award of the appraisers or refuse to accept the money and proceed with the prosecution of its exceptions to the appraisers' award, in which event the money would remain in the hands of the clerk pending final judgment. State v. Kraszyk, 240 Ind. 524, 167 N.E.2d 339 (1960).

The purpose of this act was to protect the landowner against loss and if, before the question of damages was finally determined, the condemnor was permitted to withdraw part of the assessed damages as fixed by the appraisers and which it had paid to the clerk of the court in order to get possession of the land, the purpose of the statute was defeated. State v. Kraszyk, 240 Ind. 524, 167 N.E.2d 339 (1960).

Requirement for Immediate Possession.
If the condemnor decided to take immediate possession of the lands condemned, it had to pay to the clerk of the court such assessed damages, as a condition precedent to taking possession. State ex rel. Socony Mobil Oil Co. v. Delaware Circuit Court, 245 Ind. 154, 3 Ind. Dec. 143, 196 N.E.2d 752 (1964).

Right to Withdraw Damages.
Parties defendant with any right, title or interest in the land appropriated could withdraw the sums allowed to them by the appraisers before the review of the damages were assessed by a court. State ex rel. Socony Mobil Oil Co. v. Delaware Circuit Court, 245 Ind. 154, 3 Ind. Dec. 143, 196 N.E.2d 752 (1964).

Who Entitled to Damages.
Damages alleged to have been inflicted enured to the benefit of the person who owned the lands and accrued at the time the damages were inflicted. Church v. Grand Rapids & I.R.R., 70 Ind. 161 (1880); Indiana, B. & W. Ry. v. Allen, 100 Ind. 409 (1885); Evansville & T.H.R.R. v. Nye, 113 Ind. 223, 15 N.E. 261 (1888); Sherlock v. Louisville, N.A. & C. Ry., 115 Ind. 22, 17 N.E. 171 (1888); Harshbarger v. Midland Ry., 131 Ind. 177, 27 N.E. 352, 30 N.E. 1083 (1891); Shauver v. Phillips, 7 Ind. App. 12, 32 N.E. 1131, 34 N.E. 450 (1893).

The filing of a complaint or instrument for the appropriation of land constituted a taking of the property, and the then owner of the land was entitled to the damages assessed, and his subsequent coveyance of the land did not transfer the claim for damages. Fort Wayne & S.W. Traction Co. v. Fort Wayne & W. R. Co., 170 Ind. 49, 83 N.E. 665, 16 L.R.A. (n.s.) 537 (1908).

32-24-1-11. Exceptions to assessment — Trial — Notice of filing appraisers' report — Request for payment. — (a) Any party to an action under this chapter aggrieved by the assessment of benefits or damages may file written exceptions to the assessment in the office of the circuit court clerk. Exceptions to the assessment must be filed not later than twenty (20) days after the filing of the report.

(b) The cause shall further proceed to issue, trial, and judgment as in civil actions. The court may make orders and render findings and judgments that the court considers just.

(c) Notice of filing of the appraisers' report shall be given by the circuit court clerk to all known parties to the action and their attorneys of record by certified mail. The period of exceptions shall run from and after the date of mailing. Either party may appeal a judgment as to benefits or damages as in civil actions.

(d) Twenty (20) days after the filing of the report of the appraisers, and if the plaintiff has paid the amount of damages assessed to the circuit court clerk, any one (1) or more of the defendants may file a written request for payment of each defendant's proportionate share of the damages held by the circuit court clerk. The defendants making a request for payment must also file sufficient copies of the request for service upon the plaintiff and all other defendants not joining in the request. The defendants making the request may withdraw and receive each defendant's proportionate share of the damages upon the following terms and conditions:

(1) Each written request must:
 (A) be verified under oath; and
 (B) state:
  (i) the amount of the proportionate share of the damages to which each of the defendants joining in the request is entitled;
  (ii) the interest of each defendant joining in the request; and
  (iii) the highest offer made by the plaintiff to each of the defendants for each defendant's respective interests in or damages sustained in respect to the property that has been acquired by the plaintiff.

(2) Upon the filing of a written request for withdrawal and payment of damages to any of the defendants, the circuit court clerk shall immediately issue a notice to the plaintiff and all defendants of record in the cause who have not joined in the request for payment. The notice must contain the following:
 (A) The names of the parties.
 (B) The number of the cause.
 (C) A statement that a request for payment has been filed.
 (D) A notice to appear on a day, to be fixed by the court, and show cause, if any, why the amounts requested should not be withdrawn and paid over by the circuit court clerk to those defendants requesting the amounts to be paid.
 (E) A copy of the request for payment.

If a defendant not requesting payment is a nonresident of Indiana, or if that defendant's name or residence is unknown, publication and proof of the notice and request for payment shall be made as provided in section 4 [IC 32-24-1-4] of this chapter.

(3) After a hearing held after notice of a written request made under this section, the court shall determine and order the payment by the circuit court clerk of the proportionate shares of the damages due to the defendants requesting payment. Any of the defendants may appeal an order under this subdivision within the same time and in the same manner as provided for allowable appeals from interlocutory orders in civil actions.

(4) If exceptions to the appraisers' report have been duly filed by the plaintiff or any defendant, the circuit court clerk may not make payment to any defendant of any part of the damages deposited with the clerk by the plaintiff until the defendants requesting payment have filed with the circuit court clerk a written undertaking, with surety approved by the court, for the repayment to the plaintiff of all sums received by those defendants in excess of the amount or amounts awarded as damages to those defendants by the judgment of the court upon trial held on the exceptions to the assessment of damages by the appraisers. However, the court may waive the requirement of separate surety as to any defendant who is a resident freeholder of the county in

which the cause is pending and who is owner of real property in Indiana that is liable to execution, not included in the real property appropriated by the plaintiff, and equal in value to the amount by which the damages to be withdrawn exceed the amount offered to the defendants as stated in their request or the amount determined by the court if the plaintiff has disputed the statement of the offer. A surety or written undertaking may not be required for a defendant to withdraw those amounts previously offered by the plaintiff to the defendant if the plaintiff has previously notified the court in writing of the amounts so offered. The liability of any surety does not exceed the amount by which the damages to be withdrawn exceed the amount offered to the defendants with whom the surety joins in the written undertaking. Each written undertaking filed with the circuit court clerk shall be immediately recorded by the clerk in the order book and entered in the judgment docket, and from the date of the recording and entry the written undertaking is a lien upon all the real property in the county owned by the several obligors, and the undertaking is also a lien upon all the real property owned by the several obligors in each county of Indiana in which the plaintiff causes a certified copy of the judgment docket entry to be recorded, from the date of the recording.

(5) The withdrawal and receipt from the circuit court clerk by any defendant of that defendant's proportionate share of the damages awarded by the appraisers, as determined by the court upon the written request and hearing, does not operate and is not considered as a waiver of any exceptions duly filed by that defendant to the assessment of damages by the appraisers.

(6) In any trial of exceptions, the court or jury shall compute and allow interest at an annual rate of eight percent (8%) on the amount of a defendant's damages from the date plaintiff takes possession of the property. Interest may not be allowed on any money paid by the plaintiff to the circuit court clerk:

(A) after the money is withdrawn by the defendant; or

(B) that is equal to the amount of damages previously offered by the plaintiff to any defendant and which amount can be withdrawn by the defendant without filing a written undertaking or surety with the court for the withdrawal of that amount. [P.L.2-2002, § 9.]

NOTES TO DECISIONS

ANALYSIS

In general.
Constitutionality.
Additions and improvements.
Amount of damages.
Appeal barred by agreement.
Burden of proof.
Change of venue.
Civil action.
Dismissal.
Estoppel.
Exceptions.
—Withdrawals.
Filing exceptions.
Injunction against sale of buildings.
Interest.
Inspection by jury.
Judgment.
Jurisdiction.
No appraisal.
—Appeal.
Notice of appraisers' report.
Payment.
Possession.
Presumptions on appeal.

Purpose.
Review on appeal.
Right to trial.
—Jury trials.
——Timely request.
Subsequent purchasers.
Surety.
Vacating appraisers' report.
Waiver of appeal.
Withdrawal of appraisers' report.

In General.

Where one of the defendants withdrew his share of the deposited damages as determined by the appraisers and, by reason of his failure to appear, was not awarded any damages at the trial of the defendants' exceptions to the appraisement, it was error to permit the plaintiff to withdraw the difference between its total original deposit and the amount awarded to the two defendants whose exceptions were tried. Socony Mobil Oil Co. v. State, 248 Ind. 680, 11 Ind. Dec. 539, 230 N.E.2d 530 (1967).

Proceedings in eminent domain, like other civil actions, are governed by the Indiana Rules of Trial Procedure. State v. Blount, 154 Ind. App. 580, 34 Ind. Dec. 370, 290 N.E.2d 480 (1972).

The 1975 amendment of the predecessor statute to this section contained no language implying a retrospective legislative intent, and in the absence of express language to the contrary, legislative enactments, including amendments to existing laws, are construed as being prospective in operation. State v. Denny, 409 N.E.2d 652 (Ind. App. 1980).

Constitutionality.

The four percent interest rate prescribed by the predecessor statute to this section prior to the 1975 amendment was not so low as to be unconstitutional as a deprivation of just compensation. Struble v. Elkhart County Park & Recreation Bd., 175 Ind. App. 669, 61 Ind. Dec. 466, 373 N.E.2d 906 (1978).

Additions and Improvements.

The provisions of the predecessor statute to this section and former IC 32-11-1-7 (repealed; for similar provision see IC 32-24-1-10) had to be construed together, and by such sections the propriety of further proceedings after the damages initially determined had been paid and possession passed was contemplated, and hence the court had continuing jurisdiction to provide for full and just compensation to the owner of all the property, including extensions, additions, and capital expenditures, made after the proceedings were commenced. Public Serv. Co. v. City of Lebanon, 221 Ind. 78, 46 N.E.2d 480 (1943).

Amount of Damages.

Parties who appropriated land under the right of eminent domain could have paid the damages awarded into court and had the question as to the amount of damages tried. Cleveland, C., C. & St. L.R.R. v. Nowlin, 163 Ind. 497, 72 N.E. 257 (1904); Union Traction Co. v. Basey, 164 Ind. 249, 73 N.E. 263 (1905); Indianapolis N. Traction Co. v. Dunn, 37 Ind. App. 248, 76 N.E. 269 (1905); Douglas v. Indianapolis & N.W. Traction Co., 37 Ind. App. 332, 76 N.E. 892 (1906).

When the exceptions alleged that the damages were too low, all questions as to damages could have been inquired into. Toledo & C. Interurban Ry. v. Wilson, 44 Ind. App. 213, 86 N.E. 508 (1908), reh'g overruled, 88 N.E. 864 (1909).

The trial court had full authority under this section to have the jury hear evidence on the actual amount of land appropriated by the state and to grant full, true and just compensation for all property taken in this one action, as otherwise defendants would have had to resort to an inverse condemnation action and try the question of damages piecemeal. Flesch v. State, 250 Ind. 529, 14 Ind. Dec. 475, 237 N.E.2d 374 (1968).

Appeal Barred by Agreement.

If the parties agreed that neither party should appeal from the award of damages, the agreement could have been pleaded in bar of the appeal. Southern Ind. Power Co. v. Cook, 182 Ind. 505, 107 N.E. 12 (1914).

Burden of Proof.

The burden of proof was on the landowner to prove his damages and he was entitled to open and close. Consumers' Gas Trust Co. v. Huntsinger, 12 Ind. App. 285, 40 N.E. 34 (1895); Indianapolis & Cincinnati Traction Co. v. Shepherd, 35 Ind. App. 601, 74 N.E. 904 (1905); Alberson Cem. Ass'n v. Fuhrer, 192 Ind. 606, 137 N.E. 545 (1923).

When the condemnor established the right to take, the burden of proof was on the defendant-owner in respect of the value of the property taken. Van Sickle v. Kokomo Water Works Co., 239 Ind. 612, 158 N.E.2d 460 (1959).

Change of Venue.

After appraisers were appointed and made their report, and after exceptions to such report by either or both parties presented an issue for submission to a jury as to the amount of damages, a change of venue from the county could have been taken. Clinton Coal Co. v. Chicago & E.I.R.R., 190 Ind. 465, 130 N.E. 798 (1921).

An order granting a change of venue from the county in a condemnation proceeding made prior to the appointment of appraisers was at most an irregularity, and not void.

Change of Venue. (Cont'd)
Clinton Coal Co. v. Chicago & E.I.R.R., 190 Ind. 465, 130 N.E. 798 (1921).

After the point was reached of trying the question of damages, the cause proceeded as in ordinary civil actions, and a change of venue from the county could have been had. Matlock v. Bloomington Water Co., 196 Ind. 271, 146 N.E. 852, reh'g overruled, 196 Ind. 280, 148 N.E. 198 (1925).

Civil Action.
Trials on the question of damages in appropriation proceedings have uniformly been regarded as civil actions, and trial by jury was demandable. Lake Erie, W. & St. L.R.R. v. Heath, 9 Ind. 558 (1857); Piper v. Connersville & L. Tpk. Co., 12 Ind. 400 (1859); Barrett v. Carthage Tpk. Co., 16 Ind. 105 (1861); Alberson Cem. Ass'n v. Fuhrer, 192 Ind. 606, 137 N.E. 545 (1923); Matlock v. Bloomington Water Co., 196 Ind. 271, 146 N.E. 852, reh'g overruled, 196 Ind. 280, 148 N.E. 198 (1925).

Parties aggrieved by the assessment of damages could file exceptions thereto and have a trial thereon as in civil actions. Vandalia Coal Co. v. Indianapolis & L. Ry., 168 Ind. 144, 79 N.E. 1082 (1907).

Dismissal.
In proceedings under the Eminent Domain Act of 1905, where the state had made voluntary payment of the award and had taken possession of the real estate, a dismissal of the proceeding ought not have been a matter of right but should have been subject to the discretion of the court which, as expressly provided in this section, "may make such further orders, and render such finding and judgment as may seem just," for this language contemplated judicial action other than proceeding "to issue, trial and judgment" as in civil actions. State v. Pollitt, 220 Ind. 593, 45 N.E.2d 480 (1942).

In action by the state highway commission to condemn real estate, wherein, without objection, an order was made appointing appraisers who made an award, which the state contested but subsequently paid to the clerk of court from whom defendant withdrew the money, the state could not, as a matter of right, after the money had been voluntarily paid and withdrawn, dismiss the condemnation proceedings and obtain restitution of the money paid, for while this section provided that the "cause shall further proceed to issue, trial and judgment as in civil actions," it did not make available to a condemnor every right to a plaintiff in a civil action, since the only issue there referred to was the amount of damages, and Burns' §§ 2-901 and 2-902 (since repealed; see now Rule TR. 41) were not applicable at this stage of the proceedings.

State v. Pollitt, 220 Ind. 593, 45 N.E.2d 480 (1942).

Estoppel.
Estoppel was not an available defense to landowners' failure to file exceptions to the award of the appraisers, even though the mayor stated that the landowners did not need to file exceptions while negotiations continued, where the landowners received express written notice that they had to file written objections within 20 days after the notice was filed. Samplawski v. City of Portage, 512 N.E.2d 456 (Ind. App. 1987).

Exceptions.
The filing of exceptions to the award of appraisers did not prevent the construction of the work when the law was complied with. Wabash R.R. v. Fort Wayne & S.W. Traction Co., 161 Ind. 295, 67 N.E. 674 (1903).

In a condemnation proceeding, if neither party filed exceptions within ten days after the filing of the appraisers' report, no exception could have been thereafter filed by either party. State v. Redmon, 205 Ind. 335, 186 N.E. 328 (1933).

In a condemnation proceeding by the state to secure land for highway, where the state filed exceptions within ten days after the filing of the appraisers' report, but subsequently dismissed them, the court was without jurisdiction to try issue of damages on exceptions filed by defendants subsequent to such ten days. State v. Redmon, 205 Ind. 335, 186 N.E. 328 (1933).

In condemnation proceeding, if one party filed exceptions within ten days after the filing of the appraisers' report, and did not thereafter dismiss them, permission to the other party to file exceptions after ten days was not prejudicial. State v. Redmon, 205 Ind. 335, 186 N.E. 328 (1933).

Court erred in modifying report of appraisers in eminent domain proceeding and rendering judgment under modified report, where property owners failed to except to report within ten days of its filing. State v. Rousseau, 209 Ind. 458, 199 N.E. 587 (1936).

Under the condemnation statute, the issue was formed as a matter of law upon the filing of exceptions to the appraiser's award. Van Sickle v. Kokomo Water Works Co., 239 Ind. 612, 158 N.E.2d 460 (1959).

The appellant was precluded from accepting the payment made to the clerk if he would maintain his standing in court to prosecute his exceptions, and when he chose to accept the money, he thereby waived his exceptions to the award of the appraisers in a condemnation action. Denny v. State, 244 Ind. 5, 1 Ind. Dec. 343, 189 N.E.2d 820 (1963).

An appeal from condemnation proceedings taken while exceptions to the report of ap-

Exceptions. (Cont'd)

praisers were pending was premature. Lake County Trust Co. v. Indiana Port Comm'n, 248 Ind. 362, 11 Ind. Dec. 133, 229 N.E.2d 457 (1967).

Where exceptions were not filed until after ten-day period, exceptions were properly dismissed, and fact that appraiser's report was authorized later than the ten-day period prescribed by former IC 32-11-1-9 (repealed; for similar provision see IC 32-24-1-13) had no effect on the ten-day period to file exceptions. Ray v. State, 252 Ind. 395, 18 Ind. Dec. 117, 248 N.E.2d 337 (1969).

If there are no exceptions to the appraisers' report, the appraisers' award is conclusive, but if there are exceptions to the appraisers' report, the appraisers' report becomes the complaint and the exceptions the answer in a trial to determine the damages with respect to all parties. Best Realty Corp. v. State, 74 Ind. Dec. 435, 400 N.E.2d 1204 (Ind. App. 1980).

—Withdrawals.

A party to an eminent domain action does not have an absolute right to withdraw exceptions to the appraiser's report. Daugherty v. State, 699 N.E.2d 780 (Ind. App. 1998).

In exercising its discretion to allow or deny the withdrawal of exceptions in an eminent domain action, the trial court should allow the withdrawal except in instances where injustice would result. Daugherty v. State, 699 N.E.2d 780 (Ind. App. 1998).

In making a determination as to whether or not to permit the withdrawal of exceptions in an eminent domain action, the trial court should consider the following nonexclusive factors: the length of time between the filing of the appraisers' report and the motion to withdraw, whether the withdrawing party is attempting to do so on the eve of the trial, whether the withdrawing party and trial court have been put on notice of the other party's dissatisfaction with the report, and the extent of trial preparation which has already occurred. Daugherty v. State, 699 N.E.2d 780 (Ind. App. 1998).

In an eminent domain action, where the state did not file a motion to withdraw exceptions on the eve of the trial, even though the matter had been set for mediation, and where the trial court held a hearing and allowed the landowner the opportunity to demonstrate why the withdrawal should not be allowed, there was no abuse of discretion in allowing the state to withdraw its exceptions and the granting of judgment in favor of the state. Daugherty v. State, 699 N.E.2d 780 (Ind. App. 1998).

Parties to an eminent domain action file exceptions at their own peril in that, under certain circumstances, they may not be permitted to withdraw the exceptions and terminate the litigation which they have commenced. Daugherty v. State, 699 N.E.2d 780 (Ind. App. 1998).

Filing Exceptions.

An exception to the appraisers' report had to be filed within the ten-day period from the filing of the appraisers' report. State ex rel. Agan v. Hendricks Superior Court, 250 Ind. 675, 13 Ind. Dec. 664, 235 N.E.2d 458, reh'g denied, 250 Ind. 675, 238 N.E.2d 446 (1968).

The filing of exceptions by either party is sufficient to submit the question of damages to the court or jury, and it is unnecessary that a landowner file exceptions as a condition precedent to his right of recovery, if exceptions have been filed by the condemning party. State v. Blount, 154 Ind. App. 580, 34 Ind. Dec. 370, 290 N.E.2d 480 (1972).

The statutory time period allowed for filing objection to the appraiser's award in an eminent domain proceeding could not be extended by the trial court. Southern Ind. Gas & Elec. Co.v. Decker, 261 Ind. 527, 40 Ind. Dec. 641, 307 N.E.2d 51 (1974).

Where defendants in a condemnation proceeding filed exceptions to the appraisers' report after the expiration of the 10-day period in effect at that stage of the proceedings, the subsequent amendment to this section extending the period to 20 days did not validate the failure to file timely exceptions even if the amendment would be found to apply retroactively to the cause of action and thus affect proceedings subsequent to its enactment. McGill v. Muddy Fork of Silver Creek Watershed Conservancy Dist., 175 Ind. App. 48, 60 Ind. Dec. 64, 370 N.E.2d 365 (1977).

Landowners' delivery of a written proposal regarding damages involved in the taking of their property to the mayor within five days of the filing of the appraisers' report did not constitute substantial compliance with this section; eminent domain statutes must be strictly complied with and their requirements are jurisdictional. Samplawski v. City of Portage, 512 N.E.2d 456 (Ind. App. 1987).

If no exceptions are filed within the statutory time limit, the appraisers' award becomes final and there is no issue left for trial. On the other hand, if either party files exceptions, then any party is entitled to go to trial on the exceptions and the question of damages becomes one for the jury. State v. Berger, 534 N.E.2d 268 (Ind. App. 1989).

Where only one party files exceptions, he may ordinarily, by dismissing his exceptions, eliminate all basis to go to trial, or by dismissing a part of the exceptions, such as those claiming damages to the residue, he may preclude litigation of those claims. State v. Berger, 534 N.E.2d 268 (Ind. App. 1989).

Where it is established by filing of excep-

Filing Exceptions. (Cont'd)
tions to first report of appraisers that landowner had notice of condemnation action and opportunity to be heard; court has no jurisdiction to try issue of damages where there was no timely filing of exceptions to second report since it is not essential to due process that appeal be provided at every step of proceedings. Lehnen v. State, 693 N.E.2d 580 (Ind. App. 1998).

Any party to an eminent domain action desiring to insure a trial on the question of damages should file his own timely exceptions. Daugherty v. State, 699 N.E.2d 780 (Ind. App. 1998).

Injunction Against Sale of Buildings.

In a condemnation proceeding, the court had authority under the petition for an injunction filed in the same proceeding to resolve the question of whether the state should have been enjoined from selling or disposing of the buildings upon so-called "temporary right-of-way." State v. Curtis, 241 Ind. 507, 173 N.E.2d 652 (1961).

Interest.

In condemnation proceedings, the defendant had the option of whether or not to withdraw his award. If he decided not to withdraw his award, but await the final decision of the court, he was entitled to interest from the date the condemnor took possession until the date of the final decision. State v. Young, 246 Ind. 52, 3 Ind. Dec. 570, 199 N.E.2d 694 (1964) (decision prior to 1965 amendment).

Prior to the 1961 amendment to this section, if the condemnor appealed and prevented the owner from using money tendered or paid into court, the owner was entitled to interest upon the full amount of the award as determined on appeal from the time the condemnor took possession of the property. Indiana & Mich. Elec. Co. v. Louck, 247 Ind. 24, 5 Ind. Dec. 404, 206 N.E.2d 871 (1965).

Prior to the 1961 amendment to this section, irrespective of who filed objections to the appraisers' report or who appealed from judgment of circuit court after a trial de novo on the issue of damages, interest on the amount of the court award was payable from the time of the taking by the condemnor to the time of the judgment. Indiana & Mich. Elec. Co. v. Louck, 247 Ind. 24, 5 Ind. Dec. 404, 206 N.E.2d 871 (1965).

Subsequent to the 1961 amendment and prior to the 1965 amendment, since the jury was not permitted to know the amount of the appraisers' award, they could not possibly make a determination as to whether there was any excess amount over and above the appraisers' award upon which interest should have been allowed and the allowance of inter-

est was for the court and not the jury. State v. Jordan Woods, Inc., 248 Ind. 208, 10 Ind. Dec. 337, 225 N.E.2d 767 (1967).

The purpose of awarding interest in an eminent domain proceeding is not to compensate the landowner for loss of value of his property, but rather to measure the loss caused the landowner due to the deprivation of the use of his land, and interest thus should be allowed for the period of time between the entry or physical taking by the condemnor and the payment of just compensation therefor. State v. Blackiston Land Co., 158 Ind. App. 93, 39 Ind. Dec. 32, 301 N.E.2d 663 (1973).

Provisions of this section regarding allowance of interest apply to inverse condemnation actions, and trial court properly made award of interest to run from the date on which the state entered possession. State v. Blackiston Land Co., 158 Ind. App. 93, 39 Ind. Dec. 32, 301 N.E.2d 663 (1973).

Where the state failed to notify the court in writing of the amount of the offer to purchase it made to defendants, the proviso in paragraph 6 was not met, and therefore defendants were entitled to have interest computed on the entire amount of the damage award. State v. Reuter, 170 Ind. App. 353, 54 Ind. Dec. 169, 352 N.E.2d 806 (1976); State v. Denny, 77 Ind. Dec. 748, 409 N.E.2d 652 (Ind. App. 1980).

Where jury's verdict for damages was greater than that offered by the state, it was proper to compute the interest on the difference between the jury verdict and the state's offer from the time of taking to the time of withdrawal of the state's deposit and also to compute interest on the difference between the jury's verdict and the actual amount of state funds withdrawn until the final award. State v. Turner, 67 Ind. Dec. 611, 386 N.E.2d 208 (Ind. App. 1979).

Interest should be allowed on the judgment in accordance with the provisions of this section as it existed at the time the plaintiff took possession of the property, rather than under the provisions of this section as it existed at the time of the judgment. State v. Denny, 77 Ind. Dec. 748, 409 N.E.2d 652 (Ind. App. 1980).

Even though former IC 32-11-1-8 (repealed; se this section for similar provisions) both permits a landowner to withdraw the amount of the state's final purchase order without posting surety and prohibited an award of interest on any amount that can be withdrawn without posting surety, landowners were entitled to interest for the time the money was on deposit because they could not at the time of the condemnation prior to the 1975 amendment to former IC 32-11-1-8 (repealed; see this section for similar provisions) withdraw the money without posting surety.

Interest. (Cont'd)
State v. Denny, 409 N.E.2d 652 (Ind. App. 1980).

There is no statutory authorization for the plaintiff in a condemnation action to receive interest. Tipmont Rural Elec. Membership Corp. v. City of Crawfordsville, 423 N.E.2d 697 (Ind. App. 1981).

Landowners are entitled to prejudgment interest from the date of taking in eminent domain proceedings. Dicanio v. State Bank, 493 N.E.2d 820 (Ind. App. 1986).

Inspection by Jury.
Inspection of premises by jury was proper. Pittsburgh, Ft. W. & C. Ry. v. Swinney, 59 Ind. 100 (1877).

Judgment.
If the damages assessed were paid into court, and, on the trial, the damages were reduced below the sum paid, judgment could have been rendered against the landowner for the excess. Douglas v. Indianapolis & N.W. Traction Co., 37 Ind. App. 332, 76 N.E. 892 (1906).

Where the interlocutory order appointing appraisers was reversed, judgment after trial by jury on exceptions to report of appraisers had to be reversed. Western Union Tel. Co. v. Louisville & N.R.R., 185 Ind. 690, 114 N.E. 406 (1916).

On appeal to the circuit court from an award of appraisers, the court could go further than the appraisers and could make such orders and findings and render such judgment as would constitute just compensation, and could use the statutory provisions directed to the appraisers in determining the same question submitted to the appraisers. Schnull v. Indianapolis Union Ry., 190 Ind. 572, 131 N.E. 51 (1921).

Jurisdiction.
Where defendants in a condemnation proceeding filed exceptions to the appraisers' report after the expiration of the 10-day period, their exceptions were a nullity and the jurisdiction of the trial court to try the issue of damages rested entirely on plaintiff's timely filed exceptions; when the trial court sustained plaintiff's motion to dismiss its exceptions, the trial court had no power to proceed further in the trial. McGill v. Muddy Fork of Silver Creek Watershed Conservancy Dist., 175 Ind. App. 48, 60 Ind. Dec. 64, 370 N.E.2d 365 (1977).

No Appraisal.

—Appeal.
In proceedings to condemn an electric public utility by a city, under its right of eminent domain, in which judgment was rendered in favor of the defendant utility, and plaintiff city appealed to the Supreme Court, and the record showed that no appraisal of said utility sought to have been condemned had been made, the appellate tribunal could not determine whether the utility's property was sought to be taken without just compensation and without due process of law, in view of Ind. Const., Art. 1, §§ 21, 23; U.S. Const., Amend. 14; IC 8-1-2-1 et seq. City of Lebanon v. Public Serv. Co., 214 Ind. 295, 14 N.E.2d 719, appeal dismissed, 305 U.S. 558, 59 S. Ct. 84, 83 L. Ed. 352, reh'g denied, 305 U.S. 671, 59 S. Ct. 143, 83 L. Ed. 435 (1938).

Notice of Appraisers' Report.
The 1973 amendment requiring notice of the appraisers' report to be given to known parties is not to be applied retroactively. Cordill v. City of Indianapolis, 168 Ind. App. 685, 52 Ind. Dec. 158, 345 N.E.2d 274 (1976).

Where defendants were present when the court entered an order of appropriation in a condemnation proceeding, at which time the court directed the appraisers to file their report on a specified date, the clerk was not required to serve defendants with a copy of the report either under Rule TR. 5(A) or Rule TR. 72(D). McGill v. Muddy Fork of Silver Creek Watershed Conservancy Dist., 175 Ind. App. 48, 60 Ind. Dec. 64, 370 N.E.2d 365 (1977).

Mailing of a copy of an actual appraisal report that was file stamped by the clerk by certified mail complied with this section; this provided notice not only of the filing, but also of the specific damage figures awarded by the appraisers. Samplawski v. City of Portage, 512 N.E.2d 456 (Ind. App. 1987).

Payment.
Where there was no showing of ownership of any property other than in the owner of real estate, the clerk could immediately pay all the condemnation damages held by him over to the real estate owner under this act. LaPinta v. State, 246 Ind. 512, 5 Ind. Dec. 477, 207 N.E.2d 215 (1965).

Possession.
The possession of the condemnor during the pendency of an appeal, and until compliance with the orders and judgment of the court, gave it no greater right than that of a licensee. Schnull v. Indianapolis Union Ry., 190 Ind. 572, 131 N.E. 51 (1921).

In condemnation for railroad right-of-way, the landowner, in undistributed possession of the property until payment or tender of damages, was not deprived thereof by fixing the price at which it could have been taken. Sisters of Providence v. Lower Vein Coal Co., 198 Ind. 645, 154 N.E. 659 (1926), overruled on other grounds, Joint County Park Bd. v.

Possession. (Cont'd)
Stegemoller, 228 Ind. 118, 89 N.E.2d 720 (1950).

Presumptions on Appeal.
The Supreme Court could not presume that the amount fixed by the appraiser or the trial court would be too low, in view of IC 32-11-1-8. City of Lebanon v. Public Serv. Co., 214 Ind. 295, 14 N.E.2d 719, appeal dismissed, 305 U.S. 558, 59 S. Ct. 84, 83 L. Ed. 352, reh'g denied, 305 U.S. 671, 59 S. Ct. 143, 83 L. Ed. 435 (1938). In connection with this case, see Public Serv. Co. v. City of Lebanon, 219 Ind. 62, 34 N.E.2d 20 (1941).

In a proceeding to condemn a public utility, which was appealed to the Supreme Court, such court was warranted in assuming, in the absence of some showing of fact, that the court appointed appraisers were qualified as required by statute. Southern Ind. Gas & Elec. Co. v. City of Boonville, 215 Ind. 552, 20 N.E.2d 648 (1939).

Purpose.
The evident purpose of this section, which provided that the court could make such further orders and render such findings and judgment as might have seemed just, was to enable the court to meet any contingency or situation that might have arisen, and to have provided for full and just compensation to the owners of all the property, including extensions, additions, capital expenditures and the like, made after the proceedings were commenced. City of Lebanon v. Public Serv. Co., 214 Ind. 295, 14 N.E.2d 719, appeal dismissed, 305 U.S. 558, 59 S. Ct. 84, 83 L. Ed. 352, reh'g denied, 305 U.S. 671, 59 S. Ct. 143, 83 L. Ed. 435 (1938). In connection with this case, see Public Serv. Co. v. City of Lebanon, 219 Ind. 62, 34 N.E.2d 20 (1941); Public Serv. Co. v. City of Lebanon, 221 Ind. 78, 46 N.E.2d 480 (1943).

In passing the eminent domain act, it was the intention of the legislature to expedite such proceedings by turning the possession over to the condemnor upon the payment of the appraisal and pending any future litigation in the case. State v. Marion Circuit Court, 239 Ind. 327, 157 N.E.2d 481 (1959).

This section sets forth the procedure by which the appraisers' report is to be challenged, i.e., taken "exception to." Harding v. State, 603 N.E.2d 176 (Ind. App. 1992).

Review on Appeal.
Since statutes recognized the right of appeal from final judgments in proceedings for the assessment of damages for property taken by eminent domain, in such appeal the whole case could have been reviewed as in other appeals from final judgments. State v. Wood, 219 Ind. 424, 39 N.E.2d 448 (1942).

Right to Trial.

—Jury Trials.
Trials on the question of damages in eminent domain proceedings are regarded as civil actions and a trial by jury may be demanded under appropriate circumstances. State v. City of Terre Haute, 170 Ind. App. 228, 54 Ind. Dec. 69, 352 N.E.2d 542 (1976).

——Timely Request.
Defendant in an eminent domain proceeding would have until ten days after the filing of exceptions to timely file a request for jury trial. State ex rel. Bd. of Aviation Comm'rs v. Kosciusko County Superior Court, 430 N.E.2d 754 (Ind. 1982).

Subsequent Purchasers.
While it is clear the legislature intended that known parties receive notice at both the appropriation and the valuation stage, there is no indication that the legislature intended "known parties to the action" to include subsequent purchasers, nor does the statute contemplate requiring a condemnor to conduct a second title search prior to the valuation stage to find subsequent purchasers. MDM Invs. v. City of Carmel, 740 N.E.2d 929 (Ind. App. 2000).

Surety.
Where a bond would have been required in order to withdraw an offered amount from the court, that part of the statute which forbids an interest award where the defendant could have withdrawn such amount without a bond is inapplicable. State v. Simley Corp., 169 Ind. App. 650, 53 Ind. Dec. 545, 351 N.E.2d 41 (1976).

In condemnation proceeding where landowner withdrew the amount deposited by the state and furnished bond as provided in this section and such bond was entered in judgment docket, such bond constituted a lien on all the landowner's real estate and it was not necessary to comply with either former IC 34-1-43-1 or former IC 34-1-43-2 to perfect such lien. State y. Cox, 177 Ind. App. 47, 63 Ind. Dec. 214, 377 N.E.2d 1389 (1978).

Vacating Appraisers' Report.
Trial court, after determining that the appropriation proceedings failed to meet the statutory requirements, properly vacated the appraisers' report and entered a new order appropriating the real estate and appointing appraisers. State v. Berger, 534 N.E.2d 268 (Ind. App. 1989).

Waiver of Appeal.
In a condemnation proceeding where the state has accepted a benefit from the judgment of the trial court based on the jury's

Waiver of Appeal. (Cont'd)
award of damages to landowners, the state has waived its right to appeal. State v. Kraszyk, 240 Ind. 524, 167 N.E.2d 339 (1960).

Withdrawal of Appraisers' Report.
Because this section provides that the court after hearing and determining the exceptions filed to the appraisers' report should make such further orders and render such findings and judgment as justice requires, the court acted within its statutory power in allowing the original appraisers to withdraw their written report after situation changed. State v. Smith, 260 Ind. 555, 37 Ind. Dec. 325, 297 N.E.2d 809 (1973).

Collateral References. Reviewability, on appeal from final judgment in eminent domain proceedings, of interlocutory order as affected by fact that order was separately appealable. 79 A.L.R.2d 1352.

Review of discretion as to admissibility, on issue of condemned real property, of evidence of sale prices of other real property. 85 A.L.R.2d 110.

Evidentiary effect of view by jury in condemnation case. 1 A.L.R.3d 1397.

Waiver [of jury trial]. 12 A.L.R.3d 7.

Propriety and effect, in eminent domain proceeding, of argument or evidence as to landowner's unwillingness to sell property. 17 A.L.R.3d 1449.

Propriety and effect, in eminent domain proceeding, of argument or evidence as to source of funds to pay for property. 19 A.L.R.3d 694.

Propriety and effect, in eminent domain proceeding, of instruction to the jury as to landowner's unwillingness to sell property. 20 A.L.R.3d 1081.

Propriety and effect of argument or evidence as to financial status of parties in eminent domain proceeding. 21 A.L.R.3d 936.

Admissibility, on issue of value of condemned real property, of rental value of other real property. 23 A.L.R.3d 724.

Admissibility of photographs or models of property condemned. 23 A.L.R.3d 825.

Admissibility of evidence of proposed or possible subdivision or platting of condemned land on issue of value in eminent domain proceedings. 26 A.L.R.3d 780.

Admissibility of testimony of expert, as to basis of his opinion, to matters otherwise excludible as hearsay — state cases. 89 A.L.R.4th 456.

32-24-1-12. Offer of settlement. — (a) Not later than ten (10) days before a trial involving the issue of damages, the plaintiff shall, and a defendant may, file and serve on the other party an offer of settlement. Not more than five (5) days after the date offer of settlement is served, the party served may respond by filing and serving upon the other party an acceptance or a counter offer of settlement. The offer must state that it is made under this section and specify the amount, exclusive of interest and costs, that the party serving the offer is willing to accept as just compensation and damages for the property sought to be acquired. The offer or counter offer supersedes any other offer previously made under this chapter by the party.

(b) An offer of settlement is considered rejected unless an acceptance in writing is filed and served on the party making the offer before the trial on the issue of the amount of damages begins.

(c) If the offer is rejected, it may not be referred to for any purpose at the trial but may be considered solely for the purpose of awarding costs and litigation expenses under section 14 [IC 32-24-1-14] of this chapter.

(d) This section does not limit or restrict the right of a defendant to payment of any amounts authorized by law in addition to damages for the property taken from the defendant.

(e) This section does not apply to an action brought under IC 8-1-13-19 (repealed). [P.L.2-2002, § 9.]

NOTES TO DECISIONS

Interest.

A landowner who accepts a condemnor's settlement offer of a condemnation action under this section is entitled to interest. Harding v. State, 603 N.E.2d 176 (Ind. App. 1992).

32-24-1-13. Special procedures for department of transportation.

— (a) The Indiana department of transportation or any state board, agency, or commission that succeeds the department in respect to the duties to locate, relocate, construct, reconstruct, repair, or maintain the public highways of Indiana, having the right to exercise the power of eminent domain for the public use, in its action for condemnation is not required to prove that an offer of purchase was made to the property owner in an action under this article.

(b) The court shall on the return day fixed at the time of the filing of the complaint appoint appraisers as provided by law and fix a day not later than ten (10) days after the date of the court's order for the appraisers to appear, qualify, and file their report of appraisal.

(c) If the appraisers appointed by the court fail to appear, qualify, and file their report of appraisal as ordered by the court, the court shall discharge the appraisers and appoint new appraisers in the same manner as provided in subsection (b). [P.L.2-2002, § 9.]

NOTES TO DECISIONS

ANALYSIS

Appointment of appraisers.
Day for report of appraisers.
Fair market value.
Good faith offer.
Offer to purchase.

Appointment of Appraisers.

Where the deputy attorney general was present in court when appraisers were appointed and failed to object thereto, any objection to failure to appoint appraisers within the ten-day period required by this section was waived by the state. State ex rel. Agan v. Hendricks Superior Court, 250 Ind. 675, 13 Ind. Dec. 664, 235 N.E.2d 458, reh'g denied, 250 Ind. 675, 238 N.E.2d 446 (1968).

Day for Report of Appraisers.

Where appraisers were ordered by the court to make their report at a time in excess of that set by this section, and where the parties were present and did not object thereto, such was a matter of procedure and was not jurisdictional and a party was in no position to later claim error. Ray v. State, 252 Ind. 395, 18 Ind. Dec. 117, 248 N.E.2d 337 (1969).

Fair Market Value.

The provisions of former IC 32-11-1-2.1 (repealed; for similar provision see 32-24-1-5) requiring a condemnor to make an offer based on the actual fair market value of the property as a condition precedent to condemnation, being the most recent expression of the legislature, supersede the earlier provision in this section relieving the state of the obligation to prove an offer to purchase. Decker v. State, 426 N.E.2d 151 (Ind. App. 1981).

Good Faith Offer.

Any condemnor, including the state, must make a good faith offer to purchase in the particular manner described by IC 32-11-1-2.1 before attempting to exercise its eminent domain authority. Decker v. State, 426 N.E.2d 151 (Ind. App. 1981).

Offer to Purchase.

Under this section, it was not necessary for the state to prove an offer of purchase was made. Sadlier v. State, 252 Ind. 525, 18 Ind. Dec. 516, 251 N.E.2d 27 (1969).

32-24-1-14. Costs of proceedings.

— (a) Except as provided in subsection (b), the plaintiff shall pay the costs of the proceedings.

(b) If there is a trial, the additional costs caused by the trial shall be paid as ordered by the court. However, if there is a trial and the amount of damages awarded to the defendant by the judgment, exclusive of interest and costs, is greater than the amount specified in the last offer of settlement made by the plaintiff under section 12 [IC 32-24-1-12] of this chapter, the court shall allow the defendant the defendant's litigation expenses in an amount not to exceed two thousand five hundred dollars ($2,500). [P.L.2-2002, § 9.]

NOTES TO DECISIONS

Analysis

In general.
Attorney's fees.
Damages reduced.
Fees and expenses.
—Exemption.
—Not allowed.
Matters included.

In General.

The law determined who should pay costs, and persons appointed to assess damages could not determine the question. Wabash R.R. v. Fort Wayne & S.W. Traction Co., 161 Ind. 295, 67 N.E. 674 (1903).

Since this was a special statute, it superseded and took precedence over IC 34-1-32-4 when the proceeding involved was under a statute including this section. Flesch v. State, 250 Ind. 529, 242 N.E.2d 511 (1968).

This section specifically provides for the payment of costs by the plaintiff, and in the event of contest the additional costs to have been paid as the court should adjudge; as the statute specifically created such liability, it was a special statute which took precedence over the general statute relating to costs. Flesch v. State, 250 Ind. 529, 242 N.E.2d 511 (1968).

Attorney's Fees.

The provision in former IC 32-11-1-10 (repealed; see this section for similar provisions) for litigation expenses authorized the award of attorney's fees to litigants who successfully challenge a condemning authority's valuation of property taken through inverse condemnation. City of Garrett v. Terry, 512 N.E.2d 405 (Ind. 1987).

Damages Reduced.

If, on trial of the question of damages, the damages assessed were reduced, the party appropriating the land would recover the costs of the trial. Douglas v. Indianapolis & N.W. Traction Co., 37 Ind. App. 332, 76 N.E. 892 (1906).

Fees and Expenses.

—Exemption.

Section 4 of Public Law 312-1977, which enacted former IC 32-11-1-8.1 (repealed; for similar provisoin see 32-24-1-12) and this section, exempts any project for which offers to purchase or negotiations have occurred prior to July 1, 1977 from the application of the provision allowing for litigation expenses. State v. Bircher, 446 N.E.2d 607 (Ind. App. 1983).

—Not Allowed.

Condemnees' attorneys' fees and extraordinary litigation expenses were not recoverable under the obdurate behavior or bad faith exception to the general rule of nonrecovery of attorney fees, nor under the constitutional mandate entitling condemnees to just compensation for property taken for public use, where the bad faith exception was inapplicable to the state and condemnees' argument that without the change of venue which precipitated such extra fees and expenses their property would have been taken without just compensation was unsubstantiated and too tenuous to justify the award. State v. Hicks, 465 N.E.2d 1146 (Ind. App. 1984).

Where city's last offer of settlement was $41,500.00, and award to owner of condemned property was for $41,500.00, the owner was not entitled to litigation expenses under this section because litigation expenses can only be granted if the award is greater than the last offer of settlement. City of Mishawaka ex rel. Dep't of Redevelopment v. Fred W. Bubb Funeral Chapel, Inc., 469 N.E.2d 757 (Ind. App. 1984).

Matters Included.

Although this section refers to "additional costs," there is no definition as to what a court may consider as costs, and it would appear that the legislature never intended for the word "costs" to cover every conceivable expense incurred. State v. Holder, 260 Ind. 336, 36 Ind. Dec. 331, 295 N.E.2d 799 (1973).

Prior to the 1977 amendment to former IC 32-11-1-10 (repealed; see this section for sim-

Matters Included. (Cont'd) ilar provisions), the words "additional costs," as was used in this section, did not include defendant's attorney fees and witnesses' fees.

State v. Holder, 260 Ind. 336, 36 Ind. Dec. 331, 295 N.E.2d 799 (1973); City of Indianapolis ex rel. DOT v. Central R.R., 175 Ind. App. 120, 60 Ind. Dec. 133, 369 N.E.2d 1109 (1977).

Collateral References. Relinquishment of part of land or incorporeal rights therein as affecting costs. 5 A.L.R.2d 724.

Attorney's fees as within statute imposing upon condemnor liability for "expenses," "costs," and the like. 26 A.L.R.2d 1295.

Costs in proceeding for condemning a public utility plant. 68 A.L.R.2d 392.

Liability for costs in trial tribunal in eminent domain proceedings as affected by offer or tender by condemnor. 70 A.L.R.2d 804.

Liability of state or its agency or board for costs in eminent domain proceedings. 72 A.L.R.2d 1379.

Liability, upon abandonment of eminent domain proceedings, for expenses incurred by property owner. 92 A.L.R.2d 355.

Condemnor's liability for costs of condemnee's expert witnesses. 68 A.L.R.3d 546.

32-24-1-15. Failure to pay assessed damages — Action to declare forfeiture. — (a) If the person seeking to take property under this article fails:

(1) to pay the assessed damages not later than one (1) year after the appraisers' report is filed, if exceptions are not filed to the report;

(2) to pay:

(A) the damages assessed if exceptions are filed to the appraisers' report and the exceptions are not sustained; or

(B) the damages assessed and costs if exceptions are filed to the appraisers' report and the exceptions are sustained;

not later than one (1) year after the entry of the judgment, if an appeal is not taken from the judgment;

(3) to pay the damages assessed or the judgment rendered in the trial court not later than one (1) year after final judgment is entered in the appeal if an appeal is taken from the judgment of the trial court; or

(4) to take possession of the property and adapt the property for the purpose for which it was acquired not later than five (5) years after the payment of the award or judgment for damages, except where a fee simple interest in the property is authorized to be acquired and is acquired;

the person seeking to acquire the property forfeits all rights in the property as fully and completely as if the procedure to take the property had not begun.

(b) An action to declare a forfeiture under this section may be brought by any person having an interest in the property sought to be acquired, or the question of the forfeiture may be raised and determined by direct allegation in any subsequent proceedings, by any other person to acquire the property for a public use. In the subsequent proceedings the person seeking the previous acquisition or the person's proper representatives, successors, or assigns shall be made parties. [P.L.2-2002, § 9.]

NOTES TO DECISIONS

In General.

The power of eminent domain was an attribute of sovereignty and inured in every independent state. It was superior to all property rights and extended to all property within the state. State v. Flamme, 217 Ind. 149, 26 N.E.2d 917 (1940).

Abandonment.

The acts, both of the original owners of the land and railroad company to which the land was first awarded, amounted to an abandonment of all claims under the condemnation proceedings. Coburn v. Sands, 150 Ind. 141, 48 N.E. 786 (1897).

Where the state had made no entry upon the property, but had abandoned the condemnation, it was not bound by a judgment for damages, erroneously entered in the form of a personal judgment. State v. Flamme, 217 Ind. 149, 26 N.E.2d 917 (1940).

Appurtenant Easement.

Because in subdivision (a)(4) of this section "where" means "in the event that," this section does not inflict forfeiture upon an appurtenant easement of a tract that was conveyed in fee simple, and the appurtenant easement may not be separated from the tract. Schwartz v. Castleton Christian Church, Inc., 594 N.E.2d 473 (Ind. App. 1992).

Ejectment.

Where ejectment suit was pending in which defendant denied that state had made full payment within the year required by this section, it was proper for court to deny a writ of assistance by which state sought to obtain possession of the property. State ex rel. Dep't of Nat'l Resources v. Winfrey, 419 N.E.2d 1319 (Ind. App. 1981).

Forfeiture of Rights.

Under this section, where less than a fee simple was condemned, a condemnor's rights in the condemned real estate could have been "forfeited," even after final judgment and payment of the damages, if it failed for five years to devote the land to the use for which it was condemned, and the word "forfeit" carried no suggestion of reimbursement to the condemnor of the price paid. State v. Pollitt, 220 Ind. 593, 45 N.E.2d 480 (1942).

If the state or other condemnor could, by mere inaction, have avoided taking the property originally sought to have been acquired, then it logically followed that the condemnor could have, by positive action, waived the lapse of time, abandoned its action and permitted the condemnee to immediately make such use of the premises as it saw fit, without having to wait the passage of time allowed by the statute before the condemnor forfeited its right to take the property. Pendleton v. Poor, 244 Ind. 107, 1 Ind. Dec. 506, 191 N.E.2d 3 (1963).

Forfeiture Through Nonuse.

Subsection (a)(4) of predecessor statute to this section causes the forfeiture of an appropriation through nonuse only in those cases in which an appropriation of less than a fee simple has been made, such as when a mere right-of-way has been taken. Schwartz v. Castleton Christian Church, Inc., 594 N.E.2d 473 (Ind. App. 1992).

Injunction.

In the absence of an allegation that the condemnation award had not been paid within the proper time, the complaint, in an action to enjoin the condemnor from asserting title, was insufficient as against a demurrer, unless other facts were pleaded sufficient to stay the cause of action. Russell v. Trustees of Purdue Univ., 93 Ind. App. 242, 178 N.E. 180 (1931).

Judgment Not Paid Within Year.

The provision of the statute with reference to the payment of the judgment within one year was positive and self-executing, and if payment was not so made, the condemnor was in the same position as if no appropriation or condemnation had been begun or made. State v. Flamme, 217 Ind. 149, 26 N.E.2d 917 (1940).

Where plaintiff brought a condemnation action against defendants and damages were paid into the clerk's office more than one year after the appraisers' report was filed, exceptions to which were filed by defendants but not by plaintiff, the provision of this section requiring damages to be paid "within one year after the appraisers' report is filed" unless exceptions are filed to the report does not refer solely to exceptions filed by the condemnor, but alludes equally to condemnor and condemnee so that condemnee, having filed exceptions, has waived his right to relief. Anthrop v. Tippecanoe Sch. Corp., 156 Ind.

Judgment Not Paid Within Year. (Cont'd)
App. 167, 36 Ind. Dec. 322, 295 N.E.2d 637
(1973).

Possession.

In condemnation for railroad right-of-way,
the landowner, in undisturbed possession of
the property until payment or tender of damages, was not deprived thereof by fixing the
price at which it might have been taken.
Sisters of Providence v. Lower Vein Coal Co.,
198 Ind. 645, 154 N.E. 659 (1926), overruled
on other grounds, Joint County Park Bd. v.

Stegemoller, 228 Ind. 118, 89 N.E.2d 720
(1950).

Proceeding Dismissed.

If proceeding were dismissed, the landowner was not entitled to recover incidental
costs or damages. Howard v. Illinois Cent.
R.R., 64 F.2d 267 (7th Cir. 1933).

Condemnor had the right to dismiss its
cause of action after the return of the verdict
without being liable for payment of damages
assessed. Pendleton v. Poor, 244 Ind. 107, 1
Ind. Dec. 506, 191 N.E.2d 3 (1963).

Collateral References. Condemnor's
waiver, surrender, or limitation, after award,
of rights or part of property acquired by
condemnation. 5 A.L.R.2d 724.

Liability, upon abandonment of eminent
domain proceedings, for loss incurred by property owner. 92 A.L.R.2d 355.

32-24-1-16. Right to procedures. — A person having an interest in property that has been or may be acquired for a public use without the procedures of this article or any prior law followed is entitled to have the person's damages assessed under this article substantially in the manner provided in this article. [P.L.2-2002, § 9.]

NOTES TO DECISIONS

Constitutionality.

To limit a utility, whose property interests
are substantially interfered with, to relief by
way of inverse condemnation would deny it
the right to compensation guaranteed by the
Indiana Constitution. Indiana & Mich. Elec.
Co. v. Whitley County Rural Elec. Membership Corp., 160 Ind. App. 446, 42 Ind. Dec.
390, 312 N.E.2d 503 (1974).

Adjoining Lands.

A defendant in a condemnation action may
not enlarge the appropriation made by the
condemning authority or alternatively may
not defeat the authority's right of condemnation because it elects not to condemn adjacent
land, which the condemnee may or may not
own but, if the owner is aggrieved, a remedy
is available to him under this statute.
Rockwell v. State, 260 Ind. 50, 35 Ind. Dec. 76,
291 N.E.2d 894 (1973).

Alternative Remedies.

If lands were appropriated under the right
of eminent domain, the landowner could sue
for damages or pursue the remedy given by
statute. Merchants' Mut. Tel. Co. v.
Hirschman, 43 Ind. App. 283, 87 N.E. 238
(1909).

Equitable relief is not available to enjoin an
alleged taking of private property for a public
use, duly authorized by law, when a suit for

Alternative Remedies. (Cont'd)
compensation can be brought against the government entity subsequent to the taking. Dible v. City of Lafayette, 713 N.E.2d 269 (Ind. 1999).

Annoyance and Inconvenience.
Where there was a taking, not of the real estate itself, but of rights and interests in the real estate held prior to the highway construction, the enjoyment of the rights and use of the benefits of the property were impaired and the market value diminished, and such "annoyance and inconvenience" could have been considered in determining damages. State v. Stefaniak, 250 Ind. 631, 14 Ind. Dec. 649, 238 N.E.2d 451 (1968).

Appeals.
Where plaintiff sued for damages for land already taken, defendant could not appeal from interlocutory order finding that there had been a "taking" of land. Evansville-Vanderburgh Levee Auth. Dist. v. Towne Motel, Inc., 247 Ind. 161, 7 Ind. Dec. 475, 213 N.E.2d 705 (1966).

Application.

—Sufficiency.
In a proceeding by landowner for assessment of damages for land taken by railroad, the application must sufficiently have described the property, averred its taking, and referred to the law authorizing such taking. Indianapolis & V.R.R. v. Newsom, 54 Ind. 121 (1876).

Change of Ownership.
Where railroad had acquired and was using property of another railroad which had condemned the property for right-of-way, it adopted the original appropriation and was bound to compensate the owners and bound by the judgment in the condemnation proceedings against the corporation through which it took its title. New York, C. & St. L.R.R. v. Hammond, 132 Ind. 475, 32 N.E. 83 (1892); Chicago & I. Coal Ry. v. Hall, 135 Ind. 91, 34 N.E. 704, 23 L.R.A. 231 (1893); Chicago & S.E.R.R. v. Galey, 141 Ind. 360, 39 N.E. 925 (1895); Midland Ry. v. Galey, 141 Ind. 483, 39 N.E. 940 (1895).

Date of Valuation.
Date on which value of property condemned under former IC 18-7-8-17 was provided for in former IC 32-11-1-6 (repealed; for similar provisions see IC 32-24-1-9), which stated that right to damages accrued at date of service of notice of condemnation upon owner, and not date of declaration that such property was in a blighted area; although appellant waived any question as to date by failing to object to court's instructions to appraisers to fix value as of certain date. Elson v. City of Indianapolis ex rel. Dep't of Redevelopment, 246 Ind. 337, 4 Ind. Dec. 652, 204 N.E.2d 857 (1965).

Language requiring that damages be assessed "substantially in the manner as herein provided" encompassed the date as of which those damages were to be measured, that date being the date of the service of the notice, as provided in former IC 32-11-1-6 (repealed; for similar provision see IC 32-24-1-9). State v. Blackiston Land Co., 158 Ind. App. 93, 39 Ind. Dec. 32, 301 N.E.2d 663 (1973).

Deductions for Benefits.
In an action by the state to condemn real estate for the purpose of widening, and in some places changing, the right of a highway which ran through defendant's farm, an instruction that benefits, in order to be set off against the damage to the land not taken in making the improvement, had to have been special or local or such as resulted directly or peculiarly to the particular tract of land of defendants, and that general benefits resulting to the owners in common with the public could not have been set off, was proper on the question of benefits. State v. Ahaus, 223 Ind. 629, 63 N.E.2d 199 (1945).

In order that benefits could have been set off against the damage to the land not taken as provided in this section, such benefits, if any, must have been special or local or such as resulted directly or peculiarly to the residue of the particular tract of land from which the appropriation was made. General benefits resulting to owners in common with the public or locality at large could not have been set off against damages to the residue of the land. State v. Smith, 237 Ind. 72, 143 N.E.2d 666 (1957).

Highway Commission.
Where the state highway commission threatened to take leased premises without purchase or condemnation of lessee's interest under a grant from the owners, this statute did not furnish an adequate remedy at law that would preclude the lessee from enjoining such taking. Thomas v. Lauer, 227 Ind. 432, 86 N.E.2d 71 (1949).

Instructions.
An instruction that the jury could consider "in arriving at your verdict, the value of surrounding comparable property", while a correct statement of law, was improper where there was no evidence of the value of comparable property. State v. Lincoln Memory Gardens, Inc., 242 Ind. 206, 177 N.E.2d 655 (1961).

An instruction that limited a condemnation award to the "fair market value" of the land actually taken was erroneous, the true mea-

Instructions. (Cont'd)

sure of damages having been the difference between the market value of the entire tract before the taking and the market value of the residue after the taking; and the error in giving such erroneous instruction could not have been cured by the giving of a contradictory instruction correctly stating the law. Stephenson v. State, 244 Ind. 452, 2 Ind. Dec. 278, 193 N.E.2d 369 (1963).

Interest Without Condemnation.

An inverse condemnation suit against the state under this section was applicable where an interest in land was taken for public use without having first been appropriated under the act. State v. Geiger & Peters, Inc., 245 Ind. 143, 3 Ind. Dec. 133, 196 N.E.2d 740 (1964).

Even where the electric company had no property within the newly annexed area, a franchised utility's right to serve the annexed area could not be perfected without a condemnation action where the electric company had a property interest outside the area, the value or usefulness of which would be substantially interfered with by the loss of the annexed area. Indiana & Mich. Elec. Co. v. Whitley County Rural Elec. Membership Corp., 160 Ind. App. 446, 42 Ind. Dec. 390, 312 N.E.2d 503 (1974).

Judgment.

This section contemplated a judgment for the amount assessed by the court or jury. Southern Ind. Power Co. v. Cook, 182 Ind. 505, 107 N.E. 12 (1914).

Lands Taken Without Assessment.

If entry was made and possession taken of the land of an individual for use without first having had his damages assessed and tendered, the owner could maintain an action to recover possession of the land and he could have enjoined the use of the land until his damages were assessed and tendered. Cox v. Louisville, N.A. & C.R.R., 48 Ind. 178 (1874); Midland Ry. v. Smith, 113 Ind. 233, 15 N.E. 256 (1888); Louisville, N.A. & C. Ry. v. Soltweddle, 116 Ind. 257, 19 N.E. 111, 9 Am. St. 852 (1888); Strickler v. Midland Ry., 125 Ind. 412, 25 N.E. 455 (1890); Morgan v. Lake Shore & M.S. Ry., 130 Ind. 101, 28 N.E. 548 (1891); Midland Ry. v. Smith, 135 Ind. 348, 35 N.E. 284 (1893); Louisville, N.A. & C. Ry. v. Berkey, 136 Ind. 591, 36 N.E. 642 (1894).

The fifteen-year statute of limitations applied to proceedings to assess damages for the appropriation of land. Shortle v. Louisville, N.A. & C. Ry., 130 Ind. 505, 30 N.E. 639 (1892); Shortle v. Terre Haute & I.R.R., 131 Ind. 338, 30 N.E. 1084 (1892).

Recovery of damages could have been made by landowner for lands taken without an assessment. Evansville & R.R.R. v. Charlton, 6 Ind. App. 56, 33 N.E. 129 (1893); Chicago & I. Coal Ry. v. Hall, 135 Ind. 91, 34 N.E. 704, 23 L.R.A. 231 (1893); Pittsburgh, C., C. & St. L. Ry. v. Harper, 11 Ind. App. 481, 37 N.E. 41 (1894); Kennedy v. Cleveland, C., C. & St. L. Ry., 20 Ind. App. 315, 50 N.E. 592 (1898).

Consent by landowner to the construction of a railroad over his land did not bar his right to have his damages assessed. Evansville & R.R.R. v. Charlton, 6 Ind. App. 56, 33 N.E. 129 (1893); Chicago & I. Coal Ry. v. Hall, 135 Ind. 91, 34 N.E. 704, 23 L.R.A. 231 (1893).

If persons permitted their lands to have been wrongfully appropriated, they could afterwards have had their damages assessed under this act. Vandalia Coal Co. v. Indianapolis & L. Ry., 168 Ind. 144, 79 N.E. 1082 (1907).

Limitations and Prescription.

Twenty years' adverse use of land barred the right to recover damages. Sherlock v. Louisville, N.A. & C. Ry., 115 Ind. 22, 17 N.E. 171 (1888).

The application had to be filed before the claim was barred by the statute of limitations. Midland Ry. v. Smith, 125 Ind. 509, 25 N.E. 153 (1890).

Permission for Suit.

It was not necessary to obtain permission from the state to maintain an action under this section. State v. Geiger & Peters, Inc., 245 Ind. 143, 3 Ind. Dec. 133, 196 N.E.2d 740 (1964).

Power Lines.

In action to appropriate right-of-way for power line across land, instruction that jury should determine fair market value of easement, damages if any, to land caused by taking easement, and such other damages from construction, correctly stated elements of damages. Northern Ind. Pub. Serv. Co. v. Nielson, 123 Ind. App. 199, 109 N.E.2d 442 (1952).

Remaindermen.

Remaindermen were entitled to have their damages assessed. Shortle v. Terre Haute & I.R.R., 131 Ind. 338, 30 N.E. 1084 (1892).

Right of Access.

Where a new interstate highway blocked the normal outlet to appellees' steel fabricating plant which did not abut the proposed new highway and left an insufficient alternate route, it had the effect of depriving appellees of any suitable access to their steel fabricating business. This constituted a denial of appellees' right of access to their property and was a taking of property rights which was compensable. State v. Tolliver, 246

Right of Access. (Cont'd)
Ind. 319, 5 Ind. Dec. 193, 205 N.E.2d 672 (1965).

The operator of a filling station was not entitled to damages for loss of business due to his customers being obstructed from access to his station for a year as a result of the work of widening and resurfacing of the streets upon which his station site abutted. Papp v. City of Hammond, 248 Ind. 637, 11 Ind. Dec. 468, 230 N.E.2d 326 (1967).

Although the state took no more of plaintiffs' land than the previously granted right-of-way for the reconstruction and improvement of the highway, the raising of the grade level of the highway so as to interfere with access to plaintiffs' property and cause surface water to drain from the highway on to plaintiffs' property constituted a taking for which plaintiffs were entitled to compensation. State v. Lovett, 254 Ind. 27, 21 Ind. Dec. 8, 257 N.E.2d 298 (1970).

Taking.

—In General.

A takings claim does not accrue until available state remedies have been tried and proven futile, but efforts to predict how state courts will handle a particular inverse-condemnation suit are bootless; there is no uncompensated taking, nothing to litigate under 42 U.S.C.S. § 1983, until the state has established both what it has taken, and its refusal to pay just compensation. SGB Fin. Servs., Inc. v. Consolidated City of Indianapolis-Marion County, 235 F.3d 1036 (7th Cir. 2000).

—Adjacent Property.

Where land on all sides of property in question was taken for highway purposes, placing the residence in an unorthodox position, placing the lot in a cul-de-sac, placing dwelling in violation of zoning ordinances, and reducing the value of the property substantially, the question of a compensable taking was a matter for the jury's determination. State v. Stefaniak, 250 Ind. 631, 14 Ind. Dec. 649, 238 N.E.2d 451 (1968).

—Causing Zoning Violation.

The placing of appellant's building in violation of the zoning ordinances was a "taking" and should have been considered as a compensable injury to appellant's premises. Schuh v. State, 251 Ind. 403, 15 Ind. Dec. 667, 241 N.E.2d 362 (1968).

—Found.

In a proceeding under this section for the taking of property, where it was stipulated that in 1924 a resolution was adopted for the opening of the street in question but nothing was done with respect thereto until the street was constructed over the plaintiff's property in 1967, there was sufficient evidence to support the finding of the court that a taking occurred at the latter time. City of Hammond v. Drangmeister, 173 Ind. App. 476, 58 Ind. Dec. 165, 364 N.E.2d 157 (1977).

—Portion of Street.

Where appellant brought inverse condemnation action for alleged damages suffered when state took part of road in front of his house for a new highway, it would not succeed where he was still left with a two-way street, although narrower, in front of his house that met intersecting streets at the end of his block because he did not show the injury was special and peculiar to his land and not some inconvenience suffered by the public generally. Young v. State, 252 Ind. 131, 17 Ind. Dec. 224, 246 N.E.2d 377 (1969), cert. denied, 396 U.S. 1038, 90 S. Ct. 685, 24 L. Ed. 2d 683 (1970).

Time of Accrual of Damages.

Testimony of a real estate agent that he was familiar on February 11, 1957, with real estate values in the section where the land was located, and that the defendants sustained damages in the amount of $6,000, was sufficient for the jury to base their verdict upon in concluding that the damages to defendants two days later, February 13, 1957, were in the amount of $5,500. Southern Ind. Gas & Elec. Co. v. Jones, 240 Ind. 434, 166 N.E.2d 127 (1960).

Value.

—Evidence.

Where the parties in condemnation proceeding stipulated that evidence of the value of the property as of the date of the trial might be introduced, appellant's contention that evidence of value should have been strictly limited to the date that appellees were served with notice, under this statute, or as to the date of the taking under former IC 18-7-7-17 was properly denied. City of Evansville ex rel. Dep't of Redevelopment v. Bartlett, 243 Ind. 464, 186 N.E.2d 10, reh'g denied, 243 Ind. 471, 186 N.E.2d 799 (1962).

Zoning Ordinance.

A zoning ordinance which purported to authorize unlawful and unconstitutional appropriation of property rights without payment of compensation was wholly void and could have been collaterally attacked, the property owner having been under no duty to protect himself by inverse condemnation proceedings under this statute. Indiana Toll Rd. Comm'n v. Jankovich, 244 Ind. 574, 2 Ind. Dec. 243, 193 N.E.2d 237 (1963).

32-24-1-17. Repeal of conflicting laws. — All laws and parts of laws in conflict with the provisions of this chapter are hereby repealed: provided, that this repeal shall not affect proceedings pending on April 15, 1905, but such proceedings may be completed as if this chapter had never been passed. [P.L.2-2002, § 9.]

CHAPTER 2

PROCEDURES FOR CITIES AND TOWNS

32-24-2-1. "Fiscal officer" defined. — As used in this chapter, "fiscal officer" means:

(1) the city controller of a consolidated city or second class city;

(2) the city clerk-treasurer of a third class city; or

(3) the town clerk-treasurer of a town.

[P.L.2-2002, § 9.]

Effective Dates. P.L.2-2002, § 9. July 1. 2002.

32-24-2-2. "Municipality" defined. — As used in this chapter, "municipality" means a city or town. [P.L.2-2002, § 9.]

32-24-2-3. "Property" defined. — As used in this chapter, "property" refers to real property or personal property. [P.L.2-2002, § 9.]

32-24-2-4. "Work board" defined. — As used in this chapter, "works board" means:

(1) the board of public works or the board of public works and safety of a city; or

(2) the legislative body of a town.

[P.L.2-2002, § 9.]

32-24-2-5. Alternative proceedings. — If:

(1) a municipality has the power to acquire property under this chapter; or

(2) another statute provides for proceedings by a municipality for acquiring property under this chapter;

the board exercising those powers may proceed under IC 32-24-1 instead of this chapter. [P.L.2-2002, § 9.]

NOTES TO DECISIONS

Conveyance in Lieu of Condemnation.
A conveyance in lieu of actual condemnation of real property constitutes a condemnation proceeding because it indicates an intention to acquire the property by condemnation and is tantamount to a taking under the power of eminent domain. P.C. Mgt., Inc. v. Page Two, Inc., 573 N.E.2d 434 (Ind. App. 1991).

City, which purchased a leasehold interest in lieu of condemnation, had no obligation to purchase a sublease interest where the sublease had terminated upon the city's purchase, in view of language in the sublease providing that it would terminate if the master lease terminated "for any reason." P.C. Mgt., Inc. v. Page Two, Inc., 573 N.E.2d 434 (Ind. App. 1991).

Collateral References. 26 Am. Jur. 2d Eminent Domain, §§ 17-24.
27 Am. Jur. 2d Eminent Domain, §§ 375-384.

29A C.J.S. Eminent Domain, §§ 391-416.

32-24-2-6. Applicability — Adoption of resolution — Duties of works board. — (a) This chapter applies if the works board of a municipality wants to acquire property for the use of the municipality or to open, change, lay out, or vacate a street, an alley, or a public place in the municipality, including a proposed street or alley crossings of railways or other rights-of-way.

(b) The works board must adopt a resolution that the municipality wants to acquire the property. The resolution must describe the property that may be injuriously or beneficially affected. The board shall have notice of the resolution published in a newspaper of general circulation published in the municipality once each week for two (2) consecutive weeks. The notice must name a date, at least ten (10) days after the last publication, at which time the board will receive or hear remonstrances from persons interested in or affected by the proceeding.

(c) The works board shall consider the remonstrances, if any, and then take final action, confirming, modifying, or rescinding its original resolution. This action is conclusive as to all persons. [P.L.2-2002, § 9.]

NOTES TO DECISIONS

Notice.
The "in the municipality" language of former IC 32-11-1.5-3 (repealed; see this section for similar provisions) was to be read to

include "or within four miles of the corporate limits." Vickery v. City of Carmel, 424 N.E.2d 147 (Ind. App. 1981).

32-24-2-7. List of owners or holders of property. — (a) When the final action under section 6 [IC 32-24-2-6] of this chapter is taken, the works board shall have prepared the following:

(1) A list of all the owners or holders of the property, and of interests in it, sought to be acquired or to be injuriously affected.

(2) If a street, alley, or public place is to be opened, laid out, changed, or vacated in the municipality, or within four (4) miles of it, a list of the

owners or holders of property, and of interests in it, to be beneficially affected by the work.

(b) The list required by subsection (a) may not be confined to the owners of property along the line of the proposed work but must include all property taken, benefitted, or injuriously affected. In addition to the names, the list must show, with reasonable certainty, a description of each piece of property belonging to those persons that will be acquired or affected, either beneficially or injuriously. A greater certainty in names or descriptions is not necessary for the validity of the list than is required in the assessment of taxes. [P.L.2-2002, § 9.]

32-24-2-8. Award of damages — Notice to owners. — (a) Upon the completion of the list, the works board shall award the damages sustained and assess the benefits accruing to each piece of property on the list.

(b) When the assessments or awards are completed, the works board shall have a written notice served upon the owner of each piece of property, showing the amount of the assessment or award, by leaving a copy of the notice at the owner's last usual place of residence in the municipality or by delivering a copy to the owner personally.

(c) If the owner is a nonresident, or if the owner's residence is unknown, the municipality shall notify the owner by publication in a daily newspaper of general circulation in the municipality once each week for three (3) successive weeks.

(d) The notices must also name a day, at least ten (10) days after service of notice or after the last publication, on which the works board will receive or hear remonstrances from persons with regard to the amount of their respective awards or assessments.

(e) Persons not included in the list of the assessments or awards and claiming to be entitled to them are considered to have been notified of the pendency of the proceedings by the original notice of the resolution of the works board. [P.L.2-2002, § 9.]

32-24-2-9. Appointment of guardian — Defects in proceedings. — (a) If a person having an interest in property affected by the proceedings is mentally incompetent or less than eighteen (18) years of age, the works board shall certify that fact to the municipality's attorney.

(b) The municipality's attorney shall apply to the proper court and secure the appointment of a guardian for the person less than eighteen (18) years of age or the mentally incompetent person. The works board shall give notice to the guardian, who shall appear and defend the interest of the protected person. However, if the protected person already has a guardian, the notice shall be served on that guardian. The requirements of notice to the guardian are the same as for other notices.

(c) If there is a defect in the proceedings with respect to at least one (1) interested person, the defect does not affect the proceedings except as it may concern the interest or property of those persons, and the defect does not affect any other person concerned.

(d) In case of a defect, supplementary proceedings of the same general character as those prescribed by this chapter may be initiated in order to correct the defect. [P.L.2-2002, § 9.]

32-24-2-10. Consideration of remonstrances. — (a) A person notified or considered to be notified under this chapter may appear before the works board on the day fixed for hearing remonstrances to awards and assessments and remonstrate in writing against them.

(b) After the remonstrances have been received, the works board shall either sustain or modify the awards or assessments in the case of remonstrances that have been filed. The works board shall sustain the award or assessment in the case of an award or assessment against which a remonstrance has not been filed.

(c) A person remonstrating in writing who is aggrieved by the decision of the works board may, not later than twenty (20) days after the decision is made, take an appeal to a court that has jurisdiction in the county in which the municipality is located. The appeal affects only the assessment or award of the person appealing. [P.L.2-2002, § 9.]

32-24-2-11. Appeal — Costs. — (a) The appeal may be taken by filing an original complaint in the court against the municipality within the time required by section 10(c) [IC 32-24-2-10(c)] of this chapter, setting forth the action of the works board with respect to the assessment and stating the facts relied upon as showing an error on the part of the board. The court shall rehear the matter of the assessment de novo and confirm, reduce, or increase the assessment. If the court reduces the amount of benefit assessed or increases the amount of damages awarded, the plaintiff may recover costs. If the court confirms the amount of the assessment, the plaintiff may not recover costs. The judgment of the court is conclusive, and an appeal may not be taken from the court's judgment.

(b) If upon appeal the benefits assessed or damages awarded by the works board are reduced or increased, the municipality may, upon the payment of costs, discontinue the proceedings. It may also, through the works board, make and adopt an additional assessment against all the property originally assessed in the proceeding, or that part that is benefitted, in the manner provided for the original assessment. However, such an assessment against any one (1) piece of property may not exceed ten percent (10%) of the original assessment against it.

(c) If the municipality decides to discontinue the proceedings upon payment of costs and if assessments for benefits have already been paid, the amounts paid shall be paid back to the person or persons paying them. [P.L.2-2002, § 9.]

NOTES TO DECISIONS

ANALYSIS

Temporary restraining order.
—Sewer release system.

Temporary Restraining Order.

—Sewer Release System.
A landowner is not entitled to a temporary

Temporary Restraining Order. (Cont'd)

—Sewer Release System. (Cont'd)
restraining order to prevent a city and its board of public works and safety from acquiring part of the landowner's property in implementation of a project for the construction and installation of a sewer release system where it does not seem probable that she would be able to prevail in her claim that her rights under the Fourteenth Amendment would be abrogated if the city proceeded under this chapter. Kozicki v. City of Crown Point, 560 F. Supp. 1203 (N.D. Ind. 1983).

32-24-2-12. Delivery of list to fiscal officer — Duties of fiscal officer. — (a) Upon completion of the assessment list by the works board, the list shall be delivered to the fiscal officer of the municipality. From the time the respective amounts of benefits are assessed, or if a lot or parcel has sustained both benefits and damages because of an improvement as stated in the assessment list, then the excess of benefits assessed over damages awarded constitutes a lien superior to all other liens except taxes against the respective lot or parcel.

(b) The fiscal officer of the municipality shall immediately prepare a list of the excess of benefits, to be known as the local assessment list. If the municipality is a second class city and the county treasurer collects money due the city, the local assessment list shall be delivered to the county treasurer.

(c) The duties of the fiscal officer of the municipality and county treasurer are the same as prescribed with regard to assessments for street improvement. The provisions of the statute relating to:

(1) the payment of street improvement assessments by installments on the signing of waivers and issuance of bonds and coupons in anticipation;

(2) the duties of the fiscal officer and the county treasurer in relation to them; and

(3) the enforcement of payment of assessments in proceedings for the improvement of streets by the works board;

applies to these assessments. [P.L.2-2002, § 9.]

32-24-2-13. Assessments — Due and payable — Failure to pay. — (a) The benefit assessments are due and payable to the fiscal officer or county treasurer from the time of the preparation or delivery of the assessment duplicate.

(b) If an assessment is not paid within sixty (60) days, the municipality, by its attorney, shall proceed to foreclose the liens as mortgages are foreclosed, with similar rights of redemption, and have the property sold to pay the assessments. The municipality may recover costs, with reasonable attorney's fees, and interest from the expiration of the sixty (60) days allowed for payment, at the rate of six percent (6%) per year.

(c) If the person against whom the assessment is made is a resident of the municipality, demand for payment must be made by delivering to the person personally, or leaving at the person's last or usual place of residence, a notice of the assessment and demand for payment. [P.L.2-2002, § 9.]

32-24-2-14. Use of works board funds. — The works board may determine if any part of the damages awarded shall be paid out of funds appropriated for the use of the board. However, not more than two thousand dollars ($2,000) in damages may be paid out of the municipality's funds for any improvement or condemnation except under an ordinance appropriating money for the specific improvement or condemnation. All benefits assessed and collected by the fiscal officer or county treasurer are subject to draft, in the usual manner, upon certificate by the works board in favor of persons to whom damages have been awarded. Any surplus remaining above actual awards belongs to the municipality. The works board may delay proceedings until the benefits have been collected. [P.L.2-2002, § 9.]

32-24-2-15. Certificates. — (a) Upon completion of the award of damages or whenever any time for delay as provided has expired, the works board shall make out certificates for the proper amounts and in favor of the proper persons. Presentation of the certificates to the fiscal officer of the municipality entitles the person to a warrant on the fiscal officer or the county treasurer. The certificates or vouchers shall, whenever practicable, be actually tendered to the persons entitled to them, but when this is impracticable, they shall be kept for the persons in the office of the works board. The making and fixing of the certificate is a valid and effectual tender to the person entitled to it, and the certificate must be delivered to that person on request.

(b) If a dispute or doubt arises as to which person the money shall be paid, the works board shall make out the certificate in favor of the municipality's attorney for the use of the persons entitled to it. The attorney shall draw the money and pay it into court in a proper proceeding, requiring the various claimants to interplead and have their respective rights determined.

(c) If an injunction is obtained because damages have not been paid or tendered, the works board may tender the certificate for the amount with interest from the time of entry upon the property, if any has been made, including all accrued costs. The injunction shall then be dissolved. The pendency of an appeal does not affect the validity of a tender made under this section, but the municipality may proceed with its acquisition of the property in question. However, when a lot or parcel has sustained both benefits and damages because of improvements as stated in the assessment list, only an excess of damages awarded over benefits assessed is payable under this section. [P.L.2-2002, § 9.]

32-24-2-16. Rights-of-way adjoining bodies of water. — (a) This section applies whenever the works board of a municipality located upon or adjoining a harbor connected with a navigable stream or lake, or upon any navigable channel, slip, waterway, or watercourse, wants to acquire for the use of the municipality any property for a right-of-way for seawalls, docks, or other improvement of the harbor, channel, slip, waterway or watercourse.

(b) The works board shall adopt a resolution that the municipality wants to acquire the property, describing the property that may be injuriously or beneficially affected. All proceedings necessary for the completion of and payment for any such undertaking, including notice, remonstrance, appeal, letting of and performance of contracts, assessment and collection of payment for benefits, and the determination and payment of damages to property, are the same, to the extent applicable, as those proceedings for street improvements of the municipality by its works board or other entity charged by statute with the performance of those duties on behalf of the municipality. [P.L.2-2002, § 9.]

CHAPTER 3

PROCEDURES FOR STATE GOVERNMENT

32-24-3-1. Petition filed by attorney general. — If the governor considers it necessary:

(1) to acquire property on which to construct public buildings for the state; or

(2) to acquire property adjoining state property on which buildings have been erected;

the governor may order the attorney general to file an action in the name of the state. The attorney general shall file the action in a court that has jurisdiction in the county in which the property is located. The state's petition must ask that appraisers be appointed to appraise the value of the property considered necessary to be acquired for the public uses of the state. [P.L.2-2002, § 9.]

Effective Dates. P.L.2-2002, § 9. July 1. 2002.

Opinions of Attorney General. There is no statutory limit on how far in advance of a project the power of eminent domain may be exercised except where the interest condemned is less than a fee simple; then under former IC 32-11-1-11 (repealed; for similar provisions see IC 32-24-1-15), the property must be adapted to the use for which it was taken within five years from payment of the award. 1976, No. 7, p. 19.

Collateral References. 26 Am. Jur. 2d Eminent Domain, §§ 73-87.

29A C.J.S. Eminent Domain, §§ 65-86.

32-24-3-2. Notice to owners. — Upon filing the petition, the attorney general shall provide the owners of the property the notice required by law in the commencement of a civil action. It is sufficient to make defendants to the petition all persons who are in possession of the property and those who appear to be the owners or to have any interest in the property by the tax duplicates and the records in the offices of the auditor and recorder of the county. After notice has been given, the court shall appoint three (3) resident freeholders of the county where the property is located to appraise the value of the property. [P.L.2-2002, § 9.]

32-24-3-3. Appraisers — Oath — Report. — (a) Before entering upon their duties, the appraisers shall take and subscribe an oath that they will honestly appraise the property at its fair cash value.

(b) The appraisers shall make a report of their appraisement within a time fixed by the court.

(c) If the appraisers fail for any cause to make a report within the time fixed by the court, the court may extend the time or may appoint other appraisers. [P.L.2-2002, § 9.]

Collateral References. Referee's failure to file report within time specified by statute, court order, or stipulation as terminating reference. 71 A.L.R.4th 889.

32-24-3-4. Exceptions — Filing — Trial — Costs — Venue. — (a) After the appraisers file their report, any of the defendants may, within a reasonable time fixed by the court, file exceptions to the report, alleging that the appraisement of the property, as made by the appraisers, is not the true cash value of the property. If exceptions are filed, a trial on the exceptions shall be held by the court or before a jury, if asked by either party.

(b) The circuit court clerk shall give notice of filing of the appraisers' report to all known parties to the action and their attorneys of record by certified mail.

(c) Upon the trial of the exceptions, the court may revise, correct, amend, or confirm the appraisement in accordance with the finding of the court or verdict of the jury.

(d) The court shall apportion the costs accruing in the proceedings as justice may require.

(e) Changes of venue may be had as in other cases. [P.L.2-2002, § 9.]

32-24-3-5. Method of payment by state. — When the value of the property has been finally determined by the court, the governor may provide for the amount so found and may direct the auditor of state to draw a warrant on the treasurer of state to be paid out of any fund available in favor of the clerk of the circuit court. The clerk shall receive the money and hold it in court for the use of the owners and other persons adjudged to be entitled to the money. [P.L.2-2002, § 9.]

32-24-3-6. Execution and delivery of deed. — Upon payment to the clerk of the circuit court and the filing of a receipt for the payment of the money in open court as a part of the proceedings of the cause, the court shall direct the clerk of the circuit court to:

(1) execute a deed conveying the title of the property to the state of Indiana; and

(2) deliver the deed to the governor.

[P.L.2-2002, § 9.]

CHAPTER 4

PROCEDURES FOR UTILITIES AND OTHER CORPORATIONS

32-24-4-1. Private entities who may take or condemn lands. —
(a) A person, firm, partnership, limited liability company, or corporation authorized to do business in Indiana and authorized to:
    (1) furnish, supply, transmit, transport or distribute electrical energy, gas, oil, petroleum, water, heat, steam, hydraulic power, or communications by telegraph or telephone to the public or to any town or city; or
    (2) construct, maintain or operate turnpikes, toll bridges, canals, public landings, wharves, ferries, dams, aqueducts, street railways, or interurban railways for the use of the public or for the use of any town or city;
may take, acquire, condemn, and appropriate land, real estate, or any interest in the land or real estate.

(b) A person described in subsection (a) has all accommodations, rights, and privileges necessary to accomplish the use for which the property is taken. A person acting under subsection (a) may use acquired, condemned, or appropriated land to construct railroad siding, switch, or industrial tracks connecting its plant or facilities with the tracks of any common carrier. [P.L.2-2002, § 9.]

Effective Dates. P.L.2-2002, § 9. July 1. 2002.
Cross References. Cemeteries, locating through, restrictions, injunctions, IC 23-14-44.
Opinions of Attorney General. An independently incorporated realty company affiliated with a public utility having the power of eminent domain does not itself have a statutory authority to condemn land. 1976, No. 7, p. 19.

NOTES TO DECISIONS

ANALYSIS

In general.
Abuse of discretion.
Court review.
Legislative question.
Necessity.
Priority.
Public.
Public use.
Violation of zoning regulations.
Waterworks companies.
Within procedural rules.

In General.

The right of a foreign corporation to exercise the power of eminent domain was in derogation of the common law and existed only by virtue of an affirmative grant of power. Gradison v. Ohio Oil Co., 239 Ind. 218, 156 N.E.2d 80 (1959).

Under this section, a foreign corporation authorized to do business in this state could exercise the power of eminent domain if a like domestic corporation were given such privilege. Gradison v. Ohio Oil Co., 239 Ind. 218, 156 N.E.2d 80 (1959).

A public utility qualified to exercise the power of eminent domain under this act was not required to obtain from the public service commission a certificate of convenience, economy, or necessity, as required by former IC 8-1-8-2, before appropriating and condemning a right-of-way or easement across private lands for use of its power lines. Graham Farms, Inc. v. Indianapolis Power & Light Co., 249 Ind. 498, 12 Ind. Dec. 652, 233 N.E.2d 656 (1968). But see Alabach v. Northern Ind. Pub. Serv. Co., 164 Ind. App. 471, 329 N.E.2d 645 (1975).

This section together with IC 32-11-3-2 authorizes a public utility to condemn real property interests in such quantity and amount as deemed necessary. Indianapolis Power & Light Co. v. Barnard, 175 Ind. App. 308, 60 Ind. Dec. 494, 371 N.E.2d 408 (1978).

This section provides for the legislative delegation of the power of eminent domain to certain corporations operating in the public interest and demonstrates a legislative purpose that the power conferred be limited to the acquisition of real estate interests for the public purposes therein specified. Indianapolis Power & Light Co. v. Barnard, 175 Ind. App. 308, 60 Ind. Dec. 494, 371 N.E.2d 408 (1978).

A power company was not required to obtain a permit pursuant to former IC 8-21-7-3 prior to its exercise of the power of eminent domain even though it intended to erect towers upon the condemned property. Indianapolis Power & Light Co. v. Barnard, 175 Ind.

In General. (Cont'd)
App. 308, 60 Ind. Dec. 494, 371 N.E.2d 408 (1978).

Abuse of Discretion.

In determining what was meant by the word "necessary" as it was used for condemnation of rights deemed necessary to accomplish the use for which the property was taken pursuant to this section, the court recognized that a large discretion was necessarily vested in the condemnors in determining what property and how much was necessary and that the exercise of such discretion would not have been disturbed unless "clear abuse" thereof was shown. Jensen v. Indiana & Mich. Elec. Co., 257 Ind. 599, 29 Ind. Dec. 1, 277 N.E.2d 589 (1972).

The condemning authority's exercise of its power may not be prevented unless a clear abuse of discretion is shown. Indianapolis Power & Light Co. v. Barnard, 175 Ind. App. 308, 60 Ind. Dec. 494, 371 N.E.2d 408 (1978).

Court Review.

The courts are not to infringe upon the administrative act of determining the necessity or reasonableness of the decision to appropriate and take land; rather, they are only to determine whether there is legislatively delegated legal authority which would allow the exercise of the power of eminent domain to acquire the land. Indianapolis Power & Light Co. v. Barnard, 175 Ind. App. 308, 60 Ind. Dec. 494, 371 N.E.2d 408 (1978).

Legislative Question.

All questions concerning the expediency of taking private property for public use were exclusively for the legislature. Unless the action of the legislature was arbitrary, and the use for which the property was taken was clearly private, the courts would not interfere. Dahl v. Northern Ind. Pub. Serv. Co., 239 Ind. 405, 157 N.E.2d 194 (1959).

Where the intended use was public, the necessity and expediency of the taking could have been determined by such agency and in such mode as the state might designate. They were legislative questions, no matter who might have been charged with their decisions, and a hearing thereon was not essential to due process in the sense of the Fourteenth Amendment. Dahl v. Northern Ind. Pub. Serv. Co., 239 Ind. 405, 157 N.E.2d 194 (1959).

Necessity.

The statute vested discretion in the utiltity to take or appropriate property for public use, and if in its judgment the property sought to have been appropriated was necessary to distribute electric energy to the public, the utility had the right to condemn, and its judgment therein could not have been questioned

or superseded by the courts except for fraud, capriciousness or illegality. Dahl v. Northern Ind. Pub. Serv. Co., 239 Ind. 405, 157 N.E.2d 194 (1959).

In limiting the power of appropriation to that which was necessary, it was manifest that it was the legislative purpose to prevent the abuse of the power by making appropriations for speculative, monopolistic, or other purposes, foreign to the legitimate objects contemplated by the corporating charter. Dahl v. Northern Ind. Pub. Serv. Co., 239 Ind. 405, 157 N.E.2d 194 (1959).

The power of condemnation extended to an electric company is not limited to the purpose of transmitting energy but also extends within reason to the purpose of furnishing systems reliability by establishment of a "backup" system. J.M. Foster Co. v. Northern Ind. Pub. Serv. Co., 164 Ind. App. 72, 46 Ind. Dec. 570, 326 N.E.2d 584 (1975).

"Necessary" under this section means that which is reasonably proper and useful for the purpose sought and it must be based upon a present need or a fair and reasonable future need. Ellis v. Public Serv. Co., 168 Ind. App. 269, 51 Ind. Dec. 442, 342 N.E.2d 921 (1976).

The showing of a necessity for condemnation does not require proof that no subsequent contingencies will arise during the execution of the project such as might theoretically defeat the use of the land as originally contemplated. Indianapolis Power & Light Co. v. Barnard, 175 Ind. App. 308, 60 Ind. Dec. 494, 371 N.E.2d 408 (1978).

A power company's general allegations as to the use which it intended to make of the property interest sought and the necessity of the condemnation for such use were sufficient to sustain its exercise of power. Indianapolis Power & Light Co. v. Barnard, 175 Ind. App. 308, 60 Ind. Dec. 494, 371 N.E.2d 408 (1978).

Priority.

A power company's complaint for condemnation, filed before the land was certified as an airport being used for public purposes, created a prior and existing right of the public to use the real estate for a high voltage transmission line rather than as an airport, and the subsequent certification did not defeat this right. Indianapolis Power & Light Co. v. Barnard, 175 Ind. App. 308, 60 Ind. Dec. 494, 371 N.E.2d 408 (1978).

Public.

Former IC 32-11-3-1 (repealed; see this section for similar provisions) grants the power of eminent domain to a utility to furnish energy to the "public," not to Indiana residents alone. Oxendine v. Public Serv. Co., 423 N.E.2d 612 (Ind. App. 1980).

Public Use.

The real test was whether or not the prop-

Public Use. (Cont'd)

erty sought to have been taken would have been devoted to a public use named in the statute, namely, "to furnish, supply, transport, or distribute gas, oil [or] petroleum" whether it was "to" or "for" the public. Gradison v. Ohio Oil Co., 239 Ind. 218, 156 N.E.2d 80 (1959).

Whether a use was public did not depend upon the number using the utility, but rather whether the public had the right to use it without discrimination. Gradison v. Ohio Oil Co., 239 Ind. 218, 156 N.E.2d 80 (1959).

Violation of Zoning Regulations.

As a general rule, the propriety of a taking of property by eminent domain is not defeated by the fact that the purpose for which the property is taken is a use prohibited by zoning regulations. Indianapolis Power & Light Co. v. Barnard, 175 Ind. App. 308, 60 Ind. Dec. 494, 371 N.E.2d 408 (1978).

A utility having authority from the public service commission to extend its water distribution system and well fields was not subject to regulation by the local zoning authorities. Darlage v. Eastern Bartholomew Water Corp., 177 Ind. App. 425, 64 Ind. Dec. 287, 379 N.E.2d 1018 (1978).

Waterworks Companies.

The question of whether land which a water company sought to condemn was necessary for the construction and maintenance of a reservoir was a judicial one. Indianapolis Water Co. v. Lux, 224 Ind. 125, 64 N.E.2d 790 (1946).

"Necessary land" was that which was reasonably proper, suitable and useful for the purpose sought, and it was not necessary that plaintiff show an absolute or indispensible necessity for the taking. Indianapolis Water Co. v. Lux, 224 Ind. 125, 64 N.E.2d 790 (1946).

Where, in an action by a water company to condemn land, there was evidence that the construction of a dam for the purpose of creating a reservoir raised the level of a stream approximately four and one-half feet where it flowed through defendants' land, and when the reservoir was full it permanently flooded a portion of such land and during the time of high water flooded a great part of the remainder, and that part of the land not flooded was necessary for a border around such reservoir, a necessity for the taking of the portion of the land not flooded was shown. Indianapolis Water Co. v. Lux, 224 Ind. 125, 64 N.E.2d 790 (1946).

In a proceeding by a water company to condemn land for the purpose of obtaining necessary water supply for a town, it was not necessary that the petition have alleged that the petitioner had the right to lay its pipes over and along a public highway, as defendants alleged it was necessary for the petitioner to do, as such fact was not material to the issue. Reuter v. Milan Water Co., 209 Ind. 240, 198 N.E. 442 (1935), overruled on other grounds, Joint County Park Bd. v. Stegemoller, 228 Ind. 118, 89 N.E.2d 720 (1950).

In condemnation proceedings to take land for the purpose of supplying water to a city or town, it was no objection that there was no basis for determining the amount of water that would have been taken, since the amount of water that would have been taken was a question of fact to have been determined by the appraisers' record. Reuter v. Milan Water Co., 209 Ind. 240, 198 N.E. 442 (1935), overruled on other grounds, Joint County Park Bd. v. Stegemoller, 228 Ind. 118, 89 N.E.2d 720 (1950).

A waterworks company organized under a law specifically authorizing it to exercise the power of eminent domain could exercise such power before it had obtained a franchise from the city or town it contemplated serving or before a finding of necessity or convenience by the public service commission. Reuter v. Milan Water Co., 209 Ind. 240, 198 N.E. 442 (1935), overruled on other grounds, Joint County Park Bd. v. Stegemoller, 228 Ind. 118, 89 N.E.2d 720 (1950).

In a proceeding by a water supply company to condemn land for water supply to a town, it was no defense of objectors that plaintiff had leased its proposed waterworks to the town, to have been operated by it. Reuter v. Milan Water Co., 209 Ind. 240, 198 N.E. 442 (1935), overruled on other grounds, Joint County Park Bd. v. Stegemoller, 228 Ind. 118, 89 N.E.2d 720 (1950).

Where a company was organized to supply water to a city or town, it made no difference whether the water was taken from a surface lake or stream or from a subterranean body of water. Reuter v. Milan Water Co., 209 Ind. 240, 198 N.E. 442 (1935), overruled on other grounds, Joint County Park Bd. v. Stegemoller, 228 Ind. 118, 89 N.E.2d 720 (1950).

Within Procedural Rules.

The right of eminent domain power contained in IC 32-11-3-1 was statutory in origin and within the coverage of the Indiana Rules of Procedure. Jensen v. Indiana & Mich. Elec. Co., 257 Ind. 599, 29 Ind. Dec. 1, 277 N.E.2d 589 (1972).

Collateral References. 26 Am. Jur. 2d   29A C.J.S. Eminent Domain, §§ 22-26.
Eminent Domain, §§ 17-24.

32-24-4-2. Actions allowed. — The condemnor may take, acquire, condemn, and appropriate a fee simple estate, title, and interest in an amount of land as the condemnor considers necessary for the condemnor's proper uses and purposes. However, for rights-of-way, the condemnor shall take, acquire, condemn, and appropriate an easement. [P.L.2-2002, § 9.]

NOTES TO DECISIONS

ANALYSIS

In general.
Electric companies.
Necessity.
Power companies.

In General.

A public utility qualified under this act to exercise the power of eminent domain was not required to obtain from the public service commission a certificate of convenience, economy, or necessity, as required by former IC 8-1-8-2, before appropriating and condemning a right-of-way or easement across private lands for use of its power lines. Graham Farms, Inc. v. Indianapolis Power & Light Co., 249 Ind. 498, 12 Ind. Dec. 652, 233 N.E.2d 656 (1968). But see Alabach v. Northern Ind. Pub. Serv. Co., 164 Ind. App. 471, 329 N.E.2d 645 (1975).

Former IC 32-11-3-2 (repealed; see this section for similar provisions), together with former IC 32-11-3-1 (repealed; for similar provisions see IC 32-24-4-1), authorizes a public utility to condemn real property interests in such quantity and amount as deemed necessary. Indianapolis Power & Light Co. v. Barnard, 175 Ind. App. 308, 60 Ind. Dec. 494, 371 N.E.2d 408 (1978).

Electric Companies.

A power company seeking to condemn a strip of land across a farm for the erection of a transmission line was not required to pursue a route on a direct line from the starting point to its terminal without deviation, but could make reasonable or necessary deviations. Guerrettaz v. Public Serv. Co., 227 Ind. 556, 87 N.E.2d 721 (1949).

Necessity.

"Necessary" under the predecessor statute to this section means that which is reasonably proper and useful for the purpose sought, and it must be based upon a present need or a fair and reasonable future need. Ellis v. Public Serv. Co., 168 Ind. App. 269, 51 Ind. Dec. 442, 342 N.E.2d 921 (1976).

Power Companies.

In a proceeding by a power company to condemn a strip of land across a farm for the erection of a transmission line, the complaint, which specifically described the real estate with its point of beginning, its course and terminus, was not objectionable for failing to state definitely where the line began or where it ended. Guerrettaz v. Public Serv. Co., 227 Ind. 556, 87 N.E.2d 721 (1949).

32-24-4-3. Appropriation and condemnation procedures. — The appropriation and condemnation of land and easements in land authorized under this chapter shall be made under IC 32-24-1, except as otherwise provided in this chapter. [P.L.2-2002, § 9.]

Opinions of Attorney General. An independently incorporated realty company affiliated with a public utility having the power of eminent domain does not itself have a statutory authority to condemn land. 1976, No. 7, p. 19.

32-24-4-4. Land zoned for agricultural use. — (a) This section applies to a public utility that appropriates by condemnation procedures an easement for right-of-way purposes on land zoned or used for agricultural purposes.

(b) If a public utility makes a uniform easement acquisition offer under IC 32-24-1-5 or a settlement offer under IC 32-24-1-12 in excess of five thousand dollars ($5,000), the owner of the land may elect to accept as compensation either a lump sum payment or annual payments for a period not to exceed twenty (20) years.

(c) The landowner must elect either the lump sum payment or the annual payment method at the time the landowner:

(1) accepts the public utility's offer under IC 32-24-1-5 or IC 32-24-1-12 to purchase an easement;

(2) accepts the appraisers' award; or

(3) is awarded damages by a judgment in a proceeding under this article.

The grant of easement or judgment, whichever is applicable, must state the method of payment the landowner has elected to receive.

(d) If the land is owned by more than one (1) person, the election to receive annual payments must be unanimous among all record owners to be binding upon the public utility.

(e) Selection of the lump sum method of payment irrevocably binds the landowner and the landowner's successors in interest.

(f) The annual amount payable must be equal to the lump sum payment that would have otherwise been made by the utility divided by the number of years the landowner elects to receive the annual payments plus interest at a rate agreed upon by the public utility and the landowner on the balance remaining at the end of each year. The public utility shall make the annual payment as close as practicable to the date of the landowner's acceptance of the public utility's offer or the date of the judgment granting the utility the easement. If the public utility and the landowner are unable to agree upon the interest rate, the interest rate shall be the average annual effective interest rate for all new Federal Land Bank Loans, computed on the basis of the twelve (12) month period immediately preceding the date of settlement.

(g) A landowner who withdraws the appraisers' award under IC 32-24-1-11 may receive only a lump sum payment from the clerk at that time. If the landowner is later awarded a judgment for damages that exceeds the amount of the appraisers' award, the landowner may elect either method of compensation only to the extent that the damages exceed the appraisers' award remaining to be paid by the public utility as a result of the judgment.

(h) A landowner who elects the annual payment method may terminate the election by giving notarized written notice to the public utility at least ninety (90) days before the annual date of payment. The public utility may prescribe reasonable forms for the notice and may require that these forms be used for the notice to be effective. In the event the landowner terminates this election, the public utility shall pay the landowner in a single payment the difference between the lump sum and the total of all annual payments previously paid by the public utility. Upon the landowner's receipt of this payment, the public utility's payment obligations cease.

(i) If a landowner sells the landowner's entire interest in the servient estate, the landowner shall give the public utility prompt notarized written notice of the sale, together with a copy of the deed specifying the name and address of the landowner's successor in interest. If the public utility receives the notice less than ninety (90) days before the date of an annual payment, the public utility may make this annual payment to the landowner but must make all successive payments to the landowner's successors and assigns.

(j) If a landowner sells less than the landowner's entire interest in the servient estate, the public utility may continue to make the annual payments to the landowner.

(k) A public utility shall make annual payments to the landowner only for the time the servient estate continues to be zoned or used for agricultural purposes. If the servient estate is no longer zoned or used for agricultural purposes, the public utility shall pay to the landowner the difference between the lump sum and the total of all annual payments previously paid by the public utility. Upon the landowner's receipt of this payment, the public utility's payment obligations cease.

(*l*) This section is binding upon the heirs, successors, and assigns of the landowner and the public utility.

(m) Every offer of a public utility under IC 32-24-1-5 and IC 32-24-1-12 must include the following statement in at least ten (10) point boldface type capital letters:

"IF THIS OFFER IS OVER FIVE THOUSAND DOLLARS ($5,000), YOU MAY ELECT UNDER IC 32-24-4-4 TO ACCEPT PAYMENT IN A LUMP SUM PAYMENT OR IN ANNUAL PAYMENTS FOR A PERIOD NOT TO EXCEED TWENTY (20) YEARS WITH INTEREST. IF YOU ELECT ANNUAL PAYMENTS, THEN POSSESSION WILL BE RE-QUIRED THIRTY (30) DAYS AFTER YOU HAVE RECEIVED YOUR FIRST ANNUAL PAYMENT.".

(n) Every offer of a public utility under IC 32-24-1-5 and IC 32-24-1-12 must also include a form to be used by the landowner to accept the offer that substantially contains the following:

ACCEPTANCE OF OFFER

I (We),_____ ,_____ ,_____, landowner(s) of the above described property or interest in property hereby accept the offer of $_____ made by _____ (condemnor) on this _____ day of _____, 20____. Please check one of the following if the offer is in excess of five thousand dollars ($5,000):

( ) I (We) elect to accept payment in a lump sum.

( ) I (We) elect to accept payment in annual payments for a period of _____ years with interest as determined under IC 32-24-4-4.

_____

_____

_____

_____

NOTARY'S CERTIFICATE

STATE OF _____)
) SS:
COUNTY OF _____)

Subscribed and sworn to before me this _____ day of _____, 20____. My Commission Expires: _____

_____
(Signature)

_____
(Printed) NOTARY PUBLIC.

[P.L.2-2002, § 9.]

CHAPTER 5

EMINENT DOMAIN FOR GAS STORAGE

32-24-5-1. Declaration of public interest. — Whereas, the storage of gas in subsurface strata or formations of the earth in Indiana tends to insure a more adequate supply of gas to domestic, commercial, and industrial consumers of gas in this state and materially promotes the economy of the state, the storage of gas is declared to be in public interest and for the welfare of Indiana and the people of Indiana and to be a public use. [P.L.2-2002, § 9.]

Effective Dates. P.L.2-2002, § 9. July 1. 2002.

Collateral References. 29A C.J.S. Eminent Domain, §§ 27-29, 52-55.

32-24-5-2. Right to condemn land — Lands which may be condemned — Rights acquired. — (a) A person, firm, limited liability company, municipal corporation, or other corporation authorized to do business in Indiana and engaged in the business of transporting or distributing gas by means of pipelines into, within, or through Indiana for ultimate public use may condemn:

(1) land subsurface strata or formations;

(2) other necessary land rights;

(3) land improvements and fixtures, in or on land, except buildings of any nature; and

(4) the use and occupation of land subsurface strata or formations;

for constructing, maintaining, drilling, utilizing, and operating an underground gas storage reservoir.

(b) The following rights in land may be condemned for use in connection with the underground storage of gas:

(1) To drill and operate wells in and on land.

(2) To install and operate pipelines.

(3) To install and operate equipment, machinery, fixtures, and communication facilities.

(4) To create ingress and egress to explore and examine subsurface strata or underground formations.

(5) To create ingress and egress to construct, alter, repair, maintain, and operate an underground storage reservoir.

(6) To exclusively use any subsurface strata condemned.

(7) To remove and reinstall pipe and other equipment used in connection with rights condemned under subdivisions (1) through (6).

(c) Acquisition of subsurface rights in land for gas storage purposes by condemnation under this section must be without prejudice to any subsequent proceedings that may be necessary under this section to acquire additional subsurface rights in the same land for use in connection with the underground storage. Surface rights in land necessary for the accomplishment of the purposes set forth in this section may be condemned.

(d) Except with respect to a proceeding under this chapter to:

(1) acquire the right to explore and examine a subsurface stratum or formation in land; and

(2) create the right of ingress and egress for operations connected to the acquisition;

and subject to subsection (e), as a condition precedent to the exercise of the right to condemn any underground stratum, formation, or interest reasonably expected to be used or useful for underground gas storage, a condemnor first must have acquired by purchase, option, lease, or other method not involving condemnation, the right, or right upon the exercise of an option, if any, to store gas in at least sixty per cent (60%) of the stratum or formation. This must be computed in relation to the total surface acreage overlying the entire stratum or formation considered useful for the purpose.

(e) A tract under which the stratum or formation sought to be condemned is owned by two (2) or more persons, firms, limited liability companies, or corporations must be credited to the condemnor as acquired by it for the purpose of computing the percentage of acreage acquired by the condemnor in complying with the requirement of subsection (d) if the condemnor acquires from the owner or owners of an undivided three-fourths (¾) part or interest or more of the underground stratum or formation, by purchase, option, lease, or other method not involving condemnation, the right, or right upon the exercise of an option, if any, to store gas in the stratum or formation. It is not necessary for the condemnor to have acquired any interest in the property in which the condemnee has an interest before instituting a proceeding under this chapter. [P.L.2-2002, § 9.]

NOTES TO DECISIONS

Construction.

This section, granting those engaged in the business of transporting or distributing gas authority to condemn subsurface strata, was a statutory source for the power pursued, and it was unnecessary to consider the contention that a municipality, by engaging in acts outside its statutory authority, became a public utility for regulatory purposes. Citizens Gas & Coke Util. v. Sloan, 136 Ind. App. 297, 3 Ind. Dec. 20, 196 N.E.2d 290, reh'g denied, 136 Ind. App. 311, 197 N.E.2d 312 (1964).

32-24-5-3. May not prejudice certain rights of owners and lessees — Notice to owners of gas storage stratum — Procedures for

protecting gas storage areas. — (a) The rights acquired by condemnation must be without prejudice to the rights and interests of the owners or their lessees to:

(1) execute oil and gas leases;

(2) drill or bore to any other strata or formation not condemned; and

(3) produce oil and gas discovered.

However, any drilling and all operations in connection with the drilling must be performed in a manner that protects the strata or formations condemned against the loss of gas and against contamination of the reservoir by water, oil, or other substance that will affect the use of the condemned strata or formations for gas storage purposes.

(b) If the owners of mineral rights or the owners' lessees drill into land in which gas storage rights have been condemned under this chapter, the owners of mineral rights or their lessees shall give notice to the owner of the gas storage stratum, formation, or horizon at least thirty (30) days before commencing the drilling. The notice must specify the location and nature of the operations, including the depth to be drilled. The notice must be given by United States registered or certified mail, return receipt requested, and addressed to the usual business address of the owner or owners of the gas storage stratum or formation condemned under this chapter.

(c) It is the duty of the owner of a gas storage stratum or formation to designate all necessary procedures for protecting the gas storage area. The actual costs incurred over and above customary and usual drilling and other costs that would have been incurred without compliance with the requirements shall be borne by the owner of the gas storage stratum or formation. An owner or lessee of mineral interests other than gas storage rights is not responsible for an act done under such a requirement or the consequences of this act. [P.L.2-2002, § 9.]

32-24-5-4. Limits of condemnation and appropriation. — Only the rights in land necessary for use in connection with underground storage of gas and those subsurface strata adaptable for underground storage of gas may be appropriated and condemned under this chapter. Rights in the subsurface of land constituting a part of a geological structure are deemed necessary to the operation of an underground storage reservoir in the structure. In determining the compensation to be paid to the owner of an oil producing stratum, or interest in the stratum, condemned under this chapter, proof may be offered and consideration must be given to potential recovery, if any, of oil from a stratum by secondary or other subsequent recovery processes in addition to potential recovery by a primary process. [P.L.2-2002, § 9.]

32-24-5-5. Condemnation and appropriation procedures. — The appropriation and condemnation of subsurface strata or formations in land rights in and easements in land and subsurface strata or formations authorized by this chapter must be made under IC 32-24-1. [P.L.2-2002, § 9.]

CHAPTER 6

EXCEPTIONS TO EMINENT DOMAIN ASSESSMENTS

32-24-6-1. Objections to condemnation or appropriation. — (a) A party may file a written objection in a proceeding for the condemnation or appropriation of property for public use brought by:

(1) the state of Indiana;

(2) a commission, a department, or an agency of the state;

(3) a county;

(4) a township;

(5) a city;

(6) a town; or

(7) a taxing district;

under a law of the state authorizing the assessment of damages or benefits, appraisal, compensation, condemnation, or appropriation of property for public use.

(b) A party aggrieved by:

(1) the assessment of compensation or damages;

(2) the fixing of the value of the property involved; or

(3) the fixing of benefits;

as set forth in the report of an appraiser filed in a proceeding described in subsection (a) may file written exceptions in the office of the clerk of the court in which the cause is pending within ten (10) days after the report is filed. After the objections are filed, the cause shall proceed to issue, trial, and judgment as in civil actions in accordance with the provisions of the law not in conflict with this chapter governing the procedure in eminent domain as defined in IC 32-24-1. [P.L.2-2002, § 9.]

Effective Dates. P.L.2-2002, § 9. July 1. 2002.

NOTES TO DECISIONS

Objections.

The general eminent domain act of 1905 (IC 32-11-1) applied alike to all bodies having the right to exercise the power, and where objec- tions were properly made under such statute, this section had no effect, this section being supplemental. Cemetery Co. v. Warren Sch. Tp., 236 Ind. 171, 139 N.E.2d 538 (1957).

Collateral References. 26 Am. Jur. 2d Eminent Domain, §§ 107-110.

29A C.J.S. Eminent Domain, §§ 222-225.

32-24-6-2. Notice — Running of period of exceptions. — In the exercise of the power of eminent domain, notice of filing of the appraisers' report shall be given by the clerk of the court to all known parties to the action by certified mail. Any period of exceptions after which the parties are barred from disputing the appraisal and condemnation shall run from the date of mailing. [P.L.2-2002, § 9.]

ARTICLE 25

CONDOMINIUMS

CHAPTER 1

APPLICATION OF LAW

32-25-1-1. Applicability of article. — This article applies to property if:

(1) the sole owner of the property; or

(2) all of the owners of the property;

submit the property to this article by executing and recording a declaration under this article. [P.L.2-2002, § 10.]

Effective Dates. P.L.2-2002, § 10. July 1. 2002.

32-25-1-2. Persons subject to article. — (a) The following are subject to this article and to declarations and bylaws of associations of co-owners adopted under this article:

(1) Condominium unit owners.

(2) Tenants of condominium unit owners.

(3) Employees of condominium unit owners.

(4) Employees of tenants of condominium owners.

(5) Any other persons that in any manner use property or any part of property submitted to this article.

(b) All agreements, decisions, and determinations lawfully made by an association of co-owners in accordance with the voting percentages established in:

(1) this chapter;

(2) the declaration; or

(3) the bylaws;

are binding on all condominium unit owners. [P.L.2-2002, § 10.]

NOTES TO DECISIONS

Nuisances.

Consent by the homeowners board in the action is not determinative of the issue of whether a nuisance was created. Keane v. Pachter, 598 N.E.2d 1067 (Ind. App. 1992).

CHAPTER 2

DEFINITIONS

32-25-2-1. Applicability. — The definitions in this chapter apply throughout this article. [P.L.2-2002, § 10.]

Effective Dates. P.L.2-2002, § 10. July 1. 2002.

32-25-2-2. Association of co-owners. — "Association of co-owners" means all the co-owners acting as an entity in accordance with the:
(1) articles;
(2) bylaws; and
(3) declaration.
[P.L.2-2002, § 10.]

32-25-2-3. Building. — "Building" means a structure containing:
(1) at least two (2) condominium units; or
(2) at least two (2) structures containing at least one (1) condominium unit. [P.L.2-2002, § 10.]

32-25-2-4. Common areas and facilities. — "Common areas and facilities", unless otherwise provided in the declaration or lawful amendments to the declaration, means:
(1) the land on which the building is located;
(2) the building:
  (A) foundations;
  (B) columns;
  (C) girders;
  (D) beams;
  (E) supports;
  (F) main walls;
  (G) roofs;
  (H) halls;
  (I) corridors;
  (J) lobbies;

    (K) stairs;

    (L) stairways;

    (M) fire escapes;

    (N) entrances; and

    (O) exits;

  (3) the:

    (A) basements;

    (B) yards;

    (C) gardens;

    (D) parking areas;

    (E) storage spaces;

    (F) swimming pools; and

    (G) other recreational facilities;

  (4) the premises for the lodging of:

    (A) janitors; or

    (B) persons in charge of the property;

  (5) installations of central services, such as:

    (A) power;

    (B) light;

    (C) gas;

    (D) hot and cold water;

    (E) heating;

    (F) refrigeration;

    (G) air conditioning; and

    (H) incinerating;

  (6) the:

    (A) elevators;

    (B) tanks;

    (C) pumps;

    (D) motors;

    (E) fans;

    (F) compressors;

    (G) ducts;

    (H) apparatus; and

    (I) installations;

existing for common use;

(7) community and commercial facilities provided for in the declaration; and

(8) all other parts of the property:

    (A) necessary or convenient to its:

      (i) existence;

      (ii) maintenance; and

      (iii) safety; or

    (B) normally in common use.

[P.L.2-2002, § 10.]

32-25-2-5. Common expenses. — "Common expenses" means:

(1) all sums lawfully assessed against the co-owners by the association of co-owners;

(2) expenses of:
    (A) administration;
    (B) maintenance;
    (C) repair; or
    (D) replacement;
of the common areas and facilities;
(3) expenses agreed upon as common expenses by the association of co-owners; and
(4) expenses declared common expenses by:
    (A) this chapter;
    (B) the declaration; or
    (C) the bylaws.
[P.L.2-2002, § 10.]

32-25-2-6. Common profits. — "Common profits" means the balance remaining, after the deduction of the common expenses, of all:
(1) income;
(2) rents;
(3) profits; and
(4) revenues;
from the common areas and facilities. [P.L.2-2002, § 10.]

32-25-2-7. Condominium. — "Condominium" means real estate:
(1) lawfully subjected to this chapter by the recordation of condominium instruments; and
(2) with respect to which the undivided interests in the common areas and facilities are vested in the condominium unit owners. [P.L.2-2002, § 10.]

32-25-2-8. Condominium instruments. — "Condominium instruments" means:
(1) the:
    (A) declaration;
    (B) bylaws;
    (C) plats; and
    (D) floor plans;
of the condominium; and
(2) any exhibits or schedules to the items listed in subdivision (1). [P.L.2-2002, § 10.]

32-25-2-9. Condominium unit. — "Condominium unit" means:
(1) an enclosed space:
    (A) that consists of one (1) or more rooms occupying all or part of a floor or floors in a structure of one (1) or more floors or stories, regardless of whether the enclosed space is designed:
        (i) as a residence;
        (ii) as an office;
        (iii) for the operation of any industry or business; or

(iv) for any other type of independent use; and
  (B) that has:
    (i) a direct exit to a public street or highway; or
    (ii) an exit to a thoroughfare or to a given common space leading to a thoroughfare; and
  (2) the undivided interest in the common elements appertaining to an enclosed space referred to in subdivision (1). [P.L.2-2002, § 10.]

32-25-2-10. Contractable condominium. — "Contractable condominium" means a condominium from which one (1) or more portions of the condominium real estate may be withdrawn. [P.L.2-2002, § 10.]

32-25-2-11. Co-owner. — "Co-owner" means a person who owns:
  (1) a condominium unit in fee simple; and
  (2) an undivided interest in the common areas and facilities;
in the percentage established in the declaration. [P.L.2-2002, § 10.]

32-25-2-12. Declarant. — "Declarant" means any person who:
  (1) executes or proposes to execute a declaration; or
  (2) executes an amendment to a declaration to expand an expandable condominium. [P.L.2-2002, § 10.]

32-25-2-13. Declaration. — "Declaration" means the instrument by which the property is submitted to this article. The term refers to a declaration as it may be lawfully amended from time to time. [P.L.2-2002, § 10.]

32-25-2-14. Expandable condominium. — "Expandable condominium" means a condominium to which real estate may be added. [P.L.2-2002, § 10.]

32-25-2-15. Limited common areas and facilities. — "Limited common areas and facilities" means the common areas and facilities designated in the declaration as reserved for use of:
  (1) a certain condominium unit; or
  (2) certain condominium units;
to the exclusion of the other condominium units. [P.L.2-2002, § 10.]

32-25-2-16. Majority or majority of co-owners. — "Majority" or "majority of co-owners" means the co-owners with at least fifty-one percent (51%) of the votes, in accordance with the percentages assigned in the declaration to the condominium units for voting purposes. [P.L.2-2002, § 10.]

32-25-2-17. Person. — "Person" means:
  (1) an individual;
  (2) a firm;
  (3) a corporation;

(4) a partnership;

(5) an association;

(6) a trust;

(7) any other legal entity; or

(8) any combination of the entities listed in subdivisions (1) through (7).

[P.L.2-2002, § 10.]

32-25-2-18. Property. — "Property" means:

(1) the land;

(2) the building;

(3) all improvements and structures on the land or the building; and

(4) all:

(A) easements;

(B) rights; and

(C) appurtenances;

pertaining to the land or the building. [P.L.2-2002, § 10.]

32-25-2-19. To record. — "To record" means to record in accordance with the laws of the state. [P.L.2-2002, § 10.]

32-25-2-20. Unit number. — "Unit number" means the:

(1) number;

(2) letter; or

(3) combination of numbers and letters;

designating the condominium unit in the declaration. [P.L.2-2002, § 10.]

CHAPTER 3

CLASSIFICATION OF PROPERTY

SECTION.
32-25-3-1. Common areas and facilities.

32-25-3-1. Common areas and facilities. — A condominium unit and the unit's undivided interest in the common areas and facilities constitute real property. [P.L.2-2002, § 10.]

Effective Dates. P.L.2-2002, § 10. July 1. 2002.

CHAPTER 4

OWNERSHIP INTEREST IN CONDOMINIUMS

32-25-4-1. Interest in property submitted to condominium — Conveyances — Title. — (a) If property is submitted to the condominium, each condominium unit owner is seized of:

(1) the fee simple title to;

(2) the exclusive ownership of; and

(3) the exclusive possession of;

the owner's condominium unit and undivided interest in the common areas and facilities.

(b) A condominium unit may be:

(1) individually conveyed;

(2) individually encumbered; and

(3) the subject of:

(A) ownership;

(B) possession;

(C) sale; and

(D) all types of juridic acts inter vivos or causa mortis;

as if the condominium unit were sole and entirely independent of the other condominium units in the building of which the condominium unit forms a part.

(c) Individual titles and interests with respect to condominium units are recordable. [P.L.2-2002, § 10.]

Effective Dates. P.L.2-2002, § 10. July 1. 2002.

Collateral References. Standing to bring action relating to real property of condominium. 74 A.L.R.4th 165.

32-25-4-2. Tenancy of unit. — A condominium unit may be held and owned by two (2) or more persons:

(1) as joint tenants;

(2) as tenants in common;

(3) as tenants by the entirety; or

(4) in any other real property tenancy relationship recognized under the law of the state. [P.L.2-2002, § 10.]

32-25-4-3. Undivided interests in common areas — Access to units. — (a) Each condominium unit owner is entitled to an undivided interest in the common areas and facilities as designated in the declaration. Except as provided in subsection (b), the undivided interest must be expressed as a percentage interest based on:

(1) the size of the unit in relation to the size of all units in the condominium;

(2) the value of each condominium unit in relation to the value of all condominium units in the condominium; or

(3) the assignment of an equal percentage undivided interest to each condominium unit.

An undivided interest allocated to each condominium unit in accordance with this subsection must be indicated in a schedule of undivided interests in the declaration. However, if the declaration does not specify the method of allocating the percentage undivided interests, an equal percentage undivided interest applies to each condominium unit. The total undivided interests allocated in accordance with subdivision (1) or (2) must equal one hundred percent (100%).

(b) With respect to an expandable condominium, the declaration may allocate undivided interests in the common area on the basis of value if:

(1) the declaration prohibits the creation of any condominium units not substantially identical to the condominium units depicted on the recorded plans of the declaration; or

(2) the declaration:

(A) prohibits the creation of any condominium units not described in the initial declaration; and

(B) contains a statement on the value to be assigned to each condominium unit created after the date of the declaration.

(c) Interests in the common areas may not be allocated to any condominium units to be created within any additional land until the plats and plans and supplemental declaration depicting the condominium units to be created are recorded. Simultaneously with the recording of the plats and plans for the condominium units to be created, the declarant must execute and record an amendment to the initial declaration reallocating undivided interests in the common areas so that the future condominium units depicted on the plats and plans will be allocated undivided interests in the common areas on the same basis as the condominium units depicted in the prior recorded plats and plans.

(d) Except as provided in IC 32-25-8-3, the undivided interest of the owner of the condominium unit in the common areas and facilities, as expressed in the declaration, is permanent and may not be altered without the consent of the co-owners. A consent to alteration must be stated in an amended declaration, and the amended declaration must be recorded. The undivided interest may not be transferred, encumbered, disposed of, or separated from the condominium unit to which it appertains, and any purported transfer, encumbrance, or other disposition is void. The undivided interest is considered to be conveyed or encumbered with the condominium unit to which it appertains even though the undivided interest is not expressly mentioned or described in the conveyance or other instrument.

(e) The common areas and facilities shall remain undivided. A condominium unit owner or any other person may bring an action for partition or division of any part of the common areas and facilities if the property has been removed from this chapter as provided in IC 32-25-8-12 and IC 32-25-8-16. Any covenant to the contrary is void.

(f) Each condominium unit owner:

(1) may use the common areas and facilities in accordance with the purpose for which the common areas and facilities were intended; and

(2) may not, in the owner's use of the common areas and facilities, hinder or encroach upon the lawful rights of the other co-owners.

(g) The:

(1) necessary work of:

(A) maintenance;

(B) repair; and

OWNERSHIP INTEREST IN CONDOMINIUMS

(C) replacement;

of the common areas and facilities; and

(2) the making of any additions or improvements to the common areas and facilities:

may be carried out only as provided in this chapter and in the bylaws.

(h) The association of condominium unit owners has the irrevocable right, to be exercised by the manager or board of directors, to have access to each condominium unit from time to time during reasonable hours as is necessary for:

(1) the maintenance, repair, or replacement of any of the common areas and facilities:

(A) in the condominium unit; or

(B) accessible from the condominium unit; or

(2) making emergency repairs in the condominium unit necessary to prevent damage to:

(A) the common areas and facilities; or

(B) another condominium unit.

[P.L.2-2002, § 10.]

NOTES TO DECISIONS

Owners Refusal to Grant Access.

The declaratory judgment was a proper exercise of the superior court's discretion where defendant violated plaintiff condominium corporation's declaration of horizontal regime and by-laws and the Horizontal Prop- erty Act, when defendant condominium unit owner refused to allow the condominium cor- poration to have access to her balcony to make common area repairs. Ferrell v. Dunescape Beach Club Condominiums Phase I, Inc., 751 N.E.2d 702 (Ind. App. 2001).

32-25-4-4. Contributions to association — Exceptions for units offered for sale for the first time. — (a) Except as provided in subsection (d) or (e), the co-owners are bound to contribute pro rata, in the percentages computed under section 3 [IC 32-25-4-3] of this chapter, toward:

(1) the expenses of administration and of maintenance and repair of the general common areas and facilities and, in the proper case, of the limited common areas and facilities of the building; and

(2) any other expense lawfully agreed upon.

(b) A co-owner may not exempt the co-owner from contributing toward the expenses referred to in subsection (a) by:

(1) waiver of the use or enjoyment of the common areas and facilities; or

(2) abandonment of the condominium unit belonging to the co-owner.

(c) All sums assessed by the association of co-owners shall be established by using generally accepted accounting principles applied on a consistent basis and shall include the establishment and maintenance of a replace- ment reserve fund. The replacement reserve fund may be used for capital expenditures and replacement and repair of the common areas and facilities and may not be used for usual and ordinary repair expenses of the common areas and facilities. The fund shall be:

(1) maintained in a separate interest bearing account with a bank or savings association authorized to conduct business in the county in which the condominium is established; or

(2) invested in the same manner and in the same types of investments in which the funds of a political subdivision may be invested:

(A) under IC 5-13-9; or

(B) as otherwise provided by law.

Assessments collected for contributions to the fund are not subject to gross income tax or adjusted gross income tax.

(d) If permitted by the declaration, the declarant or a developer (or a successor in interest of either) that is a co-owner of unoccupied condominium units offered for the first time for sale is excused from contributing toward the expenses referred to in subsection (a) for those units for a period that:

(1) is stated in the declaration;

(2) begins on the day that the declaration is recorded; and

(3) terminates no later than the first day of the twenty-fourth calendar month following the month in which the closing of the sale of the first condominium unit occurs.

However, if the expenses referred to in subsection (a) incurred by the declarant, developer, or successor during the period referred to in this subsection exceed the amount assessed against the other co-owners, the declarant, developer, or successor shall pay the amount by which the expenses incurred by the declarant, developer, or successor exceed the expenses assessed against the other co-owners.

(e) If the declaration does not contain the provisions referred to in subsection (d), the declarant or a developer (or a successor in interest of either) that is a co-owner of unoccupied condominium units offered for the first time for sale is excused from contributing toward the expenses referred to in subsection (a) for those units for a stated period if the declarant, developer, or successor:

(1) has guaranteed to each purchaser in the purchase contract, the declaration, or the prospectus, or by an agreement with a majority of the other co-owners that the assessment for those expenses will not increase over a stated amount during the stated period; and

(2) has obligated itself to pay the amount by which those expenses incurred during the stated period exceed the assessments at the guaranteed level under subdivision (1) receivable during the stated period from the other co-owners.

[P.L.2-2002, § 10.]

NOTES TO DECISIONS

Common Expenses.

Condominium developers who retained ownership on some units in the development were "co-owners" under the Indiana Horizontal Property Law, and, as such, were required to pay their proportionate share of common expenses regardless of the terms of the declaration and bylaws. Hatfield v. La Charmant Home Owners Ass'n, 469 N.E.2d 1218 (Ind. App. 1984), decided prior to the 1985 amendment, which added subsections (d) and (e).

CHAPTER 5
CONVEYANCE PROCEDURES

32-25-5-1. First conveyance of each unit. — (a) At the time of the first conveyance of each condominium unit:

(1) every mortgage and other lien affecting the condominium unit, including the unit's percentage of undivided interest in the common areas and facilities, must be paid and satisfied of record; or

(2) the condominium unit being conveyed and the unit's percentage of undivided interest in the common areas and facilities must be released from the mortgage or other lien by partial release.

(b) A partial release under subsection (a)(2) must be recorded. [P.L.2-2002, § 10.]

Effective Dates. P.L.2-2002, § 10. July 1. 2002.

32-25-5-2. Unpaid assessments. — (a) Except as provided in subsection (b), in a voluntary conveyance, the grantee of a condominium unit is jointly and severally liable with the grantor for all unpaid assessments against the grantor for the grantor's share of the common expenses incurred before the grant or conveyance, without prejudice to the grantee's right to recover from the grantor the amounts of common expenses paid by the grantee.

(b) The grantee:

(1) is entitled to a statement from the manager or board of directors setting forth the amount of the unpaid assessments against the grantor; and

(2) is not liable for, nor shall the condominium unit conveyed be subject to a lien for, any unpaid assessments against the grantor in excess of the amount set forth in the statement. [P.L.2-2002, § 10.]

CHAPTER 6
LIENS AND ENCUMBRANCES

32-25-6-1. Liens against individual unit owners — Multiple unit owners. — (a) After a declaration is recorded under this article and while the property remains subject to this article, a lien may not arise or be effective against the property as a whole. Except as provided in subsection (b), liens or encumbrances may arise or be created only against:

    (1) each condominium unit; and

    (2) the undivided interest in the common areas and facilities appurtenant to each unit;

in the same manner and under the same conditions as liens or encumbrances may arise or be created against any other parcel of real property.

    (b) Labor performed or materials furnished with the consent or at the request of a condominium unit owner, the owner's agent, or the owner's contractor or subcontractor may not be the basis for filing a lien under any lien law against the condominium unit or any other property of any other co-owner not expressly consenting to or requesting the performance of the labor or the furnishing of the materials. However, express consent is considered to be given by the owner of any condominium unit in the case of emergency repairs to the condominium unit. Labor performed or materials furnished for the common areas and facilities, if authorized by the association of co-owners, the manager, or board of directors in accordance with this article, the declaration, or the bylaws:

    (1) are considered to be performed or furnished with the express consent of each co-owner;

    (2) constitute the basis for the filing of a lien under any lien law against each of the condominium units; and

    (3) are subject to subsection (c).

    (c) If a lien against two (2) or more condominium units becomes effective, the owner of a condominium unit against which the lien is effective may remove the owner's:

    (1) unit; and

    (2) undivided interest in the common areas and facilities appurtenant to the unit;

from the lien by payment of the fractional or proportional amounts attributable to the unit. After the payment, discharge of the lien, or other satisfaction of the lien, the condominium unit and the undivided interest in the common areas and facilities appurtenant to the condominium unit are free and clear of the lien. A partial payment, partial satisfaction of the lien, or discharge of the lien may not prevent the lienholder from proceeding against any condominium unit and the undivided interest in the common areas and facilities appurtenant to the condominium unit that remain subject to the lien. [P.L.2-2002, § 10.]

Effective Dates. P.L.2-2002, § 10. July 1. 2002.

32-25-6-2. Easement over common areas for declarant. — Subject to any restrictions and limitations in the condominium instruments, the declarant has a transferable easement over and upon the common areas and facilities for the purpose of:

    (1) making improvements within:

      (A) the condominium; or

      (B) additional real estate;

under those instruments and this article; and

(2) doing all things reasonably necessary and proper in connection with the improvements referred to in subdivision (1). [P.L.2-2002, § 10.]

32-25-6-3. Liens arising from unpaid assessments for common expenses — Foreclosure — Suit for expenses. — (a) All sums assessed by the association of co-owners but unpaid for the share of the common expenses chargeable to any condominium unit constitute a lien on the unit effective at the time of assessment. The lien has priority over all other liens except:

(1) tax liens on the condominium unit in favor of any:

(A) assessing unit; or

(B) special district; and

(2) all sums unpaid on a first mortgage of record.

(b) A lien under subsection (a) may be filed and foreclosed by suit by the manager or board of directors, acting on behalf of the association of co-owners, under laws of Indiana governing mechanics' and materialmen's liens. In any foreclosure under this subsection:

(1) the condominium unit owner shall pay a reasonable rental for the unit, if payment of the rental is provided in the bylaws; and

(2) the plaintiff in the foreclosure is entitled to the appointment of a receiver to collect the rental.

(c) The manager or board of directors, acting on behalf of the association of co-owners, may, unless prohibited by the declaration:

(1) bid on the condominium unit at foreclosure sale; and

(2) acquire, hold, lease, mortgage, and convey the condominium unit.

(d) Suit to recover a money judgment for unpaid common expenses is maintainable without foreclosing or having the lien securing the expenses.

(e) If the mortgagee of a first mortgage of record or other purchaser of a condominium unit obtains title to the unit as a result of foreclosure of the first mortgage, the acquirer of title, or the acquirer's successors and assigns, is not liable for the share of the common expenses or assessments by the association of co-owners chargeable to the unit that became due before the acquisition of title to the unit by the acquirer. The unpaid share of common expenses or assessments is considered to be common expenses collectible from all of the co-owners, including the acquirer or the acquirer's successors and assigns. [P.L.2-2002, § 10.]

CHAPTER 7

DECLARATION

32-25-7-1. Recording — Contents of declaration. — (a) The owner of the land on which a condominium is declared shall record with the recorder of the county in which the land is situated a declaration. Except as provided in section 2 or 3 [IC 32-25-7-2 or IC 32-25-7-3] of this chapter, the declaration must include the following:

(1) A description of the land on which the building and improvements are or are to be located.

(2) A description of the building, stating:

  (A) the number of stories and basements; and

  (B) the number of condominium units.

(3) A description of the common areas and facilities.

(4) A description of the limited common areas and facilities, if any, stating to which condominium units their use is reserved.

(5) The percentage of undivided interest in the common areas and facilities appertaining to each condominium unit and its owner for all purposes, including voting.

(6) A statement of the percentage of votes by the condominium unit owners required to determine whether to:

  (A) rebuild;

  (B) repair;

  (C) restore; or

  (D) sell;

the property if all or part of the property is damaged or destroyed.

(7) Any covenants and restrictions in regard to the use of:

  (A) the condominium units; and

  (B) common areas and facilities.

(8) Any further details in connection with the property that:

  (A) the person executing the declaration considers desirable; and

  (B) are consistent with this article.

(9) The method by which the declaration may be amended in a manner consistent with this chapter.

  (b) A true copy of the bylaws shall be annexed to and made a part of the declaration.

  (c) The record of the declaration shall contain a reference to the:

  (1) book;

  (2) page; and

  (3) date of record;

of the floor plans of the building affected by the declaration. [P.L.2-2002, § 10.]

Effective Dates. P.L.2-2002, § 10. July 1. 2002.

32-25-7-2. Additional contents for expandable condominium. — (a) If a condominium is an expandable condominium, the declaration shall contain, in addition to the matters specified in section 1 [IC 32-25-7-1] of this chapter:

(1) a general plan of development showing:

  (A) the property subject to the condominium;

    (B) areas into which expansion may be made; and

    (C) the maximum number of condominium units in additional phases that may be added;

  (2) a schedule or formula for determining the percentage of undivided interests in the common areas and facilities that will appertain to each condominium unit as each additional phase is added; and

  (3) a time limit, not exceeding ten (10) years, within which the phase or phases may be added to the condominium.

(b) If additional phases are not developed within five (5) years after the recordation of the declaration, the development of additional phases is not considered to be part of:

  (1) a common scheme; and

  (2) development of the entire condominium.

[P.L.2-2002, § 10.]

32-25-7-3. Additional contents for contractable condominium. — If a condominium is a contractable condominium, the declaration shall contain, in addition to matters specified in section 1 [IC 32-25-7-1] of this chapter:

  (1) an explicit reservation of an option to contract the condominium;

  (2) a statement of any limitations on the option to contract the condominium;

  (3) a date, not later than ten (10) years after the recording of the declaration, upon which the option to contract the condominium will expire;

  (4) a statement of any circumstances that will terminate the option to contract the condominium before the expiration date referred to in subdivision (3);

  (5) a legally sufficient description of all withdrawable land;

  (6) a statement as to whether portions of the withdrawable land may be withdrawn from the condominium at different times; and

  (7) a statement of any limitations:

    (A) fixing the boundaries of portions of the withdrawable land; or

    (B) regulating the order in which the portions may be withdrawn.

    [P.L.2-2002, § 10.]

32-25-7-4. Filing and contents of floor plans. — (a) Simultaneously with the recording of the declaration, a set of floor plans of the condominium or building shall be filed in the office of the county recorder. The set of floor plans must include the following:

  (1) The relation of the condominium or building to lot lines.

  (2) The:

    (A) layout;

    (B) elevation;

    (C) location;

    (D) unit numbers; and

    (E) dimensions;

of the condominium units.

(3) The name of the condominium or building, or that it has no name.

(4) The verified statement of a registered architect or licensed professional engineer certifying that the set of floor plans is an accurate copy of portions of the plans of the building as filed with and approved by the municipal or other governmental subdivision having jurisdiction over the issuance of permits for the construction of buildings.

(b) If the set of floor plans referred to in subsection (a) does not include a verified statement by an architect or engineer that the plans fully and accurately depict the layout, location, unit numbers, and dimensions of the condominium units as built, an amendment to the declaration must be recorded before the first conveyance of any condominium unit. The amendment to the declaration must have attached to it a verified statement of a registered architect or licensed professional engineer certifying that the filed set of floor plans or the set of floor plans being filed simultaneously with the amendment fully and accurately depicts the layout, location, unit numbers, and dimensions of the condominium units as built. The set of floor plans shall:

(1) be kept by the recording officer in a separate file for each building;

(2) be indexed in the same manner as a conveyance entitled to be recorded;

(3) be numbered serially in the order of receipt;

(4) be designated "condominium unit ownership", with the name of the building, if any; and

(5) contain a reference to the:

  (A) book

  (B) page; and

  (C) date of recording;

of the amendment to the declaration.

(c) The record of the amendment to the declaration referred to in subsection (b) shall contain a reference to the file number of the set of floor plans of the building affected by the amendment to the declaration. [P.L.2-2002, § 10.]

32-25-7-5. Designation of units — Interests conveyed — Contents of deed of conveyance — Failure to conform. — (a) Each condominium unit in a building shall be designated, on the set of floor plans referred to in section 4 [IC 32-25-7-4] of this chapter, by letter, number, or other appropriate designation.

(b) Any instrument recognized by the state for the conveyance or transfer of interests in title, which describes the apartment by using the designation referred to in subsection (a) followed by the words "in (name) Condominium as recorded in Book _____, p. ____, under the date of _____, _____, of the records of _____ County, Indiana", is considered to contain a good and sufficient description for all purposes.

(c) Any conveyance or transfer of interest in title of a condominium unit is considered also to convey the undivided interests of the owner in the common areas and facilities, both general and limited, appertaining to the condominium unit without specifically or particularly referring to the undivided interests. The:

    (1) contents;
    (2) form;
    (3) method of preparation;
    (4) recording of an instrument of conveyance; and
    (5) interpretation of an instrument of conveyance;
are governed by the law of Indiana relating to real property.
    (d) Each instrument or deed of conveyance also shall include the follow-
ing:
    (1) A statement of the use for which the condominium unit is intended.
    (2) A statement of the restrictions on the use of the condominium unit.
    (3) The percentage of undivided interest appertaining to the condomin-
    ium unit in the common areas and facilities.
    (4) The amount of any unpaid current or delinquent assessments of
    common expenses.
    (5) Any other details and restrictions that:
        (A) the grantor and grantee consider desirable; and
        (B) are consistent with the declaration.
    (e) Failure to make a statement in the deed as required by subsection
(d)(4) does not:
    (1) invalidate the title conveyed by the deed; or
    (2) absolve a grantee under the deed from liability for any unpaid
    current or delinquent assessments of common expenses against a
    condominium unit on the date of its conveyance.
    (f) Upon the request of a:
    (1) condominium unit owner;
    (2) prospective grantee;
    (3) title insurance company; or
    (4) mortgagee;
the secretary or other authorized officer of the association of co-owners shall
provide, within five (5) days of the request, a statement of the amount of
current and delinquent assessments of common expenses against a particular condominium unit. [P.L.2-2002, § 10.]

    **32-25-7-6. Changes in percentage of undivided interest in com-
mon areas.** — (a) Except as provided in subsection (b), if the declaration
for a condominium is in conformity with section 2 [IC 32-25-7-2] of this
chapter, it is presumed that any owner of a condominium unit in that
condominium has consented to the changes in the percentage of undivided
interest in the common areas and facilities appertaining to the owner's unit.
    (b) An owner of a condominium unit who entered an agreement to
purchase that unit before the recordation of the declaration may not be
presumed to have consented to the changes referred to in subsection (a)
unless the owner:
    (1) was provided a copy of:
        (A) the expansion provisions; or
        (B) the declaration; and
    (2) made a written acknowledgment of the receipt of the provisions
    before entering the purchase agreement.

(c) The reallocation of percentage of undivided interests in the common areas and facilities vests when the amendment to the declaration incorporating the reallocated percentages is recorded.

(d) When the amendment to the declaration incorporating:

　(1) the addition of condominium units;

　(2) the expansion of common areas and facilities; or

　(3) both addition and expansion as described in subdivisions (1) and (2);

is recorded, all liens, including mortgage liens, are released as to the percentage of undivided interests in the common areas and facilities described in the declaration (before amendment of the declaration) and shall attach to the reallocated percentage of undivided interests in the common areas and facilities described in the amendment to the declaration as though the liens had attached to those percentage interests on the date of the recordation of the mortgage or other document that evidences the creation of the lien. The percentage interest in the common areas and facilities appertaining to additional condominium units being added by the amendment to the declaration are subject to mortgage liens and other liens upon the recordation of the amendment to the declaration. [P.L.2-2002, § 10.]

NOTES TO DECISIONS

Reallocation of Percentages.

Subsection (b) of the predecessor statute to this section pertained to "reallocation of percentage of undivided interests in common areas and facilities," and did not address reallocation of percentages when an owner enlarges his individual condominium unit; therefore, the failure of the condominium association to record the supplemental declaration did not relieve the owners of their obligation to pay the increased assessment resulting from expansion of their condominium unit. Lynn v. Windridge Co-Owners Ass'n, 743 N.E.2d 305 (Ind. App. 2001).

CHAPTER 8

ADMINISTRATION OF CONDOMINIUMS

32-25-8-1. Bylaws — Part of declaration — Modification. — The administration of every property is governed by bylaws. A true copy of the bylaws shall be annexed to and made a part of the declaration. A modification of or amendment to the bylaws is valid only if:

(1) the modification or amendment is set forth in an amendment to the declaration; and

(2) the amendment is recorded.

[P.L.2-2002, § 10.]

Effective Dates. P.L.2-2002, § 10. July 1. 2002.

32-25-8-2. Necessary provisions of bylaws. — The bylaws must provide for the following:

(1) With respect to the board of directors:

(A) the election of the board from among the co-owners;

(B) the number of persons constituting the board;

(C) the expiration of the terms of at least one-third ($^1/\!/s3$) of the directors annually;

(D) the powers and duties of the board, including whether the board may engage the services of a manager or managing agent;

(E) the compensation, if any, of the directors; and

(F) the method of removal from office of directors.

(2) The method of calling meetings of the co-owners and the percentage, if other than a majority of co-owners, that constitutes a quorum.

(3) The election from among the board of directors of a president, who shall preside over the meetings of:

(A) the board of directors; and

(B) the association of co-owners.

(4) The election of a secretary, who shall keep the minute book in which resolutions shall be recorded.

(5) The election of a treasurer, who shall keep the financial records and books of account.

(6) The maintenance, repair, and replacement of the common areas and facilities and payments for that maintenance, repair, and replacement, including the method of approving payment vouchers.

(7) The manner of collecting from each condominium owner the owner's share of the common expenses.

(8) The designation and removal of personnel necessary for the maintenance, repair, and replacement of the common areas and facilities.

(9) The method of adopting and of amending administrative rules governing the details of the operation and use of the common areas and facilities.

(10) The restrictions on and requirements respecting the use and maintenance of the condominium units and the use of the common areas and facilities that are:

(A) not set forth in the declaration; and

(B) designed to prevent unreasonable interference with the use of their respective units and of the common areas and facilities by the several co-owners.

(11) The percentage of votes required to amend the bylaws.

(12) Other provisions consistent with this article considered necessary for the administration of the property. [P.L.2-2002, § 10.]

32-25-8-3. Documents required to be recorded — Index. — (a) The following shall be recorded:

    (1) A declaration.

    (2) An amendment to a declaration.

    (3) An instrument by which this article may be waived.

    (4) An instrument affecting the property or any condominium unit.

(b) A declaration and any amendment to a declaration are valid only if the declaration or amendment is recorded.

(c) All of the laws of the state applicable to the recording of instruments affecting real property apply to the recording of instruments affecting any interest in a condominium unit.

(d) In addition to the records and indexes required to be maintained by the recording officer, the recording officer shall maintain an index or indexes in which:

    (1) the record of each declaration contains a reference to the record of each conveyance of a condominium unit affected by the declaration; and

    (2) the record of each conveyance of a condominium unit contains a reference to the declaration of the building of which the condominium unit is a part. [P.L.2-2002, § 10.]

32-25-8-4. Maintenance of offices and model units. — (a) A declarant may:

    (1) maintain:

      (A) sales offices;

      (B) management offices; and

      (C) model condominium units;

in the condominium only if the condominium instruments provide for those items; and

    (2) specify the rights of the declarant with regard to the:

      (A) number;

      (B) size;

      (C) location; and

      (D) relocation;

of the items referred to in subdivision (1).

(b) If the declarant ceases to be a condominium unit owner:

    (1) an item referred to in subsection (a)(1) that is not designated a condominium unit by the condominium instruments becomes part of the common areas and facilities; and

    (2) the declarant ceases to have any rights to the item referred to in subdivision (1) unless the item is removed promptly from the condominium real estate under a right reserved in the condominium instruments to make the removal. [P.L.2-2002, § 10.]

32-25-8-5. Prohibited alterations and structural changes. — A condominium unit owner may not make an alteration or structural change that would:

(1) jeopardize the soundness or safety of the property;

(2) reduce the value of the property; or

(3) impair any easement or hereditament;

unless the condominium unit owner has obtained the unanimous consent of all the other co-owners. [P.L.2-2002, § 10.]

32-25-8-6. Profits and expenses allocated by percentage of undivided interests. — The:

(1) common profits of the property shall be credited to; and

(2) common expenses of the property shall be charged to;

the condominium unit owners according to the percentage of the owners' undivided interests in the common areas and facilities. [P.L.2-2002, § 10.]

NOTES TO DECISIONS

Common Expenses.

Condominium developers who retained ownership on some units in the development were "co-owners" under the Indiana Horizontal Property Law, and, as such, were required to pay their proportionate share of common expenses regardless of the terms of the declaration and bylaws. Hatfield v. La Charmant Home Owners Ass'n, 469 N.E.2d 1218 (Ind. App. 1984).

32-25-8-7. Taxes and assessments. — (a) Taxes, assessments, and other charges of:

(1) the state;

(2) any political subdivision;

(3) any special improvement district; or

(4) any other taxing or assessing authority;

shall be assessed against and collected on each condominium unit. Taxes, assessments, and other charges referred to in this subsection may not be assessed and collected on the building or property as a whole.

(b) Each condominium unit shall be carried on the tax books as a separate and distinct entity for the purpose of taxes, assessments, and other charges.

(c) A forfeiture or sale of the building or property as a whole for delinquent taxes, assessments, or charges may not divest or affect the title to a condominium unit if taxes, assessments, and charges on the condominium unit are currently paid. [P.L.2-2002, § 10.]

32-25-8-8. Records of expenditures on common areas. — (a) The manager or board of directors shall keep detailed, accurate records in chronological order of the receipts and expenditures affecting the common areas and facilities, specifying and itemizing:

(1) the maintenance and repair expenses of the common areas and facilities; and

(2) any other expenses incurred.

(b) The records and the vouchers authorizing the payments shall be available for examination by the co-owners at convenient hours of weekdays. [P.L.2-2002, § 10.]

32-25-8-9. Insurance. — (a) The co-owners, through the association of co-owners, shall purchase:

(1) a master casualty policy, payable as part of the common expenses, affording fire and extended coverage in an amount consonant with the full replacement value of the improvement that in whole or in part comprises the common areas and facilities; and

(2) a master liability policy in an amount:

(A) required by the bylaws;

(B) required by the declaration; or

(C) revised from time to time by a decision of the board of directors of the association.

(b) The policy referred to in subsection (a)(2) shall cover:

(1) the association of co-owners;

(2) the executive organ, if any;

(3) the managing agent, if any;

(4) all persons acting, or who may come to act, as agents or employees of any of the entities referred to in subdivisions (1) through (3) with respect to:

(A) the condominium;

(B) all condominium unit owners; and

(C) all other persons entitled to occupy any unit or other portions of the condominium.

(c) Other policies required by the condominium instruments may be obtained by the co-owners through the association, including:

(1) worker's compensation insurance;

(2) liability insurance on motor vehicles owned by the association;

(3) specialized policies covering land or improvements on which the association has or shares ownership or other rights; and

(4) officers' and directors' liability policies.

(d) When any policy of insurance has been obtained by or on behalf of the association of co-owners, the officer required to send notices of meetings of the association of co-owners shall promptly furnish to each co-owner or mortgagee whose interest may be affected written notice of:

(1) the obtainment of the policy; and

(2) any subsequent changes to or termination of the policy.

[P.L.2-2002, § 10.]

Collateral References. Condominium association's liability to unit owner for injuries caused by third person's criminal conduct. 59 A.L.R.4th 489.

32-25-8-10. Disaster procedures. — (a) In case of fire or any other casualty or disaster, other than complete destruction of all buildings containing the condominium units:

(1) the improvements shall be reconstructed; and

(2) the insurance proceeds shall be applied to reconstruct the improvements.

(b) In the event of complete destruction of all of the buildings containing condominium units:

(1) the buildings shall not be reconstructed, except as provided in subdivision (2), and the insurance proceeds, if any, shall be divided among the co-owners:
    (A) in the percentage by which each owns an undivided interest in the common areas and facilities; or
    (B) proportionately according to the fair market value of each condominium unit immediately before the casualty as compared with the fair market value of all other condominium units;
as specified in the bylaws of the condominium; and
(2) the property shall be considered as to be removed from the condominium under section 16 [IC 32-25-8-16] of this chapter, unless by a vote of two-thirds (⅔) of all of the co-owners a decision is made to rebuild the building.

(c) If a decision is made under subsection (b)(2) to rebuild the building, the insurance proceeds shall be applied, and any excess of construction costs over insurance proceeds shall be contributed as provided in this section in the event of less than total destruction of the buildings.

(d) A determination of total destruction of the buildings containing condominium units shall be made by a vote of two-thirds (⅔) of all co-owners at a special meeting of the association of co-owners called for that purpose. [P.L.2-2002, § 10.]

32-25-8-11. Inadequate insurance. — (a) If:
    (1) the:
        (A) improvements are not insured; or
        (B) insurance proceeds are not sufficient to cover the cost of repair or reconstruction; and
    (2) the property is not to be removed from the condominium;
the co-owners shall contribute the balance of the cost of repair or reconstruction in the percentage by which a condominium unit owner owns an undivided interest in the common areas and facilities as expressed in the declaration.

(b) The amount of the contribution under subsection (a):
    (1) is assessed as part of the common expense; and
    (2) constitutes a lien from the time of assessment of the contribution as provided in IC 32-25-6-3. [P.L.2-2002, § 10.]

32-25-8-12. Classification of property after disaster and decision not to rebuild. — The following apply if, under section 10 [IC 32-25-8-10] of this chapter, it is not determined by the co-owners to rebuild after a casualty or disaster has occurred:
    (1) The property is considered to be owned in common by the condominium unit owners.
    (2) The undivided interest in the property owned in common that appertains to each condominium unit owner is the percentage of undivided interest previously owned by the owner in the common areas and facilities.
    (3) Any liens affecting any of the condominium units are considered to be transferred in accordance with the existing priorities to the percent-

age of the undivided interest of the condominium unit owner in the property.

(4) The property is subject to an action for partition at the suit of any condominium unit owner, in which event the net proceeds of sale, together with the net proceeds of the insurance on the property, if any;

    (A) are considered as one (1) fund; and

    (B) are divided among all the condominium unit owners in a percentage equal to the percentage of undivided interest owned by each owner in the property, after first paying out of the respective shares of the condominium unit owners, to the extent sufficient for the purpose, all liens on the undivided interest in the property owned by each condominium unit owner. [P.L.2-2002, § 10.]

32-25-8-13. Amendment of declaration to add additional real estate. — (a) Subject to the declaration and this chapter, a declarant may add additional real estate to an expandable condominium if an amendment to the declaration required by subsection (b) is executed in the manner described in section 3 [IC 32-25-8-3] of this chapter. The expansion is effective when the instruments required by subsection (b) are recorded.

(b) In expanding the condominium, the declarant shall:

    (1) prepare, execute, and record amendments to the condominium instruments; and

    (2) record new plats and plans under IC 32-25-7-1 and IC 32-25-7-4.

The amendment to the declaration shall assign an identifying number to each condominium unit within the real estate being added and shall reallocate undivided interests in the common areas and facilities under IC 32-25-4-3. [P.L.2-2002, § 10.]

32-25-8-14. Amendment of declaration to remove real estate. — (a) Subject to:

    (1) the declaration;

    (2) condominium instruments; and

    (3) this chapter;

a declarant may withdraw withdrawable land from a contractable condominium unless the withdrawal is prohibited by subsection (c). The contraction is effective when the instruments required by subsection (b) are recorded.

(b) In contracting the condominium, the declarant shall prepare, execute, and record an amendment to the declaration and condominium instruments:

    (1) containing a legally sufficient description of the land being withdrawn; and

    (2) stating the fact of withdrawal.

(c) If a portion of the withdrawable land was described under IC 32-25-7-3(6) and IC 32-25-7-3(7), that portion may not be withdrawn if any person other than the declarant owns a condominium unit situated on that portion of the withdrawable land. If that portion of the withdrawable land was not described under IC 32-25-7-3(6) and IC 32-25-7-3(7), none of the withdrawable land may be withdrawn if any person other than the declarant owns a condominium unit situated on that portion of the withdrawable land. [P.L.2-2002, § 10.]

32-25-8-15. Option to not expand condominium. — If a declarant reserves an option in the declaration to not expand the condominium, the declarant shall:

(1) make a full disclosure of that option to every prospective buyer in writing before the buyer enters an agreement to purchase a condominium unit; and

(2) obtain and retain an instrument acknowledging receipt of that disclosure by the prospective buyer. [P.L.2-2002, § 10.]

32-25-8-16. Removal of property from condominium — Recording of instrument — Action for partition. — (a) All of the co-owners may remove a property from this article by a recorded removal instrument if the holders of all liens affecting any of the condominium units:

(1) consent in a recorded instrument to the removal; or

(2) agree in a recorded instrument that their liens be transferred to the percentage of the undivided interest of the condominium unit owner in the property as provided in this section.

(b) If it is determined under section 10 [IC 32-25-8-10] of this chapter that all of the buildings containing condominium units have been totally destroyed:

(1) the property is considered removed from this article; and

(2) an instrument reciting the removal under section 10 of this chapter shall be recorded and executed by the association of co-owners.

(c) At the time of recording under subsection (b)(2), the property is removed from this article.

(d) Upon removal of the property from this article, the property is considered to be owned in common by the condominium unit owners. The undivided interest in the property owned in common that appertains to each condominium unit owner is the percentage of undivided interest previously owned by the owner in the common areas and facilities.

(e) Under the circumstances described in subsection (a) or in subsections (b) through (d), the property is subject to an action for partition at the suit of any condominium unit owner, in which event the net proceeds of sale, together with the net proceeds of the insurance on the property, if any:

(1) are considered as one (1) fund; and

(2) are divided among all the condominium unit owners in a percentage equal to the percentage of undivided interest owned by each owner in the property, after first paying out of the respective shares of the condominium unit owners, to the extent sufficient for the purpose, all liens on the undivided interest in the property owned by each condominium unit owner.

(f) A removal under this section does not bar the subsequent resubmission of the property to this article. [P.L.2-2002, § 10.]

CHAPTER 9

ACTIONS AND PROCEEDINGS

32-25-9-1. Compliance with articles, bylaws, and covenants — Failure to comply — Organization of association. — (a) Each condominium unit owner shall comply with:

(1) the articles of incorporation or association;

(2) the bylaws;

(3) any administrative rules adopted under:

(A) the articles of incorporation or association; or

(B) the bylaws; and

(4) the covenants, conditions, and restrictions set forth in:

(A) the declaration; or

(B) the deed to the owner's condominium unit.

(b) Failure to comply as required under subsection (a) is grounds for an action:

(1) to recover sums due;

(2) for damages;

(3) for injunctive relief; or

(4) for any other legal or equitable relief;

maintainable by the manager or board of directors on behalf of the association of co-owners or by an aggrieved co-owner.

(c) The association of co-owners may be organized as:

(1) a nonprofit corporation under:

(A) IC 23-7-1.1 (before its repeal August 1, 1991); or

(B) IC 23-17; or

(2) an unincorporated association.

[P.L.2-2002, § 10.]

Effective Dates. P.L.2-2002, § 10. July 1. 2002.

NOTES TO DECISIONS

Injunction.

Trial court abused its discretion in denying injunctive relief in an action brought by a condominium association to compel a unit owner to remove a deck constructed in violation of condominium bylaws where the court's factual findings did not show that the equities favored denial of the injunction. Cobblestone II Homeowners Ass'n v. Baird, 545 N.E.2d 1126 (Ind. App. 1989).

Collateral References. Validity and construction of regulations of governing body of condominium or cooperative apartment pertaining to parking. 60 A.L.R.5th 647.

32-25-9-2. Persons who may bring action on behalf of owners — Service of process. — (a) The board of directors, or the manager with the approval of the board of directors, may bring an action on behalf of two (2) or more of the condominium unit owners, as their respective interests appear, with respect to any cause of action relating to:

(1) the common areas and facilities; or

(2) more than one (1) condominium unit.

An action brought under this subsection does not limit the rights of any condominium unit owner.

(b) Service of process on two (2) or more condominium unit owners in any action relating to:

(1) the common areas and facilities; or

(2) more than one (1) condominium unit;

may be made on the person designated in the declaration to receive service of process. [P.L.2-2002, § 10.]

Collateral References. Standing to bring action relating to real property of condominium. 74 A.L.R.4th 165.

ARTICLE 26

FENCES

CHAPTER 1

FENCING ASSOCIATIONS

32-26-1-1. Formation of associations. — (a) Five (5) or more persons may form a fencing association if the persons are interested in:
(1) enclosing land with one (1) general fence; or
(2) doing any other work necessary to protect land and to secure crops raised on land.
(b) The enclosed land described in subsection (a) must be:
(1) improved land;
(2) used for purposes of cultivation; and
(3) situated in an area that is:
(A) definitely described by sections or subdivisions of sections; or
(B) sufficiently described by metes and bounds, and on or near any stream, watercourse, lake, pond, or marsh, and subject to overflow from any stream, watercourse, lake, pond, or marsh.
(c) The association shall adopt and subscribe articles, which must specify the name and objects of the association. [P.L.2-2002, § 11.]

Effective Dates. P.L.2-2002, § 11. July 1. 2002.
Collateral References. 35 Am. Jur. 2d Fences, §§ 1-5.

36A C.J.S. Fences, §§ 3, 4.

32-26-1-2. Election of directors — Notice. — (a) Three (3) or more members of the association may give notice of an election to choose directors for the association.
(b) The notices must:
(1) be written or printed;
(2) specify the time and location of the election; and
(3) be posted for at least ten (10) days before the election in at least five (5) public places in each township where the contemplated work will occur.
(c) The location of the election must be near the contemplated work. [P.L.2-2002, § 11.]

32-26-1-3. Number of directors. — At the election, at least five (5) of the association members shall elect by ballot at least three (3) but not more than seven (7) association members as directors of the association. [P.L.2-2002, § 11.]

32-26-1-4. Recording of articles — Contents — Rights of association — Joining association. — (a) After the election of directors, the association shall record articles of association in the office of the recorder of the county where the proposed fence will be located.
(b) The articles must specify the following:
(1) The name and objects of the association.
(2) The names of the association's officers for the first year.
(3) The character of the work proposed.

(4) The location where the fence is to be located.

(c) After recording the articles of association, the association is a body corporate and politic by the name and style adopted, with all the rights, incidents, and liabilities of bodies corporate.

(d) Any person owning land in the area may at any time become a member of the association by signing the articles of association. [P.L.2-2002, § 11.]

NOTES TO DECISIONS

In General.
Articles of association had to be recorded before corporations had a legal existence. Por-

ter v. State ex rel. Dunkleberg, 141 Ind. 488, 40 N.E. 1061 (1895).

32-26-1-5. Petition to board of commissioners — Apportionment of costs — Appointment of viewers — Notice of apportionment. —
(a) The board of directors shall petition the board of commissioners of the county where the fence is to be located.

(b) The petition must do the following:
(1) Be signed by the owners of the major part of the improved land.
(2) Give a full description of the contemplated work, specifying particularly:
(A) the points of beginning and ending of the work;
(B) the course and distances of the work;
(C) the manner and character of the gates to be placed on all public highways crossed;
(D) the nature and character of the improvement;
(E) a detailed statement of the projected cost, as accurately as the projected cost can conveniently be stated; and
(F) the description of the area to be enclosed.
(3) Request the appointment of viewers to view and apportion among the owners of real estate in the area the cost of the improvement, and all expenses that:
(A) are incurred procuring the improvement; and
(B) are considered to be necessary in maintaining the improvement for one (1) year after the completion of the fence.

(c) The apportionment of the cost and expenses incurred under this chapter must be made according to the number of acres of land owned by each landowner that is improved and used for the purposes of cultivation, as described in section 6 [IC 32-26-1-6] of this chapter.

(d) The board of commissioners, on proof that the signers of the petition own the major part of the improved land in the area, shall hear and consider the petition. If the board of commissioners decides the improvement is a public utility and is in the best interests of the owners of the lands in the area, the board of commissioners shall appoint three (3) viewers.

(e) The viewers, who may not be members of the association or interested in the proposed work, shall make the apportionments described in subsection (b) (3) among the landowners.

(f) The viewers shall be furnished:

(1) a copy of the plan and profile of the proposed work; and

(2) a certified copy of the order of the board of commissioners for their appointment.

(g) The viewers shall meet at a time and place in the area to make the apportionment as fixed by the board of commissioners.

(h) Before the apportionment begins, the owners of improved land in the area are entitled to notice of the time when and place where the viewers will begin the examination of lands and the apportionment of assessments by written or printed notices posted at the door of the courthouse of the county and five (5) public places in the area. [P.L.2-2002, § 11.]

32-26-1-6. Duties and powers of viewers. — (a) At the time and place named by the board of commissioners and fixed by the notices, the appointed viewers shall do the following:

(1) Meet and inspect the lands improved and used for cultivation in the area.

(2) Assess against the owners of the improved land the costs and expenses of the improvement. The costs and expenses shall be apportioned among them severally, according to the number of acres of improved land owned by each owner.

(3) Hear and determine any complaints at that time regarding the assessment.

(b) The appointed viewers have the authority to:

(1) hear evidence;

(2) swear and examine witnesses;

(3) reexamine any lands;

(4) cause surveys and measurements to be made; and

(5) adjourn periodically until the viewers complete the apportionment of assessments. [P.L.2-2002, § 11.]

32-26-1-7. Viewers' report. — (a) The appointed viewers, after having completed their apportionment, shall submit a written report of their work to the board of commissioners, together with a tabular statement of the assessments made.

(b) The directors of the association shall record the written report by the appointed viewers in the office of the recorder of the county.

(c) From the recording date of the written report, the assessments in the written report shall be respectively a lien on each tract of land described in the written report for the amount assessed to the tract. [P.L.2-2002, § 11.]

32-26-1-8. Annual assessments. — (a) The board of directors may make annual assessments after the first assessment for the purpose of repairing and maintaining the improvement and for other necessary expenses.

(b) The board of directors shall apportion the annual assessments among the owners and file a tabular statement of the apportionment and assessment in the recorder's office.

(c) The tabular statement of the apportionment and assessment is a lien on the tracts of land respectively assessed and may be collected in the same manner as the original assessment. [P.L.2-2002, § 11.]

32-26-1-9. Fences erected prior to 1877 — Formation of associations. — (a) If the owners of land have, under or by virtue of any law of Indiana or by mutual consent, erected a fence before March 14, 1877, as described in this chapter, the landowners may:
   (1) organize an association according to the provisions of this chapter;
   (2) file their articles of association in the office of the recorder; and
   (3) petition the board of commissioners as provided in subsection (b).
   (b) The petition must show that:
   (1) the fence was built before March 14, 1877; and
   (2) the goal of the organization is to maintain the fence in good order and repair, as though built under this chapter.
   (c) The board of commissioners shall consider the petition. If the board of commissioners is satisfied that:
   (1) the owners of the major part of the land improved and used for the purposes of cultivation enclosed by the fence signed the petition; and
   (2) the maintenance of the improvement is of public utility and for the best interests of the owners of the land in the area;
the board of commissioners shall make an order allowing the board of directors of the association to make assessments for that purpose, as provided in section 8 [IC 32-26-1-8] of this chapter.
   (d) After the directors of the association follow the steps provided in section 8 of this chapter, the association is a body corporate and politic, as though originally organized under this chapter, and has all the rights and powers granted in this chapter.
   (e) All liens that then exist in favor of any creditor that financed the improvement, or against any lands on account of the improvement, shall be preserved and may be enforced, either according to the law under which the liens were created or according to this chapter. [P.L.2-2002, § 11.]

32-26-1-10. Board of directors — Appointment of officers — Quorum. — (a) The board of directors shall appoint a president, secretary, and treasurer.
   (b) The treasurer shall give a bond:
   (1) sufficient in penalties and securities;
   (2) payable to the association by its corporate name; and
   (3) conditioned for:
      (A) the faithful discharge of the treasurer's duties; and
      (B) the safekeeping and prompt payment, according to the order of the board of directors, of all money accessible to the treasurer.
   (c) A majority of the board of directors is a quorum for the transaction of business.
   (d) Previous notice of any regular or adjourned meeting of the directors is not necessary. [P.L.2-2002, § 11.]

32-26-1-11. Board of directors — Vacancies. — If a vacancy occurs in the office of director, the other members of the board shall fill the vacancy by a pro tempore appointment from the members of the association. The appointment continues until the next annual election and until a successor is elected and qualified. [P.L.2-2002, § 11.]

32-26-1-12. Board of directors — Terms of officers. — The president, secretary, and treasurer continue in office for one (1) year and until their successors in office are elected and qualified. [P.L.2-2002, § 11.]

32-26-1-13. Board of directors — Drawing of money. — The treasurer may not draw money, except upon the order of the president and secretary. [P.L.2-2002, § 11.]

32-26-1-14. Board of directors — Settling of accounts. — Each year, before the expiration of the treasurer's term, and more often if the board of directors requires, the treasurer shall present the treasurer's vouchers and settle with the board. [P.L.2-2002, § 11.]

32-26-1-15. Supplemental assessments. — (a) If the board of directors finds that any lands that will be affected by the proposed work have been omitted from the assessment or that any mistake has occurred in the assessment, the board may order a supplemental assessment for the correction of mistakes.

(b) The owners of all lands directly affected by the supplemental assessment shall have notice of the time and place of making the supplemental assessment and of a time when and place where the owners may be heard regarding the supplemental assessment in the same manner as in respect to the original assessment.

(c) The supplemental assessment, when completed, shall be filed for record in the same manner as the original assessment.

(d) The supplemental assessment shall, from that date, be a lien on the lands described in the supplemental assessment in like manner as the original assessment. [P.L.2-2002, § 11.]

32-26-1-16. Ordering payment of assessments — Installments. — The board of directors may, without reference to the completion of the proposed work, order:

(1) the payment of the assessment in installments as it considers proper; or

(2) the payment in full at a stated time.

[P.L.2-2002, § 11.]

32-26-1-17. Enforcement of payment. — Payment of the assessments may be enforced by suit in any court with jurisdiction as for ordinary debts or by the foreclosure of the lien in any court with jurisdiction in the same manner as is provided by law for the foreclosure of mortgages and the sale of mortgaged premises for the collection of debts. [P.L.2-2002, § 11.]

32-26-1-18. Contract to lowest bidder — Purchase of existing fence. — (a) The proposed work shall be awarded by the board of directors by contract to the lowest responsible bidder, after suitable advertisements, as a whole or in sections or subdivisions as the board considers most advantageous.

(b) The board of directors may purchase any fence built along the line of the proposed fence and use the fence instead of building new fencing. [P.L.2-2002, § 11.]

32-26-1-19. Appropriation of land for construction or maintenance. — If the association wishes to appropriate any land for the construction or maintenance of any work, the association must proceed in the manner required by law for the assessment of like damages in case of the construction of railroads or other similar works. [P.L.2-2002, § 11.]

32-26-1-20. Alteration of description of proposed work — Extension. — Every association organized under this chapter with the concurrence of three-fourths (¾) of its members, expressed by resolution at any regular meeting of the association, may:

(1) correct or perfect any incorrect or imperfect description of the proposed work; or

(2) provide for the extension of the proposed work beyond the limits prescribed in the original articles of the association. [P.L.2-2002, § 11.]

32-26-1-21. Restrictions on enforcement of liens. — An association may not commence an action to enforce any lien upon land for assessments made five (5) years after the date of recording the schedule of the assessment constituting a lien, as contemplated by this chapter. Any assessment made under any former law of Indiana upon the same subject, when action is not pending for the enforcement of the assessment, is prima facie satisfied upon the record five (5) years after the recording of the schedule of the assessment. [P.L.2-2002, § 11.]

32-26-1-22. Adoption of rules — Fines and penalties. — The association may pass any rules and impose reasonable fines and penalties to insure the success of the object of the association's incorporation. The association may:

(1) employ individuals to keep the fence in repair;

(2) employ gatekeepers to attend to the gates on all public highways;

(3) employ keepers of pounds to impound and care for all stock found running at large in the area enclosed by the fence;

(4) make bylaws regulating:

(A) when stock may run at large in the enclosed area; and

(B) the number of cattle, horses, and swine each landowner or occupant of lands in the enclosed area may be allowed to permit to run at large. [P.L.2-2002, § 11.]

32-26-1-23. Prohibition against throwing down common fence. — A person may not throw down the common fence. A person who throws down a common fence shall pay to the association at least five dollars ($5) but not more than twenty dollars ($20), recoverable before any court with jurisdiction. A person who throws down a common fence is liable for all damages that accrue because of the person's actions. Damages are recoverable under this subsection in the same manner as a forfeiture. [P.L.2-2002, § 11.]

32-26-1-24. Roving stock. — It is a Class C infraction for a person to allow the person's stock to run at large in the enclosed area unless expressly permitted to do so by the board of directors of the association. A person who violates this section is liable to all persons whose lands are trespassed upon for consequential damages. [P.L.2-2002, § 11.]

Cross References. Infractions and ordinance violation enforcement proceedings, IC 34-28-5.

32-26-1-25. Poundkeepers — Duties — Sale of stock. — (a) Any stock found roving about in the enclosed area contrary to the laws or regulations of the association shall be taken up and impounded at the expense of the owner. The poundkeeper shall:

(1) if the owner is known, notify the owner, in writing, of the impounding of the stock; or

(2) if the owner is unknown, post for ten (10) days a written or printed description of the stock at the public gates of the association and three

(3) other public places in the township where the fence is located.

(b) If, after the expiration of ten (10) days, the owner fails to reclaim and pay the expenses of keeping and posting the stock and the damages caused by the stock to any owner or occupant of land in the area, the stock shall, upon ten (10) days further notice, be sold to pay the expenses and damages.

(c) If, after payment for the stock, there is a remaining balance, the balance shall be deposited in the treasury of the association for the benefit of the owner. If no claim is made for the remaining balance for six (6) months, it shall vest in the association. [P.L.2-2002, § 11.]

CHAPTER 2
ENCLOSURES, TRESPASSING ANIMALS, AND PARTITION FENCES

32-26-2-1. "Lawful fence" defined. — (a) As used in this chapter, "lawful fence" means any structure typically used by husbandmen for the enclosure of property.

(b) The term includes:

(1) a cattle guard;

(2) a hedge;

(3) a ditch; and

(4) any other structure that witnesses knowledgeable about fences testify is sufficient to enclose property. [P.L.2-2002, § 11.]

Effective Dates. P.L.2-2002, § 11. July 1. 2002.

Cross References. Construction of cattle guards in certain counties, IC 8-17-1-2.1.

Lawful partition fence, IC 32-26-9-1.

NOTES TO DECISIONS

ANALYSIS

In general.
Applicability.

In General.

It was not proper to prove, in order to show that a fence was a lawful one, that it was such as were temporarily kept in that locality for special purposes. Blizzard v. Walker, 32 Ind. 437 (1869).

Applicability.

Former version of this section applied only to outside fences and not to partition fences. Cook v. Morea, 33 Ind. 497 (1870).

Collateral References. 4 Am. Jur. 2d Animals, §§ 49-54.

35 Am. Jur. 2d Fences, §§ 6-32.

36A C.J.S. Fences, §§ 21, 23.

Injunction to restrain repeated trespasses by tearing down fences. 60 A.L.R.2d 310.

Validity of statutes requiring the construction of fences — modern cases. 87 A.L.R.4th 1129.

32-26-2-2. Domestic animal breaking into enclosure. — (a) This subsection applies in a township for which the board of county commissioners has adopted an ordinance that allows domestic animals to run at large in unenclosed public areas. If a domestic animal breaks into an enclosure or enters upon the property of another person that is enclosed by a lawful fence, the person injured by the actions of the domestic animal may recover the amount of damage done.

(b) This subsection applies in a township for which the board of county commissioners has not adopted an ordinance that allows domestic animals to run at large in unenclosed public areas. If a domestic animal breaks into an enclosure or enters upon the property of another person, it is not necessary for the person injured by the actions of the domestic animal to allege or prove the existence of a lawful fence to recover for the damage done. [P.L.2-2002, § 11.]

NOTES TO DECISIONS

ANALYSIS

In general.
Applicability.
Burden of proof.
Common law.
Lawful fence.
—Effect.

In General.

Compliance with statute by persons who took up animals in order to retain possession as against the owner was required. Frazier v. Goar, 1 Ind. App. 38, 27 N.E. 442 (1891); Forsyth v. Walch, 4 Ind. App. 182, 30 N.E. 720 (1892); Wyman v. Turner, 14 Ind. App. 118, 42 N.E. 652 (1896).

When animals were lawfully at large, they could not have been said to have been trespassing animals. Noblesville Gas & Imp. Co. v. Teter, 1 Ind. App. 322, 27 N.E. 635 (1891).

Animals which escaped from an inclosure of the owner for the purpose of confining them, and which he endeavored to recover when he learned of their escape, could not be regarded as animals running at large within the meaning of the statute. Wolf v. Nicholson, 1 Ind. App. 222, 27 N.E. 505 (1891); Stephenson v. Ferguson, 4 Ind. App. 230, 30 N.E. 714 (1892).

Applicability.

This section did not apply to inside or partition fences. Myers v. Dodd, 9 Ind. 290, 68 Am. Dec. 624 (1857); Brady v. Ball, 14 Ind. 317 (1860); Cook v. Morea, 33 Ind. 497 (1870).

Burden of Proof.

When the owner of animals claimed that

they had a right to run at large, he had to produce an order of the county board to that effect. Atkinson v. Mott, 102 Ind. 431, 26 N.E. 217 (1885).

If animals lawfully at large broke through a fence, the burden was on the landowner to show that the fence was a lawful one. Crum v. Conover, 14 Ind. App. 264, 40 N.E. 644 (1895).

Common Law.

At common law, each person was bound to keep his animals on his own lands. Williams v. New-Albany & S.R.R., 5 Ind. 111 (1854); Brady v. Ball, 14 Ind. 317 (1860); Atkinson v. Mott, 102 Ind. 431, 26 N.E. 217 (1885); Crum v. Conover, 14 Ind. App. 264, 40 N.E. 644 (1895), rehearing overruled, 14 Ind. 268, 42 N.E. 1029 (1896).

The statutes as to taking up trespassing animals superseded the common law remedies. Little v. Swafford, 14 Ind. App. 7, 42 N.E. 245 (1895).

Lawful Fence.

—Effect.

When animals were permitted to run at large, they could not have been detained when trespassing upon lands unless such animals broke through a lawful fence. Clark v. Stipp, 75 Ind. 114 (1881).

If animals were prohibited from running at large, the owner was liable for damages done by them without regard to the kind of fence they broke over. Atkinson v. Mott, 102 Ind. 431, 26 N.E. 217 (1885); Crum v. Conover, 14 Ind. App. 264, 40 N.E. 644 (1895), rehearing overruled, 14 Ind. 268, 42 N.E. 1029 (1896).

Collateral References. Personal liability of public officer for killing or injuring animal while carrying out statutory duties with respect to it. 2 A.L.R.3d 822.

Liability for injury to trespassing stock from poisonous substances on the premises. 12 A.L.R.3d 1103.

Liability of motorist for collision as affected

by attempts to avoid dog or other small animal in road. 41 A.L.R.3d 1124.

Measure, elements, and amount of damages for killing or injuring cat. 8 A.L.R.4th 1287.

Cat as subject of larceny. 55 A.L.R.4th 1080.

Liability for injuries caused by cat. 68 A.L.R.4th 823.

32-26-2-3. Tender of damages caused by domestic animal. —

(a) The owner of a domestic animal described in section 2 [IC 32-26-2-2] of this chapter may:

(1) tender to the person injured by the domestic animal:

(A) any costs that have accrued; and

(B) an amount, in lieu of damage, which equals or exceeds the amount of damages awarded by the court or by a jury in an action filed to recover damages caused by the actions of the domestic animal; or

(2) offer in writing to confess judgment for the amounts set forth in subdivision (1);
before an action filed to recover damages caused by a domestic animal described in section 2 of this chapter proceeds to trial.

(b) If the person injured by the domestic animal described in section 2 of this chapter rejects the tender or offer under subsection (a) and causes a trial for damages to proceed, the person injured:

(1) shall pay the costs of the trial; and

(2) may recover only the damages awarded.
[P.L.2-2002, § 11.]

32-26-2-4. Trespassing animal treated as stray. — Except as provided in this chapter, if a domestic animal breaks into the enclosure of a person who is not the owner of the domestic animal, the person, without regard to the season of the year:

(1) may confine the animal in the same manner as a stray animal may be confined; and

(2) shall proceed under IC 32-34-8 for stray animals.
[P.L.2-2002, § 11.]

Cross References. Estrays, taking up, IC 32-34-8.

NOTES TO DECISIONS

In General.
Animals could only have been taken up and detained as trespassing animals when they broke into an inclosure. Anderson v. Worley, 104 Ind. 165, 3 N.E. 817 (1885).

32-26-2-5. Notice to owner of stray required. — A person described in section 4 [IC 32-26-2-4] of this chapter shall, within twenty-four (24) hours after confining a stray animal, give notice to the owner of the animal, if the owner is known and can be immediately found. [P.L.2-2002, § 11.]

NOTES TO DECISIONS

In General.
In order to justify the takerup in detaining the animal, he must have given the notice required in this section. The notice must have contained a statement of the trespass and the damages assessed. Haffner v. Barnard, 123 Ind. 429, 24 N.E. 152 (1890).

Notice to owner in writing was required and if his name was unknown such fact should have been stated in the notices posted. Forsyth v. Walch, 4 Ind. App. 182, 30 N.E. 720 (1892); Wyman v. Turner, 14 Ind. App. 118, 42 N.E. 652 (1896).

32-26-2-6. Assessment of damages caused by stray. — Before posting or advertising a stray animal, a person described in section 4 [IC 32-26-2-4] of this chapter shall procure from two (2) disinterested property owners an examination and assessment of the damages caused by the stray animal with a certificate of the damages. Damages under this section may include reasonable pay for the persons making the assessment. [P.L.2-2002, § 11.]

32-26-2-7. Contents of notice to owner of stray. — A notice or advertisement described in section 6 [IC 32-26-2-6] of this chapter must specify the following:

(1) The fact of trespass in the enclosure of the person confining the stray animal.

(2) The damages assessed, including pay for the person making the assessment. [P.L.2-2002, § 11.]

NOTES TO DECISIONS

In General.

The notice had to contain a statement of the trespass and the amount of damages assessed. Haffner v. Barnard, 123 Ind. 429, 24 N.E. 152 (1890).

When personal notice was given to the owner, posting or advertising was not required. Haffner v. Barnard, 123 Ind. 429, 24 N.E. 152 (1890).

32-26-2-8. Requirements to reclaim stray. — The owner of a stray animal confined under section 4 [IC 32-26-2-4] of this chapter may demand the stray animal from the person who confined the stray animal only if the following conditions are met:

(1) The owner proceeds under IC 32-34-8-18 to prove that the stray animal is the owner's property.

(2) The owner pays the costs allowed in the case of stray animals.

(3) The owner pays the damages and the costs of assessment. [P.L.2-2002, § 11.]

Cross References. Reclaiming estrays by owners, IC 32-34-8-18.

32-26-2-9. Civil action to controvert damage assessment or deny trespass. — (a) Within five (5) days after the owner of a stray animal confined under section 4 [IC 32-26-2-4] of this chapter receives a notice under section 7 [IC 32-26-2-7] of this chapter, the owner may file a civil action to:

(1) controvert the amount of damages assessed; or

(2) deny the trespass.

(b) If the owner of a stray animal confined under section 4 of this chapter files an action under subsection (a), the cause shall be docketed for trial. [P.L.2-2002, § 11.]

32-26-2-10. Jury trial. — Either party in an action filed under section 9 [IC 32-26-2-9] of this chapter may demand a jury. [P.L.2-2002, § 11.]

32-26-2-11. Damages assessed by court — Paid before reclaiming stray. — If damages are assessed against the owner of a stray animal in a trial under this chapter, the owner must pay the damages and all costs assessed against the owner before the owner may recover the owner's property. [P.L.2-2002, § 11.]

32-26-2-12. Judgment of no trespass. — If the verdict or finding in a trial under this chapter is that the stray animal confined under section 4 [IC

32-26-2-4] of this chapter did not commit the trespass, a judgment shall be entered against the person who confined the stray animal for all costs and damages that are assessed. [P.L.2-2002, § 11.]

32-26-2-13. Sale of stray — Proceeds to cover damages. — If a stray animal confined under section 4 [IC 32-26-2-4] of this chapter is sold under IC 32-34-8, the person who confined the stray animal may retain out of the sale price of the stray animal the damages sustained by the person and the costs of assessing the damages in addition to the costs and allowances recoverable under IC 32-34-8. [P.L.2-2002, § 11.]

32-26-2-14. Unlawful fence. — In an action filed under this chapter, if the court or jury finds the fence through which a stray animal breaks is not a lawful fence, the animal shall be released to the animal's owner and the occupant of the enclosure shall pay costs and damages to the animal's owner. [P.L.2-2002, § 11.]

NOTES TO DECISIONS

In General.
    When animals were not allowed to run at large, the character of fence kept was immaterial. Atkinson v. Mott, 102 Ind. 431, 26 N.E. 217 (1885).
    If animals lawfully at large broke through a fence, the burden was on the landowner to show that the fence was a lawful one. Crum v. Conover, 14 Ind. App. 264, 40 N.E. 664 (1895), rehearing overruled, 14 Ind. App. 268, 41 N.E. 1029 (1896).

32-26-2-15. Existing fence transformed to partition fence. — When a fence that is already erected becomes a partition fence because previously unenclosed property is enclosed, the person who encloses the previously unenclosed property shall pay to the owner of the existing fence fifty percent (50%) of the value of the existing fence, as estimated by the owner of the existing fence. [P.L.2-2002, § 11.]

NOTES TO DECISIONS

ANALYSIS

In general.
Applicability.

In General.
    If the party so using such fence denied his liability, suit could have been brought to recover the value of one half of such fence before an estimate of its value was made. Bartlett v. Adams, 43 Ind. 447 (1873).

Applicability.
    This section applied only where a landowner in fencing uninclosed land joined his fence to an existing fence on the division line. Byers v. Davis, 3 Ind. App. 387, 29 N.E. 798 (1892).

32-26-2-16. Action for payment to owner of existing fence. — (a) If a person who encloses previously unenclosed property refuses to pay the owner of an existing fence under section 15 [IC 32-26-2-15] of this chapter, the owner may file a civil action for recovery of the amount due under section 15 of this chapter.

(b) This subsection applies if, before a trial under subsection (a):

(1) the person who encloses the previously unenclosed property offers to the owner of an existing fence; and

(2) the owner of the existing fence refuses to accept;
an amount equal to or larger than the damages awarded at the trial and the costs accrued up to the date of the offer. The owner of the existing fence shall pay the costs of the action and receive only the damages assessed. [P.L.2-2002, § 11.]

32-26-2-17. Consent to join new fence to existing fence. — A person who encloses property that has previously been unenclosed may not join the new fence to another person's existing fence without the consent of the owner of the existing fence. If consent to join the new fence with the existing fence is not given, each property owner shall give property that is equivalent to fifty percent (50%) of the width of a lane, or a reasonable distance, for the erection of the second fence. [P.L.2-2002, § 11.]

32-26-2-18. Prohibition against removal of fence forming partition. — This section applies to a person who ceases to use the person's property or opens the person's enclosures. A person to whom this section applies may not remove any part of the person's fence that forms a partition fence between the person's property and the enclosure of any other person until the person to whom this section applies has first given six (6) months notice of the person's intention to remove the fence to any person who may be interested in the removal of the fence. [P.L.2-2002, § 11.]

NOTES TO DECISIONS

ANALYSIS

Inclosure.
Removal of fence.

Inclosure.
To constitute an "inclosure," as used in this section, the fences, including the partition fence, had to surround some part of the land adjoining. Gundy v. State, 63 Ind. 528 (1878).

Removal of Fence.
If a party to a partition fence desired to remove it, he should have taken the same steps to ascertain its value and the point at which it would have been fairly divided, as when about to have erected such a fence. Haines v. Kent, 11 Ind. 126 (1858).

32-26-2-19. Erecting fence on another's property. — (a) This section applies to a person who, by mistake, erects a fence on the property of another person.

(b) Within six (6) months after the determination of the legal property line, a person to whom this section applies may enter upon the other person's property and remove the fence that the person to whom this section applies erected. Before entering upon the other person's property, the person to whom this section applies must pay or offer to pay to the other person reasonable damages for injury caused in passing over the property to remove the fence. [P.L.2-2002, § 11.]

NOTES TO DECISIONS

Replevin.
Fence rails and stakes unlawfully taken and used by a wrongdoer in the construction of a fence on his land became a part of the realty and could not have been replevied. Ricketts v. Dorrel, 55 Ind. 470 (1877).

32-26-2-20. Removal of fence from another's property — Exposing crops. — If the fence to be removed under section 19 [IC 32-26-2-19] of this chapter forms any part of a fence enclosing a field of another party on which there is a crop, the person to whom section 19 of this chapter applies may not remove the fence in a manner that exposes the field until the crop:

(1) has been gathered and removed, or secured from injury; or

(2) might, with reasonable diligence, have been gathered and secured.

After the conditions set forth in this section have been met, the person to whom section 19 of this chapter applies may immediately remove the fence and materials, whether or not more than six (6) months have elapsed since the legal property line was determined. [P.L.2-2002, § 11.]

CHAPTER 3

RECORDING AGREEMENTS TO ERECT AND REPAIR FENCES

32-26-3-1. Agreements for provisions outside of this chapter. — Adjoining property owners who elect to erect, repair, maintain, or pay for fences separating their lands in a manner other than that set forth under this article shall do so by written agreement. When the agreement is signed by the adjoining property owners, the agreement must be recorded in the office of the recorder in the county or counties in which the adjoining properties are situated. [P.L.2-2002, § 11.]

Effective Dates. P.L.2-2002, § 11. July 1. 2002.
Collateral References. 1 Am. Jur. 2d Adjoining Landowners, §§ 17, 21.

35 Am. Jur. 2d Fences, §§ 8, 13.
36A C.J.S. Fences, §§ 1-3.

32-26-3-2. Construction. — This chapter may not be held or construed as annulling or abrogating any subsisting legal right created under or any cause of action that arose and was fully accrued under any law or agreement if the legal right became effective before January 1, 1950. [P.L.2-2002, § 11.]

CHAPTER 4

CUTTING OF LIVE FENCES ALONG PUBLIC HIGHWAYS

32-26-4-1. Applicability — Height restrictions — Time periods for cutting. — (a) This chapter:

(1) does not apply to:

(A) a highway intersection located within a city or town; or

(B) a building of a substantial character that is located at the intersection of highways; and

(2) except for the provisions of this chapter concerning hedge fences, applies only to the intersection of a state highway with another state highway, a county highway, or a township highway.

(b) Except as provided in subsection (c), the owner of a hedge or live fence along the line of a highway shall cut and trim down the hedge or live fence to a height of not more than five (5) feet once in each calendar year.

(c) This subsection applies if a hedge, live fence, or natural growth other than a tree connects with or is found at a highway intersection, adjacent to a curve where the view of the highway may be obstructed, or at a railway right-of-way. The owner of a hedge, live fence, or other growth to which this subsection applies shall trim and maintain the hedge, live fence, or other growth at a height of not more than five (5) feet above the level of the center of the traveled road bed in the highway that adjoins the hedge, live fence, or other growth:

(1) throughout the year;

(2) for a distance of:

(A) one hundred (100) feet, if the obstruction is a hedge or live fence; or

(B) fifty (50) feet, if the obstruction consists of any other natural growths; and

(3) beginning at the intersection of the highway and continuing along the lines dividing the highways and the adjoining property.

(d) This subsection applies to a tree growing within fifty (50) feet of the intersection of a highway with:

(1) another highway; or

(2) a steam or interurban railroad.

The owner of a tree to which this subsection applies shall trim the tree so that the view at the intersection is not obstructed.

(e) Except for a natural elevation of land, an obstruction to the view at the intersection of a highway with another highway or a steam or interurban railroad that exceeds a height of five (5) feet above the center of the highway may not be maintained at the intersection.

(f) After May 22, 1933, a building may not be erected within fifty (50) feet of an intersection to which this chapter applies. [P.L.2-2002, § 11.]

Effective Dates. P.L.2-2002, § 11. July 1. 2002.

NOTES TO DECISIONS

ANALYSIS

County highways.
Evidence.
Height requirements.
Obstructions.

County Highways.

Counties owe no statutory duty to motorists to clear growth along county highways. Hurst v. Board of Comm'rs, 446 N.E.2d 347 (Ind. App. 1983), rev'd on other grounds, 476 N.E.2d 832 (Ind. 1985).

Where plaintiff involved in automobile collision maintained that county had a duty to remove vegetation obscuring the view of a roadway near a curve, there was no evidence that any of the plants listed in IC 15-3-4-1 or that any growth over five feet in height, as provided in former IC 32-10-4-1 (repealed; see

County Highways. (Cont'd)
this section for similar provisions), obstructed the view of the roadway. Harkness v. Hall, 684 N.E.2d 1156 (Ind. App. 1997).

Evidence.
In an action for damages for a railroad crossing accident, no negligence of county commissioners was shown where there was no evidence as to whether or not the commissioners had inspected the crossing, as to who owned the land on which the trees, brush, and vegetation which allegedly obstructed the view of the crossing were growing, or as to whether or not the railway or other owner were ever notified to cut such growth. Wroblewski v. Grand Trunk W. Ry., 150 Ind. App. 327, 28 Ind. Dec. 277, 276 N.E.2d 567 (1971).

Height Requirements.
The language "a height of not to exceed five feet" as used in former version of this section indicates nothing more than a duty to cut any offending growth to five feet. The statute does not impose a duty to cut below five feet if necessary to open the view. Board of Comm'rs v. Hatton, 427 N.E.2d 696 (Ind. App. 1981).

Obstructions.
Any obstructions mentioned under former version of this section had to be cut or trimmed, in conformity with this section, by owner of land upon which such obstructions existed. Wroblewski v. Grand Trunk W. Ry., 150 Ind. App. 327, 28 Ind. Dec. 277, 276 N.E.2d 567 (1971).

Collateral References. 1 Am. Jur. 2d Adjoining Landowners, §§ 15-18.
36A C.J.S. Fences, §§ 1-3.

32-26-4-2. Examination of fences — Notice to owners — Failure to comply — Assessment of costs. — (a) The trustee of each township, the county highway superintendent, the Indiana department of transportation, or other officer in control of the maintenance of a highway shall between January 1 and April 1 of each year, examine all hedges, live fences, natural growths along highways, and other obstructions described in section 1 [IC 32-26-4-1] of this chapter in their respective jurisdictions. If there are hedges, live fences, other growths, or obstructions along the highways that have not been cut, trimmed down, and maintained in accordance with this chapter, the owner shall be given written notice to cut or trim the hedge or live fence and to burn the brush trimmed from the hedge or live fence and remove any other obstructions or growths.

(b) The notice required under subsection (a) must be served by reading the notice to the owner or by leaving a copy of the notice at the owner's usual place of residence.

(c) If the owner is not a resident of the township, county, or state where the hedge, live fence, or other obstructions or growth is located, the notice shall be served upon the owner's agent or tenant residing in the township. If an agent or a tenant of the owner does not reside in the township, the notice shall be served by mailing a copy of the notice to the owner, directed to the owner's last known post office address.

(d) If the owner, agents, or tenants do not proceed to cut and trim the fences and burn the brush trimmed from the fences or remove any obstructions or growths within ten (10) days after notice is served, the township trustee, county highway superintendent, or Indiana department of transportation shall immediately:

(1) cause the fences to be cut and trimmed or obstructions or growths removed in accordance with this chapter; and

(2) burn the brush trimmed from the fences.

All expenses incurred under this subsection shall be assessed against and become a lien upon the land in the same manner as road taxes.

(e) The township trustee, county highway superintendent, or Indiana department of transportation having charge of the work performed under subsection (d) shall prepare an itemized statement of the total cost of the work of removing the obstructions or growths and shall sign and certify the statement to the county auditor of the county in which the land is located. The county auditor shall place the statement on the tax duplicates. The county treasurer shall collect the costs entered on the duplicates at the same time and in the same manner as road taxes are collected. The treasurer may not issue a receipt for road taxes unless the costs entered on the duplicates are paid in full at the same time the road taxes are paid. If the costs are not paid when due, the costs shall become delinquent, bear the same interest, be subject to the same penalties, and be collected at the same time and in the same manner as other unpaid and delinquent taxes. [P.L.2-2002, § 11.]

NOTES TO DECISIONS

ANALYSIS

In general.
Failure of evidence.
Height requirements.
Road width.

In General.
In all statutory proceedings more or less ex parte in their nature, a strict compliance with the substantial provisions of the statute was necessary to the validity of the proceedings. Poyser v. Stangland, 230 Ind. 685, 106 N.E.2d 390 (1952).

Construction of public highway across partition line did not break continuity of line so that adjoining landowners should construct half of section of fence to north, and half of section to south of such highway. Poyser v. Stangland, 230 Ind. 685, 106 N.E.2d 390 (1952).

Failure of Evidence.
Since under former version of this section county was only required to inspect railroad crossings twice a year and give notice to landowner to cut or trim any obstructions found growing, and since plaintiff in wrongful death action against railroad company failed to present any evidence as to who owned land in question, or whether land was inspected, or whether railroad or other owner was notified of obstructions found, jury would have had no reasonable evidence on which to decide liability, and question therefore was properly withheld from jury. Wroblewski v. Grand Trunk W. Ry., 150 Ind. App. 327, 28 Ind. Dec. 277, 276 N.E.2d 567 (1971).

Height Requirements.
The language "a height of not to exceed five feet" as used in former IC 32-10-4-1 (repealed) indicates nothing more than a duty to cut any offending growth to five feet. The statute does not impose a duty to cut below five feet if necessary to open the view. Board of Comm'rs v. Hatton, 427 N.E.2d 696 (Ind. App. 1981).

Road Width.
Where boundary lines have never been established by competent authority, the width of the road established by use is limited to that portion actually travelled and excludes any berm or shoulder. Board of Comm'rs v. Hatton, 427 N.E.2d 696 (Ind. App. 1981).

32-26-4-3. Action in name of state — Fee for prosecuting attorney.
— The prosecuting attorney shall prosecute a suit under section 2(e) [IC 32-26-4-2(e)] of this chapter in the name of the state on relation of the supervisor or county highway superintendent. The prosecuting attorney shall receive a fee of ten dollars ($10), collected as a part of the costs of the suit, for bringing a suit under this section. [P.L.2-2002, § 11.]

CHAPTER 5

CUTTING LIVE FENCES BETWEEN ADJOINING LANDS

32-26-5-1. Height and width restrictions — Time periods. — A hedge or other live fence grown along the lines dividing properties owned by different persons in Indiana shall be cut and trimmed down to the height of not more than five (5) feet and to a width of not more than three (3) feet once in each calendar year. [P.L.2-2002, § 11.]

Effective Dates. P.L.2-2002, § 11. July 1. 2002.
Collateral References. 1 Am. Jur. 2d Adjoining Landowners, §§ 15-18.

36A C.J.S. Fences, §§ 1-3.
Encroachment of trees, shrubbery, or other vegetation across boundary line. 65 A.L.R.4th 603.

32-26-5-2. Complaint — Notice — Failure to comply — Expenses. — (a) Upon receiving a complaint in writing signed by an owner of land adjoining a hedge or fence to which this chapter applies alleging that the owner of the fence has neglected to cut and trim the hedge or fence, the township trustee shall examine, within five (5) days after receiving the complaint, the hedge or other live fence.

(b) If the hedge or other live fence that is the subject of the complaint under subsection (a) has not been cut and trimmed, the township trustee shall give the owner of the hedge or other live fence written notice to cut and trim the hedge or other live fence and to remove the brush to the owner's property within thirty (30) days after receiving the notice.

(c) The notice required under subsection (b) must be served by reading the notice to the owner or by leaving a copy of the notice at the owner's usual place of residence. If the owner of properties divided by the hedge or other live fence is not a resident of the township where the hedge or other live fence is located, the notice shall be served by mailing a copy of the notice to the owner directed to the owner's last known post office address.

(d) If the owner or the owner's agents or tenants do not cut and trim the fences and remove the brush, the trustee shall, immediately after the expiration of thirty (30) days, cause the hedge or other live fence to be cut and trimmed and the brush removed to the owner's property.

(e) The trustee shall recover all expenses incurred under subsection (d) by bringing a suit against the owner of the property on which the hedge or live fence is situated before the county court, the circuit court, or the superior court of the county in which the hedge or other live fence is situated. Collection of the expenses and any judgment recovered shall be without relief from valuation or appraisement laws. [P.L.2-2002, § 11.]

32-26-5-3. Action in name of state — Fee for prosecuting attorney. — The prosecuting attorney shall prosecute a suit under this chapter in the name of the state on relation of a township trustee. The prosecuting attorney shall receive ten dollars ($10) collected as part of the cost of the suit, for bringing a suit under this section. [P.L.2-2002, § 11.]

CHAPTER 6
ENCLOSURE OF LAND SUBJECT TO FLOODING

32-26-6-1. Petition to enclose land with one general fence — Appointment of viewers — Apportionment of costs. — (a) The owners of real property in a county who own the major portion of the property in the county that is:

(1) improved and used for purposes of agriculture;

(2) in an area that is:

(A) definitely described by sections or subdivisions of sections; or

(B) sufficiently described by metes and bounds; and

(3) situated upon or near, and subject to overflow from:

(A) a stream;

(B) a watercourse;

(C) a lake;

(D) a pond; or

(E) a marsh;

may petition the board of commissioners of the county, asking permission to enclose the properties within one (1) general fence that has swinging gates on all public highways crossed by the fence. A petition under this subsection must set forth the kind of fence and gates desired.

(b) Upon the receipt of a petition under subsection (a), the board of county commissioners shall appoint as viewers three (3) reputable householders of the county who are not related by blood or marriage to any of the parties interested in the subject of the petition. After being sworn to faithfully and fairly perform the services required of them, the viewers shall proceed:

(1) within a reasonable time after the viewers' appointment; and

(2) after giving publication of the viewers' intention by posting written or printed notices describing the properties in the townships where the properties are located;

to inspect the properties and make an assessment against the owners of the properties for the cost of the fence.

(c) The cost of the fence shall be apportioned between the owners of the properties severally according to the number of acres of improved land owned by each owner and the benefits accruing to the owners severally because of the fence. [P.L.2-2002, § 11.]

Effective Dates. P.L.2-2002, § 11. July 1.   Waters and Waterways, §§ 225-228, 395-399.
2002.   93 C.J.S. Waters, §§ 24-30.
Collateral References. 78 Am. Jur. 2d

32-26-6-2. Submission of report by viewers — Remonstrances. —
(a) After having performed the duties required under section 1 [IC 32-26-6-1] of this chapter, the viewers shall, as soon as practicable, submit a report in writing to the board of county commissioners of the viewers' actions and a tabular statement of the viewers' assessment. The report submitted under this section is sufficient authority for the board of county commissioners to issue an order for the erection or construction of the fence and gates if there is no remonstrance against the erection of the fence and gates.

(b) If a remonstrance is made under subsection (a), the board of county commissioners may order or refuse to order the erection of the fence or gate, in the board's discretion.

(c) If the order under subsection (a) is not made because of a mistake or error committed by the viewers, other viewers may be appointed to perform the same service and submit a report. [P.L.2-2002, § 11.]

32-26-6-3. Filing of report with county auditor— Assessment for delinquent payments. — (a) A certified copy of the report of the viewers, as approved by the board of commissioners, shall be filed in the office of the county auditor.

(b) Thirty (30) days after the fence and gates described in section 1 [IC 32-26-6-1] of this chapter have been constructed, any person interested in the fence and gates may make an affidavit before the county auditor showing which property owners have not paid their several assessments. The county auditor shall enter the sums assessed against the delinquent persons upon the tax duplicate to be collected by the treasurer as other taxes are collected. When the assessments have been collected, the money shall be paid out to the property owners who have voluntarily paid the cost of the fence, in proportion to the amount of the property owners' several assessments. [P.L.2-2002, § 11.]

32-26-6-4. Employment of surveyor. — The viewers appointed under this chapter may, if necessary, employ a surveyor, who shall be paid for the surveyor's services as may be agreed upon. The board of county commissioners shall fix the compensation of the viewers for their services. The entire cost and expenses of the proceedings are a part of the cost of the erection of the fence and gates and shall be collected in the same manner. [P.L.2-2002, § 11.]

32-26-6-5. Seasonal restrictions on stock running at large. — A person who owns property enclosed under this chapter may not allow stock to run at large upon the enclosed property during the period beginning March 16 and ending December 25 of any year. [P.L.2-2002, § 11.]

CHAPTER 7

RECORDING FENCEMARKS; REMOVAL OF MARKED FENCING FROM OVERFLOWED LANDS

32-26-7-1. Blank book supplied by commissioners. — If petitioned by at least twenty (20) property owners in the county, the board of county commissioners shall furnish a blank book to the recorder of the county, paid for out of the county fund, in which the county recorder shall keep a record of marks of rails and plank fencing that are adopted by the property owners of the county. [P.L.2-2002, § 11.]

Effective Dates. P.L.2-2002, § 11. July 1. 2002.
Collateral References. 78 Am. Jur. 2d

Waters and Waterways, §§ 225-228, 395-399.
93 C.J.S. Waters, §§ 24-30.

32-26-7-2. Fee for recording mark. — The county recorder shall charge a fee in accordance with IC 36-2-7-10 for the recording of each mark from the person adopting and having the mark recorded. The recorder may not record two (2) marks that exactly correspond. [P.L.2-2002, § 11.]

32-26-7-3. Retrieving marked rails after high water. — Any person who has the person's rails or plank fencing marked and recorded as provided under this chapter may, if the rails or plank fencing are removed by high water and overflow off the person's property on to the property of another person, remove the rails and plank fencing on to the person's own property at any time of the year. The owner of the rails or plank fencing is responsible for and shall pay all damages that may be done to growing grain on the property from which the rails or plank fencing are removed or over which the rails or plank fencing are hauled. [P.L.2-2002, § 11.]

CHAPTER 8

RECOVERY OF PROPERTY MOVED BY HIGH WATER

32-26-8-1. Time limitations — Selection of arbitrator — Umpire. — (a) When the fence rails or other property of a person in Indiana are removed by high water and lodged upon the real property of another person, the owner of the fence rails or other property may proceed, within sixty (60) days after the fence rails or other property are lodged, upon the real property on which the fence rails or other property are lodged.

(b) If the owner of the real property refuses to deliver up the fence rails or other property, the parties shall each select an arbitrator, who shall examine or hear evidence upon all the circumstances and facts and determine the case.

(c) If the arbitrators selected under subsection (b) cannot agree, the arbitrators shall select an umpire. The decision of a majority of the arbitrators and the umpire is final. [P.L.2-2002, § 11.]

Effective Dates. P.L.2-2002, § 11. July 1. 2002.
Collateral References. 78 Am. Jur. 2d

Waters and Waterways, §§ 225-228, 395-399.
93 C.J.S. Waters, §§ 24-30.

32-26-8-2. Arbitrators — Oath. — Before the arbitrators proceed under section 1 [IC 32-26-8-1] of this chapter, the arbitrators must swear, before a person who may administer oaths, to discharge the arbitrators' duties faithfully, impartially, and according to law. [P.L.2-2002, § 11.]

32-26-8-3. Division of property claimed by at least 10 people. — If at least ten (10) persons claim the same property under section 1 [IC 32-26-8-1] of this chapter, the persons shall give notice to all interested persons of the time and place of the arbitration. Upon hearing all the facts and circumstances in the case, the arbitrators shall award to each person making a claim a proportion of the property as the arbitrators consider reasonable and just. [P.L.2-2002, § 11.]

32-26-8-4. Not a trespass to retrieve property. — It is not a trespass for a person to go upon the real property of another person for the purposes set forth in this chapter. A person who goes upon the real property of another person under this chapter shall go upon the route that will do the least possible injury to the real property, if it is practicable and convenient. [P.L.2-2002, § 11.]

CHAPTER 9

PARTITION FENCES

32-26-9-1. Used by adjoining property owners. — A fence that is used by adjoining property owners as a partition fence, unless otherwise agreed upon by the property owners, is considered a partition fence and shall be repaired, maintained, and paid for as provided under this chapter. [P.L.2-2002, § 11.]

Effective Dates. P.L.2-2002, § 11. July 1. 2002.

Opinions of Attorney General. Roughly speaking, as to partition fences, one should face the property at the adjoining landowner and build that half which was to the right. 1950, No. 41, p. 145.

NOTES TO DECISIONS

ANALYSIS

In general.
Animals doing damage.
Ownership of materials.
Railroad companies.
Removal of fence.
Repair.
Wire fences.

In General.

When a person who inclosed lands used the fence of an adjoining landowner so as to make it a partition fence, he became liable for one half of the value thereof. Bartlett v. Adams, 43 Ind. 447 (1873).

To constitute a fence a partition fence, it was required either to be on the line dividing the lands of different owners, or the parties must have agreed that it should be a partition fence. Byers v. Davis, 3 Ind. App. 387, 29 N.E. 798 (1892).

An oral agreement between adjoining landowners respecting the portion of a partition fence that should have been built by each landowner was not a covenant running with the land, so as to bind a subsequent purchaser without notice. Hull v. Breedlove, 89 Ind. App. 460, 165 N.E. 328 (1929).

Animals Doing Damage.

The statute relating to the recovery of damages when animals break through a lawful fence did not apply to partition fences. Myers v. Dodd, 9 Ind. 290, 68 Am. Dec. 624 (1857); Brady v. Ball, 14 Ind. 317 (1860); Cook v. Morea, 33 Ind. 497 (1870); Stephenson v. Elliott, 2 Ind. App. 233, 28 N.E. 326 (1891).

The owners of partition fences were each bound to maintain the same, and when not kept in repair, they were required to confine their animals to their own lands. Myers v. Dodd, 9 Ind. 290, 68 Am. Dec. 624 (1857); Brady v. Ball, 14 Ind. 317 (1860); Cook v. Morea, 33 Ind. 497 (1870); Stephenson v. Elliott, 2 Ind. App. 233, 28 N.E. 326 (1891).

Owners of lands were not liable for damages done by animals not under their control that passed over such lands and broke through partition fences. Cook v. Morea, 33 Ind. 497 (1870).

If the parties apportioned the fence that each was to have kept in repair, the party failing to keep his portion in repair could not recover for damages done by animals that broke through such portion. Hinshaw v. Gilpin, 64 Ind. 116 (1878); Baynes v. Chastain, 68 Ind. 376 (1879).

Animals could have been retained until damages were paid for breaking through lawful partition fences. Enders v. McDonald, 5 Ind. App. 297, 31 N.E. 1056 (1892).

Ownership of Materials.

Where the fence was wrongfully removed, the rails became personal property, and the subject of replevin by the lawful owner. Moore v. Combs, 24 Ind. App. 464, 56 N.E. 35 (1900), overruled on other grounds, Ayres v. Blevins, 28 Ind. App. 101, 62 N.E. 305 (1901).

Railroad Companies.

Fences erected by railroad companies along their rights-of-way were not partition fences. Cleveland, C., C., & I. Ry. v. Crossley, 36 Ind. 370 (1871); Jeffersonville, M. & I.R.R. v. Sullivan, 38 Ind. 262 (1871).

Removal of Fence.

Removal of fence without right gave a right of recovery to the owner. Moore v. Combs, 24 Ind. App. 464, 56 N.E. 35 (1900), overruled on other grounds, Ayres v. Blevins, 28 Ind. App. 101, 62 N.E. 305 (1901).

Repair.

Parol contracts for keeping fences in repair were valid between the parties thereto. Baynes v. Chastain, 68 Ind. 376 (1879); Burck v. Davis, 35 Ind. App. 648, 73 N.E. 192 (1905).

If the parties agreed that each should keep up one half of the fence, damages could have been assessed under the statute against the party in default. Bruner v. Palmer, 108 Ind. 397, 9 N.E. 354 (1886).

Covenants in deeds concerning the maintenance of fences ran with the land. Lake Erie & W.R.R. v. Priest, 131 Ind. 413, 31 N.E. 77 (1892); Toledo, St. L. & K.C.R.R. v. Cosand, 6 Ind. App. 222, 33 N.E. 251 (1893); Lake Erie & W.R.R. v. Power, 15 Ind. App. 179, 43 N.E. 959 (1896).

Covenants in deeds concerning the maintenance of fences ran with the land. Union Traction Co. v. Thompson, 61 Ind. App. 183, 111 N.E. 648 (1916).

Parol contracts for keeping fences in repair were valid between the parties thereto. Such a contract was not binding, however, on a purchaser without notice of such contract. Bartlett v. State ex rel. Hamilton, 186 Ind. 16, 114 N.E. 692 (1917).

Wire Fences.
Persons building wire fences could have been liable for damages on account of injuries caused by fence. Carskaddon v. Mills, 5 Ind. App. 22, 31 N.E. 559 (1892); Morrow v. Sweeney, 10 Ind. App. 626, 38 N.E. 187 (1894); McFarland v. Swihart, 11 Ind. App. 175, 38 N.E. 483, 54 Am. St. 499 (1894); Lowe v. Guard, 11 Ind. App. 472, 39 N.E. 428, 54 Am. St. R. 511 (1895); Blue v. Briggs, 12 Ind. App. 105, 39 N.E. 885 (1895).

Collateral References. 35 Am. Jur. 2d Fences, §§ 6-32.
36A C.J.S. Fences, §§ 5-12.

Encroachment of trees, shrubbery, or other vegetation across boundary line. 65 A.L.R.4th 603.

32-26-9-2. Responsibility for maintaining fences. — (a) The owner of a property that:
(1) is located outside;
(2) abuts; or
(3) is adjacent to;
the boundary of the corporate limits of a town or city shall separate the owner's property from adjoining properties by a partition fence constructed upon the line dividing or separating the properties regardless of when the properties were divided.

(b) Except as otherwise provided in this chapter, and if a division of the partition fence has not been made between the property owners for the building, repairing, or rebuilding of the partition fence:
(1) for a partition fence built along a property line than runs from north to south:
(A) the owner whose property lies to the east of the fence shall build the north half of the fence; and
(B) the owner whose land lies to the west of the fence shall build the south half of the fence; and
(2) for a partition fence built along a property line that runs from east to west:
(A) the owner whose property lies north of the fence shall build the west half of the fence; and
(B) the owner whose property lies to the south of the fence shall build the east half of the fence.

(c) Notwithstanding subsection (b), if either property owner has constructed one-half (½) of a partition fence that is not the portion required under subsection (b) and has maintained that portion of the partition fence for a period of not less than five (5) years, the property owner may continue to maintain the portion of the fence.

(d) If a property owner fails to build, rebuild, or repair a partition fence after receiving notice under this chapter, the township trustee of the township in which the property is located shall build, rebuild, or repair the fence as provided under this chapter. [P.L.2-2002, § 11.]

NOTES TO DECISIONS

ANALYSIS

In general.
Agreement of parties.

Construction.
Duty of township trustee.
Mandamus.
Separate action for damages.

In General.

Predecessor statute to this section recognized the right of adjacent landowners to contract and agree among themselves as to what portion of a line fence had to be built and kept in repair by the respective parties in interest. Bartlett v. State ex rel. Hamilton, 186 Ind. 16, 114 N.E. 692 (1917).

Since an oral agreement between the owners of adjoining lands as to the part of a partition fence each had to maintain was not a covenant running with the land so as to bind a subsequent purchaser without notice, the rights of the parties were governed by this section as though there was no agreement. Hull v. Breedlove, 89 Ind. App. 460, 165 N.E. 328 (1929).

There having been no agreement between the owners of adjoining lands as to the maintenance of an east and west partition fence between them, it was the duty of the owner of the land south of the fence to maintain the east half. Hull v. Breedlove, 89 Ind. App. 460, 165 N.E. 328 (1929).

Agreement of Parties.

In an action for a declaratory judgment to determine the rights and status of parties relative to the construction and maintenance of a partition fence between two tracts of land, title to both of which was derived by the owners thereof from a common ancestor, the evidence was sufficient to justify a finding by the court that the parties to the action had adopted the division for the maintenance of the line fence as originally made by such common ancestor and the former owner of one of the tracts from whom such ancestor purchased it subsequent to such division. Retter v. Retter, 110 Ind. App. 659, 40 N.E.2d 385 (1942).

Construction.

Former section, relating to construction and repair of fences, applied only to lands situated outside the corporate limits of any city or town. Scott v. Pandell, 124 Ind. App. 474, 118 N.E.2d 372 (1954).

Former section recognized the right of adjacent landowners to agree among themselves as to what portions of a partition fence had to be built and kept in repair by the respective landowners, and the courts have held that

such a division, even though contrary to that provided by statute, was valid and lawful. Haley v. Williams, 125 Ind. App. 377, 123 N.E.2d 921 (1954).

Duty of Township Trustee.

Where township trustee was mandated to rebuild partition fence in accordance with law and in proceeding for contempt against trustee brought by relator for failure to rebuild fence it was shown that workmen hired to rebuild fence and who had to cross relator's land refused to work under restrictions placed upon them by relator, it was proper for court to find trustee not in contempt and to order trustee to comply with mandate as soon as practicable and order relator to refrain from any action which would hinder attempts by the trustee to rebuild the fence. State ex rel. Thrasher v. Hayes, 177 Ind. App. 196, 63 Ind. Dec. 627, 378 N.E.2d 924 (1978).

Mandamus.

In mandamus action against township trustee with regard to erecting partition fence, evidence supported finding of trial court that relator did not know manner in which landowners of adjoining land and predecessors had maintained fence and that relator was not affected by such manner of maintenance. Coffman v. State ex rel. Edwards, 121 Ind. App. 90, 94 N.E.2d 547 (1950).

Separate Action for Damages.

Where plaintiff brought contempt of court proceedings against township trustee for his failure to obey mandate of court to make repairs to partition fence, and while case was on appeal plaintiff brought another action for damages resulting from trustee's failure to comply with statute and mandate, plaintiff could not, in such separate suit, seek damages for injuries occurring up to the time of commencement of the contempt proceedings since the outcome of the contempt proceedings could be determinative of the question of liability in the damage suit, but plaintiff could, in such separate suit, seek damages for injuries occurring thereafter. Thrasher v. Van Buren Tp., 182 Ind. App. 121, 71 Ind. Dec. 455, 394 N.E.2d 215 (1979).

Collateral References. Validity of statutes requiring the construction of fences — modern cases. 87 A.L.R.4th 1129.

32-26-9-3. Sharing of costs — Failure to compensate — Lawful partition fence — Crossing a ditch or creek — Construction of floodgates. — (a) A partition fence shall be built, rebuilt, and kept in

repair at the cost of the property owners whose properties are enclosed or separated by the fences proportionately according to the number of rods or proportion of the fence the property owner owns along the line of the fence, whether the property owner's title is a fee simple or a life estate.

(b) If a property owner fails or refuses to compensate for building, rebuilding, or repairing the property owner's portion of a partition fence, another property owner who is interested in the fence, after having built, rebuilt, or repaired the property owner's portion of the fence, shall give to the defaulting property owner or the defaulting property owner's agent or tenant twenty (20) days notice to build, rebuild, or repair the defaulting property owner's portion of the fence. If the defaulting property owner or the defaulting property owner's agent or tenant fails to build, rebuild, or repair the fence within twenty (20) days, the complaining property owner shall notify the township trustee of the township in which the properties are located of the default.

(c) This subsection applies if the fence sought to be established, rebuilt, or repaired is on a township line. Unless disqualified under subsection (h), the complaining property owner shall notify the trustee of the township in which the property of the complaining property owner is located of the default under subsection (b), and the trustee has jurisdiction in the matter.

(d) The township trustee who receives a complaint under this section shall:

    (1) estimate the costs for building, rebuilding, or repairing the partition fence; and

    (2) within a reasonable time after receiving the complaint, make out a statement and notify the defaulting property owner of the probable cost of building, rebuilding, or repairing the fence.

If twenty (20) days after receiving a notice under this subsection the defaulting property owner has not built, rebuilt, or repaired the fence, the trustee shall build or repair the fence. The trustee may use only the materials for the fences that are most commonly used by the farmers of the community.

(e) If the trustee of a township is disqualified to act under subsection (h), the trustee of an adjoining township who resides nearest to where the fence is located shall act on the complaint upon receiving a notice by a property owner who is interested in the fence.

(f) A lawful partition fence is any one (1) of the following that is sufficiently tight and strong to hold cattle, hogs, horses, mules, and sheep:

    (1) A straight board and wire fence, a straight wire fence, a straight board fence, or a picket fence four (4) feet high.

    (2) A straight rail fence four and one-half (4½) feet high.

    (3) A worm rail fence five (5) feet high.

(g) This subsection applies if a ditch or creek crosses the division line between two (2) property owners, causing additional expense in the maintenance of the part over the stream. If the property owners cannot agree upon the proportionate share of each property owner, the township trustee shall appoint three (3) disinterested citizens who shall apportion the partition fence to be built by each property owner.

(h) If a township trustee is:

    (1) related to any of the interested property owners; or

    (2) an interested property owner;

the trustee of any other township who resides nearest to where the fence is located shall act under this chapter.

(i) This subsection applies if a ditch or creek forms, covers, or marks the dividing line or a part of the dividing line between the properties of separate and different property owners so that partition fences required under this chapter cannot be built and maintained on the dividing line. The partition fences shall be built and maintained under this chapter as near to the boundary line as is practical, and each property owner shall build a separate partition fence on the property owner's property and maintain the fence at the property owner's cost.

(j) This subsection applies where a partition fence required under this chapter crosses a ditch or creek and it is impracticable to construct or maintain that portion of the fence that crosses the ditch or creek as a stationary fence. Instead of the portion of the fence that would cross the ditch or creek, there shall be constructed, as a part of the partition fence, floodgates or other similar structures that are sufficiently high, tight, and strong to turn hogs, sheep, cattle, mules, and horses or other domestic animals. The floodgates or other similar structures shall be constructed to swing up in times of high water and to connect continuously with the partition fences.

(k) This subsection applies if the building and maintenance of the floodgates or other similar structure required under subsection (j) causes additional expenses and the property owners cannot agree upon the character of floodgates or other similar structure, or upon the proportionate share of the cost to be borne by each property owner. The township trustee, upon notice in writing from either property owner of a disagreement and the nature of the disagreement, shall appoint three (3) disinterested citizens of the township who shall determine the kind of structure and apportion the cost of the floodgate or other structure between the property owners, taking into consideration the parts of the fence being maintained by each property owner.

(l) The determination of a majority of the arbitrators of any matter or matters submitted to them under this section is final and binding on each property owner. The compensation of the arbitrators is two dollars ($2) each, which shall be paid by the property owners in the proportion each property owner is ordered to bear the expense of a gate or structure.

(m) This subsection applies if either or both of the property owners fail to construct or compensate for constructing the structure determined upon by the arbitrators in the proportion determined within thirty (30) days after the determination. The township trustee shall proceed at once to construct the gate or structure and collect the cost of the gate or structure, including the compensation of the arbitrators, from the defaulting property owner in the same manner as is provided for ordinary partition fences. The floodgate or other structure shall be repaired, rebuilt, or replaced according to the determination of the arbitrators. [P.L.2-2002, § 11.]

Opinions of Attorney General. Former IC 32-10-9-3 (repealed; see this section for similar provisions) mandated that all partition fences must be sufficiently tight and strong to hold hogs, sheep, cattle, mules and horses regardless of whether the landowners have these animals. 1989, No. 89-19.

When a complaining landowner has given an adjoining landowner notice to build, rebuild, or repair his proportionate part of a fence and after 20 days it has not been built, rebuilt, or repaired to meet the statutory requirements of former IC 32-10-9-3 (repealed; see this section for similar provisions), the complaining landowner shall then notify the trustee of the township in which the land is located of the improvement he may desire made on the partition fence to meet the statutory requirements of this section and the trustee has jurisdiction. The trustee should determine whether the partition fence meets the statutory requirements, and if it does not, the trustee has the duty to see that the statutory requirements are enforced. 1989, No. 89-19.

NOTES TO DECISIONS

ANALYSIS

In general.
Constitutionality.
Burden of proof.
Collection of judgments.
Complaint.
Duty of township trustee.
Mandate.
Validity of assessment.

In General.

Acts 1897, ch. 122, p. 184, defining partition fences, regulating the construction thereof and providing for the enforcement of liens for the building of such fences, was construed. Tomlinson v. Bainaka, 163 Ind. 112, 70 N.E. 155 (1904); Burck v. Davis, 35 Ind. App. 648, 73 N.E. 192 (1905).

Former section required each landowner to construct not a separate partition fence along the entire length of the dividing line, but to require each to construct and maintain at his own expense on his own land a fence for one half the distance, which, when connected by a floodgate in pursuance to the provisions of this section, would have constituted a continuous partition fence. Smith v. Timmons, 77 Ind. App. 448, 132 N.E. 319 (1921).

Constitutionality.

No constitutional objections existed as to laws of this character. Collins v. Wilber, 173 Ind. 361, 89 N.E. 372 (1909).

Burden of Proof.

In an action against a landowner to recover his share of the cost of constructing a partition fence, the burden was upon him to show that his lands were within the exceptions mentioned in the statute. Deemer v. Knight, 55 Ind. App. 397, 103 N.E. 868 (1914).

Collection of Judgments.

If a personal judgment was rendered against the owner of land to recover his share of the cost of constructing a partition fence, the judgment was not void for that reason, and the collection thereof could not be enjoined. Schilling v. Quinn, 178 Ind. 443, 99 N.E. 740 (1912).

Complaint.

A complaint to enforce a lien for the cost of a fence need not have contained a copy of the contract for building the fence. Collins v. Wilber, 173 Ind. 361, 89 N.E. 372 (1909).

In a complaint by an adjoining landowner to enjoin the collection of an assessment for the erection of a partition fence on a line separating plaintiff's land from adjoining land, averments that plaintiff's land had always been in the common and uninclosed, that the fence constructed did not complete an inclosure of appellant's land, that the same would not have been of any use, value, or service to plaintiff, and that it would have been of service only to the adjoining landowner, were not sufficient to render the complaint good as against a demurrer. Ashley v. Kelley, 84 Ind. App. 303, 149 N.E. 377 (1925), rehearing denied, 84 Ind. App. 304, 150 N.E. 417 (1926).

Duty of Township Trustee.

Former section did not make a township trustee a tribunal to determine the existence of a contract between adjoining landowners regarding the maintenance of a partition fence. Bartlett v. State ex rel. Hamilton, 186 Ind. 16, 114 N.E. 692 (1917).

Mandate.

Mandate to compel township trustee to build partition fence could lie. State ex rel. Magnet v. Kemp, 141 Ind. 125, 40 N.E. 661 (1895).

Prior to the amendment of this section, a township trustee was not required, and could not have been compelled by mandamus, to construct a floodgate across a stream as part of the partition fence. State ex rel. Fielo v. Burkit, 182 Ind. 665, 108 N.E. 113 (1915).

Validity of Assessment.

The cost of erecting a partition fence could

Validity of Assessment. (Cont'd)
not have been legally assessed against an adjoining landowner where the township trustee failed to furnish such landowner an estimate of the probable expense of constructing such fence, and failed, after constructing the fence, to deliver to such adjoining owner a statement of the actual cost incurred by him in constructing the fence. Rhodes v. Dunn, 106 Ind. App. 367, 19 N.E.2d 876 (1939).

A special assessment for the construction of a partition fence could not have been enforced against the land of one of the adjoining owners where the petition for the construction of such fence was not made by such adjoining

landowner, but by her son who acted, so far as the record showed, without authority from the owner. Rhodes v. Dunn, 106 Ind. App. 367, 19 N.E.2d 876 (1939).

Although these sections had to be liberally construed in favor of the object and purposes for which they were enacted, yet there must have been a substantial compliance by the township trustee with the provisions of the act before any authority existed on his part to construct a partition fence and create a lien against the lands of any resident of the township. Rhodes v. Dunn, 106 Ind. App. 367, 19 N.E.2d 876 (1939).

32-26-9-4. Fence constructed by township trustee — Certificate of costs — Amount paid out of general fund. — (a) As soon as the township trustee has had a fence built, rebuilt, or repaired under this chapter, the trustee shall make out a certified statement in triplicate of the actual cost incurred by the trustee in the building, rebuilding, or repairing the fence. One (1) copy must be handed to or mailed to the property owner affected by the work, one (1) copy must be retained by the trustee as a record for the township, and one (1) copy must be filed in the auditor's office of the county in which the fence is located and in which the property of the property owner affected by the work is located. At the same time the trustee shall also file with the county auditor a claim against the county for the amount shown in the statement filed with the county auditor.

(b) The county auditor shall:

(1) examine the claims and statement as other claims are examined; and

(2) present the claims and statements to the board of county commissioners at the next regular meeting.

Unless there is an apparent error in the statement or claim, the board of county commissioners shall make allowance, and the county auditor shall issue a warrant for the amount claimed to the township trustee submitting the claim out of the county general fund without an appropriation being made by the county council.

(c) The amount paid out of the county general fund under subsection (b) shall be:

(1) placed by the county auditor on the tax duplicate against the property of the property owner affected by the work;

(2) collected as taxes are collected; and

(3) when collected, paid into the county general fund. [P.L.2-2002, § 11.]

NOTES TO DECISIONS

Validity of Assessment.
The cost of erecting a partition fence could not have been legally assessed against an adjoining landowner where the township trustee failed to furnish such landowner an

estimate of the probable expense of constructing such fence, and failed, after constructing the fence, to deliver to such adjoining owner a statement of the actual cost incurred by him in constructing the fence. Rhodes v. Dunn,

Validity of Assessment. (Cont'd)
106 Ind. App. 367, 19 N.E.2d 876 (1939).

A special assessment for the construction of a partition fence could not have been enforced against the land of one of the adjoining owners where the petition for the construction of such fence was not made by such adjoining landowner, but by her son who acted, so far as the record showed, without authority from the owner. Rhodes v. Dunn, 106 Ind. App. 367, 19 N.E.2d 876 (1939).

Although former version of these sections had to be liberally construed in favor of the object and purposes for which they were enacted, yet there must have been a substantial compliance by the township trustee with the provisions of the act before any authority existed on his part to construct a partition fence and create a lien against the lands of any resident of the township. Rhodes v. Dunn, 106 Ind. App. 367, 19 N.E.2d 876 (1939).

32-26-9-5. No personal liability for township trustee. — The township trustee has no personal liability for a contract the trustee makes under this chapter for building, rebuilding, or repairing fences under this chapter. The contractor shall receive payment from the township funds, which shall be reimbursed when the contract price is paid into the county treasury. [P.L.2-2002, § 11.]

32-26-9-6. Liberal construction. — This chapter shall be liberally construed in favor of the objects and purposes for which it is enacted and shall apply to all land, whether enclosed or unenclosed, cultivated or uncultivated, wild or wood lot. [P.L.2-2002, § 11.]

NOTES TO DECISIONS

In General.
The fact that adjoining land was not inclosed was no defense to an assessment for building a partition fence along one side of it, and it was immaterial that the fence constructed did not complete an inclosure of such land. Ashley v. Kelley, 84 Ind. App. 303, 149 N.E. 377 (1925), reh'g denied, 84 Ind. App. 304, 150 N.E. 417 (1926).

CHAPTER 10

SPITE FENCES AS NUISANCE

32-26-10-1. Fence over six feet in height. — A structure in the nature of a fence unnecessarily exceeding six (6) feet in height, maliciously:

    (1) erected; or

    (2) maintained;

for the purpose of annoying the owners or occupants of adjoining property, is considered a nuisance. [P.L.2-2002, § 11.]

Effective Dates. P.L.2-2002, § 11. July 1. 2002.

NOTES TO DECISIONS

In General.
A judgment for damages and a decree enjoining the maintenance of fences of a height in excess of six feet alleged to have been erected in violation of law would not be reversed for insufficiency of evidence where the

In General. (Cont'd)
evidence was sufficient that the fences unnecessarily exceeded six feet in height, and that they were each maliciously erected or maintained for the purpose of annoying the plaintiff. Grooms v. Meriweather, 79 Ind. App. 274, 137 N.E. 32 (1922).

Collateral References. 1 Am. Jur. 2d Adjoining Landowners, §§ 106-118.
36A C.J.S. Fences, § 5.

32-26-10-2. Actions for nuisance. — (a) An owner or occupant injured either in the owner's or occupant's comfort or the enjoyment of the owner's or occupant's adjoining property by the nuisance described in section 1 [IC 32-26-10-1] of this chapter may bring an action for:

(1) damages in compensation for the nuisance;

(2) the abatement of the nuisance; and

(3) all other remedies for the prevention of a nuisances.

(b) The provisions of law concerning actions for nuisance are applicable to an action under subsection (a). [P.L.2-2002, § 11.]

NOTES TO DECISIONS

Applicability.
Where the fence in question was no more than six feet tall, regardless of how unsightly the fence may have been, with its attached vinyl strips, license plates, and orange construction site fencing, it could not be a nuisance under this former IC 32-10-10-2 (repealed; see this section for similar provisions). Wernke v. Halas, 600 N.E.2d 117 (Ind. App. 1992).

ARTICLE 27

CONSTRUCTION WARRANTIES ON REAL PROPERTY

CHAPTER 1

STATUTORY HOME IMPROVEMENT WARRANTIES

32-27-1-1. Applicability. — (a) This chapter applies only to a home improvement that is made under a home improvement contract.

(b) This chapter applies only to a home improvement contract entered into after June 30, 1992. [P.L.2-2002, § 12.]

Effective Dates. P.L.2-2002, § 12. July 1. 2002.

32-27-1-2. Effective date of warranties. — The warranties defined by this chapter become effective on the warranty date. [P.L.2-2002, § 12.]

32-27-1-3. "Home" defined. — (a) As used in this chapter, "home" means an attached or detached single family dwelling.
(b) The term includes an attached garage.
(c) The term does not include:
    (1) a driveway;
    (2) a walkway;
    (3) a patio;
    (4) a boundary wall;
    (5) a retaining wall not necessary for the structural stability of the home;
    (6) landscaping;
    (7) a fence;
    (8) an offsite improvement;
    (9) an appurtenant recreational facility; or
    (10) other similar item.
[P.L.2-2002, § 12.]

32-27-1-4. "Home improvement" defined. — As used in this chapter, "home improvement" means any alteration, repair, or other modification of an existing home. [P.L.2-2002, § 12.]

32-27-1-5. "Home improvement contract" defined. — As used in this chapter, "home improvement contract" means a written agreement between a remodeler and an owner to make a home improvement. [P.L.2-2002, § 12.]

32-27-1-6. "Load bearing parts of the home" defined. — As used in this chapter, "load bearing parts of the home" means the following:
    (1) Foundation systems and footings.
    (2) Beams.
    (3) Girders.
    (4) Lintels.
    (5) Columns.
    (6) Walls and partitions.
    (7) Floor systems.
    (8) Roof framing systems.
[P.L.2-2002, § 12.]

32-27-1-7. "Major structural defect" defined. — As used in this chapter, "major structural defect" means actual physical damage to the load bearing functions of the load bearing parts of the home that:

(1) were installed, altered, or repaired by the remodeler in the course of remodeling the home; or

(2) although not installed, altered, or repaired by the remodeler, were directly damaged by the work of the remodeler;

to the extent that the home becomes unsafe, unsanitary, or otherwise unlivable. [P.L.2-2002, § 12.]

32-27-1-8. "Owner" defined. — As used in this chapter, "owner" means a person who:

(1) owns the home; and

(2) contracts with the remodeler to perform the home improvement work in the home improvement contract.

The term includes any of the owner's successors in title before the expiration of the warranties defined by this chapter. [P.L.2-2002, § 12.]

32-27-1-9. "Person" defined. — As used in this chapter, "person" means an individual, a corporation, a limited liability company, a business trust, an estate, a trust, a partnership, an association, a cooperative, or other legal entity. [P.L.2-2002, § 12.]

32-27-1-10. "Remodeler" defined. — As used in this chapter, "remodeler" means a person who contracts with an owner to alter, repair, or modify the owner's home. [P.L.2-2002, § 12.]

32-27-1-11. "Warranty date" defined. — As used in this chapter, "warranty date" means the date by which all home improvements and work under the home improvement contract have been substantially completed so the owner can occupy and use the improvement in the manner contemplated by the home improvement contract. [P.L.2-2002, § 12.]

32-27-1-12. Warranties offered by remodelers. — (a) In performing home improvements and in contracting to perform home improvements, a remodeler may warrant to the owner the following:

(1) During the two (2) year period beginning on the warranty date, the home improvement must be free from defects in workmanship or materials.

(2) During the two (2) year period beginning on the warranty date, the home improvement must be free from defects caused by faulty installation of:

(A) new plumbing systems;

(B) new electrical systems;

(C) new heating, cooling, and ventilating systems; or

(D) extended parts of existing systems.

The warranty does not cover appliances, fixtures, or items of equipment that are installed under the home improvement contract.

(3) During the four (4) year period beginning on the warranty date, the home improvement must be free from defects caused by faulty workmanship or defective materials in the roof or roof systems of the home improvement.

(4) During the ten (10) year period beginning on the warranty date, the home improvement and affected load bearing parts of the home must be free from major structural defects.

(b) The warranties provided in this section survive the passing of legal or equitable title in the home to subsequent persons. [P.L.2-2002, § 12.]

32-27-1-13. Disclaimer of warranties — Waiver — Notice. — (a) A remodeler may disclaim all implied warranties only if all of the following conditions are met:

(1) The warranties defined in this chapter are expressly provided for in the home improvement contract between a remodeler and an owner.

(2) The performance of the warranty obligations is guaranteed by an insurance policy in an amount equal to the contract price made under the home improvement contract.

(3) The remodeler carries completed operations products liability insurance covering the remodeler's liability for reasonably foreseeable consequential damages arising from a defect covered by the warranties provided by the remodeler.

(b) The disclaimer must be printed in a minimum size of 10 point boldface type setting forth that the warranties defined by this chapter replace the implied warranties that have been disclaimed by the remodeler. The owner must affirmatively acknowledge by complete signature that the owner has read, understands, and voluntarily agrees to the disclaimer.

(c) The owner must acknowledge the disclaimer of implied warranties by signing, at the time of execution of the home improvement contract, a separate one (1) page notice attached to the home improvement contract that includes the following language:

"NOTICE OF WAIVER OF IMPLIED WARRANTIES

I recognize that by accepting the express warranties and the insurance covering those warranties for the periods provided in this home improvement contract, I am giving up the right to any claims for implied warranties, which may be greater than the express warranties. Implied warranties are unwritten warranties relating to the reasonable expectations of a homeowner with regard to the remodeling and home improvement of the homeowner's home, as those reasonable expectations are defined by the courts on a case by case basis.".

(d) If there is a default of the:

(1) insurance for the performance of the warranty obligations; or

(2) completed operations products liability insurance;

the disclaimer by the remodeler is void. [P.L.2-2002, § 12.]

32-27-1-14. Actions for breach of warranty. — (a) If a remodeler breaches a warranty set forth in section 12 [IC 32-27-1-12] of this chapter, the owner may bring an action against the remodeler for:

(1) damages arising from the breach; or

(2) specific performance.

(b) If damages are awarded for a breach of a warranty set forth in section 12 of this chapter, the award may not be for more than:

(1) the actual damages that are:

(A) necessary to effect repair of the defect that is the cause of the breach; or

(B) the difference between the value of the home without the defect and the home with the defect;

(2) the reasonably foreseeable consequential damages arising from the defect covered by the warranty; and

(3) attorney's fees, if those fees are provided for in the written contract between the parties. [P.L.2-2002, § 12.]

Collateral References. Breach of warranty in sale, installation, repair, design, or inspection of septic or sewage disposal systems. 50 A.L.R.5th 417.

32-27-1-15. Warranties created by contract — No restriction on other remedies. — (a) The warranties defined in this chapter are in addition to any other rights created by contract between the parties.

(b) The remedies provided in section 14 [IC 32-27-1-14] of this chapter do not limit any remedies available in an action that is not predicated on the breach of an express or implied warranty defined by this chapter. [P.L.2-2002, § 12.]

CHAPTER 2

NEW HOME CONSTRUCTION WARRANTIES

32-27-2-1. Effective date of warranties. — The warranties defined by this chapter (or IC 34-4-20.5 or IC 32-15-7 before their repeal) become effective on the warranty date attributed to a new home. [P.L.2-2002, § 12.]

Effective Dates. P.L.2-2002, § 12. July 1. 2002.

32-27-2-2. "Initial home buyer" defined. — As used in this chapter, "initial home buyer" means a person who executes a contract with a builder to buy a new home and who:

(1) occupies the new home as its first occupant; and

(2) occupies the new home as a residence. [P.L.2-2002, § 12.]

32-27-2-3. "Major structural defect" defined. — As used in this chapter, "major structural defect" means actual damage to the load bearing part of a new home, including actual damage due to:

(1) subsidence;

(2) expansion; or

(3) lateral movement;

of the soil affecting the load bearing function, unless the subsidence, expansion, or lateral movement of the soil is caused by flood, earthquake, or some other natural disaster. [P.L.2-2002, § 12.]

32-27-2-4. "New home" defined. — (a) As used in this chapter, "new home" means a new dwelling occupied for the first time after construction.

(b) The term does not include:

(1) a detached garage;

(2) a driveway;

(3) a walkway;

(4) a patio;

(5) a boundary wall;

(6) a retaining wall not necessary for the structural stability of the new home;

(7) landscaping,

(8) a fence;

(9) nonpermanent construction material;

(10) an off-site improvement;

(11) an appurtenant recreational facility; or

(12) other similar item.

[P.L.2-2002, § 12.]

32-27-2-5. "Home buyer" defined. — (a) As used in this chapter, "home buyer" means a purchaser of a new home.

(b) The term includes any owner of the new home before the expiration of the warranties defined by this chapter. [P.L.2-2002, § 12.]

32-27-2-6. "Builder" defined. — As used in this chapter, "builder" means a person who constructs new homes for sale, including the construction of new homes on land owned by home buyers. [P.L.2-2002, § 12.]

32-27-2-7. "Warranty date" defined. — As used in this chapter, "warranty date" means the date of the first occupancy of the new home as a residence by the initial home buyer. [P.L.2-2002, § 12.]

32-27-2-8. Warranties offered by builders. — (a) In selling a completed new home, and in contracting to sell a new home to be completed, the builder may warrant to the initial home buyer the following:

(1) During the two (2) year period beginning on the warranty date, the new home will be free from defects caused by faulty workmanship or defective materials.

(2) During the two (2) year period beginning on the warranty date, the new home will be free from defects caused by faulty installation of:

   (A) plumbing;

   (B) electrical;

   (C) heating;

   (D) cooling; or

   (E) ventilating;

systems, exclusive of fixtures, appliances, or items of equipment.

   (3) During the four (4) year period beginning on the warranty date, the new home will be free from defects caused by faulty workmanship or defective materials in the roof or roof systems of the new home.

   (4) During the ten (10) year period beginning on the warranty date, the new home will be free from major structural defects.

 (b) The warranties provided in this section (or IC 34-4-20.5-8 or IC 32-15-7 before their repeal) survive the passing of legal or equitable title in the new home to a home buyer. [P.L.2-2002, § 12.]

32-27-2-9. Disclaimer of warranties — Waiver — Notice. — (a) A builder may disclaim all implied warranties only if all of the following conditions are met:

   (1) The warranties defined in this chapter are expressly provided for in the written contract between a builder and an initial home buyer of a new home.

   (2) The performance of the warranty obligations is backed by an insurance policy in an amount at least equal to the purchase price of the new home.

   (3) The builder carries completed operations products liability insurance covering the builder's liability for reasonably foreseeable consequential damages arising from a defect covered by the warranties provided by the builder.

 (b) The disclaimer must be printed in a minimum size of 10 point boldface type setting forth that the statutory warranties of this chapter are in lieu of the implied warranties that have been disclaimed by the builder, and the initial home buyer must affirmatively acknowledge by complete signature that the home buyer has read, understands, and voluntarily agrees to the disclaimer. Additionally, the initial home buyer must acknowledge the disclaimer of implied warranties by signing, at the time of execution of the contract, a separate one (1) page notice, attached to the contract, that includes and begins with the following language:

"NOTICE OF WAIVER OF IMPLIED WARRANTIES

I recognize that by accepting the express warranties and the insurance covering those warranties for the periods of time provided in this contract, I am giving up the right to any claims for implied warranties, which may be greater than the express warranties. Implied warranties are unwritten warranties relating to the reasonable expectations of a homeowner with regard to the construction of the homeowner's home, as those reasonable expectations are defined by the courts on a case by case basis.".

(c) If there is a default of either:

(1) the insurance for the performance of the warranty obligations; or

(2) the completed operations products liability insurance;

the disclaimer by the builder is void from and after the default. [P.L.2-2002, § 12.]

32-27-2-10. Actions for breach of warranty — Damages. — (a) If a builder provides and breaches a warranty set forth in section 8 [IC 32-27-2-8] of this chapter (or IC 34-4-20.5-8 or IC 32-15-7-8 before their repeal), the home buyer may bring an action against the builder for:

(1) damages arising from the breach; or

(2) specific performance.

(b) If damages are awarded for a breach of a warranty set forth in section 8 of this chapter (or IC 34-4-20.5-8 or IC 32-15-7-8 before their repeal), the award may be for not more than:

(1) the actual damages, which are either:

(A) the amount necessary to effect repair of the defect that is the cause of the breach; or

(B) the amount of the difference between the value of the new home without the defect and the value of the new home with the defect;

(2) the reasonably foreseeable consequential damages arising from the defect covered by the warranty; and

(3) attorney's fees, if those fees are provided for in the written contract between the parties. [P.L.2-2002, § 12.]

Collateral References. Breach of warranty in sale, installation, repair, design, or inspection of septic or sewage disposal systems. 50 A.L.R.5th 417.

32-27-2-11. Rights created by contract — Other remedies not limited. — (a) The warranties set forth in this chapter (or IC 34-4-20.5 or IC 32-15-7 before their repeal) are in addition to any rights created by contract between the parties.

(b) The remedies provided in section 10 [IC 32-27-2-10] of this chapter (or IC 34-4-20.5-10 or IC 32-15-7-10 before their repeal) do not limit any remedies available in an action that is not predicated upon the breach of an express or implied warranty set forth in this chapter (or IC 34-4-20.5 or IC 32-15-7 before their repeal) or otherwise existing. [P.L.2-2002, § 12.]

ARTICLE 28

LIENS ON REAL PROPERTY

CHAPTER 1

RECORD OF LIENS; DUTY TO SATISFY RECORD AFTER RELEASE OR DISCHARGE OF LIENS

32-28-1-1. Release — Discharge — Satisfaction of record. — (a) This section applies to a person, a firm, a limited liability company, a corporation, a copartnership, an association, an administrator, an executor, a guardian, a trustee, or another person who is the owner, holder, or custodian of any mortgage, mechanic's lien, judgment, or other lien recorded in Indiana.

(b) When the debt or obligation and the interest on the debt or obligation that the mortgage, mechanic's lien, judgment, or other lien secures has been fully paid, lawfully tendered, and discharged, the owner, holder, or custodian shall:

(1) release;

(2) discharge; and

(3) satisfy of record;

the mortgage, mechanic's lien, judgment, or other lien.

(c) If the release, discharge, or satisfaction is a release, discharge, or satisfaction in part, the instrument must:

(1) state on its face that the instrument is a:

(A) partial release;

(B) partial discharge; or

(C) partial satisfaction; and

(2) describe what portion of the mortgage, mechanic's lien, judgment, or other lien is released, discharged, or satisfied. [P.L.2-2002, § 13.]

Effective Dates. P.L.2-2002, § 13. July 1. 2002.

Cross References. Release of mortgages by corporation doing business in Indiana, IC 32-29-5-1.

Opinions of Attorney General. Former 32-8-1-1 (repealed; now see this section for similar provisions) applied to all corporations, including corporations located in other states. 1989, No. 89-26.

A Florida corporation was required to pay the recording fees that were provided by IC 36-2-7-10 for the release of mortgages in the state of Indiana. 1989, No. 89-26.

NOTES TO DECISIONS

ANALYSIS

In general.
Act of 1893.

Applicability.
Construction.
Evidence of payment.
Failure to release lien.

In General.

In a complaint to recover penalty, the complaint was sufficient having established the relationship of mortgagor and mortgagee, for the relationship once having been established would have been presumed to have continued until the contrary was made to appear. Spaulding v. Jones, 11 Ind. App. 562, 39 N.E. 526 (1894).

Where there had been a mistake in recording mortgage, the purchaser was entitled to a release of the mortgage, but could not recover penalty and attorney's fees since under the statute they were recoverable only upon the payment "of the debt or obligation" which "the mortgage was made to secure." Osborn v. Hocker, 160 Ind. 1, 66 N.E. 42 (1903).

If a judgment was rendered under this section for $50.00, no appeal would lie to the Appellate or Supreme Court if no question was raised except as to the amount of the judgment, IC 33-3-2-4. Hood v. Baker, 165 Ind. 562, 76 N.E. 243 (1905).

Mortgagee had no implied duty to facilitate the sale of a portion of the real estate before pursuing its right to foreclose under the mortgage. Gainer Bank v. Cosmopolitan Nat'l Bank, 577 N.E.2d 982 (Ind. App. 1991).

Act of 1893.

Acts 1893, ch. 58, p. 64, providing for the recovery of a penalty for a refusal to satisfy a mortgage on demand, was constitutional. Judy v. Thompson, 156 Ind. 533, 60 N.E. 270 (1901).

Acts 1893, ch. 58, p. 64, prior to its amendment in 1901, did not apply to corporations. Studebaker Bros. Mfg. Co. v. Morden, 159 Ind. 173, 64 N.E. 594 (1902); Southern Ind. Loan & Sav. Inst. v. Doyle, 26 Ind. App. 102, 59 N.E. 179 (1901).

Applicability.

Former 32-8-1-1 (repealed; now see this section for similar provisions) was inapplica-ble to a judgment creditor because it governed situations where the holder of a lien, judgment, or mortgage failed to release or discharge the obligation after he had been paid, and where the case involved an erroneously recorded default judgment, not the discharge of an obligation by the judgment creditor after payment on the part of the debtor, the debtor failed to state a claim under this section. Henson v. CSC Credit Servs., 830 F. Supp. 1204 (S.D. Ind. 1993), aff'd in part and rev'd in part on other grounds, 29 F.3d 280 (7th Cir. 1994).

Construction.

In order to properly construe former IC 32-8-1-2, which dealt with forfeiture for failure to release liens, it had to be read in conjunction with former 32-8-1-1 (repealed; now see this section for similar provisions). Schwartz v. Zent, 448 N.E.2d 38 (Ind. App. 1983).

Evidence of Payment.

Plaintiff successfully argued that insured could not show that the full amount had been paid at the time the trial court reviewed the petition because plaintiff argued that insured owed interest above and beyond the amount paid to the clerk. Poehlman v. Feferman, 693 N.E.2d 1355 (Ind. App. 1998).

Failure to Release Lien.

Where person who had not been paid by contractor and who had no contractual relationship with purchaser of property filed mechanic's lien long after time for filing had expired and refused to release lien after he was paid and after demand, there was sufficient evidence from which jury could infer malice and to support judgment for compensatory and punitive damages. Harper v. Goodin, 78 Ind. Dec. 182, 409 N.E.2d 1129 (Ind. App. 1980).

Collateral References. 55 Am. Jur. 2d Mortgages, §§ 1397, 1405 — 1407.

59 C.J.S. Mortgages, §§ 201, 255, 470.

32-28-1-2. Demand of release — Action for damages against mortgagor. — (a) This section applies if:

(1) the mortgagor or another person having the right to demand the release of a mortgage or lien makes a written demand, sent by registered or certified mail with return receipt requested, to the owner, holder, or custodian to release, discharge, and satisfy of record the mortgage, mechanic's lien, judgment, or other lien; and

(2) the owner, holder, or custodian fails, neglects, or refuses to release, discharge, and satisfy of record the mortgage, mechanic's lien, judg-

ment, or other lien as required under section 1 [IC 32-28-1-1] of this chapter not later than fifteen (15) days after the date the owner, holder, or custodian receives the written demand.

(b) An owner, holder, or custodian shall forfeit and pay to the mortgagor or other person having the right to demand the release of the mortgage or lien:

(1) a sum not to exceed five hundred dollars ($500) for the failure, neglect, or refusal of the owner, holder, or custodian to:

(A) release;

(B) discharge; and

(C) satisfy of record the mortgage or lien; and

(2) costs and reasonable attorney's fees incurred in enforcing the release, discharge, or satisfaction of record of the mortgage or lien.

(c) If the court finds in favor of a plaintiff who files an action to recover damages under subsection (b), the court shall award the plaintiff the costs of the action and reasonable attorney's fees as a part of the judgment.

(d) The court may appoint a commissioner and direct the commissioner to release and satisfy the mortgage, mechanic's lien, judgment, or other lien. The costs incurred in connection with releasing and satisfying the mortgage, mechanic's lien, judgment, or other lien shall be taxed as a part of the costs of the action.

(e) The owner, holder, or custodian, by virtue of having recorded the mortgage, mechanic's lien, judgment, or other lien in Indiana, submits to the jurisdiction of the courts of Indiana as to any action arising under this section. [P.L.2-2002, § 13.]

Opinions of Attorney General. Former IC 32-8-1-2 (repeled; see this section for similar provisions), concerning forfeitures for failure, neglect, or refusal to release a mortgage, applied only to any owner, holder or custodian who is a resident of Indiana. 1989, No. 89-26.

NOTES TO DECISIONS

ANALYSIS

Construction.
Construction with other laws.
Damages.
Evidence of payment.
Use of remedy.

Construction.

Predecessor provision of this section was in derogation of the common law, and therefore had to be strictly construed. Any ambiguity in its provisions had to be resolved against the penalty. Schwartz v. Zent, 448 N.E.2d 38 (Ind. App. 1983).

In order to properly construe predecessor statute of this section, it should be read in conjunction with IC 32-8-1-1, which provides that it is the duty of a lienholder to release his lien when the debt secured thereby is fully paid. Schwartz v. Zent, 448 N.E.2d 38 (Ind. App. 1983).

Construction with Other Laws.

Former IC 32-8-6-1 and former IC 32-8-1-2 (repealed; see this section for similar provisions) were repugnant to each other; in particular, the provisions pertaining to notice and damages were irreconcilable. Southwest Forest Indus. v. Firth, 435 N.E.2d 295 (Ind. App. 1982).

Damages.

Evidence held sufficient for jury to infer malice and assess compensatory and punitive damages. Harper v. Goodin, 78 Ind. Dec. 182, 409 N.E.2d 1129 (Ind. App. 1980).

Evidence of Payment.

Plaintiff successfully argued that insured could not show that the full amount had been paid at the time the trial court reviewed the petition because plaintiff argued that insured owed interest above and beyond the amount paid to the clerk. Poehlman v. Feferman, 693 N.E.2d 1355 (Ind. App. 1998).

Use of Remedy.

The remedy which former IC 32-8-1-2 (repealed; see this section for similar provisions) provides for the breach of the duty to release a judgment was intended for use by the debtor, or by one who, through the debtor, acquired a similar interest in the release of the lien, and not by those who had at most only a collateral interest in the release of the judgment. Schwartz v. Zent, 448 N.E.2d 38 (Ind. App. 1983).

CHAPTER 2

LIMITATION ON AND REINSTATEMENT OF LIENS AFTER DESTRUCTION OF RECORDS

32-28-2-1. Judgment liens — Limitation — Action for reinstatement. — (a) Except as provided in subsections (b) and (c), if the record of a judgment of an Indiana court that would otherwise be a lien upon real estate is destroyed, six (6) months after the date when the record is destroyed the judgment ceases to be a lien upon any real estate as against any right, title, lien on or interest in the real estate accruing to or acquired by any person for a valuable consideration and without notice.

(b) The record of a judgment does not cease to be a lien under subsection (a) six (6) months after the date when the record is destroyed if the judgment plaintiff or the assignee or owner of the judgment, less than six (6) months after the date when the record is destroyed, files an action to reinstate the record of the judgment in the court having jurisdiction of the record.

(c) If the plaintiff obtains a judgment or decree in the action filed under subsection (b), the filing of the action to reinstate the record preserves the lien of the judgment in the same manner and to the same extent as if the record had not been destroyed. [P.L.2-2002, § 13.]

Effective Dates. P.L.2-2002, § 13. July 1. 2002.

Cross References. Reinstatement of records, IC 5-15-2.

Title to real estate and presumptions when records of judgments are destroyed, IC 34-41-4-2

NOTES TO DECISIONS

Strict Construction.

Being in derogation of common law, predecessor statute to this chapter had to be strictly construed. Tucker v. Capital City Riggers, 437 N.E.2d 1048 (Ind. App. 1982).

Collateral References. 51 Am. Jur. 2d Liens and Encumbrances, §§ 6, 8.

7 C.J.S. Attachment, § 271.

CHAPTER 3

MECHANIC'S LIENS

32-28-3-1. Persons who may have lien — Property on which lien may be held — Priority — No-lien contracts — Recording of contract — Notice — Innocent purchasers. — (a) A contractor, a subcontractor, a mechanic, a lessor leasing construction and other equipment and tools, whether or not an operator is also provided by the lessor, a journeyman, a laborer, or any other person performing labor or furnishing materials or machinery, including the leasing of equipment or tools, for:

(1) the erection, alteration, repair, or removal of:

(A) a house, mill, manufactory, or other building; or

(B) a bridge, reservoir, system of waterworks, or other structure; or

(2) the construction, alteration, repair, or removal of a walk or sidewalk located on the land or bordering the land, a stile, a well, a drain, a drainage ditch, a sewer, or a cistern; or

(3) any other earth moving operation;

may have a lien as set forth in this section.

(b) A person described in subsection (a) may have a lien separately or jointly upon the:

(1) house, mill, manufactory, or other building, bridge, reservoir, system of waterworks, or other structure, sidewalk, walk, stile, well, drain, drainage ditch, sewer, cistern, or earth:

(A) that the person erected, altered, repaired, moved, or removed; or

(B) for which the person furnished materials or machinery of any description; and

(2) on the interest of the owner of the lot or parcel of land:

(A) on which the structure or improvement stands; or

(B) with which the structure or improvement is connected;

to the extent of the value of any labor done or the material furnished, or both, including any use of the leased equipment and tools.

(c) All claims for wages of mechanics and laborers employed in or about a shop, mill, wareroom, storeroom, manufactory or structure, bridge, reservoir, system of waterworks or other structure, sidewalk, walk, stile, well, drain, drainage ditch, cistern, or any other earth moving operation shall be a lien on all the:

(1) machinery;

(2) tools;

(3) stock;

(4) material; or

(5) finished or unfinished work;

located in or about the shop, mill, wareroom, storeroom, manufactory or other building, bridge, reservoir, system of waterworks, or other structure, sidewalk, walk, stile, well, drain, drainage ditch, sewer, cistern, or earth used in a business.

(d) If the person, firm, limited liability company, or corporation described in subsection (a) is in failing circumstances, the claims described in this section shall be preferred debts whether a claim or notice of lien has been filed.

(e) Subject to subsection (f), a contract for the construction, alteration, or repair of:

(1) a Class 2 structure (as defined in IC 22-12-1-5);

(2) an improvement on the same real estate auxiliary to a Class 2 structure (as defined in IC 22-12-1-5); or

(3) property that is:

(A) owned, operated, managed, or controlled by a:

(i) public utility (as defined in IC 8-1-2-1);

(ii) municipally owned utility (as defined in IC 8-1-2-1);

(iii) joint agency (as defined in IC 8-1-2.2-2);

(iv) rural electric membership corporation formed under IC 8-1-13-4;

(v) rural telephone cooperative corporation formed under IC 8-1-17; or

(vi) not-for-profit utility (as defined in IC 8-1-2-125);

regulated under IC 8; and

(B) intended to be used and useful for the production, transmission, delivery, or furnishing of heat, light, water, telecommunications services, or power to the public;

may include a provision or stipulation in the contract of the owner and principal contractor that a lien may not attach to the real estate, building, structure or any other improvement of the owner.

(f) A contract containing a provision or stipulation described in subsection (e) must meet the requirements of this subsection to be valid against subcontractors, mechanics, journeymen, laborers, or persons performing labor upon or furnishing materials or machinery for the property or improvement of the owner. The contract must:

(1) be in writing;

(2) contain specific reference by legal description of the real estate to be improved;

(3) be acknowledged as provided in the case of deeds; and

(4) be filed and recorded in the recorder's office of the county in which the real estate, building, structure, or other improvement is situated not more than five (5) days after the date of execution of the contract.

A contract containing a provision or stipulation described in subsection (e) does not affect a lien for labor, material, or machinery supplied before the filing of the contract with the recorder.

(g) Upon the filing of a contract under subsection (f), the recorder shall:

(1) record the contract at length in the order of the time it was received in books provided by the recorder for that purpose;

(2) index the contract in the name of the:

(A) contractor; and

(B) owner;

in books kept for that purpose; and

(3) collect a fee for recording the contract as is provided for the recording of deeds and mortgages.

(h) A person, firm, partnership, limited liability company, or corporation that sells or furnishes on credit any material, labor, or machinery for the alteration or repair of an owner occupied single or double family dwelling or the appurtenances or additions to the dwelling to:

(1) a contractor, subcontractor, mechanic; or

(2) anyone other than the occupying owner or the owner's legal representative;

must furnish to the occupying owner of the parcel of land where the material, labor, or machinery is delivered a written notice of the delivery or work and of the existence of lien rights not later than thirty (30) days after the date of first delivery or labor performed. The furnishing of the notice is a condition precedent to the right of acquiring a lien upon the lot or parcel of land or the improvement on the lot or parcel of land.

(i) A person, firm, partnership, limited liability company, or corporation that sells or furnishes on credit material, labor, or machinery for the original construction of a single or double family dwelling for the intended occupancy of the owner upon whose real estate the construction takes place to a contractor, subcontractor, mechanic, or anyone other than the owner or the owner's legal representatives must:

(1) furnish the owner of the real estate:

(A) as named in the latest entry in the transfer books described in IC 6-1.1-5-4 of the county auditor; or

(B) if IC 6-1.1-5-9 applies, as named in the transfer books of the township assessor;

with a written notice of the delivery or labor and the existence of lien rights not later than sixty (60) days after the date of the first delivery or labor performed; and

(2) file a copy of the written notice in the recorder's office of the county not later than sixty (60) days after the date of the first delivery or labor performed.

The furnishing and filing of the notice is a condition precedent to the right of acquiring a lien upon the real estate or upon the improvement constructed on the real estate.

(j) A lien for material or labor in original construction does not attach to real estate purchased by an innocent purchaser for value without notice of a single or double family dwelling for occupancy by the purchaser unless notice of intention to hold the lien is recorded under section 3 [IC 32-28-3-3] of this chapter before recording the deed by which the purchaser takes title. [P.L.2-2002, § 13; P.L.101-2002, § 5.]

Amendments. The 2002 amendment by P.L.101-2002, amending this section as enacted by P.L.2-2002, made a stylistic change; added subsection (e)(3)(A)(v), and made a related change; redesignated former subsection (e)(3)(A)(v) as (e)(3)(A)(vi); and inserted "telecommunications services" in subsection (e)(3)(B).

Effective Dates. P.L.2-2002, § 13. July 1. 2002.
    P.L.101-2002, § 5. July 1, 2002.

Indiana Law Journal. Mechanic's Liens in Indiana — The Extent of the Property and Property Interests Subject to the Lien, 36 Ind. L.J. 526.

Indiana Law Review. Survey: Property Law: Reconstructing Property Law in Indiana: Altering Familiar Landscapes, 33 Ind. L. Rev. 1405 (2000).

Res Gestae. Rules, rulings for the trial lawyer, 39 (No. 3) Res Gestae 34 (1995).

NOTES TO DECISIONS

ANALYSIS

In general.
Constitutionality.
Amount of lien.
Appeal.
Applicability.
Architects.
Attorney fees.
Bankruptcy.
Burden of showing coverage.
Calculation of award.
Comparison with employee liens.
Completion of building.
Construction.
—In general.
—Duty to record.
—Labor.
—Legal representative.
—Owner.
—Owner-occupied family dwelling.
Contractors.
Contract to purchase.
Debt.
Defenses of owner.
Destruction of building.
Developers.
Driveway.
Elements of mechanics' lien.
Entire building or lot.
Estoppel.
Failure of principal contractor to perform contract.
Fixtures.
Fringe benefit funds or unions.
Improvements.
—Economic development law.
—Labor.
—Temporary.
Insolvency or failing circumstances.
Labor.
—Fuel for machinery.
—Services provided.
Laborers.
Leased premises.

Lien not allowed.
Married women.
Materials.
—In general.
—Actual use in building.
—Consent of owner.
—Corporations.
—Credit.
—Payment to another.
—Requirements.
—Sale directly to owner.
—Structures other than buildings.
—Sureties.
—Vendor of materialman.
—When lien attaches.
Minors.
Mortgaged premises.
No-lien agreements.
Notice.
—Effect of failure to give notice.
—Exception when dealing with owner.
—Necessary averments.
—Nonresidential additions to dwellings.
—Oral notice.
—Residing elsewhere while house repaired.
—Tenants by the entireties.
—Time for giving notice.
—To owner of property.
—To person agreeing to purchase land.
—To record title holder.
Oil and gas wells.
Original construction.
Ornamental landscaping.
Pavements.
Payment to contractor.
Possession.
Preemption.
Public property.
Purpose.
Religious societies.
Repairs and alterations.
Sale of goods.
Separate contracts.

Several buildings.
Several claims.
Subcontractors.
Summary judgment.
—Inappropriate.
Supervisory services.
Tenancy by entirety.
Theory of lien.
Time for filing.
Title to materials.
Validity.
Value of services.
Waiver or release of lien.
—In general.
—Attorney fees.
—Contract provisions.
—Description of property.
—Held binding.
—Parties to waiver.
—Subcontractors.
Wells for water.
Widow's exemption.

In General.

One who asserted a mechanic's lien had the burden of bringing himself within the provisions of the statute creating the lien. Puritan Eng'r Corp. v. Robinson, 207 Ind. 58, 191 N.E. 141 (1934).

The mechanics' lien statute rested on the principle that one who furnished labor or material for the improvement of property was entitled to look to the property for his compensation. Jackson v. J.A. Franklin & Son, 107 Ind. App. 38, 23 N.E.2d 23 (1939).

A contractor's failure to secure a permit required by county ordinance prior to construction does not bar his recovery under a mechanic's lien. Johnson v. Taylor Bldg. Corp., 171 Ind. App. 674, 60 Ind. Dec. 467, 371 N.E.2d 404 (1978).

Constitutionality.

The statute providing for and regulating the acquiring of liens by mechanics was constitutional. Smith v. Newbaur, 144 Ind. 95, 42 N.E. 40, 33 L.R.A. 685 (1895); Barrett v. Millikan, 156 Ind. 510, 60 N.E. 310, 83 Am. St. 220 (1901).

The title to the Act of 1883, regulating the liens of mechanics, was broad enough to cover the provisions of the act, and amendments thereto, which gave contractors, subcontractors and corporations liens. The case of *Indianapolis Traction Co. v. Brennan*, 174 Ind. 1, 87 N.E. 215, 90 N.E. 65, 91 N.E. 503, 30 L.R.A. (n.s.) 85 (1909), and other cases asserting a different doctrine were overruled on this point. Rooker v. Ludowici Celadon Co., 53 Ind. App. 275, 100 N.E. 469 (1913); Moore-Mansfield Constr. Co. v. Indianapolis, N. & T. Ry., 179 Ind. 356, 101 N.E. 296, 44 L.R.A. (n.s.) 816 (1913).

Amount of Lien.

Where a principal contractor has furnished labor and materials for a price agreed upon by him and the owner of the property, the amount of the lien is measured and limited by the agreed price. Walker v. Statzer, 152 Ind. App. 544, 31 Ind. Dec. 496, 284 N.E.2d 127 (1972).

While former IC 32-8-3-1 (repealed; see this section for simlar provisions) does not expressly list "profit" as an item for which a mechanic's lien may be asserted, any claim for labor or materials reasonably includes some degree of profit. Ford v. Culp Custom Homes, Inc., 731 N.E.2d 468 (Ind. App. 2000).

Appeal.

In appeal from a mechanic's lien foreclosure by subcontractors, property owner on appeal could obtain no review on questions of liability on ground of absence of lienholder's notice to owners of intention to hold them personally responsible for debts and personal judgment without contractual relationship, because of failure to set out a narrative statement of the evidence in appeal brief. Dykiel v. Hilson Lumber & Supply Co., 127 Ind. App. 485, 139 N.E.2d 450 (1957).

Applicability.

The failure to identify every type of provider by specific designation is not fatal to inclusion within this section (formerly IC 32-8-3-1; see this section for similar provisions) if it is determined that the statute covers the services rendered or materials provided. Haimbaugh Landscaping, Inc. v. Jegen, 653 N.E.2d 95 (Ind. App. 1995).

If a claimant did not fall into one of the categories listed in the former mechanic's lien statute (IC 32-8-3-1, repealed; see this section for similar provisions), that claimant was not entitled to the protection of the statute. Greenland Homes, Inc. v. E & S Mktg. Resources, Inc., 227 Bankr. 710 (Bankr. S.D. Ind. 1998).

The court overrruled *In re Bluffton Casting Corp.*, 186 F.3d 857 (7th Cir. 1999) by holding that Indiana law broadly protects the rights of workers against losing wages due when an employer encounters tough economic times by moving workers to the front of the company's creditor queue with a mechanic's lien that trumps the rights of other creditors to the company's assets, and this lien protects unionized workers to the same extent it protects the rights of nonunionized workers. Faehnrich v. Bentz Metal Prods. Co., 253 F.3d 283 (7th Cir. 2001).

Architects.

An architect who drew the plans, and used them as his tools in the supervision of the remodeling of a building, was entitled to a

Architects. (Cont'd)
mechanic's lien for the labor expended in the drawing of the plans and specifications and in the supervision of the construction, and was a "laborer," within the meaning of this statute. Beeson v. Overpeck, 112 Ind. App. 195, 44 N.E.2d 195 (1942).

Architectural plans may add value to or improve real estate, for the purpose of a mechanic's lien, even though the building is never constructed. O'Hara v. Architects Hartung & Assocs., 163 Ind. App. 661, 46 Ind. Dec. 497, 326 N.E.2d 283 (1975).

Attorney Fees.
Tender of payment before trial of action to foreclose mechanic's lien was not sufficient to curtail attorney fees. Prewitt v. Londeree, 141 Ind. App. 291, 8 Ind. Dec. 327, 216 N.E.2d 724 (1966).

The award of attorney's fees in an action to foreclose a mechanic's lien is not an attempt to compensate the attorneys for all the legal services performed in connection with the lien; rather, the amount of the award is intended to reflect the amount the lienholder reasonably had to expend to foreclose the lien. Korellis Roofing, Inc. v. Stolman, 645 N.E.2d 29 (Ind. App. 1995).

Bankruptcy.
A mechanic's lien having attached to defendant's building before the institution of bankruptcy proceedings and his discharge in bankruptcy, the sale of the building in the bankruptcy proceedings did not discharge the lien, and it could have been enforced against the building in the hands of the purchaser. New Union Lumber Co. v. Good, 82 Ind. App. 492, 146 N.E. 584 (1925).

Burden of Showing Coverage.
The mechanics' lien law in derogation of the common law was strictly construed to ascertain who was within its provisions, and the burden was upon one asserting a lien to have brought himself within its provisions. William F. Steck Co. v. Springfield, 151 Ind. App. 671, 30 Ind. Dec. 333, 281 N.E.2d 530 (1972).

Indiana law places a burden upon a mechanic's lienholder who seeks to foreclose such a lien to show that the purported lien meets all statutory requirements necessary to its creation. Van Wells v. Stanray Corp., 168 Ind. App. 35, 51 Ind. Dec. 143, 341 N.E.2d 198 (1976).

The burden is upon the foreclosing lienholder to show that the purported lien meets all statutory requirements necessary to its creation. Riggins v. Sadowsky, 76 Ind. Dec. 47, 403 N.E.2d 1152 (Ind. App. 1980).

In establishing his right to foreclose, the burden is on the contractor to prove that his lien meets the statutory requirements.

Marshall County Redi-Mix, Inc. v. Matthew, 458 N.E.2d 219 (Ind. 1984).

Because the mechanic's lien is purely a creature of statute, the burden is on the party asserting the lien to bring itself clearly within the strictures of the statute. Premier Invs. v. Suites of Am., Inc., 644 N.E.2d 124 (Ind. 1994).

Calculation of Award.
Trial court could award defendant nothing on his counterclaim, calculating plaintiff's award by determining the difference between the amount recoverable by plaintiff on his mechanic's lien and the damages theoretically due defendant on his counterclaim, where the price was contractually specified. Korellis Roofing, Inc. v. Stolman, 645 N.E.2d 29 (Ind. App. 1995).

Comparison with Employee Liens.
For discussion of differences between the lien given pursuant to former IC 32-8-3-1 (repealed; now see this section for similar provisions) and the right provided for in former IC 32-8-3-9 (repealed; see IC 32-28-3-9 for similar provisions), see In re Hull, 19 Bankr. 501 (Bankr. N.D. Ind. 1982).

Completion of Building.
Liens for materials or labor could have been acquired, although the building was not completed. Scott v. Goldinhorst, 123 Ind. 268, 24 N.E. 333 (1890).

Construction.

—In General.
The spirit of the Mechanic's Lien Law was to prefer laborers as a class, and not to prefer one class over another. McElwaine v. Hosey, 135 Ind. 481, 35 N.E. 272 (1893).

Statutes of this character, being in derogation of the common law, were strictly construed in ascertaining who was within their provisions. Cincinnati, R. & M.R.R. v. Shera, 36 Ind. App. 315, 73 N.E. 293 (1905); Indianapolis N. Traction Co. v. Brennan, 174 Ind. 1, 87 N.E. 215, 90 N.E. 65, 91 N.E. 503 (1909), overruled on other grounds, Moore-Mansfield Constr. Co. v. Indianapolis, N.C. & T. Ry., 179 Ind. 356, 101 N.E. 296 (1913); Ward v. Yarnelle, 173 Ind. 535, 91 N.E. 7 (1910), overruled on other grounds, Moore-Mansfield Constr. Co. v. Indianapolis, N.C. & T. Ry., 179 Ind. 356, 101 N.E. 296 (1913); Toner v. Whybrew, 50 Ind. App. 387, 98 N.E. 450 (1912); Rader v. A.J. Barrett Co., 59 Ind. App. 27, 108 N.E. 883 (1915); Deal v. Plass, 59 Ind. App. 185, 109 N.E. 51 (1915); Gardner v. Sullivan Mfg. Co., 77 Ind. App. 60, 133 N.E. 31 (1921); Puritan Eng'r Corp. v. Robinson, 207 Ind. 58, 191 N.E. 141 (1934);

Construction. (Cont'd)

—In General. (Cont'd)
Menzenberger v. American State Bank, Inc., 101 Ind. App. 600, 198 N.E. 819 (1935).

Mechanics' lien statutes had to be strictly construed in regard to performance of designated acts whereby the owner could relieve his property from a laborer's or materialman's lien. Midland Bldg. Industries v. Oldenkamp, 122 Ind. App. 347, 103 N.E.2d 451 (1952).

This section is in derogation of the common law and should be strictly construed as to its scope. Wiggin v. Gee Co., 179 Ind. App. 631, 68 Ind. Dec. 151, 386 N.E.2d 1218 (1979).

Provisions relating to the creation, existence, or persons entitled to claim a mechanic's lien are to be narrowly construed since the lien rights created are in derogation of common law. Premier Invs. v. Suites of Am., Inc., 644 N.E.2d 124 (Ind. 1994).

—Duty to Record.
Because the former mechanic's lien statute (IC 32-8-3-1, repealed; see this section for similar provisions) used the mandatory term "shall," rather than the permissive term "may," when imposing the duty to record the notice of lien with the county recorder, there was no valid lien where the plaintiff failed to comply with this requirement. Rose & Walker, Inc. v. Swaffar, 721 N.E.2d 899 (Ind. App. 2000).

—Labor.
Enforcement of a claim for supervisory labor in the construction of property was permitted under mechanic's lien statutes, and Indiana followed the majority rule in this regard. Marcisz v. Osborne, 124 Ind. App. 574, 118 N.E.2d 378 (1954).

—Legal Representative.
The term "legal representative" was not broad enough to have included a contractor acting as an "agent," for the owner. William F. Steck Co. v. Springfield, 151 Ind. App. 671, 30 Ind. Dec. 333, 281 N.E.2d 530 (1972).

The term "legal representative" as used in the fourth paragraph of this section was not confined in its meaning to "executor or administrator." William F. Steck Co. v. Springfield, 151 Ind. App. 671, 30 Ind. Dec. 333, 281 N.E.2d 530 (1972).

—Owner.
A contractor who took title to real estate for collateral was not an owner within paragraph four, while he was constructing a dwelling for the former title holders who intended to occupy the completed family dwelling. William F. Steck Co. v. Springfield, 151 Ind. App. 671, 30 Ind. Dec. 333, 281 N.E.2d 530 (1972).

—Owner-Occupied Family Dwelling.
The term "owner-occupied ... family dwelling" as used in the third paragraph of this section means a private residence of the owner as distinguished from a residence owned and held for renting to tenant-occupants. Barker v. Brownsburg Lumber Co., 73 Ind. Dec. 592, 399 N.E.2d 426 (Ind. App. 1980).

Contractors.
Where a road contractor supplied principal contractor with steam shovel, engineer, and fireman, which men and machinery were used in grading railroad right-of-way, he had a lien against railroad for work and labor performed. Algiers, W. & W. Ry. v. Foulkes Contracting Co., 101 Ind. App. 632, 200 N.E. 438 (1936).

The contractor did not avoid the intent of the statute by having the title to the property placed in his name during the period of construction. William F. Steck Co. v. Springfield, 151 Ind. App. 671, 30 Ind. Dec. 333, 281 N.E.2d 530 (1972).

A "contractor" as the term is used in the mechanic's lien statute is a person who contracts to erect or construct a building, structure or other improvement. Premier Invs. v. Suites of Am., Inc., 644 N.E.2d 124 (Ind. 1994).

The erecting requirement of former IC 32-8-3-1 (repealed; see this section for similar provisions) was some physical act of labor in connection with the creation of a structure or improvement on land; a contractor was within the statute only if the contractor had used some physical act of labor in connection with the creation of a structure or improvement on land. Premier Invs. v. Suites of Am., Inc., 644 N.E.2d 124 (Ind. 1994).

A contractual relationship is not sufficient to bring a contractor within the protection of the mechanic's lien statute. Greenland Homes, Inc. v. E & S Mktg. Resources, Inc., 227 Bankr. 710 (Bankr. S.D. Ind. 1998).

Contract to Purchase.
Persons holding lands under a contract of purchase could not create a lien thereon that would defeat the title of the vendor. Peoples Sav., Loan & Bldg. Ass'n v. Spears, 115 Ind. 297, 17 N.E. 570 (1888); Davis v. Elliott, 7 Ind. App. 246, 34 N.E. 591 (1893); Rusche v. Pittman, 34 Ind. App. 159, 72 N.E. 473 (1904); Toner v. Whybrew, 50 Ind. App. 387, 98 N.E. 450 (1912).

A complaint to enforce a mechanic's lien was sufficient as to the purchaser of real estate if it showed that the furnishing of materials commenced prior to the time of transfer. Jeffersonville Water Supply Co. v. Riter, 138 Ind. 170, 37 N.E. 652 (1894).

If a person who held a contract for the

Contract to Purchase. (Cont'd)
purchase of land caused a building to be erected upon the land, a mechanic's lien could not have been taken as against the owner of the land upon the building or the land. Toner v. Whybrew, 50 Ind. App. 387, 98 N.E. 450 (1912).

Legal owner of real property, who had given possession of property to purchaser under conditional sales contract, which was not recorded, and who was not aware that any work was being done on the premises, could not have been bound by a mechanic's lien. Woods v. Deckelbaum, 244 Ind. 260, 1 Ind. Dec. 517, 191 N.E.2d 101 (1963).

Where vendee under conditional land contract entered into contract for the performance of certain work, such contractor could place a lien on the property to the extent of such vendee's interest in the property, but could not reach the interest of the title owner of the property where such title owner did not give his consent to such work. Miles Homes of Ind., Inc. v. Harrah Plumbing & Heating Serv. Co., 77 Ind. Dec. 587, 408 N.E.2d 597 (Ind. App. 1980).

Debt.
A lien could not exist without the existence of a debt which, under this section, it secured. The debt had to arise out of contract express or implied, but the right to the lien which the section granted was one in rem, and a lien could have been declared and foreclosed without the recovery of a personal judgment. Thus, where there was judgment in rem, but no personal judgment against joint owner of realty, lien nevertheless attached against interest of joint owner. Mann v. Schnarr, 228 Ind. 654, 95 N.E.2d 138 (1950).

Defenses of Owner.
The owner of the property could make any defense to the claim of a laborer that the contractor might have made. Merritt v. Pearson, 58 Ind. 385 (1877).

Destruction of Building.
The lien on land for materials furnished for use in a building thereon was not lost by the destruction of the building by fire before notice of intention to hold the lien was filed. Smith v. Newbaur, 144 Ind. 95, 42 N.E. 40, 33 L.R.A. 685 (1895); Bratton v. Ralph, 14 Ind. App. 153, 42 N.E. 644 (1896); Krause v. Board of Trustees, 162 Ind. 278, 70 N.E. 264, 65 L.R.A. 111, 102 Am. St. R. 203 (1904).

Developers.

Driveway.
Where crushed stone was delivered for a driveway and parking area to be used in conjunction with a commercial garage, such driveway and parking area was a structure within the scope of this section. Haugh v. Zehrner, 158 Ind. App. 409, 39 Ind. Dec. 369, 302 N.E.2d 881 (1973).

Elements of Mechanics' Lien.
The necessary allegations in a foreclosure of mechanic's lien were: 1. plaintiff had contract with defendant or owner of real estate; 2. description of real estate; 3. material was furnished and used for the building; 4. the amount due; and 5. proper notice was filed within statutory period. Prewitt v. Londeree, 141 Ind. App. 291, 8 Ind. Dec. 327, 216 N.E.2d 724 (1966).

The mechanics' lien statute did not require a contractual basis for work done, as evidenced by provisions of former IC 32-8-3-3 which, on its face, could fairly be interpreted as only requiring a mechanic to notify the landowner of the specific amount of his lien and the description of the real estate subject to the lien without regard to the existence or nonexistence of any contractual relationship between the mechanic and the landowner. Saint Joseph's College v. Morrison, Inc., 158 Ind. App. 272, 39 Ind. Dec. 244, 302 N.E.2d 865 (1973).

A mechanics' lien need not be based on a formal contract. O'Hara v. Architects Hartung & Assocs., 163 Ind. App. 661, 46 Ind. Dec. 497, 326 N.E.2d 283 (1975).

Entire Building or Lot.
The lien of a mechanic or materialman did not attach to any specific articles furnished for a building, but if it attached at all, it must have been on the entire building. Baylies v. Sinex, 21 Ind. 45 (1863).

Mechanics' liens attached to the whole lot or subdivision of land upon which the building was erected. City of Crawfordsville v. Barr, 65 Ind. 367 (1879).

Liens could not have been acquired upon parts of a building or machinery that might have been put into a building, but such liens must have been upon the entire building and the interest of the owner of the building in the real estate on which the building was situated. City of Portland v. Indianapolis Mortar & Fuel Co., 57 Ind. App. 166, 106 N.E. 735 (1914).

Estoppel.
Homeowners against whom a mechanic's lien was filed were estopped from asserting that work was completed at earlier date in light of their refusal to make payment until additional work was done. Walker v. Statzer, 152 Ind. App. 544, 31 Ind. Dec. 496, 284 N.E.2d 127 (1972).

Failure of Principal Contractor to Perform Contract.
The mechanic's lien provided by these sec-

Failure of Principal Contractor to Perform Contract. (Cont'd)
tions was not affected by the failure of the principal contractor to perform his contract. Coonse & Caylor Ice Co. v. Home Stove Co., 70 Ind. App. 226, 121 N.E. 293 (1918).

Where the owner of certain real estate entered into a contract for construction of a barn which required the contractor to furnish the labor and materials necessary therefor, and the contractor contracted with a lumber company to furnish the lumber for such construction, and delivered the lumber upon the premises in accordance with the contract, which was accepted by the contractor, the landowner could not defeat the lumber company's right to a materialman's lien for the price of the materials thus delivered by changing his mind and refusing to construct the barn, especially where the material thus ordered was of unusual dimensions. Jackson v. J.A. Franklin & Son, 107 Ind. App. 38, 23 N.E.2d 23 (1939).

Fixtures.
Chandeliers put in a building by its owner with intention on his part that they should have become a part of the realty were fixtures, so that the contractor who furnished and put them in could have had a mechanic's lien therefor. McFarlane v. Foley, 27 Ind. App. 484, 60 N.E. 357, 87 Am. St. R. 264 (1901).

Liens could have been acquired on steam heating plants under the statute. Wells v. Christian, 165 Ind. 662, 76 N.E. 518 (1906).

Where the evidence failed to show that curtains, draperies, shower curtains, and rug in bathroom were permanent fixtures, no lien attached as to such articles. Menzenberger v. American State Bank, Inc., 101 Ind. App. 600, 198 N.E. 819 (1935).

A machine owned by a company that was a portable piece of equipment and not a fixture since the company leased its facility, the machine sat on a pallet behind its facility and could be removed without substantial or permanent damage to the facility, and the machine could be used in business elsewhere. Dinsmore v. Lake Elec. Co., 719 N.E.2d 1282 (Ind. App. 1999).

Fringe Benefit Funds or Unions.
Fringe benefit funds and unions are not entitled to acquire and foreclose upon a mechanic's lien for fringe benefits which are owed to the fund under a collective bargaining agreement. Neither a union nor the fringe benefit funds are contractors or subcontractors; also, they furnish neither labor nor materials. Edwards v. Bethlehem Steel Corp., 517 N.E.2d 430 (Ind. App. 1988).

Improvements.
The former mechanic's lien statute (IC 32-

8-3-1, repealed; now see this section for similar provisions) referred only to "structures," and does not include any specific reference to "improvements". Greenland Homes, Inc. v. E & S Mktg. Resources, Inc., 227 Bankr. 710 (Bankr. S.D. Ind. 1998).

—Economic Development Law.
A mechanic's lien could attach to improvements constructed under the provisions of the economic development law (former IC 18-6-4.5-1 — IC 18-6-4.5-30) although the city held the fee simple title to the property. City of Evansville v. Verplank Concrete & Supply, Inc., 74 Ind. Dec. 151, 400 N.E.2d 812 (Ind. App. 1980).

—Labor.
While the mechanic's lien statute does not specifically make lienable work which creates an "improvement" upon land or work that "improves" land, projects involving physical labor supplied in connection with the "creation" of an improvement on the land are within the statute. Greenland Homes, Inc. v. E & S Mktg. Resources, Inc., 227 Bankr. 710 (Bankr. S.D. Ind. 1998).

—Temporary.
Advertising work, including signs and art work, cannot be construed as an "improvement" to real estate, as it is not a valuable addition that is inextricably tied to the real estate, but temporary work that will be removed after the sale of the property, and thus does not fall within the protection of the mechanic's lien statute. Greenland Homes, Inc. v. E & S Mktg. Resources, Inc., 227 Bankr. 710 (Bankr. S.D. Ind. 1998).

Insolvency or Failing Circumstances.
The statute gave a preference, where the owner of the building was in failing circumstances or insolvent, both to the laborer and to the materialman. Kulp v. Chamberlain, 4 Ind. App. 560, 31 N.E. 376 (1892).

The preference liens that were given to persons for wages without the giving of notice were limited to the class of service mentioned and to the structures named in the clause of the statute which provided therefor. Sulzer-Vogt Mach. Co. v. Rushville Water Co., 160 Ind. 202, 65 N.E. 583 (1902).

When mechanics and laborers were given liens against failing debtors without filing notices of such liens, such liens must have been enforced within a year the same as other liens were required to be enforced. Smith v. Tate, 30 Ind. App. 367, 66 N.E. 88 (1903).

The preference given to mechanics and laborers, when the debtors were in failing circumstances without filing notice of liens, applied only to claims for wages and did not include claims for materials. National Supply

**Insolvency or Failing
Circumstances.** (Cont'd)
Co. v. Stranahan, 161 Ind. 602, 69 N.E. 447
(1904).

Labor.

—Fuel for Machinery.
Neither Indiana courts nor the legislature
have expanded the meaning of "labor" to
include fuel for machinery as lienable under
the statute; plaintiff's supplying of fuel to
defendant's subcontractor for use in heavy
machinery at construction site was not "labor", and therefore plaintiff was not entitled
to a mechanic's lien for the cost of the fuel
provided. P & P Oil Serv. Co. v. Bethlehem
Steel Corp., 643 N.E.2d 9 (Ind. App. 1994).

—Services Provided.
Indiana courts have consistently construed
the term "labor" to mean "services provided."
P & P Oil Serv. Co. v. Bethlehem Steel Corp.,
643 N.E.2d 9 (Ind. App. 1994).

Laborers.
Persons performing labor for contractors
were entitled to liens on the buildings.
Merritt v. Pearson, 58 Ind. 385 (1877).

General managers of manufacturing works
were neither mechanics nor laborers. Raynes
v. Kokomo Ladder & Furn. Co., 153 Ind. 315,
54 N.E. 1061 (1899).

Laborers who performed work on a building
for a subcontractor could obtain a mechanic's
lien. Stephens v. Duffy, 41 Ind. App. 385, 81
N.E. 1154 (1907), rehearing overruled, 83
N.E. 268 (1908).

Persons who paper the walls of a house
were laborers within the meaning of the mechanic's lien statute, and could take liens for
their work. Johnson v. Spencer, 49 Ind. App.
166, 96 N.E. 1041 (1912).

Where plaintiffs, who were laborers in the
employ of defendant contractor, had entered
into a collective bargaining agreement, pursuant to which defendant promised, but subsequently failed, to pay into three funds certain wages and fringe benefits owed to
plaintiffs, the plaintiffs were "laborers" under
former IC 32-8-3-1 (repealed; see this section
for similar provisions), and thus were eligible
to exercise their lien rights to enforce a mechanic's lien to collect their wages only.
Edwards v. Bethlehem Steel Corp., 554
N.E.2d 833 (Ind. App. 1990).

Where a contractor who prepared signs,
camera art, site maps and displays did not
erect, alter, repair, move, or remove a structure or improvement on real estate and did
not provide materials for such work, he was
not a "laborer" or a person "furnishing materials," as those terms are used in the mechanic's lien statute. Greenland Homes, Inc. v. E &

S Mktg. Resources, Inc., 227 Bankr. 710
(Bankr. S.D. Ind. 1998).

Leased Premises.
Where a lease for oil and gas was forfeited
for failure to drill wells according to terms of
lease, the lien for construction of the derrick
for the lessee attached to the well. Montpelier
Light & Water Co. v. Stephenson, 22 Ind. App.
175, 53 N.E. 444 (1899); McAnally v. Glidden,
30 Ind. App. 22, 65 N.E. 291 (1902).

Inactive consent was insufficient to bind
landlord for repairs contracted for by tenant.
Woods v. Deckelbaum, 244 Ind. 260, 1 Ind.
Dec. 517, 191 N.E.2d 101 (1963).

Where the owners of the legal title of the
real estate occupied by other persons under
contract of sale were not aware through their
authorized agency that any work was being
done on the premises, such owners could not
have been bound by the mechanic's lien.
Woods v. Deckelbaum, 244 Ind. 260, 1 Ind.
Dec. 517, 191 N.E.2d 101 (1963).

Lien Not Allowed.
Liens could not have been obtained for the
use of a machine furnished a contractor to
perform work on a building, nor for labor in
keeping such machine in repair, nor for the
use of a railroad switch in loading and unloading cars. Potter Mfg. Co. v. A.B. Meyer & Co.,
171 Ind. 513, 86 N.E. 837, 131 Am. St. 267
(1909).

Married Women.
Liens acquired on the lands of a married
man did not have priority over the inchoate
interest of his wife in such lands. Bishop v.
Boyle, 9 Ind. 169, 68 Am. Dec. 615 (1857);
Mark v. Murphy, 76 Ind. 534 (1881).

Husbands had no authority to charge the
lands of their wives by authorizing the erection of buildings thereon without their consent. Johnson v. Tutewiler, 35 Ind. 353 (1871);
Capp v. Stewart, 38 Ind. 479 (1872);
Crickmore v. Breckenridge, 51 Ind. 294
(1875).

Married women could make contracts for
the improvement of their property the same
as if they were unmarried. Vail v. Meyer, 71
Ind. 159 (1880); Stephenson v. Ballard, 82
Ind. 87 (1882).

Married women could authorize their husbands to act as their agents in the improvement of their property, and thereby create
liens thereon. Jones v. Pothast, 72 Ind. 158
(1880); Thompson v. Shepard, 85 Ind. 352
(1882).

Materials.

—In General.
Persons furnishing materials to a contractor or a subcontractor, for a new building,

Materials. (Cont'd)

—In General. (Cont'd)
could acquire a lien for the value of such materials. Barker v. Buell, 35 Ind. 297 (1871); Colter v. Frese, 45 Ind. 96 (1873); Hamilton v. Naylor, 72 Ind. 171 (1880); Neeley v. Searight, 113 Ind. 316, 15 N.E. 598 (1888); Smith v. Newbaur, 144 Ind. 95, 42 N.E. 40, 33 L.R.A. 685 (1895); Trueblood v. Shellhouse, 19 Ind. App. 91, 49 N.E. 47 (1898).

Liens on land for materials furnished for a building could only have been acquired in the manner prescribed by statute. Slack v. Collins, 145 Ind. 569, 42 N.E. 910 (1896).

As a general rule, in order to have acquired a materialman's lien under this act, the materialman had to show that the material was furnished at the request of the owner of the land on which the improvement was to have been made, for the purpose of the improvement, and that it was used in construction of the improvement, and that the lien claimed was filed in the time prescribed by statute in the office of the county recorder. Jackson v. J.A. Franklin & Son, 107 Ind. App. 38, 23 N.E.2d 23 (1939).

To be within lien statute, materials must be reasonably necessary to alteration or erection of structure, must be attached as permanent fixtures and must not be essentially personal in nature, absent intention that they are to be attached as permanent fixtures. Display Fixtures Co. v. R.L. Hatcher, Inc., 438 N.E.2d 26 (Ind. App. 1982).

—Actual Use in Building.
In order to acquire a lien for materials, it must have been shown that the materials were furnished for, and were actually used in, the building. Crawford v. Crockett, 55 Ind. 220 (1876); Hill v. Sloan, 59 Ind. 181 (1877); Lawton v. Case, 73 Ind. 60 (1880); Jones v. Hall, 9 Ind. App. 458, 35 N.E. 923, 37 N.E. 25 (1894); Leeper v. Myers, 10 Ind. App. 314, 37 N.E. 1070 (1894); Farrell v. Lafayette Lumber & Mfg. Co., 12 Ind. App. 326, 40 N.E. 25 (1895); Barnett v. Stevens, 16 Ind. App. 420, 43 N.E. 661, 45 N.E. 485 (1896); Miller v. Fosdick, 26 Ind. App. 293, 59 N.E. 488 (1901); Puritan Eng'r Corp. v. Robinson, 207 Ind. 58, 191 N.E. 141 (1934).

It was not always necessary for one asserting the right to a materialman's lien to show that the material furnished actually went into the building for which it was furnished, since the circumstances in a particular case, especially where the material was furnished to the owner of a building to be used therein, might estop such owner in a foreclosure suit from invoking the general rule. Moore & Richter Lumber Co. v. Scheid, 68 Ind. App. 694, 121 N.E. 91 (1918); Coonse & Taylor Ice Co. v. Home Stove Co., 70 Ind. App. 226, 121 N.E.

293 (1918); Jackson v. J.A. Franklin & Son, 107 Ind. App. 38, 23 N.E.2d 23 (1939).

A materialman claiming a lien ordinarily had to show that his materials were furnished for, and were actually used in, the erection, alteration, or repair of the building against which the lien was asserted. Jackson v. J.A. Franklin & Son, 107 Ind. App. 38, 23 N.E.2d 23 (1939).

In order to acquire a lien under this statute, it was necessary for the materialman to show that the improvement was made by the authority of the owner of the real estate, and that he furnished the material for the building, and that such material was used in the building, and that within the time prescribed by the statute, he filed in the office of the recorder of the county the proper notice of his intentions to hold such lien, but if materials have been furnished the owner of the building, who diverted them without consent of the materialman, he would still have been entitled to a lien, even though the materials were not used in the building. Ohio Oil Co. v. Fidelity & Deposit Co., 112 Ind. App. 452, 42 N.E.2d 406 (1942).

If a materialman sold his materials without any understanding as to their application, he could assert no lien upon the building upon which they might have been used, since, in such case, he relied exclusively upon the credit of the buyer and took no security. Ohio Oil Co. v. Fidelity & Deposit Co., 112 Ind. App. 452, 42 N.E.2d 406 (1942).

A mechanic's lien was acquired only when the materials were furnished with an understanding that they were to have been used for a purpose named in the statute, and not when they were supplied under an ordinary sale on credit or on open account, although the buyer might actually have used them in the improvement. Ohio Oil Co. v. Fidelity & Deposit Co., 112 Ind. App. 452, 42 N.E.2d 406 (1942).

Where debtor and beneficial owner of the real estate indicated to creditor that it was the owner of the subject realty, and parties stipulated that materials were ordered by and delivered to the debtor, "furnishing" of the materials was sufficiently established, without proof that they were used on the realty, either through estoppel of the debtor as owner of the property to deny their use or by the presumption that materials actually delivered are used in the building. Van Wells v. Stanray Corp., 168 Ind. App. 35, 51 Ind. Dec. 143, 341 N.E.2d 198 (1976).

—Consent of Owner.
In order that a lien could have attached to real estate, under Acts 1909, ch. 116, p. 295, as amended by Acts 1921, ch. 56, p. 135, for material furnished in the construction of a building erected thereon, it was necessary that the material be furnished by authority

Materials. (Cont'd)

—Consent of Owner. (Cont'd)
and direction of the owner; something more than the inactive consent of the owner was necessary in order that such a lien could have been acquired against the real estate. Holland v. Farrier, 75 Ind. App. 368, 130 N.E. 823 (1921); Robert Hixon Lumber Co. v. Rowe, 83 Ind. App. 508, 149 N.E. 92 (1925).

Mechanic's lien could only attach to title-holder's interest when materials used on real estate were furnished under authority and direction of title holder; something more than inactive consent by such owner was necessary. Display Fixtures Co. v. R.L. Hatcher, Inc., 438 N.E.2d 26 (Ind. App. 1982).

Shopping mall lessor's awareness of construction was insufficient to establish the sort of active consent needed to maintain a mechanic's lien where the lessor received no direct benefit from the improvements. Stern & Son v. Gary Joint Venture, 530 N.E.2d 306 (Ind. App. 1988).

—Corporations.
A corporation could acquire a lien for materials. Wood v. Isgrigg Lumber Co., 71 Ind. App. 64, 123 N.E. 702 (1919).

—Credit.
Materials did not need to have been furnished on credit of building, and lien could have been acquired if they were furnished on credit of contractor. Clark v. Huey, 12 Ind. App. 224, 40 N.E. 152 (1895).

—Payment to Another.
In action for foreclosure of mechanic's lien, the lien of plaintiff-materialman was not defeated or affected by payment on the part of the owner to the contractor. Bennett v. Pearson, 139 Ind. App. 224, 8 Ind. Dec. 679, 218 N.E.2d 168 (1966).

—Requirements.
To satisfy the requirements regarding the materials furnished, (1) the materials must be sold to the property owner or his agent for that purpose; (2) the materials must be furnished for the purpose of being used in constructing the particular improvement; (3) the improvement must have been authorized by or consented to by the property owner; and (4) the materials must have actually been used in the construction. V-Line Corp. v. Federated Dep't Stores, Inc., 684 F. Supp. 213 (S.D. Ind. 1988).

—Sale Directly to Owner.
A contract between the owner and a contractor for the erection of a house and garage which contained a provision that no mechanics' liens were to be filed except such as might be filed by the contractor for labor and materials furnished by him, though duly acknowledged and recorded, did not preclude the filing of a lien by one who sold materials directly to the owner to be used in the construction of said house. Holding v. Lewis Mfg. Co., 87 Ind. App. 296, 161 N.E. 702 (1928).

—Structures Other Than Buildings.
Persons who furnished materials for erection of tank on land could have acquired lien. Parker Land & Imp. Co. v. Reddick, 18 Ind. App. 616, 47 N.E. 848 (1897).

—Sureties.
Sureties on the bond of a contractor could not acquire a lien for materials furnished by them to the contractor. Miller v. Taggart, 36 Ind. App. 595, 76 N.E. 321 (1905).

—Vendor of Materialman.
Persons selling materials to the person who furnishes them for a building could not obtain a lien for such materials. Caulfield v. Polk, 17 Ind. App. 429, 46 N.E. 932 (1897).

The statute made no provision for a lien in favor of one who simply sold materials to another who was himself but a materialman. Caulfield v. Polk, 17 Ind. App. 429, 46 N.E. 932 (1897); Totten & Hogg Iron & Steel Foundry Co. v. Muncie Nail Co., 148 Ind. 372, 47 N.E. 703 (1897).

A dealer or materialman who furnished material to another materialman had no right to a mechanic's lien on the property improved. Wood v. Isgrigg Lumber Co., 71 Ind. App. 64, 123 N.E. 702 (1919).

Where, in a contract by a building contractor for the purchase of water softeners, there was nothing in the contract to indicate that the seller contemplated the possibility of a mechanic's lien as security for the contract price, but the purchaser was at liberty to use them as he pleased and to sell them at retail, or in buildings constructed for himself or for others, it was held that the seller was not entitled to a lien therefor, notwithstanding a clause in the contract of sale reserving title in the seller until the water softeners were paid for. Puritan Eng'r Corp. v. Robinson, 207 Ind. 58, 191 N.E. 141 (1934).

A materialman supplying material to another materialman was not entitled to a mechanic's lien. City of Evansville v. Verplank Concrete & Supply, Inc., 74 Ind. Dec. 151, 400 N.E.2d 812 (Ind. App. 1980).

—When Lien Attaches.
Liens for materials dated from the time materials were furnished and had priority over other liens except liens of mechanics and other materialmen. Krotz v. A.R. Beck Lumber Co., 34 Ind. App. 577, 73 N.E. 273 (1905).

Liens of materialmen related to the time

Materials. (Cont'd)

—When Lien Attaches. (Cont'd)
when the furnishing of materials began. Lloyd v. Arney, 43 Ind. App. 450, 87 N.E. 989 (1909).

A mechanic's lien could attach under this section for labor and materials. Under such statute, claims for hauling dirt and for rent of concrete mixer would be labor and material cost, while claims for such things as workmen's [worker's] compensation payments and social security payments together with ice, lights and telephone service, would not necessarily be labor and material costs so as to be included in lien against property. Mann v. Schnarr, 228 Ind. 654, 95 N.E.2d 138 (1950).

Minors.
Mechanics' liens could not have been acquired on the property of minors. Price v. Jennings, 62 Ind. 111 (1877); Alvey v. Reed, 115 Ind. 148, 17 N.E. 265, 7 Am. St. 418 (1888).

Mortgaged Premises.
Statutory provisions formed a part of the mortgage and the mortgage lien was subject to such statutory liens as might thereafter attach to the property. Thorpe Block Sav. & Loan Ass'n v. James, 13 Ind. App. 522, 41 N.E. 978 (1895); Carriger v. Mackey, 15 Ind. App. 392, 44 N.E. 266 (1896); Building & Loan Ass'n v. Coburn, 150 Ind. 684, 50 N.E. 885 (1898); Deming-Colborn Lumber Co. v. Union Nat'l Sav. & Loan Ass'n, 151 Ind. 463, 51 N.E. 936 (1898); Stoermer v. People's Sav. Bank, 152 Ind. 104, 52 N.E. 606 (1899); Pierce v. Blair, 196 Ind. 710, 149 N.E. 560 (1925).

The legislature had power to make the claims of laborers in factories for wages preferred liens on the property over mortgages on the property. Rexing v. Princeton Window Glass Co., 51 Ind. App. 124, 94 N.E. 1031 (1911).

A mechanic's lien for supplies furnished to operate a waterworks and lighting plant had priority over a mortgage given to secure the payment of the bonds of the company. Citizens' Trust Co. v. National Equip. & Supply Co., 178 Ind. 167, 98 N.E. 865, 41 L.R.A. (n.s.) 695 (1912).

No-Lien Agreements.
An owner could not avail himself of the no-lien provisions of this section by posting the required sign after the commencement of the work. General Elec. Co. v. Fuelling, 142 Ind. App. 74, 12 Ind. Dec. 489, 232 N.E.2d 622 (1968).

Where the evidence showed that the plaintiff did not begin work on the project prior to the signing and posting of the waiver of lien contract, he was precluded from claiming he was outside the no-lien contract. Ramsey v. Peoples Trust & Sav. Bank, 148 Ind. App. 167, 23 Ind. Dec. 670, 264 N.E.2d 111 (1970).

Where the subcontractor, who agreed to do a job while under the impression that he could obtain a mechanic's lien if necessary, had already commenced work on a project, a subsequently recorded no-lien agreement was insufficient to cut off that subcontractor's rights to obtain a mechanic's lien. Imperial House of Ind., Inc. v. Eagle Sav. Ass'n, 176 Ind. App. 572, 62 Ind. Dec. 660, 376 N.E.2d 537 (1978).

Even if a no-lien agreement is more encompassing than the construction contract, that is not sufficient to present an intention that the no-lien agreement is an independent contract which is not to be construed with the construction contract. Torres v. Meyer Paving Co., 423 N.E.2d 692 (Ind. App. 1981).

No-lien contract covering work to be performed on two parcels of land was valid even though the contract provided a legal description of one parcel and only the street address of the other parcel. Carey Concrete Corp. v. Family Dollar Stores of Ind., Inc., 542 N.E.2d 1021 (Ind. App. 1989).

A no-lien contract is not invalid because of deficiencies in the legal description of the property if the description is sufficient to give the prospective lienholder notice of the real estate on which the building mentioned in the contract is to be erected, and allows him to differentiate between other no-lien contracts recorded by the same property owner. Fordeck-Kemerly Elec., Inc. v. Helmkamp, 591 N.E.2d 1035 (Ind. App. 1992).

A waiver of mechanic's liens should be supported by consideration in order to be effective, but the fact that the consideration for a no-lien contract is oral will not render the agreement unenforceable. Fordeck-Kemerly Elec., Inc. v. Helmkamp, 591 N.E.2d 1035 (Ind. App. 1992).

Where a no-lien contract was executed at some time after the master contract, it required independent consideration. Fordeck-Kemerly Elec., Inc. v. Helmkamp, 591 N.E.2d 1035 (Ind. App. 1992).

Notice.

—Effect of Failure to Give Notice.
A mechanics' lien for materials and services was held invalid for failure to give notice to the owner within fourteen days from the date of the first delivery of materials or the first labor performed. Pioneer Lumber & Supply Co. v. First-Merchants Nat'l Bank, 169 Ind. App. 406, 23 Ind. Dec. 244, 349 N.E.2d 219 (1976).

—Exception When Dealing with Owner.
A contractor who took deed to property for

Notice. (Cont'd)

—Exception When Dealing with Owner. (Cont'd)

security only was not the "owner" within the meaning of this section and did not dispense with requirement for notice. William F. Steck Co. v. Springfield, 151 Ind. App. 671, 30 Ind. Dec. 333, 281 N.E.2d 530 (1972).

—Necessary Averments.

A complaint to foreclose a mechanic's lien for the value of labor and material provided in the original construction of a single or double family dwelling which has been purchased for occupancy must either aver that the notice of intent to hold the lien was filed prior to the recording of the purchaser's deed, or aver such constructive or actual notice as is necessary to put the purchaser's status as a bona fide purchaser into question. Riggins v. Sadowsky, 76 Ind. Dec. 47, 403 N.E.2d 1152 (Ind. App. 1980).

—Nonresidential Additions to Dwellings.

Provision of this section providing the time for filing notice of intention to hold mechanics' lien on single or double family dwellings did not apply where materials were supplied for construction of a child day care center which was to be built as an addition to a private residence, but the time limits of IC 32-8-3-3 applied. Wiggin v. Gee Co., 179 Ind. App. 631, 68 Ind. Dec. 151, 386 N.E.2d 1218 (1979).

—Oral Notice.

The requirement of this section as to the recording and giving of notice of construction contract was mandatory, and the burden of proving compliance was upon owner of real estate who wished to avoid responsibility for improvements. Thus, oral notice of a "non-lien" contract was not sufficient to avoid requirements of statute. Kendall Lumber & Coal Co. v. Roman, 120 Ind. App. 368, 91 N.E.2d 187 (1950).

—Residing Elsewhere While House Repaired.

Where parties occupied house under unrecorded contract of sale, but after house burned resided elsewhere until the house was repaired, the house was "owner-occupied" within the third paragraph of this section and written notice to such occupying owner was required to enforce mechanics' lien. Barker v. Brownsburg Lumber Co., 73 Ind. Dec. 592, 399 N.E.2d 426 (Ind. App. 1980).

—Tenants by the Entireties.

Written notice of a lien addressed to husband and wife tenants by the entireties, but delivered only to the husband, did not satisfy the notice requirement of this section. Bayes v. Isenberg, 429 N.E.2d 654 (Ind. App. 1981).

—Time for Giving Notice.

In order to preserve the lien, the materialman must give notice to the owner within 14 days from the date of the first delivery, and he cannot thereafter obtain a lien by merely claiming a lien only on the materials delivered within 14 days prior to the notice or thereafter. Henderlong Lumber Co. v. Zinn, 76 Ind. Dec. 700, 406 N.E.2d 310 (Ind. App. 1980).

—To Owner of Property.

A written notice of lien rights must be provided to the owner of property subject to the lien and filed in the county recorder's office within 60 days of the date of the first delivery of material or labor performed. McCorry v. G. Cowser Constr., Inc., 636 N.E.2d 1273 (Ind. App.), aff'd, 644 N.E.2d 550 (Ind. 1994).

When a materialman agrees to supply materials and services to a contractor rather than the owners of real estate, the materialman must furnish written notice to the owners of his intention to hold a lien as a condition precedent to holding the lien. Garage Doors of Indianapolis, Inc. v. Morton, 682 N.E.2d 1296 (Ind. App. 1997).

—To Person Agreeing to Purchase Land.

Where person agreed to purchase land and, before transaction was completed and deed executed and recorded, contracted for construction of a building on such land, such person was the "owner" to whom notice should have been given by a supplier of materials, and notice to the title holder according to the public records was not sufficient. Mid Am. Homes, Inc. v. Horn, 272 Ind. 171, 72 Ind. Dec. 502, 396 N.E.2d 879 (1979).

—To Record Title Holder.

It was improper for trial court to conclude as a matter of law that plaintiff's lien was void and invalid, where plaintiff sold material and labor on credit for the original construction of a single family dwelling to builder who did not intend to occupy the residence but held legal title to the property, with defendants the intended occupants; plaintiff gave notice to builder, but not defendants; and plaintiff had neither actual nor constructive notice of the defendants' involvement in the property, defendants never becoming record title holders. Shackelford v. Rice, 659 N.E.2d 1142 (Ind. App. 1996).

Oil and Gas Wells.

A lien could have been acquired on an oil

Oil and Gas Wells. (Cont'd)
well for labor performed and fuel furnished in drilling the well. Montpelier Light & Water Co. v. Stephenson, 22 Ind. App. 175, 53 N.E. 444 (1899); Niagara Oil Co. v. McBee, 45 Ind. App. 576, 91 N.E. 250 (1910).

Notice of an intention to hold a lien on a house for a stated amount would not create a lien on a gas well situated some distance from the house. Windfall Natural Gas, Mining & Oil Co. v. Roe, 41 Ind. App. 687, 84 N.E. 996 (1908).

A mechanic's lien could not have been obtained for fuel furnished to a contractor who performed labor in drilling a gas or oil well. Mossburg v. United Oil & Gas Co., 43 Ind. App. 465, 87 N.E. 992 (1909).

Original Construction.
Labor or materials provided in conjunction with a project which is necessary and essential to the functional use of a house, mill, manufactory or other "building" may give rise to a lien even if they do not occur contemporaneously with the original construction. Haimbaugh Landscaping, Inc. v. Jegen, 653 N.E.2d 95 (Ind. App. 1995).

Ornamental Landscaping.
An ornamental landscaping project constitutes or creates a "structure" to make such projects lienable; the erecting requirement is some physical act of labor in connection with the creation of a structure or improvement on land. Haimbaugh Landscaping, Inc. v. Jegen, 653 N.E.2d 95 (Ind. App. 1995).

Pavements.
Under prior similar provisions, a pavement constructed in front of lots did not authorize the taking of a lien on the lot. Knaube v. Kerchner, 39 Ind. 217 (1872).

Payment to Contractor.
Payment in full to contractor would not defeat liens that were properly taken. Colter v. Frese, 45 Ind. 96 (1873); City of Crawfordsville v. Johnson, 51 Ind. 397 (1875); Merritt v. Pearson, 58 Ind. 385 (1877); Clark v. Huey, 12 Ind. App. 224, 40 N.E. 152 (1895).

If a laborer performed labor for a contractor on a building, such laborer could enforce a lien for the amount due him although he might have known that the contractor had been fully paid for the work before the labor was performed and that the contractor was not to receive any money for the work. Johnson v. Spencer, 49 Ind. App. 166, 96 N.E. 1041 (1912).

Possession.
Mechanics had to take notice of the rights of persons in possession of land upon which the buildings were erected. Krotz v. A.R. Beck

Lumber Co., 34 Ind. App. 577, 73 N.E. 273 (1905).

Preemption.
When a state statute relates to or interferes with the Employee Retirement Income Security Act (ERISA), the state statute will be preempted. Edwards v. Bethlehem Steel Corp., 554 N.E.2d 833 (Ind. App. 1990).

Employees' mechanic's liens filed under this chapter for unpaid vacation pay, in an attempt to enforce their rights under a collective bargaining agreement, were invalid because of the preemptive effect of § 301 of the Labor Management Relations Act of 1947, 29 U.S.C. § 185(a). Faehnrich v. Bentz Metal Prods., 231 F.3d 1029 (7th Cir. 2000).

Plaintiffs' liens that secured their unpaid vacation pay was not preempted by § 301 of the Labor Management Relations Act of 1947, 29 U.S.C.S. § 185(a), because it did not require interpretation of the collective bargaining agreement (CBA). For preemption to apply, interpretation of the CBA and not simply a reference to it was required. Faehnrich v. Bentz Metal Prods. Co., 253 F.3d 283 (7th Cir. 2001).

Public Property.
Liens could not have been taken by mechanics upon public bridges. Board of Comm'rs v. Norrington, 82 Ind. 190 (1882).

Liens could not have been acquired upon public buildings or grounds. Board of Comm'rs v. O'Connor, 86 Ind. 531 (1882); Secrist v. Board of Comm'rs, 100 Ind. 59 (1885).

Mechanics' liens could not have been acquired upon schoolhouses. Falout v. Board of Sch. Comm'rs, 102 Ind. 223, 1 N.E. 389 (1885); Jeffries v. Myers, 9 Ind. App. 563, 37 N.E. 301 (1894); Townsend v. Cleveland Fire-Proofing Co., 18 Ind. App. 568, 47 N.E. 707 (1897).

If a city purchased property upon which a mechanic's lien had been properly acquired, such lien was not discharged on the ground that such a lien could not have been acquired upon city property. City of Portland v. Indianapolis Mortar & Fuel Co., 57 Ind. App. 166, 106 N.E. 735 (1914).

Purpose.
The intended purpose of this statute was to put the owner on notice of all the outstanding indebtedness that the contractor incurred during the building of a new home. William F. Steck Co. v. Springfield, 151 Ind. App. 671, 30 Ind. Dec. 333, 281 N.E.2d 530 (1972).

The primary purpose of this section is to protect the contractor and those claiming under him from failure of the owner to provide compensation due under the contract. In re Hull, 19 Bankr. 501 (Bankr. N.D. Ind. 1982).

Purpose. (Cont'd)

A second purpose of this section is to protect real estate from secret liens that could cloud alienability of real estate. In re Hull, 19 Bankr. 501 (Bankr. N.D. Ind. 1982).

The two purposes of the former mechanic's lien statute (IC 32-8-3-1, repealed; see this section for similar provisions) were to put landowners on notice that there was a lien on their property and to put any third party buyers on notice of the encumbrance on the property. Rose & Walker, Inc. v. Swaffar, 721 N.E.2d 899 (Ind. App. 2000).

Religious Societies.

Churches or buildings belonging to religious societies were subject to mechanics' liens. Gurtemiller v. Rosengarn, 103 Ind. 414, 2 N.E. 829 (1885).

Repairs and Alterations.

In order that a lien could have been obtained for repairs, the same must have been ordered by the owner, or he must have been connected with the contract therefor. Wilkerson v. Rust, 57 Ind. 172 (1877); Woodward v. McLaren, 100 Ind. 586 (1885).

Tenants could create liens on property for repairs to the extent of their interest in the property. McCarty v. Burnet, 84 Ind. 23 (1882); McAnally v. Glidden, 30 Ind. App. 22, 65 N.E. 291 (1902); Koehring v. Bowman, 194 Ind. 433, 142 N.E. 117 (1924).

A mechanic's lien could have been held for raising a house and repairing the roof, putting in brick-work, and fixing a grate, under a notice of intention "for work and labor done and material furnished, and for the erection and construction of said building." Rhodes v. Webb-Jameson Co., 19 Ind. App. 195, 49 N.E. 283 (1898).

Sale of Goods.

There is nothing to preclude one from filing a mechanic's lien to secure a debt owed by virtue of a contract whose predominant thrust is the sale of goods. Baker v. Compton, 455 N.E.2d 382 (Ind. App. 1983).

Separate Contracts.

It was error for trial court to conclude that a valid mechanics' lien could not embrace work done under two separate contracts. Saint Joseph's College v. Morrison, Inc., 158 Ind. App. 272, 39 Ind. Dec. 244, 302 N.E.2d 865 (1973).

Several Buildings.

Liens had to be taken on each building separately, a joint lien on several buildings not being permissible. Hill v. Braden, 54 Ind. 72 (1876); Hill v. Ryan, 54 Ind. 118 (1876); McGrew v. McCarty, 78 Ind. 496 (1881). But see West v. Dreher, 73 Ind. App. 133, 126 N.E. 688 (1920).

When work was done on several buildings on the same parcel of ground, a joint lien could have been taken on the buildings. Wilkerson v. Rust, 57 Ind. 172 (1877); Crawford v. Anderson, 129 Ind. 117, 28 N.E. 314 (1891).

A single lien could have been had upon all the buildings and lands constituting a single plant, for materials used in an improvement relating to all the buildings, without specifying the particular buildings upon which the separate portions of the materials were furnished. Premier Steel Co. v. McElwaine-Richards Co., 144 Ind. 614, 43 N.E. 876 (1896).

Several Claims.

Persons could not jointly acquire liens on claims due them severally. McGrew v. McCarty, 78 Ind. 496 (1881).

This section did not invalidate the waiver of a mechanic's lien on the part of the original contractor, even though the contract was not recorded. Hammond Hotel & Imp. Co. v. Williams, 95 Ind. App. 506, 176 N.E. 154, rehearing denied, 95 Ind. App. 528, 178 N.E. 177 (1931).

Subcontractors.

Subcontractors were entitled to benefits of liens. Algiers, W. & W. Ry. v. Foulkes Contracting Co., 101 Ind. App. 632, 200 N.E. 438 (1936).

Summary Judgment.

—Inappropriate.

Where pleadings and answers to interrogatories raised a factual issue as to date of completion of work, summary judgment was properly refused. Walker v. Statzer, 152 Ind. App. 544, 31 Ind. Dec. 496, 284 N.E.2d 127 (1972).

Where a bridge constituted neither a state nor a federal public work subject to the respective statutory protections provided to those working on public projects, the plaintiff was afforded the protection of a state mechanic's lien, and reversal of the trial court's summary judgment against the plaintiff was required for a hearing on the validity of the lien and on the amount of attorneys fees to which the plaintiff was entitled. J.S. Sweet Co. v. White County Bridge Comm'n, 714 N.E.2d 219 (Ind. App. 1999).

Supervisory Services.

The benefits of Indiana's mechanic's lien statutes cannot be invoked by a real estate developer performing supervisory services but not physical labor, particularly a developer who is an equity participant in the

Supervisory Services. (Cont'd)
project. Premier Invs. v. Suites of Am., Inc., 644 N.E.2d 124 (Ind. 1994).

Tenancy by Entirety.
Liens could have been obtained upon lands held by a husband and wife as tenants by the entireties. Dalton v. Tindolph, 87 Ind. 490 (1882); Wilson v. Logue, 131 Ind. 191, 30 N.E. 1079, 31 Am. St. 426 (1882); Taggart v. Kem, 22 Ind. App. 271, 53 N.E. 651 (1899).

Real property owned by husband and wife as tenants by entirety could have been subject to mechanic's lien although wife did not sign contract where there was evidence that she had knowledge of the improvements being made and made no objection. Means v. Everitt, 131 Ind. App. 370, 167 N.E.2d 885 (1960).

Theory of Lien.
A contract was but one phase of an action to foreclose a mechanic's lien; the theory of a lien upon which foreclosure might have been had was that property had been improved by the lienor with at least the consent of the owner. Prewitt v. Londeree, 141 Ind. App. 291, 8 Ind. Dec. 327, 216 N.E.2d 724 (1966).

Time for Filing.
Where a corporation executed a contract to furnish all the materials to build a house according to plans furnished by it, including a kitchen cabinet to have been installed therein, it would have been entitled to a lien for the entire amount of the price of such materials within 60 days after the cabinet was delivered. Holding v. Lewis Mfg. Co., 87 Ind. App. 296, 161 N.E. 702 (1928).

A contract to furnish the owner with materials to complete a building, after the contractor quit, could not have been tacked to a contract with the latter so as to extend the time for filing notice of lien. Kendallville Lumber Co. v. Adams, 93 Ind. App. 141, 176 N.E. 555 (1931).

In a mechanic's lien case, the evidence was held to show that the materials were furnished to building contractor and owner under separate contracts, so as to have required a lien notice within 60 days after last delivery to contractor. Kendallville Lumber Co. v. Adams, 93 Ind. App. 141, 176 N.E. 555 (1931).

Where company supplied labor and materials to alter or modify existing construction, notice of mechanic's lien had to be filed within thirty days after the date it last supplied labor and materials; notice filed sixty days after that date was not timely. Garage Doors of Indianapolis, Inc. v. Morton, 682 N.E.2d 1296 (Ind. App. 1997).

Title to Materials.
Under this act, it was not required that the

title to materials delivered by a materialman for the construction or repair of a building had to pass to the owner of the building in order to give the materialman the right to a lien on the building. Jackson v. J.A. Franklin & Son, 107 Ind. App. 38, 23 N.E.2d 23 (1939).

Validity.
A purported lien is valid only if it meets all statutory requirements necessary to its creation and if it does, the lien is necessarily valid as against any party contesting its legal existence, whether property owner or competing creditor. Stanray Corp. v. Horizon Constr., Inc., 168 Ind. App. 164, 51 Ind. Dec. 294, 342 N.E.2d 645 (1976).

Value of Services.
One who performs labor or services is competent to testify as to the value of such services. Walker v. Statzer, 152 Ind. App. 544, 31 Ind. Dec. 496, 284 N.E.2d 127 (1972).

Waiver or Release of Lien.

—In General.
A contractor could waive the right of himself and those claiming under him to a mechanic's lien where the statute imposed no restriction on his rights. Hammond Hotel & Imp. Co. v. Williams, 95 Ind. App. 506, 176 N.E. 154, rehearing denied, 95 Ind. App. 528, 178 N.E. 177 (1931).

A contract for the waiver of mechanic's liens, like other contracts, must be supported by consideration. Urbanational Developers, Inc. v. Shamrock Eng'r, Inc., 175 Ind. App. 416, 61 Ind. Dec. 29, 372 N.E.2d 742 (1978).

The waiver provisions included in this section favor the owner and the alienability of property. In re Hull, 19 Bankr. 501 (Bankr. N.D. Ind. 1982).

—Attorney Fees.
Where a contractor was not entitled to foreclose a mechanic's lien because he waived his rights thereto, he was not entitled to recover attorneys' fees. Hammond Hotel & Imp. Co. v. Williams, 95 Ind. App. 506, 176 N.E. 154, rehearing denied, 95 Ind. App. 528, 178 N.E. 177 (1931).

—Contract Provisions.
Where a provision in a building contract waived the rights of the contractor, subcontractors, materialmen, and laborers to a mechanic's lien on the premises, which provision was not acknowledged as provided by this section, it did not prevent the acquirement and enforcement of a mechanic's lien on the premises. Hutton v. McGuire, 88 Ind. App. 163, 161 N.E. 648 (1928).

Under a contract whereby the contractor expressly agreed to waive the right to a me-

Waiver or Release of Lien. (Cont'd)

—Contract Provisions. (Cont'd)
chanic's or materialman's lien, the lien was waived as to all work done under the contract. Hammond Hotel & Imp. Co. v. Williams, 95 Ind. App. 506, 176 N.E. 154, rehearing denied, 95 Ind. App. 528, 178 N.E. 177 (1931).

—Description of Property.
The description of property in a building contract as the "northwest corner of Michigan Street and Colfax Avenue," was sufficient within the meaning of this section authorizing waiver of liens. Clarage v. Palace Theater Corp., 95 Ind. App. 443, 165 N.E. 550 (1929).

—Held Binding.
The binding effect of waiver by contract of mechanic's lien was held not defeated by the owner's failure to comply with his own independent covenants or to pay the amount due under the contract. Hammond Hotel & Imp. Co. v. Williams, 95 Ind. App. 506, 176 N.E. 154, rehearing denied, 95 Ind. App. 528, 178 N.E. 177 (1931).

—Parties to Waiver.
Where contractor waived its right to acquire or enforce a mechanic's lien in agreement made with bank which was loaning money for improvement project, which agreement was made at same time as affidavit of project owner was furnished, and all such papers were signed by same person who was an officer in both companies, contractor could not thereafter enforce mechanic's lien against project owner on ground that project owner was not a party to the agreement waiving the right to lien. King Pin Motor Lodge, Inc. v. D.J. Constr. Co., 416 N.E.2d 1317 (Ind. App. 1981).

—Subcontractors.
Prior to the amendment of this section in 1921, a direct and positive covenant in the principal contract against liens precluded all who worked or furnished material to the principal contractor from acquiring a lien.

Baldwin Locomotive Works v. Edward Hines Lumber Co., 189 Ind. 189, 125 N.E. 400, 127 N.E. 275, 13 A.L.R. 1059 (1919). If the principal contract, however, did not contain such direct and express covenant, subcontractors were not precluded from acquiring a lien. Kokomo, F. & W. Traction Co. v. Kokomo Trust Co., 193 Ind. 219, 137 N.E. 763 (1923).

A building contract providing for waiver of all liens was held to have been binding on subcontractors. Clarage v. Palace Theater Corp., 95 Ind. App. 443, 165 N.E. 550 (1929).

Even though a general contractor who complies with the requirements of this section can effectively waive the right for himself and those who work under him on a contract or provide materials for the contract to obtain a mechanic's lien, such a waiver in a contract between the owner and general contractor, in order to be effective against a subcontractor, must be direct, positive, and express, with any doubt regarding the language of the contract being construed against a waiver. In re Hull, 19 Bankr. 501 (Bankr. N.D. Ind. 1982).

Wells for Water.
In a suit by the driller of wells on defendant's premises to enforce a mechanic's lien, a complaint which alleged an agreement of defendant to pay plaintiff a specified rate per foot for the drilling, and that plaintiff drilled a well for water, and furnished the pipe, and that a lien notice was filed, was held sufficient under this section. Koch v. Fishburn, 90 Ind. App. 287, 164 N.E. 721 (1929).

Plaintiff suing to enforce a materialman's and laborer's lien for drilling wells at specified rate per foot on defendant's premises was entitled to a lien for the agreed compensation under this section, although water was not found by the driller. Koch v. Fishburn, 90 Ind. App. 287, 164 N.E. 721 (1929).

Widow's Exemption.
The widow of a decedent who did not leave an estate worth more than $500 took the estate free of mechanics' liens. Lloyd v. Arney, 43 Ind. App. 450, 87 N.E. 989 (1909).

Collateral References. 53 Am. Jur. 2d Mechanics' Liens, §§ 28-48.

56 C.J.S. Mechanics' Liens, §§ 2-19.

Right to mechanic's lien as for "labor" or "work," in case of preparatory or fabricating work done on material intended for use and used in particular building or structure. 25 A.L.R.2d 1370.

Mechanic's lien for grading, clearing, filling, landscaping, excavating, and the like. 39 A.L.R.2d 866.

Fixtures installed upon property under lease, right to mechanic's lien. 42 A.L.R.2d 685.

Right to mechanic's lien upon leasehold for supplying labor or material in attaching or installing fixtures. 42 A.L.R.2d 685.

Amount for which mechanic's lien may be obtained where contract has been terminated or abandoned by consent of parties or without fault on contractor's part. 51 A.L.R.2d 1009.

Lien for improvements made or placed on premises of another by mistake. 57 A.L.R.2d 263.

Satisfaction or enforcement of lien for improvement made or placed on premises of another by mistake. 57 A.L.R.2d 263.

Validity of statute making private property owner liable to contractor's laborers, materialmen, or subcontractors where owner fails to exact bond or employ other means of securing their payment. 59 A.L.R.2d 885.

Interest of spouse in estate by entireties as subject to lien in satisfaction of his or her individual debt. 75 A.L.R.2d 1172.

Sufficiency of notice under present statute making notice by owner of nonresponsibility necessary to prevent mechanic's liens. 85 A.L.R.2d 949.

Mechanic's lien for services in connection with subdividing land. 87 A.L.R.2d 1004.

Mechanic's lien for work under water well-drilling contract. 90 A.L.R.2d 1346.

Taking or negotiation of unsecured note of owner or contractor as waiver of mechanic's lien. 91 A.L.R.2d 425.

Swimming pool as lienable item within mechanic's lien statute. 95 A.L.R.2d 1371.

What constitutes "Commencement of building or improvement" for purpose of determining accrual of lien. 1 A.L.R.3d 822.

Charge for use of machinery, tools, or appliances used in construction as basis for mechanic's lien. 3 A.L.R.3d 573.

Right of heir or devisee to have realty exonerated from lien thereon at expense of personal estate. 4 A.L.R.3d 1023.

Mechanic's lien for work on or material for separate buildings of one owner. 15 A.L.R.3d 73.

Surveyor's work as giving rise to right to mechanic's lien. 35 A.L.R.3d 1391.

Mechanic's lien based on contract with vendor pending executory contract for sale of property as affecting purchaser's interest. 50 A.L.R.3d 944.

Removal or demolition of building or other structure as basis for mechanic's lien. 74 A.L.R.3d 386.

Release or waiver of mechanic's lien by general contractor as affecting rights of subcontractor or materialman. 75 A.L.R.3d 505.

Delivery of material to building site as sustaining mechanic's lien — modern cases. 32 A.L.R.4th 1130.

Architect's services as within mechanic's lien statute. 31 A.L.R.5th 664.

32-28-3-2. Extent of lien. — (a) The entire land upon which the building, erection, or other improvement is situated, including the part of the land not occupied by the building, erection, or improvement, is subject to a lien to the extent of the right, title, and interest of the owner for whose immediate use or benefit the labor was done or material furnished.

(b) If:

(1) the owner has only a leasehold interest; or

(2) the land is encumbered by mortgage;

the lien, so far as concerns the buildings erected by the lienholder, is not impaired by forfeiture of the lease for rent or foreclosure of mortgage. The buildings may be sold to satisfy the lien and may be removed not later than ninety (90) days after the sale by the purchaser. [P.L.2-2002, § 13.]

NOTES TO DECISIONS

ANALYSIS

In general.
Applicability.
—Contract to purchase.
Cross-claims.
Destruction of building.
Entire building or lot.
Equitable title.
Husband and wife.
Landlord and tenant.
Machinery.
Mortgages.
Necessity of notice.
Priority of liens.
Repairs and alterations.
Title.

Unimproved portion of lands.

In General.

As a general rule, a mechanic's lien could have been imposed on whatever interest an individual who contracted for work or materials might have owned in the property on which the work was done or materials used, whether the interest was legal or equitable. Fletcher Ave. Sav. & Loan Ass'n v. Roberts, 99 Ind. App. 391, 188 N.E. 794 (1934).

The legislature intended to make not only the title of the real estate subject to a mechanic's lien, but any right or interest therein as well. Potter v. Cline, 161 Ind. App. 349, 43 Ind. Dec. 446, 316 N.E.2d 422 (1974).

Applicability.

—Contract to Purchase.

Former IC 32-8-3-2 (repealed; see this section for similar provisions) did not apply to a lienholder who did not erect a building but supplied plumbing work for person purchasing land under contract. Miles Homes of Ind., Inc. v. Harrah Plumbing & Heating Serv. Co., 77 Ind. Dec. 587, 408 N.E.2d 597 (Ind. Dec. 1980).

Cross-Claims.

Where, in a suit to quiet title to certain real estate, defendants filed cross-complaint to enforce mechanic's lien for services rendered and material furnished in the erection of the building in question, the remedies invoked by defendants in their cross-complaint having been statutory and in derogation of the common law, they had to bring themselves within the provisions of the statute before they could have recovered on their claim. National Brick Co. v. Russell, 99 Ind. App. 53, 190 N.E. 614 (1934).

Destruction of Building.

The lien on land for materials furnished for use in a building thereon was not lost by the destruction of the building by fire before notice of intention to hold the lien was filed. Smith v. Newbaur, 144 Ind. 95, 42 N.E. 40, 33 L.R.A. 685 (1895); Bratton v. Ralph, 14 Ind. App. 153, 42 N.E. 644 (1896).

Entire Building or Lot.

The lien attached to the entire lot or subdivision of land upon which the building was erected. City of Crawfordsville v. Barr, 65 Ind. 367 (1879).

The lien of a mechanic extended to the entire tract upon which the building was erected although there might have been other buildings on the tract. Judah v. F.H. Cheyne Elec. Co., 53 Ind. App. 476, 101 N.E. 1039 (1913).

Equitable Title.

A mechanic could not acquire lien as against the owner of the legal title where improvements were ordered by equitable owner of land. People's Sav., Loan & Bldg. Ass'n v. Spears, 115 Ind. 297, 17 N.E. 570 (1888); Davis v. Elliott, 7 Ind. App. 246, 34 N.E. 591 (1893); Rusche v. Pittman, 34 Ind. App. 159, 72 N.E. 473 (1904); Toner v. Whybrew, 50 Ind. App. 387, 98 N.E. 450 (1912).

If a person who held a contract for the purchase of land caused a building to be erected upon the land, a mechanic's lien could not have been taken as against the owner of the land upon the building or the land. Toner v. Whybrew, 50 Ind. App. 387, 98 N.E. 450 (1912).

There might have been cases where mechanics' liens might have been taken as against the owner of property where he had contracted to sell the property and the vendee had ordered repairs done on buildings with consent and approbation of such owner. Rader v. A.J. Barrett Co., 59 Ind. App. 27, 108 N.E. 883 (1915).

A mechanic's lien could attach to an equitable interest in the property, unless a title was held under some condition which prohibited the owner of the equitable interest from placing a lien thereon. Fletcher Ave. Sav. & Loan Ass'n v. Roberts, 99 Ind. App. 391, 188 N.E. 794 (1934).

Husband and Wife.

Where a husband and wife had jointly purchased a house on contract in the form of a lease, the husband, by ordering a furnace installed therein, could have created a lien against his interest therein in favor of the contractor. Koehring v. Bowman, 194 Ind. 433, 142 N.E. 117 (1924).

Landlord and Tenant.

Tenants could create liens for repairs to the extent of their interest in the property. McCarty v. Burnet, 84 Ind. 23 (1882).

Where a lease for oil and gas was forfeited for failure to drill wells according to terms of lease, the lien for the construction of a derrick for the lessee, to have been used in the construction and operation of a gas and oil well on the leased premises, attached to the well. Montpelier Light & Water Co. v. Stephenson, 22 Ind. App. 175, 53 N.E. 444 (1899); McAnally v. Glidden, 30 Ind. App. 22, 65 N.E. 291 (1902).

If a tenant erected a building upon leased land, a mechanic's lien could have been enforced against such building. Williamson v. Shank, 41 Ind. App. 513, 83 N.E. 641 (1908).

A mechanic's lien on a leasehold estate was not destroyed by the surrender of the lease creating such estate. National Lumber Co. v. Hobbs, 74 Ind. App. 476, 129 N.E. 255 (1920).

A mechanic's lien could have been had on a building erected by a tenant on leased land. Holland v. Farrier, 75 Ind. App. 368, 130 N.E. 823 (1921).

Tenants could create liens for repairs to the extent of their interest in the property. Koehring v. Bowman, 194 Ind. 433, 142 N.E. 117 (1924).

The holder of a lease with an option to purchase had an interest in real estate to which a mechanic's lien would attach. Koehring v. Bowman, 194 Ind. 433, 142 N.E. 117 (1924).

A provision in a lease prohibiting the enforcement of any mechanic's lien "against said

Landlord and Tenant. (Cont'd)
real estate or the buildings or improvements
erected thereon" would not prevent the filing
and enforcement of a lien upon the leasehold
estate for labor done and materials furnished
in remodeling the buildings on a contract with
the tenant, as the provision was clearly for
the protection of the lessor and not available
to the lessee. Robertson v. Sertell, 88 Ind. App.
591, 161 N.E. 669 (1928).

Machinery.
A lien could have been had for machinery
furnished to repair machinery in factory. Totten & Hogg Iron & Steel Foundry Co. v.
Muncie Nail Co., 148 Ind. 372, 47 N.E. 703
(1897).

Mortgages.
A mortgage not recorded until several
months after its execution and after rights to
mechanics' liens had been created against the
property so mortgaged was inferior to such
liens although notice of them was not filed
until after the mortgage was recorded. Thorpe
Block Sav. & Loan Ass'n v. James, 13 Ind.
App. 522, 41 N.E. 978 (1895); Carriger v.
Mackey, 15 Ind. App. 392, 44 N.E. 266 (1896);
Building & Loan Ass'n v. Coburn, 150 Ind.
684, 50 N.E. 885 (1898); Deming-Colborn
Lumber Co. v. Union Nat'l Sav. & Loan Ass'n,
151 Ind. 463, 51 N.E. 936 (1898); Stoermer v.
People's Sav. Bank, 152 Ind. 104, 52 N.E. 606
(1899).
Rights of parties where a mortgage was
executed on the land during the erection of a
building, and labor was performed and material furnished both before and after the execution of the mortgage, were governed by
statute. Ward v. Yarnelle, 173 Ind. 535, 91
N.E. 7 (1910), overruled on other grounds,
Moore-Mansfield Constr. Co. v. Indianapolis,
N.C. & T. Ry., 179 Ind. 356, 101 N.E. 296
(1913).
Where a mortgagee, which was also the
owner of equitable title under deed to third
party designated by it, contracted for improvements of the mortgaged premises, the
realty was subject to mechanics' liens to the
extent of the mortgagee's interest in the premises, and the mechanics' liens were superior
to the mortgage lien. Fletcher Ave. Sav. &
Loan Ass'n v. Roberts, 99 Ind. App. 391, 188
N.E. 794 (1934).
Where suppliers and mechanics argued
that a deed executed for a bank, which was
held in escrow and later recorded, conferred
ownership of the land on the bank thereby
rendering its interest subordinate to the mechanics' liens, the trial court did not err in
finding that the deed was merely a security
device and that, therefore, the bank retained
a mortgaged lien which took priority over the
mechanics' liens because it related back to

prior mortgages. Brenneman Mechanical &
Elec., Inc. v. First Nat'l Bank, 495 N.E.2d 233
(Ind. App. 1986).

Necessity of Notice.
The holders of mortgage liens upon certain
real estate were entitled to subrogation to the
rights of claimants for labor and material
furnished for the erection of a building upon
the land, where the mortgagees acted in good
faith without notice and the mortgagor, who
was primarily liable for such claims, had an
interest in the property he was entitled to
protect. Mishawaka, St. Joseph Loan & Trust
Co. v. Neu, 209 Ind. 433, 196 N.E. 85 (1935).

Priority of Liens.
Mortgage lien and the mechanic's liens of
record were entitled to equal priority, except
to the extent that the debtor had defenses
against a lien due to possible counterclaims
and rights to setoff, since the clearly stated
purpose of the mortgage loan was for the
construction of improvements on the property
and the mechanic's lienholders who had no
prior obligation to perform services or furnish
supplies to the debtor should have known
that the loan proceeds would be used to pay
for the improvements. Venture Properties,
Inc. v. Altite Roofing, Inc., 139 Bankr. 890
(Bankr. N.D. Ind. 1990).

Repairs and Alterations.
Liens for repairs could not have been obtained when not ordered by the owner of the
land, or where he was not connected with the
contract therefor. Wilkerson v. Rust, 57 Ind.
172 (1877); Woodward v. McLaren, 100 Ind.
586 (1885).
Where work was completed in the repair of
a dwelling house and outbuildings, which
were appurtenant to the dwelling, a joint lien
could have been taken upon the dwelling with
the appurtenant outbuildings. Crawford v.
Anderson, 129 Ind. 117, 28 N.E. 314 (1891).
Liens could have been acquired for repairs
and alterations of buildings. Rhodes v. Webb-
Jameson Co., 19 Ind. App. 195, 49 N.E. 283
(1898); Montpelier Light & Water Co. v.
Stephenson, 22 Ind. App. 175, 53 N.E. 444
(1899); McAnally v. Glidden, 30 Ind. App. 22,
65 N.E. 291 (1902).

Title.
It is not necessary to prove title to the lot
upon which the lien is claimed. Potter v.
Cline, 161 Ind. App. 349, 43 Ind. Dec. 446, 316
N.E.2d 422 (1974).

Unimproved Portion of Lands.
Where at time of entering contract property
was a single parcel and was thereafter divided into 81 lots, the fact that one of such lots
contained no improvements did not prevent

Unimproved Portion of Lands. (Cont'd) that lot from being subject to the lien. Inter-City Contractors Servs., Inc. v. Consumer Bldg. Indus., Inc., 175 Ind. App. 665, 61 Ind. Dec. 476, 373 N.E.2d 903 (1978).

Collateral References. Right to mechanic's lien upon leasehold for supplying labor or material in attaching or installing fixtures. 42 A.L.R.2d 685.

32-28-3-3. Requirements to acquire lien — Statement and notice of intention. — (a) Except as provided in subsection (b), a person who wishes to acquire a lien upon property, whether the claim is due or not, must file in duplicate a sworn statement and notice of the person's intention to hold a lien upon the property for the amount of the claim:

(1) in the recorder's office of the county; and

(2) not later than ninety (90) days after performing labor or furnishing materials or machinery described in section 1 [IC 32-28-3-1] of this chapter.

The statement and notice of intention to hold a lien may be verified and filed on behalf of a client by an attorney registered with the clerk of the supreme court as an attorney in good standing under the requirements of the supreme court.

(b) This subsection applies to a person that performs labor or furnishes materials or machinery described in section 1 of this chapter related to a Class 2 structure (as defined in IC 22-12-1-5) or an improvement on the same real estate auxiliary to a Class 2 structure (as defined in IC 22-12-1-5). A person who wishes to acquire a lien upon property, whether the claim is due or not, must file in duplicate a sworn statement and notice of the person's intention to hold a lien upon the property for the amount of the claim:

(1) in the recorder's office of the county; and

(2) not later than sixty (60) days after performing labor or furnishing materials or machinery described in section 1 of this chapter.

The statement and notice of intention to hold a lien may be verified and filed on behalf of a client by an attorney registered with the clerk of the supreme court as an attorney in good standing under the requirements of the supreme court.

(c) A statement and notice of intention to hold a lien filed under this section must specifically set forth:

(1) the amount claimed;

(2) the name and address of the claimant;

(3) the owner's:

(A) name; and

(B) latest address as shown on the property tax records of the county; and

(4) the:

(A) legal description; and

(B) street and number, if any;

of the lot or land on which the house, mill, manufactory or other buildings, bridge, reservoir, system of waterworks, or other structure may stand or be connected with or to which it may be removed.

The name of the owner and legal description of the lot or land will be sufficient if they are substantially as set forth in the latest entry in the transfer books described in IC 6-1.1-5-4 of the county auditor or, if IC 6-1.1-5-9 applies, the transfer books of the township assessor at the time of filing of the notice of intention to hold a lien.

(d) The recorder shall:

(1) mail, first class, one (1) of the duplicates of the statement and notice of intention to hold a lien to the owner named in the statement and notice not later than three (3) business days after recordation;

(2) post records as to the date of the mailing; and

(3) collect a fee of two dollars ($2) from the lien claimant for each statement and notice that is mailed.

The statement and notice shall be addressed to the latest address of the owner as specifically set out in the sworn statement and notice of the person intending to hold a lien upon the property. [P.L.2-2002, § 13.]

Indiana Law Review. Judicial Developments in Business and Contract Law, 30 Ind. L. Rev. 961 (1997).

NOTES TO DECISIONS

Analysis

In general.
Description of claimant.
Description of improvements.
Description of property.
Effect of notice on third parties.
Estoppel.
Failure to margin.
Failure to release lien.
Filing and recording.
—Acknowledgment not required.
Groundless claims.
Necessity of notice.
Notice of intent.
—Verification.
—Work performed.
Property.
Public use and necessity.
Requisites and sufficiency of notice.
—Name of owner.
Separate claims.
Summary judgment.
—Inappropriate.
Tenants by entirety.
Time for filing.
—Separate contracts.
—Work incidental to contract.
Transfer of title.
Waiver.

In General.

In actions for the foreclosure of mechanics' liens, plaintiff had to prove first, that it filed its lien notice within 60 days after furnishing the last of the materials for the building in question and secondly, it must have been shown that plaintiff furnished the material for use in the particular building on which the lien was sought to have been foreclosed. Wymer v. Harrison Sheet Steel Co., 125 Ind. App. 169, 123 N.E.2d 241 (1954).

A lien will not be defeated by reason of an unintentional misstatement or a trivial error where the defect is not misleading. Rudd v. Anderson, 153 Ind. App. 11, 32 Ind. Dec. 172, 285 N.E.2d 836 (1972).

Description of Claimant.

The designation of the wrong claimant rendered a lien invalid. Mullis v. Brennan, 716 N.E.2d 58 (Ind. App. 1999).

Description of Improvements.

It was not necessary to include information as to the nature of improvements to perfect a lien under former IC 32-8-3-3 (repealed; see this section for similar provisions). Thomas J. Henderson, Inc. v. Leibowitz, 490 N.E.2d 396 (Ind. App. 1986).

Compliance with the statutory requirement of legal description, street and number, was sufficient to satisfy the purpose of former IC 32-8-3-3 (repealed; see this section for similar provisions) and a lienholder was not required to specifically identify the improvements made by him. Johnson v. Blankenship, 679 N.E.2d 505 (Ind. App. 1997), aff'd, 688 N.E.2d 1250 (Ind. 1997).

Description of Property.

The notice should have contained a reasonable definite description of the property.

Description of Property. (Cont'd)

Munger v. Green, 20 Ind. 38 (1863); Howell v. Zerbee, 26 Ind. 214 (1866); City of Crawfordsville v. Irwin, 46 Ind. 438 (1874); City of Crawfordsville v. Barr, 65 Ind. 367 (1879); Irwin v. City of Crawfordsville, 72 Ind. 111 (1880).

Where description of property was capable of being reduced to a certainty, it was sufficient. Caldwell v. Asbury, 29 Ind. 451 (1868); O'Halloran v. Leachey, 39 Ind. 150 (1872); City of Crawfordsville v. Johnson, 51 Ind. 397 (1875); Kealing v. Voss, 61 Ind. 466 (1878); City of Crawfordsville v. Barr, 65 Ind. 367 (1879); City of Crawfordsville v. Boots, 76 Ind. 32 (1881); White v. Stanton, 111 Ind. 540, 13 N.E. 48 (1887); McNamee v. Rauck, 128 Ind. 59, 27 N.E. 423 (1891); Quaack v. Schmid, 131 Ind. 185, 30 N.E. 514 (1892); Dalton v. Hoffman, 8 Ind. App. 101, 35 N.E. 291 (1893).

When a personal judgment was sought, the sufficiency of the description of the property could not have been raised by demurrer, but otherwise when it was only sought to enforce the lien. O'Halloran v. Leachey, 39 Ind. 150 (1872); City of Crawfordsville v. Barr, 65 Ind. 367 (1879).

Misdescription of property by giving wrong number of lot did not necessarily render the notice invalid. Newcomer v. Hutchings, 96 Ind. 119 (1884).

Indefinite descriptions of property in such notices could have been aided by extrinsic evidence, under proper averments. White v. Stanton, 111 Ind. 540, 13 N.E. 48 (1887); Coburn v. Stephens, 137 Ind. 683, 36 N.E. 132, 45 Am. St. 218 (1894); Maynard v. East, 13 Ind. App. 432, 41 N.E. 839, 55 Am. St. R. 238 (1895).

Including in a notice more property than was proper did not invalidate the same. Scott v. Goldinhorst, 123 Ind. 268, 24 N.E. 333 (1890).

Mistake in description of property did not render the notice invalid if the owner knew the property intended to be described. Smith v. Newbaur, 144 Ind. 95, 42 N.E. 40, 33 L.R.A. 685 (1895).

A notice describing the land upon which a mechanic's lien was sought that was defective in part was not void and a lien could have been decreed thereon upon averment and proof of the true description, the notice having been sufficient to have apprised the owner of the property intended. Stephens v. Duffy, 41 Ind. App. 385, 81 N.E. 1154 (1907), rehearing overruled, 83 N.E. 268 (1908); Windfall Natural Gas, Mining & Oil Co. v. Roe, 42 Ind. App. 278, 85 N.E. 722 (1908).

Notice of an intention to hold a lien on a house for a stated amount did not create a lien on a gas well situated some distance from such house. Windfall Natural Gas, Mining & Oil Co. v. Roe, 41 Ind. App. 687, 84 N.E. 996 (1908).

A complaint to enforce a mechanic's lien could have been amended so as to show that the building was erected on a different lot from the one described in the notice. Hillyard v. Robbins, 53 Ind. App. 107, 101 N.E. 341 (1913).

Misdescription of property in notice could have been corrected in a complaint to enforce the lien if the notice were sufficient to apprise the owner of the property who contracted to have the work done as to the property intended to be described in the notice. Deal v. Plass, 59 Ind. App. 185, 109 N.E. 51 (1915).

A liberal construction was given this section providing that a lien notice was sufficient where the land could have been identified from the description or any reference therein. Brannum-Keene Lumber Co. v. Cole, 67 Ind. App. 667, 119 N.E. 721 (1918).

A recorded lien notice under this section, although containing an imperfect description, was sufficient to enable identification of land where it was described by section, township, range, county, name of owner, extent of acreage, and nature of improvements, and owners had no other land in county. Brannum-Keene Lumber Co. v. Cole, 67 Ind. App. 667, 119 N.E. 721 (1918).

A notice of a mechanic's lien which described the real estate on which the lien claimant had performed work and furnished material was sufficient to cover defendant's leasehold interest where the complaint averred that fact, although the notice did not mention the leasehold interest. Robertson v. Sertell, 88 Ind. App. 591, 161 N.E. 669 (1928).

In a suit to foreclose a mechanic's lien, evidence establishing that the premises described in the notice as 1334 Concord Avenue, in the City of Elkhart, Indiana, and also described as lot No. 118 in Elliston's first addition to such city, showed a sufficient description of the premises involved, and the rights of third persons could not have been affected by the admission of evidence disclosing the description of the same real estate, taken from the city or town plat. Isbell Lumber & Coal Co. v. Marchesseau Plumbing Co., 104 Ind. App. 373, 11 N.E.2d 518 (1937).

Notices of mechanics' liens which described the real estate as being the "improvements on the T. H. & L. R. R. Co. Rt. of Way Tract 90 feet E & W on South & 80 ft on North, West of and adjoining Center St. off N C a of S. 18 a of N½ of S W¼ Sec. 18 N. R. L. as well as upon the Office Building, Ice Plant and Coal Yard," were sufficient as against corporation employees' lienholders, although the correct section number was 12 instead of 18, where the abbreviations used would have been easily understood by one familar with the premises.

Description of Property. (Cont'd)
Watson v. Strohl, 220 Ind. 672, 46 N.E.2d 204
(1943).

Where, in a decree foreclosing mechanic's
lien notices, the land was correctly described
and there was no appeal from the judgment
by the owner of the real estate against whom
the liens were foreclosed, such owner was
bound by the decree, and third parties dealing
with the title to the land, subsequent to the
entry of the decree, could not be heard to say
that they were misled by incorrect descriptions contained in the notices. Watson v.
Strohl, 220 Ind. 672, 46 N.E.2d 204 (1943).

Since the 1963 amendment to the predecessor statute to this section, a legal description
of the land was required, and where the legal
description contained in the notice was for an
entirely different parcel of land from that on
which house was built, the lien was invalid.
Froberg v. Northern Ind. Constr., Inc., 416
N.E.2d 451 (Ind. App. 1981).

Effect of Notice on Third Parties.
Although the notice required by former IC
32-8-3-3 (repealed; see this section for similar
provisions) often comes too late to be of benefit to the landowner, it does serve the purpose of warning third parties such as prospective purchasers, landowners, or tenants of the
existence of a lien on the property which is the
object of their attention. Cato v. David Excavating Co., 435 N.E.2d 597 (Ind. App. 1982),
overruled on other grounds, Johnson v.
Blankenship, 679 N.E.2d 505 (Ind. App.
1997).

Estoppel.
Where a party refused to make final payment because the work was allegedly incomplete, that party was later estopped from
claiming that the work was completed prior to
the additional work and that the lien was
untimely filed. Smith v. Bruning Enters., Inc.,
424 N.E.2d 1035 (Ind. App. 1981).

Failure to Margin.
Failure to margin mechanic's liens did not
invalidate the liens; natural gas storage company could not defeat the validity of contractor's liens by claiming that hypothetical third
parties were not given sufficient notice of the
liens claimed, where contractor failed to properly cross reference each oil and gas lease or
easement involved. McCartin McAuliffe Mechanical Contractor v. Midwest Gas Storage,
Inc., 685 N.E.2d 165 (Ind. App. 1997).

Failure to Release Lien.
Where person who had not been paid by
contractor, had no contractual relationship
with purchaser of property, filed mechanic's
lien long after the 60-day period had expired,
and refused to release lien after demand and

after payment, there was sufficient evidence
from which jury could infer malice and to
support judgment for compensatory and punitive damages. Harper v. Goodin, 78 Ind.
Dec. 182, 409 N.E.2d 1129 (Ind. App. 1980).

Filing and Recording.
Notices were deemed recorded from the
time of their having been filed with the recorder. Wilson v. Hopkins, 51 Ind. 231 (1875).

Liens for labor and materials were created
by the filing of a notice of an intention to hold
a lien, and not by the recording of the notice.
Adams v. Buhler, 131 Ind. 66, 30 N.E. 883
(1892); Adams v. Shaffer, 132 Ind. 331, 31
N.E. 1108 (1892); Northwestern Loan & Inv.
Ass'n v. McPherson, 23 Ind. App. 250, 54 N.E.
130 (1899).

—Acknowledgment Not Required.
The acknowledgment requirement for filings regarding alienation of property, found in
former IC 32-1-2-18 (repealed; see IC 32-21-
2-3), do not apply to mechanic's liens. Eyster
v. S.A. Birnbaum Contracting, Inc., 662
N.E.2d 201 (Ind. App. 1996).

Groundless Claims.
Trial court properly dismissed plaintiff's
action to foreclose a mechanic's lien because
the lien was untimely, and the court properly
awarded attorney's fees to the defendant because the plaintiff prosecuted its action with
knowledge that its claim was groundless, and
also because plaintiff falsified documents in
an unsuccessful attempt to prove otherwise,
but the trial court erred by trebling its award
of attorney's fees. Harco, Inc. v. Plainfield
Interstate Family Dining Assocs., 758 N.E.2d
931 (Ind. App. 2001).

Necessity of Notice.
Personal knowledge by the owner of the
performance of labor or the furnishing of
materials did not supply the notice required
by statute. Neeley v. Searight, 13 Ind. 316, 15
N.E. 598 (1888); Caylor v. Thorn, 125 Ind.
201, 25 N.E. 217 (1890); Parker v. Dillingham,
129 Ind. 542, 29 N.E. 23 (1891).

Liens of mechanics could have been acquired only by taking the steps required by
statute. Barnett v. Stevens, 16 Ind. App. 420,
43 N.E. 661, 45 N.E. 485 (1896).

The holders of mortgage liens upon certain
real estate were entitled to subrogation to the
rights of claimants for labor and material
furnished for the erection of a building upon
the land where the mortgagees acted in good
faith without notice and the mortgagor, who
was primarily liable for such claims, had an
interest in the property he was entitled to
protect. Mishawaka, St. Joseph Loan & Trust
Co. v. Neu, 209 Ind. 433, 196 N.E. 85 (1935).

Where a notice of mechanic's lien for labor

Necessity of Notice. (Cont'd)

and materials furnished described the real property benefited by such labor and materials as situated in a named city of this state, by street and number, and referred to a dwelling thereon for which such labor and materials were furnished, and the work completed, it was a sufficient description under the provisions of this section. Isbell Lumber & Coal Co. v. Marchesseau Plumbing Co., 104 Ind. App. 373, 11 N.E.2d 518 (1937).

Notice of Intent.

—Verification.

Prior to the 1967 amendment to the predecessor statute to this section, where notices of intent to hold mechanics' liens were not properly verified, as required by this section, plaintiffs could not recover, as the statutory creation of mechanics' liens were in derogation of the common law and had to be strictly construed. Aetna Glass Corp. v. Mercury Bldrs., Inc., 145 Ind. App. 286, 18 Ind. Dec. 431, 250 N.E.2d 598 (1969).

Prior to the 1967 amendment to the predecessor statute to this section, the term "verified," as used in that section, meant that the notice of intent had to be supported by an oath or affirmation in writing concerning the truth of the matters set forth in the notice, and the notarized acknowledgment of the execution of the notice was not sufficient. Aetna Glass Corp. v. Mercury Bldrs., Inc., 145 Ind. App. 286, 18 Ind. Dec. 431, 250 N.E.2d 598 (1969).

A notice of intention to hold a lien complied with the predecessor statute to this section notwithstanding the name of the person signing the notice was omitted from the jurat attached to the notice. Whitfield v. Greater S. Bend Hous. Corp., 150 Ind. App. 291, 28 Ind. Dec. 266, 276 N.E.2d 188 (1971).

—Work Performed.

Work actually called for by the contract or continuing employment performed in good faith with intention of completing the job will permit the filing of the statement of intention to hold a lien within 60 days after the performance of the last work. Potter v. Cline, 161 Ind. App. 349, 43 Ind. Dec. 446, 316 N.E.2d 422 (1974).

Property.

The term "property" as used in former IC 32-8-3-3 (repealed; see this section for similar provisions) apparently comprehends both the improvement and the land improved. Cato v. David Excavating Co., 435 N.E.2d 597 (Ind. App. 1982), overruled on other grounds, Johnson v. Blankenship, 679 N.E.2d 505 (Ind. App. 1997).

Public Use and Necessity.

The public use and necessity exception did not apply to a privately-owned public utility; while an adequate, reliable and reasonably priced supply of natural gas was essential to the public, one particular company's ownership of one particular facility was not. McCartin McAuliffe Mechanical Contractor v. Midwest Gas Storage, Inc., 685 N.E.2d 165 (Ind. App. 1997).

Requisites and Sufficiency of Notice.

Form and contents of notice were sufficient if it stated the amount, to whom, by whom, for what due, and described the premises. Simonds v. Buford, 18 Ind. 176 (1862); Coburn v. Stephens, 137 Ind. 683, 36 N.E. 132, 45 Am. St. 218 (1894); Jeffersonville Water Supply Co. v. Riter, 146 Ind. 521, 45 N.E. 697 (1897); Rhodes v. Webb-Jameson Co., 19 Ind. App. 195, 49 N.E. 283 (1898).

The notice should have stated whether the claim was due or not, but a failure to have done so was immaterial as between the original parties. Wade v. Reitz, 18 Ind. 307 (1862); Schneider v. Kolthoff, 59 Ind. 568 (1877); Albrecht v. C.C. Foster Lumber Co., 126 Ind. 318, 26 N.E. 157 (1890).

A notice was not necessarily invalid because it claimed more than was due. Harrington v. Dollman, 64 Ind. 255 (1878); Albrecht v. C.C. Foster Lumber Co., 126 Ind. 318, 26 N.E. 157 (1890).

The notice did not need to contain an itemized statement of the claim. Neeley v. Searight, 113 Ind. 316, 15 N.E. 598 (1888).

Former IC 32-8-3-3 (repealed; see this section for similar provisions) was held not to require that the notice of intention to hold a mechanic's lien shall state from whom the money is due. Cline v. Indianapolis Mortar & Fuel Co., 65 Ind. App. 383, 117 N.E. 509 (1917).

Former IC 32-8-3-3 (repealed; see this section for similar provisions) entitled a contractor working on two houses under a single contract to a lien on both houses and lots by a single notice. West v. Dreher, 73 Ind. App. 133, 126 N.E. 688 (1920).

Former IC 32-8-3-3 (repealed; see this section for similar provisions) fairly be interpreted as only requiring a mechanic to notify the landowner of the specific amount of his lien and the description of the real estate subject to the lien without regard to the existence or nonexistence of any contractual relationship between the mechanic and the landowner. Saint Joseph's College v. Morrison, Inc., 158 Ind. App. 272, 39 Ind. Dec. 244, 302 N.E.2d 865 (1973).

A notice of a mechanic's lien specifically setting forth the amount claimed, the lienholder's name and address, the property owner's name and address, and the street and

Requisites and Sufficiency of Notice. (Cont'd)

number of the lots at which the work was done, together with a legal description of the property, satisfied the statutory requirements. The lienholder was not required to refer additionally to the improvements he made to the subject property. O.J. Shoemaker, Inc. v. Board of Trustees, 479 N.E.2d 1349 (Ind. App. 1985).

A lien is valid against a purchaser by contract who had contracted for the improvements and who was notified even though the title holder who had no responsibility for the improvement was not notified. Thomas J. Henderson, Inc. v. Leibowitz, 490 N.E.2d 396 (Ind. App. 1986).

Former IC 32-8-3-3 (repealed; see this section for similar provisions) places the duty of addressing the notice on the recorder, not on the lienor, and any error the recorder makes will not affect the validity of the lien. Brownsburg Lumber Co. v. Mann, 537 N.E.2d 1386 (Ind. App. 1989).

—Name of Owner.

Listing the wrong owner of real estate on a mechanic's lien notice was not a hypertechnicality, but instead was fatal to the mechanic's lien and the lien did not attach to the real estate despite similarity in names of prior and current corporate owners of real estate. Logansport Equip. Rental, Inc. v. Transco, Inc., 755 N.E.2d 1135 (Ind. App. 2001).

Separate Claims.

Joint notices of liens could not have been filed by persons holding separate claims. McGrew v. McCarty, 78 Ind. 496 (1881).

Summary Judgment.

—Inappropriate.

Genuine issue of material fact existed as to whether liens were timely filed and whether natural gas storage company approved contractor's work on its rectifier beds, and whether the work was performed pursuant to one or two separate contracts. McCartin McAuliffe Mechanical Contractor v. Midwest Gas Storage, Inc., 685 N.E.2d 165 (Ind. App. 1997).

Tenants by Entirety.

Although property was owned by husband and wife as tenants by the entirety, a notice of intention to hold a mechanic's lien which named only the husband as owner sufficiently complied with the statute. Beneficial Fin. Co. v. Wegmiller Bender Lumber Co., 75 Ind. Dec. 71, 402 N.E.2d 41 (Ind. App.), rehearing denied, 403 N.E.2d 1150, 76 Ind. Dec. 52 (Ind. App. 1980).

Time for Filing.

Notice by a contractor to the owner had to be filed within 60 days after the completion of the building. City of Crawfordsville v. Brundage, 57 Ind. 262 (1877).

For all work done or materials furnished for the entire structure, the notice could have been filed within 60 days after the completion of the work or building. Hamilton v. Naylor, 72 Ind. 171 (1880); Lawton v. Case, 73 Ind. 60 (1880); Thomas v. Kiblinger, 77 Ind. 85 (1881); Stephenson v. Ballard, 82 Ind. 87 (1882); Patton v. Matter, 21 Ind. App. 277, 52 N.E. 173 (1898).

When only a portion of the materials was furnished or labor was performed on a building by a person, he had to file his notice within 60 days after furnishing the materials or performing the labor. Hamilton v. Naylor, 72 Ind. 171 (1880); Lawton v. Case, 73 Ind. 60 (1880); Thomas v. Kiblinger, 77 Ind. 85 (1881); Sulzer-Vogt Mach. Co. v. Rushville Water Co., 160 Ind. 202, 65 N.E. 583 (1902).

A general allegation that notice of intention to hold a lien was filed "within sixty days after furnishing the material and doing the work" was sufficient and was not controlled by special averments showing that the work was submitted to inspection at an earlier day, if it was also shown that defects were thereby disclosed which postponed its actual completion to the date alleged. Jeffersonville Water Supply Co. v. Riter, 138 Ind. 170, 37 N.E. 652 (1894).

Notice of a mechanic's lien was in time if filed within sixty days after furnishing the last of several lots of material ordered and furnished at different times where they were all supplied under one contract and used in the repair of several buildings constituting one manufacturing plant. Premier Steel Co. v. McElwaine-Richards Co., 144 Ind. 614, 43 N.E. 876 (1896).

Work done by a contractor to remedy a defect in the performance of his work, caused by his own negligence, for which he made no charge, but which was necessary to complete the performance, could have been considered the last work done for the period fixing the time for filing the lien, under the statute giving sixty days after performing the labor or furnishing the material. Conlee v. Clark, 14 Ind. App. 205, 42 N.E. 762, 56 Am. St. R. 298 (1896).

A single notice of intention to hold a mechanic's lien could have been made the basis of acquiring a lien for several different claims held by one assignee, and the notice of intention to hold a lien therefor having been filed within sixty days from the furnishing of the last item, the lien related back to and included the whole account. Trueblood v. Shellhouse, 19 Ind. App. 91, 49 N.E. 47 (1898).

Time for Filing. (Cont'd)

Acceptance of work by owner limited time for filing notice of lien. Sulzer-Vogt Mach. Co. v. Rushville Water Co., 160 Ind. 202, 65 N.E. 583 (1902).

Where the time had elapsed for filing a mechanic's lien against real estate for labor and material furnished by claimant for the construction of tanks on the land, the insertion of bricks in the tanks by the lien-claimant's employee after expiration of the time in which to assert a lien did not give the right to assert a lien. Chapman-Stein Co. v. Lippincott Glass Co., 87 Ind. App. 411, 161 N.E. 645 (1928).

Where notice of a mechanic's lien was filed within the period prescribed by statute, the fact that it was not filed within 60 days of the contract date for the completion of the work was immaterial. Robertson v. Sertell, 88 Ind. App. 591, 161 N.E. 669 (1928).

In the trial of an action to foreclose a mechanic's lien for materials furnished to be used in the construction of a house and garage, the larger part of the materials having been furnished to the contractor, and the remainder to the owner, the question whether the materials were furnished under a single contract or under separate contracts with the contractor and owner was a question of fact, and the evidence was held to show two contracts. Kendallville Lumber Co. v. Adams, 93 Ind. App. 141, 176 N.E. 555 (1931).

Where a contractor abandoned the work and it was completed by the owner, the latter purchasing materials from the same materialman, the time for filing notice of lien for the materials furnished to the contractor could not have been extended by tacking together the two accounts of the contractor and the owner. Kendallville Lumber Co. v. Adams, 93 Ind App. 141, 176 N.E. 555 (1931).

Before plaintiff would have been entitled to recover in action to foreclose mechanic's lien, he had to make a prima facie showing of compliance with this section in that his lien was filed within the statutory period. Ellis v. Auch, 124 Ind. App. 454, 118 N.E.2d 809 (1954).

Where the time elapsed for the filing of a mechanic's lien for labor and material furnished, claimant could not revive the limitation period by the doing of some act incidental thereto. Ellis v. Auch, 124 Ind. App. 454, 118 N.E.2d 809 (1954).

Where a contractor on July 30 performed additional work in response to the owner's complaint and refusal to pay and thereafter, on September 23 filed a notice of intent to hold a mechanic's lien, the trial court properly concluded that the lien was filed within 60 days of the date that the last materials and labor were expended on the job and thus the lien was timely filed. Gooch v. Hiatt, 166 Ind.

App. 521, 49 Ind. Dec. 490, 337 N.E.2d 585 (1975).

The 60-day period is computed from the date of the last furnishing of materials sold for use in constructing the particular improvement which the owner of the real estate has authorized, and which are in fact used in that construction. Van Wells v. Stanray Corp., 168 Ind. App. 35, 51 Ind. Dec. 143, 341 N.E.2d 198 (1976); Stanray Corp. v. Horizon Constr., Inc., 168 Ind. App. 164, 51 Ind. Dec. 294, 342 N.E.2d 645 (1976).

Provisions of former IC 32-8-3-3 (repealed; see this section for similar provisions) and not former IC 32-8-3-1 applied to the time for filing notice of intention to hold mechanic's lien where purpose for which materials were supplied was for construction of child day care center although it was to be constructed as an addition to a private one-family residence. Wiggin v. Gee Co., 179 Ind. App. 631, 68 Ind. Dec. 151, 386 N.E.2d 1218 (1979).

It is a generally recognized rule of law that where the time has elapsed for the filing of a mechanic's lien for labor and material furnished by a claimant, such claimant cannot revive the limitation period by the doing of some act incidental thereto. Contech Architects & Eng'rs, Inc. v. Courshon, 180 Ind. App. 77, 68 Ind. Dec. 306, 387 N.E.2d 464 (1979).

Where plaintiff did not clearly prove that work was done within the 60-day period, decision of trial judge denying the lien was proper. Contech Architects & Eng'rs, Inc. v. Courshon, 180 Ind. App. 77, 68 Ind. Dec. 306, 387 N.E.2d 464 (1979).

A subcontractor completes its work, and the 60-day period for filing a notice of intention to hold mechanic's lien commences, when the subcontractor finishes the task for which it was hired, not when it comes to pick up tools left at the job. Riddle v. Newton Crane Serv., Inc., 661 N.E.2d 6 (Ind. App. 1996).

Where an engineer believed that he had fulfilled his obligations under a contract by January, the filing of a mechanic's lien in May could not appropriately be based upon services performed in March, and the trial court erred in finding that the lien was timely filed. Abbey Villas Dev. Corp. v. Site Contractors, Inc., 716 N.E.2d 91 (Ind. App. 1999).

A notice of intention to hold mechanic's lien was not timely filed as to any work done by the plaintiff where the only work performed by the plaintiff within the 60 days prior to the filing of the notice was on a piece of portable equipment that was not a fixture. Dinsmore v. Lake Elec. Co., 719 N.E.2d 1282 (Ind. App. 1999).

—Separate Contracts.

Where labor or materials are furnished under separate contracts, even though the contracts are between the same persons, and

Time for Filing. (Cont'd)

—Separate Contracts. (Cont'd)
relate to the same building or improvement, the contracts cannot be tacked together to enlarge the time for filing a lien for what was done or furnished under either, but a lien must be filed for what was done under each contract within the statutory period after its completion. Wavetek Ind., Inc. v. K.H. Gatewood Steel Co., 458 N.E.2d 265 (Ind. App. 1984).

Where the court found that there were contracts for each of five subdivisions, not one for all five, the fact that most of the work on one of the subdivisions was completed more than sixty days prior to the filing of a creditor's notice of intent resulted in a finding that the notice was not filed timely with respect to work completed prior to that date. Greenland Homes, Inc. v. E & S Mktg. Resources, Inc., 227 Bankr. 710 (Bankr. S.D. Ind. 1998).

—Work Incidental to Contract.
The 60 day period cannot be extended through the performance of an act incidental to the contract, and the right to a mechanic's lien cannot be revived through the performance of some act incidental to the work which is not done with the intention of completing the job. Abbey Villas Dev. Corp. v. Site Contractors, Inc., 716 N.E.2d 91 (Ind. App. 1999).

Transfer of Title.
Allowance of a timely filed mechanic's lien to have been nullified by a subsequent transfer or lien would have defeated the purposes and intent of the statute. Dallas Co. v. William Tobias Studios, Inc., 162 Ind. App. 213, 44 Ind. Dec. 487, 318 N.E.2d 568 (1974).

Waiver.
Genuine issue of material fact existed as to whether mechanic's liens were waived where natural gas storage company agreed to pay contractor in consideration for contractor's waiver of mechanic's liens, but money was not paid until almost eight months after the waiver was executed and four months after the liens had been filed. McCartin McAuliffe Mechanical Contractor v. Midwest Gas Storage, Inc., 685 N.E.2d 165 (Ind. App. 1997).

Collateral References. Sufficiency of notice, claim or statement of mechanic's lien with respect to nature of work. 27 A.L.R.2d 1169.

Sale of real property as affecting time for filing notice or perfecting mechanic's lien as against purchaser's interest. 76 A.L.R.2d 1163.

Time for filing notice or claim of mechanic's lien where claimant has contracted with general contractor and later contracts directly with owner. 78 A.L.R.2d 1165.

Amendment of statement of claim of mechanic's lien as to designation of owner of property. 81 A.L.R.2d 681.

Abandonment of construction or of contract as affecting time for filing mechanic's liens or time for giving notice to owner. 52 A.L.R.3d 797.

32-28-3-4. Liens filed before March 10, 1967. — Any otherwise valid and enforceable statement and notice of intention to hold a lien filed before March 10, 1967, is valid and enforceable. [P.L.2-2002, § 13.]

32-28-3-5. "Lender" defined — Recording of statement and notice of intention — Priority among mechanic's liens — Priority of mortgage lender. — (a) As used in this section, "lender" refers to:

(1) an individual;

(2) a supervised financial organization (as defined in IC 24-4.5-1-301);

(3) an insurance company or a pension fund; or

(4) any other entity that has the authority to make loans.

(b) The recorder shall record the statement and notice of intention to hold a lien when presented under section 3 [IC 32-28-3-3] of this chapter in the miscellaneous record book. The recorder shall charge a fee for recording the statement and notice in accordance with IC 36-2-7-10. When the statement and notice of intention to hold a lien is recorded, the lien is created. The recorded lien relates back to the date the mechanic or other person began to perform the labor or furnish the materials or machinery. Except as provided in subsections (c) and (d), a lien created under this chapter has priority over a lien created after it.

(c) The lien of a mechanic or materialman does not have priority over the lien of another mechanic or materialman.

(d) The mortgage of a lender has priority over all liens created under this chapter that are recorded after the date the mortgage was recorded, to the extent of the funds actually owed to the lender for the specific project to which the lien rights relate. This subsection does not apply to a lien that relates to a construction contract for the development, construction, alteration, or repair of the following:

(1) A Class 2 structure (as defined in IC 22-12-1-5).

(2) An improvement on the same real estate auxiliary to a Class 2 structure (as defined in IC 22-12-1-5).

(3) Property that is:

(A) owned, operated, managed, or controlled by:

(i) a public utility (as defined in IC 8-1-2-1);

(ii) a municipally owned utility (as defined in IC 8-1-2-1);

(iii) a joint agency (as defined in IC 8-1-2.2-2);

(iv) a rural electric membership corporation formed under IC 8-1-13-4;

(v) a rural telephone cooperative corporation formed under IC 8-1-17; or

(vi) a not-for-profit utility (as defined in IC 8-1-2-125);

regulated under IC 8; and

(B) intended to be used and useful for the production, transmission, delivery, or furnishing of heat, light, water, telecommunications services, or power to the public. [P.L.2-2002, § 13; P.L.101-2002, § 6.]

Amendments. The 2002 amendment by P.L.101-2002, amending this section as enacted by P.L.2-2002, added subsection (d)(3)(A)(v), and made a related change; redesignated former subsection (d)(3)(A)(v) as (d)(3)(A)(vi); and inserted "telecommunications services" in subsection (d)(3)(B).

Effective Dates. P.L.101-2002, § 6. July 1, 2002.

NOTES TO DECISIONS

Builders & Mfrs. Ass'n, 109 Ind. 351, 9 N.E. 177 (1886); Neeley v. Searight, 113 Ind. 316, 15 N.E. 598 (1888); Albrecht v. C.C. Foster Lumber Co., 126 Ind. 318, 26 N.E. 157 (1890); Newhouse v. Morgan, 127 Ind. 436, 26 N.E. 158 (1891); Parker v. Dillingham, 129 Ind. 542, 29 N.E. 23 (1891); Quaack v. Schmid, 131 Ind. 185, 30 N.E. 514 (1892); Hubbard v. Moore, 132 Ind. 178, 31 N.E. 534 (1892); Adams v. Shaffer, 132 Ind. 331, 31 N.E. 1108 (1892).

Act of 1883.

The Act of 1883 requiring personal notice to the owner of property in order to obtain a lien was repealed by Acts 1891, ch. 26, p. 28. Such act was construed by the cases of Vinton v.

Construction.

The priority provisions of the former Mechanics' Lien Law (see this chapter for similar provisions) and of the former Employees' Lien Law (see IC 32-28-12 for similar provisions)

Construction. (Cont'd)

were in irreconcilable conflict, and, since the Mechanics' Lien Law was enacted many years later than the Employees' Lien Law, and made an exception to the general priority granted by the earlier act, the latter act had to prevail where the lien right had been properly perfected and enforced thereunder. Watson v. Strohl, 220 Ind. 672, 46 N.E.2d 204 (1943).

Failure to Margin.

Failure to margin mechanic's liens did not invalidate the liens; natural gas storage company could not defeat the validity of contractor's liens by claiming that hypothetical third parties were not given sufficient notice of the liens claimed, where contractor failed to properly cross reference each oil and gas lease or easement involved. McCartin McAuliffe Mechanical Contractor v. Midwest Gas Storage, Inc., 685 N.E.2d 165 (Ind. App. 1997).

Filing Without Recording.

Liens were created by the filing of notices with the recorder, whether the notices were recorded or not. Adams v. Buhler, 131 Ind. 66, 30 N.E. 883 (1892); Adams v. Shaffer, 132 Ind. 331, 31 N.E. 1108 (1892); Northwestern Loan & Inv. Ass'n v. McPherson, 23 Ind. App. 250, 54 N.E. 130 (1899).

Where notice of intention to hold a lien was filed by a mechanic or materialman as provided by law, the failure of the recorder to record it in the miscellaneous record as required, did not defeat the priority of the lien as against the holder of an intervening mortgage. Northwestern Loan & Inv. Ass'n v. McPherson, 23 Ind. App. 250, 54 N.E. 130 (1899).

Priorities.

The lien related to the time when work was commenced, or the time when materials were begun to be furnished, and had priority over subsequent liens. Fleming v. Bumgarner, 29 Ind. 424 (1868); Mark v. Murphy, 76 Ind. 534 (1881); Zehner v. Johnston, 22 Ind. App. 452, 53 N.E. 1080 (1899); Krotz v. A.R. Beck Lumber Co., 34 Ind. App. 577, 73 N.E. 273 (1905).

Where one acquired a mortgage lien on property with knowledge of the uses and purposes to which such property was applied by the owner, and with notice that under the statute the mortgaged property was subject to after acquired liens for labor and material or, in case of failing circumstances of mortgagor, to claims which would have been preferred debts, whether notice of liens should have been filed or not, such statutory provisions entered into and formed a part of the mortgage, and the mortgage lien was subject to such statutory liens as might thereafter attach to the property. Thorpe Block Sav. &

Loan Ass'n v. James, 13 Ind. App. 522, 41 N.E. 978 (1895); Carriger v. Mackey, 15 Ind. App. 392, 44 N.E. 266 (1896); Building & Loan Ass'n v. Coburn, 150 Ind. 684, 50 N.E. 885 (1898); Deming-Colborn Lumber Co. v. Union Nat'l Sav. & Loan Ass'n, 151 Ind. 463, 51 N.E. 936 (1898); Stoermer v. People's Sav. Bank, 152 Ind. 104, 52 N.E. 606 (1899); Zehner v. Johnston, 22 Ind. App. 452, 53 N.E. 1080 (1899).

Rights of parties and priority of liens when a mortgage was executed upon the land during the construction of a building, and materials were furnished and labor performed both before and after the execution of the mortgage was fixed by law. Ward v. Yarnelle, 173 Ind. 535, 91 N.E. 7 (1910), overruled on other grounds, Moore-Mansfield Constr. Co. v. Indianapolis, N.C. & T. Ry., 179 Ind. 356, 101 N.E. 296 (1913).

Mechanics' liens for work and materials furnished under contract before a mortgage to secure the money used in paying for work and materials was executed were of equal priority with one another and with the mortgage lien. McLaughlin Mill Supply Co. v. Laundry Serv., Inc., 95 Ind. App. 693, 184 N.E. 429 (1933).

A purchase-price mortgage, designated as a second mortgage, was junior to a mortgage executed on the same day for money used in paying for work and materials on the realty covered by the mortgages. McLaughlin Mill Supply Co. v. Laundry Serv., Inc., 95 Ind. App. 693, 184 N.E. 429 (1933).

In an equitable receivership proceeding, mechanic's lien claimants were not entitled to priority in the absence of allegations and proof that their liens had been determined and adjudicated or that their claims of liens were pending and unadjudicated and undetermined in suits brought in the state court in apt time, for the purpose of enforcing and foreclosing their liens. Torrington Co. v. Sidway-Topliff Co., 70 F.2d 949 (7th Cir. 1934).

In an equity receivership proceeding, a city and county were not entitled to priority of payment for taxes insofar as said taxes became a lien and were payable after the time fixed for filing claims with receivers. Torrington Co. v. Sidway-Topliff Co., 70 F.2d 949 (7th Cir. 1934).

Where each of two holders of mechanics' liens of the same class forclosed his lien on the same property without making the other a party defendant, and one of them brought suit in ejectment and to quiet title against the other lienholder, and the other filed a cross-complaint to quiet his title to the property purchased at foreclosure sale, as between the lienholders, the court properly allocated the remainder of the proceeds of sale of the property, after payment of other claims and interest in the property, in proportion to the

Priorities. (Cont'd)

amount of their respective claims. Hochstetler v. A. Allen Wilkinson Lumber Co., 107 Ind. App. 336, 24 N.E.2d 432 (1940).

A person holding title to real estate acquired through sheriff's sale resulting from foreclosure of corporation employees' liens did not have a claim prior to that of a mechanic's lienhilder because of the fact that the judgment on such corporation employees' liens was rendered prior to the date of the judgments on the mechanics' liens, where such liens had priority over the corporation employees' liens, since a judgment foreclosing a lien related back to the date of the lien. Watson v. Strohl, 220 Ind. 672, 46 N.E.2d 204 (1943).

A money judgment on a mechanic's lien has no priority over a judgment on a mortgage recorded before such judgment on the mechanic's lien was secured where the mortgagee had not been made a party therein. Mitchels Plumbing & Heating Co. v. Whitcomb & Keller Mfg. Co., 154 Ind. App. 63, 33 Ind. Dec. 458, 289 N.E.2d 138 (1972).

It was proper to grant priority to lien of materialman over that of mortgagee where materials were supplied prior to the time the property was mortgaged although the notice of lien was not given until thereafter. Beneficial Fin. Co. v. Wegmiller Bender Lumber Co., 75 Ind. Dec. 71, 402 N.E.2d 41 (Ind. App.), rehearing denied, 403 N.E.2d 1150, 76 Ind. Dec. 52 (Ind. App. 1980).

A mechanic's lien perfected prior to date of bankruptcy is, generally speaking, superior to the claim of the trustee under § 70(c)(3) of the Bankruptcy Act, former 11 U.S.C. § 110(c)(3) (now see 11 U.S.C. § 544(a)). In re Hull, 19 Bankr. 501 (Bankr. N.D. Ind. 1982).

Generally, mechanics' liens relate back in time to when materials or labor are initially furnished for construction and have priority over all liens subsequently created. Where mechanics' lien claimants have notice of a mortgage wherein the money derived from the loan is used in the construction of the improvements, the mortgage lien and mechanics' liens have equal priority. Brenneman Mechanical & Elec., Inc. v. First Nat'l Bank, 495 N.E.2d 233 (Ind. App. 1986).

Where the release of an old mortgage and the execution of a new one appear to be part of one transaction, and the new mortgage is taken and recorded simultaneously with the release of the old mortgage, the recording of the new and the cancellation of the old mortgage constitute a contemporaneous act. Under such circumstances, equity keeps the lien of the first mortgage alive for the benefit of the mortgagee. Brenneman Mechanical & Elec., Inc. v. First Nat'l Bank, 495 N.E.2d 233 (Ind. App. 1986).

Mortgage lien and the mechanic's liens of record were entitled to equal priority, except to the extent that the debtor had defenses against a lien due to possible counterclaims and rights to setoff, since the clearly stated purpose of the mortgage loan was for the construction of improvements on the property and the mechanic's lienholders who had no prior obligation to perform services or furnish supplies to the debtor should have known that the loan proceeds would be used to pay for the improvements. Venture Properties, Inc. v. Altite Roofing, Inc., 139 Bankr. 890 (Bankr. N.D. Ind. 1990).

A properly recorded and perfected mechanic's lien takes priority over a mortgage which is executed before labor or materials are first furnished for the property but recorded after labor or materials are first furnished. Greyhound Fin. Corp. v. R.L.C., Inc., 637 N.E.2d 1325 (Ind. App. 1994).

—Mechanic's Lien Over Mortgage.

Where a mortgage was executed before but not recorded until after the date a mechanic's lienholder began to furnish labor and materials, the mechanic's lien took priority, since the date on which a mortgage is recorded is dispositive for determining its priority with respect to a mechanic's lien. Eyster v. S.A. Birnbaum Contracting, Inc., 662 N.E.2d 201 (Ind. App. 1996).

—Relation Back.

Mechanic's lien statute (formerly IC 32-8-3, repealed; now see this chapter for similar provisions) unambiguously refers to the specific mechanic or other person that installed the labor and/or materials for which the mechanic's lien is claimed and does not refer to any mechanic or other person who performed any work under any contract which would permit the lien of a party that continued work of another party to relate back to the date the prior party began the work. PCL/Calumet v. Entercitement, LLC, 760 N.E.2d 633 (Ind. App. 2001).

Proof of Filing and Recording.

Where material was furnished to a contractor, the notice of an intention to acquire a mechanic's lien, given pursuant to law, did not need to contain a recital showing that notice had also been given to the owner in accordance with the law. In an action to foreclose the lien, however, it had to be averred in the complaint and proved on the trial that such notice was given. Adams v. Shaffer, 132 Ind. 331, 31 N.E. 1108 (1892).

When Deemed Recorded.

Notices were deemed recorded from the time of filing the same with the recorder. Wilson v. Hopkins, 51 Ind. 231 (1875); North-

When Deemed Recorded. (Cont'd)
western Loan & Inv. Ass'n v. McPherson, 23 Ind. App. 250, 54 N.E. 130 (1899).

Where Recorded.
The notice had to be recorded in the miscellaneous record book. Adams v. Buhler, 131 Ind. 66, 30 N.E. 883 (1892). See Wilson v.

Logue, 131 Ind. 191, 30 N.E. 1079 (1892); Adams v. Shaffer, 132 Ind. 331, 31 N.E. 1108 (1892).

As between the original parties, the recording of the notice in the wrong book was immaterial. Adams v. Shaffer, 132 Ind. 331, 31 N.E. 1108 (1892).

Collateral References. Priority as between mechanic's lien and purchase-money mortgage. 73 A.L.R.2d 1407.
Priority as between mechanic's lien and mortgage not providing for future advances

executed before effective date of mechanic's lien, as affected by fact that proceeds of the mortgage were paid, in whole or part after that date. 80 A.L.R.2d 179.

32-28-3-6. Enforcement of lien — Foreclosure. — (a) A person may enforce a lien by filing a complaint in the circuit or superior court of the county where the real estate or property that is the subject of the lien is situated. The complaint must be filed not later than one (1) year after:
(1) the date the statement and notice of intention to hold a lien was recorded under section 3 [IC 32-28-3-3] of this chapter; or
(2) subject to subsection (c), the expiration of the credit, if a credit is given.
(b) Except as provided in subsection (c), if a lien is not enforced within the time set forth in subsection (a), the lien is void.
(c) A credit does not extend the time for filing an action to enforce the lien under subsection (a)(2) unless:
(1) the terms of the credit are in writing;
(2) the credit was executed by:
(A) the lienholder; and
(B) all owners of record; and
(3) the credit was recorded:
(A) in the same manner as the original statement and notice of intention to hold a lien; and
(B) not later than one (1) year after the date the statement and notice of intention to hold a lien was recorded.
(d) If the lien is foreclosed under this chapter, the court rendering judgment shall order a sale to be made of the property subject to the lien. The officers making the sale shall sell the property without any relief from valuation or appraisement laws. [P.L.2-2002, § 13.]

Cross References. Limitations as to liens and actions to enforce mechanics' liens, IC 32-28-7-1, IC 32-28-7-2.

Lien on mine and royalties, enforcement, IC 22-10-11-16.

NOTES TO DECISIONS

In general.
Application of proceeds.
Arbitration.
Assignment of claim.

Bankruptcy of general contractor.
Commencement.
Complaint.
—Amendment.
—Amount due.
—Contract for work.

—Cross-complaints.
—Description of property.
—Filing of notice.
—Owner.
—Sufficient.
—Use of material.
Construction.
Demand for payment.
Destruction of building.
Election of remedies.
Estoppel.
Federal law.
Jurisdiction of courts.
Limitation of actions.
—In general.
—Counterclaim.
Notice.
Parties.
Setoff.
Survival of actions.
Trial.
—Findings.
—Judgment.
—Jury trial.
Waiver of lien.

In General.

No personal liability existed in favor of laborers or materialmen as against school corporations. Jefferies v. Myers, 9 Ind. App. 563, 37 N.E. 301 (1894).

A lien taken under contract made with individuals for erection of building and transfer of property to a corporation could have been enforced notwithstanding the fact the corporation never assumed the liability of the subscribers. Davis & Rankin Bldg. & Mfg. Co. v. Vice, 15 Ind. App. 117, 43 N.E. 889 (1896).

Where a receiver who had leased property by order of court thereafter accepted a surrender of the lease with the approval of the court, persons holding liens on the property for work and labor performed for lessee could not enforce their claims by the sale of the property in the hands of the receiver, but the court had equity power to order the payment of the claims by the receiver. McAnally v. Glidden, 30 Ind. App. 22, 65 N.E. 291 (1902).

The validity, existence, and enforceability of a mechanic's lien could only have been adjudicated by proceedings in courts of law for the determination and foreclosure thereof on the real estate. Torrington Co. v. Sidway-Topliff Co., 70 F.2d 949 (7th Cir. 1934).

IC 34-1-45-2, which provided that judgments were a lien upon real estate and chattels real in the county where, and only where, such judgment had been duly entered and indexed in the judgment docket from and after the time the same was entered and indexed by the clerk in the judgment docket as provided by law, was not applicable to judgments enforcing a mechanic's lien, except insofar as such a judgment included a judg-

ment for the recovery of money or costs and thereby gave a general lien on all of the property of the judgment defendant. Watson v. Strohl, 220 Ind. 672, 46 N.E.2d 204 (1943).

Application of Proceeds.

If a portion of the lands were conveyed, payments made on the claims should have been applied to the satisfaction of the liens on such conveyed lands. Dungan v. Dollman, 64 Ind. 327 (1878).

Mechanics' liens acquired subsequent to mortgage were not superior so far as the land was concerned, as no change in the law relative to the rights of mortgagees was effected by statutory enactment, save as to the buildings. Thorpe Block Sav. & Loan Ass'n v. James, 13 Ind. App. 522, 41 N.E. 978 (1895).

A mechanic's lien was not affected by the appointment of a receiver for the property, and upon the sale of the property by the receiver the lien attached to the proceeds of the sale. Totten & Hogg Iron & Steel Foundry Co. v. Muncie Nail Co., 148 Ind. 372, 47 N.E. 703 (1897).

A lienor, in event of insufficiency of funds, was entitled to no more than his pro rata share of the fund, regardless of the form his action might have assumed. Kline v. Hammond Mach. & Forge Works, 76 Ind. App. 573, 127 N.E. 220 (1920).

Arbitration.

A building contract that required the parties to submit questions in dispute to the architect was valid, and such submission, or a valid excuse, was a condition precedent to the maintenance of an action, but a provision that such architect's decision was final was void as against public policy. Maitland v. Reed, 37 Ind. App. 469, 77 N.E. 290 (1906).

Assignment of Claim.

A contractor by assignment of a building contract did not lose his right to enforce his lien, the assignee having been made a party defendant and having acquiesced and disclaimed all interest in the contract. Shapiro v. Schultz, 32 Ind. App. 219, 68 N.E. 184 (1903).

Bankruptcy of General Contractor.

Because the debtor-contractor was not a necessary party to the foreclosure action, the lienors would not have violated the automatic stay by commencing their action to enforce their liens and therefore, the time period in this section (formerly IC 32-8-3-6, repealed; now see this section for similar provisions) was not tolled by the bankruptcy of the debtor-contractor. Deluxe Sheet Metal, Inc. v. Plymouth Plastics, Inc., 555 N.E.2d 1296 (Ind. App. 1990), cert. denied, 502 U.S. 819, 112 S. Ct. 77, 116 L. Ed. 2d 50 (1991).

Commencement.

Complaint must be filed and summons issued prior to expiration of the one-year period. Valley View Dev. Corp. v. Cheugh & Schlegel of Dayton, Inc., 151 Ind. App. 450, 30 Ind. Dec. 16, 280 N.E.2d 319 (1972) (decision on facts arising before adoption of TR. 3 which provides that an action is commenced by filing a complaint).

Complaint.

—Amendment.

A complaint to enforce a mechanic's lien could have been amended so as to show that the building was erected on a different lot from the one described in the notice. Hillyard v. Robbins, 53 Ind. App. 107, 101 N.E. 341 (1913).

—Amount Due.

The complaint should have shown the amount that was due. City of Crawfordsville v. Irwin, 46 Ind. 438 (1874).

—Contract for Work.

The facts stated should have been sufficient to show a contract for doing work or furnishing materials, and that the work was done or materials were furnished under the contract. Stephenson v. Ballard, 50 Ind. 176 (1875); Adams v. Buhler, 116 Ind. 100, 18 N.E. 269 (1888).

It had to be shown by the complaint that the person to whom the materials were furnished had authority to erect the building. Ogg v. Tate, 52 Ind. 159 (1875).

—Cross-Complaints.

In action to quiet title, cross-complaint for foreclosure of mechanic's lien was held insufficient on demurrer. National Brick Co. v. Russell, 99 Ind. App. 53, 190 N.E. 614 (1934).

The courts had to treat the appellant's cross-complaint as a separate and distinct pleading, unaided by other pleadings in the case, and if it appeared on its face that it was not filed within one year from the time when notice of the lien was recorded, said lien was null and void. Grimm v. Rhoades, 129 Ind. App. 1, 149 N.E.2d 847 (1958).

—Description of Property.

The property should have been described in the complaint. City of Crawfordsville v. Barr, 65 Ind. 367 (1879).

—Filing of Notice.

The complaint had to show that the proper notice was filed. Sharpe v. Clifford, 44 Ind. 346 (1873); City of Crawfordsville v. Barr, 45 Ind. 258 (1873); City of Crawfordsville v. Irwin, 46 Ind. 438 (1874); City of Crawfordsville v. Brundage, 57 Ind. 262

(1877); City of Crawfordsville v. Boots, 76 Ind. 32 (1881).

The original notice, or a copy thereof, had to be filed with the complaint. Scott v. Goldinhorst, 123 Ind. 268, 24 N.E. 333 (1890); Davis v. McMillan, 13 Ind. App. 424, 41 N.E. 851 (1895).

Complaint was sufficient after judgment where it had been averred that the notice had been filed in less than 60 days after the materials had been furnished. Hubbard v. Moore, 132 Ind. 178, 31 N.E. 534 (1892); Indiana Mut. Bldg. & Loan Ass'n v. Paxton, 18 Ind. App. 304, 47 N.E. 1082 (1897).

Notice given to owner to render him personally liable did not need to have been made part of a complaint to enforce the lien. Adamson v. Shaner, 3 Ind. App. 448, 29 N.E. 944 (1892).

In an action to foreclose a mechanic's lien, it was not prejudicial error to strike out a paragraph of answer alleging that the cause of action was barred by the statute of limitations, since plaintiff, in order to be successful, was required to bring himself within the provisions of the statute relating to the enforcement of mechanic's liens, one provision having been that the complaint had to be filed within one year from the time when the notice of the lien had been received for recording, and it was shown that the complaint was so filed within the year. George v. Williams, 109 Ind. App. 623, 37 N.E.2d 21 (1941).

—Owner.

The complaint had to show who owned the land when the building was erected. Adams v. Buhler, 116 Ind. 100, 18 N.E. 269 (1888).

—Sufficient.

If it was shown that the work was accepted, with a promise to pay therefor, a complaint in an action to enforce a mechanic's lien was sufficient even if it failed to show a complete compliance with the terms of the original contract. Vorhees v. Beckwell, 10 Ind. App. 224, 37 N.E. 811 (1894).

Personal liability shown by facts stated in complaint would have made a complaint good. Clark v. Maxwell, 12 Ind. App. 199, 40 N.E. 274 (1895); Chicago & S.E. Ry. v. Woodard, 159 Ind. 541, 65 N.E. 577 (1902).

—Use of Material.

The complaint in an action to enforce a lien for materials had to allege that the materials were furnished for, and used, in the buildings. City of Crawfordsville v. Barr, 45 Ind. 258 (1873); Hill v. Braden, 54 Ind. 72 (1876); Hill v. Ryan, 54 Ind. 118 (1876); Crawford v. Crockett, 55 Ind. 220 (1876); Talbott v. Goddard, 55 Ind. 496 (1876); City of Crawfordsville v. Brundage, 57 Ind. 262

Complaint. (Cont'd)

—Use of Material. (Cont'd)
(1877); Leeper v. Myers, 10 Ind. App. 314, 37 N.E. 1070 (1894).

The complaint was sufficient having averred that the defendants had purchased of the plaintiffs "certain building materials" which were delivered at the building for the purpose of being used in the erection and construction of the same. Manor v. Heffner, 15 Ind. App. 299, 43 N.E. 1011 (1896).

Construction.
The statutes providing for the mechanic's lien and its enforcement were in derogation of the common law and had to be strictly construed, and anyone who sought their benefits had to bring himself within their provisions. Grimm v. Rhoades, 129 Ind. App. 1, 149 N.E.2d 847 (1958).

Demand for Payment.
Demand for payment before suit was not necessary, and payment after suit had to include costs and attorney fees. Duckwall v. Jones, 156 Ind. 682, 58 N.E. 1055, 60 N.E. 797 (1900).

Destruction of Building.
Where a building on which the contractor had expended more than he had received was accidentally destroyed before completion, the payments made by the owner which had gone into the property had to have been treated as an execution of the contract pro tanto, leaving the loss thereof to have fallen upon the owner. Krause v. Board of Trustees, 162 Ind. 278, 70 N.E. 264, 65 L.R.A. 111, 102 Am. St. R. 203, 1 Ann. Cas. 460 (1904).

Election of Remedies.
Persons could enforce liens without first pursuing their remedies against persons personally liable for the claims. Andis v. Davis, 63 Ind. 17 (1878).

Parties seeking to enforce mechanics' liens had to pursue the method provided by statute. Farmers' Loan & Trust Co. v. Canada & St. L. Ry., 127 Ind. 250, 26 N.E. 784, 11 L.R.A. 740 (1891). See also National Brick Co. v. Russell, 99 Ind. App. 53, 190 N.E. 614 (1934).

Estoppel.
Estoppel of owner to prevent enforcement of lien for improvements made on land in the possession of another person was upheld due to owner's conduct. Lengelsen v. McGregor, 162 Ind. 258, 67 N.E. 524 (1903), reh'g overruled, 162 Ind. 266, 70 N.E. 248 (1904).

Federal Law.
Indiana's mechanic's lien laws are not preempted by the Natural Gas Policy Act of 1978, 15 U.S.C. §§ 3301-3432. McCartin McAuliffe Mechanical Contractor v. Midwest Gas Storage, Inc., 685 N.E.2d 165 (Ind. App. 1997).

Jurisdiction of Courts.
There having been no provision in the statute establishing the jurisdiction of a probate court for the foreclosure of a mechanic's lien and the mechanic's lien law specifically placing such jurisdiction in the circuit and superior courts, the Marion County Probate Court had no such jurisdiction. Demma v. Forbes Lumber Co., 133 Ind. App. 204, 178 N.E.2d 455 (1961), reh'g denied, 133 Ind. App. 204, 181 N.E.2d 253 (1962).

In the opinion of the Appellate Court (Court of Appeals), the Marion County Probate Court did not have jurisdiction in a cause involving a mechanic's lien, and its proceedings in the matter were not merely erroneous but were in all respects void, the sections creating such court not having conferred such jurisdiction upon the court, jurisdiction having been vested in a circuit or superior court of the county where the property was situated. Demma v. Forbes Lumber Co., 133 Ind. App. 204, 181 N.E.2d 253 (1961).

Limitation of Actions.

—In General.
The action had to be commenced within the time specified by the statute. Close v. Hunt, 8 Blackf. 254 (1846); Schneider v. Kolthoff, 59 Ind. 568 (1877); Hamilton v. Naylor, 72 Ind. 171 (1880).

An action to enforce a lien had to be commenced within the time fixed by statute in order to obtain priority as against assignees. Kulp v. Chamberlin, 4 Ind. App. 560, 31 N.E. 376 (1892).

It was only necessary to file a complaint to enforce the lien within a year from the time of filing notice of the lien. Carriger v. Mackey, 15 Ind. App. 392, 44 N.E. 266 (1896); Moore-Mansfield Constr. Co. v. Indianapolis, N. & T. Ry., 179 Ind. 356, 101 N.E. 296, 44 L.R.A. (n.s.) 816, 1915D Ann. Cas. 917 (1913).

Failure to enforce lien within time fixed by statute did not affect other lienholders. Union Nat'l Sav. & Loan Ass'n v. Helberg, 152 Ind. 139, 51 N.E. 916 (1898); Deming-Colborn Lumber Co. v. Union Nat'l Sav. & Loan Ass'n, 151 Ind. 463, 51 N.E. 936 (1898); Stoermer v. People's Sav. Bank, 152 Ind. 104, 52 N.E. 606 (1899).

Amendment of complaint could have been made after expiration of time fixed for enforcing lien. Trueblood v. Shellhouse, 19 Ind. App. 91, 49 N.E. 47 (1898).

Persons who were given preference liens without filing notices when debtors were in failing circumstances were required to enforce their liens within one year, the same as

Limitation of Actions. (Cont'd)

—In General. (Cont'd)
other liens acquired by mechanics. Smith v. Tate, 30 Ind. App. 367, 66 N.E. 88 (1902).

The statute requiring actions to enforce mechanic's lien to have been commenced within a year from the time of recording notice of the lien did not apply where the property had passed into the hands of a receiver and had been sold before the expiration of the year, and claims were filed within the time fixed by the court. Randall v. Wagner Glass Co., 47 Ind. App. 439, 94 N.E. 739 (1911).

Benefit of notice of lien and claim of lien was lost unless suit was filed within one year. Torrington Co. v. Sidway-Topliff Co., 70 F.2d 949 (7th Cir. 1934).

—Counterclaim.
Where a bank argued that a mechanics' lien should be subordinated to all other liens due to the lienholder's failure to foreclose its lien within one year from the date of recording as required by this section, it was held that Rule TR. 13(J) removed the statute of limitations' one year bar, as the lienholder had filed a counterclaim to foreclose its lien which was a claim of priority that resulted in diminishing the bank's claim. Brenneman Mechanical & Elec., Inc. v. First Nat'l Bank, 495 N.E.2d 233 (Ind. App. 1986).

Notice.
Where all persons having an interest in the property were not served, the court could not order a sale of any interest in the property which such persons possess. Fox v. Galvin, 177 Ind. App. 654, 64 Ind. Dec. 654, 381 N.E.2d 103 (1978).

Parties.
The owner of the property when the action was commenced to enforce the lien should have been a party. Marvin v. Taylor, 27 Ind. 73 (1866); Kellenberger v. Boyer, 37 Ind. 188 (1871); Vorhees v. Beckwell, 10 Ind. App. 224, 37 N.E. 811 (1894).

A surety on the bond of a contractor given to secure the payment by him of all debts for materials and labor could not enforce a lien for materials furnished by such surety. McHenry v. Knickerbacker, 128 Ind. 77, 27 N.E. 430 (1891); Miller v. Taggart, 36 Ind. App. 595, 76 N.E. 321 (1905).

In actions by materialmen to enforce liens, the contractor was not a necessary party. Hubbard v. Moore, 132 Ind. 178, 31 N.E. 534 (1892).

In an action to enforce a mechanic's lien against the property of a married woman, the husband was a proper party defendant. Vorhees v. Beckwell, 10 Ind. App. 224, 37 N.E. 811 (1894).

Contractor was not a necessary party defendant where, in the enforcement of a lien, the owner, contractor and materialman agreed that the owner should become the debtor of the materialman and in consideration thereof the materialman's debt against the contractor was to have been released, and the contractor did not controvert such facts. Leeper v. Myers, 10 Ind. App. 314, 37 N.E. 1070 (1894).

Mortgagees had to be made parties or their rights would not have been affected. Union Nat'l Sav. & Loan Ass'n, v. Helberg, 152 Ind. 139, 51 N.E. 916 (1898); Deming-Colborn Lumber Co. v. Union Nat'l Sav. & Loan Ass'n, 151 Ind. 463, 51 N.E. 936 (1898); Stoermer v. People's Sav. Bank, 152 Ind. 104, 52 N.E. 606 (1899).

Plaintiffs whose claims were several could not join in the enforcement of mechanics' liens. Northwestern Loan & Inv. Ass'n v. McPherson, 23 Ind. App. 250, 54 N.E. 130 (1899).

If mortgagees were not made parties to a suit to foreclose a mechanic's lien commenced and judgment obtained within a year, such mortgagees could have enjoined a sale of the property under the foreclosure decree after the expiration of the year. Martin v. Berry, 159 Ind. 566, 64 N.E. 912 (1902).

Persons not made parties to actions to foreclose liens were not affected by the proceedings. Krotz v. A.R. Beck Lumber Co., 34 Ind. App. 577, 73 N.E. 273 (1905).

Setoff.
If a contractor had a claim against a materialman on account of materials furnished, the owner was not entitled to a setoff on account of such claim. Indiana Ry. v. Wadsworth, 29 Ind. App. 586, 64 N.E. 938 (1902).

Survival of Actions.
In an action to foreclose a mechanic's lien by two partners, on the death of one, the action was properly continued in the name of the surviving partner, and, on the death of the surviving partner, his administrator should have been substituted on the filing of a supplemental complaint alleging that such surviving partner had died. Kokomo, F. & W. Traction Co. v. Kokomo Trust Co., 193 Ind. 219, 137 N.E. 763 (1923).

Trial.

—Findings.
A general verdict or finding of the truth of the complaint entitled the plaintiff to a decree enforcing the lien by a sale of the property.

Trial. (Cont'd)

—Findings. (Cont'd)
Nordyke, Marmon & Co. v. Dickson, 76 Ind. 188 (1881).

—Judgment.

A judgment was sufficient when the amount due was stated and the property was ordered sold. Deming v. Patterson, 10 Ind. 251 (1858).

Special finding of facts in an action to enforce liens against several buildings for materials furnished under one contract were sufficient to sustain a judgment in foreclosure for the amount due on each building. Manor v. Heffner, 15 Ind. App. 299, 43 N.E. 1011 (1896).

—Jury Trial.

Actions to enforce mechanics' liens were not triable by jury. Albrecht v. C.C. Foster Lumber Co., 126 Ind. 318, 26 N.E. 157 (1890); Reichert v. Krass, 13 Ind. App. 348, 40 N.E. 706, 41 N.E. 835 (1895); Robertson v. Sertell, 88 Ind. App. 591, 161 N.E. 669 (1928).

Waiver of Lien.

Taking the note of the person owing the debt was not a waiver of the lien unless the note was payable in bank, in which case it was prima facie evidence of a waiver of the lien. Goble v. Gale, 7 Blackf. 218, 41 Am. Dec. 219 (1844); Millikin v. Armstrong, 17 Ind. 456 (1861); Hill v. Sloan, 59 Ind. 181 (1877); Schneider v. Kolthoff, 59 Ind. 568 (1877).

Notes given for debts due mechanics, which were not payable in bank, did not operate as a waiver of the lien in the absence of an express agreement. Rhodes v. Webb-Jameson Co., 19 Ind. App. 195, 49 N.E. 283 (1898).

A contractor could waive the right of himself and those claiming under him to the lien given by statute. Kokomo, F. & W. Traction Co. v. Kokomo Trust Co., 193 Ind. 219, 137 N.E. 763 (1923).

———

Collateral References. Public sale, what constitutes. 4 A.L.R.2d 575.

32-28-3-7. Actions to enforce liens — Sales of property to satisfy liens. — (a) A person whose lien is recorded under this chapter may be a party to an action to enforce a lien.

(b) The court may, by judgment, direct a sale of the land and building for the satisfaction of the liens and costs. The sale shall not prejudice the rights of:

(1) a prior encumbrance; or

(2) an owner or other person who is not a party to the action.

(c) If several actions are brought by different claimants and are pending at the same time, the court may order the actions to be consolidated. [P.L.2-2002, § 13.]

NOTES TO DECISIONS

ANALYSIS

In general.
Application of proceeds.
Consolidation of actions.
Findings.
Judgment.
—Sufficient.
Jury trial.

In General.

Trial courts had the inherent power to consolidate causes in proper cases to expedite the administration of justice. Trusler v. Galambos, 238 Ind. 195, 149 N.E.2d 550 (1958).

Application of Proceeds.

If a portion of the lands were conveyed, payments made on the claims should have been applied to the satisfaction of the liens on such conveyed lands. Dungan v. Dollman, 64 Ind. 327 (1878).

In the application of the proceeds of the sale of the property, the security afforded by a mortgage on the land was benefited by the erection of a building thereon but did not make subsequently perfected mechanic's lien superior thereto so far as the land was concerned, since no change in the law relative to the rights of mortgagees was effected, save as to the buildings. Thorpe Block Sav. & Loan Ass'n v. James, 13 Ind. App. 522, 41 N.E. 978 (1895).

Application of Proceeds. (Cont'd)

A mechanic's lien was not affected by the appointment of a receiver for the property, and upon the sale of the property by the receiver the lien attached to the proceeds of the sale. Totten & Hogg Iron & Steel Foundry Co. v. Muncie Nail Co., 148 Ind. 372, 47 N.E. 703 (1897).

A lienor in event of insufficiency of funds was entitled to no more than his pro rata share of the fund, regardless of the form his action might have assumed. Kline v. Hammond Mach. & Forge Works, 76 Ind. App. 573, 127 N.E. 220 (1920).

Consolidation of Actions.

The owner of the property when the suit was commenced had to be a party thereto. Marvin v. Taylor, 27 Ind. 73 (1866); Kellenberger v. Boyer, 37 Ind. 188 (1871).

When subsequent purchasers of the lands were made parties, they had to set up whatever claims they might have had that were adverse to the liens. Woollen v. Wishmier, 70 Ind. 108 (1880).

Mortgagees had to be made parties or their rights would not have been affected. Union Nat'l Sav. & Loan Ass'n v. Helberg, 152 Ind. 139, 51 N.E. 916 (1898); Deming-Colborn Lumber Co. v. Union Nat'l Sav. & Loan Ass'n, 151 Ind. 463, 51 N.E. 936 (1898); Stoermer v. People's Sav. Bank, 152 Ind. 104, 52 N.E. 606 (1899).

Plaintiffs whose claims were several could not join in the enforcement of liens but the court could consolidate separate actions. Northwestern Loan & Inv. Ass'n v. McPherson, 23 Ind. App. 250, 54 N.E. 130 (1899).

On motion, the court could consolidate actions to foreclose mechanics' liens which were being prosecuted by separate plaintiffs. Central States Gas Co. v. Parker Russell Mining & Mfg. Co., 196 Ind. 163, 142 N.E. 119 (1925).

Findings.

A general verdict or finding of the truth of the complaint entitled the plaintiff to a decree enforcing the lien by a sale of the property. Nordyke, Marmon & Co. v. Dickson, 76 Ind. 188 (1881).

Special finding of facts where proceedings were pending to enforce liens against several buildings for materials furnished under one contract were held sufficient to sustain a judgment in foreclosure for the amount due on each building. Manor v. Heffner, 15 Ind. App. 299, 43 N.E. 1011 (1896).

Judgment.

—Sufficient.

If the judgment specified the amount due, and directed a sale of the property for the payment thereof, it was sufficient. Deming v. Patterson, 10 Ind. 251 (1858).

Jury Trial.

Jury trials could not be demanded. Albrecht v. C.C. Foster Lumber Co., 126 Ind. 318, 26 N.E. 157 (1890); Reichert v. Krass, 13 Ind. App. 348, 40 N.E. 706, 41 N.E. 835 (1895); Robertson v. Sertell, 88 Ind. App. 591, 161 N.E. 669 (1928).

32-28-3-8. Insufficient proceeds from sale of property. — If the proceeds of the sale of the property subject to a lien are insufficient to pay all the claimants, the court shall order the claimants to be paid in proportion to the amount due each claimant. [P.L.2-2002, § 13.]

NOTES TO DECISIONS

In General.

A mortgage executed upon real estate prior to the beginning of work or the furnishing of materials for a house thereon was superior to the lien so far as the real estate was concerned, as the mechanic's lien law imported that prior liens were superior to the liens of such mechanics and materialmen; but for the mechanic's lien statute, however, a mortgage upon a lot would have been a prior lien upon house subsequently built. Ward v. Yarnelle, 173 Ind. 535, 91 N.E. 7 (1910), overruled on other grounds, Moore-Mansfield Constr. Co. v. Indianapolis, N.C. & T. Ry., 179 Ind. 356, 101 N.E. 296 (1913).

That the security afforded by a mortgage on land was benefited by the erection of a building on the land did not make subsequently perfected mechanics' liens superior thereto so far as the land was concerned, as no change in the law relative to the rights of mortgagees was effected by the mechanic's lien law, save as to the buildings. Thorpe Block Sav. & Loan Ass'n v. James, 13 Ind. App. 522, 41 N.E. 978 (1895).

A lienor was entitled to no more than a pro rata share of the fund under this section, whatever form his action might take. Kline v. Hammond Mach. & Forge Works, 76 Ind. App. 573, 127 N.E. 220 (1920).

32-28-3-9. Liens by persons employed by lessees — Liability of property owner. — (a) This section applies to a:

 (1) subcontractor;

 (2) lessor leasing construction and other equipment and tools, regardless of whether an operator is also provided by the lessor;

 (3) journeyman; or

 (4) laborer;

employed or leasing any equipment or tools used by the lessee in erecting, altering, repairing, or removing any house, mill, manufactory or other building, or bridge, reservoir, system of waterworks, or other structure or earth moving, or in furnishing any material or machinery for these activities.

 (b) Except as provided in section 12 [IC 32-28-3-12] of this chapter, in order to acquire and hold a lien, a person described in subsection (a) must give to the property owner, or if the property owner is absent, to the property owner's agent, written notice particularly setting forth the amount of the person's claim and services rendered for which:

 (1) the person's employer or lessee is indebted to the person; and

 (2) the person holds the property owner responsible.

 (c) Subject to subsections (d) and (e), the property owner is liable for the person's claim.

 (d) The property owner is liable to a person described in subsection (a) for not more than the amount that is due and may later become due from the owner to the employer or lessee.

 (e) A person described in subsection (a) may recover the amount of the person's claim if, after the amounts of other claims that have priority are subtracted from the amount due from the property owner to the employer or lessee, the remainder of the amount due from the property owner to the employer or lessee is sufficient to pay the amount of the person's claim.

 (f) This section applies to a person described in subsection (a) who gives written notice, to the property owner or, if the property owner is absent, to the owner's agent, before labor is performed or materials or machinery is furnished. The notice must particularly set forth the amount of:

 (1) labor the person has contracted to perform; or

 (2) materials or machinery the person has contracted to furnish;

for the employer or lessee in erecting, altering, repairing, or removing any of the buildings or other structures described in subsection (a). A person described in subsection (a) has the same rights and remedies against the property owner for the amount of the labor performed by the person or materials or machinery furnished by the person after the notice is given, as are provided in this chapter for persons who serve notice after performing the labor or furnishing the materials or machinery.

 (g) If an action is brought against a property owner under this section, all subcontractors, equipment lessors leasing equipment, journeymen, and laborers who have:

 (1) performed labor or furnished materials or machinery; and

 (2) given notice under this section;

may become parties to the action. If, upon final judgment against the property owner the amount recovered and collected is not sufficient to pay the claimants in full, the amount recovered and collected shall be divided among the claimants pro rata. [P.L.2-2002, § 13.]

NOTES TO DECISIONS

Analysis

In general.
Constitutionality.
Additional work.
Appeal.
Arbitration.
—Appeal.
—Contest.
—Rights of subcontractors.
Assignees.
Attorney fees.
Bankruptcy.
Burden of proof.
Complaints.
Construction.
Limitation of actions.
Materialmen.
Mortgages.
Owner's promise to pay for materials.
Payment to contractor.
Priority.
Public corporations.
Purpose.
Release.
—Improper.
Separate action against owner.
Subcontractors.
—In general.
—Complaint.
—Employees.
—Notice.
—Payment in full.
—Sureties.
Sufficiency of notice.
Time of filing.
Time of notice.
Waiver.

In General.

The owner could have been held liable only for what was due the contractor at the time of service of notice. Raleigh v. Tossettel, 36 Ind. 295 (1871).

Persons furnishing labor and materials could have held the owner personally liable and also enforced a lien on the property. O'Halloran v. Leachey, 39 Ind. 150 (1872); Crawford v. Crockett, 55 Ind. 220 (1876).

The giving of a notice of an intention to hold a lien did not render the owner personally liable. Crawford v. Crockett, 55 Ind. 220 (1876); Lawton v. Case, 73 Ind. 60 (1880).

Former IC 32-8-3-9 (repealed; see this section for similar provisions) favors the right of one who made improvements to realty. In re Hull, 19 Bankr. 501 (Bankr. N.D. Ind. 1982).

The right created by the personal liability section is strictly a derivative one. Coplay Cement Co. v. Willis & Paul Group, 983 F.2d 1435 (7th Cir. 1993).

Constitutionality.

The title to the Mechanics' Lien Law was broad enough to include this section, which made the owner of property personally liable for materials and work under certain conditions. Halstead v. Olney J. Dean & Co., 182 Ind. 446, 105 N.E. 903 (1914).

Additional Work.

Although the plaintiff had been paid in full for certain repair work and extras connected with a contracting job for which he sought to foreclose a mechanic's lien, the recovery was not excessive as including additional pay for such repairs and extras where the court found that the reasonable value of the work on the contract was the amount of the judgment and the defendant introduced no evidence showing deductions to which he was entitled. Central Dredging Co. v. F.G. Proudfoot Co., 87 Ind. App. 171, 158 N.E. 229 (1927).

Additional work performed by a subcontractor under order of a plumbing inspector, without direction of the owner or the general contractor, was held merely an attempt to bring to life the right to file a lien which had died because of failure to serve notice as required by this section. Koring v. Varner, 90 Ind. App. 258, 168 N.E. 582 (1929).

Appeal.

In appeal from a mechanic's lien foreclosure by subcontractors, property owner on appeal could obtain no review on questions of liability on ground of absence of lienholder's notice to owners of intention to hold them personally responsible for debts and personal judgment without contractual relationship, because of failure to set out a narrative statement of the evidence in appeal brief. Dykiel v. Hilson Lumber & Supply Co., 127 Ind. App. 485, 139 N.E.2d 450 (1957).

Arbitration.

—Appeal.

Where project owner had agreed to submit claims to arbitration, since an agreement as to those claims existed, owner did not have any basis to appeal the arbitration when it was entered because the submission of any other claims was not contemplated in the parties' agreement. Angell Enters., Inc. v.

Arbitration. (Cont'd)

—Appeal. (Cont'd)
Abram & Hawkins Excavating Co., 643 N.E.2d 362 (Ind. App. 1994).

—Contest.
A party may not contest arbitrability for the first time in its petition to vacate an arbitration award. Angell Enters., Inc. v. Abram & Hawkins Excavating Co., 643 N.E.2d 362 (Ind. App. 1994).

—Rights of Subcontractors.
Where subcontractors were in privity with the general contractor only to the extent contemplated in this section (formerly IC 32-8-3-9, repealed; now see this section for similar provisions), they could not rely upon the arbitration clause in project owner's contract with the general contractor; the subcontractors' only right to arbitration was through in-court agreement based upon the claims under this statute. Angell Enters., Inc. v. Abram & Hawkins Excavating Co., 643 N.E.2d 362 (Ind. App. 1994).

Assignees.
When, after a general assignment by a contractor for the benefit of his creditors, certain materialmen gave notice to a property owner of their intention to hold him responsible for material furnished by them to the contractor, the assignee of the contractor was entitled, as against the materialmen, to the amount agreed to have been due from the property owner for the material. Kulp v. Chamberlin, 4 Ind. App. 560, 31 N.E. 376 (1892).

Attorney Fees.
Where subcontractor's recovery was based on the personal responsibility provisions of the mechanic's lien statute, and was not, in fact, an action to enforce a lien, attorney fees were not available in subcontractor's action. McCorry v. G. Cowser Constr., Inc., 636 N.E.2d 1273 (Ind. App.), aff'd, 644 N.E.2d 550 (Ind. 1994).
A recovery based on the personal responsibility provisions of the mechanic's lien statute does not constitute a lien and therefore attorney fees are not available. McCorry v. G. Cowser Constr., Inc., 644 N.E.2d 550 (Ind. 1994).

Bankruptcy.
Where the subcontractors did not file their notices under the Mechanic's Lien Law, that they were holding the owner responsible for payment of the sums due them for work, labor and materials furnished in the construction of a filling station, until after the contractor had been adjudged a bankrupt, sub-contractors

could not acquire a superior claim and thereby obtain a preference over the other creditors of the bankrupt. Lockridge v. Brockman, 137 F. Supp. 383 (N.D. Ind. 1956).

Burden of Proof.
The burden of proof is upon an asserted mechanic's lienholder who seeks to foreclose to show that the purported lien meets all the requirements necessary to its creation. Blade Corp. v. American Drywall, Inc., 74 Ind. Dec. 416, 400 N.E.2d 1183 (Ind. App. 1980).

Complaints.
Complaints to enforce personal liabilities did not need to contain a copy of the notice served on the owner. Irwin v. City of Crawfordsville, 58 Ind. 492 (1877); School Town of Princeton v. Gebhart, 61 Ind. 187 (1878); Adamson v. Shaner, 3 Ind. App. 448, 29 N.E. 944 (1892).
Complaints to enforce a personal liability against owners of property did not need to show a right to foreclose a lien. Clark v. Maxwell, 12 Ind. App. 199, 40 N.E. 274 (1895).

Construction.
The fact that the lien section of this act used the term "all persons performing labor or furnishing materials," while in the personal liability section there was no such language, did not require a construction which would preclude one from furnishing materials only to a contractor or subcontractor for use in the construction of a building from recovering the value thereof from the owner under the maxim expressio unius est exclusio alterius, in view of the uniform judicial and legislative construction of the act persisting for many years. Nash Eng'r Co. v. Marcy Realty Corp., 222 Ind. 396, 54 N.E.2d 263 (1944).

Limitation of Actions.
Actions to enforce personal liabilities did not need to have been brought within a year after the completion of the work. School Town of Princeton v. Gebhart, 61 Ind. 187 (1878).

Materialmen.
In suit by a materialman to recover the price of material furnished to the owner of the building in question and to enforce a materialman's lien therefor, the judgment providing that plaintiffs recover from the defendant a certain sum of money, and that the judgment attach to the sum of money deposited with the county clerk as security for payment of the judgment, was not a personal judgment against the defendant. Jackson v. J.A. Franklin & Son, 107 Ind. App. 38, 23 N.E.2d 23 (1939).
A merchant or manufacturer who furnished material for a building without performing

Materialmen. (Cont'd)
any labor thereon could enforce personal liability against the owner for the value of the material under this section. Nash Eng'r Co. v. Marcy Realty Corp., 222 Ind. 396, 54 N.E.2d 263 (1944).

One who was employed in furnishing material was engaged in so doing, and a person who contracted with him to furnish the material could have been called his "employer"; and, while the phrase "services rendered" was intended to require details of the kind of labor performed and the price per hour per day, yet, in view of the early amendments to the original act, it might also have been deemed to have meant a bill of particulars for material furnished. Nash Eng'r Co. v. Marcy Realty Corp., 222 Ind. 396, 54 N.E.2d 263 (1944).

Contracts for the erection of private buildings, containing provisions that the contractor should pay for all material, afforded to unnamed materialmen a remedy as third-party beneficiaries against the contractor. Nash Eng'r Co. v. Marcy Realty Corp., 222 Ind. 396, 54 N.E.2d 263 (1944).

Materialman cannot pursue his rights under this section by intervening in action between owner and contractor where he has not given notice to owner as provided by this section. Ziegler Bldg. Materials, Inc. v. Parkison, 73 Ind. Dec. 497, 398 N.E.2d 1330 (Ind. App. 1980).

Where contract permitted owner to retain ten percent of all amounts due contractor until project was completed, but project was not completed by contractor and owner had to pay an amount in addition to the retained funds to complete the project, owner owed nothing to contractor, and therefore supplier of material to contractor had no claim against owner. Blade Corp. v. American Drywall, Inc., 74 Ind. Dec. 416, 400 N.E.2d 1183 (Ind. App. 1980).

Mortgages.
The mortgage of the bank, notwithstanding the discrepancy between the description of the note in the mortgage agreement and the note actually executed, was supported by a debt and the home buyer did not owe the contractor any monies under the construction contract, for the mortgage was full enough to direct attention to the sources of correct information in regard to it, and was such as not to mislead or deceive. Pioneer Lumber & Supply Co. v. First-Merchants Nat'l Bank, 169 Ind. App. 406, 23 Ind. Dec. 244, 349 N.E.2d 219 (1976).

Owner's Promise to Pay for Materials.
When materials were furnished for buildings of different persons without any distinction being made as to the materials used in the buildings, the owners could not have been held personally liable for such materials. Crawford v. Powell, 101 Ind. 421 (1884).

As a general rule, compliance with this section is a prerequisite to obtaining a personal judgment by a materialman against the owner of real estate, but such compliance is not required where the materialman's cause of action is predicated on the owner's promise to pay for the materials. Lawshe v. Glen Park Lumber Co., 176 Ind. App. 344, 62 Ind. Dec. 338, 375 N.E.2d 275 (1978).

Payment to Contractor.
Payment by an owner to a contractor after notice pursuant to this section constituted no defense. Indianapolis Power & Light Co. v. Todd, 485 N.E.2d 632 (Ind. App. 1985).

Priority.
Commercial property owners right to set off against retainage, for costs of settling mechanics liens and of remedying uncompleted work of general contractor, had priority over amounts available for payment to subcontractors who had issued notices of personal liability. Poindexter Excavating, Inc. v. Downey, 198 Bankr. 292 (S.D. Ind. 1996).

Public Corporations.
There could have been no personal liability created against a county for materials furnished for a public building. Secrist v. Board of Comm'rs, 100 Ind. 59 (1885).

School corporations could not have been rendered personally liable for labor or materials used or employed in erecting schoolhouses. Jefferies v. Myers, 9 Ind. App. 563, 37 N.E. 301 (1894).

Purpose.
The primary purpose of this section is to protect the owner and those claiming under the general contractor from failure of the general contractor to pay those with a right to payment under the contract. In re Hull, 19 Bankr. 501 (Bankr. N.D. Ind. 1982).

This section was not intended to provide a lien. In re Hull, 19 Bankr. 501 (Bankr. N.D. Ind. 1982).

This section was intended to be an alternative to the mechanic's lien and provided only for a right to an action in personam against the owner of the property. In re Hull, 19 Bankr. 501 (Bankr. N.D. Ind. 1982).

The personal liability section gives a subcontractor an alternative means to a mechanics' lien of shifting from himself to the owner the burden of the general contractor's financial difficulties. Coplay Cement Co. v. Willis & Paul Group, 983 F.2d 1435 (7th Cir. 1993).

The personal liability provision is designed to protect a subcontractor from the consequences of a contractor defaulting by providing to the subcontractor a means of shifting

Purpose. (Cont'd)

from himself to the owner the burden of the general contractor's financial difficulties. Mercantile Nat'l Bank v. First Bldrs. of Ind., Inc., 732 N.E.2d 1287 (Ind. App. 2000).

Release.

—Improper.

Forcing plaintiff to release liens and other evidence of entitlement to payment in Indiana, when he may not have been able to recover against defendant in a related action in Ohio, undermined the intention of the Indiana statutes; trial court's order releasing personalty liens and notice to owner of personal responsibility, were incompatible with the purpose of the statutes. John Wendt & Sons v. Edward C. Levy Co., 685 N.E.2d 183 (Ind. App. 1997).

Separate Action Against Owner.

By complying with former IC 32-8-3-9 (repealed; see this section for similar provisions), a subcontractor could enforce its claim on the funds in the hands of the owner by a separate action against the owner. In re Hull, 19 Bankr. 501 (Bankr. N.D. Ind. 1982).

When the subcontractor complied with former IC 32-8-3-9 (repealed; see this section for similar provisions) the owners then obtained the right to pay the subcontractor directly and to setoff the amount so paid from that amount due to the general contractor. In re Hull, 19 Bankr. 501 (Bankr. N.D. Ind. 1982).

Subcontractors.

—In General.

Where a subcontractor notified the owner of a building that he would hold him responsible for the amount which the original contractor was indebted to him, setting forth the amount of his claim and the services rendered, the owner by the express terms of the statute became liable therefor, not exceeding the amount he was indebted to the original contractor. Roberts v. Koss, 32 Ind. App. 510, 70 N.E. 185 (1904).

A machine company furnishing equipment to be used by a housemover in moving buildings is not a subcontractor or supplier under former IC 32-8-3-9 (repealed; see this section for similar provisions). Lee & Mayfield, Inc. v. Lykowski House Moving Eng'rs, Inc., 489 N.E.2d 603 (Ind. App. 1986).

Nothing in former IC 32-8-3-9 (repealed; see this section for similar provisions) suggested that an owner's liability was limited to the amount he owed to a contractor which had been subcontracted to the subcontractor seeking to collect his claim from the owner. Coplay Cement Co.

v. Willis & Paul Group, 983 F.2d 1435 (7th Cir. 1993).

—Complaint.

A complaint against the owner under this section for materials furnished a subcontractor did not need to allege that the general contractor was indebted to the subcontractor. Indianapolis Power & Light Co. v. Southeastern Supply Co., 146 Ind. App. 554, 21 Ind. Dec. 82, 257 N.E.2d 722 (1970).

—Employees.

The employees of a subcontractor were protected by former IC 32-8-3-9 (repealed; see this section for similar provisions); thus, they may have had a claim against the owner pursuant to this section. Indianapolis Power & Light Co. v. Todd, 485 N.E.2d 632 (Ind. App. 1985).

An owner's payment to a subcontractor does not extinguish the claims of the subcontractor's employees against the owner if the owner still owes money on the project to any party. Indianapolis Power & Light Co. v. Todd, 485 N.E.2d 632 (Ind. App. 1985).

—Notice.

In order to hold an owner personally liable, a subcontractor had to comply with the notice provisions of this section. Aetna Glass Corp. v. Mercury Bldrs., Inc., 145 Ind. App. 286, 18 Ind. Dec. 431, 250 N.E.2d 598 (1969).

Notice of a plumbing subcontractor's intent to hold property owners personally liable for amounts not received from the general contractor was inadequate where subcontractor never filed a mechanic's lien and the letter of notification simply announced the amount owed and did not make it clear that the subcontractor would be looking to the property owners for payment. SRL Plumbing & Sewer, Inc. v. Turk, 757 N.E.2d 193 (Ind. App. 2001).

—Payment in Full.

It was no defense to the claim against the owner by a materialman, who had given to the owner the notice required by this section, for materials furnished a subcontractor that the subcontractor had been paid in full by the general contractor. Indianapolis Power & Light Co. v. Southeastern Supply Co., 146 Ind. App. 554, 21 Ind. Dec. 82, 257 N.E.2d 722 (1970).

—Sureties.

A provision in a building contractor's surety bond that if the principal should fail to pay all persons who have contracts with the principal for labor and materials, they should have a direct right of action against the principal and the surety on the bond, did not limit the surety's liability to only those persons con-

Subcontractors. (Cont'd)

—Sureties. (Cont'd)
tracting with the contractor, but covered all persons selling materials to a subcontractor, in view of a preceding general provision expressing the dominant purpose of the instrument to be the faithful performance of the contract by the principal. Nash Eng'r Co. v. Marcy Realty Corp., 222 Ind. 396, 54 N.E.2d 263 (1944).

Sufficiency of Notice.
The notice to the owner under this section had to show that the work was performed for, or materials were furnished to, the contractor, and should have stated the amount due, but need not have described the premises. Gilman v. Gard, 29 Ind. 291 (1868); O'Halloran v. Leachey, 39 Ind. 150 (1872); Crawford v. Crockett, 55 Ind. 220 (1876).

Time of Filing.
Former IC 32-8-3-9 (repealed; see this section for similar provisions) permitted the same persons who would be entitled to a lien on a landowner's property to assert limited personal liability against the owner even though they were not in direct privity with the owner, but only with the general contractor; while a mechanic's lien must be filed within a specified period of time, there is no such time limitation in the personal respon-

sibility statute. McCorry v. G. Cowser Constr., Inc., 636 N.E.2d 1273 (Ind. App.), aff'd, 644 N.E.2d 550 (Ind. 1994).
While a mechanic's lien must be filed within a specified period of time, there is no such time limitation in the personal responsibility statute, which makes no mention of a lien on real estate and does not separately provide for the recovery of attorney fees. McCorry v. G. Cowser Constr., Inc., 644 N.E.2d 550 (Ind. 1994).

Time of Notice.
The notice could have been given to the owner at any time before he had paid the contractor. School Town of Princeton v. Gebhart, 61 Ind. 187 (1878).

Waiver.
Former IC 32-8-3-9 (repealed; see this section for similar provisions) was not intended to be available to the general contractor and therefore it should not be open to waiver by the contract between the owner and the general contractor. In re Hull, 19 Bankr. 501 (Bankr. N.D. Ind. 1982).
A no-lien agreement does not waive the right of a subcontractor to give notice of holding the owner personally liable since a no-lien agreement waives only the right to obtain a mechanic's lien, and this section does not involve a mechanic's lien. In re Hull, 19 Bankr. 501 (Bankr. N.D. Ind. 1982).

32-28-3-10. Foreclosure action requested by property owner. —
(a) A lien is void if both of the following occur:
(1) The owner of property subject to a mechanic's lien or any person or corporation having an interest in the property, including a mortgagee or a lienholder, provides written notice to the owner or holder of the lien to file an action to foreclose the lien.
(2) The owner or holder of the lien fails to file an action to foreclose the lien in the county where the property is located not later than thirty (30) days after receiving the notice.
However, this section does not prevent the claim from being collected as other claims are collected by law.
(b) A person who gives notice under subsection (a)(1) by registered or certified mail to the lienholder at the address given in the recorded statement and notice of intention to hold a lien may file an affidavit of service of the notice to file an action to foreclose the lien with the recorder of the county in which the property is located. The affidavit must state the following:
(1) The facts of the notice.
(2) That more than thirty (30) days have passed since the notice was received by the lienholder.
(3) That no action for foreclosure of the lien is pending.
(4) That no unsatisfied judgment has been rendered on the lien.
(c) The recorder shall:

(1) record the affidavit of service in the miscellaneous record book of the recorder's office; and

(2) certify on the face of the record any lien that is fully released.

When the recorder records the affidavit and certifies the record under this subsection, the real estate described in the lien is released from the lien. [P.L.2-2002, § 13.]

NOTES TO DECISIONS

Notice Found Insufficient.

Statement in letter, "Please file suit on your Mechanic's Lien which you filed in order that the matter may be brought to a head," such letter not being sent by registered or certified mail, was insufficient to constitute the notice required by former IC 32-8-3-10 (repealed; see this section for similar provisions). Lafayette Tennis Club, Inc. v. C.W. Ellison Bldrs., Inc., 77 Ind. Dec. 129, 406 N.E.2d 1211 (Ind. App. 1980).

Recording of Lien.

Former IC 32-8-3-11 (repealed; now see this section for similar provisions) imposed the obligation of former IC 32-8-3-3 and former IC 32-8-3-6 (both repealed; see IC 32-28-3 for similar provisions), requiring that the lien be recorded and suit be filed in the county where the property was located, because these sections all related to the same subject matter, and had to be construed consistently. Ford v. Culp Custom Homes, Inc., 731 N.E.2d 468 (Ind. App. 2000).

Slander of Title.

The filing of a notice of intention to hold a mechanic's lien by a person not entitled to such a claim and the action to foreclose the lien filed more than 30 days after the owner's notice to commence suit was malicious slander of title. Lee & Mayfield, Inc. v. Lykowski House Moving Eng'rs, Inc., 489 N.E.2d 603 (Ind. App. 1986).

32-28-3-11. Written undertaking with surety. — (a) In an action to foreclose a lien:

(1) the defendant or owner of the property subject to the lien; or

(2) any person having an interest in the property subject to the lien, including a mortgagee or other lienholder;

may file in the action a written undertaking with surety to be approved by the court.

(b) An undertaking filed under this section must provide that the person filing it will pay any judgment that may be recovered in the action to foreclose the lien, including costs and attorney's fees allowed by the court, if the claim on which the judgment is founded is found by the court to have been a lien on the property at the time the action was filed.

(c) If an undertaking is filed and approved by the court:

(1) the court shall enter an order releasing the property from the lien; and

(2) the property shall be discharged from the lien.

[P.L.2-2002, § 13.]

NOTES TO DECISIONS

Substitution of surety.

Costs.

If a bond to release the property was filed and judgment was rendered for less than $50.00, the plaintiff would have recovered

Costs. (Cont'd)
costs. Scott v. Goldinhorst, 123 Ind. 268, 24 N.E. 333 (1890).

Letters of Credit.
Plaintiff could not base a claim of harm upon the substitution of an absolute guarantee of payment, a letter of credit, for liens which had not been taken to judgment; once an irrevocable letter of credit was issued in a manner which guaranteed plaintiff payment in the event of a judgment, plaintiff could not be heard to complain of the source of the money. John Wendt & Sons v. Edward C. Levy Co., 685 N.E.2d 183 (Ind. App. 1997).

Release of Liens and Notice Improper.
Forcing plaintiff to release liens and other

evidence of entitlement to payment in Indiana, when he may not have been able to recover against defendant in a related action in Ohio, undermined the intention of the Indiana statutes; trial court's order releasing personalty liens and notice to owner of personal responsibility, were incompatible with the purpose of the statutes. John Wendt & Sons v. Edward C. Levy Co., 685 N.E.2d 183 (Ind. App. 1997).

Substitution of Surety.
Substituting a surety as the basis of the court's action in the proceeding was correct as to mechanic's liens. John Wendt & Sons v. Edward C. Levy Co., 685 N.E.2d 183 (Ind. App. 1997).

Collateral References. Security, right to require, as condition of canceling lien of record or of recording payment. 2 A.L.R.2d 1064.

32-28-3-12. Liens by persons involved with railroad construction.

— (a) This section applies to a person who:
   (1) performs work or labor such as:
      (A) grading;
      (B) building embankments;
      (C) making excavations for track;
      (D) building:
         (i) bridges;
         (ii) trestlework;
         (iii) works of masonry;
         (iv) fencing; or
         (v) other structures; or
      (E) performs work of any kind;
   in the construction or repair of a railroad or part of a railroad in Indiana; or
   (2) furnishes material for:
      (A) a bridge, trestlework, work of masonry, fence, or other structure; or
      (B) use in the construction or repair of a railroad or part of a railroad;
   in Indiana.
  (b) The work, labor, or material described in subsection (a) may be provided under a contract:
   (1) with the railroad corporation building, repairing, or owning the railroad; or
   (2) with a person, corporation, or company engaged as:
      (A) lessee;
      (B) contractor;
      (C) subcontractor; or
      (D) agent;

of the railroad corporation in the work of constructing or repairing the railroad or part of the railroad in Indiana.

(c) A person to whom this section applies may have a lien to the extent of the work or labor performed, or material furnished, or both, upon:

    (1) the right-of-way and franchises of the railroad corporation; and

    (2) the works and structures as set forth in this section that may be upon the right-of-way and franchise of the railroad corporation;

within the limits of the county in which the work or labor may be performed or the material may be furnished.

(d) A person performing work or labor or furnishing materials under a contract described in subsection (b)(2) is not required to give notice to the railroad corporation under section 9 [IC 32-28-3-9] of this chapter in order to acquire and hold a lien for labor performed or material furnished under the provisions of this section. The performance of the labor or the furnishing of the materials is sufficient notice to the railroad corporation. A lien that is acquired as set forth in this subsection shall be enforced as other mechanic's liens are enforced in Indiana.

(e) A person who, in doing business with a railroad company, has constructed a building or other improvement on a portion of the railroad right-of-way adjacent to the person's place of business may have a lien to the extent of the fair market value of the improvement on that portion of the right-of-way. The lien may be acquired and enforced:

    (1) upon abandonment of the right-of-way by the railroad company; and

    (2) against the successors in title of the railroad company.

This subsection does not apply to property that is subject to a written agreement providing for the disposition of improvements upon abandonment. Liens acquired under this subsection shall be enforced as other mechanic's liens are enforced in Indiana. [P.L.2-2002, § 13.]

NOTES TO DECISIONS

ANALYSIS

In general.
Assignment.
Complaint to enforce.
Entire road.
Fences.
Fuel.
Grading.
Payment.
Personal judgment.
Priorities.
Sale not authorized.
Subcontractors.
Well digging.

In General.

  Railroad companies could have been held liable only for the value of the materials furnished or work done, and were not controlled by the contract price for such materials and labor. Morris v. Louisville, N.A. & C.R.R., 123 Ind. 489, 24 N.E. 335 (1890).

Articles furnished for the personal use of the employees of a contractor who built a railroad were not such articles as authorized the acquiring of a lien on the road. Ferguson v. Despo, 8 Ind. App. 523, 34 N.E. 575 (1893).

Liens for materials could have been acquired only when such materials were used in constructing the railroad. Cincinnati, R. & M.R.R. v. Shera, 36 Ind. App. 315, 73 N.E. 293 (1905).

Assignment.

  If a claim against a railroad company was assigned before a lien therefor was acquired, the assignee could not perfect the lien by the filing and recording of a notice. Fleming v. Greener, 173 Ind. 260, 90 N.E. 72, 140 Am. St. R. 254, 21 Ann. Cas. 959 (1909), overruled on other grounds, Moore-Mansfield Constr. Co. v. Indianapolis, N.C. & T. Ry., 179 Ind. 356, 101 N.E. 296 (1913).

Complaint to Enforce.

Complaint to enforce lien for construction of a railroad contained necessary allegations to show jurisdiction of court and to entitle plaintiff to recover. Chapman v. Elgin, J. & E.R.R., 11 Ind. App. 632, 39 N.E. 289 (1895); Dean v. Reynolds, 12 Ind. App. 97, 39 N.E. 763 (1895).

Entire Road.

The lien created was upon the railroad as a unit, and not upon fragmentary parts thereof. Midland Ry. v. Wilcox, 122 Ind. 84, 23 N.E. 506 (1890), overruled on other grounds, 87 N.E. 719 (Ind.), 90 N.E. 73 (Ind. 1909); Farmers' Loan & Trust Co. v. Canada & St. L. Ry., 127 Ind. 250, 26 N.E. 784, 11 L.R.A. 740 (1891); Indiana, I. & I.R.R. v. Larrew, 130 Ind. 368, 30 N.E. 517 (1892).

The notice need only have been filed in the county where the materials were furnished or work done, and the lien extended to the entire line of the road, and could have been enforced in any county in which the road ran. Midland Ry. v. Wilcox, 122 Ind. 84, 23 N.E. 506 (1890); Farmers' Loan & Trust Co. v. Canada & St. L. Ry., 127 Ind. 250, 26 N.E. 784, 11 L.R.A. 740 (1890).

Fences.

Liens could have been acquired and enforced for fencing railroad. Indiana Ry. v. Wadsworth, 29 Ind. App. 586, 64 N.E. 938 (1902).

Fuel.

Liens cannot have been acquired for fuel furnished to a contractor to use in operating machinery used in the construction of a railroad. Cincinnati, R. & M.R.R. v. Shera, 36 Ind. App. 315, 73 N.E. 293 (1905).

Grading.

Grading and clearing right-of-way was such work as authorized the acquiring of a lien. Dean v. Reynolds, 12 Ind. App. 97, 39 N.E. 763 (1895).

Payment.

Payment of all due a contractor from a railroad company did not defeat the lien of a laborer. Indiana, I. & I.R.R. v. Larrew, 130 Ind. 368, 30 N.E. 517 (1892).

Payment for the construction of a section of a railroad released such section from a contract requiring the road to have been constructed by sections. Reynolds v. Louisville, N.A. & C. Ry., 143 Ind. 579, 40 N.E. 410 (1895).

Personal Judgment.

An admission by defendant railroad company that it was operating its road sustained a finding that the right-of-way of the defendant was necessary in its use as a common carrier and that a lien thereon for labor performed could not have been foreclosed and that a personal judgment ought to have been rendered in lieu of a decree of foreclosure. Pere Marquette R.R. v. Baertz, 36 Ind. App. 408, 74 N.E. 51 (1905); Pere Marquette R.R. v. Smith, 36 Ind. App. 439, 74 N.E. 545 (1905).

Priorities.

A mechanic's lien took priority over subsequent mortgage of the railroad and over the mortgage of a railroad yet to have been built as well as over holders of bonds secured by trust deed and mortgage executed to secure the bonds. Farmers' Loan & Trust Co. v. Canada & St. L. Ry., 127 Ind. 250, 26 N.E. 784, 11 L.R.A. 740 (1891).

Sale Not Authorized.

Contractors constructing railroads acquired a lien on the roadbed constructed by them, and such lien could have been enforced, but neither the road as an entirety nor its franchises could have been sold. Louisville, N.A. & C. Ry. v. Boney, 117 Ind. 501, 20 N.E. 432, 3 L.R.A. 435 (1889); Midland Ry. v. Wilcox, 122 Ind. 84, 23 N.E. 506 (1890).

Subcontractors.

Laborers for subcontractors who built railroads could have acquired liens on such roads. Ferguson v. Despo, 8 Ind. App. 523, 34 N.E. 575 (1893); Pere Marquette R.R. v. Baertz, 36 Ind. App. 408, 74 N.E. 51 (1905); Pere Marquette R.R. v. Smith, 36 Ind. App. 439, 74 N.E. 545 (1905).

Well Digging.

Digging a well for use in operating a railroad was such work as authorized the acquiring of a lien on the road. Wabash R.R. v. Achemire, 19 Ind. App. 482, 49 N.E. 835 (1898).

32-28-3-13. Notice of intention by persons involved with railroad construction. — A person who desires to acquire the lien provided for in section 12 [IC 32-28-3-12] of this chapter must give notice of the person's intention to hold the lien by causing the notice to be recorded in the recorder's office of the county in which the work was done or material furnished in the same manner and within the same time as provided in this chapter for giving notice of a mechanic's lien. A person who gives notice

within the proper time may enforce the lien in the same manner as mechanic's liens are enforced. The suit must be brought within one (1) year after the time the notice was filed in the recorder's office. [P.L.2-2002, § 13.]

Cross References. Limitation of actions to enforce liens, IC 32-8-7-1 et seq. IC 32-28-8-1.

NOTES TO DECISIONS

In General.
Notice had to be filed only in the county where the materials were furnished or work done, and no other notice was required than such as was provided by statute. Midland Ry. v. Wilcox, 122 Ind. 84, 23 N.E. 506 (1890); Farmers' Loan & Trust Co. v. Canada & St. L. Ry., 127 Ind. 250, 26 N.E. 784, 11 L.R.A. 740 (1891); Ferguson v. Despo, 8 Ind. App. 523, 34 N.E. 575 (1893).

If a claim was assigned before a lien had been acquired by the filing of a notice, the assignee could not file a notice and acquire a lien. Fleming v. Greener, 173 Ind. 260, 90 N.E. 72, 140 Am. St. R. 254, 21 Ann. Cas. 959 (1909), overruled on other grounds, Moore-Mansfield Constr. Co. v. Indianapolis, N.C. & T. Ry., 179 Ind. 356, 101 N.E. 296 (1913).

32-28-3-14. Attorney's fees. — (a) Except as provided in subsection (b), in an action to enforce a lien under this chapter, the plaintiff or lienholder may recover reasonable attorney's fees as a part of the judgment.

(b) A plaintiff may not recover attorney's fees as part of the judgment against a property owner in an action in which the contract consideration for the labor, material, or machinery has been paid by the property owner or party for whom the improvement has been constructed. [P.L.2-2002, § 13.]

NOTES TO DECISIONS

ANALYSIS

In general.
Constitutionality.
Amount and proof.
Discretion of court.
Failure to include in settlement.
—Effect.
Fees denied.
—Counterclaims.
—Recovery under personal responsibility provisions.
Fees for appeal.
Fees properly awarded.
Invalid lien.
Motion to correct errors.
No dispute as to lien.
Reasonableness of fee.
—Circumstances of case control.
—Failure to challenge.
—Fee not reasonable.
Summary judgment improper.

In General.
If the plaintiff did not recover judgment, attorney fees could not have been allowed. Bird v. Rector, Wardens, & Vestrymen, 154 Ind. 138, 56 N.E. 129 (1900).
Payment or tender after suit had to include

attorney fees. Chicago & S.E. Ry. v. Woodard, 159 Ind. 541, 65 N.E. 577 (1902).
Persons who recovered judgments under the Mechanic's Lien Law were entitled to recover a reasonable attorney fee. Beach v. Huntsman, 42 Ind. App. 205, 85 N.E. 523 (1908); Rexing v. Princeton Window Glass Co., 51 Ind. App. 124, 94 N.E. 1031 (1911).
A lien sought to have been enforced by one furnishing labor and materials at the request of the record owner of the property, after the conveyance to such owner was set aside, was not an equitable lien, but a statutory lien for the enforcement of which attorney fees were allowed. Olejniczak v. Indiana Lumber Mfg. Co., 78 Ind. App. 168, 135 N.E. 6 (1922).
Recovery by a lien claimant was not excessive because it included attorney's fees. Robertson v. Sertell, 88 Ind. App. 591, 161 N.E. 669 (1928).
Where the court found that plaintiff was estopped from and denied the right to recover attorney's fees in the foreclosure of his lien, it committed error, for the statute was mandatory and left no room for exceptions on the basis of estoppel or otherwise; having found for the appellant, the court should have allowed a reasonable attorney's fee based upon the stipulation, the amount having been de-

In General. (Cont'd)

termined by the evidence. Byerly v. Lusardi, 133 Ind. App. 315, 182 N.E.2d 4 (1962).

Attorney's fees are authorized as a part of the in rem judgment against the interests of the owner who authorizes the labor and materials. Potter v. Cline, 161 Ind. App. 349, 43 Ind. Dec. 446, 316 N.E.2d 422 (1974).

Former IC 32-8-3-14 (repealed; see this section for similar provisions) permitted attorney fees only for a valid "judgment in any sum." Complete Elec. Co. v. Liberty Nat'l Bank & Trust Co., 530 N.E.2d 1216 (Ind. App. 1988).

What constitutes a reasonable attorney's fee in an action to enforce a mechanic's lien is a question of fact, the computation of which may depend on a variety of factors, including the time and effort required, the value of the interest involved, the experience, reputation, and ability of the attorneys performing the services, and the results secured at trial. Clark's Pork Farms v. Sand Livestock Sys., 563 N.E.2d 1292 (Ind. App. 1990).

Constitutionality.

Statute authorizing attorneys' fees for enforcement of mechanic's lien did not amount to class legislation or the taking of property without compensation or due process of law. Duckwall v. Jones, 156 Ind. 682, 58 N.E. 1055, 60 N.E. 797 (1900).

Amount and Proof.

It was a matter of common knowledge that the amount of a reasonable attorney's fee, as provided by this section, depended upon the amount in controversy, the questions involved, the difficulties encountered in prosecuting the action, as well as the time and labor employed. Winslow Gas Co. v. Plost, 69 Ind. App. 611, 122 N.E. 594 (1919).

In foreclosure of a mechanic's lien, the court could not include in the judgment an attorney's fee under this section where there was no proof in respect thereof. Winslow Gas Co. v. Plost, 69 Ind. App. 611, 122 N.E. 594 (1919).

Uncontradicted, expert, opinion evidence regarding the value of attorney's services in mechanic's lien cases was not conclusive. Dunn v. Deitschel, 204 Ind. 269, 169 N.E. 529 (1930).

The trial court, in valuing attorney's services in mechanic's lien cases, could have applied its own knowledge and professional experience. Dunn v. Dietschel, 204 Ind. 269, 169 N.E. 529 (1930).

In suit to enforce a materialman's lien and to recover the price of the material furnished, it was error to render judgment for the services of plaintiff's attorney in the case, in the absence of any evidence showing the value of his services so rendered. Jackson v. J.A.

Franklin & Son, 107 Ind. App. 38, 23 N.E.2d 23 (1939).

Discretion of Court.

If no evidence is offered in proceedings in which it is proper for trial court to award reasonable attorney fees, the trial court may award such fees based on the judge's knowledge and experience in the legal profession and his decision is reviewable only for abuse of discretion. Fox v. Galvin, 177 Ind. App. 654, 64 Ind. Dec. 654, 381 N.E.2d 103 (1978).

Failure to Include in Settlement.

—Effect.

A materialman, in the absence of fraud or mistake of fact, was not entitled to recover an attorney's fee which was not included in the settlement of an account, although action had been brought on the claim to enforce the lien. Grant County Lumber Co. v. Marley, 100 Ind. App. 42, 192 N.E. 110 (1934).

Fees Denied.

—Counterclaims.

A contractor was not entitled to any attorney fees where the property owner had received a judgment on his counterclaim in excess of the contractor's judgment, wholly defeating the latter. Complete Elec. Co. v. Liberty Nat'l Bank & Trust Co., 530 N.E.2d 1216 (Ind. App. 1988).

Under former IC 32-8-3-14 (repealed; see this section for similar provisions), if a mechanic's lienor shall "recover judgment in any sum," he was entitled to recover reasonable attorney's fees. However, if a judgment on a counterclaim exceeded the judgment on the original claim, the latter judgment was defeated and the lienor was not entitled to attorney's fees. Clark's Pork Farms v. Sand Livestock Sys., 563 N.E.2d 1292 (Ind. App. 1990).

—Recovery Under Personal Responsibility Provisions.

Where subcontractor's recovery was based on the personal responsibility provisions of the mechanic's lien statute, and was not, in fact, an action to enforce a lien, attorney fees were not available in subcontractor's action. McCorry v. G. Cowser Constr., Inc., 636 N.E.2d 1273 (Ind. App.), aff'd, 644 N.E.2d 550 (Ind. 1994).

Fees for Appeal.

Contractual provision for "reasonable attorney's fees" authorized award for both trial and appellate fees. Parrish v. Terre Haute Sav. Bank, 438 N.E.2d 1 (Ind. App. 1982).

Fees Properly Awarded.

Where a developer did not prevail on its

Fees Properly Awarded. (Cont'd)
counterclaims to a contractor's action, and where the contractor's defense against the developer's claims was part and parcel of, and necessary to, the enforcement of its mechanic's lien, the trial court did not err in awarding attorney fees to the contractor. Abbey Villas Dev. Corp. v. Site Contractors, Inc., 716 N.E.2d 91 (Ind. App. 1999).

Invalid Lien.
Attorney fees may not be awarded to a mechanic seeking to enforce an invalid lien, even though otherwise entitled to damages for breach of contract. Saint Joseph's College v. Morrison, Inc., 158 Ind. App. 272, 39 Ind. Dec. 244, 302 N.E.2d 865 (1973); Froberg v. Northern Ind. Constr., Inc., 416 N.E.2d 451 (Ind. App. 1981); King Pin Motor Lodge, Inc. v. D.J. Constr. Co., 416 N.E.2d 1317 (Ind. App. 1981).

Motion to Correct Errors.
Where motion to correct errors challenged a judgment declaring mechanic's lien valid, the issue of the validity of attorney's fees was necessarily included in such challenge and the issue of attorney's fees was not waived by failure to specifically raise it in motion to correct errors. Froberg v. Northern Ind. Constr., Inc., 416 N.E.2d 451 (Ind. App. 1981).

No Dispute as to Lien.
The court committed no error in allowing the recovery of attorney's fees to appellees who filed the liens even though there was no dispute over the claims and the failure to pay the claims could not be blamed upon the appellant, for legal services had been rendered to protect their interests as appellant had filed suit upon the lien, thus precipitating action on the part of the other appellees and the statute provided for attorney's fees in situations of this sort. Byerly v. Lusardi, 133 Ind. App. 315, 182 N.E.2d 4 (1962).

Reasonableness of Fee.

—Circumstances of Case Control.
The reasonableness of the fee will turn on

the circumstances of the case. Templeton v. Sam Klain & Son, 425 N.E.2d 89 (Ind. 1981).

Trial court did not abuse its discretion in the award of attorney fees three times the amount of the judgment for plaintiff, where court found fees were reasonable considering complexity and length of case and the amount plaintiff reasonably had to expend to foreclose his lien. Johnson v. Blankenship, 679 N.E.2d 505 (Ind. App. 1997), aff'd, 688 N.E.2d 1250 (Ind. 1997).

—Failure to Challenge.
Where at every stage of the lawsuit, defendant had repeatedly asserted the lack of the trial court's power to award attorney's fees for an appeal under this section but had never challenged the reasonableness of the amount of award, defendant having failed to raise that issue on appeal was foreclosed from litigating that issue upon a petition to transfer and was bound by the amount of the award. Templeton v. Sam Klain & Son, 425 N.E.2d 89 (Ind. 1981).

—Fee Not Reasonable.
A reasonable fee for the prosecution of the claim and foreclosure of the lien alone would not be a reasonable fee for those services plus the defense of the judgment on appeal. Templeton v. Sam Klain & Son, 425 N.E.2d 89 (Ind. 1981).

Summary Judgment Improper.
Where a bridge constituted neither a state nor a federal public work subject to the respective statutory protections provided to those working on public projects, the plaintiff was afforded the protection of a state mechanic's lien, and reversal of the trial court's summary judgment against the plaintiff was required for a hearing on the validity of the lien and on the amount of attorneys fees to which the plaintiff was entitled. J.S. Sweet Co. v. White County Bridge Comm'n, 714 N.E.2d 219 (Ind. App. 1999).

Collateral References. Excessiveness or adequacy of attorneys' fees in matters involving real estate — modern cases. 10 A.L.R.5th 448.

32-28-3-15. Accepting payment with notice of payees indebtedness to another — Criminal liability. — A person who knowingly or intentionally:

(1) performs labor, supplies services, or furnishes material or machinery in the:

(A) construction;

(B) repair; or

(C) remodeling;

of a building, structure, or other work;

(2) accepts payment for the labor, services, material, or machinery furnished and supplied;

(3) at the time of receiving the payment, knows that the person is indebted to another for:

(A) labor, including the cost of renting or leasing construction and other equipment and tools, whether or not an operator is also provided by the lessor;

(B) services;

(C) material; or

(D) machinery;

used or employed in the construction, repair, or remodeling;

(4) fails:

(A) at the time of receiving the payment; and

(B) with intent to defraud;

to notify in writing the person from whom the payment was received of the existence of the outstanding indebtedness; and

(5) causes the person from whom the payment was received to suffer a loss by failing under subdivision (4) to notify the person of the existence of the outstanding indebtedness;

commits a Class D felony. [P.L.2-2002, § 13.]

Cross References. Penalties for felonies, IC 35-50-1, IC 35-50-2, IC 35-50-5-2.

NOTES TO DECISIONS

ANALYSIS

In general.
Application of act of 1921, ch. 55.
Elements.
—Knowledge and intent.

In General.

This section (formerly IC 32-8-3-15) was a criminal statute which derived from the common law offense of fraud. Miller v. State, 496 N.E.2d 592 (Ind. App.), aff'd, 502 N.E.2d 92 (Ind. 1986).

Former IC 32-8-3-15 (repealed, now see this section for similar provisions) required only that the person from whom the payment was received suffer a loss because of the defendant's actions. The statute did not require the entity seeking payment for the services or goods it provided to file a valid lien to recover the debt owed to it. Gamblin v. State, 568 N.E.2d 1040 (Ind. App. 1991).

Application of Act of 1921, ch. 55.

Acts 1921, ch. 55, § 1, which contained the words "who shall accept payment in full for the labor, services, material or machinery so

furnished," applied only when payment was made in a final settlement. Williams v. State, 89 Ind. App. 46, 165 N.E. 762 (1929).

Elements.

—Knowledge and Intent.

Although absent from the predecessor statute to this section prior to the 1978 and 1983 amendments, knowledge and intent were construed as statutory elements of the felony of receiving payment while indebted. Miller v. State, 496 N.E.2d 592 (Ind. App.), aff'd, 502 N.E.2d 92 (Ind. 1986).

The offense of receiving payment while indebted derives from the common law offense of fraud and inherently carries with it and requires proof of a mens rea element. Miller v. State, 502 N.E.2d 92 (Ind. 1986).

A felony conviction on an offense which has its roots in fraud, such as receiving payment while indebted, will not be affirmed when no intent to defraud has been proven beyond a reasonable doubt. Miller v. State, 496 N.E.2d 592 (Ind. App.), aff'd, 502 N.E.2d 92 (Ind. 1986).

The requisite criminal intent can be in-

Elements. (Cont'd)

—Knowledge and Intent. (Cont'd)
ferred from a defendant contractor accepting payments for work and materials used in the construction of a house, knowing that the materialman had not been paid. Miller v. State, 502 N.E.2d 92 (Ind. 1986).

32-28-3-16. Liens on property other than Class 2 structures and utilities — Prohibition or construction contracts. — (a) This section applies to a construction contract for the construction, alteration, or repair of a building or structure other than:

(1) a Class 2 structure (as defined in IC 22-12-1-5) or an improvement on the same real estate auxiliary to a Class 2 structure (as defined in IC 22-12-1-5); or

(2) property that is:

(A) owned, operated, managed, or controlled by a public utility (as defined in IC 8-1-2-1), a municipally owned utility (as defined in IC 8-1-2-1), a joint agency (as defined in IC 8-1-2.2-2), a rural electric membership corporation formed under IC 8-1-13-4, rural telephone cooperative corporation formed under IC 8-1-17, or a not-for-profit utility (as defined in IC 8-1-2-125) regulated under IC 8; and

(B) intended to be used and useful for the production, transmission, delivery, or furnishing of heat, light, water, telecommunications services, or power to the public.

(b) A provision in a contract for the improvement of real estate in Indiana is void if the provision requires a person described in section 1 [IC 32-28-3-1] of this chapter who furnishes labor, materials, or machinery to waive a right to:

(1) a lien against real estate; or

(2) a claim against a payment bond;

before the person is paid for the labor or materials furnished.

(c) A provision in a contract for the improvement of real estate in Indiana under which one (1) or more persons agree not to file a notice of intention to hold a lien is void. [P.L.2-2002, § 13; P.L.101-2002, § 7.]

Amendments. The 2002 amendment by P.L.101-2002, amending this section as enacted by P.L.2-2002, inserted "rural telephone cooperative corporation formed under IC 8-1-17" in subsection (a)(2)(A); and inserted "telecommunications services" in subsection (a)(2)(B).

Effective Dates. P.L.101-2002, § 7. July 1, 2002.

32-28-3-17. Prohibition on contracts subject to laws of other states. — A provision in a contract for the improvement of real estate in Indiana is void if the provision:

(1) makes the contract subject to the laws of another state; or

(2) requires litigation, arbitration, or other dispute resolution process on the contract occur in another state. [P.L.2-2002, § 13.]

32-28-3-18. Prohibition on contracts conditioning payment on obligor's receipt of payment from a third party. — (a) This section applies to a provider of labor, materials, or equipment under a contract for the improvement of real estate that conditions the right of the provider to receive payment on the obligor's receipt of payment from a third person with whom the provider does not have a contractual relationship.

(b) This section does not apply to a construction contract for the construction, alteration, or repair of the following:

(1) A Class 2 structure (as defined in IC 22-12-1-5).

(2) An improvement on the same real estate auxiliary to a Class 2 structure (as defined in IC 22-12-1-5).

(3) Property that is:

(A) owned, operated, managed, or controlled by a:

(i) public utility (as defined in IC 8-1-2-1);

(ii) municipally owned utility (as defined in IC 8-1-2-1);

(iii) joint agency (as defined in IC 8-1-2.2-2);

(iv) rural electric membership corporation formed under IC 8-1-13-4;

(v) rural telephone cooperative corporation formed under IC 8-1-17; or

(vi) not-for-profit utility (as defined in IC 8-1-2-125);

regulated under IC 8; and

(B) intended to be used and useful for the production, transmission, delivery, or furnishing of heat, light, water, telecommunications services, or power to the public.

(c) An obligor's receipt of payment from a third person may not:

(1) be a condition precedent to;

(2) limit; or

(3) be a defense to;

the provider's right to record or foreclose a lien against the real estate that was improved by the provider's labor, material, or equipment. [P.L.2-2002, § 13; P.L.101-2002, § 8.]

Amendments. The 2002 amendment by P.L.101-2002, amending this section as enacted by P.L.2-2002, added subsection (b)(3)(A)(v), and made a related change; redesignated former subsection (b)(3)(A)(v) as (b)(3)(A)(vi); inserted "telecommunications services" in subsection (b)(3)(B); and substituted "may" for "shall" in the introductory language of subsection (c).

Effective Dates. P.L.101-2002, § 8. July 1, 2002.

CHAPTER 4

FORECLOSURE AND EXPIRATION OF A MORTGAGE OR VENDOR'S LIEN

32-28-4-1. Time of expiration — Limitations on actions. — (a) A mortgage or vendor's lien upon real estate expires ten (10) years after the last installment of the debt secured by the lien becomes due, as shown by the record of the lien.

(b) An action may not be brought or maintained in the courts of Indiana to foreclose a mortgage or enforce a vendor's lien reserved by a grantor to secure the payment of an obligation secured by the mortgage or lien if the last installment of the debt secured by the mortgage or lien, as shown by the record of the mortgage or lien, has been due more than ten (10) years. However, a lien or mortgage described in this section that was created before September 1, 1982, expires twenty (20) years after the time the last installment becomes due, and an action may not be brought to foreclose the mortgage or enforce the vendor's lien when the last installment has been due more than twenty (20) years. [P.L.2-2002, § 13.]

Effective Dates. P.L.2-2002, § 13. July 1. 2002.

Cross References. Series mortgages, IC 32-29-10.

NOTES TO DECISIONS

ANALYSIS

Conditional sale.
Distinction between mortgage and note.
Mortgages.

Conditional Sale.

Where a mortgage lien on certain described real estate and personalty attached thereto had expired by limitation under the provisions of this section, a linotype machine sold on conditional sale and attached to the mortgaged premises after expiration of the mortgage could have been recovered by the conditional seller, although the real estate mortgage had not been released of record by the mortgagee. Citizens Bank v. Mergenthaler Linotype Co., 216 Ind. 573, 25 N.E.2d 444 (1940).

Distinction Between Mortgage and Note.

Where statute of limitation provided a limit of ten years for bringing action on written actions for the payment of money and 20 years upon contracts in writing other than those for the payment of money, a mortgage was governed by the 20-year provision although the note itself may have been barred by the ten-year provision. Yarlott v. Brown, 192 Ind. 648, 138 N.E. 17 (1923).

Mortgages.

An action to foreclose a mortgage made to secure the payment of a note was controlled by the twenty-year statute of limitations, even though the mortgage contained an express promise to pay the debt. Lewis v. Davis, 114 Ind. App. 715, 55 N.E.2d 119 (1944).

Collateral References. 77 Am. Jur. 2d Vendor and Purchaser, §§ 421-473.

92 C.J.S. Vendor and Purchaser, §§ 377-395.

Validity and construction of provision of mortgage or other real-estate financing contract prohibiting prepayment for a fixed period of time. 81 A.L.R.4th 423.

32-28-4-2. Expiration — Date final installment due not included.

— (a) Except as provided in section 3 [IC 32-28-4-3] of this chapter, if the record of a mortgage or lien described in section 1 [IC 32-28-4-1] of this chapter does not show when the debt or the last installment of the debt secured by the mortgage or lien becomes due, the mortgage or vendor's lien expires twenty (20) years after the date on which the mortgage or lien is executed.

(b) If the date has been omitted in a mortgage or vendor's lien, the mortgage or vendor's lien expires twenty (20) years after the date on which the mortgage or vendor's lien is recorded. Upon the request of the owner of record of real estate encumbered by a mortgage or lien that has expired under this section, the recorder of the county in which the real estate is situated shall certify on the record that the mortgage or vendor's lien is fully paid and satisfied by lapse of time, and the real estate is released from the lien. [P.L.2-2002, § 13.]

32-28-4-3. Affidavit to state date final installment due. — (a) If the record of a mortgage or vendor's lien to which this chapter applies does not show the time when the debt or the last installment of the debt secured by the mortgage or vendor's lien becomes due:

(1) the original mortgagee;

(2) the owner of the mortgage; or

(3) the owner of a vendor's lien;

may file an affidavit with the recorder of the county where the mortgage or lien is recorded, stating when the debt becomes due. An affidavit must be filed under this section not later than twenty (20) years after the date of the mortgage or lien, or, if the mortgage or lien contains no date of execution, not later than twenty (20) years from the date the mortgage or vendor's lien was recorded. Upon the filing of the affidavit, the recorder shall note in the record of the mortgage or vendor's lien that an affidavit has been filed, showing the location where the affidavit is recorded.

(b) The filing of an affidavit under subsection (a) has the same effect with respect to the duration of the lien of the mortgage or vendor's lien described in the affidavit and with respect to the time within which an action may be brought or maintained to foreclose the mortgage or vendor's lien as though the time of maturity of the debt or the last installment of the debt secured by the mortgage or vendor's lien had been stated in the mortgage or vendor's lien when recorded. The affidavit is prima facie evidence of the truth of the averments contained in the affidavit. The lien of a mortgage or vendor's lien on the real estate described in the affidavit expires twenty (20) years after the time when the debt or the last installment of the debt secured by the mortgage or vendor's lien becomes due, as shown by the affidavit. Upon the expiration of a mortgage or lien as described in this section and at the request of the real estate owner, the recorder of the county in which the affidavit is recorded shall certify on the record of the mortgage or vendor's lien that the mortgage or vendor's lien is fully paid and satisfied by lapse of time and that the real estate is released from the lien.

(c) The recorder shall charge a fee for filing the affidavit in accordance with the fee schedule established in IC 36-2-7-10. [P.L.2-2002, § 13.]

CHAPTER 5

RELEASE OF LIENS ON CONVEYANCE OF REAL ESTATE

32-28-5-1. Recording satisfaction of lien. — (a) If a grantee has satisfied a lien on real property, the grantor shall, upon the request of the grantee, record on the lien record that the lien has been satisfied.

(b) Recording on the record of a lien under subsection (a) that the lien has been satisfied operates as a complete discharge of the lien. [P.L.2-2002, § 13.]

Effective Dates. P.L.2-2002, § 13. July 1. 2002.
Cross References. Attestation of satisfaction, IC 32-29-3-1.
Release of mortgage lien, IC 32-29-1-6.
Collateral References. 55 Am. Jur. 2d Mortgages, §§ 462-472.

59 C.J.S. Mortgages, §§ 444, 478-481.
Construction of provision in real estate mortgage, land contract, or other security instrument for release of separate parcels of land as payments are made. 41 A.L.R.3d 7.

32-28-5-2. Certification that lien is satisfied. — (a) If a grantee has satisfied a lien on real property but the grantor has not recorded that the lien has been satisfied under section 1 [IC 32-28-5-1] of this chapter, the grantor shall, at the request of the grantee, certify that the lien has been satisfied. The grantor's certification shall be acknowledged by the grantor in the same manner as is required to entitle a conveyance of real property to be recorded. The grantor's certification shall be recorded by the recorder in whose office the deed is recorded, with reference to the location of the recorded deed.

(b) A recorded certification that a lien has been satisfied operates as a complete discharge of the lien. [P.L.2-2002, § 13.]

CHAPTER 6

RELEASE OF MECHANIC'S LIENS

32-28-6-1. Requirements for release — Failure to release — Affidavit stating that no foreclosure pending. — (a) If:

(1) a person owns or has an interest in real estate to which a mechanic's lien has been attached;

(2) the debt secured by the lien has satisfied or paid; and

(3) the person who owns or has an interest in the encumbered real estate demands that the lien be released;

the lienholder shall release the lien within fifteen (15) days after the demand.

(b) If the lienholder does not release the lien within fifteen (15) days after the demand, the lienholder is liable to the person who owns or has an interest in the real estate to which the mechanic's lien has been attached for the greater of:

(1) actual damages; or

(2) liquidated damages in the sum of ten dollars ($10) per day from the fifteenth day until the release or expiration of the lien.

(c) A person who owns or who has an interest in real estate to which a mechanic's lien has been attached may, at any time thirteen (13) months after the date of the filing of the notice of the lien, file in the office of the recorder of the county in which the real estate is situated an affidavit stating that no suit for the foreclosure of the lien is pending and that no unsatisfied judgment has been rendered on the lien. [P.L.2-2002, § 13.]

Effective Dates. P.L.2-2002, § 13. July 1. 2002.

NOTES TO DECISIONS

ANALYSIS

Construction with other law.
Demand for payment.

Construction with Other Law.
Former IC 32-8-6-1 (repealed; now see this section for similar provisions) and former IC 32-8-1-2 (repealed) were repugnant to each other; in particular, the provisions pertaining to notice and damages were irreconcilable.

Southwest Forest Indus. v. Firth, 435 N.E.2d 295 (Ind. App. 1982).

Demand for Payment.
It is not necessary that the word "demand" be used in making a demand before the bringing of a suit; if any word or words are used and understood by both parties to signify that a demand is being made, then that is sufficient. Southwest Forest Indus. v. Firth, 435 N.E.2d 295 (Ind. App. 1982).

Collateral References. 53 Am. Jur. 2d Mechanics' Liens, §§ 290, 295.

56 C.J.S. Mechanics' Liens, § 276.

32-28-6-2. Recording and certification of affidavit. — If a person who owns or has an interest in real estate encumbered by a mechanic's lien files the affidavit described in section 1(c) [IC 32-28-6-1(c)] of this chapter, the recorder of the county in which the encumbered real estate is situated shall immediately record the affidavit and certify on the record of the lien that the mechanic's lien is fully satisfied and that the real estate described in the mechanic's lien is released from the lien. The fee of the recorder for the filing and recording of the affidavit shall be an amount prescribed by law and shall be paid by the person filing the affidavit. [P.L.2-2002, § 13.]

CHAPTER 7
MECHANIC'S LIENS AND LIENS ON PUBLIC IMPROVEMENTS; FORECLOSURES AND EXPIRATION

32-28-7-1. Statute of limitations. — An action may not be brought or maintained in Indiana to foreclose or enforce a mechanic's lien filed under Indiana law when the debt secured by the lien, as shown by the record of the lien, has been due more than one (1) year. If the record of the lien does not show when the debt secured by the lien became due, an action to foreclose or enforce the lien may not be brought or maintained in Indiana more than one (1) year after the filing date of the lien. [P.L.2-2002, § 13.]

Effective Dates. P.L.2-2002, § 13. July 1. 2002.

Cross References. Limitation on time for enforcement, IC 32-28-3-6.

Special procedure for satisfaction of mechanics' lien on real estate, IC 32-28-6-1, IC 32-28-6-2.

NOTES TO DECISIONS

ANALYSIS

Barred action.
Construction.
Tolling.

Barred Action.

The courts had to treat the appellant's cross complaint as a separate and distinct pleading, unaided by other pleadings in the case; it appeared on its face that it was not filed within one year from the time when notice of the lien it sought to foreclose was recorded and when it was filed said lien was null and void. Grimm v. Rhoades, 129 Ind. App. 1, 149 N.E.2d 847 (1958).

Construction.

The mechanic's lien law of this state cre-

ated new rights of purely statutory origin. The statutes providing for the lien and its enforcement were in derogation of the common law and had to be strictly construed and anyone who sought their benefits had to bring himself within their provisions. Grimm v. Rhoades, 129 Ind. App. 1, 149 N.E.2d 847 (1958).

Tolling.

Literal compliance with Rule TR. 3 by filing a complaint commences the cause of action and is sufficient to toll the statute of limitations in former IC 32-8-7-1 (repealed; see this section for similar provisions). Geiger & Peters, Inc. v. American Fletcher Nat'l Bank & Trust Co., 428 N.E.2d 1279 (Ind. App. 1981).

Collateral References. 53 Am. Jur. 2d Mechanics' Liens, § 251.

56 C.J.S. Mechanics' Liens, § 275.

"Commencement of building or improvement" for purposes of determining accrual of lien, what constitutes. 1 A.L.R.3d 822.

32-28-7-2. Expiration of mechanics lien. — A mechanic's lien filed under Indiana law expires one (1) year after the debt secured by the lien becomes due, as shown by the record of the lien. If the record of the mechanic's lien does not show when the debt secured by the lien becomes due, the mechanic's lien expires one (1) year after the filing date of the lien. [P.L.2-2002, § 13.]

Cross References. Special procedure for satisfaction of mechanics' liens on real estate, IC 32-28-6-1, IC 32-28-6-2.

NOTES TO DECISIONS

ANALYSIS

Commencement of action.
Construction.
Expired lien.

Commencement of Action.

Complaint must be filed and summons issued prior to expiration of mechanic's lien. Valley View Dev. Corp. v. Cheugh & Schlegel of Dayton, Inc., 151 Ind. App. 450, 30 Ind. Dec. 16, 280 N.E.2d 319 (1972) (decision on facts arising before adoption of Rule TR. 3 which provides that an action is commenced by filing a complaint).

Construction.

The mechanic's lien law of this state created rights of purely statutory origin. The statutes providing for the lien and its enforcement were in derogation of the common law and had to be strictly construed and anyone who sought their benefits had to bring himself within their provisions. Grimm v. Rhoades, 129 Ind. App. 1, 149 N.E.2d 847 (1958).

Expired Lien.

The courts had to treat the appellant's cross complaint as a separate and distinct pleading, unaided by other pleadings in the case; it appeared on its face that it was not filed

Expired Lien. (Cont'd)
within one year from the time when notice of the lien it sought to foreclose was recorded

and when it was filed said lien was null and void. Grimm v. Rhoades, 129 Ind. App. 1, 149 N.E.2d 847 (1958).

32-28-7-3. Expiration of liens for public improvements. —
(a) Except as provided in subsection (b), the lien of an assessment for a:
  (1) street;
  (2) sewer;
  (3) sidewalk;
  (4) ditch; or
  (5) other public improvement;
expires five (5) years after the assessment (including any installment payments) is due and payable, as shown by the record creating the lien.

(b) If an assessment is payable in installments, an action to enforce the lien may be brought within fifteen (15) years after the date of the approval of the record creating the lien. After the expiration of this time period, upon the request of the owner of record of the encumbered real estate, the custodian of the record evidencing the lien, in the jurisdiction in which the real estate is situated, shall certify on the record that the lien of the assessment for street, sewer, sidewalk, ditch, or other public improvement is satisfied and released by lapse of time and that the encumbered real estate is released from the lien. [P.L.2-2002, § 13.]

NOTES TO DECISIONS

When Limitation Commences.
The limitation for foreclosing municipal improvement assessment liens was 15 years from the final approval of the assessment, as shown by the record containing and evidencing the liens. Hennessey v. Breed, Elliott & Harrison, Inc., 92 Ind. App. 165, 176 N.E. 251 (1931).

32-28-7-4. Lien enforceable — Action begun before expiration. — If
an action to enforce a lien to which this chapter applies was commenced in Indiana before the lien expired, the lien as it existed at the time the action commenced may be enforced. [P.L.2-2002, § 13.]

NOTES TO DECISIONS

ANALYSIS

Commencement of action.
Construction.

Commencement of Action.
Complaint must be filed and summons issued prior to expiration of mechanic's lien. Valley View Dev. Corp. v. Cheugh & Schlegel of Dayton, Inc., 151 Ind. App. 450, 30 Ind. Dec. 16, 280 N.E.2d 319 (1972) (decision on facts arising before adoption of TR. 3 which provides that an action is commenced by filing a complaint).

Construction.
The mechanic's lien law of this state created new rights of purely statutory origin. The statutes providing for the lien and its enforcement were in derogation of the common law and had to be strictly construed and anyone who sought their benefits had to bring himself within their provisions. Grimm v. Rhoades, 129 Ind. App. 1, 149 N.E.2d 847 (1958).

CHAPTER 8

FORECLOSURE AND EXPIRATION OF LIENS ON PUBLIC IMPROVEMENTS

SECTION.
32-28-8-1. Statute of limitations.

32-28-8-1. Statute of limitations. — (a) Except as provided in subsection (b), an action may not be brought for the foreclosure of a lien of an assessment for a:

(1) street;
(2) sewer;
(3) sidewalk;
(4) ditch; or
(5) other public improvement;

if the action is not commenced within five (5) years after the right of action accrues.

(b) If an assessment described in subsection (a) is payable in installments, an action may be brought within fifteen (15) years after the date of the final approval of the assessment as shown by the record creating the lien. [P.L.2-2002, § 13.]

Effective Dates. P.L.2-2002, § 13. July 1. 2002.

Cross References. Reopening judgment foreclosing improvement lien, IC 32-28-9-1.

NOTES TO DECISIONS

ANALYSIS

In general.
Applicability.
Construction.
Drainage assessment liens.
Drainage bonds.
Moratorium acts.
—Effect.
Remedy of landowner.
When limitation commences.

In General.

The owners of improvement assessment liens, or the holders of bonds issued upon such liens, had only the statutory rights given them. Marshall v. Watkins, 106 Ind. App. 235, 18 N.E.2d 954 (1939).

Applicability.

This section is not limited to assessments by municipal corporations but applies to assessments made by county for drainage improvements. Marshall v. Watkins, 106 Ind. App. 235, 18 N.E.2d 954 (1939).

Construction.

This section barring actions for collection of assessment liens is a general statute of limitations, and is not limited exclusively to liens

for municipal improvements. Marshall v. Watkins, 106 Ind. App. 235, 18 N.E.2d 954 (1939).

Drainage Assessment Liens.

An action to enforce a drainage assessment lien was barred by this section, when not commenced within five years after final approval of assessment, since statute expressly included "ditches." Marshall v. Watkins, 106 Ind. App. 235, 18 N.E.2d 954 (1939).

Where the lien of assessments for sewer improvements attached to the real estate on August 23, 1928, and no effort was made thereafter to enforce the collection of unwaivered assessments pursuant to law, and Barrett Law bonds were issued against the assessments as if waivers had been properly and timely executed, an action to foreclose the lien brought in April, 1939, was barred by the statute of limitations. Read v. Abe Rosenblum & Sons, 115 Ind. App. 200, 58 N.E.2d 376 (1944).

An unverified complaint filed 19 days after the final approval of an assessment roll, designated as an appeal from assessments for sewer improvements was unauthorized, and hence did not toll the running of the statute of limitations against an action to foreclose the assessment lien. Read v. Abe Rosenblum & Sons, 115 Ind. App. 200, 58 N.E.2d 376 (1944).

Drainage Bonds.

The fifteen-year limitation provided by this act applied to drainage bonds issued for payment of drainage assessments which were finally approved less than 15 years prior to proceedings to sell such land for unpaid instalment of assessment, notwithstanding the bonds were issued under a prior statute fixing the limitation at five years. Indiana Trust Co. v. Beagley, 105 Ind. App. 502, 15 N.E.2d 758 (1938).

Moratorium Acts.

—Effect.

The Moratorium Act of 1933, ch. 2, § 1, did not have the effect to suspend the running of the statute of limitations against an action on a ditch assessment lien, in view of the provision in Acts 1935, ch. 4, § 2, providing that that act should not apply to the sale of land and lots of the payment of delinquent improvement assessments, ditch assessment or any other special assessment. Marshall v. Watkins, 106 Ind. App. 235, 18 N.E.2d 954 (1939).

Remedy of Landowner.

Where action on a special improvement lien was barred by the statute of limitations, but created an apparent lien upon the owner's land, the owner's remedy was by injunction against collection or attempting to collect such assessments. Marshall v. Watkins, 106 Ind. App. 235, 18 N.E.2d 954 (1939).

In suit to enjoin the collection of drainage assessments, and for an adjudication that liens for such assessment were no longer a lien upon the assessed property, the complaint alleging that no payment had been made on the assessment instalments during the past five years and that no suit had been brought within 15 years from the date of approval of the assessments to foreclose the assessment lien was held to state a cause of action. Marshall v. Watkins, 106 Ind. App. 235, 18 N.E.2d 954 (1939).

When Limitation Commences.

The limitation for foreclosing municipal improvement assessment liens was 15 years from the final approval of the assessment, as shown by the record containing and evidencing the liens. Hennessey v. Breed, Elliott & Harrison, Inc., 92 Ind. App. 165, 176 N.E. 251 (1931).

Collateral References. 53 Am. Jur. 2d Mechanics' Liens, § 5.

64 Am. Jur. 2d Public Works and Contracts, §§ 99-103.

56 C.J.S. Mechanics' Liens, §§ 4, 11.

CHAPTER 9

LIMITING TIME FOR REOPENING JUDGMENTS FORECLOSING LIENS FOR PUBLIC IMPROVEMENTS

32-28-9-1. Statute of limitations. — If:

(1) a court with jurisdiction in Indiana renders a judgment foreclosing a public improvement lien;

(2) the sheriff of a county sells the encumbered real estate to satisfy the lien; and

(3) the sheriff has executed a sheriff's deed for the real estate to a purchaser;

an action to reopen the judgment or invalidate the deed for any cause may not be brought unless the action is filed within one (1) year after the date of the deed. [P.L.2-2002, § 13.]

Effective Dates. P.L.2-2002, § 13. July 1. 2002.

CHAPTER 10

REAL ESTATE: EMPLOYEES' LIEN ON STRIP MINES

32-28-10-1. "Strip mine" defined. — (a) As used in this chapter, "strip mine" means a tract of land on which the surface soil has been removed or is being removed or is proposed to be removed from the coal seam by one (1) group of operating machines or machinery and where mine run coal is being produced in the raw state ready for direct sale to a consumer or for transportation to a cleaning or preparation plant.

(b) The term includes the plant used for cleaning and preparing the coal for market. [P.L.2-2002, § 13.]

Effective Dates. P.L.2-2002, § 13. July 1.
2002.

32-28-10-2. Property covered by lien — Priority — Required filings — Suits. — (a) A person employed and working in and about a strip mine has a lien on:

(1) the strip mine;

(2) all machinery and fixtures connected with the strip mine; and

(3) everything used in and about the strip mine;

for labor performed within a two (2) month period preceding the lien. Except as provided in subdivision (b), this lien is superior to and has priority over all other liens. As against each other, these liens have priority in the order in which they accrued.

(b) A state tax lien is superior to and has priority over a lien described in subsection (a).

(c) A person desiring to acquire an employee lien as described in subsection (a) shall file within sixty (60) days after the time the payment became due in the recorder's office of the county where the mine is situated a notice of intention to hold a lien upon property for the amount of the claim. The person filing a lien shall state in the lien notice the amount of the claim and the name of the coal works, if known. If the person filing the lien does not know the name of the coal works, the person shall include in the notice any other designation describing the location of the mine. The recorder shall immediately record the notice in the location used for recording mechanic's liens. The recorder shall receive a fee in accordance with IC 36-2-7-10. If the mine is located in more than one (1) county, the notice of intention to hold a lien may be filed in any county where any part of the mine is located.

(d) Suits brought to enforce a lien created under this section must be brought within one (1) year after the date of filing notice of the lien in the recorder's office. All judgments rendered on the foreclosure of the liens must include:

(1) the amount of the claim found to be due;

(2) the interest on the claim from the time due; and

(3) reasonable attorney's fees.

The judgment shall be collected without relief from valuation, appraisement, or state laws. [P.L.2-2002, § 13.]

CHAPTER 11

ENGINEER'S, LAND SURVEYOR'S, AND ARCHITECT'S LIENS

32-28-11-1. Persons who may secure and enforce lien. — Registered professional engineers, registered land surveyors, and registered architects may secure and enforce the same lien that is now given to contractors, subcontractors, mechanics, journeymen, laborers, and materialmen under IC 32-28-3 and any statutes that supplement IC 32-28-3. [P.L.2-2002, § 13.]

Effective Dates. P.L.2-2002, § 13. July 1. 2002.

Res Gestae. Rules, rulings for the trial lawyer, 39 (No. 3) Res Gestae 34 (1995).

NOTES TO DECISIONS

ANALYSIS

In general.
Applicability.
Burden of showing coverage.
Construction.
Plans prepared by persons other than architects.
Real estate developers.

In General.

Architectural plans may add value to or improve real estate, for the purpose of imposing a mechanic's lien, even though the building is never constructed. O'Hara v. Architects Hartung & Assocs., 163 Ind. App. 661, 46 Ind. Dec. 497, 326 N.E.2d 283 (1975).

Applicability.

If a claimant did not fall into one of the categories listed in the former mechanic's lien statute, that claimant was not entitled to the protection of the former statute. Greenland Homes, Inc. v. E & S Mktg. Resources, Inc., 227 Bankr. 710 (Bankr. S.D. Ind. 1998).

Burden of Showing Coverage.

Because the mechanic's lien is purely a creature of statute, the burden is on the party asserting the lien to bring itself clearly within

the strictures of the statute. Premier Invs. v. Suites of Am., Inc., 644 N.E.2d 124 (Ind. 1994).

Construction.

Provisions relating to the creation, existence, or persons entitled to claim a mechanic's lien are to be narrowly construed since the lien rights created are in derogation of common law. Premier Invs. v. Suites of Am., Inc., 644 N.E.2d 124 (Ind. 1994).

Plans Prepared by Persons Other Than Architects.

A person who was not an architect had to allege facts to have brought him within the exceptions of IC 25-4-1-18. Kolan v. Culveyhouse, 144 Ind. App. 249, 17 Ind. Dec. 23, 245 N.E.2d 683 (1969).

Real Estate Developers.

The benefits of Indiana's mechanic's lien statutes cannot be invoked by a real estate developer performing supervisory services but not physical labor, particularly a developer who is an equity participant in the project. Premier Invs. v. Suites of Am., Inc., 644 N.E.2d 124 (Ind. 1994).

Collateral References. 5 Am. Jur. 2d Architects, §§ 20-22.

56 C.J.S. Mechanics' Liens, § 33.

Amount for which mechanic's lien may be obtained where contract has been terminated or abandoned by consent of parties or without fault on contractor's part — architect's services. 51 A.L.R.2d 1009.

Mechanic's lien for services in connection with subdividing land. 87 A.L.R.2d 1004.

Surveyor's work as giving rise to right to mechanic's lien. 35 A.L.R.3d 1391.

Architect's services as within mechanics' lien statute. 31 A.L.R.5th 664.

32-28-11-2. Lien secured and enforced in same manner as mechanic's lien. — A lien created under this chapter may be secured and enforced in the same manner as mechanic's liens are secured and enforced. [P.L.2-2002, § 13.]

CHAPTER 12
CORPORATE EMPLOYEES' LIENS

32-28-12-1. Property on which lien may be held — Priority. — (a) Except as provided in subsection (b), the employees of a corporation doing business in Indiana, whether organized under Indiana law or otherwise, may have and hold a first and prior lien upon:

(1) the corporate property of the corporation; and

(2) the earnings of the corporation;

for all work and labor done and performed by the employees for the corporation from the date of the employees' employment by the corporation. A lien under this section is prior to all liens created or acquired after the date of the employment of the employees by the corporation, except as otherwise provided in this chapter.

(b) An employee lien arising from the sale of real estate:

(1) is limited to a lien on the real estate; and

(2) is subject to section 3 [IC 32-28-12-3] of this chapter.

[P.L.2-2002, § 13.]

Effective Dates. P.L.2-2002, § 13. July 1. 2002.

Cross References. Exclusive priority for debts due to employees of liquidated insurers, IC 27-9-3-40.

Preferences as to wages of clerical employees of insurance companies, which become insolvent, IC 27-9-3-40.

Wages as preferred claims generally, IC 22-2-10-1.

NOTES TO DECISIONS

ANALYSIS

Comparison to mechanics lien.
Priorities.
Who entitled to lien.

Comparison to Mechanics Lien.

An employee lien under former IC 32-8-24-1 (repealed; see this section for similar provisions) was closely analogous to a nonpossessory mechanics lien under former

Comparison to Mechanics Lien. (Cont'd) IC 32-8-31-2 (repealed; see IC 32-33-10-1 through IC 32-33-10-3 for similar provisions): both liens protected those who furnished labor or services to the entity that owned the property subject to the lien, and the filing requirements for the two types of liens were identical. Ameritrust Nat'l Bank v. Domore Corp., 147 Bankr. 473 (N.D. Ind. 1992).

Priorities.

Priority and preference claims of laborers for wages over other claims of liens where the property had passed into the hands of an assignee or receiver was upheld. Shull v. Fontanet Mining Ass'n, 128 Ind. 331, 26 N.E. 790 (1891); Eversole v. Chase, 127 Ind. 297, 26 N.E. 835 (1891); Aurora Nat'l Bank v. Black, 129 Ind. 595, 29 N.E. 396 (1891); Bell v. Hiner, 16 Ind. App. 184, 44 N.E. 576 (1896), overruled on other grounds, Board of Comm'rs v. Crone, 36 Ind. App. 283, 75 N.E. 826 (1905).

The lien of a laborer for wages on corporation property was superior to an unpreferred judgment lien which was not of record 60 days before the laborer acquired his lien. Forrest v. Corey, 29 Ind. App. 159, 64 N.E. 45 (1902).

Under former IC 32-8-24-2 (repealed) valid employee liens had priority over a security interest even though it was perfected by filing with the Indiana Secretary of State two years before the recording of the employee liens with the county recorder, since the creditor's lien was not recorded or entered on the records of the county where the corporation was located or doing business for 60 days. Ameritrust Nat'l Bank v. Domore Corp., 147 Bankr. 473 (N.D. Ind. 1992).

Who Entitled to Lien.

Contractors engaged to erect buildings and to furnish materials therefor were not laborers. Anderson Driving-Park Ass'n v. Thompson, 18 Ind. App. 458, 48 N.E. 259 (1897).

A chemist was entitled to a lien for his services to a corporation. Johnson v. Citizens' Trust Co., 78 Ind. App. 487, 136 N.E. 49 (1922).

The words "work and labor" in the former version of this statute were used in their ordinary sense and were sufficiently comprehensive to include employees who worked with their heads as well as their hands. Johnson v. Citizens' Trust Co., 78 Ind. App. 487, 136 N.E. 49 (1922).

Collateral References. 53 Am. Jur. 2d Master and Servant, § 88.

55 C.J.S. Master and Servant, §§ 139-150.

Liens for severance or dismissal pay provided for by employment contract or collective labor agreement. 40 A.L.R.2d 1044.

What are "wages" within the meaning of the priority provisions of the Bankruptcy Act (11 U.S.C. § 64(a)(2)) or of state insolvency laws. 17 A.L.R.3d 374.

32-28-12-2. Filing of notice of intention to hold lien — Priority. — (a) This section does not apply to a lien acquired by any person for purchase money.

(b) Any employee wishing to acquire a lien under section 1 [IC 32-28-12-1] of this chapter upon the corporate property of any corporation or the corporation's earnings, whether the employee's claim is due or not, must file, in the recorder's office of the county where the corporation is located or doing business, notice of the employee's intention to hold a lien upon the corporation's property and earnings. The notice must state the following:

(1) The amount of the employee's claim.

(2) The date of the employee's employment.

(3) The name of the corporation.

When a notice required by this section is presented for record, the county recorder shall record the notice in the record required by law for notice of mechanic's liens. The recorder shall charge a fee for recording the notice in an amount specified in IC 36-2-7-10(b)(1) and IC 36-2-7-10(b)(2). The lien created shall relate to the time when the employee was employed by the corporation or to any subsequent date during the employee's employment, at the election of the employee. The lien has priority over all liens suffered or created after the time elected by the employee, except other employees' liens, over which the lien has no priority.

(c) If:

(1) a person other than an employee acquires a lien upon the corporate property of any corporation located or doing business in Indiana;

(2) the lien, for a period of sixty (60) days, either:

(A) remains a matter of record in the proper place specified in IC 26-1-9.1-501; or

(B) remains otherwise perfected under applicable law; and

(3) no notice of an employee's intention to hold a lien is filed by any employee of the corporation during that period;

the lien described in subdivision (1) has priority over the lien of an employee in the county where the corporation is located or doing business. [P.L.2-2002, § 13.]

Cross References. Priorities of liens, IC 32-28-3-5.
Indiana Law Review. Developments in Contract and Commercial Law, 26 Ind. L. Rev. 761 (1993).

NOTES TO DECISIONS

ANALYSIS

Description of property.
Priority.
—Bankruptcy.
—Mechanics' liens.
—Perfected security interest.

Description of Property.

Notice by an employee of an intention to hold a lien on corporation property did not need to describe the property. Forrest v. Corey, 29 Ind. App. 159, 64 N.E. 45 (1902).

Priority.

—Bankruptcy.

That lien was perfected, then subsequently satisfied by the parties through the terms of a settlement agreement, was all that was required to make the lien unavoidable by the bankruptcy trustee, and the fact that the lien was not enforced under former IC 32-8-24-3 (repealed) was irrelevant. Petr v. Wheeler (In re Florline Corp.), 190 Bankr. 342 (Bankr. S.D. Ind. 1996).

—Mechanics' Liens.

The priority provisions of the Mechanic's Lien Law (former IC 32-8-3-5, repealed) and of the former Employees' Lien Law were in irreconcilable conflict, and, since the Mechanic's Lien Law was enacted many years later than the former Employees' Lien Law, and made an exception to the general priority granted by the earlier act, the latter act had to prevail where the lien right was properly perfected and enforced thereunder. Watson v. Strohl, 220 Ind. 672, 46 N.E.2d 204 (1943).

Where corporation employee's lien was foreclosed at a time when holder of mechanic's lien still had five months within which to foreclose and without making the holder of the mechanic's lien a party, the mechanic's lien was valid against the purchaser at the foreclosure sale. Watson v. Strohl, 220 Ind. 672, 46 N.E.2d 204 (1943).

—Perfected Security Interest.

Under the former version of this section, valid employee liens had priority over a security interest even though it was perfected by filing with the Indiana Secretary of State two years before the recording of the employee liens with the county recorder, since the creditor's lien was not recorded or entered on the records of the county where the corporation was located or doing business for 60 days. Ameritrust Nat'l Bank v. Domore Corp., 147 Bankr. 473 (N.D. Ind. 1992).

32-28-12-3. Employee claim for commission due upon conveyance of real estate — Filing of notice. — (a) Notwithstanding section 2 [IC 32-28-12-2] of this chapter, an employee:

(1) whose claim is for a commission due upon the conveyance of real estate; and

(2) who wishes to acquire a lien on the real estate;
may file a notice in the recorder's office of the county in which the real estate
is located of the employee's intention to hold a lien on the real estate.

(b) A notice filed under this section must:

(1) contain the same information required for a mechanic's lien;

(2) state that the claim is due upon the conveyance of the real estate;
and

(3) be filed before the conveyance of the real estate by the corporation.

(c) The recorder of any county shall, when notice is presented for
recording under this section:

(1) record the notice in the record required by law for notice of
mechanic's liens; and

(2) charge a fee in an amount specified in IC 36-2-7-10(b)(1) and IC
36-2-7-10(b)(2).

(d) The lien created under this section must relate to:

(1) the time when the employee was employed by the corporation; or

(2) any subsequent date during the employment, at the election of the
employee;
and has priority over all liens suffered or created after the date, except other
employees' liens, over which there is no priority. [P.L.2-2002, § 13.]

32-28-12-4. Enforcement of lien. — (a) An employee having acquired a
lien under this chapter may enforce the lien by filing a complaint in the
circuit or superior court in the county where the lien was acquired at any
time within six (6) months after the date of acquiring the lien, or if a credit
is given, after the date of the credit.

(b) The court rendering judgment for the claim shall declare the claim a
lien upon the corporation's property and order the property sold to pay and
satisfy the judgment and costs, as other lands are sold on execution or
decree, without relief from valuation or appraisement laws.

(c) In an action brought under former IC 32-8-24-3 (repealed; see this
section for similar provisions), the court shall make orders as to the
application of the earnings of the corporation that are just and equitable,
whether or not the the relief is asked for in the complaint. [P.L.2-2002,
§ 13.]

Cross References. Attorney's fees, IC 32-
28-3-14.

NOTES TO DECISIONS

Attorney's Fees.

In an action to enforce the lien of an employee against corporation property, the
plaintiff could recover an attorney's fee, as the
practice for enforcing mechanics' liens was
applicable to such actions. Forrest v. Corey, 29
Ind. App. 159, 64 N.E. 45 (1902); Johnson v.
Citizens' Trust Co., 78 Ind. App. 487, 136 N.E.
49 (1922).

Bankruptcy.

That lien was perfected, then subsequently
satisfied by the parties through the terms of a
settlement agreement, was all that was required to make the lien unavoidable by the
bankruptcy trustee, and the fact that the lien
was not enforced under former IC 32-8-24-3

Bankruptcy. (Cont'd)
(repealed; see this section for similar provisions) was irrelevant. Petr v. Wheeler (In re Florline Corp.), 190 Bankr. 342 (Bankr. S.D. Ind. 1996).

32-28-12-5. Parties to actions — Consolidation. — (a) In an action brought under this chapter, all persons whose liens are recorded under section 2 [IC 32-28-12-2] of this chapter may be made parties to the action. Issues shall be made up and trials had as in other cases.

(b) The court may, when several actions are pending by different claimants to enforce liens under this chapter, order that the cases be consolidated. If the proceeds of the sale of the corporation's property or the corporation's earnings are insufficient to pay and satisfy the claimants in full, the court shall order the claimants to be paid in proportion to the amount due each, and the sale shall be made without prejudice to the rights of any prior encumbrances, owner, or other persons not parties to the action. [P.L.2-2002, § 13.]

32-28-12-6. Written undertaking. — In a proceeding commenced under this chapter, a defendant may file a written undertaking, with surety to be approved by the court, in the exercise of sound discretion, to the effect that the defendant will pay the judgments that may be recovered, and costs. An undertaking under this section releases the defendant's property from the liens created under this chapter. [P.L.2-2002, § 13.]

32-28-12-7. Applicability of laws and rules for mechanic's liens. — In all cases not specially provided for in this chapter, the law, rules, practice, and pleadings in force in reference to the enforcement of mechanic's liens apply to suits commenced under this chapter. [P.L.2-2002, § 13.]

CHAPTER 13

COMMON LAW LIENS

32-28-13-1. "Common law lien" defined. — As used in this chapter, "common law lien" means a lien against real or personal property that is not:

(1) a statutory lien;

(2) a security interest created by agreement; or

(3) a judicial lien obtained by legal or equitable process or proceedings. [P.L.2-2002, § 13.]

Effective Dates. P.L.2-2002, § 13. July 1. 2002.

32-28-13-2. "Property owner" defined. — As used in this chapter, "property owner" means the owner of record of real or personal property against which a common law lien is held under this chapter. [P.L.2-2002, § 13.]

32-28-13-3. "Public official" defined. — As used in this chapter, "public official" means an individual who holds office in or is an employee of the executive, judicial, or legislative branch of the state or federal government or a political subdivision of the state or federal government. [P.L.2-2002, § 13.]

32-28-13-4. Purpose. — (a) This chapter provides the procedure for filing and releasing a common law lien.

(b) This chapter does not create a common law lien. A common law lien does not exist against the property of a public official for the performance or nonperformance of the public official's official duty. A person asserting a common law lien must prove the existence of the lien as prescribed by the common law of Indiana. [P.L.2-2002, § 13.]

32-28-13-5. Statement of intention — Filing — Contents — Mailing to property owner — Filing by attorney. — (a) A person who wishes to record a common law lien must file with the county recorder of a county in which the real or personal property against which the common law lien is to be held is located a statement of the person's intention to hold a common law lien against the real or personal property.

(b) A statement of intention to hold a common law lien must meet all of the following requirements:

    (1) Except as provided in subsection (d), the person filing the statement must swear or affirm that the facts contained in the statement are true to the best of the person's knowledge.

    (2) The statement must be filed in duplicate.

    (3) The statement must set forth:

        (A) the amount claimed to be owed by the property owner to the lienholder;

        (B) the name and address of the lienholder;

        (C) the name of the property owner;

        (D) the last address of the property owner as shown on the property tax records of the county;

        (E) the legal description and street and number, if any, of the real property against which the common law lien is filed;

        (F) a full description of the personal property against which the common law lien is filed, including the location of the personal property; and

        (G) the legal basis upon which the person asserts the right to hold the common law lien.

(c) The recorder shall send by first class mail one (1) of the duplicate statements filed under subsection (b) to the property owner at the address listed in the statement within three (3) business days after the statement is recorded. The county recorder shall record the date the statement is mailed to the property owner under this subsection. The county recorder shall collect a fee of two dollars ($2) from the lienholder for each statement that is mailed under this subsection.

(d) The statement of intention to hold a common law lien required under subsection (b) may be verified and filed on behalf of a client by an attorney registered with the clerk of the supreme court as an attorney in good standing under the requirements of the supreme court. [P.L.2-2002, § 13.]

32-28-13-6. Notice to commence suit by property owner. — (a) A property owner may send to the lienholder a notice requiring the lienholder to commence suit on the common law lien. The notice to commence suit must be made by registered or certified mail to the lienholder at the address given in the lienholder's statement filed under section 5 [IC 32-28-13-5] of this chapter.

(b) If the lienholder fails to commence suit within thirty (30) days after receiving the notice to commence suit, the common law lien is void. To release the common law lien from the property, the property owner must comply with the requirements of section 7 [IC 32-28-13-7] of this chapter. [P.L.2-2002, § 13.]

32-28-13-7. Affidavit of service of notice to commence suit — Release from lien — Fee. — (a) If a lienholder fails to commence suit after notice to commence suit is sent under section 6 [IC 32-28-13-6] of this chapter, a property owner may file an affidavit of service of notice to commence suit with the recorder of the county in which the statement of intention to hold a common law lien was recorded. The affidavit must:

(1) include:
(A) the date the notice to commence suit was received by the lienholder;
(B) a statement that at least thirty (30) days have elapsed from the date the notice to commence suit was received by the lienholder;
(C) a statement that a suit for foreclosure of the common law lien has not been filed and is not pending;
(D) a statement that an unsatisfied judgment has not been rendered on the common law lien; and
(E) a cross-reference specifying the record of the county recorder containing the statement of intention to hold a common law lien; and
(2) have attached to it a copy of:
(A) the notice to commence suit that was sent to the lienholder under section 6 of this chapter; and
(B) the return receipt of the notice to commence suit.

(b) The property against which the lien has been filed is released from the common law lien when the county recorder:
(1) records the affidavit of service of notice to commence suit in the miscellaneous record book of the recorder's office; and
(2) certifies in the county recorder's records that the lien is released.

(c) The county recorder shall collect a fee for filing the affidavit of service of notice to commence suit under the fee schedule established in IC 36-2-7-10. [P.L.2-2002, § 13.]

32-28-13-8. Certificate of satisfaction. — (a) When a common law lien recorded under this chapter has been satisfied, the lienholder shall record a certificate of satisfaction with the recorder of the county in which the statement of intention to hold a common law lien was recorded. The certificate must specify the record of the county recorder that contains the statement of intention to hold a common law lien filed by the lienholder under section 5 [IC 32-28-13-5] of this chapter.

(b) The certificate of satisfaction recorded under this section must discharge and release the property owner from the common law lien and bar all suits and actions on the lien.

(c) The recorder shall collect a fee for recording a certificate of satisfaction under this section in accordance with the fee schedule established in IC 36-2-7-10. [P.L.2-2002, § 13.]

32-28-13-9. Civil action against lienholder. — A person who is injured by a common law lien that is recorded under section 5 [IC 32-28-13-5] of this chapter may bring a civil action against the lienholder for:

(1) actual damages;

(2) costs; and

(3) reasonable attorney's fees. [P.L.2-2002, § 13.]

ARTICLE 29

MORTGAGES

CHAPTER 1

MORTGAGE OF REAL ESTATE

32-29-1-1. Possession of real estate. — (a) This section does not apply to security interests in rents and profits arising from real estate.

(b) Unless a mortgage specifically provides that the mortgagee shall have possession of the mortgaged premises, the mortgagee is not entitled to possession of the mortgaged premises. [P.L.2-2002, § 14.]

Effective Dates. P.L.2-2002, § 14. July 1. 2002.

NOTES TO DECISIONS

ANALYSIS

In general.
Common law.
Deeds absolute on face.
Receivership.
Rents, improvements and repairs.

In General.
This section applied only to mortgages of real estate. Broadhead v. McKay, 46 Ind. 595 (1874).

Since the enactment of this section, mortgagees have had only a lien on the mortgaged premises, and they were not entitled to the possession of the same unless the mortgage specially provided therefor. Baldwin v. Moroney, 173 Ind. 574, 91 N.E. 3, 30 L.R.A. (n.s.) 761 (1910); Yarlott v. Brown, 192 Ind. 648, 138 N.E. 17 (1923).

This section affected only the right to possession during the period of the operation of the mortgage before default. Federal Land Bank v. Schleeter, 208 Ind. 9, 194 N.E. 628 (1934), reh'g denied, 208 Ind. 16, 194 N.E. 628 (1935).

Common Law.
This section changed the common law rule that upon the execution of a mortgage the mortgagee was entitled to hold the premises from the time the mortgage went into effect until payment. Jewett v. Tomlinson, 137 Ind. 326, 36 N.E. 1106 (1893); Federal Land Bank v. Schleeter, 208 Ind. 9, 194 N.E. 628 (1934), reh'g denied, 208 Ind. 16, 194 N.E. 628 (1935).

Deeds Absolute on Face.
This section was applicable to deeds abso-

lute on their face, but which were, in fact, only mortgages. Wheeler v. Ruston, 19 Ind. 334 (1862); Smith v. Parks, 22 Ind. 59 (1864).

If an absolute deed was made, which was, in fact, a mortgage, the grantor could recover possession of the lands from one who did not claim under the grantee. Parker v. Hubble, 75 Ind. 580 (1881); Sinclair v. Gunzenhauser, 179 Ind. 78, 98 N.E. 37 (1912), reh'g overruled, 100 N.E. 376 (1913).

Receivership.
The appointment of a receiver over a Chapter 11 debtor's apartment complex did not terminate the debtor's ownership of the property or the rents it generated. That appointment did nothing more than deprive the debtor of its statutory right to possession of the property; and its ownership interest continued. In re Willows of Coventry, Ltd. Partnership, 154 Bankr. 959 (Bankr. N.D. Ind. 1993).

Rents, Improvements and Repairs.
Mortgagee in possession was chargeable with rental value of property, and on redemption was entitled to have been reimbursed for all necessary repairs. Hosford v. Johnson, 74 Ind. 479 (1881).

Mortgagee in possession of premises could recover value of repairs to mortgaged property but not improvements at the expense of the redemptioners. Miller v. Curry, 124 Ind. 48, 24 N.E. 219 (1889), rehearing overruled, 124 Ind. 53, 74 N.E. 374 (1890); Horn v. Indianapolis Nat'l Bank, 125 Ind. 381, 25 N.E. 558, 9 L.R.A. 676, 21 Am. St. R. 231 (1890).

Collateral References. 55 Am. Jur. 2d Mortgages, §§ 10-14.

59 C.J.S. Mortgages, §§ 1-12.

32-29-1-2. Covenant for the payment of a sum not implied. — A mortgage may not be construed to imply a covenant for the payment of the sum intended to be secured by the mortgage so as to enable the mortgagee or the mortgagee's assignees or representatives to maintain an action for the recovery of this sum. If an express covenant is not contained in the mortgage for the payment and a bond or other separate instrument to secure the payment has not been given, the remedy of the mortgagee is confined to the real property described in the mortgage. [P.L.2-2002, § 14.]

Cross References. Series mortgages, IC 32-29-10-1 et seq.

NOTES TO DECISIONS

In General.

If there was no agreement, in or out of the mortgage, to pay the mortgage debt, the remedy was confined to the mortgaged property. Fletcher v. Holmes, 25 Ind. 458 (1865); Harrison Bldg. & Deposit Co. v. Lackey, 149 Ind. 10, 48 N.E. 254 (1897).

The term "conveyance of real estate," as used in the statutes relating to conveyances of land infant feme coverts, comprehended mortgages of real estate as well as deeds of conveyance, and before such feme covert could disaffirm her mortgage she had to restore the consideration received, although she could have disaffirmed the note secured by the mortgage, thus avoiding liability. United States Sav. Fund & Inv. Co. v. Harris, 142 Ind. 226, 40 N.E. 1072, 41 N.E. 451 (1895).

If there was no covenant in a mortgage to pay a debt, the mortgage could not have been enforced after the debt was barred. Lilly v. Dunn, 96 Ind. 220 (1884); Tennant v. Hulet, 65 Ind. App. 24, 116 N.E. 748 (1917).

Where wife jointly executed open-ended mortgage with husband, she was not personally liable for the deficiency created by a foreclosure due to husband's subsequent indebtedness unless the mortgage contained an express covenant creating personal liability

for indebtedness of both mortgagor and borrower. Citizens Bank & Trust Co. v. Gibson, 463 N.E.2d 276 (Ind. App. 1984), modified on other grounds, 490 N.E.2d 728 (Ind. 1986).

Where mortgage agreement had provided that the mortgagors would protect title to the mortgaged property against all claims and demands and would promptly discharge any liens thereon and where the mortgagee did not have total control over the disbursement of the loan proceeds, the mortgagee was under no duty to protect the mortgagors from mechanics' liens under either the agreement, custom or practice, or the relationship between itself and the mortgagors. Woodall v. Citizens Banking Co., 503 N.E.2d 427 (Ind. App. 1987).

This section (formerly IC 32-8-11-2) only states that a mortgage will not be construed as implying a covenant for the payment of a sum intended to be secured. An action for personal liability is maintainable where an express covenant for payment is contained in the mortgage. First Ind. Fed. Sav. Bank v. Hartle, 567 N.E.2d 834 (Ind. App. 1991).

In the absence of an express agreement to pay, a mortgagee's remedy is confined to foreclosure only. First Ind. Fed. Sav. Bank v. Hartle, 567 N.E.2d 834 (Ind. App. 1991).

Collateral References. Validity and construction of provision of mortgage or other real-estate financing contract prohibiting pre-

payment for a fixed period of time. 81 A.L.R.4th 423.

32-29-1-3. Sale of property by mortgagee. — A mortgage of real estate, including an instrument having the legal effect of a mortgage, may not authorize the mortgagee to sell the mortgaged property. The sale of mortgaged property by the mortgagee may only be made under a judicial proceeding. [P.L.2-2002, § 14.]

Cross References. Foreclosure of mortgages, IC 32-29-7-3.

Trustee, power to sell, IC 30-1-9-18.

NOTES TO DECISIONS

In General.

This section prohibited a power of sale in

the mortgage. Eaton & H.R.R. v. Hunt, 20 Ind. 457 (1863). See also Baldwin v. Moroney, 173

In General. (Cont'd)
Ind. 574, 91 N.E. 3, 30 L.R.A. (n.s.) 761 (1910).

A later act (June 17, 1852, IC 30-1-9-18) authorized a power of sale in trust mortgages. Eaton & H.R.R. v. Hunt, 20 Ind. 457 (1863); Sinclair v. Gunzenhauser, 179 Ind. 78, 98 N.E. 37 (1912).

The mortgagee was not forbidden to act as agent for the sale of the lands mortgaged where the agency was not created by the mortgage. Farley v. Eller, 29 Ind. 322 (1868).

Where deed was actually executed as mortgage to secure repayment, the real estate described in the deed should have been sold on execution to satisfy the amount due. Smith v. Brand, 64 Ind. 427 (1878).

When express authority was given the trustee to sell and convey, he did not need to apply to the court for authority to sell. Iles v. Martin, 69 Ind. 114 (1879).

Collateral References. Rights of holder of "first refusal" option on real property in event of sale at foreclosure or other involuntary sale. 17 A.L.R.3d 962.

32-29-1-4. Priority of mortgage for purchase money. — A mortgage granted by a purchaser to secure purchase money has priority over a prior judgment against the purchaser. [P.L.2-2002, § 14.]

Cross References. Widow, rights against purchase-money mortgage, IC 29-1-2-2(b).

NOTES TO DECISIONS

ANALYSIS

In general.
Determination of status as purchase-money mortgage.

In General.
The taking of a mortgage for purchase-money was a waiver of the equitable lien of the vendor. Harris v. Harlan, 14 Ind. 439 (1860); Mattix v. Weand, 19 Ind. 151 (1862); Wilson v. Hunter, 30 Ind. 466 (1868); Fouch v. Wilson, 60 Ind. 64, 28 Am. R. 651 (1877); Anderson v. Donnell, 66 Ind. 150 (1879); Richards v. McPherson, 74 Ind. 158 (1881), overruled on other grounds, Shaw v. Rigby, 84 Ind. 375 (1882); Robbins v. Masteller, 147 Ind. 122, 46 N.E. 330 (1897); Cassidy v. Ward, 70 Ind. App. 550, 123 N.E. 724 (1919).

A vendor of lands who neglected to take a mortgage to secure purchase-money until after the execution of a mortgage thereon to a third person, for value, without notice, was postponed to the latter. Houston v. Houston, 67 Ind. 276 (1879).

The taking of a new mortgage by a vendor for purchase-money in lieu of an old mortgage did not deprive him of his right of priority. Hanlon v. Doherty, 109 Ind. 37, 9 N.E. 782 (1887).

When a person advances the purchase price for real estate and secures that present debt and a preexisting debt with a mortgage on that real estate, consideration is sufficiently present to support the mortgage. Further, "value" is sufficiently present to establish that person as a bona fide purchaser. Huntingburg Prod. Credit Ass'n v. Griese, 456 N.E.2d 448 (Ind. App. 1983).

Determination of Status as Purchase-Money Mortgage.
The tests employed in determining whether a mortgage was a purchase-money mortgage were whether the proceeds were applied to the purchase price and whether the deed and mortgage were executed as part of the same transaction. Liberty Parts Whse., Inc. v. Marshall County Bank & Trust, 459 N.E.2d 738 (Ind. App. 1984).

32-29-1-5. Required language. — A mortgage of land that is:
(1) worded in substance as "A.B. mortgages and warrants to C.D." (here describe the premises) "to secure the repayment of" (here recite the sum for which the mortgage is granted, or the notes or other evidences of debt, or a description of the debt sought to be secured, and the date of the repayment); and
(2) dated and signed, sealed, and acknowledged by the grantor;

is a good and sufficient mortgage to the grantee and the grantee's heirs, assigns, executors, and administrators, with warranty from the grantor (as defined in IC 32-17-1-1) and the grantor's legal representatives of perfect title in the grantor and against all previous encumbrances. However, if in the mortgage form the words "and warrant" are omitted, the mortgage is good but without warranty. [P.L.2-2002, § 14.]

NOTES TO DECISIONS

ANALYSIS

In general.
After-acquired title.
Conflict of laws.
Deed absolute as mortgage.
Description.
—Debt.
—Land.
Estoppel of mortgagor.
Flaws in document.
Form.
Signature of mortgagor.

In General.

Only the mortgagee, his heirs, assigns, executors, or administrators could have had recourse on the covenants of warranty in a mortgage. Parker v. Rodman, 84 Ind. 256 (1882).

A mortgage with warranty was entitled to as much faith and confidence as a warranty deed. Rinehardt v. Reifers, 158 Ind. 675, 64 N.E. 459 (1902).

The fact that in executing a mortgage on a grain elevator situated on real estate owned by a railroad, which constituted an "interest in real estate," a chattel mortgage form was used did not change the character of the mortgage, nor estop the mortgagee from asserting that the mortgage was properly recorded in the county where the elevator was situated, in view of this section and IC 32-1-2-16. Lincoln Nat'l Bank & Trust Co. v. Nathan, 215 Ind. 178, 19 N.E.2d 243 (1939).

After-Acquired Title.

If a mortgage did not contain a warranty, an after-acquired title by the mortgagor would not have inured to the benefit of the mortgagee. Curren v. Driver, 33 Ind. 480 (1870), overruled on other grounds, Tanguey v. O'Connell, 132 Ind. 62, 31 N.E. 469 (1892).

Conflict of Laws.

Mortgages of land were governed by the laws in force at the place the land was situated. Nathan v. Lee, 152 Ind. 232, 52 N.E. 987, 43 L.R.A. 820 (1899).

Deed Absolute as Mortgage.

If the deed were made to secure a subsisting debt, it would have been held to be a mortgage. The test of whether it was a deed or a mortgage was whether it was executed to secure the payment of a debt. Hanlon v. Doherty, 109 Ind. 37, 9 N.E. 782 (1887); Voss v. Eller, 109 Ind. 260, 10 N.E. 74 (1887); Wolfe v. McMillan, 117 Ind. 587, 20 N.E. 509 (1888); Bever v. Bever, 144 Ind. 157, 41 N.E. 944 (1895); Brown v. Folette, 155 Ind. 316, 58 N.E. 197 (1900); Greenwood Bldg. & Loan Ass'n v. Stanton, 28 Ind. App. 548, 63 N.E. 574 (1902); White v. Redenbaugh, 41 Ind. App. 580, 82 N.E. 110 (1907); Beidelman v. Koch, 42 Ind. App. 423, 85 N.E. 977 (1908); Wysong v. Sells, 44 Ind. App. 238, 88 N.E. 954 (1909); Sinclair v. Gunzenhauser, 179 Ind. 78, 98 N.E. 37 (1912); Calahan v. Dunker, 51 Ind. App. 436, 99 N.E. 1021 (1912); Ward v. Tuttle, 54 Ind. App. 674, 102 N.E. 405 (1913); Voris v. Ferrell, 57 Ind. App. 1, 103 N.E. 122 (1913); Rooker v. Fidelity Trust Co., 185 Ind. 172, 109 N.E. 766 (1915); In re Aurora Gaslight, Coal & Coke Co., 64 Ind. App. 690, 113 N.E. 1012 (1916).

A deed absolute on its face could have been shown to have been executed as a mortgage. Kitts v. Willson, 130 Ind. 492, 29 N.E. 401 (1891); Scobey v. Kiningham, 131 Ind. 552, 31 N.E. 355 (1892); Pool v. Davis, 135 Ind. 323, 34 N.E. 1130 (1893); Loeb v. McAlister, 15 Ind. App. 643, 41 N.E. 1061, 44 N.E. 378 (1895), reh'g overruled, Kelso v. Kelso, 16 Ind. App. 615, 44 N.E. 1013 (1896); Mott v. Fiske, 155 Ind. 597, 58 N.E. 1053 (1900); Matchett v. Knisely, 27 Ind. App. 664, 62 N.E. 87 (1901); Greenwood Bldg. & Loan Ass'n v. Stanton, 28 Ind. App. 548, 63 N.E. 574 (1902); Calahan v. Dunker, 51 Ind. App. 436, 99 N.E. 1021 (1912); Voris v. Ferrell, 57 Ind. App. 1, 103 N.E. 122 (1913); In re Aurora Gaslight, Coal & Coke Co., 64 Ind. App. 690, 113 N.E. 1012 (1916).

Description.

—Debt.

Former IC 32-1-2-15 (repealed; see this section for similar provisions) did not require that the mortgage refer specifically to the amount of indebtedness or the notes which evidence the debt. It only required the debt to be described. Literal accuracy in describing the debt was not required. Commercial Bank v. Rockovits, 499 N.E.2d 765 (Ind. App. 1986).

Description. (Cont'd)

—Land.

In order for a mortgage to be effective, a mortgage must contain a description of the land intended to be covered. The description of the real estate must be sufficient to identify it, or it must furnish the means by which it can be identified. In re Dunn, 109 Bankr. 865 (Bankr. N.D. Ind. 1988).

Estoppel of Mortgagor.

If a mortgage contained covenants of warranty, the mortgagor was estopped to deny that he had title to the premises mortgaged. Boone v. Armstrong, 87 Ind. 168 (1882); Thalls v. Smith, 139 Ind. 496, 39 N.E. 154 (1894); Griffis v. First Nat'l Bank, 168 Ind. 546, 81 N.E. 490 (1907).

A mortgagor was estopped to aver, as against his mortgagee, that he had no title to the land mortgaged. Scobey v. Kiningham, 131 Ind. 552, 31 N.E. 355 (1892).

Flaws in Document.

Slight variation in the corporate name of the debtor, which variation did not differ from the actual corporate name until the fifth word in the name, was insufficient in itself to nullify the constructive notice gained by recording the mortgage or to render the mortgage invalid as to the corporation. Arnol & Mildred Shafer Farms, Inc. v. ITT Fin. Services—Commercial Div., 102 Bankr. 712 (Bankr. N.D. Ind.), rev'd on other grounds sub nom. United States v. Arnol & Mildred Shafer Farms, Inc, 107 Bankr. 605 (N.D. Ind. 1989).

Form.

Former IC 32-1-2-15 (repealed; see this section for similar provisions) suggested a minimum form of mortgage. However, no particular form of words is necessary to constitute a mortgage of real property and, if an instrument shows a present purpose on the part of a mortgagor to create an encumbrance or lien on specified real property as security for the payment of a debt or the performance of an obligation, it is sufficient to constitute a mortgage. In re Dunn, 109 Bankr. 865 (Bankr. N.D. Ind. 1988).

Signature of Mortgagor.

A mortgage signed by the mortgagor by his Christian name only could have been good where the surname of the grantor was otherwise shown. Zann v. Haller, 71 Ind. 136, 36 Am. R. 193 (1880).

Collateral References. Construction of provision in real estate mortgage, land contract, or other security instrument for release of separate parcels of land as payments are made. 41 A.L.R.3d 7.

32-29-1-6. Entry of satisfaction into record. — After a mortgagee of property whose mortgage has been recorded has received full payment from the mortgagor of the sum specified in the mortgage, the mortgagee shall, at the request of the mortgagor, enter in the record of the mortgage that the mortgage has been satisfied. An entry in the record showing that a mortgage has been satisfied operates as a complete release and discharge of the mortgage. [P.L.2-2002, § 14.]

Cross References. Deeds, reservation of liens, satisfaction, IC 32-28-5-1, IC 32-28-5-2.

Opinions of Attorney General. If a mortgagor, after payment of a mortgage in full, requested any mortgagee [including an out-of-state corporation] to enter satisfaction of the mortgage on the margin or other proper place in the record of such mortgage, the mortgagor was required to do so by former IC 32-8-11-5 (repealed; now see this section for similar provisions). 1989, No. 89-26.

NOTES TO DECISIONS

Renewal of mortgage.
Sufficiency of satisfaction.
Tender and demand before maturity.

In General.

The holder of a mortgage was not bound to enter satisfaction thereof until it was fully paid. Storey v. Krewson, 55 Ind. 397, 23 Am. R. 668 (1876).

Mortgagee had no implied duty to facilitate the sale of a portion of the real estate before pursuing its right to foreclose under the mortgage. Gainer Bank v. Cosmopolitan Nat'l Bank, 577 N.E.2d 982 (Ind. App. 1991).

Assignment.

In an action by the assignee against the assignor who was the payee of a promissory note secured by a mortgage on real estate, to recover damages for the alleged unlawful act of the defendant in satisfying the mortgage while the note remained unpaid, the complaint should have alleged the value of the mortgage so assigned. Fox v. Wray, 56 Ind. 423 (1877).

An entry of satisfaction by a mortgagee after he had assigned the debt secured was void. Reeves v. Hayes, 95 Ind. 521 (1884).

A mortgagee's satisfaction subsequent to an unrecorded assignment was valid as to innocent purchasers. Goldenson v. Lieberman, 73 App. 636, 127 N.E. 161 (1920).

Consideration.

As between the parties, it could have been set up that the entry of satisfaction was without consideration. Harris v. Boone, 69 Ind. 300 (1879).

Death of Mortgagee.

If the mortgage became inoperative by the death of the mortgagee, the mortgagor could have had the same declared satisfied. Murdock v. Cox, 118 Ind. 266, 20 N.E. 786 (1888).

Decree for Entry of Satisfaction.

An entry of satisfaction made by order of court only affected the parties to the proceeding. Dixon v. Hunter, 57 Ind. 278 (1877).

Courts on having decreed that a mortgage should have been entered satisfied could di-

rect the clerk to make the entry. Anderson Bldg., Loan Fund & Sav. Ass'n v. Thompson, 87 Ind. 278 (1882).

Executors and Administrators.

The administrator of the estate of a mortgagee could enter satisfaction of a mortgage. Connecticut Mut. Life Ins. Co. v. Talbot, 113 Ind. 373, 14 N.E. 586, 3 Am. St. 655 (1887).

Fraud.

When an entry of satisfaction was procured by fraud, such entry could have been set aside. Reagan v. Hadley, 57 Ind. 509 (1877); Burton v. Reagan, 75 Ind. 77 (1881).

Record as Constructive Notice.

After entry of satisfaction, the record was no longer constructive notice to parties who had no notice that the entry was improperly procured. Etzler v. Evans, 61 Ind. 56 (1878); Farmers' Bank v. Butterfield, 100 Ind. 229 (1884).

Release by Joint Mortgagee.

A release of a mortgage by one joint mortgagee did not affect the rights of the other mortgagee. Howe v. White, 162 Ind. 74, 69 N.E. 684 (1904).

Renewal of Mortgage.

Taking a new mortgage in place of an old one discharged the old mortgage. Smith v. Wells Mfg. Co., 148 Ind. 333, 46 N.E. 1000 (1897).

Sufficiency of Satisfaction.

An entry that signified that the mortgage had been fully paid was sufficient. Richards v. McPherson, 74 Ind. 158 (1881), overruled on other grounds, Shaw v. Rigby, 84 Ind. 375 (1882).

In entering satisfaction on the margin of the record, it was not necessary to describe the lands. Bryant v. Richardson, 126 Ind. 145, 25 N.E. 807 (1890).

Tender and Demand Before Maturity.

A complaint to compel satisfaction showing a tender and demand for satisfaction before maturity of the debt was had. Bowen v. Julius, 141 Ind. 310, 40 N.E. 700 (1894).

32-29-1-7. Certificate of satisfaction. — If a mortgage has been paid and satisfied by the mortgagor, the mortgagor may take a certificate of satisfaction, duly acknowledged by the mortgagee or the mortgagee's lawful agent, as required for the acknowledgment of conveyances to entitle them to be recorded. The certificate and acknowledgment shall be recorded by the recorder in whose office the mortgage is recorded, with a reference to the location of the record of the mortgage. The recorded certificate discharges and releases the mortgagor from the mortgage (or portion of the mortgage as indicated in a partial satisfaction), and bars all suits and actions on the mortgage. [P.L.2-2002, § 14.]

NOTES TO DECISIONS

In General.
Any entry showing full payment was a sufficient entry of satisfaction. Richards v. McPherson, 74 Ind. 158 (1881), overruled on other grounds, Shaw v. Rigby, 84 Ind. 375 (1882).

The release of the mortgage was not invalid on account of a misdescription of the property if the mortgage was otherwise sufficiently identified. Bryant v. Richardson, 126 Ind. 145, 25 N.E. 807 (1890).

32-29-1-8. Assignment of mortgage. — (a) Any mortgage of record or any part of the mortgage may be assigned by the mortgagee or any assignee of the mortgage, either by an assignment entered on the margin of the record, signed by the person making the assignment and attested by the recorder, or by a separate instrument executed and acknowledged before any person authorized to take acknowledgments, and recorded in the mortgage records of the county. The county recorder shall note the assignment in the margin by reference to the location where the assignment is recorded.

(b) The signature of a person on an assignment under subsection (a) may be a facsimile. The facsimile on the assignment is equivalent to and constitutes the written signature of the person for all requirements regarding mortgage assignments.

(c) Notwithstanding subsection (a), marginal assignments may be accepted at the discretion of the recorder. Except in a county that accepts marginal assignments of mortgage, an assignment of mortgage must be recorded on a separate written instrument from the mortgage. If a recorder accepts marginal assignments of mortgage, an instrument presented for recording in that county may not contain more than one (1) assignment. If a recorder allows an instrument to contain more than one (1) assignment, the fee for recording that instrument is provided in IC 36-2-7-10(b)(3).

(d) After entry is made of record, the mortgagor and all other persons are bound by the record, and the entry is a public record. Any assignee may enter satisfaction or release of the mortgage, or the part of the mortgage held by the assignee of record. [P.L.2-2002, § 14.]

NOTES TO DECISIONS

Acknowledgment.
Acknowledgment of the assignment of a mortgage was only necessary to entitle the same to record. Tulley v. Citizens' State Bank, 18 Ind. App. 240, 47 N.E. 850 (1897).

Allegation of Assignment.
A complaint by an assignee to foreclose a mortgage, which merely averred that the mortgage was indorsed to him, without stating by whom, was not good as against a

Allegation of Assignment. (Cont'd)
demurrer for defect of parties, because the
mortgagee was not made a defendant. Nichol
v. Henry, 89 Ind. 54 (1883).

Assignment of Debt.
An assignment of a debt secured by mort-
gage carried with it the mortgage security.
Garrett v. Puckett, 15 Ind. 485 (1860); Sample
v. Rowe, 24 Ind. 208 (1865); Parkhurst v.
Watertown Steam Engine Co., 107 Ind. 594, 8
N.E. 635 (1886); Baugher v. Woollen, 147 Ind.
308, 45 N.E. 94 (1896); Perry v. Fisher, 30 Ind.
App. 261, 65 N.E. 935 (1903).
Assignment of part of notes secured by a
mortgage operated as an assignment of the
mortgage pro tanto. Parkhurst v. Watertown
Steam Engine Co., 107 Ind. 594, 8 N.E. 635
(1886).

Assignment of Mortgage Without Debt.
The assignment of a mortgage without a
transfer of the debt secured conveyed no
right. French v. Turner, 15 Ind. 59 (1860);
Johnson v. Cornett, 29 Ind. 59 (1867);
Hubbard v. Harrison, 38 Ind. 323 (1871).

Effect of Statute.
Prior to the adoption of this section, parties
lost none of their rights by failing to have
assignments of mortgages recorded.
Hasselman v. McKernan, 50 Ind. 441 (1875);
Dixon v. Hunter, 57 Ind. 278 (1877); Reeves v.
Hayes, 95 Ind. 521 (1884); Citizens State
Bank v. Julian, 153 Ind. 655, 55 N.E. 1007
(1899).
On the adoption of this section, it applied to
all mortgages then of record and theretofore
equitably assigned. Connecticut Mut. Life
Ins. Co. v. Talbot, 113 Ind. 373, 14 N.E. 586, 3
Am. St. 655 (1887); Citizens State Bank v.
Julian, 153 Ind. 655, 55 N.E. 1007 (1899).

Mortgage to Secure Commercial Paper.
The assignee of a mortgage given to secure
commercial paper took the mortgage like the
paper, if for value, before maturity, free from
all the equities which might have constituted
a defense. Gabbert v. Schwartz, 69 Ind. 450
(1880).

Record.
If the assignee failed to have his assign-
ment recorded, persons could act on a release
of the mortgage executed by the mortgage.
Connecticut Mut. Life Ins. Co. v. Talbot, 113
Ind. 373, 14 N.E. 586, 3 Am. St. 655 (1887).
The assignee of a mortgage had to take
notice of all mortgages of record and of the
rights of the parties thereunder. Brower v.
Witmeyer, 121 Ind. 83, 22 N.E. 975 (1889).
If the assignment of a mortgage was not on
record, it was presumed that the mortgagee
owned the debt secured by the mortgage.
Baugher v. Woollen, 147 Ind. 308, 45 N.E. 94
(1896).
Failure to have the assignment of a mortgage recorded rendered the same ineffective
as to subsequent purchasers only. Citizens
State Bank v. Julian, 153 Ind. 655, 55 N.E.
1007 (1899); Tulley v. Citizens State Bank, 18
Ind. App. 240, 47 N.E. 850 (1897).
If the assignee of record of a mortgage
acquired title to the land and conveyed the
same, the grantee held the land free of claims
of assignees whose assignments were not recorded. Artz v. Yeager, 30 Ind. App. 677, 66
N.E. 917 (1903).
The entry of satisfaction by the mortgagee
after the assignment of the mortgage was
valid as to innocent purchasers when the
assignment was not recorded. Goldenson v.
Lieberman, 73 Ind. App. 636, 127 N.E. 161
(1920).

—Persons Protected.
The recording provisions of this section
were enacted to protect subsequent purchasers and mortgagees and not the original mortgagor. Rowe v. Small Bus. Admin., 446 N.E.2d
991 (Ind. App. 1983).

32-29-1-9. Chapter does not affect provisions on foreclosure. —
This chapter does not affect any provisions made by law relating to the
foreclosure of mortgages to the state, so far as the provisions conflict with
the provisions of this chapter. [P.L.2-2002, § 14.]

32-29-1-10. Items covered by mortgage. — (a) In addition to any
other obligation secured by a mortgage, a mortgage may also secure:
  (1) future obligations and advances up to the maximum amount stated
  in the mortgage (whether made as an obligation, made at the option of
  the lender, made after a reduction to a zero (0) or other balance, or made
  otherwise) to the same extent as if the future obligations and advances
  were made on the date of execution of the mortgage; and

(2) future modifications, extensions, and renewals of any indebtedness or obligations secured by the mortgage if and to the extent that the mortgage states that the mortgage secures those future advances, modifications, extensions, and renewals.

(b) The lien of a mortgage with respect to future advances, modifications, extensions, and renewals referred to in subsection (a) has the priority to which the mortgage otherwise would be entitled under IC 32-21-4-1 without regard to the fact that the future advance, modification, extension, or renewal may occur after the mortgage is executed. [P.L.2-2002, § 14.]

32-29-1-11. Rents and profits — Assignments — Not limited by chapter. — (a) This chapter does not limit:

(1) the right to assign, mortgage, or pledge the rents and profits arising from real estate;

(2) the right of an assignee, a mortgagee, or a pledgee to collect rents and profits for application in accordance with an assignment, a mortgage, or a pledge; or

(3) the power of a court of equity to appoint a receiver to take charge of real estate to collect rents and profits for application in accordance with an assignment, a mortgage, or a pledge.

(b) A person may enforce an assignment, a mortgage, or a pledge of rents and profits arising from real property:

(1) whether the person has or does not have possession of the real estate; and

(2) regardless of the:

(A) adequacy of the security; or

(B) solvency of the assignor, mortgagor, or pledgor.

(c) If a person:

(1) enforces an assignment, a mortgage, or a pledge of rents and profits arising from real estate; and

(2) does not have possession of the real estate;

the obligations of a mortgagee in possession of real estate may not be imposed on the holder of the assignment, mortgage, or pledge. [P.L.2-2002, § 14.]

CHAPTER 2

RECORDING OF ASSIGNMENT

32-29-2-1. Transfer or assignment in writing — Acknowledgment. — A person who transfers or assigns a mortgage within Indiana shall do so in writing by:

(1) noting the assignment or transfer on the record recording the mortgage; or

(2) separate written instrument.

A person who transfers or assigns a mortgage as described in this section shall cause the notation or written instrument to be acknowledged before an officer authorized to take acknowledgments of the execution of mortgages. [P.L.2-2002, § 14.]

Effective Dates. P.L.2-2002, § 14. July 1. 2002.

NOTES TO DECISIONS

In General.

The assignment of a note secured by mortgage was not a written assignment of the mortgage as required by this statute. Perry v. Fisher, 30 Ind. App. 261, 65 N.E. 935 (1903).

Where a mortgage was given to secure a series of bonds, which bonds were payable to the mortgagee or bearer, and the mortgagee sold some of the bonds, the purchaser thereof did not lose the security afforded by the mortgage, if he failed to record an assignment of his proportional interest in said mortgage, by reason of the provisions of Acts 1899, ch. 122, § 2, p. 191, repealed by Acts 1933, ch. 128, § 1. Kaufmann v. Millies, 106 Ind. App. 569, 18 N.E.2d 970 (1939).

Where a mortgage securing corporate bonds issued during a certain year recited that the bonds of an issue for said year were to be used "for the purpose of refunding and paying the indebtedness secured by ... mortgages and encumbrances now against said real estate," was properly recorded, purchasers of said bonds had constructive notice of the prior bonds and encumbrances of the respective holders of bonds issued during such year by reason of the recording of the mortgage. Kaufmann v. Millies, 106 Ind. App. 569, 18 N.E.2d 970 (1939).

Collateral References. 66 Am. Jur. 2d Records and Recording Laws, § 61.

59 C.J.S. Mortgages, § 201.

32-29-2-2. Instrument must contain location and address of transferee or assignee. — In order to be recorded, a written instrument that transfers or assigns a mortgage under this chapter must state the location and business address of the person to whom the mortgage is transferred or assigned. [P.L.2-2002, § 14.]

CHAPTER 3

ATTESTATION OF RELEASES; LEGALIZING PRIOR RELEASE

SECTION.
32-29-3-1. Attestation of releases.

32-29-3-1. Attestation of releases. — The release of a mortgage, lease, or other instrument required by law to be recorded written upon the margin, or upon the record, of any mortgage in Indiana by the party authorized to release the mortgage is not a valid release of the mortgage, lease, or other instrument unless the release is attested on the record by the recorder or deputy recorder of the county in which the mortgage is recorded. [P.L.2-2002, § 14.]

Effective Dates. P.L.2-2002, § 14. July 1. 2002.

CHAPTER 4

RELEASE BY STATE

SECTION.
32-29-4-1. Release and discharge by state.

32-29-4-1. Release and discharge by state. — If the mortgage records of a county in Indiana indicate that a mortgage has been executed to the state and:

(1) there is no evidence of indebtedness secured by the mortgage in the possession of the treasurer of state or auditor of state; and

(2) there is no evidence in the office of the auditor of state or treasurer of state that a loan secured by the mortgage was made;

the auditor of state may release and discharge the mortgage of record. [P.L.2-2002, § 14.]

Effective Dates. P.L.2-2002, § 14. July 1.
2002.

CHAPTER 5

RELEASE BY FINANCIAL INSTITUTIONS OR CORPORATIONS

SECTION.
32-29-5-1. Release by financial institutions
            or corporations.

32-29-5-1. Release by financial institutions or corporations. — (a) It is lawful for:

(1) the president, vice president, cashier, secretary, treasurer, attorney in fact, or other authorized representative of a national bank, state bank, trust company, or savings bank; or

(2) the president, vice president, general manager, secretary, treasurer, attorney in fact, or other authorized representative of any other corporation doing business in Indiana;

to release upon the record mortgages, judgments, and other record liens upon the payment of the debts secured by the liens.

(b) A release, when made upon the margin or face of the record of the mortgage, judgment, or other lien and attested by the recorder, clerk, or other officer having custody of the record of the lien, is a full discharge and satisfaction of the lien.

(c) The recorder of each county may require that each release, discharge, or satisfaction of a mortgage, judgment, or lien, or any partial release of any of these, be recorded on a separate written instrument. If a recorder requires the recording of each release, discharge, or satisfaction on a separate written instrument, an instrument presented for recordation in that county may not contain more than one (1) release, discharge, or satisfaction. If a recorder allows an instrument to contain more than one (1) release, discharge, or satisfaction, the fee for recording that instrument is provided in IC 36-2-7-10(b)(3).

(d) Except as provided in subsection (e), a national bank, state bank, trust company, savings bank, or other corporation may release and discharge mortgages, judgments, or other record liens by a separate written instrument signed by its:
(1) corporate name;
(2) president;
(3) vice president;
(4) cashier;
(5) secretary;
(6) treasurer;
(7) attorney-in-fact; or
(8) authorized representative.
A release under this subsection shall be recorded by the recorder, clerk, or other officer having custody of the record of the lien, with a reference on the margin of the record of the lien to the location where the release is recorded. Upon recordation, the release is a full discharge and satisfaction of the lien, or portion of the lien, as indicated in a partial release.

(e) A release by the attorney-in-fact may not be recorded until a written instrument specifically granting the attorney in fact the authority to release and discharge mortgages, judgments, or other record liens has been filed and recorded in the recorder's office of the county where the release is to be recorded. The written instrument must be in writing and signed and acknowledged by two (2) officers of the national bank, state bank, trust company, savings bank, or other corporation.

(f) A party may revoke the written instrument filed under subsection (e) by:
(1) noting on the written instrument granting the attorney in fact the authority to release mortgages and liens that this power has been revoked; or
(2) filing and recording in the recorder's office of the county where the written instrument described in subsection (e) of this section was filed, a separate written instrument signed and acknowledged by two (2) officers of the entity revoking the attorney-in-fact's authority.
The written notice of revocation described in this subsection must be attested by the recorder of the county in which the revocation is filed. The party conferring the power described in subsection (e) is bound by an act performed before written notice revoking the authority is properly attested to and filed in the county recorder's office. [P.L.2-2002, § 14.]

Effective Dates. P.L.2-2002, § 14. July 1. 2002.
Opinions of Attorney General. A Florida corporation was required to pay the recording fees that were provided by IC 36-2-7-10 for the release of mortgages in the state of Indiana. 1989, No. 89-26.

NOTES TO DECISIONS

Applicability.
Former IC 32-8-15-1 (repealed; now see this section for similar provisions) applied to powers of attorney given by national banks and corporations, and not to powers of attorney given to national banks and corporations. Sagamore Park Centre Assocs. v. Sagamore Park Properties, 200 Bankr. 332 (N.D. Ind. 1996).

Collateral References. 55 Am. Jur. 2d
Mortgages, §§ 1405-1407.
59 C.J.S. Mortgages, §§ 458, 468.

CHAPTER 6

MORTGAGE RELEASE BY TITLE INSURANCE COMPANIES

32-29-6-1. "Mortgage" defined [expires pursuant to IC 32-29-6-17].
— As used in this chapter, "mortgage" means a mortgage or mortgage lien on an interest in real property in Indiana given to secure a loan in the original principal amount of not more than one million dollars ($1,000,000). [P.L.2-2002, § 14.]

Effective Dates. P.L.2-2002, § 14. July 1.
2002.

32-29-6-2. "Mortgagee" defined [expires pursuant to IC 32-29-6-17].
— As used in this chapter, "mortgagee" means:
(1) the grantee of a mortgage; or
(2) if a mortgage has been assigned of record, the last person to whom the mortgage has been assigned of record. [P.L.2-2002, § 14.]

32-29-6-3. "Mortgage servicer" defined [expires pursuant to IC 32-29-6-17]. — As used in this chapter, "mortgage servicer" means the last person to whom a mortgagor or the mortgagor's successor in interest has been instructed by a mortgagee to send payments on a loan secured by a mortgage. A person transmitting a payoff statement is the mortgage servicer for the mortgage described in the payoff statement. [P.L.2-2002, § 14.]

32-29-6-4. "Mortagor" defined [expires pursuant to IC 32-29-6-17]. — As used in this chapter, "mortgagor" means the grantor of a mortgage. [P.L.2-2002, § 14.]

32-29-6-5. "Payoff statement" defined [expires pursuant to IC 32-29-6-17]. — As used in this chapter, "payoff statement" means a statement of the amount of:

(1) the unpaid balance of a loan secured by a mortgage, including principal, interest, and any other charges properly due under or secured by the mortgage; and

(2) interest on a per day basis for the unpaid balance.

[P.L.2-2002, § 14.]

32-29-6-6. "Person" defined [expires pursuant to IC 32-29-6-17]. — As used in this chapter, "person" means an individual, a corporation, or any other legal entity. [P.L.2-2002, § 14.]

32-29-6-7. "Record" defined [expires pursuant to IC 32-29-6-17]. — As used in this chapter, "record" means to record with the county recorder. [P.L.2-2002, § 14.]

32-29-6-8. "Title insurance company" defined [expires pursuant to IC 32-29-6-17]. — As used in this chapter, "title insurance company" means a corporation or other business entity authorized and licensed to transact the business of insuring titles to interests in real property in Indiana under IC 27. [P.L.2-2002, § 14.]

32-29-6-9. When title insurance company may execute certificate of release [expires pursuant to IC 32-29-6-17]. — An officer or appointed agent of a title insurance company may, on behalf of a mortgagor or a person who acquired from the mortgagor a lien against all or part of the property described in a mortgage, execute a certificate of release that complies with the requirements of this chapter and record the certificate of release in the real property records of each county in which the mortgage is recorded if:

(1) a satisfaction or release of the mortgage has not been executed and recorded within sixty (60) days after the date payment in full of the loan secured by the mortgage was sent in accordance with a payoff statement furnished by the mortgagee or the mortgage servicer; and

(2) the title insurance company, an officer of the title insurance company, or an agent of the title insurance company has sent to the last known address of the mortgagee or the mortgage servicer, at least thirty (30) days before executing the certificate of release, written notice of its intention to execute and record a certificate of release in accordance with this section after the expiration of the sixty (60) day period.

[P.L.2-2002, § 14.]

32-29-6-10. Contents of release [expires pursuant to IC 32-29-6-17]. — A certificate of release executed under this chapter must contain substantially all of the following:

(1) The name of the mortgagor, the name of the original mortgagee and, if applicable, the name of the mortgage servicer, the date of the mortgage, the date of recording of the mortgage, and the volume and page or instrument number for the mortgage in the real property records where the mortgage is recorded, together with similar information for the last recorded assignment of the mortgage.

(2) A statement that the mortgage was in the original principal amount of not more than one million dollars ($1,000,000).

(3) A statement that the person executing the certificate of release is an officer or a duly appointed agent of a title insurance company authorized and licensed to transact the business of insuring titles to interests in real property in Indiana under IC 27.

(4) A statement that the certificate of release is made on behalf of the mortgagor or a person who acquired a lien from the mortgagor against all or part of the property described in the mortgage.

(5) A statement that the mortgagee or mortgage servicer provided a payoff statement that was used to make payment in full of the unpaid balance of the loan secured by the mortgage.

(6) A statement that payment in full of the unpaid balance of the loan secured by the mortgage was made in accordance with the written or verbal payoff statement and received by the mortgagee or mortgage servicer, as evidenced in the records of the title insurance company or its agents by:

   (A) a bank check;

   (B) a certified check;

   (C) an escrow account check from the title company or title insurance agent;

   (D) an attorney trust account check that has been negotiated by the mortgagee or mortgage servicer; or

   (E) any other documentary evidence of payment to the mortgagee or mortgage servicer.

(7) A statement indicating that more than sixty (60) days have elapsed since the date payment in full was sent.

(8) A statement that after the expiration of the sixty (60) day period referred to in section 9 [IC 32-29-6-9] of this chapter, the title insurance company, its officers, or its agent sent to the last known address of the mortgagee or mortgage servicer, at least thirty (30) days before executing the certificate of release, notice in writing of its intention to execute and record a certificate of release as required under this section, with an unexecuted copy of the proposed certificate of release attached to the written notice.

(9) A statement that neither the title insurance company nor its officers or agent have received notification in writing of any reason why the certificate of release should not be executed and recorded after the expiration of the thirty (30) day notice period referred to in section 9 of this chapter. [P.L.2-2002, § 14.]

32-29-6-11. Certificate to be executed and acknowledged in same manner as deed [expires pursuant to IC 32-29-6-17]. — A certificate of release authorized by this chapter shall be executed and acknowledged in the same manner as required by law in Indiana for the execution and acknowledgment of a deed. [P.L.2-2002, § 14.]

32-29-6-12. Authorization of appointed agent by title company [expires pursuant to IC 32-29-6-17]. — (a) A title insurance company may authorize an appointed agent of the title insurance company to execute certificates of release under this chapter by recording a notice of authorization in the office of the county recorder for each county in which the duly appointed agent is authorized to execute and record certificates of release on behalf of the title insurance company. The notice of authorization must state the following:

(1) The name of the title insurance company that is authorizing an appointed agent to execute certificates of release on behalf of the title insurance company.

(2) The identity of the person who is an appointed agent of the title insurance company and who is authorized to execute and record certificates of release in accordance with the requirements of this chapter on behalf of the title insurance company.

(3) That the appointed agent has full authority to execute and record certificates of release in accordance with the requirements of this chapter on behalf of the title insurance company.

(b) The notice of authorization must be executed and acknowledged in the same manner as required by law in Indiana for the execution and acknowledgment of a deed.

(c) A single notice of authorization recorded in the office of a county recorder under this section constitutes the authority of the appointed agent to execute and record certificates of release in that county on behalf of the title insurance company. A separate notice of authority is not required for each certificate of release recorded by an appointed agent.

(d) The authority granted to an appointed agent by a title insurance company under this section continues until a revocation of the notice of authorization is recorded in the office of the county recorder for the county in which the notice of authorization was recorded.

(e) The delegation of authority to an appointed agent by a title insurance company under this section does not relieve the title insurance company of any liability for damages for the wrongful or erroneous execution and recording of a certificate of release by the appointed agent. [P.L.2-2002, § 14.]

32-29-6-13. Withholding release due to misstatements [expires pursuant to IC 32-29-6-17]. — A creditor or mortgage servicer may not withhold the release of a mortgage if the written mortgage payoff statement misstates the amount of the payoff and the written payoff is relied upon in good faith by an independent closing agent without knowledge of the misstatement. It is not a misstatement if the written payoff statement is not accurate as a result of a change in circumstances occurring after the issuance of the payoff statement. The release of a mortgage does not affect the ability of the creditor or mortgage servicer to collect the full amount owed without regard to a misstatement in the written payoff statement and a release of the mortgage. [P.L.2-2002, § 14.]

32-29-6-14. Acceptance of insufficient payment — No effect on creditors' or mortgage servicers' rights [expires pursuant to IC 32-29-6-17]. — The acceptance of a payment by a creditor or mortgage servicer of an amount that is not sufficient to pay the amount owed does not constitute a waiver, release, accord and satisfaction, or other impairment of the creditors or mortgage servicers rights notwithstanding any contrary instructions or restrictive endorsements. [P.L.2-2002, § 14.]

32-29-6-15. Recording and indexing of certificate of release [expires pursuant to IC 32-29-6-17]. — A certificate of release prepared, executed, and recorded in accordance with the requirements of this chapter constitutes a release of the mortgage described in that certificate of release, and the county recorder shall enter and index the certificate of release in the same manner that a release or satisfaction of mortgage is entered and indexed in the records of the county recorder. [P.L.2-2002, § 14.]

32-29-6-16. Execution and recording of a wrongful or erroneous certificate [expires pursuant to IC 32-29-6-17]. — (a) The execution and recording of a wrongful or erroneous certificate of release by a title insurance company or a duly appointed agent with authority from a title insurance company does not relieve the mortgagor, or anyone succeeding to or assuming the interest of the mortgagor, from any liability for the debt or other obligations secured by the mortgage that is the subject of the wrongful or erroneous certificate of release.

(b) Additionally, a title insurance company or an appointed agent with authority from a title insurance company that wrongfully or erroneously executes and records a certificate of release is liable to the mortgagee, or the assignee of the mortgagee if the mortgage has been assigned, for actual damages sustained due to the recording of a wrongful or erroneous certificate of release. [P.L.2-2002, § 14.]

32-29-6-17. Applicability — Expiration of chapter July 1, 2003. — (a) This chapter applies to the release of a mortgage after June 30, 2001, and before July 1, 2002, regardless of when the mortgage was created or assigned.

(b) This chapter expires July 1, 2003. [P.L.2-2002, § 14.]

CHAPTER 7

FORECLOSURE — REDEMPTION, SALE, RIGHT TO RETAIN POSSESSION

32-29-7-1. "Auctioneer" defined. — As used in this chapter, "auction-eer" means an auctioneer licensed under IC 25-6.1. [P.L.2-2002, § 14.]

Effective Dates. P.L.2-2002, § 14. July 1. 2002.

32-29-7-2. "Economically feasible" defined. — For the purposes of section 4(b) [IC 32-29-7-4(b)] of this chapter, the sale of property by the sheriff through the services of an auctioneer is "economically feasible" if the court determines that:

(1) a reasonable probability exists that, with the use of the services of an auctioneer, a valid and enforceable bid will be made at a foreclosure for a sale price equal to or greater than the amount of the judgment and the costs and expenses necessary to its satisfaction, including the costs of the auctioneer; and

(2) the reasonable probability would not exist without the use of an auctioneer. [P.L.2-2002, § 14.]

32-29-7-3. Time limitations on issuance of process — Filing of judgment and decree — Sale of premises — Notice of sale. — (a) In a proceeding for the foreclosure of a mortgage executed on real estate, process may not issue for the execution of a judgment or decree of sale for a period of three (3) months after the filing of a complaint in the proceeding. However:

(1) the period shall be:

(A) twelve (12) months in a proceeding for the foreclosure of a mortgage executed before January 1, 1958; and

(B) six (6) months in a proceeding for the foreclosure of a mortgage executed after December 31, 1957, but before July 1, 1975; and

(2) if the court finds that the mortgaged real estate is residential real estate and has been abandoned, a judgment or decree of sale may be executed on the date the judgment of foreclosure or decree of sale is entered, regardless of the date the mortgage is executed.

(b) A judgment and decree in a proceeding to foreclose a mortgage that is entered by a court having jurisdiction may be filed with the clerk in any county as provided in IC 33-17-2-3. After the period set forth in subsection (a) expires, a person who may enforce the judgment and decree may file a praecipe with the clerk in any county where the judgment and decree is filed, and the clerk shall promptly issue and certify to the sheriff of that county a copy of the judgment and decree under the seal of the court.

(c) Upon receiving a certified judgment under subsection (b), the sheriff shall, subject to section 4 [IC 32-29-7-4] of this chapter, sell the mortgaged premises or as much of the mortgaged premises as necessary to satisfy the judgment, interest, and costs at public auction at the office of the sheriff or at another location that is reasonably likely to attract higher competitive bids. The sheriff shall schedule the date and time of the sheriff's sale for a time certain between the hours of 10 a.m. and 4 p.m. on any day of the week except Sunday.

(d) Before selling mortgaged property, the sheriff must advertise the sale by publication once each week for three (3) successive weeks in a daily or weekly newspaper of general circulation. The sheriff shall publish the advertisement in at least one (1) newspaper published and circulated in each county where the real estate is situated. The first publication shall be made at least thirty (30) days before the date of sale. At the time of placing the first advertisement by publication, the sheriff shall also serve a copy of the written or printed notice of sale upon each owner of the real estate. Service of the written notice shall be made as provided in the Indiana Rules of Trial Procedure governing service of process upon a person. The sheriff shall charge a fee of ten dollars ($10) to one (1) owner and three dollars ($3) to each additional owner for service of written notice under this subsection. The fee is:

(1) a cost of the proceeding;

(2) to be collected as other costs of the proceeding are collected; and

(3) to be deposited in the county general fund for appropriation for operating expenses of the sheriff's department.

(e) The sheriff also shall post written or printed notices of the sale in at least three (3) public places in each township in which the real estate is situated and at the door of the courthouse of each county in which the real estate is located.

(f) If the sheriff is unable to procure the publication of a notice within the county, the sheriff may dispense with publication. However, the sheriff shall state that the sheriff was not able to procure the publication and explain the reason why publication was not possible.

(g) Notices under subsections (d) and (e) must contain a statement, for informational purposes only, of the location of each property by street address, if any, or other common description of the property other than legal description. A misstatement in the informational statement under this subsection does not invalidate an otherwise valid sale. [P.L.2-2002, § 14.]

Cross References. Assignment, IC 32-29-1-8, IC 32-29-2-1, IC 32-29-8-1.

Foreclosure of assigned mortgage, IC 32-29-8-1.

Foreclosures by state, IC 32-29-1-9.

Limitation of lien and action, IC 32-8-7-1, IC 32-28-7-4, IC 32-28-8-1.

Parties to action for foreclosure, IC 32-29-8-1.

Satisfaction and release, IC 32-28-1-1, IC 32-28-1-2, IC 32-29-1-6, IC 32-29-1-7, IC 32-29-3-1, IC 32-29-4-1, IC 32-29-5-1.

NOTES TO DECISIONS

ANALYSIS

Constitutionality.
Applicability.
Deficiency judgment.
Extinguishment of lien.
Forfeiture or foreclosure.
Land sale contract.
Liquidated damages.
Notice requirements.
Private sale.
Receivers.
Right of leaseholder.
Sale.
—Irregularities.

Constitutionality.

Acts 1931, ch. 90 (formerly IC 32-8-16-1 — IC 32-8-16-10) was an independent act of legislation, and did not attempt to amend an earlier act, and was not in conflict with Ind. Const., Art. 4, § 21. Home Owners' Loan Corp. v. Wise, 215 Ind. 445, 19 N.E.2d 737 (1939).

The former act was not invalid on the ground that it embraced subjects which were not contained in the title of the act, and hence not violative of Ind. Const., Art. 4, § 19. Home Owners' Loan Corp. v. Wise, 215 Ind. 445, 19 N.E.2d 737 (1939).

Applicability.

This chapter was not controlling in the foreclosure of a mortgage executed prior to the taking effect of the former act. Knapp v. Ellyson Realty Co., 211 Ind. 180, 5 N.E.2d 973 (1937).

The former act (IC 32-8-16) provided the only method of foreclosing real estate mortgages executed after its effective date, and former IC 34-2-29-1 remained in force after such date only for the purpose of procedure in foreclosure of mortgages executed prior to the effective date of the later act. Home Owners' Loan Corp. v. Wise, 215 Ind. 445, 19 N.E.2d 737 (1939).

Deficiency Judgment.

A contract seller who forecloses on his contract can obtain a deficiency judgment if he buys the property at a foreclosure sale for less than the amount still due on the contract without providing the trial court with proof that the property is worth less than the amount due at the time of sale. Arnold v. Melvin R. Hall, Inc., 496 N.E.2d 63 (Ind. 1986).

Extinguishment of Lien.

Where notice was given a bank by publication under the terms of this section, it followed that the bank received adequate notice as required by the governing statute, and thus an execution sale following publication of notice extinguished the junior lien of the bank. Hines v. Behrens, 421 N.E.2d 1155 (Ind. App. 1981).

Forfeiture or Foreclosure.

Where land sale contract is breached, the forfeiture provisions of the contract are appropriate only in circumstances in which it is found to be consonant with notions of fairness and justness under the law, otherwise the proper remedy is for the trial court to exercise its equity jurisdiction to enter a judgment of foreclosure pursuant to this section. Ogle v. Wright, 172 Ind. App. 309, 56 Ind. Dec. 460, 360 N.E.2d 240 (1977).

Where mortgagors, without request or agreement, tendered to a mortgagee a deed containing a covenant which, upon acceptance by the mortgagee, would have absolved mortgagors from any further liability on the underlying debt, and the mortgagee refused acceptance and consistently pursued its original remedy of foreclosure and a deficiency levy in the event the sale of the mortgaged property failed to satisfy the judgment on the note, no merger of the mortgage into the fee occurred and the mortgagee was entitled to foreclosure. Ellsworth v. Homemakers Fin. Serv., Inc., 424 N.E.2d 166 (Ind. App. 1981), rehearing denied, 438 N.E.2d 6 (Ind. App. 1982).

Whether a particular sum paid toward a particular contract price is minimal, and would thereby tend to support forfeiture rather than foreclosure, depends upon the totality of the circumstances surrounding the contract and its performance, and summary judgment is inappropriate. Johnson v. Rutoskey, 472 N.E.2d 620 (Ind. App. 1984).

Land Sale Contract.

A vendor's interest under a contract for sale of real property is a lien upon real estate and where purchasers have paid a substantial portion of the total contract price, the vendor could not seek forfeiture but was required to proceed with foreclosure. Skendzel v. Marshall, 261 Ind. 226, 38 Ind. Dec. 752, 301 N.E.2d 641 (1973), cert. denied, 415 U.S. 921, 94 S. Ct. 1421, 39 L. Ed. 2d 476 (1974); Tidd v. Stauffer, 159 Ind. App. 570, 41 Ind. Dec. 199, 308 N.E.2d 415 (1974).

Liquidated Damages.

Although contract for sale of real property provided that in case of default the vendor could terminate the contract and keep the payments as liquidated damages, where vendee had paid 29.7 percent of the price, a judgment of foreclosure would be the proper

Liquidated Damages. (Cont'd)
remedy. Morris v. Weigle, 270 Ind. 121, 66 Ind. Dec. 337, 383 N.E.2d 341 (1978).

Notice Requirements.
Where a temporary restraining order against a foreclosure sale was issued after the required notices of sale had been given, the subsequent dismissal of the order did not require that new notice of sale be given. Indiana Sub. Sewers, Inc. v. Hanson, 166 Ind. App. 165, 49 Ind. Dec. 91, 334 N.E.2d 720 (1975).

Private Sale.
The private sale of mortgaged farm property pursuant to an order of a federal bankruptcy court was contrary to state law, and the debtor's assignment of equity to the mortgagee bank as security did not excuse the obligation to follow Indiana foreclosure law. In re Kerns, 111 Bankr. 777 (S.D. Ind. 1990).

Receivers.
On appeal from interlocutory order denying petition for appointment of receiver in proceedings to foreclose mortgage, where complaint was filed February 15, 1935, and real estate was sold by sheriff January 8, 1936, mortgagee had burden of proving date such mortgage was executed. Polish Nat'l Alliance v. Hyzy, 210 Ind. 619, 4 N.E.2d 544 (1936).

When on January 24, 1936, petition was filed for appointment of receiver for mortgaged property which was sold January 8, 1936, under complaint in foreclosure proceeding, filed February 5, 1935, such petition was properly denied where it could not have been ascertained from such petition or record when such mortgage was executed, as it could not have been found whether there was year of redemption, and if not, under statute prohibiting sale under mortgage foreclosure within year after filing such complaint, receiver could not have been appointed. Polish Nat'l Alliance v. Hyzy, 210 Ind. 619, 4 N.E.2d 544 (1936).

Right of Leaseholder.
Lessor was denied due process by its exclusion from foreclosure action, and the foreclosure did not abolish its leasehold. Como, Inc. v. Carson Square, Inc., 648 N.E.2d 1247 (Ind. App. 1995).

Sale.

—Irregularities.
A mortgage foreclosure sale in the amount of $3,000 of property having a market value of $6,000 or more, had in the office of the sheriff instead of at the courthouse door as required by statute, would not have been set aside because of inadequacy of price and irregularity in the sale, where there was no evidence as to what price the property would have brought at a forced sale, and it was shown that the mortgagor, during the redemption period, had been unable to obtain a loan in an amount sufficient to discharge the property lien, and the sheriff accepted the higher of two bids received on the day of sale. Fox v. Jackson, 116 Ind. App. 390, 64 N.E.2d 799 (1946).

Collateral References. 55 Am. Jur. 2d Mortgages, §§ 510-521, 533-535.

59 C.J.S. Mortgages, §§ 482-491, 813-878.
Public sale, what constitutes. 4 A.L.R.2d 575.
Foreclosure of mortgage as affecting easement claimed in, over, or under property. 46 A.L.R.2d 1197.

Foreclosure sale of mortgaged real estate as a whole or in parcels. 61 A.L.R.2d 505.
Effect of foreclosure on dedication of land by mortgagor. 63 A.L.R.2d 1160.
Mortgage foreclosure forbearance statutes — modern status. 83 A.L.R.4th 243.

32-29-7-4. Sale by auction. — (a) A sheriff shall offer to sell and sell property on foreclosure in a manner that is reasonably likely to bring the highest net proceeds from the sale after deducting the expenses of the offer and sale.

(b) Upon prior petition of the debtor or any creditor involved in the foreclosure proceedings, the court in its order of foreclosure shall order the property sold by the sheriff through the services of an auctioneer if:

(1) the court determines that a sale is economically feasible; or

(2) all the creditors in the proceedings agree to both that method of sale and the compensation to be paid the auctioneer.

(c) An auctioneer engaged by a sheriff under this section shall conduct the auctioneer's activities as appropriate to bring the highest bid for the property on foreclosure. The advertising conducted by the auctioneer is in addition to any other notice required by law.

(d) The auctioneer's fee must be a reasonable amount stated in the court's order. However, if the sale by use of an auctioneer has not been agreed to by the creditors in the proceedings and the sale price is less than the amount of the judgment and the costs and expenses necessary to the satisfaction of the judgment, the auctioneer is entitled only to the auctioneer's advertising expenses plus one hundred dollars ($100). The amount due the auctioneer on account of the auctioneer's expenses and fee, if any, shall be paid as a cost of the sale from its proceeds before the payment of any other payment from the sale. [P.L.2-2002, § 14.]

NOTES TO DECISIONS

Private Sale.
The private sale of mortgaged farm property pursuant to an order of a federal bankruptcy court was contrary to state law, and the debtor's assignment of equity to the mortgagee bank as security did not excuse the obligation to follow Indiana foreclosure law. In re Kerns, 111 Bankr. 777 (S.D. Ind. 1990).

32-29-7-5. Waiver of time limitations on issuance of process. — The owner of the real estate subject to the issuance of process under a judgment or decree of foreclosure may, with the consent of the judgment holder endorsed on the judgment or decree of foreclosure, file with the clerk of the court a waiver of the time limitations on issuance of process set out in section 3 [IC 32-28-7-3] of this chapter. If the owner files a waiver under this section, process shall issue immediately. The consideration for waiver, whether or not expressed by its terms, shall be the waiver and release by the judgment holder of any deficiency judgment against the owner. [P.L.2-2002, § 14.]

Cross References. Valuation and appraisement laws, IC 34-2-28-1 — IC 34-2-28-14.

32-29-7-6. Real estate located in more than one county. — (a) If the mortgaged real estate is located in more.than one (1) county:
  (1) the court of any county the mortgaged real estate is located in has jurisdiction of an action for the foreclosure of the mortgage; and
  (2) all the real estate shall be sold in the county where the action is brought, unless the court orders otherwise.
(b) A judgment and decree granted by a court or a judge in an action for the foreclosure of the mortgaged real estate shall be recorded in the lis pendens record kept in the office of the clerk of each county where the real estate is located, unless the judgment and decree is filed with the clerk in the county as provided in IC 33-17-2-3. [P.L.2-2002, § 14.]

32-29-7-7. Redemption of real estate by owner. — Before the sale under this chapter, any owner or part owner of the real estate may redeem the real estate from the judgment by payment to the:

(1) clerk before the issuance to the sheriff of the judgment and decree; or

(2) sheriff after the issuance to the sheriff of the judgment and decree; of the amount of the judgment, interest, and costs for the payment or satisfaction of which the sale was ordered. If the owner or part owner redeems the real estate under this section, process for the sale of the real estate under judgment may not be issued or executed, and the officer receiving the redemption payment shall satisfy the judgment and vacate order of sale. However, if the real estate is redeemed by a part owner, the part owner shall have a lien on the shares of the other owners for their respective shares of the redemption money, with interest at the rate of eight percent (8%) per annum, plus the costs of redemption. The lien shall be of the same force and effect as the judgment lien redeemed by the part owner and shall be enforceable by appropriate legal proceedings. [P.L.2-2002, § 14.]

NOTES TO DECISIONS

ANALYSIS

Bankruptcy plan.
—Reinstatement of mortgage.

Bankruptcy Plan.

—Reinstatement of Mortgage.
Where a creditor obtains a judgment of foreclosure in a state court before a debtor files a petition in bankruptcy under Chapter 13, the debtor's Chapter 13 plan cannot merely provide for the payment of the arrearages and thereby reinstate the mortgage. Waterfield Mtg. Co. v. Britton, 35 Bankr. 373 (N.D. Ind. 1982).

Collateral References. Redemption rights of mortgagor making timely tender but of inadequate amount because of officer's mistake. 45 A.L.R.2d 1316.

Necessity of tender of payment by one seeking to redeem property from mortgage foreclosure. 80 A.L.R.2d 1317.

Mortgages: effect on subordinate lien of redemption by owner or assignee from sale under prior lien. 56 A.L.R.4th 703.

32-29-7-8. No requirement to offer rents, profits, or portions of real estate for sale. — In selling real estate under this chapter, the sheriff is not required to first offer the rents and profits of the real estate or separate portions or parcels of the real estate. The sheriff may offer for sale the whole body of the mortgaged real estate together with rents, issues, income, and profits of the real estate unless the court in its judgment and order of sale has otherwise ordered. If any part of the judgment, interest, or costs remains unsatisfied, the sheriff shall immediately levy the residue on the other property of the defendant. [P.L.2-2002, § 14.]

NOTES TO DECISIONS

Sale of Real Property by Parcels.
Where the sale of real property by parcels was not required in a sheriff's sale under a decree of foreclosure, the defaulting party could not complain that too much of the property was sold, that the property was not

Sale of Real Property by Parcels. (Cont'd)

sold in parcels, and that the price was inadequate where none of the bidders wished to buy separate tracts and where there were numerous judgment and tax liens against the property. York v. Miller, 167 Ind. App. 444, 50 Ind. Dec. 394, 339 N.E.2d 93 (1975).

32-29-7-9. Sheriff or agent may not purchase real estate at sale — Sheriff to pay proceeds — No relief or redemption. — (a) A sheriff or an agent of the sheriff making a foreclosure sale under this chapter may not directly or indirectly purchase property sold by the sheriff or the sheriff's agent. If the purchaser of property sold on foreclosure fails to immediately pay the purchase money, the sheriff shall resell the property either on the same day without advertisement or on a subsequent day after again advertising in accordance with this chapter, as the judgment creditor directs. If the amount bid at the second sale does not equal the amount bid at the first sale, including the costs of the second sale, the first purchaser shall be liable for:

(1) the deficiency;

(2) damages not exceeding ten percent (10%); and

(3) interest and costs;

all of which may be recovered in a court of proper jurisdiction by the sheriff.

(b) If the property is sold, the sheriff shall pay the proceeds as provided in IC 32-30-10-14. Every sale made under this chapter must be without relief from valuation or appraisement laws and without any right of redemption. [P.L.2-2002, § 14.]

NOTES TO DECISIONS

Vacation of Sheriff's Sale.

The trial court erred in denying plaintiff's request to vacate a sheriff's sale where the sheriff refused to accept the successful bidder's check due to its form, announced that a resale would take place later that day, and then sold the property at the resale to an unsuccessful bidder from the first sale for $20,000 less than the original successful bid. National Oil & Gas, Inc. v. Gingrich, 716 N.E.2d 491 (Ind. App. 1999).

32-29-7-10. Execution of deed after sale. — Immediately after a foreclosure sale under this chapter, the sheriff shall execute and deliver to the purchaser a deed of conveyance for the premises, which must be valid to convey all the right, title, and interest held or claimed by all of the parties to the action and all persons claiming under them. The sheriff shall file a return with the clerk of the court. [P.L.2-2002, § 14.]

NOTES TO DECISIONS

ANALYSIS

In general.
Due process.
—State action.

In General.

Delivery of a sheriff's deed as the result of a mortgage sale constituted mere record evidence of the purchaser's title which was perfect from the date of the sale. State Bank v. Brown, 317 U.S. 135, 63 S. Ct. 128, 87 L. Ed. 140 (1942), reh'g denied, 317 U.S. 712, 63 S. Ct. 432, 87 L. Ed. 567 (1943).

This section and the sections following gave the debtor a year from the institution of foreclosure suit within which to redeem, and terminate his rights and interest in the property at the sale, and therefore delivery of the deed by the sheriff became a ministerial act which he could have been compelled to perform. State Bank v. Brown, 317 U.S. 135, 63

In General. (Cont'd)
S. Ct. 128, 87 L. Ed. 140 (1942), reh'g denied,
317 U.S. 712, 63 S. Ct. 432, 87 L. Ed. 567
(1943).

Due Process.

—State Action.
State action existed in action by lessor

alleging trial court's judgment of foreclosure
was not applicable to it because it was not
named as a party to the action in violation of
due process, as the foreclosure was brought
pursuant to former IC 32-8-16-6 (repealed;
see this section for similar provisions). Como,
Inc. v. Carson Square, Inc., 648 N.E.2d 1247
(Ind. App. 1995).

32-29-7-11. Court appointed receiver — Continued possession by owner until sale.

— (a) If the court appoints a receiver of mortgaged property, the receiver shall take possession of the mortgaged property, collect the rents, issues, income, and profits and apply the rents, issues, income, and profits to the payment of taxes, assessments, insurance premiums, and repairs required in the judgment of the receiver to preserve the security of the mortgage debt. The receiver shall promptly file a final report with the clerk of the court and, subject to the approval of the court, account for and pay over to the clerk, subject to the further order of the court, the balance of income or other proceeds that remain in the receiver's possession.

(b) If the mortgaged property is occupied as a dwelling by the record owner of the fee simple title, the owner shall be permitted to retain possession of the mortgaged property, rent free, until the foreclosure sale if the owner continues to pay the taxes and special assessments levied against the mortgaged property and if the owner, in the judgment of the court, does not suffer waste or other damage to the property. However, if the record owner of the fee simple title does not pay the taxes and special assessments levied against the mortgaged property, the owner may retain possession of that part of the mortgaged property, not exceeding fifteen (15) acres, that is actually occupied as a dwelling by the record owner of the fee simple title, rent free, until the sale, if the owner does not, in the judgment of the court, suffer waste or other damage to the property. The owner of any crops growing on the mortgaged property at the time of the commencement of an action for foreclosure, other than the owner of fee simple title or the owner's assigns, may enter the property to care for and harvest the crops at any time within one (1) year after the filing of the foreclosure action. [P.L.2-2002, § 14.]

NOTES TO DECISIONS

ANALYSIS

Appeal.
Receiver.
—Appointment.
—Due process.
——Not shown.
——Shown.
—No basis for appointment.
—State action.

Appeal.
Where final judgment ordered foreclosure

of equitable mortgage and sale of realty, order
which denied motion to secure appointment of
receiver for rents was not interlocutory order
from which appeal could have been taken to
Supreme Court, jurisdiction over such appeal
was in appellate court. Bahar v. Tadros, 234
Ind. 302, 123 N.E.2d 189 (1954).

Receiver.

—Appointment.
This section's apparent unqualified grant of
authority to appoint a receiver, providing the

Receiver. (Cont'd)

—Appointment. (Cont'd)
mechanics of receiver's appointment, the receiver's duties, and the rights of certain owners, must be read in light of earlier statute's qualifications, and the authority for the appointment of the receiver still must be found in one of the clauses of former IC 34-1-12-1. Johnson v. La Porte Bank & Trust Co., 470 N.E.2d 350 (Ind. App. 1984).

—Due Process.

——Not Shown.
A lessee has a property interest in the leasehold that is an important interest worthy of due process protections, and when a receiver of the lessor rejected a lease, the lessee was deprived of her property interest in that lease without due process. Bowlby v. NBD Bank, 640 N.E.2d 1095 (Ind. App. 1994).

——Shown.
Where the trial court authorized receiver to retain custody and use of property pending an adjudication of any adverse claims, and lessee of seized property was given notice of this and an opportunity to have her claims of ownership heard, as to the personal property, the lessee was afforded due process protections. Bowlby v. NBD Bank, 640 N.E.2d 1095 (Ind. App. 1994).

—No Basis for Appointment.
There was no basis for the appointment of a receiver where, although the exact market value of the property was unclear, it was clear that the value exceeded the amount of the indebtedness secured by the mortgage, and because there was no evidence that the property was in danger of being lost, removed or materially injured. Johnson v. La Porte Bank & Trust Co., 470 N.E.2d 350 (Ind. App. 1984).

—State Action.
The acts of a court-appointed receiver are "state action" for due process purposes. Bowlby v. NBD Bank, 640 N.E.2d 1095 (Ind. App. 1994).

32-29-7-12. Owner may enter property to care for and harvest crops. — If the record owner of the fee simple title has the right under section 11 [IC 32-29-7-11] of this chapter to retain possession of the mortgaged premises or any part of the mortgaged premises until the foreclosure sale, the owner may, at any time within one (1) year after the commencement of the foreclosure action, enter the premises to care for and harvest any crops growing at the time of the commencement of the foreclosure action on all or part of the mortgaged premises. [P.L.2-2002, § 14.]

32-29-7-13. Redemption limited to provisions of this chapter. — There may not be a redemption from the foreclosure of a mortgage executed after June 30, 1931, on real estate except as provided in this chapter. [P.L.2-2002, § 14.]

32-29-7-14. Foreclosure of mortgage executed prior to June 30, 1931. — The laws of Indiana in force on June 29, 1931, shall apply to the foreclosure of any mortgage executed before June 30, 1931. [P.L.2-2002, § 14.]

CHAPTER 8

PARTIES TO FORECLOSURE SUIT; REDEMPTION

32-29-8-1. Mortgagee or assignee on record as defendant. — If a suit is brought to foreclose a mortgage, the mortgagee or an assignee shown on the record to hold an interest in the mortgage shall be named as a defendant. [P.L.2-2002, § 14.]

Effective Dates. P.L.2-2002, § 14. July 1. 2002.

32-29-8-2. Other parties bound to judgment. — A person who fails to:
  (1) have an assignment of the mortgage made to the person properly placed on the mortgage record; or
  (2) be made a party to the foreclosure action;
is bound by the court's judgment or decree as if the person were a party to the suit. [P.L.2-2002, § 14.]

32-29-8-3. Certain purchasers free of lien. — A person who purchases a mortgaged premises or any part of a mortgaged premises under the court's judgment or decree at a judicial sale or who claims title to the mortgaged premises under the judgment or decree, buying without actual notice of an assignment that is not of record or of the transfer of a note, the holder of which is not a party to the action, holds the premises free and discharged of the lien. However, any assignee or transferee may redeem the premises, like any other creditor, during the period of one (1) year after the sale. [P.L.2-2002, § 14.]

NOTES TO DECISIONS

ANALYSIS

Innocent purchasers.
Parties.
Redemption.

Innocent Purchasers.
  Innocent purchasers were protected against unrecorded assignments of mortgages. Connecticut Mut. Life Ins. Co. v. Talbot, 113 Ind. 373, 14 N.E. 586, 3 Am. St. 655 (1887); Baugher v. Woollen, 147 Ind. 308, 45 N.E. 94 (1896); Citizens State Bank v. Julian, 153 Ind. 655, 55 N.E. 1007 (1899); Artz v. Yeager, 30 Ind. App. 677, 66 N.E. 917 (1903).
  It was only subsequent purchasers who were affected by a failure to have the assignment of a mortgage recorded. Tulley v. Citizens State Bank, 18 Ind. App. 240, 47 N.E. 850 (1897).
  Where a deed of trust given subsequent to a mortgage, though entered in the entry book, was recorded in the miscellaneous record instead of the deed record, such entry book entry was not sufficient to put a bona fide purchaser of the mortgage on inquiry, and since he was not bound to look beyond the deed records in searching the claim of title, foreclosure of the mortgage was sufficient to bar the equity of redemption of those claiming under the trust deed although they were not

made parties to the proceeding. Sinclair v. Gunzenhauser, 179 Ind. 78, 98 N.E. 37 (1912).

Parties.
  Mortgagee, in suit for redemption of the property, was entitled not only to recover principal and interest on judgment rendered in foreclosure suit, but also attorney's fees, insurance premiums, amount paid for watchman and repairs while in possession. Hosford v. Johnson, 74 Ind. 479 (1881); Johnson v. Hosford, 110 Ind. 572, 10 N.E. 407, 12 N.E. 522 (1886).
  A purchaser at a foreclosure sale, defective because a junior mortgagee was not made a party, upon a subsequent redemption by the latter, had to account for the rents and profits, if such sale operated merely as an assignment of the first mortgage. But if the sale operated not only as an assignment of a prior mortgage, but as a foreclosure of the equity of redemption, subject to junior mortgage, purchaser standing in place of mortgagor or owner of premises was not liable to account for rents or profits. Catterlin v. Armstrong, 79 Ind. 514 (1881); Gaskell v. Viquesney, 122 Ind. 244, 23 N.E. 791, 17 Am. St. 364 (1889).
  In an action to foreclose a mortgage, the plaintiff had a right to rely upon the record in the county recorder's office as to the name of a junior mortgagee, and if the record showed no assignment of the junior mortgage, and the

Parties. (Cont'd)

junior mortgagee was a nonresident, notice by publication was sufficient, although the name of the payee of the note secured by the mortgage as set out in the record of the mortgage was not the same. Baugher v. Woollen, 147 Ind. 308, 45 N.E. 94 (1896).

The right of redemption existed only in favor of one who had an interest in the land sold, either legal or equitable, absolute or inchoate, which might have arisen by operation of law or otherwise, but it must have been an interest the security and protection of which rendered the equitable right of redemption necessary, and it must have been derived mediately or immediately from the mortgagor or judgment debtor. Anderson v. Anderson, 110 Ind. App. 577, 39 N.E.2d 806 (1942).

Redemption.

A junior mortgagee, not a party to foreclosure suit by senior mortgagee, could foreclose his mortgage and redeem by paying the amount of the senior mortgage as well as if it had not been foreclosed. McKernan v. Neff, 43 Ind. 503 (1873).

Collateral References. 55 Am. Jur. 2d Mortgages, §§ 522-524, 563-577. Gaskell v. Viquesney, 122 Ind. 244; 23 N.E. 791; 17 Am. St. 364 (1889).

59 C.J.S. Mortgages, §§ 513-516, 824-836. Mortgages: effect on subordinate lien of redemption by owner or assignee from sale under prior lien. 56 A.L.R.4th 703.

CHAPTER 9

NAME OF AND SERVICE ON PARTIES DEFENDANT IN FORECLOSURE SUITS

32-29-9-1. Name of and service on defendants. — (a) In a suit brought in a court of Indiana to:

(1) foreclose a mortgage or other lien on real estate located in Indiana; or

(2) sell real estate located in Indiana;

if the plaintiff is required to make a person a party to the suit, the plaintiff may list the person as a defendant by the name in which the person's lien or claim appears on the public records of the county in which the suit is brought.

(b) Service of summons or notice by publication to the person, described in subsection (a) is sufficient to make the court's judgment binding as to the person. [P.L.2-2002, § 14.]

Effective Dates. P.L.2-2002, § 14. July 1. 2002.

NOTES TO DECISIONS

Extinction of Lien.

Where notice was given a bank by publication under the terms of former IC 32-8-16-1, it followed that the bank received adequate notice as required by the governing statute, and thus an execution sale following publication of notice extinguished the junior lien of the bank. Hines v. Behrens, 421 N.E.2d 1155 (Ind. App. 1981).

Collateral References. 55 Am. Jur. 2d Mortgages, §§ 568-577.

59 C.J.S. Mortgages, §§ 624-634.

CHAPTER 10

TEN YEAR EXPIRATION ON LIEN OF A SERIES MORTGAGE

32-29-10-1. "Series mortgage" defined. — As used in this chapter, "series mortgage" means any mortgage, indenture of trust, or trust deed executed to create a lien on any property, whether real or personal or both, in Indiana to secure one (1) or more series of bonds, notes, or debentures. The term applies without regard to whether the total obligation to be secured is specifically defined, limited, or left open in the original security instrument. [P.L.2-2002, § 14.]

Effective Dates. P.L.2-2002, § 14. July 1. 2002.

Collateral References. 55 Am. Jur. 2d Mortgages, §§ 598-605.

32-29-10-2. "Final maturity date of the series mortgage" defined. — As used in this chapter, "final maturity date of the series mortgage" means the maturity date of the last to mature of the bonds, notes, or debentures secured by a series mortgage, as the maturity date is shown of record in the original security instrument or in a supplemental indenture subsequently recorded. [P.L.2-2002, § 14.]

32-29-10-3. "Original security instrument" defined. — As used in this chapter, "original security instrument" means the original instrument or indenture executed to evidence a series mortgage. [P.L.2-2002, § 14.]

32-29-10-4. "Supplemental indenture" defined. — As used in this chapter, "supplemental indenture" means an instrument or indenture executed to supplement the original security instrument, defining one (1) or more series of bonds, notes, or debentures secured, or to be secured, by the series mortgage, specifying property subject to the lien of the series mortgage or in another manner supplementing or amending the original security instrument. [P.L.2-2002, § 14.]

32-29-10-5. Expiration of lien. — Notwithstanding any other Indiana statute:

(1) the lien of a series mortgage expires ten (10) years after the final maturity date of the series mortgage; and

(2) an action may not be commenced in an Indiana court to enforce or to foreclose the lien of a series mortgage more than ten (10) years after the final maturity date of the series mortgage. [P.L.2-2002, § 14.]

32-29-10-6. Lien of series mortgage not impaired or injured by passage of time. — Notwithstanding any other Indiana statute, the lien of a series mortgage may not be impaired or injured by the passage of time other than as provided in section 5 [IC 32-29-10-5] of this chapter. [P.L.2-2002, § 14.]

CHAPTER 11
DUTY TO SATISFY RECORD

32-29-11-1. Release — Discharge — Satisfaction. — Unless otherwise provided in this article, if the debt or obligation, and the interest on the debt or obligation, that a mortgage secures has been fully paid, lawfully tendered, and discharged, the owner, holder, or custodian of the mortgage shall:

(1) release;

(2) discharge; and

(3) satisfy of record;

the mortgage as provided in IC 32-28-1. [P.L.2-2002, § 14.]

Effective Dates. P.L.2-2002, § 14. July 1. 2002.

ARTICLE 30
CAUSES OF ACTION CONCERNING REAL PROPERTY

CHAPTER 1
STATUTE OF LIMITATIONS IN ACTIONS CONCERNING REAL ESTATE

32-30-1-1. "Person" defined. — As used in this chapter, "person" means an individual, a partnership, an association, a limited liability company, a corporation, a business trust, a joint stock company, or an unincorporated organization. [P.L.2-2002, § 15.]

Effective Dates. P.L.2-2002, § 15. July 1. 2002.

32-30-1-2. "Contract" defined. — As used in this chapter, "contract" means an oral or a written contract. [P.L.2-2002, § 15.]

32-30-1-3. "Tort" defined. — As used in this chapter, "tort" means an injury to person or property caused by a means other than a breach of contract. [P.L.2-2002, § 15.]

32-30-1-4. "Date of substantial completion" defined. — As used in this chapter, "date of substantial completion" means the earlier of:

(1) the date upon which construction of an improvement to real property is sufficiently completed under a contract of construction, as modified by any additions, deletions, or other amendments, so that the owner of the real property upon which the improvement is constructed can occupy and use the premises in the manner contemplated by the terms of the contract; or

(2) the date of the first beneficial use of the improvement to real property or of any portion of the improvement. [P.L.2-2002, § 15.]

Cross References. Limitation of actions generally, 34-1-2-1 et seq.

NOTES TO DECISIONS

"Date of Substantial Completion."
The trial court erred in denying the defendant's motion for summary judgment where the evidence designated by the plaintiff did not support his claim that there was a genuine issue of material fact with regard to whether a condominium was substantially completed at least ten years before the initiation of the action. J.C. Spence & Assocs. v. Geary, 712 N.E.2d 1099 (Ind. App. 1999).

32-30-1-5. Statute of limitations — Deficiency in improvements. — An action to recover damages, whether based upon contract, tort, nuisance, or another legal remedy, for:

(1) a deficiency or an alleged deficiency in the design, planning, supervision, construction, or observation of construction of an improvement to real property;

(2) an injury to real or personal property arising out of a deficiency; or

(3) an injury or wrongful death of a person arising out of a deficiency;

may not be brought against any person who designs, plans, supervises, or observes the construction of or constructs an improvement to the real property unless the action is commenced within the earlier of ten (10) years after the date of substantial completion of the improvement or twelve (12) years after the completion and submission of plans and specifications to the owner if the action is for a deficiency in the design of the improvement. [P.L.2-2002, § 15.]

NOTES TO DECISIONS

In General.

This statute of repose is an absolute time limit beyond which liability no longer exists, regardless of when the cause of action accrues, and is not tolled for any reason because to do so would upset the economic balance struck by the legislature. Kissel v. Rosenbaum, 579 N.E.2d 1322 (Ind. App. 1991).

Constitutionality.

Former IC 32-15-1-2 (repealed; see this section for prior provisions) did not violate the equal protection clause of the U.S. Const., amend. 14; the privileges and immunities clause of Ind. Const., art. I, § 23; the special laws provisions of Ind. Const., art. IV, §§ 22, 23; the due process clause of the U.S. Const., amend. 14; or the open courts clause of Ind. Const., art. I, § 12. Beecher v. White, 447 N.E.2d 622 (Ind. App. 1983).

—Similar Statutes.

For a discussion of the divergent conclusions reached by other jurisdictions concerning the constitutionality of statutes similar to this statute, see Beecher v. White, 447 N.E.2d 622 (Ind. App. 1983).

Applicability of Section.

The 1977 amendment to the predecessor statute to this section covering construction deficiencies applied to construction completed prior to such amendment where party still had a year and two months in which to sue before the ten-year period elapsed. Walsh v. Halteman, 75 Ind. Dec. 595, 403 N.E.2d 894 (Ind. App. 1980).

The limitations prescribed by former IC 32-15-1-2 (repealed; see this section for prior provisions) applied to a suit based on products liability because of electrical work on home. Dodd v. Kiefer, 416 N.E.2d 463 (Ind. App. 1981).

The purpose of former IC 32-15-1-2 (repealed; see this section for similar provisions) was to establish a maximum defined time period during which architects and contractors remain residually liable for deficiencies from the construction to improvements in real property, and it was not to replace or supersede the two-year limitation for personal injury actions in former IC 34-1-2-2(1). Berns Constr. Co. v. Miller, 491 N.E.2d 565 (Ind. App. 1986), aff'd, 516 N.E.2d 1053 (Ind. 1987).

Where the real estate improvement statute of limitations is very broad in its application, barring damages based on "contract, tort, nuisance or otherwise," and the coverage of the product liability statute of limitations is much narrower because it applies only to product liability actions in which the theory of liability is negligence or strict liability in tort, and the two statutes of limitation deal with the same subject matter, therefore, according to the rules of statutory construction, the product liability statute of limitations would govern because it was more recently enacted and has a narrower scope of coverage than the real estate improvement statute of limitations. Ferguson v. Modern Farm Sys., 555 N.E.2d 1379 (Ind. App. 1990).

Former IC 32-15-1-2 (repealed; see this section for similar provisions) was applicable to an action arising from injuries sustained by a student in a high school swimming pool, commenced when the high school building was substantially completed. South Dearborn Sch. Bldg. Corp. v. Duerstock, 612 N.E.2d 203 (Ind. App. 1993).

—Construction of Real Property.

Subsection (a) of former IC 32-15-1-2 (repealed; see this section for similar provisions) was applicable to injuries resulting from deficiencies during the construction of real property, such as damages to the transmission cable of a power company, not simply those deficiencies from which injury results after the construction was completed. Northern Ind. Pub. Serv. Co. v. Fattore Constr. Co., 486 N.E.2d 633 (Ind. App. 1985), overruled on other grounds, Berns Constr. Co. v. Miller, 516 N.E.2d 1053 (Ind. 1987).

—Contractual Indemnity Claim.

Former IC 32-15-1-2 (repealed; see this section for similar provisions) did not apply to a contractual indemnity claim. South Dearborn Sch. Bldg. Corp. v. Duerstock, 612 N.E.2d 203 (Ind. App. 1993).

Applicability of Section. (Cont'd)

—Manufacturer of Defective Improvement to Real Estate.
In an action against a corporation which allegedly negligently designed, manufactured, distributed, and assembled a large capacity grain storage bin, which, once it was erected on real estate by a third party, became dislodged, causing property damage, the applicable statute of limitations was that of the products liability statute, not the real estate improvement statute. Grain Dealers Mut. Ins. Co. v. Chief Indus., Inc., 612 F. Supp. 1179 (N.D. Ind. 1985).

—Retention of Control.
One who constructs or designs an improvement but thereafter retains control or possession of it is not entitled to the statute of repose defense. Huber v. Henley, 669 F. Supp. 1474 (S.D. Ind. 1987).

Date of Substantial Completion.
In suit for negligence and products liability against electrical contractor as result of fire, a motion for summary judgment by defendant on ground that limitations had run was properly denied where only evidence was date on which electrical work was completed and date gas service was changed from contractor to first purchaser of home, since it could not be said as a matter of law that other facts might not affect the date of substantial completion. Dodd v. Kiefer, 416 N.E.2d 463 (Ind. App. 1981).

The trial court erred in denying the defendant's motion for summary judgment where the evidence designated by the plaintiff did not support his claim that there was a genuine issue of material fact with regard to whether a condominium was substantially completed at least ten years before the initiation of the action. J.C. Spence & Assocs. v. Geary, 712 N.E.2d 1099 (Ind. App. 1999).

Jury Instructions.
The inclusion of an instruction reciting the provisions of former IC 32-15-1-2 (repealed; see this section for similar provisions) was superfluous where no dispute existed as to the permissible time for filing suit. Jordan v. Talaga, 532 N.E.2d 1174 (Ind. App. 1989).

Collateral References. What statute of limitations governs action by contractee for defective or improper performance of work by private building contractor. 1 A.L.R.3d 914.

32-30-1-6. Statute of limitations — Injuries arising in ninth or tenth year after substantial completion.

— (a) Notwithstanding section 5 [IC 32-30-1-5] of this chapter, if an injury to or wrongful death of a person occurs during the ninth or tenth year after substantial completion of an improvement to real property, an action in tort to recover damages for the injury or wrongful death may be brought within two (2) years after the date on which the injury occurred, irrespective of the date of death.

(b) However, an action may not be brought more than:

(1) twelve (12) years after the substantial completion of construction of the improvement; or

(2) fourteen (14) years after the completion and submission of plans and specifications to the owner, if the action is for a deficiency in design; whichever comes first. [P.L.2-2002, § 15.]

Collateral References. What statute of limitation governs action by contractee for defective or improper performance of work by private building contractor. 1 A.L.R.3d 914.

32-30-1-7. No defense for person in actual possession of property.

— The limitation set forth in sections 5 and 6 [IC 32-30-1-5 and IC 32-30-1-6] of this chapter (or IC 34-4-20 or IC 32-15-1 before their repeal) may not be used as a defense by a person who is in actual possession or control of the real property, including an owner or a tenant, upon which an improvement has been made at the time the deficiency in the improvement constitutes the proximate cause of the injury or wrongful death for which it is proposed to bring an action. [P.L.2-2002, § 15.]

CHAPTER 2
EJECTMENT AND QUIET TITLE

32-30-2-1. Persons from whom property may be recovered. — A person having a valid subsisting interest in real property and a right to the possession of the real property may recover the real property and take possession by an action brought against the tenant in possession or, if there is not a tenant, against the person claiming the title or interest in the real property. [P.L.2-2002, § 15.]

Compiler's Notes. P.L.2-2002, § 15, which enacted Article IC 32-30 provided for "Ejectment and Quiet Title" to be the heading of both chapters IC 32-30-2 and IC 32-30-3.

Effective Dates. P.L.2-2002, § 15. July 1. 2002.

Cross References. Adverse possession, tax payment required, 32-21-7-1.
Landlord, ejectment, IC 32-30-3.
Occupying claimant law, IC 32-30-3.1.
Real party in interest to be plaintiff, IC 32-30-3-13.

NOTES TO DECISIONS

ANALYSIS

Complaint.
Estoppel.
Executor.
Findings.
Justices of the peace.
Landlords.
Leasehold.
Parties.
Partition.
Possessor.
Railroad company.

Receiver.
Right of possession.
Tenants.
Tenants.
Writ of assistance.

Complaint.

An allegation of complaint, in ejectment, that plaintiff "is the owner of the following described real estate" (describing it), although indefinite and uncertain, would be deemed cured by the judgment, in view of this section

Complaint. (Cont'd)

and IC 32-15-2-4. Sabinske v. Patterson, 100 Ind. App. 657, 196 N.E. 539 (1935).

A defective complaint in ejectment was not demurrable on the ground that the Municipal Court of Marion County had no jurisdiction of the subject-matter of the action, where it did not show on its face that the action was not a possessory one between landlord and tenant. Adams v. Holcomb, 226 Ind. 67, 77 N.E.2d 891 (1948).

Estoppel.

The rule of estoppel of a tenant in possession to deny his landlord's title did not apply when the purpose of the suit was to establish title, or where the decree sought would not only have given possession of the land but by estoppel settled the title to it. Adams v. Holcomb, 226 Ind. 67, 77 N.E.2d 891 (1948).

Executor.

An executor could have sued to recover possession of land held by the testator for a term of years. Duchane v. Goodtitle, 1 Blackf. 117 (1821).

Findings.

A conclusion of law that plaintiffs were the owners in fee simple and were entitled to possession could not stand where there was no finding that plaintiffs were entitled to the possession of the real estate in controversy, and the omission was not cured by a finding that title "rested" in plaintiffs. Jose v. Hunter, 60 Ind. App. 569, 103 N.E. 392 (1913).

Justices of the Peace.

Justices of the peace had jurisdiction in actions for the recovery of lands only when the relation of landlord and tenant existed. Blair v. Porter, 12 Ind. App. 296, 38 N.E. 874, 40 N.E. 81 (1894).

Landlords.

A landlord could bring an action for possession against a tenant who defaulted in the payment of rent under this section. Saint Germain v. Sears, Roebuck & Co., 112 Ind. App. 412, 44 N.E.2d 216 (1942).

Ejectment was a proper remedy to be used by a landlord to recover possession of the leased premises from his tenant after the expiration of the term, or for nonpayment of rent, or for forfeiture of the lease by breach of the condition thereof when it was stipulated in the lease or provided by law that the lessor should have the right to re-enter for such nonpayment of rent or breach of condition. Adams v. Holcomb, 226 Ind. 67, 77 N.E.2d 891 (1948).

Leasehold.

A leasehold constituted a "valid subsisting interest in real property," within the meaning of this section. Goodwine v. Barnett, 2 Ind. App. 16, 28 N.E. 115 (1891).

Parties.

Persons who merely claimed an interest in the land should not have been made parties defendant. Liggett v. Lozier, 133 Ind. 451, 32 N.E. 712 (1892).

Partition.

When lands were set off in partition, the person to whom the same were assigned could sue to recover possession pending an appeal. Randles v. Randles, 67 Ind. 434 (1879).

Possessor.

If the owner of lands forcibly ejected a person in possession under a claim of right, such person could recover possession by suit. Judy v. Citizen, 101 Ind. 18 (1885).

Railroad Company.

Lands unlawfully taken by a railroad company could have been recovered in an action for possession. Graham v. Columbus & I. Cent. R.R., 27 Ind. 260, 89 Am. Dec. 498 (1866); Cox v. Louisville, N.A. & C.R.R., 48 Ind. 178 (1874).

Lands unlawfully taken by a railroad company for a right of way could be recovered by suit. Terre Haute & S.E.R.R. v. Rodel, 89 Ind. 128, 46 Am. R. 164 (1883).

Ejectment would not lie against a railroad company to recover land on which its road was located and operated after public rights had intervened. Morgan v. Lake Shore & M.S. Ry., 130 Ind. 101, 28 N.E. 548 (1891); Midland R.R. v. Smith, 135 Ind. 348, 35 N.E. 284 (1893); Louisville, N.A. & C.R.R. v. Berkey, 136 Ind. 591, 36 N.E. 642 (1894).

Receiver.

A suit could be maintained in a state court to recover possession of lands from a receiver appointed by a United States court. Fort Wayne, M. & C.R.R. v. Mellett, 92 Ind. 535 (1894).

Right of Possession.

To maintain ejectment, the plaintiff must have had the right of possession. Miller v. Shriner, 87 Ind. 141 (1882).

Where defendant contended that the premises upon which he and his wife resided belonged to them, subject only to the right of plaintiff to receive a part of the net proceeds therefrom, pursuant to an agreement and arrangement between plaintiff and defendant, and plaintiff contended that she was entitled to the possession of the premises, a temporary injunction enjoining defendant from interfering with or preventing another to whom plaintiff had rented certain fields

Right of Possession. (Cont'd)

from farming such fields was improper, since by statutes of this state and adequate legal remedy for one having a right to recover possession of real estate was provided. Detamore v. Roberts, 223 Ind. 12, 57 N.E.2d 585 (1944).

An action in ejectment was one to recover the possession of real estate, maintainable by one having a valid subsisting interest therein and a right to the possession thereof. Taylor v. Phelan, 117 Ind. App. 40, 69 N.E.2d 145 (1946), overruled on other grounds, State v. LaRue's Inc., 239 Ind. 56, 154 N.E.2d 708 (1958).

Where plaintiff in an action to have a tax deed declared invalid leased the real estate to another before he filed an additional paragraph of complaint seeking possession thereof, he could not recover on such additional paragraph, for the action for possession was maintainable, when commenced, only by the tenant, and hence the portion of the judgment awarding plaintiff the possession of the property was erroneous. Taylor v. Phelan, 117 Ind. App. 40, 69 N.E.2d 145 (1946), overruled on other grounds, State v. LaRue's Inc., 239 Ind. 56, 154 N.E.2d 708 (1958).

Tenants.

A tenant at will could have maintained an action of ejectment. Buntin v. Doe ex dem. Duchane, 1 Blackf. 26 (1818).

A tenant under a lease could have recovered possession of the lands from the landlord. Huffman v. Starks, 31 Ind. 474 (1869).

Tenants.

Tenants-in-common could sue to recover lands from their cotenants. Vance v. Schroyer, 77 Ind. 501 (1881); Frakes v. Elliott, 102 Ind. 47, 1 N.E. 195 (1885).

An action by a tenant under a lease for a term of years to restrain and enjoin the landlord from entering in and upon the leased premises and from interfering in any manner with the tenant's quiet enjoyment and peaceable possession of the premises was a possessory action under this section, and injunction would not lie. Paetz v. Mix, 80 Ind. App. 449, 141 N.E. 248 (1923).

Writ of Assistance.

Courts of equity could order the issuance of a writ of assistance to put a purchaser under a decree of foreclosure in possession of the land bought. Emerick v. Miller, 159 Ind. 317, 64 N.E. 28 (1902).

The remedies given a purchaser of land at a judicial sale by writ of assistance and by any other legal action for the purpose of obtaining possession were concurrent, and either or both of such remedies could be pursued until relief is had. Wohadlo v. Szczygiel, 115 Ind. App. 560, 58 N.E.2d 759 (1945).

The failure of a purchaser of real estate at a partition sale to ask for a writ of assistance to be put in possession did not bar him from maintaining an action for possession and for damages for unlawful detention. Wohadlo v. Szczygiel, 115 Ind. App. 560, 58 N.E.2d 759 (1945).

Collateral References. Ejectment as remedy of tenant against stranger wrongfully interfering with his possession. 12 A.L.R.2d 1192.

Action to recover property of church or religious society. 20 A.L.R.2d 421.

Right of landowner who has conveyed property to third person to maintain summary possession action. 47 A.L.R.2d 1170.

Commercial leases: application of rule that lease may be canceled only for "material" breach. 54 A.L.R.4th 595.

Dispossession of one spouse under execution on judgment against the other. 58 A.L.R.2d 701.

Encroachment of trees, shrubbery, or other vegetation across boundary line. 65 A.L.R.4th 603.

32-30-2-2. Substitution of landlord for tenant in action. — If it appears in an action brought under section 1 [IC 32-30-2-1] of this chapter that the defendant is only a tenant, the landlord may be substituted as the defendant if the landlord has received reasonable notice. [P.L.2-2002, § 15.]

32-30-2-3. Legal service on nonresident. — Legal service on a defendant who is a nonresident:

(1) is considered served on the defendant if the service is made to the defendant's agent for the property and the defendant's agent resides in Indiana; or

(2) may be had by publication, as in other cases. [P.L.2-2002, § 15.]

32-30-2-4. Contents of complaint. — In an action initiated under section 1 [IC 32-30-2-1] of this chapter, the plaintiff's complaint must contain the following information:

(1) A claim that the plaintiff is entitled to the possession of the premises, including a description of the premises.

(2) The interest the plaintiff claims in the premises.

(3) That the defendant unlawfully keeps the plaintiff from possession of the premises. [P.L.2-2002, § 15.]

NOTES TO DECISIONS

ANALYSIS

In general.
Caption.
Clerical errors.
Complaint.
Description of lands.
Effect of insufficient description.
Plaintiff's title.
Possession.

In General.

A complaint was sufficient if it contained the substance of what was required by statute. Knight v. McDonald, 37 Ind. 463 (1871).

The complaint was sufficient if it stated in substance the requirements of the statute. Smith v. Kyler, 74 Ind. 575 (1881); Blake v. Minkner, 136 Ind. 418, 36 N.E. 246 (1894); Laramore v. Blumenthal, 58 Ind. App. 597, 108 N.E. 602 (1915).

Caption.

Where a complaint in ejectment was captioned "State of Indiana, Perry County," and in the body of the complaint the property was described as being in "said county," the fact that the property was in Perry County, Indiana, was sufficiently alleged. Hughes v. Windpfennig, 10 Ind. App. 122, 37 N.E. 432 (1894).

Clerical Errors.

Clerical errors in complaint were deemed corrected on appeal. Ross v. Banta, 140 Ind. 120, 34 N.E. 865, 39 N.E. 732 (1893).

Complaint.

The complaint must allege that the plaintiff is entitled to possession of the premises and that the defendant is unlawfully keeping the plaintiff from such possession. Vance v. Schroyer, 77 Ind. 501 (1881); Levi v. Engle, 91 Ind. 330 (1883); Mansur v. Stright, 103 Ind. 358, 3 N.E. 112 (1885); Simmons v. Lindley, 108 Ind. 297, 9 N.E. 360 (1886); Nitter v. Hendricks, 150 Ind. 605, 50 N.E. 748 (1898).

Description of Lands.

The complaint must have described the real estate with reasonable accuracy and have designated the county and state in which the land was situated. Leary v. Langsdale, 35 Ind. 74 (1871); Jolly v. Ghering, 40 Ind. 139 (1872); McCarnan v. Cochran, 57 Ind. 166 (1877).

The description of the lands should have been sufficient to enable an officer to identify them in executing a writ of possession. College Corner & Richmond Gravel Rd. Co. v. Moss, 92 Ind. 119 (1883); Reid v. Mitchell, 95 Ind. 397 (1884); Cunningham v. McCollum, 98 Ind. 38 (1884).

Deed filed as exhibit would not aid the description of the land in the complaint. Liggett v. Lozier, 133 Ind. 451, 32 N.E. 712 (1892).

Effect of Insufficient Description.

A demurrer would lie to a complaint when the lands were not sufficiently described. Lenninger v. Wenrick, 98 Ind. 596 (1884); Liggett v. Lozier, 133 Ind. 451, 32 N.E. 712 (1892).

Judgment would have been set aside if the description of the land was not sufficient. Boyer v. Robertson, 149 Ind. 74, 48 N.E. 7 (1897).

Plaintiff's Title.

It was sufficient to state the character of the title of the plaintiff without giving its source. McMannus v. Smith, 53 Ind. 211 (1876).

When the source of the plaintiff's title was alleged, no other could have been proved. Ragsdale v. Mitchell, 97 Ind. 458 (1884).

The plaintiff in ejectment had to recover, if at all, on the strength of his own title. Jose v. Hunter, 60 Ind. App. 569, 103 N.E. 392 (1913); White v. Suggs, 56 Ind. App. 572, 104 N.E. 55 (1914); State v. Tuesburg Land Co., 61 Ind. App. 555, 109 N.E. 530, 111 N.E. 342 (1915).

Where, in an action to recover possession of certain real estate purchased by plaintiff at sheriff's sale, upon mortgage foreclosure, the complaint alleged that plaintiff had a fee-simple title obtained by such purchase, the proof which sustained plaintiff's allegation of title through the sheriff's sale was sufficient to have sustained a judgment in favor of plaintiff, as against defendant's contention

Plaintiff's Title. (Cont'd)

that plaintiff was required to establish his fee-simple title by proof of a chain of title from the government down to his purchase. Dietrich v. Federal Land Bank, 211 Ind. 500, 5 N.E.2d 884 (1937).

Possession.

Demand for possession before suing did not need to be alleged. Hays v. Wilstach, 82 Ind. 13 (1881); McCaslin v. State ex rel. Auditor, 99 Ind. 428 (1885).

The complaint had to allege that the plaintiff was entitled to the possession of the lands. Miller v. Shriner, 87 Ind. 141 (1882); Pittsburgh, C., C. & St. L.R.R. v. O'Brien, 142 Ind. 218, 41 N.E. 528 (1895); Nutter v. Hendricks, 150 Ind. 605, 50 N.E. 748 (1898); Wilson v. Jinks, 63 Ind. App. 615, 115 N.E. 67 (1917).

If the action is between tenants in common the complaint must aver that the cotenant denies the plaintiff's right of possession. Blake v. Minkner, 136 Ind. 418, 36 N.E. 246 (1894).

A conclusion of law that plaintiffs were the owners in fee simple and were entitled to possession could not stand where there was no finding that plaintiffs were entitled to the possession of the real estate in controversy, and the omission was not cured by a finding that title "rested" in plaintiffs. Jose v. Hunter, 60 Ind. App. 569, 103 N.E. 392 (1913).

Where, in an action to recover the possession of real estate, the complaint alleged that, as a part of the consideration for the purchase of the real estate, defendants agreed to give absolute possession on a certain date, and inserted a covenant in the warranty deed, and that the defendants wrongfully failed and refused to give possession on said date, and now wrongfully and unlawfully hold possession and have kept plaintiffs out of possession since said date, the complaint was sufficient to warrant the inference that plaintiffs were entitled to the possession of such real estate, and hence it substantially complied with this section. Guckenberger v. Shank, 110 Ind. App. 442, 37 N.E.2d 708 (1941).

32-30-2-5. Answer. — The answer of the defendant to a complaint under section 4 [IC 32-30-2-4] of this chapter may contain a denial of each material statement or allegation in the plaintiff's complaint. With each denial, the defendant may give in evidence every legal or equitable defense to the action that the defendant may have. [P.L.2-2002, § 15.]

Cross References. Defenses and objections, how presented, Rule TR. 12.

Defenses, when presented, Rules TR. 6, 12(A).

Demurrers and pleas in abatement abolished, Rule TR. 7(B).

Form of pleading, Rule TR. 10.

General rules of pleading, Rule TR. 7.

Service and filing of pleadings, Rule TR. 5.

NOTES TO DECISIONS

ANALYSIS

In general.
Confession and avoidance.
Cross-complaint.
Disclaimer.
Fraud.
General denial.
Matters specially pleaded.
Reply.
Special answer.

In General.

Evidence of any defense to the lessor's action against hold-over tenants for possession of the realty was admissible under the general denial. Johnson v. Greenen, 98 Ind. App. 612, 188 N.E. 796 (1934).

A denial pleading that an interest in real estate was without right and unfounded and a cloud upon cross-complainants' title was suf-

ficient to put in issue contention that the deed and contract relied upon by cross-complainants constituted an equitable mortgage. Kerfoot v. Kessener, 227 Ind. 58, 84 N.E.2d 190 (1949).

In landlord's action against a holdover tenant for possession and damages, in which defendant filed answer in general denial and a second paragraph alleging an affirmative defense, it was not reversible error for the court to sustain a demurrer to the second paragraph of answer, since defendant could plead every defense, legal or equitable, under the general denial. Taylor Washing Mach. Co. v. Schmueser, 105 Ind. App. 392, 15 N.E.2d 116 (1938).

Confession and Avoidance.

If the defendant pleads only in confession and avoidance, he had the burden of proof. Roots v. Beck, 109 Ind. 472, 9 N.E. 698 (1887).

Cross-Complaint.

The defendant could have filed a cross-complaint and obtained affirmative relief. Emily v. Harding, 53 Ind. 102 (1876); McMannus v. Smith, 53 Ind. 211 (1876); Gilpin v. Wilson, 53 Ind. 443 (1876).

The defendant could file a cross-complaint and obtain affirmative relief. Barnes v. Union Sch. Tp., 91 Ind. 301 (1883).

Defenses to cross-complaints could be proved without being specially pleaded. Palmerton v. Hoop, 131 Ind. 23, 30 N.E. 874 (1892); Watkins v. Lewis, 153 Ind. 648, 55 N.E. 83 (1899).

In action to quiet title, defendant was not harmed by refusal to allow him to file a cross-complaint averring ownership of the land involved and seeking to have his title thereto quieted. Gwinn v. Hobbs, 72 Ind. App. 439, 118 N.E. 155 (1917).

Disclaimer.

An answer of disclaimer was not subject to demurrer. McAdams v. Lotton, 118 Ind. 1, 20 N.E. 523 (1889).

Fraud.

Although fraud as a defense could be shown under the general denial, the rule, that where the evidence under the issue formed by the general denial was equally balanced, the plaintiff must fail, did not apply, but, owing to the peculiar nature of the defense, the defendant had to establish the fraud by a fair preponderance of the evidence. J.M. Robinson, Norton & Co. v. Stalcup, 58 Ind. App. 370, 106 N.E. 395 (1914).

General Denial.

All legal or equitable defenses could have been given in evidence under a general denial. Vail v. Halton, 14 Ind. 344 (1860); Tracy v. Kelley, 52 Ind. 535 (1875); Freed v. Brown, 55 Ind. 310 (1876); Steeple v. Downing, 60 Ind. 478 (1878).

All defenses, legal or equitable, could be proved under the general denial. East v. Peden, 108 Ind. 92, 8 N.E. 722 (1886); Jackson v. Neal, 136 Ind. 173, 35 N.E. 1021 (1894); Kaufman v. Preston, 158 Ind. 361, 63 N.E. 570 (1902); Allen v. Indianapolis Oil Co., 27 Ind. App. 158, 60 N.E. 1003 (1901); Beasey v. High, 33 Ind. App. 689, 72 N.E. 181 (1904).

The statute of limitations could be proved under the general denial. Watson v. Lecklider, 147 Ind. 395, 45 N.E. 72 (1896).

In action by lessors in ejectment for default in payment of rent, it was reversible error to refuse lessees permission to show the amount and value of work performed by them in payment of rent under an agreement with lessors. Karas v. Skouras, 79 Ind. App. 99, 137 N.E. 289 (1922).

In an action involving title to land, all matters of descent, including adverse possession, were admissible under the general denial. Geiger v. Uhl, 204 Ind. 135, 180 N.E. 10 (1932).

In an action in ejectment under the answer of denial, defendant was entitled to give in evidence all his defenses, legal and equitable, to defeat plaintiff's claim. Complaint alleged that plaintiff was the owner of the described real estate. Defendant was authorized to contest that allegation by any competent evidence tending to establish that plaintiff was not the owner and not entitled to possession thereof because he held the same in trust for defendant. Any evidence of a trust relationship for defendant, whether resulting or constructive trust, was admissible under the answer of denial. Schwab v. Schwab, 130 Ind. App. 108, 162 N.E.2d 329 (1959).

In ejectment action defendant was permitted to give in evidence every defense he might have without an affirmative answer and such right applied to paragraphs of complaint which were not in ejectment. Smeekens v. Bertrand, 144 Ind. App. 656, 17 Ind. Dec. 724, 248 N.E.2d 48 (1969).

Matters Specially Pleaded.

Matter in abatement of the action must have been specially pleaded. Wilson v. Poole, 33 Ind. 443 (1870).

Matters occurring after the commencement of the suit had to be specially pleaded. Johnson v. Briscoe, 92 Ind. 367 (1883).

Reply.

Reply was not necessary in order to introduce evidence to avoid evidence on part of defense. Jackson v. Neal, 136 Ind. 173, 35 N.E. 1021 (1894).

Special Answer.

Where a bad special answer was held to be good this was cause for reversal of the judgment. Abdil v. Abdil, 33 Ind. 460 (1870).

A defendant could have set up a defense by special answer. Vanduyn v. Heppner, 45 Ind. 589 (1874).

If a general denial was pleaded the sustaining of a demurrer to a special answer was harmless. Berlin v. Oglesbee, 65 Ind. 308 (1879).

If bad special answers were held good, it was cause for reversing a judgment. Over v. Shannon, 75 Ind. 352 (1881).

The defendant could set up his defense by special answer, if he chose. Over v. Shannon, 75 Ind. 352 (1881).

If the general denial was pleaded, the sustaining of a demurrer to a good special answer was harmless. West v. West, 89 Ind. 529 (1883); Mason v. Roll, 130 Ind. 260, 29 N.E. 1135 (1892); Smith v. Pinnell, 143 Ind. 485, 40 N.E. 798 (1895); Watson v. Lecklider, 147 Ind.

Special Answer. (Cont'd)
395, 45 N.E. 72 (1896); Gibbs v. Potter, 166 Ind. 471, 77 N.E. 942 (1906); Beasey v. High, 33 Ind. App. 689, 72 N.E. 181 (1904).

Since, by this section, all defenses, legal or equitable, in an action for possession, could be made under a general denial, error could not be predicated on the action of the court in sustaining a demurrer to a paragraph of answer when another paragraph contained a general denial. Sheehan Constr. Co. v. Kuhn, 70 Ind. App. 459, 123 N.E. 442 (1919).

32-30-2-6. Defendant not required to prove possession. — The defendant is not required to prove the defendant is in possession of the premises to make a defense under this chapter. [P.L.2-2002, § 15.]

Compiler's Notes. This section provides in effect that defendant's possession of the property is not in issue under a general denial. In view of the fact that plaintiff in his complaint alleges that defendant is wrongfully in possession, it would seem that under Rule TR. 8 requiring specific admissions, denials, or averments that the pleader is without information as to the facts, this section may have been superseded.

NOTES TO DECISIONS

Analysis

In general.
Instructions to jury.

In General.
If the defendant appeared and made defense, he admitted his possession of the property. Holman v. Elliott, 86 Ind. 231 (1882); Carver v. Carver, 97 Ind. 497 (1884); Caspar v. Jamison, 120 Ind. 58, 21 N.E. 743 (1889); Weigold v. Pross, 132 Ind. 87, 31 N.E. 472 (1892).

When the defendant made defense, the burden was on him to show a lawful possession. Carver v. Carver, 97 Ind. 497 (1884); Masepohl v. Heimbach, 43 Ind. App. 632, 88 N.E. 316 (1900).

In action for ejectment and possession of real estate, where defendants by their answer denied allegations of complaint and made defense to the action, burden of proving lawful possession was upon them. Leckrone v. Lawler, 125 Ind. App. 35, 118 N.E.2d 381 (1954).

Instructions to Jury.
Where complaint alleged defendant's possession of the realty in controversy, an instruction that the general denial required plaintiff to prove such possession was harmless error, defendant's possession being established by uncontradicted evidence. Seaver v. Vonderahe, 74 Ind. App. 631, 127 N.E. 206 (1920).

32-30-2-7. Limits to recovery for use and occupation of premises. — The plaintiff may recover in an action under this chapter for the use and occupation of the premises up to the time the use or occupation is terminated by the defendant. However, the plaintiff may not recover for the use and occupation of the premises for more than six (6) years before the commencement of the action. [P.L.2-2002, § 15.]

NOTES TO DECISIONS

Analysis

In general.
Exemplary damages.
Exemption from execution.
Measure of damages.
Nominal damages.
Rents and profits.
Time for which allowed.

In General.
Under the present statute, plaintiff could sue to recover damages for injury to the land in the action for possession. Richwine v. Presbyterian Church, 135 Ind. 80, 34 N.E. 737 (1893); Cargar v. Fee, 140 Ind. 572, 39 N.E. 93 (1894).

Exemplary Damages.
Exemplary damages could be recovered in cases of wanton aggression. Hill v. Forkner, 76 Ind. 115 (1881).

Exemption from Execution.
No property was exempt from execution on

Exemption from Execution. (Cont'd)
a judgment for damages. Smith v. Wood, 83 Ind. 522 (1882).

Measure of Damages.
The measure of damages was the value of the use and occupation and not the value of the property. Vandalia R.R. v. Topping, 72 Ind. App. 694, 126 N.E. 485 (1920).

Nominal Damages.
When the plaintiff recovered possession, he was entitled to nominal damages without proof. Hill v. Forkner, 76 Ind. 115 (1881); Dobbins v. Baker, 80 Ind. 52 (1881).

Rents and Profits.
An action would lie to recover rents and profits after surrender of possession by the defendant. Huncheon v. Long, 25 Ind. App. 530, 58 N.E. 563 (1900).

In a suit for the possession of real estate, rents could be recovered up to the time of trial, and, where the complaint seeking damages only in the amount due at the time suit was commenced was not amended in the trial court to conform to proof of the amount due at the time of judgment, it was treated as so amended on appeal. Esch v. Leitheiser, 117 Ind. App. 338, 69 N.E.2d 760 (1946).

Time for Which Allowed.
Damages could be allowed until the date of trial. Dobbins v. Baker, 80 Ind. 52 (1881).

Damages for use and occupation was limited to six years unless the defendant claimed for improvements. Hyatt v. Cochran, 85 Ind. 231 (1882).

32-30-2-8. Judgment for damages — Expiration of interest before plaintiff could be put in possession of premises. — If the plaintiff's interest in the premises expires before the time in which the plaintiff could be put in possession of the premises, the plaintiff may obtain only a judgment for damages. [P.L.2-2002, § 15.]

32-30-2-9. Multiple plaintiffs or defendants. — If there are two (2) or more plaintiffs or defendants, one (1) or more of the plaintiffs may recover against one (1) or more of the defendants:
    (1) the premises or any part of the premises;
    (2) an interest in the premises; or
    (3) damages;
according to the right of the parties, but the recovery may not be for an interest greater than the interest claimed by the party. [P.L.2-2002, § 15.]

NOTES TO DECISIONS

ANALYSIS

Portion of land.
Portion of parties.

Portion of Land.
Judgments could be rendered for only a portion of the land sued for. Carver v. Carver, 97 Ind. 497 (1884).

If judgment was rendered for only a portion of the land claimed, the plaintiff could not recover the other portion in a subsequent suit on the same claim of title. Roby v. Eggers, 130 Ind. 415, 29 N.E. 365 (1891).

Portion of Parties.
A judgment could have been reversed as to one defendant and affirmed as to another. Clements v. Robinson, 54 Ind. 599 (1876); Parker v. Small, 58 Ind. 349 (1877).

A part of the plaintiffs might have recovered and the rest failed. Steeple v. Downing, 60 Ind. 478 (1878).

32-30-2-10. Petition for new trial — Under same restrictions as other civil actions. — A petition for a new trial under this chapter may be made by the party against whom judgment is rendered, or the party's heirs, assigns, or personal representatives, under the same restrictions and on the same grounds as allowed in other civil actions. [P.L.2-2002, § 15.]

32-30-2-11. Petition for new trial — Filing same as for other civil actions. — The petition for a new trial must be filed at the time provided for the filing of petitions for a new trial in other civil actions. [P.L.2-2002, § 15.]

32-30-2-12. Third person interests subject to final result of proceedings. — Third persons acquiring an interest in the subject matter of the action during the pendency of the proceedings initiated under this chapter shall take their interests subject to the final result of the proceedings. [P.L.2-2002, § 15.]

NOTES TO DECISIONS

In General.
Persons who had notice of the ejectment suit could not acquire an interest in the lands during which time allowed for a new trial which could have been asserted against the owner of the lands. Smith v. Cottrell, 94 Ind. 379 (1884).

If the plaintiff recovered, and a new trial was granted, and the defendant recovered, persons purchasing from the plaintiff before granting of the new trial were not innocent purchasers. Griswold v. Ward, 128 Ind. 389, 27 N.E. 751 (1891).

32-30-2-13. Recovery of damages when premises have been transferred to good faith purchaser. — A party who, after a new trial, proves that the party is entitled to the premises that have been transferred in good faith to a purchaser may recover the proper amount of damages against the other party, either in the same action or in a subsequent action. [P.L.2-2002, § 15.]

32-30-2-14. Judgment against tenant conclusive against landlord. — In an action against a tenant under this chapter, the judgment is conclusive evidence against the landlord who has received notice under section 2 [IC 32-30-2-2] of this chapter. [P.L.2-2002, § 15.]

32-30-2-15. Plaintiff must recover on strength of own title. — To recover through an action brought under this chapter, the plaintiff must recover on the strength of the plaintiff's own title. [P.L.2-2002, § 15.]

Cross References. Real party in interest to be plaintiff, IC 32-30-3-13.

NOTES TO DECISIONS

ANALYSIS

In general.
Adverse possession.
Commencement of action.
Equitable title.
Judicial sale.
Prior possession.
Source of title.

In General.
The plaintiff had to prove title to the land to be in himself. Stehman v. Crull, 26 Ind. 436 (1866).

The plaintiff had to prove title to the lands in controversy in himself. Hagenbuck v. McClaskey, 81 Ind. 577 (1882); Coan v. Elliott, 101 Ind. 275 (1885); Castor v. Jones, 107 Ind. 283, 6 N.E. 823 (1886); Roots v. Beck, 109 Ind. 472, 9 N.E. 698 (1887); Blake v. Minkner, 136 Ind. 418, 36 N.E. 246 (1894); Wilson v. Johnson, 145 Ind. 40, 38 N.E. 38, 43 N.E. 930 (1894); Jose v. Hunter, 60 Ind. App. 569, 103 N.E. 392 (1913).

Title in the plaintiff had to be proved, as want of title on the part of the defendant would not support claim of plaintiff. Cook v. Leggett, 88 Ind. 211 (1882); Silver Creek

In General. (Cont'd)

Cement Corp. v. Union Lime & Cement Co., 138 Ind. 297, 35 N.E. 125, 37 N.E. 721 (1893); Blake v. Minkner, 136 Ind. 418, 36 N.E. 246 (1894); Wilson v. Johnson, 145 Ind. 40, 38 N.E. 38, 43 N.E. 930 (1894); Pittsburgh, C., C. & St. L.R.R. v. O'Brien, 142 Ind. 218, 41 N.E. 528 (1895); Graham v. Lunsford, 149 Ind. 83, 48 N.E. 627 (1897); Beck v. Miller, 69 Ind. App. 1, 121 N.E. 281 (1918).

In actions of ejectment, the plaintiff had to recover, if at all, on the strength of his own title. Jose v. Hunter, 60 Ind. App. 569, 103 N.E. 392 (1913); White v. Suggs, 56 Ind. App. 572, 104 N.E. 55 (1914); State v. Tuesburg Land Co., 61 Ind. App. 555, 109 N.E. 530, 111 N.E. 342 (1915).

Adverse Possession.

Proof of title acquired by adverse possession would support an alleged title of fee simple. McWhorter v. Heltzell, 124 Ind. 129, 24 N.E. 743 (1890).

Commencement of Action.

The plaintiff must have had title at the commencement of the suit. Inge v. Garrett, 38 Ind. 96 (1871).

The plaintiff had to have title at the commencement of the action. Craig v. Bennett, 146 Ind. 574, 45 N.E. 792 (1897).

There had to be proof that the plaintiff was at the commencement of the action, entitled to possession of the land, and, if a special finding was made, there must have been a finding to that effect. Jose v. Hunter, 60 Ind. App. 569, 103 N.E. 392 (1913); Wilson v. Jinks, 63 Ind. App. 615, 115 N.E. 67 (1917).

Equitable Title.

Where the complaint alleged that the plaintiff had legal title he could not have recovered on proof of equitable title. Groves v. Marks, 32 Ind. 319 (1869).

When the plaintiff was entitled to possession, he could recover on proof of an equitable title. Burt v. Bowles, 69 Ind. 1 (1879).

If a legal title was alleged, proof of an equitable title could not be made. Stout v. McPheeters, 84 Ind. 585 (1882); Johnson v. Pontious, 118 Ind. 270, 20 N.E. 792 (1889); Ryason v. Dunten, 164 Ind. 85, 73 N.E. 74 (1905); Danforth v. Meeks, 176 Ind. 400, 96 N.E. 153 (1911); Coppock v. Austin, 34 Ind. App. 319, 72 N.E. 657 (1904); Raub v. Lemon, 61 Ind. App. 59, 108 N.E. 631 (1915).

Judicial Sale.

The introduction into evidence of the record of the judgment without a transcript of the record of the proceedings was not a sufficient showing of title in purchaser at the sheriff's sale conducted under the judgment. Glidewell v. Spaugh, 26 Ind. 319 (1866).

In pleading a record of a judgment it was not necessary to show by averments that the court had jurisdiction. Spaulding v. Baldwin, 31 Ind. 376 (1869).

A sheriff's deed of conveyance, of itself, was not evidence of the authority of the sheriff to sell or of a judgment or execution. Huddleston v. Ingels, 47 Ind. 498 (1874).

In an action by a purchaser at a sheriff's sale against a person other than the execution defendant the plaintiff must have shown that the execution defendant had title in the premises to which the judgment lien attached. Shipley v. Shook, 72 Ind. 511 (1880).

In a suit for possession where there was no finding that the commissioner appointed by the court to make the sale of the land had made a conveyance to the plaintiff the judgment should have been for the defendant. Stout v. McPheeters, 84 Ind. 585 (1882).

If the plaintiff claims title under a sale on execution he must show a valid judgment, execution or decree and deed. Richcreek v. Russell, 34 Ind. App. 217, 72 N.E. 617 (1904).

Prior Possession.

Prior possession was sufficient proof of title as against a mere intruder. Doe ex dem. Wood v. West, 1 Blackf. 133 (1821); Robinoe v. Doe ex dem. Colwell, 6 Blackf. 85 (1841).

Source of Title.

Where the plaintiff traced title to the same source from which the defendants derived it was not necessary that a patent from the United States government be shown. Pierson v. Doe ex dem. Turner, 2 Ind. 123 (1850).

The plaintiff must have traced his title to the United States or to some remote grantor in possession. Huddleston v. Ingels, 47 Ind. 498 (1874).

The plaintiff had to trace his title to the United States, or to some remote grantor in possession. Smith v. Bryan, 74 Ind. 515 (1881); Start v. Clegg, 83 Ind. 78 (1882); Peck v. Louisville, N.A. & C.R.R., 101 Ind. 366 (1885); Lafayette v. Wortman, 107 Ind. 404, 8 N.E. 277 (1886).

The title to real estate, in order to be good, must be traceable to the United States or to a grantor in possession under claim of title. Brandenburg v. Seigfried, 75 Ind. 568 (1881).

When a particular source of title was alleged, no other could be proved. Ragsdale v. Mitchell, 97 Ind. 458 (1884).

If both parties claimed under the same grantor, the title need not have been traced to the United States. McWhorter v. Heltzell, 124 Ind. 129, 24 N.E. 743 (1890); Howard v. Twibell, 179 Ind. 67, 100 N.E. 372, 1915C Ann. Cas. 93 (1913); Muncie Elec. Light Co. v. Joliff, 59 Ind. App. 349, 109 N.E. 433 (1915); Beck v. Miller, 69 Ind. App. 1, 121 N.E. 281 (1918).

32-30-2-16. Order to allow plaintiff to survey property. — After:

(1) the plaintiff has filed a motion with the court;

(2) notice has been delivered to the defendant; and

(3) a hearing at which the plaintiff has shown cause;

the court may grant an order allowing the plaintiff to enter upon the property in controversy and make a survey and admeasurement of the property for purposes of an action under this chapter. [P.L.2-2002, § 15.]

32-30-2-17. Contents and service of order to allow survey. — An order issued by a court under section 16 [IC 32-30-2-16] of this chapter must describe the property. A copy of the court order must be served upon the owner or person having occupancy and control of the property. [P.L.2-2002, § 15.]

32-30-2-18. Set off of damages for permanent improvements. — If a plaintiff in an action under this chapter is entitled to damages for withholding, using, or injuring the plaintiff's property, the defendant may set off the value of any permanent improvements made to the property to the extent of the damages, unless the defendant prefers to use the law for the benefit of occupying defendants. [P.L.2-2002, § 15.]

Cross References. Occupying claimant
law, IC 32-30-3.1.

NOTES TO DECISIONS

In general.

Under this section, the defendant could only have been allowed for improvements an amount equal to the damages assessed against him. Wernke v. Hazen, 32 Ind. 431 (1869).

When the defendant claimed for improvements, he could have been charged with the rents for more than six years. Hyatt v. Cochran, 85 Ind. 231 (1882).

32-30-2-19. Exemplary damages for wanton aggression toward property. — If a defendant has demonstrated wanton aggression concerning the property that is subject to an action under this chapter, the jury may award the plaintiff exemplary damages. [P.L.2-2002, § 15.]

NOTES TO DECISIONS

In General.

In cases of wanton aggression on the part of the defendant exemplary damages could be

awarded. Hill v. Forkner, 76 Ind. 115 (1881).

Exemplary damages could not be awarded in an action of ejectment where defendant

In General. (Cont'd)
believed he was acting under a valid right.
Vandalia R.R. v. Topping, 62 Ind. App. 657,
113 N.E. 421 (1916).

32-30-2-20. Persons who may bring action to quiet title. — An
action to determine and quiet a question of title to property may be brought
by a plaintiff who:

(1) is in possession of the property;

(2) is out of possession of the property; or

(3) has a remainder or reversion interest in the property;

against a defendant who claims title to or an interest in the real property
with a claim that is adverse to the plaintiff, even if the defendant is not in
possession of the property. [P.L.2-2002, § 15.]

Cross References. Absent heir quieting
title to interest in land, IC 32-30-3-18, IC
32-30-3-19.

Adverse possession, tax payment required,
IC 32-21-7-1.

Defect in title, proceedings to quiet when
possible claimants unknown, IC 32-30-3-5.

Landlord, ejectment, IC 32-30-3.

Occupying claimant law, IC 32-30-3.1.

Property exempt from execution, quieting
title against judgment, IC 32-30-3-20, IC 32-30-3-21.

Real party in interest to be plaintiff, IC
32-30-3-13.

Recording of decree in quiet title action, IC
32-30-3-17.

Service of process, IC 32-30-3-16.

State as party to action to quiet title, Trial
Rule TR. 17.1.

NOTES TO DECISIONS

ANALYSIS

In general.
Basis of recovery.
Color of title.
Complaint.
—In general.
—Adverse title.
—Equitable title.
—Quiet title.
—Title in general.
Cross-complaint.
Description of lands.
Easement.
Equitable defense.
Estoppel.
Fraud.
Fraudulent conveyance.
Judgment.
Jury trial.
Liens on land.
Particular types of interest.
—Easement.
—Lease.
Res judicata.
Statute of limitations.
Tax deeds.
Who may sue.
Will contest.

In General.
The action could be maintained whenever
any person was asserting a claim to the lands
that would cast a cloud upon the title of the
owner. Walter v. Hartwig, 106 Ind. 123, 6 N.E.
5 (1886); Brown v. Cody, 115 Ind. 484, 18 N.E.
9 (1888).

The establishment of an equitable title and
the right to possession in the defendant would
defeat a suit to quiet the legal title, and
plaintiff could not obtain a decree if defendant
had any valid interest in the land. Sawyer v.
Kleine, 118 Ind. App. 616, 82 N.E.2d 533
(1948).

In appeal from judgment quieting title,
since appellee complied with this section and
cited cases thereunder, it was obvious that
appellee was relying on title by adverse possession. Triplett v. Triplett, 135 Ind. App. 302,
2 Ind. Dec. 312, 193 N.E.2d 662 (1963).

Basis of Recovery.
A plaintiff in a quiet title action had to
recover on the strength of his own title. Ross,
Inc. v. Legler, 245 Ind. 655, 3 Ind. Dec. 485,
199 N.E.2d 346 (1964); Freson v. Combs, 433
N.E.2d 55 (Ind. App. 1982).

In an action to quiet title, where plaintiff
specifically describes title on which he relies,
recovery must be on title as laid. Freson v.
Combs, 433 N.E.2d 55 (Ind. App. 1982).

Color of Title.
It was proper in action to quiet title where
plaintiff relied on title by adverse possession
to put tax deed in evidence to show color of

Color of Title. (Cont'd)

title which, with subsequent events as alleged in complaint and shown by evidence, vested in plaintiff legal title to said real estate, subject to a decree in a quiet title proceeding laying at rest any adverse claim or color of title. Triplett v. Triplett, 135 Ind. App. 302, 2 Ind. Dec. 312, 193 N.E.2d 662 (1963).

Complaint.

—In General.

An allegation in the complaint that the plaintiff was the owner in fee simple and that the defendant asserted an unfounded claim of title in the premises was sufficient. Dumont v. Dufore, 27 Ind. 263 (1866); Gillett v. Carshaw, 50 Ind. 381 (1874).

If the facts stated showed the defendant to have had an interest in the land, the complaint was bad. Ragsdale v. Mitchell, 97 Ind. 458 (1884); McPheeters v. Wright, 110 Ind. 519, 10 N.E. 634 (1887); Brown v. Cody, 115 Ind. 484, 18 N.E. 9 (1888).

A complaint under this section was sufficient if it showed the plaintiff to be the owner of the lands, and that the defendant was asserting an unfounded claim thereto. American Ins. Co. v. Gibson, 104 Ind. 336, 3 N.E. 892 (1885); Johnson v. Taylor, 106 Ind. 89, 5 N.E. 732 (1886); Rausch v. Trustees of United Brethren in Christ Church, 107 Ind. 1, 8 N.E. 25 (1886); Weaver v. Apple, 147 Ind. 304, 46 N.E. 642 (1897); Brown v. Cox, 158 Ind. 364, 63 N.E. 568 (1902); Huntington v. Townsend, 29 Ind. App. 269, 63 N.E. 36 (1902); Rennert v. Shirk, 163 Ind. 542, 72 N.E. 546 (1904); Gibbs v. Potter, 166 Ind. 471, 77 N.E. 942 (1906).

In an action by a widow to quiet her title to certain real estate, in the conveyance of which she had joined with her husband while she was under twenty-one years of age, the complaint was insufficient, which failed to allege that at the time of the execution of the deed the husband was also a minor. Kennedy v. Hudkins, 140 Ind. 570, 40 N.E. 52 (1895).

The complaint had to state facts showing that the plaintiff owned an interest in the land and what that interest was. Chapman v. Jones, 149 Ind. 434, 47 N.E. 1065 (1897), reh'g overruled, 149 Ind. 440, 49 N.E. 347 (1898); Corbin Oil Co. v. Searles, 36 Ind. App. 215, 75 N.E. 293 (1905); Baxter v. Baxter, 46 Ind. App. 514, 92 N.E. 881 (1910).

Where the complaint alleged that the plaintiff was the owner of the real estate involved in fee simple and that the defendants were claiming some title or interest therein adverse to plaintiff's rights, which claims were unfounded and without right, such complaint was sufficient to meet requirements of the statute providing for action to quiet title. Lantz v. Pence, 127 Ind. App. 620, 142 N.E.2d 456 (1957).

—Adverse Title.

It was not necessary for the plaintiff to particularly describe the claim of the defendant if the complaint showed that such title or claim was adverse to or a could upon the title of the defendant. Marot v. Germania Bldg. & Sav. Ass'n, 54 Ind. 37 (1876).

A complaint which showed, prima facie, that the plaintiff was entitled to immediate possession of real estate of which the defendant was unlawfully in possession was sufficient. Rose v. Nees, 61 Ind. 484 (1878).

It was not necessary to allege what claim the defendant asserted if it was alleged that such claim was adversed to the title of the plaintiff. Stumph v. Reger, 92 Ind. 286 (1883); Rausch v. Trustees of United Brethren in Christ Church, 107 Ind. 1, 8 N.E. 25 (1886); Wilson v. Wilson, 124 Ind. 472, 24 N.E. 974 (1890); Cole v. Gray, 139 Ind. 396, 38 N.E. 856 (1894); Tolleston Club v. Clough, 146 Ind. 93, 43 N.E. 647 (1896); Chaplin v. Leapley, 35 Ind. App. 511, 74 N.E. 546 (1905).

It had to be alleged that the claim of the defendant was unfounded and adverse to the title of the plaintiff. Second Nat'l Bank v. Corey, 94 Ind. 457 (1884); Conger v. Miller, 104 Ind. 592, 4 N.E. 300 (1886); Rennert v. Shirk, 163 Ind. 542, 72 N.E. 546 (1904).

If the facts stated showed that the claim of the defendant was adverse to the title of plaintiff, it was sufficient in this respect. Kitts v. Willson, 106 Ind. 147, 5 N.E. 400 (1886).

—Equitable Title.

The plaintiff needed to only state whether his title was legal or equitable and, if equitable, state facts on which his title was based. Grissom v. Moore, 106 Ind. 296, 6 N.E. 629, 55 Am. R. 742 (1886).

When a legal title was alleged, a recovery could not be had on proof of an equitable title. Johnson v. Pontious, 118 Ind. 270, 20 N.E. 792 (1889); Coppock v. Austin, 34 Ind. App. 319, 72 N.E. 657 (1904).

Complaint was good that showed, by facts stated, an equitable title in the plaintiff. Stanley v. Holliday, 130 Ind. 464, 30 N.E. 634 (1892).

Although an action to quiet title was essentially of equitable origin, a plaintiff or counterclaim to quiet title should have disclosed whether the title claimed was legal or equitable, and if an equitable title was claimed, all the facts which went to maintain it could have been shown. Sawyer v. Kleine, 118 Ind. App. 616, 82 N.E.2d 533 (1948).

—Quiet Title.

Where a real estate development corporation entered into an "option to purchase" contract with the landowner to develop the land for residential purposes and such contract was recorded, landowner who rescinded

Complaint. (Cont'd)

—Quiet Title. (Cont'd)
the contract because of breach could seek the remedy of quiet title. Bixwood, Inc. v. Becker, 181 Ind. App. 223, 70 Ind. Dec. 264, 391 N.E.2d 646 (1979).

—Title in General.
Title in plaintiff had to be shown by the facts stated in the complaint. Darkies v. Bellows, 94 Ind. 64 (1884); Chapman v. Jones, 149 Ind. 434, 47 N.E. 1065 (1897), reh'g overruled, 149 Ind. 440, 49 N.E. 347 (1898); Dodds v. Winslow, 26 Ind. App. 652, 60 N.E. 458 (1901).

Where plaintiff specifically described the title on which he relied, recovery had to be on the title as laid in the complaint, in view of this section. Ault v. Miller, 203 Ind. 487, 181 N.E. 35 (1932).

A complaint in an action to quiet title by a husband and wife which alleged that the plaintiffs owned the land as tenants by the entirety sufficiently showed the character of their title. Bousher v. Andrews, 48 Ind. App. 664, 96 N.E. 483 (1911).

Cross-Complaint.
Cross-complaint by defendant alleging ownership of land and that plaintiff was falsely and without right asserting that he held defendant's written contract to convey the land and was prosecuting his action to enforce specific performance of the contract, thereby casting a cloud upon the defendant's title, showed a claim of an adverse interest in the land, and was good. Island Coal Co. v. Streitlemier, 139 Ind. 83, 37 N.E. 340 (1894).

A cross-complaint setting up facts of misdescription of land at judicial sale was held sufficient to support an action for quieting title. Allen v. Adams, 150 Ind. 409, 50 N.E. 387 (1898).

Description of Lands.
The description of the lands should have been definite and certain. Sharpe v. Dillman, 77 Ind. 280 (1881); Ratliff v. Stretch, 117 Ind. 526, 20 N.E. 438 (1889); Jones v. Mount, 30 Ind. App. 59, 63 N.E. 798 (1902); Brown v. Reeves & Co., 31 Ind. App. 517, 68 N.E. 604 (1903); Carr v. Huntington Light & Fuel Co., 33 Ind. App. 1, 70 N.E. 552 (1904); Monaghan v. Mount, 36 Ind. App. 188, 74 N.E. 579 (1905).

Easement.
An action could have been brought to quiet title in an easement. Davidson v. Nicholson, 59 Ind. 411 (1877).

Equitable Defense.
Where in an action to quiet title, defendant admitted a claim of an adverse interest but denied all other allegations of the complaint, she was entitled to prove any equitable defense she might have had. Sawyer v. Kleine, 118 Ind. App. 616, 82 N.E.2d 533 (1948).

Estoppel.
Consent to survey of boundary lines did not estop owner, who held property by adverse possession, from asserting title to land. Wood v. Kuper, 150 Ind. 622, 50 N.E. 755 (1898).

Fraud.
The facts averred showed fraud and were sufficient to entitle plaintiff to a judgment canceling the deed. Sherrin v. Flinn, 155 Ind. 422, 58 N.E. 549 (1900).

Fraudulent Conveyance.
An action by an administrator to set aside a fraudulent conveyance and to quiet title to decedent's real estate, could have been sustained only where it was shown that it was necessary to sell such real estate to pay the debts of the estate. Jarrell v. Brubaker, 150 Ind. 260, 49 N.E. 1050 (1898).

Judgment.
In a wife's action to quiet title to certain real estate, in which she claimed a fee-simple title under her deceased husband's will, she was not entitled to judgment quieting title to the widow's one-third interest in the real estate. Ault v. Miller, 203 Ind. 487, 181 N.E. 35 (1932).

Jury Trial.
While actions to quiet title were of equitable origin, they existed in this state by virtue of the statute and were triable by jury. Macy v. Wood, 49 Ind. App. 469, 97 N.E. 553 (1912); Folsom v. Buttolph, 82 Ind. App. 283, 143 N.E. 258 (1924).

Liens on Land.
The title of one holding under a judgment lien cannot be quieted until the tax lien thereon is discharged. Browning v. Smith, 139 Ind. 280, 37 N.E. 540 (1894); Ferris v. Berkshire Life Ins. Co., 139 Ind. 486, 38 N.E. 609 (1894).

A decree quieting title to real estate as against a life tenant will not constitute a bar to an action to enforce a lien on such real estate for taxes paid. Watson v. Lecklider, 147 Ind. 395, 45 N.E. 72 (1896).

A complaint seeking to quiet title to real estate as against tax liens and ditch assessments, admitting an amount due to be determined by the court and an offer to pay, is not a collateral attack on the tax deeds but a direct attack and the defendants having introduced the tax deeds the plaintiffs were entitled to show facts in rebuttal that ren-

Liens on Land. (Cont'd)
dered the deeds void in so far as they purported to convey title. Skelton v. Sharp, 161 Ind. 383, 67 N.E. 535 (1903).

Particular Types of Interest.

—Easement.
An action could be brought to quiet title in an easement, such as a right of way. Roush v. Roush, 154 Ind. 562, 55 N.E. 1017 (1900); Chicago & S.E.R.R. v. Grantham, 165 Ind. 279, 75 N.E. 265 (1905).

—Lease.
In an action following the forfeiture of a lease the plaintiff may show that the defendant is the grantee of a lease which has been forfeited by reason of his failure to comply with the terms of the lease. Woodward v. Mitchell, 140 Ind. 406, 39 N.E. 437 (1895).

A suit to quiet title may be maintained against one who claims title under a lease from the grantor of the plaintiff's ancestor. Island Coal Co. v. Combs, 152 Ind. 379, 53 N.E. 452 (1899).

Where a lessee has lost his rights under a lease and the lessor has commenced an action to quiet his title, the lessee cannot revive any rights in the premises by reentering. Ohio Oil Co. v. Detamore, 165 Ind. 243, 73 N.E. 906 (1905).

In a quiet title action the failure to comply with the terms of the lease is a good ground for forfeiture of the lease. Logansport & Wabash Valley Gas Co. v. Seegar, 165 Ind. 1, 74 N.E. 500 (1905).

Res Judicata.
In an action by grantee under this section, an heir of grantor might have litigated her right to the property under a clause in the deed providing that, if grantee should die without issue, the property should go to the grantor's heirs, of whom defendant was one, though the conditions upon which such right of inheritance was based had not yet arisen, and, failing to do so, is concluded by the decree adjudging title in plaintiff. Green v. Scharman, 78 Ind. App. 465, 135 N.E. 3 (1922).

Statute of Limitations.
Where that statute of limitations had run against the plaintiff's right to recover possession, a suit to quiet title was also barred. Dumont v. Dufore, 27 Ind. 263 (1866).

An action to quiet title could have been brought fifteen years after the cause of action accrued. Caress v. Foster, 62 Ind. 145 (1878).

If an action to recover possession of lands was barred by the statute of limitations, a suit to quiet title was also barred. Smith v. Bryan, 74 Ind. 515 (1881).

The suit could be brought within 15 years after the action accrued. Eve v. Louis, 91 Ind. 457 (1883); Detwiler v. Schultheis, 122 Ind. 155, 23 N.E. 709 (1890); Irey v. Markey, 132 Ind. 546, 32 N.E. 309 (1892); Sinclair v. Gunzenhauser, 179 Ind. 78, 98 N.E. 37, 100 N.E. 376 (1912).

Defense of statute of limitation of actions was provable under general denial. Watson v. Lecklider, 147 Ind. 395, 45 N.E. 72 (1896).

Tax Deeds.
The holder of a tax sale certificate is not a necessary party to a suit by one claiming under a prior tax deed and a decree quieting title in such suit is not void as to him. Shedd v. Disney, 139 Ind. 240, 38 N.E. 594 (1894).

An action to quiet title to land held under a tax deed may be brought in the superior court. Browning v. Smith, 139 Ind. 280, 37 N.E. 540 (1894).

Who May Sue.
The inchoate interest of a wife in her husband's lands could not be the subject of a suit by her to quiet title. Paulus v. Latta, 93 Ind. 34 (1884); Vandevender v. Moore, 146 Ind. 44, 44 N.E. 3 (1896).

Husbands and wives could join in actions to quiet title to the lands of the wives. Indiana, B. & W.R.R. v. Brittingham, 98 Ind. 294 (1884).

The remedy of a quiet title action for those who hold tax deeds belongs only to those holding such deeds. McDonald v. Geisendorff, 128 Ind. 153, 27 N.E. 333 (1891).

A person having possession under a contract for the sale of land may bring action to quiet title. Puterbaugh v. Puterbaugh, 131 Ind. 288, 30 N.E. 519, 15 L.R.A. 341 (1892).

A purchaser of real estate which the vendor could have claimed as exempt from sale on execution, could maintain an action to quiet title to such real estate if the same was commenced before the sheriff's sale. Moss v. Jenkins, 146 Ind. 589, 45 N.E. 789 (1897).

Real party in interest had to sue, grantor in deed could not maintain action. Chapman v. Jones, 149 Ind. 434, 47 N.E. 1065 (1897), reh'g overruled, 149 Ind. 440, 49 N.E. 347 (1898).

Persons who were either in or out of possession of land could sue to quiet the title to the land. Island Coal Co. v. Combs, 152 Ind. 379, 53 N.E. 452 (1899); Scobey v. Thompson, 10 Ind. App. 12, 37 N.E. 277 (1894).

Remaindermen could sue to have their titles quieted. Rinkenberger v. Meyer, 155 Ind. 152, 56 N.E. 913 (1900).

Mortgagees who have conveyed the lands by warranty deeds could sue to quiet the title to the lands. Indianapolis v. Board of Church Extension of United Presbyterian Church, 28 Ind. App. 319, 62 N.E. 715 (1902).

Who May Sue. (Cont'd)

Guardians who never had possession of the lands of their wards could not sue to quiet the title to such lands. Tucker v. White, 28 Ind. App. 328, 62 N.E. 758 (1902).

Where mortgage was made to nonresident to avoid taxation, owner of land could not quiet title. Callicott v. Allen, 31 Ind. App. 561, 67 N.E. 196 (1903).

Executor of a decedent's estate without either equitable or legal title could not maintain a statutory action to quiet title to realty belonging to the estate, although he alleged that he was authorized by the will to sell the real estate, and that such sale was necessary to pay debts and legacies. Simms v. Gilmore, 78 Ind. App. 244, 135 N.E. 183 (1922).

Will Contest.

Will under which title was claimed could be contested in an action to quiet title. Putt v. Putt, 149 Ind. 30, 48 N.E. 356, 51 N.E. 337 (1897).

Collateral References. Maintainability by lessee of action to quiet title to leasehold. 51 A.L.R.2d 1227.

32-30-2-21. Applicability. — This chapter applies, as far as applicable, to:

(1) cases and partition cases where the title to real estate is a genuine question; and

(2) the pleadings and evidence between parties concerning questions of title to real estate. [P.L.2-2002, § 15.]

Cross References. General provisions on procedure in quiet title actions, IC 32-30-3-13.

General provisions on procedure in partition actions, IC 32-17-4-1.

NOTES TO DECISIONS

ANALYSIS

Counter-claim and cross-complaint.
Defenses.
Effect of judgment.
Ejectment rules applicable.
General denial and special answers.
Jury trial.
Plaintiff's title.

Counter-Claim and Cross-Complaint.

Proof of an issue which was in fact a counter-claim rather than a defense could not be admissible under a general denial. Gillenwaters v. Campbell, 142 Ind. 529, 41 N.E. 1041 (1895).

The defendant in an action to quiet title to land could file a cross-complaint setting up his title and have the same adjudicated. Kraus v. Thomas, 48 Ind. App. 437, 96 N.E. 12 (1911).

Defenses.

Easement over land was not sufficient as a full defense to suit to quiet title. Messick v. Midland Ry., 128 Ind. 81, 27 N.E. 419 (1891).

Transfer of interest of plaintiff in property pending suit did not abate action. Shedd v. Disney, 139 Ind. 240, 38 N.E. 594 (1894).

Effect of Judgment.

A judgment quieting title to real estate had the effect of precluding one who was a party thereto from afterward asserting an adverse interest therein. Green v. Glynn, 71 Ind. 336 (1880).

A decree quieting title to lands prevented the parties from afterwards asserting an adverse claim held at the time of the decree. Stumph v. Reger, 92 Ind. 286 (1883); Farrar v. Clark, 97 Ind. 447 (1884); Faught v. Faught, 98 Ind. 470 (1884); Indiana, B. & W.R.R. v. Allen, 113 Ind. 308, 15 N.E. 451, 3 Am. St. R. 650 (1888); Davis v. Lennen, 125 Ind. 185, 24 N.E. 885 (1890); Satterwhite v. Sherley, 127 Ind. 59, 25 N.E. 1100 (1890); Hawkins v. Taylor, 128 Ind. 431, 27 N.E. 1117 (1891); Davis v. Barton, 130 Ind. 399, 30 N.E. 512 (1892); Tanguey v. O'Connell, 132 Ind. 62, 31 N.E. 469 (1892); Craig v. Major, 139 Ind. 624, 35 N.E. 1098 (1894); Woodward v. Mitchell, 140 Ind. 406, 39 N.E. 437 (1895); Skelton v. Sharp, 161 Ind. 383, 67 N.E. 535 (1903); Krotz v. A.R. Beck Lumber Co., 34 Ind. App. 577, 73 N.E. 273 (1905).

Claims or liens of parties on land which they failed to set up were barred by the judgment. Morarity v. Calloway, 134 Ind. 503, 34 N.E. 226 (1893); Browning v. Smith, 139 Ind. 280, 37 N.E. 540 (1894); Woodward v. Mitchell, 140 Ind. 406, 39 N.E. 437 (1895).

A decree quieting title to real estate as

Effect of Judgment. (Cont'd)
against a life tenant did not constitute a bar to an action to enforce a lien on such real estate for taxes paid, as against remaindermen, where it did not appear upon what grounds the action against the life tenant was based. Watson v. Lecklider, 147 Ind. 395, 45 N.E. 72 (1896).

Ejectment Rules Applicable.
The same rules applied to actions to quiet title as to actions for the recovery of the possession of real estate. Green v. Glynn, 71 Ind. 336 (1880).

All the rules applicable to actions of ejectment applied to actions to quiet title. Trittipo v. Morgan, 99 Ind. 269 (1884); Johnson v. Pontious, 118 Ind. 270, 20 N.E. 792 (1889).

General Denial and Special Answers.
All defenses could have been proved under a general denial. Graham v. Graham, 55 Ind. 23 (1876).

All defenses could be proved under the general denial. Sharpe v. Dillman, 77 Ind. 280 (1881); O'Donahue v. Creager, 117 Ind. 372, 20 N.E. 267 (1889); Mason v. Roll, 130 Ind. 260, 29 N.E. 1135 (1892); Watson v. Lecklider, 147 Ind. 395, 45 N.E. 72 (1896); Allen v. Indianapolis Oil Co., 27 Ind.App. 158, 60 N.E. 1003 (1901); Kaufman v. Preston, 158 Ind. 361, 63 N.E. 570 (1902); Beasey v. High, 33 Ind. App. 689, 72 N.E. 181 (1904); Chicago & S.E.R.R. v. Grantham, 165 Ind. 279, 75 N.E. 265 (1905).

Special answer could be stricken out when general denial was filed. Mason v. Roll, 130 Ind. 260, 29 N.E. 1135 (1892); Watson v. Lecklider, 147 Ind. 395, 45 N.E. 72 (1896); Beasey v. High, 33 Ind. App. 689, 72 N.E. 181 (1904).

It was not error to strike out an affirmative paragraph of answer if a general denial had been pleaded. Beasey v. High, 33 Ind. App. 689, 72 N.E. 181 (1904); Gwinn v. Hobbs, 72 Ind. App. 439, 118 N.E. 155 (1917).

Jury Trial.
Jury trial could be demanded. Trittipo v. Morgan, 99 Ind. 269 (1884); Johnson v. Taylor, 106 Ind. 89, 5 N.E. 732 (1886); Puterbaugh v. Puterbaugh, 131 Ind. 288, 30 N.E. 519, 15 L.R.A. 341 (1892); Monnett v. Turpie, 133 Ind. 424, 32 N.E. 328 (1892); Jennings v. Moon, 135 Ind. 168, 34 N.E. 996 (1893); Baxter v. Baxter, 46 Ind. App. 514, 92 N.E. 881 (1910); Macy v. Wood, 49 Ind. App. 469, 97 N.E. 553 (1912); Gwinn v. Hobbs, 72 Ind. App. 439, 118 N.E. 155 (1917); Folsom v. Buttolph, 82 Ind. App. 283, 143 N.E. 258 (1924).

Plaintiff's Title.
The plaintiff had to recover on the strength of his own title, and not on the weakness of that of his adversary. Blake v. Minkner, 136 Ind. 418, 36 N.E. 246 (1894); Graham v. Lunsford, 149 Ind. 83, 48 N.E. 627 (1897); Dodds v. Winslow, 26 Ind. App. 652, 60 N.E. 458 (1901); Krotz v. A.R. Beck Lumber Co., 34 Ind. App. 577, 73 N.E. 273 (1905); Jose v. Hunter, 60 Ind. App. 569, 103 N.E. 392 (1913); State v. Tuesburg Land Co., 61 Ind. App. 555, 109 N.E. 530, 111 N.E. 342 (1915).

32-30-2-22. No court costs if defendant disclaims interest or fails to answer. — If the defendant's answer to a complaint under this chapter disclaims any interest or estate in the property, or if the defendant does not answer the complaint and the court issues a default judgment against the defendant, the defendant may not be required to pay the plaintiff's court costs. [P.L.2-2002, § 15.]

NOTES TO DECISIONS

ANALYSIS

Action on insurance policy.
Application of section.
Costs.
Estoppel.

Action on Insurance Policy.
There could be no such pleading as a "disclaimer" in an action on a policy of windstorm insurance. Indiana Mut. Cyclone Ins. Co. v. Rinard, 102 Ind. App. 546, 200 N.E. 452 (1936).

Application of Section.
The law concerning a disclaimer by the defendant applied only to a defendant not in possession. Ragan v. Haynes, 10 Ind. 348 (1858).

The section only applied to defendants not in possession of the lands. McAdams v. Lotton, 118 Ind. 1, 20 N.E. 523 (1889); Scobey v. Thompson, 10 Ind. App. 12, 37 N.E. 277 (1894).

A disclaimer was only applicable in actions to quiet title and for partition. Walker v. Steele, 121 Ind. 436, 22 N.E. 142, 23 N.E. 271 (1889).

Costs.

If a defendant answered disclaiming any interest in the lands, and alleged that a third person was in possession thereof, he was entitled to costs. McCarnan v. Cochran, 57 Ind. 166 (1877).

If a defendant in possession filed a disclaimer, but refused to yield possession without a writ, he could be taxed with all costs. McAdams v. Lotton, 118 Ind. 1, 20 N.E. 523 (1889).

The disclaimer should have been filed when the party first appeared to entitle him to recover costs. Kitts v. Willson, 130 Ind. 492, 29 N.E. 401 (1891).

If the defendant filed a disclaimer or suf-

fered a default, he could not be taxed with costs on the ground that he acted fraudulently. Scobey v. Thompson, 10 Ind. App. 12, 37 N.E. 277 (1894).

When a defendant filed a disclaimer, the action should have been dismissed at the cost of the plaintiff. New Am. Oil & Mining Co. v. Troyer, 166 Ind. 402, 76 N.E. 253, 77 N.E. 739 (1905).

Estoppel.

When a defendant filed a disclaimer, he was estopped from afterwards asserting title to the property. New Am. Oil & Mining Co. v. Troyer, 166 Ind. 402, 76 N.E. 253, 77 N.E. 739 (1905).

32-30-2-23. Action against cotenant. — In an action by a plaintiff who is a tenant in common or joint tenant of real property against the plaintiff's cotenant, the plaintiff must show, in addition to the plaintiff's evidence of right, that defendant:

(1) denied plaintiff's right; or

(2) did some act amounting to a denial of a plaintiff's right. [P.L.2-2002, § 15.]

NOTES TO DECISIONS

ANALYSIS

Adverse possession, ouster.
Denial of possession.

Adverse Possession, Ouster.

When one tenant-in-common claimed under a deed conveying the whole estate, he would have been deemed to have ousted his cotenant. Nelson v. Davis, 35 Ind. 474 (1871).

The possession of one of several tenants-in-common is the possession of all and the statute of limitations did not run in favor of the tenant in actual possession unless that tenant disclaimed the tenancy in common and asserted a different claim and an exclusive right. Bowen v. Preston, 48 Ind. 367 (1874).

In order that the possession of a tenant-in-common was adverse to the other tenants, there had to be an actual ouster of the latter. Nicholson v. Caress, 76 Ind. 24 (1881); Patterson v. Nixon, 79 Ind. 251 (1881).

One tenant-in-common could obtain title to the whole estate by an adverse possession. English v. Powell, 119 Ind. 93, 21 N.E. 458 (1889).

The evidence to sustain an ouster by a cotenant must be stronger than that to sustain ordinary adverse possession. Price v. Hall, 140 Ind. 314, 39 N.E. 941, 49 Am. St. R. 196 (1895).

Denial of Possession.

A tenant-in-common could have maintained an action for the possession of his part of the real estate, where there was a denial of his rights by his cotenants. Bethell v. McCool, 46 Ind. 303 (1874).

Tenant-in-common suing a cotenant had to prove a denial of possession. Blake v. Minkner, 136 Ind. 418, 36 N.E. 246 (1894).

CHAPTER 3

EJECTMENT AND QUIET TITLE

32-30-3-1. Complaint — Filing — Affidavit. — (a) This section applies to all actions:

(1) in ejectment; or

(2) for the recovery of possession of real estate.

(b) At the time of filing a complaint or at any time before judgment, a plaintiff may file with the clerk of the court in which the action is filed or pending an affidavit stating the following:

(1) The plaintiff is entitled to possession of the property described in the complaint.

(2) The defendant has unlawfully retained possession of the property described in the complaint.

(3) The estimated value of the property described in the complaint.

(4) The estimated rental value of the property described in the complaint. [P.L.2-2002, § 15.]

Compiler's Notes. P.L.2-2002, § 15, which enacted Article IC 32-30 provided for "Ejectment and Quiet Title" to be the heading of both chapters IC 32-30-2 and IC 32-30-3. The provisions of IC 32-30-3 are similar to the provisions of former IC 32-6, which were codified in the 1933 edition of the Burns' Annotated Indiana Statutes, in sections of Title 3, Provisional Remedies and Special Proceedings, Chapter 13, Ejectment, and Chapter 14, Quieting Title, and correspond to provisions of Acts 1881, ch. 37; 1911, ch. 279; 1915, chs. 108 and 177; and 1935, ch. 210.

Effective Dates. P.L.2-2002, § 15. July 1. 2002.

Cross References. Ejectment, IC 32-30-3. Ejectment actions, IC 32-30-2.

NOTES TO DECISIONS

Analysis

Cooperatives.
Defective notice.
—Waiver.
Order of clerk.
Receiver.

Cooperatives.

Although ejectment is an appropriate rem- edy for removing a violating member from possession of a unit in a cooperative commu- nity, the member has a vested interest in relation to the unit, and cannot be forced to simply forfeit that interest without the trial court directing proceedings for the sale of the interest so as to insure the member's rights are adequately protected. Cunningham v. Georgetown Homes, Inc., 708 N.E.2d 623 (Ind. App. 1999).

Defective Notice.

—Waiver.
Where a vendor failed to give proper notice of intention to declare forfeiture and repossession of the property, the repossession of the property pursuant to statutory bonding procedure did not terminate nor rescind the contract. Smeekens v. Bertrand, 262 Ind. 50, 42 Ind. Dec. 74, 311 N.E.2d 431 (1974).

Order of Clerk.
Clerk's duty to issue order for possession

and sheriff's duty to approve surety on written undertaking were ministerial acts, and orders of clerk were part of cause of action. State ex rel. Allison v. Brennan, 229 Ind. 281, 97 N.E.2d 925 (1951).

Receiver.
The appointment of a receiver involved the exercise of an extraordinary equitable power which would not have been exerted where there was a full and adequate remedy at law. Meacham v. Sanders, 233 Ind. 182, 118 N.E.2d 126 (1954).

Collateral References. 25 Am. Jur. 2d Ejectment, §§ 1-5.
    28 C.J.S. Ejectment, §§ 1-33.

Air-conditioning appliance, equipment, or apparatus as fixture. 69 A.L.R.4th 359.

32-30-3-2. Order to show cause. — (a) Upon the filing of an affidavit described in section 1 [IC 32-30-3-1] of this chapter, the clerk shall issue an order for a time fixed by the judge directing the defendant to appear to controvert the affidavit or to show cause why the judge should not remove the defendant from the property and put the plaintiff in possession. The order to show cause must direct the time within which the order must be served on the defendant and set forth the date, time, and place for the hearing, which may take place no earlier than five (5) business days after the date of service on the defendant.

(b) The order to show cause must state the following:

(1) The defendant may file supporting affidavits with the court.

(2) The defendant may appear and present supporting testimony at the hearing on the order to show cause.

(3) The defendant may file with the court a written undertaking to stay the delivery of the property under this chapter.

(4) The judge may issue a judgment of possession in favor of the plaintiff if the defendant fails to appear at the hearing. [P.L.2-2002, § 15.]

NOTES TO DECISIONS

Presentation of Evidence.
Where only the defendant cooperative association was given any opportunity to present evidence before pre-judgment possession was granted, and where they were not required to first file a bond with the court in an amount

which would cover the plaintiff member's damages in the event that she was wrongfully ejected, vacation and remand was appropriate. Cunningham v. Georgetown Homes, Inc., 708 N.E.2d 623 (Ind. App. 1999).

32-30-3-3. Issuance of order for possession before hearing. — After reviewing the complaint, affidavits, and other evidence or testimony, the court may issue an order for possession before the hearing if probable cause appears that:

(1) the property is in immediate danger of destruction, serious harm, or sale to an innocent purchaser; or

(2) the holder of the property threatens to destroy, harm, or sell the property to an innocent purchaser. [P.L.2-2002, § 15.]

NOTES TO DECISIONS

Ejectment Bond.

Failure of purchasers to post bond and maintain possession did not prevent them from raising wrongful ejectment by sellers on counterclaim. Nelson v. Butcher, 170 Ind. App. 10, 53 Ind. Dec. 710, 352 N.E.2d 106 (1976).

32-30-3-4. Order shortening time for hearing on order to show cause — Temporary restraining orders. — (a) If a court issues an order of possession under section 3 [IC 32-30-3-3] of this chapter, the defendant or other person from whom possession of the property has been taken may apply to the court for an order shortening the time for hearing on the order to show cause. The court may shorten the time for the hearing and direct that the matter be heard on at least forty-eight (48) hours notice to the plaintiff. An order of possession issued under section 3 of this chapter must direct the sheriff or other executing officer to hold the property until further order of the court.

(b) If a court does not issue an order of possession under section 3 of this chapter, the court may, in addition to issuing an order to show cause, issue temporary restraining orders against the defendant as needed to preserve the rights of the parties with respect to the property and the status of the property. The court shall issue the temporary restraining orders in accordance with the rules of the supreme court governing the issuance of injunctions. [P.L.2-2002, § 15.]

32-30-3-5. Preliminary determination — Prejudgment orders. — (a) After the hearing on the order to show cause, the court shall:

(1) consider the pleadings, evidence, and testimony presented at the hearing; and

(2) determine with reasonable probability which party is entitled to possession, use, and enjoyment of the property.

The court's determination is preliminary pending final adjudication of the claims of the parties. If the court determines that the action is an action in which a prejudgment order of possession in plaintiff favor should issue, the court shall issue the order.

(b) The court may issue the prejudgment order of possession in favor of the plaintiff if the defendant fails to appear at the hearing on the order to show cause.

(c) If the plaintiff's property has a peculiar value that cannot be compensated by damages, the court may appoint a receiver to take possession of and hold the property until further order of the court. [P.L.2-2002, § 15.]

NOTES TO DECISIONS

Order Upheld.

The apparent lack of any agreement over the material terms of a purported lease was a fatal flaw for defendant's cause to establish an oral lease; plaintiff was entitled to a prejudgment possession order. Kinko's Graphics Corp. v. Townsend, 803 F. Supp. 1450 (S.D. Ind. 1992).

32-30-3-6. Order of possession — Written undertaking. — A court may not issue an order of possession in favor of a plaintiff other than an order of final judgment until the plaintiff has filed with the court a written undertaking in an amount fixed by the court and executed by a surety to be approved by the court binding the plaintiff to the defendant in an amount sufficient to assure the payment of any damages the defendant may suffer if the court wrongfully ordered possession of the property to the plaintiff. [P.L.2-2002, § 15.]

NOTES TO DECISIONS

ANALYSIS

Appeal.
Ejectment bond.
Legislative intent.
Small claims actions.
Time for filing.

Appeal.

The trial court order setting the amount of bond in an ejectment action should not have been considered as one of the kinds of court orders from which an interlocutory appeal could have been taken, since such an appeal would have caused unnecessary delay in the proceedings and would not have facilitated the administration of justice. Sholty v. Indianapolis Water Co., 255 Ind. 316, 23 Ind. Dec. 646, 263 N.E.2d 718 (1970).

Ejectment Bond.

Under a power of attorney issued by an insurance company to its agent, authorizing the agent to issue bonds to an amount not exceeding $25,000, in specified cases, including bonds issued by order of a court, the agent had authority to issue a bond in ejectment case with amount of liability open. Standard Acc. Ins. Co. v. Ayres, 217 Ind. 422, 28 N.E.2d 50 (1940).

Where only the defendant cooperative association was given any opportunity to present evidence before pre-judgment possession was granted, and where they were not required to first file a bond with the court in an amount which would cover the plaintiff member's damages in the event that she was wrongfully

ejected, vacation and remand was appropriate. Cunningham v. Georgetown Homes, Inc., 708 N.E.2d 623 (Ind. App. 1999).

Legislative Intent.

The provision of the former section pertaining to the execution of a bond by the landlord, in ejectment action against the tenant, was intended to provide a method of obtaining possession, and to give the tenant a right of action on the bond if the eviction were wrongful. Ault v. Phillips, 108 Ind. App. 535, 27 N.E.2d 379 (1940).

Small Claims Actions.

Trial court was not bound by statutory provisions on formal procedures related to evictions in landlord's claim on small claims docket, and the court properly issued order of possession, even though landlord had not executed a surety under foremr IC 32-6-1.5-6 (repealed; see this section for similar provisions). Stout v. Kokomo Manor Apts., 677 N.E.2d 1060 (Ind. App. 1997).

Time for Filing.

For an order allowing plaintiff's prejudgment possession to become effective, plaintiff, within ten (10) days from the date of entry, was required to file with the court a "written undertaking" executed by a surety (i.e., a bond) sufficient "to assure the payment of such damages as the defendant may suffer if the property has been wrongfully taken from him" or seek an appropriate extension for good cause shown. Kinko's Graphics Corp. v. Townsend, 803 F. Supp. 1450 (S.D. Ind. 1992).

32-30-3-7. Order of possession — Directed to sheriff — Contents. — The court shall direct the order of possession to the sheriff or other officer

charged with executing the order and within whose jurisdiction the property is located. The order of possession must:

   (1) describe the property;

   (2) direct the executing officer to:

     (A) seize possession of the property unless the court issued the order without notice to the parties; and

     (B) if the defendant has not filed a written undertaking as provided in section 8 [IC 32-30-3-8] of this chapter, put the plaintiff in possession of the property by removing the defendant and the defendant's personal property from the property;

   (3) have attached a copy of any written undertaking filed by the plaintiff under section 6 [IC 32-30-3-6] of this chapter; and

   (4) inform the defendant of the right to except to the surety upon the plaintiff's undertaking or to file a written undertaking for the repossession of the property as provided in section 8 of this chapter. [P.L.2-2002, § 15.]

NOTES TO DECISIONS

In General.

   The former section, authorizing the issuance of writs of possession in ejectment suits, provided a complete remedy by due course of law and barred injunctive relief by a lessee kept out of possession by the holding over of a prior tenant, on the ground of irreparable loss of profit contemplated to be made by plaintiff's use of the premises. Heugel v. Townsley, 213 Ind. 339, 12 N.E.2d 761 (1938).

32-30-3-8. Return of possession to defendant — Written undertaking. — (a) Before the hearing on the order to show cause or before final judgment, and within the time fixed in the order of possession, the defendant may require the return of possession of the property by filing with the court a written undertaking executed by a surety to be approved by the court stating that the defendant is bound in an amount determined by the court sufficient to assure the payment of costs assessed against the defendant for the wrongful detention of the property.

   (b) If a defendant files an undertaking under this section, the defendant shall:

   (1) serve a notice of filing the undertaking on the executing officer and the plaintiff or the plaintiff's attorney; and

   (2) file with the court proof of service of the notice of filing the undertaking.

   (c) If a defendant files an undertaking before the hearing on the order to show cause, the court shall terminate the hearing unless the plaintiff takes exception to the surety.

   (d) If the property is in the possession of the executing officer when the defendant files the undertaking, the court shall return possession of the property to the defendant not more than five (5) days after service of notice of the filing of the undertaking on the plaintiff or the plaintiff's attorney. [P.L.2-2002, § 15.]

NOTES TO DECISIONS

<small>ANALYSIS</small>

Construction.
Constructive eviction.
Damages.
Ejectment bond.
—Time.
Failure to file undertaking.
Motion to quash seizure order.
Voluntary vacation of premises.

Construction.

The word "execute" in the former section required delivery, and the delivery must have been of a written undertaking payable to the plaintiff. Lawless v. Johnson, 232 Ind. 64, 111 N.E.2d 656 (1953).

Constructive Eviction.

In view of the former section, landlord's action for possession for failure of tenant to pay rent did not amount to constructive eviction. Trout v. Brown, 125 Ind. App. 381, 123 N.E.2d 647 (1954).

Damages.

In action on ejectment bond, plaintiff was entitled to the damage he would have been entitled to recover in a direct action for wrongful ejectment. Ault v. Phillips, 108 Ind. App. 535, 27 N.E.2d 379 (1940).

In action on ejectment bond executed by a landlord in action against tenants, plaintiff who had been wrongfully ejected from real estate leased by him from the landlord could recover as proper elements of damage for any mental anguish, embarrassment, and humiliation suffered by him on account of the wrongful ejectment. Ault v. Phillips, 108 Ind. App. 535, 27 N.E.2d 379 (1940).

In action on ejectment bond, plaintiff, who was an evicted tenant, had the right to have the jury, in fixing the amount of recovery, instructed to consider any actual injury to his goods, resulting from such wrongful eviction, and also humiliation experienced by him from such eviction. Ault v. Phillips, 108 Ind. App. 535, 27 N.E.2d 379 (1940).

Evidence as to the rental value of premises, that defendant was in possession thereof at the time plaintiff acquired it, which possession was never surrendered, and that defendant retained possession by giving bond after plaintiff instituted suit for ejectment, was sufficient to warrant an award of damages to plaintiff. Tobin v. McClellan, 225 Ind. 335, 73 N.E.2d 679, reh'g denied, 225 Ind. 347, 75 N.E.2d 149 (1947).

Ejectment Bond.

—Time.

The court had no jurisdiction to extend the five-day period fixed by the former section for the filing of a bond by the defendant. State ex rel. Young Metal Prods., Inc. v. Lake Superior Court Room 5, 254 Ind. 285, 21 Ind. Dec. 576, 258 N.E.2d 853 (1970).

Failure to File Undertaking.

Where defendant in ejectment proceeding did not attempt to file written undertaking as required by the former section because sheriff would not accept surety, he did not comply with former statute requiring a written undertaking, and injunction would not be granted. Lawless v. Johnson, 232 Ind. 64, 111 N.E.2d 656 (1953).

Motion to Quash Seizure Order.

In an ejectment proceeding where defendant moved to quash the order issued by the clerk to the sheriff for seizure of the real estate in question, which motion the court overruled, but defendant executed the statutory undertaking, and retained possession of the real estate, he was not harmed by the overruling of his motion, and the reviewing court would not consider such ruling. Steve v. Colosimo, 211 Ind. 673, 7 N.E.2d 983 (1937).

Voluntary Vacation of Premises.

Where the tenant voluntarily vacated the premises the issue of ejectment became moot. Tenants' counterclaim for damages based solely on wrongful ejectment was not valid since the issue of wrongful eviction was not before the trial court. Haas v. Rathburn, 137 Ind. App. 172, 5 Ind. Dec. 113, 205 N.E.2d 329, reh'g dismissed, 137 Ind. App. 176, 206 N.E.2d 389 (1965).

32-30-3-9. Copies of order of possession delivered to defendant. —

(a) If a defendant or the defendant's attorney is in open court when the court issues the order of possession, a copy of the order shall be delivered to the defendant and the delivery noted in the order book.

(b) If the defendant and the defendant's attorney are not present, sufficient copies of the order shall be delivered to the sheriff or other executing officer. The executing officer shall, without delay, serve upon the defendant a copy of the order of possession by delivering the order to the defendant personally or to the defendant's agent. If the executing officer cannot find the defendant or the defendant's agent, the executing officer shall leave the order at the defendant's usual place of abode or with some person of suitable age and discretion. If the defendant and the defendant's agent do not have any known usual place of abode, the executing officer shall mail the order to the defendant's last known address. [P.L.2-2002, § 15.]

32-30-3-10. Removal of defendants after order of possession served. — If the property is in the possession or control of the defendant or the defendant's agent, the executing officer shall take the property into custody and remove the occupants from the property not earlier than forty-eight (48) hours after the order of possession is served on the defendant or the defendant's agent. [P.L.2-2002, § 15.]

32-30-3-11. Return of order of possession to court. — The executing officer shall return the order of possession with the proceedings endorsed on the order to the court in which the action is pending not more than five (5) days after taking into custody the property described in the order. [P.L.2-2002, § 15.]

32-30-3-12. Final judgment — Supercedes prior orders. — A final judgment supersedes any:
   (1) prejudgment order for possession;
   (2) temporary restraining order; or
   (3) order temporarily changing possession of property;
issued under this chapter. [P.L.2-2002, § 15.]

NOTES TO DECISIONS

ANALYSIS

In general.
Refusal to grant continuance.

In General.
  On appeal from a judgment in an ejectment case, a motion to dismiss the appeal would not have been sustained on the theory that defendant voluntarily surrendered possession of the premises in question, and that the judgment for damages was not questioned, where defendant vacated the premises after plaintiff had entered into an undertaking entitling him to possession; the questions presented by the appeal not having been moot. Walsh v. Soller, 207 Ind. 82, 190 N.E. 61, rehearing denied, 207 Ind. 87, 191 N.E. 334 (1934).

Refusal to Grant Continuance.
  In an action in ejectment, the action of the court in refusing to grant defendant a continuance on account of illness and inability to attend trial did not require the reversal of a judgment giving plaintiff immediate possession of the real estate and damages for its wrongful detention, where counsel for defendant, in argument of the motion for continuance, admitted that plaintiff was entitled to possession, and the record disclosed that the merits of the cause were fairly tried and defendant was not deprived of any substantial right. Freimann v. Gallmeier, 116 Ind. App. 170, 63 N.E.2d 150 (1945).

32-30-3-13. Persons who have rights to recover possession or quiet title in own name. — Any person having a right to:
   (1) recover the possession of; or
   (2) quiet title to;

real estate in the name of any other person has a right to recover possession or quiet title in the person's own name. An action may not be defeated or reversed if the plaintiff could have successfully maintained the action in the name of another person to inure to the plaintiff's benefit. [P.L.2-2002, § 15.]

NOTES TO DECISIONS

ANALYSIS

In general.
Purchaser at tax sale.
Tenants in common.

In General.
Prior to the adoption of this section, if lands were conveyed while in the adverse possession of a third person, a suit for possession had to be brought in the name of the grantor for the use of the grantee. Steeple v. Downing, 60 Ind. 478 (1878); Burk v. Andis, 98 Ind. 59 (1884); Peck v. Sims, 120 Ind. 345, 22 N.E. 313 (1889); Chapman v. Jones, 149 Ind. 434, 47 N.E. 1065 (1897), reh'g overruled, 149 Ind. 440, 49 N.E. 347 (1898).
Under this section, the grantee in such deeds had to bring the action to recover possession of the lands. Peck v. Sims, 120 Ind. 345, 22 N.E. 313 (1889); Chapman v. Jones, 149 Ind. 434, 47 N.E. 1065 (1897), reh'g overruled, 149 Ind. 440, 49 N.E. 347 (1898).

If lands conveyed were in possession of a tenant, the grantee had to sue for possession, although the grantor agreed to deliver possession. Holliday v. Chism, 25 Ind. App. 1, 57 N.E. 563 (1900).

Purchaser at Tax Sale.
A tax deed vested a prima facie good and valid title in the purchaser at tax sale, and a quitclaim deed from such purchaser vested the same kind of title in a purchaser from him. Murray v. Holland, 108 Ind. App. 236, 27 N.E.2d 126 (1940).

Tenants in Common.
One tenant in common could not, under this section, sue to recover the interest of his cotenant. Martin v. Neal, 125 Ind. 547, 25 N.E. 813 (1890).
A tenant in common could sue to recover possession from a trespasser. Bivens v. Henderson, 42 Ind. App. 562, 86 N.E. 426 (1908).

Collateral References. 25 Am. Jur. 2d Ejectment, §§ 63-71.
  65 Am. Jur. 2d Quieting Title, §§ 68-72.

28 C.J.S. Ejectment, § 32.
74 C.J.S. Quieting Title, §§ 52-57.

32-30-3-14. Persons named as defendants in actions — Complaint — Affidavit — Notice — Location of filing. — (a) This section applies to the following proceedings brought in a state court concerning real estate or any interest in real estate located in Indiana:
    (1) An action to:
        (A) quiet or determine title to;
        (B) obtain title or possession of; or
        (C) partition;
    real estate.
    (2) An action by an executor or administrator to:<Div align
        (A) sell real estate to satisfy the debts of a decedent; or
        (B) enforce or foreclose a mortgage or lien on real estate.
  (b) A person who institutes a proceeding described in subsection (a) may, under a circumstance set forth in subsection (c), name as a defendant any of the following individuals:
    (1) A person:
        (A) who may have an interest in real estate that is the subject of the proceeding; and

(B) whose name appears of record in a record concerning the real estate.

(2) A person who bears one of the following relationships to a former owner or encumbrancer of the real estate:

(A) Spouse.

(B) Widow or widower.

(C) Heir or devisee.

The person who institutes the proceeding does not have to know the name of a person described in subdivision (2).

(c) A person who institutes a proceeding described in subsection (a) may name an individual described in subsection (b) as a defendant if public records in the county in which the real estate that is the subject of the proceeding is located any of disclose the following circumstances:

(1) There is a break or hiatus in the record title of real estate.

(2) There exists:

(A) a defect in;

(B) an apparent defect in; or

(C) a cloud upon;

the title of the real estate due to a defective or inaccurate legal description of the real estate.

(3) There is no record that a grantor or mortgagor was unmarried when the deed to or mortgage on the real estate was executed.

(4) An instrument affecting the real estate, including a deed, will, or mortgage, was not properly executed.

(5) A mortgage, vendor's lien, or other lien or encumbrance affecting the real estate was not properly released.

(6) The person instituting the proceeding does not know:

(A) the name of another person who may claim an interest in the real estate based on the other person's relationship to a former owner, mortgagee, or encumbrancer of the real estate; or

(B) whether another person, including a person described in clause (A), who may have an interest in the real estate is alive or dead.

(d) The plaintiff in a proceeding described in subsection (a) may state the following in the complaint:

(1) The plaintiff asserts title to the real estate that is the subject of the proceeding against all other persons.

(2) The purpose of the proceeding is to quiet the title to the real estate.

(3) The plaintiff has named as defendants all persons whom the party knows may have a claim to or interest in the real estate.

(e) The plaintiff shall file with the complaint an affidavit that states the following:

(1) The complaint contains the names of all persons disclosed by public record by or through whom a claim or interest in the real estate may be asserted.

(2) The plaintiff does not know the following information about a person described in subdivision (1):

(A) Whether the person is alive or dead.

(B) The person's legal residence.

(C) The person's marital status.

(D) If the person is or has been married, the name or address of the person's spouse, widow, or widower.

(E) If the person is dead, whether the person has left any heirs or devisees.

(F) The name or legal residence of an heir or devisee.

(3) The plaintiff claims full and complete right and title in the real estate that is the subject of the proceeding described in subsection (a).

(4) The plaintiff intends to quiet title to the real estate through the proceeding.

(f) After the plaintiff files the complaint and affidavit, the plaintiff shall file an affidavit for publication of notice under IC 34-32-1.

(g) After the plaintiff files the affidavit for publication of notice described in subsection (f), the clerk of the county in which the real estate that is the subject of the proceeding described in subsection (a) is located shall publish notice of the following:

(1) The filing and pendency of the proceeding.

(2) The date on which the proceeding will take place.

(3) Designations and descriptions of any defendant whose name and legal residence are unknown.

(4) A legal description of the real estate.

(5) The purpose of the proceeding, which is to quiet title to the real estate.

(h) After the clerk publishes notice as set forth in subsection (g), the clerk shall provide proof of the publication to the court in which the proceeding described in subsection (a) is pending. Not earlier than thirty (30) days after the last publication of notice, the court may hear and determine all matters in the proceeding as if the plaintiff had known and sued all possible claimants by their proper names. All decrees, orders, and judgments issued by the court are binding and conclusive on all parties and claimants. The proceeding shall be taken as a proceeding in rem against the real estate.

(i) If the real estate that is the subject of the proceeding described in subsection (a) is located in more than one (1) county, the plaintiff may file a complaint in a court located in any county in which the real estate is located. The plaintiff may not file a complaint in more than one (1) court. The plaintiff shall publish notice of the complaint in each county in which the real estate is located. The published notice in each county shall contain the following:

(1) The legal description of the real estate that is located in that county.

(2) The other counties in which the real estate is located.

(3) Notice that a certified copy of the final judgment in the proceeding will be filed, not more than three (3) months after the judgment is entered, in the recorder's office in each county in which the real estate is located. [P.L.2-2002, § 15.]

NOTES TO DECISIONS

Persons to Whom Limited.

The statute was limited to the husband, wife, widower, widow, heir or devisee of a person or persons shown by the records of the county to have had an interest in the land. Bastin v. Myers, 82 Ind. App. 325, 144 N.E. 425 (1924).

Purpose.

The purpose of this statute was to provide a method by which the unknown "husband or wife, widower or widow, heirs or devisees of any and all persons appearing of record as a former owner or encumbrancer" might have been made a party defendant and have been bound by a decree quieting the plaintiff's title as to such husband, wife, widower, widow, heir or devisee whose name was unknown to the plaintiff. Bastin v. Myers, 82 Ind. App. 325, 144 N.E. 425 (1924).

Subject Matter to Which Limited.

The statute was limited to cases where there was one or more of the situations named in the statute, viz.: (1) A break or hiatus in the record title of the real estate; (2) A defect or apparent defect in, or cloud upon, the title of real estate on account of the defective or inaccurate description appearing in some matter of record; (3) Where it did not appear of record that a grantor or mortgagor was unmarried at the time of executing some deed or mortgage covering the land; (4) Where it appeared from the records that a deed, will, mortgage or other instrument affecting the real estate was not properly executed; (5) That a mortgage or lien affecting the land had not been properly or duly released, as disclosed by the public records of the county, "by reason whereof, some doubt may be alleged or arise as to the complete validity of the title claimed or asserted." Bastin v. Myers, 82 Ind. App. 325, 144 N.E. 425 (1924).

The complaint had to show that the action was based on one of the situations stated above. Bastin v. Myers, 82 Ind. App. 325, 144 N.E. 425 (1924).

The mere fact that it was an action to quiet title was not sufficient to authorize proceedings under this statute. Bastin v. Myers, 82 Ind. App. 325, 144 N.E. 425 (1924).

Collateral References. 65 Am. Jur. 2d Quieting Title, §§ 46-53.

74 C.J.S. Quieting Title, § 50.

32-30-3-15. Scope — Supplement to prior law. — Section 14 [IC 32-30-3-14] of this chapter may not be construed to contravene or repeal any other Indiana law concerning title to real estate or suits or actions affecting title to real estate. Section 14 of this chapter supplements laws existing on April 26, 1915. [P.L.2-2002, § 15.]

32-30-3-16. Service — First name unknown. — (a) In a suit to quiet title to real estate in a state court, the plaintiff shall serve:

(1) all resident and nonresident defendants whose residence is known; and

(2) all defendants whose residence is unknown.

(b) Service on a known defendant by:

(1) the defendant's individual name;

(2) the name by which the defendant appears of record;

(3) the name by which the defendant is commonly known; or

(4) the defendant's surname if the defendant's first name is unknown; is sufficient, legal, and binding on and against all persons claiming from, through, or under the defendant.

(c) If a plaintiff serves a defendant by the defendant's surname only, the plaintiff or the plaintiff's attorney shall file an affidavit stating that the plaintiff does not know and has not, after diligent inquiry, been able to ascertain the first name of the defendant. [P.L.2-2002, § 15.]

32-30-3-17. Entry of orders and decrees by clerk — Certification of final judgment — Quiet Title Record. — (a) The clerk of a court shall enter in the civil order book all orders and decrees in any suit to quiet the title to real estate. After a court enters final judgment in a proceeding, the clerk shall certify a copy of the final judgment and deliver the certified copy to the county recorder. The clerk shall include the costs of a transcript of the proceedings and the recording fees in the costs of the proceeding.

(b) A county recorder shall procure a substantially bound book that is the size and quality of the county deed records. The book shall be known as the "Quiet Title Record". The Quiet Title Record must contain a transcript of each proceeding and an index to each transcript. The index must contain the following:

(1) An alphabetical list of plaintiffs.

(2) The date of filing of the transcript.

(3) The date of the final judgment.

(4) The date on which the final judgment was recorded.

(5) A brief description of the real estate that was the subject of the proceeding.

(6) The book and page on which the final judgment is recorded. [P.L.2-2002, § 15.]

NOTES TO DECISIONS

Effect of Clerk's Failure.
Failure of the clerk to perform his duty under this section did not affect the decree as an adjudication of title. Skelton v. Sharp, 161 Ind. 383, 67 N.E. 535 (1903).

32-30-3-18. Presumption of death. — (a) A nonresident who, if alive, would be entitled to take and to own real estate in Indiana by descent or devise is presumed dead if the following conditions are met:

(1) The nonresident has been absent from the nonresident's last place of residence in any other state or country for seven (7) years.

(2) A spouse, parent, child, or sibling of the nonresident has not heard from the nonresident for seven (7) years.

(b) The real estate that a nonresident described in subsection (a) otherwise would have taken descends from the nonresident to the nonresident's heirs under IC 29.

(c) Title that passes under subsection (b) vests in a nonresident's heirs upon full compliance with the provisions of section 19 [IC 32-30-3-19] of this chapter. [P.L.2-2002, § 15.]

32-30-3-19. Procedure for claming property under presumption of death. — (a) A person who claims real estate under section 18 [IC 32-30-3-18] of this chapter may file a verified complaint in the circuit or superior court of the county in which the real estate is located. The complaint must:

(1) name as a defendant the nonresident who is presumed dead under section 18 of this chapter;

(2) particularly describe the real estate; and

(3) contain a statement of the facts required by section 18 of this chapter.

(b) Notice of the pendency of the action, including the date on which the court shall hear the complaint filed under subsection (a), must be published in a daily or weekly newspaper of general circulation that is printed and published in the county seat of the county in which the real estate is located. If a newspaper does not exist, notice must be published in a newspaper that is printed and published in the county in which the real estate is located. Notice must also be published in a newspaper of general circulation that is printed and published in the county seat of the county in which the defendant last resided. If a newspaper is not printed and published in that county seat, then notice must be published in a newspaper that is printed and published in the county seat nearest to the county in which the defendant last resided.

(c) Prima facie proof of publication of notice as required by subsection (b) consists of:

(1) affidavits of the publishers of the newspapers in which the notice was published; and

(2) a printed copy of the published notice.

(d) The court shall hear the complaint filed under subsection (a) not earlier than sixty-five (65) days after notice was first published under subsection (b). If the court finds that:

(1) the defendant received sufficient notice under subsection (b); and

(2) the facts alleged in the complaint are true;

the court shall enter judgment quieting the title to the real estate in favor of the plaintiff.

(e) A judgment entered under subsection (d) becomes final and absolute three (3) years after the date it was entered unless, within those three (3) years, the defendant appears and moves to vacate the judgment. [P.L.2-2002, § 15.]

32-30-3-20. Real estate exempt from sale on execution — Complaint — Quieting title. — (a) A resident householder in Indiana who may claim real estate owned by the householder exempt from sale on execution may quiet the title to the real estate against any judgment or lien.

(b) The complaint in an action described in subsection (a) must state the following:

(1) The ownership of the real estate.

(2) The existence of a judgment against the real estate.

(3) The right of the owner to claim the real estate exempt from sale on execution.

(c) In an action described in subsection (a), the title to the real estate may be quieted against a judgment whether the householder has executed the judgment or has filed a schedule claiming an exemption from sale on execution if the court finds that the owner's interest, in value, of the real estate does not at the time of the hearing exceed any mortgages, tax, or assessment on the real estate by more than seven hundred dollars ($700). [P.L.2-2002, § 15.]

NOTES TO DECISIONS

Injunction to Prevent Sale.
A landowner could invoke the jurisdiction of a court of chancery, for the purpose of arresting a threatened sale of his land upon an execution issued against the property of a

third person, even though a remedy at law to quiet title might have been available. Tomlinson v. Miller, 115 Ind. App. 469, 58 N.E.2d 358 (1944).

32-30-3-21. Real estate exempt from sale on execution — Determination of value. — At the hearing under section 20 [IC 32-30-3-20] of this chapter, the court shall determine the value of the householder's interest in the real estate and shall set forth this amount in the decree quieting the title to the real estate. While the householder owns the real estate, the amount shall be charged against any other claim of exemption made by the householder to limit the householder's exemption in the real estate from sale on execution or other final process to the amount allowed by law. [P.L.2-2002, § 15.]

NOTES TO DECISIONS

Injunction to Prevent Sale.
A landowner could invoke the jurisdiction of a court of chancery, for the purpose of arresting a threatened sale of his land upon an execution issued against the property of a

third person, even though a remedy at law to quiet title might have been available. Tomlinson v. Miller, 115 Ind. App. 469, 58 N.E.2d 358 (1944).

CHAPTER 3.1

OCCUPYING CLAIMANT

32-30-3.1-1. Recovery for improvements made by occupying claimant — Complaint. — If an occupant of real property:
(1) has color of title to the property;
(2) in good faith has made valuable improvements to the property; and
(3) after making improvements to the property is found, in a court action, not to be the rightful owner of the property;
an order may not be issued to give the plaintiff possession of the property until a complaint that meets the requirements of section 2 [IC 32-30-3.1-2]

of this chapter has been filed and the provisions of this chapter are complied with. [P.L.2-2002, § 15.]

Effective Dates. P.L.2-2002, § 15. July 1. 2002.

NOTES TO DECISIONS

In General.

The right of an occupying claimant to value of improvements was purely statutory. Chesround v. Cunningham, 3 Blackf. 82 (1832).

Recovery of claims for improvements to land could only be had by complying with statutory provisions for making such claims. Westerfield v. Williams, 59 Ind. 221 (1877).

Claims for improvements on land could only be asserted by complying with the provisions of the statute. Doren v. Lupton, 154 Ind. 396, 56 N.E. 849 (1900).

The statute provided that after the question of title had been litigated and adjudicated, in the main action, an occupying claimant who was defeated in the main action could file his cross-complaint to recover the value of the improvements made in good faith under color of title. Philbin v. Carr, 75 Ind. App. 560, 129 N.E. 19 (1920).

Where landowner conveyed to contractor who agreed to reconvey upon payment of cost of constructing building within given time, and where third party was thereafter induced to pay contractor and take quitclaim deed to property from contractor, with understanding that third party would convey to original landowner if payment was made within given period, third party had sufficient color of title to be reimbursed for improvements made to property. Bahar v. Tadros, 123 Ind. App. 570, 112 N.E.2d 754 (1953).

The rights of an occupying claimant were purely statutory under this chapter, and amounted to nothing more than the right to recover the value of improvements made in good faith under color of title when it had been adjudicated that the title under which the occupant claimed was inferior to that of another, so that statute did not apply where mortgagee did not assert title, but merely contended that transactions resulting in record title did not discharge his mortgage.

Miladin v. Istrate, 125 Ind. App. 46, 119 N.E.2d 12 (1954).

This act did not prevent the occupant of land from relying on equitable estoppel and laches to retain possession and title. Phar-Crest Land Corp. v. Therber, 251 Ind. 674, 16 Ind. Dec. 570, 244 N.E.2d 644 (1969).

This section was not the exclusive remedy for an improver who improved real estate of another erroneously believing it to be his own. Duncan v. Akers, 147 Ind. App. 511, 23 Ind. Dec. 38, 262 N.E.2d 402 (1970).

Applicability.

The occupying claimant's statute is designed to afford relief where an occupant having only color of title makes improvements to land under the belief that it is his and then learns that someone else is in truth the owner. It has no application where a true owner makes improvements and then subsequently loses his ownership through operation of law. City of Gary v. Belovich, 544 N.E.2d 178 (Ind. App. 1989).

Purchasers of real estate, who defaulted on payment due under a conditional sales contract, were the rightful owners of equitable title which was defeasible by the failure to perform the terms of the contract, and therefore did not have a cause of action under the occupying claimant's statute. Kolley v. Harris, 553 N.E.2d 164 (Ind. App. 1990).

This chapter is designed to afford relief where an occupant with only color of title makes improvements to the land believing it to be his own and then learns someone else is the true owner. Mickle v. Kirk, 558 N.E.2d 1119 (Ind. App. 1990), aff'd in part, rev'd in part on reh'g, 565 N.E.2d 1161 (Ind. App. 1991).

Color of Title.

Where a party was in possession under and pursuant to a state of facts which, of themselves, showed the character and extent of his entry and claim such facts could have constituted color of title. Bell v. Longworth, 6 Ind. 273 (1855); Vancleave v. Milliken, 13 Ind. 105 (1859).

A judicial proceeding under which possession is taken will constitute color of title although the proceeding was void. Sims v. Gay, 109 Ind. 501, 9 N.E. 120 (1886); Sedwick v. Ritter, 128 Ind. 209, 27 N.E. 610 (1891).

A sale on a school fund mortgage, though

Color of Title. (Cont'd)

void, gave the purchaser color of title. Paxton v. Sterne, 127 Ind. 289, 26 N.E. 557 (1891).

An invalid tax deed would constitute color of title. Fish v. Blasser, 146 Ind. 186, 45 N.E. 63 (1896).

A deed void on its face may give color of title as effectually as though it was regular if it contains a description sufficient to identify the land. Hitt v. Carr, 62 Ind. App. 80, 109 N.E. 456 (1915).

The doctrine of color of title is available only in cases where the instrument purporting to be a conveyance is accepted in good faith and in the honest belief that it invests title in the claimant. Philbin v. Carr, 75 Ind. App. 560, 129 N.E. 19 (1920).

Verbal statements, although accompanied by acts of ownership, and exhibitions of title papers, did not constitute color of title. Philbin v. Carr, 75 Ind. App. 560, 129 N.E. 19 (1920).

Extent of Recovery.

A claimant can only recover the value of improvements to the extent they increase the value of the property upon which they were mistakenly placed and to the extent they benefit the owner of the realty, regardless of their value to the occupying claimant. Mickle v. Kirk, 558 N.E.2d 1119 (Ind. App. 1990), aff'd in part, rev'd in part on reh'g, 565 N.E.2d 1161 (Ind. App. 1991).

Tax sale purchaser was not entitled to receive the value of an improvement made to the property which was not constructed until after his right to possession was put in issue. Mickle v. Kirk, 565 N.E.2d 1161 (Ind. App. 1991).

Lien.

Equity recognized a lien which was based upon general considerations of justice between the parties to the transaction involved. Such a lien could result by implication from a duty resting on the owner of property which was the subject-matter of the lien and the lien was completed by equity in pursuance of the maxim, "that is deemed done that ought to be done." Bahar v. Tadros, 123 Ind. App. 570, 112 N.E.2d 754 (1953).

Recovery Not Allowed.

Improvements made after defendant knew he had no title to the land could not have been allowed. Osborn v. Storms, 65 Ind. 321 (1879).

Improvements made by defendant after suit is commenced could not be allowed. Richwine v. Presbyterian Church, 135 Ind. 80, 34 N.E. 737 (1893).

Statute of Limitations.

Limitations, statute ran from time claimant was adjudged not the owner of the land. Fish v. Blasser, 146 Ind. 186, 45 N.E. 63 (1896).

Who May Recover.

If lands mortgaged to the state were forfeited, and were then sold by the mortgagor, and the purchaser made improvements, he was not entitled to the value thereof as against a purchaser from the state. Vannoy v. Blessing, 36 Ind. 349 (1871).

Foreclosure of mortgage, purchasers who obtained a deed could claim for improvements. Goodell v. Starr, 127 Ind. 198, 26 N.E. 793 (1891).

Only bona fide occupants of the land, that is, those that believed they were the lawful owners thereof, could claim for improvements. Bryan v. Uland, 101 Ind. 477, 1 N.E. 52 (1885); Richwine v. Presbyterian Church, 135 Ind. 80, 34 N.E. 737 (1893).

The owner of a determinable fee in land was not an occupying claimant, and could not recover for improvements made on the land during occupancy thereof. Pulse v. Osborn, 30 Ind. App. 631, 64 N.E. 59 (1902).

When the owner of a life estate made improvements on the land, his administrator or executor could not recover the value of the improvements from the remaindermen. Pulse v. Osborn, 30 Ind. App. 631, 64 N.E. 59 (1902).

A purchaser of land who failed to acquire title because of a prior recorded deed, but who in good faith took possession and expended large sums of money in making improvements, was a bona fide occupant. Harmon v. Scott, 78 Ind. App. 554, 133 N.E. 141 (1921).

The occupying claimant's statute includes owners who never really had title, either legal or equitable, even though they believed, in good faith, that they did. It does not include title which is defeasible. Kolley v. Harris, 553 N.E.2d 164 (Ind. App. 1990).

Collateral References. Compensation, upon eviction, for improvements made or placed on premises of another by mistake. 57 A.L.R.2d 263.

32-30-3.1-2. Complaint — Contents. — The complaint must:

(1) set forth the grounds on which the defendant seeks relief; and

(2) state, as accurately as practicable, the value of the improvements on the real property and the value of the property without the improvements. [P.L.2-2002, § 15.]

32-30-3.1-3. Trial of the issues — Assessment of value. — All issues under this chapter joined together must be tried as in other cases, and the court or jury trying the cause shall assess the following:

(1) The value of all lasting improvements made on the real property in question before the commencement of the action for the recovery of the property.

(2) The damages, if any, which the premises may have sustained by waste or cultivation through the time the court renders a judgment.

(3) The fair value of the rents and profits that may have accrued, without the improvements, through the time the court renders a judgment.

(4) The value of the real property that the successful claimant has in the premises, without the improvements.

(5) The taxes, with interest, paid by the defendant and by those under whose title to the property the defendant claims. [P.L.2-2002, § 15.]

NOTES TO DECISIONS

ANALYSIS

Amount recoverable.
Burden of proof, good faith.
Improvements not recoverable.
Rents chargeable.
Res judicata.

Amount Recoverable.

The measure of damages was the value of improvements at the time when judgment had been rendered determining the title to the land. McGill v. Kennedy, 11 Ind. 20 (1858).

The general rule is that a bona fide occupying claimant of lands was entitled to recover for improvements in the amount which he enhanced the value of the property to the owner. Thompson v. Illinois Cent. R.R., 75 Ind. App. 410, 129 N.E. 55 (1920).

Burden of Proof, Good Faith.

When an occupying claimant of land made a claim in an action of ejectment for improvements made on the land, he had the burden of proof to show that the improvements were made in good faith. Jose v. Hunter, 60 Ind. App. 569, 103 N.E. 392 (1913).

Improvements Not Recoverable.

The defendant could not have recovered for improvements made after he knew he had no title to the land. Osborn v. Storms, 65 Ind. 321 (1879).

Improvements made by the defendant after suit commenced to recover the land could not be allowed. Richwine v. Presbyterian Church, 135 Ind. 80, 34 N.E. 737 (1893).

Rents Chargeable.

If the defendant was entitled to the improvements, he was only chargeable with the rental value without the improvements. Elliott v. Armstrong, 4 Blackf. 421 (1837); Adkins v. Hudson, 19 Ind. 392 (1862).

The defendant might have been charged with rents up to the time of the trial under the occupying claimant law. Adkins v. Hudson, 19 Ind. 392 (1862).

When a claim was made for improvements, the occupant could be charged with rents for more than six years. Hyatt v. Cochran, 85 Ind. 231 (1882).

Res Judicata.

Where lessee did not by reason of his lease claim title or the value of improvements as claimant under color of title under the occupying claimant's statute in an action in ejectment brought against him by the lessor, he could not prevail in an action to quiet title or recover the value of such improvements under such statute in a subsequent action based on the lease. Kline v. Indiana Trust Co., 79 Ind. App. 466, 137 N.E. 555 (1922).

Collateral References. Measure and items of recovery for improvements mistak- enly placed or made on land of another. 24 A.L.R.2d 11.

32-30-3.1-4. Plaintiff's election. — The plaintiff in the main action for possession of the real property may pay the appraised value of the improvements to the real property, and the taxes paid, with interest, deducting the value of the rents and profits, and the damages sustained, as assessed at the trial, and take the property. [P.L.2-2002, § 15.]

NOTES TO DECISIONS

In General.
If the plaintiff paid the damages assessed in favor of the defendant, he could then have execution for possession of the land and for the damages assessed for detention thereof. Hollingsworth v. Stumph, 131 Ind. 546, 30 N.E. 525 (1892).

32-30-3.1-5. Defendant's election. — If a plaintiff fails to pay the defendant the value of the improvements to the real property established under section 4 [IC 32-30-3.1-4] of this chapter after a reasonable time fixed by the court, the defendant may take the property after paying the plaintiff the appraised value of the property, minus the value of the improvements. [P.L.2-2002, § 15.]

32-30-3.1-6. Parties to be tenants in common. — If the plaintiff does not pay the defendant the appraised value of the improvements to the real property under section 4 [IC 32-30-3.1-4] of this chapter and the defendant does not pay the plaintiff the appraised value of the real property under section 5 [IC 32-30-3.1-5] of this chapter within the time fixed by the court, the parties will be held to be tenants in common of all the real property, including the improvements, each holding an interest proportionate to the value of the party's property as determined under section 5 of this chapter. [P.L.2-2002, § 15.]

32-30-3.1-7. Color of title under judicial or tax sale. — Except when the purchaser knows at the time of the sale that the seller lacks authority to sell the property, a purchaser who in good faith, at a judicial or tax sale, purchases property that is sold by the proper person or officer has color of title within the meaning of this chapter, whether or not the person or officer had sufficient authority to sell the property. The rights of the purchaser acquired under this section pass to the purchaser's assignees or representatives. [P.L.2-2002, § 15.]

NOTES TO DECISIONS

In General.
An invalid tax deed could constitute color of title. Wiggins v. Holley, 11 Ind. 2 (1858).

Invalid tax deeds constituted color of title. Watkins v. Winings, 102 Ind. 330, 1 N.E. 638 (1885); Sims v. Gay, 109 Ind. 501, 9 N.E. 120 (1886); English v. Powell, 119 Ind. 93, 21 N.E. 458 (1889); Fish v. Blasser, 146 Ind. 186, 45 N.E. 63 (1896).

Deeds made under judicial proceedings gave color of title though the sales were void. Sims v. Gay, 109 Ind. 501, 9 N.E. 120 (1886); Goodell v. Starr, 127 Ind. 198, 26 N.E. 793 (1891); Paxton v. Sterne, 127 Ind. 289, 26 N.E.

In General. (Cont'd)
557 (1891); Sedwick v. Ritter, 128 Ind. 209, 27 N.E. 610 (1891).

A sale of land under a decree of foreclosure and the sheriff's deed thereunder were sufficient to give the purchaser and those claiming under him color of title. Goodell v. Starr, 127 Ind. 198, 26 N.E. 793 (1891).

This and the next following section are exclusive as to what constituted color of title. Philbin v. Carr, 75 Ind. App. 560, 129 N.E. 19 (1920).

32-30-3.1-8. Color of title under connected title. — An occupant of real property has color of title within the meaning of this chapter if the occupant:

(1) can show a connected title in law or equity, derived from the records of any public office; or

(2) holds the property by purchase or descent from a person claiming title derived from public records or by a properly recorded deed. [P.L.2-2002, § 15.]

NOTES TO DECISIONS

ANALYSIS

In general.
Extent of possession.
Lease for term.
Oral gift.
Prior recorded deed.
Quitclaim deed.
Verbal statements.

In General.

The definitions of "color of title" given in this and the preceding section were applicable to every case wherein the question of title was in issue. Philbin v. Carr, 75 Ind. App. 560, 129 N.E. 19 (1920).

Where, in an action to quiet title, the special findings disclosed a break in the claim of title under which plaintiff which included the land in controversy could have been considered nothing more than giving them color of title, which would have been sufficient if the findings showed actual occupancy of any part of the land the deed purported to convey, since, where color of title existed, actual possession of a part only was regarded in law as possession of the whole. Sheets v. Stiefel, 117 Ind. App. 584, 74 N.E.2d 921 (1947).

Where landowner conveyed to contractor who agreed to reconvey upon payment of cost of constructing building within given time, and where third party was thereafter induced to pay contractor and take quitclaim deed to property from contractor, with understanding that third party would convey to original landowner if payment was made within given period, third party had sufficient color of title to be reimbursed for improvements made to property. Bahar v. Tadros, 123 Ind. App. 570, 112 N.E.2d 754 (1953).

Extent of Possession.

When a person entered upon land under color of title by deed or other written instrument he acquired actual possession to the extent of the boundaries contained in the writing. Bell v. Longworth, 6 Ind. 273 (1855); Bauman v. Grubbs, 26 Ind. 419 (1866).

Where an entry was made on land under color of title, possession was taken in law to the extent of the metes and bounds described in the conveyance; and this, although the deed might have been a nullity. Worthley v. Burbanks, 146 Ind. 534, 45 N.E. 779 (1897); Moore v. Hinkle, 151 Ind. 343, 50 N.E. 822 (1898); Sinclair v. Gunzenhauser, 179 Ind. 78, 98 N.E. 37, 100 N.E. 376 (1912).

Lease for Term.

A lessee for a term of years did not have color of title entitling him to recover under the occupying claimant's statute for improvements he had made on the land prior to his ejectment by the lessor. Kline v. Indiana Trust Co., 79 Ind. App. 466, 137 N.E. 555 (1922).

Oral Gift.

An occupant to whom a grantee made an oral gift of land, and with whom he left the deed did not have color of title. Philbin v. Carr, 75 Ind. App. 560, 129 N.E. 19 (1920).

Prior Recorded Deed.

A purchaser of land who failed to acquire title because of a prior recorded deed, but who in good faith took possession and expended large sums of money in making improvements was a bona fide occupant. Harmon v. Scott, 78 Ind. App. 554, 133 N.E. 141 (1921).

Quitclaim Deed.

A quitclaim deed executed by a person having no title to a person having notice of the facts did not create color of title. Wright v. Tichenor, 104 Ind. 185, 3 N.E. 853 (1885).

Verbal Statements.

Verbal statements, although accompanied by acts of ownership and exhibitions of title papers, did not constitute color of title. Philbin v. Carr, 75 Ind. App. 560, 129 N.E. 19 (1920).

32-30-3.1-9. Recovery for lasting improvements — Claimant under color of title — Purchaser. — (a) A claimant occupying real property who has color of title may recover the value of lasting improvements to the real property made by the party under whom the claimant claims, as well as those improvements made by the occupying claimant.

(b) A person holding the premises as a purchaser, by an agreement in writing from the party having color of title, is entitled to the remedy set forth in subsection (a). [P.L.2-2002, § 15.]

NOTES TO DECISIONS

ANALYSIS

Color of title.
Lien.

Color of Title.

Where landowner conveyed to contractor who agreed to reconvey upon payment of cost of constructing building within given time, and where third party was thereafter induced to pay contractor and take quitclaim deed to property from contractor, with understanding that third party would convey to original landowner if payment was made within given period, third party had sufficient color of title to be reimbursed for improvements made to property. Bahar v. Tadros, 123 Ind. App. 570, 112 N.E.2d 754 (1953).

Lien.

Equity recognized a lien which was based upon general consideration of justice between the parties to the transaction involved. Such a lien could result by implication from a duty resting on the owner of property which was the subject-matter of the lien and the lien was completed by equity in pursuance of the maxim, "that is deemed done that ought to be done." Bahar v. Tadros, 123 Ind. App. 570, 112 N.E.2d 754 (1953).

32-30-3.1-10. Execution for possession. — A plaintiff in an action for possession of real property to which this chapter applies is entitled to an execution for the possession of the real property in accordance with this chapter, but not otherwise. [P.L.2-2002, § 15.]

NOTES TO DECISIONS

In General.

When the plaintiff paid the damages assessed in favor of the defendant for improvements, he could have a writ for possession. Hollingsworth v. Stumph, 131 Ind. 546, 30 N.E. 525 (1892); Emerick v. Miller, 159 Ind. 317, 64 N.E. 28 (1902).

This section had exclusive reference to the conditions upon which the successful plaintiff against the occupying claimant who had improved and enhanced the value of the real estate could have execution for possession, and did not apply to the original suit for possession of real estate under 34-1-48-1 et seq. Emerick v. Miller, 159 Ind. 317, 64 N.E. 28 (1902).

32-30-3.1-11. Defective sale — Writ of possession. — If any land is sold by an executor, an administrator, a guardian, a sheriff, or a commissioner of the court and afterwards the land is recovered in the proper action by:

(1) a person who was originally liable;

(2) a person in whose hands the land would be liable to pay the demand or judgment for which or for whose benefit the land was sold; or

(3) anyone making a claim under a person identified under subdivision (1) or (2);

the plaintiff is not entitled to a writ for the possession of the land without having paid the amount due, as determined under section 12 [IC 32-30-3.1-12] of this chapter (or IC 34-1-49-12 or IC 32-15-3-12 before their repeal) within the time determined by the court. [P.L.2-2002, § 15.]

NOTES TO DECISIONS

ANALYSIS

Judicial sales.
Mortgage.
Repayment by heirs.
Sheriff's sale.

Judicial Sales.
The liens of purchasers of lands at judicial sales were upheld where there was a failure of title. Jones v. French, 92 Ind. 138 (1883); Morris v. Goodwin, 1 Ind. App. 481, 27 N.E. 985 (1891).

Mortgage.
Where mortgage by administrator was set aside because of a defect in the proceedings,

the mortgagee was entitled to a lien on the land for the amount of his loan. Baker v. Edwards, 156 Ind. 53, 59 N.E. 174 (1901).

Repayment by Heirs.
When lands were sold to pay the debts of a decedent, his heirs could not have obtained the land without repaying the purchase-money received by the administrator. Walton v. Cox, 67 Ind. 164 (1879).

Sheriff's Sale.
If a sheriff's sale of land was invalid, a purchaser in good faith had a lien on the land for his purchase-money. Short v. Sears, 93 Ind. 505 (1883).

32-30-3.1-12. Adjustment of amount due. — Any defendant in the main court action for possession of real property may file a complaint setting forth the sale and title under it and any other matter allowed under this chapter. The court proceedings must assess the values, damages, and other amounts of which assessment is required under section 3 [IC 32-30-3.1-3] of this chapter. If after the main court action the plaintiff has not paid the amount assessed by the court, the court shall set a reasonable time for the plaintiff to pay the defendant. If the plaintiff does not pay the amount within the time set by the court, the court shall order the land sold without relief from valuation or appraisement laws. If the premises are sold, the defendant is entitled to receive from the proceeds of the sale the amount the defendant is due, with interest, and court costs. The plaintiff is entitled to the remainder of the proceeds of the sale. [P.L.2-2002, § 15.]

NOTES TO DECISIONS

In General.
The persons in possession as owners could file a cross-complaint and have the amount of their claims adjusted, and the court could fix

a time for the payment thereof, and direct a sale of the property, if it was not paid within the time fixed. Goodell v. Starr, 127 Ind. 198, 26 N.E. 793 (1891).

CHAPTER 4

ACTIONS FOR WASTE

32-30-4-1. Judgment for damages — Forfeiture — Eviction. —

(a) Wrongs that were previously remediable by an action of waste are remediable by a judgment for damages, forfeiture of the estate of the offending party, and eviction from the premises.

(b) A judgment of forfeiture and eviction may be given to a person who is entitled to the reversion against the tenant in possession only when the injury to the estate in reversion is adjudged:

(1) to be equal to the value of the tenant's estate or unexpired term; or

(2) to have been done in malice.

[P.L.2-2002, § 15.]

Effective Dates. P.L.2-2002, § 15. July 1. 2002.

Cross References. Ejectment, IC 32-30-2, IC 32-30-3.

NOTES TO DECISIONS

ANALYSIS

Action by guardian.
Injunction.
Joinder of parties.
Proof of waste.
Rights of tenants.
Waste by life tenant.
What constituted waste.

Action by Guardian.

A guardian could not maintain an action for waste in his own name, but the suit should have been in the name of the ward. Wilson v. Galey, 103 Ind. 257, 2 N.E. 736 (1885).

If a guardian was in possession of the lands of his ward, he could sue in his own name to prevent injury to the lands. Kinsley v. Kinsley, 150 Ind. 67, 49 N.E. 819 (1898).

Injunction.

A mortgagee could have enjoined the commission of waste when his security would have been endangered. Knarr v. Conaway, 42 Ind. 260 (1873).

A mandatory injunction would not lie against a life tenant to compel repairs and to prevent waste when it was not shown that the injury to the owner in fee could not be compensated in damages. Gleason v. Gleason, 43 Ind. App. 426, 87 N.E. 689 (1909).

Joinder of Parties.

All persons having an interest in land could join in an action to recover damages for waste and to prevent future injury. Halstead v. Coen, 31 Ind. App. 302, 67 N.E. 957 (1903); Halstead v. Sigler, 35 Ind. App. 419, 74 N.E. 257 (1905).

Proof of Waste.

It was competent to allow a witness who had knowledge of the property involved to describe the condition of the premises at the time the defendant took possession and at the time of the commencement of the suit and to give an opinion as to the value of the farm and what it would have been worth if kept in ordinarily good repair. Ferguson v. Stafford, 33 Ind. 162 (1870).

Before possession could be recovered during the continuance of a term on the account of waste, it had to be proven that the injury equaled the value of the unexpired term, or that it was done in malice. Bollenbacker v. Fritts, 98 Ind. 50 (1884); Sullivan v. O'Hara, 1 Ind. App. 259, 27 N.E. 590 (1891).

Rights of Tenants.

Tenants could only be deprived of their rights in growing crops when there was a judgment of forfeiture for waste. Sullivan v. O'Hara, 1 Ind. App. 259, 27 N.E. 590 (1891).

Waste by Life Tenant.

The sale by a life tenant of valuable trees for commercial purposes constituted waste. Modlin v. Kennedy, 53 Ind. 267 (1876); Robertson v. Meadors, 73 Ind. 43 (1880).

It was waste for a life tenant to use timber on a farm to replace buildings destroyed by lightning. Miller v. Shields, 55 Ind. 71 (1876).

What Constituted Waste.

The rule of the common law that the cutting of a standing tree was waste was not applicable in this state. Dawson v. Coffman, 28 Ind. 220 (1867).

Whether the cutting of standing trees would amount to waste depended upon the fact of its lessening the value of the estate. Dawson v. Coffman, 28 Ind. 220 (1867).

The doctrine of the common law as to waste had no application to a band of Indians in the use of a large tract of wild land granted by the United States to such band. Wheeler v. Meshing-go-me-sia, 30 Ind. 402 (1868).

32-30-4-2. Intervening estate. — Notwithstanding an intervening estate for life or years, a person who has a remainder or reversion in an estate may maintain an action for waste, trespass, or injury to the inheritance. [P.L.2-2002, § 15.]

NOTES TO DECISIONS

ANALYSIS

Joinder of causes.
Life tenants.
Persons entitled to sue.

Joinder of Causes.
Claims for waste could not have been settled in an action for partition. Stout v. Dunning, 72 Ind. 343 (1880).

Life Tenants.
Tenants for life who committed actionable waste were liable to all of the remaindermen. Stout v. Dunning, 72 Ind. 343 (1880). See also Dawson v. Coffman, 28 Ind. 220 (1867).

Owners in fee could have enjoined tenants for life from cutting and removing valuable growing timber, to the irreparable injury of the fee simple. Robertson v. Meadors, 73 Ind. 43 (1880).

Persons Entitled to Sue.
A remainderman of personal property could sue to protect his interest. Goudie v. Johnston, 109 Ind. 427, 10 N.E. 296 (1887).
Persons having a mere expectancy could not maintain an action for waste. Gwaltney v. Gwaltney, 119 Ind. 144, 21 N.E. 552 (1889).

Collateral References. Forfeiture of life estate for waste. 16 A.L.R.3d 1344.

CHAPTER 5
RECEIVERSHIPS

32-30-5-1. Grounds for appointment. — A receiver may be appointed by the court in the following cases:

(1) In an action by a vendor to vacate a fraudulent purchase of property or by a creditor to subject any property or fund to the creditor's claim.

(2) In actions between partners or persons jointly interested in any property or fund.

(3) In all actions when it is shown that the property, fund or rent, and profits in controversy are in danger of being lost, removed, or materially injured.

(4) In actions in which a mortgagee seeks to foreclose a mortgage. However, upon motion by the mortgagee, the court shall appoint a receiver if, at the time the motion is filed, the property is not occupied by the owner as the owner's principal residence and:

(A) it appears that the property is in danger of being lost, removed, or materially injured;

(B) it appears that the property may not be sufficient to discharge the mortgaged debt;

(C) either the mortgagor or the owner of the property has agreed in the mortgage or in some other writing to the appointment of a receiver;

(D) a person not personally liable for the debt secured by the mortgage has, or is entitled to, possession of all or a portion of the property;

(E) the owner of the property is not personally liable for the debt secured by the mortgage; or

(F) all or any portion of the property is being, or is intended to be, leased for any purpose.

(5) When a corporation:

(A) has been dissolved;

(B) is insolvent;

(C) is in imminent danger of insolvency; or

(D) has forfeited its corporate rights.

(6) To protect or preserve, during the time allowed for redemption, any real estate or interest in real estate sold on execution or order of sale, and to secure rents and profits to the person entitled to the rents and profits.

(7) In other cases as may be provided by law or where, in the discretion of the court, it may be necessary to secure ample justice to the parties. [P.L.2-2002, § 15.]

Effective Dates. P.L.2-2002, § 15. July 1. 2002.

Cross References. Appointment of receiver for telephone companies on petition of the public service commission, IC 8-1-19-1, IC 8-1-19-2.

Banks and trust companies, appointment as receiver authorized, IC 28-1-11-6.

Corporations for profit, appointment of receiver upon judicial dissolution, IC 23-1-47-3.

Distribution of assets under Uniform Liquidation Act, IC 30-2-7.

Financial institutions, liquidation by department of financial institutions, IC 28-1-3.1.

Insurance companies, appointment of receivers for, IC 27-8-3-18, IC 27-2-4-1.

Mortgage foreclosure, appointment of receiver in, IC 32-29-7-11.

Nonpayment of contributions, interest, penalties or damages assessed under Employment Security Act for 170 days, as cause for receivership, IC 22-4-31-1.

Partnership appointment to settle, IC 23-4-3-4 — IC 23-4-3-6.

Railroads, appointment of receivers for, IC 8-3-2-15.

NOTES TO DECISIONS

—Chattel mortgage.
—Exemption from execution.
—Insolvency.
—Junior mortgagee.
—Mortgage foreclosure.
—Receiver after decree.
Actions for loss or injury imminent.
—In general.
—Miscellaneous applications.
——Ejectment.
——Fraudulent conveyances.
——Mechanic's lien foreclosure.
——Partition.
——Title to land.
—Municipal services.
Actions by vendor.
After final judgment and pending appeal.
Ancillary to main action.
Appointment not mandatory.
Appointment not required.
Appointment pendente lite.
Appointment without notice.
Consent to powers of receiver.
Construction.
Corporations.
—In general.
—Disposition of assets.
—Imminent danger of insolvency.
——Dissension among shareholders.
—Individuals, partnerships, associations.
—Insolvency.
—Termination of franchise.
Discretion of court.
Divorce actions.
Federal courts.
Hearing on application.
Jurisdiction and venue.
Prerequisites to appointment.
Preservation of right of redemption.
Remedy at law available.
Sufficiency of original complaint.
Validation of unauthorized action.
When appointment set aside.

In General.

The court has inherent power to appoint receivers in any case where it is necessary to protect the rights of the parties and in any other cases as provided by law. McElwaine v. Hasey, 135 Ind. 481, 35 N.E. 272 (1893).

Authority to appoint receivers should not have been exercised in doubtful cases. Corbin v. Thompson, 141 Ind. 128, 40 N.E. 533 (1895).

An action could not be maintained against a life tenant solely for the appointment of a receiver because such tenant failed to pay assessments for street improvements. Hay v. McDaniel, 26 Ind. App. 683, 60 N.E. 729 (1901).

A receiver could be appointed in such cases as might have been provided by law, or where, in the discretion of the court or the judge thereof in vacation, it might have been neces-

sary to secure ample justice to the parties. Hawkins v. First Nat'l Bank, 201 Ind. 228, 165 N.E. 547 (1929).

Under former IC 34-48-1-1 (repealed; see this section for similar provisions) the court could, in its discretion, appoint a receiver under a showing that a number of actions have or might have been commenced, or that many creditors of the firm were threatening to and would institute actions against the firm, subjecting it to excessive cost and expense, resulting in dissipation of its assets. West v. Reeves, 207 Ind. 404, 190 N.E. 431 (1934).

In an application for appointment of a receiver, it was held that the complaint was amendable so as to appeal to the inherent equitable power of the court to appoint receiver. West v. Reeves, 207 Ind. 404, 190 N.E. 431 (1934).

Actions Against Life Tenants.

An action could not be maintained by a life tenant solely for the appointment of a receiver because such tenant failed to pay assessments for state improvements. Hay v. McDaniel, 26 Ind. App. 683, 60 N.E. 729 (1901).

Actions Between Partners.

—In General.

It was only in exceptional cases that a receiver would be appointed for a partnership until after a dissolution. Barnes v. Jones, 91 Ind. 161 (1883).

Receivers could not be appointed for partnerships on the mutual request of the partners. There must have been a suit and adversary parties. Pressley v. Harrison, 102 Ind. 14, 1 N.E. 188 (1885).

A receiver could not be appointed for a partnership until a summons for the defendants had been issued and delivered to the sheriff for service. Pressley v. Harrison, 102 Ind. 14, 1 N.E. 188 (1885); Tucker v. Tucker, 194 Ind. 108, 142 N.E. 11 (1924).

Where complaint was filed by one partner before a judge in vacation, asking the appointment of a receiver, and defendant, a copartner, voluntarily appeared to such action and filed his answer, without process, and submitted the same, such judge thereby acquired full and complete jurisdiction both of the subject-matter of the action and the persons of the parties, such voluntary appearance having been equivalent to the service of process. Pressley v. Lamb, 105 Ind. 171, 4 N.E. 682 (1886). Second appeal of Pressley v. Harrison, 102 Ind. 14, 1 N.E. 188 (1885).

The receiver of a partnership could only take possession of all firm assets and collect all firm debts. Wallace v. Milligan, 110 Ind. 498, 11 N.E. 599 (1887).

Actions Between Partners. (Cont'd)

—In General. (Cont'd)

If all partnership property was legally disposed of, a receiver would not be appointed to take charge of the same. Davis v. Niswonger, 145 Ind. 426, 44 N.E. 542 (1896).

An interlocutory order appointing a receiver for a partnership was properly made in a suit for accounting and dissolution of the partnership, where the appointment was made after a hearing on the merits had been pursuant to notice given defendant. Maple v. McReynolds, 208 Ind. 338, 196 N.E. 3 (1935).

A receiver should not have been appointed for the property of a partnership until the existence of the partnership was established by satisfactory proof. Hawkins v. Aldridge, 211 Ind. 332, 7 N.E.2d 34, 109 A.L.R. 1205 (1937).

In action for accounting by partners against another partner, under the evidence the court properly ordered dissolution of the partnership and appointment of receiver, as requested in defendant's answer to preserve assets, prevent dissipation thereof, and see that they were properly applied. Riedman v. Riedman, 105 Ind. App. 657, 16 N.E.2d 979 (1938).

Where a partner, sued for an accounting by other partners, asked appointment of a receiver in his answer, he could not object to the court's appointment of a receiver as requested. Riedman v. Riedman, 105 Ind. App. 657, 16 N.E.2d 979 (1938).

—Grounds for Appointment.

There must have been some misconduct or mismanagement after the dissolution of a partnership to have justified the appointment of a receiver. Bufkin v. Boyce, 104 Ind. 53, 3 N.E. 615 (1885).

Where partnership property had been conveyed in trust and a controversy arose as to its application, a receiver could be appointed. Naylor v. Sidener, 106 Ind. 179, 6 N.E. 345 (1886).

If partnership assets were being wasted or misappropriated, a receiver could be appointed in a suit for a settlement. Fink v. Montgomery, 162 Ind. 424, 68 N.E. 1010 (1903).

Appointment of a receiver to take charge of property or funds was justified when there were conflicting claims. Goshen Woolen Mills Co. v. City Nat'l Bank, 150 Ind. 279, 49 N.E. 154 (1908).

The refusal of a partner, or one of the parties jointly interested, to account for joint funds or property, and a showing that the other persons jointly interested would have been injured thereby, was sufficient ground for appointment of a receiver pendente lite.

Vogel v. Chappell, 211 Ind. 310, 6 N.E.2d 953 (1937).

Where the persons in control of a private bank were improperly conducting its business, and it was alleged to be insolvent, a partner therein could sue for an accounting and have a receiver appointed to take control of the assets of the bank. Wehmeier v. Mercantile Banking Co., 49 Ind. App. 454, 97 N.E. 558 (1912).

Actions to Foreclosure of Mortgage.

—In General.

When the mortgaged property was sufficient to pay the debt, a receiver should not have been appointed to collect the rents and profits. Sellers v. Stoffel, 139 Ind. 468, 39 N.E. 52 (1894); World Bldg., Loan & Inv. Co. v. Marlin, 151 Ind. 630, 52 N.E. 198 (1898).

Receivers could be appointed in actions to foreclose mortgages to secure the application of the rents on the mortgage debt before a sale, when the property was not sufficient to satisfy the debt secured by the mortgage. Leader Publishing Co. v. Grant Trust & Sav. Co., 182 Ind. 651, 108 N.E. 121 (1915).

When there was a provision in a mortgage authorizing the appointment of a receiver pending foreclosure, the court should have, upon proper application, appointed a receiver, on a showing of any equitable ground therefor. Hawkins v. First Nat'l Bank, 201 Ind. 228, 165 N.E. 547 (1929).

The mandatory provisions in subdivision (4) apply to motions by a mortgagee and not to motions by anyone except a mortgagee. Farver v. DeKalb County Farm Bureau, 576 N.E.2d 1361 (Ind. App. 1991).

The 1986 revision of former IC 34-48-1-1 (repealed; see this section for similar provisions) merely changed procedures involved in obtaining a previously existing remedy. As such, the fourth subdivision became applicable in all mortgage foreclosure proceedings from and after its effective date. Farver v. DeKalb County Farm Bureau, 576 N.E.2d 1361 (Ind. App. 1991).

—Chattel Mortgage.

If a petition to foreclose a chattel mortgage showed that the mortgagor was insolvent, that the mortgaged property was not sufficient in value to secure the debt, and that there was danger of its removal beyond the jurisdiction of the court, it was sufficient to authorize the appointment of a receiver of such property. Reynolds v. Quick, 128 Ind. 316, 27 N.E. 621 (1891); Leader Publishing Co. v. Grant Trust & Sav. Co., 182 Ind. 651, 108 N.E. 121 (1915).

—Exemption from Execution.

If the debtor sought to claim the rents as

Actions to Foreclosure of Mortgage. (Cont'd)

—Exemption from Execution. (Cont'd) exempt from execution, he should have made such claim in the application for the appointment of a receiver. Storm v. Ermantrout, 89 Ind. 214 (1883).

—Insolvency.

When a corporation was insolvent, or in imminent danger of insolvency, a receiver could be appointed. Howard v. Whitman, 29 Ind. 557 (1868); First Nat'l Bank v. United States Encaustic Tile Co., 105 Ind. 227, 4 N.E. 846 (1886).

When the mortgaged property was inadequate to secure the debt, and the person liable therefor was insolvent, a receiver could be appointed to take charge of the rents and profits, regardless of the insolvency of the defendant. Brinkman v. Ritzinger, 82 Ind. 358 (1882); Main v. Ginthert, 92 Ind. 180 (1883); Hursh v. Hursh, 99 Ind. 500 (1885); Reynolds v. Quick, 128 Ind. 316, 27 N.E. 621 (1891); Leader Publishing Co. v. Grant Trust & Sav. Co., 182 Ind. 651, 108 N.E. 121 (1915).

It need not have been alleged that the mortgagor was insolvent in order to have authorized the appointment of a receiver. Pouder v. Tate, 96 Ind. 330 (1884); Hursh v. Hursh, 99 Ind. 500 (1885).

A receiver may be appointed when a corporation is insolvent or in imminent danger of insolvency. Coddington v. Canady, 157 Ind. 243, 61 N.E. 567 (1901); Chicago & S.E. Ry. v. Kenney, 159 Ind. 72, 62 N.E. 26 (1901); Thayer v. Kinder, 45 Ind. App. 111, 89 N.E. 408, 90 N.E. 323 (1909).

—Junior Mortgagee.

A junior mortgagee could, in a proper case, have a receiver appointed to collect rents in an action to foreclose a senior mortgage. Buchanan v. Berkshire Life Ins. Co., 96 Ind. 510 (1883).

—Mortgage Foreclosure.

Receiver for mortgaged property should be appointed only in a clear case of necessity in order to protect the rights of others. Hickam v. Golladay, 83 Ind. App. 569, 149 N.E. 375 (1925).

In an action to foreclose and for the appointment of a receiver, a verified complaint alleging that the "mortgaged property was insufficient of value at the time to pay and discharge the debt," and describing unpaid notes secured by the mortgage and setting said notes out as exhibits, was sufficient to authorize the appointment of a receiver, without further evidence, notwithstanding the omission of figures to show the value of the mortgaged property. Stair v. Meissel, 207 Ind. 280, 192 N.E. 453 (1934).

Clauses (4) and (6) of the predecessor statute to this section, were held not to authorize the appointment of a receiver in view of former IC 34-2-29-2, providing that the owner shall be entitled to possession for one year from the date of sale. Federal Land Bank v. Schleeter, 208 Ind. 9, 193 N.E. 378, 194 N.E. 628 (1934).

Rights of mortgagor and mortgagee were not a matter of free contract; statutory regulations and public policy were controlling. Federal Land Bank v. Schleeter, 208 Ind. 9, 193 N.E. 378, 194 N.E. 628 (1934).

Where mortgaged property was insufficient to pay mortgage indebtedness, and foreclosure proceedings were instituted, any mortgage bondholders could apply for a receiver. Lowe v. Swafford, 209 Ind. 514, 199 N.E. 709, 103 A.L.R. 1222 (1936).

—Receiver After Decree.

After an appeal from a decree foreclosing a mortgage, the action could be regarded as yet pending for the purpose of an application for a receiver for the rents and profits, and the trial court, in a proper case, had authority to appoint a receiver to collect the rents pending the appeal. Brinkman v. Ritzinger, 82 Ind. 358 (1882).

When a receiver had been properly appointed under clause (4) of the predecessor statute to this section, he could be continued after decree of foreclosure. Buchanan v. Berkshire Life Ins. Co., 96 Ind. 510 (1883).

In a mortgage foreclosure proceeding, a receiver could be appointed to collect rents and profits pending the sale of the premises and during the year of redemption, if the property was in tenant's possession and was insufficient to discharge the mortgage debts. Miller v. St. Louis Union Trust Co., 202 Ind. 688, 178 N.E. 1 (1931).

Actions for Loss or Injury Imminent.

—In General.

Receivers could be appointed to take charge of personal property when there were conflicting claims thereto and there was danger of loss or injury to the property. Hellebush v. Blake, 119 Ind. 349, 21 N.E. 976 (1889); Sallee v. Soules, 168 Ind. 624, 81 N.E. 587 (1907); Hodgin v. Hodgin, 175 Ind. 157, 93 N.E. 849 (1911).

Appointment of receiver where controversy existed respecting rights and interests in property of nonresidents was held justified. Hellebush v. Blake, 119 Ind. 349, 21 N.E. 976 (1889); Galloway v. Campbell, 142 Ind. 324, 41 N.E. 597 (1895).

The plaintiff must have shown that he had an existing right in the property in order to

**Actions for Loss or Injury
   Imminent.** (Cont'd)

—In General. (Cont'd)
have had a receiver appointed. Steele v. Aspy, 128 Ind. 367, 27 N.E. 739 (1891).

Appointment by the court of a receiver was justified where there were many conflicting interests and controversy between creditors of insolvent debtor. McElwaine v. Hosey, 135 Ind. 481, 35 N.E. 272 (1893).

If there were conflicting claims to property, and there was danger of loss or injury to the same, a receiver could be appointed to take charge thereof. Mead v. Burk, 156 Ind. 577, 60 N.E. 338 (1901); Levin v. Florsheim & Co., 161 Ind. 457, 68 N.E. 1025 (1903).

Creditors could have a receiver appointed to take charge of property subject to their claims when there was danger of waste or loss of the property. Levin v. Florsheim & Co., 161 Ind. 457, 68 N.E. 1025 (1903).

Courts did not have jurisdiction to appoint a receiver for the property of an individual and seize possession of it on allegations that he was indebted to the applicant and that he was conducting himself so as to be in danger of insolvency, without a showing that the applicant had a lien on such property; former IC 34-48-1-1 (repealed; see this section for similar provisions), relative to the appointment of receivers for corporations, not being applicable. State ex rel. Lebanon Disct. Corp. v. Superior Court, 195 Ind. 174, 144 N.E. 747 (1924); Slow v. Ohio Valley Roofing Co., 198 Ind. 190, 152 N.E. 820 (1926).

Where, in an action by owners of interests in oil leases against nonresident owners for appointment of a receiver to preserve their interests therein, upon which, by operating contract, they had given plaintiff a lien, a temporary restraining order would not be availing, no other adequate remedy at law existed, waste and loss was threatened, and the emergency could not be anticipated in time for the service of notice, the appointment of a receiver without notice was not in abuse of discretion. Meyering v. Petroleum Holdings, Inc., 227 Ind. 313, 86 N.E.2d 78 (1949).

Where nonresident defendants had repeatedly promised to pay their share of expenses in operating oil leases in which they owned an interest but had not done so, and one lease was in immediate danger of being forfeited for failure to commence drilling and another leasehold was being wasted by failure to protect it by an offset well, and the operator had a lien for money advanced and was not willing to make further advancements unless defendants paid their share and could make no expenditures in excess of $1,000 without the consent of all parties, appointment of a receiver without notice for defendants' interests in order to conserve them, pending collection

of money due, was not an abuse of discretion. Meyering v. Petroleum Holdings, Inc., 227 Ind. 313, 86 N.E.2d 78 (1949).

Appointment of a receiver pending action to quiet title was proper under the facts in record, pursuant to clause three of the predecessor statute to this section. Stanley v. Gieseking, 230 Ind. 690, 105 N.E.2d 171 (1952).

—Miscellaneous Applications.

——Ejectment.
Receivers could be appointed to take charge of land and crops. Bitting v. Ten Eyck, 85 Ind. 357 (1882).

——Fraudulent Conveyances.
Where, in proceedings, ancillary to an action to set aside deeds, a petition for the appointment of a receiver pendente lite alleged that grantor executed a deed to his son with the agreement that the lands be held in trust, and recited the various things done by the son in violation of the agreement, including a conveyance of the land by the son to his wife and the subsequent execution of mortgages and leases thereon, and further alleged the insolvency of the son and wife and their refusal to reconvey after demand, and the pleadings in the action to set aside the deeds alleged that the grantor executed the deed because of threats of personal injury, intimidation and undue influence, the trial court was well within its discretion in appointing a receiver pending the determination of the rights of the parties to the main action. Ratcliff v. Ratcliff, 219 Ind. 429, 39 N.E.2d 435 (1942).

——Mechanic's Lien Foreclosure.
Where property-owners were unable to complete a house under construction, or pay off liens thereon, the appointment of a receiver in a mechanic's lien foreclosure suit came within the court's jurisdiction, and did not constitute the taking of property without due process, where the court had jurisdiction of the parties and the subject-matter, in view of former IC 34-48-1-1 (repealed; see this section for similar provisions). Flanders v. Ostrom, 206 Ind. 87, 187 N.E. 673 (1933).

In a suit by creditor for foreclosure of mechanic's lien on property which debtors were using as residence and for appointment of receiver, the appointment of a receiver could not be sustained if the allegations failed to show statutory or equitable grounds upon which it might stand. Kleinmeyer v. Sears, Roebuck & Co., 236 Ind. 663, 142 N.E.2d 918 (1957).

——Partition.
Pending a suit for partition a receiver could

Actions for Loss or Injury Imminent. (Cont'd)

—Miscellaneous Applications. (Cont'd)

——Partition. (Cont'd)
be appointed to care for the property and collect the rents. Edwards v. Dykeman, 95 Ind. 509 (1884); Rapp v. Reehling, 122 Ind. 255, 23 N.E. 68 (1889); Hodgin v. Hodgin, 175 Ind. 157, 93 N.E. 849 (1911).

——Title to Land.
Where the defendant (in an action by plaintiff for the possession of certain real estate) succeeded upon the defense that he occupied as a purchaser, and not as a tenant, the court would not appoint a receiver, upon application of the plaintiff, to take possession and collect the rents, but left the plaintiff to assert his title in the ordinary forms of procedure at law. Corbin v. Thompson, 141 Ind. 128, 40 N.E. 533 (1895).

—Municipal Services.
Where company which provided services to municipal airport was sued by person claiming default in payment under contract and sought immediate possession of the property, intervention by city in which it sought the appointment of a receiver to keep the business operating was proper. United States Aircraft Fin., Inc. v. Jankovich, 173 Ind. App. 644, 58 Ind. Dec. 401, 365 N.E.2d 783 (1977), rev'd on other grounds, 407 N.E.2d 287, 77 Ind. Dec. 262 (Ind. App. 1980).

Actions by Vendor.
A receiver may have been appointed in a suit by a vendor for purchase-money in case waste was threatened or done by the vendee. McCaslin v. State ex rel. Evans, 44 Ind. 151 (1873).

After Final Judgment and Pending Appeal.
After an appeal, the lower court could appoint a receiver, in a proper case, to take charge of the property pending the appeal. Brinkman v. Ritzinger, 82 Ind. 358 (1882).
A receiver could be appointed after the rendition of a decree, where occurrences arose which threatened the effectiveness of the decree. Chicago & S.E. Ry. v. St. Clair, 144 Ind. 371, 42 N.E. 225 (1895).

Ancillary to Main Action.
As an almost universal rule, the appointment of a receiver was not an independent action, but was ancillary to the main action. Supreme Sitting of Order of Iron Hall v. Baker, 134 Ind. 293, 33 N.E. 1128, 20 L.R.A. 210 (1893); State v. Union Nat'l Bank, 145 Ind. 537, 44 N.E. 585, 57 Am. St. R. 209 (1896); Sheridan Brick Works v. Marion Trust Co., 157 Ind. 292, 61 N.E. 666, 87 Am. St. R. 207 (1901); Hay v. McDaniel, 26 Ind. App. 683, 60 N.E. 729 (1901).
An application for appointment of a receiver did not of itself constitute a suit, but it was an interlocutory proceeding in a pending suit. Maple v. McReynolds, 208 Ind. 338, 196 N.E. 3 (1935).

Appointment Not Mandatory.
Appointment of receiver under former IC 34-48-1-1 (repealed; see this section for similar provisions) was permissive and not mandatory. Hammond Theatrical Co. v. Gregory, 208 Ind. 31, 194 N.E. 631 (1935).
Where a restraining order or an injunction could have stopped the practices complained of, the remedy of a receivership was not warranted. Lafayette Realty Corp. v. Moller, 247 Ind. 433, 8 Ind. Dec. 214, 215 N.E.2d 859 (1966).

Appointment Not Required.
There was no basis for the appointment of a receiver where, although the exact market value of the property was unclear, it was clear that the value exceeded the amount of the indebtedness secured by the mortgage, and because there was no evidence that the property was in danger of being lost, removed or materially injured. Johnson v. La Porte Bank & Trust Co., 470 N.E.2d 350 (Ind. App. 1984).

Appointment Pendente Lite.
While trial courts had wide discretionary power to appoint receivers pendente lite such powers should have been exercised only when it was clear that no other full and adequate remedy existed whereby justice between the parties could have been effected and a wrong prevented. Ziffrin v. Ziffrin, 242 Ind. 351, 179 N.E.2d 276 (1962).

Appointment Without Notice.
It was error to appoint a receiver without notice upon plaintiff's allegations without supporting facts that defendant was indebted to plaintiff and others, that defendant was without funds to pay such indebtedness and was insolvent or in danger of insolvency, that if a receiver was not appointed defendant's assets would diminish and its debts increase, creditors would be unable to collect debts, the physical assets of defendant corporation would be lost, wasted, and/or misappropriated, and other creditors would obtain an unfair advantage, that plaintiff did not have an adequate remedy at law and that an emergency existed. Inter-City Contractors Serv. v. Jolley, 257 Ind. 593, 28 Ind. Dec. 681, 277 N.E.2d 158 (1972).

Consent to Powers of Receiver.
Where respondent, in action for writ of

Consent to Powers of Receiver. (Cont'd)
mandate and prohibition to vacate order enlarging authority of receiver, claimed that relator consented to such enlargement, such consent must have appeared in the record of the case. State ex rel. Makar v. Saint Joseph Circuit Court, 242 Ind. 339, 179 N.E.2d 285 (1962).

Construction.

A statute which granted the authority to appoint a receiver was to have been strictly construed. State ex rel. Makar v. Saint Joseph Circuit Court, 242 Ind. 339, 179 N.E.2d 285 (1962).

Corporations.

—In General.

In a suit by stockholders against a corporation and the officers thereof, a receiver could be appointed. Wayne Pike Co. v. Hammons, 129 Ind. 368, 27 N.E. 487 (1891); Supreme Sitting of Order of Iron Hall v. Baker, 134 Ind. 293, 33 N.E. 1128, 20 L.R.A. 210 (1893); Thayer v. Kinder, 45 Ind. App. 111, 89 N.E. 408, 90 N.E. 323 (1909).

If the stockholders of a corporation were unable to agree upon its management, and it had no money to pay its debts, a receiver could be appointed. Sheridan Brick Works v. Marion Trust Co., 157 Ind. 292, 61 N.E. 666, 87 Am. St. R. 207 (1901).

An appointment without notice under this clause (5) of the predecessor statute to this section could be made only upon sufficient cause shown by affidavit. Orin Jessup Land Co. v. Lannes, 193 Ind. 645, 141 N.E. 454 (1923).

The power to appoint receiver for a corporation should be exercised cautiously, especially where the acts relied upon were not by law expressly made grounds for the appointment. Allied Magnet Wire Corp. v. Tuttle, 199 Ind. 166, 154 N.E. 480, 156 N.E. 558, 50 A.L.R. 252 (1926).

Where the appointment of a receiver was sought for a corporation operating a motorbus line which had taken over the bus line and the property from the purchaser of the same and assumed the purchaser's indebtedness therefor, the fact that plaintiff, as a creditor of the corporation, had a legal remedy for such indebtedness against the surety who was the original purchaser, did not necessarily defeat the suit for appointment of a receiver, since it was only a full, complete, and adequate remedy at law against the principal debtor that would prevent equity from taking jurisdiction, and not a remedy against some one else. South Side Motor Coach Corp. v. McFarland, 207 Ind. 301, 191 N.E. 147 (1934).

In a suit for appointment of receiver of an insolvent corporation, the fact that the petition requested authority be granted to the receiver to file suit to set aside a conveyance of the debtor's property did not render the petition bad for uncertainty, as being inconsistent. Merriman & Wasson Co. v. Eagle Pencil Co., 209 Ind. 421, 199 N.E. 243 (1936).

In a suit for appointment of receiver of a corporation which was in process of liquidation to wind up the affairs of the corporation in an orderly manner, under judicial supervision, the court had authority under former IC 34-48-1-1 (repealed; see this section for similar provisions) and subsection to appoint a receiver in an action instituted solely for that purpose. Specialty Furn. Co. v. Rusche, 212 Ind. 184, 6 N.E.2d 959 (1937).

The court properly appointed a limited receiver for small drugstore, for the purpose of composing differences between directors of the corporation and restoring proper management to duly elected directors. Dynamite Drugs, Inc. v. Kerch, 212 Ind. 568, 10 N.E.2d 624 (1937).

The inability of the officers and directors of a dairymen's cooperative corporation to persuade the O. P. A. to increase prices of products was not cause for the appointment of a receiver on the ground of mismanagement. Indianapolis Dairymen's Coop. v. Bottema, 226 Ind. 237, 79 N.E.2d 399 (1948).

Evidence that a corporation operating a school of beauty culture had no tangible assets, but was a going concern with approximately 90 students enrolled, that it owed no outstanding obligations other than weekly current bills, which were discounted, and that it had approximately $50,000 in securities, was insufficient to show insolvency as a ground for the appointment of a receiver pending an action against it for fraud. Royal Academy of Beauty Culture v. Wallace, 226 Ind. 383, 78 N.E.2d 32, 81 N.E.2d 534 (1948).

An individual, not a stockholder nor a lienholder, asserting an unliquidated claim for damages by reason of an alleged tort, could not have a receiver appointed for a corporation before his claim was reduced to judgment. Royal Academy of Beauty Culture v. Wallace, 226 Ind. 383, 78 N.E.2d 32, 81 N.E.2d 534 (1948).

Trial court erred in allowing fees to receiver pendente lite and to his attorney where receiver had been appointed for labor union at its request in action for injunction, as receiver had no vested interest in his appointment, and owed no duty to defend union on appeal from such action, since he was not a party to the judgment appointing him, or a necessary party to the appeal. International Union of Operating Eng'rs v. Hoisting & Portable Eng'rs, Local 103, 231 Ind. 634, 110 N.E.2d 332 (1953).

One of the prime objects of former IC 34-48-1-1 (repealed; see this section for similar

Corporations. (Cont'd)

—In General. (Cont'd)

provisions) was to afford a diligent unpaid creditor of a dissolved corporation the equitable power of the court, exercised through the agency of a receiver, ancillary to the main action, to collect, conserve, and protect the assets of the dissolved corporation until the merits of the asserted creditor's claim could be judicially established. Seaney v. Ayres, 135 Ind. App. 585, 1 Ind. Dec. 350, 189 N.E.2d 826 (1963).

Alleged acts of overreaching and of fraud alone were not sufficient grounds for a receiver in every case, they must have been of such magnitude that the survival of the corporation was imperiled. Lafayette Realty Corp. v. Moller, 247 Ind. 433, 8 Ind. Dec. 214, 215 N.E.2d 859 (1966).

Before a receiver could be appointed an emergency must have been shown to exist such that the management and operation of a corporation must have been taken over at once from those in control, irreparable damage and injury must have resulted unless a receiver was appointed and there must have been no adequate remedy otherwise available. Lafayette Realty Corp. v. Moller, 247 Ind. 433, 8 Ind. Dec. 214, 215 N.E.2d 859 (1966).

The drastic remedy of appointing a receiver was justified where the managing director of a corporation treated corporate assets and funds as his own, secretly withdrew funds from the corporate account to pay his attorney fees even during present litigation, and breached fiduciary duties. Dotlich v. Dotlich, 475 N.E.2d 331 (Ind. App. 1985).

—Disposition of Assets.

When a suit was brought against a corporation simply for an accounting and the appointment of a receiver, a sale of the corporate property should not have been ordered. Wayne Pike Co. v. Hammons, 129 Ind. 368, 27 N.E. 487 (1891).

The receiver of an insolvent building and loan association was required to list the assets of the association in its hands for taxation, and pay the taxes thereon. Board of County Comm'rs v. Marion Trust Co., 30 Ind. App. 137, 65 N.E. 589 (1902).

A receiver pendente lite, as an officer of the court, held possession of the property for the benefit of the party or parties ultimately determined to be entitled thereto, and his custody was considered to be the custody of the court. Parfenoff v. Kozlowski, 218 Ind. 154, 31 N.E.2d 206 (1941).

The appointment of a substitute receiver in the place and stead of one theretofore appointed did not change the legal custody of the property. Parfenoff v. Kozlowski, 218 Ind. 154, 31 N.E.2d 206 (1941).

—Imminent Danger of Insolvency.

Finding by trial court that without proposed loan, corporation would have difficulty continuing its normal operations did not justify appointment of a receiver pendente lite under former IC 34-48-1-1 (repealed; see this section for similar provisions). Crippin Printing Corp. v. Abel, 441 N.E.2d 1002 (Ind. App. 1982).

——Dissension Among Shareholders.

Potential or even probable shareholder deadlock is of itself an insufficient basis for appointment of receiver pendente lite, rather, appointment of a receiver is appropriate only where there is dissension between sets of stockholders owning equal amounts of stock such that there is a present danger to investors consisting of a serious suspension of or interference with conduct of business resulting in imminent danger of dissipation of corporate assets. Crippin Printing Corp. v. Abel, 441 N.E.2d 1002 (Ind. App. 1982).

—Individuals, Partnerships, Associations.

A receiver could not be appointed for a building and loan association, at the suit of a stockholder, without the recommendation of the auditor of state. Huntington County Loan & Sav. Ass'n v. Fulk, 158 Ind. 113, 63 N.E. 123 (1902).

Courts did not have jurisdiction to appoint a receiver for the property of an individual and seize possession of it on allegations and proof that he was insolvent and had transferred all his business property to a trustee for the benefit of certain creditors not including the plaintiff, without any showing that the plaintiff had a lien on the property transferred or that there was fraud in making such transfer. Slow v. Ohio Valley Roofing Co., 198 Ind. 190, 152 N.E. 820 (1926). See also Zechiel v. Firemen's Fund Ins. Co., 61 F.2d 27 (7th Cir. 1932); State ex rel. Lebanon Disct. Corp. v. Superior Court, 195 Ind. 174, 144 N.E. 747 (1924).

Act of court in appointing receiver for an agency or exchange organized by the persons contracting plan for insurance under the reciprocal plan was wholly void, appointment not being provided for by statute. Turner v. Henshaw, 86 Ind. App. 565, 155 N.E. 222 (1927).

Appointment of receiver by copartnership at instance of contract creditor could not be collaterally attacked. Zechiel v. Firemen's Fund Ins. Co., 61 F.2d 27 (7th Cir. 1932), cert. denied, 288 U.S. 602, 53 S. Ct. 387, 77 L. Ed. 978 (1933).

A receiver could be appointed for a corpora-

Corporations. (Cont'd)

—Individuals, Partnerships, Associations. (Cont'd)
tion which had taken over a motor-bus line and its equipment from the purchaser and assumed the purchaser's indebtedness therefor, in order to conserve the assets of the corporation and to prevent them from being dissipated by a multiplicity of suits. South Side Motor Coach Corp. v. McFarland, 207 Ind. 301, 191 N.E. 147 (1934).

In a suit for appointment of a receiver of an alleged insolvent corporation, the evidence was held to warrant appointment of receiver, where it showed that defendant was indebted to various creditors in large amounts, and that defendant was unable to pay its debts. Merriman & Wasson Co. v. Eagle Pencil Co., 209 Ind. 421, 199 N.E. 243 (1936).

A party asserting that a corporation was insolvent or in imminent danger of insolvency had the burden of proving that fact. Royal Academy of Beauty Culture v. Wallace, 226 Ind. 383, 78 N.E.2d 32, 81 N.E.2d 534 (1948).

In determining whether a debtor was unable to meet its obligations, the court should have allowed for reasonable use of the debtor's credit. Royal Academy of Beauty Culture v. Wallace, 226 Ind. 383, 78 N.E.2d 32, 81 N.E.2d 534 (1948).

—Insolvency.
Right of stockholders of insolvent corporation to have a receiver appointed and right of other stockholders to intervene in suit was upheld. Thayer v. Kinder, 45 Ind. App. 111, 89 N.E. 408, 90 N.E. 323 (1909).

The Lake circuit court had jurisdiction of the subject-matter of an action for the appointment of a receiver for an insolvent corporation, or a corporation in imminent danger of insolvency, which appointment could be made by the court or the judge thereof in vacation. Jefferson Park Realty Corp. v. Kelley, Glover & Vale, Inc., 105 Ind. App. 313, 12 N.E.2d 977 (1938).

Insolvency as a ground for the appointment of a receiver was the state of inability to pay debts as they fell due in the usual course of trade or business, and an excess of assets over liabilities did not of itself render the debtor solvent, for the assets might not be readily convertible into money, and, notwithstanding their supposed value, the debtor might not be able to pay the claims against him as they became due. Royal Academy of Beauty Culture v. Wallace, 226 Ind. 383, 78 N.E.2d 32, 81 N.E.2d 534 (1948).

The allegation that the president was a nonresident of Indiana and was transferring his assets and the assets of the corporation out of the state of Indiana, and that because of such transfer of assets the corporation was in imminent danger of insolvency, was not a statement of evidentiary facts sufficient to make out a case where the corporation was in imminent danger of insolvency under former IC 34-48-1-1 (repealed; see this ection for similar provisions). Second Real Estate Inv., Inc. v. Johann, 232 Ind. 24, 111 N.E.2d 467 (1953).

—Termination of Franchise.
A receiver could legally be appointed after the expiration of the three years next following the limitation of the charter of a corporation, in a suit instituted before the expiration of the three years. Lime City Bldg., Loan & Sav. Ass'n v. Black, 136 Ind. 544, 35 N.E. 829 (1893); Hatfield v. Cummings, 140 Ind. 547, 40 N.E. 53 (1893).

A receiver of the property of a corporation which had forfeited its franchise could be appointed to hold the property subject to order of the court, when necessary to aid an injunction against the further unlawful use of the property. Columbian Athletic Club v. State ex rel. McMahan, 143 Ind. 98, 40 N.E. 914, 28 L.R.A. 727, 52 Am. St. R. 407 (1895); Eel River R.R. v. State ex rel. Kistler, 155 Ind. 433, 57 N.E. 388 (1900).

Discretion of Court.
This statute gave the trial courts large discretionary power in the appointment of receivers pendente lite. Ratcliff v. Ratcliff, 219 Ind. 429, 39 N.E.2d 435 (1942).

Former IC 34-48-1-1 (repealed; see this section for similar provisions) required the court to appoint a receiver when the general conditions of subdivision (4) of the former section and any one of its six conditions (A)-(F) were met. The court has discretion whether to appoint a receiver under other subdivisions of the statute, but under subdivision (4), appointment was mandatory once the statutory conditions were met. Farver v. DeKalb County Farm Bureau, 576 N.E.2d 1361 (Ind. App. 1991).

The trial court abused its discretion by granting the petition for receivership pursuant to IC 23-1-47-1, and by failing to grant the receivership pursuant to the mandatory provisions of former IC 34-48-1-1 (repealed; see this section for similar provisions). KeyBank Nat'l Ass'n v. Michael, 737 N.E.2d 834 (Ind. App. 2000).

Divorce Actions.
In divorce actions, the court had power to appoint a receiver to take possession of defendant's property situated in the court's jurisdiction, when necessary to the protection of the plaintiff's rights. Tormohlen v. Tormohlen, 210 Ind. 328, 1 N.E.2d 596 (1936).

An application for the appointment of a receiver pendente lite was not an independent

Divorce Actions. (Cont'd)
action, but was ancillary to the main action and was not the ultimate purpose or object contemplated by the principal action. Ratcliff v. Ratcliff, 219 Ind. 429, 39 N.E.2d 435 (1942).

The authority of a divorce court to impose a receivership was not necessarily derived from the dissolution statutes (IC 31-1-11.5-7, repealed, and IC 31-1-11.5-17, repealed); a court has ample authority under former IC 34-48-1-1 (repealed; see this section for similar provisions) to appoint receivers in all cases where it is found necessary to protect the rights of all parties and to properly execute court decrees. In re Gore, 527 N.E.2d 191 (Ind. App. 1988).

Federal Courts.
The order of a state court appointing a receiver could not be collaterally attacked by a federal court on grounds of its invalidity; but the federal court could look into the receiver's conduct. In re Hawkins Mtg. Co., 66 F.2d 16 (7th Cir. 1933), cert. denied, 291 U.S. 659, 54 S. Ct. 376, 78 L. Ed. 1051 (1934).

Hearing on Application.
An application to have a receiver appointed after notice could be heard either upon oral testimony or affidavits. Pouder v. Tate, 96 Ind. 330 (1884); Hursh v. Hursh, 93 Ind. 500 (1885).

A verified complaint asking for the appointment of a receiver was evidence only of the facts alleged, and not of the conclusions stated therein. Little Wonder Light Co. v. VanSlyke, 198 Ind. 269, 153 N.E. 477 (1926).

Jurisdiction and Venue.
A change of judge could have been had in applications for the appointment of receivers. Shoemaker v. Smith, 74 Ind. 71 (1881).

Judges had the same power in vacation to appoint receivers that courts had when in session. Pressley v. Lamb, 105 Ind. 171, 4 N.E. 682 (1886); First Nat'l Bank v. United States Encaustic Tile Co., 105 Ind. 227, 4 N.E. 846 (1886); Chicago & S.E. Ry. v. Kenney, 159 Ind. 72, 62 N.E. 26 (1901).

The court could appoint a receiver of personal property within its jurisdiction and involved in a pending action, although the defendant resided in another state. Hellebush v. Blake, 119 Ind. 349, 21 N.E. 976 (1889); Galloway v. Campbell, 142 Ind. 324, 41 N.E. 597 (1895).

Judge holding court in one county could appoint a receiver in another county of the circuit. Chicago & S.E. Ry. v. St. Clair, 144 Ind. 371, 42 N.E. 225 (1895).

A superior court was unauthorized to appoint a receiver for the property of a tire company in a suit to secure such appointment by a contract creditor, in view of former IC

34-48-1-1 (repealed; see this section for similar provisions), where the appointment was not justified under an equitable rule, and was not authorized by statute. Steinbrenner Rubber Co. v. Duncan, 86 Ind. App. 218, 155 N.E. 625 (1927).

Prerequisites to Appointment.
A receiver could only be appointed in a suit where there were adverse parties, but the defendant could admit the truth of the facts stated in the application. Pressley v. Harrison, 102 Ind. 14, 1 N.E. 188 (1885); First Nat'l Bank v. United States Encaustic Tile Co., 105 Ind. 227, 4 N.E. 846 (1886); Winona, W.E. & S.B. Traction Co. v. Collins, 162 Ind. 693, 69 N.E. 998 (1904).

The plaintiff must have shown that he had a present existing right in the property at the time in order to have had a receiver appointed. Steele v. Aspy, 128 Ind. 367, 27 N.E. 739 (1891); Sheridan Brick Works v. Marion Trust Co., 157 Ind. 292, 61 N.E. 666, 87 Am. St. R. 207 (1901); Steinbrenner Rubber Co. v. Duncan, 86 Ind. App. 218, 155 N.E. 625 (1927).

A receiver could not be appointed without notice until summons was issued on the complaint in the action and delivered to the officer for service. Alexandria Gas Co. v. Irish, 152 Ind. 535, 53 N.E. 762 (1899); Winona, W.E. & S.B. Traction Co. v. Collins, 162 Ind. 693, 69 N.E. 998 (1904); Tucker v. Tucker, 194 Ind. 108, 142 N.E. 11 (1924).

A court order appointing a receiver without notice, and directing such receiver to take possession of property, without notice to, or opportunity to be heard by, those in possession, was wholly unwarranted. State ex rel. Lebanon Disct. Corp. v. Superior Court, 195 Ind. 174, 144 N.E. 747 (1924).

The appointment of a receiver under former IC 34-48-1-1 (repealed; see this section for similar provisions) and IC 34-48-1-9, without notice or appearance, was authorized only on showing by affidavit that there was no other remedy, and that an immediate necessity existed for such action. Firestone Coal Mining Co. v. Roetzel, 201 Ind. 430, 169 N.E. 465 (1930).

The court should have been satisfied of the merits of plaintiff's main action before granting petition for appointment of a receiver. Hawkins v. Aldridge, 211 Ind. 332, 7 N.E.2d 34, 109 A.L.R. 1205 (1937).

Although courts had general statutory and inherent authority to appoint receivers with notice, they clearly had no authority to appoint receivers without notice, except upon sufficient cause shown by affidavit. State ex rel. Red Dragon Diner, Inc. v. Superior Court, 239 Ind. 384, 158 N.E.2d 164 (1959).

Preservation of Right of Redemption.
When necessary to secure justice between

Preservation of Right of
Redemption. (Cont'd)

the parties, a receiver could be appointed to collect the rents and profits of lands sold on execution, during the time allowed for redemption. Connelly v. Dickson, 76 Ind. 440 (1881); Travellers Ins. Co. v. Brouse, 83 Ind. 62 (1882); Merritt v. Gibson, 129 Ind. 155, 27 N.E. 136, 15 L.R.A. 277 (1891); Harris v. United States Sav. Fund & Inv. Co., 146 Ind. 265, 45 N.E. 328 (1896); Sweet & Clark Co. v. Union Nat'l Bank, 149 Ind. 305, 49 N.E. 159 (1898); Russell v. Bruce, 159 Ind. 553, 64 N.E. 602, 65 N.E. 585 (1902).

If the mortgagor was in actual personal occupancy of the property, a receiver should not have been appointed to receive the rents during the time allowed for redemption from a foreclosure sale. Sheeks v. Klotz, 84 Ind. 471 (1882); Merritt v. Gibson, 129 Ind. 155, 27 N.E. 136, 15 L.R.A. 277 (1891); Sellers v. Stoffel, 139 Ind. 468, 39 N.E. 52 (1894); World Bldg., Loan & Inv. Co. v. Marlin, 151 Ind. 630, 52 N.E. 198 (1898).

If the property sold under a mortgage was in possession of tenants, a receiver could be appointed to collect rents during the time allowed for redemption when the lands did not sell for enough to pay the judgment. Merritt v. Gibson, 129 Ind. 155, 27 N.E. 136, 15 L.R.A. 277 (1891); Harris v. United States Sav. Fund & Inv. Co., 146 Ind. 265, 45 N.E. 328 (1896); Sweet & Clark Co. v. Union Nat'l Bank, 149 Ind. 305, 49 N.E. 159 (1898); World Bldg., Loan & Inv. Co. v. Marlin, 151 Ind. 630, 52 N.E. 198 (1898).

If the mortgaged property sold for a sufficient sum to pay the judgment and decree of foreclosure, no receiver should have been appointed on the application of the mortgagee, and if such receiver was appointed before such sale, he should have been discharged, and any rents received by him, after paying the costs of receivership, should have been paid to the one entitled to the possession of such real estate during the year allowed for redemption. World Bldg., Loan & Inv. Co. v. Marlin, 151 Ind. 630, 52 N.E. 198 (1898).

The appointment of a receiver to take charge of land during the redemption period was improper where it appeared that the value of the land exceeded the mortgage indebtedness, and there was no evidence as to the solvency or insolvency of the mortgagor. Hickam v. Golladay, 83 Ind. App. 569, 149 N.E. 375 (1925).

In a proceeding for appointment of receiver in mortgage foreclosure, the evidence was held to justify the appointment for collection of rents and profits of the mortgaged land during the year of redemption. Miller v. St. Louis Union Trust Co., 202 Ind. 688, 178 N.E. 1 (1931).

Remedy at Law Available.

A receiver would not be appointed where plaintiff had a remedy at law, unless there was a showing that the remedy at law would not be adequate or effectual. Hawkins v. Aldridge, 211 Ind. 332, 7 N.E.2d 34, 109 A.L.R. 1205 (1937).

A receiver would not be appointed to prevent the issuance of an injunction where it was not an alternative remedy at law and the action sought was to prevent the conveyance of any of appellant's assets, not just the property over which he had a lien. McKain v. Rigsby, 250 Ind. 438, 14 Ind. Dec. 360, 237 N.E.2d 99 (1968).

Sufficiency of Original Complaint.

Ordinarily, the sufficiency of the complaint in the main action could not be tested on the hearing of the application for a receiver. Bufkin v. Boyce, 104 Ind. 53, 3 N.E. 615 (1885).

If the complaint showed no right of recovery on the cause of action stated therein, a receiver would not be appointed on the application of the plaintiff. Goshen Woolen Mills Co. v. City Nat'l Bank, 150 Ind. 279, 49 N.E. 154 (1898); Hay v. McDaniel, 26 Ind. App. 683, 60 N.E. 729 (1901).

Validation of Unauthorized Action.

A consent for receiver to borrow money, which was given after the receiver had taken charge, would not give validity to a prior order authorizing the receiver to operate the business if such purported authorization was void ab initio. State ex rel. Makar v. Saint Joseph Circuit Court, 242 Ind. 339, 179 N.E.2d 285 (1962).

Where order extending authority of a receiver to authorize the operation of all of defendant's business was invalid, a cross-complaint subsequently filed by defendant's business partner, and containing allegations which would justify the appointment of a general receiver and asking that such previous appointment of a general receiver be validated could not validate the prior order. State ex rel. Makar v. Saint Joseph Circuit Court, 242 Ind. 339, 179 N.E.2d 285 (1962).

When Appointment Set Aside.

Since the appointment of a receiver was within the sound discretion of the court, and was not controlled by the agreement of the interested parties, an order appointing a receiver for a corporation could be set aside notwithstanding a majority of the stockholders had agreed that a receiver should be appointed, and were claiming that such action of the court would work a hardship on the stockholders and the receiver. Cooper v. Ferguson Willis Oil Co., 199 Ind. 742, 161 N.E. 4 (1928).

Collateral References. Tort action, appointment of receiver at instance of plaintiff in. 4 A.L.R.2d 1278.

Propriety of appointing receiver, at behest of mortgagee, to manage or operate property during foreclosure action. 82 A.L.R.2d 1075.

Funds deposited in court as subject of garnishment. 1 A.L.R.3d 936.

Appealability of order directing payment of money into court. 15 A.L.R.3d 568.

Eminent domain: payment or deposit of award in court as affecting condemnor's right to appeal. 40 A.L.R.3d 203.

Voluntary payment into court of judgment against one joint tortfeasor as release of others. 40 A.L.R.3d 1181.

Appointment or discharge of receiver for marital or community property necessitated by suit for divorce or separation. 15 A.L.R.4th 224.

Liability of corporate custodian for negligence in dealing with affairs or assets of corporation. 74 A.L.R.4th 770.

32-30-5-2. Persons who may not be appointed. — A court may not appoint:

(1) a party;

(2) an attorney representing a party; or

(3) another person interested in an action;

as a receiver in that action. [P.L.2-2002, § 15.]

NOTES TO DECISIONS

ANALYSIS

Acceptance, waiver of objection.
Agreement of parties.
Attorney for receiver.
Claimant.
Discretion of court.
Employees of parties.

Acceptance, Waiver of Objection.
Party accepting appointment as receiver in a foreclosure suit could not later object to the proceedings on the ground that he was the owner of the property involved and therefore an interested party. Lowe v. Swafford, 209 Ind. 514, 199 N.E. 709, 103 A.L.R. 1222 (1936).

Agreement of Parties.
Agreement of parties as to appointment was not binding on the court. Polk v. Johnson, 35 Ind. App. 478, 65 N.E. 536 (1902), aff'd, 160 Ind. 292, 66 N.E. 752 (1903); Durbin v. Northwestern Scraper Co., 36 Ind. App. 123, 73 N.E. 297, appeal dismissed, 165 Ind. 237, 75 N.E. 1 (1905).

Attorney for Receiver.
An attorney acting as counsel for the receiver should be held to the same standard of impartiality as that for the receiver. KeyBank Nat'l Ass'n v. Michael, 737 N.E.2d 834 (Ind. App. 2000).

Claimant.
A trust company making claim against a company for which it was acting as receiver was acting in a dual capacity in violation of former IC 34-48-1-2 (repealed; see this section for similar provisions). Saint Joseph Loan & Trust Co. v. Studebaker Corp., 66 F.2d 151 (7th Cir.), cert. denied, 290 U.S. 699, 54 S. Ct. 209, 78 L. Ed. 601 (1933).

Discretion of Court.
Excepting persons referred to in former IC 34-48-1-2 (repealed; see this section for similar provisions), the determination as to who should be appointed a receiver rested in the discretion of the court, and if an order of appointment was invalid, the same person could have been appointed a receiver under a valid order. Robinson v. Dickey, 143 Ind. 214, 42 N.E. 638 (1896).

Employees of Parties.
Employee of a party should not have been appointed. State v. Union Nat'l Bank, 145 Ind. 537, 44 N.E. 585, 57 Am. St. R. 209 (1896).

Generally speaking, the agent, employee, or attorney of party actively engaged in obtaining a receivership should not have been appointed as receiver; but this rule was not inflexible, and it was otherwise where he was a man of integrity, was experienced, outstanding, and agreed upon by parties involved in case. Cooper v. Morris, 210 Ind. 162, 200 N.E. 222 (1936).

32-30-5-3. Oath — Written undertaking. — Before beginning duties as a receiver, the receiver must:

(1) swear to perform the duties of a receiver faithfully; and

(2) with one (1) or more sureties approved by the court or judge, execute a written undertaking, payable to such person as the court or the judge directs, to the effect that the receiver will:

    (A) faithfully discharge the duties of receiver in the action; and

    (B) obey the orders of the court or judge.

[P.L.2-2002, § 15.]

NOTES TO DECISIONS

ANALYSIS

Liability of receiver.
Liability of surety.

Liability of Receiver.

Where the appointment of a receiver of a reciprocal insurance exchange, in an action of which the court had jurisdiction, was void because the exchange was not a legal entity, and the receiver received assets belonging to the subscribers to the association and appropriated them to the use of the receivership, but committed no breach of official duty, the receiver was liable in his individual capacity for the taking of the property but the surety on his bond was not. State ex rel. Stone v. United States Fid. & Guar. Co., 119 Ind. App. 63, 78 N.E.2d 881 (1948).

Liability of Surety.

Where an order appointing a receiver for a reciprocal insurance exchange was void because the exchange was not a legal entity, all further orders having to do with the attempted receivership were also void, and hence an order discharging the receiver from his bond and trust could afford the surety on his bond no protection as a defense in an action on the bond. State ex rel. Stone v. United States Fid. & Guar. Co., 119 Ind. App. 63, 78 N.E.2d 881 (1948).

32-30-5-4. Deposit and delivery of money or other things. — If it is admitted by the pleading or examination of a party that the party has in the party's possession or under the party's control any money or other thing capable of delivery, which:

    (1) is the subject of the litigation;

    (2) is held by the party as trustee for another party; or

    (3) belongs or is due to another party;

the court or the judge may order the money or thing to be deposited in court or with the clerk, or delivered to the other party, with or without security, subject to the further order of the court or the judge. [P.L.2-2002, § 15.]

NOTES TO DECISIONS

Applicability.

Former IC 34-48-1-4 (repealed; see this section for similar provisions) only applied to cases where a party by a pleading or on examination admitted that he had possession of money or other thing the subject of the controversy, belonging to or held in trust for another. Swingle v. Bank of Ind., 41 Ind. 423 (1872).

Former IC 34-48-1-4 (repealed; see this section for similar provisions) was applicable only in receivership proceedings. Snihurowycz v. AAMCO Transmissions, Inc., 418 N.E.2d 1190 (Ind. App. 1981).

32-30-5-5. Disobedience — Contempt. — If, in the exercise of its authority, a court or judge:

    (1) has ordered the deposit or delivery of money or another thing; and

    (2) the order is disobeyed;

the court or the judge, besides punishing the disobedience as contempt, may make an order requiring the sheriff to take the money or thing and deposit it or deliver it in conformity with the direction of the court or judge. [P.L.2-2002, § 15.]

32-30-5-6. Loaning of deposits — Consent. — Money deposited or paid into court or with the clerk in an action may not be loaned out unless consent is obtained from all parties having an interest in or making claim to the money. [P.L.2-2002, § 15.]

32-30-5-7. Actions of receiver. — The receiver may, under control of the court or the judge:

(1) bring and defend actions;

(2) take and keep possession of the property;

(3) receive rents; and

(4) collect debts;

in the receiver's own name, and generally do other acts respecting the property as the court or judge may authorize. [P.L.2-2002, § 15.]

Cross References. Bond upon judicial sale, IC 30-3-3-1.

Distribution of assets under Uniform Liquidation Act, IC 30-2-7.

Power of receiver to invest in obligations issued under Federal Home Loan Bank Act and National Housing Act, IC 30-1-5-1.

NOTES TO DECISIONS

ANALYSIS

Actions.
—In general.
—Foreign receivers.
—In receiver's name.
—Leave to sue receiver.
Continuation of business.
Contracts.
Control by court.
Due process.
—Insufficient.
—State action.
—Sufficient.
Jurisdiction over property.
Leases.
—Factors considered.
Possession of property.
Removal of house from realty.
Sale of property.
Third parties.

Actions.

—In General.

Receivers could usually only maintain suits where the party whose effects he received might have sued. La Follett v. Akin, 36 Ind. 1 (1871).

A receiver could sue for the conversion of property of which he had the right of possession. Kehr v. Hall, 117 Ind. 405, 20 N.E. 279 (1889).

The only rights of action which a receiver may maintain are those which resided in the debtor prior to the appointment of the receiver. State ex rel. Shepard v. Sullivan, 120 Ind. 197, 21 N.E. 1093, 22 N.E. 325 (1889).

A receiver of the effects of an insolvent debtor could not sue the sureties on a penal bond of the debtor. State ex rel. Shepard v. Sullivan, 120 Ind. 197, 21 N.E. 1093, 22 N.E. 325 (1889).

When a receiver was appointed, he alone could sue to enforce any rights connected with the receivership. Davis v. Ladoga Creamery Co., 128 Ind. 222, 27 N.E. 494 (1891); Rand v. Wright, 141 Ind. 226, 39 N.E. 447 (1895); Big Creek Stone Co. v. Seward, 144 Ind. 205, 42 N.E. 464, 43 N.E. 5 (1895); Northwestern Mut. Life Ins. Co. v. Kidder, 162 Ind. 382, 70 N.E. 489, 66 L.R.A. 89, 1 Ann. Cas. 509 (1904).

In an action by a receiver for specific performance of a contract for conveyance of lands, where the complaint alleged a direction from the court to sue and enforce the contract, sufficient authority was shown in the receiver to maintain the action. Davis v. Talbot, 138 Ind. 235, 36 N.E. 1098 (1894).

A receiver of a corporation represented the creditors thereof, and he was the proper person to maintain an action to set aside chattel mortgages on the corporate property, as the rights of the creditors in this respect became vested in the receiver. National State Bank v. Vigo County Nat'l Bank, 141 Ind. 352, 40 N.E. 799, 50 Am. St. R. 330 (1895).

Receiver of corporation represented both corporation and creditors and could maintain or defend suits in behalf of each. Franklin Nat'l Bank v. Whitehead, 149 Ind. 560, 49 N.E. 592, 39 L.R.A. 725, 63 Am. St. R. 302 (1898).

The order appointing a receiver authorized him to take charge of, and reduce to his

Actions. (Cont'd)

—In General. (Cont'd)
possession all of the property of every description belonging to the bank; it empowered him to bring and prosecute in his own name, as such receiver, all actions necessary in the discharge of his duties or to defend the same. Coddington v. Canaday, 157 Ind. 243, 61 N.E. 567 (1901).

A receiver for a corporation, appointed under the general powers of a court of equity, could assert only those rights which could have been asserted by the corporation and, on that basis only, could litigate for the benefit of the stockholders or the creditors, except where the corporation had been guilty of fraud against its creditors. Turner v. Henshaw, 86 Ind. App. 565, 155 N.E. 222 (1927).

The receiver of a corporation could maintain an action to recover assets illegally transferred without joining persons for whose benefit the action was brought. Mercantile Com. Bank v. Southwestern Ind. Coal Corp., 93 Ind. App. 313, 169 N.E. 91, 171 N.E. 310 (1929).

—Foreign Receivers.
Receivers appointed in other states could sue in this state. Metzner v. Bauer, 98 Ind. 425 (1884); Catlin v. Wilcox Silver-Plate Co., 123 Ind. 477, 24 N.E. 250, 8 L.R.A. 62, 18 Am. St. R. 338 (1890).

—In Receiver's Name.
Prior to the enactment of IC 32-4-5-1, a receiver could not have sued in his own name unless authorized by some special statute or by the order of the court appointing him. Manlove v. Burger, 38 Ind. 211 (1871); Garver v. Kent, 70 Ind. 428 (1880).

Even then, the statute regulating mutual insurance companies authorized receivers of such companies to sue in their own names. Manlove v. Burger, 38 Ind. 211 (1871).

A receiver could sue in his own name without an order of court to recover possession of property from his lessees. Pouder v. Catterson, 127 Ind. 434, 26 N.E. 66 (1891).

A receiver must show that authority has been conferred upon him, in his representative capacity, to maintain the action. Davis v. Talbot, 128 Ind. 222, 27 N.E. 494 (1891).

—Leave to Sue Receiver.
In a suit to forfeit franchise of corporation in hands of receiver, the receiver could neither sue nor be sued without leave obtained by the court which made the appointment. Wayne Pike Co. v. State ex rel. Whitaker, 134 Ind. 672, 34 N.E. 440 (1893).

When authority to sue was not denied, no proof was required. Ayres v. Foster, 25 Ind. App. 99, 57 N.E. 725 (1906); Henry v. Epstein, 50 Ind. App. 660, 95 N.E. 275 (1911).

It was not necessary to allege that the court had granted leave to sue the receiver when the complaint was filed in the court appointing him. Curtis v. Mauger, 186 Ind. 118, 114 N.E. 408 (1916).

Continuation of Business.
Where a receiver was appointed, the court had the right to direct the receiver to continue the business and to contract and to incur obligations that became a charge on the property. Blythe v. Gibbons, 141 Ind. 332, 35 N.E. 557 (1893); Heisen v. Binz, 147 Ind. 284, 45 N.E. 104 (1896); Brunner, Mond & Co. v. Central Glass Co., 18 Ind. App. 174, 47 N.E. 686, 63 Am. St. R. 339 (1897).

Where the mortgaged property was used for business purposes of such nature that a discontinuation of the business would destroy or greatly impair the value of the property, the court could authorize the receiver to carry on the business while he remained in charge. Leader Publishing Co. v. Grant Trust & Sav. Co., 182 Ind. 651, 108 N.E. 121 (1915).

Whether a receiver should be ordered to continue the business or reduce the assets to cash was a matter for the sound discretion of the trial court. Portage Brick Co. v. North Ind. Brick Co., 189 Ind. 639, 128 N.E. 847 (1920).

Contracts.
The authority of a receiver to assign a contract could only have been put in issue by a pleading under oath. Vannoy v. Duprez, 72 Ind. 26 (1880).

Contracts by receiver without court approval did not become a lien or charge against the property in the hands of the receiver, since persons dealing with the receiver were bound to know that he possessed limited powers and was constantly subject to the orders of the power which created him. Brunner, Mond & Co. v. Central Glass Co., 18 Ind. App. 174, 47 N.E. 686, 63 Am. St. R. 339 (1897).

Where the owner of real estate executed a contract to sell the same on payments and thereafter placed a mortgage thereon, on the foreclosure of such mortgage and the appointment of a receiver for the property, the purchaser was liable to the receiver for the amounts paid on the purchase-price to the mortgagor after notice of the mortgage and of the appointment of receiver. Railroadmens Bldg. Sav. Ass'n v. Rifner, 88 Ind. App. 580, 163 N.E. 236 (1928).

Control by Court.
Courts appointing receivers had entire control over the property and funds of the receivership, and the receiver could not question

Control by Court. (Cont'd)
any order of the court. Herrick v. Miller, 123 Ind. 304, 24 N.E. 111 (1890).

Ordinarily, a receiver had no discretion in the application of the funds in his hands by virtue of the receivership, but held them strictly subject to the order of the court, and to be disposed of as the court might direct, and he had no authority to determine the amounts to be allowed for the services of himself or his attorney. Citizens Trust Co. v. Wheeling Can Co., 199 Ind. 311, 157 N.E. 441 (1927).

Due Process.

—Insufficient.
Lessee has a property interest in the leasehold that is an important interest worthy of due process protections, and when a receiver of the lessor rejected a lease, the lessee was deprived of her property interest in that lease without due process. Bowlby v. NBD Bank, 640 N.E.2d 1095 (Ind. App. 1994).

—State Action.
The acts of a court-appointed receiver are "state action" for due process purposes. Bowlby v. NBD Bank, 640 N.E.2d 1095 (Ind. App. 1994).

—Sufficient.
Where the trial court authorized receiver to retain custody and use of property pending an adjudication of any adverse claims, and lessee of seized property was given notice of this and an opportunity to have her claims of ownership heard, as to the personal property, the lessee was afforded due process protections. Bowlby v. NBD Bank, 640 N.E.2d 1095 (Ind. App. 1994).

Jurisdiction over Property.
The jurisdiction of receivers over property was only coextensive with the jurisdiction of the courts appointing them. Catlin v. Wilcox Silver-Plate Co., 123 Ind. 477, 24 N.E. 250, 80 L.R.A. 62, 18 Am. St. R. 338 (1890).

A receiver had only such powers as were conferred by statute and the order of the court under which he was appointed; a receiver took all property of the debtor which constituted the subject of the action and was within the jurisdiction of the court, but he did not take property not involved in the action or not included in an order designating the particular property of which the receiver was to have charge. State ex rel. Pancol v. Cleveland, 241 Ind. 206, 171 N.E.2d 255 (1961).

A receiver had no right to property which did not belong to the debtor for whose property he was the receiver. State ex rel. Pancol v. Cleveland, 241 Ind. 206, 171 N.E.2d 255 (1961).

Leases.

—Factors Considered.
In determining whether to seek approval to reject a lease, the receiver should be guided by considerations as to whether the lease would be "unduly burdensome or imperil the fund entrusted to his care." Bowlby v. NBD Bank, 640 N.E.2d 1095 (Ind. App. 1994).

Possession of Property.
A receiver duly appointed was empowered by former IC 34-48-1-7 (repealed; see this section for similar provisions) of the statute, under the control of the court or judge thereof in vacation, to take and keep possession of the property. Chicago & S.E. Ry. v. Kenney, 29 Ind. App. 506, 68 N.E. 20 (1902).

A receiver for an insolvent, appointed for the purpose of winding up its affairs, took the property of the insolvent impressed with the then legal or equitable rights of creditors. Irwin's Bank v. Fletcher Sav. & Trust Co., 195 Ind. 669, 145 N.E. 869, 146 N.E. 909 (1924).

Removal of House from Realty.
In a suit to foreclose a mechanic's lien, the court had authority to authorize the receiver appointed in the suit to remove from the realty a small house, other than the new dwelling, which lessened the value of the realty. Flanders v. Ostrom, 206 Ind. 87, 187 N.E. 673 (1933).

Sale of Property.
Property in possession of a receiver was not subject to sale under execution. Knode v. Baldridge, 73 Ind. 54 (1880).

Receivers could not purchase for their own benefit property connected with the receivership. Herrick v. Miller, 123 Ind. 304, 24 N.E. 111 (1890).

On the foreclosure of a mortgage on personal property that was in the hands of a receiver, the court could direct that the receiver instead of the sheriff sell the property. Leader Publishing Co. v. Grant Trust & Sav. Co., 182 Ind. 651, 108 N.E. 121 (1915).

In a suit to foreclose a mechanic's lien, the court had jurisdiction to authorize the receiver appointed in the case to sell the realty. Flanders v. Ostrom, 206 Ind. 87, 187 N.E. 673 (1933).

Notwithstanding the restrictions imposed by statute, the articles of incorporation and the provisions of the stock certificates, where there were ample facts proved to justify it, preferred stockholders were entitled to an order in receivership proceedings requiring the receiver to sell the assets. Zumpfe v. Piccadilly Realty Co., 214 Ind. 282, 13 N.E.2d 715, 15 N.E.2d 362, 124 A.L.R. 1060 (1938).

Former IC 34-48-1-7 (repealed; see this section for similar provisions) inferentially

Sale of Property. (Cont'd)

recognized the power of a court to order a sale in a receivership proceeding. Zumpfe v. Piccadilly Realty Co., 214 Ind. 282, 13 N.E.2d 715, 15 N.E.2d 362, 124 A.L.R. 1060 (1938).

Third Parties.

Until the receiver was appointed and actually in possession, third parties were not affected by the order. The appointment cannot be attacked collaterally. Cook v. Citizens Nat'l Bank, 73 Ind. 256 (1881).

Persons dealing with a receiver had to take notice of his limited powers. Brunner, Mond & Co. v. Central Glass Co., 18 Ind. App. 174, 47 N.E. 686, 63 Am. St. R. 339 (1897).

32-30-5-8. Partial admission — Enforcement. — If the answer of the defendant admits part of the plaintiff's claim to be just, the court, on motion, may order the defendant to satisfy that part of the claim and may enforce the order by execution. [P.L.2-2002, § 15.]

32-30-5-9. Notice required prior to appointment. — Receivers may not be appointed in any case until the adverse party has appeared or has had reasonable notice of the application for the appointment, except upon sufficient cause shown by affidavit. [P.L.2-2002, § 15.]

NOTES TO DECISIONS

ANALYSIS

In general.
Adequate remedy at law.
Affidavit.
Affidavit in record.
Ancillary action.
Appearance of adverse party.
Necessity notice.
—Summons and appearance.
Temporary restraining order sufficient.
Without notice.
—Cause insufficient.
—Complaint.
—Court's discretion.
—Emergency.
—Evidence.
—Information and belief.

In General.

Facts, not conclusions, must have been pleaded to have alleged a sufficient cause for this act to be applied without notice. Indianapolis Mach. Co. v. Curd, 247 Ind. 657, 9 Ind. Dec. 359, 221 N.E.2d 340 (1966).

Adequate Remedy at Law.

A receiver would not be appointed where plaintiff had a remedy at law unless there was a showing that the remedy would not be adequate or effectual. Morris v. Nixon, 223 Ind. 530, 62 N.E.2d 772 (1942).

Where, in an action by an administratrix for the appointment of a receiver for a restaurant business allegedly owned by plaintiff's decedent, there was an allegation in the complaint showing that defendants, who allegedly had taken possession of the business, were insolvent or in imminent danger of insolvency, plaintiff failed to show that she did not have a complete and adequate remedy at law as provided by IC 29-1-13-10, creating liability against persons intermeddling with the property of a decedent's estate. Morris v. Nixon, 223 Ind. 530, 62 N.E.2d 772 (1942).

The provisions of this statute as to appointment of a receiver must have been strictly complied with, in absence of a verified complaint or affidavit showing that neither the ordinary procedure for appointment which required notice to be given nor an attachment or restraining order until notice could be given and a receiver appointed, was an adequate remedy. Rotan v. Cummins, 236 Ind. 394, 140 N.E.2d 505 (1957).

Affidavit.

The affidavits must have set out facts showing not only a necessity for the appointment of a receiver but must have also shown necessity for not giving notice to the adverse party. Wabash R.R. v. Dykeman, 133 Ind. 56, 32 N.E. 823 (1892); Henderson v. Reynolds, 168 Ind. 522, 81 N.E. 494, 11 L.R.A. (n.s.) 960, 11 Ann. Cas. 377 (1907); Marshall v. Matson, 171 Ind. 238, 86 N.E. 339 (1908); Mannos v. Bishop-Babcock-Becker Co., 181 Ind. 343, 104 N.E. 579 (1914); Ryder v. Shea, 183 Ind. 15, 108 N.E. 104 (1915); General Motors Oil Co. v. Matheny, 185 Ind. 114, 113 N.E. 4 (1916); Kent Ave. Grocery Co. v. George Hitz & Co., 187 Ind. 606, 120 N.E. 659 (1918).

An affidavit on "information and belief" was not sufficient to authorize the appointment of a receiver without notice. Henderson v. Reynolds, 168 Ind. 522, 81 N.E. 494, 11 L.R.A. (n.s.) 960, 11 Ann. Cas. 977 (1907); Mannos v. Bishop-Babcock-Becker Co., 181 Ind. 343, 104

Affidavit. (Cont'd)
N.E. 579 (1914); McFerran v. Grube, 182 Ind. 713, 106 N.E. 719 (1914); Ledger Publishing Co. v. Scott, 193 Ind. 683, 141 N.E. 609 (1923); Jordan v. Walker, 197 Ind. 365, 151 N.E. 2 (1926).

The statute provided that a receiver should not be appointed without notice "except upon sufficient cause shown by affidavit." This meant that facts showing sufficient cause must have been stated in a verified complaint or in affidavit or affidavits supporting a complaint. Bookout v. Foreman, 198 Ind. 543, 154 N.E. 387 (1926); State ex rel. Red Dragon Diner, Inc. v. Superior Court, 239 Ind. 384, 158 N.E.2d 164 (1959).

Where a verified complaint alleged that an emergency existed for the immediate appointment of a receiver for an alleged incompetent without notice, but no affidavits were filed, the evidence was insufficient to justify the appointment of a receiver without notice. Hizer v. Hizer, 201 Ind. 406, 169 N.E. 47 (1929).

When a receiver was appointed without notice, the only evidence under former IC 34-48-1-9 (repealed; see this section for similar provisions) which was proper to be considered by the court must have been in the form of affidavits, which also could include the verified complaint. Second Real Estate Inv., Inc. v. Johann, 232 Ind. 24, 111 N.E.2d 467 (1953).

An affidavit, which could have included or consisted of a verified complaint, was only evidence proper for appointment of a receiver without notice. Albert Johann & Sons Co. v. Berges, 238 Ind. 265, 150 N.E.2d 568 (1958).

Facts justifying relief sought must have been shown by an affidavit or verified complaint and not mere conclusions of a plaintiff, for appointment of a receiver without notice. Albert Johann & Sons Co. v. Berges, 238 Ind. 265, 150 N.E.2d 568 (1958).

Where the complaint was not verified in positive terms, but merely recited that plaintiffs believed the representations therein were "true and correct to the best of their knowledge," and where it was not accompanied by a separate affidavit alleging facts justifying dispensation from notice, the requirements of former IC 34-48-1-9 (repealed; see now this section for similar provisions) were not met and no receiver should have been appointed without notice. Environmental Control Sys. v. Allison, 161 Ind. App. 148, 43 Ind. Dec. 176, 314 N.E.2d 820 (1974).

Affidavit in Record.
The affidavits in support of the application for the appointment of a receiver without notice must have been filed and placed of record in the cause in which the receiver was appointed. Sullivan Elec. Light & Power Co. v.

Blue, 142 Ind. 407, 41 N.E. 805 (1895); Marshall v. Matson, 171 Ind. 238, 86 N.E. 339 (1908).

The rule was otherwise under the earlier statute. Eureka Lumber Co. v. Buff & Blue Oolitic Stone Co., 157 Ind. 213, 60 N.E. 1067 (1901).

The affidavits were a part of the record without a bill of exceptions under the Practice Code of 1903 (§ 2-3104, since repealed. See Rule AP 7.2 for present provisions). Marshall v. Matson, 171 Ind. 238, 86 N.E. 339 (1908).

Ancillary Action.
The consent of parties to the appointment of a receiver would not confer jurisdiction on the court when no action was pending between the parties. Pressley v. Harrison, 102 Ind. 14, 1 N.E. 188 (1885).

Except in the appointment of a receiver for a corporation because of insolvency or danger of insolvency, the action for a receiver was not and could not be an independent action, but was ancillary to an action and a part of it. Supreme Sitting of Order of Iron Hall v. Baker, 134 Ind. 293, 33 N.E. 1128, 20 L.R.A. 210 (1893); State v. Union Nat'l Bank, 145 Ind. 537, 44 N.E. 585, 57 Am. St. R. 209 (1896); Sheridan Brick Works v. Marion Trust Co., 157 Ind. 292, 61 N.E. 666, 87 Am. St. R. 207 (1901); Tucker v. Tucker, 194 Ind. 108, 142 N.E. 11 (1924); Hay v. McDaniel, 26 Ind. App. 683, 60 N.E. 729 (1901).

Appearance of Adverse Party.
The appearance requirement of former IC 34-48-1-9 (repealed; see this section for similar provisions) was met where the person whose property is placed in receivership sets out the parameters of a court's inquiry over the propriety of a receivership over his personal assets by his own pleading. In re Gore, 527 N.E.2d 191 (Ind. App. 1988).

Necessity Notice.
If the appointment of a receiver was prayed for as final relief, no other notice was required than that given of the main action. Newell v. Schnull, 73 Ind. 241 (1881); Winchester Elec. Light Co. v. Gordon, 143 Ind. 681, 42 N.E. 914 (1896).

Notice of the application would have been presumed on appeal when the record was silent. Miller v. Shriner, 86 Ind. 493 (1882).

It was an error to appoint a receiver in chambers on an allegation of emergency where no notice was given to the defendant and where there was no affidavit showing sufficient cause for an appointment without notice. Winchester Elec. Light Co. v. Gordon, 143 Ind. 681, 42 N.E. 914 (1896).

—Summons and Appearance.
There was a sufficient appearance to justify

Necessity Notice. (Cont'd)

—Summons and Appearance. (Cont'd)
the appointment of a receiver without notice where one of the partners in the firm sought to be placed in receivership appeared at the time the appointment was sought and made an answer. Pressley v. Lamb, 105 Ind. 171, 4 N.E. 682 (1886).

An appearance by a defendant to an application for the appointment of a receiver was a waiver of the service of notice. Pressley v. Lamb, 105 Ind. 171, 4 N.E. 682 (1886); First Nat'l Bank v. United States Encaustic Tile Co., 105 Ind. 227, 4 N.E. 846 (1886).

There was not a sufficient appearance to justify the appointment of a receiver where there was a paper filed purporting to be an answer signed by a nonresident and there was no appearance by the defendant or anyone assuming to act for the defendant. State v. Union Nat'l Bank, 145 Ind. 537, 44 N.E. 585, 57 Am. St. R. 209 (1896).

If a receiver was appointed without notice before the summons issued in the action was delivered to the sheriff, the appointment was void. Marshall v. Matson, 171 Ind. 238, 86 N.E. 339 (1908).

Temporary Restraining Order Sufficient.
A receiver should not have been appointed without notice where a temporary restraining order would have been ample for the protection of all interests until notice could be given and the application for a receiver determined on its merits. Henderson v. Reynolds, 168 Ind. 522, 81 N.E. 494, 11 L.R.A. (n.s.) 960, 11 Ann. Cas. 977 (1907); Ryder v. Shea, 183 Ind. 15, 108 N.E. 104 (1915); Kent Ave. Grocery Co. v. George Hitz & Co., 187 Ind. 606, 120 N.E. 659 (1918); Tucker v. Tucker, 194 Ind. 108, 142 N.E. 11 (1924); Hizer v. Hizer, 201 Ind. 406, 169 N.E. 47 (1929); Indiana Merchants Protective Ass'n v. Little, 202 Ind. 193, 172 N.E. 905 (1930); Tormohlen v. Tormohlen, 210 Ind. 328, 1 N.E.2d 596 (1936); Hawkins v. Aldridge, 211 Ind. 332, 7 N.E.2d 33, 109 A.L.R. 1205 (1937); Largura Constr. Co. v. Super-Steel Prods. Co., 216 Ind. 58, 22 N.E.2d 990 (1939).

Without Notice.

—Cause Insufficient.
A mere statement of opinion or conclusions as to such necessity, even though made under oath, would not justify the appointment of a receiver without notice. Wabash R.R. v. Dykeman, 133 Ind. 56, 32 N.E. 823 (1892); Continental Clay & Mining Co. v. Bryson, 168 Ind. 485, 81 N.E. 210 (1907); Ryder v. Shea, 183 Ind. 15, 108 N.E. 104 (1915); General Motors Oil Co. v. Matheny, 185 Ind. 114, 113 N.E. 4 (1916); Tucker v. Tucker, 194 Ind. 108,

142 N.E. 11 (1923); Hizer v. Hizer, 201 Ind. 406, 169 N.E. 47 (1929).

A receiver should not have been appointed for a corporation without notice when it had an office in the county, and it was not shown that delay would cause a destruction of property or an irreparable injury. Wabash R.R. v. Dykeman, 133 Ind. 56, 32 N.E. 823 (1892); Sullivan Elec. Light & Power Co. v. Blue, 142 Ind. 407, 41 N.E. 805 (1895); Continental Clay & Mining Co. v. Bryson, 168 Ind. 485, 81 N.E. 210 (1907); Kent Ave. Grocery Co. v. George Hitz & Co., 187 Ind. 606, 120 N.E. 659 (1918); Welfare Loan Soc'y v. Seward, 193 Ind. 541, 141 N.E. 221 (1923).

An application for the appointment of a receiver alleging that applicant had been told certain things regarding the property in controversy, and that he "believed" certain things in relation to said property, was not sufficient to establish his right to have a receiver appointed without notice, notwithstanding the fact that the application was verified by an oath that the matters and things thereon stated were true "in substance and in fact." Jordan v. Walker, 197 Ind. 365, 151 N.E. 2 (1926).

A receiver should not have been appointed for real estate without giving notice to the owner thereof, although the former owner had transferred it to his wife with the intent to avoid payment of a note, and she, with like intent, transferred it to the holder thereof at the time of the application for a receiver, where it did not appear that said holder was a nonresident, or that plaintiff's interest could not be properly protected by a restraining order. Bookout v. Foreman, 198 Ind. 543, 154 N.E. 387 (1926).

A complaint alleging that defendant's funds were being wrongfully paid out, that the income would be wasted, and that plaintiff would lose its entire security for the indebtedness, did not justify the appointment of a receiver without notice. Indiana Merchants Protective Ass'n v. Little, 202 Ind. 193, 172 N.E. 905 (1930).

In a divorce case, where it was alleged in the complaint for the appointment of a receiver to take charge of defendant's property and business that defendant was the owner of a large amount of personal property consisting of valuable blooded livestock, horses, cattle, and hogs; that he operated a large and extensive chicken hatchery, and sold chickens over a large territory of the United States, and dealt in poultry and eggs, and was the owner of property of the value of $60,000, and had an annual income of $10,000; that defendant's whereabouts were not known to plaintiff; but it was not alleged in the complaint for appointment of receiver that in his absence he did not have some competent person or persons in charge of his business, plaintiff was

Without Notice. (Cont'd)

—Cause Insufficient. (Cont'd)
not entitled to the appointment of a receiver without notice to take charge of defendant's business and property. Tormohlen v. Tormohlen, 210 Ind. 328, 1 N.E.2d 596 (1936).

Notice of an interlocutory hearing for appointment of a receiver was not dispensed with because such appointment was prayed for as a part of the final relief; nor did such fact, together with the fact that the appointment was made in open court, dispense with the necessity of showing cause by affidavit or giving defendant an opportunity to be heard, to cross-examine witnesses, and to offer countervailing evidence. Hawkins v. Aldridge, 211 Ind. 332, 7 N.E.2d 34, 109 A.L.R. 1205 (1937).

To justify a receivership without notice the defendant must have been beyond the jurisdiction of the court and there must have been a specific statement of facts, the necessity for a receiver, and a valid reason for the absence of notice. Largura Constr. Co. v. Super-Steel Prods. Co., 216 Ind. 58, 22 N.E.2d 990 (1939).

Where complaint merely alleged "that the defendant is insolvent and owes a large amount of indebtedness and claims which it is unable to pay," such allegation was not a statement of facts sufficient to authorize the court to appoint a receiver without notice or to exercise any discretion regarding such an appointment. State ex rel. Red Dragon Diner, Inc. v. Superior Court, 239 Ind. 384, 158 N.E.2d 164 (1959).

The trial court was without jurisdiction to appoint a receiver over relator, the record indicating that no notice was given to him. State ex rel. Mammoth Dev. & Constr. Consultants, Inc. v. Superior Court, 265 Ind. 573, 55 Ind. Dec. 449, 357 N.E.2d 732 (1976).

Affidavit of plaintiff alleging that he "feels" that he will not be paid, that he "feels" there is a pressing emergency, that he "knows" there are insufficient funds and he has "reason to believe" that defendant would misapply the cash assets, without alleging facts, was insufficient to support the appointment of a receiver without notice. Meek v. Steele, 174 Ind. App. 497, 59 Ind. Dec. 411, 368 N.E.2d 257 (1977).

—Complaint.
In an application for appointment of a receiver without notice, where there were no affidavits filed in support of the application, the Supreme Court could look only to the allegations of the verified complaint in determining the sufficiency of the showing of necessity for dispensing with the giving of notice. Tormohlen v. Tormohlen, 210 Ind. 328, 1 N.E.2d 596 (1936).

Facts showing cause for appointment of a receiver without notice, as provided in former IC 34-48-1-9 (repealed, see now this section for similar provisions), must have been stated in the application for appointment and in the affidavit or affidavits; mere opinions or conclusions were not sufficient. Tormohlen v. Tormohlen, 210 Ind. 328, 1 N.E.2d 596 (1936).

Under former IC 34-48-1-9 (repealed; see this section for similar provisions), before a receiver would have been appointed without notice, it must have appeared, either in the verified complaint or by affidavit, not only that there was a cause for the appointment, but that there was cause for such appointment without notice. Tormohlen v. Tormohlen, 210 Ind. 328, 1 N.E.2d 596 (1936).

In a suit for appointment for receiver without notice, it was not necessary that the verified application particularly describe the property, where it was alleged to be or about to be wasted or removed from the court's jurisdiction. H-A Circus Operating Corp. v. Silberstein, 215 Ind. 413, 19 N.E.2d 1013 (1939).

In an action for the appointment of a receiver without notice, the complaint must not only have alleged sufficient reason for the appointment of a receiver, but there must also have been a showing that an emergency was imminent requiring such appointment without notice. Morris v. Nixon, 223 Ind. 530, 62 N.E.2d 772 (1945).

Where no affidavits were filed in support of a verified complaint for the appointment of a receiver without notice, the court could look only to the allegations of fact set out in the complaint in determining the sufficiency of the showing to dispense with the necessity of notice. Morris v. Nixon, 223 Ind. 530, 62 N.E.2d 772 (1945).

Where, in an action by an administratrix for the appointment of a receiver for a restaurant business allegedly owned by plaintiff's decedent, the complaint was silent as to when defendants took possession of the business and hence contained nothing to show that plaintiff could not have reasonably anticipated the injury complained of in time to have given notice of the application for the receiver, there was no showing of diligence required to warrant the appointment of a receiver without notice. Morris v. Nixon, 223 Ind. 530, 62 N.E.2d 772 (1945).

Where, in an action for the appointment of a receiver without notice, there was no allegation that notice could not be served on defendants, and no reason was shown why a restraining order could not have been issued and served at the time the petition was filed restraining defendants from disposing of the property in question until a notice and hearing could be had on the application for appointment of the receiver, and there was no showing that such restraining order would

Without Notice. (Cont'd)

—Complaint. (Cont'd)
not have been ample to protect the property until the hearing, the appointment of a receiver without notice was error. Morris v. Nixon, 223 Ind. 530, 62 N.E.2d 772 (1945).

For the appointment of a receiver without notice, complaint had to show (1) a probability that plaintiff would be entitled to judgment, (2) that there was sufficient cause for appointment of a receiver without notice, (3) that plaintiff's rights could not be protected by a restraining order or other adequate remedy and, if shown, that it had to be further shown that the emergency necessitating the appointment could not have been given in time to give notice or that waste or loss was threatened and delay until notice could be given would defeat object of the suit. Albert Johann & Sons Co. v. Berges, 238 Ind. 265, 150 N.E.2d 568 (1958).

The court looked only to the facts stated in the verified complaint in determining the necessity of dispensing with the giving of notice; the complaint must not only have alleged facts which supported the plaintiff's right to the appointment of a receiver after notice, it must also have stated specific facts which established: (1) that an emergency existed which rendered interference necessary before there was time to give notice in order to prevent waste, destruction or loss, (2) that protection could not have been afforded in any other way, (3) that plaintiff could not reasonably have anticipated the injury in time to give notice. State ex rel. Red Dragon Diner, Inc. v. Superior Court, 239 Ind. 384, 158 N.E.2d 164 (1959).

—Court's Discretion.
The court, and not the complainant, determined whether the facts warranted the appointment of a receiver without notice. Hizer v. Hizer, 201 Ind. 406, 169 N.E. 47 (1929).

—Emergency.
A court was not justified in appointing a receiver without notice when the complaint did not show that the property or any part of the same was about to be wasted, misappropriated or removed beyond the jurisdiction of the court, and that delay might entirely defeat the object of the suit. Chicago & S.E. Ry. v. Cason, 133 Ind. 49, 32 N.E. 827 (1892); Wabash R.R. v. Dykeman, 133 Ind. 56, 32 N.E. 823 (1892); Sullivan Elec. Light & Power Co. v. Blue, 142 Ind. 407, 41 N.E. 805 (1895); Marshall v. Matson, 171 Ind. 238, 86 N.E. 339 (1908); Mannos v. Bishop-Babcock-Becker Co., 181 Ind. 343, 104 N.E. 579 (1914); General Motors Oil Co. v. Matheny, 185 Ind. 114, 113 N.E. 4 (1916).

In order to justify the appointment of a receiver without notice, the defendant must have been beyond the jurisdiction of the court or not to be found, and there must have been an emergency making it necessary to appoint a receiver to prevent waste, destruction or loss of property, or the facts must have been such that to give notice would have jeopardized the custody or control of the property which was sought by the appointment of a receiver. If a temporary restraining order against the defendant would protect the property in question, a receiver should not have been appointed without notice. Continental Clay & Mining Co. v. Bryson, 168 Ind. 485, 181 N.E. 210 (1907); Henderson v. Reynolds, 168 Ind. 522, 81 N.E. 494, 11 L.R.A. (n.s.) 960, 11 Ann. Cas. 977 (1907); Ryder v. Shea, 183 Ind. 15, 108 N.E. 104 (1915); Kent Ave. Grocery Co. v. George Hitz & Co., 187 Ind. 606, 120 N.E. 659 (1918); Orin Jessup Land Co. v. Lannes, 193 Ind. 645, 141 N.E. 454 (1923); Ledger Publishing Co. v. Scott, 193 Ind. 683, 141 N.E. 609 (1923); Tucker v. Tucker, 194 Ind. 108, 142 N.E. 11 (1924); Hizer v. Hizer, 201 Ind. 406, 169 N.E. 47 (1929).

A receiver should not have been appointed without notice except where facts existed from which an emergency arose rendering interference necessary before there was time to give notice, in order to prevent waste, destruction or loss, and on a showing that protection could not have been afforded to the applicant in any other way. Bookout v. Foreman, 198 Ind. 543, 154 N.E. 387 (1926); Morris v. Nixon, 223 Ind. 530, 62 N.E.2d 772 (1945).

Allegations that an emergency existed for the appointment of a receiver without notice, and that necessity existed for immediate appointment, were not allegations of fact justifying appointment of a receiver without notice. Hizer v. Hizer, 201 Ind. 406, 169 N.E. 47 (1929).

The appointment of a receiver without notice or appearance was authorized only on showing by affidavit that there was no other remedy, and that an immediate necessity existed for such action. Firestone Coal Mining Co. v. Roetzel, 201 Ind. 430, 169 N.E. 465 (1930).

Cause for appointing a receiver with out notice must have been evidenced by the existence of facts from which an emergency arose, rendering interference before there was time to give notice necessary in order to prevent waste, destruction, or loss, and showing that protection could not be afforded plaintiff in any other way. Tormohlen v. Tormohlen, 210 Ind. 328, 1 N.E.2d 596 (1936).

A receiver would be appointed without notice only when plaintiff could be proteced in no other way and upon a showing that plaintiff would be entitled to judgment, that immediate injury was about to be inflicted, that

Without Notice. (Cont'd)

—Emergency. (Cont'd)
there was immediate necessity for a receiver without notice, and that plaintiff could not reasonably have anticipated the injury in time to have given notice. Hawkins v. Aldridge, 211 Ind. 332, 7 N.E.2d 34, 109 A.L.R. 1205 (1937).

Where, in an action by owners of interests in oil leases against nonresident owners for appointment of a receiver to preserve their interests therein upon which, by operating contract, they had given plaintiff a lien, a temporary restraining order would not be availing, no other adequate remedy at law existed, waste and loss were threatened, and the emergency could not be anticipated in time for the service of notice, the appointment of a receiver without notice was not an abuse of discretion. Meyering v. Petroleum Holdings, Inc., 227 Ind. 313, 86 N.E.2d 78 (1949).

The receiver was appointed without notice. Such ex parte hearings were to be avoided where possible. It was only in extreme cases that a court could exercise such unusual powers. There must have existed a pressing emergency which showed that waste, loss or destruction of property would probably occur before reasonable notice could have been given and the parties heard and the lack of any other available remedy, before a court could appoint a receiver on an ex parte hearing. Fagan v. Clark, 238 Ind. 22, 148 N.E.2d 407 (1958).

—Evidence.
On an application for the appointment of a receiver without notice, the only evidence admissible was the verified complaint and the affidavits filed therewith. Sullivan Elec. Light & Power Co. v. Blue, 142 Ind. 407, 41 N.E. 805 (1895); Marshall v. Matson, 171 Ind. 238, 86 N.E. 339 (1908); General Motors Oil Co. v. Matheny, 185 Ind. 114, 113 N.E. 4 (1918); Kent Ave. Grocery Co. v. George Hitz & Co.,

187 Ind. 606, 120 N.E. 659 (1918); Hizer v. Hizer, 201 Ind. 406, 169 N.E. 47 (1929).

Oral evidence was not admissible in a proceeding for appointment of a receiver without notice, and would not have been considered on appeal. Indiana Merchants Protective Ass'n v. Little, 202 Ind. 193, 172 N.E. 905 (1930).

Facts showing cause for appointment of a receiver without notice must have been stated in the verified complaint or affidavits, and not by mere opinions or conclusions. Indiana Merchants Protective Ass'n v. Little, 202 Ind. 193, 172 N.E. 905 (1930).

The fact that a court of another state had appointed a receiver for a corporation was sufficient ground for the appointment of an ancillary receiver for intangible property of the corporation situated in this state, on a proper showing by plaintiff. H-A Circus Operating Corp. v. Silberstein, 215 Ind. 413, 19 N.E.2d 1013 (1939).

Former IC 34-48-1-9 (repealed; see this section for similar provisions) authorized the appointment of a receiver without notice, "upon sufficient cause shown by affidavit." H-A Circus Operating Corp. v. Silberstein, 215 Ind. 413, 19 N.E.2d 1013 (1939).

—Information and Belief.
To the extent that a petition for appointment of a receiver without notice was verified upon information and belief it could not be considered. Hawkins v. Aldridge, 211 Ind. 332, 7 N.E.2d 34, 109 A.L.R. 1205 (1937).

In application for appointment of receiver without notice, the verification of the complaint by plaintiff's attorneys, as follows: "That the matters and things set forth in the above and foregoing application for receiver without notice is true in substance and in fact," was not subject to the objection that the verification was based upon information and belief. H-A Circus Operating Corp. v. Silberstein, 215 Ind. 413, 19 N.E.2d 1013 (1939).

32-30-5-10. Appeal. — (a) In all cases commenced or pending in any Indiana court in which a receiver may be appointed or refused, the party aggrieved may, within ten (10) days after the court's decision, appeal the court's decision to the supreme court without awaiting the final determination of the case.

(b) In cases where a receiver will be or has been appointed, upon the appellant filing of an appeal bond:

(1) with sufficient surety;

(2) in the same amount as was required of the receiver; and

(3) conditioned for the due prosecution of the appeal and the payment of all costs or damages that may accrue to any officer or person because of the appeal;

the authority of the receiver shall be suspended until the final determination of the appeal. [P.L.2-2002, § 15.]

NOTES TO DECISIONS

ANALYSIS

In general.
Aggrieved parties.
Appealable decision.
Appeal-bond.
Bill of exceptions.
Corporation dissolved after appeal taken.
Court rule.
Exceptions.
Impairment of collateral.
Joint appeals.
Jurisdiction.
Matters reviewed.
Motion for new trial.
Motion to dismiss appeal.
Motion to set aside appointment.
Possession pending appeal.
Procedure on appeal.
Sufficiency of complaint.
Supreme and appellate courts.
Time for perfecting appeal.

In General.

An appeal may be taken from an order appointing, or refusing to appoint, a receiver. Dale v. Kent, 58 Ind. 584 (1877); Pressley v. Lamb, 105 Ind. 171, 4 N.E. 682 (1886); Wabash R.R. v. Dykeman, 133 Ind. 56, 32 N.E. 823 (1892); Daugherty v. Payne, 175 Ind. 603, 95 N.E. 233 (1911); Lewis v. Nielson, 176 Ind. 414, 96 N.E. 145 (1911); General Motors Oil Co. v. Matheny, 185 Ind. 114, 113 N.E. 4 (1916); Standard Elec. Mfg. Co. v. Tuttle, 74 Ind. App. 559, 126 N.E. 438 (1920).

When an appeal was taken from an order of court appointing or refusing to appoint a receiver, the statute regulating the taking of such appeals must have been strictly followed, as must have been the General Practice Code. Daugherty v. Payne, 175 Ind. 603, 95 N.E. 233 (1911); Lewis v. Nielson, 176 Ind. 414, 96 N.E. 145 (1911); General Motors Oil Co. v. Matheny, 185 Ind. 114, 113 N.E. 4 (1916).

The court would not consider whether there was sufficient evidence to authorize appointment of a receiver without notice when no appeal was perfected from such appointment but appeal was taken from the order appointing the receiver after notice. Stair v. Meissel, 207 Ind. 280, 192 N.E. 453 (1934).

Where a statute providing for appeal from an order appointing a receiver provided no method of perfecting the appeal, the court could look to other provisions of the code in pari materia to determine what steps should have been taken to perfect the appeal.

O'Malley v. Hankins, 207 Ind. 589, 194 N.E. 168 (1935).

Upon appeal from appointment of receiver, the court would not pass upon the sufficiency of the complaint, but only upon the sufficiency of the showing of necessity of a receiver. O'Malley v. Hankins, 207 Ind. 589, 194 N.E. 168 (1935).

An appeal from interlocutory order appointing a receiver to take charge of certain real estate and collect the rents and profits pending the litigation would have been dismissed on failure of appellant to perfect the appeal within ten days from the date of appointment of the receiver, as required by former IC 34-48-1-10 (repealed; see this section for similar provisions). Catherwood v. Morgan, 209 Ind. 260, 198 N.E. 301, 101 A.L.R. 682 (1935).

A court could appoint, without notice, a receiver for a named defendant corporation, but could not in such action adjudicate conflicting claims of third parties and the defendant for whom the receiver was appointed. Kelley, Glover, Vale Realty Co. v. Kramer, 211 Ind. 321, 6 N.E.2d 963 (1937).

Where the transcript and assignment of error was not filed in the office of the clerk of the Supreme Court until 11 days after the order of court appointing a receiver, such filing was not within the time required to perfect an appeal. Hill v. Lincoln Nat'l Bank & Trust Co., 214 Ind. 451, 15 N.E.2d 1019 (1938).

The provisions of former IC 34-48-1-10 (repealed; see this section for similar provisions) could only be intended to apply to appeals from orders relating to the appointment of a receiver and not from all orders in receivership proceedings. Poston v. Akin, 218 Ind. 142, 31 N.E.2d 638 (1941).

Aggrieved Parties.

All persons made defendants and against whom relief was sought were "aggrieved" parties within the meaning of former IC 34-48-1-10 (repealed; see this section for similar provisions) and could appeal. Marshall v. Matson, 171 Ind. 238, 86 N.E. 339 (1908).

A corporation which was not a party to a receivership proceeding, and the interests of which were not affected by the order appointing the receiver, was not an "aggrieved party," within the meaning of the statute, and could not prosecute an appeal from the interlocutory order appointing a receiver. Kelley, Glover, Vale Realty Co. v. Kramer, 211 Ind. 321, 6 N.E.2d 963 (1937).

Under former IC 34-48-1-10 (repealed; see

Aggrieved Parties. (Cont'd)
this section for similar provisions) the word "thereafter" referred back to the appointment or refusal to appoint a receiver, and the "party aggrieved" was the party aggrieved by such appointment or refusal to appoint. Poston v. Akin, 218 Ind. 142, 31 N.E.2d 638 (1941).

Appealable Decision.
Where the court appointed a receiver without notice, who was to hold and preserve the property until the date fixed "for a hearing as to whether or not the receivership herein created, without notice, shall be continued pending the determination of this action," and on the date so fixed the court ordered that "the receivership herein be and the same is hereby continued and made permanent pending the determination of the main cause of action," the order last quoted was a decision of the court appointing a receiver, with notice, from which decision an appeal within ten days would lie. Stair v. Meissel, 207 Ind. 280, 192 N.E. 453 (1934).

An appellant tacitly recognized that the order from which he sought to appeal was an interlocutory order by bringing the appeal to the Supreme Court and by filing his briefs within the time prescribed by the rules of the court for filing briefs in appeals from interlocutory orders. Poston v. Akin, 218 Ind. 142, 31 N.E.2d 638 (1941).

Where a complaint sought a judgment in a certain amount and ancillary thereto prayed that a receiver be appointed for a corporation, the order appointing the receiver was an interlocutory order, but even if it were possible to say that the original appointment of the receiver was a final order, an order denying a subsequent petition which sought only to change the personnel of the receiver could only be an interlocutory order in the receivership proceedings which was not appealable. Poston v. Akin, 218 Ind. 142, 31 N.E.2d 638 (1941).

Where appellant had been a party to the various receivership proceedings during a period of three years, it could not be said that his petition for the removal of the receiver amounted to an appeal from the original order appointing the receiver and was in substantial compliance with the requirements of the statute providing for an appeal from the original order of appointment. Poston v. Akin, 218 Ind. 142, 31 N.E.2d 638 (1941); Voorhees v. Indianapolis Car & Mfg. Co., 140 Ind. 220, 39 N.E. 738 (1895); State v. Union Nat'l Bank, 145 Ind. 537, 44 N.E. 585, 57 Am. St. R. 209 (1896).

No right of appeal existed from an order of the court refusing to vacate or set aside its original ruling appointing a receiver, in an action of mortgage foreclosure. Parfenoff v.

Kozlowski, 218 Ind. 154, 31 N.E.2d 206 (1941).

The appointment of a substitute receiver did not give a second opportunity to question the original appointment. Parfenoff v. Kozlowski, 218 Ind. 154, 31 N.E.2d 206 (1941).

When a motion to set aside and vacate an interlocutory order appointing a receiver was made, overruled, and excepted to, the appeal was not from the ruling on the motion, but from the order appointing the receiver. Parfenoff v. Kozlowski, 218 Ind. 154, 31 N.E.2d 206 (1941).

Former IC 34-48-1-10 (repealed; see this section for similar provisions) did not provide for an appeal from an interlocutory order of the court refusing to vacate the appointment of a receiver. Parfenoff v. Kozlowski, 218 Ind. 154, 31 N.E.2d 206 (1941).

While it was true that in an interlocutory appeal from an order appointing a receiver the Supreme Court was not concerned with the question of whether the complaint was sufficient to withstand demurrer, and was only interested in the sufficiency of the facts to sustain the appointment, yet the court did not need to ignore the pleadings and the rulings thereon when an examination of them disclosed that finally it had to be held that the plaintiff was entitled to no relief whatever. Hughes v. Fifer, 218 Ind. 198, 31 N.E.2d 634 (1941).

Where the appointment of a receiver was first made without notice and then notice was given with a date fixed for a hearing to confirm the appointment after such hearing, the aggrieved party had his day in court and the ten-day period for appeal under former IC 34-48-1-10 (repealed; see this section for similar provisions) was calculated from the time of such hearing after notice. Fagan v. Clark, 238 Ind. 22, 148 N.E.2d 407 (1958).

Appeal-Bond.
An appeal from the appointment of a receiver with bond filed in the same amount as required of the receiver suspended his authority. Wabash R.R. v. Dykeman, 133 Ind. 56, 32 N.E. 823 (1892); General Motors Oil Co. v. Matheny, 185 Ind. 114, 113 N.E. 4 (1916).

If a term-time appeal was taken, that was, without notice to the adverse party, the trial court had to fix the amount of the appeal-bond and approve the sureties within the term at which the order was made appointing or refusing to appoint the receiver. Daugherty v. Payne, 175 Ind. 603, 95 N.E. 233 (1911).

The filing of an approved appeal-bond in an amount less than the receiver's bond did not require a dismissal of the appeal although it did not suspend the authority of the receiver. General Motors Oil Co. v. Matheny, 185 Ind. 114, 113 N.E. 4 (1916).

Appeal-Bond. (Cont'd)

Where an appeal was taken from the appointment of a receiver, no bond was required unless to suspend the receiver's authority or to perfect an appeal without giving notice. Seymour v. M. Ewing Fox Co., 191 Ind. 510, 133 N.E. 832 (1922); Indianapolis Brew. Co. v. Bingham, 226 Ind. 137, 78 N.E.2d 432 (1948).

Where appellant perfected appeal and furnished bond to Supreme Court from order of Appellate Court appointing receiver pendente lite in action by labor union for injunction, authority of receiver was suspended by operation of law and thereafter, receiver had no authority to act as receiver or incur expenses. International Union of Operating Eng'rs v. Hoisting & Portable Eng'rs, Local 103, 231 Ind. 634, 110 N.E.2d 332 (1953).

Bill of Exceptions.

On appeal under former IC 34-48-1-10 (repealed; see this section for similar provisions) from appointment of receiver in mortgage foreclosure, failure to include bill of exceptions in the record required the dismissal of the appeal, where a consideration of the evidence was necessary. Zeplovitz v. Folk, 209 Ind. 408, 197 N.E. 915 (1935).

Corporation Dissolved after Appeal Taken.

Supreme Court did not lose jurisdiction of appeal under former IC 34-48-1-10 (repealed; see this section for similar provisions) by dissolution of corporation after appeal was granted and bond filed. O'Malley v. Hankins, 207 Ind. 589, 194 N.E. 168 (1935).

Court Rule.

Rule 2-2 [now AP. 3, 13] providing the time within which to appeal was clear and concise and covered all appeals, whether they be from final judgments or interlocutory orders, and therefore a statute fixing shorter time was within the rule, and on proper showing, an extension of time could be granted. McConnell v. Fulmer, 230 Ind. 576, 103 N.E.2d 803, 105 N.E.2d 817 (1952).

A ruling on the appointment of a receiver was an interlocutory order, and in appeal from such, if appellant's brief was not filed within the ten-day period after submission, the appeal would be dismissed; however, a petition for extension of time to file their brief, made within the ten-day period, had the effect of tolling the running time until the court acted on the petition. Cheatham v. Brunner, 244 Ind. 604, 2 Ind. Dec. 513, 194 N.E.2d 807 (1963).

In an appeal from an interlocutory order, the granting of extension of time within which to file a brief was ineffective, even though made by agreement with the other party, where the application for extension of time

was not made within time for filing the brief; and in such case the appeal must have been dismissed, since timely filing of the brief, or timely obtaining of an extension, was jurisdictional. Cheatham v. Brunner, 244 Ind. 604, 2 Ind. Dec. 513, 194 N.E.2d 807 (1963).

Exceptions.

(Exceptions not necessary under Rules TR. 46 and CR. 6. For manner of raising and method of making objections, see Rules TR. 7, 12 and 46.)

An appeal could be taken from the appointment of a receiver in vacation without an exception, as there was no provision of the code for taking an exception in vacation. Barnes v. Jones, 91 Ind. 161 (1883); Pressley v. Lamb, 105 Ind. 171, 4 N.E. 682 (1886); Wabash R.R. v. Dykeman, 133 Ind. 56, 32 N.E. 823 (1892).

As in appeals under the code, it was necessary for the party intending to take an appeal from an order appointing, or refusing to appoint a receiver to take an exception to the ruling of the count. Wabash R.R. v. Dykeman, 133 Ind. 56, 32 N.E. 823 (1892); Lime City Bldg. Loan & Sav. Ass'n v. Black, 136 Ind. 544, 35 N.E. 829 (1893); Gray v. Oughton, 146 Ind. 285, 45 N.E. 191 (1896); Chicago & S.E. Ry. v. McBeth, 149 Ind. 78, 47 N.E. 678 (1897).

If the exception was taken at the first legal opportunity, it was in time. Wabash R.R. v. Dykeman, 133 Ind. 56, 32 N.E. 823 (1892); State v. Union Nat'l Bank, 145 Ind. 537, 44 N.E. 585, 57 Am. St. R. 209 (1896); Lewis v. Nielson, 176 Ind. 414, 96 N.E. 145 (1911); Ryder v. Shea, 183 Ind. 15, 108 N.E. 104 (1915).

The exception had to be taken at the time the ruling was made appointing or refusing to appoint a receiver, if the party excepting was present when the ruling was made. Wabash R.R. v. Dykeman, 133 Ind. 56, 32 N.E. 823 (1892); Chicago & S.E. Ry. v. McBeth, 149 Ind. 78, 47 N.E. 678 (1897); Ryder v. Shea, 183 Ind. 15, 108 N.E. 104 (1915).

Impairment of Collateral.

The trial court erred in its ruling that allowed the receiver to impair plaintiff's collateral and place the plaintiff in imminent danger of injury to its collateral. KeyBank Nat'l Ass'n v. Michael, 737 N.E.2d 834 (Ind. App. 2000).

Joint Appeals.

Parties jointly appealing from order appointing a receiver must all have been affected by the appointment. McFarland v. Pierce, 151 Ind. 546, 45 N.E. 706, 47 N.E. 1 (1897).

Jurisdiction.

Where final judgment ordered foreclosure

Jurisdiction. (Cont'd)

of equitable mortgage and sale of realty, order which denied motion to secure appointment of receiver for rents was not interlocutory order from which appeal could be taken to Supreme Court; jurisdiction over such appeal was in Appellate Court. Bahar v. Tadros, 234 Ind. 302, 123 N.E.2d 189 (1954).

Matters Reviewed.

On appeal under former IC 34-48-1-10 (repealed; see this section for similar provisions) of the statute from an order appointing a receiver, no questions were considered except the right to make the appointment. Main v. Ginthert, 92 Ind. 180 (1883); Wabash R.R. v. Dykeman, 133 Ind. 56, 32 N.E. 823 (1892); Sullivan Elec. Light & Power Co. v. Blue, 142 Ind. 407, 41 N.E. 805 (1895); Continental Clay & Mining Co. v. Bryson, 168 Ind. 485, 81 N.E. 210 (1907).

On appeal from an order appointing a receiver, the sufficiency of the complaint in the action would not be determined, but it would be looked to in considering the necessity of such appointment. Hursh v. Hursh, 99 Ind. 500 (1885); Naylor v. Sidener, 106 Ind. 179, 6 N.E. 345 (1886); Wabash R.R. v. Dykeman, 133 Ind. 56, 32 N.E. 823 (1892); Supreme Sitting of Order of Iron Hall v. Baker, 134 Ind. 293, 33 N.E. 1128, 20 L.R.A. 210 (1893); Gray v. Oughton, 146 Ind. 285, 45 N.E. 191 (1896); Goshen Woolen Mills Co. v. City Nat'l Bank, 150 Ind. 279, 49 N.E. 154 (1898); Chicago & S.E. Ry. v. Kenney, 159 Ind. 72, 62 N.E. 26 (1901); Levin v. Florsheim & Co., 161 Ind. 457, 68 N.E. 1025 (1903); Guynn v. Newman, 174 Ind. 161, 90 N.E. 759 (1910).

The Supreme Court would not weigh conflicting evidence on an appeal from an order appointing a receiver. Naylor v. Sidener, 106 Ind. 179, 6 N.E. 345 (1886); Chicago & S.E. Ry. v. McBeth, 149 Ind. 78, 47 N.E. 678 (1897).

When evidence on which a receiver was appointed was entirely in writing, the Supreme Court would weigh the evidence on appeal. Sallee v. Soules, 168 Ind. 624, 81 N.E. 587 (1907).

If an appeal was taken from an order appointing a receiver without notice, no question involving the merits of the controversy could be considered on a motion to dismiss the appeal. Ryder v. Shea, 180 Ind. 574, 103 N.E. 411 (1913).

The question of the necessity of the appointment of a receiver for a corporation was for the trial court, and an appointment made would not be set aside on appeal because the motives influencing the plaintiff to make the application for a receiver were questionable or because in commencing the suit, the plaintiff acted in bad faith. Portage Brick Co. v. North Ind. Brick Co., 189 Ind. 639, 128 N.E. 847 (1920).

Motion for New Trial.

When an appeal was taken from an order appointing a receiver, a motion for a new trial was not necessary. Shoemaker v. Smith, 74 Ind. 71 (1881); Portage Brick Co. v. North Ind. Brick Co., 189 Ind. 639, 128 N.E. 847 (1920); West v. Reeves, 207 Ind. 404, 190 N.E. 431 (1934).

On appeal under former IC 34-48-1-10 (repealed; see this section for similar provisions) from judgment refusing application for a receiver for a surviving partnership, an exception to the judgment or order was sufficient to present the merits of the case without filing a motion for a new trial. Yanakeff v. George, 207 Ind. 703, 194 N.E. 329 (1935).

Proceedings to secure appointment of receiver to collect rents after final judgment was an action for money had and received and appeal from adverse ruling on the question could only be raised as error in overruling motion for new trial as provided by Burns' Stat., § 2-2403 (since repealed; for present provisions see Rule TR. 59(c)). Bahar v. Tadros, 125 Ind. App. 457, 126 N.E.2d 791 (1955).

Motion to Dismiss Appeal.

A motion to dismiss an appeal taken from an interlocutory order appointing a receiver without notice could not involve a question concerning the merits of the controversy. Ryder v. Shea, 180 Ind. 574, 103 N.E. 411 (1913).

An appeal from an order appointing a receiver without notice would not have been dismissed where the briefs and motion for dismissal presented no question as to jurisdiction, or with reference to the perfection of the appeal, or in regard to any matter that might have furnished ground for a motion to dismiss. Ryder v. Shea, 180 Ind. 574, 103 N.E. 411 (1913).

Motion to Set Aside Appointment.

When a receiver had been apointed, it was not necessary to move the court to set aside the appointment. The appeal had to be taken from the order appointing a receiver, and there was no right to appeal from a ruling of the court overruling a motion to vacate the order appointing a receiver. Wabash R.R. v. Dykeman, 133 Ind. 56, 32 N.E. 823 (1892); Continental Clay & Mining Co. v. Bryson, 168 Ind. 485, 81 N.E. 210 (1907); Ryder v. Shea, 183 Ind. 15, 108 N.E. 104 (1915).

A creditor intervening in an action regarding the appointment of a receiver may appeal from a decision making such an appointment. State v. Union Nat'l Bank, 145 Ind. 537, 44 N.E. 585, 57 Am. St. R. 209 (1896).

When such a motion was made, overruled and excepted to, the appeal was not from the ruling on the motion, but from the order

Motion to Set Aside

Appointment. (Cont'd)
appointing the receiver. State v. Union Nat'l Bank, 145 Ind. 537, 44 N.E. 585, 57 Am. St. R. 209 (1896); Continental Clay & Mining Co. v. Bryson, 168 Ind. 485, 81 N.E. 210 (1907).

If a receiver was appointed without notice to the adverse party, such party could appeal from the order making the appointment without moving to set aside such order and reserving an exception to the decision of the court on such motion. Ryder v. Shea, 183 Ind. 15, 108 N.E. 104 (1915).

Possession Pending Appeal.

If an appeal was taken in the main action, the receiver would not be enjoined from taking possession of the property during the pendency of such appeal. Chicago & S.E. Ry. v. Kenney, 29 Ind. App. 506, 68 N.E. 20 (1902).

Procedure on Appeal.

In appeals from an interlocutory order appointing receivers, the general statutory rules of procedure regulating appeals did not apply. West v. Reeves, 207 Ind. 404, 190 N.E. 431 (1934).

On appeal from an interlocutory order appointing a receiver, the verified application for appointment of a receiver and an affidavit reciting such appointment raised an issue requiring the consideration of the evidence in the case, and in the absence of such evidence from the record, the appeal would be dismissed. Zeplovitz v. Folk, 209 Ind. 408, 197 N.E. 915 (1935).

Sufficiency of Complaint.

A complaint was sufficient on appeal to sustain an order appointing a receiver, where it alleged that defendant was indebted to plaintiff and 44 other creditors, that many of such claims were in the hands of attorneys for collection, who were threatening to bring suit therefor, that defendant was without money or credit and its business was being operated at a loss, that its assets were being consumed in operating expenses, and that it was in imminent danger of insolvency, no objection having been made to such complaint in the court below. Portage Brick Co. v. North Ind. Brick Co., 189 Ind. 639, 128 N.E. 847 (1920).

In an application for appointment of a receiver under former IC 34-48-1-10 (repealed, see this section for similar provisions), the complaint, challenged for lack of facts necessary to appointment of a receiver, could be considered only insofar as it was directly involved in the interlocutory order and necessary to the judgment upon it. West v. Reeves, 207 Ind. 404, 190 N.E. 431 (1934).

On appeal from an interlocutory order appointing a receiver, the complaint remained in the trial court and was there subject to amendment so long as the case was still pending in that court. West v. Reeves, 207 Ind. 404, 190 N.E. 431 (1934).

On appeal from an interlocutory order appointing a receiver, the sufficiency of the complaint to withstand demurrer would not be tested. Hawkins v. Aldridge, 211 Ind. 332, 7 N.E.2d 34, 109 A.L.R. 1205 (1937).

Supreme and Appellate Courts.

The action of the court in appointing a receiver could be reviewed by the Supreme or Appellate Court on an appeal of the main action. Buchanan v. Berkshire Life Ins. Co., 96 Ind. 510 (1883); Hutchinson v. First Nat'l Bank, 133 Ind. 271, 30 N.E. 952, 36 Am. St. R. 537 (1892); Hay v. McDaneld, 156 Ind. 390, 59 N.E. 1064 (1901); Chicago Horseshoe Co. v. Gostlin, 30 Ind. App. 504, 66 N.E. 514 (1903).

If the Appellate Court had jurisdiction of an appeal in the main action, and the appointment of a receiver was incidental only, the appeal should have been to such court. Hay v. McDaneld, 156 Ind. 390, 59 N.E. 1064 (1901).

According to the express terms of the statute, the appeal could only be taken to the Supreme Court. Ryder v. Shea, 180 Ind. 574, 103 N.E. 411 (1913).

The Supreme Court had jurisdiction of the subject-matter of an appeal from an order appointing a receiver for a corporation, and the Appellate Court obtained jurisdiction by transfer of the case to it. Pierson v. Republic Cas. Co., 200 Ind. 350, 160 N.E. 43 (1928).

Time for Perfecting Appeal.

In all cases, the transcript must have been filed with the clerk of the Supreme Court within ten days, and the time could not be extended by agreement. Vance v. Schayer, 76 Ind. 194 (1881); Flory v. Wilson, 83 Ind. 391 (1882); Hursh v. Hursh, 99 Ind. 500 (1885); Barney v. Elkhart County Trust Co., 167 Ind. 505, 79 N.E. 492 (1906); Daugherty v. Payne, 175 Ind. 603, 95 N.E. 233 (1911).

The appeal must have been taken and perfected within ten days after the date of the order; that is, all the acts necessary to give the Supreme Court jurisdiction must have been performed within the ten days. Vance v. Schayer, 76 Ind. 194 (1881); Hursh v. Hursh, 99 Ind. 500 (1885); Wabash R.R. v. Dykeman, 133 Ind. 56, 32 N.E. 823 (1892); Barney v. Elkhart County Trust Co., 167 Ind. 505, 79 N.E. 492 (1906); Daugherty v. Payne, 175 Ind. 603, 95 N.E. 233 (1911); Lewis v. Nielson, 176 Ind. 414, 96 N.E. 145 (1911); Standard Elec. Mfg. Co. v. Tuttle, 74 Ind. App. 559, 126 N.E. 438 (1920).

In case an appeal was taken, from an interlocutory order made in vacation appointing a receiver, in the absence of the other party, notice of the appeal must have been given within the ten days. Vance v. Schayer, 76 Ind.

Time for Perfecting Appeal. (Cont'd)
194 (1881); Cole v. Franks, 147 Ind. 281, 46
N.E. 532 (1897); Barney v. Elkhart County
Trust Co., 167 Ind. 505, 79 N.E. 492 (1906);
Daugherty v. Payne, 175 Ind. 603, 95 N.E. 233
(1911); Lewis v. Nielson, 176 Ind. 414, 96 N.E.
145 (1911).

If a vacation appeal was taken and notice
was given below by serving the notice on the
appellee and the clerk of the court, this must
have been done within the ten days.
Dougherty v. Brown, 21 Ind. App. 115, 51 N.E.
729 (1898); Masters v. Abbitt, 51 Ind. App.
429, 99 N.E. 815 (1912).

The denial of an ancillary receivership to a
partition suit was an interlocutory order requiring completion of the appeal within ten
days. Gray v. Gray, 202 Ind. 485, 176 N.E. 105
(1931).

The ten-day period after the appointment of
a receiver was held by the Supreme Court to
run from the time the aggrieved party had
notice of the appointment. State ex rel. Nineteenth Hole, Inc. v. Marion Superior Court,
243 Ind. 604, 1 Ind. Dec. 254, 189 N.E.2d 421
(1963).

32-30-5-11. Receiver's complaint — Contents. — In any suit or action
by a receiver appointed by any court of record in Indiana, it is only necessary
for the receiver, in the receiver's complaint or pleading, to state:

    (1) the court;

    (2) the cause of action in which the receiver was appointed; and

    (3) the date on which the receiver was appointed.

Proof of the appointment is not required on the trial of the cause unless the
appointment is specially denied, in addition to the general denial filed in the
cause. [P.L.2-2002, § 15.]

NOTES TO DECISIONS

In General.
  If the allegations as to authority to sue were
not denied, no proof thereof was required.

Ayres v. Foster, 25 Ind. App. 99, 57 N.E. 725
(1900).

32-30-5-12. Record book — Statements of assets and liabilities. —
The clerk of the court of each county shall keep a record book suitable to
enter and record statements of assets and liabilities. [P.L.2-2002, § 15.]

32-30-5-13. Filing of claims against assets held by receiver. — All
claims against the assets in the hands of the receiver that are filed with the
receiver shall be filed by the receiver with the clerk of the court in which the
receivership is pending. The clerk shall record the claims with the statements under this chapter, resulting in a complete record of the assets and
liabilities of the receivership. [P.L.2-2002, § 15.]

32-30-5-14. Account of proceedings — Filing. — In all receiverships
pending or begun in any court, the receiver, within the time as may be fixed
by an order of the court in which the receivership is pending, shall file with
the court an account or report in partial or final settlement of the liquidation
or receivership proceedings. [P.L.2-2002, § 15.]

  Cross References. Distribution of assets
under Uniform Liquidation Act, IC 30-2-7.

NOTES TO DECISIONS

ANALYSIS

Failure to file objections to report.
Ruling of court.

Failure to File Objections to Report.

Where it was shown that appellant did not object or except to a receiver's final report within the time prescribed by statute, the Appellate Court would not consider the question of whether the court below had power to amend an interlocutory judgment in the receivership proceedings after the entry of its final judgment discharging the receiver. State ex rel. Unemployment Comp. Bd. v. Burton, 112 Ind. App. 268, 44 N.E.2d 506 (1942).

Ruling of Court.

Where claimant participated in the hearing on the issue formed by exceptions to a receiver's account the court's ruling approving the report decided that claimant's exceptions were not well taken, and former IC 34-48-4-1 (repealed; see this section for similar provisions) did not require a ruling first on the exceptions and second upon the account. United States ex rel. Smith v. Moore, 223 Ind. 455, 61 N.E.2d 461 (1945).

Court's approval of account of credits and charges filed by receiver in receivership proceedings was not a final order and could be modified at a later date by an order sustaining an objection to the final account and distribution, such order not being contrary to law. Johnson v. Jackson, 152 Ind. App. 643, 31 Ind. Dec. 636, 284 N.E.2d 530 (1972).

32-30-5-15. Contents of account. — The account or report required by section 14 [IC 32-30-5-14] of this chapter must set forth all:

(1) receipts and disbursements to the date of the accounting; and

(2) other appropriate information relative to the:

(A) administration of the receivership;

(B) liquidation of the receivership; and

(C) declaration and payment of dividends.

[P.L.2-2002, § 15.]

32-30-5-16. Order requiring account. — If an account is not filed within one (1) year after the date when the receiver took possession of the assets and effects of the receivership, any party interested may petition the court for an order requiring the filing of an account. [P.L.2-2002, § 15.]

32-30-5-17. Notice of filing account. — (a) Except as provided in subsection (d), upon the filing of an account or report, the clerk of the court in which the receivership is pending shall give notice of the date on which the account or report is to be heard and determined by the court.

(b) The clerk shall give the notice required by subsection (a) by publication, once each week for three (3) successive weeks in two (2) newspapers of general circulation published or circulated within the county.

(c) The date in the notice on which the account or report is to be heard and determined by the court shall be fixed not less than thirty (30) days after the date of the filing of the account or report.

(d) Publication is not required under this section if the receivership is ancillary to a mortgage foreclosure. [P.L.2-2002, § 15.]

32-30-5-18. Objections to account. — (a) During the thirty (30) day period referred to in section 17 [IC 32-30-5-17] of this chapter, any creditor, shareholder, or other interested party may file objections or exceptions in writing to the account or report.

(b) Any objections or exceptions to the matters and things contained in an account or report and to the receiver's acts reported in the report or account that are not filed within the thirty (30) day period referred to in section 17 of this chapter are forever barred for all purposes. [P.L.2-2002, § 15.]

32-30-5-19. Hearing. — At the expiration of the thirty (30) day period referred to in section 17 [IC 32-30-5-17] of this chapter, the court shall, without delay:

(1) proceed with the hearing and determination of the objections or exceptions;

(2) pass upon the account or report;

(3) order the payment of a partial or final dividend; and

(4) make other appropriate orders.

[P.L.2-2002, § 15.]

32-30-5-20. Approval of account — Release and discharge of receiver. — The court's approval of a receiver's partial account or report, as provided in section 14 [IC 32-30-5-14] of this chapter, releases and discharges the receiver and the surety on the receiver's bond for all matters and things related to or contained in the partial account or report. [P.L.2-2002, § 15.]

Collateral References. Effect of nonsuit, dismissal, or discontinuance of action upon previous order appointing receiver. 11 A.L.R.2d 1407.

Distinction between vacation of appointment and discharge of receiver. 72 A.L.R.2d 1075.

32-30-5-21. Settling of estate. — Upon the:

(1) court's approval of the receiver's final account or report, as provided in section 14 [IC 32-30-5-14] of this chapter; and

(2) receiver's performance and compliance with the court's order made on the final report;

the receiver and the surety on the receiver's bond shall be fully and finally discharged and the court shall declare the receivership estate finally settled and closed subject to the right of appeal of the receiver or any creditor, shareholder, or other interested party who has filed objections or exceptions as provided in section 18 [IC 32-30-5-18] of this chapter. [P.L.2-2002, § 15.]

32-30-5-22. Change of judge or venue. — (a) This section applies to any action, proceeding, or matter relating to or involving a receivership estate.

(b) Except as provided in subsections (c) and (d), a party to a proceeding described in subsection (a) is entitled to a change of judge or a change of venue from the county for the same reasons and upon the same terms and conditions under which a change of judge or a change of venue from the county is allowed in any civil action.

(c) This section does not authorize a change of venue from the county:

(1) concerning expenses allowed by the court incidental to the operation, management, or administration of the receivership estate;

(2) upon any petition or proceeding to remove a receiver; or

(3) upon the objections or exceptions to any partial or final account or report of any receiver.

(d) A change of venue is not allowed from the county of the administration of any receivership estate, or upon any petition or proceeding to remove a receiver, or upon objections or exceptions to a partial or final account or report of a receiver. [P.L.2-2002, § 15.]

Cross References. Change of venue, Trial Rule TR. 76.

NOTES TO DECISIONS

ANALYSIS

In general.
Ancillary receivership.
Change of judge.
Prohibition, jurisdiction on appeal.
Waiver of right.

In General.

In labor union's injunction action, pending which a receiver was requested, change of venue from county after appointment of receiver pendente lite and dismissal of appeal from such order did not transfer receivership from jurisdiction where action was filed. International Union of Operating Eng'rs v. Hoisting & Portable Eng'rs, Local 103, 231 Ind. 634, 110 N.E.2d 332 (1953).

Where the sole and principal relief was the appointment of a receiver upon final judgment, a change of venue from the county could have been had, but where the receiver was requested pending the action as relief ancillary to the main cause, the issue on a temporary receivership and the receivership itself remained in the court first acquiring jurisdiction. The jurisdiction of the issues in the principal cause was transferred to the court in another county to which the change of venue was taken. International Union of Operating Eng'rs v. Hoisting & Portable Eng'rs, Local 103, 231 Ind. 634, 110 N.E.2d 332 (1953).

Where relator sold automobiles of company in receivership and held the proceeds in trust, receiver's petition requesting payment of the funds was a separate triable issue having all the characteristics of a suit for an accounting in equity for funds held in trust, thus relator was entitled to change of venue from the county. State ex rel. Interstate Fin., Inc. v. Superior Court, 244 Ind. 491, 2 Ind. Dec. 345, 193 N.E.2d 909 (1963).

Ancillary Receivership.

A court from which a change of venue from the county had been taken in the main action, but which continued to have jurisdiction of an ancillary receivership because such receivership did not follow the venue of the main action when it left the county, would not have been restrained from making orders in connection with the receivership though the main action had been decided and facts could have been shown so that discharge of the receivership would have been mandatory, as decision in the main action did not ipso facto discharge the receiver and his duties continued until he was relieved of his trust by order of court. State ex rel. Miller v. Kroger, 235 Ind. 556, 135 N.E.2d 520 (1956).

A court having jurisdiction of an ancillary receivership could not take judicial knowledge of the records of another court wherein the main action had been decided though it was bound by the judgment of such court and upon receipt of a certified copy of the decree terminating the case in chief would have been obliged to order liquidation and termination of the receivership estate. State ex rel. Miller v. Kroger, 235 Ind. 556, 135 N.E.2d 520 (1956).

In an action to set aside a mortgage foreclosure judgment a change of venue from the county in the main action did not transfer ancillary receivership so that the court from which venue was changed had continuing jurisdiction to make orders in protection of and furtherance of the receivership estate, and issue contempt citations to enforce its orders. State ex rel. Miller v. Kroger, 235 Ind. 556, 135 N.E.2d 520 (1956).

The granting of a change of judge gave the special judge jurisdiction of the main cause of action and the ancillary receivership. State ex rel. Miller v. Kroger, 235 Ind. 556, 135 N.E.2d 520 (1956).

Change of Judge.

Only after the court had heard the evidence and rendered its decision did plaintiff file its motion for change of judge, and by virtue of TR. 76(C)(5), that motion came too late, since the right to seek change of venue from the judge had by then been waived. KeyBank Nat'l Ass'n v. Michael, 737 N.E.2d 834 (Ind. App. 2000).

Prohibition, Jurisdiction on Appeal.

In action in Supreme Court for writ of

**Prohibition, Jurisdiction on
Appeal.** (Cont'd)
prohibition, the Supreme Court would not consider the question of the lower court's jurisdiction, where its jurisdiction was conceded by both the defendant and the plaintiff, although suggested in the briefs and arguments of the case, since such question would have been a matter to be presented to the Supreme Court on appeal, in view of former IC 34-48-6-1 (repealed; see this section for similar provisions) and former 34-1-58-1 (repealed). State ex rel. Beemer v. Markey, 215 Ind. 534, 21 N.E.2d 400 (1939).

Waiver of Right.
Stipulation in argument that finance company would hold the funds in trust "until further determination by this court" was not a waiver of the right to a change of venue from the court as there was no reference to any waiver of any change of venue in the stipulation and language used was the language commonly used in referring to the court entertaining any proceedings. State ex rel. Interstate Fin., Inc. v. Superior Court, 244 Ind. 491, 2 Ind. Dec. 345, 193 N.E.2d 909 (1963).

CHAPTER 6

NUISANCE ACTIONS

32-30-6-1. "Agricultural operation" defined. — As used in this chapter, "agricultural operation" includes any facility used for the production of crops, livestock, poultry, livestock products, poultry products, or horticultural products or for growing timber. [P.L.2-2002, § 15.]

Effective Dates. P.L.2-2002, § 15. July 1. 2002.

32-30-6-2. "Industrial operation" defined. — As used in this chapter, "industrial operation" includes any facility used for the:
(1) manufacture of a product from other products;
(2) transformation of a material from one (1) form to another;
(3) mining of a material and related mine activities; or
(4) storage or disposition of a product or material.
[P.L.2-2002, § 15.]

Compiler's Notes. The compiler has deleted the word "added" following "As" at the beginning of this section as added by P.L.2-2002, § 15, for purposes of clarity.

32-30-6-3. "Locality" defined. — As used in this chapter, "locality":
(1) for purposes of section 9 [IC 32-30-6-9] of this chapter, means the specific area of land upon which an:
(A) agricultural operation; or
(B) industrial operation;
is conducted; and
(2) for purposes of section 10 [IC 32-30-6-10] of this chapter, means the following:

(A) The specific area of land upon which a public use airport operation is conducted.

(B) The airport imaginary surfaces as described in IC 8-21-10-8. [P.L.2-2002, § 15.]

32-30-6-4. "Public use airport operation" defined. — As used in this chapter, "public use airport operation" includes any facility used as a public use airport for the landing, take off, storage, or repair of aircraft. [P.L.2-2002, § 15.]

32-30-6-5. "Vicinity of the locality" defined. — As used in this chapter, "vicinity of the locality" means the following:

(1) Three (3) miles from the locality (as defined in section 3(2) [IC 32-30-6-3(2)] of this chapter) of a public use airport operation that serves regularly scheduled air carrier or military turbojet aircraft.

(2) One and one-half (1.5) miles from the locality of a public use airport operation that does not serve regularly scheduled air carrier or military turbojet aircraft. [P.L.2-2002, § 15.]

32-30-6-6. Nuisance. — Whatever is:

(1) injurious to health;

(2) indecent;

(3) offensive to the senses; or

(4) an obstruction to the free use of property;

so as essentially to interfere with the comfortable enjoyment of life or property, is a nuisance, and the subject of an action. [P.L.2-2002, § 15.]

Cross References. Injunctions, IC 34-26.

Opinions of Attorney General. Lowering of water levels in lakes by deepening outlets, rights and remedies. 1934, p. 126.

In addition to constituting a criminal offense, the keeping of tuberculosis cattle beyond the time allowed for marketing them, in the light of scientific knowledge concerning tuberculosis in cattle, of which the courts would upon suggestion take notice, would be injurious to public health and would essentially interfere with the comfortable enjoyment of life and property and therefor would constitute a nuisance under the predecessor statute to this section. 1937, p. 151.

NOTES TO DECISIONS

ANALYSIS

In general.
Abatement.
Action for damages.
Adult bookstore.
Animals.
Artificial gas manufacture.
Buildings.
Businesses and plants.
Complaint.
Conditional title.
Costs.
Counterclaim.
County property.
Creator of nuisance.
Damages.

Deeds and notes.
Defenses.
—In general.
—Reasonableness.
Demand.
Dock and swimming area.
Drain and watercourse obstructions.
Evidence and proof.
Health.
Highway obstructions.
Hogs.
Immediate possession, affidavit.
Independent contractors.
Instructions.
Interest in property.
Judgment.
Landfill.

Limitation of actions.
L-p gas tanks.
Measure of damages.
Motion for new trial.
Municipal property and functions.
Nature of action.
Nonresidents.
Oil and gas wells.
Parties plaintiff.
—In general.
—Mortgagee.
Pollution of streams.
Possession of property.
Prescription.
Presumed continuance.
Prior owners.
Privies.
Property attached to realty.
Property obtained by fraud.
Property subject to lien.
Property taken for taxes.
Property wrongfully levied on.
Public nuisance.
—In general.
—Private party.
Railroads.
Res judicata.
Review.
Spite fence.
Steam engines.
Stray bullet.
Summary judgment.
Surface water.
Title to property.
Unsightliness.
Venue.
Verdict.
What constitutes nuisance.
Wrongful taking.

In General.
Former sections IC 34-1-8-1, IC 34-1-8-2, IC 34-1-9-1 — IC 34-1-9-11, and IC 34-1-27-1, when construed together, contemplated that the verdict in a replevin action should determine where the right of possession to the property laid, and the value of the property, and the damages sustained by the parties lawfully entitled to its possession by reason of the wrongful taking and detention. Cohen v. Shubert, 100 Ind. App. 315, 195 N.E. 574 (1935).
A judgment in replevin action, where the right of possession was in one party and the actual possession was held by another party, could not be legally rendered in the absence of a verdict determining the right of possession, the value of the property, and the damages resulting from the wrongful taking and detention of the property, in view of former IC 34-1-8-1, IC 34-1-8-2, IC 34-1-9-1 — IC 34-1-9-11, and IC 34-1-27-1. Cohen v. Shubert, 100 Ind. App. 315, 195 N.E. 574 (1935).
Evidence showed commission of acts in vi-

olation of former IC 34-19-1-1 (repealed; see this section for similar provisions). Hendrick v. Tubbs, 120 Ind. App. 326, 92 N.E.2d 561 (1950).
An instruction that the mere fact that accident occurred while plaintiff was on defendant's premises was not proof that defendant was in any way negligent or guilty of maintaining a nuisance as charged in plaintiff's complaint, properly stated the law on this issue. White v. Evansville Am. Legion Home Ass'n, 5 Ind. Dec. 607, 207 N.E.2d 820 (Ind. App.), rev'd on other grounds, 247 Ind. 69, 210 N.E.2d 845 (1965).
Where plaintiff was not a stranger or a member of the general public but rather was a tenant, an open ditch adjoining the premises of the party was not a nuisance to her. DeMoss v. Coleman, 139 Ind. App. 346, 8 Ind. Dec. 415, 216 N.E.2d 861 (1966).
Defects in steps could not be a private nuisance where it was not an interference with property of the third party who was injured thereby. Stover v. Fechtman, 140 Ind. App. 62, 9 Ind. Dec. 691, 222 N.E.2d 281 (1966).
A nuisance is classified as public if it affects an entire community or neighborhood or as private if its effect is peculiar to an individual or a limited number of individuals. Beresford v. Starkey, 563 N.E.2d 116 (Ind. App. 1990), rev'd on other grounds, 571 N.E.2d 1257 (Ind. 1991).
When deciding whether one's use of his property is a nuisance to his neighbors, it is necessary to balance the competing interests of the landowners, using a common sense approach. Wendt v. Kerkhof, 594 N.E.2d 795 (Ind. App. 1992); Keane v. Pachter, 598 N.E.2d 1067 (Ind. App. 1992).
A person who owns or claims a possessory interest in property may properly bring a replevin action. Citizens Nat'l Bank v. Johnson, 637 N.E.2d 191 (Ind. App. 1994).

Abatement.
Abatement did not necessarily follow a recovery of damages for a nuisance. Cromwell v. Lowe, 14 Ind. 234 (1860).
A nuisance might have been adjudged such, and ordered to have been abated, either in a civil or criminal case. McLaughlin v. State, 45 Ind. 338 (1873).
In a suit by a railroad company to enjoin the abatement of stock-pens as a public nuisance, the burden of proof was on the plaintiff to show that the stock-pens, as maintained, were not a nuisance. Pittsburgh, C., C. & St. L.R.R. v. Crothersville, 159 Ind. 330, 64 N.E. 914 (1902).
Operation of sawmill on lot adjacent to that of the residence of plaintiff constituted a nuisance and cessation of operations pending appeal was not cause for dismissal, as plain-

Abatement. (Cont'd)

tiff still could press his charge for damages. Miller v. Gates, 62 Ind. App. 37, 112 N.E. 538 (1916).

Burden of proof was on city seeking to abate sidewalk nuisance. Carlisle v. Pirtle, 63 Ind. App. 475, 114 N.E. 705 (1917).

It was error to assess damages for a nuisance which the court ordered abated, where there was evidence that the evidence reduced the value of plaintiff's real estate but no evidence as to the effect on its rental value. Davoust v. Mitchell, 146 Ind. App. 536, 21 Ind. Dec. 124, 257 N.E.2d 332 (1970).

Action for Damages.

Action for damages caused by leakage of oil from pipe lines over a series of years, being on theory of nuisance, question of negligence of defendant was immaterial. Indiana Pipe Line Co. v. Christensen, 195 Ind. 106, 143 N.E. 596 (1924). See also Niagara Oil Co. v. Ogle, 177 Ind. 292, 98 N.E. 60, 42 L.R.A. (n.s.) 714, 1914D Ann. Cas. 67 (1912).

Definition of nuisance as given in former IC 34-19-1-1 (repealed; see this section for similar provisions) applied in action by father for death of son caused by nuisance. Pere Marquette R.R. v. Chadwick, 65 Ind. App. 95, 115 N.E. 678 (1917).

Adult Bookstore.

An injunction prohibiting defendant from operating an adult bookstore as a nuisance and from disseminating any publication within a county violated the first amendment of the United States Constitution as an impermissible prior restraint on publication. State ex rel. Blee v. Mohney Enters., 154 Ind. App. 244, 33 Ind. Dec. 678, 289 N.E.2d 519 (1972).

Animals.

If animals were held for damages done by them, it must have appeared that they broke through a lawful fence in order to prevent their recovery by the owner. Clark v. Stipp, 75 Ind. 114 (1881).

If animals were taken up as estrays, the law must have been complied with in order to have resisted a replevin suit on the part of the owner. James v. Fowler, 90 Ind. 563 (1883); Jones v. Clouser, 114 Ind. 387, 16 N.E. 797 (1888); Haffner v. Barnard, 123 Ind. 429, 24 N.E. 152 (1890); Frazier v. Goar, 1 Ind. App. 38, 27 N.E. 442 (1891); Forsyth v. Walch, 4 Ind. App. 182, 30 N.E. 720 (1892); Wilhelm v. Scott, 14 Ind. App. 275, 40 N.E. 537, 42 N.E. 827 (1895); Wyman v. Turner, 14 Ind. App. 118, 42 N.E. 652 (1896).

In an action for impounding animals found running at large, an answer by defendant that failed to show that he was a resident of the township at the time of the taking up of the animals, was insufficient. Frazier v. Goar, 1 Ind. App. 38, 27 N.E. 442 (1891).

An action of replevin would lie to recover the possession of the body of a dead dog. Vantreese v. McGee, 26 Ind. App. 525, 60 N.E. 318 (1901).

Artificial Gas Manufacture.

The manufacture of artificial gas for public use was not a nuisance per se, but the emission of noxious gases and fumes from a gas plant which endangered health and damages adjoining property was a private nuisance for which damages could be recovered or injunctive relief granted. Northern Ind. Pub. Serv. Co. v. Vesey, 210 Ind. 338, 200 N.E. 620 (1936).

It was both a public and private nuisance to operate an artificial gas plant emitting poisonous and destructive gases. Northern Ind. Pub. Serv. Co. v. Vesey, 210 Ind. 338, 200 N.E. 620 (1936).

Buildings.

The erection of a certain class of buildings in populous cities could have been a nuisance. Baumgartner v. Hasty, 100 Ind. 575, 50 Am. R. 830 (1885); Kaufman v. Stein, 138 Ind. 49, 37 N.E. 333, 46 Am. St. R. 368 (1894).

The erection of a building which would not of itself constitute a nuisance would not be enjoined because the use to which it was designed to be put would constitute such a nuisance. Dalton v. Cleveland, C., C. & St. L.R.R., 144 Ind. 121, 43 N.E. 130 (1896).

Landowners did not possess an easement of light, air or view, and had no legal cause for complaint for interference therewith by the lawful operation of a building on adjoining land. Wolf v. Forcum, 130 Ind. App. 10, 161 N.E.2d 175 (1959).

Landowners had an absolute right of lateral support for their land from the adjoining land and landowners had a right of action for the violation of the absolute right of lateral support of their land without reference to any act or acts of negligence by the adjoining landowner in making excavations. Wolf v. Forcum, 130 Ind. App. 10, 161 N.E.2d 175 (1959).

Businesses and Plants.

Lawful business could be so conducted as to become a nuisance. Owen v. Phillips, 73 Ind. 284 (1881); Zeppenfeld v. Franklin Motor Serv. Co., 77 Ind. App. 687, 134 N.E. 487 (1922).

In an action against a slaughter-house the fact that the smells, etc., of the particular slaughter-house blended with like smells from other slaughter-houses was no defense in a prosecution against the owner of the one particular slaughter-house. Dennis v. State, 91 Ind. 291 (1883).

Businesses and Plants. (Cont'd)

A slaughter-house located in a populous part of a city is prima facie a nuisance. Reichert v. Geers, 98 Ind. 73, 49 Am. R. 736 (1884).

Operation of liquor saloon in residential neighborhood as set forth in complaint stated a good cause of action. Haggart v. Stehlin, 137 Ind. 43, 35 N.E. 997, 22 L.R.A. 577 (1893); Kissel v. Lewis, 156 Ind. 233, 59 N.E. 478 (1901); Tron v. Lewis, 31 Ind. App. 178, 66 N.E. 490 (1903).

A slaughter-house erected or conducted in violation of an ordinance prohibiting its maintenance within the corporate limits of the town became a nuisance although it would not have been such in the absence of the ordinance. Major v. Miller, 165 Ind. 275, 75 N.E. 159 (1905).

The maintenance of a fertilizing plant near a dwelling-house could constitute a nuisance. Clendenin v. Pickett, 51 Ind. App. 283, 99 N.E. 530 (1912).

Sawmill near dwelling-house could constitute a nuisance. Miller v. Gates, 62 Ind. App. 37, 112 N.E. 538 (1916).

Where plaintiff suffered property damage as a result of a substance which seeped from her basement drain which was caused by defendants' discharge of prohibited materials into a public sewer system, defendants' actions prompted foreign matter to enter her property and cause her property damage; this constituted a nuisance negligent trespass. Lever Bros. Co. v. Langdoc, 655 N.E.2d 577 (Ind. App. 1995).

Complaint.

The description of the property in the complaint had to identify the place and kind of property with reasonable certainty. Malone v. Stickney, 88 Ind. 594 (1883); Hoke v. Applegate, 92 Ind. 570 (1884); Hall v. Durham, 117 Ind. 429, 20 N.E. 282 (1889); Wood v. Darnell, 1 Ind. App. 215, 27 N.E. 447 (1891). See also, Minchrod v. Windoes, 29 Ind. 288 (1868); Onstatt v. Ream, 30 Ind. 259, 95 Am. Dec. 695 (1868); Smith v. Stanford, 62 Ind. 392 (1878).

If the complaint showed that the plaintiff was entitled to the immediate possession of the property, and that it had been unlawfully taken and detained it was sufficient. Schenck v. Long, 67 Ind. 579 (1879); Entsminger v. Jackson, 73 Ind. 144 (1880); Johnson v. Simpson, 77 Ind. 412 (1881); Turpie v. Fagg, 124 Ind. 476, 22 N.E. 743 (1889); Ross v. Menefee, 125 Ind. 432, 25 N.E. 545 (1890).

The complaint did not need to aver that the property had not been taken for a tax, assessment or fine, or seized under the execution or attachment against the property of the plaintiff. Payne v. June, 92 Ind. 252 (1883); Turpie v. Fagg, 124 Ind. 476, 22 N.E. 743 (1889);

Andrews v. Sellers, 11 Ind. App. 301, 38 N.E. 1101 (1894).

The complaint could be verified by the agent or attorney of the plaintiff. Hall v. Durham, 117 Ind. 429, 20 N.E. 282 (1889).

In replevin action the allegation in the complaint that said defendants were now unlawfully and without right in possession of said property and were "wrongfully detaining" the same, although not in the words of the statute, to wit, "unlawfully detained" was sufficient compliance with former IC 34-21-1-1 (repealed; see this section for similar provisions). Sheets Oil Co. v. Fruehauf Trailer Co., 213 Ind. 314, 12 N.E.2d 504 (1938).

In an action of replevin, an averment in the complaint that the defendant "unlawfully holds" the property was equivalent to an averment that it was "unlawfully detained." Gould v. O'Neal, 1 Ind. App. 144, 27 N.E. 307 (1891); Buck v. Young, 1 Ind. App. 558, 27 N.E. 1106 (1891).

Conditional Title.

When the title to property was only to vest in a purchaser on conditions, the seller might have recovered the property when the conditions were not performed. Dunbar v. Rawles, 28 Ind. 225, 92 Am. Dec. 311 (1867).

Assignment of note given on sale of property on condition would not transfer title to property to assignee. Domestic Sewing Mach. Co. v. Arthurhultz, 63 Ind. 322 (1878); Hyde v. Courtwright, 14 Ind. App. 106, 42 N.E. 647 (1896).

In order to prevail in an action for replevin the owner must be entitled to possession at the time of judgment, thus where the seller under a conditional sales contract brought an action for replevin after default by the buyer then accepted further payments from the buyer he reinstated the contract thereby giving up his right to possession and therefore his right to replevin the article sold. Snyder v. International Harvester Credit Corp., 147 Ind. App. 364, 22 Ind. Dec. 398, 261 N.E.2d 71 (1970).

Costs.

Court could properly make a division of the costs, taxing against the plaintiff all costs after the return of the property illegally held. Grim v. Adkins, 21 Ind. App. 106, 51 N.E. 494 (1898).

Counterclaim.

Judgment may not be entered against the surety on a replevin bond where the judgment was on a counterclaim which was a separate and distinct matter not arising from the replevin action. Kegerreis v. Auto-Owners Ins. Co., 484 N.E.2d 976 (Ind. App. 1985).

County Property.

The board of county commissioners could

County Property. (Cont'd)

have been liable for nuisance by keeping and maintaining a pest-house in such manner and so near a dwelling-house as to be offensive. Haag v. Board of County Comm'rs, 60 Ind. 511, 28 Am. R. 654 (1878).

Where statute required county board of health to arrest the spread of contagious diseases and the board in compliance decided to build a hospital in such manner as to destroy or injure private property, it had to be shown in justification thereof either that such act was expressly authorized by statute or was plainly and necessarily implied from the powers conferred, and the burden of showing such justification was on the board. Anable v. Board of County Comm'rs, 34 Ind. App. 72, 71 N.E. 272, 107 Am. St. R. 173 (1904).

Jails in counties constructed in accordance with law could not be abated as nuisances, but the keeping of jails in such a manner as to be a nuisance could have been enjoined. Pritchett v. Board of County Comm'rs, 42 Ind. App. 3, 85 N.E. 32 (1908).

Creator of Nuisance.

The creator of a nuisance on land which it does not own can be required to abate the nuisance. Gray v. Westinghouse Elec. Corp., 624 N.E.2d 49 (Ind. App. 1993).

Damages.

If damages for detention were not claimed, the damages assessed could not have exceeded the value of the property. Hotchkiss v. Jones, 4 Ind. 260 (1853).

Time spent in commencing suit could not have been considered as an element of damages. Blackwell v. Acton, 38 Ind. 425 (1871).

If the plaintiff had possession of the property, he could not have recovered its value as damages. Blackwell v. Acton, 38 Ind. 425 (1871).

Only nominal damages could have been assessed when actual damages were not proved. Stevens v. McClure, 56 Ind. 384 (1877); Geisendorff v. Eagles, 70 Ind. 418 (1879); Robinson v. Shatzley, 75 Ind. 461 (1881).

Damages for detention of the property could have been allowed exceeding the value of the property. Washburn v. Roberts, 72 Ind. 213 (1880).

If property was unlawfully taken, the plaintiff could recover as damages his expenses in recovering the same and its use and deterioration in value. Yelton v. Slinkard, 85 Ind. 190 (1882). See also, Mitchell v. Burch, 36 Ind. 529 (1871).

Damages for detention of property was the reasonable value of its use during the time it was unlawfully detained. Farrar v. Eash, 5 Ind. App. 238, 31 N.E. 1125 (1892).

Where in a replevin action defendant was no longer in actual or constructive possession of the property, the action should have been allowed to continue to afford plaintiff his remedy by an award of damages for detention and loss of use. Lou Leventhal Auto Co. v. Munns, 164 Ind. App. 368, 47 Ind. Dec. 213, 328 N.E.2d 734 (1975).

Damages were recoverable either when the property was wrongfully taken or unlawfully detained. Northern Ind. Slurry Seal, Inc. v. K & K Truck Sales, Inc., 167 Ind. App. 440, 50 Ind. Dec. 412, 338 N.E.2d 704 (1975).

Landlord unlawfully detained the tenant's personal property by locking it in the leased apartment and excluding her from re-entering the premises to recover her belongings; therefore, the landlord was liable for the loss of property the tenant sustained due to his failure to return all of her personal items that he locked inside the leased premises, and the trial court properly awarded the tenant damages in the amount of the unreturned property. Robinson v. Valladares, 738 N.E.2d 278 (Ind. App. 2000).

Deeds and Notes.

Deeds and notes could be recovered in actions of replevin. Bush v. Groomes, 125 Ind. 14, 24 N.E. 81 (1890). See also, Wilson v. Rybolt, 17 Ind. 391, 79 Am. Dec. 486 (1861); Highnote v. White, 67 Ind. 596 (1879).

Defenses.

—In General.

Lawfulness of a business, lack of negligence in its conduct and contributing negligence are not defenses to an action for nuisance. Mowrer v. Ashland Oil & Ref. Co., 518 F.2d 659 (7th Cir. 1975).

Reasonableness of the use of land is available as a defense to an action for nuisance and presents a question for the jury. Mowrer v. Ashland Oil & Ref. Co., 518 F.2d 659 (7th Cir. 1975).

—Reasonableness.

"Reasonable use" of one's property may be a defense to a nuisance action where the use merely causes incidental injury to another, but where one uses his property for his profit so as to practically confiscate or destroy his neighbor's property, he should be compelled to respond in damages, for it can hardly be said such use is reasonable. Sherk v. Indiana Waste Sys., 495 N.E.2d 815 (Ind. App. 1986).

The mere fact a business is operated in accord with various rules and regulations does not require a finding that the use is reasonable. A determination of reasonableness of use in an action for nuisance depends upon the effect of the activity upon one's neighbors in the particular circumstances and locality, not merely upon whether one

Defenses. (Cont'd)

—Reasonableness. (Cont'd)
operates within the confines of particular authority. Sherk v. Indiana Waste Sys., 495 N.E.2d 815 (Ind. App. 1986).

Demand.
Replevin of mortgaged goods by the mortgagee could not be maintained without due demand upon the mortgagor for possession, after maturity of the debt and before the bringing of the suit. Roberts v. Norris, 67 Ind. 386 (1879).

A denial by defendant in a replevin action of plaintiff's ownership of the property and his right of possession of it amounted to a waiver of a demand. Allen B. Wrisley Distrib. Co. v. Serewicz, 145 F.2d 169 (7th Cir. 1944).

A request of plaintiff that defendant release material owned by plaintiff and located at defendant's place of business and ship it back in trucks to be provided by plaintiff (the material in question being at the defendant's plant pursuant to a contract between the parties), if a demand, was a qualified one with which defendant did not fail to comply by failure to ship back the goods, where plaintiff did not provide the trucks for that purpose. Allen B. Wrisley Distrib. Co. v. Serewicz, 145 F.2d 169 (7th Cir. 1944).

Whenever the defendant obtained wrongful possession of goods, no demand was necessary before the action for possession is commenced. Robinson v. Shatzley, 75 Ind. 461 (1881); Parrish v. Thurston, 87 Ind. 437 (1882); Deeter v. Sellers, 102 Ind. 458, 1 N.E. 854 (1885); Ahlendorf v. Barkous, 20 Ind. App. 657, 50 N.E. 887 (1898). See also, Lewis v. Masters, 8 Blackf. 244 (1846).

If the possession of goods was lawfully obtained, an action of replevin would not lie until after a demand. Torian v. McClure, 83 Ind. 310 (1882); Ledbetter v. Embree, 12 Ind. App. 617, 40 N.E. 928 (1895). See also, Underwood v. Tatham, 1 Ind. 276 (1848); Conner v. Comstock, 17 Ind. 90 (1861).

If the action failed for want of a demand, another suit could be brought after a demand. Williams v. Lewis, 124 Ind. 344, 24 N.E. 733 (1890). See also, Roberts v. Norris, 67 Ind. 386 (1879).

Dock and Swimming Area.
Because the dock and the swimming area were not in themselves indecent, offensive, or injurious to health, did not obstruct the free use of another's property, and there was no evidence the dock and swimming area were calculated to injure a stranger who merely entered the property, only the use of the dock and swimming area by the plaintiff made it injurious to his health, the dock and swimming area is not a nuisance. Beresford v. Starkey, 563 N.E.2d 116 (Ind. App. 1990), rev'd on other grounds, 571 N.E.2d 1257 (Ind. 1991).

Drain and Watercourse Obstructions.
The obstruction of a ditch in which a party had an easement for the drainage of his lands constituted a continuing nuisance and successive actions for damages could be maintained because of such continuance. Steinke v. Bentley, 6 Ind. App. 663, 34 N.E. 97 (1893).

Where the complaint showed that defendant had obstructed a watercourse by depositing sand in its channel and by erecting dams, and that defendant was continuing such deposits thereby causing the channel to be filled up several feet, when taken in connection with the allegations of injury, was sufficient as against the objections that the complaint did not show irreparable injury on account of such discharge of sand into the stream. American Plate Glass Co. v. Nicoson, 34 Ind. App. 643, 73 N.E. 625 (1905).

Evidence that owners of water-flushed toilets connected them to a tile drain which emptied into an open ditch and that the substance which flowed through the drain and ditch had a black and forbidding appearance, was polluted and filthy, and gave off an offensive odor, was sufficient to establish the fact that a nuisance had been created and was in existence, within the meaning of this statute. Bearcreek Tp. v. DeHoff, 113 Ind. App. 530, 49 N.E.2d 391 (1943).

The use of a surface water drain for the purpose of a sanitary sewer when such use would result in the creation of a nuisance was not authorized, regardless of whether or not any or all of the parties involved had been assessed for the construction of the drain. Bearcreek Tp. v. DeHoff, 113 Ind. App. 530, 49 N.E.2d 391 (1943).

Evidence and Proof.
Defense in replevin that property was in a third person had to be taken by general denial. Fruits v. Elmore, 8 Ind. App. 278, 34 N.E. 829 (1893); Aultman & Co. v. Forgey, 10 Ind. App. 397, 36 N.E. 939 (1894); Shipman Coal Mining & Mfg. Co. v. Pfeiffer, 11 Ind. App. 445, 39 N.E. 291 (1895). See also, Davis v. Warfield, 38 Ind. 461 (1872); Thompson v. Sweetser, 43 Ind. 312 (1873); Branch v. Wiseman, 51 Ind. 1 (1875).

It was not necessary for the plaintiff to prove that the property was detained by the defendant in the county where the action was brought. Robinson v. Shatzley, 75 Ind. 461 (1881); Tanner v. Mishawaka Woolen Mfg. Co., 28 Ind. App. 536, 63 N.E. 313 (1902).

Evidence was necessary on part of plaintiff to show title or right of possession. Miller v. Lively, 1 Ind. App. 6, 27 N.E. 437 (1891); Van Allen v. Smith, 11 Ind. App. 103, 38 N.E. 542

Evidence and Proof. (Cont'd)
(1894); Dederick v. Brandt, 16 Ind. App. 264, 44 N.E. 1010 (1896).

In an action of replevin where the only answer was the general denial, the plaintiff, under such issue, had to show his right of possession, and if the defendant attempted to prove his right of possession, the burden under such issue was upon him. Waterbury v. Miller, 13 Ind. App. 197, 41 N.E. 383 (1895).

Health.
A nuisance may exist in the absence of any injury to health. Yeager & Sullivan, Inc. v. O'Neill, 163 Ind. App. 466, 46 Ind. Dec. 231, 324 N.E.2d 846 (1975).

Highway Obstructions.
The obstruction of a highway was a nuisance. State v. Phipps, 4 Ind. 515 (1853); Langsdale v. Bonton, 12 Ind. 467 (1859); State v. Berdetta, 73 Ind. 185, 38 Am. R. 117 (1880); State v. Louisville, N.A. & C.R.R., 86 Ind. 114 (1882); Wolfe v. Sullivan, 133 Ind. 331, 32 N.E. 1017 (1893); American Furn. Co. v. Town of Batesville, 139 Ind. 77, 38 N.E. 408 (1894); Hall v. Breyfogle, 162 Ind. 494, 70 N.E. 883 (1904); Zimmerman v. State, 4 Ind. App. 583, 31 N.E. 550 (1892).

The erection and maintenance of a permanent building across a public street, closing it to travelers constituted by the state, but an individual had no right of action to recover damages unless he was able to show that he had sustained some particular or peculiar injury, different in kind, and not common to the general public. O'Brien v. Central Iron & Steel Co., 158 Ind. 218, 63 N.E. 302, 57 L.R.A. 508, 92 Am. St. R. 305 (1902).

Hogs.
The keeping of hogs is not a nuisance per se, but may become a nuisance by the manner in which the hogs are kept, the locality or both. Yeager & Sullivan, Inc. v. O'Neill, 163 Ind. App. 466, 46 Ind. Dec. 231, 324 N.E.2d 846 (1975).

Where operators of a hog feeding business allowed excrement and other waste materials to pile up creating offensive odors, and where they failed to take steps to eliminate the breeding and accumulation of excessive numbers of rats and flies, such acts obstructed the free use of the property of adjoining landowners. Yeager & Sullivan, Inc. v. O'Neill, 163 Ind. App. 466, 46 Ind. Dec. 231, 324 N.E.2d 846 (1975).

Immediate Possession, Affidavit.
In actions commenced in the circuit court, if the immediate possession of the property was not claimed, no affidavit or bond need have been filed. Catterlin v. Mitchell, 27 Ind. 298,

89 Am. Dec. 501 (1866); Hodson v. Warner, 60 Ind. 214 (1877).

The contents of an affidavit when immediate possession of property was claimed, must have shown that the plaintiff had no other complete and adequate remedy, in order for injunction to lie. Allen v. Winstandly, 135 Ind. 105, 34 N.E. 699 (1893).

If no affidavit was filed by the plaintiff on commencing suit, he was not entitled to the immediate possession of the property, but the trial proceeded to try title and right of possession. Andrews v. Sellers, 11 Ind. App. 301, 38 N.E. 1101 (1894).

Independent Contractors.
A contractee cannot escape liability for a nuisance it creates by hiring an independent contractor to do work which by its nature causes the nuisance. Gray v. Westinghouse Elec. Corp., 624 N.E.2d 49 (Ind. App. 1993).

Instructions.
When in action by administrators of a decedent to recover possession of certain bonds held by defendant, who had refused, on demand, to deliver them to plaintiffs, defendant answered by general denial and also claimed right of possession of the bonds under a contract with the deceased, an instruction that the burden was on defendant to prove his alleged contract with the decedent by a fair preponderance of the evidence, was proper. Warner v. Warner, 104 Ind. App. 252, 10 N.E.2d 773 (1937).

In an action for damages for infection of an accidental wound suffered by a child falling and cutting his knee while playing along a ditch containing "putrescent, poisonous, infectious and fecal matter," it was not error for the court to give to the jury an instruction consisting of the quotation of former IC 34-19-1-1 (repealed; see this section for similar provisions). City of Evansville v. Rinehart, 142 Ind. App. 164, 12 Ind. Dec. 675, 233 N.E.2d 495 (1968).

Interest in Property.
One must possess a proprietary interest in land in order to bring an action in private nuisance; where a plaintiff has no proprietary interest in the land on which his or her injuries occur, the proper cause of action lies in premises liability and not in private nuisance. Hutchens v. MP Realty Group, 654 N.E.2d 35 (Ind. App. 1995).

Judgment.
If the party in whose favor the verdict was returned had possession of the property, the judgment should have been that he was entitled to the possession thereof. Chissom v. Lamcool, 9 Ind. 530 (1857).

When there was a finding for the plaintiff,

Judgment. (Cont'd)

the judgment should have been that he recovered possession of the property, and in case a delivery could not be had, that he recovered the value thereof, with the damages for its detention. Bales v. Scott, 26 Ind. 202 (1866); Thompson v. Eagleton, 33 Ind. 300 (1870); Farrar v. Eash, 5 Ind. App. 238, 31 N.E. 1125 (1892).

If the suit was dismissed before verdict, there could have been no judgment for a return of the property. Wiseman v. Lynn, 39 Ind. 250 (1872); Hulman v. Benighof, 125 Ind. 481, 25 N.E. 549 (1890); Peffley v. Kenrick, 4 Ind. App. 510, 31 N.E. 40 (1892).

Landfill.

Where the facts found by the trial court show: (1) the conception rate of plaintiff's pigs ranged between 70% and 90% before the landfill on defendant's land began its operation; (2) the rate was reduced to 30% following the opening of the landfill; and (3) the reduction in rate of conception was due to the noise generated by the trash hauling trucks traveling to and from the landfill, the evidence and all reasonable inferences from it led inescapably to the conclusion defendant's use of its property was unreasonable in relation to plaintiff's use of his property as a hog breeding facility. Sherk v. Indiana Waste Sys., 495 N.E.2d 815 (Ind. App. 1986).

Limitation of Actions.

An action must have been brought within six years of the time that the cause of action accrued. Ohio & M.R.R. v. Simon, 40 Ind. 278 (1872); Lucas v. Marine, 40 Ind. 289 (1872).

Actions for damages on account of private nuisances had to be brought within six years after the actions accrue. Sherlock v. Louisville, N.A. & C. Ry., 115 Ind. 22, 17 N.E. 171 (1888); Peck v. City of Michigan City, 149 Ind. 670, 49 N.E. 800 (1898); Kelly v. Pittsburgh, C., C. & St. L.R.R., 28 Ind. App. 457, 63 N.E. 233, 91 Am. St. R. 134 (1902).

If a nuisance was of such a character that it continued from day to day, a cause of action because of the nuisance was not barred by the statute of limitations. May v. George, 53 Ind. App. 259, 101 N.E. 393 (1913).

L-P Gas Tanks.

Where plaintiff failed to prove that construction of L-P gas tank on neighboring land within 300 feet of his house would present a fire or explosion hazard, or that there would be traffic hazards, noise, odors, and dust, the trial court correctly found that there was no nuisance. Hays v. Hartfield L-P Gas, 159 Ind. App. 297, 40 Ind. Dec. 512, 306 N.E.2d 373 (1974).

Measure of Damages.

The measure of damages in a nuisance case is the injury to the use of the property including the depreciation in rental value. Yeager & Sullivan, Inc. v. O'Neill, 163 Ind. App. 466, 46 Ind. Dec. 231, 324 N.E.2d 846 (1975).

Motion for New Trial.

Where the issue tried by the court was the right to immediate possession, the court could apply replevin immediately after judgment was signed to the object of the suit and need not have stayed the order pending motion for a new trial. Crescent City Aviation, Inc. v. Beverly Bank, 139 Ind. App. 669, 9 Ind. Dec. 67, 219 N.E.2d 446 (1966).

Municipal Property and Functions.

Cemetery was not, per se, a nuisance. Begein v. Anderson, 28 Ind. 79 (1867).

City hospital was neither prima facie nor per se a nuisance. Bessonies v. City of Indianapolis, 71 Ind. 189 (1880).

Pump placed in street by a city for public use was held not a nuisance. Lostutter v. City of Aurora, 126 Ind. 436, 26 N.E. 184, 12 L.R.A. 259 (1891).

A municipal corporation has the right to treat as a nuisance a thing that, from its character, location and surroundings, may, or does, become a nuisance. Walker v. Jameson, 140 Ind. 591, 37 N.E. 402, 39 N.E. 869, 28 L.R.A. 679, 49 Am. St. R. 222 (1894).

Although a municipal corporation had the authority to declare what would constitute a nuisance it could not declare something to be a nuisance which in fact was not. City of Evansville v. Miller, 146 Ind. 613, 45 N.E. 1054, 38 L.R.A. 161 (1897); State ex rel. City of Indianapolis v. Indianapolis Union Ry., 160 Ind. 45, 66 N.E. 163, 60 L.R.A. 831 (1903); Rushville Natural Gas Co. v. Town of Morristown, 30 Ind. App. 455, 66 N.E. 179 (1903).

The authority of the common council of a city, as to the manner of improving streets and alleys, being an agency of the state in the exercise of legislative power, could not be controlled by the courts, and where the improvement was such that it cut off ingress and egress to and from the property, the nuisance was one which could not be abated, and there could only be one recovery for damages present and prospective, and that by the owner of the property when the injury occurred. Stein v. City of La Fayette, 6 Ind. App. 414, 33 N.E. 912 (1893).

Municipal corporations were liable for the erection and maintenance of nuisances. City of Valparaiso v. Moffitt, 12 Ind. App. 250, 39 N.E. 909, 54 Am. St. R. 522 (1895); City of New Albany v. Slider, 21 Ind. App. 392, 52 N.E. 626 (1899); City of New Albany v. Armstrong, 22 Ind. App. 15, 53 N.E. 185 (1899).

The fact that plaintiff was a resident of the

**Municipal Property and
   Functions.** (Cont'd)

city, and the city committed the acts complained of in an effort to keep its streets clean for the benefit of the public, did not destroy his right to maintain an action for damages against the city for creating a nuisance by depositing garbage and filth near plaintiff's premises of such a nature as to produce sickness. City of New Albany v. Slider, 21 Ind. App. 392, 52 N.E. 626 (1899).

Sewers that were kept and maintained so as to cause injury and damages were nuisances. City of Cannelton v. Bush, 45 Ind. App. 638, 91 N.E. 359 (1910); May v. George, 53 Ind. App. 259, 101 N.E. 393 (1913).

Where town resorted to the courts to have declared a nuisance and abated as such, a cement sidewalk which was built on a higher grade than the walks adjoining at either end, the town assumed the burden of establishing that the walk by reason of its comparative elevation, was a public nuisance, in that its use was perilous to pedestrians. Carlisle v. Pirtle, 63 Ind. App. 475, 114 N.E. 705 (1917).

Where residents of a town were given express permission by the town board to connect their toilets to a drain, and in one instance the trustees of the town put a ditch across a street so that one of the residents could tap his sewer outlet to the drain, an injunction restraining the use of the drain for the purposes of a sanitary sewer was properly issued against the town as well as against the parties who had so used it, even though the evidence disclosed that the town owned no toilets which emptied into it. Bearcreek Tp. v. DeHoff, 113 Ind. App. 530, 49 N.E.2d 391 (1943).

A municipal corporation was liable for maintaining or contributing to the maintenance of a nuisance to the same extent as was an individual, and it could be jointly liable with others for the maintenance thereof, and, in an action for that purpose, could be compelled to abate it. Bearcreek Tp. v. DeHoff, 113 Ind. App. 530, 49 N.E.2d 391 (1943).

Building owner failed to state an actionable nuisance claim against a city, since the owner's damages were not related to an alleged nuisance involving a fire which started in an adjacent vacant city-owned building but to the loss occasioned by the fire itself, and there was no allegation that the city "maintained" or "continued" the fire. Witco Corp. v. City of Indianapolis, 762 F. Supp. 834 (S.D. Ind. 1991).

Nature of Action.

Replevin was a possessory action, and the purpose thereof was to determine who should have had possession of property sought to have been replevied. Title of the property was not involved. Meyer v. Deifenbach, 100 Ind. App. 360, 193 N.E. 693 (1935).

Nonresidents.

Unless chattels were alleged to be detained in some county of this state, jurisdiction over nonresidents could not be obtained without service of process, but service could be made on the resident agents of such nonresidents. Rauber v. Whitney, 125 Ind. 216, 25 N.E. 186 (1890).

Oil and Gas Wells.

The drilling of an oil well within 152 feet of a dwelling-house would not be enjoined because of the noise, pollution of the air, danger from fire or explosion that would result from the operation of the well, or on account of water or oil from the well, where it was not shown that the gas well could not be operated in such a manner as to avoid the injuries apprehended. Windfall Mfg. Co. v. Patterson, 148 Ind. 414, 47 N.E. 2, 37 L.R.A. 381, 62 Am. St. R. 532 (1897).

In a suit by the state to enjoin an oil company from wasting public gas it was held that the facts stated in the complaint made a case of public nuisance which the state had a right to have abated by injunction. State v. Ohio Oil Co., 150 Ind. 21, 49 N.E. 809, 47 L.R.A. 627 (1898).

If the operator of gas and oil wells permitted salt water and oil to flow upon the lands of others, it could constitute a nuisance. Niagara Oil Co. v. Ogle, 177 Ind. 292, 98 N.E. 60, 42 L.R.A. (n.s.) 714, 1914D Ann. Cas. 67 (1912).

Evidence of use of barker or whistle, in connection with oil well, giving out 40 or 50 distinct sounds every minute supported finding that it was not nuisance. Meeks v. Wood, 66 Ind. App. 594, 118 N.E. 591 (1918).

Parties Plaintiff.

—In General.

An officer having been entitled, as such, to the possession of chattels, could replevy the same. Aman v. Mottweiler, 15 Ind. App. 405, 44 N.E. 63 (1896). See also, Dunkin v. McKee, 23 Ind. 447 (1864).

Joint owner of property could not replevy the same from another joint owner in possession. Bowen v. Roach, 78 Ind. 361 (1881); Robinson v. Dickey, 143 Ind. 205, 42 N.E. 679, 52 Am. St. R. 417 (1896); Bain v. Trixler, 24 Ind. App. 246, 56 N.E. 690 (1900). See also, Mills v. Malott, 43 Ind. 248 (1873).

A part owner of a chattel could maintain replevin against a person having no right therein. Bain v. Trixler, 24 Ind. App. 246, 56 N.E. 690 (1900).

Replevin bail could not replevy his property from an officer because he did not first levy on the property of the judgment defendant.

Parties Plaintiff. (Cont'd)

—In General. (Cont'd)
Miller v. Hudson, 114 Ind. 550, 17 N.E. 122 (1888).

A guardian could sue to recover possession of the chattels of his ward. Boruff v. Stipp, 126 Ind. 32, 25 N.E. 865 (1890).

—Mortgagee.
A mortgagee of chattels could have replevied the same if the debt was not paid at maturity. Recker v. Kilgore, 62 Ind. 10 (1878); Roberts v. Norris, 67 Ind. 386 (1879); Johnson v. Simpson, 77 Ind. 412 (1881).

A mortgagee of chattels could not have replevied the same from an officer who levied an execution against the mortgagor on such chattels. Olds v. Andrews, 66 Ind. 147 (1878).

Defense showing no debt owing, defeated action on mortgagee suing to recover goods. Aultman & Co. v. Forgey, 10 Ind. App. 397, 36 N.E. 939 (1894); Aultman & Co. v. Richardson, 10 Ind. App. 413, 38 N.E. 532 (1894).

Mortgages had to be properly and timely recorded to enable the mortgagee to replevy the property for nonpayment. Kahn v. Hayes, 22 Ind. App. 182, 53 N.E. 430 (1895).

Pollution of Streams.
A complaint showing defendant discharged large quantities of poisonous refuse from its pulp-mill into a creek which ran through plaintiff's land, thereby destroying a large part thereof, stated a cause of action for damages. Muncie Pulp Co. v. Keesling, 166 Ind. 479, 76 N.E. 1002 (1906); Muncie Pulp Co. v. Martin, 23 Ind. App. 558, 55 N.E. 796 (1899).

Where a corporation by the operation of a factory discharges offal into a river so as to affect injuriously the people along the river such corporation maintains a nuisance. Paragon Paper Co. v. State, 19 Ind. App. 314, 49 N.E. 600 (1898).

A person charged with depositing offal and sewage from a factory into a river may be prosecuted in an adjoining county into which such offal was carried by the current of the river. State v. Herring, 21 Ind. App. 157, 48 N.E. 598, 51 N.E. 951, 69 Am. St. R. 351 (1897).

In a complaint against the defendant for emptying into a stream refuse of acids and other unwholesome matter from its factory located on a stream above the plaintiff's farm it was not necessary to allege that the use the defendant made of the stream in carrying on its business was unreasonable or unnecessary. Muncie Pulp Co. v. Martin, 23 Ind. App. 558, 55 N.E. 796 (1899).

A city which discharged sewage without purification into a natural stream could be held liable for injury to a riparian owner injured by such disposal. City of Frankfort v. Slipher, 88 Ind. App. 356, 162 N.E. 241 (1928).

Possession of Property.
Where a written agreement concerning the manufacturing of items by defendant from materials furnished by plaintiff pursuant to the terms therein stated was in full force and had not been canceled pursuant to the provision concerning cancellation, plaintiff was not entitled to the immediate possession of materials furnished defendant and hence an action for replevin did not lie. Allen B. Wrisley Distrib. Co. v. Serewicz, 145 F.2d 169 (7th Cir. 1944).

Replevin was appropriate against any person having the unlawful possession of goods. Ferguson v. Day, 6 Ind. App. 138, 33 N.E. 213 (1893). See also, Rowell v. Klein, 44 Ind. 290, 15 Am. R. 235 (1873); Rose v. Cash, 58 Ind. 278 (1877).

It had to be shown that the defendant had possession of and unlawfully detained the property when the action was begun. Louthain v. Fitzer, 78 Ind. 449 (1884); Standard Oil Co. v. Bretz, 98 Ind. 231 (1884); Peninsular Stove Co. v. Ellis, 20 Ind. App. 491, 51 N.E. 105 (1898); West v. Graff, 23 Ind. App. 410, 55 N.E. 506 (1899); Morgan v. Jackson, 32 Ind. App. 169, 69 N.E. 410 (1904).

To sustain replevin the evidence had to show that the defendant was in actual or constructive possession of the property at the time of the commencement of the action. Louthain v. Fitzer, 78 Ind. 449 (1881); Hadley v. Hadley, 82 Ind. 75 (1882); Teeple v. Dickey, 94 Ind. 124 (1884); VanGorder v. Smith, 99 Ind. 404 (1885); Fruits v. Elmore, 8 Ind. App. 278, 34 N.E. 829 (1893); Peninsular Stove Co. v. Ellis, 20 Ind. App. 491, 51 N.E. 105 (1898); West v. Graff, 23 Ind. App. 410, 55 N.E. 506 (1899).

The plaintiff had to be entitled to the immediate possession of the property in order to maintain replevin. Whitehead v. Coyle, 1 Ind. App. 450, 27 N.E. 716 (1891); Ferguson v. Day, 6 Ind. App. 450, 27 N.E. 716 (1891); Ferguson v. Day, 6 Ind. App. 138, 33 N.E. 213 (1893); Fruits v. Elmore, 8 Ind. App. 278, 34 N.E. 829 (1893); Aultman & Co. v. Forgey, 10 Ind. App. 397, 36 N.E. 939 (1894); Jarrett v. Cauldwell, 47 Ind. App. 478, 94 N.E. 790 (1911); Woods v. Shearer, 56 Ind. App. 650, 105 N.E. 917 (1914).

Transfer before suit would not defeat action for unlawful possession. Helman v. Withers, 3 Ind. App. 532, 30 N.E. 5, 50 Am. St. R. 295 (1892).

The plaintiff had to allege and prove that he had title to, and right of possession of, the property sought to be replevied, and, if there was a failure in this regard, there could be no recovery, even though the defendant's posses-

Possession of Property. (Cont'd)
sion was wrongful. Central Trust Co. v. Duncan, 92 Ind. App. 224, 168 N.E. 506 (1929).

Conditional seller of automobile was entitled to possession as against purchaser where seller executed on back of contract an assignment of contract and interest of seller in automobile and therein guaranteed payment of the unpaid purchase price, and delivered the contract to assignee, and upon default of purchaser paid to assignee the unpaid amount of purchase price and assignee delivered contract back to seller, though evidence did not show written reassignment to seller; and judgment for the seller in an action of replevin ageinst the purchaser was proper. Meyer v. Deifenbach, 100 Ind. App. 360, 193 N.E. 693 (1935).

Prescription.
Prescription was no defense to a public nuisance. State v. Phipps, 4 Ind. 515 (1853); State v. Louisville, N.A. & C.R.R., 86 Ind. 114 (1882); Wolfe v. Sullivan, 133 Ind. 331, 32 N.E. 1017 (1893); Bissel Chilled Plow Works v. South Bend Mfg. Co., 64 Ind. App. 1, 111 N.E. 932 (1916).

The right to maintain a strictly private nuisance could be acquired by 20 years' use. Sherlock v. Louisville, N.A. & C. Ry., 115 Ind. 22, 17 N.E. 171 (1888).

Presumed Continuance.
Presumption that a nuisance would continue under the same conditions for an indefinite period arose from the fact that it was not legally abatable and was permitted to exist by authority of law. Northern Ind. Pub. Serv. Co. v. Vesey, 210 Ind. 338, 200 N.E. 620 (1936).

Prior Owners.
A purchaser of property may not sue a prior owner of the same property for nuisance based on actions that affected the same property and that were undertaken while the prior owner controlled the property. Lilly Indus., Inc. v. Health-Chem Corp., 974 F. Supp. 702 (S.D. Ind. 1997).

Privies.
The erection of a privy and vault within three and one-half feet of the dining room of an adjoining owner could be enjoined as a nuisance, without reference to the manner in which the vault was constructed or to the intention of the defendants to use disinfectants. Radican v. Buckley, 138 Ind. 582, 38 N.E. 53 (1894).

Property Attached to Realty.
Crops growing on land could have been replevied. Matlock v. Fry, 15 Ind. 483 (1860).

Articles forming part of realty could not be replevied, but when detached from the land could be recovered in such action. Moore v. Combs, 24 Ind. App. 464, 56 N.E. 35 (1900).

A complaint in replevin for a house had to allege that such house was personal property. Adams v. Tully, 164 Ind. 292, 73 N.E. 595 (1905).

Property Obtained by Fraud.
Property obtained by fraud could be replevied before it passed into the hands of innocent parties. Parrish v. Thurston, 87 Ind. 437 (1882); Brower v. Goodyear, 88 Ind. 572 (1883); Curme, Dunn & Co. v. Rauh, 100 Ind. 247 (1885); Thompson v. Peck, 115 Ind. 512, 18 N.E. 16, 1 L.R.A. 201 (1888); Adam, Meldrum & Anderson Co. v. Stewart, 157 Ind. 678, 61 N.E. 1002, 87 Am. St. R. 240 (1901); Tennessee Coal, Iron & R.R. v. Sargent, 2 Ind. App. 458, 28 N.E. 215 (1891); Levi v. Kraminer, 2 Ind. App. 594, 28 N.E. 1028 (1891); Peninsular Stove Co. v. Ellis, 20 Ind. App. 491, 51 N.E. 105 (1898); John H. Hibben Dry Goods Co. v. Hicks, 26 Ind. App. 646, 59 N.E. 938 (1901); Rauh v. Waterman, 29 Ind. App. 344, 61 N.E. 743, 63 N.E. 42 (1901); Jarrett v. Cauldwell, 47 Ind. App. 478, 94 N.E. 790 (1911); Woods v. Shearer, 56 Ind. App. 650, 105 N.E. 917 (1914).

Property Subject to Lien.
Property held by virtue of a lien could not have been taken by replevin until the lien was paid. Evansville & C.R.R. v. Marsh, 57 Ind. 505 (1877); Shappendocia v. Spencer, 73 Ind. 128 (1880).

Lienholder unlawfully deprived of possession of property could recover the same. Walls v. Long, 2 Ind. App. 202, 28 N.E. 101 (1891).

When defendant had recovered judgment for reward for finding property, he had right to retain possession until the judgment was paid and the owner was not entitled to replevy the same. Everman v. Hyman, 3 Ind. App. 459, 29 N.E. 1140 (1892).

If a lienholder obtained possession of the property with or without the consent of the owner, such owner could not maintain replevin without payment of the lien. Reardon v. Higgins, 39 Ind. App. 363, 79 N.E. 208 (1906).

If the defendant had a lien on the property, he could set the same up as a counter-claim and have the lien foreclosed. The judgment should have fixed the amount of the lien and directed a delivery of the property to the plaintiff on payment of the lien. Reardon v. Higgins, 39 Ind. App. 363, 79 N.E. 208 (1906); Shore v. Ogden, 55 Ind. App. 394, 103 N.E. 852 (1914).

Property Taken for Taxes.
Property taken for taxes could not be replevied. Adams v. Davis, 109 Ind. 10, 9 N.E. 162 (1886); Maple v. Vestal, 114 Ind. 325, 16

Property Taken for Taxes. (Cont'd)
N.E. 620 (1888); Andrews v. Sellers, 11 Ind.
App. 301, 38 N.E. 1101 (1894).

Property Wrongfully Levied On.
Replevin was appropriate against an officer
who wrongfully took possession of the chattels of another. Hadley v. Hadley, 82 Ind. 95
(1882); Allen v. Winstandly, 135 Ind. 105, 34
N.E. 699 (1893); Smith v. Downey, 8 Ind. App.
179, 34 N.E. 823, 35 N.E. 568, 52 Am. St. R.
467 (1893); Patterson v. Snow, 24 Ind. App.
572, 57 N.E. 286 (1900).

A mere levy on property without taking
possession thereof would not justify the action. Standard Oil Co. v. Bretz, 98 Ind. 231
(1884); Aman v. Mottweiler, 15 Ind. App. 405,
44 N.E. 63 (1896).

Chattels had to be exempt from execution
in order that the debtor could replevy them
from an officer levying an execution thereon.
Hartlep v. Cole, 101 Ind. 458 (1885); Louisville, E. & St. L.R.R. v. Payne, 103 Ind. 183, 2
N.E. 582 (1885).

Injunction, and not replevin, was the
proper remedy of one holding property under
bill of sale from the judgment debtor to prevent a sale of the property on execution,
where the property after levy was left in the
possession of the plaintiff without any bond,
undertaking, or agreement for return of the
property. Owens v. Gascho, 154 Ind. 225, 56
N.E. 224 (1900).

Recovery of exempt property from officer
levying on the same was upheld. Adams v.
Hessian, 11 Ind. App. 598, 39 N.E. 530 (1895).

If a writ of attachment was sent to another
county for service, and the sheriff levied the
same upon the property of a person who was
not a party to the attachment suit, such
person could maintain an action of replevin to
recover the property. Hoover v. Lewin, 56 Ind.
App. 367, 105 N.E. 400 (1914); Wood v.
Rathman, 58 Ind. App. 229, 108 N.E. 126
(1915).

Public Nuisance.

—In General.
Inherent danger is required for plaintiff to
proceed under a public nuisance theory, and
no nuisance was found because the agency
alleged to be a public nuisance was only
dangerous when used improperly. Sand Creek
Partners v. Finch, 647 N.E.2d 1149 (Ind. App.
1995).

—Private Party.
Because plaintiff, a private party, could not
show a special injury apart from that suffered
by the general public, plaintiff was precluded
from claiming a public nuisance. Hill v. Rieth-
Riley Constr. Co., 670 N.E.2d 940 (Ind. App.
1996).

Railroads.
A railroad in the street of a town was not a
nuisance. New Albany & S.R.R. v. O'Daily, 12
Ind. 551 (1859).

Owner of abutting lot could not maintain an
action for damages for unlawful obstruction
caused by construction of railroad embankment, the only effect of which was to render
more difficult access to his property, as the
injury was the same in kind as that suffered
by the community in general, differing only in
degree. Indiana, B. & W.R.R. v. Eberle, 110
Ind. 542, 11 N.E. 467, 59 Am. R. 225 (1887).

One who located his residence in a district
already wholly devoted to manufacturing purposes would be held to have anticipated the
incidental damages resulting from smoke,
gases, fumes, and noises, which must have
been regarded as damnum absque injuria,
and a bill to enjoin the operation of switch
engines in that neighborhood which were
used to transport the products of the manufacturing plants, and which steam up at
night, would not lie. Bennett v. Lake Erie &
W.R.R., 74 Ind. App. 156, 127 N.E. 777 (1920).

Where judgment was rendered based upon
the difference in the value of the properties
with the objectionable noise and illumination
and without the objectionable noise and illumination caused by establishment of railroad
yards and supported by special findings of
fact and conclusions of law that the operation
part of the railroad yards constituted a nuisance, the judgment was affirmed. Pennsylvania Cent. Transp. Co. v. Wilson, 155 Ind. App.
328, 35 Ind. Dec. 300, 292 N.E.2d 827 (1973).

Res Judicata.
The judgment entered in a replevin action
is conclusive as to all questions which were
litigated or which might have been litigated
under the issues. State Exch. Bank v. Teague,
495 N.E.2d 262 (Ind. App. 1986).

Where a bank's replevin action sought judgment on the defendant's indebtedness to it
and for possession of the collateral securing
the promissory note and defendants' claims,
on the other hand, refer to the manner in
which the bank went about securing possession of the collateral, at best, defendants
could have asserted their claims in the replevin action as permissive counterclaims under TR. 13(B), but they were not obliged to do
so, and the claims are not barred by res
judicata. State Exch. Bank v. Teague, 495
N.E.2d 262 (Ind. App. 1986).

Review.
If conflicting evidence exists regarding the
plaintiffs' claims sounding in nuisance, and
on appeal the parties merely ask the court to
reweigh the evidence, the appellate court
must affirm. Wendt v. Kerkhof, 594 N.E.2d
795 (Ind. App. 1992).

Spite Fence.

The erection of a high fence on one's own property, which shut off the view, air and light of the adjoining property, did not constitute an actionable nuisance. Giller v. West, 162 Ind. 17, 69 N.E. 548 (1904); Russell v. State, 32 Ind. App. 243, 69 N.E. 482 (1904). But a special statute made it actionable, see IC 32-10-10-1, IC 32-10-10-2.

Steam Engines.

It was not necessarily a nuisance to operate a portable steam engine, in a careful manner, in close proximity to a public highway. Wabash, St. L. & P.R.R. v. Farver, 111 Ind. 195, 12 N.E. 296, 60 Am. R. 696 (1887).

A steam engine in use which was so out of repair as to be in an unsafe condition for such use was a nuisance. Deller v. Hofferberth, 127 Ind. 414, 26 N.E. 889 (1891).

Stray Bullet.

Motel guest injured by a stray bullet from another room could not recover under a private nuisance theory because there was no evidence that the guest's use and enjoyment of the motel room was interfered with by the motel. Hopper v. Colonial Motel Props., Inc., 762 N.E.2d 181 (Ind. App. 2002).

Summary Judgment.

The conclusion that something is a per accidens nuisance, or nuisance in fact, is a conclusion to be reached only after a full review of the material facts. Summary judgment, which by definition is meant to resolve only those cases lacking material factual disputes, is therefore rarely appropriate in per accidens nuisance cases. Wernke v. Halas, 600 N.E.2d 117 (Ind. App. 1992).

Where genuine issues of material fact existed as to whether the defendant power company exercised due care in its placement and operation of a power line and whether it exceeded the scope of its easement, summary judgment on the plaintiffs' nuisance claim was precluded. Indiana Mich. Power Co. v. Runge, 717 N.E.2d 216 (Ind. App. 1999).

Surface Water.

A railroad company was not liable to a landowner for injuries caused by the accumulation of surface water on his premises by reason of the construction of embankments on its right of way. Hill v. Cincinnati, W. & M.R.R., 109 Ind. 511, 10 N.E. 410 (1887).

The rule that a landowner could dam against surface water to prevent it flowing upon his lands did not apply to waters flowing over lowlands adjacent to a stream or watercourse as a result of heavy rains, causing the stream to overflow its natural banks, which overflow water followed the course of the stream to its outlet, or, on the subsidence of

the flood, returned to the channel. Watts v. Evansville, Mt. C. & N.R.R., 191 Ind. 27, 129 N.E. 315 (1921).

The characterization of an action for the recovery of damages caused by the flow of surface water as one based on a nuisance could not circumvent the common-enemy doctrine. Pickett v. Brown, 569 N.E.2d 706 (Ind. App. 1991).

Under the common-enemy doctrine of water diversion, it is not unlawful to accelerate or increase the flow of surface water by limiting or eliminating ground absorption or changing the grade of the land. Pickett v. Brown, 569 N.E.2d 706 (Ind. App. 1991).

Title to Property.

The judgment only determined the right of possession of the property unless the title was put in issue and determined. Smith v. Mosby, 98 Ind. 445 (1884); McFadden v. Ross, 108 Ind. 512, 8 N.E. 161 (1886); Consolidated Tank Line Co. v. Bronson, 2 Ind. App. 1, 28 N.E. 155 (1891). See also, Highnote v. White, 67 Ind. 596 (1879); Kramer v. Matthews, 68 Ind. 172 (1879).

A judgment in a replevin suit concluded the plaintiffs therein as to the ownership of the property and as to its value. Smith v. Mosby, 98 Ind. 445 (1884); Whitehead v. Coyle, 1 Ind. App. 450, 27 N.E. 716 (1891); Fromlet v. Poor, 3 Ind. App. 425, 29 N.E. 1081 (1892).

Payment of judgment for the value of property vested title to the property in the defendant. McFadden v. Schroeder, 4 Ind. App. 305, 29 N.E. 491, 30 N.E. 711 (1892); Ledbetter v. Embree, 12 Ind. App. 617, 40 N.E. 928 (1895).

Unsightliness.

Standing alone, unsightliness, or lack of aesthetic virtue, does not constitute a private nuisance. If unsightliness is coupled with additional harms, however, such as pollution or a physical invasion, a private nuisance may be established. Wernke v. Halas, 600 N.E.2d 117 (Ind. App. 1992).

Venue.

An action of replevin could have been brought in any county where the defendant resided. Hodson v. Warner, 60 Ind. 214 (1877).

Actions of replevin had to be brought in the county where one of the defendants resided. Fry v. Shafor, 164 Ind. 699, 74 N.E. 503 (1905).

An action in replevin had to be brought in the county where the defendant resided, and a plea in abatement to the venue should have been sustained where such action brought in a different county, even though the property sought to be replevied was situated therein. Buck v. Young, 1 Ind. App. 558, 27 N.E. 1106 (1891); Fry v. Shafer, 164 Ind. 699, 74 N.E. 503 (1905).

Verdict.

If the property was in possession of the plaintiff, and a general verdict was returned for the defendant, without fixing the value of the property, judgment for its return could not have been rendered. Tardy v. Howard, 12 Ind. 404 (1859); Conner v. Comstock, 17 Ind. 90 (1861); McKeal v. Freeman, 25 Ind. 151 (1865).

If the verdict did not find the value of the goods and no objection was made, the omission would have been deemed waived. Wilcoxon v. Annesley, 23 Ind. 285 (1864).

If it did not appear who had possession of the property, a general verdict for the defendant was void for uncertainty. McKeal v. Freeman, 25 Ind. 151 (1865).

A general verdict or finding in favor of the plaintiff found that he was the owner of, and entitled to, the possession of the property. Rowan v. Teague, 24 Ind. 304 (1865); Crocker v. Hoffman, 48 Ind. 207 (1874); Payne v. June, 92 Ind. 252 (1883).

If the verdict was in favor of one party for all the property, the verdict need not have described the property. Anderson v. Lane, 32 Ind. 102 (1869).

The verdict must have found as to the right of possession of the property, and not have stated conclusions. Keller v. Boatman, 49 Ind. 104 (1874); Ridenour v. Beekman, 68 Ind. 236 (1879).

When title and right of possession were both in issue, a general verdict in favor of the plaintiff was sufficient. Van Gundy v. Carrigan, 4 Ind. App. 333, 30 N.E. 933 (1892).

If the plaintiff had possession and the verdict was in favor, the defendant could not object because the value of the goods was not found. Van Gundy v. Carrigan, 4 Ind. App. 333, 30 N.E. 933 (1892); Busching v. Sunman, 19 Ind. App. 683, 49 N.E. 1091 (1898).

If the verdict was in favor of the plaintiff, the value of the property should have been stated and damages assessed for its detention. Farrar v. Eash, 5 Ind. App. 238, 31 N.E. 1125 (1892).

What Constitutes Nuisance.

Anything offensive to the sight, smell, or hearing, erected or carried on in a public place, where the people dwell or pass, or have a right to pass is a nuisance at common law. Hackney v. State, 8 Ind. 494 (1857).

Whatever is injurious to health, or indecent, or offensive to the senses, or an obstruction to the free use of property, so as essentially to interfere with the comfortable enjoyment of life or property, is a nuisance. Ohio & M.R.R. v. Simon, 40 Ind. 278 (1872).

A public nuisance need not have constituted an annoyance or injury to all the citizens but only to any part of them. Moses v. State, 58 Ind. 185 (1877).

An obstruction to the free use of property, so as essentially to interfere with the comfortable enjoyment of life or property, is a nuisance. Williamson v. Yingling, 93 Ind. 42 (1884).

Whatever was offensive to sight, smell or hearing that was erected or carried on in such a manner as to materially interfere with health or the enjoyment of property was a nuisance. Haggart v. Stehlin, 137 Ind. 43, 35 N.E. 997, 22 L.R.A. 577 (1893); Kissel v. Lewis, 156 Ind. 233, 59 N.E. 478 (1901); Shroyer v. Campbell, 31 Ind. App. 83, 67 N.E. 193 (1903); Acme Fertilizer Co. v. State, 34 Ind. App. 346, 72 N.E. 1037, 107 Am. St. R. 190 (1905); Zeppenfeld v. Franklin Motor Serv. Co., 77 Ind. App. 687, 134 N.E. 487 (1922).

Not every dangerous agency was a nuisance, and we believe it could be said generally that an instrumentality maintained upon private premises could only be said to be a nuisance upon the ground that it was calculated to produce personal injuries when it was of such character, and so maintained, that it was reasonably and naturally calculated to injure the general public or strangers who might come upon the premises. Kirklin v. Everman, 217 Ind. 683, 28 N.E.2d 73 (1940); DeMoss v. Coleman, 139 Ind. App. 346, 8 Ind. Dec. 415, 216 N.E.2d 861 (1966).

A dog pen which emitted offensive odors and which contained a dog which barked excessively at night, so as to disturb the rest of neighbors, and which contained no dog house to shelter the dog from rain was a nuisance under former IC 34-19-1-1 (repealed; see this section for similar provisions). Davoust v. Mitchell, 146 Ind. App. 536, 21 Ind. Dec. 124, 257 N.E.2d 332 (1970).

A nuisance consists of an unreasonable interference with the use and enjoyment of one's property as determined by reasonable persons of ordinary sensibilities, and of ordinary tastes and habits. Yeager & Sullivan, Inc. v. O'Neill, 163 Ind. App. 466, 46 Ind. Dec. 231, 324 N.E.2d 846 (1975); Friendship Farms Camps, Inc. v. Parson, 172 Ind. App. 73, 56 Ind. 215, 359 N.E.2d 280 (1977).

It is not necessary that actual injury, physical sickness or illness result to find a nuisance. Friendship Farms Camps, Inc. v. Parson, 172 Ind. App. 73, 56 Ind. 215, 359 N.E.2d 280 (1977).

One claiming damages from a public nuisance must demonstrate that the agency as operated has more than a mere tendency to, or increased likelihood of, causing an injury; the alleged nuisance must cause injury as a reasonable and natural result of its operation. Sand Creek Partners v. Finch, 647 N.E.2d 1149 (Ind. App. 1995).

Indiana does not recognize a negligence suit based upon an allegation of annoyance

What Constitutes Nuisance. (Cont'd)
alone; annoyance-based nuisance claims are cognizable, but the annoyance at issue must be tied to some sort of concrete harm. Baker v. Westinghouse Elec. Corp., 70 F.3d 951 (7th Cir. 1995).

Defendant will only be enjoined or sanctioned for his conduct if it is unreasonable; reasonableness is ascertained by comparing the competing interests of the parties. Baker v. Westinghouse Elec. Corp., 70 F.3d 951 (7th Cir. 1995).

Wrongful Taking.
Former IC 34-21-1-1 (repealed; see this section for similar provisions) authorized damages due to a wrongful taking only, and not all damages, regardless of cause, once a wrongful taking has been established. Kegerreis v. Auto-Owners Ins. Co., 484 N.E.2d 976 (Ind. App. 1985).

Collateral References. Attracting people in such numbers as to obstruct access to the neighboring premises as nuisance. 2 A.L.R.2d 437.

Casting light on another's premises in connection with sporting events or amusements as a nuisance. 5 A.L.R.2d 705.

Coalyard as nuisance. 8 A.L.R.2d 419.

Liability of landowner on theory of nuisance for drowning of child. 8 A.L.R.2d 1254.

Playing of game as a nuisance rendering the owner or operator of park or other premises liable for injuries by ball to persons on nearby street, sidewalk or premises. 16 A.L.R.2d 1458.

Animal rendering or bone-boiling plant or business as nuisance. 17 A.L.R.2d 1269.

Keeping dogs, birds or other pets by tenant as nuisance. 18 A.L.R.2d 880; 11 A.L.R.3d 1399.

Liability for nuisance by oil, water, or the like flowing from well. 19 A.L.R.2d 1025.

Liability, based on nuisance, for property damaged by concussion from blasting. 20 A.L.R.2d 1372.

Tourist or trailer camp, motor court or motel as nuisance. 22 A.L.R.2d 774; 24 A.L.R.2d 571.

Use of phonograph, loud speaker, or other mechanical or electrical device for broadcasting music, advertising, or sales talk from business premises as nuisance. 23 A.L.R.2d 1289.

Dust as nuisance. 24 A.L.R.2d 194.

Private school as nuisance. 27 A.L.R.2d 1249.

Recovery of damages in replevin for value of use of property detained by successful party having only security interest as conditional vendor, chattel mortgagee, or the like. 33 A.L.R.2d 774.

Pollution of subterranean waters as nuisance. 38 A.L.R.2d 1265.

Pollution of water caused by operation of sewage disposal plant as nuisance. 40 A.L.R.2d 1177.

Liability on basis of nuisance for injury to or death of child caused by burning from hot ashes, cinders, or other hot waste material. 42 A.L.R.2d 930.

Landowner's liability on ground of nuisance for damages caused by overflow, seepage, or the like resulting from defect in artificial underground drain, conduit, or pipe. 44 A.L.R.2d 960.

Smoke and dust as rendering quarry, gravel pit, or like as a nuisance. 47 A.L.R.2d 490.

Cemetery or burial ground as nuisance. 50 A.L.R.2d 1324.

Public dump as nuisance. 52 A.L.R.2d 1134.

Manner of operation as affecting liability for escape without negligence of harmful gases or fumes from premises. 54 A.L.R.2d 764.

Nuisance by fishing, boating, bathing, or the like in inland lake. 57 A.L.R.2d 569.

Liability on theory of nuisance for injury to property inflicted by wild animal. 57 A.L.R.2d 1036.

Recovery of attorneys' fees as damages by successful litigant in replevin or detinue act. 60 A.L.R.2d 945.

Liability on theory of nuisance of proprietor of office or similar business premises for injury from fall due to presence of litter or debris on floor. 61 A.L.R.2d 100.

Liability on theory of nuisance of proprietor of store or similar business premises for injury from fall on floor made slippery by tracked-in or spilled water, oil, mud, snow, or the like. 62 A.L.R.2d 6.

Liability on theory of nuisance of proprietor of store, office, or similar business premises for injury from fall on ramp or inclined floor. 65 A.L.R.2d 398.

Liability on theory of nuisance for personal injury to one colliding with or falling over scale or machine dispensing merchandise or services on public sidewalk. 65 A.L.R.2d 965.

Liability on theory of nuisance of railroad for injury or damage resulting from motor vehicle striking bridge or underpass because of insufficient vertical clearance. 67 A.L.R.2d 1364.

Golf course or driving range as nuisance. 68 A.L.R.2d 1331.

Contributory negligence as defense against liability for damages from nuisance. 73 A.L.R.2d 1378.

Merry-go-round as nuisance. 75 A.L.R.2d 792.

Maintainability of replevin or similar possessory action where defendant, at time action is brought, is no longer in possession of property. 97 A.L.R.2d 896.

Keeping pigs as a nuisance. 2 A.L.R.3d 931.

Keeping poultry as nuisance. 2 A.L.R.3d 965.

Motorbus or truck terminal as nuisance. 2 A.L.R.3d 1372.

Electric generating plant or transformer station as nuisance. 4 A.L.R.3d 902.

Saloons or taverns as nuisance. 5 A.L.R.3d 989.

Abutting owner's liability for injury from ice formed on sidewalk by discharge of precipitation due to artificial conditions on premises. 18 A.L.R.3d 428.

Institution for punishment or rehabilitation of criminals, delinquents, or alcoholics as enjoinable nuisance. 21 A.L.R.3d 1058.

Gun club, shooting gallery or range, as nuisance. 26 A.L.R.3d 661.

Keeping horses as nuisance. 27 A.L.R.3d 627.

Punitive damages in actions based on nuisance. 31 A.L.R.3d 1346.

Children's playground as nuisance. 32 A.L.R.3d 1127.

Billboards and other outdoor advertising signs as civil nuisances. 38 A.L.R.3d 647.

Airport operations or flight of aircraft as nuisance. 79 A.L.R.3d 253.

Recovery in trespass for injury to land caused by airborne pollutants. 2 A.L.R.4th 1054.

Measure, elements, and amount of damages for killing or injuring cat. 8 A.L.R.4th 1287.

Telephone calls as nuisance. 53 A.L.R.4th 1153.

Tree or limb falls onto adjoining private property: personal injury and property damage liability. 54 A.L.R.4th 530.

Cat as subject of larceny. 55 A.L.R.4th 1080.

Encroachment of trees, shrubbery, or other vegetation across boundary line. 65 A.L.R.4th 603.

Liability for injuries caused by cat. 68 A.L.R.4th 823.

Liability of owner or operator of business premises for injuries from electrically operated door. 44 A.L.R.5th 525.

Liability for injury or death from collision with guy wire. 55 A.L.R.5th 177.

Liability of owner or operator of self-service filling station for injury or death of patron. 60 A.L.R.5th 379.

Determination whether zoning or rezoning of particular parcel constitutes illegal spot zoning. 73 A.L.R.5th 223.

Tower or Antenna as Constituting Nuisance. 88 A.L.R.5th 641.

Keeping of domestic animal as constituting public or private nuisance. 90 A.L.R.5th 619.

Sewage treatment plant as constituting nuisance. 92 A.L.R.5th 517.

Nudity as constituting nuisance. 92 A.L.R.5th 593.

Hog breeding, confining, or processing facility as constituting nuisance. 93 A.L.R.5th 621.

32-30-6-7. Persons who may bring action. — (a) An action to abate or enjoin a nuisance may be brought by any person whose:

(1) property is injuriously affected; or

(2) personal enjoyment is lessened;

by the nuisance.

(b) A civil action to abate or enjoin a nuisance may also be brought by:

(1) an attorney representing the county in which a nuisance exists; or

(2) the attorney of any city or town in which a nuisance exists.

(c) A county, city, or town that brings a successful action under this section (or IC 34-1-52-2 or IC 34-19-1-2 before their repeal) to abate or enjoin a nuisance caused by the unlawful dumping of solid waste is entitled to recover reasonable attorney's fees incurred in bringing the action. [P.L.2-2002, § 15.]

NOTES TO DECISIONS

Analysis

Action for public nuisance.
Definition of nuisance.
Injunction.

Life tenant.
Municipal corporations.
Person suffering special injuries.
State.

Action for Public Nuisance.

A party may bring a successful private action to abate or enjoin a public nuisance if the aggrieved party demonstrates special and peculiar injury apart from the injury suffered by the public. Blair v. Anderson, 570 N.E.2d 1337 (Ind. App. 1991).

Water flow blockage to a creek on plaintiffs' property was sufficient special injury to give standing to bring a private action to abate and enjoin a nuisance resulting from the operation or maintenance of an open dump. Blair v. Anderson, 570 N.E.2d 1337 (Ind. App. 1991).

Definition of Nuisance.

A nuisance as defined in the preceding section was a private nuisance to any person who sustained in his person or property any special injury different from the public. Kissel v. Lewis, 156 Ind. 233, 59 N.E. 478 (1901); Zeppenfeld v. Franklin Motor Serv. Co., 77 Ind. App. 687, 134 N.E. 487 (1922).

Defects in steps could not be a public nuisance without an infraction of a public right. Where steps were property not open to the public-at-large and lessee was not engaged in any business activity, the steps were not open to the public and no public nuisance was found due to disrepair of the steps. Stover v. Fechtman, 140 Ind. App. 62, 9 Ind. Dec. 691, 222 N.E.2d 281 (1966).

Injunction.

Temporary injunction prohibiting the operation of two diesel trucks at night close to plaintiff's bedroom windows was proper although there was no physical damage to plaintiff's property. Muehlman v. Keilman, 257 Ind. 100, 26 Ind. Dec. 616, 272 N.E.2d 591 (1971).

Life Tenant.

Owner of life estate could sue to abate nuisance and recover damages therefor. Price v. Grose, 78 Ind. App. 62, 133 N.E. 30 (1921).

Municipal Corporations.

A municipal corporation had no more right to maintain a nuisance than an individual would have, and for a nuisance maintained upon its property, the same liability attaches against a city, as to an individual. Haag v. Board of County Comm'rs, 60 Ind. 511, 28 Am. R. 654 (1878).

Municipal corporations could sue to have a nuisance abated. American Furn. Co. v. Town of Batesville, 139 Ind. 77, 38 N.E. 408 (1894); City of Valparaiso v. Bozarth, 153 Ind. 536, 55 N.E. 439, 47 L.R.A. 487 (1899).

A municipal corporation is liable for erecting and maintaining a nuisance, the same as a natural person. Stein v. City of La Fayette, 6 Ind. App. 414, 33 N.E. 912 (1893).

Where a son's death was caused by a nuisance maintained close to the dwelling-house and premises occupied by the father and son, although owned by the mother, the father could maintain an independent action for damages for the death of the son. Pere Marquette R.R. v. Chadwick, 65 Ind. App. 95, 115 N.E. 678 (1917).

A city which discharged sewage without purification into a natural stream could be held liable for injury to a riparian owner injured by such disposal. City of Frankfort v. Slipher, 88 Ind. App. 356, 162 N.E. 241 (1928).

Person Suffering Special Injuries.

Persons who suffered a special injury from the obstruction of a highway could have had the nuisance abated. Pettis v. Johnson, 56 Ind. 139 (1877).

State.

The state could sue to enjoin the continuance of a public nuisance. State v. Ohio Oil Co., 150 Ind. 21, 49 N.E. 809, 47 L.R.A. 627 (1898).

Collateral References. What constitutes special injury that entitles private party to maintain action based on public nuisance—modern cases.

32-30-6-8. Remedies. — If a proper case is made, the nuisance may be enjoined or abated and damages recovered for the nuisance. [P.L.2-2002, § 15.]

Cross References. Injunctions, IC 34-26.

NOTES TO DECISIONS

Damages.
Highway obstructions.
Independent contractors.
Injunction.
Joint liability.
Municipal corporations.
Private nuisance.
Property ownership.
—Not required.

Abatement After Prosecution.

—In General.
On the conviction of a person for maintaining a public nuisance, the nuisance could have been ordered abated. McLaughlin v. State, 45 Ind. 338 (1873).

—Aesthetic Injury.
In Indiana, a plaintiff who has proved a per accidens nuisance, or nuisance in fact, may recover aesthetic damages. Wernke v. Halas, 600 N.E.2d 117 (Ind. App. 1992).

—Punitive.
Where there was cooperation with all government agencies and defendant did its best to improve the operation of the shredder so as to alleviate damage, discomfort and inconvenience there was not grounds for punitive damages. Harrison v. Indiana Auto Shredders Co., 528 F.2d 1107 (7th Cir. 1975).

Complaint.
Plaintiff need not negative contributory negligence or his ability to protect himself. Niagara Oil Co. v. Ogle, 177 Ind. 292, 98 N.E. 60, 42 L.R.A. (n.s.) 714, 1914D Ann. Cas. 67 (1912).

A complaint to enjoin defendant from maintaining a private nuisance, alleging that defendant erected buildings within twenty-five rods of plaintiff's residence, that he collected in and about such buildings the carcasses of animals which were submitted to processes, whereby unwholesome, noxious, gases and odors were given off and permeated plaintiff's dwelling-house, greatly injuring plaintiff in the use of his premises, was sufficient. Clendenin v. Pickett, 51 Ind. App. 283, 99 N.E. 530 (1912); Miller v. Gates, 62 Ind. App. 37, 112 N.E. 538 (1916).

Continuance of Nuisance.
Where the nuisance was continued, one recovery did not bar subsequent actions. City of Valparaiso v. Moffitt, 12 Ind. App. 250, 39 N.E. 909, 54 Am. St. R. 522 (1895).

Damages.
The measure of damages in private nonpermanent nuisances is loss of use and it is measured in rental value. Harrison v. Indiana

Auto Shredders Co., 528 F.2d 1107 (7th Cir. 1975).

Damages for injury to health are available to a plaintiff in an action to abate a private nuisance. Rust v. Guinn, 429 N.E.2d 299 (Ind. App. 1981).

While the damages for the loss of use of property attributable to an abatable private nuisance are properly limited to the diminution in the fair market rental value, those persons harmed by the nuisances may still recover damages for losses distinct from those losses occasioned by the interference with the use of their property. Rust v. Guinn, 429 N.E.2d 299 (Ind. App. 1981).

The proper measure of damages in cases where the nuisance is found to be abatable is the injury to the use of the property determined by the depreciation in the fair market rental value during the time the nuisance existed. Keane v. Pachter, 598 N.E.2d 1067 (Ind. App. 1992).

Highway Obstructions.
In a prosecution for obstructing a highway, upon conviction, the court could order the abatement of the obstruction as a part of its judgment. Zimmerman v. State, 4 Ind. App. 583, 31 N.E. 550 (1892).

Independent Contractors.
A contractee cannot escape liability for a nuisance it creates by hiring an independent contractor to do work which by its nature causes the nuisance. Gray v. Westinghouse Elec. Corp., 624 N.E.2d 49 (Ind. App. 1993).

Injunction.
A property owner may maintain a suit to enjoin the removal of a wooden building to a place within the fire limits of a city, in violation of a city ordinance, where the house was to be located dangerously near the plaintiff's frame house. Kaufman v. Stein, 138 Ind. 49, 37 N.E. 333, 46 Am. St. R. 368 (1894).

The erection of a privy and vault within three and one-half feet of the dining room of an adjoining owner may be enjoined without reference to the manner in which the vault is constructed or to the intention of the defendant to use disinfectants. Radican v. Buckley, 138 Ind. 582, 38 N.E. 53 (1894).

A business which is a nuisance per se and one that is so conducted as to become an actual nuisance may be enjoined. Windfall Mfg. Co. v. Patterson, 148 Ind. 414, 47 N.E. 2, 37 L.R.A. 381, 62 Am. St. R. 532 (1897).

Temporary injunction prohibiting the operation of two diesel trucks at night close to plaintiff's bedroom windows was proper although there was no physical damage to plaintiff's property. Muehlman v. Keilman, 257 Ind. 100, 26 Ind. Dec. 616, 272 N.E.2d 591 (1971).

Injunction. (Cont'd)

Where the appropriate local authority has zoned the property specifically for shredder use and a permit issued, and careful and continued tests by reputable experts and public officials show meeting of required standards the operation of the shredder cannot be enjoined in the absence of an imminent hazard to health or welfare. Harrison v. Indiana Auto Shredders Co., 528 F.2d 1107 (7th Cir. 1975).

A permanent injunction is an extreme remedy and should be carefully limited to preclude only activities which are injuriously interfering with the rights of the party in whose favor the injunction is granted. Blair v. Anderson, 570 N.E.2d 1337 (Ind. App. 1991).

Joint Liability.

If the acts of several persons were separate and distinct as to time and place, but culminated in producing a public nuisance which injured the person or property of another, such persons were jointly and severally liable to the person injured. City of Valparaiso v. Moffitt, 12 Ind. App. 250, 39 N.E. 909, 54 Am. St. R. 522 (1895).

Municipal Corporations.

A municipal corporation, like a person, was liable for the erection and maintenance of a nuisance; and it could not escape liability on the ground that the person also liable for the nuisance had settled with the plaintiff for the damage he sustained. City of Valparaiso v. Moffitt, 12 Ind. App. 250, 39 N.E. 909, 54 Am. St. R. 522 (1895); City of New Albany v. Slider, 21 Ind. App. 392, 52 N.E. 626 (1899); City of New Albany v. Armstrong, 22 Ind. App. 15, 53 N.E. 185 (1899).

Private Nuisance.

It was the duty of the court to make an order of abatement whenever the interest and happiness of individuals or the community might require such nuisance to be abated in whole or in part. Maxwell v. Boyne, 36 Ind. 120 (1871).

Whether a mandatory injunction against a private nuisance will be decreed in any case is a matter largely within the discretion of the court. Shroyer v. Campbell, 31 Ind. App. 83, 67 N.E. 193 (1903).

Property Ownership.

—Not Required.

The party which causes a nuisance can be held liable, regardless of whether the party owns or possesses the property on which the nuisance originates. Gray v. Westinghouse Elec. Corp., 624 N.E.2d 49 (Ind. App. 1993).

Collateral References. Extent of relief granted against use of phonograph, loud speaker, or other mechanical or electrical device broadcasting music, advertising, or sales talk from business premises. 23 A.L.R.2d 1289.

Extent of relief in suits to enjoin quarries, gravel pits, and the like as nuisances. 47 A.L.R.2d 490.

Institution for punishment or rehabilitation of criminals, delinquents, or alcoholics as enjoinable nuisance. 21 A.L.R.3d 1058.

Keeping of dogs as enjoinable nuisance. 11 A.L.R.3d 1399.

Punitive damages in actions based on nuisance. 31 A.L.R.3d 1346.

Measure, elements, and amount of damages for killing or injuring cat. 8 A.L.R.4th 1287.

Cat as subject of larceny. 55 A.L.R.4th 1080.

Business interruption, without physical damage, as actionable. 65 A.L.R.4th 1126.

Liability for injuries caused by cat. 68 A.L.R.4th 823.

32-30-6-9. Policy toward agricultural and industrial operation. —
(a) This section does not apply if a nuisance results from the negligent operation of an agricultural or industrial operation or its appurtenances.

(b) The general assembly declares that it is the policy of the state to conserve, protect, and encourage the development and improvement of its agricultural land for the production of food and other agricultural products. The general assembly finds that when nonagricultural land uses extend into agricultural areas, agricultural operations often become the subject of nuisance suits. As a result, agricultural operations are sometimes forced to cease operations, and many persons may be discouraged from making investments in farm improvements. It is the purpose of this section to reduce the loss to the state of its agricultural resources by limiting the circumstances under which agricultural operations may be deemed to be a nuisance.

(c) For purposes of this section, the continuity of an agricultural or industrial operation shall be considered to have been interrupted when the operation has been discontinued for more than one (1) year.

(d) An agricultural or industrial operation or any of its appurtenances is not and does not become a nuisance, private or public, by any changed conditions in the vicinity of the locality after the agricultural or industrial operation, as the case may be, has been in operation continuously on the locality for more than one (1) year if:

(1) there is no significant change in the hours of operation;

(2) there is no significant change in the type of operation; and

(3) the operation would not have been a nuisance at the time the agricultural or industrial operation began on that locality. [P.L.2-2002, § 15.]

NOTES TO DECISIONS

Analysis

In general.
Affirmative defense.
Bleach operations.
Burden of proof.
Pork production.
Significant change in operation.

In General.

Former IC 34-19-1-4 (repealed; see this section for similar provisions), enacted in 1981, applied to any premises with a history of agricultural activities. Shatto v. McNulty, 509 N.E.2d 897 (Ind. App. 1987).

The policy of the legislature is clear; people may not move to an established agricultural area and then maintain an action for nuisance against farmers because their senses are offended by the ordinary smells and activities which accompany agricultural pursuits. Shatto v. McNulty, 509 N.E.2d 897 (Ind. App. 1987).

The doctrine of "coming to the nuisance," codified in this section, did not operate to preclude a nuisance action where the complained of hog operation did not begin until approximately five years after the plaintiffs had become adjacent landowners. Wendt v. Kerkhof, 594 N.E.2d 795 (Ind. App. 1992).

Coming to nuisance defense is not available where damage is due to negligent operation. Northern Ind. Pub. Serv. Co. v. Bolka, 693 N.E.2d 613 (Ind. App. 1998).

Affirmative Defense.

Provisions of former IC 32-19-1-4 (repealed; see this section for similar provisions) stating agricultural or industrial operations did not become a nuisances because of changed conditions in the vicinity of the operation consti-

tuted an affirmative defense. Molargik v. West Enters., Inc., 605 N.E.2d 1197 (Ind. App. 1993).

Since subsection of former IC 32-19-1-4 (repealed; see this section for similar provisions) stated agricultural or industrial operations did not become a nuisances because of changed conditions in the vicinity of the operation was an affirmative defense, the defendants waived any defense under that subsection for failure to plead it; the issue of whether the cause of the plaintiff's damages was an "industrial operation" within the meaning of the subsection and therefore protected by the subsection from being deemed a nuisance, must be pled pursuant to Trial Rule T.R. 8(C). Molargik v. West Enters., Inc., 605 N.E.2d 1197 (Ind. App. 1993).

Bleach Operations.

Defendant held to have demonstrated that its bleach operations did not constitute a nuisance in 1932, the date defendant began manufacturing bleach. Erbrich Prods. Co. v. Wills, 509 N.E.2d 850 (Ind. App. 1987).

Burden of Proof.

Defendant has the burden of proof on subsection (c), and has to prove that it satisfied all of the conditions of subsection (c) in order to benefit from the "coming to the nuisance" doctrine. Erbrich Prods. Co. v. Wills, 509 N.E.2d 850 (Ind. App. 1987); Laux v. Chopin Land Assocs., 550 N.E.2d 100 (Ind. App. 1990).

Since the legislators saw fit to put the exception as to negligence within a subsequent, separate, and distinct subsection (now subsection (d)), plaintiffs have the burden of proving defendant's negligence so as to stop

Burden of Proof. (Cont'd)
defendant from claiming the "coming to the nuisance" doctrine codified in subsection (c). Erbrich Prods. Co. v. Wills, 509 N.E.2d 850 (Ind. App. 1987); Laux v. Chopin Land Assocs., 550 N.E.2d 100 (Ind. App. 1990).

Pork Production.
Pork production generates odors which cannot be prevented, and so long as the human race consumes pork, someone must tolerate the smell. Former IC 34-19-1-4 (repealed; see this section for similar provisions) addressed that fundamental fact, and protects pork production when it is confined to its natural habitat, that is, rural farm communities. Shatto v. McNulty, 509 N.E.2d 897 (Ind. App. 1987).

Significant Change in Operation.
The requirement for invoking the statute is that there be no significant change in the type of operation. Since the statute supplies no definition of that term, we think it must be taken in its ordinary sense, as referring to qualities common to a number of items, individuals or activities which distinguish them as an identifiable class. It follows that merely increasing or decreasing the size or numbers of an operation will not serve to change the type of operation, thus, increasing a hog farm from 29 hogs to between 200 and 300 may not be a substantial change. Laux v. Chopin Land Assocs., 550 N.E.2d 100 (Ind. App. 1990).

Findings concerning the increase in the number of pigs and findings that the farmer constructed a facility for the hogs in the spring and summer of 1987 are not sufficient to sustain the conclusion of a significant change in the type of operation. Laux v. Chopin Land Assocs., 550 N.E.2d 100 (Ind. App. 1990).

Collateral References. Hog breeding, confining, or processing facility as constituting nuisance.

32-30-6-10. Limitation on public use airport operation as nuisance. — (a) This section does not apply if a nuisance results from the negligent operation of a public use airport operation or the operation's appurtenances.

(b) It is the purpose of this section to limit the circumstances under which a public use airport operation may be a nuisance in order to reduce the potential for the state to lose the benefits to the state's air transportation system that are provided by public use airports.

(c) A public use airport operation or any of the operation's appurtenances may not become a private or public nuisance by any changed condition in the vicinity of the locality that occurs after the public use airport operation operates continuously on the locality for more than one (1) year if the following conditions are met:

(1) The public use airport operation was not a nuisance at the time when the operation began operating at that locality.

(2) The public use airport operation is operated in accordance with the rules of the Indiana department of transportation, aeronautics section.

(3) There is no significant change in the hours of operation of the public use airport operation. [P.L.2-2002, § 15.]

CHAPTER 7
ACTIONS FOR INDECENT NUISANCES

32-30-7-1. "Indecent nuisance" defined. — As used in this chapter, "indecent nuisance" means a:

(1) place in or upon which prostitution (as described in IC 35-45-4);

(2) public place in or upon which deviate sexual conduct (as defined in IC 35-41-1-9) or sexual intercourse (as defined in IC 35-41-1-26); or

(3) public place in or upon which the fondling of the genitals of a person;

is conducted, permitted, continued, or exists, and the personal property and contents used in conducting and maintaining the place for such a purpose. [P.L.2-2002, § 15.]

Effective Dates. P.L.2-2002, § 15. July 1. 2002.

NOTES TO DECISIONS

"Owner" Construed.
Vendor of "adult relaxation center," who sold the premises under an installment sale contract, retained legal title to the real estate, and such title brought him within the parameters of this chapter. Eads v. Hill, 563 N.E.2d 625 (Ind. App. 1990).

Collateral References. Indecent exposure: What is "person". 63 A.L.R.4th 1040.

Nudity as constituting nuisance. 92 A.L.R.5th 593.

32-30-7-2. "Person" defined. — As used in this chapter, "person" has the meaning set forth in IC 35-41-1-22. [P.L.2-2002, § 15.]

32-30-7-3. "Place" defined. — As used in this chapter, "place" includes any part of a building or structure or the ground. [P.L.2-2002, § 15.]

32-30-7-4. "Prosecuting official" defined. — As used in this chapter, "prosecuting official" refers to public officials who have concurrent jurisdiction to enforce this chapter, including:

(1) the attorney general;

(2) the prosecuting attorney of the circuit in which an indecent nuisance exists;

(3) the corporation counsel or city attorney of the city (if any) in which an indecent nuisance exists; or

(4) an attorney representing the county in which an indecent nuisance exists. [P.L.2-2002, § 15.]

32-30-7-5. "Public place" defined. — As used in this chapter, "public place" means any place to which the public is invited by special or an implied invitation. [P.L.2-2002, § 15.]

32-30-7-6. Persons who may be found guilty of maintaining indecent nuisance. — The following are guilty of maintaining an indecent nuisance and may be enjoined from maintaining the indecent nuisance under this chapter:

(1) A person who uses, occupies, establishes, maintains, or conducts an indecent nuisance.

(2) The owner, agent, or lessee of any interest in an indecent nuisance.

(3) A person employed in an indecent nuisance.

[P.L.2-2002, § 15.]

32-30-7-7. Persons who may bring action. — (a) If an indecent nuisance exists, a prosecuting official or any resident of the county in which the indecent nuisance exists may bring an action to abate the indecent nuisance and to perpetually enjoin the maintenance of the indecent nuisance.

(b) If a person other than a prosecuting official institutes an action under this chapter, the complainant shall execute a bond to the person against whom complaint is made, with good and sufficient surety to be approved by the court or clerk in a sum of at least one thousand dollars ($1,000) to secure to the party enjoined the damages the party may sustain if:

(1) the action is wrongfully brought;

(2) the action is not prosecuted to final judgment;

(3) the action is dismissed;

(4) the action is not maintained; or

(5) it is finally decided that the injunction ought not to have been granted.

The party aggrieved by the issuance of the injunction has recourse against the bond for all damages suffered, including damages to the aggrieved party's property, person, or character and including reasonable attorney's fees incurred in defending the action.

(c) A person who institutes an action and executes a bond may recover the bond and reasonable attorney's fees incurred in trying the action if the existence of an indecent nuisance is admitted or established in an action as provided in this chapter.

(d) If a prosecuting official institutes an action under this chapter (or IC 34-1-52.5 or IC 34-19-2 before their repeal) and the existence of an indecent nuisance is admitted or established in the action, the governmental entity that employs the prosecuting official is entitled to all reasonable attorney's fees incurred by the entity in instituting the action. The fees shall be deposited in:

(1) the state general fund, if the action is instituted by the attorney general;

(2) the operating budget of the office of the prosecuting attorney, if the action is instituted by a prosecuting attorney;

(3) the operating budget of the office of the corporation counsel or city attorney, if the action is instituted by a corporation counsel or city attorney; or

(4) the county general fund, if the action is instituted by an attorney representing the county. [P.L.2-2002, § 15.]

32-30-7-8. Action brought in county where nuisance located — Complaint. — An indecent nuisance action must be brought in the circuit or superior court of the county in which the alleged indecent nuisance is located. The action is commenced by filing a verified complaint alleging the facts constituting the indecent nuisance. [P.L.2-2002, § 15.]

32-30-7-9. Preliminary injunction — Restraining order. — (a) After filing the complaint, a complainant may apply to the court for a preliminary injunction. The court shall grant a hearing on the complainant's motion for preliminary injunction not later than ten (10) days after it is filed.

(b) If an application for a preliminary injunction is made, the court may, on application of the complainant showing good cause, issue an ex parte restraining order restraining the defendant and all other persons from removing or in any manner interfering with the personal property and contents of the place where the indecent nuisance is alleged to exist until the decision of the court granting or refusing a preliminary injunction and until further order of the court. However, pending the court's decision, the stock in trade may not be restrained, but an inventory and full accounting of business transactions after the restraining order may be required.

(c) A restraining order issued under subsection (b) may be served by:

(1) handing to and leaving a copy of the order with a person who is:

(A) in charge of the place; or

(B) a resident of the place; or

(2) posting a copy of the order in a conspicuous place at or upon at least one (1) of the principal doors or entrances to the place.

(d) The officer serving a restraining order issued under subsection (b) shall immediately make and return into court an inventory of the personal property and contents situated in and used in conducting or maintaining alleged the indecent nuisance.

(e) Violation of a restraining order served under subsection (c) (or IC 34-1-52.5-4 or IC 34-19-2-4 before their repeal) is a contempt of court.

(f) If a restraining order is posted under subsection (c)(2), mutilation or removal of the order while it is in force is a contempt of court if the order contains a notice stating that mutilating or removing the order while it is in force is a contempt of court. [P.L.2-2002, § 15.]

32-30-7-10. Service or defendant. — (a) In an action under this chapter:

    (1) a copy of the complaint; and

    (2) a notice of the time and place of the hearing on the application for a preliminary injunction, if the complainant has applied for a preliminary injunction under section 9(a) [IC 32-30-7-9(a)] of this chapter;

shall be served upon the defendant at least five (5) days before the hearing.

    (b) The owners of the place where the alleged indecent nuisance is located may be served by posting the papers in the manner prescribed by section 9(c) [IC 32-30-7-9(c)] of this chapter for serving a restraining order.

    (c) If a defendant:

    (1) is granted a request for continuance; or

    (2) moves for a change of venue or a change of judge;

the preliminary writ shall be granted as a matter of course. [P.L.2-2002, § 15.]

32-30-7-11. Consolidation of trial with hearing for injunction. — (a) If the complainant has applied for a preliminary injunction under section 9(a) [IC 32-30-7-9(a)] of this chapter, the court may order the trial of the action on the merits to be advanced and consolidated with the hearing on the application for the preliminary injunction:

    (1) before or after the commencement of the hearing on an application for a preliminary injunction; and

    (2) upon:

        (A) application of either of the parties; or

        (B) the court's own motion.

    (b) Any evidence received upon an application for a preliminary injunction that is admissible in the trial on the merits becomes a part of the record of the trial and does not need to be repeated as to the parties at the trial on the merits. [P.L.2-2002, § 15.]

32-30-7-12. Effect of preliminary injunction. — (a) If the plaintiff has applied for a preliminary injunction under section 9(a) [IC 32-30-7-9(a)] of this chapter and, at the preliminary injunction hearing, the plaintiff proves by a preponderance of the evidence that the indecent nuisance exists as alleged in the complaint, the court shall issue a preliminary injunction, without additional bond, restraining the defendant and any other person from continuing the indecent nuisance.

    (b) If a defendant is enjoined under subsection (a) and it appears that the person owning, in control of, or in charge of the indecent nuisance received five (5) days notice of the hearing, the court shall:

    (1) declare a temporary forfeiture of the use of the real property upon which the indecent nuisance is located and the personal property located at the site; and

    (2) immediately issue an order closing the place against its use for any purpose until a final decision is rendered on the application for a permanent injunction;

unless the person owning, in control of, or in charge of the indecent nuisance shows to the satisfaction of the court, by competent and admissible evidence subject to cross-examination, that the indecent nuisance complained of has been abated by the person. [P.L.2-2002, § 15.]

NOTES TO DECISIONS

ANALYSIS

Constitutionality.
Applicability.
Burden of proof.
Evidence.
—Not sufficient.
—Sufficient.

Constitutionality.

Former IC 34-19-2-7 (repealed; see this section for similar provisions), which conditions the grant of a preliminary injunction and an accompanying temporary forfeiture upon a preponderance of the evidence standard, does not violate the Fourth and Fourteenth amendments to the federal constitution. Eads v. Hill, 563 N.E.2d 625 (Ind. App. 1990).

Applicability.

The provisions of this chapter relating the manner of service of the restraining order, notice, and the preliminary injunction, do not conflict with any of the Indiana Trial Rules. Eads v. Hill, 563 N.E.2d 625 (Ind. App. 1990).

Burden of Proof.

Once admitted, general reputation evidence shifted the burden of going forward with evidence that he did not know the business of an "adult relaxation center" to the defendant; because he failed to offer any such evidence, the presumption supported the trial court's determination that he owned an interest in the center with knowledge of the business conducted thereon. Eads v. Hill, 563 N.E.2d 625 (Ind. App. 1990).

Evidence.

—Not sufficient.

Where plaintiff did not prove by a preponderance of evidence that his remedy at law, a suit for money damages, was inadequate, and where an award of post-trial damages was sufficient to make plaintiff whole for his economic injury, the pre-trial relief in the form of a preliminary injunction was not warranted. Daugherty v. Allen, 729 N.E.2d 228 (Ind. App. 2000).

—Sufficient.

Evidence showing that the defendant was seen regularly entering, leaving and on the property at all hours of the day and night doing such things as carrying tools, Pepsis and beer, moving equipment, emptying trash cans, talking to employees, doing maintenance and collecting rent in cash from an employee, was sufficient to establish defendant owned an interest in a place upon which prostitution was conducted, permitted, continued or existed and that he knew of the activity. Eads v. Hill, 563 N.E.2d 625 (Ind. App. 1990).

32-30-7-13. Order closing indecent nuisance concurrent with restraining order. — An order issued under section 12(b)(2) [IC 32-30-7-12(b)(2)] of this chapter closing a place continues in effect while the restraining order issued under section 9(b) [IC 32-30-7-9(b)] of this chapter is in effect. If a restraining order has not been issued under section 9(b) of this chapter, the order closing the place under section 12(b)(2) of this chapter must include an order restraining the removal or interference with the personal property and contents. [P.L.2-2002, § 15.]

32-30-7-14. Service of restraining order — Inventory. — If a restraining order is issued under section 9(b) or 13 [IC 32-30-7-9(b) or IC 32-30-7-13] of this chapter:

(1) the restraining order shall be served under section 9(c) [IC 32-30-7-9(c)] of this chapter; and

(2) the inventory of the property shall be made and filed as provided in section 9(d) [IC 32-30-7-9(d)] of this chapter. [P.L.2-2002, § 15.]

32-30-7-15. Voluntary abatement — Real property. — (a) The owner of real property that has been closed or is to be closed under this chapter may appear after the filing of the complaint and before the hearing on the application for a permanent injunction and do the following:

(1) Pay all costs incurred.

(2) File a bond with sureties to be approved by the court:

(A) in the full value of the property to be ascertained by the court; and

(B) conditioned upon the owner immediately abating the indecent nuisance and preventing the indecent nuisance from being established or kept until the decision of the court is rendered on the application for a permanent injunction.

(b) If the defendant complies with subsection (a) and the court is satisfied:

(1) of the good faith of the owner of the real property; and

(2) that the owner did not know and, with reasonable care and diligence, could not have known that the real property was used as an indecent nuisance;

the court shall, at the time of the hearing on the application for the preliminary injunction, refrain from issuing an order closing the real property or restraining the removal or interference with the personal property. If a preliminary injunction has already been issued, the court shall discharge the order and deliver the property to the owners. [P.L.2-2002, § 15.]

32-30-7-16. Voluntary abatement — Personal property. — The owner of the personal property that has been restrained or is to be restrained under this chapter may appear after the filing of the complaint and before the hearing on the application for a permanent injunction and petition the court to release the personal property. If the court is satisfied that the owner:

(1) has acted in good faith; and

(2) did not know and, with reasonable care and diligence, could not have known that the personal property was used as an indecent nuisance;

the court shall, at the time of the hearing on the application for the preliminary injunction, refrain from issuing any order restraining the removal or interference with the personal property. If the preliminary injunction has been issued, the court shall discharge the order and deliver the property to the owner. [P.L.2-2002, § 15.]

32-30-7-17. Voluntary abatement — No release from judgment. — The release of any real or personal property under section 15 or 16 [IC 32-30-7-15 or IC 32-30-7-16] of this chapter does not release the property from any judgment, lien, penalty, or liability to which it is subject. [P.L.2-2002, § 15.]

32-30-7-18. Trial without delay. — An indecent nuisance action under this chapter shall be set down for trial without delay and takes precedence over all other cases except crimes, election contests, or injunctions. [P.L.2-2002, § 15.]

32-30-7-19. Evidence of reputation of property — Presumption of knowledge. — In an indecent nuisance action under this chapter, evidence of the general reputation of the place is:
    (1) admissible to prove the existence of the indecent nuisance; and
    (2) presumptive evidence that a person who:
      (A) owned;
      (B) was in control of; or
      (C) was in charge of;
    the indecent nuisance knew the indecent nuisance existed and used the place for an act constituting an indecent nuisance. [P.L.2-2002, § 15.]

32-30-7-20. Dismissal of action brought by private person. — (a) This section applies to an indecent nuisance complaint under this chapter filed by a private person.
    (b) The court shall not voluntarily dismiss the complaint unless:
    (1) the complainant and the complainant's attorney file a sworn statement setting forth the reason why the action should be dismissed; and
    (2) the dismissal is approved in writing or in open court by the prosecuting attorney of the circuit in which the alleged indecent nuisance is located.
    (c) If the judge believes that the action should not be dismissed, the judge may direct the prosecuting attorney to prosecute the action to judgment at the expense of the county.
    (d) If:
    (1) the action is brought by a private person;
    (2) the court finds that there were no reasonable grounds or probable cause for bringing said action; and
    (3) the case is dismissed either:
      (A) for the reason described in subdivision (2) before trial; or
      (B) for want of prosecution;
the costs may be taxed to the person who brought the case. [P.L.2-2002, § 15.]

32-30-7-21. Permanent injunction. — If at the permanent injunction hearing the plaintiff proves by a preponderance of the evidence that the indecent nuisance exists as alleged in the complaint, the court shall enter a judgment that perpetually enjoins:
    (1) the defendant and any other person from further maintaining the indecent nuisance at the place described in the complaint; and
    (2) the defendant from maintaining an indecent nuisance elsewhere. [P.L.2-2002, § 15.]

32-30-7-22. Admission of indecent nuisance — Effect of release — Unsold property — Costs. — (a) If the existence of an indecent nuisance is admitted or established as provided in section 21 [IC 32-30-7-21] of this chapter, the court shall enter an order of abatement as a part of the judgment in the case. The order of abatement must:

(1) direct the removal of all personal property and contents that:
  (A) are located at the place described in the complaint;
  (B) are used in conducting the indecent nuisance; and
  (C) have not already been released under authority of the court as provided in sections 15 and 16 [IC 32-30-7-15 and IC 32-30-7-16] of this chapter;
(2) direct the sale of personal property that belongs to the defendants who were notified or appeared at the hearing, in the manner provided for the sale of chattels under execution; and
(3) require one (1) of the following:
  (A) The renewal for one (1) year of any bond furnished by the owner of the real property under section 15(a)(2) [IC 32-30-7-15(a)(2)] of this chapter.
  (B) If a bond was not furnished, continue for one (1) year any closing order issued under section 12(b)(2) [IC 32-30-7-12(b)(2)] of this chapter at the time of granting the preliminary injunction.
  (C) If a closing order was not issued when the preliminary injunction was granted, direct the effectual closing of the place against its use for any purpose for one (1) year, unless sooner released.
(b) The owner of a place that has been closed and not released under bond may appear and obtain a release in the manner and upon fulfilling the requirements provided in sections 15 and 16 of this chapter.
(c) The release of property under this section does not release the property from any judgment, lien, penalty, or liability to which the property may be subject.
(d) Owners of unsold personal property and contents seized under subsection (a) may:
  (1) appear and claim the property within ten (10) days after an order of abatement is made; and
  (2) prove to the satisfaction of the court:
    (A) that the owner is innocent of any knowledge of the use of the property; and
    (B) that with reasonable care and diligence the owner could not have known of the use of the property.
(e) If an owner meets the requirements set forth in subsection (d), the unsold personal property and contents shall be delivered to the owner. Otherwise, the unsold personal property and contents shall be sold as provided in this section.
(f) The officer who removes and sells the personal property and contents under subsection (e) may charge and receive the same fees as the officer would receive for levying upon and selling similar property on execution.
(g) If an order of abatement requires the closing of a place under subsection (a)(3)(C), the court shall allow a reasonable sum to be paid for the cost of closing the place and keeping it closed. [P.L.2-2002, § 15.]

32-30-7-23. Violation of injunction or restraining order — Contempt. — In case of:
  (1) the violation of any injunction or closing order granted under this chapter;

(2) the violation of a restraining order issued under this chapter; or

(3) the commission of any contempt of court in proceedings under this chapter;

the court may summarily try and punish the offender. The trial may be upon affidavits or either party may demand the production and oral examination of the witnesses. [P.L.2-2002, § 15.]

32-30-7-24. Proceeds of sale. — (a) All money collected under this chapter shall be paid to the county treasurer.

(b) The proceeds of the sale of the personal property under section 22 [IC 32-30-7-22] of this chapter, or as much of the proceeds as necessary, shall be applied in payment of the costs of the action and abatement, including the complainant's costs. [P.L.2-2002, § 15.]

32-30-7-25. Indecent nuisance by tenant. — (a) This section applies to a tenant or occupant of a building or tenement, under a lawful title, who uses the place for acts that create an indecent nuisance.

(b) The owner of a place described in subsection (a) may void the lease or other title under which the tenant or occupant holds. The use of the place to create an indecent nuisance, without any act of the owner of the place, causes the right of possession to revert and vest in the owner. Without process of law, the owner may make immediate entry upon the premises. [P.L.2-2002, § 15.]

CHAPTER 8

ACTIONS FOR DRUG NUISANCES

32-30-8-1. "Nuisance" defined. — As used in this chapter, "nuisance" means:

(1) the use of a property to commit an act constituting an offense under IC 35-48-4; or

(2) an attempt to commit or a conspiracy to commit an act described in subdivision (1). [P.L.2-2002, § 15.]

Effective Dates. P.L.2-2002, § 15. July 1. 2002.

32-30-8-2. "Property" defined. — (a) As used in this chapter, "property" means a house, a building, a mobile home, or an apartment that is leased for residential or commercial purposes.

(b) The term includes:

(1) an entire building or complex of buildings; or

(2) a mobile home park;

and all real property of any nature appurtenant to and used in connection with the house, building, mobile home, or apartment, including all individual rental units and common areas.

(c) The term does not include a hotel, motel, or other guest house, part of which is rented to a transient guest. [P.L.2-2002, § 15.]

32-30-8-3. "Tenant" defined. — (a) As used in this chapter, "tenant" means a person who leases or resides in a property.

(b) The term does not include a person who:

(1) owns a mobile home;

(2) leases or rents a site in a mobile home park for residential use; and

(3) resides in a mobile home park.

[P.L.2-2002, § 15.]

32-30-8-4. Persons who may bring action. — An action to abate a nuisance under this chapter may be initiated by any of the following:

(1) The prosecuting attorney of the circuit where the nuisance is located.

(2) The corporation counsel or city attorney of a city in which a nuisance is located.

(3) An attorney representing a county in which a nuisance is located.

(4) The property owner.

[P.L.2-2002, § 15.]

32-30-8-5. Notice — Contents — Delivery — Evidence of nuisance. — (a) A person initiating an action under this chapter to abate a nuisance existing on a property shall, at least forty-five (45) days before filing the action, provide notice to:

(1) each tenant of the property; and

(2) the owner of record;

that a nuisance exists on the property.

(b) The notice required under this section must specify the following:

(1) The date and time the nuisance was first discovered.

(2) The location on the property where the nuisance is allegedly occurring.

(c) The notice must be:

(1) hand delivered; or

(2) sent by certified mail;

to each tenant and the owner of record.

(d) A person initiating an action to abate a nuisance under this chapter shall:

(1) when notice is provided under this section, produce all evidence in the person's possession or control of the existence of the nuisance; and

(2) if requested by the owner, assist the owner in the production of witness and physical evidence. [P.L.2-2002, § 15.]

32-30-8-6. No notice if owner initiates or joins action. — If the owner of record of a property that is the subject of an action under this chapter initiates or joins in the action under this chapter, the requirement under section 5 [IC 32-30-8-5] of this chapter to provide notice at least forty-five (45) days before filing does not apply to the action. [P.L.2-2002, § 15.]

32-30-8-7. Notice — Rules of Trial Procedure — Posting. — (a) Notice of a complaint initiating an action under this chapter must be made as provided in the Indiana Rules of Trial Procedure.

(b) Except in an action under this chapter in which the owner of record of the property that is the subject of the action initiates or joins the action as a party, the person who initiates an action under this chapter, not later than forty-eight (48) hours after filing a complaint under this chapter, shall post a copy of the complaint in a conspicuous place on the property alleged by the complaint to be a nuisance. [P.L.2-2002, § 15.]

32-30-8-8. Service by mail. — (a) If the defendant has not been personally served with process despite the exercise of due diligence, the person initiating an action under this chapter, not more than twenty (20) days after the filing of a complaint and the filing of an affidavit that personal service on the defendant cannot be had after due diligence, may cause a copy of the complaint to be mailed to the defendant by certified mail, restricted delivery, return receipt to the clerk of court requested. Service is considered completed when the following are filed with the court:

(1) Proof of the mailing.

(2) An affidavit that a copy of the complaint has been posted on the property alleged to be a nuisance.

(b) This subsection does not apply to transient guests of a hotel, motel, or other guest house. All tenants or residents of a property that is used in whole or in part as a business, home, residence, or dwelling who may be affected by an order issued under this chapter must be:

(1) provided reasonable notice as ordered by the court having jurisdiction over the nuisance action; and

(2) afforded an opportunity to be heard at all proceedings in the action.

(c) Notice of lis pendens shall be filed concurrently with the initiation of an action under this chapter. [P.L.2-2002, § 15.]

32-30-8-9. Scheduling of hearing. — (a) Except as otherwise provided under rules adopted by the Indiana supreme court, upon the filing of a complaint initiating an action under this chapter, the court shall schedule a hearing not later than twenty (20) days after the filing date.

(b) Service of process must be made upon the owner of the property that is alleged in the notice filed under section 5 [IC 32-30-8-5] of this chapter to be a nuisance at least five (5) days before the hearing. If service cannot be completed in time to give the owner the minimum notice required by this subsection, the court may set a new hearing date. [P.L.2-2002, § 15.]

32-30-8-10. Equitable remedies. — The court may issue an injunction or order other equitable relief under this chapter regardless of whether an adequate remedy exists at law. [P.L.2-2002, § 15.]

32-30-8-11. Ejection of tenant. — Notwithstanding any other provision of law, and in addition to or as a component of a remedy ordered under section 10 [IC 32-30-8-10] of this chapter, the court, after a hearing, may order a tenant that created a nuisance on the property leased by the tenant to vacate the property within seventy-two (72) hours after the issuance of the order. [P.L.2-2002, § 15.]

32-30-8-12. Order of restitution or possession. — (a) The court, after a hearing under this chapter, may grant a judgment of restitution or the possession of the property to the owner if:
    (1) the owner and tenant are parties to the action; and
    (2) the tenant has failed to obey an order issued under section 10 or 11 [IC 32-30-8-10 or IC 32-30-8-11] of this chapter.
  (b) If the court orders the owner to have possession of the property, the court shall require the sheriff to execute the order of possession not later than five (5) days after the order is issued.
  (c) If the owner is awarded possession of the property, the owner may seek an order from the court allowing removal of a tenant's personal property under IC 32-31-4. [P.L.2-2002, § 15.]

32-30-8-13. Plan for correction. — In an action under this chapter, the court may order the owner of the property to submit for court approval a plan for correction to ensure, to the extent reasonably possible, that the property will not again be used for a nuisance if the owner:
    (1) is a party to the action; and
    (2) knew of the existence of the nuisance.
[P.L.2-2002, § 15.]

32-30-8-14. No proof of knowledge by defendant. — Except as provided in section 13 [IC 32-30-8-13] of this chapter, the court may order appropriate relief under this chapter without proof that a defendant knew of the existence of the nuisance. [P.L.2-2002, § 15.]

32-30-8-15. Evidence of reputation and discontinuance. — In any action brought under this chapter:
    (1) evidence of the general reputation of the property is admissible to corroborate testimony based on personal knowledge or observation, or evidence seized during the execution of a search and seizure warrant, but is not sufficient to establish the existence of a nuisance under this chapter; and
    (2) evidence that the nuisance had been discontinued at the time of the filing of the complaint or at the time of the hearing does not bar the

imposition of appropriate relief by the court under sections 10 through 14 [IC 32-30-8-10 or IC 32-30-8-14] of this chapter. [P.L.2-2002, § 15.]

CHAPTER 9

ACTIONS AGAINST COTENANTS

SECTION.
32-30-9-1. Actions by joint tenants, tenants
        in common, tenants in copar-
        cenary.

32-30-9-1. Actions by joint tenants, tenants in common, tenants in coparcenary. — A claimant who is a joint tenant, tenant in common, or tenant in coparcenary may maintain an action against the claimant's cotenant or coparcener, or the cotenant's or coparcener's personal representatives, for receiving more than the cotenant's or coparcener's just proportion of the rents, profits, or other in kind payments. [P.L.2-2002, § 15.]

Effective Dates. P.L.2-2002, § 15. July 1. 2002.

NOTES TO DECISIONS

ANALYSIS

Improvements.
Purchasing adverse interest.
Rents.
Suing third party.

Improvements.

If a husband expended money on land owned by his wife while he occupied it, it would be presumed that he improved for her benefit and he could not recover from her nor could he improve the property and charge his cotenants or wards. Lane v. Taylor, 40 Ind. 495 (1872).

Where one tenant makes valuable and lasting improvements upon the common property without the knowledge or consent of his cotenant, he cannot compel such cotenant to contribute anything toward the payment of such improvements. Elrod v. Keller, 89 Ind. 382 (1882); Harry v. Harry, 127 Ind. 91, 26 N.E. 562 (1891).

Where one tenant in common makes necessary, valuable and lasting improvements he is entitled to compensation when the land is partitioned. Parish v. Camplin, 139 Ind. 1, 37 N.E. 607 (1894).

Purchasing Adverse Interest.

One or more cotenants could not purchase a lien on the common property and thus acquire title to their other cotenants' interests in the land and at most could only be entitled to contribution from those other cotenants for their portion of the lien. Jennings v. Moon, 135 Ind. 168, 34 N.E. 996 (1893).

The purchase of an outstanding title by one of two cotenants is not void but the right of the other cotenant is limited to sharing in the benefits of such purchase upon the contribution of, or offer to contribute, his proportionate part of the purchase money. Stevens v. Reynolds, 143 Ind. 467, 41 N.E. 931, 52 Am. St. R. 422 (1895).

Rents.

A tenant-in-common was only liable to account to a cotenant for rents when he excluded such cotenant from possession, or received rent from third person. Crane v. Waggoner, 27 Ind. 52, 89 Am. Dec. 493 (1866); Humphries v. Davis, 100 Ind. 369 (1885); Carver v. Coffman, 109 Ind. 547, 10 N.E. 567 (1887); Carver v. Fennimore, 116 Ind. 236, 19 N.E. 103 (1888); Bowen v. Swander, 121 Ind. 164, 22 N.E. 725 (1889); Schissel v. Dickson, 129 Ind. 139, 28 N.E. 540 (1891); Ryason v. Dunten, 164 Ind. 85, 73 N.E. 74 (1905); McCrum v. McCrum, 36 Ind. App. 636, 76 N.E. 415 (1905); Overturf v. Martin, 170 Ind. 308, 84 N.E. 531 (1908), overruled on other grounds, Stauffer v. Kesler, 191 Ind. 702, 127 N.E. 803 (1920); Geisendorff v. Cobbs, 47 Ind. App. 573, 94 N.E. 236 (1911).

If a tenant-in-common occupied lands under a bona fide claim of entire ownership, he would only be liable to account for the rental value of the premises as they were at the time he took possession. Carver v. Fennimore, 116 Ind. 236, 19 N.E. 103 (1888); Hannah v. Carver, 121 Ind. 278, 23 N.E. 93 (1889).

Where one tenant-in-common possessed

Rents. (Cont'd)
the entire premises without any agreement between his cotenants and himself as to the possession, or any demand on their part to enjoy the premises with him, the tenant in possession was not bound to account to the others for mere use and occupation. Price v. Andrew, 104 Ind. App. 619, 10 N.E.2d 436 (1937).

Where a coal mine was owned by two tenants-in-common, and one of such tenants took possession of the mine and operated it and took coal therefrom and sold it in the market, and received a profit therefrom after the expense of mining and marketing had been deducted from the sale price, the other cotenant was entitled to an accounting as to the profits of the mining operations by the other cotenant. Price v. Andrew, 104 Ind. App. 619, 10 N.E.2d 436 (1937).

Suing Third Party.
One tenant-in-common could not sue alone to recover rents from a third party. Dorsett v. Gray, 98 Ind. 273 (1884).

Collateral References. Contribution and similar rights as between cotenants where one pays the other's share of sum owing on mortgage or other lien. 48 A.L.R.2d 1305.

Accountability of cotenants for rents and profits or use and occupation. 51 A.L.R.2d 388.

Right of surviving spouse to contribution, exoneration or other reimbursement out of decedent's estate respecting lien on estate by joint tenancy. 76 A.L.R.2d 1004.

Rights in proceeds of insurance on property held jointly with right of survivorship, where one of joint owners dies pending payment of proceeds. 4 A.L.R.3d 427.

Cotenant taking cotenancy property. 17 A.L.R.3d 1394.

CHAPTER 10

MORTGAGE FORECLOSURE ACTIONS

32-30-10-1. "Auctioneer" defined. — As used in this chapter, "auctioneer" means an auctioneer licensed under IC 25-6.1. [P.L.2-2002, § 15.]

Effective Dates. P.L.2-2002, § 15. July 1. 2002.

32-30-10-2. "Economically feasible" defined. — For purposes of section 9 [IC 32-30-10-9] of this chapter, the sale of a property through the services of an auctioneer is "economically feasible" if the court determines that:

(1) a reasonable probability exists that, with the use of the services of an auctioneer, a valid and enforceable bid will be made at a foreclosure for a sale price equal to or greater than the amount of the judgment and

the costs and expenses necessary to its satisfaction, including the costs of the auctioneer; and

(2) the reasonable probability would not exist without the use of an auctioneer. [P.L.2-2002, § 15.]

32-30-10-3. Action in county where property located. — (a) If a mortgagor defaults in the performance of any condition contained in a mortgage, the mortgagee or the mortgagee's assigns may proceed in the circuit court of the county where the real estate is located to foreclose the equity of redemption contained in the mortgage.

(b) If the real estate is located in more than one (1) county, the circuit court of any county in which the real estate is located has jurisdiction for an action for the foreclosure of the equity of redemption contained in the mortgage. [P.L.2-2002, § 15.]

Cross References. Assignment, IC 29-1-8, IC 32-29-2-1.

Foreclosure of assigned mortgage, IC 32-29-1-9.

Foreclosures by state, IC 32-8-11-8.

Limitation of lien and action, IC 32-28-7-1 — IC 32-28-7-4, IC 32-28-8-1.

Mortgages executed after June, 1931, sale and redemption, IC 32-29-7-6 — IC 32-29-7-14.

Mortgages executed subsequent to July 1, 1957, time for execution, IC 32-29-7-3.

Mortgages in general, IC 32-29-1-1.

Satisfaction and release, IC 32-28-1-1, IC 32-28-1-2, IC 32-29-1-6, IC 32-29-1-7, IC 32-29-3-1, IC 32-29-4-1, IC 32-29-5-1.

State as party to action foreclosing mortgage, Trial Rule TR. 17.1.

Indiana Law Review. Is a Power of Sale in a Mortgage Valid in Indiana? 5 Ind. L.J. 293.

NOTES TO DECISIONS

ANALYSIS

General Provisions

Application of section.
Death of mortgagor.
Default justifying foreclosure.
Description of property.
Discretion of court.
Foreclosure in attachment.
Indemnity mortgage.
Judgment upon the debt.
Jurisdiction and venue.
Limitation of actions.
Record.
Rights of mortgagee.
Rights of purchasers.
Sale subject to mortgage.

Unenforceability of Debt

In general.

Complaint to Foreclose

In general.
Description of property.
Exhibits.
Instalment due.
Paragraphing.
Paragraphs.
Record.

Liens and Priorities

Failure to set up lien.

Parties to Suits

Assignees and trustees.
Lien claimants.
Mortgagees.
Mortgagor.
Owner of fee.
Receivers.
Wives of parties.

GENERAL PROVISIONS

Application of Section.

This section applied to the foreclosure of mortgages on land. Leader Publishing Co. v. Grant Trust & Sav. Co., 182 Ind. 651, 108 N.E. 121 (1915).

Death of Mortgagor.

The recovery of a judgment upon notes secured by a mortgage was no bar to another action to foreclose the mortgage, for a judgment upon mortgage indebtedness neither

GENERAL PROVISIONS (Cont'd)

Death of Mortgagor. (Cont'd)
merged nor impaired the mortgage lien, and could be enforced against the property of a decedent, even after the expiration of the year from the death of the decedent. Kohli v. Hall, 141 Ind. 411, 40 N.E. 1060 (1895).

Default Justifying Foreclosure.
Where a mortgage provided that the failure to pay any one instalment when due would make the entire debt then payable the failure to pay one instalment allowed a bill of foreclosure to be filed. Andrews v. Jones, 3 Blackf. 440 (1834); Jones v. Schulmeyer, 39 Ind. 119 (1874).

Mortgages could have been foreclosed as each instalment of the debt secured became due. Hunt v. Harding, 11 Ind. 245 (1858); Crouse v. Holman, 19 Ind. 30 (1862).

Foreclosure could have been brought after a failure to pay interest due. Smart v. McKay, 16 Ind. 45 (1861).

The debt secured, or some part thereof, must have been due before a foreclosure could have been had. Trayser v. Trustees of Ind. Asbury Univ., 39 Ind. 556 (1872).

There could be no foreclosure of a mortgage where there was no agreement in the mortgage to pay a debt. Brick v. Scott, 47 Ind. 299 (1874).

There had to be a debt which could be enforced before a mortgage could be foreclosed. Gregory v. Van Voorst, 85 Ind. 108 (1882); Lilly v. Dunn, 96 Ind. 220 (1884); Orr v. White, 106 Ind. 341, 6 N.E. 909 (1886); Fort Wayne Trust Co. v. Sihler, 34 Ind. App. 140, 72 N.E. 494 (1904).

If a mortgage provided that, on failure to perform an act, the whole debt secured should become due, the mortgage could have been foreclosed on failure to perform that act. Buchanan v. Berkshire Life Ins. Co., 96 Ind. 510 (1883); Moore v. Sargent, 112 Ind. 484, 14 N.E. 466 (1887); Kohli v. Hall, 141 Ind. 411, 40 N.E. 1060 (1895).

Averments of complaint in action to foreclose a mortgage for failure to pay instalments as they became due were held sufficient when the complaint was first attacked on appeal. Kohli v. Hall, 141 Ind. 411, 40 N.E. 1060 (1895).

A mortgage could be foreclosed on default of payment of annual interest without a provision in the mortgage to that effect. Perry v. Fisher, 30 Ind. App. 261, 65 N.E. 935 (1903).

Where a mortgage provided for the payment, at the mortgagee's option, on the first day of each month a late charge of 4% of all payments over fifteen days past due, the tender within the grace period of a payment more than fifteen days past due, unaccompanied by the late charge demanded by the mortgagee, was insufficient to prevent a default in the terms of the mortgagee and the mortgagee was declare the balance of the mortgage due and to foreclose. Bowery Sav. Bank v. Layman, 142 Ind. App. 170, 12 Ind. Dec. 670, 233 N.E.2d 492 (1968).

Description of Property.
The complaint must have contained a definite description of the mortgaged property. Magee v. Sanderson, 10 Ind. 261 (1858); Nolite v. Libbert, 34 Ind. 163 (1870); Bowen v. Wood, 35 Ind. 268 (1871); Rapp v. Thie, 61 Ind. 372 (1878); Bayless v. Glenn, 72 Ind. 5 (1880).

Discretion of Court.
Foreclosure is strictly within the equitable discretion of the trial court. Dorothy Edwards Realtors, Inc. v. McAdams, 525 N.E.2d 1248 (Ind. App. 1988).

Foreclosure in Attachment.
A mortgage could be foreclosed in an attachment suit. Sharts v. Awalt, 73 Ind. 304 (1881).

Indemnity Mortgage.
A mere indemnity mortgage could not have been foreclosed until the mortgagee had been injured by his suretyship. Ellis v. Martin, 7 Ind. 652 (1856); Eagle Ins. Co. v. Lafayette Ins. Co., 9 Ind. 443 (1857).

Where an indemnity mortgagor promised to pay a debt when due and he failed to do so the person indemnified could have foreclosed the mortgage before paying the debt. Gunel v. Cue, 72 Ind. 34 (1880).

A mortgage given by a principal to his surety to secure the debt as well as to indemnify him could have been foreclosed by the creditor. Loehr v. Colborn, 92 Ind. 24 (1883); Mitchell v. Fisher, 94 Ind. 108 (1884); Plaut v. Storey, 131 Ind. 46, 30 N.E. 886 (1892).

If an indemnity mortgagor promised to pay a debt when due, and he failed to do so, the person indemnified could foreclose the mortgage before paying the debt. Malott v. Goff, 96 Ind. 496 (1884); Reynolds v. Shirk, 98 Ind. 480 (1884); Goff v. Hedgecock, 144 Ind. 415, 43 N.E. 644 (1896).

Judgment Upon the Debt.
The taking of judgment upon the debt secured did not prevent a subsequent foreclosure of the mortgage. Hensicker v. Lamborn, 13 Ind. 468 (1859); Jenkinson v. Ewing, 17 Ind. 505 (1861); Holmes v. Hinkle, 63 Ind. 518 (1878).

Jurisdiction and Venue.
Where mortgaged lands covered in one mortgage were located in different counties the court of either county had jurisdiction to

GENERAL PROVISIONS (Cont'd)

Jurisdiction and Venue. (Cont'd)
foreclose the mortgage. Holmes v. Taylor, 48 Ind. 169 (1874).

Superior courts had jurisdiction to foreclose mortgages. Noerr v. Schmidt, 151 Ind. 579, 51 N.E. 332 (1898); Vaught v. Knue, 64 Ind. App. 467, 115 N.E. 108 (1917).

The circuit court of a county wherein real estate was situated had jurisdiction of a suit to foreclose a mortgage on said real estate, although the mortgagor had died, and his estate was being administered in another county. Hawkins v. First Nat'l Bank, 201 Ind. 228, 165 N.E. 547 (1929).

Limitation of Actions.
An action to foreclose a mortgage could have been maintained at any time within 20 years after the action accrued. Catterlin v. Armstrong, 101 Ind. 258 (1885); Leonard v. Binford, 122 Ind. 200, 23 N.E. 704 (1890).

The mortgage could have been continued in force by an agreement therein to pay the debt, after the debt was barred by the statute of limitations. Bridges v. Blake, 106 Ind. 332, 6 N.E. 833 (1886).

So long as any portion of the debt secured was unpaid, and not barred by the statute of limitations, the mortgage could have been enforced. Bottles v. Miller, 112 Ind. 584, 14 N.E. 728 (1887); Daugherty v. Wheeler, 125 Ind. 421, 25 N.E. 542 (1890).

Record.
A complaint to foreclose against one who purchased the land subject to the mortgage need not have alleged that the mortgage had been recorded. Garrett v. Puckett, 15 Ind. 485 (1860).

Where the mortgagor had not sold his equity of redemption it was not necessary to aver in the complaint against such mortgagor that the mortgage had been recorded. Culph v. Phillips, 17 Ind. 209 (1861).

Where the foreclosure involved subsequent purchasers the complaining must have al-
leged that the mortgage had been recorded or that the purchaser had notice of the mortgage. Peru Bridge Co. v. Hendricks, 18 Ind. 11 (1862); Faulkner v. Overturf, 49 Ind. 265 (1872).

Rights of Mortgagee.
Mortgagor cannot frustrate the clear statutory and contractual rights of a mortgagee by the simple expediency of the execution and delivery of an unwanted deed. Ellsworth v. Homemakers Fin. Serv., Inc., 424 N.E.2d 166 (Ind. App. 1981), rehearing denied, 438 N.E.2d 6 (Ind. App. 1982).

Mortgagee had no implied duty to facilitate the sale of a portion of the real estate before pursuing its right to foreclose under the mortgage. Gainer Bank v. Cosmopolitan Nat'l Bank, 577 N.E.2d 982 (Ind. App. 1991).

Rights of Purchasers.
Where a mortgage was foreclosed on the note last due and a sale had there could have been no foreclosure as to prior as against a purchaser who had no notice that such notes were unpaid. Minor v. Hill, 58 Ind. 176, 26 Am. R. 71 (1877).

If a mortgage was foreclosed on the note last due, and a sale was had, there could have been no foreclosure as to prior notes as against a purchaser not having notice that such notes were unpaid, but otherwise if he had notice. Hill v. Minor, 79 Ind. 48 (1881).

The purchaser at a foreclosure sale could maintain an action to have the mortgage foreclosed as against the grantee of the mortgagor and have the land sold if the decree is not satisfied within the time allowed. Goodell v. Starr, 127 Ind. 198, 26 N.E. 793 (1891).

Sale Subject to Mortgage.
When a party purchases property subject to a mortgage, he takes the land charged with the payment of the debt, and the land becomes the primary source of payment of the mortgage debt. Dorothy Edwards Realtors, Inc. v. McAdams, 525 N.E.2d 1248 (Ind. App. 1988).

UNENFORCEABILITY OF DEBT

In General.
If the debt secured could not be enforced, the mortgage could not be foreclosed. Fort
Wayne Trust Co. v. Sihler, 34 Ind. App. 140, 72 N.E. 494 (1904).

COMPLAINT TO FORECLOSE

In General.
A complaint to foreclose a mortgage which sought to fix personal liability for the mortgage debt on a purchaser from the mortgagor, by reason of a contract on his part for such payment, had to allege that the mortgaged
land had been conveyed to such purchaser. An averment that the defendant purchased the mortgaged premises was not sufficient. Hammons v. Bigelow, 115 Ind. 363, 17 N.E. 192 (1888).

A complaint by heirs to foreclose a mort-

COMPLAINT TO FORECLOSE (Cont'd)

In General. (Cont'd)
gage executed to the ancestor, which failed to allege that no debts were owing by the ancestor's estate, and that no letters of administration were granted, was bad. Brunson v. Henry, 140 Ind. 455, 39 N.E. 256 (1894).

It was not necessary to allege in a complaint in an action against an administrator and the heirs of a decedent to foreclose a mortgage executed by such decedent that a claim therefor had been filed against his estate; if a claim therefor had not been filed such fact should have been pleaded. Noerr v. Schmidt, 151 Ind. 579, 51 N.E. 332 (1898).

Description of Property.
The complaint should have contained a definite description of the mortgaged premises. Swatts v. Bowen, 141 Ind. 322, 40 N.E. 1057 (1895); Godfrey v. White, 32 Ind. App. 265, 69 N.E. 688 (1904).

The description of a town lot was not too indefinite to furnish the means of identification of same. Kelley v. Houts, 30 Ind. App. 474, 66 N.E. 408 (1903).

Exhibits.
The complaint need not have shown that the mortgage had been recorded but the original mortgage and note, or a copy thereof, must have been filed with the complaint. Cook v. White, 47 Ind. 104 (1874).

Copy of note and mortgage should have been made part of the complaint. Roche v. Moffitt, 107 Ind. 58, 3 N.E. 940 (1885).

Instalment Due.
In an action to foreclose a mortgage for failure to pay instalments as they came due, the averments of the complaint were sufficient as showing the mortgage debt due and unpaid, when the complaint was first attacked on appeal. Kohli v. Hall, 141 Ind. 411, 40 N.E. 1060 (1895).

Paragraphing.
A one paragraph complaint was sufficient although there were a number of notes involved. Collins v. Frost, 54 Ind. 242 (1876); Firestone v. Klick, 67 Ind. 309 (1879).

Paragraphs.
One paragraph of a complaint to foreclose a mortgage was all that was necessary, although there were a number of notes. Buck v. Axt, 85 Ind. 512 (1882); Hannon v. Hilliard, 101 Ind. 310 (1885); Mansfield v. Shipp, 128 Ind. 55, 27 N.E. 427 (1891).

Record.
As to subsequent purchasers, it should have been alleged that the mortgage was recorded, or that the purchaser had notice thereof. Stockwell v. State ex rel. Johnson, 101 Ind. 1 (1884); Schmidt v. Zahrndt, 148 Ind. 447, 47 N.E. 335 (1897).

A complaint to foreclose against the mortgagor, or a purchaser subject to the mortgage, need not have alleged that the mortgage was recorded. Mann v. State ex rel. Lee, 116 Ind. 383, 19 N.E. 181 (1888).

LIENS AND PRIORITIES

Failure to Set up Lien.
Persons made parties to foreclosure suits had to set up their liens or claims, as, on failure to do so, they were bound by the decree rendered. Ulrich v. Drischell, 88 Ind. 354 (1882); Woodworth v. Zimmerman, 92 Ind. 349 (1883); Masters v. Templeton, 92 Ind. 447 (1884); Barton v. Anderson, 104 Ind. 578, 4 N.E. 420 (1886); Bundy v. Cunningham, 107 Ind. 360, 8 N.E. 174 (1886); Adair v. Mergentheim, 114 Ind. 303, 16 N.E. 603 (1888); De Haven v. Musselman, 123 Ind. 62, 24 N.E. 171 (1890); Davis v. Barton, 130 Ind. 399, 30 N.E. 512 (1892); Miller v. Hardy, 131 Ind. 13, 29 N.E. 776 (1892); English v. Aldrich, 132 Ind. 500, 31 N.E. 456, 32 Am. St. R. 270 (1892); O'Brien v. Moffitt, 133 Ind. 660, 33 N.E. 616 (1893); Becker v. Tell City Bank, 142 Ind. 99, 41 N.E. 323 (1895); Maynard v. Waidlich, 156 Ind. 562, 60 N.E. 348 (1901); Dixon v. Eikenberry, 161 Ind. 311, 67 N.E. 915, 68 L.R.A. 323 (1903); Pilliod v. Angola Ry. & Power Co., 46 Ind. App. 719, 91 N.E. 829 (1910); Heaton v. Grant Lodge No. 335,

I.O.O.F., 55 Ind. App. 100, 103 N.E. 488 (1913); White v. Suggs, 56 Ind. App. 572, 104 N.E. 55 (1914).

A senior mortgagee could claim no right to money realized by the foreclosure of a junior mortgage and a sale thereon as his remedy was to foreclose his senior mortgage. Firestone v. State ex rel. Liggett, 100 Ind. 226 (1884).

Where the holder of a senior mortgage was made a party defendant to an action brought by a junior mortgagee to foreclose his mortgage, and the complaint only called in question such liens as had accrued since the mortgage in suit was executed, the judgment therein that the mortgage sued on was the prior lien on the premises did not bar the right of the senior mortgagee, who simply filed a general denial and allowed judgment to be taken by default, to have his mortgage subsequently foreclosed. English v. Aldrich, 132 Ind. 500, 31 N.E. 456, 32 Am. St. R. 270 (1892).

Where a creditor took a mortgage on land, it

LIENS AND PRIORITIES (Cont'd)

Failure to Set up Lien. (Cont'd)
then having been apparent that certain prior judgment liens could be fully paid from other land covered by such liens, the right to re-quire such payment would have continued and would have been protected as against such judgment liens. Bank of Commerce v. First Nat'l Bank, 150 Ind. 588, 50 N.E. 566 (1898).

PARTIES TO SUITS

Assignees and Trustees.
If an assignee sued to foreclose and the assignment was not in writing, the assignor should have been a party. Nichol v. Henry, 89 Ind. 54 (1883); Green v. McCord, 30 Ind. App. 470, 66 N.E. 494 (1903).

The trustee in bankruptcy of the mortgagor was a necessary party. Griffin v. Hodshire, 119 Ind. 235, 21 N.E. 741 (1889).

Where a trustee, who represented beneficiaries, was in court, the decree rendered bound them in so far as it affected the trust property. Robertson v. Van Cleave, 129 Ind. 217, 26 N.E. 899, 29 N.E. 781, 15 L.R.A. 68 (1891).

Assignee was a necessary party in an assignment by mortgagor for benefit of creditors. Hutchinson v. First Nat'l Bank, 133 Ind. 271, 30 N.E. 952, 36 Am. St. R. 537 (1892).

Lien Claimants.
The holder of a junior note need not have been made a party to a foreclosure action brought by the holder of a senior note. Harris v. Harlan, 14 Ind. 439 (1860).

Where a prior mortgagee had notice of a junior mortgage or other subsequent encumbrance he was bound to make the holder of such mortgage or encumbrance a party or the proceedings would not have been binding as to such junior claimants. Murdock v. Ford, 17 Ind. 52 (1861); Holmes v. Bybee, 34 Ind. 262 (1870); McKernan v. Neff, 43 Ind. 503 (1873).

In a complaint to foreclose a mortgage any person could be joined as a defendant to answer as to his interest but the complaint must have shown that the person so joined had, or claimed to have had, some interest in the matter in controversy. Martin v. Noble, 29 Ind. 216 (1867).

If junior encumbrancers were not made parties, their rights were not affected. Hosford v. Johnson, 74 Ind. 479 (1881); Catterlin v. Armstrong, 79 Ind. 514 (1881); Kelley v. Houts, 30 Ind. App. 474, 66 N.E. 408 (1903).

All persons claiming liens on the lands were proper parties to suits of foreclosure. Stockwell v. State ex rel. Johnson, 101 Ind. 1 (1884); Yorn v. Bracken, 153 Ind. 492, 55 N.E. 257 (1899).

All persons claiming any interest in the land should have been made parties to the suit. Yorn v. Bracken, 153 Ind. 492, 55 N.E. 257 (1899).

Mortgagees.
If a mortgage was given to secure the claims of several persons, all such persons should have been parties plaintiff. Goodall v. Mopley, 45 Ind. 355 (1873); Cain v. Hanna, 63 Ind. 408 (1878).

All the owners of a mortgage could join in a suit of foreclosure although they held separate claims. Aetna Life Ins. Co. v. Finch, 84 Ind. 301 (1882); Cressler v. Brewer, 186 Ind. 185, 114 N.E. 449 (1916).

Mortgagor.
The mortgagor was not a necessary party to the foreclosure suit where he had sold his equity of redemption prior to the commencement of the suit unless the mortgagee desired a personal judgment against the mortgagor. Stevens v. Campbell, 21 Ind. 471 (1863).

If the mortgagor had conveyed the property, he was not a necessary party unless a personal judgment was desired against him. Petry v. Ambrosher, 100 Ind. 510 (1885), overruled on other grounds, Pugh v. Highley, 152 Ind. 252, 53 N.E. 171 (1899); West v. Miller, 125 Ind. 70, 25 N.E. 143 (1890).

Owner of Fee.
The owners of parcels of mortgaged property were necessary parties to a suit to foreclose the mortgage. Day v. Patterson, 18 Ind. 114 (1862).

All owners of the fee of the mortgaged premises were necessary parties-defendant to the action. Curtis v. Gooding, 99 Ind. 45 (1884); Petry v. Ambrosher, 100 Ind. 510 (1885), overruled on other grounds, Pugh v. Highley, 152 Ind. 252, 53 N.E. 171 (1899); Pauley v. Cauthorn, 101 Ind. 91 (1885); Daugherty v. Deardorf, 107 Ind. 527, 8 N.E. 296 (1886); Watts v. Julian, 122 Ind. 124, 23 N.E. 698 (1890); Goodell v. Starr, 127 Ind. 198, 26 N.E. 793 (1891); Jackson v. Weaver, 138 Ind. 539, 38 N.E. 166 (1894); Armstrong v. Hufty, 156 Ind. 606, 55 N.E. 443, 60 N.E. 1080 (1899).

The owner of property against which the foreclosure of a street assessment lien was sought was a necessary party to the proceeding, and any judgment and decree therein to which he was not a party was void as to him. Coddington v. Nees, 72 Ind. App. 141, 125 N.E. 657 (1920).

Receivers.
In an action on promissory note and to

PARTIES TO SUITS (Cont'd)

Receivers. (Cont'd)
foreclose a mortgage securing the note, an order of the circuit court to permit the receiver of an insolvent bank, appointed by such circuit court, to be made a party defendant was broad enough to include any issue that might be litigated in said suit; and where there was a failure to take a personal judgment against the receiver in the foreclosure proceedings, the judgment in that case was a bar to a claim filed against the receiver, based on the note and mortgage. Mutual Benefit Life Ins. Co. v. Bachtenkircher, 209 Ind. 106, 198 N.E. 81, 104 A.L.R. 1135 (1935).

Wives of Parties.
The wife of a purchaser of mortgaged property was a proper party to a suit of foreclosure. Watt v. Alvord, 25 Ind. 533 (1865).

Collateral References. Acceptance of past-due interest as waiver of acceleration clause in mortgage. 97 A.L.R.2d 997.

Validity and enforceability of due-on-sale real-estate mortgage provisions. 61 A.L.R.4th 1070.

32-30-10-4. Agreements for payment of sum secured. — If there is not an express agreement in the mortgage or a separate instrument for the payment of the sum secured by the mortgage, the remedy of the mortgagee is confined to the property mortgaged. [P.L.2-2002, § 15.]

NOTES TO DECISIONS

In General.
In a suit of foreclosure of a mortgage which was not accompanied by any agreement in writing by the mortgagor to pay the debt the relief was confined to the mortgaged property. Fletcher v. Holmes, 25 Ind. 458 (1865).

If a voidable obligation was disaffirmed, a mortgage given to secure such obligation could only be enforced against the property mortgaged. United States Sav. Fund & Inv. Co. v. Harris, 142 Ind. 226, 40 N.E. 1072, 41 N.E. 451 (1895).

If there was an express promise in the mortgage to pay the debt, such promise rendered the mortgagors personally liable. Vansell v. Carrithers, 33 Ind. App. 294, 71 N.E. 158 (1904).

32-30-10-5. Remedies. — In rendering judgment of foreclosure, the courts shall:

(1) give personal judgment against any party to the suit liable upon any agreement for the payment of any sum of money secured by the mortgage; and

(2) order the mortgaged premises, or as much of the mortgaged premises as may be necessary to satisfy the mortgage and court costs, to be sold first before the sale of other property of the defendant.

The judgment is satisfied by the payment of the mortgage debt, with interest and costs, at any time before sale. [P.L.2-2002, § 15.]

Cross References. Judgment on foreclosure of mortgage, IC 32-30-12.
Redemption before sale, IC 32-29-7-7.

Time period which must elapse before execution, IC 32-29-7-3.

NOTES TO DECISIONS

ANALYSIS

Appraisement laws.
Garnishment.
Heirs and administrator.
Husband and wife.

Lien not extinguished.
Married woman's interest.
No personal judgment.
Order of sale.
Part of debt not due.

Receivership.
Replevin bail.

Appraisement Laws.
In an action to foreclose a chattel mortgage, where the notes secured waived valuation laws, but the mortgage did not, and the judgment was that the mortgage be foreclosed and the property sold according to law, to pay and satisfy the indebtedness, the judgment would not be reversed, there having been no objection as to its form, on the ground that the judgment was for the sale of the mortgaged property without relief. Mansfield v. Shipp, 128 Ind. 55, 27 N.E. 427 (1891).

Garnishment.
The legislature's prohibition of a "levy of execution" includes garnishment, which is an auxiliary means of execution. National City Bank v. Morris, 717 N.E.2d 934 (Ind. App. 1999).

Heirs and Administrator.
If the suit was against heirs and an administrator, a personal judgment over against the administrator should not have been rendered. Newkirk v. Burson, 21 Ind. 129 (1863).

Husband and Wife.
If a husband and wife purchased land and a deed was executed to them jointly, and they executed a mortgage to secure the payment of the purchase-money, and the mortgage contained an express agreement to pay the debt, a personal judgment could have been rendered against both husband and wife on the foreclosure of the mortgage. Kelley v. York, 183 Ind. 628, 109 N.E. 772 (1915).
A joint promise by husband and wife to pay a mortgage debt, found only in the mortgage, was as binding as if found in the secured notes. Noble County Bank v. Waterhouse, 89 Ind. App. 94, 163 N.E. 119 (1928).

Lien Not Extinguished.
A judgment of foreclosure was a continuation of the mortgage lien. Lapping v. Duffy, 47 Ind. 51 (1874).
The foreclosure of a mortgage did not extinguish its lien, but was a continuation thereof. Evansville Gas-Light Co. v. State ex rel. Reitz, 73 Ind. 219, 38 Am. R. 129 (1881).

Married Woman's Interest.
In a suit to foreclose a mortgage in which defendant's wife was joined as an encumbrancer, a provision in the decree that in case the property was purchased by the wife she should have the right to credit her mortgage indebtedness on the purchase price after paying in a sum sufficient to discharge in full the prior liens was not improper and the part of the decree directing the sale of the undivided two-thirds of the realty in the first instance and reserving the remainder for defendant's wife as and for her inchoate interest in the real estate was proper. State Bank v. Backus, 160 Ind. 682, 67 N.E. 512 (1903).

No Personal Judgment.
If there was no personal judgment, the decree was operative only for the purpose of selling the mortgaged property, and could not have been the basis of an action. Lipperd v. Edwards, 39 Ind. 165 (1872).

Order of Sale.
Where tracts of mortgaged land had been sold by the mortgagor and the mortgage was subsequently foreclosed the court should have ordered the tract yet owned by the mortgagor to be sold first and that the tracts conveyed away be sold inversely as to the dates of their conveyance. Houston v. Houston, 67 Ind. 276 (1879); Hahn v. Behrman, 73 Ind. 120 (1880).
The mortgaged property had to be sold before other property could be levied on. Thomas v. Simmons, 103 Ind. 538, 2 N.E. 203, 3 N.E. 381 (1885); Mitchell v. Ringle, 151 Ind. 16, 50 N.E. 30, 68 Am. St. R. 212 (1898).
Mortgagee is not permitted to sell the mortgaged premises and apply the proceeds to satisfy the judgment; instead, the judgment of foreclosure shall order the mortgaged property sold by the sheriff. Patterson v. Grace, 661 N.E.2d 580 (Ind. App. 1996).

Part of Debt Not Due.
A personal judgment could not have been legally rendered for instalments which were not due. Skelton v. Ward, 51 Ind. 46 (1875).
A personal judgment could not be rendered for the portion of the mortgage debt not due. Gall v. Fryberger, 75 Ind. 98 (1881).

Receivership.
In an action to foreclose a real estate mortgage, where the practically undisputed evidence showed that the mortgage debtor was in possession of the land in controversy and that she was solvent, and there was no evidence to show that there was any insurance, taxes, or assessments due against the land, and that the mortgage debtor had property out of which the balance due on the mortgage debt could be paid, a receiver should not have been appointed to take charge of the mortgaged property during the year of redemption. Glendenning v. Prudential Ins. Co., 210 Ind. 121, 1 N.E.2d 599 (1936).

Replevin Bail.
Replevin bail could have been entered for the stay of execution as in other judgments. Allen v. Parker, 11 Ind. 504 (1859); Niles v. Stillwagon, 22 Ind. 143 (1864).
A judgment rendered in foreclosure without

Replevin Bail. (Cont'd)
stay of execution except on the amount due was not erroneous and upon entering the proper replevin bail for the whole judgment, and paying each successive instalment as the stay thereon expired, so that no execution should issue, the defendant was entitled to stay of execution on each instalment from the time when it fell due according to the terms of the contract. Allen v. Parker, 11 Ind. 504 (1859); Skelton v. Ward, 51 Ind. 46 (1875).

32-30-10-6. Recording satisfaction of mortgage. — Upon:
(1) the foreclosure of a recorded mortgage in a court of any county having jurisdiction in Indiana; and
(2) the payment and satisfaction of the judgment as may be rendered in the foreclosure proceeding;
the prevailing party shall immediately after satisfaction of the judgment record the satisfaction of the mortgage on the records of the recorder's office of the county where the property is located. The record in foreclosure and satisfaction must show that the whole debt, secured by the mortgage, has been paid. The recorder must be paid a fee of not more than the amount specified in IC 36-2-7-10(b)(1) and IC 36-2-7-10(b)(2) in each case of foreclosure requiring satisfaction. [P.L.2-2002, § 15.]

Cross References. Foreclosure by state, IC 32-29-1-9
Satisfaction of mortgages generally, IC 32-28-1-1, IC 32-28-1-2, IC 32-29-1-6, IC 32-29-1-7, IC 32-29-3-1, IC 32-29-4-1, IC 32-29-5-1

NOTES TO DECISIONS

ANALYSIS

Order of court.
School-fund mortgages.

Order of Court.
In a proper case, the court could order its clerk to enter satisfaction of a mortgage. Anderson Bldg., Loan Fund & Sav. Ass'n v. Thompson, 87 Ind. 278 (1881).
Where the county clerk, on receiving the proceeds arising from the foreclosure sale under a school-fund mortgage, failed to release the mortgage as required by this section, the court could, in proceedings for that purpose, direct the clerk to enter satisfaction thereof. State ex rel. Woodward v. Smith, 85 Ind. App. 56, 152 N.E. 836 (1926).

School-Fund Mortgages.
Where the sheriff received the money paid under school-fund mortgage foreclosure proceedings in behalf of the school fund, and paid the same to the clerk of the county, it was the duty of the clerk to release the mortgage, as provided by this section. State ex rel. Woodward v. Smith, 85 Ind. App. 56, 152 N.E. 836 (1926).
The failure of the county clerk to release a school-fund mortgage after receiving the amount due under it, which amount was realized from the foreclosure sale of one of the tracts of land covered by the mortgage, did not render the other tract liable for the debt. State ex rel. Woodward v. Smith, 85 Ind. App. 56, 152 N.E. 836 (1926).

32-30-10-7. Order regarding agreement for the payment of the sum secured. — If there is an express written agreement for the payment of the sum of money that is secured by a mortgage or a separate instrument, the court shall direct in the order of sale that the balance due on the mortgage and costs that may remain unsatisfied after the sale of the mortgaged premises be levied on any property of the mortgage-debtor. [P.L.2-2002, § 15.]

NOTES TO DECISIONS

Deficiency Judgment.

—Proof of Market Value.

A contract seller who forecloses on his contract can obtain a deficiency judgment if he buys the property at a foreclosure sale for less than the amount still due on the contract without providing the trial court proof that the property is worth less than the amount due at the time of sale. Arnold v. Melvin R. Hall, Inc., 496 N.E.2d 63 (Ind. 1986).

Requiring each mortgagee to provide independent proof of market value as a condition to obtaining a deficiency judgment would engraft a provision which misplaces the burden of proof. Arnold v. Melvin R. Hall, Inc., 496 N.E.2d 63 (Ind. 1986).

—Vendor/Mortgagee Purchasing Property.

Absent some evidence that the fair market value of the property at the time of the foreclosure sale was less than the balance of the debt then due, whether because of waste, a general economic decline, or some other cause not attributable to the conduct of the vendor/mortgagee, who purchased the property at the foreclosure sale, was not entitled to collect a deficiency judgment. Arnold v. Melvin R. Hall, Inc., 481 N.E.2d 409 (Ind. App. 1985).

Effect of Personal Judgment.

While a mere judgment of foreclosure, without any personal judgment for the debt or the residue of the debt after applying the proceeds of the sale, loses vitality after the property is sold, the failure of the court to direct that any deficiency should be levied of any property of the mortgaged debtor does not affect the validity of the personal judgment obtained by the mortgagee. An execution may issue without an express order in the judg-

ment and upon the decree the residue may be collected. Mid-West Fed. Sav. Bank v. Epperson, 579 N.E.2d 124 (Ind. App. 1991).

Guarantee of Loan by Borrowers.

Where the loan agreement contained a number of paragraphs assuring that the loan would be guaranteed by the borrowers, and the accompanying promissory notes identified the mortgagors by name as the borrowers, there was evidence to support the conclusion that the mortgagors were personally liable for the indebtedness. McCool v. Decatur County Bank, 480 N.E.2d 596 (Ind. App. 1985).

Junior Mortgagee, General Executions.

Where property covered by both senior and junior mortgages were exhausted by proceedings under the senior mortgage, and in a foreclosure proceeding the junior mortgagee obtained a decree that he recover of and from the defendant, mortgagors, a certain sum of money together with attorney's fee and costs, former version of this section did not take away from such junior mortgagee the right to have a general execution issued and levied upon other property of the mortgagors. Taylor v. Hadnott, 210 Ind. 26, 199 N.E. 228 (1936).

Lien on Personal Property.

Execution issued on decree of foreclosure of a mortgage was a lien on the personal property of the mortgage debtor. Willson v. Binford, 54 Ind. 569 (1876).

Prerequisites to Levy.

There had to be a sale under the decree, and the balance due on the judgment ascertained, before other property of the mortgagor could be levied on. Thomas v. Simmons, 103 Ind. 538, 2 N.E. 203, 3 N.E. 381 (1885); Mitchell v. Ringle, 151 Ind. 16, 50 N.E. 30, 68 Am. St. R. 212 (1898).

Decrees for junior liens could be levied on other property when the land was sold under a decree for a senior lien. Nix v. Williams, 110 Ind. 234, 11 N.E. 36 (1887).

Res Judicata.

If there was a personal judgment against the defendant, a subsequent action would not lie for a balance due on the note after a sale of the mortgaged property. Marshall v. Stewart, 65 Ind. 243 (1878).

32-30-10-8. Issuance of order of sale — Sale by sheriff — Proceeds.

— (a) The copy of the court's order of sale and judgment shall be issued and certified by the clerk under the seal of the court to the sheriff.

(b) After receiving the order under subsection (a), the sheriff shall proceed to sell the mortgaged premises, or as much of the mortgaged premises as is necessary to satisfy the judgment, interest, and costs. If any part of the judgment, interest, and costs remain unsatisfied after the sale of the mortgaged premises, the sheriff shall proceed to sell the remaining property of the defendant. If the mortgaged property is located in more than one (1) county, a common description of the property, the sale of the property, and the location of the sale must be advertised in each county where the property is located. [P.L.2-2002, § 15.]

Cross References. Time which must elapse before issuance of execution, IC 32-29-7-3.

NOTES TO DECISIONS

ANALYSIS

In general.
Chattel mortgage.
Date of title.
Death of defendant.
Exemption.
Manner and place of sale.
Sheriff's deed.

In General.

It was not necessary to make a formal levy of the order of sale. Ewing v. Hatfield, 17 Ind. 513 (1861).

Issuing a copy of the decree without an order of the plaintiff did not affect the validity of the sale. Sowles v. Harvey, 20 Ind. 217, 83 Am. Dec. 315 (1863).

The directions of the decree as to sale must have been followed whether the decree was proper or not. Langsdale v. Mills, 32 Ind. 380 (1869).

Chattel Mortgage.

The statutes, providing for the foreclosure of mortgages and directing who should make a sale of the property, applied to mortgages on land, and did not apply to mortgages of personal property, and when a mortgage on chattels was foreclosed, the court could direct who should make the sale. Leader Publishing Co. v. Grant Trust & Sav. Co., 182 Ind. 651, 108 N.E. 121 (1915).

Date of Title.

The title of purchasers related back to the date of the mortgage. Bateman v. Miller, 118 Ind. 345, 21 N.E. 292 (1889); Paxton v. Sterne, 127 Ind. 289, 26 N.E. 557 (1891); Jarrell v. Brubaker, 150 Ind. 260, 49 N.E. 1050 (1898).

Death of Defendant.

A copy of the decree could have been issued, and a sale made thereunder after the death of the defendant, without a proceeding of revival. Kellogg v. Tout, 65 Ind. 146 (1879).

Exemption.

The lands should have been offered in parcels the same as if the sale were on an ordinary execution. Piel v. Brayer, 30 Ind. 332, 95 Am. Dec. 699 (1868).

The mortgaged property could not have been claimed as exempt from sale under the exemption laws. Love v. Blair, 72 Ind. 281 (1880).

Manner and Place of Sale.

On the foreclosure of a mortgage the rents and profits must have been first offered for sale but the sheriff's notice of sale need not have stated that fact. Brownfield v. Weicht, 9 Ind. 394 (1857).

If the lands were situated in different counties, prior to the 1995 amendments to this chapter, each tract must have been sold in the county where situated. Holmes v. Taylor, 48 Ind. 169 (1874).

The rents and profits must first be offered for sale before the fee in the property is offered. Carpenter v. Russell, 129 Ind. 571, 29 N.E. 36 (1891).

Mortgagee is not permitted to sell the mortgaged premises and apply the proceeds to satisfy the judgment; instead, the judgment of foreclosure shall order the mortgaged property sold by the sheriff. Patterson v. Grace, 661 N.E.2d 580 (Ind. App. 1996).

Sheriff's Deed.

A sheriff's deed giving the names of the mortgagors and owners of the land sold, and such a description of the judgment and decree that there could be no mistake in its identification as the one authorizing the sale of the premises, was sufficient. Carpenter v. Russell, 129 Ind. 571, 29 N.E. 36 (1891).

32-30-10-9. Sale at auction. — (a) A sheriff shall sell property on foreclosure in a manner that is reasonably likely to bring the highest net proceeds from the sale after deducting the expenses of the offer and sale.

(b) Upon prior petition of the debtor or a creditor involved in the foreclosure proceedings, the court in its order of foreclosure shall order the property sold by the sheriff through the services of an auctioneer if:

(1) the court determines that a sale is economically feasible; or

(2) all the creditors in the proceedings agree to both that method of sale and the compensation to be paid the auctioneer.

(c) An auctioneer engaged by a sheriff under this section shall conduct the auctioneer's activities as appropriate to bring the highest bid for the property on foreclosure. The advertising conducted by the auctioneer is in addition to any other notice required by law.

(d) The auctioneer's fee must be a reasonable amount stated in the court's order. However, if the sale by use of an auctioneer has not been agreed to by the creditors in the proceedings and the sale price is less than the amount of the judgment and the costs and expenses necessary to the satisfaction of the judgment, the auctioneer is entitled only to the auctioneer's advertising expenses plus one hundred dollars ($100). The amount due to the auctioneer on account of the auctioneer's expenses and fee, if any, must be paid as a cost of the sale from the proceeds before the payment of any other payment. [P.L.2-2002, § 15.]

32-30-10-10. Concurrent action for the same debt prohibited. — A plaintiff may not:

(1) proceed to foreclose the mortgagee's mortgage while the plaintiff is prosecuting any other action for the same debt or matter that is secured by the mortgage or while the plaintiff is seeking to obtain execution of any judgment in any other action; or

(2) prosecute any other action for the same matter while the plaintiff is foreclosing the mortgagee's mortgage or prosecuting a judgment of foreclosure. [P.L.2-2002, § 15.]

NOTES TO DECISIONS

Judgment Upon the Debt.

A personal judgment could have been taken, and execution enforced against the other property of the debtor, without a waiver of the mortgage lien. Applegate v. Mason, 13 Ind. 75 (1859).

The taking of judgment on the debt secured did not prevent a foreclosure of the mortgage when no execution had been issued.

Hensicker v. Lamborn, 13 Ind. 468 (1859); Jenkinson v. Ewing, 17 Ind. 505 (1861); Holmes v. Hinkle, 63 Ind. 518 (1878).

The recovery of a personal judgment on the debt secured did not prevent the recovery of another personal judgment on foreclosure of the mortgage. Duck v. Wilson, 19 Ind. 190 (1862).

32-30-10-11. Payment of principal and interest due by defendant — Dismissal. — (a) If:

(1) a complaint is filed for the foreclosure of a mortgage;

(2) any interest or installment of the principal is due, but no other installments are due; and

(3) the defendant pays the court the principal and interest due, with costs, at any time before final judgment;

the complaint must be dismissed.

(b) If the defendant pays the court the principal and interest due after the final judgment, the proceedings on the final judgment must be stayed. However, the stay may be removed upon a subsequent default in the payment of any installment of the principal or interest after the payment is due.

(c) In the final judgment, the court shall direct at what time and upon what default any subsequent execution shall issue. [P.L.2-2002, § 15.]

NOTES TO DECISIONS

ANALYSIS

Amount due.
Interest defaulted.
Liability of bail.
Personal judgment.
Requisites of decree.
Series of notes.
Set-off.
Staying execution.
Staying proceedings.

Amount Due.

Where there was no acceleration clause apparent within the executed documents, only those payments on which the defendants had defaulted were due at the time of trial. Patterson v. Grace, 661 N.E.2d 580 (Ind. App. 1996).

Interest Defaulted.

Mortgages could be foreclosed for the non-payment of interest when the same was due. Perry v. Fisher, 30 Ind. App. 261, 65 N.E. 935 (1903).

Liability of Bail.

Persons becoming bail when only a portion of the instalments were due were only liable for what was due when bail was entered. Skelton v. Ward, 51 Ind. 46 (1875).

Personal Judgment.

A personal judgment could not have been rendered for that portion of the debt not due. Skelton v. Ward, 51 Ind. 46 (1875); Gall v. Fryberger, 75 Ind. 98 (1881).

Requisites of Decree.

When only a portion of the mortgage debt was due, the decree should have specified such amount, also the amount and times when other portions would have become due, and directed when execution might have issued. Allen v. Parker, 11 Ind. 504 (1859);

Thompson v. Davis, 29 Ind. 264 (1868); Skelton v. Ward, 51 Ind. 46 (1875).

Series of Notes.

Where the holder of a mortgage secured by several notes had foreclosed for the last note due only he could not again foreclose for the residue of such notes as against a person who had purchased the mortgaged premises at the first foreclosure without notice that the previous notes had not been paid. Minor v. Hill, 58 Ind. 176, 26 Am. R. 71 (1877).

A mortgage which secures several notes maturing at different times and which was foreclosed as to the last note due may again be foreclosed for the remaining notes as against a person who has purchased the equity of redemption after the foreclosure with full knowledge that the prior notes were unpaid and who assumed to pay them as part of the purchase-money. Hill v. Minor, 79 Ind. 48 (1881).

Set-Off.

When any amount was allowed to the defendant as damages or set-off, it ought to have been applied to the amount due. Brown v. Shirk, 75 Ind. 266 (1881).

Staying Execution.

Execution could have been stayed on each instalment as the same became due. Allen v. Parker, 11 Ind. 504 (1859); Niles v. Stillwagon, 22 Ind. 143 (1864).

Staying Proceedings.

Where the record disclosed that the defendants had posted a cash bond with the trial court after judgment in an amount that exceeded principal, interest and costs, the trial court was required to stay the proceedings, subject to being enforced upon a subsequent default by the defendants. Patterson v. Grace, 661 N.E.2d 580 (Ind. App. 1996).

32-30-10-12. Sale of property in parcels. — (a) In cases under this chapter, the court shall ascertain whether the property can be sold in parcels. If the property can be sold in parcels without injury to the interest of the parties, the court shall direct that only as much of the premises be sold as will be sufficient to pay the amount due on the mortgage, with costs, and the judgment shall remain and be enforced upon any subsequent default, unless the amount due is paid before execution of the judgment is completed.

(b) If the mortgaged premises cannot be sold in parcels, the court shall order the whole mortgaged premises to be sold. [P.L.2-2002, § 15.]

NOTES TO DECISIONS

ANALYSIS

In general.
Distribution of surplus.
Interest on instalments.
Lands conveyed by mortgagor.
Order.
Sale in parcels injurious.
Subsequent term.
Violation of order.

In General.

When only a portion of the debt was due, the court should have inquired as to the divisibility of the premises, and, if divisible, order only enough to have been sold to satisfy the amount due. Wainscott v. Silvers, 13 Ind. 497 (1859); Brugh v. Darst, 16 Ind. 79 (1861); Piel v. Brayer, 30 Ind. 332, 95 Am. Dec. 699 (1868); Knarr v. Conaway, 42 Ind. 260 (1873); Griffin v. Reis, 68 Ind. 9 (1879).

If the entire debt was due, the court need not have inquired as to the divisibility of the property. Benton v. Wood, 17 Ind. 260 (1861); Piel v. Brayer, 30 Ind. 332, 95 Am. Dec. 699 (1868); Shotts v. Boyd, 77 Ind. 223 (1881).

A sale of real estate by a sheriff in a mortgage foreclosure proceeding, in solido, instead of in parcels, was not void, but voidable, and an action would lie to set aside the sale, if brought within a reasonable time, and such reasonable time was not necessarily confined to the redemption period. Security Sav. & Loan Ass'n v. Morgan, 106 Ind. App. 437, 20 N.E.2d 707 (1939).

Where the sheriff sold real estate in a mortgage foreclosure proceeding in solido, when it was susceptible of sale in parcels, and the sale was made without defendant's knowledge and in his absence, it was improper. Security Sav. & Loan Ass'n v. Morgan, 106 Ind. App. 437, 20 N.E.2d 707 (1939).

In suit to set aside a default judgment in mortgage foreclosure proceeding and to cancel sheriff's deed to purchaser, the finding of the court, supported by evidence, that the real estate sold consisted of parcels susceptible of separate sale and that plaintiff was not present at the sale and had no knowledge thereof, and the sale was without his consent, and suit was brought by plaintiff the day following plaintiff's obtaining knowledge of such facts, and the purchaser refused, prior to the expiration of the year of redemption, plaintiff's request for permission to redeem certain parcels of land sold; held to warrant judgment in favor of plaintiff. Security Sav. & Loan Ass'n v. Morgan, 106 Ind. App. 437, 20 N.E.2d 707 (1939).

Distribution of Surplus.

Where a senior mortgagee had foreclosed his mortgage and the sale of the land resulted in a surplus the junior mortgagee was entitled to have the surplus applied against his mortgage. West v. Shryer, 29 Ind. 624 (1868).

A senior mortgagee could not claim the surplus on a sale under a junior mortgage, the mortgagor being entitled to such surplus. Firestone v. State ex rel. Liggett, 100 Ind. 226 (1884).

Where there was a surplus over the amount of the debt after the sale of land on a senior mortgage such surplus would be applied to a junior mortgage on the same land before it could be given to the owner of the land. Clapp v. Hadley, 141 Ind. 28, 39 N.E. 504, 50 Am. St. R. 308 (1895).

The trial court's judgment was contrary to law where it allowed mortgagee to keep the property after paying off the lien granted to mortgagors for their equity in the property, or to sell the property herself and retain any surplus. Patterson v. Grace, 661 N.E.2d 580 (Ind. App. 1996).

Interest on Instalments.

Interest on instalments not due should not have been charged after the time when the proceeds of sale might have been applied in payment of the same. Greenman v. Pattison, 8 Blackf. 465 (1847).

Lands Conveyed by Mortgagor.

When any of the lands had been sold by the

Lands Conveyed by Mortgagor. (Cont'd)
mortgagor, such lands should have been ordered sold in the inverse order of their conveyance by the mortgagor, and lands held by him should have been sold before the sale of those conveyed. Houston v. Houston, 67 Ind. 276 (1879).

Order.
If only a portion of the property was ordered sold, the order should have specified such portion. Brugh v. Darst, 16 Ind. 79 (1861).

Sale in Parcels Injurious.
When it was found that the premises could not have been sold in parcels without injury to the parties, the whole could have been ordered sold in a body. Firestone v. Klick, 67 Ind. 309 (1879).

Subsequent Term.
The court, at a term subsequent to rendering the decree, could have made an order as to the divisibility of the premises. Hannah v. Dorrell, 73 Ind. 465 (1881).

Violation of Order.
Where a sheriff sold land as an entirety, without offering it in parcels in violation of a decree adjudging the land to be susceptible of division and ordering a certain part thereof to be first sold in satisfaction of judgment, the sale was voidable and could have been set aside. Meriwether v. Craig, 118 Ind. 301, 20 N.E. 769 (1889).

32-30-10-13. Endorsement of execution — Sale of equity of redemption prohibited. — If an execution is issued on a judgment recovered for a debt secured by mortgage of real property, the plaintiff shall endorse on the execution a brief description of the mortgaged premises. However, the equity of redemption may not be sold on the execution of judgment. [P.L.2-2002, § 15.]

NOTES TO DECISIONS

ANALYSIS

Applicability of section.
Equity of redemption.

Applicability of Section.
This section applied to executions issued on judgments where there was no foreclosure of the mortgage, and a sale under an execution issued on a judgment of foreclosure was not void, although the execution was not indorsed as this section required. Mitchell v. Ringle, 151 Ind. 16, 50 N.E. 30, 68 Am. St. R. 212 (1898).

Equity of Redemption.
The equity of redemption could not have been sold on an ordinary judgment and execution for the mortgage debt. Linville v. Bell, 47 Ind. 547 (1874).
The equity of redemption of mortgaged property could not be sold on an ordinary judgment and execution for the mortgage debt, although the required indorsement was not made on the execution. Boone v. Armstrong, 87 Ind. 168 (1882); Pence v. Armstrong, 95 Ind. 191 (1883); Reynolds v. Shirk, 98 Ind. 480 (1884).

32-30-10-14. Application of proceeds of sale. — The proceeds of a sale described in IC 32-29-7 or section 8 or 12(b) [IC 32-30-10-8 or IC 32-30-10-12(b)] of this chapter must be applied in the following order:
(1) Expenses of the offer and sale, including expenses incurred under IC 32-29-7-4 or section 9 [IC 32-30-10-9] of this chapter (or IC 34-1-53-6.5 or IC 32-15-6-6.5 before their repeal).
(2) The amount of any property taxes on the property sold:
    (A) that are due and owing; and
    (B) for which the due date has passed as of the date of the sheriff's sale.
The sheriff shall transfer the amounts collected under this subdivision to the county treasurer not more than ten (10) days after the date of the sheriff's sale.

(3) Any amount of redemption where a certificate of sale is outstanding.

(4) The payment of the principal due, interest, and costs not described in subdivision (1).

(5) The residue secured by the mortgage and not due.

(6) If the residue referred to in subdivision (5) does not bear interest, a deduction must be made by discounting the legal interest.

In all cases in which the proceeds of sale exceed the amounts described in subdivisions (1) through (6), the surplus must be paid to the clerk of the court to be transferred, as the court directs, to the mortgage debtor, mortgage debtor's heirs, or other persons assigned by the mortgage debtor. [P.L.2-2002, § 15.]

CHAPTER 11

LIS PENDENS

32-30-11-1. Lis pendens record. — Each clerk of the circuit court shall keep a book in the office of the clerk called the "lis pendens record". The lis pendens record is a public record. [P.L.2-2002, § 15.]

Effective Dates. P.L.2-2002, § 15. July 1. 2002.

NOTES TO DECISIONS

ANALYSIS

Abuse of process.
Judicial sales.

Abuse of Process.

A case for abuse of process sufficient to survive summary judgment was made, where lawyers representing a personal injury plaintiff pursued a second lis pendens which caused the sale of defendants' real property to collapse, after a trial court had ruled lawyers were not entitled to file lis pendens and had ordered a prior notice removed. National City Bank v. Shortridge, 689 N.E.2d 1248 (Ind. 1997).

Judicial Sales.

One who purchased real estate at execution sale and received a sheriff's deed therefor to satisfy judgment, in a suit by bank on notes and to set aside conveyance as fraudulent, in which lis pendens notice was given, as required by statute, had a superior title to one claiming title under a deed executed by a sheriff at judicial sale under judgment for purchaser in suit on notes and to set aside conveyance as fraudulent, where the latter suit was instituted after the giving of the lis pendens notice in the prior suit. First State Bank v. Cunningham, 103 Ind. App. 310, 7 N.E.2d 537 (1937).

32-30-11-2. Suits commenced upon a bond payment to the state. — (a) This section applies to a suit commenced upon a bond payable to the state in any of the courts of Indiana or in a district court of the United States sitting in Indiana.

(b) The plaintiff in the case shall file with the clerk of the circuit court a written notice containing:

    (1) the title of the court; and

    (2) the names of all parties to the suit and a statement that the suit is upon an official bond. [P.L.2-2002, § 15.]

32-30-11-3. Enforcement of certain interests in real estate. —

(a) This section applies to a person who commences a suit:

    (1) in any court of Indiana or in a district court of the United States sitting in Indiana;

    (2) by complaint as plaintiff or by cross-complaint as defendant; and

    (3) to enforce any lien upon, right to, or interest in any real estate upon any claim not founded upon:

        (A) an instrument executed by the party having the legal title to the real estate, as appears from the proper records of the county, and recorded as required by law; or

        (B) a judgment of record in the county in which the real estate is located, against the party having the legal title to the real estate, as appears from the proper records.

(b) The person shall file, with the clerk of the circuit court in each county where the real estate sought to be affected is located, a written notice containing:

    (1) the title of the court;

    (2) the names of all the parties to the suit;

    (3) a description of the real estate to be affected; and

    (4) the nature of the lien, right, or interest sought to be enforced against the real estate. [P.L.2-2002, § 15.]

NOTES TO DECISIONS

ANALYSIS

Condemnation proceedings.
Foreclosure notice.
Jurisdiction.
Lis pendens.
Sufficient interest.

Condemnation Proceedings.

In condemnation proceeding where landowner withdrew the amount deposited by the state and furnished bond as provided in former IC 32-11-1-8 (repealed) such bond became a judgment lien on all the property owned by the landowner and former IC 34-34-1-3 (repealed; see this section for similar provisions) had no application thereto. State v. Cox, 177 Ind. App. 47, 63 Ind. Dec. 214, 377 N.E.2d 1389 (1978).

Foreclosure Notice.

Former IC 34-34-1-3 (repealed; see this section for similar provisions) did not require that a separate written notice of a pending suit be filed with the clerk of the circuit court if the action was founded upon "an instrument executed by the party having the legal title to the real estate" which was duly recorded, because the commencement of a foreclosure action itself provided constructive notice to pendente lite claimants. Mid-West Fed. Sav. Bank v. Kerlin, 672 N.E.2d 82 (Ind. App. 1996).

Jurisdiction.

Where the plaintiff's underlying suit was for breach of contract against the defendants, the third-party plaintiff was not a defendant in the dispute, and the court had no in personam jurisdiction over her. Sheehan v. Mahoney Chevrolet-Olds, Inc., 23 F. Supp. 2d 926 (N.D. Ind. 1998).

Lis Pendens.

A claim to the title of real estate under a contract for the real estate's purchase is the kind of interest that requires filing a lis pendens notice under the statute to protect third parties; therefore, where the lis pendens notice was properly filed under former IC

Lis Pendens. (Cont'd)
34-34-1-3 (repealed; see this section for similar provisions), it was absolutely privileged so that summary judgment was properly granted for defendant on plaintiff's claim that the lis pendens notice slandered their title to the real estate. Trotter v. Indiana Waste Sys., 632 N.E.2d 1159 (Ind. App. 1994).

The purpose of a lis pendens notice is to provide the machinery whereby a person with an interim claim to property that is not otherwise recorded or perfected may put his claim upon public records, so that third parties dealing with the defendant will have constructive notice of it. Sheehan v. Mahoney Chevrolet-Olds, Inc., 23 F. Supp. 2d 926 (N.D. Ind. 1998).

Sufficient Interest.
Where property owners had unrecorded deed granting them a private easement over a road on which a developer was proposing to grant additional easements, property owners had sufficient interest to file a lis pendens notice. Curry v. Orwig, 429 N.E.2d 268 (Ind. App. 1981).

In order for a plaintiff to utilize the doctrine of lis pendens, the property that was described for the purpose of invoking lis pendens had to be at the very essence of the controversy, and it was insufficient that successful payment of the damages could be derived from the sale of the property, since such would only constitute an indirect effect on the property. Sheehan v. Mahoney Chevrolet-Olds, Inc., 23 F. Supp. 2d 926 (N.D. Ind. 1998).

Collateral References. Duration of operation of lis pendens as dependent upon diligent prosecution of suit. 8 A.L.R.2d 986.

New or successive notice of lis pendens in same or new action after loss or cancellation of original notice. 52 A.L.R.2d 1308.

Lis pendens as applicable to suit for separation or dissolution of marriage. 65 A.L.R.4th 522.

Waivability of bar of limitations against criminal prosecution. 78 A.L.R.4th 693.

32-30-11-4. Duties of clerk. — The clerk shall:

(1) record a notice filed under section 2 or 3 [IC 32-30-11-2 or IC 32-30-11-3] of this chapter in the lis pendens record; and

(2) note upon the record the day and hour when the notice was filed and recorded. [P.L.2-2002, § 15.]

32-30-11-5. Duties of sheriff or coroner. — (a) This section applies when a sheriff or coroner of a county in Indiana:

(1) seizes upon real estate or an interest in real estate by virtue of a writ of attachment; or

(2) levies upon real estate or an interest in real estate by virtue of an execution issued to the sheriff or coroner from any court other than the court of the county in which the sheriff or coroner resides.

(b) At the time of the seizure or levy, the sheriff or coroner shall file with the clerk of the circuit court of the county a written notice setting forth:

(1) the names of the parties to the proceedings upon which the writ of attachment or execution is founded; and

(2) a description of the land seized or levied upon.

The notice shall be recorded, as provided for in section 4 [IC 32-30-11-4] of this chapter.

(c) The sheriff or coroner shall state, in the return to the attachment or execution, that notice has been filed. The sheriff or coroner is allowed a fee of fifty cents ($0.50) to be taxed as costs for making and filing the notice. However, the sheriff or coroner is not required to file the notice until the attachment or execution plaintiff provides the money to pay the clerk for filing and recording the notice. [P.L.2-2002, § 15.]

Notice of Levy.
Whenever a sheriff levied a writ of attachment on real estate, he should have filed with the clerk of the circuit court of the county a notice of such levy, no matter in what county the writ of attachment was issued. First Nat'l Bank v. Farmers & Merchants Nat'l Bank, 171 Ind. 323, 86 N.E. 417 (1908).

If a sheriff who seized real estate under a writ of attachment failed to file a notice of such seizure as required by statute, the pendency of the attachment suit was not constructive notice of the suit. First Nat'l Bank v. Farmers & Merchants Nat'l Bank, 171 Ind. 323, 86 N.E. 417 (1908).

32-30-11-6. Index of notices. — Upon filing and recording the notices described in this chapter, the clerk shall index the notices by the names of each party whose interest in the real estate might be affected by the suit, attachment, or execution. The clerk shall maintain entries for each notice listing:

(1) the plaintiff versus the names of all the defendants; and

(2) each defendant whose real estate is sought to be affected at the suit of the plaintiff. [P.L.2-2002, § 15.]

32-30-11-7. Final determination adverse to party enforcing interest — Discharge of interest. — Upon the final determination of any suit brought:

(1) for the purposes described in section 2 or 3 [IC 32-30-11-2 or IC 32-30-11-3] of this chapter; and

(2) adversely to the party seeking to enforce a lien upon, right to, or interest in the real estate;

the court rendering the judgment shall order the proper clerk to enter in the lis pendens record a satisfaction of the lien, right, or interest sought to be enforced against the real estate. When the entry is made, the real estate is forever discharged from the lien, right, or interest. [P.L.2-2002, § 15.]

32-30-11-8. Certificate of dismissal or satisfaction. — (a) This section applies when:

(1) an attachment is dismissed or the judgment rendered on it is satisfied; or

(2) the execution is satisfied without a sale of the lands seized or levied upon, or upon a redemption of the real estate within the time allowed by law after a sale of the real estate upon execution.

(b) The clerk of the court that issued the attachment or execution shall make a certificate of the dismissal or satisfaction and:

(1) enter the certificate upon the lis pendens record, if the appropriate record is kept in that clerk's office; or

(2) forward the certificate to the county in which the real estate is located, to be recorded in the lis pendens record of that county.

(c) When the certificate is entered or recorded, the real estate is discharged from the lien of attachment or execution. [P.L.2-2002, § 15.]

32-30-11-9. Notices ineffective until filed. — (a) This section applies to the following:

(1) Suits described in section 2 or 3 [IC 32-30-11-2 or IC 32-30-11-3] of this chapter.

(2) The seizure of real estate under attachments and the levy of real estate under execution in the cases mentioned in section 5 [IC 32-30-11-5] of this chapter.

(b) Actions referred to in subsection (a) do not:

(1) operate as constructive notice of the pendency of the suit or of the seizure of or levy upon the real estate; or

(2) have any force or effect as against bona fide purchasers or encumbrancers of the real estate;

until the notices required by this section are filed with the proper clerk. [P.L.2-2002, § 15.]

NOTES TO DECISIONS

ANALYSIS

Bona fide encumbrancers.
Common-law rule abrogated.
Condemnation proceedings.
Duty of interested party.
Person holding legal title.
Persons in possession.
Persons not bound.
Purchasers and mortgagees.
Purpose and effect of lis pendens.
Sheriff failing to file notice.

Bona Fide Encumbrancers.

To constitute bona fide encumbrancers, judgment creditors must have acted in good faith without actual or constructive notice of the execution lien and have given value, and where the undisputed facts establish the judgment creditors did not give new consideration or otherwise change their position in reliance upon the lis pendens record, because there was no reliance by them, they do not qualify as bona fide encumbrancers protected by former IC 34-34-1-9 (repealed; see this section for similar provisions). Geller v. Meek, 496 N.E.2d 103 (Ind. App. 1986).

The mere act of docketing a judgment does not render a judgment creditor a bona fide encumbrancer. Geller v. Meek, 496 N.E.2d 103 (Ind. App. 1986).

Common-Law Rule Abrogated.

At common law, a person purchasing land during the pendency of an action concerning the title thereof took notice of such action, and took subject to the decree or judgment rendered therein. Wilson v. Hefflin, 81 Ind. 35 (1881); Randall v. Lower, 98 Ind. 255 (1884); Rothschild v. Leonhard, 33 Ind. App. 452, 71 N.E. 673 (1904); First Nat'l Bank v. Farmers & Merchants Nat'l Bank, 171 Ind. 323, 86 N.E. 417 (1908); Schaffner v. Voss, 46 Ind. App. 551, 93 N.E. 235 (1910). See also, Ray v. Roe ex rel. Brown, 2 Blackf. 258, 18 Am. St. R.

159 (1829); Green v. White, 7 Blackf. 242 (1844); Britz v. Johnson, 65 Ind. 561 (1878).

Since the enactment of this statute, this rule has been abrogated, and "until the proper notice required by this act has been filed with the proper clerk," no one was bound to take notice of pending actions relating to real estate. Pennington v. Martin, 146 Ind. 635, 45 N.E. 1111 (1897); First Nat'l Bank v. Farmers & Merchants Nat'l Bank, 171 Ind. 323, 86 N.E. 417 (1908); Cleveland, C., C. & St. L.R.R. v. Beck, 84 Ind. App. 380, 139 N.E. 705 (1923).

Condemnation Proceedings.

In a proceeding to condemn lands for public purposes, a lis pendens notice must have been filed in order to bind purchasers for value without notice of the proceeding. Cleveland, C., C. & St. L.R.R. v. Beck, 84 Ind. App. 380, 139 N.E. 705 (1923).

Duty of Interested Party.

A contract purchaser who had not recorded the land contract nor filed a lis pendens notice of a suit against him by the vendor was not entitled to notice of a tax sale of the property; the auditor is not required to check court records to see who might have an interest in any particular property. Kohlman v. Blomberg, 584 N.E.2d 566 (Ind. App. 1992).

Person Holding Legal Title.

Persons holding the legal title to land and whose title appeared of record did not need to file lis pendens notices. Dunnington v. Elston, 101 Ind. 373 (1885); Rothschild v. Leonhard, 33 Ind. App. 452, 71 N.E. 673 (1904).

Persons in Possession.

Where a bank paid out money on deposit after notice of a suit contesting the ownership thereof, it did so at its peril. Pearce v. Dill, 149 Ind. 136, 48 N.E. 788 (1897).

Persons Not Bound.

Lis pendens in second suit against same parties as in first suit was held ineffective as to persons acquiring title between dismissal of first suit and commencement of second. Carr v. Stebbins, 292 F. 747 (7th Cir. 1923), cert. denied, 263 U.S. 721, 44 S. Ct. 230, 68 L. Ed. 524 (1924).

Where plaintiff in attachment did not file a lis pendens notice, the attachment sale was invalid as against a purchaser from the owner of the attached property, who was not made a party. Fountain Trust Co. v. Rinker, 98 Ind. App. 249, 182 N.E. 709 (1932).

Purchasers and Mortgagees.

Mortgagees who acquired their alleged rights from defendant, pendente lite, were bound by a decree declaring the conveyance fraudulent and void as to plaintiff and ordering a sale of the property to pay his claim. Wild v. Noblesville Bldg., Loan Fund & Sav. Ass'n, 153 Ind. 5, 53 N.E. 944 (1899); Farmers

Bank v. First Nat'l Bank, 30 Ind. App. 520, 66 N.E. 503 (1903).

Purpose and Effect of Lis Pendens.

Purpose of lis pendens notice was to enable court to give effective relief in pending suit without having to bring upon the record as parties those who might become successors in interest to the present parties during the pendency of the suit, as the effect was to make all such successors abide by the outcome of the suit as fully as if they were parties. Carr v. Stebbins, 292 F. 747 (7th Cir. 1923), cert. denied, 263 U.S. 721, 44 S. Ct. 230, 68 L. Ed. 524 (1924).

Sheriff Failing to File Notice.

If a sheriff who seized real estate under a writ of attachment failed to file a notice of such seizure, as required by statute, the pendency of the attachment suit was not constructive notice of the suit. First Nat'l Bank v. Farmers & Merchants Nat'l Bank, 171 Ind. 323, 86 N.E. 417 (1908).

32-30-11-10. Recording lis pendens orders. — (a) This section applies to orders granted by any court or judge in any cause or proceeding, whether upon a hearing or ex parte, that affect the disposition of real estate.

(b) Orders described in subsection (a) may be recorded in the lis pendens record kept in the office of the clerk of the county in which the real estate affected is located.

(c) An order recorded under subsection (b) shall be notice of the matters set forth in the order to all persons that are or may become interested in the real estate, and the provisions of the order take effect upon the real estate against any subsequent disposition of the real estate. [P.L.2-2002, § 15.]

CHAPTER 12

JUDGMENTS IN MORTGAGE AND LIEN ACTIONS

32-30-12-1. Time for payment or other act not required. — It is not necessary in any action upon a mortgage or lien to give time for:

(1) the payment of money; or

(2) performing any other act.

Final judgment may be given in the first instance. [P.L.2-2002, § 15.]

Effective Dates. P.L.2-2002, § 15. July 1. 2002.

Cross References. Foreclosure and judgment, IC 32-29-7.

NOTES TO DECISIONS

ANALYSIS

Instalments not due.
Sale of property.

Instalments Not Due.

A decree which gave the plaintiff the right to direct the sale of different pieces of property on foreclosure was erroneous as the court

Instalments Not Due. (Cont'd)

should have directed the order of sale in the decree. Knarr v. Conway, 42 Ind. 260 (1873).

Where only part of the debts in a mortgage foreclosure were due the court could only direct, as to instalments not due, at what time and upon what default any subsequent executions should issue. Skelton v. Ward, 51 Ind. 46 (1878).

A personal judgment for a debt not due was not void, although clearly erroneous, and was not subject to collateral attack. Gall v. Fryberger, 75 Ind. 98 (1881).

Sale of Property.

In a judgment for money due upon a mortgage payable in instalments and for the sale of the mortgaged property it should have appeared that the court made inquiry as to whether the mortgaged land could have been sold in parcels before ordering the sale of the whole property. Wainscott v. Silvers, 13 Ind. 497 (1859); Griffin v. Reis, 68 Ind. 9 (1879).

Where only part of the notes secured by the mortgage were due the court must have specified by metes and bounds the particular portion of the land to be sold where the land was found to have been susceptible of division. Brugh v. Darst, 16 Ind. 79 (1861).

The provision of a statute which required that in sales of land consisting of several lots, tracts, or parcels only as much land as was necessary to satisfy the judgment should be sold applied to sales on mortgage foreclosures. Piel v. Braye, 30 Ind. 332, 95 Am. Dec. 699 (1868).

32-30-12-2. Sale of property. — In the foreclosure of a mortgage, the sale of the mortgaged property shall be ordered in all cases. [P.L.2-2002, § 15.]

NOTES TO DECISIONS

In General.

Where a deed was in fact only a mortgage it was to be foreclosed as any other mortgage. Smith v. Brand, 64 Ind. 427 (1878).

When deeds absolute were only mortgages, they had to be foreclosed as other mortgages. Lowe v. Turpie, 147 Ind. 652, 44 N.E. 25, 47 N.E. 150, 37 L.R.A. 233 (1896).

CHAPTER 13
PURCHASE OF PROPERTY SUBJECT TO JUDGMENT

32-30-13-1. Defective title — Purchaser subrogated to rights of creditor. — If, upon the sale of real or personal property of a debtor, the title of the purchaser is invalid as to all or any part of the property by reason of any defect in the proceedings or want of title, the purchaser may be subrogated to the rights of the creditor against the debtor, to the extent of the money paid and applied to the debtor's benefit. [P.L.2-2002, § 15.]

Effective Dates. P.L.2-2002, § 15. July 1. 2002.

NOTES TO DECISIONS

In General.

The doctrine of subrogation rested upon the maxim that no one should have been enriched by another's loss, and could have been in-

In General. (Cont'd)

voked wherever justice and good conscience demanded its application, in opposition to the technical rules of law, which liberated securities with the extinguishment of the original debt. Home Owners Loan Corp. v. Henson, 217 Ind. 554, 29 N.E.2d 873 (1940).

The right of subrogation was not founded upon contract, expressed or implied, but upon principles of equity and justice, and included every instance in which one party, not a mere volunteer, paid a debt for another, primarily liable, and which, in good conscience, should have been paid by the latter. Home Owners Loan Corp. v. Henson, 217 Ind. 554, 29 N.E.2d 873 (1940).

Failure of Title.

Purchase-money was not recoverable from the execution creditor for failure of title to the land. Dunn v. Frazier, 8 Blackf. 432 (1847); Neal v. Gillaspy, 56 Ind. 451, 26 Am. R. 37 (1877); Lewark v. Carter, 117 Ind. 206, 20 N.E. 119, 3 L.R.A. 440, 10 Am. St. R. 40 (1889).

If the debtor had no title to the land sold, the purchaser could have recovered the purchase-money from the debtor. Preston v. Harrison, 9 Ind. 1 (1857); Hawkins v. Miller, 26 Ind. 173 (1866); Weakley v. Conradt, 56 Ind. 430 (1877); Weaver v. Guyer, 59 Ind. 195 (1877); Westerfield v. Williams, 59 Ind. 221 (1877).

Where several parcels of real estate were sold upon foreclosure as an entirety, for an entire sum of money and the purchaser failed to get title to a part only of the parcels sold, the rule of caveat emptor was applicable, and no correct rule could be prescribed for the measure of the purchaser's damages, if such partial failure of title afforded him any cause of action against the mortgagor or judgment defendant. Parker v. Rodman, 84 Ind. 256 (1882).

Judgment Against Holder of Equitable Title.

If a judgment creditor bought in at execution sale the property in which the debtor had only an equitable interest, the legal title being in the debtor's wife, he acquired a lien on the property as against all persons except bona fide purchasers without notice. Hosanna v. Odishoo, 208 Ind. 132, 193 N.E. 599, reh'g denied, 208 Ind. 144, 195 N.E. 72 (1935).

Knowledge of Judgment Lien.

If one purchased real estate from a judgment debtor and the debtor's wife, with knowledge of litigation in which the property was bought in by the judgment creditor at a defective execution sale, and with knowledge that the judgment was in fact unsatisfied, due to the wife's holding the legal title, he took the land subject to lien of the judgment creditor, since the purchaser was not a "bona fide purchaser without notice." Hosanna v. Odishoo, 208 Ind. 132, 193 N.E. 599, reh'g denied, 208 Ind. 144, 195 N.E. 72 (1935).

Prior Secret Equities.

If a judgment creditor bid in land on an execution sale, he was protected from prior secret equities, the same as if a stranger had made the purchase. Pugh v. Highley, 152 Ind. 252, 53 N.E. 171, 44 L.R.A. 392, 71 Am. St. R. 327 (1899); Union Cent. Life Ins. Co. v. Dodds, 155 Ind. 365, 58 N.E. 258 (1900); Dodds v. Winslow, 26 Ind. App. 652, 60 N.E. 458 (1901); Krotz v. A.R. Beck Lumber Co., 34 Ind. App. 577, 73 N.E. 273 (1905).

Purchaser's Grantee.

Where land sold at sheriff's sale upon execution was misdescribed in the levy, return and notice, or, a foreclosure of a mortgage, where the decree was void for want of notice, and the land was misdescribed in the decree and sheriff's deed, the purchaser receiving a sheriff's deed nevertheless took color of title, which he could convey, and the right of subrogation to the rights of the judgment or mortgage creditors passed to his assignees. Ray v. Detchon, 79 Ind. 56 (1881).

Sale Invalid.

The purchaser under a decree of foreclosure was subrogated to the rights of the creditor when the sale was invalid. Bodkin v. Merit, 102 Ind. 293, 1 N.E. 625 (1885).

Satisfaction of judgment could have been set aside when sale was invalid. Milburn v. Phillips, 143 Ind. 93, 42 N.E. 461, 52 Am. St. R. 403 (1895); Mehrhoff v. Diffenbacher, 4 Ind. App. 447, 31 N.E. 41 (1892).

Sale Set Aside.

Where a sale was set aside the purchaser had a lien on the land for the purchase-money. Seller v. Lingerman, 24 Ind. 264 (1865); Short v. Sears, 93 Ind. 505 (1883).

If the sale was set aside, the purchaser was subrogated to the lien of the creditor. Short v. Sears, 93 Ind. 505 (1883); Paxton v. Sterne, 127 Ind. 289, 26 N.E. 557 (1891); Milburn v. Phillips, 143 Ind. 93, 42 N.E. 461, 52 Am. St. R. 403 (1895); Reed v. Kalfsbeck, 147 Ind. 148, 45 N.E. 476, 46 N.E. 466 (1896).

32-30-13-2. Vacating satisfaction of judgment. — If the judgment is entered satisfied, in whole or in part, by reason of a sale referred to in section 1 [IC 32-30-13-1] of this chapter, the purchaser, upon notice to the parties to the proceeding and upon motion, may have the satisfaction of the judgment vacated in whole or in part. [P.L.2-2002, § 15.]

32-30-13-3. Purchaser's lien. — A purchaser of property referred to in section 1 [IC 32-30-13-1] of this chapter, if the proceedings are defective or the description of the property sold is imperfect, also has a lien to the same extent on the property sold as against all persons except bona fide purchasers without notice. [P.L.2-2002, § 15.]

32-30-13-4. Creditor not required to refund purchase money. — This chapter may not be construed to require the creditor to refund the purchase money by reason of the invalidity of any sale. [P.L.2-2002, § 15.]

CHAPTER 14
VALIDATION OF CERTAIN JUDGMENTS RELATING TO LAND TITLES

32-30-14-1. Record of proceedings not required. — Unless requested, a clerk is not required to make a complete record of the proceedings in actions to quiet title. A record of the judgment in such cases, when properly recorded in the office of the county recorder, is sufficient. [P.L.2-2002, § 15.]

Effective Dates. P.L.2-2002, § 15. July 1. 2002.

CHAPTER 15
STATUTE OF LIMITATIONS

32-30-15-1. Statute of limitations. — Unless otherwise provided in this title or another law, a cause of action concerning real property must be brought within the time specified in IC 34-11. [P.L.2-2002, § 15.]

Effective Dates. P.L.2-2002, § 15. July 1, 2002.

ARTICLE 31
LANDLORD-TENANT RELATIONS

CHAPTER 1

GENERAL PROVISIONS

32-31-1-1. Tenancy at will. — (a) A tenancy at will may be determined by a one (1) month notice in writing, delivered to the tenant.

(b) A tenancy at will cannot arise or be created without an express contract. [P.L.2-2002, § 16.]

Effective Dates. P.L.2-2002, § 16. July 1. 2002.
Indiana Law Review. Survey: Property Law: Reconstructing Property Law in Indiana: Altering Familiar Landscapes, 33 Ind. L. Rev. 1405 (2000).

NOTES TO DECISIONS

ANALYSIS

Construction of leases.
Creation of tenancies at will.
Termination of tenancies at will.

Construction of Leases.
A lease should be construed so as to give effect to the intention of the parties. Burdick Tire & Rubber Co. v. Heylmann, 79 Ind. App. 505, 138 N.E. 777 (1923).

Creation of Tenancies at Will.
Tenancies at will could only be created by express contracts. Bright v. McOuat, 40 Ind. 521 (1872).

Termination of Tenancies at Will.
Tenancies at will existed at the will of both parties and either could terminate the same at pleasure. Pidgeon v. Richards, 4 Ind. 374 (1853); Knight v. Indiana Coal & Iron Co., 47 Ind. 105, 17 Am. R. 692 (1873).

Notice to quit was necessary in tenancies at will. Coomler v. Hefner, 86 Ind. 108 (1882); Barth v. Pittsburgh, C., C. & St. L. Ry., 175 Ind. 554, 93 N.E. 535 (1911).

Collateral References. 49 Am. Jur. 2d Landlord and Tenant, §§ 65-81.

51C C.J.S. Landlord and Tenant, §§ 26-183.

Landlord and tenant: respective rights in excess rent when landlord relets at higher rent during lessee's term. 50 A.L.R.4th 403.

Specificity of description of premises as affecting enforceability of lease. 73 A.L.R.4th 236.

Implied warranty of fitness or suitability in commercial leases—modern status. 76 A.L.R.4th 928.

What constitutes abandonment of residential or commercial lease — modern cases. 84 A.L.R.4th 183.

Provision in lease as to purpose for which premises are to be used as excluding other uses. 86 A.L.R.4th 259.

Landlord's liability to third person for injury resulting from attack off leased premises by dangerous or vicious animal kept by tenant. 89 A.L.R.4th 374.

Coverage of leases under state consumer protection statutes. 89 A.L.R.4th 854.

32-31-1-2. Tenancy from month to month. — A general tenancy in which the premises are occupied by the express or constructive consent of the landlord is considered to be a tenancy from month to month. However, this section does not apply to land used for agricultural purposes. [P.L.2-2002, § 16.]

Cross References. See Oil and Gas Interests, IC 32-23-7, IC 32-23-9.

NOTES TO DECISIONS

ANALYSIS

Applicability.
Construction of leases.
Estate for years.
Miscellaneous tenancies.
Occupation by servant.
Occupation under contract to purchase.
Oil and gas leases.
Tenancy at sufferance.
Tenancy at will.
Tenancy from year to year.
Tenant holding over.
—New term.

Applicability.
The statutory law of tenancies from year to year or month to month should not have been made the law controlling in personal service employment contracts, or in services following the termination of such contracts by efflux of time, when no tenancy was involved. Jenkins v. King, 224 Ind. 164, 65 N.E.2d 121, 163 A.L.R. 397 (1946).

Where a tenant under a written lease for a term of two years continued to occupy the premises after the expiration of the lease with the consent of the owner who accepted rent thereafter, a tenancy for another year was created, and this statute relating to general tenancies did not apply. Marcus v. Calumet Breweries, Inc., 117 Ind. App. 603, 73 N.E.2d 351 (1947).

Construction of Leases.
A lease was construed in the light of the statutes on the subject of landlord and tenant

which were regarded as if written into and constituting a part of the contract. Templer v. Muncie Lodge I.O.O.F., 50 Ind. App. 324, 97 N.E. 546 (1912).

Tenancies from month to month could have been created by agreement that the tenant should occupy the property for successive periods of one month each, or the parties could simply enter into a general tenancy agreement, in which case the law stepped in and made the tenancy for successive periods of one month each. Weiss v. City of South Bend, 118 Ind. App. 105, 74 N.E.2d 925 (1947).

Estate for Years.
When the term of a tenancy was fixed and certain, it was not a tenancy from year to year, but it was an estate for years. Brown's Adm'rs v. Bragg, 22 Ind. 122 (1864); Bright v. McOuat, 40 Ind. 521 (1872); Rothschild v. Williamson, 83 Ind. 387 (1882).

When a tenant under a lease exercised the privilege to extend the term for a definite period, a new term was created and not a tenancy from year to year. Remm v. Landon, 43 Ind. App. 91, 86 N.E. 973 (1909); Remm v. Landon, 44 Ind. App. 430, 89 N.E. 523 (1909).

Miscellaneous Tenancies.
Whenever there was an agreement to pay rent, there existed the relation of landlord and tenant. Hopkins v. Ratliff, 115 Ind. 213, 17 N.E. 288 (1888).

Where one claimed to be the lessor, and the one in possession acquiesced in the claim and paid rent, the presumption was that the rela-

Miscellaneous Tenancies. (Cont'd)

tionship of landlord and tenant existed and this presumption would prevail unless overcome by countervailing evidence. Howe v. Gregory, 2 Ind. App. 477, 28 N.E. 776 (1891).

Granting the exclusive use of premises for a consideration created a tenancy. Heywood v. Fulmer, 158 Ind. 658, 32 N.E. 574, 18 L.R.A. 491 (1892).

Lease for year and as long as parties may agree created tenancy. Dunphy v. Goodlander, 12 Ind. App. 609, 40 N.E. 924 (1895); Mullen v. Pugh, 16 Ind. App. 337, 45 N.E. 347 (1896).

Modification of written lease for definite time by parol agreement for indefinite period created tenancy. City of Michigan City v. Leeds, 24 Ind. App. 271, 55 N.E. 799 (1899).

Occupation by Servant.

Occupation by a servant of the premises of his employer in connection with the performance of service did not make such servant a tenant. Chatard v. O'Donovan, 80 Ind. 20, 41 Am. R. 782 (1881); Heffelfinger v. Fulton, 25 Ind. App. 33, 56 N.E. 688 (1900).

Occupation Under Contract to Purchase.

Occupation of land under a contract of purchase would not create the relation of landlord and tenant unless the contract was absolutely void. Newby v. Vestal, 6 Ind. 412 (1855); Miles v. Elkin, 10 Ind. 329 (1858); Kratemayer v. Brink, 17 Ind. 509 (1861); Mattox v. Hightshue, 39 Ind. 95 (1872); Fall v. Hazelrigg, 45 Ind. 576, 15 Am. R. 278 (1874).

Oil and Gas Leases.

Contract by landowner with corporation whereby latter was to have exclusive right to bore for natural gas on the former's land and was to have paid certain sum annually did not under the facts of the case create a tenancy from year to year. Hancock v. Diamond Plate Glass Co., 162 Ind. 146, 70 N.E. 149 (1904); Consumers' Gas Trust Co. v. Littler, 162 Ind. 320, 70 N.E. 363 (1904); Carr v. Diamond Plate Glass Co., 162 Ind. 694, 70 N.E. 1112 (1904); Consumers' Gas Trust Co. v. Crystal Window Glass Co., 163 Ind. 190, 70 N.E. 366 (1904); Consumers' Gas Trust Co. v. Ink, 163 Ind. 174, 71 N.E. 477 (1904); Consumers' Gas Trust Co. v. Worth, 163 Ind. 141, 71 N.E. 489 (1904); Ohio Oil Co. v. Detamore, 165 Ind. 243, 73 N.E. 906 (1905); Shenk v. Stahl, 35 Ind. App. 493, 74 N.E. 538 (1905); Lafayette Gas Co. v. Kelsay, 164 Ind. 563, 74 N.E. 7 (1905); Hancock v. Diamond Plate Glass Co., 37 Ind. App. 351, 75 N.E. 659 (1905); New Am. Oil & Mining Co. v. Troyer, 166 Ind. 402, 76 N.E. 253, 77 N.E. 739 (1905); Indiana Rolling Mill Co. v. Gas Supply & Mining Co., 37 Ind. App. 154, 76 N.E. 640 (1906); Zeigler v. Dailey, 37 Ind. App. 240, 76 N.E. 819 (1906).

Tenancy at Sufferance.

A tenancy at sufferance existed when the tenant came into possession lawfully, but held over without right after his right of possession ceased. Work v. Brayton, 5 Ind. 396 (1854); Coomler v. Hefner, 86 Ind. 108 (1882).

Tenancies at sufferance were created by mere permission to use premises without the payment of rent. Carger v. Fee, 140 Ind. 572, 39 N.E. 93 (1894).

Where plaintiff, interpreting this section on tenancies at will, asserted that the concept of tenancy at sufferance is no longer valid in Indiana, the court of appeals noted that IC 32-7-1-7 (repealed; see IC 32-31-1-8 for similar provisions) evidenced the concept's continued viability. Lafary v. Lafary, 522 N.E.2d 916 (Ind. App. 1988).

Tenancy at Will.

When a tenancy at will existed, it was at the will of both parties, and either could terminate it at pleasure. Pidgeon v. Richards, 4 Ind. 374 (1853); Knight v. Indiana Coal & Iron Co., 47 Ind. 105, 17 Am. R. 692 (1873).

A tenancy at will could only have been created by an express contract. Bright v. McOuat, 40 Ind. 521 (1872).

Notice to quit was necessary in tenancies at will. Coomler v. Hefner, 86 Ind. 108 (1882); Barth v. Pittsburgh, C., C. & St. L. Ry., 175 Ind. 554, 93 N.E. 535 (1911).

Tenancy from Year to Year.

When premises were occupied with the assent of the landlord, without any agreement as to the duration of term, it was a tenancy from year to year. Ross v. Schneider, 30 Ind. 423 (1868); Tolle v. Orth, 75 Ind. 298, 39 Am. R. 147 (1881); Swan v. Clark, 80 Ind. 57 (1881); Rothschild v. Williamson, 83 Ind. 387 (1882); Coomler v. Hefner, 86 Ind. 108 (1882); Barrett v. Johnson, 2 Ind. App. 25, 27 N.E. 983 (1891); Elliott v. Stone City Bank, 4 Ind. App. 155, 30 N.E. 537 (1892); Indianapolis, D. & W. Ry. v. First Nat'l Bank, 134 Ind. 127, 33 N.E. 679 (1893); Kleespies v. McKenzie, 12 Ind. App. 404, 40 N.E. 648 (1895); Ridgeway v. Hannum, 29 Ind. App. 124, 64 N.E. 64 (1902).

A parol lease for more than three years created a tenancy from year to year. Railsback v. Walke, 81 Ind. 409 (1882); Nash v. Berkmeir, 83 Ind. 536 (1882).

Renting for an indefinite period with rent to be paid monthly created a tenancy from year to year. Rothschild v. Williamson, 83 Ind. 387 (1882); Elliott v. Stone City Bank, 4 Ind. App. 155, 30 N.E. 537 (1892).

A time lease irregularly executed, under this section, became a tenancy from year to year. Bereolos v. Roth, 74 Ind. App. 100, 124 N.E. 410 (1919).

Parol contract, attempting to create life estate by father in favor of his son, created a

Tenancy from Year to Year. (Cont'd)
tenancy from year to year where son took possession of the premises thereunder. Hoppes v. Hoppes, 190 Ind. 166, 129 N.E. 629 (1921).

Where receipts for rent were each for the term of one month from the first day of the month, and were each accepted and retained by the tenant, the court might reasonably have inferred that they expressed the contract between the parties as to the length of the tenancy, and that it was a tenancy from month to month, and not from year to year. Webster v. Pressley, 77 Ind. App. 247, 133 N.E. 508 (1922).

Where a tenant held over under a lease providing that the tenant should have the privilege of another term of five years if the parties could agree on the rental, and there was no agreement as to the rent, a tenancy from year to year was created, if the landlord accepted the same rent as provided in the lease. Magee v. Indiana Bus. College, 89 Ind. App. 640, 166 N.E. 607, 167 N.E. 918 (1929).

Tenant Holding Over.

When a tenant for a year or more held over after the expiration of his term, and paid rent, a tenancy from year to year was created. That is, he became a tenant for another year. Thiebaud v. First Nat'l Bank, 42 Ind. 212 (1873); Tolle v. Orth, 75 Ind. 298, 39 Am. R. 147 (1881); Montgomery v. Board of Comm'rs, 76 Ind. 362, 40 Am. R. 250 (1881); Coomler v. Hefner, 86 Ind. 108 (1882); Kleespies v. McKenzie, 12 Ind. App. 404, 40 N.E. 648 (1895); Alleman v. Vink, 28 Ind. App. 142, 62 N.E. 461 (1902); Ridgeway v. Hannum, 29 Ind. App. 124, 64 N.E. 44 (1902); Remm v. Landon, 43 Ind. App. 91, 86 N.E. 973 (1909); Habich v. University Park Bldg. Co., 177 Ind. 193, 97 N.E. 539 (1912); Akron Milling Co. v. Leiter, 57 Ind. App. 394, 107 N.E. 99 (1914).

A subtenant in possession and holding over under a lease subject to renewal, but which had not been renewed, was not a tenant from year to year. Mason v. Kempf, 11 Ind. App. 311, 38 N.E. 230 (1894).

A tenant who remained in possession of a dwelling house after the expiration of the rental period was not relieved of liability for the rent for the succeeding rental period because of an unexpressed purpose on his part to retain possession only until he could procure another house. Alleman v. Vink, 28 Ind. App. 142, 62 N.E. 461 (1902); Burdick Tire & Rubber Co. v. Heylmann, 79 Ind. App. 505, 138 N.E. 777 (1923).

If a tenant for three years held over at the end of his term, with the consent of the landlord, he became a tenant from year to year under the terms expressed in the contract under which he entered into possession.

Ridgeway v. Hannum, 29 Ind. App. 124, 64 N.E. 44 (1902).

A tenant, holding over pending negotiations for a new lease, did not become a tenant at will. Magee v. Indiana Bus. College, 89 Ind. App. 640, 166 N.E. 607, 167 N.E. 918 (1929).

This section (formerly IC 32-7-1-3) does not apply when the tenant holds over after the expiration of the lease and pays rent; these conditions do not create a general tenancy, but rather, these conditions create a tenancy for one year. Houston v. Booher, 647 N.E.2d 16 (1995).

In the absence of an agreement to the contrary, when a tenant holds over beyond the expiration of the lease and continues to make rental payments, and the lessor does not treat the tenant as a trespasser by evicting him, the parties are deemed to have continued the tenancy under the terms of the expired lease. Rueth v. Quinn, 659 N.E.2d 684 (Ind. App. 1995).

—New Term.

When a tenant for a fixed period less than one year remained in possession of the property beyond that period, with the consent, express or implied, of the landlord, it created a tenancy for another term equal in time to the one under which he previously held. Bright v. McOuat, 40 Ind. 521 (1872); Thiebaud v. First Nat'l Bank, 42 Ind. 212 (1873); Rothschild v. Williamson, 83 Ind. 387 (1882); Bollenbacker v. Fritts, 98 Ind. 50 (1884); McNatt v. Grange Hall Ass'n, 2 Ind. App. 341, 27 N.E. 325 (1891); Kleespies v. McKenzie, 12 Ind. App. 404, 40 N.E. 648 (1895); Remm v. Landon, 43 Ind. App. 91, 86 N.E. 973 (1909).

When the tenant had the option to hold for another term, but did not exercise his privilege, his holding over did not create a new term the same as his old term. Thiebaud v. First Nat'l Bank, 42 Ind. 212 (1873); Montgomery v. Board of Comm'rs, 76 Ind. 362 (1881); Barnett v. Feary, 101 Ind. 95 (1885).

If a landlord notified a tenant during his term that if he held over, his rent would have been so much per month, and the tenant held over without notice of an acceptance of the proposition of the landlord, a new term was not created. Lautman v. Miller, 158 Ind. 382, 63 N.E. 761 (1902).

Where, after expiration of five-year lease which provided for termination "at once and without further notice," tenant held over with landlord's consent, the lease was extended for one year subject to termination at end of year without notice; and holding over for successive years did not create a general tenancy or one from year to year. Walsh v. Soller, 207 Ind. 82, 190 N.E. 61, rehearing denied, 207 Ind. 87, 191 N.E. 334 (1934).

Holding over by tenant unlawfully did not

Tenant Holding Over. (Cont'd)

—New Term. (Cont'd)
create a new term. Chicago & S.E.R.R. v. Perkins, 12 Ind. App. 131, 38 N.E. 487 (1895).

A tenancy at will, held by the tenant under a written contract with the owner, terminated on the death of the owner. Sabinske v. Patterson, 100 Ind. App. 657, 196 N.E. 539 (1935).

32-31-1-3. Tenancy from year to year. — A tenancy from year to year may be determined by a notice given to the tenant not less than three (3) months before the expiration of the year. [P.L.2-2002, § 16.]

NOTES TO DECISIONS

ANALYSIS

In general.
Construction with other law.
Failure to pay rent.
Improvements.
Notice.

In General.

When there was a general tenancy, and the rent was payable at stated times, three months' notice before the end of the year was necessary to terminate the tenancy. Barrett v. Johnson, 2 Ind. App. 25, 27 N.E. 983 (1891); Elliott v. Stone City Bank, 4 Ind. App. 155, 30 N.E. 537 (1892); Hammond v. Jones, 41 Ind. App. 32, 83 N.E. 257 (1908).

A notice by lessor before the expiration of the year that lessee could not hold over in a lease of tenancy for year and as long as parties might agree, was sufficient. Dunphy v. Goodlander, 12 Ind. App. 609, 40 N.E. 924 (1895).

A tenancy from month to month or from one period to another of less than three months' duration required a notice equal to the term of tenancy. Lautman v. Miller, 158 Ind. 382, 63 N.E. 761 (1902).

The failure of a landlord to give the required statutory notice to quit made his action for possession subject to a plea in abatement as a premature action. Jones v. Evanoff, 114 Ind. App. 318, 52 N.E.2d 359 (1944).

Construction With Other Law.

Mobile home lease was properly terminated without cause, under the provisions of IC 16-41-27-30, which did not conflict with former IC 32-7-1-3 (repealed; see this section for similar provisions). Barber v. Echo Lake

Mobile Home Community, 759 N.E.2d 253 (Ind. App. 2001).

Failure to Pay Rent.

A tenancy from year to year could have been terminated by a ten days' notice for failure to pay rent. Leary v. Meier, 78 Ind. 393 (1881).

In a tenancy to terminate on failure to pay rent, notice was unnecessary when rent was not paid when due. Thomas v. Walmer, 18 Ind. App. 112, 46 N.E. 695 (1897); Ingalls v. Bissot, 25 Ind. App. 130, 57 N.E. 723 (1900).

Improvements.

Where improvements were made by tenant to leasehold after receiving notice to terminate, such improvements were made at the tenant's own risk and he was not entitled to reimbursement. Speiser v. Addis, 78 Ind. Dec. 750, 411 N.E.2d 439 (Ind. App. 1980).

Notice.

Failure of all co-owners of leased property to sign a "Notice to Quit" did not render the notice defective where there was evidence from which an agency relationship between the signers of the notice and the other co-owners could be inferred. Pilotte v. Brummett, 165 Ind. App. 403, 48 Ind. Dec. 305, 332 N.E.2d 834 (1975).

Where a mobile home park tenant's lease expressly provided that his tenancy might be determined for violation of posted rules, his tenancy was terminated upon his violation of the posted rules and a resultant notice to quit, and he was not entitled to one month's advance notice pursuant to this section. Halliday v. Auburn Mobile Homes, 511 N.E.2d 1086 (Ind. App. 1987).

Collateral References. What 12-month period constitutes "year" or "calendar year" as used in public enactment, contract, or other written instrument. 5 A.L.R.3d 584.

Commercial leases: application of rule that lease may be canceled only for "material" breach. 54 A.L.R.4th 595.

32-31-1-4. Tenancy of not more than three months. — (a) This section applies to a tenancy of not more than three (3) months which, by express or implied agreement of the parties, extends from one (1) period to another.

(b) Notice to the tenant equal to the interval between the periods is sufficient to determine a tenancy described in subsection (a). [P.L.2-2002, § 16.]

32-31-1-5. Termination of tenancy from year to year — Form of notice. — The following form of notice may be used to terminate a tenancy from year to year:

(insert date here)

To (insert name of tenant here):

You are notified to vacate at the expiration of the current year of tenancy the following property: (insert description of property here).

(insert name of landlord here)

[P.L.2-2002, § 16.]

NOTES TO DECISIONS

In General.

Service of notice to quit by reading the same to the tenant was insufficient. Jenkins v. Jenkins, 63 Ind. 415, 30 Am. R. 229 (1878).

If the notice apprised the tenant of the premises demanded, it was sufficient. Epstein v. Greer, 78 Ind. 348 (1881).

32-31-1-6. Termination of lease for failure to pay rent. — If a tenant refuses or neglects to pay rent when due, a landlord may terminate the lease with not less than ten (10) days notice to the tenant unless:

(1) the parties otherwise agreed; or

(2) the tenant pays the rent in full before the notice period expires. [P.L.2-2002, § 16.]

NOTES TO DECISIONS

ANALYSIS

In general.
Computation of time.
Demand.
Dispossession without action.
Forfeiture as termination of tenancy.
Forfeiture provision in lease.
Portion payable in crops.
Rent payable in advance.
Tenancy from year to year.
Waiver of forfeiture.
When rent due.

In General.

Where lessor entered premises upon non-payment of rent, the lease authorizing him to do so, lessee's trustee in bankruptcy could not pay rent and demand reinstatement of lease.

Robertson v. Langdon, 72 F.2d 148 (7th Cir. 1934).

Computation of Time.

If notice to quit was served on the thirteenth of a month, the ten days would not expire until the end of the twenty-third of the month. Cheek v. Preston, 34 Ind. App. 343, 72 N.E. 1048 (1905).

Demand.

In an action to have a lease declared forfeited for failure to pay rent, the allegation that "the plaintiff just before sunset, duly demanded payment of $120, the amount due on the premises," was a sufficient allegation to show a demand. Faylor v. Brice, 7 Ind. App. 551, 34 N.E. 833 (1893).

Dispossession Without Action.

A landlord had no right by force to repossess his own real estate, even though the tenant had terminated the tenancy. Calef v. Jesswein, 93 Ind. App. 514, 176 N.E. 632 (1931).

A landlord had the right to take peaceable possession of his premises from a defaulting tenant. Calef v. Jesswein, 93 Ind. App. 514, 176 N.E. 632 (1931).

A lessor who served ten days' notice on the tenant to quit was not required to institute an action to recover possession of the premises in order that possession be transferred from the lessee to the lease. Calef v. Jesswein, 93 Ind. App. 514, 176 N.E. 632 (1931).

The lessee's failure to pay rent due within ten days after being served with ten days' notice to quit terminated the lease. Calef v. Jesswein, 93 Ind. App. 514, 176 N.E. 632 (1931).

Forfeiture as Termination of Tenancy.

When a tenant was removed from the premises for nonpayment of rent, he was released from payment of rent accruing under his contract after the termination of his tenancy. Campbell v. Nixon, 2 Ind. App. 463, 28 N.E. 107 (1891).

Forfeiture Provision in Lease.

Notice was not required when forfeiture was provided in the lease for nonpayment of rent. Thomas v. Walmer, 18 Ind. App. 112, 46 N.E. 695 (1897).

Failure to pay rent did not work a forfeiture of the lease unless it was so expressed in the lease. Templer v. Muncie Lodge I.O.O.F., 50 Ind. App. 324, 97 N.E. 546 (1912).

Portion Payable in Crops.

If a portion of the rent was payable in money at stated times, and a portion payable in a part of the crops, the entire tenancy could not have been terminated by a ten days' notice. Ricketts v. Richardson, 85 Ind. 508 (1882).

Rent Payable in Advance.

This section was not applicable where there was an agreement that the rent had to be paid in advance. Royse v. Gray, 79 Ind. App. 483, 134 N.E. 217 (1922).

Tenancy from Year to Year.

Tenancies from year to year could have been terminated by a ten days' notice for failure to pay rent. Leary v. Meier, 78 Ind. 393 (1881).

Waiver of Forfeiture.

A receipt of rent after it was due waived the right to claim a forfeiture for nonpayment. Hill v. Nisbet, 100 Ind. 341 (1885); Merrell v. Garver, 54 Ind. App. 514, 101 N.E. 152 (1913).

When Rent Due.

In the absence of a special contract, rent did not become due until the end of the term. Watson v. Penn, 108 Ind. 21, 8 N.E. 636, 58 Am. R. 26 (1886); Indianapolis, D. & W. Ry. v. First Nat'l Bank, 134 Ind. 127, 33 N.E. 679 (1893); Cowan v. Henika, 19 Ind. App. 40, 48 N.E. 809 (1897).

Collateral References. Necessity and sufficiency of demand for rent under lease sought to be forfeited for nonpayment. 31 A.L.R.2d 321.

Relief against forfeiture for nonpayment of rent. 31 A.L.R.2d 321.

Right of landlord legally entitled to possession to dispossess tenant without legal process. 6 A.L.R.3d 177.

Waiver of statutory demand-for-rent due or of notice-to-quit prerequisite of summary eviction of lessee for nonpayment of rent-modern cases. 31 A.L.R.4th 1254.

Landlord's duty, on tenant's failure to occupy, or abandonment of, premises, to mitigate damages by accepting or procuring another tenant. 75 A.L.R.5th 1.

32-31-1-7. Failure to pay rent — Form of notice. — The following form of notice may be used when a tenant fails or refuses to pay rent:

(insert date here)

To (insert name of tenant here):

You are notified to vacate the following property not more than ten (10) days after you receive this notice unless you pay the rent due on the property within ten (10) days: (insert description of property here).

(insert name of landlord here)

[P.L.2-2002, § 16.]

NOTES TO DECISIONS

In General.

Service of notice to quit by reading the same to the tenant was insufficient. Jenkins v. Jenkins, 63 Ind. 415, 30 Am. R. 229 (1878).

If the notice apprised the tenant of the premises demanded, it was sufficient. Epstein v. Greer, 78 Ind. 348 (1881).

Collateral References. Right of landlord legally entitled to possession to dispossess tenant without legal process. 6 A.L.R.3d 177.

32-31-1-8. Termination of lease — When notice not required. —

Notice is not required to terminate a lease in the following situations:

(1) The landlord agrees to rent the premises to the tenant for a specified period of time.

(2) The time for the determination of the tenancy is specified in the contract.

(3) A tenant at will commits waste.

(4) The tenant is a tenant at sufferance.

(5) The express terms of the contract require the tenant to pay the rent in advance, and the tenant refuses or neglects to pay the rent in advance.

(6) The landlord-tenant relationship does not exist.

[P.L.2-2002, § 16.]

NOTES TO DECISIONS

ANALYSIS

In general.
Advance notice.
—Not required.
Applicability.
Bankruptcy.
Definite term.
Indefinite term.
Rent payable in advance.
Tenancy at sufferance.
Title of landlord denied.
Waiver of default.

In General.

If a new term was created by the tenant holding over at the end of the term, notice to quit was not necessary to terminate such new term. Whetstone v. Davis, 34 Ind. 510 (1870).

Where a tenant held over under a written lease providing that at the expiration thereof, "the same shall terminate at once without further notice," no further notice to quit was required. Walsh v. Soller, 207 Ind. 82, 190 N.E. 61, rehearing denied, 207 Ind. 87, 191 N.E. 334 (1934).

Notice to quit was unnecessary where the

lease was for specified time. Johnson v. Greenen, 98 Ind. App. 612, 188 N.E. 796 (1934).

Where the children of tenants at will, after the death of their parents, continued to hold possession of the land after demand for possession and payment of rent therefor, they were no more than tenants at sufferance, and not entitled to notice to quit prior to action against them by the owner for possession of the land. Sabinske v. Patterson, 100 Ind. App. 657, 196 N.E. 539 (1935).

It was not necessary for vendor of realty sold on oral conditional sales contract to give notice to quit to purchaser before terminating contract for default since no relationship of landlord and tenant existed. Edwards v. Sheehan Constr. Co., 124 Ind. App. 182, 115 N.E.2d 750 (1953).

Advance Notice.

—Not Required.

Where a mobile home park tenant's lease expressly provided that his tenancy might be determined for violation of posted rules, his tenancy was terminated upon his violation of

Advance Notice. (Cont'd)

—Not Required. (Cont'd)
the posted rules and a resultant notice to quit, and he was not entitled to one month's advance notice pursuant to former IC 32-7-1-3. Halliday v. Auburn Mobile Homes, 511 N.E.2d 1086 (Ind. App. 1987).

Applicability.
This section, providing that no notice to quit was necessary where the relation of landlord and tenant did not exist, had no application to a situation between a vendor and vendee where the vendor had habitually accepted payments in the contract after the due date, and the principles of equity and fair dealing were controlling. Chambers v. Boatright, 132 Ind. App. 378, 177 N.E.2d 600 (1961).

This section (formerly IC 32-7-1-7) is a limitation on the landlord's obligation to give notice and is inapplicable to the situation involving a tenant's notice to his landlord. Edward Rose of Ind. v. Fountain, 431 N.E.2d 543 (Ind. App. 1982).

Bankruptcy.
Oral month-to-month lease with rent payable in advance was terminated as a matter of Indiana law when Chapter 7 bankruptcy debtor failed to pay rent. In re Salzer, 52 F.3d 708 (7th Cir. 1995), cert. denied, 516 U.S. 1177, 116 S. Ct. 1273, 134 L. Ed. 2d 219 (1996).

Definite Term.
When the tenancy was for a definite term, notice to quit was not necessary. McClure v. McClure, 74 Ind. 108 (1881); Barrett v. Johnson, 2 Ind. App. 25, 27 N.E. 983 (1891); Mason v. Kempf, 11 Ind. App. 311, 38 N.E. 230 (1894); Chicago & S.E.R.R. v. Perkins, 12 Ind. App. 131, 38 N.E. 487 (1895); Lautman v. Miller, 158 Ind. 382, 63 N.E. 761 (1902); Millington v. O'Dell, 35 Ind. App. 225, 73 N.E. 949 (1905); Grimes v. Muzzillo, 83 Ind. App. 368, 148 N.E. 425 (1925).

In view of this section, a tenancy for a definite period terminated on the expiration of such period and the tenant was not entitled to notice to quit. Grimes v. Muzzillo, 83 Ind. App. 368, 148 N.E. 425 (1925).

Indefinite Term.
If the tenancy was to terminate on the happening of a contingency, the tenancy terminated when the contingency accrued without notice. Clark v. Rhoads, 79 Ind. 342 (1881); Scott v. Willis, 122 Ind. 1, 22 N.E. 786 (1889); Smith v. Devoe, 69 Ind. App. 282, 121 N.E. 661 (1919).

Notice was sufficient when lessor, before the expiration of the year, gave notice that

lessee could not hold over where lease provided that the agreement was to run as long as lessor and lessee agreed, but when they did not agree, lessor was to have full possession at once. Dunphy v. Goodlander, 12 Ind. App. 609, 40 N.E. 924 (1895).

In a lease to terminate on failure to pay rent, notice was not necessary if rent was not paid. Thomas v. Walmer, 18 Ind. App. 112, 46 N.E. 695 (1897); Ripley v. Lemcke, 43 Ind. App. 336, 87 N.E. 237 (1909).

Rent Payable in Advance.
When rent was payable in advance and was not paid when due, an action for possession would lie without a notice to quit. McNatt v. Grange Hall Ass'n, 2 Ind. App. 341, 27 N.E. 325 (1891); Ingalls v. Bissot, 25 Ind. App. 130, 57 N.E. 723 (1900); Ripley v. Lemcke, 43 Ind. App. 336, 87 N.E. 237 (1909); Brown v. Thompson, 45 Ind. App. 188, 90 N.E. 631 (1910); Templer v. Muncie Lodge I.O.O.F., 50 Ind. App. 324, 97 N.E. 546 (1912); Whitcomb v. Indianapolis Traction & Term. Co., 64 Ind. App. 605, 116 N.E. 444 (1917); Royse v. Gray, 79 Ind. App. 483, 134 N.E. 217 (1922); Karas v. Skouras, 79 Ind. App. 99, 137 N.E. 289 (1922).

In an action to recover the possession of real estate, wherein the evidence was in conflict as to the length of the tenancy agreed upon between plaintiff and defendants, and as to whether there was a stipulation that rent was to be paid in advance, such evidence was insufficient to establish conclusively any one of the provisions of this section, which rendered unnecessary the service of a notice to quit on lessees. Gabier v. Coleman, 111 Ind. App. 57, 40 N.E.2d 387 (1942).

Where, in an action to recover the possession of real estate, it was contended by plaintiff that a tenancy from month to month existed between him and defendants, and that a failure of defendants to pay rent on a certain date when due operated to terminate the tenancy, and hence no notice to quit was necessary, the burden was upon plaintiff to establish such facts, in order to dispense with the necessity of written notice to terminate the lease within the provision of this section. Gabier v. Coleman, 111 Ind. App. 57, 40 N.E.2d 387 (1942).

Where a written lease from month to month required rental payments in advance for each month, and provided that upon failure to pay such rent when due the lease should terminate, and, possession be yielded without notice or demand, lessees, who failed to pay any rent after the expiration of the first month's tenancy, were not entitled to a notice to quit or demand before a suit in ejectment would lie against them. Saint Germain v. Sears, Roebuck & Co., 112 Ind. App. 412, 44 N.E.2d 216 (1942).

Rent Payable in Advance. (Cont'd)

Where by the terms of the lease the rent was payable in advance on the fifteenth day of each month, and the failure to so pay would work a forfeiture, and demand for payment was waived, an action for possession would have been under this section without demand for rent or notice to quit. Michael v. Mitchell, 118 Ind. App. 18, 73 N.E.2d 363 (1947).

Where the lease provided for payment of rent in advance, and absent a waiver or estoppel, a failure to have paid rent on the due date constituted a default of the lease and provided the lessor with the option of terminating the lease without notice to quit to the lessee. Lafayette Car Wash, Inc. v. Boes, 258 Ind. 498, 30 Ind. Dec. 725, 282 N.E.2d 837 (1972).

Under Indiana law, when there is a month-to-month tenancy with rent due in advance each month, the tenancy is terminated when the rent has not been paid when due, and in those circumstances the landlord is not required to give any notice to quit prior to initiating repossession of the property. Kipp v. Depoy, 29 Bankr. 466 (Bankr. N.D. Ind. 1983).

Tenancy at Sufferance.

Tenants at sufferance were not entitled to notice to quit. Carger v. Fee, 140 Ind. 572, 39 N.E. 93 (1894).

Where daughter and her husband were given permission to enter and use part of land in the expectation that they would purchase the land, it was at best a tenancy at sufferance and no notice to quit was necessary. Wallace v. Roger, 182 Ind. App. 256, 71 Ind. Dec. 705, 395 N.E.2d 274 (1979).

Where plaintiff, interpreting former IC 32-7-1-2 on tenancies at will, asserted that the concept of tenancy at sufferance is no longer valid in Indiana, the court of appeals noted that this section evidences the concept's continued viability. Lafary v. Lafary, 522 N.E.2d 916 (Ind. App. 1988).

Title of Landlord Denied.

If the tenant denied the title of the landlord, notice to quit or demand for possession was not necessary. Sims v. Cooper, 106 Ind. 87, 5 N.E. 726 (1886); Tobin v. Young, 124 Ind. 507, 24 N.E. 121 (1890).

Waiver of Default.

Cashing by the lessor of a check given by the lessee in payment of late rent instalment payments constituted a waiver of any default for late payment of rent. Kimmel v. Cockrell, 161 Ind. App. 659, 44 Ind. Dec. 143, 317 N.E.2d 449 (1974).

32-31-1-9. Service of notice. — (a) Notice required under sections 1 through 7 [IC 32-31-1-1 through IC 32-31-1-7] of this chapter may be served on the tenant.

(b) If the tenant cannot be found, notice may be served on a person residing at the premises. The person serving the notice must explain the contents of the notice to the person being served.

(c) If a person described in subsection (b) is not found on the premises, notice may be served by affixing a copy of the notice to a conspicuous part of the premises. [P.L.2-2002, § 16.]

Cross References. Ejectment, IC 32-30-3.

NOTES TO DECISIONS

In General.

The notice had to be served by delivering the same to the tenant if found, and if not found, to some one residing on the premises. Jenkins v. Jenkins, 63 Ind. 415, 30 Am. R. 229 (1878); Epstein v. Greer, 78 Ind. 348 (1881).

Service of notice to quit by reading the same to the tenant was insufficient. Jenkins v. Jenkins, 63 Ind. 415, 30 Am. R. 229 (1878).

If the notice apprised the tenant of the premises demanded, it was sufficient. Epstein v. Greer, 78 Ind. 348 (1881).

32-31-1-10. Conveyance by landlord of real estate. — A conveyance by a landlord of real estate or of any interest in the real estate is valid without the attornment of the tenant. If the tenant pays rent to the landlord before the tenant receives notice of the conveyance, the rent paid to the landlord is good against the grantee. [P.L.2-2002, § 16.]

NOTES TO DECISIONS

ANALYSIS

In general.
Gas lease.

In General.
On sale of leased premises, the vendee was entitled to the rents accruing after the sale, unless paid to the vendor before notice of the sale. Sampson v. Grimes, 7 Blackf. 176 (1844); Page v. Lashley, 15 Ind. 152 (1860); Carley v. Lewis, 24 Ind. 23 (1865).

The purchaser of leased premises succeeded to all the rights of the vendor under the lease. Bowen v. Roach, 78 Ind. 361 (1881); Heavilon v. Farmers Bank, 81 Ind. 249 (1881); Swope v. Hopkins, 119 Ind. 125, 21 N.E. 462 (1889).

When the leased premises were sold, the tenant became the tenant of the purchaser, in the absence of an agreement to the contrary. Kellum v. Berkshire Life Ins. Co., 101 Ind.

455 (1885); Swope v. Hopkins, 119 Ind. 125, 21 N.E. 462 (1889); Ream v. Goslee, 21 Ind. App. 241, 52 N.E. 93 (1893); Hammond v. Jones, 41 Ind. App. 32, 83 N.E. 257 (1908).

Where grantor agreed to give grantee immediate possession, it could not be said that the grantee accepted the tenant as his own and waived the right of possession and the grantor was liable to the grantee for all sums expended necessarily by the grantee in obtaining possession. Williams v. Frybarger, 9 Ind. App. 558, 37 N.E. 302 (1894); Gibbs v. Ely, 13 Ind. App. 130, 41 N.E. 351 (1895).

Gas Lease.
Where an owner of land executed a gas lease, and afterward conveyed the land, the grantee was entitled to the rents maturing after the conveyance. Chandler v. Pittsburgh Plate Glass Co., 20 Ind. App. 165, 50 N.E. 400 (1898).

Collateral References. Applicability of doctrine of estoppel to deny title in action by tenant to recover rentals previously paid to one mistakenly believed to be owner of property. 57 A.L.R.2d 350.

32-31-1-11. Attornment by tenant to stranger. — The attornment of a tenant to a stranger is void and does not affect the possession of the landlord unless:

(1) the landlord consents to the attornment; or

(2) the attornment is made under a judgment at law or the order or decree of a court. [P.L.2-2002, § 16.]

NOTES TO DECISIONS

In General.
An attornment was the acknowledgment by the tenant of a new landlord. Cressler v. Williams, 80 Ind. 366 (1881).

32-31-1-12. Remedy of sublessee. — A sublessee has the same remedy under the original lease against the chief landlord as the sublessee would have had against the immediate lessor. [P.L.2-2002, § 16.]

32-31-1-13. Remedy of alienee of lessor or lessee. — An alienee of a lessor or lessee of land has the same legal remedies in relation to the land as the lessor or lessee. [P.L.2-2002, § 16.]

NOTES TO DECISIONS

ANALYSIS

Assignment of lease.
Breach before transfer.
Conveyance of premises.

Assignment of Lease.
An administrator of a deceased tenant was not released from liability to pay rent by an assignment of the lease. Carley v. Lewis, 24 Ind. 23 (1865).

Assignment of Lease. (Cont'd)

When a lease was not assignable without the consent of the lessor, he may have claimed a forfeiture of the lease if it was assigned without his consent. Indianapolis Mfg. & Carpenters Union v. Cleveland, C., C. & I. Ry., 45 Ind. 281 (1873).

The assignee of an oil and gas lease was liable for the performance of the conditions therein stipulated where such assignment was made in writing and was accepted and held by assignee as the sole and exclusive owner thereof. Breckenridge v. Parrott, 15 Ind. App. 411, 44 N.E. 66 (1896); Edmonds v. Mounsey, 15 Ind. App. 399, 44 N.E. 196 (1896); Hardison v. Mann, 20 Ind. App. 404, 50 N.E. 899 (1898); Vandalia Coal Co. v. Underwood, 55 Ind. App. 91, 101 N.E. 1047 (1913).

Consent by the lessor to the assignment of a lease did not release the lessee from liability for rent although rent was accepted from the assignee. Jordan v. Indianapolis Water Co., 159 Ind. 337, 64 N.E. 680 (1902).

Breach Before Transfer.

At common law, the transferee of the reversion could not enforce a forfeiture of the term under a power of reentry for breach of the lessee's covenant contained in the lease, and, in the absence of a statutory provision enlarging the right of such transferee, he could not enforce a forfeiture that was in existence at the time of the transfer where the lessor had done no act to indicate his purpose of avoiding the lease by reason of the breach. Michael v. Mitchell, 118 Ind. App. 18, 73 N.E.2d 363 (1947).

Conveyance of Premises.

Rents followed the lands into the hands of a vendee, and the lessor could have sued the lessee on his covenant to pay rent, or follow the land. Carley v. Lewis, 24 Ind. 23 (1865).

If, on the conveyance of lands, the grantor was to remain in possession for a stated time, he was entitled to receive the rents for such time. Goodwin v. Hudson, 60 Ind. 117 (1877).

The vendee of leased lands succeeded to all the rights of the vendor under the lease. Allen v. Shannon, 74 Ind. 164 (1881); Bowen v. Roach, 78 Ind. 361 (1881); Kennard v. Harvey, 80 Ind. 37 (1881); Heavilon v. Farmers Bank, 81 Ind. 249 (1881); Swope v. Hopkins, 119 Ind. 125, 21 N.E. 462 (1889).

Covenants to pay rent or royalty ran with the land, and vendees were entitled to all rents accruing after the conveyance. Breckenridge v. Parrott, 15 Ind. App. 411, 44 N.E. 66 (1896); Edmonds v. Mounsey, 15 Ind. App. 399, 44 N.E. 196 (1896); Chandler v. Pittsburgh Plate Glass Co., 20 Ind. App. 165, 50 N.E. 400 (1898); Indiana Natural Gas & Oil Co. v. Hinton, 159 Ind. 398, 64 N.E. 224 (1902).

32-31-1-14. Rents from lands granted for life. — Rents from lands granted for life or lives may be recovered as other rents. [P.L.2-2002, § 16.]

NOTES TO DECISIONS

In General.

Rents due to a life tenant at his death were collectible by his personal representatives, and undue rents went to the remainderman. Henry v. Stevens, 108 Ind. 281, 9 N.E. 356 (1886); Lowrey v. Reef, 1 Ind. App. 244, 27 N.E. 626 (1891); Frame's Estate v. Frame, 48 Ind. App. 481, 96 N.E. 35 (1911).

Life tenants could sell growing crops and the purchaser could gather the same after the death of the tenant. Shaffer v. Stevens, 143 Ind. 295, 42 N.E. 620 (1896).

32-31-1-15. Rents dependent on the life of another person. — A person entitled to rents dependent on the life of another person may recover arrears unpaid at the death of the other person. [P.L.2-2002, § 16.]

NOTES TO DECISIONS

ANALYSIS

In general.
Growing crops.

In General.

Rents accruing before the death of the lessor went to his personal representative, and the rents accruing afterwards went to his heirs. Watson v. Penn, 108 Ind. 21, 8 N.E. 636, 58 Am. R. 26 (1886); Henry v. Stevens, 108 Ind. 281, 9 N.E. 356 (1886); Lowrey v. Reef, 1 Ind. App. 244, 27 N.E. 626 (1891); Frame's Estate v. Frame, 48 Ind. App. 481, 96 N.E. 35 (1911).

If lands were devised for life, subject to a lease, the rents accruing after the death of the devisee went to the reversioner. Watson v.

In General. (Cont'd)
Penn, 108 Ind. 21, 8 N.E. 636, 58 Am. R. 26 (1886).

Claims against a deceased lessor could not be set off against rents that accrued after the death of the lessor. Bell v. Bitner, 33 Ind. App. 6, 70 N.E. 549 (1904).

Growing Crops.
The lessee of a tenant for life was entitled to the crops growing at the death of the lessor. Dorsett v. Gray, 98 Ind. 273 (1884); Lowrey v. Reef, 1 Ind. App. 244, 27 N.E. 626 (1891).

Life tenants could sell growing crops, and the purchaser could gather the same after the death of the tenant. Shaffer v. Stevens, 143 Ind. 295, 42 N.E. 620 (1896).

32-31-1-16. Executor or administrator of estate of decedent. — An executor or administrator of the estate of a decedent, whether a testator or intestate:

(1) has the same remedies to recover rents; and

(2) is subject to the same liabilities to pay rents;

as the decedent. [P.L.2-2002, § 16.]

NOTES TO DECISIONS

ANALYSIS

In general.
Right to rent.

In General.
Executors or administrators could not have leased lands for a term beyond the time when their control over the lands would cease. Burbank v. Dyer, 54 Ind. 392 (1876).

Lease for years was personal estate and went to the personal representative of a deceased lessor. Mark v. North, 155 Ind. 575, 57 N.E. 902 (1900); Shipley v. Smith, 162 Ind. 526, 70 N.E. 803 (1904); Spiro v. Robertson, 57 Ind. App. 229, 106 N.E. 726 (1914).

Right to Rent.
Rents accruing before the death of the lessor went to his estate, and those accruing afterward went to his heirs. Lowrey v. Reef, 1 Ind. App. 244, 27 N.E. 626 (1891).

Administrators could not collect rents accruing after the death of their decedents. McClead v. Davis, 83 Ind. 263 (1882).

32-31-1-17. Occupant of land without contract. — An occupant of land without special contract is liable for the rent to any person entitled to receive the rent. [P.L.2-2002, § 16.]

NOTES TO DECISIONS

ANALYSIS

In general.
Contract to purchase.
Former law.
Members of family.
Oral conditional sales contract.
Tenants in common.

In General.
Where one used and occupied the land of which others were tenants in common, the law implied a promise to them to pay a reasonable value for the use of the premises. Estep v. Estep, 23 Ind. 114 (1864).

If possession of land was taken without the consent of the owner, the occupant would have been liable for rents. Winings v. Wood, 53 Ind. 187 (1876).

Contract to Purchase.
The occupant of land under an absolutely void contract of purchase was liable for rent. Mattox v. Hightshue, 39 Ind. 95 (1872); Shirk v. Stafford, 31 Ind. App. 247, 67 N.E. 542 (1903).

Contract to purchase with conversion to pay rent upon default gave rise to liability by assignee of purchaser for occupation and use. Baltes Land, Stone & Oil Co. v. Sutton, 25 Ind. App. 695, 57 N.E. 974 (1900).

Former Law.
Prior to the enactment of the predecessor statutes to this section, there could not have been a recovery for the use and occupation of real estate unless the relation of landlord and tenant existed. Newby v. Vestal, 6 Ind. 412 (1855); Miles v. Elkin, 10 Ind. 329 (1858); Nance v. Alexander, 49 Ind. 516 (1875); Pitts-

Former Law. (Cont'd)

burgh, C. & St. L. Ry. v. Thornburgh, 98 Ind. 201 (1884).

Members of Family.

This section did not apply to a person who lived as a member of the family of the tenant of land under a contract. Tinder v. Davis, 88 Ind. 99 (1882).

Where husband and wife lived together as a family in the wife's house, there was no implied agreement to have made the husband the tenant of the wife and liable for the payment of rent. Gardner v. Gardner, 29 Ind. App. 449, 64 N.E. 637 (1902).

Oral Conditional Sales Contract.

Award of trial court of damages to vendor of real estate under oral conditional sales contract resulting from default of purchaser and wrongful occupancy of said real estate was not excessive. Edwards v. Sheehan Constr. Co., 124 Ind. App. 182, 115 N.E.2d 750 (1953).

Tenants in Common.

Tenants in common were only liable to cotenants for rents when they excluded such cotenants from possession or collected rents from third persons. Humphries v. Davis, 100 Ind. 369 (1885); Carver v. Coffman, 109 Ind. 547, 10 N.E. 567 (1887); Carver v. Fennimore, 116 Ind. 236, 19 N.E. 103 (1888); Bowen v. Swander, 121 Ind. 164, 22 N.E. 725 (1889); Davis v. Hutton, 127 Ind. 481, 26 N.E. 187, 1006 (1891).

The owner of an undivided interest in land could maintain an action for partition against his cotenant in common notwithstanding the tenant in common held a valid tax lien upon such undivided interest. The lien in such cases attached to the part set off to the lien debtor when partition was complete and in such case no tender of the amount of the lien was necessary. Schissel v. Dickson, 129 Ind. 139, 28 N.E. 540 (1891).

Collateral References. Validity, construction, and effect of statute or lease provision expressly governing rights and compensation of lessee upon condemnation of leased property. 22 A.L.R.5th 327.

32-31-1-18. Death of life tenant — Recovery of rent. — If a life tenant who has demised any lands dies on or after the day on which rent is due and payable, the executor or administrator of the life tenant's estate may recover from the under tenant the whole rent due. If the life tenant dies before the day on which rent is due:

(1) the executor or administrator of the life tenant's estate may recover the proportion of rent that accrued before; and

(2) the remainderman may recover the the proportion of rent that accrued after;

the life tenant's death. [P.L.2-2002, § 16.]

NOTES TO DECISIONS

Crops.

The lessee of a tenant for life was entitled to the crops growing at the time of death of the lessor. Dorsett v. Gray, 98 Ind. 273 (1884); Henry v. Stevens, 108 Ind. 281, 9 N.E. 356 (1886); Lowrey v. Reef, 1 Ind. App. 244, 27 N.E. 626 (1891); Shaffer v. Stevens, 143 Ind. 295, 42 N.E. 620 (1896); Murray v. Cazier, 23 Ind. App. 600, 53 N.E. 476 (1899), rehearing overruled, 23 Ind. App. 604, 55 N.E. 880 (1900); Frame's Estate v. Frame, 48 Ind. App. 481, 96 N.E. 35 (1911); Jennings v. Hembree, 71 Ind. App. 370, 124 N.E. 876 (1919).

If a life tenant contracted with a person to cultivate a part of land for a portion of the crop, the former directing what parts of her land should be cultivated and the way in which it was to be done, and the life tenant died before the crop was harvested, the part of the crop that would go to the life tenant if alive belonged to her estate. Frame's Estate v. Frame, 48 Ind. App. 481, 96 N.E. 35 (1911).

Where a life tenant rented certain land to a tenant, the rent to have been paid by a fixed share of the crop raised, which was to have been gathered and delivered to the life tenant at harvest time, and the life tenant died before the crop was harvested, the life tenant's share went to the remainderman. Jennings v. Hembree, 71 Ind. App. 370, 124 N.E. 876 (1919).

**32-31-1-19. Rent paid as part of crop, rent in kind, or cash rent —
Recovery.** — (a) In a case where a tenant agrees under contract to pay as
rent:

(1) a part of the crop raised on the leased premises;

(2) rent in kind; or

(3) a cash rent;

the landlord may have a lien on the crop raised under the contract for
payment of the rent. If the tenant refuses or neglects to pay or deliver to the
landlord the rent when it is due, the landlord may enforce the lien by selling
the crop.

(b) A landlord who desires to acquire a lien on a crop raised under a
contract on leased premises must file a financing statement under IC
26-1-9.1-501 at least thirty (30) days before the crop matures and during the
year in which the crop is grown. The financing statement must:

(1) give notice of the landlord's intention to hold a lien upon the crop for
the amount of rent due;

(2) specifically set forth the amount claimed; and

(3) describe the lands on which the crop is being grown with sufficient
precision to identify the lands.

(c) A lien created under this section relates to the time of filing and has
priority over all liens created thereafter. However, a tenant may, after giving
written notice to the landlord or the landlord's agent, remove the tenant's
portion of the crop from the leased premises and dispose of the tenant's
portion of the crop when the rent is to be paid in part of the crop raised. If
the tenant does not give written notice to the landlord, the tenant may
remove not more than one-half (½) of the crop growing or matured.
[P.L.2-2002, § 16.]

NOTES TO DECISIONS

ANALYSIS

Conversion by landlord.
Custom of neighborhood.
Filing of notice.
—"Crops as rent" lease.
Mortgage by tenant to landlord.
Priority of lien.
Purchases from tenant.
Right to crops.
Tillage prevented.
When landlord's rights vest.

Conversion by Landlord.

Upon conversion of crops by landlord,
breach of covenants in lease could not be
pleaded in defense of action for value of crops.
Crowe v. Kell, 7 Ind. App. 683, 35 N.E. 186
(1893).

Conversion of crops by landlord gave rise to
liability to tenant or his assignee. Dale v.
Jones, 15 Ind. App. 420, 44 N.E. 316 (1896).

Custom of Neighborhood.

It might have been agreed that rent should

have been payable out of the crop according to
the custom of the neighborhood. Clem v. Martin, 34 Ind. 341 (1870).

Filing of Notice.

Since the amendment of this section in
1923, the landlord under an agricultural lease
could obtain a lien on the crops for cash rent
not then due by filing in the recorder's office
notice to that effect 30 days before the maturity of the crops. Simpson v. Jones, 85 Ind.
App. 35, 147 N.E. 922 (1925), rehearing denied, 85 Ind. App. 38, 152 N.E. 294 (1926).

—"Crops as Rent" Lease.

A lease of farmland which provides that a
tenant shall pay, as rent, a certain number of
bushels of grain per acre does not vest any
title to the crops in the landlord. A landlord
desiring to hold a lien on crops raised under a
"crops as rent" lease must file notice of his
intention to hold a lien. Montgomery County
Farm Bureau Coop. Ass'n v. Deseret Title
Holding Corp., 513 N.E.2d 193 (Ind. App.
1987).

Mortgage by Tenant to Landlord.

The execution by a tenant to the landlord of a mortgage on the crop did not abrogate a lien created by lease in favor of the landlord on such crop. Steele v. Moore, 54 Ind. 52 (1876).

Priority of Lien.

A landlord's lien will be prior to an unperfected security interest, even though the security interest was filed first, if the landlord at the time of filing the landlord's lien did not have actual notice of the earlier unperfected security interest. Franklin Bank & Trust Co. v. Mithoefer, 552 N.E.2d 39 (Ind. App. 1990), aff'd, 563 N.E.2d 551 (Ind. 1991).

Purchases from Tenant.

Purchasers of crops from a tenant were bound to take notice of the lien given the landlord by statute. Kennard v. Harvey, 80 Ind. 37 (1881); Shelby v. Moore, 22 Ind. App. 371, 53 N.E. 842 (1899); Campbell v. Bowen, 22 Ind. App. 562, 54 N.E. 409 (1899); Gifford v. Meyers, 27 Ind. App. 348, 61 N.E. 210 (1901).

Right to Crops.

If the term of the tenancy was uncertain, the tenant was entitled to crops that he planted, but if he knew when he planted that the tenancy would end before the crops would mature, the owner of the land was entitled to the crops. Rasor v. Qualls, 4 Blackf. 286, 30 Am. Dec. 658 (1837); Heavilon v. Farmers Bank, 81 Ind. 249 (1881); Dorsett v. Gray, 98 Ind. 273 (1884); Hall v. Durham, 117 Ind. 429, 20 N.E. 282 (1889); Shaffer v. Stevens, 143 Ind. 295, 42 N.E. 620 (1896).

Forfeiture of lease by violating conditions of leasing by tenant did not constitute forfeiture of tenant to gather or sell his share of the crops. Collier v. Cunningham, 2 Ind. App. 254, 28 N.E. 341 (1891).

If a landlord had a lien on a crop for rent, the tenant could not remove or sell the crop until the rent was paid, nor could he claim the crop as exempt from execution. Keim v. Myers, 44 Ind. App. 299, 89 N.E. 373 (1909).

Notice given by a tenant to his landlord of his intention to sell his part of the crops, as provided by this section, did not work a release of the landlord's lien on the crops for rent. Simpson v. Jones, 85 Ind. App. 35, 147 N.E. 922 (1925), rehearing denied, 85 Ind. App. 38, 152 N.E. 294 (1926).

Former IC 32-7-1-18 (repealed; see this section for similar provisions) did not require the landlord's lien to be limited to one-half the crop grown on the premises. Peoples State Bank v. Thompson, 462 N.E.2d 1068 (Ind. App. 1984).

Tillage Prevented.

Where rent was payable of percentage of crops raised and three dollars an acre for land untilled, and rains washed it out, tenant was not liable for tilled acreage, but was liable for three dollars per acre for land that was not attempted by the tenant to have been tilled. Monnett v. Potts, 10 Ind. App. 191, 37 N.E. 729 (1894).

Rent payable in crops, tillage of land prevented by excessive rains, liability of tenant for rent. Monnett v. Potts, 10 Ind. App. 191, 37 N.E. 729 (1894).

When Landlord's Rights Vest.

If the landlord was to receive his share of the crop in the field, title was vested in him when the crop matured, although undivided. Hart v. State ex rel. Baker, 29 Ind. 200 (1867).

When rent was payable in part of the crop in the field, the tenant had the right of possession of the whole until division was made. Cunningham v. Baker, 84 Ind. 597 (1882); Gordon v. Stockdale, 89 Ind. 240 (1883); Chicago & W.M. Ry. v. Linard, 94 Ind. 319, 48 Am. R. 155 (1884); Shaffer v. Stevens, 143 Ind. 295, 42 N.E. 620 (1896).

If the tenant was to deliver the share of the crop of the landlord to him, the title of the landlord in his share vested as soon as it was separated from that of the tenant. Scott v. Ramsey, 82 Ind. 330 (1882); Cunningham v. Baker, 84 Ind. 597 (1882); Chicago & W.M. Ry. v. Linard, 94 Ind. 319, 48 Am. R. 155 (1884).

32-31-1-20. Regulation of rent for private real property — Act of general assembly required — Exception for low or moderate income housing . — (a) This section does not apply to privately owned real property for which government funds or benefits have been allocated from the United States government, the state, or a political subdivision for the express purpose of providing reduced rents to low or moderate income tenants.

(b) Regulation of rental rates for privately owned real property must be authorized by an act of the general assembly. [P.L.2-2002, § 16.]

CHAPTER 2

RECORDING LEASES LONGER THAN THREE YEARS

32-31-2-1. Time for recording lease after execution. — Not more than forty-five (45) days after its execution, a lease of real estate for a period longer than three (3) years shall be recorded in the Miscellaneous Record in the recorder's office of the county in which the real estate is located. [P.L.2-2002, § 16.]

Effective Dates. P.L.2-2002, § 16. July 1. 2002.
Cross References. Recording letters of attorney, executory contracts for the sale or purchase of land, IC 32-21-3-4.

Collateral References. 66 Am. Jur. 2d Records and Recording Laws §§ 63, 64, 84.
51C C.J.S. Landlord and Tenant § 220.

32-31-2-2. Lease void for failure to record. — If a lease for a period longer than three (3) years is not recorded within forty-five (45) days after its execution, the lease is void against any subsequent purchaser, lessee, or mortgagee who acquires the real estate in good faith and for valuable consideration. [P.L.2-2002, § 16.]

CHAPTER 3

SECURITY DEPOSITS

32-31-3-1. Applicability. — (a) This chapter applies to rental agreements for dwelling units located in Indiana.

(b) This chapter does not apply to any of the following arrangements unless the arrangement was created to avoid application of this chapter:

(1) Residence at a rental unit owned or operated by an institution that is directly related to detention or the provision of medical, maternity home care, education, counseling, religious service, geriatric service, or a similar service.

(2) Occupancy under a contract of sale of a rental unit or the property of which the rental unit is a part if the occupant is the purchaser or a person who succeeds to the purchaser's interest.

(3) Occupancy by a member of a fraternal or social organization in the part of a structure operated for the benefit of the organization.

(4) Transient occupancy in a hotel, motel, or other lodging.

(5) Occupancy by an employee of a landlord whose right to occupancy is conditional upon employment in or about the premises.

(6) Occupancy by an owner of a condominium unit or a holder of a proprietary lease in a cooperative.

(7) Occupancy under a rental agreement covering property used by the occupant primarily for agricultural purposes. [P.L.2-2002, § 16.]

Compiler's Notes. Section 2 of P.L.277-1989, effective July 1, 1989, enacted prior to the recodification of this title by P.L.2-2002, provided: "Rental agreements entered into before July 1, 1989, remain valid and may be terminated, completed, consummated, or enforced as though this act had not been enacted." Section 1 of P.L.277-1989 addded a new chapter to former article IC 32-7, Landlord-Tenant Relations, IC 32-7-5, Security Deposits.

Effective Dates. P.L.2-2002, § 16. July 1. 2002.

Indiana Law Review. 1994 Developments in Property Law, 28 Ind. L. Rev. 1041 (1995).

NOTES TO DECISIONS

Construction.
Statute is in derogation of common law and must be strictly construed. Pinnacle Properties v. Saulka, 693 N.E.2d 101 (Ind. App. 1998).

32-31-3-2. "Cooperative housing association" defined. — As used in this chapter, "cooperative housing association" means a consumer cooperative that provides dwelling units to its members. [P.L.2-2002, § 16.]

32-31-3-3. "Landlord" defined. — As used in this chapter, "landlord" means:
(1) the owner, lessor, or sublessor of a rental unit or the property of which the unit is a part; or
(2) a person authorized to exercise any aspect of the management of the premises, including a person who directly or indirectly:
(A) acts as a rental agent; or
(B) receives rent or any part of the rent other than as a bona fide purchaser. [P.L.2-2002, § 16.]

32-31-3-4. "Owner" defined. — (a) As used in this chapter, "owner" means one (1) or more persons in whom is vested all or part of the legal title to property.
(b) The term includes a mortgagee or contract purchaser in possession. [P.L.2-2002, § 16.]

32-31-3-5. "Person" defined. — As used in this chapter, "person" means an individual, a corporation, an association, a partnership, a governmental entity, a trust, an estate, or any other legal or commercial entity. [P.L.2-2002, § 16.]

32-31-3-6. "Rent" defined. — As used in this chapter, "rent" includes all payments made to a landlord under a rental agreement except a security deposit, however denominated. [P.L.2-2002, § 16.]

32-31-3-7. "Rental agreement" defined. — As used in this chapter, "rental agreement" means an agreement together with any modifications, embodying the terms and conditions concerning the use and occupancy of a rental unit. [P.L.2-2002, § 16.]

32-31-3-8. "Rental unit" defined. — As used in this chapter, "rental unit" means:
>   (1) a structure, or the part of a structure, that is used as a home, residence, or sleeping unit by:
>>   (A) one (1) individual who maintains a household; or
>>   (B) two (2) or more individuals who maintain a common household; or
>   (2) any grounds, facilities, or area promised for the use of a residential tenant, including the following:
>>   (A) An apartment unit.
>>   (B) A boarding house.
>>   (C) A rooming house.
>>   (D) A mobile home space.
>>   (E) A single or two (2) family dwelling.

[P.L.2-2002, § 16.]

32-31-3-9. "Security deposit" defined. — (a) As used in this chapter, "security deposit" means a deposit paid by a tenant to the landlord or the landlord's agent to be held for all or a part of the term of the rental agreement to secure performance of any obligation of the tenant under the rental agreement.
>   (b) The term includes:
>>   (1) a required prepayment of rent other than the first full rental payment period of the lease agreement;
>>   (2) a sum required to be paid as rent in any rental period in excess of the average rent for the term; and
>>   (3) any other amount of money or property returnable to the tenant on condition of return of the rental unit by the tenant in a condition as required by the rental agreement.
>   (c) The term does not include the following:
>>   (1) An amount paid for an option to purchase under a lease with option to purchase, unless it is shown that the intent was to evade this chapter.
>>   (2) An amount paid as a subscription for or purchase of a membership in a cooperative housing association incorporated under Indiana law. [P.L.2-2002, § 16.]

32-31-3-10. "Tenant" defined. — As used in this chapter, "tenant" means an individual who occupies a rental unit:
>   (1) for residential purposes;

(2) with the landlord's consent; and

(3) for consideration that is agreed upon by both parties.
[P.L.2-2002, § 16.]

32-31-3-11. Jurisdiction. — (a) The following courts have original and concurrent jurisdiction in cases arising under this chapter:

(1) A circuit court.

(2) A superior court.

(3) A county court.

(4) A municipal court.

(5) A small claims court.

(b) A case arising under this chapter may be filed on the small claims docket of a court that has jurisdiction. [P.L.2-2002, § 16.]

32-31-3-12. Termination of rental agreement — Return of security deposit. — (a) Upon termination of a rental agreement, a landlord shall return to the tenant the security deposit minus any amount applied to:

(1) the payment of accrued rent;

(2) the amount of damages that the landlord has suffered or will reasonably suffer by reason of the tenant's noncompliance with law or the rental agreement; and

(3) unpaid utility or sewer charges that the tenant is obligated to pay under the rental agreement;

all as itemized by the landlord with the amount due in a written notice that is delivered to the tenant not more than forty-five (45) days after termination of the rental agreement and delivery of possession. The landlord is not liable under this chapter until the tenant supplies the landlord in writing with a mailing address to which to deliver the notice and amount prescribed by this subsection. Unless otherwise agreed, a tenant is not entitled to apply a security deposit to rent.

(b) If a landlord fails to comply with subsection (a), a tenant may recover all of the security deposit due the tenant and reasonable attorney's fees.

(c) This section does not preclude the landlord or tenant from recovering other damages to which either is entitled.

(d) The owner of the dwelling unit at the time of the termination of the rental agreement is bound by this section. [P.L.2-2002, § 16.]

Indiana Law Review. 1993 Developments in Indiana Property Law, 27 Ind. L. Rev. 1285 (1994).

1994 Developments in Property Law, 28 Ind. L. Rev. 1041 (1995).

NOTES TO DECISIONS

ANALYSIS

Failure to request relief.
Notice requirement.
—Erroneous assessment.
—Itemization.
—Satisfied.
Other damages.
—Attorney fees.

Tenant's mailing address.
Tenant's prior obligation.
Time of termination of lease agreement.

Failure to Request Relief.
    Evicted tenant who did not ask trial court for any relief from landlord's retention of her pre-paid rent or her security deposit was not denied relief for any improperly retained

Failure to Request Relief. (Cont'd)
funds by judgment granting landlord possession. Stout v. Kokomo Manor Apts., 677 N.E.2d 1060 (Ind. App. 1997).

Notice Requirement.

—Erroneous Assessment.
When a landlord erroneously calculates the tenant's damages, and the tenant was entitled to a return of all or part of his deposit, the landlord has not complied with the notice requirement of the statute, and the tenant is entitled to recover the security deposit due and reasonable attorney fees. Rueth v. Quinn, 659 N.E.2d 684 (Ind. App. 1995).

—Itemization.
Where landlord made a claim for damages when he filed his small claims action, but never itemized the damages he had or would reasonably suffer by reason of his tenant's noncompliance or estimate the amounts attributable for each item of damage, he did not substantially comply with the notice requirement imposed by former IC 32-7-5-12 (now see this section for similar provisions) and former IC 32-7-5-14. Chasteen v. Smith, 625 N.E.2d 501 (Ind. App. 1993).

—Satisfied.
Letter that informed tenant that landlord was keeping tenant's security deposit and applying it to unpaid rent was sufficient information to provide tenant with the opportunity to challenge the costs for which the deposit was being used. Figg v. Bryan Rental Inc., 646 N.E.2d 69 (Ind. App. 1995).

Other Damages.
While this section (formerly IC 32-7-5-12; now see this section for similar provisions) does not prevent landlords from pursuing their claims for "other damages," which could include claims for amounts in excess of the security deposit or other types of damages not specified in this section, the clear intent of IC 32-7-5-15 is that if a landlord fails to provide the requisite notice within the 45-day period for compliance with notice requirements there are no "other damages" to collect. Duchon v. Ross, 599 N.E.2d 621 (Ind. App. 1992).

Amount due mortgage company for the late closing of sale of house was damages that landlord reasonably suffered because of the tenants' noncompliance with their agreement to vacate the premises by a specified date, which the landlord is permitted to apply against the security deposit. Rueth v. Quinn, 659 N.E.2d 684 (Ind. App. 1995).

Landlord properly deducted cleaning and painting charges from tenant's security deposit as damages resulting from tenant's non-compliance with rental agreement where tenant failed to steam clean the carpet upon vacating and left marks on the walls of the apartment. Castillo-Cullather v. Pollack, 685 N.E.2d 478 (Ind. App. 1997), transfer denied, 698 N.E.2d 1187 (Ind. 1998).

—Attorney Fees.
Attorney fees were properly awarded to landlord who complied with the statutory notice requirement, where the fees were authorized under the terms of the lease agreement. Greasel v. Troy, 690 N.E.2d 298 (Ind. App. 1997).

Tenant's Mailing Address.
In order to establish a landlord's liability under this section (formerly IC 32-7-5-12; now see this section for similar provisions), a tenant must show that he provided the landlord with a written record of an address, which was intended to be his forwarding address. Deckard Realty & Dev. v. Lykins, 688 N.E.2d 1319 (Ind. App. 1997).

Three of four tenants failed to provide landlord with a written record of their forwarding address; therefore, the trial court erred in granting summary judgment in their favor in suit for return of their security deposit. Deckard Realty & Dev. v. Lykins, 688 N.E.2d 1319 (Ind. App. 1997).

Where one tenant left an address which was on file on a post it note taken down four months before commencement of lease, the note also indicated it was the tenant's father's address, and tenant was successfully served at the address, a trier of fact could reasonably conclude this was the tenant's forwarding address. Deckard Realty & Dev. v. Lykins, 688 N.E.2d 1319 (Ind. App. 1997).

Tenant's Prior Obligation.
Tenant's obligation under this section (formerly IC 32-7-5-12; now see this section for similar provisions) to provide the landlord with a mailing address prior to the running of the 45-day notice period against the landlord, applies to all provisions of the Security Deposits statutes containing this 45-day notice requirement, including former IC 32-7-5-14. In this context, "supply" means to provide or deliver the mailing address to the landlord, and where undisputed evidence established that tenants did not supply landlord with their mailing address, the 45-day notice period never commenced running, permitting landlord to properly deduct damages from the tenant's security deposit. Raider v. Pea, 613 N.E.2d 870 (Ind. App. 1993).

Time of Termination of Lease Agreement.
Where plaintiff surrendered the premises when he tore up the lease and defendant

Time of Termination of Lease Agreement. (Cont'd)
accepted this surrender when it relet the premises, the lease agreement terminated on the day defendant relet the premises. Mileusnich v. Novogroder Co., 643 N.E.2d 937 (Ind. App. 1994).

32-31-3-13. Security deposit — Uses. — A security deposit may be used only for the following purposes:

(1) To reimburse the landlord for actual damages to the rental unit or any ancillary facility that are not the result of ordinary wear and tear.

(2) To pay the landlord for:

(A) all rent in arrearage under the rental agreement; and

(B) rent due for premature termination of the rental agreement by the tenant.

(3) To pay for the last payment period of a residential rental agreement if a written agreement between the landlord and the tenant stipulates that the security deposit will serve as the last payment of rent due.

(4) To reimburse the landlord for utility or sewer charges paid by the landlord that are:

(A) the obligation of the tenant under the rental agreement; and

(B) unpaid by the tenant.

[P.L.2-2002, § 16.]

NOTES TO DECISIONS

ANALYSIS

Actual damages.
Itemized list of damages.
Proof required.

Actual Damages.

The liquidated damages due to purchasers of house from landlord because the house was not available for their possession due to tenants' failure to surrender possession was damages which landlord reasonably suffered because of the tenants' noncompliance with their agreement to vacate the premises by a specified date, which landlord was permitted to apply against the security deposit; but the landlord could not arbitrarily pay the purchasers more than required by contract and apply the payment to the tenant's security deposit. Rueth v. Quinn, 659 N.E.2d 684 (Ind. App. 1995).

Itemized List of Damages.

Since the landlord kept the security deposit for accrued rent due to the tenant's premature termination of the rental agreement, but failed to send the tenant a letter itemizing the accrued rent due to his premature termination of the rental agreement, the landlord was prevented from collecting this amount and had to return the tenant's security deposit in full. Skiver v. Brighton Meadows, 585 N.E.2d 1345 (Ind. App. 1992).

Proof Required.

Former IC 32-7-5-13 (repealed; see this section for similar provisions) did not prohibit a landlord from using a security deposit to enforce cleaning and painting provisions of a rental agreement and did not require landlord to prove that any damage to carpets and walls exceeded the ordinary wear and tear expected as a result of normal use. Castillo-Cullather v. Pollack, 685 N.E.2d 478 (Ind. App. 1997), transfer denied, 698 N.E.2d 1187 (Ind. 1998).

32-31-3-14. Time for return of security deposit and itemized list of damages. — Not more than forty-five (45) days after the termination of occupancy, a landlord shall mail to a tenant an itemized list of damages claimed for which the security deposit may be used under section 13 [IC 32-31-3-13] of this chapter. The list must set forth:

(1) the estimated cost of repair for each damaged item; and

(2) the amounts and lease on which the landlord intends to assess the tenant.

The landlord shall include with the list a check or money order for the difference between the damages claimed and the amount of the security deposit held by the landlord. [P.L.2-2002, § 16.]

Indiana Law Review. 1992 Developments in Indiana Property Law, 26 Ind. L. Rev. 1113 (1993).

1994 Developments in Property Law, 28 Ind. L. Rev. 1041 (1995).

NOTES TO DECISIONS

ANALYSIS

Estimated costs of repair.
Attorney fees.
Failure to send list.
Itemization.
Notice.
—Commencement of time period.
—Sufficient.
Tenant's prior obligation.
Termination of lease.

Estimated Costs of Repair.

Direction of former IC 32-7-5-14 (repealed; see this section for similar provisions) was explicit and mandatory. It said the landlord "shall" mail an itemized list of damages "including" the estimated costs of repair and the list "must" be accompanied by payment for the excess deposit (if any). Landlord's letter was plainly inadequate under the statute since the letter provided that costs for repairs had not been determined. Duchon v. Ross, 599 N.E.2d 621 (Ind. App. 1992).

Attorney Fees.

Attorney fees were properly awarded to landlord who complied with the statutory notice requirement, where the fees were authorized under the terms of the lease agreement. Greasel v. Troy, 690 N.E.2d 298 (Ind. App. 1997).

Failure to Send List.

Since the landlord kept the security deposit for accrued rent due to the tenant's premature termination of the rental agreement, but failed to send the tenant a letter itemizing the accrued rent due to his premature termination of the rental agreement, the landlord was prevented from collecting this amount and had to return the tenant's security deposit in full. Skiver v. Brighton Meadows, 585 N.E.2d 1345 (Ind. App. 1992).

Itemization.

Where landlord made a claim for damages when he filed his small claims action, but never itemized the damages he had or would reasonably suffer by reason of his tenant's noncompliance or estimate the amounts attributable for each item of damage, he did not substantially comply with the notice requirement imposed by former IC 32-7-5-12 and former IC 32-7-5-14 (now see this section for similar provisions). Chasteen v. Smith, 625 N.E.2d 501 (Ind. App. 1993).

Letter sent by landlord to tenant which itemized as damages material for two doors, material to fix the bathroom, material for a "kit" room, labor costs, and court costs, and set forth specific dollar amounts attributable to each, and further provided that landlord was claiming $600 for two months accrued rent, accomplished the purpose of the notice provision to inform the tenant that the landlord was keeping the security deposit and for what reason. Meyers v. Langley, 638 N.E.2d 875 (Ind. App. 1994).

Strict reading of code does not allow for substantial or partial compliance by landlord with itemization of damages notice requirement. Pinnacle Properties v. Saulka, 693 N.E.2d 101 (Ind. App. 1998).

Notice.

—Commencement of Time Period.

Where a tenant vacates the premises and the lease agreement terminates at a later date, the period within which the landlord must provide notice of damages does not commence until the date that the lease terminates. Figg v. Bryan Rental Inc., 646 N.E.2d 69 (Ind. App. 1995).

—Sufficient.

Letter that informed tenant that landlord was keeping tenant's security deposit and applying it to unpaid rent was sufficient information to provide tenant with the opportunity to challenge the costs for which the deposit was being used. Figg v. Bryan Rental Inc., 646 N.E.2d 69 (Ind. App. 1995).

Former IC 32-7-5-14 (repealed; see this section for similar provisions) was satisfied where landlord sent notice to tenant indicating that she was being charged for cleaning her apartment and informed her of the amount of the deduction from her security

Notice. (Cont'd)

—Sufficient. (Cont'd)
deposit. Castillo-Cullather v. Pollack, 685 N.E.2d 478 (Ind. App. 1997), transfer denied, 698 N.E.2d 1187 (Ind. 1998).

Where landlord listed items in her statement of damages but assigned no estimated costs to them, indicating her intent to assess only carpet damage costs against tenant, and retain the entire amount of the security deposit, landlord's failure to assign cost estimates to the other items did not render the statement insufficient. Greasel v. Troy, 690 N.E.2d 298 (Ind. App. 1997).

Landlord complied with the statutory requirement where the itemized list of damages contained in the letter to the tenant contained the itemized costs of repairing the damaged items, because the landlord was not required to substantiate the alleged damages in order to comply with the notice provisions of the statute. Schoknecht v. Hasemeier, 735 N.E.2d 299 (Ind. App. 2000).

Tenant's Prior Obligation.
Tenant's obligation under former IC 32-7-5-12 to provide the landlord with a mailing address prior to the running of the limitations period is also applicable to this section (formerly IC 32-7-5-14; now see this section for similar provisions). Raider v. Pea, 613 N.E.2d 870 (Ind. App. 1993).

Termination of Lease.
Lease agreement terminated on the day that landlord responded to tenant's demand letter by sending him an accounting of his security agreement. Figg v. Bryan Rental Inc., 646 N.E.2d 69 (Ind. App. 1995).

Date tenants surrendered premises, and landlord accepted their surrender, was when the lease agreement terminated for the purpose of determining whether letter regarding deposit was timely, where there had been an oral agreement to extend the lease, and tenants held over. Rueth v. Quinn, 659 N.E.2d 684 (Ind. App. 1995).

32-31-3-15. Failure of landlord to provide notice of damages. —
Failure by a landlord to provide notice of damages under section 14 [IC 32-31-3-14] of this chapter constitutes agreement by the landlord that no damages are due, and the landlord must remit to the tenant immediately the full security deposit. [P.L.2-2002, § 16.]

Indiana Law Review. 1992 Developments in Indiana Property Law, 26 Ind. L. Rev. 1113 (1993).

1993 Developments in Indiana Property Law, 27 Ind. L. Rev. 1285 (1994).

NOTES TO DECISIONS

ANALYSIS

Effect of noncompliance.
Failure to send list.
Other damages.

Effect of Noncompliance.
While former IC 32-7-5-12 does not prevent landlords from pursuing their claims for "other damages," which could include claims for amounts in excess of the security deposit or other types of damages not specified in that section, the clear intent of this section (formerly IC 32-7-5-15; now see this section for similar provisions) is that if a landlord fails to provide the requisite notice within the 45-day period for compliance with notice requirements there are no "other damages" to collect. Duchon v. Ross, 599 N.E.2d 621 (Ind. App. 1992).

Where tenants relinquished possession and the statutory period passed, the landlord effectively agreed with the tenants that no damages were due, and the agreement was binding upon him even though his lawsuit to

obtain possession and damages was still pending. Chasteen v. Smith, 625 N.E.2d 501 (Ind. App. 1993).

Where defendant did not provide plaintiff with an itemized list of damages as required by the statute or any other explanation for failure to return plaintiff's deposit, and the failure to comply with the notice of damages requirement constituted an agreement by the landlord that no damages were due, defendant was required to remit plaintiff his full security deposit plus any attorney fees incurred. Mileusnich v. Novogroder Co., 643 N.E.2d 937 (Ind. App. 1994).

Failure to comply totally with notice provision constitutes agreement that no damages are due. Pinnacle Properties v. Saulka, 693 N.E.2d 101 (Ind. App. 1998).

Failure to Send List.
Since the landlord kept the security deposit for accrued rent due to the tenant's premature termination of the rental agreement but failed to send the tenant a letter itemizing the accrued rent due to his premature termina-

Failure to Send List. (Cont'd)
tion of the rental agreement, the landlord was prevented from collecting this amount and had to return the tenant's security deposit in full. Skiver v. Brighton Meadows, 585 N.E.2d 1345 (Ind. App. 1992).

Other Damages.
Where the landlord provides the notice re-quired in order to apply the security deposit to damages expressly allowed by the statute, the landlord may also seek to recover any "other damages" to which he is entitled under the lease agreement. Otherwise, if the required notice is not given, the landlord has implicitly agreed that there are no "other damages" to collect. Miller v. Geels, 643 N.E.2d 922 (Ind. App. 1994).

32-31-3-16. Liability of landlord for failure to comply. — A landlord who fails to comply with sections 14 and 15 [IC 32-31-3-14 and IC 32-31-3-15] of this chapter is liable to the tenant in an amount equal to the part of the deposit withheld by the landlord plus reasonable attorney's fees and court costs. [P.L.2-2002, § 16.]

Indiana Law Review. 1992 Developments in Indiana Property Law, 26 Ind. L. Rev. 1113 (1993).

NOTES TO DECISIONS

Attorney Fees.
Statutes serve public policy of insuring equal access to courts despite relative financial conditions of parties, and fact that party awarded attorney fees is represented by non-profit legal organization is of no moment, although award of fees in such a case should be made to organization so as not to provide windfall to client. Pinnacle Properties v. Saulka, 693 N.E.2d 101 (Ind. App. 1998).

Collateral References. Landlord's liability to third party for repairs authorized by tenant. 46 A.L.R.5th 1.

32-31-3-17. Waiver of chapter void. — A waiver of this chapter by a landlord or tenant is void. [P.L.2-2002, § 16.]

32-31-3-18. Landlord to provide tenant names and addresses — Manager of dwelling unit — Agent for service of process, notice and demands. — (a) A landlord or a person authorized to enter into a rental agreement on behalf of the landlord shall disclose and furnish to the tenant in writing at or before the commencement of the rental agreement the names and addresses of the following:

(1) A person residing in Indiana who is authorized to manage the dwelling unit.

(2) A person residing in Indiana who is reasonably accessible to the tenant and who is authorized to act as agent for the owner for purposes of:

(A) service of process; and

(B) receiving and receipting for notices and demands.

A person who is identified as being authorized to manage under subdivision (1) may also be identified as the person authorized to act as agent under subdivision (2).

(b) This section is enforceable against any successor landlord, owner, or manager.

(c) A person who fails to comply with subsection (a) becomes an agent of each person who is a landlord for purposes of:

(1) service of process and receiving and receipting for notices and demands; and

(2) performing the obligations of the landlord under law or the rental agreement.

(d) If the information required by subsection (a) is not disclosed at the beginning of the rental agreement, the tenant shall be allowed any expenses reasonably incurred to discover the names and addresses required to be furnished. [P.L.2-2002, § 16.]

32-31-3-19. Liability of landlord after giving notice of conveyance. — (a) Unless otherwise agreed, if a landlord conveys, in a good faith sale to a bona fide purchaser, property that includes a dwelling unit subject to a rental agreement, the landlord is relieved of liability under law or the rental agreement as to events occurring after written notice to the tenant of the conveyance. However, for one (1) year after giving notice of the conveyance, the landlord remains liable to the tenant for the security deposit to which the tenant is entitled under section 14 [IC 32-31-3-14] of this chapter unless:

(1) the purchaser acknowledges that the purchaser has assumed the liability of the seller by giving notice to the tenant; and

(2) upon conveyance the seller transfers the security deposit to the purchaser.

(b) Unless otherwise agreed, a manager of a dwelling unit is relieved of any liability the manager might have under law or the rental agreement as to events occurring after written notice to the tenant of the termination of the manager's management. [P.L.2-2002, § 16.]

CHAPTER 4

MOVING AND STORAGE OF TENANT'S PROPERTY

32-31-4-1. "Exempt property" defined. — As used in this chapter, "exempt property" means personal property that is any of the following:

(1) Medically necessary for an individual.

(2) Used by a tenant for the tenant's trade or business.

(3) Any of the following, as necessary for the tenant or a member of the tenant's household:

(A) A week's supply of seasonably necessary clothing.

(B) Blankets.

(C) Items necessary for the care and schooling of a minor child. [P.L.2-2002, § 16.]

Effective Dates. P.L.2-2002, § 16. July 1.
2002.

32-31-4-2. Removal of tenant's personal property — Court order.
— (a) If a landlord is awarded possession of a dwelling unit by a court under
IC 32-30-2, the landlord may seek an order from the court allowing removal
of a tenant's personal property.

(b) If the tenant fails to remove the tenant's personal property before the
date specified in the court's order issued under subsection (a), the landlord
may remove the tenant's personal property in accordance with the order and
deliver the personal property to a warehouseman under section 3 [IC
32-31-4-3] of this chapter. [P.L.2-2002, § 16.]

32-31-4-3. Delivery of tenant's personal property to warehouseman — Notice to tenant — Release of exempt property.
— (a) If a
tenant has failed to remove the tenant's personal property under section 2
[IC 32-31-4-2] oof this chapter, a landlord may deliver the personal property
to a warehouseman if notice of both of the following has been personally
served on the tenant at the last known address of the tenant:

(1) An order for removal of personal property issued under section 2 [IC
32-31-4-2] of this chapter.

(2) The identity and location of the warehouseman.

(b) At the demand of the owner of the exempt property, the warehouseman shall release the exempt property to the owner without requiring
payment from the owner at the time of delivery.

(c) A waiver of the provisions of section 1 [IC 32-31-4-1] of this chapter or
subsection (b) by contract or otherwise is void. [P.L.2-2002, § 16.]

32-31-4-4. Warehouseman's lien — Tenant's right to claim property.
— (a) A warehouseman that receives property under this chapter
holds a lien on all of that property that is not exempt property to the extent
of the expenses for any of the following incurred by the warehouseman with
respect to all of the property, whether exempt or not exempt:

(1) Storage.

(2) Transportation.

(3) Insurance.

(4) Labor.

(5) Present or future charges related to the property.

(6) Expenses necessary for preservation of the property.

(7) Expenses reasonably incurred in the lawful sale of the property.

(b) A tenant may claim the tenant's property at any time until the sale of
the property under section 5 [IC 32-31-4-5] of this chapter by paying the
warehouseman the expenses described in this section. [P.L.2-2002, § 16.]

32-31-4-5. Tenant's failure to claim property — Sale of property by warehouseman.
— If a tenant does not claim the tenant's property within
ninety (90) days after receiving notice under section 3 [IC 32-31-4-3] of this
chapter, a warehouseman may sell the property received under this chapter
under IC 26-1-7-210(2). [P.L.2-2002, § 16.]

CHAPTER 5

RENTAL AGREEMENTS; RIGHT OF ACCESS

32-31-5-1. Applicability — Waiver void. — (a) This chapter applies only to a rental agreement entered into or renewed after June 30, 1999.

(b) This chapter applies to a landlord or tenant only if the rental agreement was entered into or renewed after June 30, 1999.

(c) A waiver of this chapter by a landlord or tenant, including a former tenant, by contract or otherwise, is void. [P.L.2-2002, § 16.]

Effective Dates. P.L.2-2002, § 16. July 1. 2002.

NOTES TO DECISIONS

Prospective Application.

The lockout statute was inapplicable to the lease agreement between the parties, because their agreement was executed before June 30, 1999, and the legislature did not intend for the statute to be applied retroactively. Robinson v. Valladares, 738 N.E.2d 278 (Ind. App. 2000).

32-31-5-2. Applicability of definitions. — Except as otherwise provided in this chapter, the definitions in IC 32-31-3 apply throughout this chapter. [P.L.2-2002, § 16.]

32-31-5-3. "Dwelling unit" defined. — (a) As used in this chapter, "dwelling unit" means a structure or part of a structure that is used as a home, residence, or sleeping unit.

(b) The term includes the following:

(1) An apartment unit.

(2) A boarding house unit.

(3) A rooming house unit.

(4) A manufactured home (as defined in IC 22-12-1-16) or mobile structure (as defined in IC 22-12-1-17) and the space occupied by the manufactured home or mobile structure.

(5) A single or two (2) family dwelling.

[P.L.2-2002, § 16.]

32-31-5-4. Thirty days written notice before modification of rental agreement. — Unless otherwise provided by a written rental agreement between a landlord and tenant, a landlord shall give the tenant at least thirty (30) days written notice before modifying the rental agreement. [P.L.2-2002, § 16.]

32-31-5-5. Tenant's personal property — Protections. — (a) Except as provided in IC 16-41-27-29, IC 32-31-3, or IC 32-31-4, a landlord may not:
   (1) take possession of;
   (2) remove from a tenant's dwelling unit;
   (3) deny a tenant access to; or
   (4) dispose of;
a tenant's personal property in order to enforce an obligation of the tenant to the landlord under a rental agreement.
   (b) The landlord and tenant may agree in a writing separate from the rental agreement that the landlord may hold property voluntarily tendered by the tenant as security in exchange for forbearance from an action to evict. [P.L.2-2002, § 16.]

32-31-5-6. Abandonment — Interference with tenant's access to or possession of dwelling unit — Tenant's termination of essential services. — (a) This section does not apply if the dwelling unit has been abandoned.
   (b) For purposes of this section, a dwelling unit is considered abandoned if:
   (1) the tenants have failed to:
      (A) pay; or
      (B) offer to pay;
   rent due under the rental agreement; and
   (2) the circumstances are such that a reasonable person would conclude that the tenants have surrendered possession of the dwelling unit.
An oral or written rental agreement may not define abandonment differently than is provided by this subsection.
   (c) Except as authorized by judicial order, a landlord may not deny or interfere with a tenant's access to or possession of the tenant's dwelling unit by commission of any act, including the following:
   (1) Changing the locks or adding a device to exclude the tenant from the dwelling unit.
   (2) Removing the doors, windows, fixtures, or appliances from the dwelling unit.
   (3) Interrupting, reducing, shutting off, or causing termination of any of the following to a tenant:
      (A) Electricity.
      (B) Gas.
      (C) Water.
      (D) Other essential services.
   However, the landlord may interrupt, shut off, or terminate service as the result of an emergency, good faith repairs, or necessary construction. This subdivision does not require a landlord to pay for services described in this subdivision if the landlord has not agreed, by an oral or written rental agreement, to do so.
   (d) A tenant may not interrupt, reduce, shut off, or cause termination of:
   (1) electricity;

(2) gas;

(3) water; or

(4) other essential services;

to the dwelling unit if the interruption, reduction, shutting off, or termination of the service will result in serious damage to the rental unit. [P.L.2-2002, § 16.]

Cross References. Emergency possessory orders, IC 32-31-6.

NOTES TO DECISIONS

Applicability.
The lockout statute was inapplicable to the lease agreement between the parties, because their agreement was executed before June 30, 1999, and the legislature did not intend for the statute to be applied retroactively. Robinson v. Valladares, 738 N.E.2d 278 (Ind. App. 2000).

CHAPTER 6

EMERGENCY POSSESSORY ORDERS

32-31-6-1. Applicability of definitions. — The definitions in IC 32-31-3 and IC 32-31-5 apply throughout this chapter. [P.L.2-2002, § 16.]

Effective Dates. P.L.2-2002, § 16. July 1. 2002.

32-31-6-2. Jurisdiction of small claims docket to grant emergency possessory order. — The small claims docket of a court has jurisdiction to grant an emergency possessory order under this chapter. [P.L.2-2002, § 16.]

32-31-6-3. Right to file a petition for an emergency possessory order. — The following may file a petition for an emergency possessory order under this chapter:

(1) A tenant, if the landlord has violated IC 32-31-5-6.

(2) A landlord, if the tenant has committed or threatens to commit waste to the rental unit. [P.L.2-2002, § 16.]

32-31-6-4. Petition for order — Requirements. — A petition for an order under this chapter must:

(1) include an allegation specifying:

(A) the violation, act, or omission caused or threatened by a landlord or tenant; and

(B) The nature of the specific immediate and serious:
    (i) injury;
    (ii) loss; or
    (iii) damage;
that the landlord or tenant has suffered or will suffer if the violation, act, or omission is not enjoined; and
    (2) be sworn to by the petitioner.
[P.L.2-2002, § 16.]

Cross References. Denial or interference of landlord by court order with tenant's right to access or possession; termination of essential services by tenant, IC 32-31-5-6.

32-31-6-5. Court review of petition — Scheduling of emergency hearing.

— If a tenant or a landlord petitions the court to issue an order under this chapter, the court shall immediately do the following:
    (1) Review the petition.
    (2) Schedule an emergency hearing for not later than three (3) business days after the petition is filed. [P.L.2-2002, § 16.]

32-31-6-6. Emergency hearing — Remedies.

— (a) At the emergency hearing, if the court finds:
    (1) probable cause to believe that the landlord has violated or threatened to violate IC 32-31-5-6; and
    (2) that the tenant will suffer immediate and serious injury, loss, or damage;
the court shall issue an emergency order under subsection (b).
  (b) If the court makes a finding under subsection (a), the court shall order the landlord to do either or both of the following:
    (1) Return possession of the dwelling unit to the tenant if the tenant has been deprived of possession of the dwelling unit.
    (2) Refrain from violating IC 32-31-5-6.
  (c) The court may make other orders that the court considers just under the circumstances, including setting a subsequent hearing at the request of a party to adjudicate related claims between the parties. [P.L.2-2002, § 16.]

32-31-6-7. Waste — Court findings — Remedies.

— (a) As used in this section, "waste" does not include failure to pay rent.
  (b) At the emergency hearing, if the court finds:
    (1) probable cause to believe that the tenant has committed or threatens to commit waste to the rental unit; and
    (2) that the landlord has suffered or will suffer immediate and serious:
      (A) injury;
      (B) loss; or
      (C) damage;
the court shall issue an order under subsection (c).
  (c) If the court makes a finding under subsection (b), the court shall order the tenant to do either or both of the following:
    (1) Return possession of the dwelling unit to the landlord.
    (2) Refrain from committing waste to the dwelling unit.

(d) The court may make other orders that the court considers just under the circumstances, including setting a subsequent hearing at the request of a party to adjudicate related claims between the parties. [P.L.2-2002, § 16.]

Cross References. Termination of essential services by tenant, IC 32-31-5-6.

32-31-6-8. Summons — Continuance of emergency hearing. — (a) If a petition is filed under this chapter, the clerk shall issue to the respondent a summons to appear at a hearing. The summons must:

(1) give notice of the date, time, and place of the hearing; and

(2) inform the respondent that the respondent must appear before the court to answer the petition.

(b) The clerk shall serve the respondent with the summons to appear in accordance with Rule 4.1 of the Rules of Trial Procedure.

(c) The court shall not grant a continuance of the emergency hearing except upon clear and convincing evidence that manifest injustice would result if a continuance were not granted. [P.L.2-2002, § 16.]

32-31-6-9. Subsequent hearing — Scope of remedies. — If the court sets a subsequent hearing under section 6(c) or 7(d) [IC 32-31-6-6(c) or IC 32-31-6-7(d)] of this chapter, the court may do the following at the subsequent hearing:

(1) Determine damages.

(2) Order return of a tenant's withheld property.

(3) Make other orders the court considers just under the circumstances. [P.L.2-2002, § 16.]

32-31-6-10. Subsequent claims between parties. — The adjudication of an emergency possessory claim under section 6(b) or 7(c) [IC 32-31-6(b) or IC 32-31-6-7(c)] of this chapter does not bar a subsequent claim a party may have against the other party arising out of the landlord and tenant relationship unless that claim has been adjudicated under section 9 [IC 32-31-6-9] of this chapter. [P.L.2-2002, § 16.]

CHAPTER 7

TENANT OBLIGATIONS

32-31-7-1. Applicability. — (a) Except as provided in subsection (b), this chapter applies only to dwelling units that are let for rent after June 30, 2002.

(b) This chapter does not apply to dwelling units that are let for rent with an option to purchase. [P.L.92-2002, § 1.]

Effective Dates. P.L.92-2002, § 1. July 1, 2002.

32-31-7-2. Applicability of definitions. — The definitions in IC 32-31-3 apply throughout this chapter. [P.L.92-2002, § 1.]

32-31-7-3. "Rental premises" defined. — As used in this chapter, "rental premises" includes all of the following:
(1) A tenant's rental unit.
(2) The structure in which the tenant's rental unit is a part. [P.L.92-2002, § 1.]

32-31-7-4. Waiver void. — A waiver of the application of this chapter by a landlord or tenant, by contract or otherwise, is void. [P.L.92-2002, § 1.]

32-31-7-5. Maintenance and use of property. — A tenant shall do the following:
(1) Comply with all obligations imposed primarily on a tenant by applicable provisions of health and housing codes.
(2) Keep the areas of the rental premises occupied or used by the tenant reasonably clean.
(3) Use the following in a reasonable manner:
    (A) Electrical systems.
    (B) Plumbing.
    (C) Sanitary systems.
    (D) Heating, ventilating, and air conditioning systems.
    (E) Elevators, if provided.
    (F) Facilities and appliances of the rental premises.
(4) Refrain from defacing, damaging, destroying, impairing, or removing any part of the rental premises.
(5) Comply with all reasonable rules and regulations in existence at the time a rental agreement is entered into. A tenant shall also comply with amended rules and regulations as provided in the rental agreement.
This section may not be construed to limit a landlord's obligations under this chapter or IC 32-31-8. [P.L.92-2002, § 1.]

32-31-7-6. Delivery of property to landlord. — At the termination of a tenant's occupancy, the tenant shall deliver the rental premises to the landlord in a clean and proper condition, excepting ordinary wear and tear expected in the normal course of habitation of a dwelling unit. [P.L.92-2002, § 1.]

32-31-7-7. Actions by landlord. — (a) A landlord may bring an action in a court with jurisdiction to enforce an obligation of a tenant under this chapter.
(b) Except as provided in subsection (c), a landlord may not bring an action under this chapter unless the following conditions are met:
(1) The landlord gives the tenant notice of the tenant's noncompliance with a provision of this chapter.

(2) The tenant has been given a reasonable amount of time to remedy the noncompliance.

(c) If the noncompliance has caused physical damage that the landlord has repaired, the landlord shall give notice specifying the repairs that the landlord has made and documenting the landlord's cost to remedy the condition described in the notice.

(d) A landlord is not required to comply with the notice requirements of this section to bring an action under subsection (a) if the tenant's occupancy of the rental premises has terminated.

(e) This section may not be construed to limit a landlord's or tenant's rights under IC 32-31-3, IC 32-31-5, or IC 32-31-6.

(f) If the landlord is the prevailing party in an action under this section, the landlord may obtain any of the following, if appropriate under the circumstances:

(1) Recovery of the following:

(A) Actual damages.

(B) Attorney's fees and court costs.

(2) Injunctive relief.

(3) Any other remedy appropriate under the circumstances.
[P.L.92-2002, § 1.]

CHAPTER 8

LANDLORD OBLIGATIONS UNDER A RENTAL AGREEMENT

32-31-8-1. Applicability. — (a) Except as provided in subsection (b), this chapter applies only to dwelling units that are let for rent after June 30, 2002.

(b) This chapter does not apply to dwelling units that are let for rent with an option to purchase. [P.L.92-2002, § 2.]

Effective Dates. P.L.92-2002, § 2. July 1, 2002.

32-31-8-2. Applicability of definitions. — The definitions in IC 32-31-3 apply throughout this chapter.
[P.L.92-2002, § 2.]

32-31-8-3. "Rental premises" defined. — As used in this chapter, "rental premises" includes all of the following:

(1) A tenant's rental unit.

(2) The structure in which the tenant's rental unit is a part.
[P.L.92-2002, § 2.]

32-31-8-4. Waivers void. — A waiver of the application of this chapter by a landlord or tenant, by contract or otherwise, is void. [P.L.92-2002, § 2.]

32-31-8-5. Maintenance of property. — A landlord shall do the following:

(1) Deliver the rental premises to a tenant in compliance with the rental agreement, and in a safe, clean, and habitable condition.

(2) Comply with all health and housing codes applicable to the rental premises.

(3) Make all reasonable efforts to keep common areas of a rental premises in a clean and proper condition.

(4) Provide and maintain the following items in a rental premises in good and safe working condition, if provided on the premises at the time the rental agreement is entered into:

(A) Electrical systems.

(B) Plumbing systems sufficient to accommodate a reasonable supply of hot and cold running water at all times.

(C) Sanitary systems.

(D) Heating, ventilating, and air conditioning systems. A heating system must be sufficient to adequately supply heat at all times.

(E) Elevators, if provided.

(F) Appliances supplied as an inducement to the rental agreement. [P.L.92-2002, § 2.]

32-31-8-6. Actions by tenants — Relief. — (a) A tenant may bring an action in a court with jurisdiction to enforce an obligation of a landlord under this chapter.

(b) A tenant may not bring an action under this chapter unless the following conditions are met:

(1) The tenant gives the landlord notice of the landlord's noncompliance with a provision of this chapter.

(2) The landlord has been given a reasonable amount of time to make repairs or provide a remedy of the condition described in the tenant's notice. The tenant may not prevent the landlord from having access to the rental premises to make repairs or provide a remedy to the condition described in the tenant's notice.

(3) The landlord fails or refuses to repair or remedy the condition described in the tenant's notice.

(c) This section may not be construed to limit a tenant's rights under IC 32-31-3, IC 32-31-5, or IC 32-31-6.

(d) If the tenant is the prevailing party in an action under this section, the tenant may obtain any of the following, if appropriate under the circumstances:

(1) Recovery of the following:

(A) Actual damages and consequential damages.

(B) Attorney's fees and court costs.

(2) Injunctive relief.

(3) Any other remedy appropriate under the circumstances.

(e) A landlord's liability for damages under subsection (d) begins when:

(1) the landlord has notice or actual knowledge of noncompliance; and

(2) the landlord has:

(A) refused to remedy the noncompliance; or

(B) failed to remedy the noncompliance within a reasonable amount of time following the notice or actual knowledge;

whichever occurs first. [P.L.92-2002, § 2.]

ARTICLE 32

TIME SHARES AND CAMPING CLUBS

CHAPTER 1

APPLICATION

32-32-1-1. Applicability of article. — This article does not apply to the following:

(1) The sale of not more than twelve (12) time shares or camping club memberships in a time share project or camping site project, unless the developer offers to sell time shares or camping club memberships in other projects in the same subdivision and the total number of the shares offered for sale exceeds twenty-six (26) in a period of twelve (12) months.

(2) The sale or transfer of a time share or camping club membership by an owner who is not the developer, unless the time share or camping club membership is sold in the ordinary course of business of that owner.

(3) Any transfer of a time share or camping club membership by deed instead of foreclosure or as a result of foreclosure of the time share or camping club membership.

(4) A gratuitous transfer of a time share or camping site.

(5) A transfer of a time share or camping club membership by devise or descent or a transfer to an inter vivos trust, unless the method of disposition is adopted for the purpose of evading this chapter. [P.L.2-2002, § 17.]

Effective Dates. P.L.2-2002, § 17. July 1. 2002.

CHAPTER 2

DEFINITIONS

32-32-2-1. Applicability of definitions. — The definitions in this chapter apply throughout this article. [P.L.2-2002, § 17.]

Effective Dates. P.L.2-2002, § 17. July 1. 2002.

32-32-2-2. Camping club. — "Camping club" means any enterprise, other than one that is tax exempt under Section 501 of the Internal Revenue Code, that has as its primary purpose camping or outdoor recreation that involves or will involve camping sites. [P.L.2-2002, § 17.]

Collateral References. Right to assets of voluntarily dissolved lodge or club. 70 A.L.R.4th 897.

32-32-2-3. Camping club member. — "Camping club member" means any person, other than the developer or lender, who purchases a camping club membership. [P.L.2-2002, § 17.]

32-32-2-4. Camping club membership. — (a) "Camping club membership" means an agreement evidencing a purchaser's title to, interest in, or right or license to use for more than thirty (30) days the camping or outdoor recreation facilities of a camping club.

(b) The term does not include an agreement of a camping or outdoor recreation facility that expires within three hundred sixty-five (365) days after the execution date of the agreement. [P.L.2-2002, § 17.]

32-32-2-5. Camping site. — "Camping site" means a space that:
(1) is designed and promoted for the purpose of locating a trailer, tent, tent trailer, pickup camper, or other similar device used for land based portable housing; and
(2) is the subject of a camping club membership.
[P.L.2-2002, § 17.]

32-32-2-6. Developer. — "Developer" means any person who engages in the business of creating or selling its own time shares or camping club memberships. [P.L.2-2002, § 17.]

32-32-2-7. Director. — "Director" refers to the director of the division appointed under IC 4-6-9-2. [P.L.2-2002, § 17.]

32-32-2-8. Division. — "Division" refers to the consumer protection division of the office of the attorney general created by IC 4-6-9-1. [P.L.2-2002, § 17.]

32-32-2-9. Exchange company. — "Exchange company" means any person owning or operating an exchange program. [P.L.2-2002, § 17.]

32-32-2-10. Exchange program. — (a) "Exchange program" means any arrangement allowing owners to exchange occupancy rights with persons owning other time shares or camping club memberships.

(b) The term does not include an arrangement in which all of the occupancy rights that may be exchanged are in the same time share property or camping site. [P.L.2-2002, § 17.]

32-32-2-11. Offer. — "Offer" means any advertised inducement, solicitation, or attempt to encourage any person to acquire a time share or camping club membership other than as security for an obligation. [P.L.2-2002, § 17.]

32-32-2-12. Participant. — "Participant" means any person who, by means of a verbal or written purchase, exchange, or leasing agreement, acquires a right to occupy a time share unit from a developer, purchaser, exchange company, rental or management company, or any other person or organization. [P.L.2-2002, § 17.]

32-32-2-13. Person. — "Person" means a natural person, a corporation, a government, a governmental subdivision or agency, a business trust, an estate, a trust, a partnership, an association, a joint venture, or another legal or commercial entity. [P.L.2-2002, § 17.]

32-32-2-14. Project. — "Project" means the real property, which must contain more than one (1) unit, in which time shares or camping sites are created by a single instrument or set of instruments. [P.L.2-2002, § 17.]

32-32-2-15. Project manager. — "Project manager" means any person:
(1) who coordinates the sale of time shares or camping club memberships; and
(2) to whom sales agents and representatives are responsible. [P.L.2-2002, § 17.]

32-32-2-16. Purchaser. — "Purchaser" means any person, other than the developer or lender, who purchases a time share or camping club membership. [P.L.2-2002, § 17.]

32-32-2-17. Representative. — (a) "Representative" means a person who is not a seller and who, on behalf of a developer, induces other persons to attend a sales presentation.

(b) The term does not include a person who only performs clerical tasks, arranges appointments set up by others, or prepares or distributes promotional materials. [P.L.2-2002, § 17.]

32-32-2-18. Seller. — "Seller" means a developer or any other person or agent or employee of a developer who offers time shares or camping club memberships to the public. [P.L.2-2002, § 17.]

32-32-2-19. Substantially completed. — "Substantially completed" means that:

(1) all roadways, utilities, amenities, furnishings, appliances, structural components, and mechanical systems of buildings and premises are completed and provided as represented in the time share instrument or agreement or camping club membership agreement; and

(2) the premises are ready for occupancy and the proper governmental authority has caused to be issued a certificate of occupancy, if a certificate of occupancy is required. [P.L.2-2002, § 17.]

32-32-2-20. Time share. — "Time share" means the right to use and occupy a unit on a periodic basis according to an arrangement allocating this right among various time share participants. [P.L.2-2002, § 17.]

Collateral References. Regulation of time-share or interval ownership interests in real estate. 6 A.L.R.4th 1288. Property taxation of residential time-share or interval-ownership units. 80 A.L.R.4th 950.

32-32-2-21. Time share instrument. — "Time share instrument" means any document creating or regulating time shares, excluding any law, ordinance, or governmental regulation. [P.L.2-2002, § 17.]

32-32-2-22. Time share participant. — "Time share participant" has the meaning set forth in section 12 [IC 32-32-2-12] of this chapter. [P.L.2-2002, § 17.]

32-32-2-23. Unit. — "Unit" means each portion of a time share project or each camping site that is designated for separate use. [P.L.2-2002, § 17.]

CHAPTER 3

TIME SHARES AND CAMPING CLUBS

32-32-3-1. Developers — Registration requirement — Penalties for failure to register. — (a) Before a developer may offer to sell any time shares or camping club memberships in this state, the developer must register with the division under this section.

(b) A person who applies for registration under this section shall submit an application in the manner provided by the division and shall disclose the following information under oath:

(1) The names and addresses of all officers, project managers, marketing agencies, advertising agencies, and exchange companies who are actively involved in soliciting or selling time share units or camping club memberships.

(2) The name and address of each person who owns an interest of ten percent (10%) or more in the registrant, except for reporting companies under the Securities Exchange Act of 1934.

(3) A copy of the document in which the time share project or camping club project is created.

(4) A preliminary title report for the time share project or camping club project and copies of the documents listed as exceptions in the report showing any encumbrances.

(5) Copies of and instructions for escrow agreements, deeds, and sales contracts.

(6) Documents that show the current assessments for property taxes on the time share project or camping club project.

(7) A copy of bylaws or similar instrument that creates any community ownership relationship.

(8) Copies of all documents that will be given to a participant who is interested in participating in a program for the exchange of occupancy rights among time share participants or camping club members, and copies of the documents that show acceptance of the time share or camping club membership in the program.

(c) A developer who knowingly or intentionally offers to sell any time shares or camping club memberships in this state before registering with the division under this section commits a Class D felony. [P.L.2-2002, § 17.]

Compiler's Notes. The federal Securities Exchange Act of 1934, referred to in subdivision (b)(2), appears as various sections throughout 15 U.S.C.

Effective Dates. P.L.2-2002, § 17. July 1. 2002.

Cross References. Penalties for felonies, IC 35-50-1, IC 35-50-2, IC 35-50-5-2.

32-32-3-2. Amendment of document by developer — Filing requirement. — Any amendment by the developer of the provisions of the document that created the time share or camping club membership, or of the articles of incorporation, trust, or bylaws, must be filed with the division. [P.L.2-2002, § 17.]

32-32-3-3. Registration fee. — (a) A time share or camping site developer who applies for registration under section 1 [IC 32-32-3-1] of this chapter shall pay a one (1) time registration fee of two hundred fifty dollars ($250).

(b) Each July 1 after a developer applies for registration under section 1 of this chapter, the developer shall file an update to the registration. The developer shall pay an additional fifty dollars ($50) for each yearly refiling under this subsection.

(c) The fees collected under this section shall be used, in addition to funds appropriated by the general assembly, for the administration and enforcement of this chapter. [P.L.2-2002, § 17.]

32-32-3-4. Information subject to inspection as public records. — All registration statements and information required to be filed under this chapter with the division are subject to IC 5-14-3. [P.L.2-2002, § 17.]

32-32-3-5. Membership agreement. — A time share project and camping club project must be created by a time share instrument or camping club membership agreement. The membership agreement must include the following provisions:

(1) A legal description of the time share project or camping club project that transfers an interest in real property.

(2) The name and location of the time share project or camping club project.

(3) A system of identification of the time periods assigned to time shares by letter, name, number, or any combination of letters, names, or numbers.

(4) Provisions for assessment of the expenses of the time share project or camping club project and an allocation of those expenses among the time share participants or camping club members.

(5) A procedure to add units to the time share project or camping club project.

(6) Provisions for maintenance of the time share units or camp sites.

(7) Provisions for management of the time share project or camping club project.

(8) A procedure to amend the time share instrument or the camping club membership agreement.

(9) A description of the rights of the purchaser relating to the occupancy of the time share unit or camping site. [P.L.2-2002, § 17.]

32-32-3-6. Transfer of interest in membership — Written contract. — A transfer of an interest in a time share unit or camping club membership shall be by written contract that includes or incorporates by reference the following provisions:

(1) A legal description of the time share unit or camping site that transfers an interest in real property.

(2) The name and location of the time share unit or camping site.

(3) A system of identification of the time periods assigned to time shares by letter, name, number, or any combination of letters, names, or numbers.

(4) Provisions for assessment of the expenses of the time share project or camping club project and an allocation of those expenses among the time share participants or camping club members.

(5) Provisions for maintenance of the time share units or camping sites.

(6) Provisions for management of the time share project or camping club project.

(7) A description of the rights of the time share participant or camping club member relating to the occupancy of the time share unit or camping site. [P.L.2-2002, § 17.]

Collateral References. Property taxation of residential time-share or interval-ownership units. 80 A.L.R.4th 950.

32-32-3-7. Right of cancellation — Notice of cancellation. — (a) A purchaser has the right to cancel a camping club membership or time share purchase within seventy-two (72) hours after the execution of the sales contract, excluding Sundays and legal holidays as set forth in IC 1-1-9-1. The right of cancellation shall be set forth conspicuously in boldface type on the first page of any time share instrument or camping club membership agreement and immediately above the signature of the purchaser on any sales contract. In each case, the cancellation clause must include an explanation of the conditions and manner of exercise of the cancellation right. The right of cancellation may not be waivable by any purchaser. The developer shall furnish to each purchaser a form, as prescribed by the agency, for the exercise of the right.

(b) To cancel a camping club membership or time share purchase, a consumer must give notice of cancellation by mail or telegraphic communication or as otherwise allowed by this subsection. The notice is effective on the date postmarked or when transmitted from the place of origin. Any written notice of cancellation delivered other than by mail or telegraph is effective at the time of delivery at the place of business of the developer or escrow agent designated in the form of notice of cancellation. [P.L.2-2002, § 17.]

32-32-3-8. Performance bond or escrow account required. — The attorney general may require:

(1) that a developer file a performance bond with the division; or

(2) that all or part of the money collected from the consumer as part of a purchase of a time share instrument or camping club membership, including closing costs and exchange company membership fees, be placed and held in escrow until the particular time share unit or camping site to which the time share or camping club membership relates is substantially completed and ready for occupancy. [P.L.2-2002, § 17.]

32-32-3-9. Unavailability of unit — Remedies. — If a time share unit or camping site is not available for a period to which the owner is entitled by schedule or by confirmed reservation and the developer is responsible for the unavailability of the unit or site, the participant is entitled at the participant's election to be provided:

(1) a comparable unit or site for the period; or

(2) monetary compensation for the loss of use of the time share unit or camping site. [P.L.2-2002, § 17.]

32-32-3-10. Leasehold interest. — (a) If the interest of the developer in a project is a leasehold interest, the lease, unless otherwise determined by the division, must provide that:

(1) the lessee must give the association notice of termination of the lease for any default by the lessor; and

(2) the lessor, upon the bankruptcy of the lessee, shall enter into a new lease with the association upon the same terms and conditions as were contained in the lease with the developer.

(b) The division may require the developer to execute a bond or other type of security for the payment of the lease obligation. [P.L.2-2002, § 17.]

32-32-3-11. Action for partition — Judicial sale — Waiver or subordination of rights. — An action for partition of a time share unit or camping site may not be maintained except as provided in the time share instrument. If a time share or camping site is owned by two (2) or more persons, an action may be brought for the judicial sale of the time share or camping site. A provision in a time share instrument for the waiver or subordination of the right of partition or any other right characteristic of a tenancy in common is valid. [P.L.2-2002, § 17.]

32-32-3-12. Exchange of occupancy rights — Written notice to members — Certification by members prior to execution of contract — Accuracy of information. — (a) A developer, or exchange company if the exchange company is dealing directly with the participants or camping club members, that offers a program for the exchange of occupancy rights among time share participants or camping club members or with the purchasers or members in other time share or camping club projects, or both, shall give in writing to the camping club members or time share participants the following information:

(1) The name and address of the exchange company offering the exchange program.

(2) A statement indicating whether the exchange company or any of its officers or directors has any legal or beneficial interest in any interest of the developer or managing agent in any plan to sell time shares or camping club memberships included in the program and, if so, the name, location, and nature of the interest.

(3) A statement that the time share participant's or camping club member's contract with the exchange company is a contract separate and distinct from the contract to purchase the time share or camping club membership, unless the exchange company and the developer or an affiliate of the developer are the same.

(4) A statement indicating whether the participant's or member's participation in the exchange project is dependent upon the continued inclusion of the plan to sell time shares or camping club memberships in the program.

(5) A statement indicating whether the purchaser's or member's membership or participation in the exchange program is voluntary or mandatory.

(6) A complete and accurate description of the following:

(A) The terms and conditions of the purchaser's contractual relationship with the company and the procedure by which changes in the contractual relationship and may be made.

(B) The procedure to qualify for and make exchanges.

(C) All limitations, restrictions, and priorities of the program, including limitations on exchanges based on the seasons of the year, the size of units, or levels of occupancy. The written description of the limitations, restrictions, and priorities given under this clause must be printed in boldface type and, if the limitations, restrictions, and priorities are not uniformly applied by the program, must include a clear description of the manner in which they are applied.

(7) A statement, which must be printed on all promotional brochures, pamphlets, advertisements, and other materials disseminated by the exchange company that indicate the percentage of confirmed exchanges, to the effect that:

(A) the percentage of confirmed exchanges is a summary of the requests for exchanges received by the exchange company in the most recent annual reporting period; and

(B) the percentage does not indicate the probability of a purchaser or members being confirmed to any specific choice since availability at individual locations may vary.

(8) A statement indicating whether exchanges are arranged on the basis of available space and whether there are any guarantees of fulfilling specific requests for exchanges.

(9) A statement indicating whether and under what circumstances a participant or member, in dealing with the exchange company, may lose the right to use and occupy a time share unit or camping site in any properly applied for exchange without being provided with substitute accommodations by the company.

(10) A statement of the fees to be paid by participants or members in the program, including a statement indicating whether any fees may be changed by the exchange company, and if so, the circumstances under which those changes may be made.

(11) The name and address of the site of each time share or camping club project included in the program.

(b) The information required by subsection (a) must be delivered to the camping club member or time share participant before the execution of:

(1) any contract between the camping club member or time share participant and the exchange company; or

(2) the contract to purchase the time share or camping club membership.

(c) Upon receipt of the information required by subsection (a), the camping club member or time share participant shall certify in writing that the member or participant has received the information from the developer.

(d) Except as otherwise provided in this section, the information required by subsection (a) must be accurate as of thirty (30) days before the date on which the information is delivered to the participant or member. [P.L.2-2002, § 17.]

32-32-3-13. Division's right to receive, investigate, and prosecute complaints — Collection of evidence — Issuance of subpoenas. — (a) The division may receive, investigate, and prosecute complaints concerning persons subject to this chapter.

(b) The director may subpoena witnesses and send for and compel the production of books, records, papers, and documents of time share or camping club developers who are subject to registration under this chapter for the furtherance of any investigation under this chapter. The circuit or superior court located in the county where the subpoena is to be issued shall enforce any subpoena by the attorney general. In addition, the attorney general may issue a civil investigative demand as provided by IC 4-6-3. [P.L.2-2002, § 17.]

32-32-3-14. Penalties and remedies for violations. — A person who violates this chapter commits a deceptive act and is subject to the penalties and remedies provided in IC 24-5-0.5. Any action by the attorney general for violations of this chapter may be brought in the circuit or superior court of Marion County. [P.L.2-2002, § 17.]

32-32-3-15. Assurance of voluntary compliance. — In the administration of this chapter, the attorney general may execute an assurance of voluntary compliance with a time share developer in existence on September 1, 1985, in the same manner as provided in IC 24-5-0.5-7(a), except that no filing with the court is required in order for the assurance to be effective under this chapter. [P.L.2-2002, § 17.]

ARTICLE 33

LIENS ON [PERSONAL] PROPERTY

CHAPTER 1
BLACKSMITH'S LIENS

32-33-1-1. Shoeing horses, repairing vehicles. — (a) A person who, at the request of an owner or an owner's authorized agent:

(1) shoes or causes to be shod by the person's employees a horse, a mule, an ox, or other animal; or

(2) repairs or causes to be repaired by the person's employees, a vehicle; has a lien upon the animal shod or vehicle repaired for the person's reasonable charge for shoeing the animal or repairing the vehicle.

(b) A lien conferred by this chapter takes the precedence of all other liens or claims upon the animal shod or the vehicle repaired that are not duly recorded before the recording of a claim for the lien conferred by this chapter. However, a lien may not attach to the animal shod or the vehicle repaired if the property has changed ownership before the filing of the lien. [P.L.2-2002, § 18.]

Compiler's Notes. The heading of this article as enacted by P.L.2-2002, § 18, was "Liens on Real Property." The compiler has substituted the bracketed word "Personal" for "Real" in heading of this article to reflect its content.

Effective Dates. P.L.2-2002, § 18. July 1. 2002.

NOTES TO DECISIONS

Statute Required.
Common law liens, such as a blacksmith's lien, are creatures of statute, and, when there is no express statute authorizing a lien on land, an instrument purporting to do so is void. Terpstra v. F & M Bank, 483 N.E.2d 749 (Ind. App. 1985).

Collateral References. 51 Am. Jur. 2d Liens and Encumbrances, §§ 5, 20, 21.
53 C.J.S. Liens, § 4.

32-33-1-2. Filing of claim — Recordation. — A claim for a lien under this chapter must be filed within sixty (60) days after the shoeing of a horse, a mule, an ox or other animal, or the repairing of a vehicle. The claim must be filed with the recorder of the county in which the owner of the animal or vehicle resides. A claim for a lien under this chapter must be in writing, setting forth the person's intention to claim a lien upon the animal or vehicle for the charges for shoeing or repairing. However, this lien must be recorded in the miscellaneous record book in the recorder's office of the county. The recorder shall charge a fee in accordance with IC 36-2-7-10 for recording the lien. [P.L.2-2002, § 18.]

32-33-1-3. Claim requirements — Expiration of claim. — A claim for lien under this chapter must:

(1) state the name and residence of the person claiming the lien;

(2) the name of the owner of the animal or vehicle sought to be charged with the lien;

(3) a description sufficient for identification of the animal or vehicle upon which the lien is claimed; and

(4) the amount due the claimant, as near as may be, over and above all legal set-offs.

A claim for lien filed with the recorder of the county under section 2 [IC 32-33-1-2] of this chapter expires and becomes void and of no effect if suit is not brought to foreclose the lien within three (3) months after filing the claim under section 2 of this chapter. [P.L.2-2002, § 18.]

Cross References. Limitation of foreclosure actions, IC 32-28-4-1 — IC 32-28-4-3, IC 32-28-7-1 — IC 32-28-7-4, IC 32-28-8-1.

32-33-1-4. Foreclosure. — A lien under this chapter may be foreclosed in any circuit or superior court in the county in which the lien is recorded under section 2 [IC 32-33-1-2] of this chapter. [P.L.2-2002, § 18.]

32-33-1-5. Attorney fees. — If the plaintiff recovers on a claim and a lien is foreclosed under this chapter, the plaintiff shall recover and the court may allow a reasonable fee for plaintiff's attorney for bringing and prosecuting the cause of action, all of which shall be recovered from the defendant, and the property in controversy may be sold as in case of sales in foreclosure of chattel mortgages. [P.L.2-2002, § 18.]

Cross References. Attorney's fees, IC 32-28-3-14.

CHAPTER 2

BOATS AND OTHER WATERCRAFT LIENS

32-33-2-1. Liability. — All boats, vessels, and watercraft of every description found in the waters of Indiana, including wharf boats and floating warehouses that are used for storing, receiving, and forwarding freights and that may be removed from place to place at the pleasure of the owner or owners of the watercraft, are liable for the following:

(1) A debt contracted within Indiana by the master, owner, agent, clerk, or consignee of the watercraft:

(A) on account of supplies furnished for use of the master, owner, agent, clerk, or consignee;

(B) on account of work done or service rendered for the master, owner, agent, clerk, or consignee by boatmen, mariners, laborers, or other persons; or

(C) on account of work done or materials furnished in building, repairing, fitting out, furnishing, or equipping the boat, vessel, wharf boat, floating warehouse, or watercraft.

(2) All demands or damages arising out of:

(A) a contract of affreightment made either within or outside Indiana;

(B) a willful or negligent act of the master, owner, or agent of the master or owner done in connection with the business of the boat, vessel, wharf boat, floating warehouse, or other watercraft either within or outside Indiana; or

(C) a contract relative to the transportation of persons or property entered into by the master, owner, agent, clerk, or consignee either within or outside Indiana.

(3) An injury to a person or property by the boat, vessel, wharf-boat, floating warehouse, or other watercraft, or by the owners, officers, or crew, done in connection with the business of the boat, vessel, wharf boat, floating warehouse, or other watercraft either within or without outside Indiana. [P.L.2-2002, § 18.]

Effective Dates. P.L.2-2002, § 18. July 1. 2002.

NOTES TO DECISIONS

Lessees.

Persons furnishing supplies to boats had a lien thereon although the boat was run by a lessee. Lawrenceburgh Ferry-Boat v. Smith, 7 Ind. 520 (1856).

Loss of Lien.

Where a debt had been incurred in building a steamboat, and the boat had left the state and been absent nine years, the lien was not lost by the delay in enforcing it. Such lien was not lost unless there had been unreasonable neglect and delay, operating to the prejudice of third parties, after opportunities had existed to enforce the lien. If the defendant claimed there was unreasonable delay in enforcing the lien, the facts showing such unreasonable delay had to have been set up by answer. The lien could have been enforced although no notice of the lien was given as required by the Registry Laws of the United States. Sinton v. Steamboat R.R. Roberts, 46 Ind. 476 (1874).

Maritime Liens.

The statute regulating liens on boats did not extend to maritime liens arising under contracts made and broken in another state. Steamboat J.P. Tweed v. Richards, 9 Ind. 525 (1857); Coplinger v. Steamboat David Gibson, 14 Ind. 480 (1860).

The courts of this state had no jurisdiction to enforce maritime liens against boats. Ballard v. Wiltshire, 28 Ind. 341 (1867).

Such courts, however, could enforce liens against boats for the building and fitting out of the same. Wyatt v. Stuckley, 29 Ind. 279 (1868); Sinton v. Steamboat R.R. Roberts, 34 Ind. 448, 7 Am. R. 229 (1874); Sinton v. Steamboat R.R. Roberts, 46 Ind. 476 (1874).

Masters of Boats.

Masters of boats had power to bind the owners thereof for necessaries furnished for the use of the boat. Holcroft v. Halbert, 16 Ind.

Masters of Boats. (Cont'd)
256 (1861); Sinton v. Steamboat R.R. Roberts, 46 Ind. 476 (1874).

Ordinance Fixing Wharfage Rate.
An ordinance of a city fixing a rate of wharfage did not need to prescribe the manner of enforcing the lien therefor against boats. Coal-Float v. City of Jeffersonville, 112 Ind. 15, 13 N.E. 115 (1887).

Collateral References. 12 Am. Jur. 2d Boats and Boating, §§ 21, 29-31.

53 C.J.S. Liens, §§ 4-9, 11.

Wharfinger's liability as warehouseman for injury to or destruction of stored goods from floods, heavy rains, or the like. 60 A.L.R.2d 1097.

Res ipsa loquitur with respect to personal injuries or death on or about ship. 1 A.L.R.3d 642.

Liability for injury to or death of passenger in connection with a fire drill or abandonment-of-ship drill aboard a vessel. 8 A.L.R.3d 650.

Right to recover for death of seaman as affected by Jones Act. 22 A.L.R.3d 852.

Presumption and burden of proof where subject of bailment is destroyed or damaged by windstorm or other meteorological phenomena. 43 A.L.R.3d 607.

Construction and effect of provision of homeowner's, premises, or personal liability insurance policy covering or excluding watercraft. 26 A.L.R.4th 967.

Recovery, under Jones Act (46 USCS Appx sec. 688) or seaworthiness doctrine, by seaman or maritime worker injured in boarding or leaving ship. 108 A.L.R. Fed. 264.

32-33-2-2. Property subject to. — A claim growing out of a cause set forth in section 1 [IC 32-33-2-1] of this chapter, whether arising out of contracts made or broken within or outside Indiana, or wrongs or injuries done or committed within or outside Indiana, is a lien upon the boat, vessel, or other watercraft, and upon the apparel, tackle, or furniture and appendages, including barges and lighters, that belong to the owners of the boat, vessel, or other watercraft and are used with the boat, vessel, or other watercraft at the time the action is commenced. [P.L.2-2002, § 18.]

32-33-2-3. Priority. — A lien provided for in section 2 [IC 32-33-2-2] of this chapter takes preference of any claims against the boat itself or all or any of its owners, masters, or consignees growing out of any other cause than those set forth in section 1 of this chapter and, as between themselves, mariners' and boatmens' wages shall be first preferred. [P.L.2-2002, § 18.]

32-33-2-4. Proceedings to enforce. — (a) Any person aggrieved by a cause set forth in section 1 [IC 32-33-2-1] of this chapter may have an action against the boat, vessel, or other watercraft in the county where the boat, vessel, or other watercraft may be found, or against the owners of the boat, vessel, or other watercraft, to enforce a lien provided for in section 2 [IC 32-33-2-2] of this chapter.

(b) If the complaint in the action shows:

(1) the particulars of the demand;

(2) the amount due; and

(3) a demand made upon the owner, master, clerk, or consignee and refusal of payment, and verified by the affidavit of the plaintiff or other person in the plaintiff's behalf;

an order of attachment shall be issued by the clerk against the boat, vessel, or other watercraft and the tackle and furniture of the boat, vessel, or other watercraft. The order of attachment must be directed, executed, and returned as an order of attachment in other cases. [P.L.2-2002, § 18.]

NOTES TO DECISIONS

In General.
An attachment could have been enforced against a boat for injuries done by the same through the negligence of the persons in charge of the boat. Lusk v. Davis, 27 Ind. 334 (1866).
The courts of the state had no jurisdiction to enforce maritime liens against boats. Ballard v. Wiltshire, 28 Ind. 341 (1867).

Courts of this state could enforce liens against boats for building and fitting out of the same. Wyatt v. Stuckley, 29 Ind. 279 (1868); Sinton v. Steamboat R.R. Roberts, 34 Ind. 448, 7 Am. R. 229 (1874); Sinton v. Steamboat R.R. Roberts, 46 Ind. 476 (1874).

Collateral References. Construction and application of state statutes or rules of court predicating in personam jurisdiction over nonresidents or foreign corporations on making or performing a contract within the state. 23 A.L.R.3d 551.

32-33-2-5. Proceedings — Judgment — Execution. — In all actions contemplated in section 4 [IC 32-33-2-4] of this chapter, all or any of the persons having demands described in section 4 of this chapter may join in a complaint against the boat, vessel, or other watercraft either at the commencement of the action or at any time afterwards, before judgment, upon filing the requisite complaint and affidavit. [P.L.2-2002, § 18.]

32-33-2-6. Judgment rendered by execution. — In an action under this chapter, proceedings shall be had and judgment rendered and enforced by execution or other proper means. [P.L.2-2002, § 18.]

32-33-2-7. Discharge of attachment — Restitution of boat — Judgment to be rendered against all defendants. — (a) If the defendant master, owner, or consignee, before final judgment, gives a written undertaking payable to the plaintiff, with surety to be approved by the clerk or sheriff, to the effect that the defendant will perform the judgment of the court, the attachment shall be discharged and restitution made of the boat, vessel, or other watercraft.

(b) A person who executes a written undertaking under subsection (a) shall, by order of the court, be made a defendant in the action instead of the boat, vessel, or other watercraft, and the action shall proceed to final judgment as in ordinary actions in personam. If a recovery is had by any of the plaintiffs, judgment shall be rendered against all defendants for the sum recovered. [P.L.2-2002, § 18.]

NOTES TO DECISIONS

In General.
The execution of a bond to obtain a release of a boat was not a waiver of any objections to the attachment. Carson v. Steamboat Talma, 3 Ind. 194 (1851).
When an attachment was discharged by the giving of a bond, the judgment rendered should have been a personal one against the obligors in the bond. Lawrenceburgh Ferry-Boat v. Smith, 7 Ind. 520 (1856).
When an attachment was released by giving bond, other persons could not have be-

In General. (Cont'd) come parties to the proceedings for the pur-

pose of enforcing their claims. Scott v. McDonald, 27 Ind. 33 (1866).

32-33-2-8. Service of summons. — In cases arising under section 1 [IC 32-33-2-1] of this chapter, the summons may be served upon:

(1) the officer or consignee making the contract;

(2) if the officer or consignee cannot be found, upon the clerk;

(3) if neither the officer, the consignee, nor the clerk can be found, upon any other officer of the boat, vessel, or watercraft, or any person having charge of the boat, vessel, or watercraft; or

(4) if the summons cannot be served under subdivision 1, 2, or 3, by affixing a copy of the summons in some conspicuous place in the boat, vessel, or watercraft. [P.L.2-2002, § 18.]

CHAPTER 3

CLEANING LIEN FOR SERVICES ON AND STORAGE OF CLOTHING AND HOUSEHOLD GOODS

32-33-3-1. Lien — Written receipt — Sale — Property placed in storage exempt. — (a) A person doing any cleaning, glazing, washing, alteration, repair, or furnishing any materials or supplies for or upon any garment, clothing, wearing apparel, or household goods has a lien on the item for the reasonable value of the unpaid work, labor or material, and supplies used. The lien may be foreclosed in the manner provided by this chapter if at the time of receiving the clothing, garment, wearing apparel, or household goods a written receipt is given to the person or customer leaving the item.

(b) Any garment, clothing, wearing apparel, or household goods remaining in the possession of a person, firm, partnership, limited liability company, or corporation;

(1) on which cleaning, pressing, glazing, or washing has been done; or

(2) upon which alterations or repairs have been made, or on which materials or supplies have been used or furnished;

for a period of at least ninety (90) days after the cleaning, pressing, glazing, or washing has been done, the alterations or repairs have been made, or the materials or supplies have been used or furnished may be sold to pay the reasonable or agreed charges and the costs of notifying the owner or owners. However, the person, firm, partnership, limited liability company, or corporation to whom the charges are payable and owing must first notify the owner or owners of the time and place of the sale.

(c) Property that is to be placed in storage after any of the services or labors referred to in subsection (a) or (b) is not affected by this section. [P.L.2-2002, § 18.]

Effective Dates. P.L.2-2002, § 18. July 1.
2002.

Collateral References. 51 Am. Jur. 2d
Liens and Encumbrances, § 10.
53 C.J.S. Liens, §§ 4-9.

32-33-3-2. Sale — Notice — Applicability to warehouses. — (a) This section does not apply to persons, firms, partnerships, limited liability companies, or corporations operating as warehouses or warehousemen.

(b) All garments, clothing, wearing apparel, or household goods:

(1) that are placed in storage; or

(2) on which any of the services or labors mentioned in section 1 [IC 32-33-3-1] of this chapter have been performed and that have then been placed in storage by agreement;

and that remain in the possession of a person, firm, partnership, limited liability company, or corporation without the reasonable or agreed charges having been paid for a period of ninety (90) days may be sold to pay the charges if the person, firm, partnership, limited liability company, or corporation to whom the charges are payable first notifies the owner or owners of the items placed in storage of the time and place of sale. [P.L.2-2002, § 18.]

Cross References. Warehouseman's lien, IC 32-33-14-1 — IC 32-33-14-3.

32-33-3-3. Notice of sale. — The mailing of a letter that has a return address, that is addressed to the owner at the owner's address given at the time of delivery of the article to a person, firm, partnership, limited liability company, or corporation to render any of the services or labors set forth in section 1 [IC 32-33-3-1] of this chapter, and that states the time and place of sale constitutes notice for the purposes of section 2 of this chapter. The notice must be given at least thirty (30) days before the date of sale. The cost of posting or mailing letters under this section shall be added to the charges. [P.L.2-2002, § 18.]

32-33-3-4. Proceeds of sale — Payment of over-plus. — The person, firm, partnership, limited liability company, or corporation to whom the charges are payable shall:

(1) from the proceeds of sale, deduct the charges due plus the costs of notifying the owner;

(2) hold the over-plus, if any, subject to the order of the owner;

(3) immediately after the sale mail to the owner at the owner's address, if known, a notice of the sale and the amount of over-plus, if any, due the owner; and

(4) at any time within twelve (12) months after the sale, upon demand by the owner, pay to the owner the sums or over-plus. [P.L.2-2002, § 18.]

32-33-3-5. Posting of notice. — All persons, firms, partnerships, limited liability companies, or corporations taking advantage of this chapter must keep posted in a prominent place in their receiving office at all times two (2) notices that must read as follows:

"All articles cleaned, pressed, glazed, laundered, washed, altered, or repaired and not called for in ninety (90) days shall be sold to pay charges," and "If any articles are stored by agreement and the charges are not paid for ninety (90) days, the articles shall be sold to pay charges."

[P.L.2-2002, § 18.]

CHAPTER 4

HOSPITAL LIENS

32-33-4-1. Lien on judgment for personal injuries. — A person, a firm, a partnership, an association, a limited liability company, or a corporation maintaining a hospital in Indiana or a hospital owned, maintained, or operated by the state or a political subdivision of the state is entitled to hold a lien for the reasonable value of its services or expenses on any judgment for personal injuries rendered in favor of any person, except a person covered by:

(1) the provisions of IC 22-3-2 through IC 22-3-6;

(2) the federal worker's compensation laws; or

(3) the federal liability act;

who is admitted to the hospital and receives treatment, care, and maintenance on account of personal injuries received as a result of the negligence of any person or corporation. In order to claim the lien, the hospital must at the time or after the judgment is rendered, enter, in writing, upon the judgment docket where the judgment is recorded, the hospital's intention to hold a lien upon the judgment, together with the amount claimed. [P.L.2-2002, § 18.]

Effective Dates. P.L.2-2002, § 18. July 1. 2002.

Cross References. Judgment lien, IC 34-1-45-2.

Collateral References. 51 Am. Jur. 2d Liens and Encumbrances, §§ 36-38.

41 C.J.S. Hospitals, §§ 13, 15.

Liability of one requesting medical practitioner or hospital to furnish services to third party for cost of services, absent express understanding to pay. 34 A.L.R.3d 176.

Construction, operation, and effect of statute giving hospital lien against recovery from tortfeasor causing patient's injuries. 16 A.L.R.5th 262.

32-33-4-2. Priority of lien. — The lien provided for in section 1 [IC 32-33-4-1] of this chapter is junior and inferior to all claims for attorney's fees, court costs, and all other expenses contracted for or incurred in the recovery of claims or damages for personal injuries as described in this chapter. [P.L.2-2002, § 18.]

Cross References. Attorney's fees, IC 32-28-3-14.

32-33-4-3. Lien on cause of action related to illness or injuries — Applicability — Assignability — Reduction of lien. — (a) A person, a firm, a partnership, an association, a limited liability company, or a corporation maintaining a hospital in Indiana or a hospital owned, maintained, or operated by the state or a political subdivision has a lien for all reasonable and necessary charges for hospital care, treatment, and maintenance of a patient (including emergency ambulance services provided by the hospital) upon any cause of action, suit, or claim accruing to the patient, or in the case of the patient's death, the patient's legal representative, because of the illness or injuries that:

(1) gave rise to the cause of action, suit, or claim; and

(2) necessitated the hospital care, treatment, and maintenance.

(b) The lien provided for in subsection (a):

(1) except as provided in subsection (c), applies to any amount obtained or recovered by the patient by settlement or compromise rendered or entered into by the patient or by the patient's legal representative;

(2) is subject and subordinate to any attorney's lien upon the claim or cause of action;

(3) is not applicable to accidents or injuries within the purview of:

(A) IC 22-3;

(B) 5 U.S.C. 8101 et seq.; or

(C) 45 U.S.C. 51 et seq.;

(4) is not assignable; and

(5) must first be reduced by the amount of any medical insurance proceeds paid to the hospital on behalf of the patient after the hospital has made all reasonable efforts to pursue the insurance claims in cooperation with the patient.

(c) If a settlement or compromise that is subject to subsection (b)(1) is for an amount that would permit the patient to receive less than twenty percent (20%) of the full amount of the settlement or compromise if all the liens created under this chapter were paid in full, the liens must be reduced on a pro rata basis to the extent that will permit the patient to receive twenty percent (20%) of the full amount. [P.L.2-2002, § 18.]

NOTES TO DECISIONS

Applicability.

Because all parties received their fair shares under former IC 32-8-26-3 (repealed; see this section for similar provisions), the rules subordinating the hospital lien to plaintiffs' attorney's fees under former IC 32-8-26-3(b)(2) and costs under former IC 32-8-26-3(c) did not apply. Community Hosp. v. Carlisle,

Applicability. (Cont'd)
648 N.E.2d 363 (Ind. App. 1995).

Comparative Fault of Patient.
The hospital's lien was not subject to reduction by former IC 34-4-33-12 (repealed) of the Comparative Fault Act. National Ins. Ass'n v. Parkview Mem. Hosp., 590 N.E.2d 1141 (Ind. App. 1992).

Interest of Lienholder.
The former hospital lien statute did not provide subrogation rights to hospitals, but rather a specific interest in property otherwise accruing to the patient for the amount of the treatment rendered by the hospital. With a properly perfected lien, the hospital had a direct right in the insurance proceeds and other settlement funds paid to the patient by the person claimed to be liable for the patient's injuries. National Ins. Ass'n v. Parkview Mem. Hosp., 590 N.E.2d 1141 (Ind. App. 1992).

—Effect of Recovery of Pro Rata Share.
Where a hospital, at which an automobile accident victim received treatment, obtained a default judgment for the entire amount owed to it by the accident victim and subsequently received a pro rata share under former IC 32-8-26-3(c) (repealed; see this section for similar provisions) of the amount recovered by the accident victim against the tortfeasor, the remainder of the amount owed

by the accident victim continued to exist after the hospital's lien was released for a reduced amount. Cullimore v. St. Anthony Medical Ctr., 718 N.E.2d 1221 (Ind. App. 1999).

Notice of Lien.
Where the undisputed evidence showed that the patient's attorney had actual knowledge of the hospital's lien, even though defendant/hospital may have operated under the mistaken belief that a different attorney was the proper legal representative that should have been served with notice, the attorney's actual knowledge of the lien, along with the absence of any prejudice to either party, supported summary judgment in defendant/hospital's favor. Stephens v. Parkview Hosp., Inc., 745 N.E.2d 262 (Ind. App. 2001).
One purpose inherent in the former Indiana Hospital Lien Act was to ensure that legal counsel for the patient had notice of the lien. Tankersley v. Parkview Hosp., 761 N.E.2d 886 (Ind. App. 2002).

Preemption.
The former hospital lien statute requiring hospitals to seek reimbursement first from medical insurers rather than auto, workers' compensation, or liability insurers did not apply where the insurer in question was Medicare because the state statute was preempted by federal law. Parkview Hosp. v. Roese, 750 N.E.2d 384 (Ind. App. 2001).

Collateral References. Construction, operation, and effect of statute giving hospital lien against recovery from tortfeasor causing patient's injuries. 16 A.L.R.5th 262.

32-33-4-4. Perfection of lien — Filing of claim — Notice — Contest.
— (a) To perfect the lien provided for in section 3 [IC 32-33-4-3] of this chapter, the hospital must file for record in the office of the recorder of the county in which the hospital is located, within one hundred eighty (180) days after the person is discharged, a verified statement in writing stating:

(1) the name and address of the patient as it appears on the records of the hospital;

(2) the name and address of the operator of the hospital;

(3) the dates of the patient's admission to and discharge from the hospital;

(4) the amount claimed to be due for the hospital care; and

(5) to the best of the hospital's knowledge, the names and addresses of anyone claimed by the patient or the patient's legal representative to be liable for damages arising from the patient's illness or injury.

(b) Within ten (10) days after filing the statement, the hospital shall send a copy by registered mail, postage prepaid:

(1) to each person claimed to be liable because of the illness or injury at the address given in the statement;

(2) to the attorney representing the patient if the name of the attorney is known or with reasonable diligence could be discovered by the hospital; and

(3) to the department of insurance as notice to insurance companies doing business in Indiana.

(c) The filing of a claim under subsections (a) and (b) is notice to any person, firm, limited liability company, or corporation that may be liable because of the illness or injury if the person, firm, limited liability company, or corporation:

(1) receives notice under subsection (b);

(2) resides or has offices in a county where the lien was perfected or in a county where the lien was filed in the recorder's office as notice under this subsection; or

(3) is an insurance company authorized to do business in Indiana under IC 27-1-3-20.

(d) The filing of a verified statement under subsection (a) constitutes filing of a lien under section 1 [IC 32-33-4-1] of this chapter if the statement is filed before the issuance of the judgment.

(e) A person desiring to contest a lien or the reasonableness of the charges claimed by the hospital may do so by filing a motion to quash or reduce the claim in the circuit court in which the lien was perfected, making all other parties of interest respondents. [P.L.2-2002, § 18.]

NOTES TO DECISIONS

Lack of Notice.
Where the undisputed evidence showed that the patient's attorney had actual knowledge of the hospital's lien, even though defendant/hospital may have operated under the mistaken belief that a different attorney was the proper legal representative that should have been served with notice, the attorney's actual knowledge of the lien, along with the absence of any prejudice to either party, supported summary judgment in defendant/hospital's favor. Stephens v. Parkview Hosp., Inc., 745 N.E.2d 262 (Ind. App. 2001).

Former IC 32-8-26-4(c) (repealed; see this section for similar provisions) may have accomplished constructive notice under former certain circumstances, but it did not impute notice to an attorney who had not been served under former IC 32-8-26-4(b) and who did not otherwise have actual notice. Tankersley v. Parkview Hosp., 761 N.E.2d 886 (Ind. App. 2002).

Collateral References. Construction, operation, and effect of statute giving hospital lien against recovery from tortfeasor causing patient's injuries. 16 A.L.R.5th 262.

32-33-4-5. Endorsement — Fee — Filing. — (a) The recorder of the county shall endorse on the statement filed under section 4(a) [IC 32-33-4-4(a)] of this chapter the date and hour of filing.

(b) The recorder shall charge a fee for filing the claim in accordance with the fee schedule established in IC 36-2-7-10.

(c) The department of insurance shall adopt rules under IC 4-22-2 to:

(1) provide for the filing of lien notices mailed to the department by hospitals under section 4(b)(3) [IC 32-33-4-4(b)(3)] of this chapter;

(2) provide insurance companies with reasonable and timely access to the information contained in the lien notices filed with the department under section 4(b)(3) of this chapter; and

(3) provide a system for filing and for cross-referencing lien releases mailed under section 7 [IC 32-33-4-7] of this chapter with lien notices filed under section 4(b)(3) of this chapter. [P.L.2-2002, § 18.]

32-33-4-6. Validity — Release — Satisfaction — Jurisdiction — Venue. — (a) A lien perfected under section 4 [IC 32-33-4-4] of this chapter is valid unless the lienholder executes a release of the lien under section 7 [IC 32-33-4-7] of this chapter.

(b) The release or settlement of a claim with a patient by a person claimed to be liable for the damages incurred by the patient:

(1) after a lien has been perfected under section 4 of this chapter; and

(2) without obtaining a release of the lien;

entitles the lienholder to damages for the reasonable cost of the hospital care, treatment, and maintenance.

(c) Satisfaction of a judgment rendered in favor of the lienholder under subsection (b) is satisfaction of the lien.

(d) An action by the lienholder must be brought in the court having jurisdiction of the amount of the lienholder's claim and may be brought and maintained in the county of residence of the lienholder. [P.L.2-2002, § 18.]

NOTES TO DECISIONS

Settlement with Patient.

The former version of this section entitled a hospital as lienholder to damages where a settlement is made by the party liable for the plaintiff's injuries through his insurer after the hospital's lien is perfected and before it is released. Because the party liable had notice of the lien, the party liable and his insurer should have satisfied the lien before issuing the settlement proceeds to the patient. As a result of this failure, the trial court properly found the hospital was entitled to judgment against them. National Ins. Ass'n v. Parkview Mem. Hosp., 590 N.E.2d 1141 (Ind. App. 1992).

Collateral References. Construction, operation, and effect of statute giving hospital lien against recovery from tortfeasor causing patient's injuries. 16 A.L.R.5th 262.

32-33-4-7. Release of perfected lien — Filing of certificate — Notice to department of insurance. — (a) To release a lien perfected under section 4 [IC 32-33-4-4] of this chapter, the operator of the hospital to whom the lien has been paid must file with each recorder in whose office the notice of the hospital lien was filed an executed certificate:

(1) stating that the claim filed by the hospital for treatment, care, and maintenance has been paid or discharged; and

(2) authorizing the recorder to release the lien.

The hospital shall bear the expense of obtaining a release.

(b) Upon receipt of the certificate, the recorder shall enter in the margin of the record of the lien and the entry book a memorandum of the filing and the date the certificate was filed. This entry constitutes a release of lien for which the recorder shall receive the fee prescribed in IC 36-2-7-10.

(c) If the amount of a lien has been satisfied or paid and subsequently a demand for a release of the lien is made, the lienholder is liable to the person, firm, limited liability company, or corporation against whose interest the lien has been filed for ten dollars ($10) for each day that the lien remains in effect after the fifteenth day after the demand for a release of the lien was made.

(d) The operator of the releasing hospital shall mail a copy of the release of lien certificate required under subsection (a) to the department of insurance within ten (10) days after the certificate was filed with the recorder. [P.L.2-2002, § 18.]

32-33-4-8. Personal injury claims — Hospital without right to determine liability or approve settlement. — This chapter does not give any hospital a right:
(1) of action to determine liability; or
(2) to approve a compromise or settlement;
for injuries sustained by any person covered by this chapter. [P.L.2-2002, § 18.]

NOTES TO DECISIONS

Interest of Lienholder.
The former hospital lien statute did not provide subrogation rights to hospitals, but rather a specific interest in property otherwise accruing to the patient for the amount of the treatment rendered by the hospital. With a properly perfected lien, the hospital had a direct right in the insurance proceeds and other settlement funds paid to the patient by the person claimed to be liable for the patient's injuries. National Ins. Ass'n v. Parkview Mem. Hosp., 590 N.E.2d 1141 (Ind. App. 1992).

Collateral References. Construction, operation, and effect of statute giving hospital lien against recovery from tortfeasor causing patient's injuries. 16 A.L.R.5th 262.

CHAPTER 5

AMBULANCE LIENS

32-33-5-1. "Emergency ambulance services" defined. — As used in this chapter, "emergency ambulance services" has the meaning set forth in IC 16-18-2-107. [P.L.2-2002, § 18.]

Effective Dates. P.L.2-2002, § 18. July 1.
2002.

32-33-5-2. "Provider" defined. — As used in this chapter, "provider" means a provider of emergency ambulance services other than a hospital. [P.L.2-2002, § 18.]

32-33-5-3. Lien for provision of emergency ambulance services — Applicability. — (a) A provider has a lien for all reasonable and necessary charges for the provision of emergency ambulance services to a patient upon any cause of action, suit, or claim accruing to the patient, or in the case of the patient's death, the patient's legal representative, because of the illness or injuries that:

(1) gave rise to the cause of action, suit, or claim; and

(2) necessitated the provision of emergency ambulance services.

(b) The lien:

(1) applies to any amount obtained or recovered by the patient by settlement or compromise rendered or entered into by the patient or by the patient's legal representative;

(2) is subject and subordinate to any attorney's lien upon the claim or cause of action; and

(3) is not applicable to accidents or injuries within the purview of:

(A) IC 22-3;

(B) 5 U.S.C. 8101 et seq.; or

(C) 45 U.S.C. 51 et seq.

[P.L.2-2002, § 18.]

32-33-5-4. Perfection — Verified written statement — Notice — Motion to quash. — (a) To perfect a lien under this chapter, the provider must file in the office of the recorder of the county, within sixty (60) days after the provision of services, a verified statement in writing that includes the following:

(1) The name and address of the patient.

(2) The name and address of the provider.

(3) The date services were provided.

(4) The amount claimed to be due.

(5) To the best of the provider's knowledge, the names and addresses of anyone claimed by the patient or by the patient's legal representative to be liable for damages arising from the illness or injury.

(b) Within ten (10) days after filing the statement, the provider shall send a copy by registered mail, postage prepaid:

(1) to each person claimed to be liable because of the illness or injury at the address given in the statement; and

(2) to the attorney representing the patient if the name of the attorney is known or with reasonable diligence could be discovered by the provider.

(c) The filing of a claim under subsection (a) is notice to any person, firm, limited liability company, or corporation that may be liable because of the illness or injury, if the person, firm, limited liability company, or corporation:

(1) receives notice under subsection (b); or

(2) resides or has offices in a county where the lien was perfected or in a county where the lien was filed in the recorder's office as notice under this subsection.

(d) A person desiring to contest a lien or the reasonableness of the charges claimed by the provider may do so by filing a motion to quash or reduce the claim in the circuit court in which the lien was perfected, making all other parties of interest respondents. [P.L.2-2002, § 18.]

32-33-5-5. Endorsement of statement — Fee for filing. — (a) The recorder shall endorse on the statement filed under section 4 [IC 32-33-5-4] of this chapter the date and hour of filing.

(b) The recorder shall charge a fee for filing the statement in accordance with the fee schedule established in IC 36-2-7-10. [P.L.2-2002, § 18.]

32-33-5-6. Validity — Release — Satisfaction — Jurisdiction — Venue. — (a) A lien perfected under section 4 [IC 32-33-5-4] of this chapter is valid unless the lienholder executes a release of the lien under section 7 [IC 32-33-5-7] of this chapter.

(b) The release or settlement of a claim with a patient by a person claimed to be liable for the damages incurred by the patient:

(1) after a lien has been perfected under section 4 of this chapter; and

(2) without obtaining a release of the lien;

entitles the lienholder to damages for the reasonable cost of the services provided.

(c) Satisfaction of a judgment rendered in favor of the lienholder under subsection (b) is satisfaction of the lien.

(d) An action by the lienholder shall be brought in the court having jurisdiction of the amount of the lienholder's claim and may be brought and maintained in the county of residence of the lienholder. [P.L.2-2002, § 18.]

32-33-5-7. Release — Recordation of release — Liability for failure to release after demand. — (a) To release a lien perfected under section 4 [IC 32-33-5-4] of this chapter, the provider to whom the lien has been paid must file with the recorder in whose office the notice of the lien was filed an executed certificate:

(1) stating that the claim filed by the provider for the provision of emergency ambulance services has been paid or discharged; and

(2) authorizing the recorder to release the lien.

The provider shall bear the expense of obtaining a release.

(b) Upon receipt of the certificate, the recorder shall enter in the margin of the record of the lien and the entry book a memorandum of the filing and the date the certificate was filed. This entry constitutes a release of lien for which the recorder shall receive the fee prescribed in IC 36-2-7-10.

(c) If the amount of a lien has been satisfied or paid and subsequently a demand for a release of the lien is made, the lienholder is liable to the person, firm, limited liability company, or corporation against whose interest the lien has been filed for ten dollars ($10) for each day that the lien remains in effect after the fifteenth day after the demand for a release of the lien was made. [P.L.2-2002, § 18.]

32-33-5-8. Personal injury claims — Provider without right to determine liability or approve settlement. — This chapter does not give any provider a right:

(1) of action to determine liability; or

(2) to approve a compromise or settlement;

for injuries sustained by any person covered by this chapter. [P.L.2-2002, § 18.]

CHAPTER 6

INNKEEPER'S LIENS

32-33-6-1. Lien on luggage or other articles of value — Sale — Residue of proceeds — Deposit of residue with county treasurer — Sale as bar to action — Balance due. — (a) The owner or keeper of any hotel, inn, boardinghouse, eating facility, lodging house, or restaurant has a lien upon any trunk, valise or baggage, or other article of value brought into the hotel, inn, boardinghouse, eating facility, lodging house, or restaurant by a person for any and all proper charges due from the person for food, lodging, entertainment, or other accommodation.

(b) The owner or keeper referred to in subsection (a) may detain the trunk, valise or baggage, or other articles of value until the amount of the charge is fully paid. If the charges are not paid within sixty (60) days after the charges accrued, the owner or keeper may sell the trunk, valise or baggage, or other article of value at public auction after giving ten (10) days notice of the time and place of the sale by publication of notice in a newspaper of general circulation in the county in which the hotel, inn, boardinghouse, eating facility, lodging house, or restaurant is situated. In addition, the owner or keeper must at least ten (10) days before the sale mail a copy of the notice addressed to the person at:

(1) the person's post office address if known to the owner or keeper; or

(2) the address registered by the person with the owner or keeper if the owner or keeper is required to keep a register under IC 16-41-29.

(c) After satisfying the lien out of the proceeds of a sale under this section together with any costs that may have been incurred in enforcing the lien, the residue of the proceeds of the sale, if any, must be paid on demand by the owner or keeper to the person not more than six (6) months after the sale. If the residue is not demanded within six (6) months after the date of the sale, the residue or remainder shall be deposited by the owner or keeper with the county treasurer of the county in which the hotel, inn, boardinghouse, eating facility, lodging house, or restaurant is situated, together with a statement of:

(1) the owner's or keeper's claim;

(2) the amount of costs incurred in enforcing the lien;

(3) a copy of the published notice; and

(4) the amount received from the sale of the trunk, valise or baggage, or other article of value sold at the sale.

(d) The residue deposited under subsection (c) shall be accredited to the general revenue funds of the county by the county treasurer subject to the right of the person or the person's representatives to reclaim the residue at any time within three (3) years after the date of the deposit with the county treasurer.

(e) A sale under this section is a bar to any action against the owner or keeper for the recovery of the trunk, valise or baggage, or other article of value or of the value of the trunk, valise or baggage, or other article of value, or for any damage growing out of the failure of the person to receive the trunk, valise or baggage, or other article of value.

(f) However, if the proceeds of a sale after deducting any costs that may have been incurred in enforcing the lien are not sufficient to discharge the owner's or keeper's charges, the balance remains due and owing, and the owner or keeper may commence an action at law against the person for any balance due. [P.L.2-2002, § 18.]

Effective Dates. P.L.2-2002, § 18. July 1. 2002.

NOTES TO DECISIONS

ANALYSIS

In general.
Constitutionality.
Indictment.

In General.
The enactment of the former Employees' Lien statute by implication abrogated the common law lien in favor of innkeepers in Indiana, so that an innkeeper had no lien on a piano and stool in the possession of a guest which was not owned by said guest. Nicholas v. Baldwin Piano Co., 71 Ind. App. 209, 123 N.E. 226 (1919).

Constitutionality.
The Fourteenth Amendment limits only governmental action, and the detention of plaintiffs' personal property by the operators of a mobile home park who acted under the authority of the Indiana innkeepers lien, as applied to mobile homes, former IC 13-1-7-33, did not constitute state action. Jenner v. Shepherd, 665 F. Supp. 714 (S.D. Ind. 1987).

Indictment.
In charging the removal of baggage for the purpose of defrauding a hotel or boarding-house keeper, it did not need to have been alleged that such removal was with the intent to commit such fraud. State v. Engle, 156 Ind. 339, 58 N.E. 698 (1900).

CHAPTER 7

LIABILITY OF HOTELS FOR LOSS OF PROPERTY OF GUESTS

32-33-7-1. "Guest" defined. — As used in this chapter, "guest" includes a transient guest, permanent guest, tenant, lodger, or boarder. [P.L.2-2002, § 18.]

Effective Dates. P.L.2-2002, § 18. July 1. 2002.

32-33-7-2. Safe provided for valuables — Liability for loss — Dollar limit — Assumption of liability in writing. — If:

    (1) the proprietor or manager of a hotel, an apartment hotel, or an inn provides a safe in a convenient place for the safekeeping of any money, jewels, ornaments, furs, bank notes, bonds, negotiable security, or other valuable papers, precious stones, railroad tickets, articles of silver or gold, or other valuable property of small compass belonging to or brought in by the guests of the hotel, apartment hotel, or inn;

    (2) the proprietor or manager notifies the guests by posting in a public and conspicuous place and manner at the place of registration of the hotel, apartment hotel, or inn or in each guest room a notice stating that a safe place is provided in which the articles may be deposited; and

    (3) the guest neglects or fails to deliver the guest's property to the person in charge of the office for deposit in the safe;

the hotel, apartment hotel, or inn and proprietor or manager are not liable for any loss of or damage to the property sustained by the guest or other owner of the property, whether the loss or damage is occasioned by the neglect of the proprietor or manager or of the proprietor's or manager's agents or otherwise.

    (b) If a guest delivers property to the person in charge of the office for deposit in a safe, the hotel, apartment hotel, or inn and its manager or proprietor are not liable for the loss or damage of the property sustained by the guest or other owner of the property in any amount exceeding six hundred dollars ($600), whether the loss or damage is occasioned by the negligence of the proprietor or manager or by the proprietor's or manager's agents or otherwise, notwithstanding that the property may be of greater value, unless the proprietor or manager has entered into a special agreement in writing agreeing to assume additional liability. [P.L.2-2002, § 18.]

Compiler's Notes. As enacted by P.L.2-2002, § 18, this section contained a subsection designation (b) but no subsection designation (a).

NOTES TO DECISIONS

ANALYSIS

Applicability.

Guest construed.

Applicability.

A band member's claims for damages for stolen band instruments was not governed by this section where the band equipment was not brought onto the premises as a consequence of any guest or quasi-guest capacity of members of the band, but for the performance of contractual services for the hotel, and the equipment was in the lounge stage area, not in band members' rooms or in their vehicles. Rambend Realty Corp. v. Backstreets Band, 482 N.E.2d 741 (Ind. App. 1985).

Guest Construed.

"Guest," as used in the context of the former version of this section, ordinarily referred to one who was a paying patron of the inn or hotel, and denoted one who was staying at the inn for his own purposes as opposed to the

Guest Construed. (Cont'd)
business purposes of the inn. Rambend Realty

Corp. v. Backstreets Band, 482 N.E.2d 741 (Ind. App. 1985).

Collateral References. 40 Am. Jur. 2d Hotels, Motels and Restaurants, §§ 126-130.

43A C.J.S. Inns, Hotels and Eating Places, §§ 13, 20, 36-48.

Liability of hotel, motel, summer resort, or private membership club or association operating swimming pool, for injury or death of guest or member, or of member's guest. 1 A.L.R.3d 963.

Statutory limitations upon innkeeper's liability as applicable where guest's property is lost or damaged through innkeeper's negligence. 37 A.L.R.3d 1276.

Liability for negligence of doorman or similar attendant in parking patron's automobile. 41 A.L.R.3d 1055.

32-33-7-3. Limitation of liability — Dollar limit — Assumption of greater liability. — Except as provided in section 2 [IC 32-33-7-2] of this chapter, the hotel, apartment hotel, or inn and its proprietor or manager are not liable for the loss of or damage to personal property, other than merchandise samples or merchandise for sale, brought into the hotel, apartment hotel, or inn by any guest, exceeding two hundred dollars ($200) in value, whether the loss or damage is occasioned by the negligence of the proprietor or manager or the proprietor's or manager's agents or otherwise, unless the manager or proprietor has contracted in writing to assume greater liability. This limitation of liability also applies with respect to the liability for the safekeeping of any luggage or other personal property left in any hotel, apartment hotel, or inn to be checked in any checkroom operated by the hotel, apartment hotel, or inn, whether the luggage or other personal property is brought in by and belongs to a guest or belongs to a person who is not a guest. [P.L.2-2002, § 18.]

NOTES TO DECISIONS

ANALYSIS

Applicability.
Guest construed.
Moving van.

Applicability.
A band member's claims for damages for stolen band instruments was not governed by the former version of this section where the band equipment was not brought onto the premises as a consequence of any guest or quasi-guest capacity of members of the band, but for the performance of contractual services for the hotel, and the equipment was in the lounge stage area, not in band members' rooms or in their vehicles. Rambend Realty Corp. v. Backstreets Band, 482 N.E.2d 741 (Ind. App. 1985).

Guest Construed.
"Guest," as used in the context of the former version of this section, ordinarily refered to one who was a paying patron of the inn or hotel, and denoted one who was staying at the inn for his own purposes as opposed to the business purposes of the inn. Rambend Realty Corp. v. Backstreets Band, 482 N.E.2d 741 (Ind. App. 1985).

Moving Van.
A motel guest's moving van and its contents parked in an outside parking lot were not subject to the former version of this section. Plant v. Howard Johnson's Motor Lodge, 500 N.E.2d 1271 (Ind. App. 1986).

32-33-7-4. Liability for merchandise samples or merchandise for sale. — A hotel, an apartment hotel, or an inn and its proprietor or manager are not liable for the loss of or damage to any merchandise samples or

merchandise for sale, whether the loss or damage is occasioned by the negligence of the proprietor or manager or the proprietor's or manager's agents or otherwise, unless:

    (1) the guest or other owner has given prior written notice of having brought the merchandise into the hotel and of the value of the merchandise; and

    (2) the receipt of the notice has been acknowledged in writing by the proprietor, manager, or other agent.

However, the liability of the hotel, apartment hotel, inn, or the proprietor or manager may not exceed four hundred dollars ($400) unless the manager or proprietor of the hotel, apartment hotel, or inn has contracted in writing to assume a greater liability. [P.L.2-2002, § 18.]

NOTES TO DECISIONS

Analysis

In general.
Notice to hotel.

In General.
   Where jewelry salesman turned in bags of jewelry samples which were placed in the manager's office when he was checking into the hotel but he remained silent as to the contents or the value of such bags, and such jewelry samples were missing upon presentation of his claim stub the following morning, the only remedy of such salesman was under the statute limiting liability to $400 for merchandise samples lost by the negligence of the manager of the hotel and that liability only existed after written notice had been given and no greater liability existed unless upon agreement between the hotel patron and manager, therefore no recovery could have

been had for the value of the jewelry. Eichberg & Co. v. Van Orman Ft. Wayne Corp., 248 F.2d 758 (7th Cir. 1957), cert. denied, 356 U.S. 927, 78 S. Ct. 716, 2 L. Ed. 2d 759 (1958).

Notice to Hotel.
   Sufficient notice under the Indiana Innkeepers Statute requires more than the mere statement that merchandise is being brought into a hotel or inn. Numismatic Enters. v. Hyatt Corp., 797 F. Supp. 687 (S.D. Ind. 1992).

   A safe deposit record could not be construed as sufficient notice under the Indiana Innkeepers Statute because it did not inform the hotel of the fact that the plaintiffs were bringing their merchandise into the hotel or the estimated value thereof. Numismatic Enters. v. Hyatt Corp., 797 F. Supp. 687 (S.D. Ind. 1992).

32-33-7-5. Liability after guest has departed. — In case of loss or damage to any property left by a guest after the guest has departed from any hotel, apartment hotel, or inn and ceased to be a guest, the liability of the proprietor is that of "gratuitous bailee" and may not exceed one hundred dollars ($100). [P.L.2-2002, § 18.]

   Cross References. Sale of unclaimed articles by hotel, IC 32-34-2-1.

32-33-7-6. Liability for property in transit. — In case of loss of or damage to any property while in transit to or from any hotel, apartment hotel, or inn on behalf of a guest, the liability of the proprietor is limited to two hundred dollars ($200), whether the loss or damage is occasioned by the negligence of the proprietor or the proprietor's agents or otherwise, unless:

    (1) the guest has given prior written notice of the value of the property; and

    (2) the receipt of the notice has been acknowledged in writing by the proprietor, manager, or other agent.

However, the liability of the hotel, apartment hotel, or inn may not exceed four hundred dollars ($400), unless the proprietor has contracted in writing to assume a greater liability. [P.L.2-2002, § 18.]

Collateral References. Liability of hotel, motel, or similar establishment for damage to or loss of guest's automobile left on premises. 52 A.L.R.3d 433.

CHAPTER 8
LIVESTOCK CARE AND FEEDING LIENS

SECTION.
32-33-8-1. Lien — Rights and remedies.

32-33-8-1. Lien — Rights and remedies. — The keeper of a livery stable or a person engaged in feeding horses, cattle, hogs, and other livestock:

(1) has a lien upon the livestock for the feed and care bestowed by the keeper upon the livestock; and

(2) has the same rights and remedies as are provided for those persons having, before July 24, 1853, by law, a lien under IC 32-33-9. [P.L.2-2002, § 18.]

Effective Dates. P.L.2-2002, § 18. July 1. 2002.

NOTES TO DECISIONS

ANALYSIS

Loss of possession.
Notice of sale.
Priorities.
Scope of lien.
When lien attaches.
Who entitled to lien.

Loss of Possession.

Temporary removal of animals from the possession of the keeper did not affect his right to a lien. Walls v. Long, 2 Ind. App. 202, 28 N.E. 101 (1891).

If a liveryman had a lien on animals for care and feed, his lien was lost when he parted with the possession of the animals, and he could not transfer such lien and possession to another person. Glascock v. Lemp, 26 Ind. App. 175, 59 N.E. 342 (1901); Reardon v. Higgins, 39 Ind. App. 363, 79 N.E. 208 (1906).

Notice of Sale.

Notice of the time and place of the sale of property by a liveryman to satisfy his lien was required by statute and notice that a sale would be made "on the ___ day of ___, 1877," was not a notice of the time and place of sale. Shappendocia v. Spencer, 73 Ind. 128 (1880).

Priorities.

The lien created by this section was subordinate to a prior recorded mortgage. Hanch v. Ripley, 127 Ind. 151, 26 N.E. 70, 11 L.R.A. 61 (1890).

The lien for feeding and caring for a colt after the execution of a mortgage thereon was superior to the lien of the mortgage where the mortgagee had notice that the colt was placed in the agister's hands for more than a year for care. Woodard v. Myers, 15 Ind. App. 42, 43 N.E. 573 (1896).

Scope of Lien.

Grower payments based on age and appearance of chicken pullets to be paid not later than 21 days after the pullets were removed were not part of the lien under the former version of this section. Yoder Feed Serv. v. Allied Pullets, Inc., 171 Ind. App. 692, 56 Ind. Dec. 122, 359 N.E.2d 602 (1977).

The lien granted to livery stable keepers and others caring for livestock stands, regardless of the bailee's reliance or nonreliance upon the provisions of former IC 32-8-30-9, which required a bailee to issue a receipt stating that the property might "be sold for charges." Stookey Holsteins, Inc. v. Van Voorst, 117 Bankr. 402 (Bankr. N.D. Ind. 1989).

When Lien Attaches.

Liens on animals attached from the time the care and feed was furnished. Walls v. Long, 2 Ind. App. 202, 28 N.E. 101 (1891).

Who Entitled to Lien.

The former section applied only to persons who were engaged in the business of feeding animals. Conklin v. Carver, 19 Ind. 226 (1862).

Keepers of livery stables had a lien on animals left with them, for their care and feed. Adams Express Co. v. Black, 62 Ind. 128 (1878); Shappendocia v. Spencer, 73 Ind. 128 (1880); Walls v. Long, 2 Ind. App. 202, 28 N.E. 101 (1891).

Where keeper refused offer of approximate amount of feed bill and refused to release pullets without payment of a substantially larger amount, he lost his lien and acted illegally in refusing to release pullets. Yoder Feed Serv. v. Allied Pullets, Inc., 171 Ind. App. 692, 56 Ind. Dec. 122, 359 N.E.2d 602 (1977).

Collateral References. 38 Am. Jur. 2d Garages and Filling and Parking Stations, §§ 138-152.

3A C.J.S. Animals, §§ 348.1-348.6.

CHAPTER 9

MECHANIC'S AND TRADESMAN'S LIENS

32-33-9-1. Sale. — If a person entrusts to a mechanic or tradesman materials to construct, alter, or repair an article of value, the mechanic or tradesman, if the construction, alteration, or repair is completed and not taken away and the mechanic's or tradesman's fair and reasonable charges not paid, may, after sixty (60) days after the charges became due:

(1) sell the article of value; or

(2) if the article of value is susceptible of division, without injury, may sell as much of the article of value as is necessary to pay the charges. [P.L.2-2002, § 18.]

Effective Dates. P.L.2-2002, § 18. July 1. 2002.

Cross References. Lien for repair of motor vehicles, IC 32-33-10-5 — IC 32-33-10-10.

NOTES TO DECISIONS

ANALYSIS

In general.
Credit given for charges.
Mill owners.
Priorities.
Surrender of possession.

In General.

When property was delivered by one person to another for the purpose of having work done thereon, the person doing such work usually had a lien on the property for his charges. Hanna v. Phelps, 7 Ind. 21, 63 Am. Dec. 410 (1855); East v. Ferguson, 59 Ind. 169 (1877); Shaw v. Ferguson, 78 Ind. 547 (1881); Holderman v. Manier, 104 Ind. 118, 3 N.E. 811 (1885); Watts v. Sweeney, 127 Ind. 116, 26 N.E. 680, 22 Am. St. 615 (1891).

The former section was not applicable to property left in pledge. Rosenzweig v. Frazer, 82 Ind. 342 (1881).

The former section did not declare a lien, but provided for enforcing a lien given by the common law. Watts v. Sweeney, 127 Ind. 116, 26 N.E. 680, 22 Am. St. 615 (1891).

It would seem that the common law lien of a mechanic for repairing motor vehicles has

In General. (Cont'd)

been superseded by the law creating a statutory lien thereon. See Burns' § 43-801 et seq. (since repealed and replaced by IC 32-8-31-1 et seq.). Nicholas v. Baldwin Piano Co., 71 Ind. App. 209, 123 N.E. 226 (1919).

In Indiana the common law artisan's lien has been bolstered by statutes, such as this chapter, which provide various rights and remedies to the artisan's lienholder. This fact alone, however, does not foreclose a bailee from relying upon the rights and remedies provided at common law to enforce his artisan's lien. (Decided under former IC 32-8-30.) Midwest Commerce Banking Co. v. Stookey Holsteins, Inc., 112 Bankr. 942 (Bankr. N.D. Ind. 1990).

Credit Given for Charges.

If a credit was given for the charges of the mechanic beyond the time when the chattel was to have been returned to the owner, then no lien existed. Tucker v. Taylor, 53 Ind. 93 (1876).

Mill Owners.

Mill owners had a lien for their charges on lumber sawed by them, and could enforce such lien against any lumber remaining in their possession for any balance due for sawing a larger lot of lumber. Bierly v. Royse, 25 Ind. App. 202, 57 N.E. 939 (1900).

Priorities.

Liens of execution on chattels left with mechanics for repairs were superior to the mechanic's lien. McCrisaken v. Osweiler, 70 Ind. 131 (1880).

Mortgage lien was inferior to that of the mechanic, subsequently acquired, when by the very nature of things, the repairs would have been anticipated as becoming necessary. Watts v. Sweeney, 127 Ind. 116, 26 N.E. 680, 22 Am. St. 615 (1891).

The claims of employees in factories for wages were first and preferred liens on the personal property in such factories. Rexing v. Princeton Window Glass Co., 51 Ind. App. 124, 94 N.E. 1031 (1911).

Surrender of Possession.

A voluntary surrender of possession by the mechanic of the property to the owner was a wiaver of the lien. Tucker v. Taylor, 53 Ind. 93 (1876); Holderman v. Manier, 104 Ind. 118, 3 N.E. 811 (1885); Welker v. Appleman, 44 Ind. App. 699, 90 N.E. 35 (1909).

A temporary surrender of possession of the property, without any intention of waiving the lien, was not a waiver of the lien. Walls v. Long, 2 Ind. App. 202, 28 N.E. 101 (1891); Welker v. Appleman, 44 App. 699, 90 N.E. 35 (1909).

Collateral References. 53 Am. Jur. 2d Mechanics' Liens, §§ 28-48.

56 C.J.S. Mechanics' Liens, §§ 2-19.

Bailee's lien for work on goods as extending to other goods of the bailor in his possession. 25 A.L.R.2d 1037.

Priority as between lien for repairs and the

like, and right of seller under conditional sales contract. 36 A.L.R.2d 198.

Priority as between artisan's lien and chattel mortgage. 36 A.L.R.2d 229.

Priority as between mechanic's lien and purchase-money mortgage. 73 A.L.R.2d 1407.

32-33-9-2. Notice of sale. — Before a sale under section 1 [IC 32-33-9-1] of this chapter, the mechanic or tradesman must give notice of the amount due and the time and place of the sale by mailing a certified or registered letter, return receipt requested, to the last known address of the entrusting person or owner at least thirty (30) days before the date of the sale. [P.L.2-2002, § 18.]

NOTES TO DECISIONS

In General.

Under a prior similar provision, if the value was $10.00 or more, the notice had to be published in a county newpaper, as provided in the statute. Shappendocia v. Spencer, 73 Ind. 128 (1880).

When the sale was regular, the purchaser obtained a complete title to the property. Watts v. Sweeney, 127 Ind. 116, 26 N.E. 680, 22 Am. St. 615 (1891).

32-33-9-3. Proceeds of sale. — (a) The proceeds of a sale that takes place under section 1 [IC 32-33-9-1] of this chapter, after payment of charges for construction or repair and for giving notice by registered or certified mail, shall be:

    (1) returned to the entrusting person or owner if the identity and mailing address of the entrusting person or owner are known; or

    (2) deposited with the treasurer of the county in which the construction or repair work was performed.

  (b) If the entrusting person or owner does not:

    (1) claim the article within the thirty (30) days before the date of the sale;

    (2) pay for the construction, alteration, or repair; and

    (3) provide reimbursement for the expenses of notification;

the mechanic or tradesman may proceed with the sale according to the terms of the notice. [P.L.2-2002, § 18.]

32-33-9-4. Applicability. — Except as provided in section 5 [IC 32-33-9-5] of this chapter, this chapter applies to all cases of personal property on which the bailee or keeper has, by law, a lien for any feed or care by the bailee or keeper provided on the property. However, in cases where the person liable dies before the expiration of sixty (60) days after the charges accrued, the sale may not be made until at least sixty (60) days after the date of the person's death. [P.L.2-2002, § 18.]

NOTES TO DECISIONS

Factors.
Factors had liens on property consigned to them for their charges and advances, and could retain the same out of the proceeds of sale. Mooney v. Musser, 45 Ind. 115 (1873); Shaw v. Ferguson, 78 Ind. 547 (1881).

Collateral References. Bailee's duty to insure bailed property. 28 A.L.R.3d 513.

32-33-9-5. Property of a perishable nature — Sale date. — For personal property described in section 4 [IC 32-33-9-4] of this chapter, if the property bailed or kept is:

    (1) horses;

    (2) cattle;

    (3) hogs;

    (4) other livestock; or

    (5) other property covered in this chapter that is of a perishable nature and will be greatly injured by delay;

the person to whom the charges may be due may, after the expiration of thirty (30) days after the charges become due, proceed to dispose of as much of the property as may be necessary, as provided in this chapter. [P.L.2-2002, § 18.]

32-33-9-6. Additional compensation for keeping and care of property. — Additional compensation for keeping and taking care of property referred to in section 5 [IC 32-33-9-5] of this chapter, if necessarily incurred, may be taken from the proceeds of sale under section 5 of this chapter as part of the charges. [P.L.2-2002, § 18.]

32-33-9-7. Forwarding and commission merchant — Public auction. — A forwarding and commission merchant having a lien upon goods that may have remained in store for at least one (1) year may proceed to advertise and sell at public auction as much of the goods as may be necessary to pay the amount of the lien and expenses, according to the provisions of this chapter. [P.L.2-2002, § 18.]

NOTES TO DECISIONS

In General.
Property left for storage was subject to a lien of the keeper for his charges. Pribble v. Kent, 10 Ind. 325, 71 Am. Dec. 327 (1858).

32-33-9-8. Exclusive trademark. — All mechanics, tradesmen, or bailees taking advantage of this chapter, at the time of the entrusting, must issue a receipt to the person entrusting the article to them. The receipt must conspicuously state, "All articles left on the premises after work is completed may be sold for charges.". [P.L.2-2002, § 18.]

NOTES TO DECISIONS

ANALYSIS

Common law lien.
Scope of lien.

Common Law Lien.
The former version of this section did not purport to require all bailees to issue receipts to their bailors; it only required those bailees taking advantage of the provisions of this chapter to issue such receipts. The section did not preclude a bailee from asserting a common law lien if he had not issued a receipt to the bailor upon entrustment and had not taken advantage of the provisions of the former version of this chapter in enforcing his lien. Midwest Commerce Banking Co. v. Stookey Holsteins, Inc., 112 Bankr. 942 (Bankr. N.D. Ind. 1990).

Scope of Lien.
The lien granted under former IC 32-8-29-1 to livery stable keepers and others caring for livestock stood, regardless of the bailee's reliance or nonreliance upon the provisions of this section. Stookey Holsteins, Inc. v. Van Voorst, 117 Bankr. 402 (Bankr. N.D. Ind. 1989).

CHAPTER 10

MOTOR VEHICLES LIEN FOR REPAIR, STORAGE, SERVICE, AND SUPPLIES FOR CERTAIN MOTOR VEHICLES AND EQUIPMENT

32-33-10-1. "Construction machinery and repair" defined. — As used in this chapter, "construction machinery and equipment" includes all classes and types of machinery and equipment used in road construction, road maintenance, earth moving, and building construction work. [P.L.2-2002, § 18.]

Effective Dates. P.L.2-2002, § 18. July 1. 2002.

32-33-10-2. "Farm machinery" defined. — As used in this chapter, "farm machinery" means all types of tractors, implements, and machinery used in the operation and maintenance of farms. [P.L.2-2002, § 18.]

32-33-10-3. "Motor vehicle" defined. — (a) As used in this chapter, "motor vehicle" means every vehicle and device in, upon, or by which persons or property is, or may be, moved, transported, or drawn upon public highways.
(b) The term includes:
(1) self-propelled vehicles; and
(2) vehicles and devices drawn or propelled by other vehicles, devices, trucks, and tractors. [P.L.2-2002, § 18.]

32-33-10-4. "Person" defined. — As used in this chapter, "person" includes a natural person, a firm, a copartnership, an association, a limited liability company, and a corporation. [P.L.2-2002, § 18.]

NOTES TO DECISIONS

In General.
An employee lien under former IC 32-8-24-1 (repealed) was closely analogous to a nonpossessory mechanics lien under former IC 32-8-31-2 (repealed; see this section for similar provisions): both liens protected those who furnished labor or services to the entity that owned the property subject to the lien, and the filing requirements for the two types of liens were identical. Ameritrust Nat'l Bank v. Domore Corp., 147 Bankr. 473 (N.D. Ind. 1992).

32-33-10-5. Lien. — A person engaged in:
(1) repairing, storing, servicing, or furnishing supplies or accessories for motor vehicles, airplanes, construction machinery and equipment, and farm machinery; or
(2) maintaining a motor vehicle garage, an airport or repair shop for airplanes, or a repair shop or servicing facilities for construction machinery and equipment and farm machinery;
has a lien on any motor vehicle or airplane or any unit of construction machinery and equipment or farm machinery stored, repaired, serviced, or maintained for the person's reasonable charges for the repair work, storage, or service, including reasonable charges for labor, for the use of tools, machinery, and equipment, and for all accessories, materials, gasoline, oils, lubricants, and other supplies furnished in connection with the repair, storage, servicing, or maintenance of the motor vehicle, airplane, unit of construction machinery and equipment, or farm machinery. [P.L.2-2002, § 18.]

Indiana Law Journal. Certificate of Title as Notice of Liens Upon Motor Vehicles, 25 Ind. L.J. 316, 348.

NOTES TO DECISIONS

ANALYSIS

In general.
Constitutionality.
Common law lien.
—In general.
—Legislative intent.
—Statute required.
Conditional vendee.
—Priority.
Lien not acquired.
Priorities.

In General.

In an action to replevin an automobile truck wherein defendant in his cross complaint claimed a lien for repairs and supplies, a fact alleged in the cross complaint could properly have been considered in connection with the evidence in determining the character of supplies furnished by defendant for the truck and entering into the amount of his alleged lien. Partlow-Jenkins Motor Car Co. v. Stratton, 71 Ind. App. 122, 124 N.E. 470 (1919).

One who stored an automobile at the request of the mortgagee in possession thereof, and gave statutory notice, had a lien for the storage. Hoosier Fin. Co. v. Campbell, 86 Ind. App. 62, 155 N.E. 836 (1927).

In an action to recover possession of an automobile held by mechanic to secure payment for repairs, who filed notice of mechanic's lien, the evidence was held not to sustain verdict in favor of the owner of the automobile. Hueseman v. Neaman, 97 Ind. App. 586, 187 N.E. 696 (1933).

Constitutionality.

Enforcement of a mechanic's lien for repairs to a motor vehicle under this section, under former IC 9-9-5-6, or under common law was not state action so as to invoke the due process clause of the Fourteenth Amendment. Phillips v. Money, 503 F.2d 990 (7th Cir. 1974), cert. denied, 420 U.S. 934, 95 S. Ct. 1141, 43 L. Ed. 2d 409 (1975).

Where the voluntary surrender of the motor vehicle to a mechanic for the performance of authorized repairs results in a legal property interest in the mechanic in the form of a lien with actual possession, it is not a violation of due process to allow the mechanic to retain possession and to impose on the car owner the burden of initiating litigation to resolve the dispute. Phillips v. Money, 503 F.2d 990 (7th Cir. 1974), cert. denied, 420 U.S. 934, 95 S. Ct. 1141, 43 L. Ed. 2d 409 (1975).

Common Law Lien.

—In General.

The former sections and former IC 9-9-5-6, pertaining to liens for repairing automobiles, were declaratory of the common law, and provided additional remedies, and there might have been a common law lien for repairing automobiles. Grusin v. Stutz Motor Car Co., 206 Ind. 296, 187 N.E. 382 (1933).

—Legislative Intent.

Nothing in the former version of this section indicates a legislative intent to limit either the garageman's common law remedy or that provided in former IC 9-9-5-6. Hendrickson & Sons Motor Co. v. Osha, 165 Ind. App. 185, 48 Ind. Dec. 83, 331 N.E.2d 743 (1975).

—Statute Required.

Common law liens, such as a garageman's lien, are creatures of statute, and, when there is no express statute authorizing a lien on land, an instrument purporting to do so is void. Terpstra v. F & M Bank, 483 N.E.2d 749 (Ind. App. 1985).

Conditional Vendee.

—Priority.

Where a lien was sought to have been enforced for repairs made on an automobile at the instance of the conditional vendee, without authority of the conditional vendor, if the work done on the machine was not necessary for its preservation, the lien for the repairs did not take priority over the right of the conditional vendor to the property, under a contract of sale requiring the vendee to keep the automobile free from liens, although the contract required the vendee to make all repairs necessary to keep it in first class condition. Atlas Sec. Co. v. Grove, 79 Ind. App. 144, 137 N.E. 570 (1922).

The conditional vendee of an automobile could not, as against the conditional vendor, create a lien for labor thereon or parts furnished and put upon the automobile where the conditional contract of sale provided against such acts of the vendee without the consent of the vendor, and knowledge or consent of the vendor to such repairs was not shown; and this rule applied in favor of the assignee of the vendor, to which assignment the vendee, consented. Madison Remedial Loan Ass'n v. Wells, 79 Ind. App. 266, 137 N.E. 769 (1923).

Lien Not Acquired.

Person who towed vehicle and kept it in storage was entitled to a lien under IC 9-22-5-15 for services rendered, but since he did not file notice of lien with the county recorder, he did not acquire a lien pursuant to this section and was not entitled to attorney's fees under this section. Jones v. Harner, 684 N.E.2d 560 (Ind. App. 1997).

Priorities.

A lien on motor buses for labor and materi-als furnished in repair of said motor buses, under the former sections, was not superior to other liens or to title previously acquired. Bowen v. Kokomo Omnibus Co., 87 Ind. App. 245, 161 N.E. 298 (1928).

Persons furnishing tires and repairs to motor vehicles were not entitled to a lein under the former sections where they did not allege that the owners of the title or of liens previously acquired consented thereto. Bowen v. Kokomo Omnibus Co., 87 Ind. App. 245, 161 N.E. 298 (1928).

Collateral References. 38 Am. Jur. 2d Garages and Filling and Parking Stations, §§ 138-152.

61A C.J.S. Motor Vehicles, §§ 743-759.

Bailee's lien for work on goods as extending to other goods of the bailor in his possession. 25 A.L.R.2d 1037.

Priority as between lien for motor vehicle repairs and the like, and right of seller under conditional sales contract. 36 A.L.R.2d 198.

Priority as between artisan's lien and chattel mortgage on automobile. 36 A.L.R.2d 229.

Priority of lien for storage of motor vehicle. 48 A.L.R.2d 916.

Lien for storage of motor vehicle. 48 A.L.R.2d 894; 85 A.L.R.3d 199.

Lien for towing or storage, ordered by public officer, of motor vehicle. 85 A.L.R.3d 199.

What constitutes use of vehicle "in the automobile business" within exclusionary clause of liability policy. 56 A.L.R.4th 300.

Loss of garageman's lien on repaired vehicle by owner's use of vehicle. 74 A.L.R.4th 90.

32-33-10-6. Filing of notice — Amount claimed — Description — Deadline.

— (a) A person seeking to acquire a lien upon a motor vehicle, an airplane, a unit of construction machinery and equipment, or farm machinery, whether the claim to be secured by the lien is then due or not, must file in the recorder's office of the county where:

(1) the repair, service, or maintenance work was performed; or

(2) the storage, supplies, or accessories were furnished;

a notice in writing of the intention to hold the lien upon the motor vehicle, airplane, unit of construction machinery and equipment, or farm machinery for the amount of the person's claim.

(b) A notice filed under subsection (a) must specifically state the amount claimed and give a substantial description of the motor vehicle, airplane, unit of construction machinery and equipment, or farm machinery upon which the lien is asserted.

(c) Any description in a notice of intention to hold a lien filed under subsection (a) is sufficient if by the description the motor vehicle, airplane, unit of construction machinery and equipment, or farm machinery can be identified.

(d) A notice under subsection (a) must be filed in the recorder's office not later than sixty (60) days after the performance of the work or the furnishing of the storage, supplies, accessories, or materials. [P.L.2-2002, § 18.]

NOTES TO DECISIONS

ANALYSIS

Priority over other liens.
Time for filing.

Priority over Other Liens.

A valid storage lien under former IC 32-8-31-3 would have priority over a perfected security interest. Charlie Eidson's Paint &

Priority over Other Liens. (Cont'd)
Body Shop v. Commercial Credit Plan, Inc., 146 Ind. App. 209, 20 Ind. Dec. 2, 253 N.E.2d 717 (1969).

Time for Filing.
Although automobile repairman did not obtain valid lien for repairs because lien was filed after time provided in former IC 32-8-

31-1, he nevertheless obtained a valid lien for storage when he kept the automobile after failure of the owner to pay the repair bill and take possession and he filed his lien within 60 days after furnishing such storage. Charlie Eidson's Paint & Body Shop v. Commercial Credit Plan, Inc., 146 Ind. App. 209, 20 Ind. Dec. 2, 253 N.E.2d 717 (1969).

32-33-10-7. Manner of recordation — Fee. — (a) The recorder of the county where a notice of intention to hold a lien is filed under section 6 [IC 32-33-10-6] of this chapter shall record the lien in the manner provided by law for the recording of mechanic's liens.

(b) The recorder shall receive a fee in accordance with IC 36-2-7-10 for the recording. [P.L.2-2002, § 18.]

32-33-10-8. Foreclosure — Filing deadline. — (a) A lien provided for in this chapter may be foreclosed, as equitable liens are foreclosed, in the circuit or superior court of the county where the motor vehicle, airplane, unit of construction machinery and equipment, or farm machinery is located.

(b) The complaint for foreclosure of a lien under subsection (a) must be filed not later than one (1) year after the notice of intention to hold the lien is recorded. [P.L.2-2002, § 18.]

NOTES TO DECISIONS

ANALYSIS

Conditional vendee.
Nature of action.

Conditional Vendee.
Where a lien was sought to be foreclosed upon an automobile for repairs made at the instance of the conditional vendee, under a contract of purchase which required the purchaser to make all repairs necessary to keep the automobile in first class condition, and to keep it free from liens, the burden was upon plaintiff to allege and prove that the repairs were necessary to keep the automobile in first class condition, they they were made with the

consent of the conditional vendor, and that conditional vendee was the agent of conditional vendor in having the repairs made. Atlas Sec. Co. v. Grove, 79 Ind. App. 144, 137 N.E. 570 (1922).

Nature of Action.
An action for the foreclosure of a mechanic's lien was of an equitable character and in the nature of a proceeding in rem. The venue of the action was in the county where the equipment was located when the action was commenced. Flesch v. Circle City Excavating & Rental Corp., 137 Ind. App. 695, 6 Ind. Dec. 606, 210 N.E.2d 865 (1965).

Collateral References. Airplane or other aircraft as "motor vehicle" or the like within statute providing for constructive or substituted service of process on nonresident motorist. 36 A.L.R.3d 1387.

Motor scooter as within policy provisions relating to automobiles or motorcycles. 43 A.L.R.3d 1400.

Lien for towing or storage, ordered by public officer, of motor vehicle. 85 A.L.R.3d 199.

32-33-10-9. Attorney's fees. — In a suit brought for the enforcement of a lien under section 8 [IC 32-33-10-8] of this chapter in which the plaintiff recovers judgment in any sum, the plaintiff may also recover reasonable attorney's fees as a part of the judgment in the action. [P.L.2-2002, § 18.]

32-33-10-10. Construction with other law. — This chapter may not be construed to repeal, modify, or amend IC 9-22-5-14 or IC 9-22-5-15. [P.L.2-2002, § 18.]

CHAPTER 11

TRANSFER, MOVING, AND STORAGE LIENS

32-33-11-1. Lien on goods. — A transferman, a drayman, or any other person, firm, limited liability company, or corporation that is engaged in:

(1) packing for shipment or storage; or

(2) transferring, hauling, or conveying from place to place;

goods, merchandise, machines, machinery or other articles of value is entitled to a lien under this chapter for money paid for freight, storage or demurrage charges on the goods, merchandise, machines, machinery or other articles of value or for erecting machines, machinery, stacks or other equipment. The lien is imposed upon the goods, merchandise, machines, machinery, or other articles of value that are packed, hauled, transferred, conveyed, or erected, for charges for the hauling, packing, transferring, conveying, or erecting or for money paid for freight, storage, or demurrage on the goods, merchandise, machines, machinery, or other articles of value. [P.L.2-2002, § 18.]

Effective Dates. P.L.2-2002, § 18. July 1. 2002.

NOTES TO DECISIONS

ANALYSIS

Scope of lien.
Waiver.

Scope of Lien.

Since the former version of this section clearly limited lien to charges directly relating to object transported, party seeking payment of expenses for transport of fork lift could not also demand payment of additional sums due on contracts separate from contract to move fork lift. Tucker v. Capital City Riggers, 437 N.E.2d 1048 (Ind. App. 1982).

Waiver.

Property subject to lien under the former version of this section could not be held hostage for unrelated debts, and an attempt to do so waived the lien. Tucker v. Capital City Riggers, 437 N.E.2d 1048 (Ind. App. 1982).

Collateral References. 78 Am. Jur. 2d Warehouses, §§ 112-126.

93 C.J.S. Warehousemen and Safe Depositories, §§ 63-69.

Validity, construction, and application of state statute giving carrier lien on goods for transportation and incidental storage charges. 45 A.L.R.5th 227.

32-33-11-2. Notice — Amount claimed — Description of property — Agent — Possession during pendency of lien.

— (a) A transferman, drayman, or any other person, firm, limited liability company, or corporation that is engaged in:

(1) packing for shipment or storage; or

(2) transferring, hauling, or conveying from place to place;

goods, merchandise, machinery, machines, or other articles of value and that wishes to acquire a lien on any of this property for money paid for freight, storage, or demurrage charges or for erecting machines, machinery, stacks, or other equipment, whether the claim is due or not, may, at any time within sixty (60) days after performing the labor or the payment of money described in section 1 [IC 32-33-11-1] of this chapter, file in the recorder's office of the county a notice of intention to hold a lien upon the property for the amount of the claim.

(b) The notice filed under subsection (a) must state the amount claimed and provide a substantial description of the property. The description of the property in a notice filed under subsection (a) must be sufficient to identify the property.

(c) The party ordering the work done or charges paid or advanced, shall, for the purpose of enforcing this lien, be considered prima facie the agent of all persons having or claiming any interest in the work done or charges paid or advanced but not a matter of record, if the person has knowledge of the performance of the services or the making of the expenditures.

(d) The lienor may keep possession of the goods during the pendency of the lien or an action on the lien unless otherwise ordered by the court. [P.L.2-2002, § 18.]

NOTES TO DECISIONS

Mandatory Nature of Section.

The language of the former version of this section is mandatory and indicates that compliance with notice requirement is a prereq-uisite to acquisition or creation of lien. Tucker v. Capital City Riggers, 437 N.E.2d 1048 (Ind. App. 1982).

32-33-11-3. Recordation — Fee — Priority.

— (a) The recorder shall record the notice of intention to hold a lien filed under section 2(a) [IC 32-33-11-2(a)] of this chapter, when presented, in the miscellaneous record book. The recorder shall receive fees in accordance with IC 36-2-7-10.

(b) All liens created in this manner:

(1) relate to the date the labor was begun or money advanced; and

(2) have priority over all liens suffered or created after that date. [P.L.2-2002, § 18.]

32-33-11-4. Enforcement of lien — Filing of complaint — Time prescribed — Sale.

— (a) A person that has a lien under this chapter may

enforce the lien by filing the person's complaint in the circuit or superior court of the county in which the lien is filed, at any time within one (1) year after the notice is received for record under section 2(a) [IC 32-33-11-2(a)] of this chapter by the recorder of the county.

(b) If the lien is not enforced within the time prescribed by this section, the lien is void. If the lien is enforced as provided in this chapter, the court rendering judgment shall order the sale to be made, and the officers making the sale shall sell the property without relief whatever from valuation or appraisement laws. [P.L.2-2002, § 18.]

Collateral References. Security, right to require, as condition of canceling lien of record or of recording payment. 2 A.L.R.2d 1064.

Public sale, what constitutes. 4 A.L.R.2d 575.

32-33-11-5. Attorney's fees. — (a) In all suits brought for the enforcement of a lien under the provisions of this chapter, if the plaintiff or lienholder recovers a judgment in any sum, the plaintiff or lienholder may recover reasonable attorney's fees.

(b) Attorney's fees awarded under subsection (a) shall be entered by the court as a part of the judgment in the suit for the enforcement of the lien. [P.L.2-2002, § 18.]

32-33-11-6. Notification in writing — Intention to hold lien — Sale — Notice — Proceeds — Priority — Exclusion of perishable goods. — (a) In addition to the lien provided for in section 1 [IC 32-33-11-1] of this chapter, a person, firm, limited liability company, or corporation that ships, transfers, hauls, or conveys goods, merchandise, machines, machinery, or other articles of value for another person is entitled to a lien:

(1) upon goods, merchandise, machines, machinery, or other articles of value:
(A) shipped;
(B) transferred;
(C) hauled; or
(D) conveyed;
for the other person; and

(2) to cover charges that the other person owes the person, firm, limited liability company, or corporation for goods, merchandise, machines, machinery, or other articles of value previously:
(A) shipped;
(B) transferred;
(C) hauled; or
(D) conveyed;
by the person, firm, limited liability company, or corporation for the other person.

(b) To obtain a lien under this section, a person, firm, limited liability company, or corporation must do the following:

(1) Notify the other person in writing that if the other person fails to pay the person, firm, limited liability company, or corporation for

shipping, transferring, hauling, or conveying goods, merchandise, machines, machinery, or other articles of value, the person, firm, limited liability company, or corporation may obtain a lien upon goods, merchandise, machines, machinery, or other articles of value subsequently:

    (A) shipped;

    (B) transferred;

    (C) hauled; or

    (D) conveyed;

by the person, firm, limited liability company, or corporation for the other person.

(2) File an intention to hold a lien with a county recorder as provided in section 2 [IC 32-33-11-2] of this chapter.

  (c) A sale of property subject to a lien acquired under this section may not take place under section 4 [IC 32-33-11-4] of this chapter:

    (1) for at least thirty-five (35) days after the date the person, firm, limited liability company, or corporation that has obtained the lien takes possession of the property; and

    (2) unless the person, firm, limited liability company, or corporation that has obtained the lien notifies:

      (A) the person that had the property shipped, transferred, hauled, or conveyed;

      (B) the consignee of the property; and

      (C) a secured party that has a perfected security interest in the property;

of the date, time, and location of the sale at least ten (10) days before the date the sale occurs.

  (d) A sale of property subject to a lien acquired under this section may not be concluded if the largest amount bid for the property is not at least equal to the total amount of all outstanding obligations secured by perfected security interests in the property. The proceeds of the sale of property subject to a lien under this section shall be applied as follows:

    (1) First, to a secured party that has a perfected security interest in the property in an amount equal to the amount of the perfected security interest.

    (2) Second, to the discharge of the lien acquired under this section.

    (3) Third, to the legal owner of the property.

If the highest bid for the property does not at least equal the total amount of all outstanding obligations secured by a perfected security interest in the property, the person, firm, limited liability company, or corporation that obtained the lien on the property under this section shall release the property to the legal owner of the property if the legal owner pays the person, firm, limited liability company, or corporation the amount due for shipping, transferring, hauling, or conveying the property that does not include an amount charged for property that the person, firm, limited liability company, or corporation previously shipped, transferred, hauled, or conveyed.

  (e) A person, firm, limited liability company, or corporation that obtains a lien under this section:

(1) is liable to a secured party that has a security interest in property covered by the lien:

   (A) if the person, firm, limited liability company, or corporation violates this section; and

   (B) for damages and expenses, including reasonable attorney's fees, incurred by the secured party in enforcing the secured party's rights; and

(2) is not liable to a consignee of property for damages that the consignee incurs because the person, firm, limited liability company, or corporation obtained a lien on the property under this section.

(f) A perfected security interest in property has priority over a lien obtained under this section.

(g) A lien may not be acquired under this section upon perishable goods. [P.L.2-2002, § 18.]

Collateral References. Validity, construction, and application of state statute giving carrier lien on goods for transportation and incidental storage charges. 45 A.L.R.5th 227.

32-33-11-7. Construction with other law. — This chapter may not be construed as repealing any other law in force on May 31, 1921, concerning liens or the foreclosure of liens. This chapter is intended to be supplemental to all laws in force on May 31, 1921, concerning liens and the foreclosure of liens. [P.L.2-2002, § 18.]

CHAPTER 12
MECHANIZED AGRICULTURAL SERVICES LIEN

32-33-12-1. Amount of lien — Filing of financing statement — Notice — Shifting of lien to purchase price — Attachment — Enforcement. — (a) The owner or operator of a machine or tool used in threshing or hulling grain or seeds or in the plowing, disking, or cultivating of land for the production of crops or in the combining, picking, or baling of crops has a lien upon the grain or seed threshed or hulled with the machine or upon the crops produced or prepared for market or storage by the plowing, disking, cultivating, combining, baling, or picking to secure payment to the owner or operator of the machine or tool by the owner of the crops produced or partially produced by the service, as may be agreed upon.

(b) If the charges for the services referred to in subsection (a) are not agreed upon, the amount of the lien must equal charges that are reasonable for the work.

(c) The owner or operator of the machine must file in the proper place specified in IC 26-1-9.1-501 a financing statement giving notice of the lien. The notice must designate the following:

(1) The name of the person for whom the work was done.

(2) The amount due for the service.

(3) The particular crops covered by the lien.

(4) The place where the crops are located.

(5) The date on which the work was done.

(d) The notice required in subsection (c) must be filed not later than:

(1) thirty (30) days after the completion of the work, if the work was plowing, disking, or cultivating; and

(2) ten (10) days after the completion of the work if the work was combining, baling, or picking.

(e) If the party for whom the work was done desires to sell or deliver the crops, the party must notify the consignee or purchaser that the account for service of the machine has not been paid, and the lien given on the crops shifts from the crops to the purchase price of the crops in the hands of the purchaser or consignee specified.

(f) If the crops are sold or consigned with the consent and knowledge of the party entitled to a lien on the crops, the lien does not attach to the crops or to the purchase price of the crops unless:

(1) the party entitled to the lien personally notifies the purchaser of the lien; and

(2) the sale is made within the ten (10) day period immediately following the date of the performance of the work.

This lien may be enforced as other liens are enforced. [P.L.2-2002, § 18.]

Effective Dates. P.L.2-2002, § 18. July 1. 2002.

Collateral References. 51 Am. Jur. 2d Liens and Encumbrances, § 20.

56 C.J.S. Mechanics' Liens, §§ 30, 31.

32-33-12-2. Attachment — Innocent purchaser or dealer. — A lien provided for in this chapter does not attach to crops in the hands of an innocent purchaser or dealer in the usual course of trade unless all of the notices provided for in section 1 [IC 32-33-12-1] of this chapter have been given. [P.L.2-2002, § 18.]

CHAPTER 13

WATCHMAKER AND JEWELER LIENS

32-33-13-1. Amount of lien. — A person, firm, limited liability company, or corporation engaged in performing work upon any watch, clock, or jewelry for a price has a lien upon the watch, clock, or jewelry upon which the person, firm, limited liability company, or corporation performs the work for the amount of any account that may be due for the work. [P.L.2-2002, § 18.]

Effective Dates. P.L.2-2002, § 18. July 1.
2002.

Collateral References. 51 Am. Jur. 2d
Liens and Encumbrances, §§ 20, 37.
53 C.J.S. Liens, §§ 4-9.

32-33-13-2. Materials — Written notice to owner — Proceeds of sale — Notice. — (a) A lien provided for in section 1 [IC 32-33-13-1] of this chapter includes the value or agreed price, if any, of all materials furnished by the bailees for hire in connection with the work, whether added to the article or otherwise.

(b) If the account remains unpaid for one hundred twenty (120) days after completing the work, the bailees for hire may give written notice to the owner, specifying the amount due and informing the owner that:

(1) the payment of the amount within thirty (30) days will entitle the owner to redeem the property;

(2) if the property is not redeemed within the thirty (30) day period, the bailee for hire may give a second and similar notice; and

(3) if the owner does not redeem the property not later than fifteen (15) days after the second notice is given, the bailee for hire may sell the article at a bona fide public or private sale to satisfy the account.

(c) The proceeds of a sale under subsection (b), after paying the expenses of the sale, shall be applied in liquidation of the indebtedness secured by the lien and the balance, if any, shall be paid over to the owner.

(d) The notice under subsection (b) may:

(1) be served by mail directed to the owner's last known address; or

(2) be posted in two (2) public places in the town or city where the property is located, if the owner or the owner's address is not known. The notice must be written or printed. [P.L.2-2002, § 18.]

32-33-13-3. Enforcement by other action. — This chapter does not preclude the remedy of enforcing the lien by any other action provided by law. [P.L.2-2002, § 18.]

CHAPTER 14

WAREHOUSEMAN'S LIEN

32-33-14-1. Amount of lien — Possession. — (a) All persons, firms, limited liability companies, and corporations engaged in the business of storing, warehousing, and forwarding goods, wares, and merchandise have a lien upon all goods, wares, and merchandise left with them for storage, warehousing, or forwarding, to the extent of the:

(1) value of the services of storage, warehousing, or forwarding;

(2) fair and reasonable charges for transporting the goods, wares, and merchandise to the place of storage, warehousing, or forwarding; and

(3) fair and reasonable charges for packing, crating, and otherwise placing the goods, wares, and merchandise in condition to be stored, warehoused, or forwarded.

(b) However, the goods subject to a lien under this section must remain in the possession of the person, firm, limited liability company, or corporation engaged in the business. [P.L.2-2002, § 18.]

Effective Dates. P.L.2-2002, § 18. July 1. 2002.

Cross References. Storage of household goods, lien, IC 32-33-3-2.

NOTES TO DECISIONS

Common Law Lien.
It would seem that the former version of this statute abrogated the common law lien for storage. Nicholas v. Baldwin Piano Co., 71 Ind. App. 209, 123 N.E. 226 (1919).

Collateral References. 78 Am. Jur. 2d Warehouses, §§ 112-126.

93 C.J.S. Warehousemen and Safe Depositories, §§ 63-69.

32-33-14-2. Sale at public auction — Public notice. — (a) If goods, wares, or merchandise have remained in the possession of a person, firm, limited liability company, or corporation described in section 1 [IC 32-33-14-1] of this chapter for a period of at least six (6) months without the payment of the charges due, the goods, wares, or merchandise, or as much of the goods, wares, or merchandise as is necessary, may be sold at public auction to pay the amount of the lien and the expenses of the sale.

(b) Before a sale under subsection (a), the person, firm, limited liability company, or corporation described in section 1 of this chapter must give public notice of the time and place of the sale by advertisements set up for a period of ten (10) days in three (3) public places in the city or township in which the goods, wares, or merchandise are located. One (1) of the advertisements must be:

(1) displayed in a conspicuous part of the place of business of the person, firm, limited liability company, or corporation; or

(2) if the value of the article or articles is at least ten dollars ($10), published for three (3) weeks successively in a newspaper published in the county or city in which the goods are located.

(c) The notice given under subsection (b) must:

(1) state the time, place, and date of sale;

(2) give a general description of the goods to be sold; and

(3) state the name of the person to whom a receipt for the goods was issued. [P.L.2-2002, § 18.]

32-33-14-3. Proceeds of sale. — The proceeds of a sale under section 2 [IC 32-33-14-2] of this chapter, after payment of all lien charges, together with the expenses of notice and sale, shall, if the owner is absent from the sale, be deposited with the county treasurer of the county in which the sale occurred. A receipt shall be issued for the proceeds. The proceeds are subject to the order of the person legally entitled to the proceeds. [P.L.2-2002, § 18.]

CHAPTER 15

ELECTRONIC HOME ENTERTAINMENT EQUIPMENT LIEN

32-33-15-1. Amount of lien. — A person who engages in the business of altering or repairing electronic home entertainment equipment has a lien on that equipment to the extent of the reasonable value of labor performed and materials used for which the person has not been paid. [P.L.2-2002, § 18.]

Effective Dates. P.L.2-2002, § 18. July 1. 2002.
Collateral References. 51 Am. Jur. 2d Liens and Encumbrances, §§ 20, 37.

53 C.J.S. Liens, §§ 4-9.
57 C.J.S. Mechanics' Liens, § 30.

32-33-15-2. Sale at auction. — If the lienholder has not been paid within sixty (60) days after payment becomes overdue, the lienholder may sell the equipment at auction if:

(1) the equipment is still in the lienholder's possession; and

(2) the lienholder complies with section 3 [IC 32-33-15-3] of this chapter. [P.L.2-2002, § 18.]

32-33-15-3. Notice of sale — Foreclosure by judicial proceeding — Notice published in newspaper. — (a) Before a lienholder may sell the equipment, the lienholder must, by certified mail, return receipt requested, notify the owner and any person whose security interest is perfected by filing concerning the following:

(1) The lienholder's intention to sell the equipment thirty (30) days after the owner's receipt of the notice.

(2) A description of the equipment to be sold.

(3) The time and place of the sale.

(4) An itemized statement describing the value of labor and materials provided and for which the lienholder has not been paid.

(b) If upon receipt of the notice the owner informs the lienholder in writing of the owner's objections regarding the quality of the workmanship or an alleged overcharge, the lienholder must foreclose by judicial proceeding.

(c) If there is no return of the receipt or if the postal service returns the notice as being nondeliverable, the lienholder shall publish notice of the lienholder's intention to sell the equipment in a newspaper of general circulation in the place where the equipment is being held for sale by the lienholder. The notice must include a description of the equipment and name of its owner. [P.L.2-2002, § 18.]

32-33-15-4. Proceeds of sale in excess of lien amount. — If the sale is for a sum greater than the amount of the lien, any excess shall be paid to the owner and any prior lienholder. [P.L.2-2002, § 18.]

CHAPTER 16

LIENS ON DIES, MOLDS, FORMS, AND PATTERNS

32-33-16-1. "Customer" defined. — As used in this chapter, "customer" means any individual or entity who contracts with or causes a fabricator to use a die, mold, form, jig, or pattern to manufacture, assemble, or otherwise make a product. [P.L.2-2002, § 18.]

Effective Dates. P.L.2-2002, § 18. July 1. 2002.

32-33-16-2. "Fabricator" defined. — As used in this chapter, "fabricator" means any individual or entity, including a tool or die maker, who:

(1) manufactures or causes to be manufactured, assembles, or improves a die, mold, form, jig, or pattern for a customer; or

(2) uses or contracts to use a die, mold, form, jig, or pattern to manufacture, assemble, or otherwise make a product for a customer. [P.L.2-2002, § 18.]

32-33-16-3. Amount of lien. — (a) A fabricator has a lien, dependent on possession, on any die, mold, form, jig, or pattern in the fabricator's possession belonging to the customer for the amount due the fabricator from the customer for fabrication work performed with the die, mold, form, jig, or pattern.

(b) A fabricator may retain possession of the die, mold, form, jig, or pattern until the amount due is paid. [P.L.2-2002, § 18.]

32-33-16-4. Notice. — (a) Before enforcing a lien under this chapter, notice in writing must be given to the customer, whether delivered personally or sent by certified mail to the last known address of the customer.

(b) The notice required under subsection (a) must:

(1) state that a lien is claimed for the damages set forth or attached for the amount due for fabrication work or for making or improving the die, mold, form, jig, or pattern; and

(2) include a demand for payment. [P.L.2-2002, § 18.]

32-33-16-5. Sale. — If the lienholder has not been paid the amount due within sixty (60) days after the notice provided for in section 4 [IC 32-33-16-4] of this chapter, the lienholder may sell the die, mold, form, jig, or pattern at auction if:

(1) the die, mold, form, jig, or pattern is still in the lienholder's possession; and

(2) the lienholder complies with section 6 [IC 32-33-16-6] of this chapter. [P.L.2-2002, § 18.]

32-33-16-6. Notice to customer and secured parties — Objections — Complaint to foreclose — Notice published in newspaper. — (a) Before a lienholder may sell the die, mold, form, jig, or pattern, the lienholder must, in writing, by certified mail, return receipt requested, notify the customer and any person whose security interest is perfected by filing of the following:

(1) The lienholder's intention to sell the die, mold, form, jig, or pattern thirty (30) days after the customer's receipt of the notice.

(2) A description of the die, mold, form, jig, or pattern to be sold.

(3) The time and place of the sale.

(4) An itemized statement for the amount due.

(b) If upon receipt of this notice the customer informs the lienholder in writing of the customer's objections regarding the amount due, the lienholder may file a complaint to foreclose the lien.

(c) If there is no return of the receipt of mailing, or if the postal service returns the notice as being nondeliverable, the lienholder must publish notice of the lienholder's intention to sell the die, mold, form, jig, or pattern in a newspaper of general circulation in the county where the die, mold, form, jig, or pattern is being held for sale by the lienholder. The notice must include a description of the die, mold, form, jig, or pattern and the name of the customer. [P.L.2-2002, § 18.]

32-33-16-7. Proceeds of sale in excess of lien amount. — If the sale is for a sum greater than the amount of the lien plus all reasonable expenses of the sale, any excess shall be paid to the customer and any prior lienholder. [P.L.2-2002, § 18.]

32-33-16-8. Sale prohibited if in violation of federal patent or copyright law. — A sale may not be made under this chapter if the sale would be in violation of any right of a customer under federal patent or copyright law. [P.L.2-2002, § 18.]

32-33-16-9. Action for replevin. — This chapter does not bar a customer from bringing action for replevin under IC 32-35-2. [P.L.2-2002, § 18.]

CHAPTER 17

CORPORATE EMPLOYEE'S LIENS

SECTION.
32-33-17-1. Liens on personal property of cor-
      poration.

32-33-17-1. Liens on personal property of corporation. — Unless otherwise provided in this article, corporate employee liens on personal property of a corporation for all work and labor done and performed by the employees of a corporation are governed by IC 32-28-12. [P.L.2-2002, § 18.]

Effective Dates. P.L.2-2002, § 18. July 1.
2002.

CHAPTER 18

COMMON LAW LIENS

SECTION.
32-33-18-1. Filing and releasing common law
      liens.

32-33-18-1. Filing and releasing common law liens. — The procedures for filing and releasing common law liens on personal property are governed by IC 32-28-13. [P.L.2-2002, § 18.]

Effective Dates. P.L.2-2002, § 18. July 1.
2002.

CHAPTER 19

DUTY TO SATISFY RECORD

SECTION.
32-33-19-1. Release, discharge, and satisfac-
      tion of record.

32-33-19-1. Release, discharge, and satisfaction of record. — Unless otherwise provided in this article, if the debt or obligation, including interest on the debt or obligation, that a lien on personal property secures has been fully paid, lawfully tendered, and discharged, the owner, holder, or custodian of the mortgage shall:
  (A) release;
  (B) discharge; and
  (C) satisfy of record;
the mortgage as provided in IC 32-28-1. [P.L.2-2002, § 18.]

Effective Dates. P.L.2-2002, § 18. July 1.
2002.

ARTICLE 34

LOST OR UNCLAIMED PERSONAL PROPERTY

CHAPTER 1

UNCLAIMED PROPERTY ACT

32-34-1-1. Applicability. — (a) This chapter does not apply to any property held, due, and owing in a foreign country and arising out of a foreign transaction.

(b) This chapter does not apply to:

(1) stocks;

(2) dividends;

(3) capital credits;

(4) patronage refunds;

(5) utility deposits;

(6) membership fees;

(7) account balances; or

(8) book equities;

for which the owner cannot be found and that are the result of distributable savings of a rural electric membership corporation formed under IC 8-1-13, a rural telephone cooperative corporation formed under IC 8-1-17, or an agricultural cooperative association formed under IC 15-7-1.

(c) This chapter does not apply to unclaimed overpayments of utility bills that become the property of a municipality under IC 36-9-23-28.5.

(d) This chapter does not apply to deposits required by a municipally owned utility (as defined in IC 8-1-2-1).

(e) This chapter does not apply to a business to business credit memorandum or a credit balance resulting from a business to business credit memorandum. [P.L.2-2002, § 19.]

Effective Dates. P.L.2-2002, § 19. July 1. 2002.

Cross References. Escheat of estates, IC 29-1-17-12.

Collateral References. 1 Am. Jur. 2d Abandoned, Lost and Unclaimed Property, §§ 1-45.

Modern status of rules as to ownership of treasure trove as between finder and owner of property on which found. 61 A.L.R.4th 1180.

32-34-1-2. Short title. — This chapter may be cited as the "unclaimed property act". [P.L.2-2002, § 19.]

32-34-1-3. "Administrator" defined. — As used in this chapter, "administrator" means the administrator of the unclaimed property law of another state. [P.L.2-2002, § 19.]

32-34-1-4. "Apparent owner" defined. — As used in this chapter, "apparent owner" means a person whose name appears on the records of a holder as the person entitled to property held, issued, or owing by the holder. [P.L.2-2002, § 19.]

32-34-1-5. "Business association" defined. — As used in this chapter, "business association" means the following:

(1) A corporation.

(2) A limited liability company.

(3) A joint stock company.

(4) An investment company.

(5) A partnership.

(6) A business trust.

(7) A trust company.

(8) A savings association.

(9) A savings bank.

(10) An industrial bank.

(11) A land bank.

(12) A safe deposit company.

(13) A safekeeping depository.

(14) A bank.

(15) A banking organization.

(16) A financial organization.

(17) An insurance company.

(18) A mutual fund.

(19) A credit union.

(20) A utility.

(21) A for profit or nonprofit business association consisting of two (2) or more individuals. [P.L.2-2002, § 19.]

32-34-1-6. "Domicile" defined. — As used in this chapter, "domicile" means the following:

(1) The state of incorporation of a corporation.

(2) The state of the principal place of business of a holder other than a corporation. [P.L.2-2002, § 19.]

32-34-1-7. "Financial institution" defined. — As used in this chapter, "financial institution" means a depository financial institution that is organized or reorganized under Indiana law, the law of another state, or United States law. The term includes any of the following:

(1) A commercial bank.

(2) A trust company.

(3) A savings bank.

(4) A savings association.

(5) A credit union.

(6) An industrial loan and investment company.

(7) Any other entity that has powers similar to the powers of an entity described in subdivisions (1) through (6). [P.L.2-2002, § 19.]

32-34-1-8. "Holder" defined. — As used in this chapter, "holder" means a person obligated to deliver or pay to the owner property that is subject to this chapter. [P.L.2-2002, § 19.]

32-34-1-9. "Insurance company" defined. — As used in this chapter, "insurance company" means an association, a corporation, or a fraternal or mutual benefit organization, whether or not for profit, that is engaged in the business of providing insurance, including the following:

(1) Accident insurance.
(2) Burial insurance.
(3) Casualty insurance.
(4) Credit life insurance.
(5) Contract performance insurance.
(6) Dental insurance.
(7) Fidelity insurance.
(8) Fire insurance.
(9) Health insurance.
(10) Hospitalization insurance.
(11) Illness insurance.
(12) Life insurance (including endowments and annuities).
(13) Malpractice insurance.
(14) Marine insurance.
(15) Mortgage insurance.
(16) Surety insurance.
(17) Wage protection insurance.
[P.L.2-2002, § 19.]

32-34-1-10. "Last known address" defined. — (a) As used in sections 26, 32, and 43 [IC 32-34-1-26, IC 32-34-1-32, and IC 32-34-1-43] of this chapter, "last known address" means a description of the location of the apparent owner's residence or business sufficient for the purpose of the delivery of mail or the receipt of a communication by other means known to the holder.

(b) As used in sections 21 and 37 [IC 32-34-1-21 and IC 32-34-1-37] of this chapter, "last known address" means a description indicating that the apparent owner was located within Indiana, regardless of whether the description is sufficient to direct the delivery of mail. [P.L.2-2002, § 19.]

32-34-1-11. "Mineral" defined. — As used in this chapter, "mineral" means any of the following:

(1) Gas.
(2) Oil.
(3) Coal.
(4) Other gaseous, liquid, and solid hydrocarbons.
(5) Shale.
(6) Oil shale.
(7) Cement material.
(8) Sand and gravel.
(9) Road material.
(10) Building stone.
(11) Chemical substance.
(12) Gemstone.

(13) Metallic, fissionable, and nonfissionable ores.
(14) Colloidal and other clay.
(15) Steam and other geothermal resource.
(16) Any other substance defined as a mineral under Indiana law.
[P.L.2-2002, § 19.]

32-34-1-12. "Mineral proceeds" defined. — As used in this chapter, "mineral proceeds" means proceeds currently payable and unclaimed and, upon the abandonment of those proceeds, all proceeds that would have become payable, including the following:
(1) Obligations to pay resulting from the extraction, production, or sale of minerals, including the following:
(A) Net revenue interests.
(B) Royalties.
(C) Overriding royalties.
(D) Extraction and production payments.
(E) Joint operating agreements.
(F) Pooling arrangements.
(2) Obligations for the acquisition and retention of a mineral lease, including the following:
(A) Bonuses.
(B) Delay rentals.
(C) Shut-in royalties.
(D) Minimum royalties.
[P.L.2-2002, § 19.]

32-34-1-13. "Money order" defined. — (a) As used in this chapter, "money order" includes an express money order and a personal money order on which the remitter is the purchaser.
(b) The term does not include the following:
(1) A bank money order on which the remitter is the purchaser.
(2) A bank money order or any other instrument sold by a banking or financial institution if the seller has obtained the name and address of the payee. [P.L.2-2002, § 19.]

32-34-1-14. "Owner" defined. — (a) As used in this chapter, "owner" means:
(1) a person who has a legal or an equitable interest in property subject to this chapter; or
(2) the person's legal representative.
(b) The term includes the following:
(1) A depositor in the case of property that is a deposit.
(2) A beneficiary in the case of property that is a trust other than a deposit in trust.
(3) A creditor, claimant, or payee in the case of other property. [P.L.2-2002, § 19.]

32-34-1-15. "Person" defined. — As used in this chapter, "person" means an individual, a corporation, a business trust, an estate, a trust, a partnership, an association, a joint venture, a government, a governmental subdivision, agency, or instrumentality, a public corporation, a joint or common owner, or any other legal or commercial entity. [P.L.2-2002, § 19.]

Opinions of Attorney General. The Public Employees' Retirement Fund, a retirement system supported by the State of Indiana, is not a "person" or other entity, as defined in the former Unclaimed Property Act, which must transfer State benefit warrants to the Property Custody Fund after a presumption of abandonment arises. 1983, No. 83-4, p. 21.

32-34-1-16. "Political subdivision" defined. — (a) As used in section 47 [IC 32-34-1-47] of this chapter, "political subdivision" includes any Indiana municipality, county, civil township, civil incorporated city or town, public school corporation, university or college supported in part by state funds, or any other territorial subdivision of the state recognized or designated in any law, including the following:

(1) Judicial circuits.

(2) A public utility entity not privately owned.

(3) A special taxing district or entity.

(4) A public improvement district authority or entity authorized to levy taxes or assessments.

(b) The term does not include any retirement system supported entirely or in part by the state. [P.L.2-2002, § 19.]

32-34-1-17. "Property" defined — Applicability of section. — (a) This section does not apply to section 24 [IC 32-34-1-24] of this chapter.

(b) As used in this chapter, "property" means an interest in intangible personal property, except an unliquidated claim, and all income or increment derived from the interest, including an interest that is referred to as or evidenced by:

(1) money, a check, a draft, a deposit, an interest, or a dividend;

(2) a credit balance, a customer overpayment, a gift certificate, a security deposit, a refund, a credit memorandum, an unpaid wage, an unused airline ticket, mineral proceeds, or an unidentified remittance;

(3) stock and other ownership interest in a business association;

(4) a bond, debenture, note, or other evidence of indebtedness;

(5) money deposited to redeem stocks, bonds, coupons, and other securities or to make distributions;

(6) an amount due and payable under the terms of an insurance policy; and

(7) an amount distributable from a trust or custodial fund established under a plan to provide:

(A) health;

(B) welfare;

(C) pension;

(D) vacation;

(E) severance;

(F) retirement;

(G) death;

(H) stock purchase;

    (I) profit sharing;

    (J) employee savings;

    (K) supplemental unemployment insurance; or

    (L) similar;

benefits.

  (c) The term does not include transactions between business entities and:

    (1) a motor carrier (as defined in IC 8-2.1-17-10); or

    (2) a carrier (as defined in 49 U.S.C. 13102(3)).

[P.L.2-2002, § 19.]

32-34-1-18. "State" defined. — As used in this chapter, "state" means a state of the United States, the District of Columbia, the Commonwealth of Puerto Rico, or any territory or insular possession subject to the jurisdiction of the United States. [P.L.2-2002, § 19.]

32-34-1-19. "Utility" defined. — As used in this chapter, "utility" means a person that owns or operates for public use any plant, equipment, property, franchise, or license for the transmission of communications or for the production, storage, transmission, sale, delivery, or furnishing of electricity, water, steam, or gas. [P.L.2-2002, § 19.]

32-34-1-20. Indication of interest in property — Insurance policy maturation or termination — Presumption of abandonment. — (a) For purposes of this section, an indication of interest in the property by the owner:

    (1) does not include a communication with an owner by an agent of the holder who has not identified in writing the property to the owner; and

    (2) includes the following:

      (A) With respect to an account or underlying shares of stock or other interest in a business association or financial organization:

        (i) the cashing of a dividend check or other instrument of payment received; or

        (ii) evidence that the distribution has been received if the distribution was made by electronic or similar means.

      (B) A deposit to or withdrawal from a bank account.

      (C) The payment of a premium with respect to a property interest in an insurance policy.

      (D) The mailing of any correspondence in writing from a financial institution to the owner, including:

        (i) a statement;

        (ii) a report of interest paid or credited; or

        (iii) any other written advice;

relating to a demand, savings, or matured time deposit account, including a deposit account that is automatically renewable, or any other account or other property the owner has with the financial institution if the correspondence is not returned to the financial institution for nondelivery.

      (E) Any activity by the owner that concerns:

(i) another demand, savings, or matured time deposit account or other account that the owner has with a financial institution, including any activity by the owner that results in an increase or decrease in the amount of any other account; or
(ii) any other relationship with the financial institution, including the payment of any amounts due on a loan;
if the mailing address for the owner contained in the financial institution's books and records is the same for both an inactive account and for a related account.

(b) The application of an automatic premium loan provision or other nonforfeiture provision contained in an insurance policy does not prevent the policy from maturing or terminating if the insured has died or the insured or the beneficiary of the policy otherwise has become entitled to the proceeds before the depletion of the cash surrender value of the policy by the application of those provisions.

(c) Property that is held, issued, or owed in the ordinary course of a holder's business is presumed abandoned if the owner or apparent owner has not communicated in writing with the holder concerning the property or has not otherwise given an indication of interest in the property during the following times:

(1) For traveler's checks, fifteen (15) years after issuance.
(2) For money orders, seven (7) years after issuance.
(3) For consumer credits, three (3) years after the credit becomes payable.
(4) For gift certificates, three (3) years after December 31 of the year in which the gift certificate was sold. If the gift certificate is redeemable in merchandise only, the amount abandoned is considered to be sixty percent (60%) of the certificate's face value.
(5) For amounts owed by an insurer on a life or an endowment insurance policy or an annuity contract:
(A) if the policy or contract has matured or terminated, three (3) years after the obligation to pay arose; or
(B) if the policy or contract is payable upon proof of death, three (3) years after the insured has attained, or would have attained if living, the limiting age under the mortality table on which the reserve is based.
(6) For property distributable by a business association in a course of dissolution, one (1) year after the property becomes distributable.
(7) For property or proceeds held by a court or a court clerk, other than property or proceeds related to child support, five (5) years after the property or proceeds become distributable. The property or proceeds must be treated as unclaimed property under IC 32-34-3. For property or proceeds related to child support held by a court or a court clerk, ten (10) years after the property or proceeds become distributable.
(8) For property held by a state or other government, governmental subdivision or agency, or public corporation or other public authority, one (1) year after the property becomes distributable.
(9) For compensation for personal services, one (1) year after the compensation becomes payable.

(10) For deposits and refunds held for subscribers by utilities, one (1) year after the deposits or refunds became payable.

(11) For stock or other interest in a business association, five (5) years after the earlier of:

(A) the date of the last dividend, stock split, or other distribution unclaimed by the apparent owner; or

(B) the date of the second mailing of a statement of account or other notification or communication that was:

(i) returned as undeliverable; or

(ii) made after the holder discontinued mailings to the apparent owner.

(12) For property in an individual retirement account or another account or plan that is qualified for tax deferral under the Internal Revenue Code, three (3) years after the earliest of:

(A) the actual date of the distribution or attempted distribution;

(B) the distribution date as stated in the plan or trust agreement governing the plan; or

(C) the date specified in the Internal Revenue Code by which distribution must begin in order to avoid a tax penalty.

(13) For a demand, savings, or matured time deposit, including a deposit that is automatically renewable, five (5) years after maturity or five (5) years after the date of the last indication by the owner of interest in the property, whichever is earlier. Property that is automatically renewable is considered matured for purposes of this section upon the expiration of its initial period, unless the owner has consented to a renewal at or about the time of the renewal and the consent is in writing or is evidenced by a memorandum or other record on file with the holder.

(14) For all other property, the earlier of five (5) years after:

(A) the owner's right to demand the property; or

(B) the obligation to pay or distribute the property;

arose.

(d) Property is payable or distributed for purposes of this chapter notwithstanding the owner's failure to make demand or present an instrument or a document otherwise required to receive payment. [P.L.2-2002, § 19.]

32-34-1-21. Property subject to custody of Indiana. — Except as provided in another state statute, property located in Indiana or another state is subject to the custody of this state as unclaimed property if the property is presumed abandoned and if:

(1) the last known address of the apparent owner, as shown on the records of the holder, is in Indiana;

(2) the records of the holder do not reflect the identity of the person entitled to the property and it is established that the last known address of the person entitled to the property is in Indiana;

(3) the records of the holder do not reflect the last known address of the apparent owner and it is established that:

(A) the last known address of the person entitled to the property is in Indiana; or

(B) the holder is a domiciliary or a government or governmental subdivision or agency of this state and has not previously paid or delivered the property to the state of the last known address of the apparent owner or other person entitled to the property;

(4) the last known address of the apparent owner, as shown on the records of the holder, is in a state that does not provide for the escheat or custodial taking of the property and the holder is a domiciliary or a government or governmental subdivision or agency of this state;

(5) the last known address of the apparent owner, as shown on the records of the holder, is in a foreign country and the holder is a domiciliary or a government or governmental subdivision or agency of this state;

(6) the transaction out of which the property arose occurred in Indiana, the holder is a domiciliary of a state that does not provide for the escheat or custodial taking of the property, and the last known address of the apparent owner or other person entitled to the property is:

(A) unknown; or

(B) in a state that does not provide for the escheat or custodial taking of the property; or

(7) the property is a traveler's check or money order:

(A) purchased in Indiana; or

(B) for which the issuer of the traveler's check or money order has its principal place of business in Indiana and the issuer's records:

(i) do not show the state in which the instrument was purchased; or

(ii) show that the instrument was purchased in a state that does not provide for the escheat or custodial taking of the property. [P.L.2-2002, § 19.]

32-34-1-22. Charges on property presumed abandoned. — (a) A holder may not deduct a charge from property that is presumed abandoned if the charge is imposed because the owner failed to claim the property within a specified time unless:

(1) there is a valid and enforceable written contract between the holder and the owner that allows the holder to impose the charge; and

(2) the holder regularly imposes the charge, and the charge is not regularly reversed or otherwise canceled.

(b) If a holder described in this section is a financial institution, the dormancy charges of the department of financial institutions apply. [P.L.2-2002, § 19.]

32-34-1-23. Evidence of an obligation — Burden of proof — Defenses. — (a) A record that a check, draft, or similar instrument was issued is prima facie evidence of an obligation.

(b) If the attorney general claims property from a holder who is also the issuer, the attorney general's burden of proof as to the existence and amount of the property and the abandonment of the property is satisfied by showing the following:

(1) That the instrument was issued.

(2) That the required period of time of abandonment has passed.

(c) For purposes of this section, the defenses of:

(1) payment;

(2) satisfaction;

(3) discharge; and

(4) want of consideration;

are affirmative defenses that must be established by the holder. [P.L.2-2002, § 19.]

32-34-1-24. Property in safe deposit box or other depository. — If:

(1) tangible or intangible property that is held in a safe deposit box or any other safekeeping depository in Indiana in the ordinary course of the holder's business; or

(2) the proceeds resulting from the sale of the property described in subdivision (1) as authorized by other law;

remain unclaimed by the owner for more than five (5) years after expiration of the lease or rental period on the box or other depository, the property or proceeds are presumed abandoned. [P.L.2-2002, § 19.]

32-34-1-25. Voluntary dissolution — Filing of notice. — Any:

(1) business association;

(2) banking organization; or

(3) financial institution;

that is organized under Indiana law or created in Indiana and that undergoes voluntary dissolution shall file a notice of the voluntary dissolution with the attorney general not later than ten (10) days after the adoption by the members or shareholders of the resolution to dissolve. [P.L.2-2002, § 19.]

32-34-1-26. Report to attorney general by holder of unclaimed property — Notice to apparent owner — Extension of time for filing report. — (a) A holder of property that is presumed abandoned and that is subject to custody as unclaimed property under this chapter shall report in writing to the attorney general concerning the property. Items of value of less than fifty dollars ($50) may be reported by the holder in the aggregate.

(b) For each item with a value of at least fifty dollars ($50), the report required under subsection (a) must be verified and must include the following:

(1) Except with respect to traveler's checks and money orders, the apparent owner's:

(A) name, if known;

(B) last known address, if any; and

(C) Social Security number or taxpayer identification number, if readily ascertainable.

(2) In the case of the contents of a safe deposit box or other safekeeping depository of tangible property:

(A) a description of the property;

(B) the place where the property is held and may be inspected by the attorney general; and

(C) any amount that is owed to the holder.

(3) The date:

(A) the property became payable, demandable, or returnable; and

(B) of the last transaction with the apparent owner with respect to the property.

(4) Other information that the attorney general requires by rules adopted under IC 4-22-2 as necessary for the administration of this chapter.

(c) If:

(1) a holder of property that is presumed abandoned and that is subject to custody as unclaimed property is a successor to another person who previously held the property for the apparent owner; or

(2) the holder has changed its name while holding the property;

the holder shall file with the report required by subsection (a) the former names of the holder, if any, and the known name and address of any previous holder of the property.

(d) The report required by subsection (a) must be filed as follows:

(1) The report of a life insurance company must be filed before May 1 of each year for the calendar year preceding the year in which the report is filed.

(2) All other holders must file the report before November 1 of each year to cover the year preceding July 1 of the year in which the report is filed.

(e) The holder of property that is presumed abandoned and that is subject to custody as unclaimed property under this chapter shall, not more than one hundred twenty (120) days or less than sixty (60) days before filing the report required by subsection (a), send written notice to the apparent owner of the property stating that the holder is in possession of property subject to this chapter if:

(1) the holder has a record of an address for the apparent owner that the holder's records do not show as inaccurate;

(2) the claim of the apparent owner is not barred by the statute of limitations; and

(3) the value of the property is at least fifty dollars ($50).

(f) Before the date of filing the report required by subsection (a), the holder may request the attorney general to extend the time for filing the report. The attorney general may grant the extension upon a showing of good cause. The holder, upon receipt of the extension, may make an interim payment on the amount the holder estimates will ultimately be due. The making of an interim payment under this subsection suspends the accrual of interest on the amount.

(g) The holder shall file with the report an affidavit stating that the holder has complied with this section. [P.L.2-2002, § 19.]

32-34-1-27. Delivery of unclaimed property to attorney general. —
(a) Except as provided in subsections (b) and (c), on the date a report is filed

under section 26 [IC 32-34-1-26] of this chapter, the holder shall pay or deliver to the attorney general the property that is described in the report as unclaimed.

(b) In the case of an automatically renewable deposit, if at the time of delivery under subsection (a) a penalty or forfeiture in the payment of interest would result from the delivery of the property, the time for delivery is extended until the earliest date upon which a penalty or forfeiture would not result.

(c) Tangible property held in a safe deposit box or other safekeeping depository may not be delivered to the attorney general until one hundred twenty (120) days after the date the report describing the property under section 26 of this chapter is filed.

(d) If the property reported to the attorney general is a security or security entitlement under IC 26-1-8.1, the attorney general may make an endorsement, instruction, or entitlement order on behalf of the apparent owner to invoke the duty of the issuer or its transfer agent or the securities intermediary to transfer or dispose of the security or the security entitlement in accordance with IC 26-1-8.1.

(e) If the holder of property reported to the attorney general is the issuer of a certificated security, the attorney general has the right to obtain a replacement certificate under IC 26-1-8.1-405, and an indemnity bond is not required.

(f) An issuer, the holder, and any transfer agent or other person acting under the instructions of and on behalf of the issuer in accordance with this section are not liable to the apparent owner and must be indemnified against the claims of any person in accordance with section 29 [IC 32-34-1-29] of this chapter. [P.L.2-2002, § 19.]

32-34-1-28. Publication of notice — Exceptions. — (a) Except as provided in subsection (e), the attorney general shall publish a notice not later than November 30 of the year immediately following the year in which unclaimed property has been paid or delivered to the attorney general.

(b) Except as provided in subsection (c), the notice required by subsection (a) must be published at least once each week for two (2) successive weeks in a newspaper of general circulation published in the county in Indiana of the last known address of any person named in the notice.

(c) If the holder:
(1) does not report an address for the apparent owner; or
(2) reports an address outside Indiana;
the notice must be published in the county in which the holder has its principal place of business within Indiana or any other county that the attorney general may reasonably select.

(d) The advertised notice required by this section must be in a form that, in the judgment of the attorney general, will attract the attention of the apparent owner of the unclaimed property and must contain the following information:
(1) The name of each person appearing to be an owner of property that is presumed abandoned, as set forth in the report filed by the holder.

(2) The last known address or location of each person appearing to be an owner of property that is presumed abandoned, if an address or a location is set forth in the report filed by the holder.

(3) A statement explaining that the property of the owner is presumed to be abandoned and has been taken into the protective custody of the attorney general.

(4) A statement that information about the abandoned property and its return to the owner is available, upon request, from the attorney general, to a person having a legal or beneficial interest in the property.

(e) The attorney general is not required to publish the following in the notice:

(1) Any item with a value of less than fifty dollars ($50).

(2) Information concerning a traveler's check, money order, or any similar instrument. [P.L.2-2002, § 19.]

NOTES TO DECISIONS

Missing Persons.
 Nothing within former IC 32-9-1 grants the trial court the authority to require the expenditure of funds for an investigation or reward for a missing person. Baggett v. Attorney Gen., 525 N.E.2d 616 (Ind. App. 1988).

32-34-1-29. Payment or delivery in good faith — Custody of property — Affidavit of holder — Reimbursement for expenses. — (a) For purposes of this section, payment or delivery is made in good faith if:

(1) payment or delivery was made in a reasonable attempt to comply with this chapter;

(2) the holder was not a fiduciary in breach of trust with respect to the property and had a reasonable basis for believing, based on the facts known at the time, that the property was abandoned; and

(3) there is not a showing that the records under which the delivery was made did not meet reasonable commercial standards of practice in the industry.

(b) Upon the payment or delivery of property to the attorney general, the state assumes custody and responsibility for the safekeeping of the property. A holder who pays or delivers property to the attorney general in good faith is relieved of all liability with respect to the property after the payment and delivery.

(c) A holder who has paid money to the attorney general under this chapter may later make payment to a person who, in the opinion of the holder, appears to be entitled to the payment. The attorney general shall promptly reimburse the holder for the payment without imposing a fee or other charge if the holder files proof of payment and proof that the payee was entitled to the payment. If any reimbursement is sought for a payment made on a negotiable instrument, including a traveler's check or money order, the holder must be reimbursed upon filing proof that:

(1) the instrument was duly presented; and

(2) the payment was made to a person who appeared to be entitled to the payment.

The holder must be reimbursed for the payment made even if the payment was made to a person whose claim was barred under section 41 [IC 32-34-1-41] of this chapter.

(d) A holder who has delivered property, including a certificate of any interest in a business association, but not including money, to the attorney general under this chapter may reclaim the property without paying a fee or other charge if the property is still in the possession of the attorney general, upon filing proof that the apparent owner has claimed the property from the holder.

(e) The attorney general may accept the holder's affidavit as sufficient proof of the holder's right to recover the money and the property under this section.

(f) If the holder pays or delivers property to the attorney general in good faith and later:

(1) another person claims the property from the holder; or

(2) another state claims the money or property under that state's laws relating to escheat or abandoned or unclaimed property;

the attorney general, upon written notice of the claim, shall defend the holder against the claim and indemnify the holder against any liability on the claim.

(g) Property removed from a safe deposit box or other safekeeping depository is received by the attorney general subject to the holder's right to be reimbursed for the cost of the opening and reasonable expenses incurred in determining the current addresses of any owners for whom the last previous address contained in the holder's records appears to be inaccurate. The property is subject to any valid lien or contract providing for the holder to be reimbursed for unpaid rent or storage charges. The attorney general shall reimburse or pay the holder out of the proceeds remaining after deducting the attorney general's cost of selling the property. [P.L.2-2002, § 19.]

32-34-1-30. Dividends and interest. — (a) If property, other than money, is paid or delivered to the attorney general under this chapter, the owner is entitled to receive from the attorney general any dividends, interest, or other increments realized or accruing on the property at or before delivery to the attorney general.

(b) The owner is not entitled to receive dividends, interest, or other increments accruing after delivery of the property to the attorney general under this chapter unless the property was paid or delivered under section 39(b) [IC 32-34-1-39(b)] of this chapter. [P.L.2-2002, § 19.]

32-34-1-31. Sale of property by attorney general. — (a) Except as provided in subsections (b) and (c), the attorney general, not later than three (3) years after the receipt of abandoned property, shall sell the property to the highest bidder at a public sale in a city in Indiana that, in the judgment of the attorney general, affords the most favorable market for the property. The attorney general may decline the highest bid and reoffer the property for sale if, in the judgment of the attorney general, the bid is insufficient. If, in the judgment of the attorney general, the probable cost of the sale exceeds the value of the property, the attorney general is not required to offer the property for sale. A sale held under this section must be preceded, at least three (3) weeks before the sale, by one (1) publication of notice in a newspaper of general circulation published in the county in which the property is to be sold.

(b) If the property is of a type that is customarily sold on a recognized market or that is subject to widely distributed standard price quotations, and if, in the opinion of the attorney general, the probable cost of a public sale to the highest bidder would:

(1) exceed the value of the property; or

(2) result in a net loss;

the attorney general may sell the property privately, without notice by publication, at or above the prevailing price for the property at the time of the sale.

(c) Securities shall be sold as soon as reasonably possible following receipt. If a valid claim is made for any securities in the possession of the attorney general, the attorney general may:

(1) transfer the securities to the claimant; or

(2) pay the claimant the value of the securities as of the date the securities were delivered to the attorney general.

Notice of the sale of securities is not required. Securities listed on an established stock exchange must be sold at prices prevailing at the time of the sale on the stock exchange. Other securities may be sold over the counter at prices prevailing at the time of sale or by any other method the attorney general considers reasonable.

(d) A purchaser of property at a sale conducted by the attorney general under this chapter takes the property free of all claims of the owner or previous holder and of all persons claiming through or under them. The attorney general shall execute all documents necessary to complete the transfer of ownership.

(e) A person does not have a claim against the attorney general for any appreciation of property after the property is delivered to the attorney general, except in a case of intentional misconduct or malfeasance by the attorney general. [P.L.2-2002, § 19.]

32-34-1-32. Property custody fund. — (a) The property custody fund is established. Any money received by the attorney general under section 39(b) [IC 32-34-1-39(b)] of this chapter shall be delivered to the treasurer of state for deposit in the property custody fund. Subject to any claim of the owner allowed by the attorney general under this chapter, the money shall be held in the property custody fund for safekeeping until the date the money is presumed abandoned under sections 20 and 24 [IC 32-34-1-20 and IC 32-34-1-24] of this chapter and transferred to the abandoned property fund established by section 33 [IC 32-34-1-33] of this chapter in accordance with this section.

(b) The attorney general shall specify in the notice required by section 28 [IC 32-34-1-28] of this chapter the latest date the apparent owner may claim the property from the property custody fund. Notice must also be mailed to each person having a last known address listed in the report to the attorney general filed under section 26 [IC 32-34-1-26] of this chapter.

(c) Except as provided in subsection (d), not later than twenty-five (25) days after the date specified in the notice published under subsection (b), the treasurer of state, upon order of the attorney general, shall transfer the principal of the property to which the notice relates from property custody fund to the abandoned property fund.

(d) The attorney general may allow a claim of the apparent owner before the principal of the property in the property custody fund is transferred to the abandoned property fund under subsection (c). After the elapse of the twenty-five (25) days referred to in subsection (c), the funds are considered abandoned property instead of property received under section 39(b) of this chapter for purposes of this chapter. [P.L.2-2002, § 19.]

32-34-1-33. Abandoned property fund. — (a) The abandoned property fund is established. Except as provided in subsection (b) and section 32 [IC 32-34-1-32] of this chapter, money received by the attorney general under this chapter, including the proceeds from the sale of abandoned property under section 31 [IC 32-34-1-31] of this chapter, shall be transferred by the attorney general to the treasurer of state for deposit in the abandoned property fund.

(b) Money received under this chapter that was originally drawn from a fund under the control of a local unit of government shall be transferred to the fund from which the money was originally drawn. [P.L.2-2002, § 19.]

32-34-1-34. Costs — Transfer to common school fund — Claims and refunds — Earnings and Interest. — (a) Except as provided in section 42(d) [IC 32-34-1-42(d)] of this chapter, the treasurer of state shall, on order of the attorney general, pay the necessary costs of the following:

(1) Selling abandoned property.

(2) Mailing notices.

(3) Making publications required by this chapter.

(4) Paying other operating expenses and administrative expenses, including:

(A) salaries and wages reasonably incurred by the attorney general in the administration and enforcement of this chapter; and

(B) costs incurred in examining records of the holders of property and in collecting the property from the holders.

(b) If the balance of the principal of the abandoned property fund established by section 33 [IC 32-34-1-33] of this chapter exceeds five hundred thousand dollars ($500,000), the treasurer of state may, and at least once each fiscal year shall, transfer to the common school fund of the state the balance of the principal of the abandoned property fund that exceeds five hundred thousand dollars ($500,000).

(c) If a claim is allowed or a refund is ordered under this chapter that is more than five hundred thousand dollars ($500,000), the treasurer of state shall transfer from the state general fund sufficient money to make prompt payment of the claim. There is annually appropriated to the treasurer of state from the state general fund the amount of money sufficient to implement this subsection.

(d) Before making a deposit into the abandoned property fund, the attorney general shall record the following:

(1) The name and last known address of each person appearing from the holder's reports to be entitled to the abandoned property.

(2) The name and last known address of each insured person or annuitant.

(3) The number, the name of the corporation, and the amount due concerning any policy or contract listed in the report of a life insurance company.

(e) Except as provided in subsection (f), earnings on the property custody fund and the abandoned property fund shall be credited to each fund.

(f) On July 1 of each year, the interest balance in the property custody fund established by section 32 [IC 32-34-1-32] of this chapter and the interest balance in the abandoned property fund shall be transferred to the state general fund. [P.L.2-2002, § 19.]

32-34-1-35. Investment of moneys in fund — Claims, costs, and expenses. — (a) The treasurer of state shall keep safely the money in the property custody fund established by section 32 [IC 32-34-1-32] of this chapter and the abandoned property fund established by section 33 [IC 32-34-1-33] of this chapter. The money may not be transferred or assigned except as specifically authorized and directed in this chapter. At any time, upon certification of the attorney general and the treasurer of state that there is cash on deposit in either fund in excess of the cash requirements of the fund anticipated for the next succeeding semiannual fiscal period, the state board of finance may authorize the treasurer of state to invest and reinvest the money as authorized for other funds of the state by IC 5-13, including the purchase of certificates of deposit. However, an investment may not be made in a certificate of deposit with a maturity or redemption date that is more than six (6) months after the date of purchase, subscription, or deposit. Any interest or other accretions derived from investments made under this subsection become a part of the fund from which the money was invested.

(b) A sufficient amount of money from the abandoned property fund is appropriated to the treasurer of state to pay claims, costs, and expenses ordered paid from the abandoned property fund under this chapter.

(c) A sufficient amount of money from the property custody fund is annually appropriated to the treasurer of state to pay claims ordered paid from the property custody fund under this chapter. [P.L.2-2002, § 19.]

32-34-1-36. Claim form — Payment — Time for filing claim. — (a) A person, except another state, claiming an interest in property paid or delivered to the attorney general may file a claim on a form prescribed by the attorney general and verified by the claimant.

(b) Not later than ninety (90) days after a claim is filed under subsection (a), the attorney general shall:

(1) consider the claim; and

(2) give written notice to the claimant that the claim is granted or that the claim is denied in whole or in part.

(c) Not later than thirty (30) days after a claim is allowed, the attorney general shall pay over or deliver to the claimant the property, or the net proceeds of the sale of property if the property has been sold by the attorney general, together with any additional amount to which the claimant may be entitled under section 30 [IC 32-34-1-30] of this chapter.

(d) A holder who pays the owner for property that has been delivered to the state and that, if claimed from the attorney general by the owner, would be subject to an increment under section 30 of this chapter shall recover the amount of the increment from the attorney general.

(e) A person may file a claim under subsection (a) at any time within twenty-five (25) years after the date on which the property was first presumed abandoned under this chapter, notwithstanding the expiration of any other time specified by statute, contract, or court order during which an action or a proceeding may be commenced or enforced to obtain payment of a claim for money or recovery of property. [P.L.2-2002, § 19.]

32-34-1-37. Recovery of property by another state. — (a) At any time within twenty-five (25) years after the date on which the property was presumed abandoned under this chapter, notwithstanding the expiration of any other time specified by statute, contract, or court order during which an action or proceeding may be commenced or enforced to obtain payment of a claim for money or recovery of property, another state may recover the property if any of the following subdivisions apply:

(1) All of the following apply:

(A) The property was delivered to the custody of this state because the records of the holder did not reflect the last known address of the apparent owner when the property was presumed abandoned under this chapter.

(B) The other state establishes that the last known address of the apparent owner or other person entitled to the property was in that state.

(C) Under the laws of that state the property escheated to or was subject to a claim of abandonment by that state.

(2) The property was paid or delivered to the custody of this state because the laws of the other state did not provide for the escheat or custodial taking of the property, and under the laws of that state subsequently enacted, the property has escheated to or become subject to a claim of abandonment by that state.

(3) All of the following apply:

(A) The records of the holder did not accurately identify the owner of the property.

(B) The last known address of the owner is in the other state.

(C) Under the laws of the other state, the property escheated to or was subject to a claim of abandonment by that state.

(4) The property was subject to custody by this state under section 21(7) [IC 32-34-1-21(7)] of this chapter and, under the laws of the state

of domicile of the holder, the property has escheated to or become subject to a claim of abandonment by that state.

(5) All of the following apply:

(A) The property is a sum payable on a traveler's check, money order, or similar instrument that was delivered into the custody of this state under section 21(7) of this chapter.

(B) The instrument was purchased in the other state.

(C) Under the laws of the other state, the property escheated to or is subject to a claim of abandonment by that state.

(b) A claim of another state to recover escheated or abandoned property must be presented in a form prescribed by the attorney general. The attorney general shall consider the claim and give written notice not more than ninety (90) days after the presentation of the claim to the other state that the claim is granted or denied in whole or in part. The attorney general shall allow the claim upon a determination that the other state is entitled to the abandoned property under subsection (a).

(c) The attorney general shall require another state, before recovering property under this section, to agree to indemnify this state and its officers and employees against any liability on a claim for the property. [P.L.2-2002, § 19.]

32-34-1-38. Actions against the attorney general. — A person who, under this chapter:

(1) has been aggrieved by a decision of the attorney general; or

(2) has filed a claim that has not been acted upon within ninety (90) days after its filing;

may maintain an original action to establish the claim in a court with jurisdiction and name the attorney general as a defendant. [P.L.2-2002, § 19.]

32-34-1-39. Attorney general may decline property — Property delivered before presumed abandoned. — (a) The attorney general may decline to receive property reported under this chapter if the attorney general considers the property to have a value less than the expenses of the notice and the sale of the property.

(b) A holder, with the written consent of the attorney general and upon conditions and terms prescribed by the attorney general, may report and deliver property before the property is presumed abandoned. Property delivered to the attorney general under this subsection must be held in the property custody fund established under section 32 [IC 32-34-1-32] of this chapter, and the property is not presumed abandoned until the property otherwise would be presumed abandoned under this chapter. [P.L.2-2002, § 19.]

32-34-1-40. Destruction or disposal of property. — (a) If the attorney general determines after an investigation that property delivered under this chapter does not have any substantial commercial value, the attorney general may destroy or otherwise dispose of the property at any time.

(b) An action or a proceeding may not be maintained against the state, an officer of the state, or the holder for or on account of any acts taken by the attorney general under this section, except for acts constituting intentional misconduct or malfeasance. [P.L.2-2002, § 19.]

32-34-1-41. Expiration of time to make claim — Limitations period. — (a) The expiration of any time specified by contract, statute, or court order, during which:

(1) a claim for money or property can be made; or

(2) an action or a proceeding may be commenced or enforced to obtain payment of a claim for money or to recover property;

does not preclude the money or property from being presumed abandoned or affect any duty to file a report or to pay or deliver abandoned property to the attorney general as required by this chapter.

(b) An action or a proceeding may not be commenced by the attorney general to enforce the provisions of this chapter more than ten (10) years after the holder:

(1) specifically reported the property to the attorney general; or

(2) gave express notice to the attorney general of a dispute regarding the property.

In the absence of a report, the period of limitations is tolled. The period of limitations is also tolled by the filing of a false or fraudulent report. [P.L.2-2002, § 19.]

32-34-1-42. Verified reports — Examination of records — Estimates when records insufficient. — (a) The attorney general may require a person who has not filed a report, or a person who the attorney general believes has filed an inaccurate, an incomplete, or a false report, to file a verified report in a form prescribed by the attorney general stating the following:

(1) Whether the person is holding any unclaimed property reportable or deliverable under this chapter.

(2) Describing any property not previously reported or as to which the attorney general has made inquiry.

(3) Specifically identifying and stating the amounts of property that may be in issue.

(b) The attorney general, at reasonable times and upon reasonable notice, may examine the records of a person to determine whether the person has complied with this chapter. The attorney general may conduct the examination even if the person believes the person is not in possession of any property reportable or deliverable under this chapter. When making an examination under this chapter, the attorney general may retain attorneys, appraisers, independent actuaries, independent certified public accountants, or other professionals and specialists as examiners.

(c) The attorney general may examine the records of an agent, including a dividend disbursing agent or transfer agent, of a business association that is the holder of property presumed abandoned if the attorney general has given the notice required by subsection (b) to both the business association and the agent at least ninety (90) days before the examination.

(d) If an examination of the records of a person under subsection (b) results in the disclosure of property reportable and deliverable under this chapter, the attorney general may assess the cost of the examination against the holder at the rate of two hundred dollars ($200) a day for each examiner. The cost of an examination of the records of an agent of a business association under subsection (c) may be imposed only against the business association.

(e) If a holder fails to maintain the records required under section 43 [IC 32-34-1-43] of this chapter and the available records of the holder are insufficient to permit the preparation of a report, the attorney general may require the holder to report and pay an amount that may reasonably be estimated from any available records of the holder or on the basis of any other reasonable estimating technique that the attorney general may select. [P.L.2-2002, § 19.]

32-34-1-43. Records maintained by holder — Records maintained by certain business associations. — (a) Except as provided in subsection (b) and subject to any rules adopted by the attorney general under IC 4-22-2, a holder required to file a report under section 26 [IC 32-34-1-26] of this chapter for any property for which the holder has the last known address of the owner shall maintain a record of the information required to be in the report for at least ten (10) years after the property becomes reportable.

(b) A business association that sells in Indiana traveler's checks, money orders, or other similar written instruments, other than third party bank checks on which the business association is directly liable, or that provides those instruments to others for sale in Indiana, shall maintain a record of outstanding instruments indicating the state and date of issue for at least three (3) years after the date the property is reportable. [P.L.2-2002, § 19.]

32-34-1-44. Exchange of information with other states — Enforcement of other state laws — Confidentiality of certain records — Attorney general's audit reports. — (a) The attorney general may enter into an agreement with other states to exchange information relating to unclaimed property or the possible existence of unclaimed property. The agreements may permit other states, or a person acting on behalf of a state, to examine records as authorized in section 42 [IC 32-34-1-42] of this chapter. The attorney general may, by rule, require the reporting of information needed to enable compliance with any agreements made under this section and prescribe the form.

(b) The attorney general may join with other states to seek enforcement of this chapter against a person who is or may be holding property reportable under this chapter.

(c) At the request of another state, the attorney general may commence an action on behalf of the administrator of the other state to enforce in Indiana the unclaimed property laws of the other state against a holder of property subject to escheat or a claim of abandonment by the other state, if the other state has agreed to pay expenses incurred by the attorney general in maintaining the action.

(d) The attorney general may request that the attorney general of another state or any other attorney commence an action in that state on behalf of the attorney general. The attorney general may retain another attorney to commence an action in Indiana on behalf of the attorney general. This state shall pay all expenses, including attorney's fees, in maintaining an action under this subsection. With the attorney general's approval, the expenses and attorney's fees may be paid from money received under this chapter. The attorney general may agree to pay the person bringing the action attorney's fees based in whole or in part on a percentage of the value of any property recovered in the action. Expenses or attorney's fees paid under this subsection may not be deducted from the amount that is subject to the claim by the owner under this chapter.

(e) Any documents and working papers obtained or compiled by the attorney general or the attorney general's agents, employees, or designated representatives in the course of conducting an audit under section 42 of this chapter are confidential and are not public records except:

(1) when used by the attorney general to maintain an action to collect unclaimed property or otherwise enforce this chapter;

(2) when used in joint audits conducted with or under agreements with other states, the federal government, or other governmental entities; or

(3) under subpoena or court order.

The documents and working papers may be disclosed to the abandoned property office of another state for that state's use in circumstances equivalent to those described in this subsection if the other state is bound to keep the documents and papers confidential.

(f) The attorney general's final completed audit reports are public records, available for inspection and copying under IC 5-14-3. A final report may not contain confidential documentation or working papers unless an exception under subsection (e) applies. [P.L.2-2002, § 19.]

32-34-1-45. Failure to pay or deliver property — Accrual of interest — Penalties. — (a) A holder that fails to pay or deliver the property within the time required by this chapter shall pay to the attorney general interest for the time the holder is delinquent. Interest shall accrue under this subsection at the following rates:

(1) The annual interest rate for a period of one (1) year or less after the time required by this chapter for payment or delivery of the property is:

(A) the one (1) year Treasury Bill rate published in the *Wall Street Journal* or its successor on the third Tuesday of the month in which the remittance was due; plus

(B) one (1) percentage point.

(2) The interest rate for each year after the initial year to which subdivision (1) applies is:

(A) the one (1) year Treasury Bill rate published in the *Wall Street Journal* or its successor on the third Tuesday of the month immediately preceding the anniversary; plus

(B) one (1) percentage point.

As used in this subdivision, "anniversary" means the anniversary of the date on which the property was originally due to be paid or delivered under this chapter.

(b) A holder who fails to render any report or perform other duties required under this chapter shall pay a civil penalty of one hundred dollars ($100) for each day for the first fifteen (15) days that the report is withheld or the duty not performed. After the first fifteen (15) days, the holder shall pay a civil penalty of the greater of:

(1) one hundred dollars ($100) a day for each additional day, not to exceed five thousand dollars ($5,000); or

(2) ten percent (10%) of the value of the property at issue, not to exceed five thousand dollars ($5,000).

Upon a showing by the holder of good cause sufficient in the discretion of the attorney general to excuse the failure, the attorney general may waive the penalty in whole or in part.

(c) A holder who knowingly or intentionally fails to pay or deliver property to the attorney general as required under this chapter shall pay an additional civil penalty equal to ten percent (10%) of the value of the property that must be paid or delivered under this chapter. If the attorney general believes it is in the best interest for the administration of this chapter, the attorney general may waive the penalty in whole or in part.

(d) A holder who willfully refuses, after written demand by the attorney general, to pay or deliver property to the attorney general as required under this chapter commits a Class B misdemeanor. [P.L.2-2002, § 19.]

Cross References. Penalties for misdemeanors, IC 35-50-1, IC 35-50-3, IC 35-50-5-2.

32-34-1-46. Agreements to locate, deliver or recover property — Unenforceable agreements — Compensation. — (a) This subsection does not apply to an owner's agreement with an attorney to file a claim as to identified property or to contest the attorney general's denial of a claim. An agreement by an owner that:

(1) has the primary purpose of paying compensation to locate, deliver, recover, or assist in the recovery of property presumed abandoned under this chapter; and

(2) is entered into not earlier than the date the property was presumed abandoned and not later than twenty-four (24) months after the date the property is paid or delivered to the attorney general;

is void and unenforceable.

(b) An agreement by an owner that has the primary purpose of locating, delivering, recovering, or assisting in the recovery of property is valid only if:

(1) the fee or compensation agreed upon is not more than ten percent (10%) of the amount collected, unless the amount collected is fifty dollars ($50) or less;

(2) the agreement is in writing;

(3) the agreement is signed by the apparent owner;

(4) the agreement clearly sets forth:

(A) the nature and value of the property; and

(B) the value of the apparent owner's share after the fee or compensation has been deducted; and

(5) the agreement contains the provision set forth in subsection (d).

(c) This section does not prevent an owner from asserting at any time that an agreement to locate property is otherwise invalid.

(d) This subsection applies to a person who locates, delivers, recovers, or assists in the recovery of property reported under this chapter for a fee or compensation. An advertisement, a written communication, or an agreement concerning the location, delivery, recovery, or assistance in the recovery of property reported under this chapter must contain a provision stating that, by law, any contract provision requiring the payment of a fee for finding property held by the attorney general for less than twenty-four (24) months is void, and that fees are limited to not more than ten percent (10%) of the amount collected unless the amount collected is fifty dollars ($50) or less.

(e) Subsections (b)(4) and (d) do not apply to attorney's fees.

(f) If an agreement covered by this section:

(1) applies to mineral proceeds; and

(2) contains a provision to pay compensation that includes a portion of the underlying minerals or any mineral proceeds not then presumed abandoned;

the provision is void and unenforceable.

(g) An agreement covered by this section that provides for compensation that is unconscionable is unenforceable except by the owner. An owner who has agreed to pay compensation that is unconscionable, or the attorney general on behalf of the owner, may maintain an action to reduce the compensation to a conscionable amount. The court may award reasonable attorney's fees to an owner who prevails in the action. [P.L.2-2002, § 19.]

32-34-1-47. Cooperation with attorney general. — All officers, agencies, boards, bureaus, commissions, divisions, and departments of the state, including any body politic and corporate created by the state for public purposes, and every political subdivision of the state shall do the following:

(1) Cooperate with the attorney general upon the attorney general's request to further the purposes of this chapter.

(2) Make their records available to the attorney general for the purposes of discovering property that is presumed to be abandoned under this chapter.

(3) Compile from their records, upon the attorney general's request, reports that would aid the attorney general in identifying the holders of property presumed to be abandoned under this chapter and in discovering property that is presumed to be abandoned. [P.L.2-2002, § 19.]

32-34-1-48. Employment of independent consultants by attorney general. — The attorney general may employ the services of any independent consultants and other persons possessing specialized skills or knowledge that the attorney general considers necessary or appropriate for the administration of this chapter, including consultants in the following areas:

(1) Upkeep.

(2) Management.

(3) Sale.

(4) Conveyance of property.

(5) Determination of any sources of unreported abandoned property. [P.L.2-2002, § 19.]

32-34-1-49. Duties that arose before July 1, 1996. — This chapter does not relieve a holder of a duty that arose before July 1, 1996, to report, pay, or deliver property. Except as provided in section 41(b) [IC 32-34-1-41(b)] of this chapter, a holder that did not comply with the law in effect before July 1, 1996, is subject to the applicable enforcement and penalty provisions that existed and that are continued in effect for the purpose of this section. [P.L.2-2002, § 19.]

32-34-1-50. Construction of chapter. — This chapter shall be applied and construed to effectuate its general purpose to make uniform the law with respect to the subject of this chapter among states enacting it. [P.L.2-2002, § 19.]

32-34-1-51. Enforcement of chapter. — The attorney general may maintain an action in a court of competent jurisdiction to enforce this chapter. [P.L.2-2002, § 19.]

32-34-1-52. Adoption of rules by attorney general. — The attorney general may adopt rules under IC 4-22-2 to carry out the purposes of this chapter. [P.L.2-2002, § 19.]

CHAPTER 2

SALE OF UNCLAIMED PROPERTY IN HOTELS

32-34-2-1. Unclaimed articles — Notice of sale. — (a) After a proprietor, manager, or lessee of a hotel in Indiana holds an unclaimed article for at least three (3) months, whether or not a receipt or check for the article was given to the person who left the article, the proprietor, manager, or lessee may sell the article at a public auction, and, out of the proceeds, retain any balance due from the person leaving the article, the expenses of advertising the sale, and the expenses of the sale.

(b) A proprietor, manager, or lessee may not sell the article until:

(1) notice of the sale is sent to the owner by mail, if the name and address of the owner are known; and

(2) two (2) weeks after the publication of a notice of the sale is made in a newspaper published at or nearest the place where the article was left and where the sale will take place.

(c) The notice must contain a description of the article and the time and place of the sale.

(d) A proprietor, manager, or lessee shall record the amount received at the sale for each article sold and the balance, if any, remaining after the balance due and the expenses of the sale have been paid.

(e) At any time within one (1) year after the sale, a proprietor, manager, or lessee shall refund the balance referred to in subsection (d) to the owner of the article or to the owner's heirs or assigns upon presentation of satisfactory proof of ownership. [P.L.2-2002, § 19.]

Effective Dates. P.L.2-2002, § 19. July 1. 2002.

Collateral References. 40 Am. Jur. 2d Hotels, Motels and Restaurants, §§ 79, 145-148.

43A C.J.S. Inns, Hotels, and Eating Places, § 41.

Statutory limitations upon innkeeper's liability as applicable where guest's property is lost or damaged through innkeeper's negligence. 37 A.L.R.3d 1276.

32-34-2-2. Balance from sale. — If the balance is not claimed by the owner within one (1) year after the sale conducted under section 1 [IC 32-34-2-1] of this chapter, the balance must be paid to the county treasurer for the use of the school fund. [P.L.2-2002, § 19.]

CHAPTER 3

UNCLAIMED MONEY IN POSSESSION OF A COURT CLERK

32-34-3-1. "Clerk" defined. — As used in this chapter, "clerk" means any person performing the duties of a clerk of any court, whether designated specifically as the clerk of that court or not. [P.L.2-2002, § 19.]

Effective Dates. P.L.2-2002, § 19. July 1. 2002.

32-34-3-2. Collection — Deposit in abandoned property fund. — (a) Except for money related to child support, the attorney general may collect all money that remains in the office of a clerk for at least five (5) years after being distributable without being claimed by the person entitled to the money.

(b) The attorney general may collect all money related to child support that remains in the office of a clerk for at least ten (10) years after being distributable without being claimed by the person entitled to the money.

(c) Clerks shall deliver the money described in subsections (a) and (b) to the attorney general upon demand, and the attorney general shall:

(1) make a record of the money collected; and

(2) turn it over to the treasurer of state.

(d) The treasurer of state shall deposit the money in the abandoned property fund established by IC 32-34-1-31. [P.L.2-2002, § 19.]

32-34-3-3. Claims — Payment. — (a) Within five (5) years after a sum of money is deposited in the abandoned property fund in accordance with section 2(d) [IC 32-34-3-2(d)] of this chapter, a person may make a claim to the money by filing an application in the court whose clerk originally held the sum. The claimant shall give at least ten (10) days prior notice of the proceedings on the claim to the attorney general, who may appear in the proceedings to represent the interests of the state.

(b) If the proof presented by the claimant satisfies the court that the claim is valid, the court shall order payment of the money to the claimant. If presented with a certified copy of the court's order, the attorney general shall direct the treasurer to return the sum of money to the clerk, who shall present the money to the claimant. [P.L.2-2002, § 19.]

32-34-3-4. Title to unclaimed funds — Time limit on claims. — (a) If a sum of money remains in the abandoned property fund for at least five (5) years after the date the money is deposited in the fund under section 2(d) [IC 32-34-3-2(d)] of this chapter without any order directing the return of the money:

(1) title to the sum vests in and escheats to the state; and

(2) the sum shall be distributed as part of the common school fund.

(b) Any claimant who does not file an application with the court within five (5) years after the sum is deposited in the unclaimed funds account is barred from asserting a claim. [P.L.2-2002, § 19.]

32-34-3-5. Failure to deliver to attorney general — Action against clerks. — The attorney general may bring an action against a clerk who fails to deliver a sum of money to the attorney general upon demand under section 2 [IC 32-34-3-2] of this chapter. In that action, the attorney general may recover from the clerk, individually or upon the clerk's bond, the sum demanded plus a ten percent (10%) penalty. The sum demanded plus the penalty is collectible without relief from valuation or appraisement laws. [P.L.2-2002, § 19.]

CHAPTER 4

UNCLAIMED PROPERTY IN POSSESSION OF REPOSSESSORS OF MOTOR VEHICLES OR WATERCRAFT

32-34-4-1. "Creditor" defined. — As used in this chapter, "creditor" means the person who has lawfully repossessed a vehicle. [P.L.2-2002, § 19.]

Effective Dates. P.L.2-2002, § 19. July 1. 2002.

32-34-4-2. "Debtor" defined. — As used in this chapter, "debtor" means the person from whom a vehicle is repossessed. [P.L.2-2002, § 19.]

32-34-4-3. "Value" defined. — As used in this chapter, "value" means the amount of money that a reasonable person would estimate a willing buyer would pay for an item of personal property. [P.L.2-2002, § 19.]

32-34-4-4. "Vehicle" defined. — As used in this chapter, "vehicle" means a motor vehicle or a watercraft. [P.L.2-2002, § 19.]

32-34-4-5. Property worth at least $10. — (a) If items of personal property having an estimated aggregate value of at least ten dollars ($10) are discovered within a vehicle that has been lawfully repossessed, the creditor must notify the debtor as follows:

(1) The notice must be written.

(2) The notice must list each item of personal property having an estimated value greater than five dollars ($5).

(3) The notice must include the estimated aggregate value of all of the items of personal property.

(4) The notice must include a statement that if the debtor does not claim the property within thirty (30) days after the notice was sent, the personal property will become the property of the creditor with no right of redemption by the debtor.

(5) The notice must be sent by certified mail.

(b) If the debtor does not claim the items of personal property included in a notice given under subsection (a) not more than thirty (30) days after the notice was mailed, the items of personal property become the property of the creditor with no right of redemption by the debtor. [P.L.2-2002, § 19.]

32-34-4-6. Property worth less than $10. — If items of personal property having an aggregate value of less than ten dollars ($10) are discovered within a vehicle that has been lawfully repossessed, the items of personal property are the property of the creditor with no right of redemption by the debtor. [P.L.2-2002, § 19.]

CHAPTER 5

PROPERTY LOANED TO MUSEUMS

32-34-5-1. "Lender" defined. — As used in this chapter, "lender" means a person whose name appears on the records of a museum as the person legally entitled to, or claiming to be legally entitled to, property held by the museum. [P.L.2-2002, § 19.]

Effective Dates. P.L.2-2002, § 19. July 1. 2002.

32-34-5-2. "Lender's address" defined. — As used in this chapter, "lender's address" means the most recent address of a lender as shown on the museum's records pertaining to property on loan from the lender. [P.L.2-2002, § 19.]

32-34-5-3. "Loan" defined. — As used in this chapter, "loan" means a deposit of property not accompanied by a transfer of title to the property. [P.L.2-2002, § 19.]

32-34-5-4. "Museum" defined. — As used in this chapter, "museum" means an institution located in Indiana that:
    (1) is operated by a person primarily for education, scientific, historic preservation, or aesthetic purposes; and
    (2) owns, borrows, cares for, exhibits, studies, archives, or catalogs property. [P.L.2-2002, § 19.]

32-34-5-5. "Permanent loan" defined. — As used in this chapter, "permanent loan" means a loan of property to a museum for an indefinite period. [P.L.2-2002, § 19.]

32-34-5-6. "Person" defined. — As used in this chapter, "person" means an individual, a nonprofit corporation, a trustee or legal representative, the state, a political subdivision (as defined in IC 36-1-2-13), an agency of the state or a political subdivision, or a group of those persons acting in concert. [P.L.2-2002, § 19.]

32-34-5-7. "Property" defined. — As used in this chapter, "property" means a tangible object under a museum's care that has intrinsic historic, artistic, scientific, or cultural value. [P.L.2-2002, § 19.]

32-34-5-8. "Undocumented property" defined. — As used in this chapter, "undocumented property" means property in the possession of a museum for which the museum cannot determine the owner by reference to the museum's records. [P.L.2-2002, § 19.]

32-34-5-9. Mailing of notice. — A notice given by a museum under this chapter must be mailed to the lender's last known address by certified mail. Proper notice is given if the museum receives proof of receipt of the notice not more than thirty (30) days after the notice was mailed. [P.L.2-2002, § 19.]

32-34-5-10. Notice by publication. — (a) A museum may give notice by publication under this chapter if the museum does not:

(1) know the identity of the lender;

(2) have an address last known for the lender; or

(3) receive proof of receipt of the notice by the person to whom the notice was sent within thirty (30) days after the notice was mailed.

(b) Notice by publication under subsection (a) must be given at least once a week for two (2) consecutive weeks in a newspaper of general circulation in:

(1) the county in which the museum is located; and

(2) the county of the lender's last known address, if the identity of the lender is known. [P.L.2-2002, § 19.]

32-34-5-11. Contents of notice. — In addition to any other information that may be required or seem appropriate, a notice given by a museum under this chapter must contain the following:

(1) The name of the lender, if known.

(2) The last known address of the lender.

(3) A brief description of the property on loan.

(4) The date of the loan, if known.

(5) The name of the museum.

(6) The name, address, and telephone number of the person or office to be contacted regarding the property. [P.L.2-2002, § 19.]

32-34-5-12. Acquisition of title. — A museum may acquire title in the following manner to property that is on permanent loan to the museum or that was loaned for a specified term that has expired:

(1) The museum must give notice that the museum is terminating the loan of the property.

(2) The notice that the loan of the property is terminated must include a statement containing substantially the following information:

"The records at (name of museum) indicate that you have property on loan to it. The museum hereby terminates the loan. If you desire to claim the property, you must contact the museum, establish your ownership of the property, and make arrangements to collect the property. If you do not contact the museum, you will be considered to have donated the property to the museum.".

(3) If the lender does not respond to the notice of termination within one (1) year after receipt of the notice by filing a notice of intent to preserve an interest in the property on loan, clear and unrestricted title is transferred to the museum three hundred sixty-five (365) days after the notice was received. [P.L.2-2002, § 19.]

32-34-5-13. Acquisition of title to undocumented property. — A museum may acquire title to undocumented property held by the museum for at least seven (7) years as follows:

(1) The museum must give notice that the museum is asserting title to the undocumented property.

(2) The notice that the museum is asserting title to the property must include a statement containing substantially the following information:

> "The records of (name of museum) fail to indicate the owner of record of certain property in its possession. The museum hereby asserts title to the following property: (general description of property). If you claim ownership or other legal interest in this property, you must contact the museum, establish ownership of the property, and make arrangements to collect the property. If you fail to do so within three (3) years, you will be considered to have waived any claim you may have had to the property.".

(3) If a lender does not respond to the notice within three (3) years by giving a written notice of intent to retain an interest in the property on loan, the museum's title to the property becomes absolute. [P.L.2-2002, § 19.]

32-34-5-14. Application of conservation measures to property on loan without lender's permission. — Unless there is a written loan agreement to the contrary, a museum may apply conservation measures to property on loan to the museum without the lender's permission or formal notice:

(1) if:

(A) action is required to protect the property on loan or other property in the custody of the museum; or

(B) the property on loan is a hazard to the health and safety of the public or the museum staff; and

(2) if:

(A) the museum is unable to reach the lender at the lender's last known address within three (3) days before the time the museum determines action is necessary; or

(B) the lender does not respond or will not agree to the protective measures the museum recommends and does not terminate the loan and retrieve the property within three (3) days. [P.L.2-2002, § 19.]

32-34-5-15. Lien on property for costs of application of conservation measures. — If a museum applies conservation measures to property under section 14 [IC 32-34-5-14] of this chapter or with the agreement of the lender, unless the agreement provides otherwise, the museum:

(1) acquires a lien on the property in the amount of the costs incurred by the museum; and

(2) is not liable for injury to or loss of the property if the museum:

(A) had a reasonable belief at the time the action was taken that the action was necessary to protect the property on loan or other property in the custody of the museum, or that the property on loan was a hazard to the health and safety of the public or the museum staff; and (B) exercised reasonable care in the choice and application of conservation measures. [P.L.2-2002, § 19.]

32-34-5-16. Presumption of gift to museum of certain property. — Property that:

(1) is found in or on property controlled by the museum;

(2) is from an unknown source; and

(3) might reasonably be assumed to have been intended as a gift to the museum;

is conclusively presumed to be a gift to the museum if ownership of the property is not claimed by a person or individual within ninety (90) days after its discovery. [P.L.2-2002, § 19.]

CHAPTER 6

TRANSFER OF PROPERTY INTERESTS IN MOLDS

32-34-6-1. Applicability. — (a) This chapter does not apply where a fabricator retains title to and possession of a die, mold, form, jig, or pattern.

(b) This chapter does not grant a customer any rights, title, or interest to a die, mold, form, jig, or pattern. [P.L.2-2002, § 19.]

Effective Dates. P.L.2-2002, § 19. July 1. 2002.

32-34-6-2. "Customer" defined. — As used in this chapter, "customer" means an individual or entity who contracts with or causes a fabricator:

(1) to fabricate, cast, or otherwise make a die, mold, form, jig, or pattern; or

(2) to use a die, mold, form, jig, or pattern to manufacture, assemble, or otherwise make a product. [P.L.2-2002, § 19.]

32-34-6-3. "Fabricator" defined. — As used in this chapter, "fabricator" means an individual or entity, including a tool or die maker, who:

(1) manufactures, causes to be manufactured, assembles, or improves a die, mold, form, jig, or pattern for a customer; or

(2) uses a die, mold, form, jig, or pattern to manufacture, assemble, or otherwise make a product for a customer. [P.L.2-2002, § 19.]

32-34-6-4. "Within three (3) years after the last prior use" defined. — As used in this chapter, "within three (3) years after the last prior use" includes any period after the last prior use of a die, mold, form, jig, or pattern, regardless of whether the period was before July 1, 1994. [P.L.2-2002, § 19.]

32-34-6-5. Transferal of rights to fabricator. — If a customer does not take possession of the customer's die, mold, form, jig, or pattern from a fabricator within three (3) years after the last prior use of the die, mold, form, jig, or pattern, the customer's rights, title, and interest in the customer's die, mold, form, jig, or pattern are transferred to the fabricator pursuant to the procedures of this chapter for purposes of destruction of the die, mold, form, jig, or pattern. [P.L.2-2002, § 19.]

32-34-6-6. Destruction by fabricator — Notice. — (a) After the three (3) year period specified in section 4 [IC 32-34-6-4] of this chapter has expired, a fabricator may choose to have all rights, title, and interest in the die, mold, form, jig, or pattern transferred to the fabricator for purposes of destruction. A fabricator seeking a transfer under this subsection must send written notice by registered mail, return receipt requested, to:
    (1) the customer's address as set out in any written agreement between the fabricator and the customer; and
    (2) the customer's last known address;
indicating that the fabricator intends to terminate the customer's rights, title, and interest by having the rights, title, and interest transferred to the fabricator under this chapter.
  (b) If a customer:
    (1) does not take possession of the particular die, mold, form, jig, or pattern within ninety (90) days after the date on which the notice was sent under subsection (a); or
    (2) does not make other contractual arrangements with the fabricator for taking possession or for storage of the die, mold, form, jig, or pattern;
all rights, title, and interest of the customer to the mold transfer by operation of this chapter to the fabricator for the purpose of destruction. The fabricator may then destroy the die, mold, or form. [P.L.2-2002, § 19.]

32-34-6-7. Validity of written agreements and laws concerning unfair competition. — Nothing in this chapter affects:
    (1) a written agreement between the fabricator and customer concerning possession of the die, mold, form, jig, or pattern; or
    (2) any right of the customer under federal patent or copyright law or any state or federal law pertaining to unfair competition. [P.L.2-2002, § 19.]

Collateral References. Construction and effect of provision of employment contract giving employer right to inventions made by employee. 66 A.L.R.4th 1135.

Copyrightability of sculptural works. 83 A.L.R. Fed. 845.

CHAPTER 7

TRANSFER OF PROPERTY INTERESTS IN SILK SCREENS

32-34-7-1. Applicability. — (a) This chapter does not apply where a silk screen maker or silk screen user retains title to and possession of a silk screen.

(b) This chapter does not grant a customer any rights or title to or interest in a silk screen. [P.L.2-2002, § 19.]

Effective Dates. P.L.2-2002, § 19. July 1. 2002.

32-34-7-2. "Customer" defined. — As used in this chapter, "customer" means an individual or entity that causes another individual or entity to make a silk screen or to use a silk screen to manufacture, assemble, or make a product. [P.L.2-2002, § 19.]

32-34-7-3. "Silk screen maker" defined. — As used in this chapter, "silk screen maker" means an individual or entity that makes a silk screen. [P.L.2-2002, § 19.]

32-34-7-4. "Silk screen user" defined. — As used in this chapter, "silk screen user" means an individual or entity that uses a silk screen to manufacture, assemble, or make a product. [P.L.2-2002, § 19.]

32-34-7-5. Transfer of customer's rights, title, and interest. — If a customer does not take possession of the customer's silk screen from a silk screen maker or silk screen user within three (3) years after the silk screen's last use, the customer's rights, title, and interest in the customer's silk screen are transferred to the silk screen maker or silk screen user pursuant to the procedures of this chapter for purposes of destruction of the silk screen. [P.L.2-2002, § 19.]

32-34-7-6. Destruction of silk screen by maker or user — Notice to customer — Transfer of rights. — (a) After the three (3) year period specified in section 5 [IC 32-34-7-5] of this chapter has expired, a silk screen maker or silk screen user may choose to have all rights, title, and interest in any silk screen transferred to the silk screen maker or silk screen user for purposes of destruction. A silk screen maker or silk screen user seeking a transfer under this subsection must send written notice by registered mail, return receipt requested, to:

(1) the customer's address as set out in any written agreement between the silk screen maker or silk screen user and the customer; and

(2) the customer's last known address;

indicating that the silk screen maker or silk screen user intends to terminate the customer's rights, title, and interest by having all the rights, title, and interest transferred to the silk screen maker or silk screen user under this chapter.

(b) If a customer:

(1) does not take possession of the particular silk screen within ninety (90) days after the date on which the notice was sent under subsection (a); or

(2) does not make other contractual arrangements with the silk screen maker or silk screen user for taking possession or for storage of the silk screen;

all rights, title, and interest of the customer to the silk screen transfer by operation of this chapter to the silk screen maker or silk screen user for the purpose of destruction. The silk screen maker or silk screen user may then destroy the silk screen. [P.L.2-2002, § 19.]

32-34-7-7. Effect on other agreements and rights. — This chapter does not affect:

(1) a written agreement between the silk screen maker or silk screen user and the customer concerning possession of the silk screen; or

(2) any rights of the customer under federal patent or copyright law or any state or federal law pertaining to unfair competition. [P.L.2-2002, § 19.]

32-34-7-8. Silk screens in existence on June 1, 1983. — For silk screens in existence on June 1, 1983, the three (3) year period specified in this chapter begins on the last date that the silk screen was used, regardless of whether that date was before June 1, 1983. [P.L.2-2002, § 19.]

CHAPTER 8

FINDING STRAYS OR PROPERTY ADRIFT

32-34-8-1. Advertisement. — A person who finds a stray horse, mule, ass, sheep, hog, cattle, or goat, or any other article of value, shall, within five (5) days after finding the animal or article, advertise the animal or article in writing in three (3) of the most public places in the township where the animal or article was found, stating the time the animal or article was found and giving a description of the animal or article. [P.L.2-2002, § 19.]

Effective Dates. P.L.2-2002, § 19. July 1. 2002.

Cross References. Advertising, fee, IC 32-34-8-6, IC 32-34-8-14, IC 32-34-8-30.

Animals, running at large, IC 15-2.1-21-8.

Boats and timber, taking up, IC 32-9-5-1 — IC 32-34-9-9, IC 32-34-9-10 — IC 32-34-9-13.

Estrays, taking up, IC 32-26-2-4 — IC 32-26-2-13.

Fence law, trespassing animals, IC 32-26-2-1 et seq.

NOTES TO DECISIONS

In General.

Persons who took up animals as estrays had to comply with the provisions of the statute in order to retain possession of the property as against the owner. Burton v. Calaway, 20 Ind. 469 (1863); James v. Fowler, 90 Ind. 563 (1883); Haffner v. Barnard, 123 Ind. 429, 24 N.E. 152 (1890); Frazier v. Goar, 1 Ind. App. 38, 27 N.E. 442 (1891); Forsyth v. Walch, 4 Ind. App. 182, 30 N.E. 720 (1892); Wyman v. Turner, 14 Ind. App. 118, 42 N.E. 652 (1896).

It was the statutory duty of road supervisors to cause certain specified domestic animals found running at large to be impounded. Frazier v. Goar, 1 Ind. App. 38, 27 N.E. 442 (1891); Wilhelm v. Scott, 14 Ind. App. 275, 40 N.E. 537, 42 N.E. 827 (1895); Wyman v. Turner, 14 Ind. App. 118, 42 N.E. 652 (1896); Beeson v. Tice, 17 Ind. App. 78, 45 N.E. 612, 46 N.E. 154 (1896).

Collateral References. 4 Am. Jur. 2d Animals, §§ 46-48.

3A C.J.S. Animals, §§ 123-136.

Liability of governmental entity for damage to motor vehicle or injury to person riding therein resulting from collision between vehicle and domestic animal at large in street or highway. 52 A.L.R.4th 1200.

32-34-8-2. Report to court — Appraisal. — (a) If the owner does not claim the property described in section 1 of this chapter within fifteen (15) days after the date the property is found, the finder shall report the property to a court with jurisdiction in the county where the property was found.

(b) The court shall issue a warrant to three (3) householders of the neighborhood not related to the finder (unless persons not related to the finder are not available) directing any two (2) of the householders to appraise the property. The appointed householders shall appraise the property and provide in writing to the court a report containing the following information:

(1) A clear description of the property.

(2) The householders' valuation of the property.

(3) A declaration under oath that the appraisal and description were made without partiality, favor, or affection. [P.L.2-2002, § 19.]

Cross References. Adrift property, report
to justice, IC 32-34-8-8.
  Fees of appraiser, IC 32-34-8-29.

32-34-8-3. Oath of finder. — The finder must, at the time the house-holders make the report required by section 2(b) [IC 32-34-8-2(b)] of this chapter, state under oath that the finder has no knowledge that the marks, brands, or appearance of the property have been altered by the finder or any other person since the property was lost, except for the changes stated in the householders' written report. [P.L.2-2002, § 19.]

32-34-8-4. Impounding. — The finder of an unclaimed stray horse, mule, or ass that is at least two (2) years of age shall take the animal to the pound of the proper county and keep the animal at the pound from 11 a.m. until 3 p.m. on the first day of each of the two (2) succeeding terms of the circuit court after finding the stray. [P.L.2-2002, § 19.]

32-34-8-5. Court's and clerk's duties. — A court receiving the property report prepared under section 2(b) [IC 32-34-8-2(b)] of this chapter shall, within ten (10) days, transmit to the clerk of the circuit court a copy of the description and valuation of the property, together with the proper fee. The clerk shall enter the description and appraisal in a book to be kept for that purpose. [P.L.2-2002, § 19.]

32-34-8-6. Advertising — Publication in newspapers — Fee. — Property described in section 1 [IC 32-34-8-1] of this chapter that is greater than ten dollars ($10) in value must be advertised in a newspaper of the county, if there be one, and if not, in a paper in Indiana nearest the county where the property was found. The clerk shall forward to the printer a copy of the register that is marked on the outside, "Stray Property," together with a fee of one dollar ($1) out of which the printer shall pay postage. [P.L.2-2002, § 19.]

32-34-8-7. When title vests in finder. — If the provisions of this chapter are complied with, title to:
  (1) an article described in section 1 [IC 32-34-8-1] of this chapter that is not more than twelve dollars ($12) in value and that remains unclaimed or unproven by the owner within ninety (90) days after the property is found; or
  (2) a stray animal described in section 1 of this chapter that is equal to or less than ten dollars ($10) in value and that remains unclaimed or unproven by the owner within one (1) year after the property is found;
vests in the finder. [P.L.2-2002, § 19.]

32-34-8-8. Report to court — When required. — If:

(1) an article described in section 1 [IC 32-34-8-1] of this chapter has an appraised value greater than twelve dollars ($12) and is not claimed and proven within ninety (90) days after the day the article is found; or

(2) a stray animal other than a horse, a mule, or an ass has an appraised value greater than ten dollars ($10) and is not claimed and proven within six (6) months after the animal is found;

the finder shall report that information to a court with jurisdiction where the property was initially found not later than five (5) days after the expiration of the time specified in this section. [P.L.2-2002, § 19.]

32-34-8-9. Sale by sheriff. — (a) The court shall issue a warrant to the sheriff to sell the property at auction, giving ten (10) days notice in writing of the time and place of sale and describing the property to be sold.

(b) The sheriff shall, within five (5) days after the sale, return the order and proceeds of sale to the court, retaining one dollar ($1) for the sheriff's services.

(c) The court shall immediately pay over to the county treasurer the proceeds of sale, after deducting the proper amount to be paid to the finder, fifty cents ($0.50) for the fee of the judge of the court and, for every mile that the judge must travel in making the return, a sum for mileage equal to that sum per mile paid to state officers and employees.

(d) The court shall receive from the treasurer duplicate receipts and file one (1) receipt in the office of the clerk of the circuit court and one (1) receipt with the county auditor. [P.L.2-2002, § 19.]

NOTES TO DECISIONS

In General.
If the taker up improperly refuses to deliver the property to the constable for sale, he will be considered a trespasser from the beginning and liable to the owner of the property for its value. Burton v. Calaway, 20 Ind. 469 (1863).

32-34-8-10. Animals worth over twenty dollars — Sale. — (a) If a horse, a mule, or an ass that has an appraised value greater than twenty dollars ($20) remains unclaimed or unproven twelve (12) months after the date the horse, mule, or ass was found, the finder shall deliver the horse, mule, or ass to the sheriff of the proper county on the first day of the term of the circuit court after the expiration of the twelve (12) month period.

(b) The sheriff shall sell the horse, mule, or ass delivered under subsection (a) at a public sale.

(c) After retaining one dollar ($1) for the sheriff's services and paying to the finder the charges as provided by this chapter, the sheriff shall pay the proceeds of the sale to the treasurer of the county within five (5) days after the sale.

(d) The sheriff shall receive from the treasurer duplicate receipts and file one (1) receipt in the clerk's office and the other receipt with the county auditor. [P.L.2-2002, § 19.]

32-34-8-11. County stray fund. — The county treasurer shall enter all sums paid under this chapter to the credit of the county stray fund. [P.L.2-2002, § 19.]

NOTES TO DECISIONS

In General.
When the title to such moneys vested absolutely in the county, it became a part of the common school fund. Board of Comm'rs v. State ex rel. Att'y Gen., 92 Ind. 353 (1883).

32-34-8-12. Finder's fee. — (a) The finder's fee is as follows:
   (1) For each horse, mule or ass, one dollar ($1).
   (2) For each head of neat cattle, fifty cents ($0.50).
   (3) For each sheep, goat, or hog more than six (6) months old, ten cents ($0.10).
   (b) If the owner reclaims and proves the property before the property is posted, the finder is allowed half of the appropriate amount listed in subsection (a). [P.L.2-2002, § 19.]

32-34-8-13. Reasonable sum for finding and caring for property. — (a) The finder of an article described in section 1 [IC 32-34-8-1] of this chapter is allowed a reasonable sum, as determined by a court with jurisdiction where the property was initially found.
   (b) Either the claimant or the finder may have a jury determine what amount is just and reasonable for finding and taking care of the property. [P.L.2-2002, § 19.]

32-34-8-14. Fees. — (a) If the property described in section 13 [IC 32-34-8-13] of this chapter is greater than three dollars ($3) in value, the finder of the property shall pay to the court, at the time of reporting, fifty cents ($0.50) for the judge of the court, fifty cents ($0.50) for the clerk, and one dollar ($1) for the printer where printing is required.
   (b) If the value of the property described in section 13 of this chapter is less than three dollars ($3), the court may not make a return to the clerk and the fee is twenty-five cents ($0.25). [P.L.2-2002, § 19.]

32-34-8-15. Register of stray animals. — (a) The clerk shall keep a register of stray animals and found articles.
   (b) If several strays or articles are found by one (1) person, there may be only one (1) entry, one (1) advertisement, one (1) fee of the clerk, and one (1) fee of the judge. [P.L.2-2002, § 19.]

32-34-8-16. Pay for keeping property. — If found property is sold or reclaimed, the finder is allowed just and reasonable compensation for keeping the property as determined by the court with jurisdiction where the property was initially found. The finder shall:
   (1) keep account of the time a stray animal is kept by the finder; and
   (2) state the time to the court under oath.
[P.L.2-2002, § 19.]

NOTES TO DECISIONS

In General.

The owner of an estray could not maintain an action in the circuit court to recover the same from the takerup who had complied with the provisions of the estray law until such owner had proved his ownership before a justice of the peace, and paid or tendered the legal charges for keeping the animal. Logan v. Marquess, 53 Ind. 16 (1876).

Compliance with law by persons who take up animals running at large in order to retain possession as against the owner. Frazier v. Goar, 1 Ind. App. 38, 27 N.E. 442 (1891); Forsyth v. Walch, 4 Ind. App. 182, 30 N.E. 720 (1892); Wilhelm v. Scott, 14 Ind. App. 275, 40 N.E. 537, 42 N.E. 827 (1895); Wyman v. Turner, 14 Ind. App. 118, 42 N.E. 652 (1896).

32-34-8-17. Services of animal. — (a) If an animal is found under the provisions of this chapter and worked by the finder, a reasonable compensation shall be allowed for the services of the animal. The compensation shall be deducted from the cost of keeping the animal.

(b) The finder, if required, shall verify, under oath, the time the animal worked. [P.L.2-2002, § 19.]

32-34-8-18. Owner's reclamation. — (a) At any time before sale, the owner may have the property by proving ownership in the court where the finding was reported under this chapter and paying the charges required by this chapter.

(b) At any time up to two (2) years after the date of sale, the owner may reclaim the money paid into the treasury by proper proof before the county auditor. [P.L.2-2002, § 19.]

Cross References. Reclamation of estrays, IC 32-26-2-8.

32-34-8-19. Place and time of taking up. — (a) Except as provided in subsection (c), a person may not:

(1) take up any horse or stock under this chapter except at the person's place of residence; or

(2) drive any horse or stock out of the woods and take them up under this chapter.

(b) Except as provided in subsection (c), an animal may not be taken up under this chapter between the first day of April and the first day of November unless the animal is found in the enclosure of the person who takes up the animal.

(c) When any animal may be in the act of escaping from the owner, it may be taken up at any time, wherever found. [P.L.2-2002, § 19.]

NOTES TO DECISIONS

Indictment.

An indictment charging the unlawful taking up of animals between April 1 and November 1 had to specify the time when the animals were taken up. Greene v. State, 79 Ind. 537 (1881).

32-34-8-20. Removal from county. — The finder, until the finder becomes the property's owner, may not take the found property or allow the property to be taken out of the county where the property was found for longer than three (3) days at any time. [P.L.2-2002, § 19.]

Cross References. Criminal conversion,
IC 35-43-4-3.

32-34-8-21. Fatted hogs. — (a) Fatted hogs that are found may, at the option of the finder, be killed one (1) month after posting.

(b) If fatted hogs are killed under subsection (a), the finder shall, immediately after killing the hogs, pay the hogs' appraised values, deducting costs and charges (to be liquidated as in other cases) to the county treasurer for the use of the owner. [P.L.2-2002, § 19.]

32-34-8-22. Stock hogs. — Stock hogs that are found may, at the option of the finder, be purchased by the finder, six (6) months after posting, at the hogs' appraised value, deducting the costs allowed by this chapter for finding the hogs but without an allowance for keeping the hogs. [P.L.2-2002, § 19.]

32-34-8-23. Reclamation of wrecked cargo or baggage — Advertising. — (a) Sections 1 through 22 [IC 32-34-8-1 through IC 32-34-8-22] of this chapter do not apply to property described in this section.

(b) If, upon any navigable waters within or bordering Indiana, cargo that is shipped as freight, the baggage of passengers, or a part of either of a vessel is cast adrift, afloat, or ashore by a wreck, accident, or mischance of the vessel, the cargo or part of the cargo found and secured by a person may be reclaimed by the captain, clerk, or officer navigating the vessel, the super cargo, or the owner or agent of the owner of the cargo or baggage.

(c) If the property described in this section is not claimed within seven (7) days after the property is found, the finder of the property shall advertise the property as required for articles described in section 1 [IC 32-34-8-1] of this chapter. [P.L.2-2002, § 19.]

Cross References. Advertising property,
IC 32-34-8-1, IC 32-34-8-6.

32-34-8-24. Proof — Payment. — A person who finds property described in section 23 [IC 32-34-8-23] of this chapter shall surrender the property to a claimant upon proof, or circumstances satisfactory to the finder, of the right of the claimant to the property, and after the payment by the claimant of reasonable compensation for services or expenses in connection with the finding and preserving of the property. [P.L.2-2002, § 19.]

32-34-8-25. Recovery of property by claimant — Proceedings before court. — If a person with possession of the property refuses to return the property to the claimant or claims unreasonable compensation for the services and expenses in the finding and preservation of the property, the claimant may have a summary proceeding before:

    (1) the court where the property was reported under this chapter if the property was reported; and

(2) any court with jurisdiction where the property is located if the property was not reported to a court under this chapter;
for the recovery of the property. [P.L.2-2002, § 19.]

32-34-8-26. Affidavit and summons. — (a) The claimant must file before the court specified under section 25 [IC 32-34-8-25] of this chapter an affidavit of the facts attending the wreck or accident, enumerating as nearly as possible the articles or packages in the possession of the finder and the claimant's right to recover the property.

(b) The court shall summon the person who found or is in possession of the property to appear before the court at a place and at the earliest practicable time, as designated in the writ, but not more than three (3) days after the date of the writ. [P.L.2-2002, § 19.]

32-34-8-27. Trial — Amount of compensation — Writ for delivery of property. — (a) The court shall hear and determine the matters in controversy in the most speedy manner practicable, as other proceedings are determined before the court.

(b) The court may fix the amount of compensation the claimant must pay and award a writ, or writs, for the delivery of the property to the claimant upon payment of the compensation. [P.L.2-2002, § 19.]

32-34-8-28. Trial procedure — Continuances — Appeals. — (a) The trial described in section 27 [IC 32-34-8-27] of this chapter is governed by the Indiana rules of trial procedure, except as to continuances.

(b) Appeals may be taken by either party upon the same terms and under the same rules as appeals in other civil cases are taken. [P.L.2-2002, § 19.]

32-34-8-29. Appraiser — Compensation. — An appraiser appraising property in accordance with section 2 [IC 32-34-8-2] of this chapter shall receive compensation for the appraisal services in the sum of fifty cents ($0.50) to be paid the same manner as other expenses involved in the finding of strays. [P.L.2-2002, § 19.]

Collateral References. 4 Am. Jur. 2d, §§ 46-48.
3A C.J.S. Animals, §§ 123-136.

CHAPTER 9

DRIFTING BOATS AND TIMBER

32-34-9-1. "Timber" defined. — As used in this chapter, "timber" means trees, whether standing, down, or prepared for sale, sawlogs and all other logs, cross and railroad ties, boards, planks, staves and heading, and other trees cut or prepared for market. [P.L.2-2002, § 19.]

Effective Dates. P.L.2-2002, § 19. July 1. 2002.

32-34-9-2. Boats and timber — Finding — Fees — Sale. — (a) A person who finds and secures any boats, fleets of timber, rafts, platforms, sawlogs, or other logs or trees prepared for the purpose of sale, or any cross or railroad ties, boards, planks, staves, heading, or other timber prepared for market that is the property of another and that is found adrift in the waters of Indiana without a boom or other arrangement provided by the owner to preserve the logs or timber below the point at which they are found, whether the logs or timber have a brand or not, is entitled to receive from the owner the following compensation:

(1) For each freight boat or other heavy boat, two dollars ($2) per ton for all cargo.

(2) For each jack-boat, skiff, or canoe, one dollar ($1).

(3) For each fleet of timber, fifty dollars ($50).

(4) For each raft of not less than forty (40) logs, fifteen dollars ($15).

(5) For each platform of at least ten (10) logs, four dollars ($4).

(6) For each sawlog or other log or tree prepared for sale, fifty cents ($0.50).

(7) For each cross or railroad tie, fifteen cents ($0.15).

(8) For boards or planks caught in rafts or a large body:

(A) one dollar ($1) per one thousand (1,000) board feet for a quantity twenty thousand (20,000) board feet or less; or

(B) fifty cents ($0.50) per one thousand (1,000) board feet for a quantity greater than twenty thousand (20,000) board feet.

(9) For loose and scattered boards or planks, five dollars and fifty cents ($5.50) per one thousand (1,000) board feet.

(10) For staves and heading, four dollars ($4) per one thousand (1,000) pieces that are merchantable.

(b) The compensation due under subsection (a) is payable by the owner, if required, upon the delivery to the owner of the logs or timber.

(c) The finder has a lien upon the property found for the charges provided in subsection (a).

(d) If the owner of the property fails to pay the compensation due under subsection (a) within sixty (60) days after the day the property is found, the property may be sold at the request of the person to whom the compensation is due by a constable, sheriff, or other officer of the county in which the property was found. The sale must be at the courthouse door at public auction to the highest bidder, upon thirty (30) days written or printed notice that gives the time and place of sale and a written or printed description of the property and any marks or brands on the property. The notice of the sale must be posted at the front door of the courthouse of the county in which the sale is to be made and at two (2) other public places in the county where the property is located. It is the duty of the constable or other officer making the sale to pay to the finder the finder's legal fees and charges after deducting the constable's or other officer's commission. The commission charged may be the same as if the constable or other officer had sold the same property under execution. If any sale money remains after payment of the charges and fees described in this section, the constable or other officer shall pay the remainder to the clerk of the circuit court in the county in which the sale occurred and obtain a receipt for the amount. If the constable or other officer fails to perform the constable's or other officer's duties under this chapter, the constable or other officer is liable on the constable's or other officer's official bond to the party aggrieved.

(e) If the owner, within one (1) year after the date of the sale, appears before the county judge of the county where the money is deposited with the clerk and establishes the owner's right to the satisfaction of the court to the money, the money must, upon the order of the county judge, be paid over to the owner by the clerk; otherwise, it shall be paid into the common school fund of Indiana.

(f) This chapter may not be construed to permit a person to recover under subsection (a) for any fleet of timber, raft or platform, sawlog, or other log or tree prepared for the purpose of sale, or any cross or railroad tie, board, plank, stave, heading, or other timber prepared for the market that is above any boom or other arrangement made by the owner to preserve the logs or timber. [P.L.2-2002, § 19.]

Collateral References. 52 Am. Jur. 2d Logs and Timber, §§ 102, 103.   54 C.J.S. Logs and Logging, § 36.

32-34-9-3. Fleets, rafts, or platforms — Fees for keeping. — A person who finds a fleet, raft or platform, as described in this chapter, is entitled to reasonable compensation for keeping and caring for the property in addition to the fees set forth in section 1 [IC 32-34-9-1] of this chapter. The compensation may not exceed the following rates:

(1) For each fleet, four dollars ($4) per day.
(2) For each raft, one dollar ($1) per day.
(3) For each platform, fifty cents ($0.50) per day.
[P.L.2-2002, § 19.]

32-34-9-4. Logs prepared for sale — Fees for keeping. — If a person finds any sawlog or other log or trees prepared for sale as described in this chapter and the property remains in the person's possession more than thirty (30) days after the time the person found the property to the time the owner offers to pay the charges described in section 1 [IC 32-34-9-1] of this chapter, the finder is entitled to charge, in addition to the fee set forth in section 1 of this chapter, twenty-five cents ($0.25) for every sawlog or other log or tree prepared for sale that remains in the person's possession as described in this section. [P.L.2-2002, § 19.]

32-34-9-5. Finder misconduct — Responsible to owner for value. — If the finder of any property described in this chapter:

(1) hides the property;

(2) allows the property to get aground so that the finder cannot immediately, upon the demand of the property's owner or the owner's agents, put the property afloat; or

(3) fails to put the property afloat upon demand;

the finder may not collect or receive any compensation for finding or caring for the property and, in addition to any other duties imposed by this chapter, is responsible to the owner for the value of the property as if the property were afloat. [P.L.2-2002, § 19.]

32-34-9-6. Timber dealer — Brand. — A person, firm, or corporation that deals in timber in any form is considered a timber dealer and may adopt a brand in the manner and with the effect described in this chapter. [P.L.2-2002, § 19.]

32-34-9-7. Brand — Manner of adopting. — (a) A timber dealer desiring to adopt a brand may do so by the execution of a writing in the following form:

Brand — Notice is hereby given that I (or we, as the case may be) have adopted the following brand in my (or our) business as a timber dealer: (Here insert the words, letters, figures, etc., constituting the brand, or if the brand is any device other than words, letters, or figures, insert a facsimile of the brand.) Dated this _____ day of _____ A.D. _____.

(b) The writing must be acknowledged or proved for the record in the same manner as deeds are acknowledged or proven and must be recorded in the office of the clerk of the county in which the timber dealer maintains a principal office or place of business.

(c) A copy of the writing must be posted at the timber dealer's principal place of business, at the courthouse door in the county where the timber dealer carries on business, and at the public places in the county. [P.L.2-2002, § 19.]

Cross References. Livestock brands, IC 15-5-14-1 — IC 15-5-14-14.

32-34-9-8. Brand — Exclusive trademark — Property. — A brand adopted in accordance with this chapter is the exclusive trademark of the person adopting the brand, and the brand constitutes property under IC 35-41-1-23. [P.L.2-2002, § 19.]

32-34-9-9. Brand — How stamped on timber. — A person who owns a brand shall cause the brand to be plainly stamped, branded, or otherwise impressed upon each piece of timber upon which the brand is placed. [P.L.2-2002, § 19.]

32-34-9-10. Sale of trees — Statute of frauds. — A contract for the sale of standing trees or standing timber may not be enforced by a legal action unless the contract or some memorandum of the contract is in writing and signed by the person to be charged or the person's duly authorized agent. [P.L.2-2002, § 19.]

32-34-9-11. Brand passes title. — (a) If timber is branded by the seller or by another person with the seller's consent with the brand of the purchaser or another person or corporation, the title to the timber passes at once to the person or corporation whose brand is placed on the timber.

(b) Placement of a brand on timber as described in subsection (a) does not affect the rights of the contracting parties regarding the payment of the purchase money for the timber. [P.L.2-2002, § 19.]

32-34-9-12. Brands and trademarks adopted under law prior to March 11, 1901. — (a) This chapter does not affect the validity and effect of a brand or trademark adopted and recorded under the law in effect before March 11, 1901.

(b) A brand or trademark described in subsection (a) is valid for all purposes, civil and criminal, as if the brand or trademark had been adopted and recorded under this chapter. [P.L.2-2002, § 19.]

32-34-9-13. Penalty for violations of chapter. — (a) If timber prepared for market is found on any of the streams of Indiana, the timber shall be held and disposed of as provided in this chapter. The finder of the timber shall receive as compensation for the finder's services only the fees provided for in section 2 [IC 32-34-9-2] of this chapter.

(b) A person who knowingly violates this section commits a Class D felony. [P.L.2-2002, § 19.]

Cross References. Penalties for felonies, IC 35-50-1, IC 35-50-2, IC 35-50-5-2.

CHAPTER 10
SALE OF ABANDONED WATERCRAFT

32-34-10-1. "Marina operator" defined. — As used in this chapter, "marina operator" means a person, a firm, a corporation, a limited liability company, a municipality, or another unit of government that is engaged in the business of operating a marina. [P.L.2-2002, § 19.]

Effective Dates. P.L.2-2002, § 19. July 1. 2002.

32-34-10-2. Sale — Marina operator's recovery of expenses. — A marina operator may:

(1) sell a watercraft that has been left without permission at the marina for more than six (6) months; and

(2) recover the operator's reasonable maintenance, repair, dockage, storage, and other charges if the conditions set forth in section 3 [IC 32-34-10-3] of this chapter are met. [P.L.2-2002, § 19.]

32-34-10-3. Notice to owner. — The minimum six (6) month period specified in section 2 [IC 32-34-10-2] of this chapter begins the day written notice is sent by the marina operator to the last known address of the owner of the watercraft or personally delivered to the owner of the watercraft. If the notice is mailed, the marina operator must send notice by certified mail, return receipt requested. Notice, by mail or personally delivered, must include a description of the watercraft and a conspicuous statement that the watercraft is at the marina without permission of the marina. [P.L.2-2002, § 19.]

32-34-10-4. Sale — Requirements. — To sell a watercraft and recover charges under section 2 [IC 32-34-10-2] of this chapter, a marina operator must do all of the following:

(1) Perform a search of watercraft titles for the name and address of the owner of the watercraft and the name and address of any person holding a lien or security interest on the watercraft. The search required by this subdivision must be conducted in the following order:

(A) First, in the records of the state of registration as indicated on the exterior of the watercraft.

(B) Second, in the United States Coast Guard registration records maintained by the National Vessel Documentation Center.

(C) Third, in the records of the bureau of motor vehicles.

(2) After receiving the results of the search required by subdivision (1), give notice by certified mail, return receipt requested, or in person, to the last known address of the owner of the watercraft, to any lien holder with a perfected security interest in the watercraft, and to all other persons known to claim an interest in the watercraft. The notice must include an itemized statement of the charges, a description of the watercraft, a demand for payment within a specified time not less than ten (10) days after receipt of the notice, and a conspicuous statement that unless the charges are paid within that time, the watercraft will be advertised for sale and sold by auction at a specified time and place.

(3) Advertise that the watercraft will be sold at public auction in conformity with the provisions of IC 26-1-7-210 and IC 26-1-2-328. The advertisement of sale must be published once a week for two (2) consecutive weeks in a newspaper of general circulation in the county where the watercraft has been left without permission. The advertisement must include a description of the watercraft, the name of the person on whose account the watercraft is being held, and the time and place of the sale. The sale must take place at least fifteen (15) days after the first publication. If there is no newspaper of general circulation where the sale is to be held, the advertisement must be posted at least

ten (10) days before the sale in not less than six (6) conspicuous places in the neighborhood of the proposed sale.

(4) Conduct an auction sale, not less than thirty (30) days after the return receipt is received by the marina operator, on the marina property where the watercraft was left without permission.

(5) Provide a reasonable time before the sale for prospective purchasers to examine the watercraft.

(6) Sell the watercraft to the highest bidder.

(7) Immediately after the auction sale, execute an affidavit of sale in triplicate on a form prescribed by the bureau of motor vehicles stating:

(A) that the requirements of this section have been met;

(B) the length of time that the watercraft was left on the marina property without permission;

(C) the expenses incurred by the marina operator, including the expenses of the sale;

(D) the name and address of the purchaser of the watercraft at the auction sale; and

(E) the amount of the winning bid.

[P.L.2-2002, § 19.]

32-34-10-5. Purchaser — Affidavit of sale. — Upon payment of the bid price by the purchaser, the marina operator shall provide the purchaser with the affidavit of sale described in this chapter. [P.L.2-2002, § 19.]

32-34-10-6. Affidavit of sale — Proof of ownership and right to possession. — The affidavit of sale under this chapter constitutes proof of ownership and right to possession under IC 9-31-2-16. [P.L.2-2002, § 19.]

32-34-10-7. Certificate of title — Issuance. — After the purchaser:

(1) presents the bureau of motor vehicles with the affidavit of sale;

(2) completes an application for title; and

(3) pays any applicable fee;

the bureau shall issue to the purchaser a certificate of title to the watercraft. [P.L.2-2002, § 19.]

32-34-10-8. Proceeds of sale. — If a boat is sold under this chapter for an amount of money that is greater than the charges owed to the marina operator plus all reasonable expenses of sale, the marina operator shall pay the excess in the following order:

(1) For the satisfaction of obligations held by secured parties with respect to the watercraft, in the order in which security interests in the watercraft were perfected.

(2) To the owner of the watercraft.

[P.L.2-2002, § 19.]

ARTICLE 35

CAUSES OF ACTION CONCERNING PERSONAL PROPERTY

CHAPTER 1

STATUTE OF LIMITATIONS

32-35-1-1. Time limit for claim. — Unless otherwise provided in this title or another law, a cause of action concerning personal property must be brought within the time periods specified in IC 34-11. [P.L.2-2002, § 20.]

Effective Dates. P.L.2-2002, § 20. July 1. 2002.

CHAPTER 2

REPLEVIN

32-35-2-1. Action for possession. — If any personal goods, including tangible personal property constituting or representing choses in action, are:

> (1) wrongfully taken or unlawfully detained from the owner or person claiming possession of the property; or
>
> (2) taken on execution or attachment and claimed by any person other than the defendant;

the owner or claimant may bring an action for the possession of the property. [P.L.2-2002, § 20.]

Effective Dates. P.L.2-2002, § 20. July 1, 2002.

NOTES TO DECISIONS

ANALYSIS

Affidavit not filed.
Appearance.
Complaint.
Description of property.
Immediate delivery not claimed.
Justices' courts.
Proof of detention.

Affidavit Not Filed.

If no affidavit was filed, the case proceeded to trial as to the title and right of possession of the property. Andrews v. Sellers, 11 Ind. App. 301, 38 N.E. 1101 (1894).

Appearance.

An appearance and going to trial without objection cured any defects in the affidavit. Smith v. Emerson, 16 Ind. 355 (1861).

Complaint.

A complaint sworn to could stand for both a complaint and affidavit. Cox v. Albert, 78 Ind. 241 (1881); Louisville, E. & St. L.R.R. v. Payne, 103 Ind. 183, 2 N.E. 582 (1885). See also Minchrod v. Windoes, 29 Ind. 288 (1868).

If no affidavit was filed to obtain immediate possession of the property, the complaint need not have alleged that the property was not taken for a tax or assessment. Andrews v. Sellers, 11 Ind. App. 301, 38 N.E. 1101 (1894).

Description of Property.

The complaint had to describe the property with sufficient certainty. Malone v. Stickney, 88 Ind. 594 (1883); Hoke v. Applegate, 92 Ind. 570 (1884); Hall v. Durham, 117 Ind. 429, 20 N.E. 282 (1889); Wood v. Darnell, 1 Ind. App. 215, 27 N.E. 447 (1891). See also Minchrod v. Windoes, 29 Ind. 288 (1868); Onstatt v. Ream, 30 Ind. 259, 95 Am. Dec. 695 (1868); Smith v. Stanford, 62 Ind. 392 (1878).

Immediate Delivery Not Claimed.

If an immediate delivery of the property was not claimed, no affidavit or bond need have been filed. Catterlin v. Mitchell, 27 Ind. 298, 89 Am. Dec. 501 (1866); Hodson v. Warner, 60 Ind. 214 (1877).

Justices' Courts.

The predecessor to this section did not apply to justices' courts. Green v. Aker, 11 Ind. 223 (1858).

Proof of Detention.

When possession of the property was not claimed before the trial, proof need not have been made of the detention of the property in the county where suit was brought. Robinson v. Shatzley, 75 Ind. 461 (1881).

Collateral References. Allegations in affidavit with respect to defendant's possession or with respect to relief requested as affecting maintainability of replevin or similar posses-sory action where defendant, at time action is brought, is no longer in possession of property. 97 A.L.R.2d 896.

32-35-2-2. Immediate delivery. — A plaintiff may, at the time of issuing the summons, or at any time before final judgment, claim the immediate delivery of property described in section 1 [IC 32-35-2-1] of this chapter. [P.L.2-2002, § 20.]

32-35-2-3. Filing of affidavit. — If a plaintiff claims delivery under section 2 [IC 32-35-2-2] of this chapter, the plaintiff or someone representing the plaintiff shall file an affidavit. [P.L.2-2002, § 20.]

32-35-2-4. Affidavit — Requirements. — An affidavit filed under section 3 [IC 32-35-2-3] of this chapter must:
  (1) show that the plaintiff is:
    (A) the owner of the property; or
    (B) lawfully entitled to the possession of the property;
  (2) show that:
    (A) the property was not:
      (i) taken for a tax, assessment, or fine under a statute; or
      (ii) seized under an execution or attachment against the property of the plaintiff; or
    (B) if the property was seized under an execution or attachment, the property was exempt by statute from seizure;
  (3) show that the property:
    (A) has been wrongfully taken and is unlawfully detained by the defendant; or
    (B) is unlawfully detained;
  (4) include a particular description of the property;
  (5) state the estimated value of the property; and
  (6) identify the county in which the property is believed to be detained. [P.L.2-2002, § 20.]

32-35-2-5. Controverting affidavit. — If a plaintiff files an affidavit under section 3 [IC 32-35-2-3] of this chapter, the clerk shall issue an order for a time fixed by the judge directing the defendant to appear for the purpose of controverting plaintiff's affidavit or to otherwise show cause why:
  (1) a prejudgment order for possession should not issue; and
  (2) the property should not be delivered to plaintiff. [P.L.2-2002, § 20.]

32-35-2-6. Hearing. — (a) An order issued under section 5 [IC 32-35-2-5] of this chapter must set forth the date, time, and place for the hearing and direct the time within which service shall be made upon the defendant.
  (b) The hearing shall be scheduled not sooner than five (5) days, Sundays and holidays excluded, after the date of service. [P.L.2-2002, § 20.]

32-35-2-7. Order to show cause — Requirements. — An order to show cause issued under section 5 [IC 32-35-2-5] of this chapter must inform the defendant that:
  (1) the defendant may:
    (A) file affidavits on the defendant's behalf with the court;

(B) appear and present testimony on the defendant's behalf at the time of the hearing; and

(C) file with the court a written undertaking to stay the delivery of the property in accordance with this article; and

(2) if the defendant fails to appear, plaintiff may be granted a judgment of possession. [P.L.2-2002, § 20.]

32-35-2-8. Court's issuance of order for possession. — The court may issue an order for possession under this chapter after examining the complaint, affidavits, and other evidence or testimony that the court may require. [P.L.2-2002, § 20.]

32-35-2-9. Issuance of order for possession prior to hearing. — The court may issue an order for possession under this chapter before the hearing if probable cause appears that any of the following subdivisions apply:

(1) The defendant gained possession of the property by theft or criminal conversion.

(2) The property consists of one (1) or more negotiable instruments or credit cards.

(3) By reason of specific, competent evidence shown by testimony within the personal knowledge of an affiant or witness, the property is:

(A) perishable, and will perish before any noticed hearing can be had;

(B) in immediate danger of destruction, serious harm, concealment, removal from Indiana, or sale to an innocent purchaser; or

(C) held by a person who threatens to destroy, harm, or conceal the property, remove the property from Indiana, or sell the property to an innocent purchaser. [P.L.2-2002, § 20.]

32-35-2-10. Issuance of order without notice — Efforts made to give notice — Reasons why notice cannot be given. — Before the court may issue an order for possession without notice under section 12 [IC 32-35-2-12] of this chapter, the plaintiff or the plaintiff's attorney must file an affidavit or certificate showing:

(1) the efforts, if any, that have been made to give notice; and

(2) the reasons why notice of the application for the order cannot be given. [P.L.2-2002, § 20.]

32-35-2-11. Shortening of time until hearing. — (a) If an order of possession was issued before a hearing under this chapter (or IC 34-1-9.1-4 or IC 34-21-4-4 before their repeal), the defendant or other person from whom possession of the property was taken may apply to the court for an order shortening the time for hearing on the order to show cause.

(b) The court may, upon an application made under subsection (a):

(1) shorten the time until the hearing; and

(2) direct that the matter shall be heard on not less than forty-eight (48) hours notice to the plaintiff. [P.L.2-2002, § 20.]

32-35-2-12. Order of possession issued without notice — Sheriff to hold property until further order of court. — An order of possession issued under this chapter without notice shall direct the sheriff or other executing officer to hold the property until further order of the court. [P.L.2-2002, § 20.]

32-35-2-13. Temporary restraining order. — Under any of the circumstances set forth in this chapter, or instead of the immediate issuance of an order of possession under this chapter, the judge may, in addition to issuing a preliminary order, issue a temporary restraining order directed to the defendant prohibiting certain acts with respect to the property if the issuance of the order appears to be necessary for the preservation of the rights of the parties and the status of the property. [P.L.2-2002, § 20.]

32-35-2-14. Hearing on preliminary order — Preliminary determination on right to possession. — Upon the hearing on the preliminary order under this chapter, the court shall:
    (1) consider the showing made by the parties appearing; and
    (2) make a preliminary determination which party, with reasonable probability, is entitled to possession, use, and disposition of the property, pending final adjudication of the claims of the parties. [P.L.2-2002, § 20.]

32-35-2-15. Prejudgment order of possession. — If the court determines, in an action under this chapter, that a prejudgment order of possession in the plaintiff's favor should issue, the court shall issue the order. [P.L.2-2002, § 20.]

32-35-2-16. Property of peculiar value — Appointment of receiver. — If the property claimed by the plaintiff in an action under this chapter has a peculiar value that cannot be compensated by damages, the court may, instead of issuing an order of possession, appoint a receiver to take possession of and hold the property until further order of the court. [P.L.2-2002, § 20.]

32-35-2-17. Defendant's failure to appear — Final judgment. — If the defendant in an action under this chapter fails to appear, the court may enter its final judgment with respect to possession as in other cases where there is a default for a failure to appear. [P.L.2-2002, § 20.]

32-35-2-18. Order as final judgment in action. — An order of possession issued under this chapter must:
    (1) be directed to the sheriff or other officer charged with the execution of the order within whose jurisdiction the property is believed to be located;
    (2) describe the property to be seized; and
    (3) direct the executing officer to:
      (A) seize the property if it is found;

(B) take the property into custody; and

(C) deliver the property to the plaintiff, unless:

(i) the order was issued without notice; or

(ii) the defendant files a written undertaking in accordance with section 7(1)(C) [IC 32-35-2-7(1)(C)] of this chapter within a time fixed by the court. [P.L.2-2002, § 20.]

NOTES TO DECISIONS

ANALYSIS

Abatement.
Description of property.
Jurisdiction of court.
Jurisdiction of sheriff.
Receiver for nonresident.

Abatement.

Trial on issue of abatement did not adjudicate title to property. Robinson v. Teeter, 10 Ind. App. 698, 38 N.E. 222 (1894).

Description of Property.

The order should have contained a description of the property. Magee v. Siggerson, 4 Blackf. 70 (1835).

The object of the specific description of the property required by former IC 34-21-4-11 (repealed; see this section for similar provisions) was to enable the proper officer to take the property and deliver it to the plaintiff. Sheets Oil Co. v. Fruehauf Trailer Co., 213 Ind. 314, 12 N.E.2d 504 (1938).

In action of replevin, the description of the property in the complaint as "One Fruehauf Trailer now in possession of defendants in" a named garage in a named city of this state, was sufficient. Sheets Oil Co. v. Fruehauf Trailer Co., 213 Ind. 314, 12 N.E.2d 504 (1938).

Jurisdiction of Court.

Failure of a sheriff to make return of service of a writ did not affect the jurisdiction of the court. Sterrett v. Timmons, 21 Ind. App. 343, 52 N.E. 464 (1899).

Jurisdiction of Sheriff.

Sheriffs could not go outside of their counties to serve writs of replevin. Dederick v. Brandt, 16 Ind. App. 264, 44 N.E. 1010 (1896).

Receiver for Nonresident.

The court could appoint a receiver of the property pending the action though defendant was a nonresident of the state. Hellebush v. Blake, 119 Ind. 349, 21 N.E. 976 (1889).

Collateral References. Voluntary dismissal of replevin action by plaintiff as affecting defendant's right to judgment for the return or value of the property. 24 A.L.R.3d 768.

32-35-2-19. Final judgment. — If the order issued in an action under this chapter is a final judgment:

(1) the court does not need to fix a time for the defendant to file a written undertaking;

(2) the order must direct immediate delivery to the plaintiff;

(3) a copy of any written undertaking filed by the plaintiff must be attached to the order; and

(4) the order must inform the defendant that the defendant has the right to:

(A) except to the surety upon the undertaking; or

(B) file a written undertaking for the redelivery of the property as provided in section 7(1)(C) [IC 32-35-2-7(1)(C)] of this chapter. [P.L.2-2002, § 20.]

NOTES TO DECISIONS

Approval of Bond.
If the officer received and acted on the bond, it was a sufficient approval thereof. Hartlep v. Cole, 120 Ind. 247, 22 N.E. 130 (1889).

Costs and Damages.
Attorneys' fees and expenses of the plaintiff in attending court could not be recovered in an action on the bond. Davis v. Crow, 7 Blackf. 129 (1844); Miller v. Hays, 26 Ind. 380 (1866); Blackwell v. Acton, 38 Ind. 425 (1871); Consolidated Tank Line Co. v. Bronson, 2 Ind. App. 1, 28 N.E. 155 (1891).

The damages recovered could not exceed the penalty of the bond. Kellar v. Carr, 119 Ind. 127, 21 N.E. 463 (1889).

Costs made by the plaintiff could be recovered in an action on the bond. Kellar v. Carr, 119 Ind. 127, 21 N.E. 463 (1889).

Where, in action on replevin bond, there was no evidence of the value of the property or of its use while in the possession of the plaintiff in the replevin action, the plaintiff in the action on the bond could recover only nominal damages. Holcomb & Hoke Mfg. Co. v. Watts, 91 Ind. App. 695, 170 N.E. 861 (1930).

Cure of Defects in Bond.
Defective bonds were cured by statute. Lemert v. Shaffer, 5 Ind. App. 468, 31 N.E. 1128, 32 N.E. 788 (1892); Rauh v. Waterman, 29 Ind. App. 344, 61 N.E. 743, 63 N.E. 42 (1901). See also Yeakle v. Winters, 60 Ind. 554 (1877); Philippi Christian Church v. Harbaugh, 64 Ind. 240 (1878).

Dismissal of Replevin Suit.
If the suit was dismissed on a compromise, no action would lie on the bond. Hollinsbee v. Ritchey, 49 Ind. 261 (1874); Gerard v. Dill, 96 Ind. 101 (1884).

If the plaintiff dismissed his suit, he could show, in a suit on the bond, that he had a lien on the property to mitigate the damages. McFadden v. Ross, 108 Ind. 512, 8 N.E. 161 (1886).

Dismissal of a suit was a breach of the bond to prosecute with effect. Peffley v. Kenrick, 4 Ind. App. 510, 31 N.E. 40 (1892); Rauh v. Waterman, 29 Ind. App. 344, 61 N.E. 743, 63 N.E. 42 (1901).

Estoppel of Parties.
Parties to the bond were estopped to say that there was no action pending, or that the bond was invalid, or that the parties had no interest therein. Trueblood v. Knox, 73 Ind. 310 (1881); McFadden v. Fritz, 110 Ind. 1, 10 N.E. 120 (1887); Hartlep v. Cole, 120 Ind. 247, 22 N.E. 130 (1889); Ringgenberg v. Hartman, 124 Ind. 186, 24 N.E. 987 (1890). See also Sammons v. Newman, 27 Ind. 508 (1867).

Judgment in Replevin Suit.
When there was a judgment against the plaintiff, there was a breach of his bond for which an action would lie. Brown v. Parker, 5 Blackf. 291 (1840); Wheat v. Catterlin, 23 Ind. 85 (1864); Wiseman v. Lynn, 39 Ind. 250 (1872); Peffley v. Kenrick, 4 Ind. App. 510, 31 N.E. 40 (1892).

If the defendant obtained judgment, he could sue on the bond for the value of the property though such value was not fixed by the verdict. Whitney v. Lehmer, 26 Ind. 503 (1866); Yelton v. Slinkard, 85 Ind. 190 (1882).

There had to be a judgment for a return of the property before the sureties were liable on the bond for a failure to return it. Thomas v. Irwin, 90 Ind. 557 (1883); Foster v. Bringham, 99 Ind. 505 (1885).

When there was a trial and judgment, the judgment was conclusive between the parties in an action on the bond. Woods v. Kessler, 93 Ind. 356 (1883); Smith v. Mosby, 98 Ind. 445 (1884); McFadden v. Fritz, 110 Ind. 1, 10 N.E. 120 (1887); Jackson v. Morgan, 167 Ind. 528, 78 N.E. 633 (1906); Shaver v. Kappellas, 83 Ind. App. 338, 146 N.E. 858 (1925). See also Smith v. Lisher, 23 Ind. 500 (1864); Denny v. Reynolds, 24 Ind. 248 (1865); Carr v. Ellis, 37 Ind. 465 (1871); Landers v. George, 49 Ind. 309 (1874).

If no damages were fixed by the verdict, and judgment for a return of the property or its value as specified in the verdict so rendered, and such judgment was paid, no action would lie on the bond. Jackson v. Morgan, 49 Ind. App. 376, 94 N.E. 1021 (1911), overruled on other grounds, Wade v. Culp, 107 Ind. App. 503, 23 N.E.2d 615 (1939).

Mitigation of Damages.
The return of the property after suit on the bond could be considered in mitigation of damages. June v. Payne, 107 Ind. 307, 7 N.E. 370, 8 N.E. 556 (1886).

When the title to the property was not determined in the action, the defendants, in a suit on the bond, could prove in mitigation of

Mitigation of Damages. (Cont'd)
damages that the obligees in the bond were not the owners of the property. Hulman v. Benighof, 125 Ind. 481, 25 N.E. 549 (1890); Consolidated Tank Line Co. v. Bronson, 2 Ind. App. 1, 28 N.E. 155 (1891); Robinson v. Teeter, 10 Ind. App. 698, 38 N.E. 222 (1894); Rauh v. Waterman, 29 Ind. App. 344, 61 N.E. 743, 63 N.E. 42 (1901). See also Stockwell v. Byrne, 22 Ind. 6 (1864); Wiseman v. Lynn, 39 Ind. 250 (1872); Allis v. Nanson, 41 Ind. 154 (1872).

Where there was judgment against plaintiff for return of property, and suit was brought on bond for failure to return, defendant could show he had a valid subsisting lien on the property in mitigation of damages. Consolidated Tank Line Co. v. Bronson, 2 Ind. App. 1, 28 N.E. 155 (1891).

Recitals in Bond.
The recital in the bond as to the value of the property was conclusive on the obligors. Wiseman v. Lynn, 39 Ind. 250 (1872).

In case of an increase of variance between complaint and recitals in copy of bond filed, the complaint controlled. Blackburn v. Crowder, 108 Ind. 238, 9 N.E. 108 (1886).

Time for Executing Bond.
If the property was taken by the officer on Saturday, Sunday was not included in the 24 hours given to execute a bond. Link v. Clemmens, 7 Blackf. 479 (1845).

Who May Sue on Bond.
An officer holding an execution, and the execution plaintiffs could sue on a bond given to the officer, when he had judgment for a return of the property to him. Thomas v. Irwin, 90 Ind. 557 (1883). See also Walls v. Johnson, 16 Ind. 374 (1861).

Only parties to the suit could sue on the bond. Pipher v. Johnson, 108 Ind. 401, 9 N.E. 376 (1886).

32-35-2-20. Final judgment supersedes all other orders. — Any:

(1) order for possession;

(2) temporary restraining order;

(3) prejudgment order for possession; or

(4) other preliminary transfer of possession;

issued under this article (or IC 34-1-9.1 or IC 34-21 before their repeal) is superseded by the final judgment rendered in an action under this chapter. [P.L.2-2002, § 20.]

32-35-2-21. Surety bond for value of property. — (a) Except as provided in subsection (c), the court may not issue an order of possession, with or without notice, in the plaintiff's favor in an action under this chapter until the plaintiff has filed with the court a written undertaking:

(1) in an amount fixed by the court; and

(2) executed by a surety to be approved by the court;

to the effect that the plaintiff and the surety are bound to the defendant for the value of the property, as determined by the court, along with other damages the defendant may suffer if the property has been wrongfully taken from the defendant.

(b) The amount of the bond may not be less than the value of the property.

(c) If the defendant has failed to appear and final judgment is entered, no written undertaking is required. [P.L.2-2002, § 20.]

32-35-2-22. Return of property to defendant — Defendant bound by written undertaking. — (a) In an action under this chapter, the defendant:

(1) at any time before the hearing on the preliminary order; or

(2) if final judgment has not been entered, within the time fixed in the order of possession;

may require the return of the property upon filing with the court a written undertaking executed by a surety to be approved by the court.

(b) The written undertaking must provide that the defendant is bound:

(1) as to the value of the property, as determined by the court, for the delivery of the property to the plaintiff, if delivery is ultimately ordered; and

(2) for the payment to plaintiff of the sum that may be recovered against the defendant in the action for the defendant's wrongful detention of the property. [P.L.2-2002, § 20.]

32-35-2-23. Notice of written undertaking to plaintiff by defendant — Proof of service. — At the time of filing an undertaking under section 22 [IC 32-35-2-22] of this chapter, the defendant must:

(1) serve upon the executing officer and the plaintiff or the plaintiff's attorney a notice of filing of the undertaking; and

(2) file proof of service of the notice referred to in subdivision (1) with the court. [P.L.2-2002, § 20.]

32-35-2-24. Termination of proceedings upon filing of undertaking — Exception taken to surety. — If the defendant files an undertaking under section 22 [IC 32-35-2-22] of this chapter before the hearing of the order to show cause, proceedings under the order to show cause terminate, unless exception is taken to the surety. [P.L.2-2002, § 20.]

32-35-2-25. Delivery of property to defendant after filing of undertaking — Time requirements. — If the property is in the custody of the executing officer at the time the defendant files an undertaking under section 22 [IC 32-35-2-22] of this chapter, the property shall be redelivered to the defendant not later than five (5) days after the date of service of notice of the filing of the undertaking upon the plaintiff or the plaintiff's attorney. [P.L.2-2002, § 20.]

32-35-2-26. Action against officer — Bond to indemnify officer against loss. — (a) If:

(1) any officer, by virtue of any writ of attachment or execution lawfully issued to the officer, attaches or levies upon any personal property as the property of the attachment or execution defendant; and

(2) any other person, firm, limited liability company, or corporation brings an action in replevin against the officer for the possession of any part of the property attached or levied upon;

as soon as process is served upon the officer, the officer may notify the attachment or execution plaintiff, if a resident of the officer's county, and if not a resident of the officer's county, then the attorney of the plaintiff, in writing, of the replevin suit, giving a general description of the property claimed by the replevin plaintiff in the suit, and may demand of the attachment or execution plaintiff a bond to indemnify the officer against any loss for attorney's fees incurred in the defense of the replevin suit and payment of any judgment for damages and costs.

(b) Upon failure of the attachment or execution plaintiff to execute the bond to the officer within five (5) days after the time of service of the notice described in subsection (a) with good and sufficient surety, the officer may deliver up any part of the property sued for in the replevin suit to the replevin plaintiff.

(c) If the bond demanded under subsection (a) is not given and the officer delivers the property to the replevin plaintiff, the attachment or execution plaintiff is estopped from maintaining any action whatever against the officer for the value of the property delivered up or for damages for failing to make any defense in the replevin suit. However, if the action in replevin is pending in the circuit court, the bond shall be approved by the clerk of the circuit court. [P.L.2-2002, § 20.]

NOTES TO DECISIONS

ANALYSIS

In general.
Writ sent to another county.

In General.
A third party making claim to property in possession of constable under writ of attachment could assert his claim by bringing an independent action in replevin, unless he had received the statutory notice from the constable before commencing the action. Patterson v. Snow, 24 Ind. App. 572, 57 N.E. 286 (1900).

Writ Sent to Another County.
Where a writ of attachment was sent to the sheriff of another county, and he levied upon property claimed by a person who was not a party to the action, the provisions of former IC 34-21-6-1 (repealed; see this section for similar provisions) did not apply, and the person who claimed the property taken under the writ could have recovered the same by an action of replevin. Hoover v. Lewin, 56 Ind. App. 367, 105 N.E. 400 (1914).

32-35-2-27. Delivery of order of possession in open court. — If the defendant or the defendant's attorney is in open court at the time the order of possession is issued under this chapter, a copy of the order shall be delivered promptly to the defendant and the delivery shall be noted in the order book. [P.L.2-2002, § 20.]

32-35-2-28. Service of copies of order of possession. — If the defendant and the defendant's attorney are not present in open court when the order of possession is issued under this chapter, sufficient copies of the order shall be delivered to the sheriff or other executing officer. The executing officer shall, without delay, serve upon the defendant a copy of the order of possession:
(1) by delivering the order of possession to:
(A) the defendant personally; or
(B) the defendant's agent from whose possession the property is taken;
(2) if the defendant or the defendant's agent cannot be found, by leaving it at the usual place of abode of either with some person of suitable age and discretion; or
(3) if neither the defendant nor the defendant's agent has any known usual place of abode, by mailing it to the defendant's last known address. [P.L.2-2002, § 20.]

32-35-2-29. Property taken into custody upon service of order of possession. — (a) Upon serving on the defendant a copy of the order of possession under section 28 [IC 32-35-2-28] of this chapter, the executing officer, except as provided in subsection (b), shall immediately take the property into custody if the property is in the possession or control of the defendant or the defendant's agent.

(b) If the property is a housetrailer, recreational vehicle, motor or mobile home, or boat and is being used as the principal dwelling of a defendant, at the expiration of forty-eight (48) hours after the order of possession is served, the officer shall immediately remove the property's occupants and take the property into custody. [P.L.2-2002, § 20.]

32-35-2-30. Property in building or enclosure — Recovery of property — Minimizing damage to building or enclosure. — If the property or any part of the property that is subject to an order of possession issued under this chapter is:
    (1) in a building or enclosure; and
    (2) not voluntarily delivered;
the executing officer shall cause the building or enclosure to be broken open in a manner the officer reasonably believes will cause the least damage to the building or enclosure and take possession of the property. [P.L.2-2002, § 20.]

NOTES TO DECISIONS

Constable.
    Former IC 34-1-9-9 did not authorize a constable to break open a building to execute a writ of replevin. State ex rel. McPherson v. Beckner, 132 Ind. 371, 31 N.E. 950, 32 Am. St. R. 257 (1892).

32-35-2-31. Executing officer — Maintenance of property — Expenses. — An executing officer who has taken property subject to an order of possession issued under this chapter shall:
    (1) keep it in a secure place; and
    (2) deliver it to the party entitled to the property upon receiving actual, reasonable, and necessary expenses for keeping the property. [P.L.2-2002, § 20.]

32-35-2-32. Executing officer's note upon order of possession — Return of order of possession to court. — After taking property subject to an order of possession issued under this chapter, an executing officer shall:
    (1) note the executing officer's proceedings in writing upon the order of possession; and
    (2) return the order of possession to the court in which the action is pending;
within five (5) days after taking the property mentioned in the order. [P.L.2-2002, § 20.]

32-35-2-33. Judgment for plaintiff — Delivery of property — Damages. — In an action to recover the possession of personal property, judgment for the plaintiff may be for:

(1) the delivery of the property, or the value of the property in case delivery is not possible; and

(2) damages for the detention of the property.

[P.L.2-2002, § 20.]

Cross References. Rules of procedure for original actions including writs of mandate and prohibition, Rule O.A. 1.

Judgments, generally, see Trial Rules TR. 13(M), 54, 55, 58.
Capacity to sue, Trial Rule TR. 17.

NOTES TO DECISIONS

In General.
This statute abolished writs of mandate in the circuit and superior courts, but not for the Supreme and Appellate Courts. State ex rel. Kensinger v. Cox, 193 Ind. 519, 141 N.E. 225 (1923).

In an action to replevy and to recover damages for the unlawful detention of a motor truck, the value of the truck should have been determined by deducting from its market value, as shown by the evidence, the sum still due from plaintiff on its purchase-price; and plaintiff's damages should have been measured by the value of the use of the truck, as shown by the evidence, from the time it was taken possession of by defendant until the date of the trial of the cause. General Motors Truck Co. v. Perry, 99 Ind. App. 357, 192 N.E. 720 (1934).

In an action by a conditional vendor to replevy motor vehicles, a repairman's judgment, as to the value of the vehicles which were the subject of the conditional sale, was limited to the amount of the repairman's equity therein, which consisted of labor and materials furnished in the repair of the vehicles. Yellow Mfg. Acceptance Corp. v. Linsky, 99 Ind. App. 691, 192 N.E. 715 (1934).

Former IC 34-21-9-1 (repealed; see this section for similar provisions) was enacted to protect parties from injury by the unwarranted usurpation of jurisdiction and the dignity of the sovereign state by preserving integrity of its judicial system and to prevent controversy between coordinate courts. State ex rel. Kunkel v. Circuit Court, 209 Ind. 682, 200 N.E. 614 (1936).

Extraordinary writs are issued only in cases of emergency. State ex rel. Nineteenth Hole, Inc. v. Marion Superior Court, 242 Ind. 604, 1 Ind. Dec. 254, 189 N.E.2d 421 (1963).

While the supreme court has authority to issue writs of mandate or prohibition naming the court of appeals as the respondent court, such a writ is an extraordinary remedy viewed with extreme disfavor. State ex rel. Civil City of S. Bend v. Court of Appeals, 273 Ind. 551, 76 Ind. Dec. 735, 406 N.E.2d 244 (1980).

Attorneys' Fees.
The general rule that in the absence of statute or contract providing therefor, attorneys' fees are neither allowable as costs nor recoverable as an item of damages, is applicable to prohibition proceedings. Kanizer v. State, 600 N.E.2d 982 (Ind. App. 1992).

Common-Law Remedy.
Mandamus was in no sense an equitable proceeding, but was a common-law remedy to compel performance of a legal duty. State ex rel. Beard v. Jackson, 168 Ind. 384, 81 N.E. 62

Common-Law Remedy. (Cont'd)
(1907); Steiger v. State ex rel. Fields, 186 Ind. 507, 116 N.E. 913 (1917).

Mandamus did not lie to enforce a mere equitable right. State ex rel. Spindler v. Scheiman, 179 Ind. 502, 101 N.E. 713 (1913).

Under former IC 34-21-9-1 (repealed; see now this section for similar provisions), a complaint and summons took the place of the common-law writ of mandamus; but the remedial character of the statutory action for mandate was the same as that given by the common-law writ. Gruber v. State ex rel. Welliver, 196 Ind. 436, 148 N.E. 481 (1925).

Damages for Detention.

In a suit on a replevin bond the plaintiff was entitled to recover damages of a reasonable charge to cover expenses for the keeping of the horses which had been the subject of the replevin suit. Davis v. Crow, 7 Blackf. 129 (1844).

In replevin, if the property was not found, or the plaintiff could not give bond, and was successful, the jury must have found the value of the property, as well as damages for the detention. Chissom v. Lamcool, 9 Ind. 530 (1857).

Where some of the goods ordered to be returned have been damaged and have deteriorated in value the party to whom the property was awarded is entitled to damages for such deterioration in value. Yelton v. Slinkard, 85 Ind. 190 (1882).

In an action of replevin for recovery of a horse, the measure of damages for the detention thereof was the value of the use of the animal during the entire period of detention. Farrar v. Eash, 5 Ind. App. 238, 31 N.E. 1125 (1832).

A judgment in replevin for the value of the property and damages for its detention was valid under former IC 34-21-9-1 (repealed; see this section for similar provisions), even if appellant had the right to collaterally attack it, where there was a finding that the property had been unlawfully disposed of by appellant and could not be redelivered. Shaver v. Kappellas, 83 Ind. App. 338, 146 N.E. 858 (1925).

Where plaintiff testified that his gross income from his sawmill equipment was $300 per day but that after payment of expenses and salaries his profit per day came to between $50 and $75, damages of $3,000 for ten days wrongful detention of his equipment was erroneous because, while lost profits may be considered as a legitimate element of damages for wrongful detention of property, plaintiff should not receive a windfall in the form of that portion of lost income representing expenses saved by defendant's breach. Wolff v. Slusher, 161 Ind. App. 182, 43 Ind. Dec. 250, 314 N.E.2d 758 (1974).

Where in a replevin action defendant was no longer in actual or constructive possession of the property, the action should have been allowed to continue to afford plaintiff his remedy by an award of damages for detention and loss of use. Lou Levanthal Auto Co. v. Manns, 164 Ind. App. 368, 47 Ind. Dec. 213, 328 N.E.2d 734 (1975).

Damages are recoverable either when the property is wrongfully taken or unlawfully detained. Northern Ind. Slurry Seal, Inc. v. K & K Truck Sales, Inc., 167 Ind. App. 440, 50 Ind. Dec. 412, 338 N.E.2d 704 (1975).

Landlord unlawfully detained the tenant's personal property by locking it in the leased apartment and excluding her from re-entering the premises to recover her belongings; therefore, the landlord was liable for the loss of property the tenant sustained due to his failure to return all of her personal items that he locked inside the leased premises, and the trial court properly awarded the tenant damages in the amount of the unreturned property. Robinson v. Valladares, 738 N.E.2d 278 (Ind. App. 2000).

Dismissal of Action.

There could be no judgment for the return of property where the plaintiff dismissed his action before a finding was announced by the court or a verdict returned by the jury. Wiseman v. Lynn, 39 Ind. 250 (1872).

A defendant was not entitled to a dismissal of the suit upon his verified disclaimer, filed as an answer. Choen v. Porter, 66 Ind. 194 (1879).

If the action was dismissed before verdict, no judgment for a return of the property could be rendered. Hulman v. Benighof, 125 Ind. 481, 25 N.E. 549 (1890); Peffley v. Kenrick, 4 Ind. App. 510, 31 N.E. 40 (1892).

A judgment in replevin for the return of property was none the less binding between the parties because the action was dismissed by the plaintiff. The dismissal was a practical confession by the plaintiff that he had no claim to the property. McFadden v. Schroeder, 4 Ind. App. 305, 29 N.E. 491, 30 N.E. 711 (1892).

Distinction Between Mandate and Prohibition.

Prohibition and mandate were related remedies, prohibition being used to prevent a court from doing something which it had no power to do and mandate to require it to do something which it was required to do. State ex rel. William H. Block Co. v. Marion Superior Court, 221 Ind. 228, 47 N.E.2d 139 (1943).

Effect of General Denial.

General denial submitted by defendant in replevin action placed in issue entire question

Effect of General Denial. (Cont'd)
of right to possession of property, including question of damages for taking or detention of such property. It was not necessary that defendant submit proof of damages where, as in instant case, plaintiff-appellant proved defendant's case. Fineberg v. Clark, 137 Ind. App. 528, 6 Ind. Dec. 185, 210 N.E.2d 260 (1965).

Excessiveness.
In replevin action for recovery of mortgaged chattels, judgment for plaintiff, on verdict wherein jury fixed value of each chattel, was not excessive on ground of loss of property already delivered to plaintiff, where order clearly provided that defendants be given credit on the judgment for value of all property originally taken by sheriff and delivered to plaintiff. Mullet v. Blaine, 105 Ind. App. 666, 16 N.E.2d 981 (1938).

Ex Rel. Proceedings.
Under the predecessor statute to this section, an action for mandate should have been brought in the name of the state on relation of the party in interest. State ex rel. Clifton v. Schortemeier, 197 Ind. 669, 151 N.E. 613 (1926); Hoosier Chem. Works, Inc. v. Brown, 200 Ind. 535, 165 N.E. 323 (1929); Greene v. Holmes, 201 Ind. 123, 166 N.E. 281 (1929).

The predecessor statute to this section, requiring that actions for mandate be brought in the name of the state on relation of the party in interest, was mandatory. Board of Public Safety v. Walling, 206 Ind. 540, 187 N.E. 385 (1933).

It was legally impossible for an action of mandate to be prosecuted by one in his individual and personal capacity, It must have been brought in the name of the state of Indiana on his relation. Becker v. Stanley, 228 Ind. 429, 92 N.E.2d 851 (1950); Danker v. Dowd, 230 Ind. 19, 101 N.E.2d 191 (1951).

Action brought by the state on the relation of "Alcoholic Beverage Commission" was not brought on the relation of any entity as required by statute, because there was no such entity. The alcoholic beverage commission of Indiana had been abolished, and the Indiana alcoholic beverage commission had replaced it. State ex rel. Alcoholic Beverage Comm'n v. Davis, 229 Ind. 182, 96 N.E.2d 338 (1951).

Petition for writ of mandamus not prosecuted in name of state of Indiana on relation of interested party had to be denied. Woolum v. State, 232 Ind. 703, 114 N.E.2d 561 (1953).

Original actions of mandate and prohibition in the Supreme Court must have been brought in the name of the state of Indiana on the relation of the party in interest, it being legally impossible for an action of mandate to be prosecuted by one in his individual and personal capacity; therefore, the petition for writ of mandate and prohibition entitled state

election board, etc., would be dissolved. State Election Bd. v. Johnson Circuit Court, 242 Ind. 568, 180 N.E.2d 540 (1962).

A motion to dismiss a writ of prohibition was sustained since the action was improperly brought in that it was not filed in the name of the state of Indiana on the relation of the party as provided by statute. Supreme Court ex rel. Demoss v. Daviess Circuit Court, 243 Ind. 182, 183 N.E.2d 607 (1962).

The enactment of the Indiana Rules of Procedure on January 1, 1970 repealed all procedural statutes and rules in conflict therewith and hence the form of action for seeking a writ of mandate after that date was controlled by TR. 17(A)(2) which abolished the "ex rel." action under the predecessor statute to this section and allowed the action for mandate to be brought in the name of the person for whose benefit the action was intended. Gillespie v. Gilmore, 159 Ind. App. 449, 41 Ind. Dec. 24, 307 N.E.2d 480 (1974).

Since the plaintiffs' complaint was prosecuted in their individual capacities rather than in the name of the state on relation of the party in interest as required by statute, dismissal of the action was appropriate. Pitts v. Mills, 165 Ind. App. 646, 48 Ind. Dec. 627, 333 N.E.2d 897 (1975).

Injunctions.
An injunction is not available against an individual citizen in an original action before the supreme court. State ex rel. Clay Community Sch. v. Parke Circuit Court, 271 Ind. 266, 70 Ind. Dec. 646, 392 N.E.2d 804 (1979).

Lower Court Powers.

—In General.
Alternative writs of mandate were abolished so far as actions in circuit courts were concerned, and if a complaint in such action alleged facts which showed that plaintiff was entitled to any relief at all, it was sufficient to withstand a demurrer. State ex rel. Wyman v. Hall, 191 Ind. 271, 131 N.E. 821 (1921).

In a mandamus proceeding to compel a township trustee to establish a high school, the fact that the state tax board, not a party to the action, might refuse to authorize the bond issue would not defeat plaintiff's right to judgment for mandate. Gushwa v. State ex rel. Oster, 206 Ind. 237, 189 N.E. 129 (1934).

The remedy of a defendant charged with the same traffic violation in two city courts of the same county was to seek in the circuit court a writ to enjoin the proceeding in the second court, rather than by a writ of prohibition from the Supreme Court. State ex rel. Wireman v. City Court of Lafayette, 249 Ind. 490, 11 Ind. Dec. 734, 230 N.E.2d 776 (1967).

A circuit court had authority to grant mandamus to compel an inferior court to grant a

Lower Court Powers. (Cont'd)

—In General. (Cont'd)
proper motion for change of venue from the judge. Goshen City Court v. State ex rel. Carlin, 153 Ind. App. 342, 32 Ind. Dec. 624, 287 N.E.2d 591 (1972).

—Administrative Agencies.
Trial courts have the power to issue writs of prohibition and mandamus to administrative agencies in appropriate cases, such as where constitutional due process rights are being denied. State ex rel. Pickard v. Superior Court, 447 N.E.2d 584 (Ind. 1983).

—Appeal.
Respondents' appeal in an action for mandate had to be dismissed, where the assignments of error named as appellees no one but the relators as individuals. Board of Public Safety v. Walling, 206 Ind. 540, 187 N.E. 385 (1933).

—Criminal Courts.
The power to issue writs of mandate and prohibition in aid of appellate jurisdiction was vested in all courts with appellate jurisdiction as a necessary incident to the exercise of such jurisdiction without aid of a statute. State ex rel. Gillette v. Niblack, 222 Ind. 290, 53 N.E.2d 542 (1944).
Jurisdiction was vested in the criminal court of Marion county to mandate any inferior tribunal, which included the Marion county municipal court, to perform any act which the law enjoined in connection with an appeal to such criminal court. State ex rel. Gillette v. Niblack, 222 Ind. 290, 53 N.E.2d 542 (1944).
Since the Marion criminal court was a court of original jurisdiction, it acquired jurisdiction in prosecution for vehicle taking, where jeopardy had not attached, regardless of fact that affidavit, charging same offense, was then pending in Indianapolis Municipal Court and prohibition against criminal court would not be granted. State ex rel. Tucker v. Rabb, 232 Ind. 244, 111 N.E.2d 802 (1953).

Mandate.

—In General.
Phrase in judgment that "the court does mandate" an agency to do something did not transform the judgment into a writ of mandate. Blinzinger v. Americana Healthcare Corp., 466 N.E.2d 1371 (Ind. App. 1984).

—Prerequisites.
A party requesting mandate must have a clear and unquestioned legal right to the relief sought, and must show that the respondent has an absolute duty to perform the act

demanded. State ex rel. J.A.W. v. Indiana Juvenile Parole Comm., 581 N.E.2d 989 (Ind. App. 1991); State, ex rel. J.A.W. v. Indiana Juvenile Parole Comm., 585 N.E.2d 729 (Ind. App. 1992).

—Remedy at Law.
Where an adequate remedy at law is available, the extraordinary remedy of mandate should not be imposed to compel performance of an act. State ex rel. J.A.W. v. Indiana Juvenile Parole Comm., 581 N.E.2d 989 (Ind. App. 1991).

Motion to Modify Overruled.
On appeal by defendant in replevin action, contention, in support of assigned error in overruling motion to modify judgment, that judgment should have been for appellant in certain form was sufficiently answered by the fact that the motion did not request the court to render such judgment. Mullet v. Blaine, 105 Ind. App. 666, 16 N.E.2d 981 (1938).

Possession of Property.
If the party in whose favor a verdict was returned had possession of the property, the judgment should have been that such party was the owner of, and entitled to the possession of, the property. Chissom v. Lamcool, 9 Ind. 530 (1857).
Under this statute, the plaintiff in a replevin action, first, was entitled to get the property of which he claimed possession. However, if the property could not be delivered to the plaintiff, then he was entitled to its value. State ex rel. Sanders v. Circuit Court, 243 Ind. 343, 182 N.E.2d 781 (1962).
Where, in an action of replevin, the property was already in possession of the plaintiff at the time of the finding and judgment in her favor, it was not necessary that the finding of the court should assess the plaintiff's damages or establish the value of the property. If the omission, however, was an error, it was in favor of the defendants and they could not complain. Van Gundy v. Carrigan, 4 Ind. App. 333, 30 N.E. 933 (1892); Busching v. Sunman, 19 Ind. App. 683, 49 N.E. 1091 (1898).
A verdict or finding in replevin must have shown possession by defendant at time of commencement of the suit. Peninsular Stove Co. v. Ellis, 20 Ind. App. 491, 51 N.E. 105 (1898).
The trial court did not reach a conclusion contrary to law where it determined there was no wrongful taking or detention of a semi dump trailer attached to a semi tractor, where the tractor was delivered to the county sheriff pursuant to court order and subsequently delivered to the alleged wrongdoer, where the alleged wrongdoer promptly surrenders possession to the rightful owner upon demand. Northern Ind. Slurry Seal, Inc. v. K & K Truck

Possession of Property. (Cont'd)
Sales, Inc., 167 Ind. App. 440, 50 Ind. Dec. 412, 338 N.E.2d 704 (1975).

Relation to Injunctions.
Some points of similarity may be noticed between the extraordinary remedial process of prohibition and the extraordinary remedy of courts of equity by injunction against proceedings at law. However, an injunction against proceedings at law is directed only to the parties litigant, without in any manner interfering with the court, while a prohibition is directed to the court itself, commanding it to cease from the exercise of a jurisdiction to which it has no legal claim. The former remedy affects only the parties, the latter is directed against the forum itself. Kanizer v. State, 600 N.E.2d 982 (Ind. App. 1992).

Remand for Modification.
Where the judgment was indefinite and did not so finally settle and adjudicate the controversy between the parties and the judgment not being in the alternative, the cause was remanded with instructions to modify the judgment by specifying which of the items of personal property the court found to have been "unlawfully sold and disposed of," which items were found to lack "proper care" and which items "have been allowed to deteriorate and depreciate in value" and to further modify the decree by finding and decreeing the return of the property or the value thereof in case delivery could not be had, and the amount the appellee should have recovered upon the basis of such modified findings. Randolph v. Sanders, 130 Ind. App. 41, 161 N.E.2d 772 (1959).

Replevin Bond.
If a verdict in replevin fixed the value of the property but no damages were assessed, and judgment was rendered for the defendant for the return of the property or for the value thereof, and the judgment was paid, no action would lie on the bond for damages. Jackson v. Morgan, 167 Ind. 528, 78 N.E. 633 (1906).

Matters litigated in a replevin suit could not be retried in a suit on the replevin bond. Lindsey v. Hewitt, 42 Ind. App. 573, 86 N.E. 446 (1908).

If the plaintiff had possession of the property, and the defendant obtained judgment, he could sue on the bond for failure to return the property, although the value of the property was not stated in the verdict. Lindsey v. Hewitt, 42 Ind. App. 573, 86 N.E. 448 (1908).

Res Judicata.
A judgment against the plaintiff, in an action of replevin, rendered solely because of his having failed to make and prove a lawful demand on the defendant for surrender of the goods, was no bar to a subsequent action of replevin, by the plaintiff, against the defendant for the goods; and where in the latter action, the recovery in the former was pleaded in bar, the facts could properly have been replied, and could be proved by parol evidence. Roberts v. Norris, 67 Ind. 386 (1879).

Persons not parties were not affected by judgment. Koehring v. Aultman, Miller & Co., 7 Ind. App. 475, 34 N.E. 30, 35 N.E. 30 (1893).

Judgments rendered in actions of replevin were conclusive between the parties as to the damages for the taking or detention of the property. Jackson v. Morgan, 167 Ind. 528, 78 N.E. 633 (1906).

In an action of replevin, all damages for the taking or detention of the property must have been included in the judgment, and the judgment became res judicata as to all damages that might have been included therein. Jackson v. Morgan, 167 Ind. 528, 78 N.E. 633 (1906); Shaver v. Kappellas, 83 Ind. App. 338, 146 N.E. 858 (1925).

A judgment in replevin to the effect that the plaintiff was entitled to certain stock certificates was not res judicata against an assignee of the certificates, who was not a party to the action and who took title prior to the action, although the assignee had notice of the plaintiff's claim and the plaintiff had no knowledge of the assignment. Schwegman v. Neff, 218 Ind. 63, 29 N.E.2d 985 (1940).

Stay Pending Appeal.
Where circuit court mandated the board of tax commissioners to approve appropriation ordinance of city and denied a motion for stay pending appeal, it was proper for the court of appeals to grant a stay pending completion of the appeal. State ex rel. Civil City of S. Bend v. Court of Appeals, 273 Ind. 551, 76 Ind. Dec. 735, 406 N.E.2d 244 (1980).

Title to Property.
A replevin action determined only the right to possession of the property. Highnote v. White, 67 Ind. 596 (1879); Kramer v. Matthews, 68 Ind. 172 (1879).

Where a complaint for replevin alleged ownership of the property the judgment was conclusive to the question of ownership. Smith v. Mosby, 98 Ind. 445 (1884).

Judgments in actions of replevin only determined the right of possession, unless the title was distinctly put in issue. McFadden v. Ross, 108 Ind. 512, 8 N.E. 161 (1886); Consolidated Tank Line Co. v. Bronson, 2 Ind. App. 1, 28 N.E. 155 (1891).

Where the plaintiff is entitled to the possession of the property in controversy by reason of his title to such property a judgment in his favor affirms the plaintiff's title and his right to possession. Whitehead v. Coyle, 1 Ind. App. 450, 27 N.E. 716 (1891).

Title to Property. (Cont'd)

The judgment in a replevin action is conclusive as to all questions that were or might have been litigated under the issues including the question of ownership. Fromlet v. Poor, 3 Ind. App. 425, 29 N.E. 1081 (1892).

As a general rule, where the value of the property in dispute was fixed by the verdict of the jury or finding of the court, and a judgment was rendered for the amount of such value, and the judgment was paid, the title to the property became vested in the party against whom the judgment was rendered. If the owner elected to take a judgment on the replevin bond and collected it, he had thereby abandoned his right to the property, and the title passed as fully as if it had been transferred by purchase. McFadden v. Schroeder, 4 Ind. App. 305, 29 N.E. 491, 30 N.E. 711 (1892); Ledbetter v. Embree, 12 Ind. App. 617, 40 N.E. 928 (1895).

Collateral References. 49 C.J.S. Judgments § 1 et seq.

Recovery of damages in replevin for value of use of property detained by successful party having only security interest as conditional vendor, chattel mortgagee, or the like. 33 A.L.R.2d 774.

Recovery of attorneys' fees as damages by successful litigant in replevin or detinue action. 60 A.L.R.2d 945.

Recovery of value of property in replevin or similar possessory action where defendant, at time action is brought, is no longer in possession of property. 97 A.L.R.2d 896.

Judgment granting or denying writ of mandamus or prohibition as res judicata. 21 A.L.R.3d 206.

Mandamus to compel disciplinary investigation or action against physician or attorney. 33 A.L.R.3d 1429.

Summary judgment in mandamus or prohibition cases. 3 A.L.R.3d 675.

Venue of mandamus proceeding against public officer. 48 A.L.R.2d 423.

32-35-2-34. Judgment for defendant — Return of property — Damages. — In an action to recover the possession of personal property, if the property has been delivered to the plaintiff and the defendant claims a return of the property, judgment for the defendant may be for:

(1) the return of the property, or its value, in case return is not possible; and

(2) damages for the taking and withholding of the property.

[P.L.2-2002, § 20.]

NOTES TO DECISIONS

Judgment for Return.

If the value of the property was not assessed, or the evidence failed to show who had possession of the property, a judgment of return could not have been rendered. Conner v. Comstock, 17 Ind. 90 (1861).

If the finding was for the plaintiff the judgment should have been in the alternative for possession of the property or the value thereof together with damages for detention. Bales v. Scott, 26 Ind. 202 (1866); Thompson v. Eagleton, 33 Ind. 300 (1870).

If no judgment was rendered for a return of the property, no judgment for its value could be rendered. Foster v. Bringham, 99 Ind. 505 (1885).

On a judgment for a return of the property, a return should have been made without demand, in a reasonable time, the property having been in as good a condition as when taken. June v. Payne, 107 Ind. 307, 7 N.E. 370, 8 N.E. 556 (1886).

In cases appealed from justices of the peace, judgment for the value of the property could not be rendered in case a return could not be had. Van Meter v. Barnett, 119 Ind. 35, 20 N.E. 426 (1889); Everman v. Hyman, 3 Ind. App. 459, 29 N.E. 1140 (1892); Woodard v. Myers, 15 Ind. App. 42, 43 N.E. 573 (1896).

When there was to be a return of the property, the judgment should have been for such return, or the value of the property, if a return could not be had. Farrar v. Eash, 5 Ind. App. 238, 31 N.E. 1125 (1892).

Under former IC 34-21-9-2 (repealed; see this section for similar provisions), a judgment in replevin was proper where it provided for the return of the property, but where the defendant had disposed of the property, judgment in the alternative could be given for the value of the property, plus damages for

Judgment for Return. (Cont'd)
detention. Shaver v. Kappellas, 83 Ind. App. 338, 146 N.E. 858 (1925).

Title to Property.
If the plaintiff failed to prove title in himself, the defendants were entitled to a joint judgment. Dixon v. Duke, 85 Ind. 434 (1882).

Where a justice of the peace sustained the defendant's plea in abatement that the defendant have the return of the property described in the complaint, there was no adjudication as to the ownership of the property. Robinson v. Teeter, 10 Ind. App. 698, 38 N.E. 222 (1894).

32-35-2-35. Jury to assess value of property and damages. — In actions for the recovery of specific personal property, the jury must assess:

(1) the value of the property; and

(2) the damages for the taking or detention of the property;

when the jury's verdict results in a judgment for the recovery or return of the property. [P.L.2-2002, § 20.]

ARTICLE 36

PUBLICITY

CHAPTER 1

RIGHTS OF PUBLICITY

32-36-1-1. Applicability. — (a) This chapter applies to an act or event that occurs within Indiana, regardless of a personality's domicile, residence, or citizenship.

(b) This chapter does not affect rights and privileges recognized under any other law that apply to a news reporting or an entertainment medium.

(c) This chapter does not apply to the following:

(1) The use of a personality's name, voice, signature, photograph, image, likeness, distinctive appearance, gestures, or mannerisms in any of the following:

(A) Literary works, theatrical works, musical compositions, film, radio, or television programs.

(B) Material that has political or newsworthy value.

(C) Original works of fine art.

(D) Promotional material or an advertisement for a news reporting or an entertainment medium that:

    (i) uses all or part of a past edition of the medium's own broadcast or publication; and

    (ii) does not convey or reasonably suggest that a personality endorses the news reporting or entertainment medium.

(E) An advertisement or commercial announcement for a use described in this subdivision.

(2) The use of a personality's name to truthfully identify the personality as:

    (A) the author of a written work; or

    (B) a performer of a recorded performance;

under circumstances in which the written work or recorded performance is otherwise rightfully reproduced, exhibited, or broadcast.

(3) The use of a personality's:

    (A) name;

    (B) voice;

    (C) signature;

    (D) photograph;

    (E) image;

    (F) likeness;

    (G) distinctive appearance;

    (H) gestures; or

    (I) mannerisms;

in connection with the broadcast or reporting of an event or a topic of general or public interest. [P.L.2-2002, § 21.]

Effective Dates. P.L.2-2002, § 21. July 1. 2002.

Res Gestae. Indiana: A celebrity-friendly jurisdiction, 43 (No. 9) Res Gestae 24 (2000). Spreading its wings and coming of age:

With an Indiana's law as a model, the state-based Right of Publicity is ready to move to the federal level, 45 (No. 4) Res Gestae 31 (2001).

32-36-1-2. "Commercial purpose" defined. — As used in this chapter, "commercial purpose" means the use of an aspect of a personality's right of publicity as follows:

(1) On or in connection with a product, merchandise, goods, services, or commercial activities.

(2) For advertising or soliciting purchases of products, merchandise, goods, services, or for promoting commercial activities.

(3) For the purpose of fundraising.
[P.L.2-2002, § 21.]

32-36-1-3. "Name" defined. — As used in this chapter, "name" means the actual or assumed name of a living or deceased natural person that is intended to identify the person. [P.L.2-2002, § 21.]

32-36-1-4. "News reporting or an entertainment medium" defined.
— As used in this chapter, "news reporting or an entertainment medium" means a medium that publishes, broadcasts, or disseminates advertising in the normal course of its business, including the following:
    (1) Newspapers.
    (2) Magazines.
    (3) Radio and television networks and stations.
    (4) Cable television systems.
[P.L.2-2002, § 21.]

32-36-1-5. "Person" defined. — As used in this chapter, "person" means a natural person, a partnership, a firm, a corporation, or an unincorporated association. [P.L.2-2002, § 21.]

32-36-1-6. "Personalty" defined. — As used in this chapter, "personality" means a living or deceased natural person whose:
    (1) name;
    (2) voice;
    (3) signature;
    (4) photograph;
    (5) image;
    (6) likeness;
    (7) distinctive appearance;
    (8) gesture; or
    (9) mannerisms;
has commercial value, whether or not the person uses or authorizes the use of the person's rights of publicity for a commercial purpose during the person's lifetime. [P.L.2-2002, § 21.]

32-36-1-7. "Right of publicity" defined. — As used in this chapter, "right of publicity" means a personality's property interest in the personality's:
    (1) name;
    (2) voice;
    (3) signature;
    (4) photograph;
    (5) image;
    (6) likeness;
    (7) distinctive appearance;
    (8) gestures; or
    (9) mannerisms.
[P.L.2-2002, § 21.]

32-36-1-8. Written consent for use of right of publicity — Athlete agent — Student athlete — Endorsement contract — Failure to provide notice. — (a) A person may not use an aspect of a personality's right of publicity for a commercial purpose during the personality's lifetime or for one hundred (100) years after the date of the personality's death without having obtained previous written consent from a person specified in section 17 [IC 32-36-1-17] of this chapter.

(b) A written consent solicited or negotiated by an athlete agent (as defined in IC 25-5.2-1-2) from a student athlete (as defined in IC 25-5.2-1-2) is void if the athlete agent obtained the consent as the result of an agency contract that:

(1) was void under IC 25-5.2-2-2 or under the law of the state where the agency contract was entered into;

(2) was voided by the student athlete under IC 25-5.2-2-8 or a similar law in the state where the agency contract was entered into; or

(3) was entered into without the notice required under IC 35-46-4-4 or a similar law in the state where the agency contract was entered into.

(c) A written consent for an endorsement contract (as defined in IC 35-46-4-1.5) is void if notice is not given as required by IC 35-46-4-4 or a similar law in the state where the endorsement contract is entered into. [P.L.2-2002, § 21.]

32-36-1-9. Jurisdiction. — A person who:

(1) engages in conduct within Indiana that is prohibited under section 8 [IC 32-36-1-8] of this chapter;

(2) creates or causes to be created within Indiana goods, merchandise, or other materials prohibited under section 8 of this chapter;

(3) transports or causes to be transported into Indiana goods, merchandise, or other materials created or used in violation of section 8 of this chapter; or

(4) knowingly causes advertising or promotional material created or used in violation of section 8 of this chapter to be published, distributed, exhibited, or disseminated within Indiana;

submits to the jurisdiction of Indiana courts. [P.L.2-2002, § 21.]

32-36-1-10. Liability for violations of this chapter. — A person who violates section 8 [IC 32-36-1-8] of this chapter may be liable for any of the following:

(1) Damages in the amount of:

(A) one thousand dollars ($1,000); or

(B) actual damages, including profits derived from the unauthorized use;

whichever is greater.

(2) Treble or punitive damages, as the injured party may elect, if the violation under section 8 of this chapter is knowing, willful, or intentional. [P.L.2-2002, § 21.]

32-36-1-11. Profits — Establishing amount. — In establishing the amount of the profits under section 10(1)(B) [IC 32-36-1-10(1)(B)] of this chapter:

(1) the plaintiff is required to prove the gross revenue attributable to the unauthorized use; and

(2) the defendant is required to prove properly deductible expenses. [P.L.2-2002, § 21.]

32-36-1-12. Damages — Injunctive relief. — In addition to any damages awarded under section 10 [IC 32-36-1-10] of this chapter, the court:
(1) shall award to the prevailing party reasonable attorney's fees, costs, and expenses relating to an action under this chapter; and
(2) may order temporary or permanent injunctive relief, except as provided by section 13 [IC 32-36-1-13] of this chapter. [P.L.2-2002, § 21.]

32-36-1-13. Enforcement of injunction against news reporting or entertainment medium. — Injunctive relief is not enforceable against a news reporting or an entertainment medium that has:
(1) contracted with a person for the publication or broadcast of an advertisement; and
(2) incorporated the advertisement in tangible form into material that has been prepared for broadcast or publication. [P.L.2-2002, § 21.]

32-36-1-14. Impoundment. — (a) This section does not apply to a news reporting or an entertainment medium.
(b) During any period that an action under this chapter is pending, a court may order the impoundment of:
(1) goods, merchandise, or other materials claimed to have been made or used in violation of section 8 [IC 32-36-1-8] of this chapter; and
(2) plates, molds, matrices, masters, tapes, negatives, or other items from which goods, merchandise, or other materials described in subdivision (1) may be manufactured or reproduced.
(c) The court may order impoundment under subsection (b) upon terms that the court considers reasonable. [P.L.2-2002, § 21.]

32-36-1-15. Destruction of certain items. — (a) This section does not apply to a news reporting or an entertainment medium.
(b) As part of a final judgment or decree, a court may order the destruction or other reasonable disposition of items described in section 14(b) [IC 32-36-1-14(b)] of this chapter. [P.L.2-2002, § 21.]

32-36-1-16. Property rights. — The rights recognized under this chapter are property rights, freely transferable and descendible, in whole or in part, by the following:
(1) Contract.
(2) License.
(3) Gift.
(4) Trust.
(5) Testamentary document.
(6) Operation of the laws of intestate succession applicable to the state administering the estate and property of an intestate deceased personality, regardless of whether the state recognizes the property rights set forth under this chapter. [P.L.2-2002, § 21.]

32-36-1-17. Person who may exercise rights. — (a) The written consent required by section 8 [IC 32-36-1-8] of this chapter and the rights and remedies set forth in this chapter may be exercised and enforced by:

(1) a personality; or

(2) a person to whom the recognized rights of a personality have been transferred under section 16 [IC 32-36-1-16] of this chapter.

(b) If a transfer of a personality's recognized rights has not occurred under section 16 of this chapter, a person to whom the personality's recognized rights are transferred under section 18 [IC 32-36-1-18] of this chapter may exercise and enforce the rights under this chapter and seek the remedies provided in this chapter. [P.L.2-2002, § 21.]

32-36-1-18. Death of intestate personality — Interest in personality's recognized rights. — (a) Subject to sections 16 and 17 [IC 32-36-1-16 and IC 32-36-1-17] of this chapter, after the death of an intestate personality, the rights and remedies of this chapter may be exercised and enforced by a person who possesses a total of not less than one-half (½) interest of the personality's recognized rights.

(b) A person described in subsection (a) shall account to any other person in whom the personality's recognized rights have vested to the extent that the other person's interest may appear. [P.L.2-2002, § 21.]

32-36-1-19. When deceased personality's rights terminate. — If:

(1) a deceased personality's recognized rights under this chapter were not transferred by:

(A) contract;

(B) license;

(C) gift;

(D) trust; or

(E) testamentary document; and

(2) there are no surviving persons as described in section 17 [IC 32-36-1-17] of this chapter to whom the deceased personality's recognized rights pass by intestate succession;

the deceased personality's rights set forth in this chapter terminate. [P.L.2-2002, § 21.]

32-36-1-20. Supplemental nature of rights and remedies. — The rights and remedies provided for in this chapter are supplemental to any other rights and remedies provided by law. [P.L.2-2002, § 21.]

ARTICLE 37

COPYRIGHT

CHAPTER 1

APPLICATION

SECTION.
32-37-1-1. Applicability.

32-37-1-1. Applicability. — This article does not apply to the following:
(1) A contract between a performing rights society and:
  (A) a broadcaster licensed by the Federal Communications Commission;
  (B) a cable television operator or programmer; or
  (C) another transmission service.
(2) An investigation by a law enforcement agency.
(3) An investigation by a law enforcement agency or other person concerning a suspected violation of IC 24-4-10-4, IC 35-43-4-2, or IC 35-43-5-4(11). [P.L.2-2002, § 22.]

Effective Dates. P.L.2-2002, § 22. July 1. 2002.

CHAPTER 2

DEFINITIONS

SECTION.
32-37-2-1. Applicability of definitions.
32-37-2-2. Copyright owner.
32-37-2-3. Performing rights society.

SECTION.
32-37-2-4. Proprietor.
32-37-2-5. Royalty.

32-37-2-1. Applicability of definitions. — The definitions in this chapter apply throughout this article. [P.L.2-2002, § 22.]

Effective Dates. P.L.2-2002, § 22. July 1. 2002.

32-37-2-2. Copyright owner. — (a) "Copyright owner" means the owner of a copyright, enforceable under 17 U.S.C. 101 et seq., of a nondramatic musical work.
(b) The term does not include the owner of a copyright in a motion picture or an audiovisual work, or in part of a motion picture or an audiovisual work. [P.L.2-2002, § 22.]

32-37-2-3. Performing rights society. — (a) "Performing rights society" means an association or a corporation that licenses the public performance of nondramatic musical works on behalf of copyright owners.
(b) The term includes the following:
(1) The American Society of Composers, Authors, and Publishers (ASCAP).
(2) Broadcast Music, Inc. (BMI).
(3) SESAC, Inc.
[P.L.2-2002, § 22.]

32-37-2-4. Proprietor. — "Proprietor" means the owner of:
(1) a professional office;
(2) a retail establishment;
(3) a restaurant;
(4) a bar;
(5) a tavern; or
(6) an establishment similar to an establishment listed under subdivisions (1) through (5);
that is located in Indiana, in which the public may assemble, and in which nondramatic musical works may be performed, broadcast, or otherwise transmitted. [P.L.2-2002, § 22.]

32-37-2-5. Royalty. — "Royalty" means a fee payable to a performing rights society for public performance rights. [P.L.2-2002, § 22.]

CHAPTER 3

CONTRACT REQUIREMENTS

32-37-3-1. Information to be provided by performing rights society. — (a) At least seventy-two (72) hours before the execution of a contract between a performing rights society and a proprietor, the performing rights society shall provide the proprietor with the following written information:
(1) A schedule of the rates and terms of royalties under the contract.
(2) A toll free telephone number from which the proprietor may obtain answers to inquiries concerning musical works and copyright owners represented by the performing rights society.
(3) Notice that the performing rights society is in compliance with:
(A) state and federal law; and
(B) orders of courts having jurisdiction over:
(i) rates and terms of royalties; and
(ii) the licensing for public performance of copyrighted nondramatic musical works.
(b) At the request of the proprietor or a representative of the proprietor, not less than seventy-two (72) hours before the execution of a contract between a performing rights society and a proprietor, the performing rights society shall provide the proprietor with the following additional information or specify how the proprietor may, at the proprietor's expense, obtain the following additional information:
(1) The most recent available list of the members or affiliates represented by the society.
(2) The most recent available list of the copyrighted musical works in the performing rights society's repertory. [P.L.2-2002, § 22.]

Effective Dates. P.L.2-2002, § 22. July 1.
2002.

32-37-3-2. Contract — Writing signed by parties — Information to be included. — A contract executed, issued, or renewed in Indiana between a performing rights society and a proprietor must be in a writing signed by the parties and must include the following information:

(1) The name and business address of the proprietor.

(2) The name and address of the performing rights society.

(3) The name and location of each place of business to which the contract applies.

(4) The duration of the contract.

(5) The schedule of rates and terms of the royalties to be collected under the contract, including, if applicable, the sliding scale or schedule or the increase or decrease of the rates during the term of the contract. [P.L.2-2002, § 22.]

CHAPTER 4

PROHIBITIONS

SECTION.
32-37-4-1. Acts prohibited by performing
          rights society.

32-37-4-1. Acts prohibited by performing rights society. — A performing rights society or an agent or employee of a performing rights society may not:

(1) enter into a contract unless the contract is executed in accordance with the provisions of this article;

(2) enter a proprietor's business premises to discuss a contract for the performance of copyrighted works or the payment of royalties without first disclosing:

(A) that the individual is an agent of a performing rights society; and

(B) the purpose of the discussion;

(3) engage in any coercive conduct, act, or practice that substantially disrupts a proprietor's business; or

(4) use or attempt to use any unfair or deceptive act or practice in dealing with a proprietor. [P.L.2-2002, § 22.]

Effective Dates. P.L.2-2002, § 22. July 1.
2002.

CHAPTER 5

REMEDIES

SECTION.
32-37-5-1. Remedies.

32-37-5-1. Remedies. — A person who suffers a loss as a result of a violation of this article may:

(1) bring an action to recover:
   (A) actual damages; and
   (B) reasonable attorney's fees;
(2) seek an injunction; and
(3) seek any other remedy available at law or in equity.
[P.L.2-2002, § 22.]

Index

CONDOMINIUMS —Cont'd

Records.
Common areas and facilities.
Receipts and expenditures affecting, §32-25-8-8.
Removal of property from provisions.
Right of co-owners, §32-25-8-16.
Taxation, §32-25-8-7.

CONFIDENTIALITY OF INFORMATION.

Lost and unclaimed property.
Unclaimed property act.
Confidentiality of certain records, §32-34-1-44.

CONFLICT OF LAWS.

Eminent domain.
Repeal of conflicting provisions, §32-24-1-17.
Mortgages.
Effect on other provisions relating to, §32-29-1-9.
TOD securities registration, §32-17-9-8.

CONFLICTS OF INTEREST.

Receivers.
Persons who may not be appointed, §32-30-5-2.

CONSENT.

Publicity rights.
Written consent for commercial use of aspect of personality's right of publicity, §32-36-1-8.

CONSERVATION.

Easements, §§32-23-5-1 to 32-23-5-8.
See EASEMENTS.

CONSIDERATION.

Statute of frauds.
Consideration need not be stated, §32-21-1-2.

CONSTRUCTION AND INTERPRETATION.

Disclaimer of property interests.
Official comments of probate code study commission as guide, §32-17-7-19.
Easements.
Conservation easements, §32-23-5-1.
Fences.
Partition fences, §32-26-9-6.
Fraudulent transfers, §32-18-2-21.
Principles of law and equity to supplement provisions, §32-18-2-20.
Lost and unclaimed property.
Unclaimed property act, §32-34-1-50.
Marketable title for real property, §§32-20-1-1, 32-20-1-2.
Property.
Disclaimer of property interests.
Official comments of probate code study commission as guide, §32-17-7-19.
Recodification of 2002, §§32-16-1-3 to 32-16-1-9.

CONTEMPT.

Nuisances.
Indecent nuisances.
Violation of injunction or restraining order, §32-30-7-23.
Receivers.
Deposit and delivery of money and other things.
Disobedience of order, §32-30-5-5.

CONTINUANCES.

Strays.
Wrecked cargo or baggage.
Recovery by claimant, §32-34-8-28.

CONTRACTS.

Actions.
Statute of frauds.
Written contracts as prerequisites to certain actions, §32-21-1-1.
Copyright royalties, §§32-37-3-1, 32-37-3-2.
Fencing associations.
Award of contracts, §32-26-1-18.
Mechanics' liens.
No-lien provisions or stipulations, §32-28-3-1.
Void contract provisions, §§32-28-3-16, 32-28-3-17.
Molds.
Transfer of property interests in molds.
Validity of written agreements, §32-34-6-7.
Oil and gas.
Cancellation of contracts and leases, §§32-23-8-1 to 32-23-8-4.
Estates in land.
Right to contract unaffected, §32-23-7-8.
Silk screens.
Transfer of property interests in.
Effect on written agreements, §32-34-7-7.
Statute of frauds.
General provisions, §§32-21-1-1 to 32-21-1-16.
See STATUTE OF FRAUDS.
Time shares and camping clubs.
Exchange of occupancy rights.
Certification by members prior to execution of contract, §32-32-3-12.
Transfer of interest in membership.
Written contract, §32-32-3-6.
Writing.
Statute of frauds.
General provisions, §§32-21-1-1 to 32-21-1-16.
See STATUTE OF FRAUDS.

CONVEYANCES.

Acknowledgments, §32-21-1-11.
Recordation.
See RECORDATION.
Aliens, §32-22-2-6.
Rights generally, §§32-22-2-2, 32-22-2-3, 32-22-2-5.

INDEX 794

CONVEYANCES —Cont'd
Attorneys at law.
 Requisites for conveyance of land by
  attorney, §32-21-1-14.
Condominium units, §§32-25-5-1,
  32-25-5-2.
 Instrument or deed of conveyance,
  §32-25-7-5.
Fee simple interest, §32-17-1-2.
Fraudulent transfers, §§32-18-2-1 to
  32-18-2-21.
 See FRAUDULENT TRANSFERS.
Grantor and another named as
  grantees, §§32-21-10-1 to 32-21-10-3.
 Authorized, §§32-21-10-2, 32-21-10-3.
 Definition of person, §32-21-10-1.
 Effect, §§32-21-10-2, 32-21-10-3.
Greater estate than tenant possesses.
 Effect of conveyance, §32-17-2-5.
Ink scroll.
 Private seal or ink scroll not required to
  validate, §32-21-1-12.
Joint tenants and tenants in common.
 Partition.
  Sale of indivisible land, §32-17-4-15.
Landlord and tenant.
 Effect of conveyance by landlord,
  §32-31-1-10.
 Security deposits.
  Liability of landlord after giving notice
   of conveyance, §32-31-3-19.
Mentally ill.
 Limitations on persons who may convey
  real property, §§32-22-1-1, 32-22-1-5.
Minors.
 Limitations on persons who may convey
  real property, §32-22-1-1.
 Disaffirmance of sale, §32-22-1-2.
 Married persons under age eighteen,
  §§32-22-1-3, 32-22-1-4.
Persons who may convey real property.
 Limitations, §§32-22-1-1 to 32-22-1-5.
Priority of recorded transactions,
  §§32-21-4-1 to 32-21-4-3.
Psychologically affected property,
  §§32-21-6-1 to 32-21-6-6.
Recordation, §§32-21-2-1 to 32-21-4-3.
 See RECORDATION.
Residential real estate sales disclosure,
  §§32-21-5-1 to 32-21-5-13.
 See RESIDENTIAL REAL ESTATE
  SALES DISCLOSURE.
Revocable at will of grantor.
 Provision void as to subsequent
  purchasers from grantor, §§32-21-1-7,
  32-21-1-9.
Revocable at will of person other than
  grantor.
 Subsequent conveyance by person granted
  power.
  Validity, §§32-21-1-8, 32-21-1-9.
Seals.
 Private seal or ink scroll not required to
  validate, §32-21-1-12.

CONVEYANCES —Cont'd
Tax sale surplus disclosure, §§32-21-8-1
  to 32-21-8-6.
COORDINATE SYSTEM, §§32-19-1-1 to
  32-19-4-4.
Description of land, §§32-19-1-4,
  32-19-1-5, 32-19-3-1.
 Reliance by purchaser or mortgagee not
  required, §32-19-3-2.
Designation, §32-19-1-1.
Geodetic adviser, §§32-19-4-1, 32-19-4-2.
 Funding of activities, §32-19-4-3.
Geodetic control monuments, §32-19-2-2.
Ordinances.
 Prohibiting alteration of monuments,
  §32-19-4-4.
Plane coordinates, §32-19-2-1.
Use of terms, §32-19-1-6.
Zones, §32-19-1-2.
 Descriptions by national ocean
  survey/national geodetic survey.
  Adoption, §32-19-1-3.
COPYRIGHT ROYALTIES, §§32-37-1-1 to
  32-37-5-1.
Actions.
 Remedies for violations, §32-37-5-1.
Applicability of provisions.
 Exceptions, §32-37-1-1.
Attorneys' fees.
 Actions for violations, §32-37-5-1.
Contracts, §§32-37-3-1, 32-37-3-2.
Damages.
 Remedies for violations, §32-37-5-1.
Definitions, §§32-37-2-1 to 32-37-2-5.
Exceptions to provisions, §32-37-1-1.
Injunctions.
 Remedies for violations, §32-37-5-1.
Performing rights society.
 Contract with proprietor, §§32-37-3-1,
  32-37-3-2.
 Defined, §32-37-2-3.
 Prohibited acts, §32-37-4-1.
Remedies for violations, §32-37-5-1.
Statute of frauds.
 Contracts to be in writing, §32-37-3-2.
COPYRIGHTS.
Royalties, §§32-37-1-1 to 32-37-5-1.
 See COPYRIGHT ROYALTIES.
CORONERS.
Lis pendens record.
 Duties, §32-30-11-5.
CORPORATE EMPLOYEES' LIENS,
  §§32-28-12-1 to 32-28-12-7.
Enforcement, §32-28-12-4.
 Parties to actions, §32-28-12-5.
 Practice and pleading, §32-28-12-7.
 Undertaking to release property,
  §32-28-12-6.
Entitlement to, §32-28-12-1.
Limitation of actions.
 Enforcement actions, §32-28-12-4.
Notice, §§32-28-12-2, 32-28-12-3.

FLOODS —Cont'd
Enclosure of land subject to flooding —Cont'd
Petition by landowners, §32-26-6-1.
Viewers, §32-26-6-1.
 Compensation, §32-26-6-4.
 Report, §§32-26-6-2, 32-26-6-3.
 Surveyor, employment of, §32-26-6-4.
Fences.
Enclosure of land subject to flooding, §§32-26-6-1 to 32-26-6-5.
Recordation of fencemarks.
 Removal of marked fencing from overflowed lands, §32-26-7-3.
Recovery of property moved by high water, §§32-26-8-1 to 32-26-8-4.
FORECLOSURE.
Blacksmith's liens, §32-33-1-4.
Fencing associations.
Assessments.
 Enforcement of payment, §32-26-1-17.
Mechanics' liens.
Limitation of actions, §32-28-7-1.
Mortgages, §§32-29-7-1 to 32-29-9-1.
See MORTGAGES.
Motor vehicles.
Liens for repair, storage, service and supplies, §32-33-10-8.
Attorneys' fees, §32-33-10-9.
Public improvements.
Liens on.
 Limitation of actions, §32-28-8-1.
FORFEITURES.
Waste.
Judgment of forfeiture, §32-30-4-1.
FORMS.
Acknowledgments.
Armed forces members, §32-21-9-1.
Deed or mortgage, §32-21-2-7.
Eminent domain.
Notice of offer to purchase, §32-24-1-5.
Notice requiring defendants to appear, §32-24-1-6.
Offer to purchase, §32-24-1-5.
Public utilities.
 Offer and acceptance of offer for agricultural land, §32-24-4-4.
Home improvement warranties.
Disclaimer of implied warranties.
 Notice of waiver of implied warranties, §32-27-1-13.
Landlord and tenant.
Notices.
 Nonpayment of rent, §32-31-1-7.
 Termination of tenancy from year to year, §32-31-1-5.
New home construction warranties.
Disclaimer of implied warranties.
 Notice of waiver of implied warranties, §32-27-2-9.
FRAUD.
Fraudulent transfers, §§32-18-2-1 to 32-18-2-21.
See FRAUDULENT TRANSFERS.

FRAUD —Cont'd
Statute of frauds, §§32-21-1-1 to 32-21-1-16.
See STATUTE OF FRAUDS.
FRAUDS, STATUTE OF.
General provisions, §§32-21-1-1 to 32-21-1-16.
See STATUTE OF FRAUDS.
FRAUDULENT TRANSFERS, §§32-18-2-1 to 32-18-2-21.
Applicability of act, §32-18-2-1.
Assets.
Defined, §32-18-2-2.
Property not included, §32-18-2-12.
Construction and interpretation, §32-18-2-21.
Principles of law and equity to supplement provisions, §32-18-2-20.
Debts.
Defined, §32-18-2-5.
Obligations not included, §32-18-2-12.
Definitions, §§32-18-2-2 to 32-18-2-11.
Limitation of actions, §32-18-2-19.
Remedies of creditors, §32-18-2-17.
Value.
When deemed given, §32-18-2-13.
Voidable transfers or obligations, §32-18-2-18.
When transfer fraudulent, §§32-18-2-14, 32-18-2-15.
When transfer made, §32-18-2-16.
FUNDS.
Lost and unclaimed property.
Unclaimed property act.
 Abandoned property fund, §§32-34-1-33 to 32-34-1-35.
 Property custody fund, §§32-34-1-32, 32-34-1-35.
Strays.
County stray fund, §32-34-8-11.
FUTURE INTERESTS.
Conditions subsequent.
Possibility of reverter or rights of entry for breach of.
 Limitations on, §§32-17-10-1 to 32-17-10-3.

G

GEODETIC ADVISER, §§32-19-4-1, 32-19-4-2.
Funding of activities, §§32-19-4-3.
GHOST IN THE ATTIC STATUTE.
Psychologically affected real property, §§32-21-6-1 to 32-21-6-6.
GIFTS.
Museums.
Property loaned to museums.
 Presumption of gift to museum of certain property, §32-34-5-16.

JURISDICTION —Cont'd
Partition.
Investment of sale proceeds, §32-17-5-5.
Publicity rights.
Indiana courts, §32-36-1-9.

JURY.
Replevin.
Assessment of value of property and damages for taking and detention, §32-35-2-35.

L

LANDLORD AND TENANT.
Abandonment of dwelling unit.
What constitutes, §32-31-5-6.
Access by tenant.
Emergency possessory orders generally, §§32-31-6-1 to 32-31-6-10.
Interference with, §32-31-5-6.
Alienee of lessor or lessee.
Remedies, §32-31-1-13.
Attornment.
By tenant to stranger, §32-31-1-11.
Conveyance by landlord.
Validity without attornment, §32-31-1-10.
Conveyances.
Effect of conveyance by landlord, §32-31-1-10.
Security deposits.
Liability of landlord after giving notice of conveyance, §32-31-3-19.
Death.
Executor or administrator of estate of decedent.
Rights and liabilities, §32-31-1-16.
Life tenant.
Recovery of rent, §32-31-1-18.
Person on whose life rents dependent.
Recovery of arrears unpaid at death, §32-31-1-15.
Definitions.
Emergency possessory orders.
Applicable definitions, §32-31-6-1.
Obligations of landlord, §§32-31-8-2, 32-31-8-3.
Obligations of tenant, §§32-31-7-2, 32-31-7-3.
Rental agreements, §§32-31-5-2, 32-31-5-3.
Security deposits, §§32-31-3-2 to 32-31-3-10.
Ejectment.
General provisions, §§32-30-2-1 to 32-30-2-23, 32-30-3-1 to 32-30-3-21.
Emergency possessory orders,
§§32-31-6-1 to 32-31-6-10.
Definitions.
Applicable definitions, §32-31-6-1.
Emergency hearing.
Continuance, §32-31-6-8.
Scheduling, §32-31-6-5.

LANDLORD AND TENANT —Cont'd
Emergency possessory orders —Cont'd
Jurisdiction.
Small claims docket, §32-31-6-2.
Petition.
Requirements, §32-31-6-4.
Review by court, §32-31-6-5.
Who may file, §32-31-6-3.
Remedies, §32-31-6-6.
Subsequent hearing, §32-31-6-9.
Subsequent claims between parties, §32-31-6-10.
Subsequent hearing, §32-31-6-9.
Summons, §32-31-6-8.
Executors and administrators.
Rights and liabilities, §32-31-1-16.
Forms.
Notices.
Nonpayment of rent, §32-31-1-7.
Termination of tenancy from year to year, §32-31-1-5.
Liens.
Crops.
Recovery of rent, §32-31-1-19.
Maintenance of premises.
Landlord obligations, §32-31-8-5.
Tenant obligations, §32-31-7-5.
Notice.
Nonpayment of rent, §§32-31-1-7 to 32-31-1-9.
Obligations of landlord.
Notice of noncompliance as prerequisite to enforcement action, §32-31-8-6.
Obligations of tenant.
Notice of noncompliance as prerequisite to action to enforce, §32-31-7-7.
Rental agreements.
Modification, §32-31-5-4.
Tenancy from year to year.
Termination, §32-31-1-5.
Nuisances.
Drug nuisances.
Ejection of tenant, §32-30-8-11.
Order of restitution or possession, §32-30-8-12.
Indecent nuisances.
Effect of indecent nuisance by tenant, §32-30-7-25.
Obligations of landlord, §§32-31-8-1 to 32-31-8-6.
Actions by tenant to enforce, §32-31-8-6.
Applicability of provisions, §32-31-8-1.
Definitions, §§32-31-8-2, 32-31-8-3.
Maintenance of property, §32-31-8-5.
Notice of noncompliance.
Prerequisite to enforcement action, §32-31-8-6.
Remedies of tenant for noncompliance, §32-31-8-6.
Waiver of provisions void, §32-31-8-4.
Obligations of tenant, §§32-31-7-1 to 32-31-7-7.
Actions by landlord to enforce, §32-31-7-7.
Applicability of provisions, §32-31-7-1.

LOST AND UNCLAIMED PROPERTY
—Cont'd
Unclaimed property act —Cont'd
State departments and agencies.
Cooperation with attorney general,
§32-34-1-47.
State of Indiana.
Property subject to custody of,
§32-34-1-21.
Watercraft.
Drifting boats and timber, §§32-34-9-1 to
32-34-9-13.
Repossessors of motor vehicles or
watercraft.
Unclaimed property in possession of,
§§32-34-4-1 to 32-34-4-6.
Sale of abandoned watercraft,
§§32-34-10-1 to 32-34-10-8.

M

MAIL.
Museums.
Property loaned to museums.
Notice, §32-34-5-9.

MARINAS.
Sale of abandoned watercraft.
Generally, §§32-34-10-1 to 32-34-10-8.
Marina operator.
Defined, §32-34-10-1.
Recovery of expenses, §32-34-10-2.

MECHANICS' LIENS, §§32-28-3-1 to
32-28-3-18.
Actions.
Enforcement of liens, §§32-28-3-6,
32-28-3-7.
Attorneys' fees.
Actions to enforce liens, §32-28-3-14.
Contracts.
No-lien provisions or stipulations,
§32-28-3-1.
Void contract provisions, §§32-28-3-16,
32-28-3-17.
Enforcement of liens.
Actions, §§32-28-3-6, 32-28-3-7.
Expiration, §32-28-7-2.
Enforcement of lien.
Commencement of action before lien
expired, §32-28-7-4.
Extent of lien, §32-28-3-2.
Foreclosure.
Limitation of actions, §32-28-7-1.
Foreclosure of liens.
Notice to file action to foreclose,
§32-28-3-10.
Written undertaking in actions to
foreclose, §32-28-3-11.
Housing.
Original construction, §32-28-3-1.
Leases.
Forfeiture of lease for rent.
Lien not impaired, §32-28-3-2.

MECHANICS' LIENS —Cont'd
Limitation of actions.
Enforcement of liens, §32-28-3-6.
Mortgages.
Foreclosure.
Lien not impaired, §32-28-3-2.
Notice.
Foreclosure of liens.
Notice to file action to foreclose,
§32-28-3-10.
Notice of indebtedness.
Failure to give, §32-28-3-15.
Notice to owner, §32-28-3-9.
Personal property.
Sale, §32-33-9-2.
Railroads.
Persons performing work or furnishing
materials in construction,
§§32-28-3-12, 32-28-3-13.
Statement and notice of intention to hold
lien upon real property, §§32-28-3-3 to
32-28-3-5.
Parties, §32-28-3-9.
Enforcement actions, §32-28-3-7.
Personal property, §§32-33-9-1 to
32-33-9-8.
Perishable property.
Applicability of provisions, §32-33-9-4.
Sale, §§32-33-9-5, 32-33-9-6.
Sale, §32-33-9-1.
Forwarding and commission merchant,
§32-33-9-8.
Notice, §32-33-9-2.
Perishable property, §§32-33-9-5,
32-33-9-6.
Proceeds, §32-33-9-3.
Persons entitled to lien, §32-28-3-1.
Priorities, §32-28-3-1.
Railroads.
Persons performing work or furnishing
materials in construction,
§§32-28-3-12, 32-28-3-13.
Recordation.
Statement and notice of intention to hold
lien upon real property, §§32-28-3-3,
32-28-3-5.
Release, §§32-28-6-1, 32-28-6-2.
Sales.
Personal property, §§32-33-9-1 to
32-33-9-8.
Satisfaction of lien, §32-28-3-7.
Insufficient proceeds, §32-28-3-8.
**Statement and notice of intention to
hold lien upon real property,**
§32-28-3-3.
Recordation, §§32-28-3-3, 32-28-3-5.
Validity and enforceability, §32-28-3-4.
Third parties.
Obligor's receipt of payment from third
person.
Effect on right to record or foreclose
lien, §32-28-3-18.
Waiver.
Void contract provisions, §32-28-3-16.

MORTGAGES —Cont'd
Foreclosure —Cont'd
Definitions, §§32-29-7-1, 32-29-7-2,
 32-30-10-1, 32-30-10-2.
Dismissal of complaint.
 Principal and interest paid by
  defendant, §32-30-10-11.
Dwelling.
 Record owner may continue possession
  until sale, §32-29-7-11.
Executions.
 Endorsement of execution, §32-30-10-13.
Judgments and decrees.
 Filing, §32-29-7-3.
 Real estate located in more than one
  county, §32-29-7-6.
 Remedies, §32-30-10-5.
Jurisdiction.
 Real estate located in more than one
  county, §32-29-7-6.
Limitation of actions, §§32-28-4-1 to
 32-28-4-3.
Mechanics' liens.
 Lien not impaired, §32-28-3-2.
Mortgage executed prior to June 30, 1931.
 Applicable law, §32-29-7-14.
Parties.
 Mortgagee or assignee of record as
  defendant, §32-29-8-1.
 Naming, §32-29-9-1.
 Parties bound to judgment, §32-29-8-2.
 Service on, §32-29-9-1.
Receiver appointed by court, §32-29-7-11.
Redemption of real estate by owner,
 §§32-29-7-7, 32-29-7-9, 32-29-7-13.
Remedies, §32-30-10-5.
Sale, §32-29-7-3.
 Auction, §§32-29-7-4, 32-30-10-9.
 Deed executed after sale, §32-29-7-10.
 Notice, §32-29-7-3.
 Order of sale, §§32-30-10-8, 32-30-12-2.
 Parcels, §32-30-10-12.
 Payment of proceeds by sheriff,
  §32-29-7-9.
 Proceeds, §§32-29-7-10, 32-30-10-8,
  32-30-10-14.
 Purchase by sheriff or agent prohibited,
  §32-29-7-9.
 Purchasers free of lien, §32-29-8-3.
 Real estate located in more than one
  county, §32-29-7-6.
 Redemption, §§32-29-7-7, 32-29-7-9,
  32-29-7-13.
 Rents and profits of real estate not
  required to be offered first,
  §32-29-7-8.
 Sheriff to sell, §32-30-10-8.
Satisfaction of mortgage.
 Recording, §32-30-10-6.
Time limitation on issuance of process,
 §32-29-7-3.
 Waiver, §32-29-7-5.
Venue, §32-30-10-3.
Items mortgage may cover, §32-29-1-10.

MORTGAGES —Cont'd
Joint tenants and tenants in common.
Partition.
 Sale of indivisible land, §32-17-4-15.
Judgments.
Action upon mortgage, §32-30-12-1.
Foreclosure.
 Remedies, §32-30-10-5.
Priority over prior judgment against
 purchaser, §32-29-1-4.
Jurisdiction.
Foreclosure.
 Real estate located in more than one
  county, §32-29-7-6.
Mechanics' liens.
Foreclosure of mortgage.
 Lien not impaired, §32-28-3-2.
Notice.
Foreclosure.
 Sale, §32-29-7-3.
Parties.
Foreclosure.
 Mortgagee or assignee of record as
  defendant, §32-29-8-1.
 Naming, §32-29-9-1.
 Parties bound to judgment, §32-29-8-2.
 Service on, §32-29-9-1.
Pledges of rents and profits.
Provisions not to limit, §32-29-1-11.
Possession of premises, §32-29-1-1.
Priority of recorded transactions,
 §§32-21-4-1 to 32-21-4-3.
**Priority over prior judgment against
 purchaser,** §32-29-1-4.
Receivers.
Foreclosure, §32-29-7-11.
Recordation.
Assignment or transfer of mortgage,
 §§32-29-2-1, 32-29-2-2.
Conveyances generally, §§32-21-2-1 to
 32-21-4-3.
See RECORDATION.
Releases, §32-29-11-1.
Attestation, §32-29-3-1.
Certificate of satisfaction.
 Effect, §32-29-1-7.
Corporations, §32-29-5-1.
Entry of satisfaction into record,
 §32-29-1-6.
Financial institutions, §32-29-5-1.
State of Indiana, §32-29-4-1.
Title insurance companies, §§32-29-6-1 to
 32-29-6-17.
See ABSTRACT AND TITLE
 INSURANCE.
Sales.
Sale of mortgaged property by mortgagee,
 §32-29-1-3.
Satisfaction, §32-29-11-1.
Certificate of satisfaction, §32-29-1-7.
Entry into record, §32-29-1-6.
Foreclosure.
 Recording of satisfaction of mortgage,
  §32-30-10-6.

RESTITUTION.
Nuisances.
Drug nuisances.
Order of restitution or possession,
§32-30-8-12.

RIGHT OF ENTRY.
Conditions subsequent.
Possibility of reverter or rights of entry
for breach of.
Limitations on, §§32-17-10-1 to
32-17-10-3.
Eminent domain, §§32-24-1-3, 32-24-1-5.
Fences.
Recovery of property moved by high
water, §32-26-8-4.

ROYALTIES.
Copyright royalties, §§32-37-1-1 to
32-37-5-1.
See COPYRIGHT ROYALTIES.

RULE AGAINST PERPETUITIES.
Statutory rule against perpetuities,
§§32-17-8-1 to 32-17-8-6.
Applicability of provisions, §32-17-8-1.
Exceptions, §32-17-8-2.
Effective date of provisions, §32-17-8-1.
Exceptions to provisions, §32-17-8-2.
General statement of rule, §32-17-8-5.
Reformation of instruments by court,
§32-17-8-6.
Time of creation of nonvested property
interest or power of appointment.
Determination, §32-17-8-4.
Validity of nonvested property interest or
power of appointment, §32-17-8-3.

RULES AND REGULATIONS.
Lost and unclaimed property.
Unclaimed property act, §32-34-1-52.

S

SAFE DEPOSIT BOXES.
Lost and unclaimed property.
Unclaimed property act.
Property in safe deposit box or other
depository, §32-34-1-24.

SALES.
Abandoned watercraft, §§32-34-10-1 to
32-34-10-8.
Boats.
Abandoned watercraft, §§32-34-10-1 to
32-34-10-8.
Electronic home entertainment
equipment lien, §§32-33-15-2 to
32-33-15-4.
Fabricators' liens, §§32-33-16-5 to
32-33-16-8.
Lost and unclaimed property.
See LOST AND UNCLAIMED
PROPERTY.
Mechanics' liens.
Satisfaction of lien, §32-28-3-7.
Insufficient proceeds, §32-28-3-8.

SALES —Cont'd
Mortgages.
Sale of mortgaged property by mortgagee,
§32-29-1-3.
Real property.
Disclosure.
Psychologically affected property,
§§32-21-6-1 to 32-21-6-6.
Residential real estate sales disclosure,
§§32-21-5-1 to 32-21-5-13.
See RESIDENTIAL REAL ESTATE
SALES DISCLOSURE.
Tax sale surplus disclosure, §§32-21-8-1
to 32-21-8-6.
Psychologically affected property,
§§32-21-6-1 to 32-21-6-6.
Residential real estate sales disclosure,
§§32-21-5-1 to 32-21-5-13.
See RESIDENTIAL REAL ESTATE
SALES DISCLOSURE.
Tax sale surplus disclosure, §§32-21-8-1 to
32-21-8-6.
Strays, §§32-34-8-9, 32-34-8-10.
Transfer, moving and storage liens,
§§32-33-11-4, 32-33-11-6.
Warehouseman's lien, §§32-33-14-2,
32-33-14-3.
Watchmaker and jeweler liens,
§32-33-13-2.
Watercraft.
Abandoned watercraft, §§32-34-10-1 to
32-34-10-8.

SEALS AND SEALED INSTRUMENTS.
Conveyances.
Private seal or ink scroll not required to
validate, §32-21-1-12.

SECURITIES REGULATION.
Registration.
TOD securities registration, §§32-17-9-1 to
32-17-9-15.
See TOD SECURITIES
REGISTRATION.
TOD securities registration, §§32-17-9-1
to 32-17-9-15.
See TOD SECURITIES REGISTRATION.

SERVICE OF PROCESS.
Boats and other watercraft.
Liens.
Service of summons, §32-33-2-8.
Common law liens.
Notice to commence suit, §32-28-13-6.
Affidavit of service, §32-28-13-7.
Ejectment.
Nonresident, §32-30-2-3.
Order of possession, §§32-30-3-9 to
32-30-3-11.
Order to allow plaintiff to survey
property, §32-30-2-17.
Landlord and tenant.
Nonpayment of rent.
Notice, §32-31-1-9.
Nuisances.
Drug nuisances, §32-30-8-9.
Service by mail, §32-30-8-8.